Yearbook on
International
Communist Affairs
1985

Yearbook on International Communist Affairs 1985

Parties and Revolutionary Movements

EDITOR:	Richard F. Staar
ASSISTANT EDITOR:	Margit N. Grigory

AREA EDITORS

Thomas H. Henriksen	•	Africa
William Ratliff	•	The Americas
Ramon H. Myers	•	Asia and the Pacific
Richard F. Staar John B. Dunlop	•	Eastern Europe and the Soviet Union
James H. Noyes	•	The Middle East
Dennis L. Bark	•	Western Europe

HOOVER INSTITUTION PRESS
Stanford University, Stanford, California

The text of this work is set in Times Roman;
display headings are in Melior. Typeset by
Harrison Typesetting, Inc., Portland, Oregon.
Printed and bound by Braun-Brumfield, Inc.,
Ann Arbor, Michigan.

The Hoover Institution on War, Revolution and Peace, founded at
Stanford University in 1919 by the late President Herbert Hoover,
is an interdisciplinary research center for advanced study on
domestic and international affairs in the twentieth century. The
views expressed in its publications are entirely those of the
authors and do not necessarily reflect the views of the staff,
officers, or Board of Overseers of the Hoover Institution.

Hoover Press Publication 327

International Standard Book Number 0-8179-8271-X
International Standard Serial Number 0084-4101
Library of Congress Catalog Number 67-31024

Contents

Preface ix

Party Congresses xi

Register of Communist Parties xii

Introduction xxvii

AFRICA

Introduction (*Thomas H. Henriksen*) 1
Angola (*Richard E. Bissell*) 4
Benin (*Michael S. Radu*) 8
Congo (*Michael S. Radu*) 10
Ethiopia (*Peter Schwab*) 12
Lesotho (*Wallace H. Spaulding*) 15
Mozambique (*Thomas H. Henriksen*) 16
Nigeria (*Jack H. Mower*) 21
Réunion (*Hilarie Slason*) 22
Senegal (*Jack H. Mower*) 25
South Africa (*Sheridan Johns*) 26
Sudan (*Marian Leighton*) 32
Zimbabwe (*Richard W. Hull*) 37

THE AMERICAS

Introduction (*William Ratliff*) 41
Argentina (*Mark Falcoff*) 45
Bolivia (*William Ratliff*) 49
Brazil (*Carole Merten*) 51
Canada (*Alan Whitehorn*) 55
Chile (*Paul E. Sigmund*) 59
Colombia (*Daniel L. Premo*) 61
Costa Rica (*Lowell Gudmundson*) 68
Cuba (*George Volsky*) 71
Dominican Republic (*George Volsky*) 77
Ecuador (*David Scott Palmer*) 79
El Salvador (*Thomas P. Anderson*) 81

Grenada (*Timothy Ashby*) 85
Guadeloupe (*Brian Weinstein*) 87
Guatemala (*Daniel L. Premo*) 89
Guyana (*William Ratliff*) 96
Haiti (*Brian Weinstein*) 99
Honduras (*Thomas P. Anderson*) 100
Jamaica (*Robert J. Alexander*) 102
Martinique (*Brian Weinstein*) 104
Mexico (*Marian Leighton*) 106
Nicaragua (*Thomas P. Anderson*) 110
Panama (*Marian Leighton*) 115
Paraguay (*Paul H. Lewis*) 119
Peru (*Sandra Woy-Hazleton*) 120
Puerto Rico (*George Volsky*) 128
Suriname (*William Ratliff*) 129
United States (*Harvey Klehr*) 130
Uruguay (*Martin Weinstein*) 135
Venezuela (*Carole Merten*) 137

ASIA AND THE PACIFIC

Introduction (*Ramon H. Myers*) 141
Afghanistan (*Ruth* and *Anthony Arnold*) 143
Australia (*Christine A. Gould* and *Michael Morell*) 155
Bangladesh (*Douglas C. Makeig*) 157
Burma (*Alice Straub* and *Jon A. Wiant*) 161
China (*Stephen Uhalley, Jr.*) 164
India (*Douglas C. Makeig*) 179
Indonesia (*Jeanne S. Mintz*) 187
Japan (*John F. Copper*) 190
Kampuchea (*Stephen J. Morris*) 194
Korea: Democratic People's Republic of Korea (*Tai Sung An*) 197
Laos (*Arthur J. Dommen*) 207
Malaysia and Singapore (*Jeanne S. Mintz*) 210
Mongolia (*Colleen E. Foraker*) 216
Nepal (*Chitra Krishna Tiwari*) 219
New Zealand (*Michael Morell* and *Christine A. Gould*) 222
Pakistan (*Douglas C. Makeig*) 224
Philippines (*Leif Rosenberger*) 228
Sri Lanka (*Barbara Reid*) 233
Thailand (*Clark D. Neher*) 235
Vietnam (*Douglas Pike*) 238

EASTERN EUROPE AND THE SOVIET UNION

Introduction (*John B. Dunlop* and *Richard F. Staar*) 245
Albania (*Nikolaos A. Stavrou*) 250
Bulgaria (*John D. Bell*) 263

Czechoslovakia (*Zdeněk Suda*) 275
Germany: German Democratic Republic (*Michael J. Sodaro*). 285
Hungary (*Bennett Kovrig*) 295
Poland (*Arthur R. Rachwald*) 305
Romania (*Walter M. Bacon, Jr.*) 318
Union of Soviet Socialist Republics (*R. Judson Mitchell*) 333
Yugoslavia (*Ivan Avakumovic*) 367
Council for Mutual Economic Assistance (*Aurel Braun*) 373
Warsaw Treaty Organization (*Aurel Braun*) 382
International Communist Organizations (*Wallace H. Spaulding*) 387
    World Marxist Review 387
    Front Organizations 387
Soviet Propaganda Themes (*John J. Karch*). 391

THE MIDDLE EAST

Introduction (*James H. Noyes*) 399
Algeria (*John Damis*). 402
Bahrain (*Wallace H. Spaulding*). 403
Egypt (*Glenn E. Perry*). 404
Iran (*Sepehr Zabih*) 408
Iraq (*John F. Devlin*) 412
Israel (*Glenn E. Perry*) 414
    Palestine Communist Party (*Glenn E. Perry*) 418
Jordan (*Naseer H. Aruri*). 422
Lebanon (*Nikola B. Schahgaldian*). 425
Morocco (*John Damis*) 430
Saudi Arabia (*Wallace H. Spaulding*) 432
Syria (*Glenn E. Perry*) 433
Tunisia (*John Damis*) 437
Yemen: People's Democratic Republic of Yemen (*Robert W. Stookey*) 438

WESTERN EUROPE

Introduction (*Dennis L. Bark*). 443
Austria (*Frederick C. Engelmann*) 451
Belgium (*Martin O. Heisler*) 454
Cyprus (*T. W. Adams*). 458
Denmark (*Eric S. Einhorn*) 462
Finland (*Peter Grothe*) 467
France (*Michael J. Sodaro*) 469
Germany: Federal Republic of Germany and West Berlin (*Eric Waldman*) 475
Great Britain (*Richard Sim*) 484
Greece (*D. G. Kousoulas*) 487
Iceland (*Eric S. Einhorn*). 490
Ireland (*Richard Sim*) 495
Italy (*Giacomo Sani*) 496
Luxembourg (*Eric Waldman*) 502

Malta (*J. G. E. Hugh*) 503
Netherlands (*Robert I. Weitzel*) 509
Norway (*Marian Leighton*) 514
Portugal (*H. Leslie Robinson*) 520
Spain (*H. Leslie Robinson*) 523
Sweden (*Peter Grothe*) 527
Switzerland (*Eric Waldman*) 530
Turkey (*Frank Tachau*) 533

Select Bibliography 535

Index of Biographies 555

Index of Names 557

Index of Subjects 577

Preface

This edition of the *Yearbook*, the nineteenth consecutive one, includes profiles by 79 contributors, covering 106 parties and revolutionary movements as well as ten international communist fronts, two regional organizations (the Council for Mutual Economic Assistance and the Warsaw Pact), and Soviet foreign propaganda. In addition, twelve biographic sketches of prominent communist leaders follow individual profiles. The names and affiliations of contributors are given at the end of each essay.

The *Yearbook* offers data on the organization, policies, activities, and international contacts during all of calendar 1984 of communist parties and Marxist-Leninist movements throughout the world. Information has been derived primarily from published sources, including official newspapers and journals, as well as from radio transmissions monitored by the U.S. Foreign Broadcast Information Service. Dates cited in the text without indicating a year are for 1984.

Whether to include a party or group that espouses a quasi-Marxist-Leninist ideology, yet may not be recognized by Moscow as "communist," always remains a problem. It applies specifically to certain among the so-called national liberation movements and, more important, even to some ruling parties. In making our decisions, the following criteria have been considered: rhetoric, the organizational model, participation in international communist meetings and fronts, and adherence to the USSR's foreign policy line. It seems realistic to consider the regime of Nicaragua, for example, in the same category as that of Cuba. On the other hand, despite its radicalism, Libya obviously remains less aligned. The ruling parties in the so-called "vanguard revolutionary democracies" appear to be clearly affiliated with the world communist movement. They also are discussed in the Introduction.

Our thanks go to the librarians and staff at the Hoover Institution for checking information and contributing to the bibliography. The latter was compiled by the *Yearbook* assistant editor, Mrs. Margit N. Grigory, who also prepared the index of names and remained in contact with contributors. Finally, we welcome two new members of the editorial board, John B. Dunlop (USSR) and James H. Noyes (Middle East).

Richard F. Staar
Hoover Institution

*   *   *

The following abbreviations are used for frequently cited publications and news agencies:

CSM	*Christian Science Monitor*
FBIS	*Foreign Broadcast Information Service*
FEER	*Far Eastern Economic Review*
IB	*Information Bulletin* (of the *WMR*)
JPRS	*Joint Publications Research Service*
NYT	*New York Times*

WMR	*World Marxist Review*
WP	*Washington Post*
WSJ	*Wall Street Journal*
YICA	*Yearbook on International Communist Affairs*
ACAN	Agencia Central Americano Noticias
ADN	Allgemeiner Deutscher Nachrichtendienst
AFP	Agence France-Presse
ANSA	Agenzia Nazionale Stampa Associata
AP	Associated Press
BTA	Bulgarska Telegrafna Agentsiya
ČETEKA	Československá Tisková Kancelář
DPA	Deutsche Presse Agentur
KPL	Khaosan Pathet Lao
MENA	Middle East News Agency
MTI	Magyar Távirati Iroda
NCNA	New China News Agency
PAP	Polska Agencja Prasowa
UPI	United Press International
VNA	Vietnam News Agency

Party Congresses

Country	Congress	Date (1984)
Brazil	7th	January
West Germany	7th	6–8 January
Austria	25th	13–15 January
Spain (PC)	1st	13–15 January
Sri Lanka	12th	27–29 January
Thailand	5th	February
Luxembourg	24th	4–5 February
Netherlands	extraordinary	4–5, 12, 27 February
Belgium (Flemish Wing)	1st regional	18–19 February
(Wallonian Wing)	1st regional	December 1983
Costa Rica (PCC)	14th	10–11 March
(PVP)	14th	8 April
(PVP)	15th	15–16 September
Dominican Republic	3d	15–17 March
Poland	nat'l conference	16–18 March
Norway (NKP)	18th	30 March–2 April
Guadeloupe	8th	27–29 April
Malta	extraordinary	18–25 May
Finland (SKP)	20th	25–27 May
West Berlin (SEW)	7th	25–27 May
Cape Verde (PAIGC)	2d	June
Chile	16th	before 14 June
Congo (PCT)	3d	27–30 July
Burundi (UPRONA)	2d	after 18 July
Saudi Arabia	2d	August 1983
Zimbabwe (ZANU)	5th	8–12 August
Ethiopia (WPE)	1st	6–10 September
Senegal (PIT)	2d	28–30 September
Australia (SPA)	5th	28 September–1 October
(CPA)	28th	4 November
Colombia	14th	7–11 November
Romania	13th	19–22 November
Jamaica (WP)	3d	14–21 December
South Africa	6th	December
Palestine	1st	1984

Register of Communist Parties

Status: * ruling   # unrecognized
              + legal   0 proscribed

Country: *Party(ies)/Date Founded*	Mid-1984 *Population (est.)* *(World Factbook)*	Communist Party *Membership* *(claim or est.)*	Party Leader *(sec'y general)*	Status	Last *Congress*	Last Election *(percentage of vote;* *seats in legislature)*
AFRICA (12)						
Angola Popular Movement for the Liberation of Angola (MPLA), 1956 (MPLA-PT, 1977)	7,770,000	31,000 cl.	José Eduardo dos Santos	*	First Extraord. Dec. 1980	(1980); all 203 MPLA approved
Benin People's Revolutionary Party of Benin (PRPB), 1975	3,910,000	no data	Mathieu Kerekou	*	Second 13–15 Nov. 1979	(1984); all 196 PRPB approved
Congo Congolese Labor Party (PCT), 1969	1,745,000	8,685 est.	Denis Sassou-Ngouesso (chairman)	*	Third 27–30 July 1984	95.0 (1984); all 153 PCT approved
Ethiopia Workers' Party of Ethiopia (WPE), 1984	31,998,000	30,000 est.	Mengistu Haile Mariam	*	First (Const.) 6–10 Sept. 1984	n/a
Lesotho Communist Party of Lesotho (CPL), 1962	1,474,000	no data	Jacob M. Kena	0	Sixth May 1982	n/a
Mozambique Front for the Liberation of Mozambique (FRELIMO), 1962	13,413,000	130,000 cl.	Samora Moisés Machel (chairman)	*	Fourth 26–29 Apr. 1983	(1977); all 226 FRELIMO approved

Country / Party	Population	Membership		Leader	Last Congress	Electoral Data
Nigeria Socialist Working People's Party (SWPP), 1978	88,148,000	no data	0	Dapo Fatogun	First Nov. 1978	(1983)
Réunion Réunion Communist Party (PCR), 1959	535,000	10,000 cl.	+	Paul Vergès	Fifth 12–14 July 1980	32.73 (1983); 16 of 45 (local assembly); none in Paris
Senegal Independence and Labor Party (PIT), 1981	6,541,000	no data	+	Amath Dansoko (elected at congress)	Second 28–30 Sept. 1984	0.5 (1983); none
South Africa South African Communist Party (SACP), 1921	31,688,000	no data	0	Moses Mabhida	Sixth Dec. 1984, in London	n/a
Sudan Sudanese Communist Party (SCP), 1946	21,103,000	1,500 est.	0	Muhammad Ibrahim Nugud Mansur	Fourth (legal) 31 Oct. 1967	n/a
Zimbabwe Zimbabwe African National Union (ZANU-PF), 1963	8,325,000	no data	*	Robert Mugabe (president)	Fifth 8–12 Aug. 1984	71.0 (1984); 58 of 100 (57 of 80 reserved for blacks)
TOTAL	216,650,000	211,185				

THE AMERICAS (29)

Country / Party	Population	Membership		Leader	Last Congress	Electoral Data
Argentina Communist Party of Argentina (PCA), 1918	30,097,000	70,000 est.	+	Athos Fava	Extraord. 5–6 Sept. 1983	1.3 (1983); none
Bolivia Communist Party of Bolivia (PCB), 1950	6,037,000	300 est.	+	Jorge Kolle Cueto	Fourth Apr. 1979	(1980)

Country: Party(ies)/Date Founded	Mid-1984 Population (est.) (World Factbook)	Communist Party Membership (claim or est.)	Party Leader (sec'y general)	Status	Last Congress	Last Election (percentage of vote; seats in legislature)
Brazil	134,380,000					
Brazilian Communist Party (PCB), 1960 (Communist Party of Brazil, 1922)		8,000 est.	Giocondo Dias	#	Seventh (called National Meeting of Communists) Jan. 1984	(1985)
Canada	25,142,000					
Communist Party of Canada (CPC), 1921		2,500 est.	William Kashtan	+	Twenty-fifth 13–15 Feb. 1982	0.05 (1984); none
Chile	11,655,000					
Communist Party of Chile (CPC), 1922		20,000 est.	Luis Corvalán	0	Sixteenth June 1984 (clandestine in Chile and abroad)	n/a
Colombia	28,248,000					
Communist Party of Colombia (PCC), 1930		12,000 est.	Gilberto Vieira	+	Fourteenth 7–11 Nov. 1984	1.2 (1982); 3 of 199
Costa Rica	2,693,000					
Popular Vanguard Party (PVP), 1931		3,500 est. (prior to split)	Humberto Vargas Carbonell	+	Fourteenth 8 Apr. 1984 Fifteenth 15–16 Sept. 1984	3.2 (1982); 4 of 57 (United People's Coalition)
Costa Rican People's Party (PPC), split from PVP, 1984		no data	Manuel Mora Valverde	+	Fourteenth 10–11 Mar. 1984	n/a
Cuba	9,995,000					
Cuban Communist Party (PCC), 1965		434,143 cl.	Fidel Castro Ruz	*	Second 17–20 Dec. 1981	(1981); all 499 PCC approved
Dominican Republic	6,416,000					
Dominican Communist Party (PCD), 1944		750 est.	Narciso Isa Conde	+	Third 15–17 Mar. 1984	7.1 (1982); none

Country / Party (founded)	Population	Membership	Status	Party Leader	Last Congress	Last Election
Ecuador Communist Party of Ecuador (PCE), 1928	9,091,000	500 est.	+	René Mauge Moskera	Tenth 27–29 Nov. 1981	3.6 (1984); 2 of 71 (Broad Leftist Front. FADI) 4.0 (1984) in pres. elec. for Mauge, FADI cand.
El Salvador Communist Party of El Salvador (PCES), 1928 (one of five in FMLN)	4,829,000	500 est.	0	Shafik Jorge Handal	Sixth Aug. 1970	n/a (1984)
Grenada Maurice Bishop Patriotic Movement (MBPM), 1984	113,000	no data	+	Kenrick Radix	n/a	5.0 (1984); none
Guadeloupe Communist Party of Guadeloupe (PCG), 1958	332,000	3,000 est.	+	Guy Daninthe	Eighth 27–29 Apr. 1984	22.6 (1983); 11 of 41 (local assembly); 1 of 3 in Paris
Guatemala Guatemalan Party of Labor (PGT), 1950	7,956,000	750 est.	0	Carlos González	Fourth Dec. 1969	(1984)
Guyana People's Progressive Party (PPP), 1950	837,000	200 est.	+	Cheddi Jagan	Twenty-first 31 July–2 Aug. 1982	19.5 (1980); 10 of 65
Haiti Unified Party of Haitian Communists (PUCH), 1968	5,805,000	no data	0	René Théodore	First late 1978 or early 1979	(1984)
Honduras Honduran Communist Party (PCH), 1954 (one of six in the MHR, 1982)	4,424,000	no data	0	Rigoberto Padilla Rush (expelled in Oct.?)	Third Mar. 1977	(1981)
Jamaica Workers' Party of Jamaica (WPJ), 1978	2,338,000	50 est.	+	Trevor Munroe	Third 14–21 Dec. 1984	(1983)

Country: Party(ies)/Date Founded	Mid-1984 Population (est.) (World Factbook)	Communist Party Membership (claim or est.)	Party Leader (sec'y general)	Status	Last Congress	Last Election (percentage of vote; seats in legislature)
Martinique Martinique Communist Party (PCM), 1957	330,000	1,000 est.	Armand Nicolas	+	Eighth 12–13 Nov. 1983	9.07 (1983); 4 of 41 (local assembly); none in Paris
Mexico United Socialist Party of Mexico (PSUM), 1981	77,659,000	40,800 cl.	Pablo Gómez Alvarez	+	Second 9–14 Aug. 1983	4.3 (1982); 17 of 400
Nicaragua Nicaraguan Socialist Party (PSN), 1939	2,914,000	250 est.	Luis Sánchez Sancho	+	Tenth Oct. 1973	1.3 (1984); 2 of 96
Sandinista Front of National Liberation (FSLN), 1960		4,000 cl.	Bayardo Arce Castano (coord. of Political Committee)	*		67.0 (1984); 61 of 96
Panama People's Party of Panama (PPP), 1943	2,101,000	35,000 cl.	Rubén Darío Souza	+	Sixth 8–10 Feb. 1980	(1984); none
Paraguay Paraguayan Communist Party (PCP), 1928	3,623,000	3,500 est.	Antonio Maidana (arrested 1980)	0	Third 10 Apr. 1971	(1973)
Peru Peruvian Communist Party (PCP), 1930	19,157,000	5,000 est.	Jorge del Prado	+	Eighth Extraord. 27–31 Jan. 1982	2.8 (1980); 2 of 60
Puerto Rico Puerto Rican Communist Party (PCP), 1934	3,196,520	125 est.	Frank Irrizarry	+	unknown	(1984)
Suriname Revolutionary People's Party (RVP), 1981	370,000	100 est.	Edward Naarendorp	+	First 1981	n/a

Country / Party	Population	Membership		Leader	Last Congress	Electoral data
United States Communist Party USA (CPUSA), 1919	236,413,000	17,500 cl.	+	Gus Hall	Twenty-third 10–13 Nov. 1983	0.01 (1984); none
Uruguay Communist Party of Uruguay (PCU), 1920	2,926,000	7,500 est.	0 (permitted within Broad Front)	Rodney Arismendi	Twentieth Dec. 1970	6.0 (1984); none (Broad Front coalition, 21% of vote)
Venezuela Communist Party of Venezuela (PCV), 1931	18,552,000	4,000 est.	+	Jesús Faría	Sixth 8–11 Aug. 1980	2.0 (1983); 3 of 195
TOTAL	657,629,520	674,968				

ASIA AND THE PACIFIC (21)

Country / Party	Population	Membership		Leader	Last Congress	Electoral data
Afghanistan People's Democratic Party of Afghanistan (PDPA), 1965	14,448,000	120,000 cl.	*	Babrak Karmal	Nat'l Conf. 14–15 Mar. 1982	(1978) (Rev. Council in power since Apr. 1978)
Australia Communist Party of Australia (CPA), 1920	15,462,000	1,500 est.	+	Judy Mundey	Twenty-eighth 4 Nov. 1984	(1984); none
Socialist Party of Australia (SPA), 1971		1,000 est.	+	Peter Dudley Symon	Fifth 28 Sept.–1 Oct. 1984	(1984); none
Bangladesh Communist Party of Bangladesh (CPB), 1948	99,585,000	3,000 est.	+	Muhammed Farhad	Third Feb. 1980	(1981)
Burma Burmese Communist Party (BCP), 1939	36,196,000	3,000 cl.	0	Thakin Ba Thein Tin (CC chmn.)	Second 20 July 1945 (last known)	n/a

Country: Party(ies)/Date Founded	Mid-1984 Population (est.) (World Factbook)	Communist Party Membership (claim or est.)	Party Leader (sec'y general)	Status	Last Congress	Last Election (percentage of vote; seats in legislature)
China	1,034,907,000					
Chinese Communist Party (CCP), 1921		over 40,000,000 cl.	Hu Yaobang	*	Twelfth 1–11 Sept. 1982	(1981); all 3,202 CCP approved
India	746,388,000					
Communist Party of India (CPI), 1928		478,500 cl.	C. Rajeswara Rao	+	Twelfth 21–28 Mar. 1982	2.71 (1984); 6 of 544
Communist Party Marxist (CPM), 1964		271,500 cl.	E. M. S. Namboodiripad	+	Eleventh 26–31 Jan. 1982	5.96 (1984); 22 of 544
Indonesia	169,442,000					
Indonesian Communist Party (PKI), 1920 (split)		250 est. (in exile, combined est.)	Jusuf Adjitorop (pro-Beijing faction) Sadiatjaya Sudiman (pro-Moscow faction)	0	Seventh Extraord. Apr. 1962	n/a
Japan	120,017,467					
Japan Communist Party (JCP), 1922		480,000 cl.	Tetsuzo Fuwa	+	Sixteenth 27–31 July 1982	9.43 (1983); 26 of 511
Kampuchea	6,118,000					
Kampuchean People's Revolutionary Party (KPRP), 1951		700 est.	Heng Samrin	*	Fourth 26–29 May 1981	99.0 (1981); all 117
Democratic Kampuchea (DK), or Kampuchean Communist Party (KCP), 1960		no data	Pol Pot	0	unknown	n/a
Korea (North)	19,630,000					
Korean Workers' Party (KWP), 1949		3,000,000 cl.	Kim Il-song	*	Sixth 10–15 Oct. 1980	100 (1982); all 615 KWP approved
Laos	3,732,000					
Lao People's Revolutionary Party (LPRP), 1955		35,000 est.	Kaysone Phomvihane	*	Third 27–30 Apr. 1982	(Dec. 1975) Supreme People's Assembly (all 45 appointed by LPRP)

Country / Party (founded)	Population	Party membership	Leader	Status	Last congress	Elections (% vote; seats)
Malaysia Communist Party of Malaya (CPM), 1930	15,330,000	1,100 est.	Chin Peng	0	1965 (last known)	n/a
Communist Party of Malaysia (MCP), 1983		800 est.	Ah Leng	0	unknown	n/a
Mongolia Mongolian People's Revolutionary Party (MPRP), 1921	1,860,000	76,240 cl.	Jambyn Batmonh	*	Eighteenth 26–31 May 1981	99.0 (1981); all 370 MPRP approved
Nepal Nepal Communist Party (NCP), 1949 (factions)	16,578,000	5,000 est. (75% pro-Beijing and neutral)	Man Mohan Adhikary	0	Third 1968	n/a
New Zealand Communist Party of New Zealand (CPNZ), 1921	3,238,000	50 est.	Richard C. Wolfe	+	(1984) (first since 1966)	none
Socialist Unity Party (SUP), 1966		100 est.	George Jackson	+	Sixth 22–24 Oct. 1982	0.5 (1984); none
Pakistan Communist Party of Pakistan (CPP), 1948	96,628,000	under 200 est.	Imam Ali Nazish	0 (since 1954)	First (cland.) 1976	n/a
Philippines Philippine Communist Party (PKP), 1930	55,528,000	8,000 est.	Felicismo Macapagal	#	Eighth 1980	n/a
Communist Party of the Philippines, Marxist-Leninist (CPP-ML), 1968		30,000 cl.	Rafael Baylosis	0	Re-establishment 26 Dec. 1968	n/a
Singapore Communist Party of Malaya, branch (CPM), 1930	2,531,000	200 est.	Chin Peng	0	unknown	n/a
Sri Lanka Communist Party of Sri Lanka (CPSL), 1943	15,925,000	6,000 est.	Kattorge P. Silva	+	Twelfth 27–29 Jan. 1984	1.9 (1977); 1 of 168

Country: Party(ies)/Date Founded	Mid-1984 Population (est.) (World Factbook)	Communist Party Membership (claim or est.)	Party Leader (sec'y general)	Status	Last Congress	Last Election (percentage of vote; seats in legislature)
Thailand Communist Party of Thailand (CPT), 1942	51,724,000	1,200 est.	Virat Angkhatha-vorn (active leader)	0	Fifth (cland.) Feb. 1984	n/a
Vietnam Vietnamese Communist Party (VCP), 1930	59,030,000	1,730,214 cl.	Le Duan	*	Fifth 27–31 March 1982	97.9 (1981); all 496 approved by Father-land Front
TOTAL	2,584,297,467	46,253,554				

EASTERN EUROPE AND USSR (9)

Country: Party(ies)/Date Founded	Mid-1984 Population (est.) (World Factbook)	Communist Party Membership (claim or est.)	Party Leader (sec'y general)	Status	Last Congress	Last Election (percentage of vote; seats in legislature)
Albania Albanian Party of Labor (APL), 1941	2,906,000	122,000 cl.	Enver Hoxha	*	Eighth 1–8 Nov. 1981	99.9 (1982); all 250 Democratic Front
Bulgaria Bulgarian Communist Party (BCP), 1903	8,969,000	825,876 cl.	Todor Zhivkov	*	Twelfth 31 Mar.–4 Apr. 1981	99.9 (1981); all 400 Fatherland Front
Czechoslovakia Communist Party of Czecho-slovakia (KSC), 1921	15,420,000	1,623,000 cl.	Gustáv Husák	*	Sixteenth 6–10 Apr. 1981	99.0 (1981); all 350 National Front
Germany: German Democratic Republic Socialist Unity Party (SED), 1946	16,717,000	2,202,277 cl.	Erich Honecker	*	Tenth 11–16 Apr. 1981	99.9 (1981); all 500 National Front

Country / Party (founded)	Population	Party membership	Party leader		Last party congress	Last election
Hungary Hungarian Socialist Worker's Party (HSWP), 1956	10,681,000	232,000 cl.	János Kádár	*	Twelfth 24–27 Mar. 1980	99.3 (1980): all 352 Patriotic People's Front
Poland Polish United Workers' Party (PUWP), 1948	36,887,000	2,186,000 cl.	Wojciech Jaruzelski	*	Ninth Extraord. 14–20 July 1981	99.5 (1980); all 460 Fatherland Front
Romania Romanian Communist Party (PCR), 1921	22,683,000	3,400,000 cl.	Nicolae Ceaușescu	*	Thirteenth 19–22 Nov. 1984	98.5 (1980); all 369 Front of Socialist Democracy and Unity
USSR Communist Party of the Soviet Union (CPSU), 1898	274,860,000	18,500,000 cl.	Konstantin U. Chernenko (Feb. 1984)	*	Twenty-sixth 23 Feb.–4 Mar. 1981	99.9 (1984); all 1,500 CPSU approved (71.4% of 1,500 are CPSU members)
Yugoslavia League of Communists of Yugoslavia (LCY), 1920	22,997,000	2,500,000 cl.	Dimče Belovski (secretary of the Presidium)	*	Twelfth 26–29 June 1982	–(1982); all 308 Socialist Alliance (all LCY approved)
TOTAL	412,120,000	31,591,153				

MIDDLE EAST (13)

Country / Party (founded)	Population	Party membership	Party leader		Last party congress	Last election
Algeria Socialist Vanguard Party (PAGS), 1920	21,351,000	450 est.	Sadiq Hadjeres (first secretary)	0	Sixth Feb. 1952	n/a
Bahrain Bahrain National Liberation Front (NLF/B), 1955	409,000	negligible	Yusuf al-Hassan al-Ajajai	0	unknown	n/a
Egypt Egyptian Communist Party (ECP), 1921	47,049,000	500 est.	Farid Mujahid	0	First (held in Egypt) Sept. 1980	n/a

Country: Party(ies)/Date Founded	Mid-1984 Population (est.) (World Factbook)	Communist Party Membership (claim or est.)	Party Leader (sec'y general)	Status	Last Congress	Last Election (percentage of vote; seats in legislature)
Iran Communist Party of Iran (Tudeh Party), 1941 (dissolved May 1983)	43,820,000	2,000 est. (early 1983)	Nureddin Kianuri (imprisoned) Ali Khavari (provisional leader in exile)	0	1965	3.0 (1980); 0 of 270
Iraq Iraqi Communist Party (ICP), 1932	15,000,000	no data	Aziz Muhammad	0	Third 4–6 May 1976	n/a
Israel Communist Party of Israel (CPI, "Rakah"), 1948 (Palestine Communist Party, 1922)	4,235,000 (incl. E. Jerusalem)	1,500 est.	Meir Vilner	+	Nineteenth 11–14 Feb. 1981	3.4 (1984); 4 of 120
Jordan Communist Party of Jordan (CPJ), 1951	2,689,000	1,000 est.	Fa'iq Muhammad Warrad	0	Second Dec. 1983	n/a
Lebanon Lebanese Communist Party (LCP), 1924	2,601,000	15,000 cl.	George Hawi	+	Fourth 1979	(1972)
Morocco Party of Progress and Socialism (PPS), 1974	23,565,000	30,000 cl.	'Ali Yata	+	Third 25–27 Mar. 1983	2.30 (1984); 2 of 306
Palestine Communist Party (PCP), 1982	4,500,000 Palestinians	200 est.	Bashir al-Barghuti (presumed)	0 but tolerated	First presumably in 1984	n/a
Saudi Arabia Communist Party of Saudi Arabia (CPSA), 1975	10,794,000	negligible	Ahmad Musa	0	Second Aug. 1983	n/a

Country / Party	Population	Party membership		Leader	Last party congress	Last election; seats
Syria Syrian Communist Party (SCP), 1944	10,400,000	5,000 est.	+	Khalid Bakhdash	Fifth May 1980	0.0 (1981); none
Tunisia Tunisian Communist Party (PCT), 1934	6,970,000 (1984 census)	2,000 est.	+	Muhammad Harmel (first secretary)	Eighth Feb. 1981	0.78 (1981); none
Yemen (PDRY) Yemen Socialist Party (YSP), 1978	2,147,000	26,000 cl.	*	Ali Nasir Muhammad al-Hasani	Second Extraord. 12–14 Oct. 1980	–(1978); all 111 YSP approved
TOTAL	195,530,000	83,650				

WESTERN EUROPE (23)

Country / Party	Population	Party membership		Leader	Last party congress	Last election; seats
Austria Communist Party of Austria (KPO), 1918	7,579,000	12,000 est.	+	Franz Muhri	Twenty-fifth 13–15 Jan. 1984	0.66 (1983); none
Belgium Belgian Communist Party (PCB/KPB), 1921	9,872,000	10,000 est.	+	Louis van Geyt	Twenty-fourth Mar. and Dec. 1982 (two stages)	2.3 (1981); 2 of 212
Cyprus Progressive Party of the Working People (AKEL), 1941 (Communist Party of Cyprus, 1922)	662,000	14,000 cl.	+	Ezekias Papaioannou	Fifteenth 13–15 May 1982	32.8 (1981); 12 of 35 Greek Cypriot seats
Denmark Communist Party of Denmark (DKP), 1919	5,112,000	10,000 est.	+	Poul Emanuel (secretary)	Twenty-seventh 12–15 May 1983	0.7 (1984); none
Finland Finnish Communist Party (SKP), 1918	4,873,000	50,000 cl.	+	Aarno Aitamurto	Twentieth 25–27 May 1984	14.0 (1983); 27 of 200
France French Communist Party (PCF), 1920	55,600,000	610,000 cl.	+	Georges Marchais	Twenty-fourth 3–7 Feb. 1982	16.2 (1981); 44 of 491

Country: Party(ies)/Date Founded	Mid-1984 Population (est.) (World Factbook)	Communist Party Membership (claim or est.)	Party Leader (sec'y general)	Status	Last Congress	Last Election (percentage of vote; seats in legislature)
Germany: Federal Republic of Germany	59,387,000 (ex. W. Berlin)					
German Communist Party (DKP), 1968		50,482 cl.	Herbert Mies	+	Seventh 6–8 Jan. 1984	0.2 (1983); none
Great Britain	56,023,000					
Communist Party of Great Britain (CPGB), 1920		16,000 est.	Gordon McLennan	+	Thirty-eighth 12–15 Nov. 1983	0.03 (1983); none
Greece	9,984,000					
Communist Party of Greece (KKE), 1921		42,000 est.	Kharilaos Florakis	+	Eleventh 15–18 Dec. 1982	10.9 (1981); 13 of 300
Communist Party of Greece–Interior (KKE-I), 1968		12,000 est.	Yiannis Banias	+	Third 17–23 May 1982	1.3 (1981); none
Iceland	239,000					
People's Alliance (AB), 1968		3,000 est.	Svavar Gestsson	+	Biennial Congr. Nov. 1983	17.3 (1983); 10 of 60
Ireland	3,575,000					
Communist Party of Ireland (CPI), 1933		500 est.	James Stewart	+	Eighteenth 14–16 May 1982	–(1982); none
Italy	56,998,000					
Italian Communist Party (PCI), 1921		1,700,000 cl.	Alessandro Natta (since June 1984)	+	Sixteenth 2–6 Mar. 1983	29.9 (1983); 198 of 630
Luxembourg	366,000					
Communist Party of Luxembourg (CPL), 1921		600 est.	René Urbany	+	Twenty-fourth 4–5 Feb. 1984	5.0 (1979); 2 of 59
Malta	329,599					
Communist Party of Malta (CPM), 1969		100 est.	Anthony Vassallo	+	Extraordinary 18–25 May 1984	–(1981); none
Netherlands	14,437,000					
Communist Party of the Netherlands (CPN), 1909		10,000 est.	Elli Izeboud	+	Extraordinary 4, 5, 12, 27 Feb. 1984	1.9 (1982); 3 of 150

Country / Party	Population	Membership	Leader		Congress	Last election
Norway						
Norwegian Communist Party (NKP), 1923	4,145,000	500 est.	Hans I. Kleven	+	Eighteenth 30 Mar.–2 Apr. 1984	0.3 (1981); none
Workers' Communist Party (AKP), 1973		1,000 est.	Paal Steigan	+	Third 4–5 Apr. 1983	0.7 (1981); none
Portugal						
Portuguese Communist Party (PCP), 1921	10,045,000	200,000 est.	Álvaro Cunhal	+	Tenth 8–11 Dec. 1983	18.0 (1983); 44 of 250
San Marino						
Communist Party of San Marino (PCS), 1941	22,000	300 est.	Ermenegildo Gasperoni	+	Tenth 1980	24.3 (1983); 15 of 60
Spain						
Spanish Communist Party (PCE), 1920	38,435,000	84,000 est.	Gerardo Iglesias	+	Eleventh 14–18 Dec. 1983	3.8 (1982); 4 of 350
Communist Party (PC), 1984		25,000 cl.	Ignacio Gallego	+	First 13–15 Jan. 1984	n/a
Sweden						
Left Party Communists (VPK), 1921	8,335,000	17,500 cl.	Lars Werner	+	Twenty-sixth 20–24 Nov. 1981	5.6 (1982); 20 of 349
Communist Workers' Party (APK), 1977		5,000 cl.	Rolf Hagel	+	Twenty-seventh 1983	0.1 (1982); none
Switzerland						
Swiss Labor Party (PdAS), 1921	6,477,000	4,500 est.	Armand Magnin	+	Twelfth 21–22 May 1983	0.9 (1983); 1 of 200
Turkey						
Communist Party of Turkey (TCP), 1920	50,207,000	negligible	Haydar Kutlu	0	Fifth Oct. or Nov. 1983	n/a
West Berlin						
Socialist Unity Party of West Berlin (SEW), 1949	2,000,000	4,500 est.	Horst Schmitt	+	Seventh 25–27 May 1984	0.7 (1981); none
TOTAL	404,702,599	2,882,982				
GRAND TOTAL	4,470,929,586	81,697,492				

INTERNATIONAL FRONT ORGANIZATIONS

Organization (10)	Year Founded	Headquarters	Claimed Membership	Affiliates	Countries
Afro-Asian Peoples' Solidarity Organization	1957	Cairo	unknown	87	–
Christian Peace Conference	1958	Prague	unknown	–	ca. 80
International Association of Democratic Lawyers	1946	Brussels	25,000	–	ca. 80
International Organization of Journalists	1946	Prague	180,000	–	120 plus
International Union of Students	1946	Prague	10,000,000	120	112
Women's International Democratic Federation	1945	East Berlin	200,000,000	135	117
World Federation of Democratic Youth	1945	Budapest	150,000,000	ca. 270	123
World Federation of Scientific Workers	1946	London	500,000	ca. 40	70 plus
World Federation of Trade Unions	1945	Prague	ca. 206,000,000	92	81
World Peace Council	1950	Helsinki	unknown	–	142 plus

Introduction
The Communist World, 1984

In an article published by *Agitator* (September 1984), the first deputy chief of the International Department in the Central Committee of the Communist Party of the Soviet Union (CPSU) gave the number of countries in which communist parties are active as 95, with a total membership of "almost 80 million."[1] Although the latter figure is the same as that for 1983, the former represents a drop of two (presumably North Yemen and Somalia). Nothing further has been heard about communist movements in those countries.

The Prague-based monthly *Problems of Peace and Socialism*—an English-language edition of which appears in Canada under the title *World Marxist Review*—continues to serve as the sole international press organ that speaks for most of the communist parties. A recent conference sponsored by the journal met at Prague on 4–6 December 1984, with representatives from 91 parties in attendance. Two of these requested that their names not be mentioned, probably because they fear publicity (many listed operate underground).[2] The French and Yugoslav comrades did not send delegations to this meeting of Soviet-line and independent Marxist parties.

Among the 89 listed, several are not recognized as full-fledged communist parties by Moscow: the MPLA–Workers' Party in Angola, the People's Democratic Party of Afghanistan, the National Liberation Front of Bahrain, the Benin People's Revolutionary Party, the People's Revolutionary Party of Kampuchea, the Independence Congress Party of Madagascar, the Yemen Socialist Party, the Congolese Labor Party, and the Worker's Party of Ethiopia. All of these, with the possible exception of the movement in Madagascar, appear to fall into the category of "vanguard" parties that may develop over time and be accepted as communist.[3]

The Prague meeting heard calls for a world conference, the last having been held in 1969 at Moscow. The delegate from Argentina, Óscar Arévalo, stated that a meeting of twelve Latin American parties at Buenos Aires on 6–7 July 1984 had proposed a "world forum." East German leader Erich Honecker referred to this suggestion at a plenum of his ruling party's Central Committee on 22 November and indicated a willingness to initiate "consulations about a world meeting of communist and workers' parties."[4]

The CPSU's attitude has been somewhat less than forthright regarding a new world congress, and it is a matter of record that many independent-minded movements would boycott such a gathering: the Dutch, French, Italian, Japanese, Swedish, and Yugoslav are examples, not to mention the Albanian, Chinese, and North Korean. The total count is unavailable. However, the official communist daily in Poland claimed that "more than 60 parties are now in favor of holding such a world congress."[5]

The Register of Communist Parties above includes two parties per country if Moscow recognizes both. This appears to be the case in Australia, India, New Zealand, Sweden, and Spain.[6] Several of the movements operate on geographic territories that have no national sovereignty, like Guadeloupe, Martinique, Palestine, Puerto Rico, Réunion, and West Berlin. Also listed are several "vanguard revolutionary democratic" movements: Afghanistan, Angola, Bahrain, Benin, Congo, Ethiopia, Kampuchea, Mozambique, and South Yemen. In one case, the Commission for the Organization of the Party of the Working People of Ethiopia (COPWE) transformed itself into the Ethiopian Workers' Party, a step toward full-fledged acceptance as a ruling communist movement.

We have presented the Register by geographic region. The mid-1984 population estimates all come from the same source.[7] The party membership figures represent either an official claim of the party or an estimate as of 31 December 1984 provided by the profile contributor. The Register also includes the names of current party leaders; the status of each movement (ruling, legal, unrecognized, proscribed); the dates of national conferences or congresses; and the electoral showing of the party at the most recent elections.

In summary, only fifteen countries are ruled by communist parties (about 75 million of the global 80 million members), and of these ten belong to the "socialist commonwealth" as well as holding full membership in the Council for Mutual Economic Assistance. This, for the most part pro-Soviet core, numerically represents less than half of the world communist movement. The other five ruling parties are Albania, China, Laos (considered part of the socialist commonwealth), North Korea, and Yugoslavia. These communist and workers' parties attempt to identify with and infiltrate national liberation movements, several of which already have been captured.[8]

During the year under review, communists left the government of France. The same thing happened in Bolivia; in the "free world" only Martinique and San Marino still have communist cabinet members. The bans imposed on the Tudeh Party of Iran and on all political movements by Nigeria during 1983 still remain in force. Communist organizations in Iraq and Honduras became illegal, whereas in Panama the party attained legality in 1984.

Membership has remained about the same in China (40 million or half the world total), although the current verification campaign may reduce that figure. The CPSU gained 213,000, whereas the Polish United Workers' Party lost 141,000 members. No data were released by Albania and, hence, the conclusion is that membership remained the same. Over the past two years, the League of Communists of Yugoslavia grew by 346,000, which reversed a decline of almost 50,000 before that period of time.

The 120,000 membership claimed for Afghanistan appears suspect, when the same source asserts that 60 percent, or 72,000, of these individuals serve in the armed forces.[9] Western estimates of the *total* indigenous military are about 40,000. A national conference in Angola made preparations for the ruling movement's Second Congress, to be held in December 1985. Some 500 delegates attended from all eighteen provinces.[10] No current membership figures have been released. The same applied to the newly founded Workers' Party of Ethiopia, established in September 1984, the size of which can only be estimated.

Throughout parts of Western Europe, the communist parties have suffered membership decline. In Austria, the party lost an estimated 4,000 and in Switzerland 500 members. About 100,000 individuals left the French party, and 30,000 in its Italian counterpart.[11] Only in Greece (plus 14,500) and Portugal (plus 13,000) did the respective movements make gains. Otherwise, numbers remained fairly stable. Highlights of other developments, by geographic area, follow.

Africa South of the Sahara. The most significant development has been establishment of a workers' party in Ethiopia, as mentioned in the foregoing, after five years of preparation. The new secretary general stated that "the objective of our future struggle is the building of socialism" (Addis Ababa domestic service, 6 September 1984). Seven of the eleven Politburo members are military men. However, the number of Cubans propping up the regime has dropped from 20,000 in 1977 to about 9,000 a year ago. Some of them have been transported to Angola, where the total has reached about 35,000 men.[12]

The Zimbabwe African National Union (ZANU) held its Fifth Congress in August and elected President Robert Mugabe to the vacant position of first secretary. He pledged to transform the country into a one-party, socialist state along Marxist-Leninist lines and later announced that the first general elections since independence five years ago would be held in March 1985.[13] A congress of the Congolese Labor Party (PCT) re-elected its secretary general and added five of his supporters to the Politburo in July.

Only in Mozambique did a split occur in the leadership, stable over the past fifteen years. President Moisés Samora Machel, who also heads the ruling FRELIMO party, dismissed three hard-line Marxists from his cabinet in June. They had been in charge of interior, security, and natural resources. As a result of Mozambique's agreement with the Republic of South Africa, the latter country's communist party lost its staging bases for guerrillas.[14]

These insurgents have been reduced to several hundred in number. However, the South African movement (SACP) held its Sixth Congress in London at some unspecified time in December 1984. A declaration described its role in the "revolutionary union," headed by the African National Congress, which is controlled by the SACP. A new party statute was adopted, a new Central Committee elected, and the same secretary general retained.[15]

The Americas. Three regional conferences were held during the year under review. Representatives of twelve parties, mostly from the Caribbean, met in Guyana on 2–4 March; a larger group from 21 countries in Central America and the Caribbean gathered in Havana from 11 to 13 July; a meeting in Buenos Aires on 6–7 July attracted delegates from thirteen parties, mainly from the South American continent.[16] All of them evaluated the Reagan administration's policies as warlike and gave unanimous support to the Soviet foreign policy line.

Cuba remains the only outright communist-ruled country in the Americas. During the year, it received an estimated $4 billion in economic aid and another billion in military assistance from the USSR alone. The Cuban party will hold its Third Congress in December 1985 at Havana.[17] A long-range development program, being worked out with the Soviet bloc, should receive formal approval at that time.

Some military equipment used by the estimated 6,000 to 8,000 communist guerrillas[18] in El Salvador comes from the USSR via Cuba and Nicaragua. Insurgents boycotted presidential elections in March (and the runoff in May) and continued acts of sabotage. The fighting has taken an estimated 50,000 lives during the past five years. Parliamentary elections are scheduled for March 1985.

Nicaragua now has a ruling ideology, namely Marxism-Leninism, although officially it is still a "revolutionary democracy" according to the Soviets.[19] Sandinista candidate Daniel Ortega Saavedra became president, with 67 percent of the vote in the November elections. Two-thirds of the congressional seats also were taken by the same de facto communist movement. The editor of *La Prensa* moved to Costa Rica, charging "a monstrous level of censorship."[20] The spiritual leader of the opposition is Archbishop Miguel Obando y Bravo. The country's economy has deteriorated, burdened with a foreign debt of more than $4 billion. Despite these difficulties, the regime still exports revolution.

The Sendero Luminoso (Shining Path) group in Peru has already caused about 5,000 deaths, approximately equal to its total membership. It is alleged to be a Maoist organization that uses widespread terror, as does the Tupac Amaru Revolutionary Movement. The Peruvian Communist Party is a prominent member of the (Marxist) United Left Coalition, an umbrella organization that is now the second-largest political group in the country.

Chile also has experienced considerable violence, wrought principally by the Movement of the Revolutionary Left (MIR) and the Manuel Rodríguez Patriotic Front, the latter with unofficial links to the communist party. The latter recently issued a leaflet calling upon the Chilean armed forces to oppose the Pinochet government.[21] Underground communists belong to the Popular Democratic Movement, which preaches both violence and nonviolent struggle.

The Maurice Bishop Patriotic (formerly the New Jewel) Movement participated in the November elections in Grenada, winning only 5 percent of the vote. Communists in Uruguay, although not legalized, won a fourth of the 21 percent vote for the leftist Broad Front Coalition. In Venezuela the largest communist party, the Movement to Socialism, received only 4 percent in municipal elections. The CPSU delegation that visited Caracas presumably discussed this matter.[22]

Asia and the Pacific. The Central Committee of the Chinese Communist Party (CCP) announced on 20 October 1984 its intention to press forward with urban economic reforms. Proclaiming the new "responsibility system" in the countryside a great success, the CCP pledged to carry reform into the cities. Toward that end, party cadres will be instructed to develop new "guidance" planning, make more effective use of price and tax levers, remove the government from management, and raise technological and managerial standards in all urban enterprises.[23]

Three days before the year's end, USSR first deputy prime minister I. V. Arkhipov signed three economic agreements with the People's Republic of China. They reportedly will increase the volume of trade between the two largest communist-ruled states to the equivalent of $6 billion over the next five years and provide new Soviet investments, technology, and economic advisers.[24] Although political relations still remain tense because of Moscow's refusal to comply with Beijing's three major demands—removal of troops from its northern border, withdrawal from Afghanistan, and cessation of support for Vietnam in

Kampuchea—the Chinese have been able to negotiate an important economic pact, but this does not mean that communist party relations will be resumed in the near future.

On 21 December, Deng Xiaoping and British prime minister Margaret Thatcher affixed their signatures to a treaty that legitimizes the return of Hong Kong to the PRC in 1997 under the principle of "one country—two systems." This event represented a great victory for Deng as leader of communist China, and there is no doubt that he also hopes to do the same with Taiwan.

In September, the North Koreans invited the chairman of Japan's Socialist Party for a visit, opening the way to new overtures for expanded economic relations between Pyongyang and Tokyo.[25] Talks began the following month on economic cooperation between North and South Korea. Although the first round was interrupted by defection of a Soviet student at Panmunjom, the two states agreed to continue the negotiations in 1985.

On 8 September, Pyongyang announced a new joint venture law, thus giving official approval for more trade with the West. This move clearly signaled a major shift away from the previous closed-door policy based on self-reliance. Notably, Pyongyang guarantees protection of investment and earnings by foreign partners as well as remittance of part of their wages and dividends abroad (Articles 4, 17, 22).[26]

During the March elections in the Philippines, more than 60 government troops were killed in ambushes by the New People's Army (NPA), the armed wing of the Communist Party of the Philippines (CPP). Throughout the year, the NPA stepped up its attacks, up to company strength. Broader contacts between the CPP and its urban front organizations seem to have borne fruit, as sporadic killings increased greatly in the fall. Current assessments of NPA strength vary, although most observers agree that its military activities have accelerated. Army officers in Manila now claim that the NPA has embarked on a strategy of "encircling the cities" and expanded its activities on a wide range of fronts in order to stretch the government's military forces.[27]

Nineteen eighty-four marked the fortieth anniversary of Ho Chi Minh's proclamation on Vietnam's independence from France and the tenth anniversary of North Vietnam's conquest of South Vietnam, making possible the forced reunification of a country that had been divided for 21 years. Despite appalling economic problems, the Hanoi leadership continued to display steadfast determination to unify Indochina under its hegemony.[28] With strong backing from the Kremlin, which now supplies Hanoi with advanced Mi-24 Hind combat helicopters, Su-22 swing-wing fighter aircraft, missile-attack boats, tanks, and a variety of surface-to-air missiles, Vietnamese troops began their winter offensive in late December, bent on crushing Kampuchean guerrilla resistance located around four major refugee camps along the border with Thailand.

As the war in Afghanistan enters its sixth year, the half-dozen major Mujahedeen groups are becoming increasingly unified. They are learning to use weapons like the SAM-7 antiaircraft missile and small ground-to-ground rockets. Even though Soviet forces carpet-bomb villages and assault valleys with helicopter-borne commandos, there are strong Mujahedeen bases less than ten miles from Kabul.[29] Since the Soviet invasion and its reliance on the tactics of "migratory genocide," between 250,000 and 1 million people have died, more than 2.5 million others live as refugees in Pakistan, and another 1.5 million exist under similar conditions in Iran.[30]

Eastern Europe and the Soviet Union. The deaths of Secretary General Andropov in February and Defense Minister Ustinov in December 1984, two ranking members of the Politburo, underscored the passing of the "old guard" from the CPSU leadership. Despite the fact that younger candidates were available—namely, Gorbachev (53) and Romanov (61)—the new secretary general, Konstantin Chernenko came from the same generation as his predecessor.[31]

Gorbachev has been identified as the second secretary, where he becomes vulnerable as the heir apparent and deputy to Chernenko. The latter's ideology can be described as neo-Stalinist, and during 1984 the cult of Stalin was indeed revived.[32] Examples include the readmission of Vyacheslav M. Molotov to the CPSU in July and the enticement of Stalin's daughter back to the Soviet Union from England, perhaps in preparation for the anniversary celebration of VE Day in May 1985.

Romanov, the other prime contender, had been brought to Moscow by Andropov. The protégé's "program" appears to be patterned after that of his benefactor: police methods, discipline, military-industrial expansion. "Romanov is more brutal, less likely to rock the boat" than Gorbachev.[33] The former reportedly controls the defense establishment and the military-industrial complex, which places him in a strong position.

The situation throughout Eastern Europe is not much better. The top leaders, with the exception of Ceauşescu in Romania and Jaruzelski in Poland, are also in their seventies. Neither Albania nor Yugoslavia belongs to the Soviet-dominated military alliance, the Warsaw Treaty Organization,[34] which has been used as an instrument of control by the USSR since its inception in 1955.

Of the two maverick states mentioned above, only Yugoslavia holds associate membership in the Council for Mutual Economic Assistance (CMEA), by means of which the USSR exercises economic leverage throughout Eastern Europe. At the mid-June 1984 economic summit meeting in Moscow, the Soviet attempt to force closer integration met with opposition from several countries that want better relations with the West.

However, when Erich Honecker of East Germany announced a visit to the Federal Republic of Germany, the USSR prevailed upon him to cancel the trip in early September. Less than one week later, Bulgarian leader Todor Zhivkov followed suit.[35] Only Romanian party/government head Nicolae Ceauşescu traveled to Bonn in mid-October, seemingly in defiance of Soviet wishes.

It is with Poland that the USSR has most of its problems. The party/government leader is a career military officer, an absolutely unique phenomenon for a communist-ruled state. It probably makes the Kremlin uncomfortable, and that may be why an 800-man Soviet military mission, under Gen. S. F. Shcheglov, is located in Warsaw.[36] Decisionmakers in Moscow would prefer a party apparatus worker to head the Polish communist movement, which remains in disarray.

Middle East. Throughout this region, communist parties participated in only two elections: they won the same four seats in Israel and two in Morocco. Due to continuing warfare between Iran and Iraq, the movements there were subjected to increased dispersal and repression. Splintered and harassed, the few hundred party members in Egypt witnessed arrests and trials of their leaders. The largely expatriate organizations of Saudi Arabia and Bahrain pursued a shadowy existence, the former holding a congress about which nothing is known.

Only in Lebanon,[37] despite a new estimate that halves the party membership, and "Palestine" did one hear more about communist activities. The ruling (South) Yemen Socialist Party claimed an increase of 7,000 in its membership, strengthened by expanded military/economic ties with the USSR. A statement issued by an unspecified number of "fraternal" parties from Arab countries repeated anti-American and anti-Israel propaganda of the kind that usually emanates from Moscow. The meeting presumably had been convened in either Damascus or Beirut.[38]

North Yemen (YAR), where oil reportedly has been discovered, showed its continuing ability to obtain military aid from both sides: the United States and the USSR. The Soviet Union has supplied the country with 75 percent of the equipment for its air force, from 85 to 90 percent for the army, and almost 70 percent for the navy. At the same time, the YAR maintains strong Western links and indispensable relations with moderate Arab countries. In October, President Ali Abdullah Salih visited Moscow and signed a twenty-year treaty of friendship and cooperation with the USSR, which clearly recognized the YAR's nonalignment.[39]

Western Europe. This region is still affected by Eurocommunism. In Finland, the communist party evicted all pro-Soviet hard-liners from the Central Committee on 26 May 1984. The movement in France, which has only about 15 percent of the national vote (a drop of 5 points), also has shown signs of disaffection with the Soviets. The Greeks and Spaniards each have two parties, one loyal to Moscow, the other not. The Italians are independent, and only the Austrians, Cypriots, Danes, Luxembourgeois, West Germans, and Portuguese remain faithful to Moscow.[40]

As mentioned above, at midyear the French Communist Party (PCF) decided to withdraw from the coalition government with the Socialist Party. The PCF will hold its next party congress during 6–10 February 1985 in Paris. When the Italian party asked for one of the two seats allocated to Italy on the executive commission of the European Economic Community (EEC), Socialist Prime Minister Bettino Craxi turned them down.[41] The well-advertised "opening to the left" appears to be dead in both France and Italy.

During 1984, communist parties no longer held cabinet posts in either Iceland or Finland. The expulsion of Stalinists from the Finnish party will be reviewed at an extraordinary congress, scheduled for March 1985. The CPSU is concerned, as indicated by comments appearing in print toward the end of the year. The party in the United Kingdom is involved in a possible split, resulting from the expulsion by the Eurocommunist leadership of 22 members for "factional ultra-left propaganda."[42]

Among the smaller West European communist parties, only that in San Marino holds as much as one-fourth of the seats (15 of 60) in the legislature. The Cypriot party has been notified by President Spyros Kyprianou that his political movement will no longer cooperate with it.[43] In the Netherlands, a group of orthodox Marxist-Leninists split off in February to form the pro-Soviet Alliance of Communists. A major division in the Norwegian party appears to be the reason for an extraordinary congress in the spring of 1985.

International Communist Front Organizations. During 1984 the Soviet-line international fronts continued their preoccupation with the "world peace" campaign, placing special emphasis on American intermediate-range nuclear missiles in Western Europe. With the deployment of such weapons systems in the Federal Republic of Germany, the United Kingdom, and Italy at the end of December 1983, however, the campaign took a dual approach: pressing for removal of these missiles and preventing emplacement of those scheduled for Belgium and the Netherlands in 1985. The religious and other pacifists, the ecologists, and members of the more truly nonaligned peace movement continued to clash with the Soviet-oriented groups over such a one-sided approach as well as on the status of "unofficial" dissident peace groups in the Eastern bloc, such disagreements coming to a head at the European Nuclear Disarmament meeting during July in Perugia, Italy.[44]

The main secondary emphasis of the fronts appeared to have centered upon Third World developments, most characteristically the call for a New International Economic Order to redress the alleged imbalance in the West's relations with most of Africa, Asia, and Latin America. This campaign was linked to that of world peace, both directly and indirectly in the call for "nuclear-free zones" in the Third World as well as in Europe. Other themes included the "liberation" of the Palestinian and South African peoples, support for the Greek Cypriots, and defense of the Nicaraguan "people" and government.

Highlights of international front organizational activity in 1984 included congresses held by the International Union of Students (IUS), the Afro-Asian Peoples' Solidarity Organization (AAPSO), and the International Association of Democratic Lawyers (IADL) in April, May, and October, respectively. Also, three large preparatory committee meetings for the IUS–World Federation of Democratic Youth (WFDY)–cosponsored World Youth Festival (scheduled for Moscow, summer 1985) were held. Major front personnel changes during the year included new secretaries general for the IUS and WFDY as well as a new president-designate for the AAPSO.

Richard F. Staar
Hoover Institution

NOTES

1. V. V. Zagladin, "Mezhdunarodnaia zhizn': Na perednem krae bor'by – kommunisty," *Agitator*, no. 17 (September 1984): 39. The same figures had been given in *Pravda*, 5 June 1984, p. 4.

2. Moscow radio, 7 December 1984; Foreign Broadcast Information Service, *Daily Report: Soviet Union* (Washington, D.C., hereafter *FBIS-SOV*), 10 December 1984, p. BB/1; also listed in *Rudé právo* (Prague), 7 December 1984.

3. A list of twenty such "vanguard parties" appears in table 1.3 of Richard F. Staar, *USSR Foreign Policies After Détente* (Stanford: Hoover Institution Press, 1985), pp. 14–15.

4. Diarios y Noticias, Buenos Aires, 7 July 1984; ADN, East Berlin, 22 November 1984; cited by Kevin Devlin, "New Moves for a World Communist Conference," *RAD Background Report*, no. 221 (Munich: Radio Free Europe Research, 20 December 1984), pp. 2–3.

5. Sylwester Szafarz, in *Trybuna ludu* (Warsaw), 24 February 1984; cited by Devlin, "New Moves," pp. 4–6.

6. The older Spanish Communist Party (PCE) is criticized for having "lost its positions catastrophically as a consequence of its deviation from Marxism-Leninism and its orientation toward so-called Eurocommunism" (V. V. Zagladin in *Rudé právo*, 18 August 1984, p. 6; *FBIS-SOV*, 23 August 1984, p. BB/5.

7. U. S. Central Intelligence Agency, *World Factbook, 1984* (Washington, D.C., 1984), 274 pp.

8. "Soviet World Outlook" (chapter 1), in Staar, *USSR Foreign Policies*, pp. 3–20.

9. "Torzhestva v Kabule," *Pravda*, 11 January 1985, p. 4.

10. "Konferentsiia MPLA," ibid., 15 January 1985, p. 4.

11. Roger Ricklefs, "Party of Paradox: French Communists Lose Votes, Members but Remain Powerful," *WSJ*, 18 January 1985, pp. 1, 13.

12. *U.S. News & World Report*, 23 January 1984, p. 34; James Brooks in *NYT*, 22 January 1985, on Angola.

13. *NYT*, 24 January 1985.

14. B. Drummond Ayres, Jr., "U.S. Is Planning to Aid Mozambique's Military," ibid., 17 January 1985.

15. Tass dispatch from London; "Forum kommunistov," *Pravda*, 8 January 1985, p. 5.

16. Statement in ibid., 8 August 1984, p. 4.

17. Ibid., 29 December 1984, p. 4.

18. *NYT*, 29 January 1985.

19. Openly stated by Bayardo Arce, one of the nine junta leaders, at a meeting with the pro-Soviet communist party (PSN) in Managua. Transcript published by *La Vanguardia* (Barcelona), 31 July 1984, pp. 3, 8–9.

20. *NYT*, 4 and 11 January 1985.

21. Gaston Vargas, "Two Words," Moscow radio in Spanish to Chile, 14 December 1984; *FBIS-SOV*, 17 December 1984, p. K/3.

22. Tass report in *Pravda*, 15 December 1984, p. 4.

23. *Beijing Review* 27, no. 44 (29 October 1984): 3–16. See also Robert Delfs, "Free-market Communism," *Far Eastern Economic Review*, 25 October 1984, pp. 51–52.

24. *NYT*, 30 December 1984.

25. Charles Smith, "A Thaw in the North?" *Far Eastern Economic Review*, 4 October 1984, pp. 30–32.

26. "Pyongyang Warns of Capitalist Contamination While Seeking Trade With West," *Vantage Point: Developments in North Korea* 8, no. 10 (October 1984): 14. For a copy of the new law, see pp. 15–18.

27. Guy Sacerdoti, "Red 'Army' on the March," *Far Eastern Economic Review*, 28 June 1984, pp. 40–41.

28. David Jenkins, "A Country Adrift . . . ," ibid., 8 November 1984, pp. 25–32.

29. "Afghan Rebels Grow Stronger as War Wears On," *San Francisco Sunday Examiner & Chronicle*, 30 December 1984.

30. Craig Karp, *A 5-Year Summary: Afghan Resistance and Soviet Occupation*, special report no. 118 (Washington, D.C.: Department of State), December 1984, 4 pp.

31. Staar, "The Decision-Making Process" (Chapter 2), *USSR Foreign Policies*, pp. 21–42.

32. *Times* (London), 7 May 1984.

33. Zbigniew K. Brzezinski in *WSJ*, 24 September 1984.

34. Richard F. Staar, "Soviet Relations with East Europe," *Current History* 83, no. 496 (November 1984): 353–56.

35. Ibid., pp. 386–87.

36. Article by Gen. Leon Dubicki, defector from Poland, in *WSJ*, 4 June 1984, p. 24.

37. "Prizyv livanskikh kommunistov," *Pravda*, 1 January 1985, p. 4.

38. Tass dispatch from Beirut; "Zaiavlenie kommunisticheskikh i rabochikh partii arabskikh stran," ibid., 19 July 1984, p. 4.

39. Ibid., 11 October 1984, p. 1.

40. *Economist* (London), 2 June 1984, pp. 36–37.

41. *Est et ouest* (Paris), September 1984, pp. 7–10; *WSJ*, 2 January 1985.

42. M. Kostikov and V. Mikhailov in *Pravda*, 13 December 1984, p. 4; *Morning Star* (London), 18 December 1984, p. 2.

43. Tass report over Moscow radio, 23 December 1984; *FBIS-SOV*, 31 December 1984, p. G4.

44. See *Yearbook on International Communist Affairs, 1984*, pp. 434–35, for background.

AFRICA

Introduction

Party congresses, consolidation, factionalism, and setbacks characterized Marxist ruling parties, revolutionary movements, and communist parties in sub-Saharan Africa during 1984. In Ethiopia, for example, the former military officers began the organizational consolidation by forming a party. In Mozambique, factionalism surfaced in the Marxist-Leninist party for the first time in fifteen years. Party congresses were held in Zimbabwe, Senegal, and the People's Republic of Congo. The South African party held a congress in London.

From an organizational standpoint, the most significant event took place in Ethiopia, where a vanguard Marxist-Leninist party was established. The widespread Ethiopian famine helped to obscure this major political development. Preparations for organizing such a party had been under way since 1979 when the Commission to Organize the Party of the Working People of Ethiopia (COPWE) was created. COPWE itself evolved from the military personnel who overthrew Emperor Haile Selassie in 1974 with the intention of building a socialist state on the principles of Marx and Lenin. After deliberating from 6 to 10 September, the Third Congress of COPWE, which served as the new party's constituent congress, established the Workers' Party of Ethiopia (WPE) on 10 September. Mengistu Haile Mariam, who headed COPWE, became secretary general of the WPE. Mariam stated that "the objective of our future struggle is the building of socialism" (Addis Ababa domestic service, 6 September). The military continues to play a major role in the WPE as it did in COPWE. Seven of the eleven members of the Politburo are military men, and the Provisional Military Administrative Council, or Dergue, remains in place, with Mengistu at its head.

The Zimbabwe African National Union (ZANU) held its first party congress in twenty years in August amidst bitter political infighting based more on personality and ethnicity than on ideology. Attended by more than 6,000 delegates, the congress adopted a new charter, or constitution, which tripled the membership of the Central Committee to 90. A fifteen-member Politburo replaced the National Executive and supersedes the cabinet, which was reduced in size and authority. The new party structures greatly strengthened the position of Robert Mugabe, who was also unanimously re-elected to the party leadership with new titles of first secretary and president. Mugabe thus obtained a party mandate to transform Zimbabwe into a one-party, ZANU-controlled regime. Although he reaffirmed his commitment to establishing a one-party socialist state along Marxist-Leninist lines, he pledged that this goal would be achieved "in the fullness of time and in accordance with the law and the constitution" (*CSM*, 13 August). ZANU is founding an ideological institute, called the Chitepo College of Marxism and Leninism.

In the People's Republic of Congo, the July congress of the Congolese Party of Labor (PCT) resulted in a shift of power toward the president, Denis Sassou-Ngouesso. The new PCT Politburo expanded its membership from ten to thirteen. Five of the new members are viewed as Sassou-Ngouesso loyalists. Other signs pointed to a strengthening of Sassou-Ngouesso's position. He was, for example, appointed chief of government as well as being president, chief of state, and party chairman. There also appeared a loss of power for the civilians in the party and government in favor of the military party members. The PCT signed an agreement with the Communist Party of the Soviet Union (CPSU) for the training of cadres to exchange experiences (AFP, Paris, 8 March; *FBIS*, 9 March).

A national election took place in the People's Republic of Benin on 31 July. All 196 members of the National Revolutionary Assembly were elected from lists of candidates put forward by the ruling and sole legal party, the Revolutionary Party of the People of Benin (PRPB). Benin president General Mathieu Kerekou, selected by the party's Central Committee as the only candidate, was re-elected for another five-year term. Retaining the defense portfolio, Kerekou appointed a new cabinet.

Within Mozambique's Marxist-Leninist party, the Front for the Liberation of Mozambique (FRELIMO), the first high-level split within the leadership in fifteen years occurred. In June, President Samora Moisés Machel dismissed three hard-line Marxist cabinet members—the ministers of interior, security, and natural resources. All three had held office only since May 1983. The dismissals seemed to grow from opposition to abuses of power by the military and police. During meetings of the Central Committee and the People's Assembly in April, harsh criticism was leveled at those responsible for arbitrary arrest and prolonged imprisonment without due process of the courts. The dismissal of the interior minister, Armando Emilio Guebuza, also resulted from his issuing a regulation requiring a travel pass for Mozambicans to travel outside the cities. These tough measures by the military and police could be viewed as efforts to stem an opposition guerrilla force, the Mozambique National Resistance (MNR), which has spread to all of the country's ten provinces.

The spreading war inside Mozambique also resulted in a serious setback for the South African Communist Party (SACP). Under increasing pressure from the MNR, which received support from the Republic of South Africa, Mozambique entered into the Nkomati Accord with Pretoria. This agreement represented not only a reversal of FRELIMO's international stance in Mozambique's relations with its powerful neighbor but also a switch in FRELIMO's support for the African National Congress (ANC). The ANC is closely affiliated with the SACP. Maputo hoped that the agreement, which forbade either Mozambique or South Africa to support insurgent groups opposed to the respective governments, would bring about a collapse of the MNR. This did not happen, but the agreement pulled the rug from beneath the ANC. It lost its staging bases on Mozambican soil, and its forces were reduced to a handful from several hundred within a few weeks. But the ANC still continued its sabotage operations within South Africa.

The SACP's Sixth Congress met in London at some unspecified time in December 1984. A declaration described its role in the "revolutionary union," headed by the ANC, which is controlled by the SACP. A new party statute was adopted, a new Central Committee elected, and the same secretary general, Moses Mabhida, retained.

In neighboring Lesotho, the partial lifting of a 1970 ban on the Communist Party of Lesotho (CPL) in 1984 allowed it to take part in the country's elections but without much success. Although the CPL has supported the government's foreign policy against the Republic of South Africa's policies, it has been critical of the government's "undemocratic and unpopular" domestic policy (Tass, Moscow, 4 May 1982; *FBIS*, 10 May 1982). The CPL remains very pro-Soviet and very anti-PRC. The profile on the CPL in the 1985 *YICA* marks a reappearance of coverage of this party, which had been deleted several years ago due to lack of information.

On the island of Réunion, which is a French overseas department, the Réunion Communist Party (PCR) continued to lose support among voters in 1984. Réunion voters had expected more autonomy from France and greater economic growth from the ruling Socialist-Communist alliance in mainland France. When these hopes failed to materialize, voters turned against the PCR in elections. The PCR also experienced strained relations with Réunion Federation of the Socialist Party and broke relations with the Progressive Left Movement. When the French Communist Party quit the Mitterrand cabinet, the PCR could more easily attack the policies of the French government.

In Angola, the Central Committee of the ruling Marxist-Leninist party, the Popular Movement for the Liberation of Angola–Labor Party (MPLA-PT), convened its fourteenth ordinary session in late June. The Central Committee also met frequently in extraordinary sessions during the year to discuss issues presented in the talks with the Republic of South Africa and the United States. Tension and factional splits characterized many of these meetings, as President José Eduardo dos Santos sought to maintain his coalition as he moved toward a settlement with Pretoria and Washington over the presence of some 25,000

Cuban troops in Angola and a solution to the question of independence for Namibia. Acute resistance to negotiating with South Africa came from Central Committee member and Minister of Foreign Affairs Paulo Jorge, who saw the negotiations as a sacrifice of "international duties." His removal from office on 20 October has been interpreted by some observers as a weakening of the doctrinaire faction in the MPLA-PT (Luanda domestic service, 21 October; *FBIS*, 22 October).

The MPLA-PT continued to face a serious challenge in the countryside from the guerrilla forces of Jonas Savimbi's National Union for the Total Independence of Angola, which operates over much of the country but whose strength remains in the south. There were also scattered reports of military incidents involving Holden Roberto's National Front for the Liberation of Angola in the northeast region of the country. The guerrilla warfare has taken its toll not only in lives but also in agricultural and industrial productivity. The MPLA-PT sought to arrest this trend by promoting the First Congress of the National Union of Angola in August. Dos Santos also sought allies abroad, as he signed protocols with the communist parties of Yugoslavia, Romania, and Poland (Luanda domestic service, 13 April; *FBIS*, 16 April).

Conditions for the Socialist Working People's Party (SWPP), Nigeria's Marxist party, were difficult to determine. There was scant reportage of its activities. The crackdown by the military government on political corruption may also have hindered open SWPP movements. In Senegal, however, the Independence and Labor Party (PIT) held its Second Congress, with 835 delegates attending. The congress denounced the existence of French military bases in Senegal and called for a united front against the Socialist Party government of Abdou Diouf.

Across the continent another communist party also strove to broaden its base of support. The Sudanese Communist Party (SCP), although illegal and pitted in opposition to the government of Jaafar Numeiri, reached out to gain support. It joined the newly formed National Salvation Front in August, which is made up of the Democratic Unionist Party, the 'Umma Party, and the Popular Army for the Liberation of Sudan. The front advocates formation of a provisional government for the purpose of instituting basic liberties, the rule of law, and a nonaligned foreign policy. It of course is dedicated to overthrowing Numeiri. The front's foreign policy statements are in line with those of the radical Arab communist parties, and it denounces "U.S. imperialism" and "Zionist aggression." In December the SCP participated in a gathering of world communist parties in Prague under the auspices of the journal *Problems of Peace and Socialism* (*World Marxist Review*). The position of the Numeiri government remains precarious, and the SCP is poised to exploit any political crises in the Sudan.

Another group operating in Sudan, the Sudanese People's Liberation Movement, defines itself as a Marxist-Leninist movement. It has joined in the fighting in southern Sudan, many of whose inhabitants seek autonomy or independence from the northern-based Moslem rule.

Elsewhere in sub-Saharan Africa and in the contiguous oceans, there occurred events of interest not covered in the following country profiles. These happenings are noted briefly here so as to provide a comprehensive overview. Little was reported, for instance, of the Communist Party of Mauritius. This year, however, its chairman, Leetoraj Chundramun, cabled a message of congratulations to Nicolae Ceauşescu, general secretary of the Romanian Communist Party, on the party's fortieth anniversary (*Scînteia*, Bucharest, 31 August; *FBIS*, 6 September). On another island in the Indian Ocean, to the north of Mauritius, a more significant series of events took place. On the Seychelles, the USSR, East Germany, North Korea, and Libya moved to support the regime of Albert F. Rene and a group of hard-line communist sympathizers who seized power in 1977. The Soviets have a disproportionately large embassy on the islands and are apparently making plans to undertake a naval base there (*Businessweek*, 19 November).

In the Atlantic Ocean off the west coast of Africa, the Soviet Union is also building an air and naval base on the island-nation of São Tomé and Principe. Using such bases in the Democratic Republic of São Tomé and Principe, the Soviets could keep tabs on the U.S. Polaris and Trident nuclear submarine fleet in the South Atlantic. These bases could replace those lost in the Republic of Guinea. Island bases also afford the advantage of isolating counterrevolutionary forces more easily than on the mainland (*Washington Times*, 13 September).

The Revolutionary Council of Guinea-Bissau, which has been ruling the country since a coup d'etat on 14 November 1980, continued to move in a leftward direction. An April 1984 report in the *World Marxist Review* of its first extraordinary congress, held in November 1981, stated that the congress of the African

Party for the Independence of Guinea and Cape Verde Island (PAIGC) resolved to take steps to correct past mistakes of the party. It further resolved "to apply everywhere the principles of democratic centralism and collective leadership, unity and struggle, revolutionary democracy, criticism and self-criticism."

On the mainland, the West African country of Bourkina Fasso (formerly Upper Volta) continued its movement to the radical political left. Captain Thomas Sankara, who seized power on 4 August 1983, announced the creation of Committees for the Defense of the Revolution, which are modeled on the neighborhood committees used in Cuba. He also formed the National Council of the Revolution, with the participation of other left-wing parties. In a speech before the United Nations on 4 October, President Sankara criticized the United States for imperialism and referred to Washington's aggression in Central America and the Caribbean (*Intercontinental Press*, 29 October).

Thomas H. Henriksen
Hoover Institution

Angola

Population. 7,770,000
Party. Popular Movement for the Liberation of Angola–Labor Party (Movimento Popular de Libertição de Angola–Partido do Trabalho; MPLA-PT)
Founded. 1956 (renamed 1977)
Membership. Ca. 31,000
Chairman. José Eduardo dos Santos
Secretariat. 9 members: José Eduardo dos Santos, Lucio Lara, Roberto António de Almeida, Julião Mateus Paulo, Henrique de Carvalho Santos Onambwe, Maria Mambo Cafe, Santana André Pitra, Afonso van Duném (one seat is vacant)
Central Committee. 75 members (before December 1982 purges)
Status. Ruling party
Last Congress. First Extraordinary, December 1980, in Luanda
Last Election. 1980; all 203 candidates MPLA-PT approved
Auxiliary Organizations. National Union of Angola (UNTA), MPLA Youth (JMPLA), Organization of Angolan Women (OMA)
Publications. *A Célula* (MPLA-PT political journal), *A Voz do Trabalhador* (UNTA monthly), *Diário da República* (government daily)

The ruling Marxist-Leninist political party of Angola, the Popular Movement for the Liberation of Angola–Labor Party (MPLA-PT), was founded as the MPLA in 1956. The party, established to overthrow the Portuguese colonial rule in Angola, was led for the most part by urban-based *mesticos* and intellectuals. Recruitment in the rural areas began only after 1960, and the urban leadership retained control. The initial leaders of the MPLA were known as much for being poets as politicians and included Viriato da Cruz, Mario de Andrade, and Agostinho Neto. The MPLA drew its non-African support primarily from the Portuguese Communist Party. From that base, it obtained support, both moral and material, from leftist groups in Western Europe and governments in Eastern Europe.

During the anticolonial war, the MPLA was careful to maintain its structure as a coalition organization. Ideological wars within the MPLA were common, with various factions departing the scene; most notable were those headed by Gentil Viana, Joaquim Pinto de Andrade, and Daniel Chipenda. Finding a physical base was difficult, too. The MPLA was forced out of Zaire by the presence of Holden Roberto's National Front for the Liberation of Angola (Frente Nacional de Libertação de Angola; FNLA) and out of Congo (Brazzaville) after aligning itself with a losing domestic political faction. It found an uneasy base in Lusaka, Zambia, from which it conducted remarkably ineffective guerrilla warfare against the Portuguese. In the 1974–1975 period, however, the MPLA was catapulted into power in Luanda by virtue of being favored by significant factions in the ruling military junta in Lisbon, by its educated cadres' rapid organization of urban Angolans, and by virtue of receiving massive external support from Cuba and the Soviet Union in the military showdown with the two other major factions in Angolan politics, the FNLA and Jonas Savimbi's National Union for the Total Independence of Angola (União Nacional para e Independencia Total de Angola; UNITA).

Organization and Leadership. The MPLA and its Central Committee monopolize political power in the areas of the country under the control of the central government. Day-to-day control is exercised by a much smaller group, the Political Bureau, headed by the president, currently José Eduardo dos Santos, who replaced Agostinho Neto on the latter's death in late 1979. In the period since 1980, a vast political infrastructure has been created on paper, consisting of a People's Assembly, provincial assemblies, and a number of electoral colleges meant to represent the various constituencies appropriate to a Marxist-Leninist state.

The Central Committee held its fourteenth ordinary session in late June (*FBIS*, 21 June), but the group also met repeatedly in extraordinary sessions during the year to deal with the issues of controversy in the talks with South Africa and the United States. The year under review was unusual in that the various splits between factions of the MPLA resulted in little overt political bloodshed, but dos

Santos was busy keeping his coalition together as he moved closer to a settlement with South Africa and the United States. On 18 April, for instance, the Central Committee met in Luanda to deal with misunderstandings surrounding the Joint Military Commission agreement with South Africa. A major declaration was issued the following day to reassure political cadres that the leadership knew what it was doing. The Central Committee reasserted its goals in the South African talks: to "search for a just and honorable peace which reestablishes the full sovereignty of the People's Republic of Angola throughout the national territory and which also creates conditions for a just and internationally accepted settlement of the Namibian question" (ibid., 20 April). Another extraordinary session was held on 24 July as it became clear the cooperation agreement with the South Africans was falling apart (ibid., 25 July).

Various attempts were made to stir up divisions within the MPLA Central Committee. UNITA propaganda, for instance, accused the MPLA of being a "racist movement," meaning that the MPLA discriminated against blacks. A clandestine broadcast charged that the real leadership came entirely from whites and half-castes: Franca Ndalo in the army, Henrique Teles Carreira in the air force, Herminio Escoricio in the petroleum field, Bento Ribeiro in the Ministry of Industry and Energy, and Paulo Teixeira Jorge in the Foreign Ministry (ibid., 7 June). But the greatest cause of dissension came from the sacrifice of "internationalist duties" entailed in negotiating with the South Africans. Resistance to that course came from Central Committee member and Minister of Foreign Affairs Paulo Jorge (ibid., 22 October); he was removed from office on 20 October, a move interpreted by many as a weakening of the doctrinaire Marxist faction in the MPLA.

Mass Organizations. The MPLA took the lead in creating various mass support groups for the regime, especially among youth, women, trade unionists, and various militia groups, even before creating constitutional assemblies. In 1984, there was an evident slackening of emphasis in this area, as attention moved toward strengthening state institutions. An exception to this was the First Congress of UNTA held 11–17 April (ibid., 13–18 April). The closing speech by President dos Santos made clear the priorities of the regime: rather than focus on heroic ideological endeavors, he stressed the need "to increase production and productivity" (ibid., 18 April). Otherwise, there were curious developments in mass organizations. At the 21 July conference of the Methodist church, Roberto de Almeida, Central Committee secretary for ideology, congratulated the church members on their solidarity with the MPLA regime: "What is most important is the common characteristic which makes each of us an Angolan citizen before being a Marxist, Christian, or atheist" (ibid., 23 July).

Domestic Affairs. The domestic realities of Angola since obtaining independence in 1975 have been chaos and war. Economic and social conditions have deteriorated as a result, and draconian control mechanisms have not tamed a situation many observers considered out of control.

Sociopolitical problems in Angola are bound up in the decade-old civil war between the MPLA and UNITA. The latter group controls somewhere between one-third and two-thirds of the country and has the ability to cause significant damage in the heart of Luanda; in 1984, for instance, a bombing disrupted Luanda's power supplies for an entire week, car bombs were delivered to the Cuban troop barracks in Huambo, and mines aimed at Soviet shipping were placed in the harbor of Luanda. In one sense, the problem stems from deeply ingrained ethnic divisions among the Angolan people, especially the thorough alienation of the Ovimbundu people from the MPLA, first through the defection of Daniel Chipenda from the MPLA and in recent years through the highly capable organization of UNITA by Jonas Savimbi. The position of UNITA was enhanced during 1984 with the call by Savimbi for extensive urban warfare against the MPLA (ibid., 1 May), which was followed by considerable evidence that UNITA was capable of doing so.

The economic scene remained bright only in the area of oil production, although even that came under attack with a UNITA bombing (for the first time) of a pipeline in Cabinda province (AFP, 15 July). The minister of petroleum asserted that production had already reached the 1985 target level of 200,000 barrels per day, even as rumors were regularly emanating from Europe and New York that various foreign oil companies were planning to pull out of onshore production as a result of security problems. The rest of the economy remained a shambles, however, gaining greatest publicity through a highly publicized trial of a major ring of diamond smugglers involving pilots, producers, and bureaucrats. The ringleaders were given the death penalty. The infrastructure continued to suffer: the port at Porto Amboim in Cuanza Sul province was scheduled to be closed because the loading dock had rotted and could no longer support cranes (*FBIS*, 13 July).

Dos Santos responded to these problems with major efforts in the area of strengthening state mechanisms. He urged the People's Assembly, meeting in Luanda in late January, to pay close attention to "inefficiency, lack of discipline, and negligence" (ibid., 26 January). In February, dos Santos summarily replaced three provincial commissioners, in Cabinda, Zaire, and Uige (ibid., 3 February). In May, dos Santos created a ministerial-level Defense and Security Council, which was to meet at least every week (ibid., 2 May). In July, Bento Ribeiro, the minister of industry, was replaced by Henrique de Carvalho Santos Onambwe (ibid., 9 July). Finally, the People's Assembly was called into session again in July to consider a wide range of developmental issues (ibid., 26 July).

International Relations. The foreign policy of Angola since independence has been characterized by dependence on Cuba and the Soviet Union. The October 1976 treaty of friendship and cooperation between Moscow and Luanda, valid for twenty years and committing both sides to the closest cooperation between political parties, was the axis around which Angola constructed its foreign relations. The MPLA's claims to be an authentic Marxist-Leninist party were confirmed by that agreement, even more so than by the cooperation agreements with Cuba signed in July 1976. Of course, the Cuban agreements—and subsequent unpublicized agreements—have constituted equally important steps in terms of concrete cooperation. Recent estimates suggest that about 25,000 Cuban military advisers and support personnel are in Angola, along with nearly 5,000 civilian advisers and technicians.

The maintenance of these ties with other communist states and parties results in a constant exchange of high-level visits. For example, the Soviet health minister signed a cooperation agreement in Luanda during a March visit (ibid., 20 March). A delegation from the Supreme Soviet, led by the deputy chairman of the USSR Supreme Soviet Presidium, visited Angola in August (ibid., 24–28

August). The Cuban first vice-minister for foreign relations was in Luanda for consultations 27 June–1 July (ibid., 2 July). Foreign Minister Hun Sen of Kampuchea visited Luanda in mid-June and signed a general accord of cooperation (ibid., 22 June). Consultations with Bulgaria were frequent, partly as a result of the Bulgarian Joint Commission meetings in April (ibid., 27 April), and included visits by the Bulgarian defense minister, 5–8 May, and the chairman of the Bulgarian Council of Ministers, 29 June–3 July (ibid., 7–10 May, 3 July). Dos Santos himself took a working vacation to Yugoslavia, Romania, and Poland in April (ibid., 3–15 April). And finally, a fisheries agreement was signed with the Soviet Union in January, providing for the usual exchange of fish for technical assistance (ibid., 16 January).

Some numbers on longer-term exchanges were released by the Angolans during the year. During a visit by dos Santos to Havana in March, the joint communiqué indicated that 200,000 Cubans had served in Angola during the prior decade (ibid., 20 March). It was also revealed that the number of Angolan students in Czechoslovakia was decreasing, with the return of twenty technical students to Angola in July. They had constituted "the majority of the Angolan students who left for Czechoslovakia in 1979, the year of cadre training" (ibid., 6 July).

Ties with non-Marxist states took on a new cast in 1984. Aggressive efforts by the United States to formalize solutions to the regional conflicts in southern Africa drew the MPLA into major new formulations of ties with the West. At one level, the MPLA was under severe pressure because of UNITA's success in obtaining "quasi-recognition" from governments negotiating the freedom of hostages seized by UNITA (ibid., 8 March, 21 May). Dos Santos undertook a brief trip to France, Spain, and Italy in September to repair ties (ibid., 17 September). Relations with Portugal deteriorated badly during 1984, as UNITA was given an increasingly prominent presence in Lisbon and Angolan complaints to Prime Minister Mário Soares of Portugal went largely unanswered. In August, Foreign Minister Paulo Jorge called the relationship with Portugal "in crisis" (ibid., 10 August). His replacement calmed that relationship to some degree.

A striking departure occurred in ties with South Africa. In talks held on the Cape Verde Islands in January (ibid., 24 January), the United States brokered some of the disagreements between South Africa and Angola. Then, in Lusaka on 16 February, the two countries agreed to create a joint commission to demilitarize the southern provinces of Angola, thus allowing for the removal of South African forces from the area, and presumably ending activity by the South-West African People's Organization in the region. During March, the two countries conducted joint military patrols to enforce their agreement (WP, 3 April). There had even been armed clashes, with fatalities on both sides (FBIS, 20 March). The Soviet Union was not pleased with these developments, as press comment in Moscow indicated (see commentary in Selskaia zhizn; in FBIS, 3 April). The agreement with South Africa ran into problems in the summer, with the two sides exchanging charges in August (FBIS, 2 August). In September, though, dos Santos maintained that the agreement remained alive despite the continuing presence of South African forces: "There are at present two battalions, but at moments of tension this number could rise to five. Nevertheless, the dialogue is continuing, because since January there has been no more fighting between our Angolan forces and those of South Africa." (Ibid., 19 September.)

Another fascinating breakthrough came in ties with the United States. Ties looked bleak when Angola sided with the Soviet Union in boycotting the Los Angeles Olympics, after initially indicating it would participate (ibid., 5 and 26 June). In October, however, the MPLA finally indicated it would link the withdrawal of Cuban troops to a settlement in Namibia, after resisting the concept for three years (WP, 14 October; NYT, 3 November). The principal domestic obstacle, Foreign Minister Paulo Jorge, was dismissed at the same time (WP, 23 October). At that point, with the prospect of procedural talks involving Angola, South Africa, and the United States in the wind, UNITA denounced the talks and threatened additional attacks on Luanda if not included in the negotiations.

Richard E. Bissell
Georgetown University

Benin

Population. 3,910,000
Party. Revolutionary Party of the People of Benin (Parti de la révolution populaire du Bénin; PRPB)
Founded. 1975
Membership. 200 (claimed)
Chairman. Mathieu Kerekou
Politburo. 13 members
Central Committee. 45 members
Status. Ruling party
Last Congress. Second, 13–15 November 1979
Last Election. 1984, all 196 members PRPB approved
Auxiliary Organizations. Revolutionary Defense Organizations, Youth Revolutionary Organization (ORJB), Women's Revolutionary Committee (CRFB)
Publications. *Ehuzu* (government daily)

Benin's most important internal event during 1984 was the election for the National Revolutionary Assembly (ANR), on 31 July. All 196 ANR members were elected from a list of candidates presented by the ruling and sole legal party, the Revolutionary Party of the People of Benin (PRPB). General Mathieu Kerekou, president of both the PRPB and the People's Republic of Benin, defined the nature of the election and the expectations of the regime from the electorate: "...the political censure is entirely in the hands of the masses who are expected to judge each candidate freely, publicly, and openly at the level of their electoral bases by referring to objective criteria based on social practice, militancy, revolutionary commitment, faithfulness, and real devotion to the just and noble cause of the Beninese people and their democratic and popular revolution" (*FBIS*, 2 May). Clearly these "objective" criteria for the selection of parliament members were strictly a matter of ideological definition, which is why the PRPB had selected them in April.

Following his selection as the only candidate by the party's Central Committee on 28 July, Mathieu Kerekou was elected president of Benin for another five-year term. Kerekou's re-election further strengthened his control over the country and the party and demonstrated his ability to manipulate the Marxist-Leninist party organization for his personal political ends. Moreover, in light of Benin's traditional instability until Kerekou's takeover in 1972, Kerekou's survival in power indicates a unique political acumen.

Once re-elected, Kerekou appointed his new cabinet—the National Executive Council's Permanent Committee. The most important positions are occupied by the following:

1. Captain Edouard Zodehougan, minister delegate to the president in charge of interior, security, and territorial administration. The previous occupant of this position (the second most important in the country), Martin Dohou Azonhiho, continued to fall from grace and became prefect of Mono province.

2. Affo Frederic Assogba, who replaced Tiamiou Adjibabe as minister of foreign affairs.

3. Michel Alladaye, one of the main leaders of the 1972 coup that brought Kerekou to power, who retained his position of secondary importance as minister of secondary and higher education.

President Kerekou continued to retain the defense portfolio, as he has since 1972. The most prominent Beninese politician who was promoted in terms of influence, if not formal position, was Guiriguissou Gado. One of Kerekou's most trusted aides, he moved from minister of public works to minister of transportation.

Economically, Benin remains a poor country, burdened with a proportionally huge bureaucracy and dependent on foreign, mostly French, aid. An extraordinary meeting of the Central Committee of the PRPB convened on 14 July. Even Kerekou admitted that the economic situation "continues to worsen every year" (ibid., 19 July). This situation occurred despite the increased production of oil and, since 1984, of natural gas from the Seme fields.

During 1984 Benin maintained its close ties with Libya. In turn Libya provided a small amount of aid and significant rhetorical support for Kerekou. Ties were strengthened by the warm reception given to rebel pro-Libyan forces in Chad and the anti-Israeli hostility that continued to emanate from Porto-Novo. In addition, a Soviet antisubmarine warfare vessel visited Cotonou on 4 September and was met by the chief of the general staff, General Woizan (ibid., 6 September). However, Benin retains close ties with China. In June, then–foreign minister Adjibade visited Beijing. As if to balance close ties with China and even closer ties with the Soviet bloc, on 31 May Benin established formal diplomatic ties with Nicaragua—a statement replete with anti-U.S. overtones.

The PRPB, whose original statutes were written by East German advisers, defines itself as a "vanguard" party and functions as a typical communist party. Its Politburo is officially "elected" by a Central Committee whose members are in turn proposed by the Politburo and voted for by an electorate with no alternative choices. Moreover, the Congress, officially the supreme body of the PRPB, is convened by the Politburo, and its delegates are decided by the Politburo.

"Democratic centralism" is the policymaking method of the PRPB. In practice this means that decisions made by the leadership cannot be challenged by the rank and file. To an essential extent the PRPB leadership is self-perpetuating, which explains the surprising durability of the Kerekou leadership.

The PRPB controls the country primarily through the military. Since 1972 the military has been under the increasingly tight leadership of Mathieu Kerekou and a fluctuating but always small number of close friends dependent upon his patronage abilities. In addition, a number of civilian radicals, easily recruited from among the disproportionately large Beninese intelligentsia and lacking their own power base, provide the regime with loyal and relatively competent technical support, including ministerial positions.

The PRPB maintains a system of social control centered around a number of "mass organizations," the most important of which are the Revolutionary Defense Organizations (patterned on Cuba's Committees for the Defense of the Revolution), the Youth Revolutionary Organization, and the Women's Revolutionary Committee. The PRPB also regulates the limited media outlets: the only national newspaper, *Ehuzu*; the radio station, Voice of the Revolution; and the television network.

Michael S. Radu
Hoover Institution

Congo

Population. 1,745,000
Party. Congolese Party of Labor (Parti congolaise du travail; PCT)
Founded. 1968
Membership. 8,685 (1984)
Chairman. Denis Sassou-Ngouesso
Politburo. 13 members: Denis Sassou-Ngouesso, Camille Bongou, Louis Sylvain Goma, Ange Edouard
   Poungui, Lekounzou-Itihi Ossetoumba, Jean-Michel Bokamba-Yangguma, Pierre Nze, Raymond
   Damasse Ngollo, François Xavier Katali, Jean Ganga-Zandzou, Hilaire Mounthault, Antoine Ndinga-
   Oba, Bernard Combo-Matsiona
Central Committee. 60 members
Status. Ruling and sole legal party
Last Congress. Third, 27–30 July 1984, in Brazzaville
Last Election. 1984, 95 percent, all 153 members PCT approved
Auxiliary Organizations. Congolese Trade Union Confederation (CSC), Revolutionary Union of Con-
   golese Women (URFC), Union of Congolese Socialist Youth (UJSC)
Publications. *Mwezi* (daily), *Etumba* (weekly)

Party and Domestic Affairs. The PCT congress of 27–30 July was the major domestic event in
the Congo during 1984. It resulted in a dramatic
shift of power toward the president, Denis Sassou-
Ngouesso, as well as a generational change at the
top of the Congolese political system.

Membership in the new PCT Politburo increased
from ten to thirteen. Five of the thirteen are new
members and Sassou-Ngouesso loyalists. Sassou-
Ngouesso, in addition to being president, chief of
state, and party chairman, was appointed chief of
government. The office of prime minister was
retained, but its importance is negligible. This
was substantiated by the appointment of Ange
Edouard Poungui, a technocrat without any political or party base.

Since its inception, the PCT has been divided
between civilian ideologues and radical military
men. In 1984 the former began to lose power. Jean
Pierre Thystere Tchikaya, a civilian and the main
ideologue of the party until 1984, was purged from
all functions. This included his second-ranked Pol-

itburo position. Pierre Nze, another civilian radical, retained his Politburo membership but lost his
position as foreign minister.

The generational change within the dominant
radical military group was underscored by the removal of Louis Sylvain Goma from the prime ministership. Goma was a colleague at the French military academy of former presidents Marien
Ngouabi, Alfred Raoul, and Yhombi Opango. He
served as prime minister for over eight years.
Florent Tsiba, one of the main authors of the 1979
coup that brought Sassou-Ngouesso to power, was
also purged.

These changes transformed the Congo into a
personalistic system with all powers, including the
Ministries of Defense and Internal Security, concentrated in the hands of the president. In light of
these changes, it is highly unlikely that Sassou-
Ngouesso's position will be challenged soon or that
his new five-year term as party chairman and president will not be completed. The figure given for
total party membership is impossible to confirm,

but it is clear that the PCT has succeeded in expanding its membership and that most of the new members are loyal to the present leadership.

Threats to the PCT regime are limited, and the opposition is forced to operate primarily in exile. The newly formed opposition umbrella organization, the Patriotic Congolese Movement–Common Front (MPC-FC) was limited to ineffective demands for former president Yhombi Opango's freedom. Opango was jailed without trial after his overthrow in 1979 and was guarded at the Pointe Noire airbase by Cuban and Soviet bloc guards; he now lives under restriction in his native village.

Meaningful participation in the Congo's decisionmaking process is also extremely limited. The 23 September elections for the National Assembly and president were a formality since all candidates were on the PCT list. The official results, which indicate 95 percent of the voters in favor of that list, were to be expected.

Ideology. The nature of internal political shifts in Congolese leadership appears to be personal rather than ideological; however, considering the equal Marxist-Leninist commitment of all factions involved, there are indications of a hardening of the Congolese ideological stance. PCT Central Committee member Jean Royal Kississou-Boma published an article in the *World Marxist Review* (April) on the agricultural policies of Marxist regimes and claimed that "the record of history testifies that socialism has been steadily overcoming the difficulties in agricultural development." He cited Cuba, the USSR, and Bulgaria as examples of such accomplishments. Moreover, the multiplication of party-to-party ties between the PCT and various Soviet bloc communist parties (for example, an agreement with the Soviet party in March, which provided for the training of cadres) also indicates growing encouragement by the PCT of ideological orthodoxy.

Auxiliary Organizations. The PCT is expanding its influence and control over all aspects of the country's social and economic life through a number of organizations. The most important of these are the Congolese Trade Union Confederation, the Revolutionary Union of Congolese Women, and the Union of Congolese Socialist Youth. In addition, the PCT controls all the Congolese media outlets, such as the national radio, Voice of the Congolese Revolution (VRC); the main newspaper, *Etumba*; and the television network.

International Views and Contacts. The greater leadership and party confidence exhibited during 1984 and particularly during the congress also translated into a more active foreign policy. This policy continued the existing trends of good trade relations with the West, particularly with France, and increasingly pro-Soviet diplomacy and public rhetoric.

In May, Cuban foreign minister Isidoro Malmierca Peoli paid a week-long visit to the Congo and further strengthened the ties between the two countries that date from 1963. The joint communiqué published at the end of the visit included the usual condemnations of the United States and expressions of "militant solidarity" with the Salvadoran rebels, Nicaragua, and related causes. Similar rhetoric was manifest in the joint statement signed by the Congo and Bulgaria during the visit to Brazzaville by Bulgarian prime minister Grisha Filipov in July.

In African affairs, the Congo concentrated on strengthening ties with other Marxist-Leninist regimes and playing a significant role in the affairs of Chad. The first aspect was underscored by publicity surrounding Mozambican president Moisés Samora Machel's visit to Brazzaville. His statement, "I have come to learn from you how to conduct revolution in an Africa still affected by colonialist economic exploitation" (*FBIS*, 11 April), clearly indicated his interest in the Congo's ability to attract and retain Western investments while pursuing a consistently anti-Western diplomacy. Nevertheless, the Congolese managed to wrap their acceptance of Mozambique's cooperation with South Africa in a thick layer of anti–South African rhetoric. Machel's visit resulted in the signing of a treaty of friendship and cooperation between the Congo and Mozambique. This was another step toward the formation of a diplomatic axis of African revolutionary regimes, for it added one more element to the existing treaties of this kind between the Congo and Angola, Benin, Guinea, Cuba, the USSR, and various East European regimes.

Congolese diplomacy in Chad, an area of particular interest for Sassou-Ngouesso, took another turn in October, when a conference of the Chadian factions convened in Brazzaville. However, the event only emphasized the intractable nature of Chadian politics and had no discernible impact.

Biography. *Ange Edouard Poungui.* Prime Minister Poungui was born in 1942 and trained as an economist. Poungui was a leader of the Congolese Revolutionary Youth (JRC) during the 1960s and became a PCT Politburo member first under the Ngouabi presidency (1968–1977). He was later purged and became the Congo's representative at the International Monetary Fund as well as president of the Central African Central Bank. Between 1971 and 1973 Poungui was finance minister under Ngouabi. Following the 1984 congress, he became a Politburo member again and prime minister.

Michael S. Radu
Hoover Institution

Ethiopia

Population. 31,998,000
Party. Workers' Party of Ethiopia (WPE)
Founded. 10 September 1984
Membership. 30,000–50,000 (*WP*, 11 September; WPE Constituent Congress, 10 September), with a primary core of 2,000 members and 14,000 fulltime officials
Secretary General. Mengistu Haile Mariam
Politburo. 11 full members: Mengistu Haile Mariam, Fikre-Selassie Wogderess, Fisseha Desta, Tesfaye Gebre Kidan, Berhanu Bayih, Legesse Asfaw, Addis Tedlay, Hailu Yimenu, Amanuel Amde Michael, Shimelis Mazengia, Alenu Abebe; 6 alternate members
Secretariat. 8 members: Fisseha Desta, Legesse Asfaw, Shimelis Mazengia, Fasika Sidelil, Shewandagn Belete, Wubeset Desie, Ashagre Yigletu, Embibel Ayele
Central Committee. 136 full members, 64 alternate members
Status. Ruling party
Last Congress. Constituent, 6–10 September 1984, in Addis Ababa
Last Election. N/a
Auxiliary Organizations. All-Ethiopian Peasants' Association; Kebelles; All-Ethiopia Trade Union; Revolutionary Ethiopia's Women's Association; Revolutionary Ethiopia's Youth Association
Publications. *Serto Ader*, *Meskerem*, *Addis Zemen*, *Ethiopian Herald*, *Negarit Gazeta*

A vanguard political party was established in Ethiopia on 10 September. Preparations for its establishment had been under way since 1979 when the Commission to Organize the Party of the Working People of Ethiopia (COPWE) was created. The constitution of the Workers' Party of Ethiopia (WPE) concludes the first decade of the revolution and sets the stage for moving Ethiopia more firmly into an orthodox Marxist-Leninist framework. One of its first priorities will be the effort to deal with the famine that is presently overwhelming the country. More than 6 million people are estimated to be affected by hunger.

Leadership and Party Organization. After deliberating from 6 to 10 September, the Third Congress of COPWE, which served as the WPE's Constituent Congress, established a vanguard Marxist-Leninist party on 10 September. According to Mengistu Haile Mariam, the WPE's secretary general, "It will serve us as a scientific guideline for our struggle in implementing the plan to hasten the construction of the new society . . . The objective of our future struggle is the building of socialism" (Addis Ababa domestic service, 6 September). Grigori Romanov, the head of the Soviet delegation to the Constituent Congress and member of the Politburo and secretary of the Soviet party's (CPSU) Central Committee, maintained that "the formation of the WPE is a major victory . . . Aims can only achieve their goal through a party . . . that will unwaveringly follow its basic line. That Ethiopia's progress . . . under the vanguard leadership of the party will be further secured is unquestionable." (Ibid., 7 September.) Konstantin Chernenko, general secretary of the CPSU, stressed that the formation of the WPE "is a fundamental step in the development process of Ethiopia's revolution" (*Pravda*, 11 September). Among those attending the establishment of the WPE in Addis Ababa were Sam Nujoma, the president of Namibia's South-West African People's Organization; East Germany's Erich Honecker; Kenyan president Daniel arap Moi; Ali Nasir Muhammad al-Hasani of South Yemen; Prime Minister Robert Mugabe of Zimbabwe; President Samora Machel of Mozambique; and President José Eduardo dos Santos of Angola. Representatives of most socialist countries also attended.

Although the creation of the WPE represents a move in the direction of increased civilian participation in the ongoing socialist revolution, some contradictions to pure Marxist orthodoxy continue. Seven of the eleven members of the Politburo and 20 percent of the Central Committee are from the military (*NYT*, 11 September). And though the WPE replaces COPWE, the Provisional Military Administrative Council, or Dergue, remains in place, with Mengistu retaining the leadership of that military organization. Thus, the Dergue presumably will continue to play a political role in Ethiopia that may overshadow the WPE. For if the WPE was to be *the* vanguard political entity in Ethiopia, there would have been no need to retain the organization of the Dergue. Still, as East Germany's Erich Honecker stated, "The funding of the WPE is the culmination of the revolutionary struggle of the Ethiopian people" (*Neues Deutschland*, 6 September).

Domestic Party Affairs. In preparation for the development of the WPE, by September COPWE organizations had been established at 33 regional levels, 70 subregional levels, and 240 district levels. After the party was set up, these organizations turned into WPE organizations. In addition, political training schools were established on a regional basis, and Marxist political theory was incorporated into the educational curriculum throughout the educational system. The theoretical newspaper of WPE, *Meskerem*, was upgraded and expanded to allow more people access to it (AFP, 24 January). It is clear that the attempt to ensure ideological unity and organizational cohesion between the party and the people was a major priority of the political leadership. The propaganda apparatus, the political and educational structures, and the media were utilized to prepare the population for the transformation of COPWE into the Leninist WPE. The Soviet Union, and other members of the socialist commonwealth, provided Ethiopia several hundred ideological teachers to prepare the way for the establishment of the WPE. All this was done to smooth the way for the new party, which "will become the sole instrument to effect the realization of communism" (*CSM*, 15 February).

Auxiliary Organizations. The primary responsibility of the five auxiliary organizations throughout the year was to assist Ethiopia's Relief and Rehabilitation Commission in dealing with the effects of the drought and famine that struck Ethiopia in 1983. Although the organizations also played a large role in preparing the population for the creation of the WPE, the intensity of the famine forced them to shift their resources, particularly their human resources, to attending to the consequences of the famine. With an estimated 6 million Ethiopians affected by the worst drought and famine ever to hit Ethiopia, the Ethiopian government was forced to turn to international relief agencies and foreign governments to cope with the disaster (*NYT*, 28 October, 4 November). The United States, through its Agency for International Development (AID), provided $130 million in food aid, while Western relief agencies donated another $120 million in food (ibid., 3 and 11 November). And although the USSR has provided Ethiopia with about $4 billion in weapons since 1978, in 1984 it provided only about $3 million in food aid. The Soviet Union has sent trucks to help in the distribution of food to the hungry, but it has not felt compelled to allocate much food. Some of the East European states have, however, contributed some $30 million worth of food aid, most particularly Bulgaria, which pledged $12.7 million (ibid., 11 November). The international effort was helped by the showing of newsreel footage on major television stations in Great Britain and the United States, which elicited millions of dollars in donations from citizens of both countries. International governments and private agencies worked with the Ethiopian Red Cross, the Relief and Rehabilitation

Commission, and the auxiliary organizations to organize the distribution of donated food. The Ethiopian government has sought to organize and work with all international agencies "and to give top priority to food shipments at its ports" (ibid., 3 November). And, as Mengistu stated, "We are touched by the humanitarian outpouring which the people of [the United States and Europe] demonstrated" (ibid., 17 November).

International Views, Positions, and Activities. Mengistu Haile Mariam visited Moscow 30 March to 1 April. During this time he held talks with Konstantin Chernenko, Foreign Minister Andrei Gromyko, and Defense Minister Dimitri Ustinov. Discussion revolved around the establishment of the WPE and the continuing military cooperation of the two states. Chernenko maintained that the visit was "yet another important proof of the full-blooded and dynamic cooperation between the Soviet Union and Ethiopia" (Tass, 30 March). A few days prior to the visit, Ethiopia and the USSR signed a Joint Development Protocol in which the Soviet Union agreed to aid Ethiopia in programs embracing agriculture, industry, mining, energy production, irrigation development, and trade. To this end, the USSR approved for 1984–1986 development loans and grants totaling $384 million. (Addis Ababa domestic service, 13 March.)

Relations with East Europe were also strengthened. In April a military protocol was signed with Bulgaria in which Bulgaria agreed to increase military aid to Ethiopia. Earlier János Kádár of Hungary met an Ethiopian delegation led by Fisseha Desta in an effort to develop interparty and interstate relations (MTI, 8 March).

Although relations with Cuba continued on the economic and educational levels, the Cuban military garrison in Ethiopia was reduced from 13,000 to 3,000 troops. The two primary reasons were the very limited military activity with Somalia in the Ogaden and the inability of Ethiopia to continue supporting the troops. (*NYT*, 25 January.) Sudanese president Jaafar Numeiri accused Ethiopia of waging a secret war against his country by helping Sudanese rebels trying to overthrow his government. Discussions between the two countries, brokered by Egypt, were canceled by Ethiopia in March because, according to the Ethiopian foreign minister, the United States and the Sudan were in "collusion and conspiracy" against Ethiopia (ibid., 12 March). At the time of the aborted meeting, the United States announced that it would increase its military aid to the Sudan to protect it against security threats from Ethiopia. In May Ethiopia's chargé d'affaires in Washington, Tesfaye Demeke, sought and received political asylum in the United States, maintaining that he had become "isolated within a government established with Soviet power and perpetuated with Soviet arms" (ibid., 8 May). Three months earlier, Ethiopia had expelled four U.S. diplomats from Addis Ababa, accusing them of fomenting domestic discontent. The United States responded in kind, but one of those expelled, the commercial counselor, Gelagay Zawde, requested and received political asylum. On 1 June Ethiopia's Olympic Committee announced that it would not participate at the Olympics held in Los Angeles. In 1984 Ethiopia established diplomatic relations with Nicaragua and the Ivory Coast.

Ethiopia's intermittent battles with Somalia in the Ogaden continued, but on a vastly reduced level. In the north, however, the liberation movements in Eritrea and the Tigre Popular Liberation Front dramatically increased their attacks against Ethiopian troops in Eritrea and Tigre. According to Assefau Bariamikael of the Eritrean Liberation Front–Revolutionary Council, "Support is broader than ever" (*Avanti*, Rome, 17 September). Although Ethiopia, with its Soviet, Cuban, East German, and South Yemeni allies, continues to maintain control over both regions, its position has deteriorated since 1983. To some degree this is a result of the famine, which has hit the regions of Wello, Tigre, and Eritrea particularly hard.

Peter Schwab
State University of New York
College at Purchase

Lesotho

Population. 1,474,000
Party. Communist Party of Lesotho (CPL)
Founded. 1962
Membership. No data
Leadership. R. Mataji (chairman), Jacob M. Kena (secretary general), John Motloheloa (secretary), Jacob Mosotho (1982 spokesman)
Status. Semilegal (see below)
Last Congress. No data
Last Election. N/a
Auxiliary Organizations. International front affiliates probably auxiliary to the ruling Basotho National Party (BNP) rather than the CPL (see below)
Publications. None known

The 1970 ban on CPL activities was "partially lifted" in 1984 so that the party could take part in the country's forthcoming elections, and the organization currently describes itself as the only communist party operating openly in southern Africa (*Rand Daily Mail*, Johannesburg, 2 October). The improved status of the CPL is apparently related to the notation by Tass as early as mid-1982 that although the party was then underground, it supported the "positive elements" of the government's foreign policy while criticizing its "undemocratic and unpopular" domestic policy (Tass, Moscow, 4 May 1982; *FBIS*, 10 May 1982). But it appeared even more related to the turn of the government toward the communist bloc noted a year later (*Arab News*, Jidda, 20 June 1983). Currently, the CPL sees itself as a possible junior partner to the BNP in a post-election government (*Rand Daily Mail*, 2 October).

The CPL was formerly noted as having its primary support from Basotho workers in South Africa (*Political Handbook of the World*, 1982–83, p. 292), but since partial legalization it has been reported as having strength in the capital city of Maseru as well as in certain parts of southern Lesotho (*Rand Daily Mail*, 2 October). The CPL is strongly pro-Soviet and anti-Chinese and, of course, opposed to the government of South Africa (ibid., Tass, Moscow, 4 May 1982; *FBIS*, 10 May 1982).

In October 1983, with the launching of the Lesotho Peace and Solidarity Committee (LPSC), the country's affiliate of the World Peace Council (WPC) was taken over by the ruling BNP, whose secretary general, Vincent M. Makhele, became LPSC chairman (*Peace Courier*, Helsinki, December 1983, p. 8). At the time of the WPC's 1980 congress, the Lesotho affiliate had been dominated by the opposition Basotho Congress Party (BCP) (World Peace Council, *List of Members, 1980–1983*, Helsinki, p. 90). By April 1984, the Student Council of Lesotho, another probable BNP auxiliary, given the conditions of the time, had been admitted to the International Union of Students (*Komsomolskaia pravda*, Moscow, 17 April), another major international communist front organization.

In August 1984, V. M. Makhele, who had just been appointed Lesotho's foreign minister, led a BNP delegation to the USSR (*Sovetakan Ayastan*, Erevan, 1 September).

Wallace H. Spaulding
McLean, Virginia

Mozambique

Population. 13,413,000
Party. Front for the Liberation of Mozambique (Frente de Libertação de Moçambique; FRELIMO)
Founded. 1962
Membership. 110,323 (*African Communist*, 4th Quarter, 1983)
Secretary General. Samora Moisés Machel
Politburo. 11 members: Samora Moisés Machel, Marcelino dos Santos, Joaquim Alberto Chissano, Alberto Chipande, Armando Emilio Guebuza, Jorge Rebelo, Mariano de Araújo Matsinhe, Sebastião Marcos Mabote, Jacinto Soares Veloso, Mário de Graça Machungo, José Óscar Monteiro
Secretariat. 6 members: Samora Moisés Machel, Marcelino dos Santos, Joaquim Alberto Chissano, Jorge Rebelo, Armando Panguene, José Luís Cabaço
Central Committee. 118 members
Status. Ruling party
Last Congress. Fourth, 26–29 April 1983, in Maputo
Last Election. 1977; won all 226 seats in the National People's Assembly
Auxiliary Organizations. Organization of Mozambican Women (Organização da Mulher Moçambicana); Mozambique Youth Organization
Publications. *Notícias* (daily); *O Tempo* (weekly); *Diário de Moçambique* (daily); *Domingo* (Sunday paper); *Voz da Revolução* (Central Committee organ)

FRELIMO assumed power in the southeast African country of Mozambique in 1975 after successfully waging a ten-year guerrilla war for independence from Portugal. With the collapse of Portuguese rule, FRELIMO proclaimed an independent People's Republic of Mozambique. (For more detail on the origins and background of FRELIMO, see *YICA*, 1982, p. 37.) FRELIMO is the country's sole political party, and its eleven-man Politburo is the country's most important body.

Because of continuing and major setbacks in Mozambique's economy and in the war against internal opposition, FRELIMO embarked on a significant change in foreign policy by negotiating a treaty with the Republic of South Africa and by joining the International Monetary Fund and the World Bank. Further evidence of these same problems also appeared in cabinet shuffles and in the first apparent fissures within the FRELIMO leadership in fifteen years.

Organization and Leadership. The trajectory of FRELIMO's political orientation has moved leftward since its founding in 1962. By its Second Congress (1968), FRELIMO had adopted many aspects of standard communist organizations. For example, it adhered to democratic centralism, cell structure, self-criticism, and Marxian phraseology. The radicalization process brought internal feuds and assassinations as the extreme left wing consolidated its hold over the nationalist front. The most prominent murder involved Eduardo Mondlane, the first president of FRELIMO. A troika replaced the assassinated Mondlane for six months until Samora Moisés Machel emerged as president as well as head of the guerrilla army.

In 1977 the Third Congress approved the Central Committee's recommendation to transform FRELIMO into a "Marxist-Leninist vanguard party." Even before this announced change, FRELIMO had already structured its organization along typical communist party lines. The Central Committee (now 118 members), for example, is approved by the congress and is to carry out its policies. The Politburo, as in most communist structures, shapes policy for FRELIMO. Many of its members also have ministerial portfolios and as such have seats on the Council of Ministers—the government's cabinet. Mozambique's constitution views the National Assembly as the country's highest legislative organ. Delegates come from throughout the country and are chosen by an elaborate election process every five years. FRELIMO also introduced local, district, and provincial assemblies. Constitutional provisions empower President Machel (who is also head of the party) to appoint provincial governors and members of the Council of Ministers, among others. Additionally, the president has the power to annul decisions made by the provincial assemblies. The Third Congress abolished the office of vice-president. In a practice unique to Mozambique, high FRELIMO officials have been relieved of ministerial duties and dispatched to posts as provincial or district leaders for periods of time. They also serve as first secretaries of the party in their areas. The practice of strong appointed district administrators follows from the Portuguese tradition.

The first high-level and public split within the FRELIMO leadership in fifteen years occurred in the year under review. In June, President Machel dismissed three hard-line Marxist cabinet members: Interior Minister Armando Emilio Guebuza, Security Minister Mariano Matsinhe, and Natural Resources Minister José Carlos Lobo (*NYT*, 17 June). Former Justice Minister José Óscar Monteiro, a Politburo member, replaced Guebuza, who kept his position on the Politburo. A senior official in the Ministry of Justice, Ossumane Ali Dauto, assumed the title of minister of justice. In September Machel appointed Guebuza, who holds the military rank of lieutenant general, to the position of minister in the office of the president. Matsinhe, who also retained his seat on the Politburo, became governor of Niassa province. He was replaced as minister of security by Sergío Vieira, a former assistant to the president as well as a past minister of agriculture, governor of Niassa, and vice-minister of defense. Lobo received the position of a vice-minister of foreign affairs and was replaced by the state secretary of hydrocarbons, Abdul Magid Osman. All three had been in office only since May 1983. This reshuffling appeared to stem from a serious opposition to abuses of power by the police and military (for details see the Domestic Affairs section of this profile).

Mass Organizations. Like other organizations involved in political or guerrilla struggle, FRELIMO made special appeals to several segments of the population during the war for independence. Women, for example, received much attention. FRELIMO continued this focused appeal after assuming power. According to its pronouncements, the Organization of Mozambican Women (OMM) seeks to liberate women from their traditional standing and to increase their economic and political opportunities in addition to publicizing and implementing the party line in the country as a whole. The OMM is particularly against child marriage, polygamy, and the bride-price. Formed in 1973, it is the oldest and most active of the mass organizations. One source reported that by 1980 it was firmly established throughout Mozambique (Allen Isaacman and Barbara Isaacman, *Mozambique: From Colonialism to Revolution, 1900–1982*, Boulder, Colo.: Westview Press, 1983, p. 127). In November the OMM held its fourth major gathering.

The party also set up the Mozambique Youth Organization (OJM) after the Third Party Congress (1977). Its charter called for attention to the need to mobilize Mozambicans between the ages of 18 and 35. The OJM initiated campaigns in urban areas against what it termed "bourgeois habits." The third mass organization is the Production Councils, which were formed in 1976 but extended beyond Maputo only after the Third Party Congress. The mission of the Production Councils is to mobilize workers to participate "in an active, collective, and conscious way in the discussion and resolution of their problems, especially in relation to production and productivity" (*Notícias*, 12 November 1976). The goal was to establish these councils in all factories, mills, and foundries. FRELIMO plans also called for the establishment of national organizations for artists and journalists, but the progress of this objective has been slow.

The People's Forces for the Liberation of Mozambique (FPLM). Following independence, FRELIMO began the transformation of its guerrilla forces into a conventional army, seeking help from the Soviet Union, East Germany, and North Korea. With an estimated 15,000 regular troops raised by a nationwide draft, the FPLM's original mission called for it to be used as a defense force and a mobilizing cadre to spread the party's message. At a celebration in 1983 marking his fiftieth birthday, Machel, who holds the military title of field marshal, announced a five-year goal for the army. By 1988, the army, he said, "must be the most modern in Africa in terms of study, combat and production" (Maputo domestic service, 30 September 1983; *FBIS*, 3 October 1983).

The astounding success since 1982 of the Mozambique National Resistance (MNR), which had originally been perceived as a disorganized band, has sorely tested the FPLM and kept it off balance despite repeated government claims that it has smashed the MNR's fighting capacities and inflicted huge casualties on its forces. Formed initially from former black and white soldiers in the Portuguese colonial army, the MNR has picked up its own momentum. Initially, it received white Rhodesian support and then South African aid. To combat its opposition, FRELIMO turned to its communist allies. Soviet military assistance, however, has been perceived as ineffective. According to one report, Moscow has refused to renegotiate early post-independence arms agreements and continues to supply costly and unneeded conventional equipment, such as tanks and jet aircraft. A lack of morale in the army, which is 75 percent conscripts, has also hampered an effective counterinsurgency campaign against the MNR (*CSM*, 18 October).

The military success of the MNR during the course of the year accounted for FRELIMO's negotiations with South Africa and a growing confidence among MNR officials, who stated that their forces were present in all ten provinces of Mozambique (see interview with Armando Khembo Gumbe dos Santos, secretary of information for the MNR, and Artur Vilankulu, executive director of Friends of Mozambique, *Washington Times*, 19 September). Guerrilla raids and sabotage continued as the year closed. MNR forces made determined efforts to cut the Tete highway running from Zimbabwe to Malawi through the northwestern province of Tete (*Guardian*, London, 6 December).

Domestic Affairs. The leadership changes noted above were reported as a response by the top level of the FRELIMO party to charges of abuses of

military and police power, including arbitrary arrests and punishments. Although such changes very well could stem from hidden motives of the party elite, the shuffles reportedly developed from issues raised with unexpected force during the party's Central Committee meeting on 19–21 April and at the People's Assembly session on 24–27 April (Maputo domestic service, 24 April; *FBIS*, 26 April). Both gatherings passed resolutions criticizing the SNASP (security police), regular police, soldiers, and local officials for arbitrary detentions without trial. The country's highest court, the Revolutionary Military Tribunal, also came in for criticism for its lack of due-process procedures (*Guardian*, 24 April).

These charges and the resulting changes were reminiscent of 1981 when President Machel launched a so-called legality campaign to curb excesses by the police and military. That campaign resulted in the dismissal of several SNASP agents. But in 1984 the consequences reached into the Politburo itself. During a speech on 12 May, Machel singled out Armando Guebuza, Mariano Matsinhe, and Sebastião Mabote. Machel expressed concern that abuses by the police and others hurt the government's struggle against the MNR. In another speech, in the city of Nampula in late May, Machel received prolonged applause when he stated that "in our cities, the police now act worse than the colonial police" (Maputo domestic service, 24 May; *FBIS*, 25 May).

As sketched above, the reshuffle took place in mid-June. Despite presidential criticism of his actions, Mabote, the vice-minister of defense, kept his post. The dismissal of Guebuza from the Ministry of the Interior can be viewed as the first public split in the FRELIMO leadership since the tensions of the guerrilla war with Portugal brought on fractures, dismissals, and political assassinations, culminating in the murder of FRELIMO's first president, Eduardo Mondlane. Guebuza's fall from grace probably owed as much to his role in the organization and implementation of Operation Production as to any other factor. Operation Production accounted for the forced expulsion of tens of thousands of unemployed from the major urban areas in 1983. Mozambican newspaper coverage was openly critical of the removals, for they resulted in unfair consequences and were undertaken without due process in sending urban dwellers to the remote provinces of Niassa and Cabo Delgado. Preparations were inadequate and some of the exiled starved to death (*Notícias*, 12 July). To make matters worse for Guebuza, he was held responsible for the introduction early in the year of a strict new regulation that required a pass for travel from one town to another. A circular letter from the Ministry of the Interior laid down firm guidelines for issuance of the internal passes (Maputo domestic service, 29 February; *FBIS*, 1 March).

The harshness of police and military actions against Mozambican civilians represented one sign among many of the poor military posture of the FRELIMO forces. Another sign was FRELIMO's attempt to raise the level of vigilance among urban dwellers and to enlist them on the government's side. One such effort was made when Jorge Rebelo, Politburo member and first secretary of Maputo, launched an organizational campaign by establishing brigades to reactivate the people's militia and vigilante groups in the city (Maputo domestic service, 4 May; *FBIS*, 7 May).

Economic problems continued to plague Mozambique's development. After coming to power, FRELIMO launched an all-encompassing radicalization of the economy by state ownership and state planning. A ten-year plan, approved in 1981, called for "victory over underdevelopment" in just one decade. It envisioned an increase in gross national product of 17 percent each year for the next ten years and an agricultural expansion of fivefold by 1990. Such growth rates had no precedent anywhere in the world. Realization, according to FRELIMO planners, could be achieved only through big development projects, with a total budget of $10 billion. Accordingly, huge state farms and large industrial facilities received approval and resources for agricultural production as well as steel, chemical, fertilizer, and aluminum production. The overly ambitious goals spelled disaster.

The Fourth Congress, held in April 1983, came too late to head off a rapidly collapsing economy. It called a halt to further new big projects and signaled a victory for small and private farming over state-run agriculture. But the ten-year plan is still theoretically the development blueprint. Elements within the leadership look to the nonaggression pact with South Africa and the continuing rapprochement with the West and international financial institutions, in part, to provide the funds for big projects ("Mozambique," *Quarterly Economic Review of Tanzania, Mozambique*, Annual Supplement, 1984, p. 24).

In an address to the annual meeting of the People's Assembly in April, Machel admitted governmental mistakes but criticized managers in the state-run companies for their salary increases. He attacked the management, stating: "Our companies work badly or don't work at all" (*Guardian*, 28 April).

The year 1984 saw no diminution in the economic slide. In fact, the government early in the year, in effect, declared bankruptcy by requesting a rescheduling of debt payments totaling $862 million. Because most French and Italian debt matures after 1986, the United Kingdom was the largest creditor nation affected; it was followed by Brazil and Portugal. FRELIMO's policies, mismanagement, drought, and the continuing war in the countryside against the MNR forced Maputo to look for foreign aid for food.

Hunger again stalked the land. In 1983 some 100,000 people died as famine swept through much of Mozambique. Early in 1984 about 100,000 refugees from hunger poured across the border into Zimbabwe (*NYT*, 26 February). Another year of drought exacerbated the conditions leading to successive poor harvests. Mozambique's food crisis, however, also results from other factors. Part of the explanation lies with FRELIMO policies of disrupting peasant agriculture to promote large-scale farming cooperatives or state farms. Another factor in the continuing famine rests with the widespread antigovernment insurgency. With little incentive, rural families ate their seeds rather than storing them to plant in the future. United Nations officials looked toward a grim food shortage in the first half of 1985 (ibid., 18 November).

FRELIMO's economic woes caused a reassessment and an apparent turn to the West to obtain development in the past few years. But Mozambique has retained its close ties with the Soviet bloc. FRELIMO officials made a number of trips abroad. President Machel visited the People's Republic of China (17–21 July), North Korea (22–24 July), Vietnam (25–27 July), Romania (22–24 August), and Bulgaria (25–27 August) in search of financial assistance. In Bucharest, Machel met East German president Erich Honecker, as well as Romanian leaders. His trips resulted in considerable offers of assistance, especially for consumer goods. Consumer items are vital to provide incentives to the Mozambican peasantry to produce agricultural goods.

Visitors from communist countries also made trips to the People's Republic of Mozambique, and a

Soviet fleet made its annual stop in Maputo's harbor. For example, a delegation of Soviet party officials headed by R. Kh. Abdullayev, secretary of the Uzbek Communist Party Central Committee, visited Mozambique in June. This delegation made its trip in accordance with plans for party links between the Soviet party and FRELIMO (*Pravda*, 6 June; *FBIS*, 8 June).

Mozambique also concluded an agreement on cooperation in fishing with the Soviet Union. Under its provisions, the Soviets will provide three fishing vessels and help Maputo establish fishing cooperatives. Jointly the two countries are to estimate the fisheries resources of Mozambican coastal waters (Moscow radio, 13 August; *FBIS*, 14 August). The USSR consul general in Beira announced the granting of a new credit line to Mozambique (Maputo domestic service, 21 May; *FBIS*, 22 May). Mozambique and the Soviet Union also signed a medical cooperation agreement for the 1985–1987 period. The agreement continued previous arrangements whereby the USSR sent doctors to Mozambique and Maputo dispatched health specialists to the Soviet Union to gain experience in fighting infectious diseases (Maputo domestic service, 24 October; *FBIS*, 25 October).

Breaking with established policy, FRELIMO also sought, successfully, to join the World Bank and the International Monetary Fund (Maputo domestic service, 24 September; *FBIS*, 26 September). Unable to renegotiate its debts, FRELIMO turned to the Club of Paris of Western creditors; they insisted that Mozambique first join the World Bank and the IMF. Subsequently, Western creditors agreed to reschedule Mozambique's foreign debts. Under the provisions worked out by the Club of Paris, Mozambique will begin paying off the debt in 1990 and will have six years to complete payment (Maputo radio, 29 October; *FBIS*, 30 October). Mozambique also published a new, long-expected foreign investment law in August. It guaranteed new investments against nationalization. A proviso did lay down exceptional instances for seizure, but in these cases compensation would be paid, according to the law. Disputes are to be arbitrated through the International Chamber of Commerce.

International Affairs. Reversals in domestic economic policy were exceeded in 1984 by a startling turnaround in Mozambique's relations with its powerful neighbor, the Republic of South Africa. In March, Mozambique reluctantly signed the Nkomati Accord with South Africa (for the full text of the accord, see *Rand Daily Mail*, Johannesburg, 17 March). As a determined foe of South African racial policies, FRELIMO's switch came about because of its own deteriorating military position. Maputo hoped that the nonaggression pact, which forbade either Mozambique or South Africa to support insurgent groups opposed to the respective governments, would bring about the collapse of the MNR. In fact, the MNR stepped up its sabotage and insurgency campaign, forcing FRELIMO in October to sign a cease-fire agreement directly with the rebels (*NYT*, 5 October). FRELIMO officials accused the South Africans of secretly still supporting the MNR, but Pretoria denied this and pressed FRELIMO to deal directly with the MNR. This culminated in the cease-fire agreement but not in any lessening of the fighting, which continued to the end of the year without sign of slowing.

The rapprochement with South Africa also entailed economic development assistance for improving the Mozambican transportation network. Soon after the signing of the Nkomati Accord, Mozambique signed a trilateral agreement with South Africa and Portugal for the supply of electricity to South Africa (Johannesburg domestic service, 2 May; *FBIS*, 3 May). In spite of several such cooperative ventures between Mozambique and South Africa, relations between the two states remained strained at year's end.

The end of the year did witness improved relations between FRELIMO and the African National Congress (ANC), the chief opponent in exile of the South African government. Under the conditions of the Nkomati Accord, Mozambican authorities ordered armed police to raid the homes of ANC members to confiscate weapons and detain activists shortly after the signing of the accord (*NYT*, 26 March). One of the homes raided was that of Joe Slovo, a prominent party figure in the ANC. Mozambique reported that it expelled some 800 members of ANC and reduced its presence to a ten-man office in the capital (*Economist*, 2 June).

Publications. Since independence FRELIMO has controlled the country's print and broadcast media. The party depends on two publications to carry its written message—the daily paper *Notícias* and the weekly magazine *O Tempo*. In 1981 the government launched two more national-circulation newspapers: *Diário de Moçambique* in Beira, the country's second largest city, and a Sunday paper, *Domingo* (for additional background, see *YICA*, 1982, pp. 41–42). Another publication, *Voz da Revolução*, a paper of the Central Commit-

tee, deals with Marxist theory and FRELIMO policies.

Thomas H. Henriksen
Hoover Institution

Nigeria

Population. 88,148,000
Party. Socialist Working People's Party (SWPP)
Founded. 1963
Membership. No data
Secretary General. Dapo Fatogun
Politburo. 4 members: Chaika Anozie (chairman), Wahab Goodluck (deputy chairman), Hassan Sunmonu (president, Nigerian Labour Congress), Lasisi A. Osunde
Secretariat. No data
Central Committee. No data
Status. Proscribed
Last Congress. First, December 1965
Last Election. November 1983, SWPP ineligible
Auxiliary Organizations. No data
Publications. *New Horizon*

The year under review was a slow one for the SWPP. The military coup of 31 December 1983 brought into power another federal military government, which promptly banned all political parties and all political activity. Information about the SWPP and its members has been scant. The military government has clamped down on trade union activities to the extent that the Nigerian Labour Congress (NLC) has been quiescent. None of the SWPP leaders has been reported as having attended international Marxist gatherings, nor have any of them published articles in the international communist press. A contributing factor to this lack of activity has been the turmoil within Nigeria itself. The military government arrested hundreds of politicians and has brought many to trial for corruption and malfeasance. Scores of civil servants in both the central and the state governments have been

fired. A new currency was introduced, causing short-term dislocation. Overriding all else has been a dramatic loss of petroleum revenues, which Nigeria needs for its foreign exchange. Oil revenues were $22.4 billion in 1980 but fell to $9.6 billion in 1983, with 1984 not much better (*CSM*, 29 February). Communal violence erupted once again, this time in the Yola area. It is estimated that over a thousand people died in rioting associated with the Maitatsina Moslem sect.

Given this unsettled situation under a strong military government it is not surprising that the SWPP, the NLC, and the party's auxiliary organizations kept out of the public eye.

Jack H. Mower
Washington, D.C.

Réunion

Population. 535,000
Party. Réunion Communist Party (Parti communiste réunionnais; PCR)
Founded. 1959
Membership. 10,000 claimed (September 1981); 2,000 estimated (*YICA*, 1982, p. xvi)
Secretary General. Paul Vergès
Politburo. 12 members: Julien Ramin; remaining members unknown
Secretariat. 6 members: Paul Vergès, Elie Hoarau, Jean-Baptiste Ponama; remaining members unknown
Central Committee. 32 members: Bruny Payet, Roger Hoarau, Daniel Lallemand, Hippolite Piot, Ary Yee Chong Tchi-Kan, Laurence Vergès, Laurent Vergès; remaining members unknown
Status. Legal
Last Congress. Fifth, 12–14 July 1980, in Le Port
Last Election. March 1984, partial municipal election; June 1984, European Parliament, 29.8 percent, 1 deputy; December 1984, partial cantonal election, 25.5 percent
Auxiliary Organizations. Anticolonialist Front for Réunion Autonomy, Réunion Front of Autonomous Youth, Réunion Peace Committee, Réunion General Confederation of Workers (CGTR), Committee for the Rally of Réunionese Youth (CORJ), Réunion Union of Women (UFR), Réunion General Union of Workers in France (UGTRF), Réunion General Confederation of Planters and Cattlemen (CGPER)
Publications. *Témoignages* (daily); *Travailleur réunionnais* (semimonthly), published by CGTR; *Combat réunionnais* (periodicity unknown), published by UGTRF

The island of Réunion is a French overseas department and as such is an integral part of the French Republic. It is governed by a Paris-appointed prefect (who is the senior local official), a 36-member General Council, and a 45-member Regional Assembly. It is represented in the French parliament by three deputies and three senators. The PCR, a small party that gathers most of its support from sugarcane cutters and workers in the Le Port area, was founded in Le Port in 1959, when the Réunion Federation of the French Communist Party became autonomous. The PCR advocates increased autonomy without complete independence from France.

During 1984 the PCR continued to lose strength among voters. The ruling Socialist-Communist alliance in power in mainland France between May 1981 and July 1984, when the communists left the coalition, dashed the hopes of many voters, who saw no fundamental social changes and an aggravation of the economic crisis since the left took power

(*Témoignages*, 6–7 July). PCR candidate Laurent Vergès lost a partial municipal election in Saint-André in March—the General Council had annulled the March 1983 election because of electoral pressure on the voters—and Jean-Paul Virapoullé, the city's mayor since 1972, was re-elected (*Le Monde*, 12 September). In the European Parliament election in June, the PCR's electoral percentage continued to drop, as the party received only 29.8 percent of the vote compared with 32.7 percent in the March 1983 municipal election and 33 percent in the 1979 European Parliament election (*Témoignages*, 25 June). PCR candidate Elie Hoarau, who received only 25.5 percent of the vote was defeated in his bid for counselor of Saint-Pierre in a December partial cantonal election (*Le Monde*, 4 December).

Poor economic conditions and unemployment remain the major problems facing Réunion and the PCR, and the party continued its efforts to revitalize the economy, primarily the agricultural sector, and stimulate employment and development. (Réunion has an agricultural economy based primarily on sugarcane, which comprises 90 percent of its exports. Its exports cover only 14 percent of its imports. A drought in the southern and western regions of the island decreased sugarcane production [*Témoignages*, 31 March–1 April, 11–12 and 17 August] and the decision of the European Community [EC] to raise the price of a ton of sugar one percent weakened its competitiveness [ibid., 16 January].) Party Secretary General Paul Vergès proposed planting maize to replace some sugarcane in order to diversify the island's crops (ibid., 24 February) and revitalize the agricultural sector of the economy. The PCR, with the CGTR and the CGPER, led campaigns against sugarcane plantation and factory owners to ensure that the planters received the second installment of their sugar indemnity, which had been delayed.

A deputy to the European Parliament since 1979, Vergès visited Brussels several times throughout the year to sensitize the EC to the agricultural problems France's overseas departments faced. In January he tried to get an advance deduction from the EC for semiblanched rice entering Réunion (ibid., 19 January). Later, in August, he criticized the EC's threat of imposing price regulations instead of quotas on rum because it would create competition between Réunionese and British rum and force Réunion to lower its prices (ibid., 21 August).

In the battle against unemployment, the PCR cited a report from the National Institute of Statistics and Economic Studies that said that there would be 100,000 unemployed workers in Réunion by 1988 (ibid., 12 January). The party emphasized the differences between France and Réunion, quoting various statistics to show that policies for mainland France did not apply in the island. While only 29 percent of France's population is under 20 years of age, 47 percent of Réunion's population is (ibid., 5 January). Unemployment in Réunion is 30 percent compared to 9 to 12 percent in France (ibid., 7–8 January). Layoffs in Réunion rose 2.5 percent during the period January–May compared with 1983 figures (ibid., 30 June–1 July). The PCR endorsed the concept of giving the unemployed at least two weeks of work on development projects every two months (ibid., 19 April).

Although the PCR favors increased autonomy, it continued to criticize French government efforts at decentralization. In 1984 the Regional Assembly adopted its first budget and received responsibility for the island's committees for economic and social affairs; culture, education, and environment; regional loans; and audiovisual communication (ibid., 22 March). Paul Vergès stated that the French government had good intentions for decentralizing its overseas departments but did not come through with the necessary funds. The Regional Assembly's budget, he said, was merely a transfer of funds without new credits (ibid., 12 January). Regional Assembly President Mário Hoarau, a PCR member, added that the idea of decentralization was dragging because reality did not correspond to the legislators' will; for example, he cited, the state gave only 1 million francs to the Regional Assembly for culture in 1984, while it had given the regional administrative structure previously responsible for culture 13–14 million (*Le Monde*, 12 September).

In October, the Committee for the Rally of Réunionese Youth, an organization close to the PCR, organized violent demonstrations to protest decreased school aid and the institution of new criteria to determine recipients of that aid. The government had decreed during the summer that the same guidelines used for French mainland students should apply in Réunion, which had previously had a more advantageous system for alloting aid. The unrest subsided after the government announced a 12 million franc supplementary credit for the students to defray school lunch costs (ibid., 25 October).

In October the PCR proposed two options to balance the electoral representation between rural and urban cantons. One option was to double the number of general counselors and redraw cantonal boundaries so that each canton contained 7,900 to 8,600 people. A second proposal was to keep the same number of cantons and general counselors but to regroup smaller communes into one and split several urban cantons. (Ibid., 22 October.)

Party Organization and Leadership. PCR secretary general since 1959, Paul Vergès is a member of the party's Secretariat, a deputy to the European Parliament, and mayor of Le Port. He also heads the Réunion Intercommunal Syndicate for Multiple Vocations, which is a grouping of PCR communes (except Sainte-Rose) established in late 1983 (ibid., 11 April). According to the French daily *Le Monde* (12 September), Vergès's popularity has waned within the party since the European elections because he has adopted the image of a "notable" and charismatic revolutionary and because fellow PCR members have charged him with nepotism. (His son Laurent ran the electoral battle for Saint-André in March, and his other son heads the intercommunal syndicate of communist municipalities.)

Secretariat member Elie Hoarau serves concurrently as secretary of the Réunion Peace Committee, secretary general of the CGTR, and a member of the World Peace Council. He is also mayor of Saint-Pierre and chief editor of the party's newspaper, *Témoignages*. Bruny Payet, a member of the party's Central Committee, serves concurrently as president of the Réunion Peace Committee, head of the CGTR and first deputy mayor of Sainte-Marie. Payet is also a member of the World Peace Council and the World Federation of Trade Unions' General Council. Ary Yee Chong Tchi-Kan, a member of the Central Committee, heads the youth sector of the party. Other PCR members holding elected office are Mário Hoarau (president of the Regional Assembly and mayor of Saint-Leu), Lucet Langenier (mayor of Sainte-Suzanne), and Central Committee member Roger Hoarau (regional counselor). Other noteworthy PCR members are Laurent and Laurence Vergès, Julien Ramin, Jean St-Marc, Roland Robert, Daniel Lallemand, and Hippolite Piot.

Prominent leaders within the PCR auxiliary organizations are Angelo Lauret, who serves as president of the CGPER, and Isnelle Amelin, president of the UFR.

Domestic Policies and Activities. The major goals of the PCR are to achieve autonomy for Réunion from France, a more balanced economy, and redressment of inequalities between social benefits in France and on the island. It contends that policies for France cannot apply to Réunion and has emphasized the necessity for an increased number of development projects on the island. The PCR dedicated 1984 to youth mobilization and the fight against unemployment and illiteracy (*Témoignages*, 10 February).

The PCR opposes integration of French overseas departments into the EC and contends that the French government should pay the price of that policy (that is, freight costs from Réunion to Europe to keep Réunionese goods competitive). It also opposes the accession of Spain and Portugal into the EC because of the disadvantage it would give to Réunion's agricultural products. (Ibid., 19–20 May.) As in 1983, the PCR continued to call for the closure of the South African consulate in Saint-Denis. In August the UFR again organized a demonstration against racism and apartheid in South Africa. (Ibid., 5 July, 7 August.)

Relations between the PCR and the Réunion Federation of the Socialist Party (SP) became increasingly strained as the year progressed. The PCR accused the SP of emphasizing its leaders' anticommunist attitudes, the weakening of its communist allies, and the recentering of the left (ibid., 11 October). Although the PCR had submitted reform proposals during the three years that the French Communist Party (PCF) participated in the Socialist-led government, when the PCF quit the cabinet in July, the PCR could more easily attack government policies (*Le Monde*, 12 September). By October—and the submission of the 1985 budget in the French parliament—the PCR was criticizing the government for its policies of nondevelopment in Réunion and its decreases in the budget for the overseas departments (*Témoignages*, 11 October).

In August, the PCR broke relations with the Progressive Left Movement (MPG). It charged that the MPG had systematically excluded the PCR deputy mayor of Sainte-Marie and the party from municipal management (ibid., 29 August).

International Affairs. The PCR has a strong interest in regional developments in the Indian Ocean and keeps in close contact with neighboring communist parties, as well as communist parties in France and other French overseas departments. The PCR opposes apartheid in South Africa, supports the liberation struggles of the Namibian people and the African National Congress, and endorses the actions of the Palestine Liberation Organization. It favors the creation of a zone of peace in the Indian Ocean and has repeatedly called for the removal of military forces from the region.

Hilarie Slason
Falls Church, Virginia

South Africa

Population. 31,688,000
Party. South African Communist Party (SACP)
Founded. 1921
Membership. No data
General Secretary. Moses Mabhida
Leading Organs. Composition unknown
Status. Proscribed
Last Congress. Sixth Conference, December 1984, in London
Last Election. N/a
Auxiliary Organizations. None
Publications. *African Communist* (quarterly published in East Germany)

After 31 years of illegal existence, the South African Communist Party (SACP) continues its exile and underground activities in close alliance with the country's dominant nationalist movement, the African Nationalist Congress (ANC), also proscribed and operating in similar circumstances. The SACP was formally constituted clandestinely in 1953 as the successor to the Communist Party of South Africa, the continent's first Marxist-Leninist party (1921), which was dissolved by a majority of its leadership in 1950 under the threat of a ban by the ruling Nationalist Party.

With roots primarily among the minority English-speaking workers who had opposed participation in World War I and had greeted the Bolshevik Revolution enthusiastically, the Communist Party of South Africa undertook from its inception to include workers of all races in its ranks. Only in the late 1920s and early 1930s did it successfully become a predominantly African party by attracting African workers to its ranks—at the same time that many of its white members deserted or were purged in the wake of sectarian divisions centering around the application of Comintern prescriptions for a South African "native republic." Overcoming its factionalism in the late 1930s on a rising tide of antifascism, the Communist Party of South Africa

expanded its membership to include Indians and coloureds, as well as Afrikaners. Its prestige and visibility were enhanced by the active roles taken by prominent party members both in trade unions catering to black and white semiskilled and unskilled workers and in African and Indian political organizations contesting discriminatory government policies. During the war and afterward in the 1940s, white party members contested selected parliamentary, provincial, and municipal elections in Cape province and the Witwatersrand, winning only in the late 1940s against liberal United Party candidates running in Cape parliamentary constituencies restricted to African voters removed from the common roll in 1936. Membership in the Communist Party of South Africa was never more than several thousand, but in its own eyes (and those of government authorities) it was in the forefront of militant antigovernment politics and labor agitation. It was in this spirit that the newly elected Nationalist government passed the Suppression of Communism Act in 1950.

Habituated to harassment but unprepared for clandestine existence, a majority of the Central Committee hurriedly dissolved South Africa's first nonracial political party immediately before the act became operative. Party members of all races con-

Senegal

Population. 6,541,000
Party. Independence and Labor Party (Parti de l'indépendance du travail; PIT)
Founded. 1957
Membership. No data
Secretary General. Seydou Cissoko (until congress); Amath Dansoko
Politburo. 14 members: Seydou Cissoko, Amath Dansoko, Samba Dioulde Thiam, Maguette Thiam, Mady Danfaka, Sadio Camara, Seydou Ndongo, Semou Pathe Gueye, Makhtar Mbaye, Bouma Gaye, Mohamed Laye (names of other three not known)
Secretariat. 7 members: Seydou Cissoko, Amath Dansoko, Semou Pathe Gueye, Maguette Thiam, Samba Dioulde Thiam, Mady Danfaka, Makhtar Mbaye
Central Committee. 55 members
Status. Legal
Last Congress. Second, 28 September–2 October 1984, in Dakar
Last Election. 1983, 0.5 percent, no seats
Auxiliary Organizations. Women's Democratic Union
Publications. *Daan Doole*, *Gestu*

The major event of the year for the PIT was the party's second annual conference, which met in Dakar, 28 September–2 October. In attendance were 835 delegates and numerous international guests. Soviet representatives were Mikhail P. Gabdulin, chief editor of the Soviet party journal *Agitator*, and Ye. N. Korendyasov, a senior official of the Soviet Central Committee. Trifon Pashov of the Bulgarian Central Committee also attended. Other international guests included representatives from the communist parties of Lebanon, Czechoslovakia, France, Egypt, the Sudan, India, Guyana, Greece, and East Germany. The major work of the conference was the election of officers. In addition to those listed above, the conference elected a ten-member Central Control Commission. (The names of the members were not released.) The conference denounced the existence of French bases in Senegal and called for a united front against the present government. Abdou Diouf and his Socialist Party remain very much in control in Senegal, and there was little information on the domestic activities of the PIT. The *World Marxist Review* (June) reported that the PIT has formed a new women's group, the Women's Democratic Union of Senegal.

An article by Semou Pathe Gueye appeared in the July issue of the *World Marxist Review* and one by Seydou Cissoko in the December issue. Both articles attacked the activities of the Socialist International in Senegal and considered the cooperation of Western socialists and the present Senegalese government a menace to the true interests of the Senegalese.

Jack H. Mower
Washington, D.C.

tinued to participate in antigovernment politics and trade union activity, despite banning and prosecution by the government. The focus of their activities was the components of the multiracial Congress Alliance, headed by the ANC but also including white, coloured, and Indian organizations as well as the multiracial South African Congress of Trade Unions (SACTU) established in 1955, the same year as the Congress of the People met to adopt the Freedom Charter, a generally phrased call for an end to apartheid, the extension of full democratic rights to South Africans of all races, and substantial economic restructuring involving selected government takeovers of banks and major industries. In 1953, leading Communists had met secretly in Johannesburg to reorganize into the South African Communist Party (SACP), which did not, however, reveal its underground existence publicly until mid-1960 in the wake of the post-Sharpeville disturbances and the banning of the ANC.

Shortly thereafter the leadership of the SACP joined with a portion of the ANC leadership that had also gone underground to create Umkhonto We Sizwe, a clandestine military organization dedicated to selective sabotage of government installations and communications facilities. SACP leaders and cadres, like their ANC counterparts, were ill-prepared for the abrupt shift from the nonviolent strategies that had been the hallmarks of both organizations since their inception. Sabotage was initiated in December 1961, links were made with African nationalist supporters and communist allies outside the country, and rudimentary clandestine networks were established. The nascent underground organizational centers of Umkhonto We Sizwe and the SACP were destroyed by the Nationalist government through its unrelenting use of draconian security legislation and increasingly sophisticated and forceful police tactics. In the recent assessment of an SACP spokesman, "Activity outside our borders was forced upon us, unwillingly, in the worst period of our movement's decimation in the early 1960s. After the period of the Rivonia trial and the mass arrests, imprisonments and torture of our militants, our movement had been brought close to ineffectiveness. Had it remained totally restricted to work only within the country, it was our judgment then that it might well be totally extinguished. It was decided to commence the building of an apparatus outside the country, to take on the task of rebuilding an organization out of the remnants of the wreckage—an organization which would once again function within our country but with fraternal assistance and support of personnel and organization abroad." (*African Communist*, no. 98, pp. 11–12.) It is within this dual underground and exile setting that the SACP has operated for the past two decades—working for the reconstitution of an effective organization within South Africa while the majority of its longtime leaders have worked overseas in African and European capitals in collaboration with ANC leaders who also escaped from South Africa. The 1960s were particularly difficult years, marked by occasional sharp differences as the two organizations grappled with the harsh exigencies of exile and the uncertainties of finding viable strategies for re-establishing a presence in their distant homeland. But by the mid-1970s the SACP and the ANC began to make their presence felt again within South Africa, facilitated by renewed militancy of the black majority within and the opening of friendly proximate havens with the collapse of Portuguese and Rhodesian power. Militants of Umkhonto, recruited primarily within South Africa but trained primarily outside the country, stepped up armed attacks on selected military, industrial, and administrative targets, while ANC and SACP members joined with other activists in expanding mass-based political challenges to unpopular government policies and in encouraging the further spread of black trade union activity. In the estimation of the party journal, "The external leadership has done what it set out to do—in part at least. It has created the conditions for a return of the organizations and their leadership to South Africa. It has fought a way back, via propaganda and underground organization; and it has fought a way back via foreign training and cross-border return of the armed forerunners of the peoples' liberation forces." (Ibid., p. 13.)

Organization and Leadership. The SACP has been without a national chairman since the death in September 1983 in London of Dr. Yusef Dadoo, a 74-year-old Indian medical practitioner who had held the post since 1972. The general secretary, Moses Mabhida, a 61-year-old longtime African trade unionist, has held this position since 1979. Like Dr. Dadoo, who became a communist in 1939, Mabhida also joined the party during its period of legality (1942). Also like Dr. Dadoo, Mabhida went into exile in the early 1960s, taking up a fulltime post with Umkhonto We Sizwe until his election as SACP general secretary. Other members of the Political Bureau and Central Committee have not been publicly identified; writers for party publications adopt *noms de plume*. In the continuing circumstances of multicontinent exile and ruthless domestic persecution, it is impossible to determine either the size and national composition of SACP membership or whether the aging and apparently dominant external leadership is being renewed by younger additions. Yet it is clear that the SACP in exile has attracted younger blacks whose militancy was forged in the 1976 Soweto demonstrations. This recent cadre has undoubtedly provided both new middle-level leaders to work with the older members and established multiracial leadership in the major exile headquarters as well as determined militants who have returned home to more dangerous assignments in underground cells within South Africa, almost certainly concentrated in the major urban centers of Transvaal, Cape, and Natal, where organized black militancy is most evident.

Both within South Africa and in exile, the SACP centers much attention on the ANC, which from its foundation in 1912 has been open to Africans from across the political spectrum. Since the late 1920s, African Communists have been active within the ANC, although in the early 1930s and again in the late 1940s and late 1950s, elements of the ANC membership challenged communist involvement on the intertwined grounds of the multiracialness of party membership and the extracontinental origin of its ideology. It was within this stance that the Africanist dissidents broke with the ANC in 1959 to form the Pan Africanist Congress (PAC), but the ANC leadership continued to accept Communists as full participants at all levels of the organization. In the wake of the banning of the ANC in 1960, the shared underground and exile experience of the ANC and SACP contributed to a new closeness, with lines being further blurred by the 1969 decision of the exiled ANC leadership to accept non-Africans as members. Immediately prominent non-African Communists were made members of key ANC bodies, joining prominent African SACP members who had long been active in the senior councils of the ANC. Prominent SACP members have continued to serve in visible ANC positions, with Mabhida, for example, acting as ANC representative in Mozambique and leading an ANC delegation to Swaziland in May to discuss the sensitive question of ANC activities with the Swazi government. In the assessment of Oliver Tambo, the president of the ANC, "The relationship between the ANC and the SACP is not an accident of history, nor is it a natural and inevitable development. For, as we can see, similar relationships have not emerged in the course of liberation struggles in other parts of Africa . . . our alliance is a living organism that has grown out of struggle. We have built it out of our separate and common experiences . . . Our organizations have been able to agree on fundamental strategies and tactical positions while retaining our separate identities . . . Within our revolutionary alliance each organization has a distinct and vital role to play. A correct understanding of these roles and respect for their boundaries has ensured the survival and consolidation of our cooperation and unity." (*Sechaba*, September 1981, pp. 4–5.) In the perspective of the late Dr. Dadoo, "The ANC and the SACP personify the two complementary streams of revolutionary consciousness and revolutionary organization. They are complementary because in South Africa the struggle for national liberation insistently requires organized participation by the working class and its political vanguard, the Communist Party, and the struggle for socialism just as insistently requires a powerful movement for the freedom of the oppressed nations and races, a movement led by the ANC . . . The front of the fighters for the victory of the national-democratic revolution is led by the . . . ANC . . . , a vanguard movement which includes Africans, coloureds, Indians, and the most courageous, far-sighted and increasingly democratic-minded section of the white community . . . the South African Communist Party expresses the interests of the proletariat, which acts not only within the national-democratic front, but also carries on its own class struggle. Its goals do not conflict with the goals of the national-democratic revolution, but go beyond these, to the prospect of a radical restructuring of the society on socialist lines." (*WMR*, December 1982, pp. 18, 24.)

To realize its aims, the SACP determinedly guards its separate identity and organization; in the formulation of Mabhida, "We are autonomous in all respects, having our own structure, leadership, information and communication services, finances and officials. It would not be possible for us to make a proper contribution to the struggle if we lost any piece of our independence and capacity for self-determination." (*African Communist*, no. 92, p. 82.) In the view of the Central Committee of the SACP, "We must answer the enemy's offensive against our Party by devoting even greater efforts to strengthen it organizationally and to reinforce its role not only as a constituent part of the liberation alliance but also as the independent political vanguard of our proletariat" (ibid., no. 96, p. 58).

Domestic Activities and Attitudes. In the wake of the Nkomati Accord between South Africa and Mozambique, the SACP and its allies have been confronted with both immediate difficulties and promising long-term opportunities. The agreement caught the SACP by surprise—"One of the tragedies of today's dilemma is that Mozambique signed the Nkomati Accord without adequate consultation with all the parties concerned. It appeared to be an individual decision reached unilaterally . . . No one could possible [*sic*] pretend that the Accord has not adversely affected our freedom to operate. Of all the valuable acts of international aid our movement has received from many countries, the facilities accorded to us by Mozambique in the past have been amongst the most important. Now these facilities have been severely restricted, in some spheres totally withdrawn. But of themselves, they do not demand of us any new policies. It was never our strategy to seek to conduct the struggle of our country's liberation outside of its borders . . . If the curtailment of facilities in Mozambique is to have any long-term influence on our movement, it will be simply to lend urgency to the pace of this process of fighting our way back into the country; and thus to expedite the date at which an internal revolutionary leadership is once again established—this time securely surrounded by an armed cadre and an aroused and supportive population . . . For in South Africa's freedom struggle, then, there is now intense pressure to meet the long-term challenge and re-establish the centers of our movement clearly within the borders of South Africa. It is a formidable challenge; but not more formidable than that faced in 1960—and accomplished—of resurrecting our movement from the ashes of defeat." (Ibid., no. 98, pp. 11, 13, 15.)

The SACP sees circumstances as promising for its daunting tasks of rebuilding its organization within the country and channeling and sharpening popular resistance to apartheid and the Nationalist government. "Within South Africa today, every aspect of our people's struggle contrasts sharply with the bleak days of 1960. Today there is everywhere widespread readiness for the struggle, which flares up repeatedly in a myriad of local actions by workers, peasants, squatters, students, house-holders, professionals and politicians. Everywhere, on a local level, there are respected and trusted local spokesmen and leaders, together with local organizations who fill the vacuum created by the 1960 setbacks. And there is now the evidence everywhere of the existence of an armed force of guer-

rillas, freedom fighters, operating within the country and surviving amongst the people 'like fish in water.' This is not to claim that every mass popular resistance in township or factory is organized by the ANC. Far from it. But the ANC's presence is there, everywhere; its influence and reputation, upheld and spread by the external leadership, give coherence, unity and self-confidence to every popular movement. To this extent, the external ANC leadership has fulfilled a large part of its task—the essential part—of sponsoring the spirit of mass resistance amongst the people, without which there can be no safe basis for a rebuilt organization. And the SACP has played its full part in all this." (Ibid., p. 12.)

In this perspective the SACP viewed the 1983 creation of the United Democratic Front (UDF) as especially promising. "The UDF has the potential of drawing together the mass struggles raging in the urban centers and the pockets of resistance in the rural areas, particularly in the hated Bantustans. The growth of regional branches of the UDF is a sign that the broad popular front is beginning to take on a structured and organized form and its shape and content is beginning to acquire definition. The urgent and fundamental task facing all genuine revolutionaries and patriots is to build upon this achievement and not to allow petty differences to stand in the way of creating the broadest possible opposition and resistance to race rule in all forms." (Ibid., no. 96, p. 37.) As the UDF evolved, a party spokesman diagnosed potential dangers: "The very emergence of the UDF and its fast rate of development created an excitement which drew the leadership of many of the affiliated organizations into the UDF campaigns at the expense of the affiliates themselves. There has also been the problem of police harassment and intimidation, the distribution of false leaflets by the enemy, arrests and bannings, the attempt to project the UDF as a 'front of the ANC.' All this is aimed at isolating the UDF from the masses. Another problem is that the base of the UDF is largely urban, yet repression is at its worst in rural areas. These and many other problems are cause for concern and their solution is not always easy." (Ibid., no. 98, p. 31.)

The UDF as a sign of a "broad popular front" includes not only workers and peasants, but also components of the black middle strata. In the estimation of the SACP, elements from this group, the emerging administrative and business strata in the Bantustans, the African middle class outside of the Bantustans, and the coloured and Asian middle class, are all targets of government blandishments to join as "collaborators" in sustaining white domination; at the same time "the mobilisation of the broadest possible contingent of black social forces against racial rule continues to be a revolutionary imperative in our country . . . The middle strata by their very nature do not always play a consistent role in a struggle and, especially in one with a national context, tend to shy away from revolutionary radicalism in favor of old-style bourgeois nationalism. But although we are always called upon to guard against the spread of petit-bourgeois ideology within the liberation alliance, the winning over to our side of larger and larger groups from amongst the middle strata remains a revolutionary necessity." Within this perspective the SACP enthusiastically supported the boycott of the new Indian and coloured legislative chambers created by the new South African constitution. "The overwhelming spirit of rejection of these collaborationist maneuvers which has already been demonstrated by the coloured and Indian masses must be maintained and reinforced. The struggle against the Bantustans and the new constitutional proposals is indivisible." (Ibid., p. 48–50.)

The main focus, however, of SACP activity remains the working class. In a deathbed message, the late Dr. Dadoo asserted, "Today, almost as never before, the South African workers are on the march. In this field a great responsibility rests on our Party. We are the revolutionary party of the working class, whose clear role is that of the vanguard in the fight for socialism. The working class, in essence the black working class in our country, is the pivotal force in the struggle for a revolutionary overthrow of the entire apartheid system. As such our Party must place its main focus and emphasis in organising, uniting and giving clear guidance to this class, which forms the backbone of our struggle. Included in this task is assessing our strength and weakness in the trade union movement as a whole, assessing (re-defining if necessary) the role of SACTU, and ensuring our future working in this field meets the demands of the time." (Ibid., p. 21.)

Taking up Dr. Dadoo's concern in a meeting immediately after his death, the Central Committee elaborated SACP policy toward the burgeoning black trade union movement. High priority continued to be given to the creation of a single national union federation. Despite the SACP's preferences for industrial unions over general workers' unions and for nonregistered unions over registered unions, the SACP urged that differences on matters of organization and responses to government legislation should not block moves towards unity. It also recognized that SACTU could not be expected to become the central organization for black workers. "It is for all practical purposes treated by the regime as an illegal conspiracy. It is therefore clear that in present conditions SACTU can no longer operate in the old way; more especially it cannot realistically advance the aim of winning the immediate formal affiliation of the emerging trade unions. In other words, in the quest for the creation of a new trade union center, SACTU does not compete with the existing organs. At the same time SACTU has a vital role to play in ensuring that the principles upon which it was founded continue to inspire and give direction to the growing forces of trade unionism within the country . . . It is clearly more vital than ever for SACTU to carry out its historic role to influence the trade union movement to move in a radical and democratic direction and to ensure that the united trade union center which is being striven for, will be built in the image of SACTU. To carry out this task it is necessary that SACTU strengthen itself organizationally. In collaboration with all the constituents of the Congress Alliance, it is called upon to intensify propaganda with an emphasis on the main content of revolutionary unionism. The unorganized must be organized. The vast army of unemployed workers both in the towns and in the countryside must be mobilized to express their protest and anger about their plight and the plight of their families. The negative features in the Labor Relations Act must be exposed and a cry must go out from the organized trade union movement to demand their repeal." (Ibid., pp. 55–56.)

Despite what are regarded as encouraging circumstances generally within the black population, the SACP remains wary about certain types of black activism. Not only are Bantustan leaders attacked—"the so-called Bantustan states must be completely destroyed and their administrations overthrown as a part of the struggle for the total liberation of every inch of our people's soil" (ibid., p. 47)—but politicians supporting the black consciousness stance and trade unionists eschewing political activity are also castigated. In particular, the National Forum is faulted for improper "class" analysis and criticism of the ANC, the Freedom Charter, and the SACP; it is viewed as a "'broad alliance' of the Trotskyite and Black Consciousness organizations." Its "anti-C.P. stance is part of a broader perspective, namely rejection of the existing socialist world, especially the Soviet Union.

This anti-communism and anti-Sovietism leads them straight into a political desert and, because they have no firm allies internationally, they end up being political grasshoppers." (Ibid., no. 98, pp. 23, 32.) In analogous fashion, Joe Foster, general secretary of the Federation of South African Trade Unions, continues to be attacked for "his syndicalist approach and his ignoring of the role and history of the Communist Party in South Africa" (ibid., p. 49). Similarly, scholars and activists publishing Marxist analyses in academic journals within South Africa are criticized for their reliance upon the "new philosophers" such as Nicos Poulantzes and Louis Althusser rather than relying upon the "classics" and especially Lenin. In the eyes of one SACP commentator, "It is those forces amongst the intelligentsia who have lost touch with the reality of the struggle for state power who are most active in trying to build a new 'workers' party.' Inevitably, their activities and arguments are bringing to light their basic anti-communism. The people recognize anti-communism when it emanates from the racist regime, and they will come to recognize it in any new garb." In considering the tasks of the SACP in the trade union movement, a party worker contends: "On the ideological front, the Party must wage an offensive which must include first and foremost the spreading of Marxist-Leninist ideas among workers. At the same time we must combat the proliferation of ultra-left and rightist ideas. This task demands the improvement of our ideological and propaganda machinery to ensure that when socialist ideas are discussed and debated (and they are being discussed and debated heatedly at this stage of our struggle), the Party's voice is clearly heard." (Ibid., no. 99, pp. 80, 109.)

International Views and Activities. The SACP continues to find a source of its strength, according to the last testament of the late Dr. Dadoo, in "the unswerving loyalty and respect our Party has for the CPSU [Communist Party of the Soviet Union]" (ibid., no. 96, p. 20). In this vein the SACP has been unusually concerned about what it views as a rising campaign of anti-Sovietism. "Hostility, or even neutrality, towards the Soviet Union and other countries of existing socialism can only undermine the struggle for national liberation, peace and social progress in South Africa, Africa and the world. The enemy of our enemy is our friend, not for opportunistic reasons, but because Soviet policies have been firmly rooted in the principles of Marxism-Leninism and proletarian internationalism. Ever since 1917 the Soviet Union has shown itself to be the most consistent ally in the struggle against imperialism, for national independence, peace and social progress. At a time when the racists and imperialists are leaving no stone unturned to destabilize the socialist bloc and destroy the monumental achievements of the October Revolution, it is the duty of all genuine revolutionaries to make it unmistakably clear that they have the correct attitude towards the Soviet Union and are ready to come to its defense." (Ibid., no. 98, pp. 18–19.) In the Central Committee's international resolution adopted in September 1983, the SACP was characterized as an "integral part of the world communist movement," which "despite some differences . . . remains the most cohesive and united international force fighting for peace, democracy, national liberation and socialism. It is the duty of all communist workers' parties to strive for greater unity and cohesion in our ranks. There is an urgent need to work for the convening of an international conference of the world communist movement. We shall continue to develop and deepen bilateral relations with communist and workers' parties and support the holding of regional conferences of fraternal parties." (Ibid., no. 96, p. 64.) Elsewhere in the resolution the Central Committee fully endorsed Soviet positions on a range of international issues, with particular attention to Soviet proposals for nuclear limitation and disarmament. The SACP has bitterly attacked the close links between the United States and South Africa, asserting that the "Reagan-Botha axis threatens peace and social progress" (ibid., no. 99, pp. 17–30), and Fidel Castro's speech upon the return of the bodies of Cubans killed in Grenada was reprinted in full in the SACP quarterly (ibid., no. 97, pp. 74–90). Reports of direct contacts with fraternal parties were limited to coverage of the awarding of the Order of the People's Republic of Bulgaria to General Secretary Mabhida in April, but undoubtedly SACP leaders maintained links with the CPSU and other allied parties in Eastern Europe, Cuba, and Vietnam. It is also likely that the SACP continued contacts with some or all of the eleven other Marxist-Leninist parties in Africa with which it had identified in recent years.

Publications. For 25 years the SACP has published in exile its quarterly, *African Communist*, "in the interests of African solidarity, and as a forum for Marxist-Leninist thought throughout our Continent." Distributed from an office in London that sells other party publications, *African Communist* is printed in the German Democratic Republic. An analogous arrangement is in place for the publication of *Sechaba*, the monthly magazine of the ANC. The ANC and its allies also produce publications in other European and African centers of activity.

Both the SACP and the ANC smuggle their publications into South Africa to supplement locally produced underground literature, including banned Marxist-Leninist classics. SACP propaganda pamphlets and stickers also have made their appearance in connection with May Day and the boycott campaign against coloured and Indian electoral participation.

"Radio Freedom, Voice of the African National Congress and Umkhonto We Sizwe, the People's Army" supplements the clandestine publications, broadcasting on shortwave frequencies for several hours daily from government-owned stations in Angola, Ethiopia, Madagascar, and Tanzania.

Sheridan Johns
Duke University

Sudan

Population. 21,103,000
Party. Sudanese Communist Party (al-Hizb al-Shuyu'i al-Sudani; SCP)
Founded. 1946
Membership. 5,000–10,000 members before 1971; present number estimated at 1,500
Secretary General. Muhammad Ibrahim Nugud Mansur
Politburo. 6 members: Muhammad Ibrahim Nugud Mansur, Ali al-Tijani al-Tayyib Babikar (number-two leader, arrested November 1980), Dr. Izz-al Din Ali Amir, Sulayman Hamid, Al-Gazuli (Jizuli) Said Uthman, Muhammad Ahmad Sulayman (Suleiman)
Secretariat. 7 members: Muhammad Ibrahim Nugud Mansur, Ali al-Tijani al-Tayyib Babikar, Dr. Izz-al Din Ali Amir, Abu al-Qasim (Gassim) Muhammad, Sulayman Hamid, Al-Gazuli Said Uthman, Muhammad Ahmad Sulayman
Central Committee. 12 members: in addition to 7 listed above, Sudi Darag, Khad(i)r Nasir, Abd-al-Majid Shakak, Hassan Gassim al-Sid (World Peace Council Presidential Committee member and World Federation of Trade Unions [WFTU] staff member), Ibrahim Zakariya (secretary general of WFTU)
Other Prominent SCP Members. Sharif Dishoni (former party spokesperson), Ahmad Salim (member of Prague-based Editorial Council of *World Marxist Review*)
Status. Illegal
Last Congress. Fourth, October 1967, in Khartoum
Last Election. N/a
Auxiliary Organizations. Democratic Federation of Sudanese Students (DSFS; affiliated with International Union of Students), Sudanese Youth Union, Sudan Workers' Trade Union Federation (SWTUF; operates with quasi-official standing), Sudanese Defenders of Peace and Democracy (presumably a World Peace Council affiliate)
Publications. No formal newspaper, although SCP propagates its views through clandestinely distributed leaflets

A small group of intellectuals at Khartoum University founded the SCP in 1946. Communist elements soon infiltrated the White Flag League (the first modern Sudanese nationalist body), and the SCP broadened its appeal to include railway workers and peasants. On the basis of its ties with the railway workers, the SCP made inroads into the SWTUF, which was established in 1950. In 1951 the SCP was a leading force, along with the SCP-influenced Gezira Tenants' Union, in the Anti-Imperialist Front, the leader of the popular struggle for Sudanese independence from Britain.

During the immediate post-independence period, the SCP maintained a high degree of political activism. Its activist role increased even further as the price of cotton (Sudan's major export crop) plummeted and triggered socioeconomic discontent and political chaos in the country. Meanwhile, in 1955, a group called the Anyanya (Scorpion) launched a rebellion in the southern Sudan that was aimed at securing autonomy and perhaps even secession for the region. The southerners, who constitute 25–30 percent of the country's population, belong primarily to black, non-Arabic-speaking Christian and animist tribes. They resented their subordination to the Moslem Arabs of the north and charged, in addition, that the already more prosperous north was receiving the lion's share of economic development funds.

The SCP was the only political party in Sudan to oppose the military regime that seized power in a coup d'etat in November 1958. The country's new ruler, General Ibrahim Abbud, promptly arrested all the SCP leaders he could locate. He also banned all trade unions, some of which were rallying points for the SCP. The party members still at large were forced underground. The Abbud regime, however, foundered because of its increasingly obvious inability to bring the war in the south under control. A popular revolt and a general political strike erupted in 1964, providing the SCP an opportunity to organize workers, peasants, students, professionals, and intelligentsia in the north against the regime's policies.

A parliamentary government supplanted the junta, and in 1965 some SCP officials were elected to the parliament. However, the new coalition government came to regard the Communists as a threat and denied them their parliamentary seats. Once again, the SCP was forced underground.

Deteriorating economic conditions (especially the bottoming out of the cotton market) sparked still another political crisis and created one more opportunity for the SCP to enter the political arena. On 25 May 1969, Colonel Jaafar Numeiri seized control of Sudan in a virtually bloodless coup. The victory of Numeiri and his SCP allies represented a triumph for the left against powerful economic interests and foreign capital in Sudan. The new regime nationalized the banks, brought foreign trade under state control, imposed control over strategic economic resources, and adopted other measures "to wrench Sudan from . . . neocolonial dependence" (*African Communist*, no. 98, 1984, p. 67). Khartoum also hosted the first international conference in solidarity with the "liberation struggles" of African peoples.

In 1970 the SCP's popularity and prestige reached an all-time high. With a membership totaling 5,000 to 10,000, it was the strongest and best-organized communist party in the Middle East or Africa. The party consisted of roughly three factions: the orthodox Moscow-oriented group (led by Abd al-Khaliq Mahjub until his execution in 1971), a pro-Chinese revolutionary communist faction, and a group professing "local Sudanized Marxism" without links to any outside powers.

Numeiri's failure to fulfill his dream of creating a socialist paradise in Sudan doomed his alliance with the SCP. The continuing reliance of Sudan on cotton exports and on Western financial support prompted Numeiri to move rightward economically. This shift not only sparked political differences between himself and the SCP but also generated an intraparty split over the question of support for his regime.

The SCP's advocacy of "revolution by stages"—first "national democratic" and then "socialist"—enabled the moderate faction to accept Numeiri's drift to the right and his plan to dissolve the SCP into his newly created Sudan Socialist Union (SSU). The SSU was to be the country's only political organization. The SCP's more radical faction (strongly represented by pro-communist army officers) opposed Numeiri's moves to the right. Leftist officers evidently masterminded an abortive 1971 coup attempt, which had the effect of alienating Numeiri even further from his former SCP allies. He outlawed the SCP and rounded up and liquidated most of its leaders, including Mahjub and Shafieh Ahmed Sheik, head of the Sudanese Workers' Union. Others were forced into exile.

Following the 1971 coup, two distinct wings of the SCP emerged. A controversy developed over the proper role of the army in a revolution. One faction argued that the army must take the lead.

Followers of Mahjub, however, contended that only the working class could spearhead a successful revolution in Sudan. The Mahjub thesis emphasized the staggering obstacles to a successful revolution: the economic dominance of "Western imperialism"; the enormous strength of counterrevolutionary, traditionalist forces; and the religious, ethnic, and other factional divisions among the geographic regions of the country, which allegedly were exploited by the "imperialists" and Sudanese reactionary groups. In Mahjub's view, a revolution that had support only from the army would fail to overcome all these social and economic obstacles. Only a revolution led by the working class and backed by a strong organization of all Sudanese democratic-revolutionary forces could succeed.

In 1972 Numeiri managed to end the seventeen-year-old Anyanya rebellion, which had severely drained Sudan's economy and military resources. He created a Ministry of Southern Affairs, headed by SCP Central Committee member Joseph Garang, to work out a plan for regional autonomy. This plan became the basis of a settlement, signed in the Ethiopian capital of Addis Ababa, which unified the three southern provinces into a single autonomous region, established a regional assembly and executive council, promised the impoverished south an economic development program and a more equitable share of national income, and arranged for the incorporation of the Anyanya guerrilla units into the Sudanese army.

On this fundamental dispute in Sudan between the richer north and the poorer south, the SCP was the only Sudanese political party to propose regional autonomy for the south. It has advocated broad autonomy—the right of the southerners to enjoy their own religion, language, and customs—within the context of a unified, democratic Sudan. However, the SCP also has attempted to exploit the problems of the south and of sectarian politics in order to enhance its status.

Numeiri's grant of relative autonomy to the south greatly eased the country's regional tensions, but in the early 1980s violence flared anew. Some of the Anyanya never had reconciled themselves to the Addis Ababa accords and had reverted to guerrilla warfare. External developments also affected the course of events in southern Sudan.

In August 1981 Ethiopia, Libya, and South Yemen signed a tripartite pact in Aden after close consultation with the Soviet Union and Cuba. The pact was aimed at undermining pro-Western governments in the Middle East and Africa. Sudan has become a major target of this campaign. Sudanese rebels receive sanctuary in camps along the Ethiopian side of the frontier, from where they launch crossborder raids into Sudan. Libya and South Yemen provide arms, training, and logistical and financial support for this effort, and Soviet and Cuban military and intelligence personnel in Ethiopia apparently play a coordinating role. According to Muhammad Abd al-Qadir, first secretary of the central leadership of the SSU, the Soviets and Cubans have worked to unify various Sudanese groups opposed to Numeiri's regime in order to pool their efforts (Sudan News Agency, 7 August).

In May 1983 a southern army battalion based in the upper Nile town of Bor mutinied against orders that would have replaced it with northerners. The orders contravened the spirit, if not the letter, of the Addis Ababa accords, which had stipulated that military and administrative duties by northerners in the south would be minimized. When the army attacked the Bor garrison, the battalion resisted and then left to join the guerrilla groups in the area. A former army commander, Colonel John Garang, also joined the guerrillas. He is a member of the Dinka, the dominant tribe in southern Sudan, and is no relation to Joseph Garang. By July 1983 Colonel Garang, who holds a doctorate in agronomy from Iowa State University, had organized the guerrillas into the Sudanese People's Liberation Movement (SPLM), of which he is chairman. He also serves as commander-in-chief of the SPLM's military wing, known as the Sudanese People's Liberation Army (SPLA). The SPLA, which may have as many as 10,000 fighters, arms and trains its recruits at facilities just across the Sudanese border in Ethiopia and is creating a political infrastructure among its supporters inside Sudan.

In addition to the SPLA, a group known as Anyanya II, has emerged in the southern Sudan. It advocates succession from the north and creation of an independent state in the south. Thus, its objective differs from that of the SPLA, which calls for a fusing of the struggle of northerners and southerners against Numeiri's regime.

A pamphlet issued by the SPLM describes it as "Marxist-Leninist" and as aspiring to become the "sole people's political organization" in Sudan. According to the pamphlet, the SPLA is committed to conventional as well as guerrilla warfare and to sabotage of vital installations, communications, facilities, and other government property. (Ibid., 4 March.) Joseph Oduho, former regional minister of southern Sudan and now head of the Political and

Foreign Affairs Committee of the SPLM, announced that "the aim of our fight is the creation of a united and Socialist Sudan, which can only be achieved by a lengthy revolutionary armed struggle." He added that the SPLA controlled virtually the entire rebel movement in southern Sudan, including Anyanya I and II, which "had degenerated as a result of a total lack of political and military leadership into small uncontrolled groups indulging in gangsterism." (*Le Monde*, Paris, 27 April.)

The SPLM's stated intention to overthrow "the Khartoum regime set up by the northern and southern bourgeoisie" (*Washington Times*, 12 June) and to create a unified socialist Sudan coincides with the avowed goal of the SCP. Indeed, General Omar Mohammed al-Tayeb, Sudan's first vice-president, accused the SCP, which is based in the north, of coordinating its activities with the southern-based SPLM. "The conspiracy is aimed at both southern and northern Sudan," he states. (*Intercontinental Press*, 16 April, p. 196.)

Garang's movement reaped a windfall when Numeiri announced in June 1983, in the aftermath of the Bor rebellion, a redivision of southern Sudan into its three constituent provinces. This cancellation of the key provision of the Addis Ababa accords was attacked by southerners as a ploy to divide and rule their tribes. On the heels of this move came Numeiri's announcement, in September 1983, of the introduction of shari'a, the Islamic code of law, into Sudan. The non-Moslems of southern Sudan regarded this move as a direct assault upon their Christian and tribal religions.

Still another issue exacerbated relations between northern and southern Sudan around this time. The Numeiri regime called in Western experts to develop recently discovered oil deposits in the south and to build the 217-mile Jonglei Canal to increase the flow of the White Nile. The southerners believed that these projects would deprive them of their oil and water resources, which would be diverted to the north and, in the case of oil, abroad. In February 1984 the SPLA attacked local headquarters of the Chevron Company, killing three foreign oil workers and wounding seven others. Subsequent guerrilla attacks on French engineers excavating the Jonglei Canal brought work on that project to a virtual halt. Oil exploration also appears to be at a standstill.

During a speech on 2 March to commemorate Libya's national day, Libyan leader Moammar Khadafy declared that his country was "allied with the popular revolution in the southern Sudan"

(ibid.). Exactly two weeks later, a Soviet-made Libyan bomber carried out an air raid on the Sudanese city of Omdurman, attacking, among other targets, the building that houses the radio station. Citing the raid and the growing unrest inside Sudan, which he believed to be foreign inspired, Numeiri clamped a state of emergency on the country on 29 April. He told a Saudi Arabian publication on 9 May that "Sudan is faced with foreign aggression . . . and its aim is clearly to impose Marxism-Leninism on southern Sudan as a step toward imposing it on all Sudan. The terrorist organization led by John Garang in southern Sudan has said so frankly . . . Pockets of the Marxist plot which started in some southern areas are trying to infiltrate the north through the remnants of the Sudanese Communist Party in order to operate among the workers and instigate them to stop work and paralyze the country's economy." (*Ukaz*, Jidda, 13 May.)

Domestic Attitudes and Activities. Despite its illegal status, the SCP retains considerable influence among intellectuals, students (especially at the University of Khartoum), railway workers, sympathizers in the armed forces, and cotton growers. The SCP has particular strength in the trade unions. Communist inroads also are visible among the 2–3 million disgruntled refugees in Sudan. In addition, the SCP maintains links with some Sudanese refugees in Ethiopia.

In an effort to broaden its base, the SCP joined the newly formed National Salvation Front (Jabhat al-Inqaz al-Watani) in August. Sudanese opposition sources in London stated that the new front consists of the SCP, the Democratic Unionist Party (al-Hizb al-Ittihadi al-Demuqrati), the 'Umma Party (Hizb al-Ummah), the Popular Army for the Liberation of Sudan (al-Jaysh al-Sha'bi li Tahrir al-Sudan), and several other figures and organizations in northern and southern Sudan (*Al-Watan*, Kuwait, 21 August). The front's charter calls for bringing "those gambling with the fate of the country" to task, an obvious reference to the Numeiri regime. It advocates formation of "a provisional government that rules the country for three years for the purpose of instituting basic liberties, sovereignty of law, and a free, independent and nonaligned foreign policy." The provisional government would be responsible for formulating a draft constitution that would protect human rights, religious freedom (within the basic confines of an Islamic society), and democratic institutions. Planned economic development and "solidarity with the oppressed countries in defending their rights and interests in the face of the international economic forces" are also put forth as basic objectives.

Inclusion of the SCP in the new National Salvation Front caps a prolonged effort by the party to forge alliances with other political groups in Sudan. Party spokesmen believe that a broad front of all "progressive," democratic groups is necessary to free the country from what the SCP calls Numeiri's unjust and corrupt military dictatorship (interview with Fatima Ibrahim, *Al-Yasar al-'Arabi*, Paris, no. 58, October 1983, pp. 12–13).

The SCP takes a predictable Third World Marxist line on what ails the Sudanese economy. Foreign capitalists have been allowed by Numeiri to capture the economy and have co-opted and corrupted the Numeiri government, making it an accomplice in the crime of amassing riches at the expense of the downtrodden Sudanese people. In a late 1983 interview, SCP member Fatima Ibrahim referred to Numeiri as the "10 percenter," for allegedly skimming 10 percent off all state revenues and commercial transactions for himself. She also criticized Numeiri's wife for being a "millionairess." (Ibid.) In addition, the SCP contends that the "new administrative bourgeoisie" in Khartoum has caved in to the International Monetary Fund's demands for austerity policies. These policies, in turn, have caused the standard of living of the workers and peasants to plummet.

International Views. The SCP closely parrots the radical Arab communist line on Middle Eastern politics. "U.S. imperialism" and the "Zionist aggression" of Israel are the villains. The Communists in Sudan also condemn moderate Arab countries such as Egypt for siding with the U.S.-Israeli "strategic alliance." The SCP chides the United States for its arms sales to Sudan and criticizes both the Numeiri government and Washington for making threats against Libya. The SCP reiterated these in June 1983 at a meeting of twelve Arab communist and workers' parties (*IB*, September 1983, pp. 24–28). On 7 November 1983 the SCP joined eight other Middle Eastern and North African communist parties in issuing an appeal to "all the progressive and patriotic forces in the Arab world, and also in the camp of our people's friends" to further their unity "against U.S. imperialism, Zionism, and Arab reaction." The appeal was issued in Prague. (Ibid., January, p. 27.)

In December the SCP participated in a gathering of world communist parties in Prague under the auspices of the journal *Problems of Peace and Socialism* (*World Marxist Review*). These gatherings occur periodically (the last was in 1981) to assess the international situation and formulate communist strategies and tactics for the coming years. (*Rudé právo*, Prague, 7 December.)

Faced with a growing challenge to his rule both from within and outside Sudan, Numeiri has made several concessions. In September he lifted the national state of emergency, suspended the activities of the special martial law courts set up under the emergency decree, and reversed his decision to redivide southern Sudan into three separate administrative regions. On 30 October the government announced that it had concluded a provisional peace treaty with "a powerful splinter faction of the SPLM" (UPI, 30 October). The position of the Numeiri regime remains precarious, however, and the SCP stands poised to exploit any opportunities that may arise in the course of a new political crisis in the country.

Marian Leighton
Defense Intelligence Agency

Zimbabwe

Population. 8,325,000
Party. Zimbabwe African National Union (ZANU)
Founded. 1963
Membership. No data
First Secretary and President. Robert Mugabe
Politburo. 15 members: Robert Mugabe, Simon Muzenda (holds 2 seats), Maurice Nyagumbo, Enos Nkala, Herbert Ushewokunze, Emmerson Munangagwa, Nathan Shamuyarira, Didymus Mutasa, Dzingai Mutumbuka, Teurai Ropa Nhongo, Ernest Kadungura, Sydney Sekeremayi, Rex Nhongo, Josiah Tongamirai
Central Committee. 90 members
Status. Ruling party
Last Congress. Fifth, 8–12 August 1984
Last Election. 1980, 71 percent, 57 of 100 seats
Auxiliary Organizations. People's Militia
Publications. *Moto*; ZANU has strong influence in all Zimbabwan media.

ZANU is the ruling party of the Republic of Zimbabwe. Though not an avowedly communist party, it professes to be Marxist in ideology. It was formed in 1963 by the African nationalist Ndabaningi Sithole after he split from Joshua Nkomo's Zimbabwe African Peoples' Union (ZAPU). Robert Mugabe, a Marxist, became ZANU secretary general under Sithole's presidency. In the later 1960s, ZANU launched a guerrilla war against the white-dominated Rhodesian government of Prime Minister Ian Smith. Much of ZANU's logistical and training support came from the People's Republic of China. After a bitter power struggle in 1974, Mugabe was elected to replace Sithole as party president. Internal leadership struggles continued, but by the time of the peace negotiations in Geneva in 1976, Mugabe had gained almost complete control. At the Geneva conference, the frontline states forced Moscow-supported Nkomo and his ZAPU into a Patriotic Front (PF) alliance with Mugabe and ZANU in order to present a stronger, more united opposition to the Rhodesian regime.

This fragile fabric of unity began to unravel in February 1980 when Nkomo-led ZAPU contested the pre-independence elections as a separate party. ZANU won a stunning landslide, gaining 57 of the 100 parliamentary seats to ZAPU's 20. Mugabe emerged as prime minister when Zimbabwe achieved independence from Britain in 1980. ZANU's strength derives mainly from the majority Shona people, while ZAPU's support comes overwhelmingly from the Ndebele, who constitute only 18 percent of the population.

After independence, the two parties formed a coalition government, but this collapsed in early 1982 after Nkomo spurned Mugabe's call for a merger into a single party. In February, Mugabe sacked Nkomo from his cabinet post, along with other ZAPU ministers, accusing them of stockpiling arms in preparation for a coup. ZAPU and ZANU have since been in an adversarial relationship.

Organization and Leadership. ZANU is directed by a 90-member Central Committee, under the presidency of Robert Mugabe, who is also the country's prime minister and minister of defense and of national security.

The first party congress in twenty years was convened in August 1984. It was held amid bitter political infighting based more on personality and ethnicity than on ideology. More than 6,000 delegates attended and adopted a new charter, or constitution, for the party. By its terms, the Central Committee was tripled in size to 90 members. The National Executive was abolished and replaced by a 15-member Politburo. As the party's supreme executive organ, the Politburo will rule the Central Committee and, ultimately, the entire country. It will supervise all government ministries and agencies. In many respects, it supersedes the cabinet, which has been reduced in size and authority. The Politburo's membership has been drawn from the ranks of the Central Committee by Prime Minister Mugabe and not by a body within the Central Committee. (*FBIS*, 10 August.) The party congress also created five standing committees that will handle broad questions of public policy and seek to turn the resolutions of the party congress into comprehensive programs. Each committee chairperson is appointed by the Politburo and holds a cabinet portfolio. Thus, real power in Zimbabwe now lies with the ZANU Politburo, though ultimate authority rests with Prime Minister Mugabe, serving as party head. (*Africa News*, 27 August.)

Robert Mugabe's position in both government and party has been greatly strengthened and more centralized as a result of the new party structure. He was unanimously re-elected to the party leadership, with new titles of first secretary and president (*FBIS*, 12 August). Mugabe will now push for the creation of a powerful executive presidency for the government, modeled after that of Mozambique. The party congress gave Prime Minister Mugabe a firm mandate to transform the nation into a one-party, ZANU-controlled regime. Mugabe also reaffirmed his commitment to the establishment of a one-party socialist state based on Marxist-Leninist lines. (*NYT*, 9 August.) However, he pledged this would be achieved "in the fullness of time and in accordance with the law and the constitution." (*CSM*, 13 August.)

At the party congress, Mugabe introduced a "Leadership Code of Conduct," aimed at curbing corruption and nepotism and at instilling greater ideological discipline. It would also discourage party officials from amassing wealth in the private sector. (*FBIS*, 10 August.) The Marxist prime minister is concerned that too many ZANU officials are engaging in capitalistic activities inimical to the country's socialist goals.

ZANU remains a party dominated by the Shona ethnic group, which comprises approximately 80 percent of the population. Mugabe would like to attract more Ndebele, and in 1984 there were several defections to ZANU by prominent ZAPU officials, including a cabinet minister. However, the overwhelming majority of the Ndebele have remained in ZAPU, the major opposition party. ZANU's Central Committee thus continues to be dominated by Shona speakers. Key positions on the Politburo are held by Mugabe's own Zezuru clan of Shona. (*NYT*, 14 August.) ZANU is in the process of establishing an ideological institute, called the Chitepo College of Marxism and Leninism. It has also begun a militia training program for local party leaders to teach them to protect themselves from guerrilla "dissidents." This will complement a program that has already trained more than 8,000 private citizens. (*Herald*, 21 May.)

ZANU's professed Marxism has been substantially diluted since the end of the liberation struggle and its elevation as the ruling party. Mugabe has become more cautious and pragmatic in his policies. He is committed to a mixed economy, has refrained from expropriating private property, and pays fair market prices for all government acquisitions. ZANU tolerates the white-dominated private sector because it is so vital to the economy. The highly influential agricultural minister is a prominent, nonideological white farmer. The country is in desperate need of foreign capital and has therefore permitted considerable foreign equity control over locally based enterprises. However, ZANU seeks greater state control and the progressive expansion of the state in economic development. Toward that end, the government has purchased the major newspapers, a large bank, and a pharmaceutical company and has created a state-owned minerals marketing board. But the drought and lack of capital have stalled its program to resettle 165,000 families on two-thirds of the commercial land presently under white ownership. Also, modest efforts to form agricultural cooperatives have been blocked by prominent civil servants who have a stake in the private sector. In the area of social services and education, the government has introduced free health care for people on low incomes and free education at the primary school level. State agricultural, industrial, and trading schemes have been delayed because of high capital costs. Indeed, the drought, a costly guerrilla war in Matabeleland, and declines in world mineral and commodity prices have caused a deterioration in public revenue and forced severe cuts in socialist programs. This has heightened the power struggle between the fiscal conservatives, or pragmatists, and the "scientific socialist" radicals. The former remained in control of economic matters, but the radicals' influence over purely political questions continues to grow. Nevertheless, it is unlikely that Mugabe will make any direct moves against foreign business interests for fear it might further weaken the economy.

ZANU's major publication, *Moto*, tends to reflect the more militant Marxist wing. The government-owned radio and television services are now under ZANU party domination. The country's major dailies, once privately held by a South African–based conglomerate, are under strong ZANU editorial influence. The government continues to be sensitive to negative reporting by foreign correspondents. It has broadened its links with the East through agreements with the Soviet, Bulgarian, and East German news agencies. Recently, the Bulgarian government presented Zimbabwe with a large library of publications for the new ideological institute.

Domestic Affairs. Zimbabwe's population is deeply and bitterly divided over fundamental questions of power and of national purpose and direction. This is reflected in ambivalence and contradictions in economic theory, in development strategy, and in dealings with foreign diplomats and business people. The whites, numbering approximately 100,000 (down from 240,000 in 1980), are generally against ZANU's socialist policies but grudgingly cooperate. They are internally divided, and many have bolted from Ian Smith's Republic Front to form their own Conservative Alliance, which has steadily gained seats in parliament. But whites are less active in parliament, which itself is becoming less relevant as political power and decisionmaking shift to Mugabe and the ZANU Politburo. However, key white farmers and industrialists still exert considerable behind-the-scenes influence in the economic realm, as do a number of multinational corporations, particularly Heinz and Lonrho.

ZANU's relations with ZAPU, the major opposition party, remain extremely tense and bitter. The number and magnitude of violent interparty clashes increased dramatically in 1984. Several officials in both parties were assassinated, notably Senator Moven Ndhlovu, a prominent ZANU Central Committee member. (*NYT*, 12 November.) In November, Mugabe sacked the last two ZAPU officials from his cabinet in retaliation for the Ndhlovu death. This move ended the ZANU/ZAPU government coalition, formed after independence in 1980. (*Economist*, London, 17 November.)

Anti-ZANU activity has greatly escalated since Nkomo's removal from the cabinet in early 1982. Nearly 15 percent of the 35,000-strong National Army (most ZAPU supporters) have deserted and returned to bush guerrilla warfare. Military armories have been attacked, farms have been burned, whites as well as blacks have been killed or kidnapped, and nearly a quarter of the air force was destroyed by a guerrilla raid on a major airbase. In the first half of 1983, the government retaliated brutally, using the ill-disciplined, North Korean–trained Fifth Brigade. Numerous ZAPU officials in Matabeleland were detained, and several thousand Ndebele villagers and ZAPU functionaries were killed or wounded. After severe criticism and accusations of atrocities by the clergy and foreign press, the violence subsided and the Fifth Brigade was withdrawn. In early 1984, the military action in Matabeleland was resumed out of government fear that the "dissident" activity would spread to the Central Midlands province. The ensuing turmoil, compounded by the severe drought, disrupted the local economy and caused massive hunger and malnutrition. Mugabe blamed the insurgency on ZAPU leader Joshua Nkomo. By May, the level of violence had subsided, the curfew was lifted, and the brigade was again withdrawn. But the violence in Matabeleland placed enormous constraints on the ability of ZAPU and ZANU, Ndebele and Shona, to deal with each other on economic and political levels. The military operation has also alienated prominent church leaders who had supported ZANU during the struggle for independence.

The strife in Matabeleland has left ZAPU weak and internally divided. ZAPU held its first party congress in nine years in late 1984 (*WP*, 13 October). But it was clear that Nkomo had lost considerable support among youth. Moreover, the leadership had been weakened by the death of its popular vice-president, Josiah Chinamano, and the defection to ZANU of Callistus Ndlovu, a government minister. Moreover, Mugabe had succeeded in persuading a number of local ZAPU committees in Matabeleland to defect. (*Africa Confidential*, 5 September.)

ZANU's relations with the tiny opposition party, the United African National Congress (UANC), did not improve, even though on 4 September the government released from detention its leader, former Zimbabwan prime minister Bishop Abel Muzorewa (*Africa News*, 3 December).

International Views and Positions. ZANU and the Zimbabwe government officially adhere to a policy of nonalignment. The government has obtained loans from such Western multinational agencies as the World Bank and the International Monetary Fund. Its most important trade agreements are still with the European Community's (EC's) Lome II Convention, the Generalized System of Preferences (with the United States and others), and arrangements with the Republic of South Africa. The latter is still its major trade partner. (*CSO Quarterly Digest*, June 1984.) The assistance of such Western international lending institutions has given the capitalist countries considerable leverage over the direction of Zimbabwe's fiscal and monetary policies. With the exception of the People's Republic of China, aid from Marxist countries has been meager by comparison. In January, ZANU and the Bulgarian Communist Party renewed a two-year cooperation protocol for agricultural development, and the Chinese have cooperated on a recently completed state-owned clothing factory.

On the African continent, Zimbabwe enjoys close relations with Marxist Ethiopia and Mozambique. Officially, it supports the Nkomati Accord between Mozambique and South Africa, but vows not to enter into a similar agreement with the South Africans (*FBIS*, 15 August). Zimbabwe accuses South Africa of destabilizing activities in southern Africa and of propagandizing Zimbabwe's population through the government-owned Radio Truth, which is beamed into turbulent Matabeleland.

Zimbabwe plays a leading role in the Southern African Development Coordination Conference (SADCC) and the eighteen-member Preferential Trade Agreement (PTA) with central and eastern African countries. Prime Minister Mugabe is currently chairman of SADCC and a prominent Zimbabwan economist is executive secretary of the PTA. Moreover, the Reserve Bank of Zimbabwe acts as a clearinghouse in the settlement of financial accounts of PTA member-states.

Zimbabwe continues to support the South-West African People's Organization and its Soviet-supported effort to achieve Namibian independence. It is also an active member of the Organization of African Unity and supports movements aimed at establishing a multiracial socialist government in South Africa.

Richard W. Hull
New York University

THE AMERICAS

Introduction

Revolutionary violence and electoral politics were uppermost in the thoughts and actions of Latin American Marxist-Leninists during 1984. In some countries Marxist-Leninists maintained organizational unity within parties and built (or maintained) broadly based coalitions; in some states personal and policy rivalries split organizations, weakened or precluded coalitions, and generally reduced the domestic impact of the communist left.

The revolutionary violence, which ranged from civil war to isolated terrorist actions, occurred mainly in Central America and in the Andean countries stretching from Colombia to Chile. Electoral politics were important in even more states, from most of the largest—including Argentina and Brazil—to island-nations as small as Grenada in the Caribbean. In Mexico conditions favored an expanded electoral role for the left, but intraparty strife prevented the Communists from taking real advantage of the opening.

Communist and workers groups held three major regional conferences during the year. The first, which brought together twelve parties and organizations mainly from the Caribbean, convened in Georgetown, Guyana, from 2 through 4 March; the second brought delegates from 21 countries of Central America and the Caribbean to Havana on 11–13 June; and the third brought thirteen, mainly South American, parties together on 6–7 July in Buenos Aires. All three issued statements evaluating the current situation and reasserting the line that the Reagan administration in Washington has stepped up its warlike policies in the region.

The activities and prospects for Marxist-Leninist groups in Latin America—Central America above all—were influenced by international interests and involvement in the region. The Soviet Union and Cuba provided military, economic, and other aid to Nicaragua, and the latter in turn continued to assist the Salvadoran guerrillas. The United States, on the other hand, increased its military and economic aid to the government in San Salvador after the Salvadoran presidential election early in the year brought Christian Democrat José Napoleón Duarte to power. The United States also provided "covert" support for anti-government guerrillas fighting the Sandinista government in Nicaragua. Discussions by the so-called Contadora countries (Mexico, Panama, Colombia, Venezuela) designed to reduce this international role in the region led in July to a draft treaty to reduce tensions by regional disarmament. Nicaragua accepted the draft, but the United States and its Central American allies considered the wording too vague to guarantee equally the interests of all parties concerned, and the Contadora officials soon began working on a revision.

Cuba remained the most important Marxist-Leninist country in the Western Hemisphere, in part because of its own geographical position so close to the United States and in part because of its ties to the Soviet bloc. The Cuban economy improved somewhat during 1984, though Castro admitted in October that a "spirit of fraternal cooperation" guaranteed the island's economic survival. Cuba receives at least $4 billion in economic aid and about $1.7 billion in military aid each year from the Soviet Union alone.

Cuba worked out a sixteen-year development policy with the Soviet bloc toward the end of the year, with the following goals: (1) concentrate investment and production on goods that will increase exports or decrease imports; (2) diversify exports and increase sales to the West; (3) hold back investment in health, housing, and education; and (4) postpone major expansion of the consumer market. The sugar harvest of 8 million tons brought in about $4 billion, nearly three-quarters of all export revenues. But Cuba's debt to the West is $3 billion and to the Soviet bloc $9 billion. (*Los Angeles Times*, 31 December.) Cuba has long claimed particular success in its health and education programs, which now will be cut back until the year 2000, but recent studies show that the earlier claims were much inflated (*WSJ*, 10 December).

Revolutionary warfare was most advanced in El Salvador, Nicaragua, and Peru. El Salvador remained a focus of attention throughout the year. The Farabundo Martí Front of National Liberation (FMLN)—the Salvadoran guerrillas—and its Democratic Revolutionary Front (FDR) political arm continued their civil war against the government of El Salvador. The FMLN's fortunes rose and fell periodically during the year, but at the end of December it was not appreciably nearer victory or defeat than it had been at the beginning of the year.

The FMLN/FDR boycotted the presidential elections held in March, with a runoff in May, just as they had the congressional elections two years earlier. This meant that electoral competition was limited to parties ranging from the far right—represented by Roberto d'Aubuisson and his ARENA party—to the moderate left of the Christian Democrats led by Duarte. Duarte won the presidency and seemed to have the support of the top leaders of the military; his inauguration in June raised some hopes for an end to the war, which by early 1985 had taken 50,000 lives in just over five years. Duarte's successful trip through the United States and Europe increased international support for his efforts, not least economic and military aid from the United States.

Limited breakthroughs were made after Duarte's inauguration—including a prisoner exchange—though face-to-face talks did not occur with the guerrillas until mid-October amidst national and international euphoria over the prospects for peace in the land. At the meeting, Duarte and FMLN/FDR leaders skirted their fundamental differences but did set up a joint commission. Fighting continued at a high pitch immediately after the meeting, with both government and guerrillas suffering serious defeats, while economic losses directly attributable to guerrilla sabotage rose to approximately U.S. $1 billion. When the commission met at the end of November, the critical issues re-emerged—among them FMLN demands for a new constitution, a reorganization of the military, and a formula for sharing political power—immediately dousing hopes of a quick breakthrough, which few serious observers had expected in any event. After the November meeting a Christmas/New Year's truce was agreed upon and with few exceptions adhered to. But fears that Duarte would "sell out" to the guerrillas increased within the military and on the political right. A plot against the life of Archbishop Arturo Rivera y Damas, an outspoken advocate of the negotiations, reflected rising tensions and the improbability of any serious discussions before the congressional elections scheduled for March 1985 in which the Christian Democrats hope to take majority control from the right.

In Nicaragua under the Sandinistas, Marxism-Leninism was the ruling ideology. In February the government announced that it would hold a presidential election on 4 November. The government immediately ruled out the participation of any groups or the 15,000 or so individuals involved in the guerrilla war; Sandinista leaders regularly refused even to talk with the rebels, though they did so when a Miskito Indian leader expressed interest at the end of the year (*NYT*, 17 October; and see below). The main opposition would have come from the Democratic Coordination Group led by former Sandinista junta member Arturo Cruz, who went into exile at the end of 1981. After repeated discussions with Sandinista officials, and some experience trying to campaign in Nicaragua (see *Los Angeles Times*, 26 September), Cruz concluded that guarantees of a free election were inadequate and refused to participate, a judgment seconded by one of the Sandinistas' first and strongest allies, former Venezuelan president and current vice-president of the Socialist International, Carlos Andres Pérez (*WSJ*, 11 January 1985). Sandinista presidential candidate Daniel Ortega Saavedra, the top leader in the government, won the election for a six-year term with 67 percent of the vote, and Sandinist candidates took 61 of the 96 congressional seats.

While the Sandinista government claimed allegiance from most of the people, evidence increased of rising opposition to the government. Pedro Joaquín Chamorro, the editor of *La Prensa*, Nicaragua's only opposition newspaper, moved to Costa Rica in December, charging that censorship had "reached a monstrous level" in the country (*NYT*, 4 January 1985). Archibishop Miguel Obando y Bravo, once the spiritual leader of the Sandinist opposition to Somoza, has now become the "spiritual leader of the junta's opposition" (*NYT Magazine*, 18 November); the Roman Catholic church dismissed one Jesuit and threatened to defrock several others, all among the "liberation theology" priests in Nicaragua, who refused to follow Pope John Paul II's directive to give up their positions in the Sandinist government. Dissident Miskito Indian leader Brooklyn Rivera tried to negotiate an understanding with the government on behalf of his people at the end of the year but gave up, charging that the Sandinists "keep killing us, persecuting us and destroying our traditional villages" (*NYT*, 16 December).

The Sandinist economy near the end of 1984 was described as "an economic hodgepodge that is inefficient, insolvent and infested with rule-breaking schemes and scams"; Nicaragua had a thriving black market and an escalating foreign debt of more than $4 billion (*Los Angeles Times*, 26 November).

The Sandinist government, which continued to receive military and economic aid from the Soviet bloc, was also under pressure from abroad. This came mainly from guerrillas the United States had supported with more than $73 million in aid between 1981 and early 1984 when Congress cut their assistance. The two main rebel forces are the Democratic Revolutionary Alliance (ARDE), with an estimated 5,000 fighters in southern Nicaragua, headed by former Sandinista hero Edén Pastora—who was nearly killed during the year in a bombing attack at a press conference—and the Democratic National Front (FDN), with between 10,000 and 15,000 guerrillas, mostly in northern Nicaragua, headed by Adolfo Calero and including Alfonso Robelo and some other former ARDE members who broke with Pastora last year. In October the U.S. Congress set aside $14 million, which will be made available to the guerrillas in March 1985 if released by both houses. In early January both Chamorro and Cruz came out in favor of continued U.S. aid to the rebels (*NYT*, 4 January 1985). A month later the U.S. government reportedly was considering encouraging the two groups to form an umbrella organization that could openly receive U.S. aid (ibid., 3 February 1985). The United States came under heavy international criticism for not accepting the Contadora draft (see above), and for its roles in mining Nicaraguan harbors and preparing a manual on guerrilla warfare that circulated among anti-Sandinist guerrillas. Nicaragua took the mining incident to the World Court, but the United States refused to participate in the case, arguing that international relations are not a narrow legal matter, but a political problem and along with collective security and self-defense are not appropriate for judicial resolution; the United States charged that in taking this case the court was giving up judicial restraint (ibid., 19 January 1985).

Peru, torn by a large foreign debt ($13.5 billion), inflation of 125 percent, and nearly 50 percent unemployment, provided the setting for some of the most vicious fighting in the Americas, but also the broadest and in many respects most fascinating leftist political alliance. It still houses the largest number of Soviet advisers on the continent—600. The Sendero Luminoso guerrillas—who number between 2,000 and 7,000—originated in a Maoist group during the early 1960s. The Shining Path war has caused more than 5,000 deaths; in 1984, 64 officials of all parties, including ten mayors, were killed, and infrastructure losses due to sabotage amounted to about $15 million. Several other smaller groups turned to guerrilla warfare during the year, most importantly the Tupac Amaru Revolutionary Movement. During 1984 the Peruvian government responded to increasing attacks by declaring thirteen provinces emergency zones under military control and launched a more repressive counterinsurgency program that has touched nonviolent groups as well and been criticized by Amnesty International.

The Peruvian Communist Party is the most important member of the critically important United Left (IU) coalition, which has been described as an "umbrella organization for the Marxist left." The IU won 30 percent of the vote in the 1983 municipal elections—securing the mayoralty of Lima and top offices in other municipalities—and emerged as the second largest political group in the country.

Violence also increased in Chile, where the main groups were the Movement of the Revolutionary Left (MIR) and the Manuel Rodríguez Patriotic Front, with unofficial links to the Communist Party of Chile (PCC). The Popular Democratic Movement, which includes the PCC, the Almeyda faction of the Socialist Party, and the MIR, endorses both violent and nonviolent struggle. This puts the front and its parties at odds with the much broader Democratic Alliance, which includes major portions of the Socialist Party as well as Christian Democrats and others. At the end of the year the government responded to rising leftist terrorism with increased censorship and repression.

Other countries with significant levels of Marxist-Leninist-inspired violence included Guatemala, Honduras, Ecuador, Bolivia, and Venezuela. The government of Colombia finally negotiated an indefinite suspension of military conflict with the country's four main guerrilla groups, though differences of interpretation, charges, and countercharges flared up and factions within each guerrilla organization refused to go along with the agreement and continued to fight with government troops.

Communist parties and other Marxist-Leninist groups participated in—or tried to participate in—nonviolent political activities in many countries. Marxist groups in Ecuador participated in the January elections and took a total of 10.4 percent of the presidential vote and won 6 of the 71 seats in congress. Among the Marxist participants, the communist party–dominated Broad Left Front won 3.6 percent of the presidential vote and two congressional seats, the Maoist Popular Democratic Movement won 6.1 percent and three seats, and the pro-Cuban Socialist Front won 0.7 percent and one seat. After the election, the Communists became part of the Progressive Parliamentary Front, the main opposition group in congress.

In Bolivia, where inflation had soared to between 2,000 and 3,000 percent by the end of the year, the communist party held two cabinet posts until the end of the year—the only such ministerial appointments held by Communists in a non-Marxist-Leninist government in South America—and exerted pressure on the government through its leading role in the Bolivian Labor Central (COB). By the end of the year the divergent lines followed by the COB and the government played a part in forcing the Communists out of the cabinet.

The Communist Party of Argentina, which supported the Peronist presidential candidates in 1973 and 1983, tried unsuccessfully to build a broad popular front. The Brazilian Communist Party, weakened by the withdrawal of its founder and other party members, openly carried out a program calling for direct presidential elections and its own legalization. The Communist Party of Brazil, though involved in more disruptive activities, also sought legalization. The communist Popular Vanguard Party (PVP) in Costa Rica continued to be rent asunder by a power struggle between its founder, Manuel Mora Valverde, who eventually had to found the new Costa Rican People's Party, and a more radical faction in the PVP. In Panama, the People's Party became legal; when it could not form an alliance for the 1984 presidential election, it participated with little success on its own, stressing its allegiance to the positions of the late Panamanian leader Omar Torrijos.

The Maurice Bishop Patriotic Movement participated in the election in Grenada in November, winning 5 percent of the vote and no seats in congress. The Communist Party of Uruguay, though not yet legalized, participated in the November elections through stand-in candidates in the leftist Broad Front coalition, which won 21 percent of the vote. The PCU won 25 percent of the left's vote. Only about half of the eligible Venezuelans turned out for municipal elections. The largest communist party, the Movement to Socialism, took only 4 percent. The United Left Coalition, which included the Venezuelan Communist Party—currently shaken by an internal power struggle—did worse. Communist parties in Guadeloupe and Martinique, the latter going through an internal shake-up as well, continued to be active in their respective political systems. Cheddi Jagan's People's Progressive Party in Guyana continued as the main opposition to the ruling and increasingly unpopular People's National Congress, applying some pressure through congress and an increasingly powerful role in the organized labor movement.

The Communist Party USA (CPUSA) charged that "fascist-oriented individuals" have taken over the Republican Party. The party focused its attention in 1984 on the presidential campaign. The party ran its own candidates—Gus Hall for president and Angela Davis for vice-president. The CPUSA was on the ballot in 22 states and got 35,561 votes, down almost a quarter from four years ago. But the party also gave de facto support to the Democratic Party, voicing particular support for Jesse Jackson. CPUSA criticism of U.S. foreign policy was invariably in line with that of the Soviet Union. The Socialist Workers' Party (SWP) has been shaken in the past year by purges and internal upheaval. Party membership has dropped from about 2,000 several years ago to less than 1,000 at the beginning of 1985. The SWP has adopted an increasingly positive attitude toward the Soviet Union.

William Ratliff
Hoover Institution

Argentina

Population. 30,097,000
Party. Communist Party of Argentina (Partido Comunista de la Argentina; PCA)
Founded. 1918
Membership. 70,000 (estimated); 200,000 (claimed)
Secretary General. Athos Fava
Politburo. 8 members: Athos Fava, Jorge Pereyra, Rubens Iscaro, Fernando Nadra, Óscar Arévalo, Irene Rodríguez, Luis Heller, Hugo Ojeda
Central Committee. 92 members, 33 alternates
Status. Legal
Last Congress. Extraordinary, 5–6 September 1983
Last Election. 1983, 1.3 percent, no representation
Auxiliary Organizations. Communist Youth; local branch of World Peace Council; Committee in Solidarity with Nicaragua; the party effectively controls the Argentine Permanent Assembly on Human Rights.
Publications. *¿Qué Pasa?* (weekly)

In 1984 Argentina returned to civilian rule for the first time in seven years. In elections held the previous October (see *YICA*, 1984, pp. 82–83), Dr. Raúl Alfonsín of the Radical Civic Union decisively defeated the candidate of the presumptively majoritarian Peronist party, which had dominated electoral politics for nearly forty years.

Alfonsín had ridden to power on a program that offered something to everybody, capturing votes from left, right, and center. The magnitude of his success can be fully understood, however, only with reference to two factors. First, this was the first truly open presidential contest since 1946 in which the Peronist ticket was not headed by the movement's founder, Gen. Juan D. Perón, who died in office in 1974. Second, because Alfonsín was a relatively minor political figure in the final years of the last Peronist government (1973–1976), he was free of all association with the corruption and violence that marked it and the military juntas that succeeded it (1976–1983). He was thus ideally positioned to appeal to the 7 million new voters who had reached maturity since 1976 and who wished to turn an entirely new page in their nation's history.

The new government took office in December 1983, in an atmosphere of optimism and even euphoria, even though it confronted an economic crisis unprecedented in the nation's history. The eye of the storm was an accumulated foreign debt of more than $43 billion, about half of which would fall due during 1984. During his first six months, Alfonsín recurred to the time-tested formulas of Latin American populism—wage increases and artificially imposed ceilings on prices. The result was a shortage of many articles of prime necessity and an annual inflation rate approaching 700 percent (compared with 434 percent in 1983). After lengthy delays, by the end of the year the government had finally conceded the need to reach an understanding with several hundred foreign private creditors (largely Western banks) and to sign a letter of intent with the International Monetary Fund. This evidently presaged a long period of retrenchment, austerity, and the very "recessionary solutions" that Alfonsín had loudly insisted during his presidential campaign he would never impose upon Argentines.

Two other aspects of the Argentine scene in 1984 are of relevance here. Peronism's first, unexpected electoral defeat inflicted upon that movement a psychological shock of major proportions, unleashing angry recriminations that served only to accentuate existing divisions within its leadership and also within the labor movement it has long dominated. Further, the restoration of democracy in Argentina made it easier for communist and other left-wing parties to operate in the full light of day, without fear of police harassment such as had characterized the previous period. While this meant greater visibility, it did not necessarily point to greater influence. The left generally performed poorly in the 1983 elections (see ibid., 1984, p. 82) and, with the exception of the PCA, may actually have benefited indirectly from aspects of military repression, whose principal burden fell not upon it but its longtime rival, the Peronists. Further, as the party naturally associated with Argentina's principal trading partner, the Soviet Union, the Communists in all likelihood benefited from a certain official benevolence as well as from a reported 5 percent royalty upon all Soviet commercial transactions with the country (see ibid., 1984, pp. 83–84).

Leadership and Party Organization. There were no changes in this area. Central Committee member Alfredo Varela died on 25 February.

Domestic Party Affairs. The PCA spent 1984 attempting to redefine its role in the new context of Argentine politics. Towards the new government it initially struck a pose of conditional support; as Secretary General Athos Fava never tired of repeating in the numerous interviews he gave to Eastern bloc journalists, "We have achieved bourgeois democracy, with all of the advantages and restrictions involved in this kind of change" (*Rabotnichesko delo*, Sofia, 31 July; *FBIS*, 10 August). But, he warned, "the achievement of constitutional government, no matter how good its intentions, would not mean a complete victory for the democratic forces in the country" (*Rabotnichesko delo*, 30 May; *FBIS*, 11 April). This would require a national front to include all political parties "both democratic and popular" to confront the nation's enemies, who, it was alleged, "have shown signs of regrouping." (Havana international service, 14 April; *FBIS*, 20 April.)

In effect, the PCA was returning to a very old tactic—the construction of a popular front with "bourgeois-democratic" parties, in which it would supposedly be the linchpin and balance wheel. The PCA has actually achieved this objective only once

before, when it cosponsored the Democratic Union in 1946; that coalition, however, was defeated in the presidential elections of that year, never to reassemble. The present environment seems even less promising because forming a popular front requires the party to split the Alfonsín government (in which it professed to find some "progressive" elements [*Rabotnichesko delo*, 30 March; *FBIS*, 11 April]) or, at any rate, to unite elements within the Alfonsín government to its own political organizations.

Moreover, the new administration has not been slow to utilize the resources of incumbency to forge a broad front of its own. In May it obtained a joint expression of support from all the major parties in the country, a document that the PCA refused to sign because it was too moderate and because PCA representatives had not been invited to participate in its formulation (Diarios y Noticias [DYN], 7 June; *FBIS*, 12 June). In effect, the party newspaper, *¿Qué Pasa?*, was reduced to criticizing individual policies or members of the administration and of the president's party in Congress—for excessive timidity, conservatism, or support for the United States. In particular it objected to the government's agreement with the International Monetary Fund; its lifting of price controls; its wage policies; its cautious handling of the trials of former military leaders; and its foreign policy, which has called for equidistance between the superpowers, whose moral equivalence the PCA repeatedly denies (*IB*, July). Since the party persisted in pointing to the greater danger of a "repressive apparatus which still exists" (*Rabotnichesko delo*, 31 July; *FBIS*, 10 August), this begged the question of precisely what its relationship to the administration might really be. The PCA seems to be positioning itself to reap the harvest of disillusion at some point in the future.

Of equal importance was the party's relationship with Peronism, which despite its defeat in the 1983 elections still controls the Senate, several provincial governorships, a substantial minority of seats in the Chamber of Deputies, and (of greatest moment) most of the labor movement. After two decades of antagonism, the Communists apparently determined that Peronism's hold on the laboring classes was unshakable and sought instead to bore from within. This explains, among other things, the PCA's endorsement of the Peronist presidential ticket in 1973 and again in 1983. Neither in victory (1973) nor defeat (1983) has the PCA reaped any particular advantage.

Quite obviously, the leaderless disarray in which

Peronism presently finds itself raises expectations among the left. In an interview, Fava asserted that Peronism was beset by a basic contradiction between its "working-class and popular base . . . and its conciliatory, obstructive, and anti-Communist right wing." Having led the party to a series of defeats, the Peronist leadership, he said, was "in a very profound crisis." (*IB*, October.) Among the Peronist "masses," he professed to espy inclinations toward "anti-imperialism . . . the proletarian ideology . . . [and a rejection of] bourgeois nationalism." Within the movement itself, he asserted, "the Communists represent a new element." (DYN, 6 November; *FBIS*, 8 November.) Such brave claims have been made before, only to be invalidated by the facts or by purges within the Peronist movement; nonetheless, in the present context they seem somewhat more plausible. Only the future will show to what degree the PCA—as well as other organized political forces of the left—can take advantage of the apparent decomposition of Peronism.

Auxiliary and Front Organizations. In 1984 the importance of certain left-wing organizations controlled wholly or in part by the PCA declined because the presence of a democratic government momentarily defused their primary issues. This was particularly the case with some human rights organizations, most notably the Argentine Permanent Assembly on Human Rights. On the other hand, two wholly controlled party fronts—the Committee in Solidarity with Nicaragua and the Argentine branch of the World Peace Council—were exceptionally active in public demonstrations, petitions, and fund drives. However, much of their resonance derived not so much from any implicit public sympathy for communism as for their very explicit anti-Americanism, a sentiment strong in Argentina in all seasons and among almost all political sectors, exceptionally so since the war with Great Britain in 1982, in which the United States sided with Argentina's adversary.

International Views, Positions, and Activities. In keeping with the new political environment in Argentina, the international aspects of PCA activity intensified in 1984. In April a Festival of the Communist Press was celebrated in Buenos Aires; in July the PCA hosted a two-day meeting of top-ranking communist leaders from nine South American countries convoked to study the crucial problems of the region. In attendance were representatives from Bolivia, Brazil, Chile, Colombia, Ecuador, Panama, Paraguay, Peru, Uruguay, and Venezuela (as well as from the Sandinistas and an "observer" from the Communist Party of Cuba). Relations between the PCA and the Sandinistas were predictably close; in November it was announced that 120 Communist Youth members would travel to Nicaragua to assist in the coffee harvest.

There were no significant changes in relations between Argentina and the Soviet Union (see *YICA*, 1984, pp. 83–84). A delegation from the People's Republic of China, led by Foreign Minister Wu Xueqian visited the country in July. The importance of the mission was underlined by the fact that never before had a Chinese official of comparable rank been to Argentina. Romania agreed to provide YPF, the Argentine state oil company, with equipment to expand refining facilities in Luján de Cuyo and La Plata in exchange for a specialized list of cereals and other agricultural products.

Secretary General Fava visited the German Democratic Republic in May, where he was received with full honors by Erich Honecker.

Other Leftist Groups. The Revolutionary Communist Party (PCR), a splinter faction of the PCA outlawed by the military government (1976–1983) was relegalized and announced its first political rally in nearly eight years.

Mario Firmenich, exiled head of the Montoneros, one of three urban guerrilla groups operating in Argentina during the mid-1970s, was arrested in Rio de Janeiro in February and returned to Argentina by Brazilian authorities in October to stand trial. Apart from Firmenich and Ricardo Obregón Cano, former governor of Córdoba province and a Montonero sympathizer, no other guerrilla chieftains had been apprehended and charged by the new government.

There appeared to be little public sympathy for Firmenich, though the reactions to his return were somewhat mixed.

Peronist leader Carlos Grosso was quick to insist that Firmenich "did not belong" in his movement, although he saw no reason why he might not eventually re-enter Argentine politics, as long, he said, as Firmenich agreed to play by the rules. The Frente de Izquierda Popular (FIP), led by Trotskyist-Peronist Jorge Abelardo Ramos, was far more categorical, allowing that "the solution to the plight of the 'disappeared' begins with the unmasking of the terrorists" and insisting that neither Firmenich nor Fernando Vaca Narvaja (a Montonero leader still at large) were Peronists (*La Nación*, 7 December; *JPRS*, 9 January 1985). Another Peronist leader from the more "traditional" wing of the party, Guillermo Patricio Kelly, accused Firmenich of being nothing but "a terrorist working for P-2 [Propaganda Due, an Italian-Brazilian-Argentine Masonic lodge associated with important elements of the international underworld on both sides of the Atlantic] . . . and that he has always worked for the Mafia, not for the national [Peronist] cause" (*Buenos Aires Herald*, 16 February; *FBIS*, 17 February).

For his part, Firmenich was far from contrite. Though admitting that he and his comrades had committed "errors," he denied that "all of the responsibility is ours." He boasted that the Montoneros were not finished as a movement merely because of his incarceration and promised that they would continue to wage battle in the "anti-oligarchical and anti-imperialist cause." He also warned the new government that it was "marching in the wrong direction" and that persecution of "popular militants" could lead to a crisis. He denied that his arrest would automatically promote Vaca Narvaja to leadership of the movement, which, he claimed, was collective. Significantly, in the same statement he alleged that some 5,000 Montoneros had fallen "during the period of repression"; if true, this would mean that estimates of the organization's size offered earlier by the military were less exaggerated than many thought. (Noticias Argentinas, 23 February; *FBIS*, 27 February.)

Precisely how active the Montoneros remained within Argentina was the subject of conflicting (and often highly questionable) reports. A purported summit between them and the leaders of the supposedly defunct Revolutionary People's Army (ERP) was reported in the newspaper *La Nueva Provincia* (Bahía Blanca) in April, almost immediately to be denied by the minister of interior himself (Noticias Argentinas, 14 April; *FBIS*, 18 April). The popular tabloid *Crónica* reproduced a communiqué purportedly of Montonero authorship, announcing intentions to execute ten public figures, including a bishop, a journalist, and a federal judge (DYN, 7 September; *FBIS*, 10 September). Allegations of a Montonero meeting in Bahía Blanca later proved groundless (Telam, 1 November; *FBIS*, 2 November).

Perhaps more interesting were the number of former Montoneros or sympathizers who came forward to repudiate their previous belief in violence.

One of the best-selling books of 1984 was Pablo Guissani's *Montoneros, soberbia armada* (Montoneros, armed arrogance), which among other things documented an important Cuban role in Argentina's informal civil war in 1974–1976.

Mark Falcoff
American Enterprise Institute

Buenos Aires Meeting, July 1984. A meeting of the communist parties of South America brought delegations from twelve communist parties together on 5–7 July 1984 in Buenos Aires, Argentina, under the sponsorship of the Communist Party of Argentina. "Observers" attended from Cuba and Nicaragua. The official concluding statement of that meeting was published in *IB* (October).

The statement warned that "humanity is in danger" because of the "warmongering policy of U.S. imperialism," the "common enemy" of people throughout the world who are striving for national liberation and social emancipation. Imperialist policy is "principally manifested in the preparations for deadly chemical and star wars." In the Americas, imperialist designs have resulted in such aggressive armed actions as the "barbarous invasion" of Grenada, taking over the "training and leadership of the genocidal army of El Salvador," "interventionist plots" against Nicaragua and continued efforts to "punish" Cuba for its revolution because it is "a powerful stimulus for the democratic, anti-imperialist and revolutionary struggle" of the continent. The imperialist offensive also is seen in an anticommunist "psychological war" through the mass media to "influence the minds of the people and confuse and divide them." Also, recent events demonstrate that "foreign debt has become a modern weapon of blackmail and political and economic enslavement." The United States' aggressive policy has even forced the peace-loving Soviet Union to divert funds from national development to defensive armament.

But the document also noted that positive changes have occurred in the Americas in "the last few years." Everything suggests that profound and revolutionary changes are imminent, "an essential condition for their realization being the struggle for democracy, for real freedoms, for self-determination and peaceful coexistence." These have included growing actions by peasants, urban and rural middle strata, and even part of the national bourgeoisie, Christian masses, and the Catholic church. There have been "important successes in the development of the democratic process" in Bolivia (where the government included communist ministers), Argentina (where an election was held), and Brazil (where an election was promised by the end of the year). Gains were also fought for and made in Colombia (where the government and guerrillas agreed to a cease-fire), Ecuador, Venezuela, Peru, and other countries. A "new stage of liberation" began in Central America with the victory of the Sandinista revolution.

The delgates concluded by reaffirming a statement of the 1975 Havana meeting of communist parties, that the communist parties of South America are "an integral and active part of the world communist movement and adhere firmly to the principles of Marxism-Leninism and proletarian internationalism." The unity of the working-class movement and international solidarity "are an imperative of our epoch and strengthen each other."

The official delegations at the Buenos Aires meeting were Argentina: Communist Party of Argentina; Bolivia: Communist Party of Bolivia; Brazil: Brazilian Communist Party; Colombia: Communist Party of Colombia; Chile: Communist Party of Chile; Ecuador: Communist Party of Ecuador; Guyana: People's Progressive Party; Panama: People's Party of Panama; Paraguay: Paraguayan Communist Party; Peru: Peruvian Communist Party; Uruguay: Communist Party of Uruguay; Venezuela: Communist Party of Venezuela. Observers were from Cuba: Communist Party of Cuba; and Nicaragua: Sandinista National Liberation Front.

William Ratliff
Hoover Institution

Bolivia

Population. 6,037,000
Party. Communist Party of Bolivia (Partido Comunista de Bolivia; PCB)
Founded. 1950
Membership. 300 (estimated)
Secretary General. Jorge Kolle Cueto
Party Leaders. Marcos Domic, Simón Reyes, Horst Grebe López, Carlos Carvajal, Aldo Flores
Status. Legal
Last Congress. Fourth, April 1979
Last Elections. 1980. The People's Democratic Union, the electoral coalition supported by the PCB, won 47 of the 130 seats in the lower house; these elections were nullified by a military coup; in October 1982, the parliament was allowed to meet; the PCB held two ministries until November—Labor and Mines.
Auxiliary Organizations. Communist Youth of Bolivia
Other Marxist-Leninist Parties. Maoist PCB Marxist-Leninist (PCB/ML), with estimated 150 members, led by Óscar Zamora; Trotskyist Revolutionary Workers Party (POR), with estimated 50 members in three factions led by Hugo González Moscoso, Guillermo Lora Escobar, and Amadeo Arze

The democratic regime of President Hernán Siles Suazo, as head of the Popular Democratic Union (UDP), which took office in October 1982, remained in power throughout 1984. Two PCB members who headed the Ministries of Mines and Labor were described as "the two most effective cabinet ministers" in the Siles government (*WSJ*, 2 March). Some government critics continued to argue that the PCB was the dominant influence in the government. The president was kidnapped for ten hours in June by dissident army officers and narcotics policemen who said they wanted to "clean out the Communists" (*NYT*, 12 August). But the PCB position became increasingly untenable as the year progressed and the inflation rate (in December) reached 2,000–3,000 percent. The deteriorating economic situation, marked by shortages of staples, food riots, strikes, and general unrest in the labor movement and society, created conflicts between the PCB as a member of the UDP government and the party as the largest element in the Bolivian Labor Federation (COB), which was highly critical of government economic policies. The tensions were brought to a head in the contrasting emergency economic programs prepared by the UDP and the COB. In November, in the wake of increasing unrest in the military and labor movement—what one non-PCB minister called "the anarchization of democracy"—the government and opposition agreed to hold general elections in June 1985. The PCB left the government in a general cabinet shake-up in January 1985.

The PCB relationship to the government was elaborated at party plenary sessions. Kolle Cueto stated at the beginning of the year that the PCB maintained its previous support for political democratization in the country and stressed the need for "a front made up of social classes represented by their political and party representatives who are interested in the people's democratic and anti-imperialist project which is proposed by the UDP for this period." Clearly, he concluded, the PCB still regards the UDP as the best option for the liberation of the Bolivian masses at this time. (Cadena Panamericana, La Paz, 1 February; *FBIS*, 2 February.) Thus at the beginning of the year the PCB led a campaign to bring the Movement of the Revolutionary Left (MIR), which had withdrawn from the government in 1983, back into the government in 1984. But PCB objectives, as Kolle Cueto explained in February, included the formation of a new government coalition that would incorporate other leftist political and social forces as well, thus expanding the political base of the government (*Hoy*, 23 February).

Tensions within the party and between the party and President Siles increased during the year, as noted above. Much of this was centered in the COB. Juan Lechin Oquendo, the non-PCB executive sec-

retary of the federation, noted that PCB members in the COB had disagreements with PCB members in the government (Cadena Panamericana, 12 March; *FBIS*, 13 March). Prominent PCB member Simón Reyes, a national deputy and COB official, said there was no contradiction between the strikes called by the COB and the organization's firm support for constitutional government, but added that "our support for the democratic process does not mean that we totally agree with the government's policy because there are contradictory positions within the ruling coalition." He concluded, "We are ready to defend the democratic process to the end. However, we do not want democracy to be an object that you can hold and look at, but to resolve the problems of the workers and the country. We want democracy in order to attain development." (Noticias Argentinas, Buenos Aires, 7 July; *FBIS*, 10 July.) But PCB participation in the government undoubtedly was the primary reason for the setback the party suffered at the COB congress in September, when the party lost three of its seven leadership positions. What the vote actually demonstrated, according to PCB congressman Marcos Domic, was the defeat of the "ultras," the POR (Lara), which failed to win a position on the new COB executive committee, and the Maoist PCB/ ML, which "only got some seats through their dissidents." Domic added that no other part of the labor movement has even 10 percent of the strength of the PCB. "The great loser at the congress was not the PCB," he concluded. "It was the working class, because the new executive committee does not reflect the composition of the COB." (*Latin America Weekly Report*, 28 September.)

The PCB attended a conference of communist parties convened in Buenos Aires in July and, both then and on other occasions, condemned the "warlike" schemes of the Reagan administration in El Salvador, Nicaragua, and throughout the world (e.g., PCB post-conference statement carried on Cadena Panamericana, 10 July; *FBIS*, 12 July; and comments of Felipe Rodríguez in *WMR*, October). There were reports during the year that as many as 500 radical Bolivian leftists had been trained for guerrilla warfare in Cuba and returned home to train guerrilla groups in the country (*WSJ*, 2 March), possibly to defend the Siles government if and when the rightists tried to overthrow it or possibly to act on their own. U.S. intelligence reported that President Siles is increasingly surrounded by radical leftists, including many Communists and some Cubans (*Washington Times*, 1

August). The Soviet Union has expanded its ties to the Bolivian government through aid to tin and other mining/industrial projects and, reportedly, by appointing a new military attaché at the embassy whose assignment is to promote Soviet arms sales to Bolivia (*WSJ*, 2 March).

The POR was active during the year despite its failure to win a seat on the executive committee of the COB. It won student elections at the main national university early in the year and controls the Siglo XX Miners Union, the most aggressive labor organization in the country.

William Ratliff
Hoover Institution

Brazil

Population. 134,380,000
Party. Brazilian Communist Party (Partido Comunista Brasileiro; PCB); originally Communist Party of Brazil (Partido Comunista do Brasil; PCdoB); name changed in 1960
Founded. 1922
Membership. 8,000 (Army Intelligence; *Veja*, 24 October)
Secretary General. Giocondo Dias
National Executive Committee (also referred to as National Committee for Legalization of the PCB). 12 members: Giocondo Dias, Hercules Correa, Givaldo Siqueira, Almir Neves, Salomaõ Malina, Teodoro Melo, Roberto Freire, Ivan Pinheiro, José Paulo Neto, Regis Frati, Paulo Elisario, Sergio Moraes
Central Committee (formerly National Leadership Collective, now referred to as National Provisional Committee). Reportedly will have 101 members; 66 members elected in January
Status. Illegal, but now openly seeking legalization as a party in formation
Last Congress. Seventh, January 1984; called National Meeting of Communists
Last Election. N/a
Publications. *Voz da Unidade*

The Electoral College, which met on 15 January 1985, was expected to choose Tancredo Neves, candidate of a broad opposition coalition, to succeed Gen. João Baptista Figueiredo as president of Brazil. In line with the military government's plans for a gradual return to democracy, the college had been carefully packed to ensure the victory of an approved civilian candidate from the official Social Democratic Party (Partido Demócrata Social; PDS). A combination of events made the upset possible; among the most important was the climate created by an extraordinary opposition campaign that put millions of demonstrators in the streets demanding direct presidential elections (*diretas já*). The PCB participated visibly in the *diretas* demonstrations and campaign rallies of the opposition candidate. Also present at those events were the red flags of two 1960s splinters of the PCB: the originally pro-Chinese, now pro-Albanian, Communist Party of Brazil (PCdoB) and the former guerrilla organization 8 October Revolutionary Movement (Movimento Revolucionário 8; MR-8). Freedom and Struggle (Liberdade e Luta; Libelu) and Socialist Youth Foundation (Alicerce da Juventude Socialista) are two Trotskyist groups that form the left wing of the Worker's Party (Partido dos

Trabalhadores; PT); the PT worked diligently on the diretas movement but refused to support any candidate for indirect elections. The new Communist Revolutionary Party (Partido Revolucionário Comunista; PRC) also called for a resumption of the diretas demonstrations.

Leadership and Party Organization. In January, the PCB held its Seventh Congress, called the National Meeting of Communists to avoid legal problems. Sixty-six members were elected to the National Provisional Committee, including three federal and three state deputies from the opposition Party of the Brazilian Democratic Movement (Partido do Movimento Democrático Brasileiro; PMDB). Six members were returned to the National Executive Committee, and six new members were elected. (*O Estado de São Paulo*, 11 February.)

The congress reaffirmed the principles of unity and collective leadership: "Democratic centralism is not questioned but its true and radical application, free of distortions . . . is a political necessity . . . the working class needs a party organization where the freest exchange of ideas is combined with united and centralized concrete actions" (Salomão Malina, *Que Pasa*, 18 April; *IB*, July). In the same article, Malina speaks of the debilitating effects on the party of the defections of founder Luiz Carlos Prestes and the São Paulo state leadership: "The decision not to resort to administrative measures but rather to rely on persuasion and tolerance led to a certain stagnation; all energy was directed at resolving internal questions in the ranks of the Brazilian communists." Apparently neither Prestes nor David Capistrano Filho's group in São Paulo were actually expelled—they "placed themselves outside the ranks" (*O Estado de São Paulo*, 11 February; *Folha de São Paulo*, 29 May; *JPRS*, 14 March, 9 June). The São Paulo dissidents publish the newspaper *A Esquerda*.

Domestic Affairs. The political resolution approved by the congress, "A Democratic Alternative to the Brazilian Crisis," stresses the paramount importance of securing the party's legalization. The document maintains that only on a footing of equality and equal responsibility with other parties can the PCB work effectively for necessary structural changes: restoring democracy, ending dependence on imperialism, breaking the power of monopolies

and landowners, and opening the road to socialism. Achieving this, according to the resolution, will require a democratic regime of the masses with ample channels for expression, such as grass-roots organizations, political parties, and public institutions. The proletariat will have the task of assuring solid unity among the patriotic national forces. At the same time, the working class must preserve its own identity, its political, ideological, and organizational independence. That will guarantee the cohesion and consistency of the coalition: "Only the hegemony of the proletariat will make the transition to socialism possible; it is inseparable from the leading and guiding role of the Communist Party." (Noé Gertel, "The Communist Alternative," *WMR*, August.)

In addition to the election of a national constituent assembly, the "Democratic Alternative" proposes a number of immediate initiatives, including abolition of antidemocratic laws; recognition of full freedom of party and political organization; guarantees of labor unions' right to unhindered activity and autonomy; urgent enactment of antimonopoly laws; channeling of investment into areas that enlarge domestic markets and create jobs; moratorium on debt and interest payments while the crisis persists; rescheduling of debts at fixed rates; cost of living and productivity adjustments for wages; trade union administration of welfare; and price controls on essential goods and services (ibid.).

Although the PCB operates openly as a party in formation, it has been subjected to minor harassment, and the struggle for legalization has been uphill. In October, *Voz da Unidade* offices were raided, and Executive Committee members Regis Frati and Salomão Malina were detained briefly, accused of reorganizing the illegal PCB (Radio Bandeirantes, São Paulo, 16 October; *FBIS*, 17 October). Justice Minister Ibrahim Abi-Ackel vetoed publication of the PCB's statutes, program, and manifesto in the official gazette, citing the party's ties with foreign governments as a constitutional impediment. Publication in the official gazette is a prerequisite for party registration by the Supreme Electoral Court (TSE). Deputy Roberto Freire, deputy leader of the PMDB in congress and a member of the PCB Executive Committee, had the documents inserted in the congressional diary, but the substitute was not acceptable to the TSE. The PCB will appeal the justice minister's decision. Tancredo Neves does not oppose legalization of the PCB but said a constitutional reform will be necessary, "a problem for congress, not the president" (*O Estado de São Paulo*, 20 July).

Red flags and symbols of the PCB, PCdoB, and the MR-8 were a minor scandal during the diretas demonstrations but became a major issue at the opposition rallies for Tancredo Neves. After serious government and military threats, the leftists were persuaded to leave the offending flags at home. (The illegal parties do not figure as part of the Democratic Alliance supporting Neves; this comprises only the PMDB, the large bloc of PDS dissidents called the Liberal Front, and Leonel Brizola's Democratic Labor Party [PDT].)

Auxiliary and Front Organizations. The PCB-supported labor confederation, Congress of the Working Classes (Congreso das Clases Trabalhadores; Conclat), continued to take a more conservative line politically than the rival Single Labor Central (Central Unica dos Trabalhadores; CUT), controlled by the PT with support from the Labor Pastorate of the Catholic church. Conclat, which also represents the PMDB, PDT, and PCdoB, vetoed the CUT proposal for a general strike on 25 April, the day of the congressional vote on an amendment to restore direct presidential elections. Following the defeat of the amendment, Conclat participated in the initial CUT attempts to revive diretas demonstrations but soon desisted in favor of the opposition unity candidate for indirect elections. In the most important union election in 1984, the Conclat slate, headed by Joaquim dos Santos Andrade, defeated a CUT challenge for control of the São Paulo metallurgical workers' union. (This should not be confused with the slightly smaller but more militant metallurgical union of São Bernardo do Campo, a São Paulo suburb. The São Bernardo union gained fame with its strikes in 1980 and became the base of Luis Ignácio "Lula" da Silva's PT.)

In an army seminar on communist infiltration in Brazil, Jo Rezende was accused of having links with the PCB. Rezende, who heads a movement among members of National Housing Bank cooperatives protesting unfair mortgage adjustments, denied the charge. (*Veja*, 24 October.) His group was very active in the diretas campaign. During the same seminar, Gen. Iris Lustosa warned of PCB infiltration in the army (ibid.). Executive Committee member Hercules Correa had said earlier that since PCB plans no longer include a military

"putsch," "we have stopped doing any work in the armed forces" (*Correio Braziliense*, 17 June; *JPRS*, 23 July).

International Views. Executive Committee member Teodoro Melo attended a meeting of communist leaders from thirteen Latin American countries in Buenos Aires on 6–7 July. A final communiqué from the meeting denounced "the mounting and multifaceted economic, military, political and diplomatic aggressiveness of Yankee imperialism against Cuba, and the brazen interventionism in Nicaragua." It added that U.S. policy in the region is tied to the staggering debt of the countries: "This shows that the region is being affected by a new stage of the militaristic campaign sponsored by the Reagan administration, which, under the pretext of an outrageous anti-communism . . . has led the world to the brink of nuclear war." Pointing out that this policy "contrasts with repeated Soviet peace proposals," the statement noted that such a policy has also been opposed by an "anti-militaristic outcry throughout the world." All the delegations reiterated their firm support for "the just cause of the Argentine people to recover the Malvinas islands, which were usurped by the Anglo-Yankee aggression." (Diarios y Noticias, Buenos Aires, 7 July; *FBIS*, 10 July.)

In his analysis of the PCB's political resolution, Noé Gertel inserts the "Brazilian crisis" into a regional context:

The Sandinista revolution in Nicaragua . . . is being consolidated and the people's war is widening in El Salvador against the puppet regime propped up by U.S. bayonets . . . Headway has been made by democratic forces in Bolivia and Argentina and there is growing working class resistance to the reactionary regimes in Uruguay and Chile . . . The USA's Latin American policy is in deep crisis, while the shows of strength, such as the treacherous invasion of Grenada and the aggression against Nicaragua, are only a reflection of that policy's hollowness.

The Reagan administration's attempts to contain the revolutionary movement, block the aspirations of the developing nations . . . and enter into open confrontation with the socialist world are a deadly threat to the human race . . . In this situation, we feel it is our duty to mobilize large sections of public opinion to cut short the aggressive designs of North American imperialism. [*WMR*, August.]

Communist Party of Brazil. Aurélio Peres, a PCdoB labor leader and federal deputy (PMDB), described the PCdoB as a "legitimate, authentic, Stalinist, nonrevisionist party." In the Saõ Paulo metallurgical union elections, he felt justified in supporting Andrade, a center leftist, because he was the candidate of Conclat, "which shelters all the Communists." The CUT, according to Peres, is PT, "an inconsequential, predominantly Trotskyist front . . . Things are easy for them now because they can raise the banner of class struggle, an opportunity denied the illegal parties." (*O Estado de Saõ Paulo*, 8 April.)

Reflecting the new opposition strategies, and its own hopes for eventual legalization, the PCdoB has been generally nonviolent in 1984. However, the PCdoB- and PT-dominated Committee Against Unemployment invaded the offices of the National Employment System in Saõ Paulo with 800 men, women, and children demanding jobs and benefits. After six days, Governor Franco Montoro (PMDB) decided to starve them out, but Cardenal Paulo Evaristo Arns, archbishop of Saõ Paulo, visited the invaders and had food sent in. (Ibid., 21–26 August.)

In October, police raided PCdoB training centers in Saõ Paulo and Campos do Jordaõ and detained party members for questioning in several cities. Arrests were also made at the offices of the party weekly, *Tribuna de Luta Operária*, in Goiania. (Saõ Paulo offices of *Tribuna* were destroyed by fire in April, presumably set by right-wing terrorists.) The Saõ Paulo training school, the Center of Social Studies and Research, is linked, according to police, to the Institute of People's and Workers' Political Culture, a front for the PCdoB Central Committee (Radio Bandeirantes, Saõ Paulo, 27 October; *FBIS*, 1 November). Army Intelligence reports a membership of 7,000 for the PCdoB (*Veja*, 24 October).

Trotskyist Groups. Alicerce and Libelu form the left wing of the PT and would seem to be active in the party's heavy involvement with organization of the urban unemployed; slum dwellers (*favelados*); migrant farmworkers; and landless peasants (*sem terra*). The Land Pastorate of the Catholic church cooperates with the PT on rural work, much of it related to instigation and support of land invasions. (There are differences within the church regarding these tactics, and the Vatican document on liberation theology [text in *O Globo*, 30 August] did little to settle them. Conservative clergy interpreted the paper as a condemnation of liberation theology; progressives saw it as a justification.)

PT president Luis Ignácio "Lula" da Silva, the only labor leader invited personally to the fifth anniversary celebration of the Sandinista revolution, said in Managua that "the Nicaraguan revolution is a hope for the peoples of the Third World" (*O Estado de Saõ Paulo*, 21 July). A few days earlier, during an official visit to Havana, he commented that "the Cuban experience, with all the progress achieved in the social field, despite being a poor country without resources and wealth, could be repeated in Brazil if it were a well-run country" (*Folha de Saõ Paulo*, 18 July; *FBIS*, 20 July).

Other Organizations. The name of the MR-8 appeared almost daily in the press, but always simply as one of the illegal parties waving flags at diretas demonstrations, the PMDB convention, and opposition rallies. In April, individuals claiming to be policemen raided and vandalized the Brasilia offices of the party's weekly, *Hora do Povo*. According to Army Intelligence, the MR-8 has 1,500 members (*Veja*, 24 October).

The PRC was founded on 21 June, the sixtieth anniversary of the death of Lenin. According to Ozeas Duarte, a "representative" of the PRC Central Committee, "The PRC repudiates alliances with the bourgeoisie and has no doubt that violence will be necessary to bring the working class to power." The PRC advocates street protests, clashes with police, and a general strike. Party statutes consider social democracy an antilabor concept; Trotskyism a "personal willed deviation"; and PCB tenets as "dissembled reformism nourished by Stalinism." The PRC has no international connections with parties or countries and, under present circumstances, does not seek legalization. (*Jornal do Brasil*, 8 July; *FBIS*, 12 July.) At the army seminar mentioned above, José Genoino, a PT deputy from Saõ Paulo, was cited as leader of the PRC. Genoino denied the charges (*Veja*, 24 October).

Carole Merten
Miami, Florida

Canada

Population. 25,142,000
Parties. Communist Party of Canada (CPC); Communist Party of Canada (Marxist-Leninist) (CPC-ML); Revolutionary Workers' League (RWL); Trotskyist League (TL); Forward Readers Group (FRG)
Founded. CPC: 1921; CPC-ML: 1970; RWL: 1977
Membership. CPC: 2,500 (estimated); CPC-ML: 500–1,000; RWL: several hundred
Secretary General. CPC: William Kashtan; CPC-ML: Hardial Bains; RWL: John Riddell
Central Committee. CPC: 20 members
Status. Legal
Last Congress. CPC: Twenty-fifth, 13–15 February 1982, in Toronto; CPC-ML: Fourth, 3 April 1982, in Montreal; RWL: Fifth, 27 December 1983–1 January 1984
Last Federal Election. 4 September 1984; CPC: 52 candidates, average vote 162; RWL: 5 candidates, average vote 127; no representatives
Auxiliary Organizations. CPC: Communist Party of Quebec, Canadian Peace Congress, Conseil québecois de la paix, Association of United Ukrainian Canadians, Congress of Canadian Women, Young Communist League; CPC-ML: People's Front Against Racist and Fascist Violence, Revolutionary Trade Union Opposition, Democratic Women's Union of Canada, East Indian Defence Committee, West Indian People's Organization, Communist Youth Union of Canada (M-L); RWL: Young Socialist Organizing Committee, Comité de la jeunesse révolutionnaire
Publications. CPC: *Canadian Tribune, Pacific Tribune, Combat, Communist Viewpoint, Le Communiste, Rebel Youth, Jeunesse militante, Nouvelle revue internationale*; CPC-ML: *Marxist-Leninist, Le Marxiste-Leniniste, Voice of the Youth, Voice of the People, West Indian, Lok Awaz, Etincelle, RTUOC Weekly Bulletin, Democratic Women, People's Front Bulletin, Canadian Student, BC Worker*; RWL: *Socialist Voice, Lutte ouvrière, New International* (copublished with U.S. counterpart); TL: *Sparticist Canada*

Several Marxist-Leninist parties and groups operate legally in Canada. The oldest and largest is the CPC. Since its founding in 1921, the CPC has been consistently pro-Moscow in alignment. The CPC-ML, founded in 1970, is pro-Albanian. Several Trotskyist groups exist, including the RWL, the TL, and the FRG.

Pierre Trudeau's resignation as both prime minister and leader of the Liberal Party paved the way for the historic Conservative landslide victory in the September federal elections. The combined vote for all communist parties was in the vicinity of 0.1 percent of the vote. No candidates were elected. The parties have been increasingly active in municipal elections, notably in Vancouver, Winnipeg, and Toronto, and several members have won election.

The Canadian economy continued to be mired in its worst recession since the Great Depression of the 1930s. The federal government, along with most provincial governments, continued to legislate cutbacks in social services and to impose wage restrictions.

The testing of the U.S. cruise missile continued to be a catalyst for the peace movement. On

28 April over 100,000 persons in Vancouver marched in a peace walk and the Peace Petition Caravan presented to Parliament a petition with 400,000 signatures calling for Canada to become a nuclear-free zone.

Communist Party of Canada. Headquartered in Toronto, the CPC ran 52 candidates in the 1984 federal elections and received just over 8,000 votes, up from the 1980 but down slightly from the 1979 elections. The CPC noted that while its membership is unaltered, its composition has undergone change. The party has been successful in recruiting among new immigrants and youth (*Communist Viewpoint*, June). It has also seen membership increases in Quebec and Saskatchewan (*Canadian Tribune*, 10 September). It has set a goal of a 5 percent overall increase in membership and a 10 percent increase in readership for the party newspaper (ibid., 9 January). The Young Communist League has pledged to double its membership (*Communist Viewpoint*, June). During the election campaign 750,000 copies of the CPC platform were printed (*Canadian Tribune*, 23 July). On 23–25 November, the Canadian Peace Congress, along with the Conseil québecois de la paix and the World Peace Council, sponsored a disarmament conference in Toronto (ibid., 5 November, 3 December). In December, William Kashtan, party general secretary, and William Stewart, party labor secretary, attended a board meeting in Prague of the journal *World Marxist Review*. The Twenty-sixth Congress of the CPC is scheduled to be held in Toronto 5–8 April 1985.

The CPC notes that Canada, severely affected by the economic crisis, has seen an intensification of the class struggle and that united efforts are required to prevent a turn to the right (ibid., 3 September). New antilabor legislation, government cutbacks in social services, and attacks upon the universality of welfare programs should all be opposed (ibid., 3 December). Noting that both the Liberal and Progressive Conservative parties have swung to the right, the CPC, nevertheless, warned that the Conservatives were the "American party in Canada" (ibid., 2 April, 2 July, 3 September) and, if elected, would increase the militarization of the country. The CPC, consequently called for a minority government in which a coalition of progressive forces would hold the balance of power (ibid., 16 July).

The CPC observes that most progressive and socialist-minded Canadians are New Democratic Party (NDP) supporters and thus gives "critical support" to the NDP (ibid., 3 September). Though critical of past NDP provincial governments' anti-labor legislation and the NDP's drift to the right, the CPC calls for cooperation with the NDP, particularly in municipal politics (ibid., 10 September). Accordingly, Communists have run under the label Committee of Progressive Electors in Toronto and Vancouver and the Labour Election Committee in Winnipeg. Some have been successful in the last two cities.

The CPC has been highly critical of the new Conservative government of Brian Mulroney in Ottawa and depicts him as "selling out" Canada in his efforts to weaken the National Energy Program and the Foreign Investment Review Agency (ibid., 19 November, 17 December). The CPC also criticizes proposals to implement deregulation and to increase military spending (ibid., 21 May, 10 December). It warns that the Canadian people voted against the Liberals rather than for the political right (ibid., 10 September). The CPC calls for extensive "nationalization" with "democratic control" and a reduction in the hours of work without a decline in pay (ibid., 27 February) as methods for economic recovery.

Viewing the increased disarray within the Parti québecois (PQ) government in Quebec, the CPC suggests that the PQ has gone from "a respectable petit-bourgeois and independentist party" to an "even more respectable neo-conservative nationalist party" (ibid., 10 December). It calls for a new "mass labor" party in the province.

In general, the CPC favors any efforts at Canadianization of the economy (*Communist Viewpoint*, March). The CPC points out that Canadian economic woes are accentuated by Canada's dependence on the United States. It noted the continued U.S. pressures to keep Canada a "resource hinterland" and the sharpening of relations between the United States and Canada in the last months of the Trudeau era (ibid., June). The CPC approves the recent actions of the Canadian section of the United Auto Workers union in pushing first for full autonomy and then full independence from its U.S.-based international parent organization (*Canadian Tribune*, 17 and 24 December). The CPC also opposes efforts to extend free trade with the United States and calls instead for a nationalization of U.S. branch plants in Canada (ibid., 13 February, 26 March).

The CPC warns that we have entered a more critical stage internationally where civilization itself is at stake (ibid., 15 October). Under Reagan, according to the CPC, the United States has shifted its strategy, abandoned détente, and gone over to a cold war, confrontationist policy of preparing for war. There has been a "super escalation" of the arms race (ibid., 5 November). American aims are to achieve military superiority so as to destroy socialism. The CPC suggests that world peace, more than ever before, is a priority task and observes the growing size of the peace movement. The recent addition of key Canadian labor organizations to the peace cause is welcomed. The party urges that efforts be made to annul the cruise missile–testing agreement and have Canada declared a weapons-free zone (ibid., 13 and 20 February). The CPC calls for a more independent foreign policy and Canadian withdrawal from NATO, the North American Air Defense Command (NORAD), and the Defense Production Sharing Agreement.

In general, the CPC continues to echo Soviet positions in foreign affairs and reiterates the call for a convening of an international conference of communist and workers' parties (ibid., 17 December).

Communist Party of Canada (Marxist–Leninist). The CPC-ML, headquartered in Montreal, perceives that the "capitalist-revisionist crisis" has deepened and that the bourgeoisie have launched an all-out ideological attack against the workers. The CPC-ML believes that although objective conditions are ripe for revolution, subjective conditions lag (*Marxist-Leninist*, 29 September). Since there can be no third road between the dictatorship of the bourgeoisie and the dictatorship of the proletariat, the party calls on workers to reject the "class-collaborationist" schemes of "labour-aristocrats" and to reject all demands for concessions in salaries and services. Efforts should be made to resist the shifting of the burden of the crisis onto the backs of the working class. Instead, the party's slogan is "Make the Rich Pay for the Crisis" (ibid., 13 December).

For the first time since the CPC-ML's founding in 1970, the party did not contest a federal election. Instead it called for mass militant demonstrations in place of the "bourgeois election fraud" (*People's Front Bulletin* 1, no. 2). The CPC-ML rejects pressure to unite with revisionists. The NDP is portrayed as a bourgeois party with a "socialist mask" that, when in power, fosters "state monopoly capitalism." The PQ is characterized as seeking to split people by "reactionary narrow nationalism and chauvinism." Increased restrictions on immigration (*West Indian*, 1–15 June) and student visas, police harassment of minorities, and "super exploitation" of immigrants provide evidence, according to the CPC-ML, that there is a growing tendency towards fascism and state-fostered racism. Racism is portrayed as a phenomenon fostered by the rich, not the people (ibid.). Canada is seen as becoming increasingly a "military-bureaucratic state machine" that is escalating its attacks on "progressive and democratic organizations." Such an intensified bourgeois offensive necessitates that the "people" militantly defend themselves against such assaults. (*Marxist-Leninist*, 7 December.) The CPC-ML asserts that fascists and racists have no right to speak or organize and has endeavored to block right-wing speaking engagements and Defence Department recruitment meetings at several universities. The CPC-ML has also organized "militant pickets" around visiting warships, military recruiting centers, and military parades. CPC-ML militancy has frequently led to scuffles, arrests, and fines. The party has called on activists "to step up the mass struggle," and a growing number of members have been arrested. Last year's arson attack on the party's headquarters and bookstore in British Columbia caused serious damage, but the CPC-ML remains resolute in its call for "revolutionary violence" as the means for establishing a communist regime.

On the international scene, the CPC-ML sees inter-imperialist contradictions as sharpening and says the "imperialist" United States and the "social-imperialist" USSR are becoming increasingly aggressive and preparing for war to redivide the world (*Voice of the People*, March/April). The CPC-ML dismisses disarmament talks as "fraudulent" and maintains they will not lessen the arms race. Both superpowers are seen as endeavoring to intimidate smaller states into joining the "aggressive" military blocs. The recent turmoil in India is, in part, explained as due to Soviet and American efforts to incite communal violence and seek domination over the subcontinent. (*Lok Awaz*, 1 November.) Noting with dismay the Mulroney government's actions as leading to increased U.S. domination of Canada (*Marxist-Leninist*, 7 December), the CPC-ML calls on Canada to regain its sovereignty by reducing the "U.S. imperialist domination of Canada," by withdrawing from NATO and NORAD, by refusing to test cruise missiles, and by declaring "neutrality." Canada should also desist from efforts to transform the Caribbean states into "neo-colonies of Canadian imperialism" (*West Indian*, November/December

1983). Albania is held up as the only state pursuing a proper course of action.

Revolutionary Workers' League. The RWL belongs to the Trotskyist Fourth International. It ran five candidates in the federal election. None was elected. Steve Penner was appointed to the newly created post of executive secretary. Though on the whole supporting the union-based reformist NDP in English Canada, the RWL is nevertheless critical of the "pro-capitalist" NDP leadership and calls for the NDP to take a more socialist and pro-Quebec position. While several RWL members have been expelled from the NDP, the RWL still claims that most of the delegates at the Fifth RWL Convention were also members of the NDP (*Socialist Voice*, 30 January).

The RWL sees Quebec as an oppressed nation, and while previously conceding some positive role for the "bourgeois-nationalist" PQ, the RWL criticizes the recent antilabor measures of the PQ government and its declining commitment to Quebec sovereignty (ibid., 3 December). Believing the PQ to be in the midst of disintegration, the RWL proposes the creation of a new Quebec labor party. While calling for increased labor militancy on wage concessions, the party views the renewed stress on Canadian nationalism in union ranks as "reactionary" and weakening international working-class unity (ibid., 19 November).

According to the RWL, the danger of war is caused, not by the USSR, but by U.S. imperialism. It suggests that the center of confrontations, war, and revolution today is Central America (ibid., 16 January) and that protracted U.S. imperialist war in the region "is the single most important issue" (ibid., 16 and 30 January, 22 October). The RWL demands a withdrawal of all U.S. troops and arms and calls for support of the Cuban and Nicaraguan revolutionary regimes (ibid., 19 November). It deplored the U.S. invasion of Grenada.

Trotskyist League. Although critical of the Stalinist degeneration of the USSR caused by a parasitic leadership caste, the TL claims the USSR and Cuba, nevertheless, should be defended from attacks. It sees Central America as a key realm of activity. Believing in "permanent revolution," it calls for a military victory in El Salvador and urges that the "vacillating petty-bourgeois nationalist" Sandinistas consolidate and complete the revolution (*Sparticist Canada*, November). Accordingly, it calls upon both Cuba and the Soviet Union to in-

crease aid given to Nicaragua (ibid., March). It warns that détente is an illusion and that the United States is preparing for an invasion of both Nicaragua and Cuba (ibid., January, November).

While conceding Quebec's right to independence, it is critical of the allegedly progressive character of Québecois nationalism and instead favors "bi-national class unity" within Canada and joint "U.S./Canadian working class unity" towards a "continental socialist revolution." The TL denies that the RWL is revolutionary, noting that the RWL is unwilling to use violence and supports the "anticommunist and pro-capitalist" NDP (ibid., March). The TL also alleges that the RWL has lost almost 75 percent of its membership since 1977 (ibid., March). The TL warns that the struggle against fascism is "crucial" (ibid., January).

The Forward Readers Group. The FRG chooses to operate within the NDP. Despite the "liberal-reformist" course the NDP pursues, the NDP is still portrayed as having a class base (*Forward*, November/December). The FRG calls on the NDP to become bolder in its commitment to socialism and to a program of class struggle and in its demands for Canada's withdrawal from NATO and NORAD. It views with alarm suggestions that the NDP might abandon its opposition to these military alliances. The FRG, in general, supports the Left-Caucus's efforts to steer the NDP on a more left-wing course. While critical of the ouster of several members of the RWL from the NDP, the FRG notes that the RWL is increasingly operating as a party, not a league. In foreign policy, the FRG sees U.S. actions in Central America as constituting the "gravest danger to the entire world." (Ibid., November/December.)

Other Marxist-Leninist Groups. Several ex-members of the Parti communiste ouvrièr (Workers Communist Party) now publish the Marxist-Leninist review *Libération*. Still other ex-members of the WCP, calling themselves the Collectif de militantes et de militants pour le socialisme, publish *Bulletin de liaison*. The Socialist Challenge Organization, a pro–Fourth International group, publishes *Socialist Challenge*. The International Socialists publish the Trotskyist-leaning *Workers' Action*. The Committee for a New Beginning publishes a mimeographed news sheet entitled *Network*.

Alan Whitehorn
Royal Military College of Canada

Chile

Population. 11,655,000
Party. Communist Party of Chile (Partido Comunista de Chile; CPC)
Founded. 1922
Membership. 20,000 (estimated)
Secretary General. Luis Corvalán
Politburo. 20 members (clandestine and in exile)
Secretariat. 5 members (clandestine and in exile)
Status. Illegal, but operates through Popular Democratic Movement
Last Congress. Sixteenth, June 1984, held clandestinely in Chile and simultaneously outside the country; resolutions and declarations published subsequently
Last Election. 1973, 16 percent, 23 of 150 seats
Auxiliary Organizations. Communist Youth (illegal), National Trade Union Coordinating Committee (CNS; headed by a Christian Democrat), Popular Democratic Movement (MDP; organized in September 1983)
Publications. *El Siglo* (clandestine), appears sporadically

The partial political opening in Chile that began in 1983 continued during 1984, until President Augusto Pinochet imposed a state of siege (martial law) on 6 November. The CPC is illegal, but it functions both through underground cells and through two legal front organizations, the MDP and the CNS, or Coordinadora—the heads of which, in both cases, are members of other parties. The party continues, as it has since September 1980, to endorse "all forms of struggle, both violent and nonviolent"—a shift from its earlier policy of the *via pacifica*, or parliamentary road to power.

The MDP includes, in addition to the CPC, the Almeyda faction of the Socialist Party; the Movement of the Revolutionary Left (MIR), with which the CPC had been at odds over the violence issue during the Allende period; and Chispa, a tiny Socialist splinter group. The MDP is headed by Manuel Almeyda, the brother of Allende's foreign minister, Clodomiro Almeyda, a Socialist leader now living in exile in East Berlin. In February the MDP held a public meeting in Santiago attended by 7,000 people. The MDP president was subsequently arrested under the Internal Security Law for making illegal public declarations during the meeting.

Other factions of the Socialist Party are members of the Democratic Alliance (AD), the broad opposition coalition ranging from socialists and Christian leftists through the Radical and Christian Democratic parties to representatives of the self-styled Republican Right. The issue of endorsement of violence sharply separates the AD from the MDP. Within the AD the socialist groups advocate cooperative relations with the MDP, but the centrist and rightist groups oppose any formal links. Aware of these internal divisions, the Pinochet government continues to press the AD to define itself on the communist issue.

A number of rightist groups emerged in Chile in late 1983, but efforts to bring them together in a single coalition met with only mixed success. In June one of those groups, the Independent Democratic Union (UDI), attempted to secure a court decision declaring the MDP illegal because it violated the 1980 constitution, which outlaws "totalitarian parties" based on doctrines of "the class struggle." However, since the constitutional provision has not been activated through an implementing law, no action was taken.

In the trade union area, 1983 also saw the organization of the National Workers Command (CNT), which coordinated the monthly protest movements that rocked Chile from May to November of that year. Composed principally of the CNS, the Christian Democratic–influenced Democratic Workers Union (UDT), and the powerful Copper Workers Federation, the CNT suffered internal divisions in 1984 relating to the issue of whether and when to call an anti-Pinochet general strike. The copper workers and the UDT were dubious about its prospects for success, but the CNS pressed for action. There were also disputes about the distribution of voting power, as well as bad feelings resulting from the victory of the more anticommunist candidates in the elections to the Trade Union Department of the Christian Democratic Party. The protest movement continued in 1984, but the internal divisions within the CNT and public disagreements with the AD over the nature and timing of the protests reduced the dynamism of the movement. In addition, the government continued to point to cooperation between the CNT and the MDP as evidence of communist control of the protests.

The communist endorsement of violence in 1980 was related, in the view of many observers, to the emergence in 1984 of a new *violentista* group in Chile, the Manuel Rodríguez Patriotic Front (FPMR). Named after a guerrilla hero of the revolution against Spain in the early nineteenth century, this underground group was composed of young revolutionaries linked to the communist party but not acting in its name. Along with the long-standing terrorist actions of the MIR, the activities of the FPMR contributed to a marked escalation of terrorism in Chile during 1984. According to the *Washington Post* (13 April), there were 130 bombings and acts of sabotage in the first three months of 1984. By November that number had risen to over 400 (*Boston Globe*, 20 November). In the last part of the year, the nature of MIR and FPMR terrorism changed. Instead of the occasional predawn bombing of commercial establishments or electric transmission towers, bombings now took place during daylight hours in places where there were likely to be civilian casualties. In late October, there were also two cases of the use by the FPMR of remote-control car bombs against installations of the national police (carabineros) that resulted in a number of police casualties. Pinochet cited the killing of the carabineros when he imposed martial law on 6 November. He argued that the escalation of violence required strong countermeasures. The government claimed that it had proof that the FPMR members had been trained in Cuba and used sophisticated equipment that could only have been smuggled into the country from abroad. The Communists denied that the FPMR was a party group, but the issuance of communiqués through CPC-controlled media as well as what appeared to be links between those accused of being FPMR activists and the CPC indicated that it was operating under party guidance.

The most important CPC activity in 1984 was the holding of a clandestine national convention in Chile in early June, along with a simultaneous meeting outside the country of representatives of party members living in exile (Radio Moscow, 14 June; *FBIS*, 16 July). The two meetings discussed the same preparatory documents, endorsed a statement favoring "the most diverse forms of struggle, whether peaceful or violent, depending on the occasion and the resources available to the people," and elected a Central Committee, which in turn designated the members of the Political Commission (Politburo) and re-elected Luis Corvalán as secretary general. Reflecting the continuing line of the CPC, the congress rejected any dialogue with Pinochet and announced that a "critical and self-critical analysis of the period following the 11 September 1973 coup" had turned the party "into a revolutionary organization which is continuously more stable and open." At the same time the congress called for more cooperation between the MDP and the AD and other opposition sectors.

Yet in October when an AD committee of lawyers proposed a consensus document on human rights and democracy that could be endorsed by all those opposed to the government, the CPC attacked it for accepting the 1980 constitution as a basis for negotiation. Similar statements were made by the MDP and the MIR (*FBIS*, 24, 26, and 27 October). In turn the Socialist members of the AD criticized the CPC for its public endorsement of violence, another example of the continuing split between the CPC and major sectors of the Socialist Party, including those headed by Carlos Briones, Allende's former interior minister, and exile groups associated with former senator Carlos Altamirano (who during the Allende period had advocated a more "revolutionary" line than had the CPC).

With the opposition disunited and terrorism on the increase, Pinochet felt strong enough to retreat on an earlier promise to advance the date of congressional elections, which he had reluctantly endorsed in September 1983 under pressure from his new interior minister, Sergio Onorre Jarpa. In August, Pinochet held a series of interviews with foreign press representatives to announce that he would remain in office until 1989 and that the original date of 1990 for congressional elections would be observed. He did not rule out possible re-election by plebiscite until 1997. In early November Pinochet reimposed strict censorship, expelled the correspondent of the United Press, and announced that all foreign correspondents would be required to secure removal of their credentials. The interior minister also denied permission to the head of the church-sponsored Vicariate of Solidarity to re-enter the country (he was a Spanish citizen) and forbade publication of Archbishop Juan Francisco Fresno's statements following an inspection of a shantytown that had been raided by the police. Leftist leaders were shipped off to internal exile in the extreme north and south of the country, and a state of martial law was imposed that effectively undercut a protest rally scheduled for 27 November. In effect, the partial political opening of the preceding eighteen months was ended, and repression was reimposed.

The Communists, of course, were able to continue to function despite these measures since they had an effective clandestine organization. The other groups, however, were limited in their capacity to maintain their activities under a state of siege. Critics in and out of Chile, including the U.S. Department of State, pointed to the danger of a resulting political polarization, which would give the CPC the leadership of the opposition movement. As the year ended, the AD and other opposition groups were reassessing their strategy and attempting to adjust to the new wave of government persecution, while the Communists were reported to be preparing for renewed activities at the end of March 1985 that would enable them to assert a leading role in the anti-Pinochet struggle.

Paul E. Sigmund
Princeton University

Colombia

Population. 28,248,000
Party. Communist Party of Colombia (Partido Comunista de Colombia; PCC)
Founded. 1930
Membership. 12,000 (estimated)
General Secretary. Gilberto Vieira
Executive Committee. 14 members: Jesús Villegas, Alvaro Vásquez, Jaime Caicedo, Teofilo Forero, Mario Upegui, Gustavo Osorio, Manuel Cepeda, Carlos Romero, Roso Osorio, Angelino Garzón, Hernando Hurtado, José Arrizola, Alvaro Mosquera, Miller Chacón
Central Committee. 80 members
Status. Legal
Last Congress. Fourteenth, 7–11 November 1984
Last Elections. 1984: municipal and state assembly, 2.0 percent; 1982: presidential, 1.2 percent; congressional, 1.2 percent, 1 of 114 senators, 3 of 199 representatives

Auxiliary Organizations. Trade Union Confederation of Workers of Colombia (CSTC), claims 300,000 members; Federation of Agrarian Syndicates; Communist Youth of Colombia (JUCO), claims 2,000 members

Publications. *Voz Proletaria* (weekly), 40,000 circulation; *Documentos Políticos*, theoretical journal, 5,000 circulation; Colombian edition of *World Marxist Review*, 2,000 circulation; JUCO publishes a monthly supplement to *Voz Proletaria*.

The communist movement in Colombia has undergone various transformations in both name and organization since the party's initial formation in December 1926. The PCC was publicly proclaimed on 17 July 1930. In July 1965, a schism within the PCC between pro-Soviet and pro-Chinese factions resulted in the latter's becoming the Communist Party of Colombia, Marxist-Leninist (PCC-ML). Only the PCC has legal status. It has been allowed to participate in elections under its own banner since 1972. In 1984, the PCC participated in municipal council and departmental assembly elections as the leading member of a leftist coalition called the Democratic Front Command, which received 2.0 percent of the total popular vote.

According to U.S. intelligence sources, the PCC has 12,000 members. Although the party contends that its ranks have increased in recent years, the 1982 and 1984 elections suggest that the party's growth has been less rapid than its leaders had hoped, especially in the larger cities. The PCC exercises only marginal influence in national affairs.

The highest party authority is the congress, convened at four-year intervals. Gilberto Vieira, the general secretary of the PCC, is 75. A major source of the party's influence is its control of the CSTC, which is a member of the Soviet-front World Federation of Trade Unions. The PCC attempts to influence the CSTC through the Federation of Agrarian Syndicates, which functions as a part of the CSTC.

The PCC's youth organization, the JUCO, operates through the National Youth Coordinating Committee, where it plays an active role in promoting party policy among university and secondary school students.

Guerrilla Warfare. Although not a serious threat to the government, guerrilla warfare has been a feature of Colombian life since the late 1940s; the current wave began in 1964. The four main guerrilla organizations are the Revolutionary Armed Forces of Colombia (FARC), long controlled by the PCC; the M-19, a guerrilla organization that began as the armed hand of the National Popular Alliance (ANAPO); the pro-Chinese People's Liberation Army (EPL), which is the guerrilla arm of the PCC-ML; and the Castroite National Liberation Army (ELN). A fifth group, the small, urban, Trotskyist-oriented Workers' Self-Defense Movement (ADO), conducted no major operations in 1984.

Domestic peace has been a primary goal of President Belisario Betancur since he began his four-year term in August 1982. His efforts to negotiate a peaceful solution to Colombia's long-standing guerrilla problem met with historic success in 1984. Negotiations between guerrilla leaders and the Colombian Peace Commission culminated in truce agreements in March and August. Under the accords, the FARC agreed to a one-year cease-fire, effective 28 May, while the M-19, EPL, and ADO agreed to suspend armed activity indefinitely after 30 August. Neither agreement requires the guerrillas to surrender their weapons, nor did the government make any explicit commitment to withdraw troops from those areas affected by guerrilla violence. The pact with the FARC affirmed the government's willingness to encourage adoption by the Colombian congress of agrarian reform and laws designed to broaden the electoral representation of opposition political forces and their access to the news media. The agreement with the M-19, EPL, and ADO called for the convening of a "great national dialogue" in which the country's various political forces will participate with full representation (*Intercontinental Press*, 12 November).

Despite this historic breakthrough, guerrilla violence has not been eliminated. According to Colombian military sources, nineteen soldiers and 82 guerrillas died in armed clashes in the first five months following the May cease-fire (EFE, 24 September). The ELN and splinter groups within the FARC and M-19 have refused to negotiate with the government and continue their guerrilla operations in an effort to sabotage the peace agreements. On 2 December, President Betancur urged the ELN and other guerrillas still fighting to accept the Amnesty Law promulgated in December 1982 and to participate in the pacification process (*El Espectador*, 3 December).

According to the FARC's principal leader, Manuel Marulanda Vélez, the movement has "4,000 or 5,000" men operating on 27 fronts. Each of the FARC's rural fronts is composed of two columns, numbering about 200 men. The FARC has expanded its areas of influence in recent years to include portions of the departments of Huila, Caquetá, Tolima, Cauca, Boyacá, Santander, Antioquia, Valle, Meta, and Cundinamarca and the intendancy of Arauca. The FARC's general headquarters is located somewhere in the border zone between Caquetá and Huila. Jacobo Arenas is Marulanda's second-in-command. Other members of FARC's central staff are Jaime Guaraca, Alfonso Cano, and Raúl Reyes. Although Marulanda has never confirmed officially that FARC is the armed wing of the PCC, it is widely believed that the leadership mechanisms and general policy of the FARC are determined by the PCC's bylaws, and political resolutions emitted at various party congresses and plenums are presumably transmitted to the fronts through Marulanda's directives.

Prior to the March truce agreement, the FARC intensified its actions in the middle Magdalena region. In a communiqué sent to news media in Bucaramanga, the FARC warned that it would not suspend its military operations "until both a truce and a cease-fire are agreed upon" (*El Tiempo*, 1 February). Military sources accused the FARC of bringing in additional guerrillas from southern Colombia "to sabotage peace programs in the area and to win support for the PCC in the elections" (*El Espectador*, 29 January). According to official reports, in early February FARC columns operating in the middle Magdalena region murdered over 30 peasants for being army informants (*El Tiempo*, 14 February).

In August, FARC leaders accused the army of hindering the cease-fire process and asked for the direct intervention of congress to prevent disruption of the process (*El Espectador*, 10 August). In response to repeated charges that the FARC has continued with kidnappings aand extortions, Marulanda stated in September that "many of the crimes charged to the FARC are committed by deserters from the various fronts operating in the areas where FARC groups are known to be located." Marulanda also denied that the FARC is dependent on any foreign ideology. He describes the movement as "a nationalist, autonomous, and independent organization that makes its own decisions without any logistical and financial support from Cuba or the USSR" (*El Tiempo*, 30 September).

On 6 October, FARC's general command reiterated its support for the government's peace efforts and presented an eighteen-page document establishing the bases for FARC to become a political party "that will openly struggle for the Colombian people's social demands" (ibid., 7 October).

Dissension within FARC's general command surfaced in February over the status of peace negotiations with the government. In a clandestine communiqué, the Ricardo Franco Urban Front criticized FARC's general staff, especially Jacobo Arenas and Alfonso Cano, for becoming "a bureaucratic and administrative apparatus" (*El Siglo*, 18 February). In May, FARC dissidents claimed credit for bombing several U.S. diplomatic and commercial buildings in Bogotá in which two people were killed and eleven injured (*El Espectador*, 24 May). Marulanda denounced the bombings and said that the Ricardo Franco group, which calls itself a part of the FARC, "has nothing to do with our movement" (ibid., 29 May). In October, the Ricardo Franco Front reiterated its position to continue "at war" and charged the FARC with "continuing to conduct kidnappings" and "insisting on arming and training an army that will be ready for a civil war" (*FBIS*, 19 October). The declaration echoed earlier allegations by Colombian military intelligence sources who revealed FARC documents that contained a plan "to create a self-styled people's army with over 36,000 men" (AFP, 5 October). In December, the front criticized the PCC and accused Gilberto Vieira of "playing a dirty trick on the party" through his condemnation of the front's activities. The front also attacked Arenas for his alleged responsibility for the disappearance of dissident FARC leaders (*El Tiempo*, 17 December).

Domestic Attitudes and Activities. The PCC recognizes the experience of the Communist Party of the Soviet Union as an ideological source, but it also takes "maximum account of the national characteristics and revolutionary and democratic traditions of the Colombian people." This has enabled the party to devise its own tactics, which combine diverse forms of struggle ranging from electoral campaigns to guerrilla warfare. According to Vieira, "We Communists want to advance by democratic means, by what we call action and the mass struggle, and not only by means of elections, which are only one part of the process." Vieira claims that the PCC has failed to become an important factor in the electoral process because of Colombia's deeply rooted bipartisan tradition.

In an analysis of the March elections during the Central Committee's plenum in April, Jaime Caicedo noted that the united left forces of the Democratic Front had "improved their position" in comparison with 1982. However, he stressed the PCC must increase its efforts to raise the level of work among the masses and to strengthen its authority among the population at large (*Pravda*, 20 April). According to Vieira, the forms of struggle in Colombia cannot be permanently changed without modifying the "antidemocratic structure" of the political system. He said the party would seek to solidify the foundations of the Democratic Front through "agreements and cooperation with various circles of leftist forces." He added that the prospect of attaining peace depends in part "on a realistic movement of political reform of the obsolete two-party system" (ibid., 31 May). At a plenary meeting of the Central Committee on 22–23 June, the party included among its most urgent tasks "the struggle for reforms aimed at liquidating the exclusive monopoly of the traditional ruling parties in Colombia's political life" (*Voz Proletaria*, 28 June).

The PCC defines its political line and organizes its activity on the basis of work among the masses. Party statements criticize "adventurist and terrorist practices" that militate against the unity of the masses and weaken the prospects of the popular movement. The PCC views as one of its principal tasks the attainment of unified activity by the working class and overcoming the 1947 split in the trade union movement, which Vieira attributes to "agents of U.S. imperialism supported by the local reactionary regime" (*Pravda*, 31 May). At a festival marking the fifty-fourth anniversary of the party, Manuel Cepeda spoke of the need to create a mass party through the union of the working class, the peasantry, and the intelligentsia. He called on progressive parties and organizations to "unite under the banner of the Democratic Front" (ibid., 24 July).

Propaganda plays an important role in the party's activity. Cepeda, who serves as director of *Voz Proletaria*, wrote of the "need to raise the whole of our propaganda and information work to a higher political and ideological level . . . so as to clarify the meaning of the PCC's strategy, tactics, slogans, and initiatives." Among the issues of key importance in implementing the party's political line, he cited: (1) the establishment of a broad anti-imperialist and antimonopoly front; (2) the leadership of the working class and the role of the PCC in the struggle for democratic change; (3) creative application of the principles and ideas of Marxism-Leninism in Colombia's concrete conditions; (4) exposure of the lies about the Soviet Union and existing socialism; (5) rebuffs to the ruling classes' reactionary ideology; and (6) criticism of reformist and pseudo-revolutionary doctrines (*WMR*, August).

The PCC considers the peace agreement between the government and the FARC "an important step toward stabilizing the internal situation in the country." In a communiqué issued on 3 April, the party endorsed President Betancur's announcement of a cease-fire pact. Reservations within the Central Committee about the effectiveness of the agreement under existing socioeconomic conditions in Colombia, along with concern over the legal and political limitations on Betancur's ability to implement the structural reforms set forth in the pact, resulted in a series of disagreements and the resignation of Humberto Criales de la Rosa from the committee. Vieira subsequently confirmed that Criales had opposed various aspects of the party's policies and had "maintained deeply mistaken opinions" (*El Tiempo*, 26 April).

In July, Vieira expressed optimism over the announced peace agreement with the M-19, EPL, and ADO. However, he added that in order to consolidate the truce, the government should lift the state of siege imposed on 1 May following the assassination of Justice Minister Rodrigo Lara Bonilla (*Voz Proletaria*, 12 July). The party dismissed intelligence reports of the FARC's military reorganization as "a ruse that seeks to undermine the national peace process." Vieira also denied accusations that the PCC and the FARC follow orders from Havana and Moscow (*El Siglo*, 2 October). The PCC considered the EPL's and the M-19's withdrawal from the National Dialogue Commission in November "a source of concern for those interested in the national policy of peace and democratic opening." Hernando Hurtado said that the PCC would urge both groups to rejoin the commission "in order not to defeat the democratization process" (*FBIS*, 29 November).

An estimated 800 delegates attended the PCC's Fourteenth Congress, including foreign delegations from the Soviet Union and Cuba. The documents and declarations approved by the congress indicate that the strategy and tactics of the PCC will continue to be a combination of all forms of mass struggle. In reviewing the current economic and political situation in Colombia, Vieira emphasized the country's "dependence on imperialism in the economic, technological, military, cultural, and financial spheres." He called on the party to "reject U.S. diktat," to achieve unity of action among the working class and democratic circles, and to "implement progressive transformations in Colombia in the interests of the working people." He stated that if an agreement is reached on a democratic peace, the guerrilla movement will be able to take an active part in the organization and political education of the broad peasant and urban masses. (*Pravda*, 9 November.)

Angelino Garzón, who succeeded Juan Pastor Pérez as president of the CSTC upon the latter's death in July, addressed the congress on the importance of extending the PCC's ties with the broad popular masses, the Communists' efforts to strengthen worker unity, and the activization of party work among the trade unions, youth, and in rural areas (ibid., 10 November). José Arrizola spoke about the party's task in strengthening its propaganda effort. The congress approved a declaration committing the party to work for greater access to radio and television. (Ibid., 8 November.) At present, only one Bogotá radio station broadcasts twice daily a 45-minute news program compiled by journalists associated with the PCC (*WMR*, August).

International Views and Positions. The PCC faithfully follows the Soviet line in its international positions. According to Vieira, the party is engaged primarily in the struggle for the emancipation of the Colombian people. However, the PCC insists that it is impossible to remain neutral in the "great international struggle" between socialism and capitalism. The party therefore "enthusiastically" supports the socialist countries and particularly the Soviet Union "because it defends genuine socialism, despite its imperfections" (*Cromos*, 23 November 1982). At the same time, the party claims that it is not dependent on Moscow, Havana, or "any foreign place," nor does it serve as the agent for the international policy of any foreign country. The PCC wants a Colombian international policy that is "independent and autonomous."

According to Vieira, Colombia is beset externally by the "threat of U.S. imperialist adventurism." While he sees the expansionist course of U.S. aggression directed against all of Latin America, it is of special significance for Colombia "because of its proximity to Central America" (*Pravda*, 30 May). Nevertheless, the PCC considers that under President Betancur there has been a shift for the

better in Colombia's official stand on a number of international issues. Party statements have been highly supportive of Betancur's active participation in the organization of the Contadora group and of his efforts to improve Colombia's relations with Cuba and Nicaragua. The party feels that Colombia's entry into the nonaligned movement could lead to "a change of the traditional line of submitting to U.S. imperialism conducted by the local oligarchy" (*WMR*, August).

Political declarations approved by the Fourteenth Congress expressed "serious anxiety" over "President Reagan's aggressive military policy," the growing involvement of American imperialism in El Salvador's civil war, and the United States' undeclared war against Nicaragua. The PCC reaffirmed its support for the Cuban revolution and proclaimed solidarity with the Nicaraguan people in their struggle against U.S. interventionism.

The Maoists. The PCC-ML is firmly pro-Chinese, although recently the party has looked more toward Albania for political guidance (*Intercontinental Press*, 12 November). Its present leadership hierarchy is not clearly known. The PCC-ML has an estimated membership of one thousand. Unlike the PCC, it has not attempted to obtain legal status, and its impact on national life is insignificant. Its official news organ is *Revolución*. The Marxist-Leninist League of Colombia publishes the monthly *Nueva Democracia*. PCC-ML statements are sometimes found in Chinese publications and those of pro-Chinese parties in Europe and Latin America.

The PCC-ML's guerrilla arm, the EPL, was the first to attempt a revolutionary "people's war" in Latin America. The EPL has conducted only limited operations since 1975, although according to Colombian intelligence it still has an estimated 350 guerrillas organized into four fronts. The EPL operates mainly in the departments of Antioquia and Córdoba, with urban support networks in Bogotá, Medellín, Montería, Bucaramanga, Barrancabermeja, Cali, and Florencia. The EPL is headed by Francisco Caraballo. Other prominent members of the EPL's general staff are Ernesto Rojas, Óscar William Calvo, and Bernardo Gutiérrez. The EPL carried out twenty attacks on various *corregimientos* and villages during February and early March in a resurgence of actions in Antioquia and Córdoba (*El Tiempo*, 20 March). In March, the EPL issued a communiqué supporting with "full enthusiasm" the guidance of the PCC-ML regarding the dialogue and multilateral truce proposed to the Peace Commission (*El Espectador*, 30 March). Bernardo Gutiérrez warned in June that the EPL was "still at war" and that it would continue to conduct military actions until it concluded an agreement with the Peace Commission that established "specific goals" (*El Tiempo*, 10 June). On 23 August, the EPL concluded a cease-fire agreement with the government approved by the Twelfth Congress of the PCC-ML. The national command ordered all EPL units to cease offensive military actions and to release all hostages as of 30 August. Rojas said that during the cease-fire the group would "extend its political efforts within the different sectors of the rural and urban masses" (*El Espectador*, 24 August). In October, Rojas announced that eight EPL guerrillas had died in clashes with the army since 24 August and warned that "the truce might be broken due to the army's violations of the agreements." He added that a "guerrilla summit" would be held in November to unify views on the democratic opening. (EFE, 17 October.)

In an interview on 1 November, Rojas said the PCC-ML/EPL is prepared to "play the democratic game" because at this time "the conditions do not exist to make the change to socialism." The movement has proposed the election of a constituent assembly to transform Colombia's bipartisan system (AFP, 1 November). On 13 November, the EPL withdrew from the "national dialogue," complaining that the dialogue had been "overtaken by bureaucracy" and that the Peace Commission had become "practically inoperative" (*El Espectador*, 14 November). In December, Óscar Calvo charged that the EPL was being "harassed" by the army and that guerrilla territory was "not being respected according to the peace agreements." On 20 December, Calvo announced that the EPL would return to the "national dialogue" in January 1985, providing that the government complied with its agreements (EFE, 18 and 21 December).

The Independent Revolutionary Workers' Movement (MOIR) has aspired since 1971 to become the first mass-based Maoist party in Latin America. Its leadership and organization are independent of those of the PCC-ML. The MOIR has no military branch and has been unable to strengthen its political position in recent elections. MOIR lists received only 22,815 votes (0.04 percent) in the 1984 elections. The MOIR's general secretary is Francisco Mosquera. Other prominent leaders are Marcelo Torres, Avelino Niño, and Diego Betancur Alvarez, son of the president.

The M-19. The M-19, which first appeared in January 1974 as the self-proclaimed armed branch of ANAPO, takes its name from the contested presidential election of 19 April 1970. Since 1976, the M-19 has been actively involved in Colombia's guerrilla movement, pursuing "a popular revolution of national liberation toward socialism." Resolutions adopted by the M-19 at its Eighth National Conference in August 1982 defined the group as a "political-military organization" that seeks to "lead the masses on all levels of their economic, political, and military struggle" (*Intercontinental Press*, 12 November). Estimates on the movement's size range from 900 to 5,000. In recent years, the M-19 has concentrated its activities in Caquetá, Meta, and in the Putumayo intendancy area in southern Colombia. In March, the M-19 issued a communiqué announcing that it would resume operations in the departments of Valle, Cauca, and Nariño "because it has been impossible to attain peace in Colombia despite all efforts" (*El Siglo*, 17 March).

The M-19's leadership hierarchy was severely weakened in 1983 when the movement's principal leader, Jaime Bateman Cayón, was killed in a plane crash. Bateman has been succeeded by Ivan Marino Ospina, with Alvaro Fayad moving up to second-in-command. Other members of the M-19's high command are Carlos Pizarro, Antonio Navarro, Rosemberg Pabón, and Andrés Amarales. Several additional changes in leadership occurred in 1984. In March, the high command expelled Gustavo Arias Londoño for leading the M-19's Southern Front in an unauthorized attack on Florencia in Caquetá, in which some 40 persons died. Members of the Southern Front subsequently denounced Marino and Fayad as "traitors to the revolutionary cause" and announced that Arias had been chosen "sole commander of the M-19" (ibid., 17 March). Arias and his followers now constitute a dissident faction of the M-19 and refuse to recognize the August cease-fire. On 10 August, Carlos Toledo Plata, ex-ANAPO congressman and one of the M-19's founders, was killed by unidentified gunmen in his hometown of Bucaramanga.

The M-19 held out for what it considered a "broader peace agreement" than that reached by the government with the FARC. In April, the M-19's high command distributed a "Proposal for National Dialogue" in which it called for "a democratic opening to achieve the people's participation in the great national decisions" (EFE, 23 April). For the M-19, the peace accord signed with the government on 24 August constitutes an agreement to end hostilities in order to open the way to a "national dialogue."

During a December meeting with Marino in Mexico City, President Betancur accused the M-19 of "irregularities" in compliance with the truce. For his part, Marino reasserted the M-19's determination to move ahead with the peace process. He reaffirmed the M-19's condemnation of kidnapping, blackmail, and extortion and added that his meeting with the president had "permitted the reaffirmation of the need to intensify national dialogue as a basic mechanism to seek the basis for a lasting and stable government." (FBIS, 10 December.)

Since mid-December, the army and M-19 columns have been fighting intermittently in the jurisdiction of Corinto, in northwest Cauca. M-19 leaders have admitted to mining the areas around its camps in San Pablo and Yarmal, prompting Colombia's acting defense minister to accuse the M-19 of establishing an "independent republic" (AFP, 18 and 20 December). In a letter to President Betancur, the M-19 high command reaffirmed its "desire to dialogue" in order to prevent a disruption of the cease-fire (EFE, 24 December). In an effort to prevent any further clashes, the head of Colombia's Peace and Verification Commission agreed to meet with M-19 leaders.

The National Liberation Army. The ELN was formed in Santander in 1964 under the inspiration of the Cuban revolution. It undertook its first military action in January 1965. Once recognized as the largest and most militant of the guerrilla forces operating in Colombia, the ELN has never recovered from the toll exacted on its leadership and urban network by an army offensive in 1973. According to Colombian intelligence, the ELN has approximately 350 men organized into four fronts. It operates mainly in Arauca intendancy and the northeastern sector of Caquetá. Except for FARC and M-19 dissidents, the ELN is the only guerrilla movement that did not sign a cease-fire agreement with the government in 1984. In an August communiqué, ELN leaders vowed to continue fighting. They denounced leaders of the guerrilla movements that signed a peace agreement as "infamous traitors to the revolutionary cause." The ELN continues to

assert that "only through revolutionary violence can power by the people be reached" (AFP, 25 August).

Peace Prospects. During the past year, a climate of peace has been achieved in some regions of Colombia such as the middle Magdalena area, the FARC's former theater of operations. In others, such as Valle, Antioquia, Caldas, and Córdoba, the ELN and dissident guerrilla factions continue sporadic actions.

While most analysts agree that armed clashes with the guerrillas have fallen sharply since the cease-fire, kidnappings and extortion based on the threat of kidnapping have increased. In recent years, kidnapping has taken on the dimensions of a national industry, and it is difficult to determine whether guerrillas or common criminals are responsible for any particular crime (WP, 11 September).

Not everyone is pleased with President Betancur's efforts. Some army officers are reported to be unhappy at the cease-fire, which they feel rewards terrorism. The guerrillas have not surrendered their weapons, and several small rebel groups have refused to negotiate with the government. Moreover, there is considerable uncertainty over what form the "national dialogue" is to take. Its vagueness has left Betancur open to political attacks from both sides. According to the chairman of the Peace and Verification Commission, the national dialogue will be conducted through a series of round-table discussions that will study different social problems. For the M-19 and other guerrilla groups, the dialogue is seen as an opening to undertake the political mobilization of the millions of Colombians who did not vote in the last presidential elections. If guerrilla leaders are allowed to form political movements that can run candidates in the 1986 general elections, the cease-fire may hold.

A tenuous truce has been achieved with Colombia's major guerrilla groups. However, the guerrilla forces remain armed in their rural encampments in various departments. The army is still deployed in wide parts of the countryside. Both the army and the guerrillas have reported cease-fire violations by the other side. It remains to be seen how far the government can meet the guerrillas' demands for social policies to improve the lot of peasant farmers and urban poor. The congress, which has already voted to reject participation in the "national dialogue," is unlikely to approve any of the political and economic reforms Betancur has pledged to put forward under the truce accords. If the country's traditional political groups are unwilling or financially unable to deal effectively with the causes of the problem within a reasonable period, Betancur's laudable peace efforts could be destroyed, and Colombia may once again be confronted by a resurgence of guerrilla activity. For the moment, however, most officials, guerrilla leaders, and outside observers remain prudently optimistic that Colombia can sustain the peace initiatives advanced in 1984.

Daniel L. Premo
Washington College

Costa Rica

Population. 2,693,000

Party. Popular Vanguard Party (Partido Vanguardia Popular; PVP). Splinter faction led by ex-party leader Manuel Mora Valverde disputes the party name, but reportedly now goes by the name of the Costa Rican People's Party (Partido del Pueblo Costarricense; PPC) (*FBIS*, 2 October). Other secondary leftist parties are the Movement of the New Republic (Movimiento de la Nueva República; MNR), until mid-1984 known as the Revolutionary People's Movement, and the Costa Rican Socialist Party (Partido Socialista Costarricense; PSC). A left splinter group is the National Patriotic Committee (Comité Patriótico Nacional; COPAN). All formed part of the leftist electoral coalition, United People (Pueblo Unido; PU), in the 1978 and 1982 elections. For the 1986 elections, Patriotic Alliance (Alianza Patriótica; AP) has recently been formed, joining the PPC, MNR, PSC, and the new Radical Democratic Party (Partido Radical Democrático; PRD), but excluding for the moment the PVP and some of its related COPAN sympathizers (ibid.).

Founded. PVP: 1931; MNR: 1970; PSC: 1972; COPAN: mid-1970s

Membership. PVP: variously estimated at 3,500 prior to the recent splits or 5,000 "cells" with over 10,000 members (*La Nación*, San José, 27 December 1983)

President. PVP: Arnoldo Ferreto Segura

Secretary General. PVP: Humberto Vargas Carbonell; PPC: Manuel Mora Valverde

Undersecretary General. PVP: Óscar Madrid (Madrigal?) Jiménez (?); PPC: Eduardo Mora Valverde

Central Committee. PVP: 35 members, 15 alternates; PPC: 35 members, 15 alternates

Status. Legal; the Vargas-Ferreto faction is now legally recognized as the PVP by the Supreme Electoral Tribunal. The Mora or PPC faction has not yet been legally recognized and often continues to use the same party name (PVP) in its public declarations.

Last Congress. PVP: Fourteenth, 8 April 1984; Fifteenth, 15–16 September 1984, in San José, attended by 216 delegates; PPC: Fourteenth, 10–11 March 1984, in San José

Last Election. 1982 PU coalition won 3.2 percent of presidential vote; 4 of 57 national deputies

Auxiliary Organizations. Unitary Workers Central (Central Unitaria de Trabajadores; CUT); General Workers Confederation (Confederación General de Trabajadores; CGT); National Peasants Federation (Federación Campesina Nacional; FCN); Costa Rican Peace and Solidarity Council (an umbrella group made up of some 50 union and solidarity committees)

Publications. PVP: *Libertad Revolucionaria* (weekly); PPC: *Libertad* (weekly)

The PVP was founded in 1931 as a group of students, intellectuals, and workers by its leader of 52 years, Manuel Mora Valverde. While originally a splinter group of the Reformist Party of the 1920s, the PVP gained its start in national politics from the 1934 Atlantic banana workers' strike against United Fruit Company. The banana workers' union formed at this time remains the principal bastion of PVP support; a limited number of public employees and student groups have been added more recently. Since its founding the PVP has won a small number of seats in the national congress; PVP deputies are often leading professionals and academics, and their legislative concerns have anticipated the major parties' initiatives in health, education, and housing.

In November 1983, at the Third Extraordinary Congress of the party, a major split developed, leading to the purge in December of Manuel Mora Valverde and his supporters by parliamentary leader Arnoldo Ferreto Segura and ex-legislator Humberto Vargas Carbonell. Vargas became general secretary and Ferreto was eventually named PVP president after Mora angrily rejected this largely honorific post. The Central Committee maneuvering that led to the purge was opposed by Mora and his followers, and the dust has yet to settle from this unexpected shake-up within left-wing politics.

Domestic Activities. In the electoral campaigns of 1978 and 1982, the PVP formed part of the PU ticket, led by Rodrigo Gutiérrez, a physician.

The two junior members of the PU coalition are outgrowths of early 1970s university radical movements, with little if any mass base of support. Recently, a new left-wing coalition, the Patriotic Alliance (AP), has been launched with a view to the 1986 elections. However, this group appears to exclude the official PVP, as presently led by Vargas and Ferreto, while it has added a left-liberal party, the PRD, led by several ex-ministers of the administration of Rodrigo Carazo (1978–1982). The PU coalition was continuously plagued by internal divisions, and its various successors will undoubtedly be even more split, as is evident in the very founding of the AP. The electoral prospects for the left in 1986 appear bleak indeed.

PVP affairs during 1984 were almost totally dominated by the falling-out and mutual recriminations emanating from the unprecedented high-level purges of late 1983. Other issues of importance to the party and its various factions included the prolonged banana workers' strike against the United Fruit Company's successor, the Compañía Bananera de Costa Rica, the role of the United States in influencing Costa Rican relations with Nicaragua, and the various assassination attempts and border fighting in Costa Rica traceable to the war between the Sandinistas and the *contras*.

Infighting and rhetorical dueling over the proprietorship of the official party name began immediately after Manuel Mora's December 1983 ouster and has continued unabated since then. On 9 January Mora returned from a trip to Cuba and was feted in San José by a large group of his followers. At this gathering an attempt was made to remove Arnoldo Ferreto as parliamentary leader and Central Committee executive secretary, as well as several other lower-level officials who had supported the Vargas-Ferreto line. All of these measures were rejected out of hand by Ferreto as no more than the whims of a "fraudulent assembly" (*FBIS*, 12 January, 1 February). However, in a clear response to this show of popular support for Mora, Vargas and Ferreto expelled four veteran Central Committee members, Eduardo Mora (Manuel's brother), José Merino, César Solano, and Lenin Chacón. The expulsion of Chacón, party secretary general of the San José sectional committee and one of the organizers of the welcoming rally for Mora, showed just how deep the rift had become. In a largely empty conciliatory gesture, Vargas accepted Manuel Mora's resignation as PVP president but insisted that he was still a member of the party's Political Commission and Directorate (ibid., 3 February).

Reacting to Mora and his followers' continued use of the party name and their occupation of party printing facilities, and perhaps fearing a negative ruling by the electoral authorities, Vargas and Ferreto first attempted to register their group as the Costa Rican Communist Party (Partido Comunista Costarricense) with the Supreme Electoral Tribunal, without formally ceding the existing party name to the Mora faction. Mora himself claimed this to be evidence of his opponents' "desperation" in the face of imminent defeat, while Ferreto denied having initiated any such move. (Ibid., 9 February.) However, to the surprise of many, in February the Civil Registry's electoral office quickly granted legal recognition to the Vargas-Ferreto slate as the official PVP; this was confirmed by the Supreme Electoral Tribunal in June (ibid., 22 February, 4 June).

Having been rebuffed by the electoral authorities, Mora took a page out of his opponents' book by attempting to register his group as the Costa Rican Communist Party (Partido Comunista Costarricense), while appealing the tribunal's decision against him. The appeal was rejected, first for lack of signatures and then several times as part of the tribunal president's rather banal attempt to instruct his fellow citizens in the antidemocratic evils of Marxism-Leninism and the dictatorship of the proletariat (ibid., 21 June, 22 and 23 August, 5 and 14 September, 7 November). Reacting to this double defeat, Mora commented bitterly that "the Popular Vanguard Party is still the Popular Vanguard Party, because the party belongs to its members, and it is the members who decide on the party's present and future plans, not any government tribunal" (ibid., 6 July). Subsequently, the Mora faction has frequently used the label of the Costa Rican People's Party (PPC), although formal legal recognition is still pending.

The organizational struggle led to three purported party congresses during the year. In the midst of the electoral registration battle, both sides convened congresses; Mora in early March and Ferreto in early April (*Libertad*, 16–22 March; *FBIS*, 12 April). At the latter gathering Manuel Mora was finally expelled from the official PVP along with his brother Eduardo, and new levels of accusatory rhetoric were reached (*FBIS*, 12 April, 29 June). Each of these rival congresses was termed the PVP's fourteenth. In mid-September, at the time originally scheduled for the Fourteenth Congress, the official PVP convened its Fifteenth Congress, with 216 delegates attending, in San José, to further consolidate positions after what Vargas admitted was "truly a purge" (ibid., 18 September).

On the whole, the official PVP faction was greatly weakened and isolated by the purge. The newly formed AP coalition, led in part by the Mora brothers and certain progressive former politicians from the major parties, has attracted both the PSC and MNR to its side and appears to exclude the official PVP. Vargas and Ferreto have responded by criticizing the AP for premature interest in electoral matters and lack of a broad participatory framework, stopping short, however, of any rejection of eventual cooperation. (Ibid., 24 May, 18 September, 2 October.)

Local interpretations of the origin of the split/ purge have not progressed beyond those reported in last year's profile (*YICA*, 1984, p. 107). Manuel Mora continues to suggest that the Vargas faction is made up of "hard-liners" preparing for guerrilla

warfare as part of a general Central American conflagration. Vargas responded by ridiculing the Mora brothers' alleged appeal to the bourgeoisie and its mass media in an effort to convince the workers' class enemy that the PPC deserves support since it would pose no threat to the bourgeoisie's interest. Vargas saw this as further proof of the "divisionists' reformism and opportunism." (*FBIS*, 2 February, 6 and 26 March.) Elements of the local media continued to interpret the Moras as representing the more cautious, united-front line, allegedly favored by Fidel Castro, a longtime friend of the Mora brothers, versus an adventurist, pro-Soviet faction bent on military provocation throughout Central America (*La República*, San José, 11 April; *FBIS*, 19 April). However, this line of thought has been the standard view of the bourgeois press so studiously courted by the Moras, the former intent on denouncing all "hard-liners," real or imaginary, and the latter bent on regaining control of the party. Neither has offered firm evidence regarding events either before or after the December 1983 purge. Whatever the origins and motives for the schism, it has hardly increased the left's capacity for either military adventurism or political influence in the short run.

The obsession of party leaders with purges and counterpurges limited their role in ongoing national and international debates and conflicts during 1984. Of these, only two generated much interest on the part of the left: a lengthy midyear banana workers' strike on the southern coast and the multifaceted role of the United States and its anti-Nicaraguan positions within Costa Rican politics.

The banana workers' strike was called in July against the Compañía Bananera and lasted some 72 days, the longest strike in Costa Rican history. When it finally ended, police had killed one worker, the company had made no major concessions, and it had threatened to withdraw completely from the country. Like past PVP-led banana workers' strikes, the 1984 strike was an economic failure, but a political success in highlighting its central role in what threatened to become a nationalist *cause célèbre*. The 3,000 workers who had gone on strike in July for a 57 percent wage increase after two years of frozen salary levels were being dismissed at a rate of 50 per day in December, after 800 had been laid off in October for four months and at least 600 permanently dismissed in the first half of December alone. The government issued orders to the company to stop dismantling its facilities and was negotiating for the acquisition of some 2,000–

3,000 hectares of banana plantations that the company claimed had been irretrievably damaged owing to the prolonged strike. (*Central America Report*, 14 December; *Latin America Regional Reports, Mexico and Central America*, 17 August, 21 September; *FBIS*, 12 September.) As the strike movement waned in late August and early September, President Luis Alberto Monge angrily accused PVP deputies of attempting to prolong it to subvert law and order in the region and force a more serious confrontation with the company (*FBIS*, 20 August).

International Views and Positions. Throughout 1984 the various PVP factions and leaders repeatedly denounced what they saw as U.S. interventionism in Costa Rican affairs intended to facilitate *contra* operations from Costa Rican soil, if not open conflict with Nicaragua. Events, when added to U.S. ambassador Curtin Winsor's remarkably frequent verbal faux pas, gave many an occasion for such denunciations. The alleged Sandinista attacks on Costa Rican territory early in May led to large-scale peace demonstrations in San José on 15 May, led by major party progressives and ex-presidents, but with the enthusiastic support of the PVP. Moreover, the attempt on the life of Edén Pastora at the end of May led to an early flurry of accusations of left complicity with Sandinista operatives, but just as quickly spawned speculation regarding possible rightist designs on Pastora's life. (*Central America Report*, 11 and 18 May; *FBIS*, 4, 7, 11, 14, 23, and 30 May; *La Nación Internacional*, San José, 17–23 May; *Tico Times*, San José, 18 May; *Miami Herald*, 5, 6, and 31 May, 1 and 2 June; *NYT*, 1 June.)

Ambassador Winsor's statements and standing offer of "development" assistance by the U.S. Army Corps of Engineers along the sensitive northern border region were cause for repeated PVP denunciations of his "imperialist, interventionist, and militarist" intent and role in local politics, as well as public rebukes by ruling party officials on at least one occasion (*FBIS*, 2, 16, 17, and 22 November 1983; 13 March, 22 May, 6 and 27 July, 3 and 15 August, 9 and 29 October; *Tico Times*, 27 January). The left also denounced the planned installation of an extremely powerful radio station in northern Costa Rica. Although technically under Costa Rican ownership, and thus skirting the constitutional prohibition of foreign ownership of the mass media, the station (Radio Impacto) was being heavily financed by the United States and would broadcast, with repeater stations in Honduras and El Salvador, heavy doses of Voice of America programming throughout the Nicaraguan border region and beyond to the rest of Central America. Broadbased opposition to this development, as well as the ambassador's aggressive advocacy of such an allegedly Costa Rican initiative, offers fertile ground for PVP anti-imperialist rhetoric and action in the immediate future. (*FBIS*, 22 May, 18 September, 2 and 9 October.)

Lowell Gudmundson
Florida International University

Cuba

Population. 9,995,000
Party. Communist Party of Cuba (Partido Comunista de Cuba; PCC)
Founded. 1965
Membership. 434,143 (*WMR*, July 1981)
First Secretary. Fidel Castro Ruz

Politburo. 14 members: Fidel Castro Ruz, Raúl Castro Ruz (second secretary), Juan Almeida Bosque, Ramiro Valdés Menéndez, Guillermo García Frías, José Ramón Machado Ventura, Blas Roca Calderío, Carlos Rafael Rodríguez, Pedro Miret Prieto, Sergio del Valle Jiménez, Armando Hart Dávalos, Jorge Risquet Valdés, Julia Camacho Aguilera, Osmany Cienfuegos Gorrián; 10 alternate members
Secretariat. 8 members: Fidel Castro Ruz, Raúl Castro Ruz, Pedro Miret Prieto, Jorge Risquet Valdés, Lionel Soto Prieto, José Ramón Machado Ventura, Jesús Montané Oropesa, Julio Rizo Alvarez
Central Committee. 148 members, 77 alternates (*Granma*, 5 April 1981)
Status. Ruling party
Last Congress. Second, 17–20 December 1981
Last Election. 1981, all 499 representatives PCC approved
Auxiliary Organizations. Union of Young Communists (Unión de Jóvenes Comunistas; UJC), Union of Cuban Pioneers (Unión de Pioneros de Cuba; UPC), Federation of Cuban Women (Federación de Mujeres Cubanas; FMC), Committees for the Defense of the Revolution (Comités de Defensa de la Revolución; CDR), Confederation of Cuban Workers (Confederación de Trabajadores de Cuba; CTC), National Association of Small Farmers (Asociación Nacional de Agricultores Pequeños; ANAP)
Publications. *Granma* (six days a week), official organ of the Central Committee; *Juventud Rebelde* (daily), organ of the UJC

The Cuban leadership had two principal concerns in 1984, the "Year of the Twenty-fifth Anniversary of the Triumph of the Revolution"—relations with the United States and the domestic economy. There was a slight improvement in the first and no betterment in the second, seen from the perspective of Havana.

Leadership and Party Organization. The PCC, possibly temporarily, played a much smaller role in domestic and foreign actions by the Cuban regime, or at least its "leading" role as the overseeing organization was not emphasized by the media. But party life is expected to pick up in 1985 as the PCC prepares for its Third Congress, scheduled for December in Havana. There were no changes in top party or government leaders in Cuba. As in the past, President Fidel Castro dominated the scene. Although Castro spoke of the future with increasing frequency, there were no indications that a second level of leaders was in the wings to ease the work burden of the Castro generation now in power— men who are or are approaching 60 years of age— let alone to replace it. The leitmotiv of many speeches by Castro was a plan for the development of the country for the next fifteen years. The year 2000 was being dangled in the minds of Cubans as the beginning of a period of material well-being, in the same way as the year 1975 was mentioned by Castro during the first years in power. But the improvements promised by Cuban leaders were not to be a result of any drastic changes of the system, or even within the system. Castroism—judging by the pronouncements of the "maximum leader"—was to continue being a fairly standard copy of the Soviet model, albeit with a tropical character. The tropical

paradigm of Marxism-Leninism continued to be a highly personalized rule of a charismatic *caudillo*, with a dispirited populace going through the motions of serious productive endeavors.

Cuba did not launch any new foreign policy initiatives at least overtly, although it organized the First Consultative Meeting of Anti-Imperialist Organizations of the Caribbean and Central America, held under party auspices in Havana 11–13 June, with 29 groups represented. (The meeting's announced objective was to counteract the Reagan administration's "warmongering policy in the region as part of the anticommunist crusade that the United States is promoting throughout the world" [*Granma*, 1 July].) To be sure, Cuba continued to maintain close political ties with various ruling and nonruling Marxist-Leninist parties, whose leaders visited Havana regularly. But again here the visits, and those of Cuban party leaders to foreign lands (in February Castro attended the funeral of Yuri A. Andropov in Moscow and met with Konstantin Chernenko), appeared to be perfunctory encounters devoid of urgent purpose or of any particular meaning.

One reason for the lack of revolutionary élan in Cuba could be the physical deterioration of Cuban towns noticed by foreign observers. Homes in the poorest parts of Havana "are grim and crowded" with three generations having to live together because of the housing shortage, noted one journalist. "There has been little new construction for a full generation, only deterioration." (*WSJ*, 15 August.)

The creation of what Castro called the Program of the Communist Party of Cuba was the main task mentioned in the official convocation issued by the

Central Committee for the Third Congress. The congress, after making a "critical analysis" of the fulfillment of the objectives set by the Second Congress, "will define the main tasks for the next five-year period and outline the main course of Cuban society's development through the year 2000. The Central Committee of the Party considers that the conditions exist to set down the Program of the Communist Party of Cuba." The program will make of Castro a Lenin-like figure, indicated the convocation (signed by Castro himself). The program will reassert the correctness of the socialist course chosen by the revolutionary people of Cuba and will set forth the outlook of their secure future.

Among other points to be discussed by the congress, the convocation said, would be resolutions dealing with economic management, improvements in local government, and "the development of socialist democracy and socialist legality." There will be one delegate per 350 party members and candidates, and 30 percent of the delegates will be workers linked directly to production. (*Granma*, 2 January 1985.)

Cuban Armed Forces. According to Havana, the strengthening of Cuban military forces so in evidence in 1984 was part of its defensive preparedness against a possible U.S. landing. In February, Castro announced that the Territorial Troop Militia, a paramilitary force created 1 May 1980, was a million strong. "If the United States wants to invade, it would have to kill all of the Cuban people," he said. (Ibid., 2 February.) With 225,000 regular members of the armed forces and 190,000 reservists, together with the million men and women in the militia, Cuba could have about 15 percent of its people under arms. A Pentagon study published in 1984 found that counting its combined forces, Cuba was one of the most militarized nations in the world. With Soviet military aid estimated at $1.7 billion annually for the past three years, Cuban forces were the second largest in the Western Hemisphere, larger than those of Brazil, Mexico, or Canada. (*NYT*, 2 May.)

According to the Pentagon, the Soviet Union has been stepping up its military assistance to the Castro regime since 1983. Among the most important weapons delivered to the Havana government in 1984 were twelve new jet interceptors, including seven MiG-21s and five MiG-23s, 22 military helicopters, 100 tanks, eleven multiple rocket launchers, and 83 antitank guns. Other Soviet matériel shipped to Cuba in recent months included at least 30 surface-to-air missiles and eleven self-propelled antiaircraft guns. The Cuban Navy, the report said, received three Turya-class patrol hydrofoils and one 4,500-ton floating drydock. The study, which did not mention a more recently arrived Koni-class frigate and a diesel-powered Foxtrot submarine, said that Cuba's military forces were made up of 25 divisions with 950 tanks, with an air force of more than 270 jet combat aircraft and a navy with three submarines. The Soviets maintain near Havana an intelligence-gathering complex, apparently equipped with electronic devices; the complex, the report said, was "the most extensive Soviet facility of this type outside the USSR." (*Miami Herald*, 3 April.)

The Economy. In a speech closing the 27–28 December session of the National Assembly of People's Power, President Castro stated that Cuba's economy grew by 7.4 percent in 1984. But other statements and data disclosed in the course of the year indicate clearly that in fact the Cuban economy deteriorated further in 1984 and that the growth was much smaller than claimed. In December 1983, Havana estimated that in 1984 growth would be between 4.0 and 4.5 percent and that the 1984 budget surplus would be 221.7 million pesos. (One peso is officially quoted in Cuba at about $1.20, although its value on the free exchange market is $0.50.) The final budget figures were not announced by Havana, but the 1985 budget was estimated in December at 7.9 billion pesos, with a surplus of 15.8 million pesos. (*Granma*, 1 and 20 January 1985.)

In February, Castro stated that the "Cuban economy is going to be affected by a setback in the sugar plan." At the same time, Havana disclosed that the housing construction plan would not be fulfilled. In April Cuba had to request a hundred Western banks and governments to renegotiate its debt, which totals $2.8 billion (as it did in 1983), according to the head of the Cuban National Bank, who estimated 1984 losses in income from convertible currency would be about $1 billion because, as he put it, of the "crisis in the sugar market" (ibid., 15 April). Less than a month later, Havana reported that sugar production in 1984 would be 1 million tons less than planned because of rains and disorganization in the sugar industry.

As described by foreign observers, the economy was plagued by shortages of consumer goods and spare parts for transportation and industrial machinery. "The signs of the country's hard-currency dearth are everywhere: in the factories bereft of modern equipment and limping along on old machinery; in the sad disrepair of Havana's buildings, many of them reflections of architectural beauty and bygone affluence; in the old Chevies and Plymouths dating back to the 1940s and 1950s that chug along the streets" (*WSJ*, 11 July). The same source estimated Cuba's Western debt, payments of which were rescheduled, at $3.5 billion. In addition, it said Cuba owed the Soviet bloc, principally the Soviet Union, some $9 billion.

Another indication of the considerable problems in the economy came during November when Havana reported on coordination of the Cuban economic plans with those of the Soviet bloc nations. "The Cuban economy depends mainly on the sale of sugar, whose buying power today in the capitalist markets is lower than 50 years ago: thus without assistance from the Council for Mutual Economic Assistance [CMEA] . . . Cuba would be condemned to starvation" (*Granma*, 11 November). The Havana newspaper also said that in the current five-year plan (1980–1985), the government had doubled the country's military outlays. Cuban dependence on the Soviet bloc was not only greater, but also was to extend through the end of this century. In October, Cuba and the USSR signed a broad cooperation agreement to run up to the year 2000. Under an agreement with East Germany, between 1986 and 1990 East Berlin would assist in refurbishing Havana, including its infrastructure. Plans were also announced in Cuba to begin building before the year 2000 a subway in the capital, a project to be undertaken with Soviet bloc assistance.

Faced with collapsing sugar prices, growing foreign debt, and the shortfall in the production of exportable goods, the Castro government proposes to carry out an analysis of its current economic policies with the view of arriving at a plan of action that would take the country through the next five-year plan (1986–1990) to the end of the century. One rationale for that review was given by Castro during the October meeting of CMEA held in Havana. Cuba "has not been able to meet its obligations assumed in the trade agreements with Soviet bloc countries," Castro said. Thus, he continued, it was necessary not only to raise the degree of the country's self-sufficiency in food and import less from the Soviet bloc, but also to increase exports of Cuban agricultural products to the bloc nations. "We must first meet the commitments to the socialist countries and then to the rest of the countries in the

hard currency area," Castro said in a December speech. He noted that among the bloc countries Cuba had the lowest percentage of trade with hard currency nations, some 15 percent. (Ibid., 12 December.) In the same address, the communist leader noted the country was annually using almost 3 million tons of oil, worth over $500 million, to produce electricity, and that all crude oil was imported from the Soviet Union, over a distance of more than 10,000 kilometers. Castro said that these shipments would have to decline and that in the future Cuba would have to rely primarily on nuclear-powered generators, one of which was under construction near Cienfuegos, with two others being planned. In all, he said, Cuba received 10 million tons of Soviet petroleum a year, more than 95 percent of the country's needs, at a cost of over $2 billion.

The most detailed explanation of the Cuban economic situation was given by Castro in a lengthy speech on 29 December at the close of the regular three-day session of the National Assembly of the People's Power (Cuba's parliament), which among a few measures approved a new housing law (that makes most Cuban owners of the houses and apartments they live in and permits them to freely sell or rent them), and a labor code. Castro disclosed that in 1984 Cuba produced 8.2 million tons of sugar, its main product, about 700,000 tons less than planned. But this sizable output underscored the country's precarious economic situation, he indicated. In late December, he said the price of sugar on the international market dropped below 4 cents a pound, whereas in 1959, the year the revolutionary government came into power, it was more than 5 cents. At that time, he continued, a ton of sugar bought 6 tons of crude oil; today to buy the same ton 3 tons of sugar were needed. In all, the total value of the sugar production at the current prices would cover only some 25 percent of the country's fuel needs.

World prices for Cuba's second exportable product, nickel, were also lower on the world market than in 1983, Castro said, admitting that the country had not met its nickel production plan. The same was true of the third export, citrus fruit, "We fell short in three strategic export products," Castro said. "We increased imports."

Cuba must increase its exports, Castro said, because in the next five years it would receive from the Soviet Union goods, services, and credits valued at approximately 20 billion rubles. To plan repayment of that assistance, he said, the top leadership of the country had met (apparently secretly) on 22–24 November to analyze the country's management and pledged to work hard during one year and came up with solutions to be approved by the Third Congress in December 1985. One decision taken by the meeting was to prioritize investments to ensure exports to socialist countries. To do this, Castro said, appropriations on the social side of the budget would be cut drastically. Among the cuts he mentioned was housing construction and "many social programs." He commented: "The situation is tense. The goals are difficult, and they demand effort and real savings." (Ibid., 13 January 1985.)

Foreign Relations. For the first time, the Cuban news media began referring to military and civilian losses in Angola, where the Castro government continued to maintain a military force of close to 30,000 and several thousand civilians. In March, when President José Eduardo dos Santos of Angola visited Cuba, Havana said that over 150,000 Cubans had worked in Angola in military and civilian capacities since Cuba's 1975 military intervention in support of the Marxist regime. According to some Western reports, during the past nine years some 3,000 Cubans have been killed or wounded in Angola. In 1984, the reports said, Cuban troops became increasingly involved in the country's civil war, in which pro-Western guerrillas, supported by South Africa, have been fighting forces of the Luanda government, trained and propped up by Cuban units. In November, Angola was reported ready to cut the number of Cuban troops in that country from 30,000 to 10,000 and to redeploy those remaining far from its southern borders if South Africa would grant independence to South-West Africa (*NYT*, 2 November).

On the other hand, there were no reports of withdrawal of Cuban troops from Ethiopia, where the Cubans are believed to be engaged principally in training Ethiopian units. In December, Mengistu Haile Mariam, Ethiopia's top leader, met with Castro in Havana, where the two signed an agreement on cooperation between the PCC and the Workers' Party of Ethiopia. Another Marxist African leader to visit Cuba was Joaquim Chissano, foreign minister of Mozambique and member of the Politburo of the ruling Marxist party of that country, who in late November signed several economic treaties with the Havana government.

U.S.-Cuban Relations. The United States looms large on Cuba's foreign affairs horizon. Not only does Havana consider Washington its chief adversary, but it also believes that the United States could be a powerful factor in improving economic conditions on the island should it choose to change its policy toward the Castro government. In recent years, after two decades of defiance toward the United States, and frequently what appeared to be disinterest in improving relations with it, Castro has been giving signals of wanting to normalize these ties. He has been indicating that normalization on his terms, the posture he has maintained in the 1970s, is no longer a prerequisite for beginning bilateral talks. But Cuba has been very sensitive to any hardening of the American posture. For a long while after the October 1983 U.S. invasion of Grenada, Havana acted as though convinced that President Reagan would order a similar action against Cuba.

In December the United States and Cuba, after more than four years of negotiations, signed an agreement for the repatriation to Cuba of 2,746 Cuban criminals and mental patients who came to this country in the 1980 boatlift from the Cuban port of Mariel. Although the first efforts to negotiate the repatriation of the undesirable *Marielitos* were made late in 1980, it was not until 1984 that the talks got under way seriously. Cuba requested a suspension of the conversations, which took place in New York, during the final weeks of the presidential campaign. The agreement was the first between the two governments since the Reagan administration took office.

Castro expressed satisfaction over the agreement. After noting that both sides agreed to meet again in six months, he said: "Both sides are to be congratulated for having worked hard, carefully and diligently. An important, real, and objective change has taken place during the past four years: the present U.S. administration—whose hostility to our revolution is well known—nonetheless adopted measures against groups, once trained by the CIA, that engaged in terrorist attacks on Cuban personnel in the United States." (*Granma*, 23 December.)

While the White House officially stated that the 14 December agreement did not alter the cool, if not hostile, U.S.-Cuban relationship, privately some administration officials and one Cuban diplomat indicated that the technical accord might serve as a starting point to ease tension between the two countries.

Beginning in February 1985, 100–150 undesirables will be sent to Cuba monthly from the United States and up to 20,000 Cuban emigrants will be allowed to enter the United States annually. To process these relatives of Cubans in this country, the United States will increase its diplomatic staff in Havana by ten more consuls in the U.S. Interests Section.

Among the areas of disagreement between Washington and Havana, the most important are Cuba's military ties with the Soviet Union; Cuban support to Salvadoran guerrillas; the Cuban military presence in Angola and Nicaragua; the U.S. economic and trade embargo on Cuba; U.S. spy plane overflights of Cuban territory; the U.S. naval base in Guantánamo; and the U.S.-supported anti-Castro Radio Martí.

George Volsky
University of Miami

Havana Conference, June 1984. The First Consultative Meeting of Anti-imperialist Organizations of the Caribbean and Central America was held in Havana on 11–13 June 1984 under the sponsorship of the PCC. The meeting brought together official delegations from 28 parties, fronts, and other organizations in 21 countries. The official declaration of the meeting was published in the PCC organ *Granma* (15 June) and in *IB* (September).

The document opened by stating that the peoples of Central America and the Caribbean have long been separated by colonialism, which has been "reinforced by U.S. imperialism in the last few decades." The people's movement has only gradually overcome some of the problems of plunder, lack of communication, and disinformation. "Above all," it asserted, "we recognize that we are brothers and sisters because we are confronting the same enemy, which oppresses and exploits us. Now, faced with U.S. imperialism's aggressive policy, [we] need close unity, diverse means of rapid communication, mutual support, encouragement and shared criticism in order to survive, struggle and win."

The Reagan administration has launched a "politico-economic and military plan aimed at crushing the anti-colonialist and anti-imperialist people's movement, wiping out socialism in Cuba by means of military aggression, overthrowing the Sandinist People's Revolution and choking the Salvadoran and Guatemalan rebellions." It operates by "neocolonialism and annexation," by military maneuvers and "increasing the military forces of the puppet dictatorships at its service, and through the International Monetary Fund, controlling the impoverished economies of the region." The delegates

"confirmed the interdependence that exists between our people's struggles and the international situation."

The document condemned U.S. "attacks on the heroic Sandinist People's Revolution in Nicaragua; its occupation of Honduras; and the military, political and economic aid it has given to the genocidal dictatorship of El Salvador." It called for "support for the heroic Guatemalan people" and independence for Puerto Rico and denounced plans for the "establishment of a military force in the eastern Caribbean under U.S. control." While conditions in most countries were simply noted in passing, three paragraphs were devoted to conditions in Grenada, said to be currently occupied by an "illegal servile puppet regime and its U.S. masters." According to the document, "the defeat of the Grenadian revolution constituted a serious setback for the Caribbean and world revolutionary process," although the participants expressed their conviction that "sooner or later" the Grenadian people would again be free.

The delegates elaborated objectives designed to make the Caribbean a "zone of peace." These were (1) "the dismantling of all the foreign military bases that exist in the region, a ban on setting up new ones, and the elimination of nuclear weapons"; (2) "the stopping of all acts of economic, political and military aggression . . . through economic blockades or the manipulation of international credit agencies and the halting of direct and indirect actions aimed at destabilizing governments"; (3) "a ban on the use of mercenaries in acts of aggression and the prohibition of recruiting and training mercenaries"; (4) an end to "colonial and foreign domination" in some countries; (5) "non-interference and non-intervention in the internal affairs of the states of the region, and respect for sovereignty and territorial integrity"; (6) "an end to military maneuvers in the region that are against the peoples' interests"; and (7) abrogation of bilateral or multilateral military treaties between countries in the area and other countries. The meeting concluded "by calling on all the peoples in the region to be firmly united and to redouble the struggle without quarter for true independence, freedom, peace and social progress."

Countries and organizations represented at the meeting were Antigua: Antigua Caribbean Liberation Movement; Bahamas: Vanguard Nationalist and Socialist Party of the Bahamas; Barbados: Movement for National Liberation; Cuba: Communist Party of Cuba; Curacao: Curacao Socialist Movement; Dominica: United Dominica Labor

Party and Dominica Liberation Movement; Dominican Republic: delegation of the United Left of the Dominican Republic (including Socialist Bloc, Dominican Communist Party, Party of the Dominican Working People, and Anti-Imperialist Patriotic Union); El Salvador: Farabundo Martí National Liberation Front and Revolutionary Democratic Front; Grenada: Maurice Bishop Patriotic Movement; Guadeloupe: Communist Party of Guadeloupe; Guatemala: Guatemalan National Revolutionary Unity; French Guiana: Socialist Party of Guiana; Guyana: People's National Congress and People's Progressive Party; Haiti: Unified Party of Haitian Communists; Jamaica: Workers' Party of Jamaica; Martinique: Martinique Communist Party and Martinique Progressive Party; Nicaragua: Sandinista National Liberation Front; Puerto Rico: Puerto Rican Socialist Party; St. Lucia: Progressive Labor Party and Workers' Revolutionary Movement; San Vicente: Movement for National Unity and United People's Movement; Trinidad and Tobago: February 18th Movement and People's Popular Movement.

William Ratliff
Hoover Institution

Dominican Republic

Population. 6,416,000
Party. Dominican Communist Party (Partido Comunista Dominicano; PCD)
Founded. 1944
Membership. 500–1,000
Secretary General. Narciso Isa Conde
Central Committee. 27 members
Status. Legal
Last Congress. Third, 15–17 March 1984
Last Election. 1982, 7.1 percent, no representation
Auxiliary Organizations. No data
Publications. *Hablan los Comunistas* (weekly)

The economic problems besetting the Dominican Republic occupied the attention of the country's Marxist groups, which in 1984 tried, unsuccessfully, to capitalize on widespread popular discontent with sharp price increases for food, gasoline, medicines, and other imported goods. The Dominican Marxist left, which was accused by the government of President Jorge Blanco of instigating (together with the extreme right) bloody riots in April, was as divided as ever.

Some 30 extreme left organizations, most with a handful of members each, are known to be operating legally in the country. The secretary general of the ruling left-of-center Dominican Revolutionary Party (PRD), José Francisco Peña Gómez, mayor of Santo Domingo and a vice-president of Socialist International, attributed the weakness of the Dominican Marxists to the strength of the nation's democracy and a lively and free exchange of ideas in the media. In an interview, Dr. Peña Gómez said that many of the young Dominicans who are being invited as students to the Soviet bloc countries return home disillusioned by the lack of the freedom of expression there. In all there are said to be about 5,000 members of leftist organizations in the Dominican Republic, frequently quarreling, changing allegiance, and forming new "parties" or "movements."

Regarded as the leading Marxist organization in the country is the Dominican Communist Party (PCD), a pro-Soviet and pro-Cuban group, whose secretary general has been for years Narciso Isa Conde. The PCD held its Third Congress in March in Santo Domingo (the second was held in 1979). The congress re-elected Isa Conde, and ratified the party's "policy of unity" of the Dominican left, even though Isa Conde, in a report he read in the name of the Central Committee, cited difficulties still to be overcome before a unity group, the Left Front, could play a more effective role in the country's political life. He said that political relations among different leftist groups have improved considerably and that "much of the left is no longer devoting its efforts to mutual destruction." (*Listin Diario*, Santo Domingo, 26 March.)

In his re-election, Isa Conde received 216 votes out of a total of 280 valid ballots. Although Silvano Lora, another leader, received 234 votes, he did not become secretary general because the party determined that its Central Committee had decided who would occupy the post rather than the delegates to the Congress. Eight new members of the Central Committee were chosen, bringing the total to 27. They were Odalis Martínez, Fausto Collado, Nelson Pérez Marte, Alfredo Pierre, Daniel Santana, Fausto López, Domingo Rosario, Tancredo Vargas, and Lourdes Contreras. Three communist leaders who recently questioned the work of the PCD leadership, Braulio Torres, Luis Salce, and Raúl Cuevas, were not re-elected to the Central Committee. By a vote of 80 to 59 they were censored. Two members of the PCD were expelled from the organization supposedly for defaming party leaders. Rafael Pimentel and Arístides Arroyo told reporters that a "series of internal problems that have affected the PCD for some time had gotten worse and had degenerated into occupation of some local offices by an 'armed group' and the dissolution of one of the principal committees in the capital." (Ibid., 28 March.)

There were other internal problems after the congress. Isa Conde conceded that there were "differences" within the PCD leadership and a "division" within leftist labor unions (*Hablan los Comunistas*, 28 July–4 August). Leftist groups were also attacked by former president Juan Bosch, at one time their strong supporter and the leader of his own leftist organization, the Dominican Liberation Party (Partido de Liberación Dominicana; PLD).

Bosch accused them of being directed from abroad and of paying large salaries to their leaders. They denied the charges. Whatever his salary, Isa Conde traveled widely. He visited Cuba, Panama, Nicaragua, and most of the Soviet bloc countries, usually accompanied by several Central Committee members. He was also detained several times by the police.

The Dominican Leftist Front (Frente de Izquierda Dominicana), formed in June 1983, includes the Socialist Bloc (Bloque Socialista; BS), the PCD, the Dominican Workers Party (Partido de Trabajadores Dominicanos), the Anti-imperialist Patriotic Union (Union Patriótica Anti-Imperialista), the Revolutionary Communist League (Liga Comunista Revolucionaria), and the Movement for Socialism (Movimiento pro Socialismo). The BS comprises the Socialist Party (Partido Socialista), the Socialist Workers Movement (Movimiento Socialista de Trabajadores), and the Communist Workers Nucleus (Núcleo Comunista de Trabajadores).

While the left was not expected to have much impact on the 1986 presidential election, some observers believe it could disturb the electoral process by fanning popular discontent over deepening economic problems, which are not expected to improve in 1985. The problems facing President Blanco were many: the country's main export is sugar, but earnings barely cover production costs; unemployment is estimated at 40 percent of the nation's labor force; half of the population of 6.4 million is under the age of sixteen, and the population growth rate is 2.7 percent, one of the highest in Latin America; the country owes $2.4 billion, and its foreign commerce depends on subsidies from the International Monetary Fund, which requires sacrifices for its loans.

On the political front, the PRD was divided and could lose the election if Juan Bosch forms a pact with the conservative Reformist Party (Partido Reformista) of former president Joaquín Balaguer, which some believe possible, even though the two former chief executives were political enemies a decade ago. To complicate matters politically, more than a dozen non-Marxist parties are maneuvering for a place in a series of multiparty electoral alliances.

The most traumatic event of 1984 was the April riots in Santo Domingo. Officials and residents of the capital were caught by surprise by the three days of food-price rioting, which left 55 people dead and 150 wounded and caused widespread damage. The

April price increases were the result of austerity conditions the IMF imposed in the second year of a three-year $400 million loan. All Dominican dealings with the IMF have been widely publicized for years by the country's media. The national perception, which the left has endeavored to deepen, has been that IMF terms for granting loans, which are renegotiated annually, are unusually harsh, considering the Dominican Republic's precarious economic condition.

The Dominican Republic and Romania established diplomatic relations at the ambassadorial level on 25 July. The two governments, according to a joint communiqué, expressed their "conviction that the establishment of diplomatic relations will contribute to promoting the relations between the Socialist Republic of Romania and the Dominican Republic in numerous areas in their mutual interest and in the interest of the cause of peace and international cooperation" (*Scînteia*, Bucharest, 25 July).

George Volsky
University of Miami

Ecuador

Population. 9,091,000
Party. Communist Party of Ecuador (PCE, pro-Moscow), Communist Party of Ecuador, Marxist-Leninist (PCE-ML, pro-Beijing), Revolutionary Socialist Party of Ecuador (PSRE, pro-Havana)
Founded. PCE: 1928, PCE-ML; 1972; PSRE: 1962
Membership. PCE: 500; PCE-ML: 100; PSRE: 200 (all estimated)
Secretary General. PCE: René Mauge Moskera
Central Committee. PCE: 8 members: Milton Jijón Saavedra, José Solís Castro, Efraín Alvarez Fiallo, Bolívar Bolanos Sánchez, Ghandi Burbano Burbano, Xavier Garaycoa Ortíz, Alfredo Castillo, Freddy Almeidau
Status. Legal
Last Congress. PCE: Tenth, 27–29 November 1981, in Guayaquil
Last Election. 29 January 1984; PCE's electoral front, 3.6 percent, 2 of 71 seats; PCE-ML: 6.1 percent, 3 of 71 seats
Auxiliary Organizations. PCE: Ecuadorean Workers Confederation (CTE), comprises about 20 percent of organized workers; Ecuadorean University Students Federation (FEUE)
Publications. No data

In 1984 Ecuador continued to experience economic difficulties due largely to declining oil prices, the lingering negative impact on agriculture of severe weather in 1983, and substantial increases in foreign debt repayment requirements. In the midst of Ecuador's worst economic recession in almost twenty years, citizens went to the polls to vote for candidates at all levels of government. The signals the results gave were mixed; center-left social democrats were victors in most provincial and local elections and substantially increased their numbers in Ecuador's unicameral congress. Marxist candidates also fared better than in the past. The presidency, however, was narrowly won by the center-right Social Christian candidate León Febres Cordero. With congress and the executive branch controlled by different parties, tension and crisis were almost guaranteed. While an early confrontation between congress and the executive over appointment of supreme court justices was resolved, general strikes called by the Sole Workers Front (FUT) in October 1984 and January 1985 put the new administration on notice that its four-year tenure in office would not be an easy one. During the year, Marxist parties and unions followed their recent pattern in Ecuador's open political system of continuing to grow in organizational capacity.

Domestic Activities. Nevertheless, the Marxist parties did not heed PCE chief René Mauge's call for a united front in the 29 January elections. Apparently they believed that they could win more congressional seats by running on their own (*YICA*, 1984, p. 119). This strategy paid dividends, as Mauge's Moscow-oriented Broad Left Front (FADI) captured 3.6 percent of the presidential vote and 2 congressional seats (compared to 1 in the 1979–1984 period). Jaime Hurtado and his Maoist Popular Democratic Movement (MDP) surprised everyone by winning 6.1 percent of the presidential vote for a fourth-place finish and 3 seats in the congress. Manuel Salgado Tamayo of the pro-Havana Socialist Front (FS) finished last of the nine presidential candidates with 0.7 percent of the vote, but did gain a seat in the congress. (*El Universo*, Guayaquil, 2 April; *Times of the Americas*, 29 February.) Thus the Marxist parties together accounted for 10.4 percent of the total presidential vote in January of 2,573,486 and 6 of congress's 71 seats, as compared to only 2 of 69 seats in the 1979 elections.

Mauge requested his FADI supporters to vote for Rodrigo Borja's candidacy in the 6 May runoff elections among the two top presidential vote getters (since no candidate received a majority in the first round). FADI also joined with Borja's Democratic Left (ID) and three other center-left parties to form a Progressive Parliamentary Front. The coalition won 38 seats: ID 24; FADI 2; Popular Democracy—former president Osvaldo Hurtado's party—3; Francisco Huerta's Democratic Party (PD) 6; and the Ecuadorean Roldós Party (PRE) of supporters of former president Jaime Roldós 3. This group comprised a majority for the opposition in congress, and committed itself, among other objectives, to work "to improve and defend the viability of the constitutional system" and to "oppose measures limiting the role of the state in the country's economic life." (*El Universo*, Guayaquil, 26 July.)

Jaime Hurtado's MDP, on the other hand, requested its supporters to cast blank ballots in the May presidential runoff election and to persuade others to do likewise (ibid., 2 April). Of the 2,912,565 votes cast in the runoff, 9.6 percent were either blank or spoiled (*FBIS*, 10 May). The MDP, along with the FS, the Guayaquil-based Concentration of Popular Forces (CFP) with seven seats, and the Alfarist Radical Front (FRA) of Cecilia Calderón with six seats, chose to maintain their independent positions in congress—a total of seventeen representatives (*El Universo*, 2 April). With the 1984 elections the first in which Ecuador's estimated 447,189 adult illiterates had the right to vote, the MDP captured a substantial portion of them with a surprising show of strength in some rural highland provinces (*Latin America Regional Report*, 2 March; *Visión*, 16 January).

The political ferment and economic difficulties in Ecuador during the year contributed to a sharp increase in politically inspired violence. Between 27 February and 28 March a strike of oil workers and local leaders in two jungle provinces led to eight wounded, seven bridges destroyed, and the temporary rupturing of the country's main oil pipeline. The issue was regionalism, a local perception that the benefits accruing to the country from oil production were not finding their way back to the people and the region that produced them. The government was forced to declare a state of emergency in the region for ten days, with temporary military occupation to protect the oil-producing and -transporting infrastructure. (*FBIS*, 8, 9, 16, and 28 March.) In other incidents, 157 were detained in street demonstrations in Quito during elementary and secondary school strikes in February (ibid., 17 February); two were wounded and arms were taken in an attack on a military customs post in Quito in March (ibid., 30 March); one was killed in Guayaquil in a clash between supporters and opponents of the mayor in September (ibid., 7 September); a bomb explosion damaged the Guayaquil home of ID leader Fernando Larrea in October (ibid., 13 October); and another bomb exploded in congress in November (ibid., 30 November). An attempted general strike by the FUT and the National Union of Teachers (UNE) on 31 October fizzled after it was declared illegal by the new Febres Cordero administration (ibid., 2 November). However, a second national strike on 9–10 January 1985 in response to the government's increase in food, transport, and gasoline prices was more effective. Quito was brought to a standstill and casualties were high—seven killed, 50 wounded, and 500 arrested (*Latin America Weekly Report*, 18 January 1985).

Ecuador's first guerrilla organization, Alfaro Lives! (*YICA*, 1984, p. 119), moved from symbolic actions to several incidents suggesting increased organizational capacity. These included the occupation of the Ecuadorean news agency and the explosion of a leaflet bomb in the main square of Quito in May (*FBIS*, 7, 29 May). The arrest of eleven members of the group in June and the capture and extradition of the group's alleged leader, Rosa Mireya Cárdenas, ended most of the organization's operations—at least temporarily. Statements by the captured leader suggested that the organization was beginning to expand its operations to include kidnappings, jailbreaks, and the search for financial support for these operations from abroad. She indicated that she had been in touch with Nicaraguan authorities and representatives of the Colombian guerrilla organization, M-19. (Ibid., 6 September.)

International Views and Activities. In foreign affairs, the normalization of relations with Cuba, reduced to the chargé d'affaires level in 1981 after the removal by the Cuban government of its nationals who had sought refuge in the Ecuadorean Embassy in Havana, was agreed to on 24 January and completed on 20 March with the arrival of the new Cuban ambassador (ibid., 26 January, 21 March). Outgoing President Hurtado also visited the People's Republic of China in May (ibid., 22 May). The new Febres Cordero administration requested the departure of a Nicaraguan diplomat after he had visited a border area in Esmeraldas province in which some unrest had been reported (ibid., 17 December). PCE leader René Mauge met in Buenos Aires in July with the heads of twelve other South American communist parties. Their final communiqué noted, among other concerns, their absolute denouncement of "Yankee imperialism against Cuba and the brazen interventionism in Nicaragua" and "U.S. policy tied to the staggering debt of the countries of the region . . . bent on maintaining dependency and backwardness" (ibid., 10 July).

The two-month confrontation between the executive and legislative branches and ensuing crisis from October to December over selection of supreme court justices indicated that democracy in Ecuador would be in for some rough sledding in coming months, even though a compromise was eventually worked out in this case. A combination of factors would be likely to give Marxist organizations in Ecuador continued opportunities to increase their appeal and their support: President Febres Cordero's populist style and his commitment to conservative economic principles; the left and left-center opposition's control of congress; continuing debt repayment obligations (estimated at 23 percent of the budget for fiscal year 1985 [ibid., 16 October]); and low world prices for Ecuador's exports.

David Scott Palmer
Foreign Service Institute

El Salvador

Population. 4,829,000

Party. The Farabundo Martí Front of National Liberation (Frente Farabundo Martí de Liberación Nacional; FMLN) is the armed Marxist-Leninist movement currently at war with government forces. It is composed of the following movements, with their leaders indicated: the Popular Liberation Forces (Fuerzas Populares de Liberación; FPL), Leonel González, with Dimas Rodríguez second in command; the Popular Revolutionary Army (Ejército Popular Revolucionario; ERP), Joaquín Villalobos, with Ana Guadalupe Martínez second in command; the Armed Forces of National Resistance (Fuerzas Armadas de Resistencia Nacional; FARN, often abbreviated to RN), Fermán Cienfuegos (real name Eduardo Sancho Casteneda); the Communist Party of El Salvador (Partido Comunista de El Salvador; PCES), Shafik Jorge Handal; the Central American Revolutionary Workers' Party (Partido Revolucionario de Trabajadores Centroamericanos; PRTC), Roberto Roca. These participate equally in the governing body known as the United Revolutionary Directorate (Directorio Revolucionario Unificada; DRU).

The Political Arm. The Democratic Revolutionary Front (Frente Democratico Revolucionario; FDR), an umbrella group of those opposing the government and headquartered in Mexico City, has representation from the five DRU groups, but its president is Guillermo Manuel Ungo of the National Revolutionary Movement (Movemiento Nacional Revolucionario; MNR), a social-democratic party. The Popular Social Christian Movement (Movemiento Popular Social Cristiano; MPSC), a breakaway group from the Christian Democrats, headed by Rubén Ignacio Zamora Rivas, is also represented.

Founded. FDR: 1980

Membership. N/a

The Political-Diplomatic Commission of the FDR. This commission is a virtual government in exile, chaired by Dr. Ungo, and includes Rubén Zamora (MPSC), Fabio Castillo (PRTC), Mario Aguiñada Carranza (PCES), José Napoleón Rodríguez Ruiz (FARN), Salvador Samayoa (FPL), Ana Guadalupe Martínez (ERP), and Héctor Oqueli.

Status. Illegal

Publications. Newspapers: *Venceremos* and *Senal de Libertad* (both in Mexico City); clandestine radio stations: Radio Venceremos and Radio Martí

Although the PCES is the oldest of the Marxist movements, it was the last to join the armed struggle. The first guerrilla bands of the FPL entered the field in 1970 under Salvador Cayetano Carpio, who committed suicide last year in Managua. They were followed in 1972 by the ERP and FARN, with the small PRTC and the PCES entering into combat in 1979 and 1980, respectively. The overthrow of the military dictatorship in October 1979 brought chaos that soon plunged the country into a civil war between the FMLN, supported by Nicaragua, Cuba, and the Soviet Union, and government forces supported by the United States. National elections in 1984, in which the FDR declined to participate, resulted in victory of the Christian Democrats and the installation in June of José Napoleón Duarte as national president, but did little to end the continuing civil war.

Party Organization. On 16 December 1983 the FMLN groups announced their intention to function as a single force, a move long opposed by the late Salvador Cayetano Carpio. A breakaway group from the FPL called the Revolutionary Workers' Movement–Salvador Cayetano Carpio (Movemiento Obrero Revolucionario; MOR-SCC) was formed in December 1983 to oppose the FMLN, but it remains insignificant (*Intercontinental Press*, 23 January). In May the ERP renamed its political

arm the Salvadoran Revolutionary Party (Partido Revolucionario Salvedoreño; PRS), but the leadership of the PRS is identical to that of the ERP. In May the PCES held its fourth plenum, meeting in rebel-held territory.

The Civil War. The war for control of El Salvador continued to take its toll. By the government's own count, it had suffered 15,000 casualties between January 1981 and January 1984 (Radio Venceremos, 28 January; *FBIS*, 30 January). FMLN casualties can only be guessed at, but are probably lower. Including civilians, some 50,000 persons have died in the violence that began in 1980.

With U.S. aid, the regular army has built itself up to a strength of 48,000 effectives. To keep pace, the FMLN, which previously relied on volunteers, has been forced to use impressment in the fifth of the country that it controls in order to maintain itself at a strength of 15,000 (*This Week Central America and Panama*, 8 October). The FMLN buys arms or receives them in donations from sympathetic countries, but the State Department estimates that 50 percent are captured from government forces (*WP*, 28 March).

The previous year ended disastrously for government forces. For the last twelve days of 1983, heavy fighting resulted in over 500 government casualties. On 30 December 1983, the FMLN, led by Dimas Rodríguez, overran the Fourth Brigade headquarters at El Paraiso, Chalatenango department, inflicting an estimated 600 casualties, including over a hundred dead. The same day, FMLN forces routed the garrison guarding the strategic Cuscatlan bridge and destroyed the bridge. On 14 January, the rebels launched an attack on Chalatenango City itself, but were repelled with heavy losses. A second FMLN offensive in February centered on the eastern part of the country, particularly the department of San Miguel. The rebels seized several towns temporarily and shot down two government helicopters. The government did, however, capture Eliseo Godínez, near Santa Ana. Godínez was commander of the FMLN Feliciano Ama Southwestern Front. (Radio Cadena Sonora, San Salvador, 2 February; *FBIS*, 6 February.)

The fighting continued into March, the month of the elections, with the government mounting an offensive in San Vicente department, using aerial bombardment and attempting to win back territory in Morazán, where the rebels continued to hold San Fernando, Perquín, and Torola. In the same month, the rebels besieged Suchitoto, north of the capital, and assaulted the garrison at San Miguel, the major city of the eastern part of the country. On election day the FMLN seized Tejutepeque and San Vicente in Cabañas department.

But by May, the war appeared to be turning around. Lt. Col. Domingo Monterrosa, the commander of government forces in Chalatenango, claimed that he had the FMLN "on the run" (*WSJ*, 25 May). In June the government did appear to be gaining the upper hand. Even the longtime rebel stronghold of Perquín fell on 17 June to government forces without a fight. Then, on 28 June, the rebel forces overran the site of the Cerrón Grande dam and seized the country's most important electrical station, killing 80 government troops. But the FMLN victory turned into defeat when the army stormed back into the area by helicopter and retook the strategic site ten hours after it had been seized. Although the FMLN had threatened to blow up the facility if attacked, it retreated, leaving the installation intact. (*Latin America Regional Report*, 13 July.) Unable to regain the initiative, the FMLN contented itself with cutting power lines and attempting to sabotage the cotton harvest.

It was expected that the coming of the dry season in October would see a major FMLN thrust, but preparations for the peace talks, which took place on 15 October, blunted enthusiasm for war on both sides. As soon as the talks were over, the govern-

ment went on the offensive in both Morazán and Chalatenango. During the drive in Morazán, a helicopter carrying Colonel Monterrosa and three other top commanders was either shot down or crashed accidentally, and all aboard were killed. As Monterrosa was regarded as the government's top commander, his death gave a psychological advantage to the rebels. Joaquín Villalobos, who commands the FMLN Modesto Ramírez Central Front, then launched his own counterattack in Chalatenango. Heavy fighting continued into November. In early December, a bitter battle broke out around Chinchontepec volcano in the eastern region, with several hundred casualties on both sides (AP, 4 December).

The Elections. As had been the case in the March 1982 Constituent Assembly elections, the FDR attempted to ignore the national elections of 25 March and the subsequent presidential runoff elections in May. Guillermo Ungo declared that the elections would "not be a solution" (DPA, Hamburg, 9 February; *FBIS*, 10 February). But despite insistence by the FDR that it would not actively boycott the elections, local FMLN commanders disrupted road traffic and seized voter identity cards. The election was simply not held in the 40 municipalities controlled by the rebels. (*WP*, 26 March.) Afterwards, the FDR characterized the elections as a failure.

Negotiations. The FDR had long insisted that it was eager for unconditional negotiations, and during 1983 its representatives had met on several occasions with representatives of the Salvadoran government and with U.S. special envoys Richard Stone and Henry Kissinger, but these talks had produced no result. In February the FDR repeated its call for a postponement of the planned elections, the formation of a broad-based provisional government, the abolition of the 1983 constitution, the purging in the armed forces of those guilty of atrocities, and the return of all exiles (DPA, Hamburg, 9 February; *FBIS*, 10 February). As a gesture of good will, the FDR arranged in June the exchange of Col. Adolfo Castillo, the army chief of staff who was their prisoner, for eight rebels. Also freed was Dr. Eduardo Vides Casanova, the brother of the defense minister.

In Panama City in July, Guillermo Ungo once again openly called for dialogue, but rejected further meetings outside of El Salvador, insisting that future talks must take place within the country

(Havana international service, 9 July; *FBIS*, 10 July). This desire for negotiations was reiterated in a Radio Martí broadcast of 5 August (*FBIS*, 6 August). The next month, José Napoleón Duarte, the new president, began a series of low-level contacts with the FDR (*This Week Central America and Panama*, 24 September). On 9 October, four days after another prisoner exchange, Duarte announced that he would be willing to meet the rebel leaders in El Salvador on 15 October at La Palma, Chalatenango, a site within rebel territory. Ungo at once responded favorably and asked that Belisario Betancur, the president of Colombia, be invited to be the neutral observer. Duarte rejected this, but both sides agreed on Msgr. Arturo Rivera y Damas, archbishop of San Salvador.

To the La Palma meeting, the FDR-FMLN sent Dr. Ungo, Rubén Zamora, Facundo Guardado y Guardado (head of the Bloque Popular Revolucionaria), and Fermán Cienfuegos. Joaquín Villalobos had also been expected to attend, but was unable to arrive in time. They met with Duarte and the government delegation for six and a half hours, with the archbishop acting as moderator. The subsequent communiqué did not mention the major issues separating the two sides: power sharing and whether the rebels could keep their arms during a transition period. The major point announced was that a permanent peace commission of four members from each side would be established, and that further talks would be held. In November, Salvador Samayoa, Héctor Oqueli, and Óscar Acevedo of the FDR participated in a television debate with government leaders held in Los Angeles, California (Knight Ridder Service, 15 November). Then on 30 November, the joint commission held its first meeting at Ayagualo near San Salvador. The FMLN-FDR delegation was headed by Rubén Zamora, who took a hard-line position, insisting upon power sharing between the government and rebels, the establishment of a provisional government, a purge of right-wing elements in the army, and an eventual integration of the rival armed forces. The government refused to discuss these conditions. An agreement was reached that both sides would keep all roads open to civilian traffic between 22 December and 3 January 1985. On 12 December the rebels announced a unilateral truce for the Christmas and New Year's holidays and released 43 prisoners of war (*WP*, 12 December). The government agreed to take part in the truce the next day.

Foreign Contacts. In addition to travels directly related to the negotiating process, Dr. Ungo traveled to Lisbon for a conference on Latin America in June, while the same month Rubén Zamora met with U.S. political figure Jesse Jackson in Panama. Mario Aguiñada traveled to Bogotá in July. Rubén Zamora, Ana Guadalupe Martínez, and Salvador Samayoa headed the FDR delegation to a meeting of European and Latin American foreign ministers discussing the Central American situation in Costa Rica in late September. Shafik Handal went to East Germany in August and was welcomed by communist party leader Erich Honecker, who promised solidarity with the FDR-FMLN.

Biography. *Joaquín Villalobos.* Villalobos was born in 1952 and began his career as a student leader for the PCES. In 1971 he assisted in the formation of the ERP as an underground movement of PCES members. In 1975 a leadership dispute erupted within the ERP as to whether to continue ties to the PCES. Villalobos then ordered the execution of the ERP's leader, Roque Dalton García, and broke with the PCES. In 1978 he was instrumental in forging links to the Popular League of 28 February, a group with mass participation capable of sustaining the activities of the ERP, which is now subsumed into the PRS. He is commander of the ERP and secretary general of the PRS, as well as commanding the Modesto Ramírez Central Front.

Thomas P. Anderson
Eastern Connecticut State University

Grenada

Population. 113,000
Party. Maurice Bishop Patriotic Movement (MBPM)
Founded. 27 May 1984
Membership. No data
Chairman. Kenrick Radix
Leading Organs. No data
Status. Legal
Last Congress. None
Last Election. 3 December 1984, 5 percent, no seats
Auxiliary Organizations. The Maurice Bishop and Martyrs of October 19, 1983, Memorial Foundation; The Grenada Foundation
Publications. *The Indies Times* (weekly), *The Democrat* (biweekly)

The New Jewel Movement (NJM)—vanguard party of Grenada's deposed People's Revolutionary Government (PRG)—was reborn on 27 May as the Maurice Bishop Patriotic Movement (MBPM). Named after the Grenadian prime minister executed by a rival faction of the PRG prior to the U.S.-led intervention of 25 October 1983, the MBPM renewed ties with the Soviet bloc and leftist organizations in the West that had been cultivated by the PRG. Invoking the image of Maurice Bishop as a martyred hero, the MBPM entered candidates for thirteen of the fifteen parliamentary seats being contested in Grenada's 3 December national election. Campaigning on a socialist platform advocating renationalization of local businesses and land, the MBPM failed to capture a single seat, winning only 5 percent of the 41,000 votes cast.

Leadership and Party Organization. On 21 January the Maurice Bishop and Martyrs of October 19, 1983, Memorial Foundation was established by ex-PRG officials Kenrick Radix (minister of industrial development, labor, and legal affairs), George Louison (minister of agriculture, rural development, and cooperatives), and Lyden Ramdhanny (minister of tourism). Radix, a law partner of Maurice Bishop, had been one of the founders of the NJM in the early 1970s, and both he and Louison were also members of the NJM Central Committee and the Politburo. The Memorial Foundation served as an organizational and fundraising vehicle for the disintegrated Grenadian left prior to formal launching of the MBPM at a rally commemorating both Bishop's birthday and the 150th anniversary of the abolition of slavery in the British empire (*Granma Weekly Review*, 8 July; *JPRS*, 25 September).

Kenrick Radix was elected chairman of the MBPM steering committee, the membership of which included Einstein Louison (brother of George), a graduate of the Soviet Union's Vystrel Military Academy and ex–chief of staff of the People's Revolutionary Army. Formation of the MBPM led to a split among survivors of the Bishop regime. Social Democrats such as Ramdhanny and Fennis Augustine (ex-PRG high commissioner in London) publicly disassociated themselves from the MBPM, citing differences over key issues (Caribbean News Agency, 3 June; *FBIS*, 6 June).

Activities of the Memorial Foundation and the MBPM caused friction with the interim government of Grenada, which was referred to as a "puppet" of the Americans (*Rudé právo*, 5 May; *FBIS*, 10 May). Officials of the interim administration accused MBPM supporters of sabotaging electrical generating plants and attempting to disrupt the 3 December election by stealing voter registration cards. Following his party's defeat at the polls, Kenrick Radix accused the United States of rigging the elections by buying votes and falsifying ballots (*Grenadian Voice*, 8 December).

Auxiliary and Front Organizations. The MBPM maintains extensive international ties through official support groups in the United States, Canada, Britain, Sweden, and Cuba. The New York–based Grenada Foundation, Inc., chaired by the PRG's former ambassador to the Organization of American States, Dessima Williams, was formed in June for the purpose of "assisting and supporting Grenada's struggle for sovereignty and genuine independence." Supporters of the Grenada Foundation included Congressman John Conyers, Pete Seeger, and the American Association of Jurists (*News Release*, The Grenada Foundation, 19 June). In July, the Grenada Foundation and the National Black United Front (NBUF) sponsored a visit to the United States of the mother and sisters of Maurice Bishop. During the course of the tour, Mrs. Bishop was presented with the annual Maurice Bishop Pan African Award at the NBUF national convention following the keynote address by U.S. presidential candidate Jesse Jackson. In May, Mrs. Bishop had traveled to Havana to help launch the Maurice Bishop Award sponsored by Casa de las Americas (*Indies Times*, 18 August). On 13 March—fifth anniversary of Grenada's Marxist coup d'etat—the Toronto, Canada, chapter of the Maurice Bishop and Martyrs of October 19, 1983, Memorial Foundation was inaugurated by former PRG press secretary Don Rojas along with a tape-recorded statement of support from Congressman Ronald Dellums (*Intercontinental Press*, 2 April). During the election campaign, the MBPM distributed $20,000 to families of islanders killed during the army coup of 19 October 1983. Party spokesmen said that the money came from "friendship societies" in North America and Europe. (Car-

ibbean News Agency, 23 October; *FBIS*, 24 October.)

International Views, Positions, and Activities. In addition to establishing support organizations in the West, the MBPM rebuilt the NJM's ties with the Soviet bloc. Relations with Cuba are particularly strong, reflecting the fact that the MBPM leadership is composed of survivors of the Bishop, or Castroite, wing of the NJM as opposed to the Coard, or Stalinist, wing that deposed Maurice Bishop. Fidel Castro invited Alimenta Bishop, mother of the slain prime minister, to share the platform with him during the annual May Day celebration in Havana (*Intercontinental Press*, 25 June). Under the auspices of the Maurice Bishop and Martyrs of October 19, 1983, Memorial Foundation, seven Grenadian students were sent to Cuba during 1984 and a limited number of Cuban scholarships were offered to primary and secondary school children on the island (Caribbean News Agency, 23 October; *FBIS*, 24 October). In June, the MBPM joined 28 other regional leftist parties at the Consultative Meeting of Anti-Imperialist Organizations of the Caribbean and Central America, held in Havana. Following the meeting, Kenrick Radix thanked the Cubans for their support, promising that "we will rise again one day to seize our own future and to continue the internationalism for which Maurice Bishop and other revolutionaries were renowned" (*Granma Weekly Review*, 8 July; *JPRS*, 25 September).

In April, MBPM official Don Rojas visited East Germany, Hungary, Czechoslovakia, and Bulgaria, attending a conference of the International Union of Students in the last country. Rojas remained a member of the Executive Committee of the International Organization of Journalists (IOJ) and IOJ regional secretary for the Caribbean (*Rudé právo*, 5 May; *FBIS*, 10 May). The extent of the MBPM's relations with the Soviet Union is unknown, although the Soviet media referred to the party as "a continuation of the New Jewel Movement Party," which was continuing "the just struggle for the liberation of the Grenadian people" (Moscow domestic service, 3 August; *FBIS*, 7 August). The MBPM's international stance continues to follow the pro-Soviet line articulated by the NJM. The party considers itself a follower of the doctrines espoused by Maurice Bishop, whom it calls a "true socialist, a true Marxist-Leninist" (*Rudé právo*, 5 May, *FBIS*, 10 May).

Regardless of the MBPM's poor showing in the Grenadian national elections, the party finished the year as a successfully reorganized revolutionary movement that will not easily disappear from the island's political arena. The MBPM made little attempt to conceal its Leninist orientation, as proclaimed by a party spokesman who said that "very soon [Grenada] will be liberated by a second revolution which, according to the laws of history, is inevitable" (Havana domestic service, 30 May; *FBIS* 1 June).

Timothy Ashby
Arlington, Virginia

Guadeloupe

Population. 332,000
Party. Communist Party of Guadeloupe (Parti communiste guadeloupéen; PCG)
Founded. 1958 (1944 as section of French Communist Party)
Membership. 3,000
Secretary General. Guy Daninthe
Politburo. 12 members
Central Committee. 48 members
Status. Legal
Last Congress. Eighth, 27–29 April 1984
Last Election. 1983, 22.6 percent, 11 of 41 seats in local assembly; 1 of 3 in Paris
Auxiliary Organizations. General Confederation of Guadeloupan Workers (Confédération générale des travailleurs guadeloupéens; CGTG), Union of Guadeloupan Women (Union des femmes guadeloupéenes; UFG), Union of Guadeloupan Youth (UJCG)
Publications. *L'Entincelle* (PCG), *Madras* (UFG)

Although the PCG was founded in 1944 as a section of the French Communist Party (PCF), it now emphasizes its 1958 independence. The reasons are the growing sense of separatism in Guadeloupe and attacks on the party from both the traditional right and the newer nationalists. The move toward independence in New Caledonia during 1984 encouraged the latter. An increasingly difficult economic situation threatened all parties because none had a solution.

Leadership and Party Organization. Between 27 and 29 April 1984 the PCG's Eighth Congress met in Pointe-à-Pitre, its stronghold. The meeting marked the fortieth anniversary of the party and also the seventieth birthday of Hégésippe Ibéné, the most active of the founders. Three hundred delegates from Guadeloupe and its island dependencies were joined by representatives of communist parties in Martinique, Cuba, French Guyana, Guyana, Trinidad and Tobago, Jamaica, Venezuela, France, St. Lucia, and the Soviet Union. Perhaps for the first time a representative of the Unified Communist Party of Haiti was present. The Haitian representative addressed the delegates.

The congress approved the political goals of the party; namely, "democratic and popular autonomy" as a stage on the road to eventual independence and socialism. Guadeloupans residing in France asked for a resolution favoring independence, but the leadership insisted the island was not ready for it. In their view, independence would pull Guadeloupe into other forms of economic dependence.

A second major concern of the congress was the state-owned Beauport sugar mill. The government had decided to close it, but protests from the PCG and others gave it a new, albeit short, lease on life. Beauport is the last large mill.

Delegates re-elected Guy Daninthe as secretary general, but as in the previous year, he did not dominate the party. Other members of the Central Committee such as Christian Céleste signed statements of the Central Committee, and the island's communist deputy to the French National Assembly, Ernest Moutoussamy, was quoted and depicted in *L'Etincelle* more often than Daninthe. Moutoussamy published a novel, *Il pleure dans mon pays* (The tears of my country). Another leading member of the party, Dr. Henri Bangou, longtime mayor of the most important city, Pointe-à-Pitre, published two books, *Aliénation et sociétés post-esclavagistes aux Antilles* and *Le Parti socialiste français et la décolonisation*.

The affiliated CGTG held its Seventh Congress 23–25 March, and its leaders echoed the concerns of the PCG. The 35 percent rate of unemployment (*NYT*, 6 June) was a source of particular anxiety. On 9–10 June party members celebrated the fortieth anniversary of *L'Etincelle*.

Domestic Affairs. The party was challenged and humiliated on the issue of independence. The challenge came from movements claiming to represent the true aspirations of the masses. The newspaper *Combat Ouvrier* attacked the PCG for alleged passivity toward France. The terrorist group Caribbean Revolutionary Alliance (ARC) and the Movement for an Independent Guadeloupe (MPGI) expressed their disdain for the Communists, and the more conservative nationalists of the Union for the Liberation of Guadeloupe (UPLG) accused the PCG of contributing to transforming Guadeloupe from a colony, which might have gotten its independence, into a department of France in 1946. Departmental status made independence all the more difficult to achieve, in their view. UPLG members traveled to the United States and Canada to explain their ideas about independence. A visit to the island of American ambassador to France Evan Galbraith angered all these parties because he supported a continuing French presence. *Le Monde* (20 September) published evidence of more direct foreign involvement. The Libyans allegedly support the ARC and the MPGI, according to the French newspaper, and they are reportedly promoting the spread of Islam in order to weaken French control.

Put on the defensive by the ARC, which was officially outlawed in May, the UPLG, and others, the communist leadership continued to claim that the way to independence must be carefully prepared. It denounced the dozens of explosions set off by the ARC and others during the year. On 26 April bombs went off in twelve towns, for example, and four persons were killed by explosions the night of 24–25 July. An automobile belonging to a party member was set on fire by a bomb.

The party was humiliated when police arrested two of its young members for alleged possession of explosive devices. Embarrassed party leaders denounced terrorism and dissociated themselves from the two, who belonged to the UJCG. Guy Daninthe declared in *L'Etincelle* (7 July) that the party was absolutely opposed to terrorism and was not responsible for the independent acts of individuals who happen to be members of the PCG. Despite the disclaimers, police searched UJCG headquarters as well as the house of a member of the Central Committee.

The PCG, on the other hand, seemed surprisingly indifferent to elected local institutions such as the new Regional Council and the old General Council. It is in the minority, but the Regional Council now has significant powers as a result of the Mitterrand government's policy of decentralization. Municipal elections were held in three towns, and the PCG lost each one.

On 17 June voters went to the polls to elect delegates to the European Parliament. Unlike the Communist Party of Martinique (PCM), which supported the list of candidates presented by the PCF, the PCG called for total abstention. The reasons given were that in the view of the party, the Common Market is a capitalist, imperialist grouping to which Guadeloupe was linked against the will of the people. Only 15 percent of eligible Guadeloupans voted, an abstention rate almost as high as that in Martinique.

The change in government in France and the refusal of the PCF to join the new cabinet of Prime Minister Laurent Fabius was greeted with official indifference by the PCG. Leaders said that the test of any French government is what it does to save the sugar industry in the island. The PCG pledged to ally itself with all forces of the left.

Auxiliary Organizations. At the end of December 1983 the UJCG held a solidarity week with the peoples of the Caribbean and Central America. The UJCG rally was addressed by three Haitians. The CGTG, headed by Claude Morvan, called several strikes and expressed its opposition to the threatened closing of the Beauport sugar mill. The UFG met on 11 March to celebrate the International Day of Women. It debated the economic situation in Guadeloupe and expressed concern about the ever declining sugar industry and the ever increasing rate of unemployment.

The small Socialist Revolution Group issued similar statements, but it does not appear to be affiliated with the PCG.

International Views. The favorite target of the PCG remained the United States. For example, the party claimed a CIA agent killed Maurice Bishop, late prime minister of Grenada. Between 2 and 4 March, PCG delegates joined with other Marxist-Leninist parties in Georgetown, Guyana, to denounce the American occupation of Grenada. Guy Daninthe and Deputy Moutoussamy participated in a march for peace in Paris on 28 October.

Brian Weinstein
Howard University

Guatemala

Population. 7,956,000
Party. Guatemalan Party of Labor (Partido Guatemalteco del Trabajo; PGT)
Founded. 1950
Membership. 750 (estimated)
General Secretary. Carlos Gonzáles
Leading Bodies. No data
Status. Illegal
Last Congress. Fourth, December 1969
Last Election. N/a
Auxiliary Organizations. Guatemalan Autonomous Federation of Trade Unions (FASGUA); Patriotic Youth of Labor (JPT)
Publications. No data

The communist party in Guatemala, renamed the Guatemalan Party of Labor in 1950, originated in the predominantly communist-controlled Socialist Labor Unification founded in 1921. The PGT operated legally between 1951 and 1954, playing an active role in the administration of President Jacobo Arbenz. Outlawed in 1954 following the overthrow of Arbenz, it has since operated underground. Internal disagreements over the proper role of armed struggle culminated in a major party schism in 1978

and the formation of a Leadership Nucleus Cell that carries out independent guerrilla actions. Although the PGT has some influence among students, intellectuals, and workers, its role in national affairs is insignificant. According to U.S. intelligence sources, the PGT's several factions contain fewer than 800 members.

The Guatemalan political scene was highlighted in 1984 by the election of a Constituent Assembly in July. The assembly has been charged with drafting a new constitution in anticipation of general elections promised for 1985. General Óscar Majía Víctores, who replaced Gen. Efraín Ríos Montt in a palace coup in August 1983, announced that the assembly would also draft a law to regulate the 1985 elections, which he called "a step toward the return to constitutional rule" (*Prensa Libre*, 5 July). Meanwhile, the struggle continues between various Marxist-led guerrilla groups and counterinsurgency operations by the military.

The systematic repression used to control the guerrilla threat from 1981 to 1983 has given way under Mejía to a program of resettlement and pacification in the Indian highlands, with "security" organized by the armed forces and guaranteed by local civil defense militia. While Guatemala's military government prepares the groundwork for a transition to civilian rule, ongoing human rights abuses belie claims of imminent democratization.

Guerrilla and General Violence. As part of their counterinsurgency strategy, recent military governments in Guatemala have downplayed the importance of guerrilla and communist operations. Press censorship continued in 1984. Apart from official army communiqués and local press reports, in which guerrilla groups are not identified by name, news about guerrilla and clandestine party activity is found in bulletins and political manifestos issued by the various guerrilla organizations and opposition movements and infrequent statements by church and human rights groups.

Four guerrilla groups have been active in Guatemala in recent years. The Revolutionary Armed Forces is the military arm of the PGT (see below). The Rebel Armed Forces (Fuerzas Armadas Rebeldes; FAR) was originally a military commission of the PGT when it was formed in 1962. Three fronts were established, one made up of PGT members, one led by rebel army officers from an abortive 1960 uprising, and one made up of student (mostly PGT) youth. The FAR split in 1965. The army officer front left, and the student front disintegrated. In 1966 the remainder of the FAR split from the PGT, taking with it most of the party's youth. In the late 1970s, FAR developed considerable influence in the trade union movement, and its activists played a key role in the formation of the Central Nacional de Trabajadores (CNT) and the broad-based National Committee for Labor Unity, both of which have been subjected to heavy repression since 1978. Former FAR members have provided

the founding nucleus for Guatemala's other major guerrilla groups.

FAR was active in 1984 primarily in the remote Petén region. It is believed to have fewer than 200 members, plus several hundred sympathizers. According to the FAR's principal commander, Pablo Monsanto, a popular revolutionary war is "the best way to develop a broad and flexible national front" (Havana international service, 7 February; *FBIS*, 8 February). FAR spokesman Modesto Betancur criticized the elections as a "political maneuver" sponsored by the United States in "a false show of democracy." He called for an intensification of the revolutionary war to achieve the FAR's objective of a "patriotic, popular, and democratic government" (Havana international service, 28 March; *FBIS*, 4 April). In April, Monsanto reaffirmed FAR's support for the Contadora group's efforts because "it is the Latin American alternative to Washington's warmongering stance in Central America" (Havana international service, 22 April; *FBIS*, 24 April). In September, Monsanto said that the revolutionary movement in Guatemala was taking measures "to overcome its political and military shortcomings" through greater coordination and centralization. He admitted that the political arm of the "democratic movement" has suffered heavy leadership losses and is now active mainly abroad (*Granma*, Havana, 18 September).

A third guerrilla organization is the Armed People's Organization (Organización del Pueblo en Armas; ORPA), many of whose founders split from FAR in 1972. ORPA prepared for eight years before launching its first military actions in September 1979. ORPA's principal leader is Gaspar Ilón, one of the few survivors of a PGT rural guerrilla front smashed in 1961. Unlike the Guerrilla Army of the Poor (EGP), ORPA has no mass organizations and operates primarily as a military entity. Other guerrilla leaders have criticized ORPA's lack of political organization, which they claim has reduced its overall effectiveness. Although ORPA claimed credit for attacks on police garrisons in the capital in January, the movement has never fully recovered from the destruction of its urban network in late 1981. In April, ORPA members managed to evade tight security in Guatemala City and launch a damaging mortar attack on the Army Computer Center and Honor Guard headquarters. ORPA's rural fronts continue to operate in the southwestern part of Guatemala, especially in the departments of San Marcos, Suchitepéquez, Quetzaltenango, and Sololá.

ORPA intensified its armed activity in March and April, inflicting "heavy" casualties on army troops engaged in a counterinsurgency offensive in Suchitepéquez (Havana international service, 25 March, 8 April; *FBIS*, 27 March, 11 April).

The army launched a counterinsurgency drive in San Marcos in late July, mobilizing some 8,000 troops with air support. According to an army report, ORPA's founder and second-in-command, Rosalio De León Escobar, was among the twenty guerrillas killed on 8 August in a skirmish near the Mexican border (DPA, 9 August; *FBIS*, 10 August). For its part, ORPA claimed to have inflicted 122 casualties on army troops during clashes in San Marcos and Suchitepéquez from 20 July to 7 August (*Prensa Libre*, 22 August). ORPA leader Julio García subsequently claimed that the army had launched its offensive in San Marcos to offset ORPA's propaganda and recruiting activities in the area. He added that ORPA had "successfully defended" its positions of influence in the southwestern foothills and coastal plain. (Havana international service, 21 September; *FBIS*, 25 September.)

The largest and most active of Guatemala's guerrilla organizations is the Guerrilla Army of the Poor (Ejército Guerrillero de los Pobres; EGP). The EGP's founders broke from FAR in the 1960s mainly because of differences over policy toward the Indian population. The EGP proper was formed in 1972. After a long period of only sporadic operations, the EGP began its phase of "continuous military actions" in 1980. It now operates on seven fronts and is the only guerrilla group to have a truly national organization. The EGP has an estimated 1,500 combatants, although some of its leaders claim as many as 3,000. The EGP operates primarily in the Indian highland departments of Quiché, Huehuetenango, Alta and Baja Verapaz, and Chimaltenango. The EGP's major activities in 1984 are discussed below.

In February 1982, Guatemala's four major guerrilla groups proclaimed the Guatemalan National Revolutionary Unity alliance (URNG). The URNG's political platform promised to end repression, racial discrimination, and economic domination by the rich; guaranteed the establishment of a truly representative government; and adopted a nonaligned foreign policy. There is less agreement among the groups on the question of how to combine political and military work. The URNG declared that the only path open to the Guatemalan people was a "revolutionary people's war." To this end, it called for the formation of "a great front of

patriotic unity." In response to the URNG's request, Guatemalan exiles in Mexico City organized the Committee of Patriotic Unity (Comité Guatemalteco de Unidad Patriótica; CGUP). The CGUP is headed by Luis Tejera Gómez and contains representative leaders from the primary opposition political forces in Guatemala, including the United Revolutionary Front (FUR), the Democratic Front Against Repression, and the Directorate of the National Committee of Labor Unity. On 27 September, FUR announced the formation of the Popular Front, a coalition of leftist movements that received a combined total of less than 10 percent of the popular vote on 1 July and occupies only one seat in the Constituent Assembly (*El Gráfico*, 28 September).

In a communiqué released in Havana on the second anniversary of its founding, the URNG claimed "increasing coordination between the political and military branches of the people's revolutionary war at the operational level" (Havana international service, 7 February; *FBIS*, 8 February). According to URNG member Andrea Ramírez, guerrilla forces in Guatemala successfully parried army offensives launched in 1983 against EGP and ORPA strongholds. The URNG claims to have since managed to reactivate the guerrilla struggle in urban sectors and in the central highlands and to have organized new battlefronts along the Mexican border (Havana international service, 16 April; *FBIS*, 20 April). The URNG announced in August that guerrilla forces carried out 84 military actions in the previous five months, inflicting "over 500 casualties" (Havana international service, 28 August; *FBIS*, 29 August). General Mejía admitted that guerrillas had "attempted to renew" their activities in the country's main departments. He cited clashes in San Marcos in which guerrillas claimed to have inflicted 49 casualties on the army in the first week of August (military sources reported that 24 guerrillas and only five soldiers had been killed) (ACAN, 13 August; *FBIS*, 13 August). Mejía also accused Cuba of continuing its military and logistical support to guerrilla groups and vowed that "subversion will be defeated."

In September, Gen. Roberto Lobos Zamora, deputy chief of state, claimed that guerrilla activity had been "neutralized even in the most troubled areas of the interior," although he admitted that military patrols were still tracking rebels in the border areas (*El Gráfico*, 7 September). General Lobos subsequently stated that the government had no intention of initiating a dialogue with the guerrillas since there already exists an amnesty law. He added that as a temporary government, the military "can neither commit nor mortgage the nation's security." He reiterated that the rebels have been "decimated" and those still operating in the highlands are under "constant pressure" (*Prensa Libre*, 16 October). The Defense Ministry reported on 4 November that the army killed fourteen guerrillas in clashes north of Nebaj, Quiché Department (ibid., 5 November). For its part, the URNG issued a press bulletin stating that guerrillas had inflicted 37 casualties on government troops during skirmishes in Huehuetenango and Quiché in December (ibid., 4 January 1985).

Politically motivated killings involving leftist groups and right-wing paramilitary organizations have been a common feature of Guatemalan life since the mid-1960s. The systematic assassination of people in opinion-making positions by self-proclaimed death squads, such as the Secret Anticommunist Army, has decimated university faculties, student associations, rural cooperatives, trade unions, peasant leagues, and the leadership of moderate and left-of-center political organizations. Assassinations and "disappearances" continued in 1984, although it is generally agreed that urban death squad activity, which church and human rights organizations have charged is directly controlled by the government, declined somewhat in 1982 after Ríos Montt came to power. Groups such as Guatemala's Human Rights Commission, the Peasants Unity Committee (CUC), and the Democratic Front Against Repression issued periodic communiqués charging the government with mass murders, attacks on refugee camps, kidnappings, and increased repression in general in 1984.

A rash of politically inspired kidnappings and disappearances early in the year prompted church and university officials to voice their concern to General Mejía over escalating violence. Their discussions led to the formation on 29 March of a Peace Commission to look into human rights violations. In May, the rector of San Carlos University threatened to resign as chairman of the Peace Commission in protest over the alleged kidnapping of 30 persons during a three-week period (Havana international service, 24 May; *FBIS*, 31 May). For the fourth year, Guatemalan workers decided against parading on 1 May in protest over the repressive campaign waged against union leaders (DPA, 30 April; *FBIS*, 1 May). On 6 May, the head of the National Committee of Labor Unity reported that 26 members of the workers' movement had been abducted since the first of the year and were presumed murdered (Havana international service, 6 May; *FBIS*, 8 May).

In August, the government rejected statements by a United Nations' human rights official who expressed concern over the increase in politically oriented violence. General Mejía dismissed Guatemala's poor human rights image worldwide as "the result of misinformation and the distortion of national reality" (IPS, Rome, 14 August; *FBIS*, 16 August). In September, Guatemala's Human Rights Commission charged that over 500 people had been the victims of political kidnappings in 1984 (*Uno Mas Uno*, Mexico City, 29 September; *FBIS*, 4 October). The murder of three prominent citizens in October, including a deputy of the Constituent Assembly, prompted the government to report the existence of a "macabre plan" to increase unrest and "to prevent the continuation of the democratic process" (ACAN, 27 and 28 October; *FBIS*, 29 October). General Mejía subsequently claimed that recent violence had been carried out by groups intent on tarnishing the government's image and "delaying our return to constitutional rule." He suggested the possibility that murders were being perpetrated by leftists, specifically "the Communists and various subversive groups at San Carlos University" (*Prensa Libre*, 31 October). Amnesty International's report on Guatemala for 1983 expressed concern that Guatemala's regular security and military forces, as well as paramilitary groups acting under government orders or with official complicity, "have continued to be responsible for massive violations of human rights, including large-scale tortures, disappearances, and extrajudicial executions" (ACAN, 24 October; *FBIS*, 26 October). Government spokesmen complained of Amnesty International's "well-known lack of impartiality." In contrast, Guatemala's foreign minister termed "90 percent positive" a preliminary report drafted by the United Nations Commission on Human Rights. While the report states that many of the charges of human rights violations that were presented could not be proved, it also concludes that "violence and disappearances constitute a permanent fact of life in Guatemala" (ACAN, 4 December; *FBIS*, 5 December).

Leadership and Organization. Little information is available on PGT leaders or structure. Since 1972, two general secretaries and nineteen ranking members of the Central Committee have "disappeared," apparently the victims of assassination. In

1978, the leadership split over the question of the proper role of armed struggle in the revolutionary process. The dissident faction, known as the PGT-Leadership Nucleus (PGT-LN), is headed by Mario Sánchez. According to Sánchez, the party itself must become the Communists' organ for armed revolutionary struggle. The Moscow-oriented faction of the PGT is headed by Carlos Gonzáles. Other prominent members of the PGT's Central Committee are Antonio Castro, Otto Sánchez, Rigoberto López, Pedro Martínez, Daniel Ríos, José Cardoza Aguilar, Antonio Fuentes, Pedro Gonzalo Torres, and Pablo Hernández.

Student agitators are active at the secondary and university levels but disclaim direct affiliation with the PGT. Student leaders supported by the PGT have been unsuccessful in recent years in gaining control of the influential Association of University Students (AEU), although the AEU's statements on domestic issues tend to be strongly critical of the government and its inability to control right-wing extremists. In August, the AEU asked the special United Nations liaison on human rights to pressure local authorities to investigate the fate of "hundreds" of people in Guatemala who have been arrested and are missing, including numerous student leaders and university professors (Havana international service, 19 August; *FBIS*, 21 August). Members of the PGT's youth arm are believed to be active in the Robín García Student Front and other student organizations created to combat the government at the political level.

The PGT also controls the clandestine Guatemalan Autonomous Federation of Trade Unions (FASGUA), an umbrella organization of some 50 small unions before the government drove it underground. FASGUA affiliated with the communist-front World Federation of Trade Unions in October 1974. The PGT also exercises some influence within the National Committee for Labor Unity (CNUS). The CNUS, which had the support of some 70 member unions, was the most important voice for organized labor in Guatemala until the late 1970s.

Domestic Attitudes and Activities. It is difficult to determine whether the PGT's Central Committee met on a regular basis during 1984. Similarly, there are few sources that reveal the content of any political resolutions that may have been adopted. In order to characterize the PGT's attitudes on domestic and foreign issues, it is necessary to rely on statements of party leaders made in foreign

publications or in occasional interviews published abroad. Clandestine bulletins attributed to the PGT appear occasionally in Guatemala, but their authenticity is questionable.

For over 27 of the party's 34 years of existence, it has been forced to work underground and subjected to varying levels of persecution. Despite such adverse conditions, the party claims a steady increase in influence among the masses, especially among workers, peasants, and other sectors of the population that it says are "suffering from capitalist oppression and exploitation."

Since its Fourth Congress in 1969, the PGT has adhered to the position that the revolution can triumph only through the use of force. Until May 1981, however, the party did not commit itself fully to armed struggle. The Political Commission of the Central Committee viewed as an important step the formation of the URNG and declared that no political-military organization on its own can achieve a revolutionary war of the people as a whole against the military. PGT leaders' unwillingness to devote themselves exclusively to developing the military potential of the party has been the source of internal dissension and has led to a number of splits in recent years. No faction is strong militarily, although the group headed by Gonzáles maintains international ties with the Soviet bloc and residual influence in the trade union and student movements.

According to Rigoberto López, the PGT's primary tasks in 1984 were "to consolidate its ranks" to encourage as much as possible "the consolidation of a joint vanguard of the Guatemalan revolution" (*WMR*, January). Although generally supportive of the URNG's efforts to achieve a revolutionary alliance, the PGT fears that the revolutionary movement is in danger of becoming isolated from the masses. While Carlos Gonzáles acknowledges that the rapprochement of the major revolutionary organizations, including the PGT, has entered "a phase of consolidation," the party continues to favor the formation of "a single revolutionary front" and "renewed efforts to achieve tactical and strategic unity" under the aegis of the PGT. According to the Central Committee, it is the party's task to "consolidate the relations between the party and the people's masses and to establish an alliance of all revolutionary forces" (*IB*, July 1983). In keeping with the revolutionary popular war strategy agreed upon within the URNG, the PGT seeks to combine its military action with political work among the masses. In López's view, the working class is "very active" in the struggle against the military dictatorship, although opportunities for legal trade union activities are admittedly limited. Nevertheless, the party claims that the level of working-class consciousness "has risen perceptibly" as a result of semilegal and clandestine action (*WMR*, January).

In August, General Mejía announced that the military government would guarantee the participation of the PGT in the 1985 general elections "as long as it fulfills the legal requirements." Responding through the local press, the PGT ruled out the possibility of registering in order to take part openly in the electoral process. The party reaffirmed that the main obstacle to any form of participation by "revolutionary and progressive sectors" in any elections is "the absolute lack of electoral guarantees that stem from a process of genocide" (*Prensa Libre*, 24 August).

International Positions and Contacts. The PGT's positions on international issues follow those of the USSR closely. According to Otto Sánchez, Guatemalan Communists view strengthening the party's solidarity with the Soviet Union and other socialist countries as their primary international duty. The party maintains that by steadfastly supporting the USSR, the international working class "strengthens its solidarity with all the peoples fighting for political emancipation, economic independence, democracy, peace and socialism" (*WMR*, April 1979).

The party views as a priority task the defense of the Sandinista revolution against U.S. aggression. The PGT condemns the use of Honduran territory "as a bridgehead for armed intervention against Nicaragua and El Salvador" and calls for the dismantling of U.S. military bases (ibid., July).

In a message to the Soviet party on the anniversary of the October Revolution, Gonzáles expressed the PGT's support for the "peace-loving policy of the Soviet Union and other socialist countries aimed at disarmament and the elimination of tension in international relations" (*Pravda*, 9 November).

The Guerrilla Army of the Poor. The EGP emerged out of discussions among former FAR members in exile. The first contingent of the EGP entered Guatemala in January 1972, and military operations began in November 1975. The EGP's membership is believed to have increased from an initial 300 to an estimated 1,500 in 1984. Six independent commands operate in the countryside, and one in Guatemala City. The movement's rural fronts were most active in 1984 in the mountainous regions of Quiché, Huehuetenango, and to a lesser extent in Chimaltenango. The EGP's commander-in-chief is Rolando Morán, 52, whose revolutionary career began in the ranks of the PGT. He later joined the FAR and then helped found the EGP. Julián Pérez was a frequent spokesman for the EGP in 1984.

The EGP's principal thesis is that the revolutionary war in Guatemala cannot be conceived without the mass participation of the people. In the absence of legal means for change, EGP leaders believe that securing the support and active participation of Guatemala's large Indian population is decisive. The incorporation of the Indians into the people's war and the promotion of guerrilla methods of struggle by Indians in an effort to achieve their liberation is viewed by EGP theorists as Guatemala's fundamental contribution to revolution in Latin America.

According to EGP leader Carmelo Díaz, the EGP does not have separate political and military organizations. The movement consists of groups that conduct political work and also serve as combat units. According to Díaz, guerrillas operate in urban areas in commando-type combat groups in detachments of 20 to 30 men. For attacks on military barracks and rural operations, the EGP has specially trained groups numbering about 80 men (*YICA*, 1984, p. 137). In recent years, the EGP's rural fronts have relied heavily on peasants to supply food and provide information concerning troop movements and actions taken by local civil militia. It is widely believed that the government's pacification program involving the forced resettlement of entire villages and the organization of civil patrols on a massive scale has succeeded in denying to guerrillas much of the rural support network they had established in Quiché, Huehuetenango, and San Marcos.

EGP leaders now admit to making tactical errors in 1981 and early 1982. The movement's support in the Indian highlands in 1981 led it to believe that it could move quickly from the propaganda-harassment stage to one of general insurrection against the isolated Romeo Lucas García regime. In addition, the guerrilla offensive in El Salvador and the U.S. campaign against Nicaragua influenced the leadership to accelerate the pace of the "popular revolutionary war." The EGP admits that it was caught off guard by the 1982 coup and the effectiveness of the subsequent counterinsurgency campaign launched by the Ríos Montt government. The

EGP was poorly prepared to defend its rural support bases or to evacuate peasants from the main areas of conflict. Guerrilla strategy now is to concentrate once again on small-scale attacks. According to Julián Pérez, the EGP is "in a phase of struggle for territory, people, and power, which will require us to intensify our organizational efforts" (Havana international service, 30 January; *FBIS*, 1 February).

For much of 1984 the EGP concentrated its operations in Quiché, where it claimed responsibility for numerous attacks on military patrols and garrisons. In actions commemorating the founding of the movement, EGP rebels inflicted 33 casualties on army troops during the period from 6 to 20 January (*El Nuevo Diario*, Managua, 25 January). According to a news dispatch, the EGP claimed to have killed 67 and wounded 19 army personnel in actions in Quiché and Huehuetenango during August (*El Gráfico*, 13 September). In November, the EGP issued a communiqué accusing the army of bombing the civilian population in Quiché "to make its counterinsurgency campaign more effective." EGP leaders charged that during August and September "a total of 1,585 persons were either murdered, kidnapped, disappeared or were arrested by the Guatemalan Army" (*FBIS*, 7 November).

In a communiqué issued in San José in December, the EGP charged that the government had intensified its indiscriminate bombing of villages in Quiché and Chimaltenango. According to the report, the army is also "promoting a slander, misinformation, and psychological warfare campaign to cover up its responsibility in the destruction of villages, the burning of crops, and the kidnappings and disappearances of people" (AFP, 11 December; *FBIS*, 13 December).

While the combined strength of guerrilla forces continues to represent a serious threat to Guatemala's stability, the advantage appears to have shifted perceptibly in favor of the military government in 1984. The army's prolonged and systematic counterinsurgency program has exacted a heavy toll on the guerrilla groups that make up the URNG and forced the EGP and ORPA to retreat from their former strongholds in Quiché, Huehuetenango, and San Marcos. General Mejía told reporters in July that civilian rule was now possible because the guerrilla movement has been "wiped out" after a two-year offensive. He also conceded that "many innocent people who had nothing to do with it" were killed (*NYT*, 8 July).

The cost in human lives and suffering to Guatemala's Indian population has been staggering. Entire populations have been displaced in the regions most severely affected by the violence. In Quiché alone, an estimated 80 percent of the population at the village level has been displaced since 1981. Many of those unable to resettle in other regions of the country have sought refuge in Mexico or are located in displaced persons camps maintained by the army. Widows and orphans are scattered through the highlands. According to private Guatemalan relief sources, at the municipal and village levels in Quiché approximately 20 percent of the population consists of widows and another 25 percent are orphans with at least one parent and in many cases both parents deceased. Victims of the violence are still suffering from a severe lack of food, clothing, medical attention, and housing. Lack of communication and transportation hampers relief efforts in many communities, some of which can be reached only by army helicopter or on foot.

The number of Guatemalan refugees in Mexico is estimated in the tens of thousands. The problem of their eventual resettlement in an already impoverished countryside must be taken into consideration in assessing the potential for further social and political strife. Despite progress in 1984 toward "democratization" of the political process, guerrilla warfare and general political violence are certain to remain part of the Guatemalan scene for the immediate future.

Daniel L. Premo
Washington College

Guyana

Population. 837,000
Parties. People's Progressive Party (PPP); Working People's Alliance (WPA)
Founded. PPP: 1950; WPA: organized in 1973, became formal party in 1979
Membership. PPP: 100 leaders and several hundred militants above non-Marxist rank and file (estimated); WPA: 30 leaders (estimated)
General Secretary. PPP: Cheddi Jagan
Politburo. PPP, 12 members: Cheddi Jagan, Janet Jagan, Ram Karran, Feroze Mohamed, Pariag Sukhai, Clinton Collymore, Narbada Persaud, Isahak Basir, Rohit Persaud, Cyril Belgrave, Reepu Daman Persaud, Harry Persaud Nokta; WPA, 5 members: Clive Thomas, Walter Omawale, Moses Bhagwan, Eusi Kawayana, Rupert Roopnarine
Status. Legal but harassed
Last Congress. PPP: Twenty-first, 31 July–2 August 1982
Last Election. 1980. PPP: 19.46 percent, 10 of 65 seats in national assembly, and 35 of 169 seats in regional democratic councils; the WPA boycotted the elections.
Auxiliary Organizations. PPP: Progressive Youth Organization (PYO), Women's Progressive Organization (WPO)
Publications. PPP: *Mirror* (weekly), *Thunder* (quarterly); WPA: *Dayclean* (weekly)

Guyana remains under the rule of Forbes Burnham and his People's National Congress (PNC) party, both overwhelmingly returned to power in the fraudulent 1980 elections. The depressed economy continued to deteriorate during 1983. Political opposition to the government came chiefly from the PPP and secondarily from the WPA and several other small parties, despite some harassment by the government.

Cheddi Jagan remained the dominant opposition voice in Guyana, and the PPP was still primarily (but not exclusively) the party of the nation's Indo-Guyanese population. (The PNC is largely the political organization of the Afro-Guyanese population.) The PPP, founded in 1950, has been a professed Marxist-Leninist party only since 1969 and now is "in the process of transforming from a mass but organizationally loose party into a Leninist party of the new type." One of the distinguishing characteristics of the PPP is the relatively small number of top party leaders who have any significant knowledge of Marxism-Leninism and their

ignorance of the indifference of most Indo-Guyanese to that ideology.

Jagan and the PPP receive strong backing from the PYO, which is described as a "training ground for young Communists." The PYO, under the leadership of First Secretary Navin Chandarpal, is a member of the World Federation of Democratic Youth. The WPO is led by Janet Jagan, Gail Teixeira, and Indra Chandarpal. Both PPP auxiliaries focus on problems of employment and education and social and other issues.

The PPP maintained its ongoing critique of the PNC. Moses Nagamootoo, a member of the PPP Executive Committee, accused the PNC of carrying out a "4-F" policy: resorting to fraud to stay in office, using force to crush the working-class struggle, resorting to fear against the workers as the largest employer, and using food as a weapon to starve the people into submission (*Mirror*, Georgetown, 22 July). A *Mirror* editorial (9 December) charged that the PNC government had produced the severe economic crisis, with a high cost of living and infinitesimal wage increases, the mass migration of Guyanese to other countries, and a huge debt burden that has caused a shortage of foreign exchange as well as of essential foods and other products. If things do not change, according to Jagan, "the country will continue to stagnate, sink deeper into the economic/financial crisis and drift into the imperialist orbit" (ibid., 15 April).

Specific points of concern to the PPP in 1984 were the two devaluations—25 percent in January and 10 percent in October—which the PPP suggests may be a "piece-meal" program to meet stipulations of the International Monetary Fund (ibid., 14 October); a slide in agriculture and a fouled-up food distribution system (ibid., 28 October, 11 November); and a continuing decline in educational standards (ibid., 7 October).

The PPP, as "the Marxist-Leninist vanguard party of Guyana," calls for a political program based on the "three broad pillars of anti-imperialism, socialist orientation and democracy" (ibid., 30 September). The party advocates a National Patriotic Front government to bring about an anti-imperialist "revolutionary People's Democracy." More specifically, the national crisis must be overcome by "a comprehensive programme and policies ensuring democracy at all levels, political, social and industrial; ending discrimination, corruption and extravagance; separating party from state; deepening the content of anti-imperialism politically, economically and culturally; redistributing the national income in favor of the poor working people; raising political and ideological consciousness based on working class (Marxist-Leninist) ideology; having the working class and peasantry play the leading and guiding role; making the parliament function as a truly deliberative body; strengthening all-round ties with the socialist community of states." (Ibid., 9 December.) In an interview (Caribbean News Agency [CANA], Bridgetown, 10 October), he added, "Marxist-Leninists believe in the mastery of all forms of struggle. The method or combination of methods will be determined by the circumstances at any given time."

Perhaps the most important domestic development of the year came on the domestic front when PNC control over the national Trades Union Congress (TUC) was broken. Again in 1984 Jagan refused to speak at the TUC May Day rally in Georgetown, charging that the confederation refused to give adequate leadership positions to non-government unions (*Mirror*, 22 April). Prior to the annual TUC Conference on 25–30 September, the six-union antigovernment movement led by the PPP, which had a minority position on the TUC Executive Committee, proposed sharing seats equally with the PNC forces, but the proposal was rejected. At the September conference the antigovernment forces won a majority position in what the PPP called the first free and secret vote in twenty years. The victory by the six-union movement, which included the two largest sectors of the working class, the sugar and bauxite workers, was successful because it was backed by nearly twenty votes from the PNC-controlled unions. The antigovernment forces won key offices long held by PNC members, including the presidency (George Daniels of the Public Service Union) and three vice-presidencies as well as the posts of organizing secretary and treasurer. (Ibid., 7 October.) "The lesson of the TUC elections," according to the *Mirror* (14 October), "is that in any genuine free and fair elections, the ruling PNC wouldn't have a chance!" The four major tasks of the TUC after the election, according to the PPP, are (1) to unite against the intrigues of imperialism; (2) ensure that national income and state revenues are distributed in favor of the working people; (3) seek revolutionary solutions, not pro-imperialist "remedies"; and (4) work for a political solution to the national crisis (ibid., 7 October). According to Jagan, "The trade unions will serve the workers only when the latter begin to think of themselves not as individuals fighting separate employers, but as a class—the working class fighting the capitalist class—and when they arm themselves with working class ideology—Marxism-Leninism" (ibid., 25 November).

The PPP consistently adopted international positions that paralleled those taken by the Soviet Union (*WMR*, April)—for example, claims that the United States is a "rotten society" filled with unscrupulous exploiters, depraved elements, drug traffickers, racists, fascists, mercenaries, and the like (*Mirror*, 25 March); charges that the United States interfered in the Grenadian election (CANA, 4 December); and support for Nicaragua against alleged threats from the United States (*Mirror*, 18 November). Jagan played host to a conference of Caribbean leftist parties on 2–4 March (see below).

Among the major trips abroad by PPP officials were those by Cheddi Jagan to the Soviet Union in July and to Cuba in December. The PPP denied charges that Cuba was involved in trying to set up a coalition including the PPP and the PNC (CANA, 8 December).

The WPA. The WPA, now affiliated with the Socialist International, adopted some more moderate domestic and international positions during 1984 and came under fire from the PPP for so doing (*Mirror*, 20 May). The party concluded that the trade unions "struck their first real blow against the dictatorship's control" at the September TUC conference. The new hope for the union movement came because of several developments of recent years, among them the breakdown of "old racial camps," the constructive policies of the four- and six-union movements, and of Cheddi Jagan at the September conference (*Dayclean*, Georgetown, 13 October).

Conference of Caribbean Communist and Revolutionary Parties. Twelve parties and organizations from eleven countries convened in Georgetown, Guyana, from 2 through 4 March. The conference, held at Freedom House on the invitation of PPP leader Cheddi Jagan, was called to "exchange views on the current situation in the area after the U.S. invasion of Grenada" (*Granma*, English edition, 25 March). Jagan explained that the PNC in Guyana was not invited because at the time the Caribbean "consultations" were initiated in 1972, Burnham's party did not qualify for membership. The PPP leader added that the PNC "has been taking different positions from time to time." (*Mirror*, 11 March.)

The parties and organizations attending were the Movement for National Liberation (MONALI) of Barbados; the Cuban Communist Party; Action Committee for a Socialist Movement (ACSAM) of Curaçao; the Dominican Liberation Movement Alliance; the People's Progressive Party of Guyana; the Communist Party of Guadeloupe; the Workers' Party of Jamaica; the Martinique Communist Party; the United People's Movement of St. Vincent and the Grenadines; the Workers' Revolutionary Movement of St. Lucia; the February 18th Movement and the People's Popular Movement of Trinidad and Tobago.

The official communiqué (text in *Mirror*, 11 March; *Granma*, 25 March) noted the following points discussed at the conference:

1. "...the Grenada tragedy introduced a renewed emphasis on the use of force by U.S. imperialism as a solution to the Region's problems."

2. "...the deteriorating economic situation and the declining living standards of the Caribbean peoples are endangering peace and security in the Region...the Reagan-sponsored Caribbean Basin Initiative is basically an instrument aimed at creating a military/political bloc linked to imperialism and against the interests of the peoples of the Region."

3. "...the need to counter the U.S. imperialist military offensive...all participants re-iterated their whole-hearted support and solidarity with the people of Nicaragua and with the revolutionary forces of El Salvador, led by the FMLN/FDR. Firm support and solidarity was also re-affirmed with the people and Government of Cuba...emphasis was made on the necessity to step up the fight for world peace and to make the Caribbean a Zone of Peace."

4. "All delegates expressed their firm repudiation of U.S. military bases in the Region, against all aggressive military maneuvers, Washington's increased militarization of the Region and in particular the proposed Washington sponsored and controlled Eastern Caribbean Sub-Regional Interventionist Army."

5. "Participants...highly appreciated the positive stand taken by the Governments of Guyana, Trinidad and Tobago, the Bahamas and Belize for the dignified and sovereign stand in their rejection of the criminal invasion of Grenada."

6. "Delegates expressed deep regret at the death of Maurice Bishop and his colleagues...recognized the heroic resistance put up by patriotic Grenadians and Cuban internationalist workers...and agreed to protest vigorously against the illegal occupation of Grenada and insist on the recognition of the Human Rights of all Grenadian citizens."

William Ratliff
Hoover Institution

Haiti

Population. 5,805,000 (about 1 million outside Haiti)
Party. Unified Party of Haitian Communists (Parti unifie des communistes haïtiens; PUCH)
Founded. 1934 (PUCH, 1968)
Membership. Secret
Secretary General. René Théodore
Leading Bodies. No data
Status. Illegal
Last Congress. First, 1978 (?)
Last Election. N/a
Auxiliary Organizations. No data
Publications. *Boukan* (sporadic), *Haïti-Progrès*, edited by Ben Dupuy, in New York, serves as an outlet or forum for PUCH sympathizers.

Intellectuals such as the novelist Jacques Roumain founded the Haitian communist party fifty years ago in 1934, and it has remained a small, now clandestine and exile, organization of professors and writers. In 1949 the government banned all parties; in 1968 the party changed its name to United Party of Haitian Communists. The following year President François Duvalier made it a crime punishable by death to belong to a communist party or to engage in activity called communist.

The party operates in a very ephemeral way in Montreal, New York, Havana, and Paris, with delegates appearing from time to time at meetings or congresses of other communist parties. It has been called a "head without a body" because of its small leadership group of intellectuals and the absence of a mass membership. During the elections to the 59-member National Assembly in February, there was no sign of PUCH activity, which, in any case, would have been severely repressed. In May all political parties were, once again, banned.

Leadership and Party Organization. René Théodore is the general secretary of PUCH, and he resides in Havana. There may have been a congress in 1978 within Haiti, as the party has claimed, but more significant meetings take place in Havana, Montreal, and other centers of Haitian intellectuals. Ulrick Joly, labor leader and member of the Central Committee of PUCH, died in France. He was liberated from a Haitian prison in 1973 after the American ambassador was kidnapped.

Domestic Party Affairs. PUCH has no voice in Haiti and is overshadowed by other opposition parties whose leaders, committed to Western-style democracy, have been systematically harassed by the government of President Jean-Claude Duvalier. Outside Haiti alleged sympathizers such as Ben Dupuy, editor of *Haïti-Progrès*, call for unification of the opposition on the left and condemn those they label on the right. (For an example of the debate of exiles, see Jean-Louis Firmin, "Pour l'édification de Ben Dupuy," in *Haïti-Observateur*, New York, 10–17 August, p. 7.)

In an interview in Havana with a Hungarian journalist, René Théodore analyzed the demonstrations and spontaneous riots in May. He claimed that PUCH members were involved: "Our activists, operating illegally and using mainly the means of verbal agitation, are denouncing the dictatorship in increasingly wider circles; our decisions and appeals from the 'underground' are reaching party members." (*FBIS*, 11 July.)

International Views. A representative of the PUCH attended the Eighth Congress of the Communist Party of Guadeloupe (PCG) in April; the representative addressed the congress in Creole. He attacked the Duvalier regime and blamed the United States for the longevity of the regime. The representative also attacked the activities of the International Monetary Fund as an agent of international capitalism and American interests. Haitians, who may be resident in Guadeloupe, attended meetings of other Guadeloupan communist organizations. *Boukan*, called a publication of PUCH, sent a message of solidarity to the PCG newspaper, *L'Etincelle*.

Brian Weinstein
Howard University

Honduras

Population. 4,424,000
Major Marxist-Leninist Movement. Honduran Revolutionary Movement (Movimiento Hondureño Revolucionario; MHR)
Founded. 1982
Membership. No data
Governing Body. The National Unified Directorate (Directorio Nacional Unificado; DRU) of the MHR is composed of representatives of several small parties. These parties are the Honduran Communist Party (Partido Comunista Hondureño; PCH), whose secretary general until October was Rigoberto Padilla Rush, and whose national political commission head is Mario Sosa Navarro; Lorenzo Zelaya People's Revolutionary Front (Frente Popular Revolucionario; FPR-LZ) under Efraín Duarte; Movement of Revolutionary Unity (Movimiento de Unidad Revolucionario; MUR); Popular Liberation Movement (Movimiento de Liberación Popular; MLP) commonly called the Cinchoneros and led by Raúl López; the Morazanista Front of Honduran Liberation (Frente Morazanista de Liberación Hondureña; FMLH), whose spokesman is Fernando López; and the Revolutionary Party of Central American Workers (Partido Revolucionario de Trabajadores Centroamericanos; PRTC).
Status. All MHR-DRU organizations are illegal.
Publications. *Vanguardia Revolucionaria* (PCH monthly)

The PCH is by far the oldest constituent unit of the MHR. It was originally established in the 1920s, but disappeared during the dictatorship of Tiburcio Carías Andino. It was reconstituted in 1954, but was declared illegal in 1957. Since that time it has been periodically persecuted by the government. In 1982, PCH Secretary General Rigoberto Padilla was forced to flee to Cuba to avoid arrest. This set off a power struggle within the PCH, which appears to be continuing.

Honduras, the most desperately poor and backward of the Central American nations, for a long time avoided any violent left-wing activity, but its strategic location, bordering on such strife-torn areas as Guatemala, El Salvador, and Nicaragua has led to increasing internal tension and some insurgent activities. Its location has also led to the establishment of extensive U.S. military bases in the country. Some fourteen airfields, two radar stations, and a major training base have been constructed by the United States. This North American military presence has in turn furnished cause for a great deal of local resentment, with many demonstrations taking place in the major cities. The MHR groups have sought to take advantage of the anti-Yankee sentiment in their own propaganda and have attempted sabotage against the installations.

The one major attempt at an insurgency was stifled in 1983 when a group of more than a hundred PRTC members staged an armed invasion from Nicaragua under the leadership of Dr. José María Reyes Matos. The guerrillas were crushed by the military, and Reyes was killed in September 1983. This failure was a severe blow to the Marxists, who have not since that time been able to mount a major attack.

Domestic Party Affairs. The most singular event to occur within the PCH during the year was the expulsion of Rigoberto Padilla Rush from his post as secretary general and from the Central Committee of the party. This was announced in *Vanguardia Revolucionaria*, which is distributed clandestinely in Honduras, on 9 October. The action was taken by the Central Committee because of a rule of the party that all Central Committee members must live in Honduras. The monthly went on to denounce some party leaders who live abroad and "take advantage of their leadership status to obtain funds and live comfortably." (ACAN, Panama City, 9 October; *FBIS*, 10 October.)

This should not be seen as necessarily marking the definitive departure of Padilla from the PCH, as he has proved a remarkably durable political figure. Only five days after his ouster, he gave a lengthy interview to Cuban radio, which continued to style him secretary general of the PCH. The interview itself was a blistering attack upon the government of President Roberto Suazo Córdova, which had been elected in 1981. Padilla accused the president of doing nothing in the face of the economic crisis and pointed out "his outrageous defeatism toward the dictates of the Yankee Pentagon." He noted that "increased movement among the masses in Honduras" and in particular the anti-Yankee May Day demonstration that drew 150,000 to Tegucigalpa. He also pointed out that the Catholic church and patriotic elements within the armed forces had also rejected the government's "treacherous and defeatist behavior." (Havana international service, 14 October; *FBIS*, 15 October.)

Guerrilla Activity and Repression. The Honduran public security forces, which are a part of the armed forces, cracked down relentlessly on suspected subversive elements and managed to keep the MHR groups confused and demoralized. A raid on 9 May in Juticalpa municipality brought about the arrest of Santos Rigoberto Arce. The security forces claimed that this broke up a PCH-backed group called the Revolutionary People's Command, which had been planning terrorist attacks. (Cadena Audio Video, Tegucigalpa, 23 May; *FBIS*, 25 May.) A dawn raid on the town of El Progreso on 9 June resulted in the arrest of 24 persons accused of subversive activity. A few days later, Dr. Elisenda Portabeela Esquefa, a Spanish Catalan physician working with the Salvadoran refugees in Honduras, was shot and killed by the Honduran army. She was accused of being a Basque terrorist working with subversive elements in Honduras. (*This Week Central America and Panama*, 18 June.)

The most spectacular guerrilla action of the year was the seizure on 17 September of a Tegucigalpa radio station by armed members of the FMLH. They broadcast a message to the Honduran people denouncing the Suazo government as "treacherous and corrupt" and urged the people to rise up against it. Bombs, many of which failed to go off, were also planted around the capital and its airport, evidently by the same group. (Cadena Audio Video, Tegucigalpa, 17 September; *FBIS*, 18 September.)

The relative lull in subversive activity, compared with the two previous years, probably indicates a change in tactics among the parties of the MHR, rather than their collapse. The massive North American presence and the intense nationalist resentment against it have made it possible for the Marxists to infiltrate unions, church organizations, and peace groups in the guise of working for the common patriotic goal of expelling the Yankees. If resentment against the United States builds, it may prove the necessary springboard for a new guerrilla movement.

At the same time, the debilitating effects of internal feuds within the various Marxist movements cannot be discounted as a reason for their recent inactivity. MHR unity exists chiefly on paper, and there appears to be very little real coordination among the movements.

Thomas P. Anderson
Eastern Connecticut State University

Jamaica

Population. 2,338,000
Party. Workers' Party of Jamaica (WPJ)
Founded. 1978
Membership. 50 (estimated)
Secretary General. Trevor Munroe
Leading Bodies. No data
Status. Legal
Last Congress. Third, 14 December 1984
Last Election. 1983, WPJ boycotted
Auxiliary Organizations. Young Communist League, Committee of Women for Progress, University and Allied Workers Union, National Union of Democratic Teachers
Publications. *Struggle*

The growing deterioration of the economic and social situation in Jamaica found expression in 1972 in the victory of the democratic-socialist People's National Party (PNP), headed by Michael Manley. The PNP government remained in power until 1980, when the opposition, the Jamaica Labor Party (JLP) won a landslide victory and its leader, Edward Seaga, became prime minister.

In December 1983, two years before constitutionally mandated, Seaga called an election. The PNP boycotted the elections because Seaga had not brought the electoral rolls up to date, as he had promised to do before new elections were called. The result was that the JLP won all seats in parliament.

Both the PNP and the WPJ agitated throughout the year for new elections. Seaga, however, made it clear in September that he would not call elections soon and emphasized that the constitutional term of the incumbent parliament did not expire until 1989 (*Latin America Regional Report*, 2 November).

Meanwhile the economic and social situation of Jamaica remained critical. In July the Seaga government received an International Monetary Fund loan of U.S. $143.5 million, but at the cost of agreeing to a severe austerity program (ibid., 20 July). In August, unemployment reached an estimated 26.3 percent, and inflation, after two years of decline, was running at 20 percent (*CSM*, 30 August).

Leadership and Organization. The WPJ appears to have the Moscow franchise in Jamaica. The rival Jamaica Communist Party, organized in 1975 by Chris Lawrence, did nothing of note in 1984. The WPJ grew out of the Workers' Liberation League, organized in the early 1970s by Dr. Trevor Munroe, a member of the political science department of the Jamaican branch of the University of the West Indies. It was formally established as a political party in December 1979. During the Manley era, the WPJ gave critical support to the PNP government. It backed PNP candidates in the 1980 elections, but subsequently sought to distance itself somewhat from the PNP.

The Third Congress of the WPJ opened in Kingston on 14 December. In attendance were more than 250 representatives of WPJ organizations and delegations from fifteen foreign communist and workers' parties, including representatives from the International Information Department of the Central Committee of the Soviet party.

In delivering the WPJ Central Committee's report, Trevor Munroe called on Jamaican Communists to struggle even more actively for peace in the Caribbean and the world. Munroe denounced the United States for militarism and called for a withdrawal of U.S. forces from Grenada and an end to U.S. interference in Nicaragua. He demanded the resignation of the Seaga government and proposed the formation of a temporary government to organize elections. In conclusion, Munroe stressed that the WPJ will continue to be the vanguard of the Jamaican people in their struggle for full independence and a better life. The WPJ will continue to be guided by the principles of Marxism-Leninism and proletarian internationalism and to fight selflessly for peace, democracy, and social progress. (*Pravda*, 15 December; *FBIS*, 26 December.)

In an article in the December 1983 issue of *World Marxist Review*, WPJ Central Committee member Anthony Harriot expounded at length on the organizational techniques of the party. The principal vehicles for recruitment are "party study groups," which investigate ideological principles and methods of practical struggle; the Nelson Mandela Workers Education Seminars, held in Kingston by Trevor Munroe, which acquaint "the audience with its [the WPJ's] proposals and demands"; and "party support groups," which "usually grow out of the study groups but differ from the latter in that they are directed toward concrete actions. They assist the primary party organizations in fundraising, distribution of the party newspaper *Struggle*, and will play a major role in our election campaigns."

The WPJ is highly selective in accepting new members. Harriot said that the party accepts less than 50 percent of those who apply. The WPJ concentrates its recruiting efforts "on the organized working class," that is, the members of the JLP's and the PNP's labor unions. Harriot added that "special importance is attached to ensuring that all party members have a clear idea of our policy's objectives" and that "the WPJ pays constant attention to the qualitative ideological and political upgrading of its membership." He did, however, indicate a problem: "Even advanced sympathizers of our party limit themselves to attending rallies and meetings, and carrying out specific tasks from time to time. This, in our view, is a manifestation of the deep misconception that it is leaders and not the masses who make history."

Domestic Attitudes and Activities. During 1984, the WPJ carried out a number of specific campaigns. One of these was an attempt to mobilize sugar workers to "bring the most serious pressure on the government to keep open the three state-owned sugar factories due for closure." The WPJ argued that the only "language this government understands is pressure." The factory closings were part of the Seaga government's program to rationalize the sugar industry. (Caribbean News Agency, Bridgetown, 19 April.)

The position of the WPJ regarding the knotty problem of the road to power appears somewhat equivocal. The WPJ does not appear to endorse the guerrilla war approach that Moscow seems to have recommended to some of its Latin American allies. In his article in the *World Marxist Review* (December 1983), Anthony Harriot wrote: "It is necessary to ensure a correct approach to the problem of gaining power. A policy in this area which is not well-thought-out can lead to the loss of a realistic perspective and encourage adventurist tendencies, which also means a weakening of the party's influence among the masses. It is a grave and costly error to attempt to seize power in periods of consolidation of capitalist power, but equally grave is the missed chance at social revolution." Herriot concluded that "it requires scientific prevision and organizational preparation to avoid both mistakes. In addition, we are not seeking to gain mass support at any cost, since this eventuality weakens the party."

International Views, Positions, and Activities. The WPJ maintains more or less close relations with other pro-Soviet parties, particularly those in the Caribbean region. In November, Trevor Munroe visited Cuba and conferred with Fidel Castro. The visit was reportedly designed to improve relations between the Jamaican and Cuban parties, which had been strained because of differing views of the events that led to the U.S. invasion of Grenada (Caribbean News Agency, Bridgetown, 3 November).

Trevor Munroe and the WPJ had a close relationship with Bernard Coard, leader of the faction of the New Jewel Movement in Grenada that ousted and then killed Maurice Bishop. Munroe argued that the fundamental blame for the crisis in the New Jewel Movement lay with Bishop. It was Bishop's refusal to accept that he represented only a minority of the party that led to his deposition and house arrest. Though admitting that this was not sufficient justification for execution, Munroe claimed that "what the membership of the New Jewel Movement voted for on October 13 was that disciplinary measures should be applied, because not only did the

Comrade not accept the decision of the Party, which he had always accepted in the past when he was a minority and which principle he had always preached, but instead and on top of that now had begun to actually incite the people against other Party leaders and against the Party." (*Intercontinental Press*, 28 May.)

Earlier in the year, the WPJ participated in a meeting of communist and revolutionary parties in Georgetown, Guyana, called by the People's Progressive Party of Guyana, to discuss the impact of the Grenadian invasion on the Caribbean area. In addition to the representatives of the WPJ and the host party, there were delegations present from Cuba, Barbados, Curacao, Dominica, Guadeloupe, Martinique, St. Vincent, St. Lucia, and Trinidad and Tobago. (*Granma Weekly Review*, Havana, 25 March.)

Of significance is that overseas pro-Moscow parties sought throughout the year to maintain contact with the PNP. A delegation from the Soviet party attended the PNP's annual convention in September (*Pravda*, 6 September), and the East German party sent a message (*Neues Deutschland*, East Berlin, 19 September). Michael Manley visited Cuba and conferred with Castro only two weeks after Trevor Munroe's visit.

Revolutionary Marxist League. The third and smallest Marxist-Leninist organization in Jamaica is the Revolutionary Marxist League (RML). It was organized in the late 1970s and identifies itself as Trotskyist. It is, however, aligned with the Revolutionary Socialist League in the United States, which repudiates the traditional Trotskyist position that the Soviet Union and other Soviet bloc states remain "workers' states." The RML advocated abstention in the 1980 general elections. Its Second Congress met in 1982 and was attended by a representative of its U.S. counterpart. At that meeting, the two groups proclaimed their intention of forming an "international tendency" within the Trotskyist movement. The RML, like the Communist Party of Jamaica, did little to attract attention during the year.

Robert J. Alexander
Rutgers University

Martinique

Population. 330,000
Party. Martinique Communist Party (Parti communiste martiniquais; PCM)
Founded. 1921 (PCM, 1957)
Membership. Under 1,000
Secretary General. Armand Nicolas
Politburo. 3 members
Secretariat. 4 members
Central Committee. 33 members
Status. Legal
Last Congress. Eighth, 12–13 November 1983
Last Election. 1983, 9.07 percent, 4 of 41 seats in local assembly; none in Paris
Auxiliary Organizations. Union of Women of Martinique (Union des femmes de la Martinique), General Confederation of Martinican Workers (Confédération générale du travail; CGTM)
Publications. *Justice* (weekly)

Growing dissension within the PCM over the issue of autonomy versus independence for Martinique led to the most serious discord among the leadership since the party was founded in 1921. One result was the sudden appearance of another communist party led by two members of the Regional Council, the most important elected body in the island. The PCM watched the decline of the left in France with dismay but refused to break its local alliance with the Socialist and Progressive parties. The party rejoiced in the move toward decentralization that the Conseil Régional represented but lamented its own weakening position in the island. Sensitive to demands for autonomy or independence from France, the PCM insisted that since 1957 it has not received orders from the French Communist Party (PCF).

Leadership and Party Organization. Since the Eighth Congress in November 1983, General Secretary Armand Nicolas has fought off demands from within the party for a radical position on independence. After heated debate, the congress voted for autonomy with the possibility of independence in the distant future, but dissidents called for immediate independence. The section committee of the town of Schoelcher refused to celebrate the alliance of the left partly due to this issue, and the Politburo dissolved it. Two PCM members of the Regional Council, Dany Emmanuel and Léandre Marimoutou, refused to vote according to party directives, and the Central Committee asked them to resign. They did resign from the party but refused to resign from the Regional Council to which they had been elected in 1983, thus threatening the slim leftist majority.

All section committees with the exception of Trinité condemned the two renegades. The dissidents there published a declaration favoring independence and were promptly expelled from the party. Some members of the editorial board of the party newspaper, *Justice*, quit in protest.

Armand Nicolas invoked the principle of democratic centralism in vain, and in October the party held an assembly to re-establish discipline among members of the Central Committee, section committees, and cell bureaus.

Dissidents who had been expelled from the party created the Communist Party for Independence and Socialism (Parti communiste pour l'indépendance et le socialisme), but it is too early to judge its influence.

In the elections to the European Parliament on

17 June, the PCM supported the French Communist Party list, which included Paul Vergès of Réunion, another overseas department. Only 30 percent of those eligible voted, and the communist list collected 5.75 percent of those votes.

Domestic Party Affairs. The PCM rejoiced in the new powers of the Regional Council, where an alliance of Socialists, Communists, and Aimé Césaire's Progressive Martinique Party (PPM) held a bare majority of 21 of a total of 41 seats. Césaire continued to head the council, and Armand Nicolas served as vice-president. The French law of 2 August confirmed the powers and responsibilities of the council over land, resources, and culture. PCM support for the Regional Council contrasted with its criticism of the less important General Council, where the PCM is in the minority. The General Council of Martinique was accused of corruption and mismanagement by the French General Accounting Office.

At the beginning of the year, the PCM explicitly supported the government of François Mitterrand and celebrated the local unification of the left in a public meeting on 29 February. After the change in government in France and the subsequent PCF refusal to be part of the new cabinet of Prime Minister Laurent Fabius, the PCM took pains to emphasize its independence from the French party and its support for the local union of the left. Nonetheless, toward the end of the year PCM criticism of the Socialist-led government increased.

Elected communist officials met with the prefect of Martinique, named by the Mitterrand government, to express their concern about the banana industry, other economic matters, and the imprisonment of Marc Pulvar, a labor leader accused of murder. The PCM joined the government in denouncing the terrorism of the Caribbean Revolutionary Alliance (ARC), which had set bombs in Guadeloupe. The PCM expressed its outrage when the ARC openly named two Martiniquans as enemies. The PCM supported government attempts to increase autonomy and severely criticized demands for immediate independence on the grounds that the masses of Martinique were not ready for it. In partial municipal elections, the PCM claimed victory in one town.

Auxiliary Organizations. The CGTM, which is headed by Philibert Duféal, initiated several short strikes. Martiniquan workers in France, who belong to the General Confederation of Workers there, decided to organize themselves, and this action may establish a link between Martiniquans in France and Martiniquan workers. The Union of Women of Martinique, headed by Solange Fitte-Duval, held its Fourth Congress on 16 September. Among the many issues discussed were the differences in rights of women in the metropole and in Martinique. For example, a woman worker in Martinique is allowed five days' maternity leave compared with fifteen days' leave in France.

International Views. The CPM sent a delegation to Georgetown, Guyana, for a meeting of twelve Marxist-Leninist organizations and parties on 2–4 March. Participants denounced the American invasion of Grenada and expressed concern about the political evolution of Central America.

On 10–13 June in Havana PCM representatives participated in the first meeting of the Anti-imperialist Organization of the Caribbean and Central America, which also denounced the United States.

Although Moscow and Paris remained the most important world capitals for the PCM, the party newspaper, *Justice*, published an unusually cordial article about China.

In January, *Justice* journalists met to explore ways to improve the newspaper. Ex-Maoists published the newspaper *APAL*, or *Asé pléré an nou lité*, which is Creole for "Stop complaining and let's fight."

Brian Weinstein
Howard University

Mexico

Population. 77,659,000
Party. Unified Socialist Party of Mexico (Partido Socialista Unificado de Mexico; PSUM)
Founded. 1919 (PSUM, 1981)
Membership. 40,800 (*IB*, no. 15)
Secretary General. Pablo Gómez Alvarez
Political Commission. 21 members: Pablo Gómez Alvarez, Sabino Hernández Tellez, Gilberto Rincon Gallardo Meltiz, Manuel Stephens García, Jorge Alocer Villanueva, Rolando Cordera Campos, Ivan García Solis, Arnaldo Martínez Verdugo, Eduardo Montes Manzano, Pablo Pascual Moncayo, Marcos Leonel Posadas Segura, Gerardo Unzueta Lorenzana, Miguel Angel Velasco Muñoz, Leopoldo Arthur Whaley Martínez, Valentín Campa Salazar, Eduardo González Ramírez, Adolfo Sánchez Rebolledo. (A Central Committee plenum in November 1984 voted to expand the Political Commission from 17 to 21 members [*Pravda*, 13 November]. The names of the four new members were unavailable at the time of writing.)
Secretariat. 7 members: Pablo Gómez Alvarez, Sabino Hernández Tellez, Gilberto Rincon Gallardo Meltiz, Manuel Stephens García, Jorge Alocer Villanueva, Jesús Sosa Castro, José Woldenberg Karakowsky
Central Committee. 75 members
Status. Legal
Last Congress. Second, 9–14 August 1983
Last Elections. 1982; 3.5 percent of vote for president; 4.3 percent of the vote for, and 17 of 400 seats in, the legislature

Auxiliary Organizations. Youth/Student Section of the PSUM, Independent Center of Agricultural Workers and Peasants (CIOAC), Sole National Union of University Workers (SUNTU), Single Union of Workers of the Nuclear Industry

Publications. *Asi Es* (weekly)

The PSUM, recognized by the Soviet Union as the official communist party of the country, was formed in 1981 as the product of a fusion between the Mexican Communist Party (Partido Comunista Mexicano; PCM) with four smaller groups. They are the Popular Action Movement (Movimiento de Acción Popular; MAP), the Mexican People's Party (Partido Popular Mexicano; PPM), the Revolutionary Socialist Party (Partido Socialista Revolucionario; PSR), and the Socialist Action and Unity Movement (Movimiento de Acción y Unidad; MAUS).

Domestic Views and Activities. Since its Second Congress in August 1983, the PSUM has been consumed with two major issues: the leadership struggle within the party and the search for a strategy and allies in the campaign for the federal elections of July 1985. The intraparty leadership crisis was rooted in the fact that the PSUM was the offspring of two separate political movements—one grouped around the PCM and the other around the PPM. The struggle, which focused on the size and composition of the PSUM's leading organs (the Secretariat and the Political Commission), degenerated into "exhausting, harsh debates and difficult negotiations in the top echelon, which have kept the present secretary general, Pablo Gómez, at a virtual impasse . . . The internal struggle is so emotional that it is the main factor for disruption fostered by our enemies." (*Proceso*, Mexico City, 20 August.)

Resistance to the decisions adopted by the Second Congress, both with regard to leaders selected and policies adopted, became obvious even before the conclave ended. A lengthy resolution put out by the Second Plenum of the PSUM's Central Committee on 4–6 November 1983 addressed these problems. According to the resolution, "it became evident that there was a need to eliminate . . . the compartmentalized type of leadership, wherein there still persist alignments . . . that originate directly or indirectly in all the organizations that merged in November 1981. Our Second Congress was a step forward, not only for the development of the PSUM's political line, but also because it afforded a more clear-cut realization that . . . [compartmentalized] leadership hampers the fulfillment of the unified goals that gave rise to the PSUM. The party's rank and file demand a leadership capable of . . . operating as a single agency and directing the entire party in a collective fashion, and not merely segments thereof." The resolution denounced "sectarianism" and "factionalism" and called for the development of "internal democracy" in the party. (*Asi Es*, 11–17 November 1983.)

The persistence of the crisis within the party was illustrated graphically during the Third Plenum in January. Roberto Jaramillo Flores, the staunchly pro-Soviet former leader of the PSR, contended that the PSUM had virtually ejected him because of his refusal to dissolve the PSR as a separate organization and failed to take his seat at the plenum. Shortly after the plenum ended, Political Commission member Arnaldo Martínez Verdugo discussed the PSUM's organizational problems in an interview with *Uno Mas Uno* (21 January). He conceded that the unification process that joined the PCM with the other components of the new PSUM was never expected to "go great guns" or be "idyllic," and he predicted more "very tense moments" on intraparty issues. Martínez Verdugo characterized the PSUM as "viable, but immature." What was to be done? In Martínez Verdugo's words, "The time must come when the PSUM selects its own leaders, independent of the role they played in other organizations [before the merger] . . . All the contributing elements of the PSUM are not sufficiently considered when drawing up positions."

Jaramillo, not surprisingly, rendered a much harsher judgment on the PSUM's internal difficulties. On 25 June, an article in *Uno Mas Uno* stated: "According to Roberto Jaramillo—the most recent defector from the . . . PSUM—the irresponsibility, charlatanism, and ambitions of the . . . PCM have ruined leftist unity in this country and turned the PSUM into 'a weak party involved in a permanent internal struggle, a party in crisis, a party that is merely a house of cards that can be blown away.'" Jaramillo has focused his energies on obtaining legal registration for the PSR from the Federal Electoral Commission.

The leadership crisis in the PSUM evidently came to a head at the Sixth Plenum on 22–23 July. A special edition of the party organ, *Asi Es*, published the full transcript of the proceedings. It was obvious from the debates that the intraparty strife seriously hampered the party's effectiveness as a political force. The participants at the plenum bewailed the failure to implement many of the programs set forth by the party's Second Congress—a failure attributed to "insufficient . . . agreement on extremely important aspects of our policy" and to "the lack of participation . . . on the party's various leadership levels, but especially in . . . the Political Commission, in which outstanding leaders failed to participate because of their disagreement with the results of the Congress." It was resolved "to deploy the necessary effort to restore to the Political Commission outstanding leaders who have decided to cease participating in it." (*JPRS*, 84–136, 13 December.) Jaramillo apparently was the leader most on the minds of those at the plenum.

The plenum noted the close connection between the party's internal struggle and its inability to accomplish its political objectives. The discussants emphasized that "our internal situation is not a quarrel among us, at least not that alone. It is a problem of a national nature." (Ibid.) Central Committee member Raymundo Cardenas declared that "with the activity being carried out by the government's PRI [Institutional Revolutionary Party] and the National Action Party [PAN; the chief opposition party], we shall be left on the sidelines completely if we don't . . . give another loud ring of the bell, so to speak . . . I maintain that those who do not do everything that should be done internally to achieve unity will be condemned by history." Another participant in the debate, Olac Fuentes, reiterated the need for "recognition of the plurality that exists in the party" —a recognition that had to be realized by means of "proportionality in representation and integration in leadership." (Ibid.)

In concluding, the plenum established a special commission to prepare a proposal "on the formation and operation of the Political Commission and the Secretariat" (ibid.). It was agreed that these internal matters had to be resolved in order for the PSUM to compete effectively in the political campaign leading up to the 1985 Mexican elections.

"Unity of the left" became the battle cry for the PSUM's electoral strategy. Complementing the party's efforts to structure its leadership in a manner more representative of the elements comprising it was its effort to seek allies along the leftist political spectrum—and perhaps beyond—to challenge the PRI.

The question of the PSUM's electoral strategy became acute as a result of dramatic developments on the Mexican political scene, which has been dominated totally by the PRI for more than 50 years. In the early 1980s, the downhill slide of Mexico's economy and the growing disenchantment among Mexicans with the corruption and undemocratic nature of the PRI paved the way for a rapid rise to influence of the PAN. A conservative, capitalist-oriented organization, the PAN has close links with the church hierarchy and with business interests, particularly in northern and northwestern Mexico. It is strongly entrenched in some of the country's most industrially developed and politically significant states.

Having never lost a presidential or gubernatorial election or faced a genuinely viable opposition force, the PRI suffered a jolt in the summer of 1983, when PAN candidates won 5 of 61 contested legislative seats and 9 of 105 municipal posts in five Mexican states. Among those elected by the PAN were the mayors of the state capitals of Chihuahua and Durango and the city of Ciudad Juarez on the U.S.-Mexican border. (*WP*, 17 August.) The PRI voided the results of some of the summer elections and went on to win a number of other municipal contests during the autumn—often through vote rigging. Disturbances broke out in several towns in protest against the PRI's fraud.

The erosion of Mexico's political stability and the growing competition between the PRI and the PAN (labeled by the PSUM as the two principal "bourgeois" parties) opened new perspectives for the Communists. The PSUM was faced with both a challenge and an opportunity to enhance its position in the country. The resolution of the party's Second Plenum, in November 1983, spelled out the necessity to "defeat the PRI and unmask the PAN" and to counteract the polarization between the two parties that threatened to "put the socialist alternative on the sidelines" (*Asi Es*, 11–17 November 1983). The party pledged itself "to defeat the government's social and economic policy" and declared that "the struggle for political democracy is an essential task of PSUM." The document cautioned that "preventing our party's isolation is one of the present terms for its development" and called for an attempt "to approach and unite all the forces of the national left. This effort must be made by upholding the PSUM's program . . . but at the same time seeking means that will allow for the permanent cooperation of various parties and groups that accept unity of action in principle." (Ibid.)

Two major obstacles lay in the path of the PSUM's attempt to forge a broad leftist alliance.

One was the Law on Political Organizations and Electoral Processes, which stipulated that any party participating in an alliance would lose its registration with the Federal Election Commission. The PSUM pledged its determination to amend or eliminate this regulation, which it castigated as "undemocratic" and "unconstitutional." The other obstacle to unity involved resistance from factions within the PSUM itself, notably among Alejandro Gascon Mercado, former leader of the PPM, and his followers. Several of the leftist groups that the PSUM majority regarded as potential allies were looked upon by Gascon as virtual satellites of the PRI. In particular, he criticized the Popular Socialist Party (PPS) and the Socialist Workers Party (PST) as groups that sported a socialist veneer while colluding with the PRI to sell out the working class. Moreover, Gascon objected to the PSUM's decision to support candidates of other leftist parties in various local elections—a decision that was tantamount to "riding on the coattails of the other organizations" (*Uno Mas Uno*, 15 October).

Viewing the Mexican political scene at the start of 1984, the PSUM's Third Plenum issued a document stating that "the left, especially the PSUM, never had such favorable terrain—fertilized by the economic disaster and the crisis of the PRI bureaucracy—in order to develop its concepts among the working masses and become a basic force in the Mexican political spectrum" (ibid., 22 January). General Secretary Gómez delivered a lengthy report to the plenum that outlined the crisis facing the PRI and the duties and tasks of the PSUM in the upcoming electoral contests.

"By continuing to resist the implementation of new political reforms that would pave the way for a trend toward the rise of a multiparty system, the government is fostering the polarization of the electorate around two parties," said Gómez. "In all municipalities, the principle of proportional representation has degenerated into the simple appointment of municipal councillors by the parties, in obvious violation of the constitution." Outlining his party's goals, Gómez declared that "the PSUM proposes a democratic multiparty parliamentary system under which the government would not control elections but would itself be under the full control of a freely elected national chamber of representatives. It is also fighting for democracy in the trade unions and other mass organizations, for democratic municipalities and city councils, for the right to form political and trade union organizations, for democratic mass media, schools and universities."

Perhaps most important, "the PSUM must lead the working people's struggles if it is to succeed in elections. It follows that electoral support for the PSUM depends on the level and quality of the people's political awareness. And this means that the immediate task of the PSUM is to accelerate the development of the class consciousness of the proletariat, which is still low, and to revive the revolutionary traditions of the peasantry. The emphasis must be on work in the trade union and peasant movements." (*IB*, June.)

In March the PSUM was instrumental in coordinating a "national civic strike" of some one hundred Mexican leftist organizations to protest "the injustice and the difficult economic situation" perpetuated by the government. The PSUM's National Struggle March, as it was called, took place in Mexico City and in about twenty other cities throughout the country. Interviewed on 4 March by the newspaper *El Dia*, General Secretary Gómez said: "This is not the time for internal disputes within the PSUM, but the time for a struggle alongside the working people." Rolando Cordera, the coordinator of the PSUM's deputies in the legislature, told the marchers in Mexico City that "the PSUM is here to fight for labor union democracy and to separate the unions from the PRI." He called for free and secret elections in the trade unions. The national civic strike was the second of its kind; the first, held in October 1983, led to clashes in Mexico City and the port of Acapulco between police and leftist workers and students.

On 20 June the PSUM signed a declaration of unity with four other leftist parties (PPS, PST, the Communist Left Unity, and the Socialist Current) to work together in the struggle for "peace, solidarity, and anti-imperialism, and to develop a broad mass movement to prevent nuclear war." They also pledged to press for rectification of "the unfair and unbearable conditions affecting international economic relations, particularly in the financial and trade relations between our countries and the developed capitalist economies" (*Excelsior*, 4 July). Alliances with other leftist groups for the purpose of waging electoral contests continued to elude the PSUM, however. The lack of progress in this sphere was due partly to the electoral law, which effectively barred the formation of a broad leftist coalition and partly to the stubbornness and ineptitude of the PSUM and some of its would-be allies.

Meanwhile the PRI continued to engage in electoral fraud in widely scattered local balloting, and PAN supporters who believed their candidates had been cheated of victory increasingly turned to violence. An ominous event occurred around Christmas, when riots erupted in the town of Piedras Negras, just across the Rio Grande from Eagle Pass, Texas. Supporters of PAN refused to accept the PRI's contention that their candidate had been defeated in a municipal election. They set fire to the town hall and the police station and blocked travel across the bridge spanning the Rio Grande; at least one person was killed in the disturbances.

The incident in Piedras Negras provided a bitter foretaste of the trouble awaiting the PRI if it resorted to large-scale fraud in the federal elections of July 1985. At stake were seven state governorships, all the seats in the lower house (Chamber of Deputies) of the federal legislature, and a substantial number of municipal posts. As 1984 came to a close, the PSUM, still divided internally into competing factions, was poised to contest the elections, which many political observers regarded as a possible watershed in Mexican history.

International Views and Activities. The PSUM's international activities have focused heavily on developments in the hemisphere. In the autumn of 1983, not long after the party's Second Congress, Gómez headed delegations to the Soviet Union and Nicaragua; the timing suggested that the Soviets may have assigned the PSUM specific tasks in the international support campaign waged by the communist states on behalf of the Sandinistas.

The resolution of the party's Second Plenum, in November 1983, stated:

The PSUM Central Committee is of the opinion that

the United States' military intervention in Grenada constitutes an unspeakable aggression against the sovereignty of that Caribbean state, a provocation against socialist Cuba, united by solidarity with the Grenadian people, and a flagrant violation of . . . international law . . . The militarist escalation has now reached an alarming climax; the Reagan government is continuing to prepare overtly for aggression against Nicaragua . . . We are aware of the consequences for Mexico of a widespread war in Central America . . . In view of this fact, solidarity with the struggles in Central America and the Caribbean is the PSUM's prime internationalist obligation . . . It is time for popular mobilization, for solidarity with the Grenadian people, for the defense of Nicaragua and Cuba, for support to the Salvadoran rebels, and for curbing the repression and genocide in Guatemala. [*Asi Es*, 11–17 November.]

In May the PSUM sponsored a festival of solidarity with the revolutionary struggles in Central America (*Pravda*, 22 May). The party gave sustained and positive media coverage to the Contadora negotiations aimed at bringing peace to Central America and reducing the U.S. military presence there.

In December the PSUM participated in a meeting of communist parties in Czechoslovakia under the auspices of the Prague-based journal *Problems of Peace and Socialism* (*World Marxist Review*). Such meetings are held periodically to assess the international situation and plan future strategies and tactics.

Marian Leighton
Defense Intelligence Agency

Nicaragua

Population. 2,914,000
Party. Sandinista Front of National Liberation (Frente Sandinista de Liberación Nacional; FSLN)
Founded. 1960
Membership. 4,000 card-carrying members; 200,000 supporters (estimated)

National Directorate. 9 members (all participate equally): Humberto Ortega Saavedra, Daniel Ortega Saavedra, Tomás Borge Martínez, Jaime Wheelock Román, Henry Ruiz Hernández, Bayardo Arce Castano, Carlos Núñez Téllez, Luis Carrion Cruz, Víctor Manuel Tirado López

Central Government Leadership Committee. 9 members: Dora María Téllez (political secretary)

Political Committee of the FSLN. 3 members: Bayardo Arce Castano (coordinator), Jaime Wheelock Román, Humberto Ortega Saavedra

Status. Ruling party

Main State Organs. National Junta of Government, 3 members: Daniel Ortega (coordinator), Sergio Ramírez Mercado, Rafael Córdova Rivas. (As the result of national elections on 4 November 1984, Daniel Ortega became president-elect, and Sergio Ramírez vice-president-elect.) Cabinet includes Humberto Ortega (defense), Tomás Borge (interior), Father Miguel d'Escoto Brockman (foreign affairs), Jaime Wheelock (agrarian reform), Carlos Tunnerman Bernheim (education, until 11 July when he became ambassador to the United States and was replaced by Father Fernando Cardenal Martínez), Father Ernesto Cardenal Martínez (culture), Joaquín Cuadra Chamorro (finance), Henry Ruiz (planning).

Last Election. 4 November 1984; presidential race, 63 percent; Constituent Assembly, 63 percent, 61 of 96 seats

Auxiliary Organizations. Sandinista Defense Committees (Comités de Defensa Sandinista; CDS), estimated membership 300,000 in 8,500 local and regional chapters, secretary general, Letitia Herrera; Sandinista Youth (Juventud Sandinista 19 de Julio), under Carlos Carrión; Association of Nicaraguan Women (Asociación de Mujeres Nicaraguenses), led by Glenda Monterey; Sandinista Workers' Central (Central Sandinista de Trabajadores), secretary general, Lucio Jiménez; Association of Farmworkers (Asociación de Trabajadores del Campo), under Edgardo García

Other Marxist Parties. Several small leftist parties combine with the FSLN to form the Patriotic Revolutionary Front. These are the Moscow-oriented communist group formed in 1937 and known as the Nicaraguan Socialist Party (Partido Socialista Nicaraguense; PSN), secretary general, Luis Sánchez; the anti-Soviet Communist Party of Nicaragua (Partido Comunista Nicaraguense; PCN), headed by Eli Altamirano; the Popular Christian Social Party (Partido Popular Social Cristiano; PPSC); and the Popular Action Movement–Marxist-Leninist (Movemiento Acción Popular; MAP-ML). The non-Marxist Independent Liberal Party is also part of the front.

After years of struggle, the Sandinista movement seized power in July 1979, overthrowing the dictatorship of Anastasio Somoza Debayle. Distrusting and fearing the United States, the FSLN-dominated government soon brought in large numbers of Cuban and Russian advisers and moved to the left, establishing a literacy campaign, land reform, and government control over much of the private sector. Since 1982 the Managua regime has constantly been harassed by counterrevolutionaries (*contras*) based in Honduras and Costa Rica and backed by the United States. This harassment has helped to bring about a permanent state of crisis and occasioned government restrictions on freedom of the press and other personal liberties. Press censorship was very severe until the beginning of the election campaign when it was loosened to some extent, but after the campaign closed, it once again became so harsh that it caused the editor of the

opposition *La Prensa* to choose exile in protest (*NYT*, 22 December).

Domestic Problems. Under the FSLN, Nicaragua has experienced a declining economy. Production has fallen off badly, and the government has been forced to import $20 million worth of basic grains (ibid., 1 July). The value of the currency continued to decline, with the córdoba being worth only half a U.S. penny on the black market. The external debt has reached $4 billion, and even the extreme-left PSN accused the FSLN of leading the country into bankruptcy (*This Week Central America and Panama*, 23 July). However, although government mismanagement of the 55 percent of the economy it controls is partly to blame, U.S. pressure and capital flight have also played a role in the decline. Faced with these problems, the government moved increasingly toward central planning, a move said to be favored by Henry Ruiz and opposed by Jaime Wheelock (*Latin America Regional Report*, 17 February). An increase in Soviet economic support was also expected to help the country avoid collapse.

The War with the Contras. The main effect of the border war has been to give the government an excuse for a greater mobilization of society. In January the conscription law announced in 1983 went into effect, raising the strength of the Sandinista People's Army (Ejército Popular Sandinista; EPS) strength to 30,000, with another 100,000 serving in the militia. The main contra group, the Democratic National Front (Frente Democrático Nacional; FDN), launched a major offensive in March, causing heavy fighting in the departments of Madriz, Jinotega, and Nueva Segovia. FDN aircraft, based in Honduras, shot up Chinandega and a number of smaller towns, and mines were laid in Nicaraguan harbors, causing damage to several ships, including Soviet freighters. At the same time, "Piranha" motorboats, also based in Honduras, staged coastal raids, striking a patrol boat and damaging the oil storage facilities at the major Pacific port of Corinto. So severe were the motorboat attacks that half the population of Corinto had to be evacuated to safer territory. Nicaragua protested these attacks at the United Nations, where the country has a seat on the Security Council, claiming that the United States was directly involved in aggressive acts. FDN attacks and border skirmishes with Honduran forces continued throughout the year, but the FDN failed to make any significant gains or to hold a single municipality.

In the Costa Rica border region, another group, known as ARDE, was active during the first half of the year. However, a split in the ranks of the organization, which saw Alfonso Robelo and other prominent supporters join forces with the FDN, the nearly fatal assassination attempt on the life of the main ARDE military leader, Edén Pastora, and a fierce June offensive of the EPS, combined to bring about the virtual demise of the organization. In July, Pastora, recovering from his wounds, announced in Washington that he was abandoning the armed struggle and would work for peaceful change in Nicaragua (ibid., 13 July). He reversed this stance in September, but has initiated little military activity (ibid., 21 September).

There continued to be talk that the FSLN was considering the import of Soviet MiG-21s or other high-performance fighters to bolster Nicaragua's virtually nonexistent air force. Across from the capital on Lake Managua at Punta Huete, the government continued work on a military airfield that Robelo claimed was being readied to receive the MiG fighters (Radio Impacto, San José, 4 August; *FBIS*, 6 August). In November, information was leaked from the U.S. government that a Soviet freighter was on its way to Nicaragua with crates similar to those used to transport MiGs. The ship docked at Corinto on 7 November, amid rumors of impending war with the United States should the fighters really be on board. The Sandinistas called for a general mobilization, while denying, correctly as it turned out, the presence of jet aircraft on the freighter. Twenty thousand students preparing to help with the coffee harvest were diverted to military duty and armed. The militia was totally mobilized, and a state of emergency decreed.

Negotiation Efforts. Although tensions continued high all year between Nicaragua on one hand and the United States and Honduras on the other, efforts for a negotiated settlement were under way. Through the good offices of the Mexican government, talks between Deputy Foreign Minister Víctor Hugo Tinoco and U.S. special envoy Harry Shlaudeman were held at Manzanillo, Mexico, and this led to a meeting in Managua in early June between U.S. secretary of state George Shultz and junta coordinator Daniel Ortega. The results appeared disappointing, and afterward Ortega declared that the "United States' aggressive stance has not changed" (Managua domestic service, 30 June; *FBIS*, 2 July). During July, representatives of the United States and Nicaragua continued to meet at Manzanillo, and that same month Nicaragua announced that it accepted in principle the peace and cooperation plan proposed by the Contadora group of Latin American countries, which called for a demilitarization of the region. As the United States had informally suggested that it would accept the plan if Managua did so, Washington was placed in a difficult position. It feared that demilitarization of the region would lead to Nicaraguan hegemony. Washington finally denounced the acceptance as duplicitous, a move that resulted in a major propaganda coup for the FSLN. (*This Week Central America and Panama*, 1 October.)

On 3 October, Daniel Ortega, accompanied by Miguel d'Escoto and Carlos Tunnerman, met in New York City with Langhorne Motley, U.S. assistant secretary of state for inter-American affairs, and Harry Shlaudeman to discuss relations between the two countries. Afterwards Ortega addressed the General Assembly of the United Nations.

Following his election, Daniel Ortega announced his desire to meet personally with President Reagan, but the White House rebuffed the offer, preferring to continue the ongoing talks at Manzanillo, the eighth session of which took place in late November (UPI, 18 November).

One aspect of the contra war was that many Miskito Indians of the Atlantic Coast region had joined contra forces, claiming ethnic persecution by the FSLN. But in September a meeting was arranged by Senator Edward Kennedy between Miskito leader Brooklyn Rivera and Daniel Ortega in Managua. After a series of discussions, Ortega announced that he would release all Miskito political prisoners, officially recognize Rivera's group, Misurasata, as speaking for the Miskito people, negotiate with the group over autonomy and Indian rights and allow them a free press (ibid., 21 October). However, by the end of the year, the talks had broken down over the issue of autonomy, and in early January 1985 Rivera left Nicaragua.

Relations with the Church. Relations between the Sandinista government and the Roman Catholic church remained strained. One issue was the pope's demand that the four priests occupying high government posts resign either their priestly functions or their government ministries. This the priests have rejected. Trouble also arose with the arrest of the missionary priest Luis Amado Peña in July for allegedly aiding the contras. Ten foreign priests who led a protest against his arrest were expelled from Nicaragua, despite protests from the papacy and Miguel Obando y Bravo, the archbishop of Managua, who has long been critical of Sandinista policies. In an attempt to improve relations with the Catholic church, Minister Secretary of the Junta Rodrigo Reyes led a delegation to the Vatican on 3 September, meeting with high church officials. The conversations were evidently unsuccessful, and in December the Jesuit order expelled Fernando Cardenal from its ranks.

The Elections. On 22 February, Daniel Ortega announced that national elections for president, vice-president, and a Constituent Assembly would be held on 4 November. On 27 February the FSLN announced that Daniel Ortega would be its candidate for president with Sergio Ramírez as his running mate. The electoral law was promulgated by the Council of State on 28 March. It stipulated that there would be a six-year term of office for those elected and that the campaign would begin 8 August and close on 31 October. It dropped a proposal that a party would need 5,000 valid signatures to register, and it gave each party fielding a presidential candidate 1.5 million córdobas for that campaign and 4.5 million for the assembly campaign. To enable the parties to campaign, the state of emergency was lifted on 20 July, and a decree of 6 August re-established civil rights, habeas corpus, and partially lifted media censorship.

Besides the FSLN, six parties fielded candidates in the election. These were the PSN, the PCN, PPSC, MAP-ML, the Independent Liberals, and the Democratic Conservatives. A Democratic Coordination Group composed of the Social Democrats, Christian Democrats, and the Constitutional Liberals at first declared its intention to present ex–government member Arturo Cruz as its candidate. Cruz, however, declared that he would run only if exiled leaders such as Adolfo Calero of the FDN were allowed to return, a demand the government refused. Cruz also insisted on guarantees of freedom of movement and assembly, sufficient campaign time, equal access to the media, international observers, and assurances that the winner, whoever he might be, would be allowed to take office (*CSM*, 26 September). The deadline to register parties was 25 July, but when the Democratic Coordination Group had not registered by that date, it was extended to 4 August. This date also passed, but on 15 August, Cruz dropped his demands concerning the exiles and was given until 25 August to register his candidacy. He did not register and announced his intention to campaign as a "noncandidate," which the government informed him it would not allow. (*Economist*, London, 25 August.) The government then moved to strip the three parties backing him of their legal status. Despite this, negotiations continued, with meetings being held chiefly in Brazil. In the end, however, Cruz insisted that there would not be sufficient time to campaign and demanded that the elections be postponed, which the Sandinistas refused to do, leaving the matter at that point.

The meaning of the election stirred up considerable debate within Sandinista circles. A frequent question was whether an opposition party would be allowed to run the country if elected. Tomás Borge declared that there would be "total freedom for the electoral process; no freedom to destroy the revolution" (*Latin America Regional Report*, 17 July). Daniel Ortega said that if another party won, it would be allowed to govern, but would "face problems" (*La Prensa*, 18 January), but Bayardo Arce, in a secret speech, admitted that the purpose of the elections was to "disarm the international bourgeoisie" and that they were "an expedient in order to deprive our enemies of an argument" rather than a real contest for power (*This Week Central America and Panama*, 22 October).

Despite the government subsidies, the various parties complained that the Sandinistas monopolized the electoral process. The fifteen minutes per party per day allotted to them on radio were insufficient to counteract the constant barrage of propaganda from the government. The PSN newspaper *Avance* (1 August) charged that the election had "only one face." The Liberal Party candidate, Virgilio Godoy Rivas, charged that the government had interfered with the movement of his supporters and that the Sandinistas had a monopoly on the news media (*This Week Central America and Panama*, 20 October). Shortly thereafter, Godoy announced that the Liberals were withdrawing from the election, but the government did not recognize this withdrawal, and the Independent Liberal Party remained on the ballot.

In the election of 4 November, Ortega took 63 percent of the vote. He was sworn in for the six-year term on 10 January 1985. The Sandinistas also won 61 seats in the Constituent Assembly. The Liberals and the Democratic Conservatives each collected about 10 percent of the vote, and the small Marxist parties ran far behind. (*NYT*, 6 November; *WP*, 15 November.) Of those eligible to participate in the elections, 75 percent actually voted.

International Activities. The FSLN leadership continued to be prodigious travelers during the year. Daniel Ortega went to Moscow for the funeral of Yuri Andropov in February, and again in late March, after which he visited North Korea. He returned with Miguel d'Escoto and Henry Ruiz to Moscow in June as part of a tour through Eastern bloc countries that also took them to Czechoslovakia and East Germany. Daniel's brother Humberto had visited Russia and East Germany in April and attended Mexico's independence day celebrations in September. Sergio Ramírez traveled to Iran and Libya in March, to Colombia, Venezuela, and Panama to discuss the Contadora effort in July, and to Quito for Ecuador's presidential inauguration in August. Henry Ruiz was also in Quito in January for an economic conference and in March toured Bulgaria and the Soviet Union. Jaime Wheelock went to Brazil, Argentina, and Peru on a tour of

agrarian projects in February and to East Germany in August to discuss buying agricultural supplies. Carlos Tunnerman set out for East Germany, Austria, and Spain to discuss education projects in March, and Bayardo Arce visited Italy, France, Spain, Portugal, and West Germany in June to discuss economic matters and was an observer at a meeting of the Socialist International in Brazil in September. Ernesto Cardenal also went to Spain in March for a writers' conference and to Brussels in October for the so-called people's trial of Ronald Reagan. Carlos Núñez visited several West European countries in September, and Luis Carrión went to East Germany in October. While in the United States for U.N. meetings, Daniel Ortega also spoke to students of Harvard Law School on 8 October and subsequently went to Atlanta to visit with Mayor Andrew Young. The most frustrated traveler was Tomás Borge, who was scheduled for a lecture tour in the United States in January, but was denied a visa. He went to Paris in February, however, for the funeral of Argentine writer Julio Cortázar and toured Libya and the Eastern bloc countries in September.

Numerous diplomatic visitors and guests continued to arrive in Managua. In April, Nicaragua played host to the First International Labor Union Meeting for Peace, and in May the labor ministers of the nonaligned bloc of countries arrived for their Third International Conference. Olof Palme, the Swedish premier, arrived on 9 February for an official visit. He was followed by Regis Debray, foreign policy adviser to the president of France, and by U.S. political figure Jesse Jackson in June. Foreign Minister Stefan Olszowski of Poland made a state visit 18–20 September, and Australian foreign minister Bill Hayden came to meet Humberto Ortega on 12 October. The next day, Socialist International President Willy Brandt came for a two-day visit.

Biographies. *Bayardo Arce Castano.* Arce was born in 1949 and first made contact with the FSLN in 1969. In 1971 he joined the underground movement in León. A member of the Prolonged Popular War faction of the FSLN, he was named to the united Sandinista directorate in March 1979. He was chief political officer on the northern front during the final offensive against Somoza. He was named coordinator of the political committee following the triumph of the revolution. (David Nolan, *The Ideology of the Sandinistas and the Nicaraguan*

Revolution, Coral Gables, Fla.: University of Miami, 1984.)

Carlos Núñez Téllez. Núñez was born in León in 1951, the son of an artisan, and joined the FSLN in 1971. He was a Sandinista organizer in León and later in Managua. A member of the Proletarian Tendency, he joined the Sandinista directorate in March 1979. He participated in the siege of Managua in the last months of the war. After the victory, he became president of the Council of State. (Ibid.)

Thomas P. Anderson
Eastern Connecticut State University

Panama

Population. 2,101,000
Party. People's Party of Panama (Partido del Pueblo; PPP)
Founded. 1943
Membership. 750 (estimated)
Secretary General. Rubén Darío Sousa (alternate spelling Souza)
Politburo. (Incomplete listing): César Agusto De Leon Espinosa, Miguel Antonio Porcella Peña, Anastacio E. Rodríguez, Clito Manuel Souza Batista, Ruperto Luther Trottman (international secretary). Other prominent members are Felix Dixon (Editorial Council representative) and Carlos Chang Marin (*Critica*, April 1980).
Central Committee. 26 members
Status. Legal
Last Congress. Sixth, 8–10 February 1980
Last Election. 1984; no representatives
Auxiliary Organizations. Panama Peace Committee, People's Party Youth, National Center of Workers of Panama, Union of Journalists of Panama, Federation of Panamanian Students, and National Union of Democratic Women
Publications. *Unidad* (weekly)

The year 1984 began with the surprise resignation, in February, of President Ricardo de la Espriella, evidently for his refusal to stack his cabinet with favorites of the National Guard and to permit the military to meddle in the upcoming electoral process. Espriella was replaced by Vice-President Jorge Illueca.

Panama voted in May for a president, two vice-presidents, and 67 members of a new national legislature. This was the first free election after sixteen years of military rule. The two major presidential candidates were Nicolás Ardito Barletta, whom his opponents portrayed as a creature of the National Guard (now known as the Panama Defense Forces; PDF), and 83-year-old Dr. Arnulfo Arias Madrid, a three-time former president. Each time Arias took office, he had been ousted by the Guard—most recently in 1968, when Torrijos deposed him in a coup only eleven days after Arias assumed the presidency. Arias pledged that if he won the 1984 elections, he would trim the PDF's power by transferring its immigration, customs, and police functions to civilian agencies.

Barletta, a longtime vice-president of the World Bank and resident of the United States, ran as the candidate of the official Democratic Revolutionary Party (DRP) and its three partners in a coalition called the National Democratic Union. Arias, who received his higher education at Harvard, was the standard-bearer of the Authentic Panamenista Party and other groups in a coalition labeled the Alliance of Democratic Opposition.

The PPP attempted to create an electoral alliance composed of groups that shared its avowed objective of perpetuating the legacy of Torrijos—a non-aligned foreign policy, a mixed economy, and a strong pro-labor stance. Sousa told a meeting of the party's middle-level officials in late January that the proposed alliance should revolve around "democracy and the rescue of our natural resources and sovereignty" (read: return of the Panama Canal)—ideas that had been tested since Torrijos came to power. "In other words," said Sousa, "we, the Panamanian Communists, make a historic commitment to continue perfecting the Torrijist ideals, which have brought independence, well-being, and respect to the country, and to pursue with renewed intensity the effort of honest Panamanians to eradicate . . . corruption, which the Panamanian workers view with great indignation." (*Critica*, Panama City, 31 January.)

Having failed to establish an electoral alliance, the PPP fielded its own candidates in the election: Dr. Carlos del Cid, an attorney, for president; César De Leon, a professor of history and philosophy, for first vice-president; and Julio Bermudez, the founder and secretary general of the National Confederation of Peasant Settlements (CONAC), for second vice-president. On 30 March Bermudez and Carlos Chang Marin, another important party official, presented the PPP's electoral platform. Twelve goals were enumerated: (1) expansion of the people's democratic rights; (2) defense of labor benefits; (3) a code to protect the family; (4) creation and development of Indian districts; (5) consolidation of the multisector, or mixed, model of economy; (6) a plan of investments and financing for national development; (7) overall agrarian reform to provide food; (8) defense of natural resources and the environment; (9) strict adherence to the anticolonial features of the Torrijos-Carter treaties; (10) educational reform in line with the socioeconomic needs and the culture of the nation; (11) defense forces

that march alongside the people; and (12) a non-aligned foreign policy committed to peace (Panama City domestic service, 30 March).

About a month later, Bermudez read a virulently anti-American statement that Sousa had drafted: "U.S. imperialism and its national lackeys have united in order to annul all these measures of social progress and divert the democratic course of national liberation that General Torrijos chartered. Efforts have been made to align our country with the U.S. war, intervention, and aggression, particularly in . . . Central America." The Reagan administration, according to the statement, promotes enmity against "the Sandinistas and the Salvadoran revolutionaries," supports "the bloody dictatorship of Honduras," and carries out plans for "violating the Canal's neutrality and ceding our territory to be used as a base and support for these wicked actions so that imperialism can continue dominating and exploiting all our peoples and their natural resources." As a result, "we Panamanian Communists have determined to fully participate in the coming elections with the purpose of defending the Torrijist, democratic, anti-imperialist orientation to keep its social achievements and make its further advance possible." (Ibid., 27 April.)

A more detailed picture of the PPP's strategy and tactics was revealed during a forum held on 11 April at the University of Panama in which the candidates running for election participated. Speaking on behalf of the PPP, Carlos del Cid explained that "as Marxist-Leninists, our final objective is to build a Communist society in Panama. But the establishment of a Socialist system that will subsequently be transformed into a Communist region . . . must respond . . . to specific objectives and subjective conditions in the society. All of these conditions have yet to mature in the country. That is why . . . we must first pass through what we call the democratic phase of national liberation." Del Cid went on to advocate the creation of a "democratic front of national liberation, which would be made up of social forces such as the working class, the peasants, the small bourgeoisie . . . the middle class, and the nationalist bourgeoisie. These would express themselves through various political and party organizations that represent their interests." Del Cid did not disclose whether the PPP would insist on playing the dominant role in such a coalition of "progressive" social forces. Among the socioeconomic goals that del Cid set out for Panama were industrialization, distribution of national income in favor of workers and "popular sectors," and the introduction of more advanced forms of economic production and organization. He declared that Panama needed foreign capital and foreign investments in the current phase of economic development. He emphasized the PPP's commitment to "ideological pluralism," popular participation in government and economic planning, and "progressive democracy." Del Cid reiterated the party's call for a "diversification of the country's international relations" and stressed the need for an "international struggle" to modify the Torrijos-Carter treaties to ensure Panama's complete independence and sovereignty over the canal. (Sistema de Television Educativa, Panama City, 11 April.)

Barletta defeated Arias by the razor-thin margin of 1,700 votes (*NYT*, 20 May). Arias's supporters charged fraud, and some street violence erupted. The PPP can be expected to give at least tacit support to Barletta, so long as he moves to fulfill his campaign pledge to keep the military out of politics and consolidate civilian democracy in Panama. Carlos Chang Marin, an important PPP official, summed up the party's attitude toward the PDF when he stated that any president of Panama would have to work with the PDF in order to govern, but that the relationship could have a "progressive orientation" if the military would support programs to improve the lot of the workers and peasants (*La Prensa*, Panama City, 5 March).

The Soviet daily *Pravda* published a Tass dispatch from Panama reporting on a statement of Sousa's to a PPP Central Committee plenum. According to the report, Sousa criticized "the attempt by the local oligarchy, in alliance with American imperialism, to consign to oblivion the legacy of Panama's distinguished leader, Omar Torrijos." *Pravda* also disclosed that the plenum had decided to hold the Eighth National Congress of the PPP in 1985.

Auxiliary Organizations. On 3 September 1982, President de la Espriella granted legal status to the Panama Peace Council. At its most recent congress (23 September 1982), Dr. Camilo O. Pérez (a vice-president of the World Peace Council; WPC) was appointed president, and a presidium of 33 members was reappointed. It included "representatives of political parties, mass organizations, and the regional presidents of this organization" (*Peace Courier*, September 1982). Influential members of the Peace Council include Nathaniel Hill Arboleda (a WPC secretary) and Ruperto

Luther Trottman (international secretary of the PPP). A PPP official, Marta Matamoros, serves as international secterary of the National Union of Democratic Women, which is an affiliate of the Women's International Democratic Federation. Although the PPP lost its complete control over the International Union of Students affiliate, the Federation of Panamanian Students (Federación des Estudiantes de Panama; FEP) in the late 1960s, it remains very influential in this organization. The FEP is especially active at the University of Panama.

In a communiqué issued in May, the secretary general of the FEP deplored the worsening socioeconomic problems in the country and the U.S. intervention in Central America. Aside from its continuing association with the FEP, the PPP has formed its own student affiliate, the Frente Reformista Universitaria.

The PPP's youth affiliate, the People's Party Youth, is an arm of the World Federation of Democratic Youth, one of the Soviet Union's principal international front groups. Pastor Falconett, secretary of the PPP's youth movement, was interviewed on 10 March on Havana radio. He alleged that the Reagan administration was violating the Panama Canal treaties and was using military forces assigned exclusively to protect the canal for aggressive actions in El Salvador, Grenada, and elsewhere.

The PPP's trade union affiliate, the Federación Sindical de Trabajadores, was disbanded by Torrijos in 1968. However, the party is influential in the World Federation of Trade Unions affiliate, the Central Nacional de Trabajadores.

International Positions. During a speech at the Karl Marx conference held in April 1983 in East Germany, Sousa stated that the PPP was linked by its Marxist-Leninist heritage to the "democratic struggle of the international labor class," the "national liberation movement," and the "defense of world peace." Sousa called the USSR the "vanguard" of this struggle. The Reagan administration, he said, through its "bellicose" policies was trying to circumvent the Torrijos-Carter treaties and promote U.S. "imperialism" in Central America. (*Neues Deutschland*, East Berlin, 14 April 1983.) The PPP Politburo pledged on 7 September 1983 to continue Torrijos's efforts to achieve "diplomatic independence," "internationalism," and "nonalignment." The Politburo affirmed PPP solidarity with

Nicaragua and the revolutionary struggle in El Salvador, Guatemala, and other Central American nations. It approved the Contadora group's principles of "self-determination," "peace," and "nonintervention." (*La Prensa*, 16 September 1983.)

The PPP expressed strong opposition to the continued existence of the School of the Americas, a military training facility that was to be closed under the terms of the Torrijos-Carter treaties. Rubén Darío Paredes, Torrijos's successor as head of the National Guard, wanted Panama to run the school rather than close it down, but it finally went out of existence on 1 October. Other positions taken by the PPP have included statements of support for Soviet and Cuban foreign policy and for the revolutionary process in Central America. Secretary General Sousa received the Soviet Order of Friendship and a medal from the Bulgarian Communist Party on the occasion of his sixtieth birthday.

As far back as January 1975, when Moscow still shunned revolutionary violence in Central and South America, the Soviet party's theoretical journal, *Kommunist*, published a strident article by Sousa claiming that the "liberation" struggle in Latin America had reached a turning point and that the region had become a "sociopolitical volcano." Sousa participated in a meeting in Buenos Aires in July with top-ranking communist leaders of twelve other Latin American countries. The conclave, presided over by the general secretary of the Communist Party of Argentina, welcomed delegations from the Cuban Communist Party and the Sandinista National Liberation Front of Nicaragua as observers. Billing the conference as a forum for the discussion of political and economic trends in the hemisphere, the participants issued a communiqué on 7 July that cited the need for coordinated action against "the aggressive and belligerent policy of the U.S. administration" (which was contrasted with "repeated Soviet peace proposals") and on behalf of "all democratic demands" throughout the South American continent. Among specific grievances listed in the communiqué were "the mounting and multifaceted economic, military, political and diplomatic aggressiveness of Yankee imperialism against Cuba" and the "brazen interventionism in Nicaragua." The communiqué expressed firm support for "the just cause of the Argentine people to recover the Malvinas [Falklands] islands, which were usurped by the Anglo-Yankee aggression." (Diarios y Noticias, Buenos Aires, 7 July.)

The PPP participated in the meeting of world communist parties held in Czechoslovakia in December under the sponsorship of the journal *Problems of Peace and Socialism* (*World Marxist Review*). These meetings, the last of which took place in December 1981, constitute a forum for the international communist movement as it assesses its current situation and plans strategies for the future. (*Rudé právo*, Prague, 7 December.)

Other Leftist Parties. In 1974 a group called the Tendencia or Fracción broke away from the PPP. It was formed by PPP youth leaders and members of the leadership of the FEP. This organization held its first congress in 1978. Although little is known about its recent activities, it had about 1,500 members and sympathizers in 1984 (*World Factbook*, 1984). Another party that was not very active in 1984 was the Maoist Communist Party/Marxist-Leninist. During 1982 this party launched a violent attack on the PPP, accusing it of being nonrevolutionary, collaborationist, and acting against the interests of the people.

Another leftist party, the Socialist Workers' Party (PST), was officially recognized on 26 September 1983 after it had gathered more than 30,000 signatures. Virgilio Arauz was recognized as the party's legal representative. The PST was the only major party that opposed the constitutional referendum of 29 April 1983 (*Critica*, 26 September 1983). In May of that year, the party came out against the candidacy of General Paredes for president in the elections scheduled for 1984 and invited the PPP to break with the National Guard and the DRP's presidential candidate and create a left-wing coalition with a joint PST-PPP presidential candidate. When this plan faltered, the PST chose Ricardo Barria as its own presidential candidate.

During a television program in which the various candidates for president were interviewed, Barria was asked how his party planned to carry out its announced intentions to nationalize the Panama Canal and the banks, expropriate private businesses, and close down the military garrisons. He replied that "we do not need the Defense Forces . . . [they] are not defending us, they are defending U.S. imperialism . . . The Defense Forces . . . allow military men to train here in order to go to crush the . . . Salvadoran and Nicaraguan peoples." He added that "we will not obtain the canal through treaties, nor through laws, but through our struggle." Among other topics that Barria addressed was the country's foreign debt. He declared that "we cannot pay that debt because it is coming out of the pockets of the Panamanian workers and people." (Sistema de Television Educativa, 11 April.) In October 1983 the PST participated in a demonstration at the U.S. Embassy in Panama City to protest the invasion of Grenada.

The Workers' Revolutionary Party (PRT), a Trotskyist organization, was declared legal in October 1983 after gathering the requisite 30,000 signatures. The party's legal representative is its president, Graciela J. Dixon; its secretary general is Dr. Egbert Wetherborne. The party nominated Dr. José Renan Esquivel as its presidential candidate in the 1984 elections and formed an alliance with several trade union groups under the name United People's Front (FREPU). The PRT professed a commitment to Torrijist goals and called upon the PPP and PST to reject the candidate of the National Guard and the official DRP and seek an alternative among the leftist parties. In February the PRT issued a communiqué that was tantamount to "a plague on both your houses" curse at the mainline candidates: "The two oligarchic alliances differ only in form. Dr. Arias would follow the Reagan administration's backward style, while Dr. Barletta would help to maintain its interests and those of the Panamanian bourgeoisie with an even greater executive efficiency than would the 80-year-old leader. Neverthe-

less, both groups . . . represent interests that are entirely opposed to those of the poor and working people in our country . . . Both alliances represent only more hunger, unemployment, unsanitary conditions, political repression, and the submission of our country to U.S. imperialist plans." The communiqué declared that "it is neither possible nor admissible for parties . . . that are known for defending . . . the poor and exploited to join forces with the established bourgeois and oligarchic electoral alliances. Therefore, our PRT appeals . . . to the People's Party, the Socialist Workers' Party, the Tendency . . . and other progressive sectors that have hopeless illusions about the reformist measures of the last decade . . . to join the FREPU." The FREPU was described as consisting of "the most active and rational members of the organized workers' movements, many neighborhood and community organizations, organized Christian sectors, Indians, progressive professionals, students, and two political parties that seek to defend the interests of the exploited . . . classes: the Independent Party of the Working Class (PICO) and our PRT." (*Ya*, Panama City, 14 February.)

Marian Leighton
Defense Intelligence Agency

Paraguay

Population. 3,623,000
Party. Paraguayan Communist Party (PCP)
Founded. 1928
Membership. 3,500 (estimated)
Secretary General. Antonio Maidana
Leading Bodies. No data
Status. Illegal
Last Congress. Third, 10 April 1971
Last Election. N/a
Auxiliary Organizations. No data
Publications. *Adelante* (underground daily)

During 1984 Gen. Alfredo Stroessner's long-established dictatorship began showing signs of strain. Stroessner is now 72 and is reportedly in poor health. There is much speculation in Paraguay about his successor. That has not only raised the hopes of the opposition parties, but has created fissures inside the two main institutions that support the regime: the military and the Colorado Party. It remains to be seen how much the PCP can profit from this situation.

The PCP is outlawed and has lost its most able leaders in recent years. Its secretary general, Antonio Maidana, was kidnapped in Buenos Aires four years ago and is presumably being held incommunicado in one of Stroessner's jails. The party has not found another forceful leader to replace him. In addition, its attempts to gain entry into the National Accord, a coalition of the four chief opposition parties, have repeatedly been rebuffed.

Nevertheless, the Paraguayan government accuses the PCP of having a hand in any disturbances that occur, such as the rash of peasant land seizures that broke out in mid-1984 in the provinces of Alto Paraná, Canendiyú, Caaguazú, San Pedro, and Guairá. In Alto Paraná, where the first peasant invasions took place, the government calmed the situation by purchasing the acreage and forming a peasant colony; but as other invasions broke out in nearby provinces, it took a tougher line, blaming communist subversives for the outbreaks and moving to dislodge the squatters. (*Latin America, Southern Cone Report*, 7 September.)

Some evidence of PCP success in infiltrating the National Accord surfaced in early 1984 when the Salvadoran guerrilla front announced the arrival of a contingent of 122 Paraguayans from the Popular Colorado Movement (MOPOCO) to join their cause. The MOPOCO, an anti-Stroessner splinter of the Colorado Party in exile, is one of the four parties composing the National Accord. The group's leader, Fidelio Chavez, announced that their purpose was to "break the chains of capitalist exploitation to begin the construction of socialism" (*FBIS*, 31 May).

Paul H. Lewis
Tulane University

Peru

Population. 19,157,000
Party. Peruvian Communist Party (Partido Comunista Peruano; PCP)
Founded. 1928
Membership. 5,000
Secretary General. Jorge del Prado
Central Committee. 15 members: Gustavo Espinoza Montesinos, Guillermo Herrera, Asunción Caballero Mendez, Jorge del Prado, Oliver Vila, Isidoro Gamarra, Roberto Rojas, Valentín Pacho, Julián Serra, Jaime Figueroa, Víctor Checa, Antonio Torres Andrade, César Alva, Carlos Bonino, Alfonso Barrantes Lingán
Status. Legal
Last Congress. Eighth Extraordinary, 27–31 January 1982, in Lima

Last Election. 1980, 2.8 percent, 2 of 60 seats
Auxiliary Organizations. General Confederation of Peruvian Workers (CGTP)
Publications. *Unidad*

The PCP is an important component of the United Left (IU) coalition, which in 1984 became a major political force in the nation. In the November 1983 municipal elections, the IU won 30 percent of the national vote and emerged as the second largest political group behind the social-democratic American Popular Revolutionary Party (APRA), which polled 34 percent, and well ahead of the government party, Popular Action (AP), and its coalition partner, the rightist Popular Christian Party (PPC). Most significantly, the IU won the mayoralty of Lima and captured top positions throughout the nation, including the municipalities of Ica, Cuzco, Huaráz, Huancayo, and Puno. Much of the political climate of Peru in 1984 was conditioned by the upcoming 1985 presidential and general elections. The Marxist coalition's chances of significant gains in the national congress are quite strong, given its success in organizing at the local level and the continuing crisis of confidence in the ability of the government of Fernando Belaúnde Terry to cope with a stagnating economy and the deteriorating sociopolitical conditions manifested in a guerrilla war that has claimed over 5,000 lives in four years.

Political Parties. The IU is a coalition of political parties, popular fronts, and individuals who identify with the IU as a party per se. Formed in 1980, the components of IU and the members of its National Directive Committee include the Moscow-line PCP led by Jorge del Prado; the social-democratic Revolutionary Socialist Party (PSR) of Enrique Bernales; the Revolutionary Communist Party (PCR) led by Manuel Dammert; the Maoist front, National Unity of the Revolutionary Left (UNIR), led by Jorge Hurtado; the Unified Mariateguista Party (PUM)—a recent union of several groups including the Revolutionary Vanguard (VR), Revolutionary Movement of the Left (MIR), and a faction of the PCR—headed by Javier Diez Canseco; and the Trotskyist Worker, Peasant, Student, and Popular Front (FOCEP) led by Genero Ledesma. As an umbrella organization for the Marxist left, the IU has managed to maintain outward unity, constraining the seemingly endemic sectarian divisions of the left to maneuvering within the coalition. The organic looseness of the coalition

has provided a place for leftist independents to participate and allowed small regional parties to adhere to the IU's national political policy. One of its members described the IU as "an alliance of socialist hegemony, a revolutionary political front that represents the grand historical possibility of unifying the national democratic movement with Marxism and socialism . . . to construct a Peruvian nation on a nonaligned, independent, and democratic base" (*Quehacer*, December 1983, p. 91). Adherents define the IU in terms of the political space it occupies—it is not a party, but a new type of political formation, a movement that not only combines parties but attracts independent participants.

A principal source of unity is IU leader Dr. Alfonso Barrantes Lingán. As a student at San Marcos University, Barrantes was president of APRA's university federation. He joined the PCP in 1960, but when the Sino-Soviet split divided the Peruvian party, he became an "independent" Marxist-Leninist. An affable individual who despises sectarianism, Barrantes is admired and trusted by all Marxist groups. And as a Christian who frequently quotes the Bible and respects family and tradition, he has supporters among the non-Marxist left as well. (Ibid., p. 94.)

Barrantes's first year as the continent's only Marxist mayor was one of mixed success. He and his party mediated squatter land invasions, street vendor occupations, and municipal workers' wage demands with little help from the central government or Aprista councilmen, whose obstructionism was denounced as "electorally motivated" by IU leaders (*Resumen Semanal*, 1–12 January, p. 1, 24 February–1 March, p. 2, 13–19 April, p. 6). The lack of government funds caused severe difficulties for all municipalities, which were prohibited from collecting their own taxes or from changing personnel. The IU surmounted these problems by mobilizing citizens to assist with self-help projects and by soliciting funds from international agencies. Barrantes, for example, implemented his campaign promises on nutrition "to provide a glass of milk a day for children under five and pregnant women" with money raised on a European trip in December 1983 (ibid., 23–29 December 1983, p. 4).

Mayor Barrantes was the unanimous choice for president on the IU ticket since he most clearly represents unity within the coalition. But the selection of the two vice-presidential candidates presented a critical problem. Initially, PCP leader Jorge del Prado and Cusqueño poet Luis Nieto (PUM) were chosen, but within 24 hours they had been dropped. Though perhaps representative of the partisan alignments within the IU, they were electorally risky since they firmly identified the IU with Soviet orthodoxy (*Latin America Weekly Report*, [*LAWR*], 19 October, p. 4). Officially the PCP "asked del Prado to decline with the objective of bettering the composition of the ticket, making possible an outside candidate" (*Resumen Semanal*, 5–11 October, p. 2). The IU's final ticket included Enrique Bernales, PSR secretary general, and Agustín Haya de la Torre of the Popular Democratic Union (UDP) as vice-presidential candidates. Del Prado was placed at the head of the Senate list and César Barrera (UNIR) led the deputy list for Lima. The IU's electoral formula provides five candidates for each of the parties on the Senate list (40) and twenty independent spots. On the deputy list for Lima there are four places for each of the parties within the IU and eight independent spots. (*Caretas*, 15 October, p. 17.)

In addition to the parties that formally make up the IU, several small parties will cooperate with the IU for the elections. These include the left of center Popular Action–Socialist (APS) and the National Integration Party (PADIN), which will have candidates on lists in various provinces, and numerous splinter groups that will instruct their followers to vote for the IU. Only one communist party will participate separately from the IU, the Trotskyist Socialist Workers Party (PST) of Ricardo Napuri. Although the IU accepts all who want to participate in a Marxist alliance, the Trotskyists have consistently presented sectarian problems that IU leaders seek to avoid.

The IU is not expected to win the 1985 elections, but it is doubtful that the front-runner, APRA, will win enough votes (50 percent of all valid votes) to avoid a runoff. The IU's electoral strength, approximately one-third of the voters, will definitely have an impact on the formation of the governing coalition for the last half of the decade. Most likely, APRA will ally with a portion of the AP, but there are factions in both the IU and APRA that would favor an accommodation along social-democratic lines.

Domestic Affairs. The IU's appeal and its chances of achieving a position of national influ-

ence are directly related to the crisis facing the present Peruvian government. At the end of 1984, Peru was more than $345 million in arrears on a $13.5 billion debt, the servicing of which accounted for one-third of the year's budget (*LAWR*, 14 December, p. 2). Almost every statistic for the year was gloomy. Growth in 1984 was just over 2 percent in real terms, domestic savings were at 1950s levels, new investment loans were only 16 percent of the 1983 level, and inflation raged at 125 percent (ibid., 26 October, p. 8). The stagnating economy produced a nonagricultural unemployment rate of 15 percent, while underemployment hovered at 50 percent as one-third of the population received less than the minimum wage (ibid., 9 November, p. 2). The situation is such that it is estimated Lima has the largest underground economy in the world (*WSJ*, 15 August). President Belaúnde has been unwilling, however, to take further austerity moves, such as increasing the gasoline tax, for fear of social and political repercussions. He has also been unwilling to trim military expenditures, which accounted for 25 percent of the 1984 budget compared with 15 percent for social services (Americas Watch, *Abdicating Democratic Authority: Human Rights in Peru*, October, p. 16; *Latin America Regional Report* [*LARR*], 9 November, p. 2).

Contending solutions to the nation's financial crisis are at the center of the partisan debate. Each party's campaign program revolves around questions of government spending, growth priorities, taxation policy, foreign trade, and national currency matters. In contrast to the internationalist, free-trade, private enterprise–oriented economic policy of the Belaúnde administration, the IU proposes an economic plan that (1) emphasizes basic needs through planning and nationalization, which will encourage economic redistribution as opposed to growth stimulation; (2) encourages a revitalization of state enterprises and industrial communities; (3) decreases dependence on imports by placing priority on agricultural development and selective import controls to encourage national reactivation; (4) emphasizes greater state control over foreign currency transactions and supports a selective moratorium on the foreign debt; and (5) supports the armed forces' defense needs within an overall diplomatic structure that reduces the risk of external aggression (*LAWR*, 9 November, pp. 4–5, 30 November, pp. 6–7).

On the whole, labor unrest during 1984 was less than in the previous year in terms of the number of strikes, but the number of workers affected increased drastically due to the magnitude of the stoppages (*LARR*, 9 November, p. 2). The most important were the two general strikes (22 March and 29 November) called jointly by the four major labor confederations: the communist CGTP, the Velasquista Confederation of Workers of the Peruvian Revolution (CTRP), the Christian Democratic National Workers' Central (CNT), and the Aprista Confederation of Peruvian Workers (CTP). Both strikes were declared illegal by the minister of labor because the demands, such as a freeze on gasoline prices and the declaration of a national agrarian emergency, were deemed political because they were not wage related. The government suspended constitutional guarantees for three days in order to "protect people, property, and the right to work." To this end it offered a transportation bonus to all who went to work, had armed police drive the state-owned buses, and allowed a two-hour tolerance in arriving at work without salary reductions. (*Resumen Semanal*, 16–23 March, p. 3.)

From the organizers' perspective the 22 March strike, the fifth national strike since 1980, was quite successful. *El Observador* claimed that 60 percent of workers throughout Peru struck in "the fullest rejection of the government and its economic policy of hunger and misery." The size of the strike was second only to the 1977 strike that brought the military's move toward democracy. In the provinces, the strike was almost total, with 95 percent of the work force observing the strike in Cuzco, 97 percent in Iquitos, 90 percent in Chiclayo, 90 percent in Tacna, and 80 percent in Huancayo (*Resumen Semanal*, 16–23 March, p. 1–2). The secretary general of the CGTP, Valentín Pacho, said that 90 percent of all unionized workers observed the 29 November strike despite government intimidation (ibid., 30 November–6 December, p. 1; *LAWR*, 7 December, p. 11).

Union demonstrations during both strikes were dispersed by force, with scores wounded and hundreds detained. In March at a gathering in front of the CGTP headquarters in Lima, PCP leader Jorge del Prado was seriously wounded when he was struck in the chest by a tear gas grenade. An IU deputy and the mayor of Huancayo were also wounded, as police broke up a union rally. The IU alleged that labor, neighborhood, and political leaders had been deliberately stopped and physically abused by the military and the police. Although over 500 persons were detained, IU members believed there was a certain amount of selectivity involved since the IU mayors of San Juan de Miraflores and San Martín de Porres and leftist journalists were sought out and arrested. Moreover, they claimed that the aggression against del Prado was intentional, and delegates in parliament asked for Interior Minister Luis Percovich's resignation (*Resumen Semanal*, 23–29 March, p. 2). The government's hard-line attitude toward the legal left is rooted in part in a perception of a direct link between the Communists in parliament, who are seeking power electorally, and the Communists in the highlands, who are seeking power through armed rebellion.

Terrorist Activities. In 1980 the Peruvian Communist Party of the Shining Path of Mariategui (Sendero Luminoso) launched an armed struggle in the Andean highlands. With a Maoist commitment to a long-term rural rebellion and idealized notions of native communism, Sendero represents a militant messianism that is uniquely Peruvian. An offshoot of political-guerrilla groups formed in the early 1960s and associated peripherally with the Maoist PCP–Red Flag, the group was nurtured for eighteen years in the isolated university town of Ayacucho under the tutelage of Dr. Abimael Guzmán Reyenoso. Sendero is ideologically anti-Soviet and anti-Chinese (having been more attuned to the Gang of Four); it eschews any international connections of influence. After carefully establishing a political base in Indian communities, in 1980 Sendero initiated a campaign of violence against all representatives of authority. It created liberated zones in which it imposed its antitechnological, subsistence peasant model by brutal methods, destroying farm equipment, crops, closing regional markets, and killing informers and reluctant supporters. Sendero's tactics and goals both alienated it from the legal and parliamentary left and set in motion a repressive response from the state. In two years the number of provinces under the control of the military, the emergency zone, has grown to thirteen, as the government seeks to eliminate the guerrilla threat of Sendero.

Nevertheless, the number of attacks, the violence, and the atmosphere of chaos and disorder have mounted, and the consequences have had an important impact upon the nation. As of November, it was estimated that 5,017 persons had been killed in the internal war, 2,657 of them between July 1983 and July 1984 (ibid., 8–15 November, p. 2; *LAWR*, 3 August, p. 2). Despite a lull in the early part of the year, in May, June, and July Sendero launched its most costly attacks yet on the national infrastructure. It blew up a section of the oil pipeline from the Amazon to the Pacific Coast, causing a five-day interruption (*FBIS*, 31 May). It knocked out six bridges connecting the central highlands to Lima and downed eight high-tension towers in the Mantaro Valley, which blacked out one-third of the nation in July. It attacked seven towers in November. The sabotage accounted for an estimated $15 million lost on electricity alone in 1984. (*LAWR*, 3 August, p. 2; *Resumen Semanal*, 2–8 November, p. 1.) Manufacturing and agricultural enterprises were also targets: cotton storehouses were torched in Canete (*LAWR*, 3 August, p. 2); a trainload of zinc and lead concentrate was derailed in June (ibid., 6 July, p. 5); and in November a convoy of copper was hit, and a palm oil mill and a plantation of the crop substitution program were destroyed (*Resumen Semanal*, 2–8 November, p. 1).

Armed clashes involving Sendero also escalated in frequency and in numbers of participants during this period. According to police sources, attacks were perpetrated by bands of "hundreds," and the deaths attributed to these incidents were higher than those of previous years. From 22 to 24 June police estimated 500 guerrillas and peasants participated in armed actions, leaving 150 dead, including nine civil guards (*LAWR*, 6 July, p. 8).

The strength of Sendero forces continues to be a matter of debate, with 1984 estimates varying from 2,000 to 7,000 (Americas Watch, *Abdicating Democratic Authority*, p. 63). Yet estimates suggest that over 1,000 Senderistas had been killed, with 3,500 taken prisoner (*OIGA*, 9 July; *JPRS*, 9 August, p. 70). This total implies that Sendero has either greatly expanded its support, or others are acting under the cover of Sendero, and/or the majority killed and arrested are not Senderistas.

The apparent ability of Sendero to operate simultaneously in many different locations and the spread of attacks to areas outside of Ayacucho led to speculation that the rebellion had entered a new stage of influence with the opening of a second front in the coca-growing areas of Tingo Maria. Increased violence in the jungle region at least reflects a coincidence of interests as hostility to the U.S. and Peruvian governments' coca crop substitution program leads peasants to join in attacks on authorities; but whether these attacks are initiated by Sendero, drug traffickers, or an alliance of the two is uncertain (*LAWR*, 17 August, pp. 8–9; *WSJ*, 10 August).

Sendero is not the only group committed to armed struggle in Peru. In the north attacks and communiqués have been made by the PCP–Puka Llacta and Huaycacholo, both of which profess support for the aims of Sendero. But the most significant development in 1984 came with the emergence of the Tupac Amaru Revolutionary Movement (MRTA). Isolated attacks had been attributed to this new group as early as November 1983, when it was formed from splits in the PSR with the PSR–Marxist-Leninist leading the movement. According to *Caretas* (9 October, p. 14), at a meeting on 9 June to celebrate the nineteenth anniversary of the initiation of the 1965 guerrilla campaign, various MIR factions, including MIR-IV Etapa, MIR-PERU, MIR Yahuarina, and Insurgencia Política, joined the Tupac Amaru movement and agreed to begin armed actions. The leaders of the movement are said to be Marco Antonio Turkaowsky and Ernesto Montes Aliaga (*FBIS*, 21 September). The MRTA's operations have been noticeably different from Sendero Luminoso's. It publicizes its actions and distributes propaganda. Claiming to be the heir of the 1965 guerrillas, it is ideologically more in the mainstream of the Peruvian communist movement: it does not view the USSR as an imperialist nation, it does not attack the parliamentary left, and it identifies U.S. capitalism as the enemy (*OIGA*, 15 October, p. 24).

The appearance of the Tupac Amaru group has presented a dilemma for the parliamentary Marxist left. The IU's relationship to the MRTA becomes important because, as *Caretas* (22 October, p. 29) explained, the willingness to initiate an armed struggle "is used by outsiders to condemn Marxists and by insiders to define 'purists.'" Most members of the coalition adhere to the thesis that revolutionary violence is indispensable for destroying repressive regimes. Thus, Jorge del Prado said the PCP "tacitly supports the Tupac Amaru movement's political actions on making public its repudiation of the administration's economic policy" (*FBIS*, 5 October). The MRTA's targets have underscored its opposition to Belaúnde's pro-U.S. policies—the U.S. Embassy, Sears, and two wire services (*OIGA*, 1 October, p. 8, 15 October, p. 24).

But the IU has consistently rejected the methods of Sendero, arguing that indiscriminate terrorism erodes popular support and that democratic options are currently available to the masses. The looseness of the coalition has so far prevented any rupture on this issue, and the IU's commitment to democratic, electoral politics separates it decisively from the groups that have launched armed struggles. Despite the government's claims and beliefs, there is no evidence of any ties between the IU and Sendero. A Senderista prisoner in El Fronton referred to the IU as "being on the reactionary bandwagon . . . they are legitimizing this rotten corrupt state . . . therefore they are our enemies" (*El Diario de Marka*, 16 December 1983; *JPRS*, 16 February, p. 119). In fact the IU's acceptance of the electoral path to power has made it a target of Sendero violence since the 1983 municipal elections placed IU mayors in many central highland towns. For example, in November, the IU district mayor of Huanuco was assassinated in front of the town's inhabitants, prompting Jorge del Prado to denounce the "series of crimes and wave of terror in the country against IU leaders. All of these assassinations," he suggested, "form part of an escalation that can do nothing but serve the elements of reaction." (*Resumen Semanal*, 2–8 November, pp. 1–2.) Since 1980, 64 officials of all parties have been killed, including ten mayors in 1984; others have resigned after receiving death threats (*FBIS*, 24 September).

Not only does Sendero have few ties with political groups in the country, it also appears to have little significant international support. Once again, despite the government's continued references to outside influences, the only evidence is that photocopied pamphlets of Sendero's few pronouncements are being sold in Europe by various revolutionary communist groups (*Resumen Semanal*, 19–25 October, p. 3; *LAWR*, 19 October, p. 12). It is more likely that these groups are inspired by the success of Sendero and are making money on the sale of literature than that they are influencing the Peruvian guerrillas. Sendero's needs from the outside are few, its strength has been in its total self-reliance. Americas Watch (*Abdicating Democratic Authority*, p. 66) noted that Sendero's weapons included dynamite robbed from mines (95 cases were stolen in 1984, according to *NYT*, 1 September), arms stolen from soldiers, and traditional weapons of Ayacucho.

The Peruvian government's response to Sendero has primarily been efforts to develop an effective counterinsurgency strategy. The result has been the escalation of violence and spread of militarization, with the concomitant weakening of democratic guarantees. The IU coalition has been a consistent critic of the government's policy on four counts: (1) the tendency to link all opposition with subversion; (2) the reluctance to view the solution to the Andean rebellion within a social-economic framework; (3) the pursuit of a "dirty war" of counterinsurgency; and (4) the refusal of the government to seek a political alternative to the mounting violence.

Throughout the year efforts by IU politicians to challenge the government publicly, whether in parliament or in the street, were subjected to charges of "subversion." Deputies were suspended from the parliament for questions that were "disrespectful," and IU leaders, members, and sympathizers were selectively stopped for identification checks, detained at peaceful demonstrations, and arrested on charges that were several years old. The former editor of the leftist newspaper *El Diario* and the secretary general of a provincial federation of peasants were jailed for eight months for participating in a strike two years before (*Resumen Semanal*, 20–26 April, p. 7). Important popular organizations were disbanded by the government. The National Agrarian Confederation (CNA), its twenty regional peasant federations, and the 150 agrarian leagues formed by the agrarian reform were denied public registration in November. Although the government claimed this was to improve agricultural development, the IU saw it merely as a way to break a powerful opposition group (ibid., 2–8 November, p. 3). Finally, political marches were virtually banned. In August, a march for "peace and justice" sponsored by the IU, CGTP, and other labor and professional organizations to protest terrorism and to ask that human rights be respected in the antiterrorist struggle was canceled when the government took the unprecedented measure of placing the city of Lima under military control. Ostensibly to protect the public order, the organizations involved viewed the move as one calculated to provoke disorder and called off the rally. (*FBIS*, 27 August.)

Early in 1984 there was hope that the new head of the Political-Military Command would bring about some changes. Quechuan-speaking Gen. Adrián Huamán Centeno promised to seek socioeconomic assistance as well as use military means to address the emergency zone's problems. In addition, he said, he would cooperate with the public prosecutor's office in investigating human rights violations and the prosecution of any police or military responsible. But the new tactics were never really tried. Huamán received only $2 million of his requested $20 million for aiding agriculture, and by August he had been dismissed, in large part because of his continued emphasis on socioeconomic solutions in the face of the government's preference for "pacification" (*Resumen Semanal*,

24–30 August, p. 2, 31 August–6 September, pp. 1–2). In fact, after Sendero's June-July offensive, there was a major change in the counterinsurgency campaign. The police were relieved of their duties, and 6,000 soldiers, marines, and airmen were mobilized in the emergency zone. The armed forces were granted nationwide control over all antisubversive activities, and a news commission was created to control counterintelligence information as well as to provide material for the daily press (*LAWR*, 27 July, p. 9, 24 August, p. 2). In addition, rural militias were organized to provide armed, round-the-clock patrols for outlying communities, although critics quickly warned that such a move would only increase the number of civilian casualties (ibid., 21 September, p. 8).

Indeed, the government came under greater suspicion of waging a "dirty war." According to Amnesty International, Peru was the only country in Latin America where illegal executions and the number of disappeared had increased from 1983 (ibid., 2 November, p. 7). IU Deputy Javier Diez Canseco took information documenting 200 disappeared persons to the U.N. Working Group on Forced Disappearances, and the district attorney of Ayacucho said that in February over 1,500 allegations had been made about disappeared persons (*Intercontinental Press*, 9 July; Americas Watch, *Abdicating Democratic Authority*, p. 102). Officials dismissed human rights organizations' reports as leftist propaganda and the "most effective arm of Sendero Luminoso" (*Caretas*, 9 October, pp. 29–30; *Intercontinental Press*, 9 July), but as evidence of torture in illegal detention centers and of mass graves continued to appear, the Peruvian weekly *Caretas* (29 October, p. 8) urged the government and the population to respect the principle of human dignity and to punish atrocities on all sides.

The number of dead and disappeared had reached almost a numbing level in 1984, but a series of events in August shocked the nation nonetheless. Within the span of a few days, evidence was disclosed implicating the police in the death of peasant leader and PSR party member Jesús Oropesa; a journalist, Jamie Ayala, disappeared after last being seen walking into the Marine barracks in Huanta; the government publicly acknowledged that police had killed six missionaries; and 50 tortured and mutilated bodies were found by the attorney general's staff as they searched for individuals who had "disappeared" (*Resumen Semanal*, 24–30 August, pp. 2–3).

Demands for changes in the government's policy had increased with the election of many opposition mayors in 1983. Upon taking office, Ayacucho's mayor, Leonor Zamora (PADIN), wanted an open meeting on terrorism and violence, a dialogue that would include Sendero (ibid., 30 December 1983–5 January 1984, p. 1). The military command banned any such meeting at the time. But as fighting terror with terror had proved unsuccessful and its image had been so tarnished, both internally and internationally, in late 1984 the government became willing to discuss the possibility of a dialogue, an alternative that it had so quickly dismissed earlier. The president of the Chamber of Deputies, Elias Mendoza, said he favored all initiatives, and both the prime minister and minister of justice indicated they would be disposed to talk with valid negotiators. President Belaúnde, walking a political tightrope so as not to endanger his party's chances in the 1985 elections, wanted to appear willing to pursue all alternatives. However, he indicated that any dialogue with the rebels would be conditional: "We will talk with Sendero when they have a command, as is the case in Colombia. In our case, with whom do we talk? We can not talk with those who hide their faces." (Ibid., 2–8 November, p. 2, 8–15 November, p. 1.) Interestingly enough, the Aprista candidate, Alán García, the nominee with the best chance of winning in 1985, has been the most cautious about dialogue, as he felt it would be dangerous to treat the government and Sendero as equals (ibid., 8–15 November, p. 1). Meanwhile, the major concern of the IU coalition at the end of 1984 was not the basis for negotiation with the terrorists, but rather trying to assure that the elections scheduled for 1985 are actually held.

International Relations. Relations with the Soviet Union are cordial and important to Peru. Officials are careful when discussing foreign influences on Sendero Luminoso to differentiate between official support and nebulous international conspiracies, and they tend to blame the current situation on the latter (*Caretas*, 9 October, p. 29). When President Belaúnde visited Washington and the United Nations in October, he was concerned more about the international economic situation than about Moscow's role in hemispheric problems (*NYT*, 30 December).

On the occasion of the PCP celebration of the fifteenth anniversary of Peru's establishment of diplomatic relations with the USSR, it was noted that trade balances with that country were advantageous to Peru and debt renegotiations were successfully in place. The deal with the USSR provided for $320 million to be paid over eight years; $95 million of this was to be in manufactured products or raw materials. The first shipment, 2,500 zinc disks for batteries, worth $2,850,000, left Peru on 19 June. Other products selected for in-kind payment include denim, chicken, canned tomatoes, coffee, cocoa, and fish flour (*FBIS*, 21 June). The PCP was apprehensive that the government would yield to pressure from the International Monetary Fund "to restrict, reduce or cancel" Peru's relations with the socialist countries (*Unidad*, 9 February; *JPRS*, 21 March, p. 74). These ties are significant. There are 600 Soviet civilian and military personnel in Peru, making it the largest contingent of Soviet advisers on the continent (*Washington Times*, 12 June). Soviet financial assistance and technology are instrumental to the Olmos hydroelectric and irrigation projects and the Paita fish-processing factory (*FBIS*, 16 February). In addition to commercial and military ties, over a thousand Peruvian students are studying in the Soviet Union, and the USSR maintains cultural centers in eleven major Peruvian cities (*Washington Times*, 12 June).

Peru maintains relations with many socialist bloc nations, and in June the government received a delegation from Poland headed by the vice-president of the Polish parliament, offering technology and economic aid to reactivate and modernize agriculture and mining enterprises (*Resumen Semanal*, 1–7 June, p. 5).

Peru has also established ties with the People's Republic of China. A delegation headed by Liao Hanxing, vice-chairman of the Standing Committee of the National People's Congress, spent one week in Peru with the objective of "strengthening commercial and cultural ties because the axis of activity is shifting from the Atlantic to Pacific." In welcoming the visitors, Sandro Mariategui, president of the Committee on Foreign Affairs, stated that Peru is "more Asiatic than Western." China is interested in Peru's copper and iron in exchange for manufactured goods and technology. (*FBIS*, 6 April.)

The IU has greatly extended its international connections. In June several mayors went on a trip to Spain, France, Germany, Switzerland, and Great Britain to work out interchanges and establish financial assistance arrangements (*Resumen Semanal*, 15–21 June, p. 4). Barrantes himself made two European trips, one in December 1983 to negotiate economic assistance and the other in November 1984 to promote his understanding of foreign relations as a presidential candidate.

The PCP has continued to maintain ties and good relations with other communist parties around the world. Secretary General Jorge del Prado visited Cuba, Nicaragua, and Armenia in 1984. Most important has been the PCP's support for the Nicaraguan liberation process. In May, 28 labor, political, social, and popular organizations called for participants to join in a continental march to Nicaragua for the fifth anniversary of the Sandinista victory (ibid., 18–24 May, p. 4). In July, Valentín Pacho, secretary general of the CGTP, attended a regional communist party meeting in Buenos Aires. Topics of discussion included the foreign debt of the various nations, U.S. aggression, and common support against military or right-wing coups. Representatives from thirteen nations agreed "to coordinate regional action to confront the aggressive and belligerent policy of the US administration" and "to support all democratic demands of the continent." (*FBIS*, 10 July.)

Sandra Woy-Hazleton
Miami University

Puerto Rico

Population. 3,196,520
Party. Puerto Rican Socialist Party (Partido Socialista Puertorriqueño; PSP); Puerto Rican Communist
   Party (Partido Comunista Puertorriqueño; PCP)
Founded. PSP: 1971; PCP: 1934
Membership. PSP: 150 (estimated): PCP: 125 (estimated)
Secretary General. PSP: vacant; PCP: Franklin Irrizarry
Leading Bodies. No data
Status. Legal
Last Congress. PSP: Second, 1979; PCP: none known
Last Elections. 1984; PSP: 0.3 percent, no representatives
Auxiliary Organizations. No data
Publications. PSP: *Claridad* (weekly)

It was significant that during the heated 1984 campaign for governor of Puerto Rico, the island's highest office, the role of Marxist organizations went virtually unreported by the media. That these groups were practically ignored by the local press, radio, and television was not a result of deliberate bias. Rather, it was simply recognition by independent observers of the increasing irrelevance of the minuscule Marxist groupings in the political life of Puerto Rico. The island's residents seemed in 1984 to be concerned more with current economic problems than with the future political status of Puerto Rico.

Puerto Rico is a commonwealth of the United States. Federal funds account for one-third of its gross domestic product, against 11 percent for the states, and Puerto Ricans pay no federal taxes. Relations with Washington directly affect the island's economy because federal budget cuts could make the plight of Puerto Rico's unemployed even harder. According to official statistics, unemployment is 21 percent, and some 60 percent of the population is eligible for poverty aid.

In some 30 years as a U.S. commonwealth, Puerto Rico's politics have been dominated by three political parties, two large and one small. For the past eight years, the governor of Puerto Rico was Carlos Romero Barceló, leader of the New Progressive Party (NPP), which favors statehood for the island. On 6 November Romero Barceló was defeated by the candidate of the Popular Democratic Party (PDP), Rafael Hernández Colón, which favors retaining the present commonwealth status (also called "free associate state"). Taking office on 2 January 1985, Hernández Colón called for better relations with the Reagan administration. He assumed the governorship at a time when relations with Washington appeared to be at a low ebb. The governor's identification with the liberal wing of the national Democratic Party might make his dealings with the White House more strained than those of his more conservative predecessor, generally seen as an ally of the Republican Party.

The victory of Hernández Colón was practically assured by a split in NPP ranks and the candidacy of the outgoing mayor of San Juan, Hernán Padilla, who abandoned the party when it nominated Romero Barceló. In the gubernatorial race, Hernández Colón won 808,986 votes (47.8 percent); Romero Barceló 756,100 (44.7 percent); Padilla 67,361 votes (3.9 percent); and the candidate of the Puerto Rican Independent Party (PIP), Fernando Martín, 60,333 votes (3.5 percent).

Puerto Rico's Marxists—the majority by peaceful means, a few clandestine extremists by violence—have been seeking independence. The weaker than expected showing of the PIP, which in recent elections received about 5 percent of the popular vote, showed that pro-independence forces—and the Marxists—have been losing ground among Puerto Ricans.

The principal Marxist group is the Puerto Rican Socialist Party, a pro-Cuban organization with some 150 members. Its leader and former secretary general, Juan Mari Bras, is a personal friend of Fidel Castro, whom he frequently visits in Havana. In late 1982, the 57-year-old Mari Bras resigned his position, which he had held for many years, and the organization has been reorganizing its top leadership since. The PSP publishes the weekly newspaper *Claridad* in San Juan and advocates the establishment of Puerto Rico as a socialist state.

Equally small, some 125 members strong, is the Puerto Rican Communist Party, a pro-Moscow group closely associated with the Communist Party USA. Even smaller in membership are two Trotskyist parties, the International Workers' League and the Puerto Rican Socialist League. A Puerto Rican, Andrea González, was candidate for vice-president of the United States on the Socialist Workers Party (SWP) ticket. She visited the island during the summer and said that one of the purposes of her trip was to "cut through the disinformation [that] the people of the United States have been subjected to regarding events in Puerto Rico." She said that "the big news media spread the idea that no one in Puerto Rico is opposed to colonialism and militarization. They never report on the activities of the independence movement." (*Intercontinental Press*, 17 September.)

The operations of clandestine, Marxist-oriented terrorist groups, both on the island and on the U.S. mainland, were less noticeable in 1984. The main group, which in the past ten years claimed responsibility for well over a hundred bombings in various mainland cities, is the Armed Forces of National Liberation (Fuerzas Armadas de Liberación Nacional; FALN), which is said to have fewer than two dozen members. While the incidence of bombings attributed to and claimed by the FALN has declined in recent years, investigators do not consider that it and other such groups have become extinct and believe they could resume their activities at any time.

George Volsky
University of Miami

Suriname

Population. 370,000
Party. 25 February Movement or Standvaste (25FM), pro-government; Communist Party of Suriname (CPS), pro-Albanian; Revolutionary People's Party (RVP, by its Dutch initials), pro-Cuban
Founded. 25FM: 1983; CPS: 1981; RVP: 1981
Membership. 25FM: 200 (estimated); CPS: 25 (estimated); RVP: 100 (estimated)
Leadership. 25FM: Desi Bouterse, Harvey Naarendorp, Etienne Boevereen, Paul Bhagwandaas; CPS: Bram Mehr; RVP: Edward Naarendorp, Glenn Sankatshing, Lothar Boksteen
Status. All regular party activity has been suspended since the 1980 coup.
Last Congress. 25FM: First, 12 May 1984; CPS: First, 24 July 1981

Suriname gained independence from the Netherlands in 1975. On 25 February 1980 the country's democratic government was overthrown by a military coup that brought Lt. Col. Desi Bouterse to power. After a moderate beginning, Bouterse adopted a leftist line and thwarted alleged coup attempts in December 1982 and in January and November 1983 that resulted in the murders of at least twenty prominent Surinamese intellectual, political, and labor leaders. The developments in 1982 led to the suspension of critical aid from the Netherlands and the United States. The economy has deteriorated, and foreign reserves have dried up. Negotiations with the International Monetary Fund have led to demands that the massive public sector (45 percent of the national work force) be reduced and a devaluation (of up to 30 percent) be instituted. These demands have led Bouterse to try to regain aid from the Netherlands or find other sources of funding from the Soviet bloc.

On 12 May the Bouterse government held the first congress of the 25 February Movement, which had been established the previous November. At the inaugural congress Bouterse said the 25FM would have the characteristics of a vanguard socialist party with mass membership. Movement leaders were appointed, and seven sections were set up: youth, women, production, labor, defense, propaganda, and foreign relations. (*Latin American Caribbean Report*, 15 June.)

In August Lt. Col. Bouterse lifted the state of emergency he had imposed in December 1982, and in December 1984 the government announced a transition to democracy would begin on 1 January 1985. The transition program is scheduled to last for 27 months. A 31-seat national assembly will be made up of fourteen representatives from the armed forces, eleven from the labor unions, and six from private industry and business. The government will be appointed by the national assembly. (*FBIS*, 10 and 13 December.)

According to terms reached with the Soviet Union in mid-1984, the Surinamese News Agency will disseminate Tass reports in Suriname. The Soviet Union has constructed radio facilities that enabled the Surinamese government to begin three shortwave broadcasts per week to Europe. The People's Republic of China has given Suriname an interest-free loan of U.S. $12 million to construct an indoor sports stadium in Paramaribo. Brazil continues to provide military equipment to the Surinamese in exchange for Surinamese products. Bouterse visited Nicaragua in July for the fifth anniversary of the Nicaraguan revolution. The Guyana-Cuba Friendship Society celebrated its tenth anniversary. Foremost among the exile groups are the Suriname Liberation Council, set up in the Netherlands by former Surinamese president Henk Chin-a-Wen after he was removed from office in early 1982, and the Amsterdam People's Resistance under the leadership of former minister Andre Haakmat.

William Ratliff
Hoover Institution

United States

Population. 236,413,000
Party. Communist Party USA (CPUSA)
Founded. 1919
Membership. 17,500 (claimed)
Secretary General. Gus Hall

Politburo. 10 members: Henry Winston, George Meyers, Charlene Mitchell, James Jackson, Arnold Bechetti, Mike Zagarell, Helen Winter, John Pittman, James West, James Steele
Central Committee. 83 members
Status. Legal
Last Congress. Twenty-third Convention, 10–13 November 1983, Cleveland, Ohio
Last Election. 1984 presidential, under 0.1 percent
Auxiliary Organizations. United States Peace Council, National Alliance Against Racist and Political Repression, Trade Unionists for Action and Democracy, National Congress of Unemployed Organizations, Young Communist League, Women for Racial and Economic Equality
Publications. *Daily World*, *Political Affairs*, *People's World*

The CPUSA is the largest and oldest Marxist-Leninist organization in the United States. Founded in 1919, it achieved its greatest influence in the 1930s when its membership was close to 100,000, and it played a significant role in the labor movement. Following World War II, as the cold war developed and domestic anticommunism increased, the party began to decline. In the early 1950s a substantial number of party cadres went underground to avoid government persecution. The party lost all but a few thousand of its members after the revelations of Stalin's crimes by the Soviet government in the late 1950s. Since then, it has remained a marginal group in American life, although there have been steady and modest gains in membership in the past decade.

Leadership and Party Organization. The party's leader, Gus Hall, has been at the helm since 1959, giving him a longer tenure than any previous general secretary. Among the other party leaders are Henry Winston (national chairman), Arnold Bechetti (national organizational secretary), Sid Taylor (treasurer), George Meyers (labor), Si Gerson (political action), James Jackson, Charlene Mitchell (Afro-American affairs), Mike Zagarell (editor, *Daily World*), and James West (chairman, Central Review Commission). Party leaders in key states include Jarvis Tyner (New York), Rick Nagin (Ohio), Sam Webb (Michigan), Helvi Savola (Minnesota), and Maurice Jackson (Maryland–D.C.).

At the party's Twenty-third Convention in 1983, Hall insisted that Communists become more visible in their activities, decrying a "right opportunist" tendency to hide their presence and focus on mere reform. A persistent theme in the party press throughout 1984 was that the CPUSA should become more visible. There were claims that party petitioners seeking ballot status for the 1984 elections were receiving a positive response. Hall insisted that the public reception was at least two to

three times better than in 1980. Party leaders emphasized the attention the Hall candidacy received from reporters, the public, and local groups and claimed that the CPUSA was "speaking to millions" through its activities, including large ads in the *New York Times* (*Daily World*, 21 June).

Domestic Party Affairs. The party's main focus during the year was the presidential election. The Communists' major goal was the defeat of the Reagan administration. Gus Hall noted that while the administration was not fascist, "fascist-oriented individuals" had taken over the Republican Party and written the "most war-oriented, anti-labor, racist platform in the history of U.S. politics" (*NYT*, 23 September). This meant that all communist resources had to be devoted to defeating Reaganism.

The party's tactics led it along two different tracks. The first was to run its own candidates, Gus Hall and Angela Davis, for president and vice-president. They ran as the most implacable Reagan opponents in the race. The Hall-Davis ticket was on the ballot in 22 states and Washington, D.C., one fewer than in 1980. Its total vote was 35,561 (10,000 fewer than four years before), with 4,672 in Illinois, 4,826 in Connecticut, and 4,671 in Alabama. Local and state party candidates got votes ranging from 1,000–2,000 in statewide races in Illinois and Michigan to some 50,000 for candidates to the University of Illinois Board of Trustees.

The party recognized, however, that it represented no credible electoral alternative to Reagan; as a result it gave de facto support to the Democratic Party while criticizing it for various shortcomings. Hall argued that Communists had no illusions that the Democratic Party could be transformed into a truly progressive force, but he admitted that most people, including labor and blacks, had opted to work in that party and not in a third party. He insisted that the Communists respected that judgment and believed that progressive forces in the

Democratic Party had to concentrate on pressuring Walter Mondale to move to the left. The party saw its own role as a leftist spur to Mondale; the sharper the division between him and Reagan, the more votes he would get (*Political Affairs*, July).

According to the Communists, the mobilization of labor, youth, the elderly, farmers, blacks, Hispanics, women, and the peace movement could defeat Reagan. The party gave enthusiastic support to Jesse Jackson's campaign. His insulting remarks about American Jews were excused as slips for which he had sincerely apologized. The party denounced Louis Farrakhan's anti-Semitic statements but argued that linking the controversial Moslem minister and Jackson supporter to Jackson was a ploy by the anti-Semitic right wing and was part of an effort to distract attention from Jackson's issues and to smear him (*Daily World*, 2 February, 3 July). Angela Davis claimed that Jackson's platform demands "played a historic role in moving the candidates in a more progressive direction" and lauded Geraldine Ferraro's nomination as "a historic first for our country" (*NYT*, 19 August).

Just before the election, Hall claimed the party's goal had been achieved; blacks, women, Hispanics, and the peace and union movements had for the first time taken an independent stand, and their leaders would soon have to find a way to form a new political party (*Daily World*, 1 November). This optimistic note continued even in the face of a Republican landslide. Hall interpreted the election to mean "no swing to the right and no new political realignment." Voters opposed Reaganism but had voted for Reagan because they "see the presidency as a figurehead" (ibid., 9 November). Henry Winston insisted that the party's position had been vindicated: "Our people, and first of all our working class, won new positions in the fight for a reversal" of Reaganism. He attributed the Democrats' defeat to their refusal to distinguish themselves from Reagan and reminded everyone that just as Richard Nixon had been ousted from office two years after his massive victory, the same fate could befall Reagan (ibid., 21 November).

On domestic issues the CPUSA has called for a massive jobs program, a six-hour day with no cut in pay, an increase in the minimum wage, expansion of affirmative action programs, deep cuts in the military budget, and restoration of social programs (*Political Affairs*, July). Hall called for ending tax benefits for the wealthy, eliminating income taxes on those making less than $30,000 a year, and

terminating interest payments on the federal debt (*Daily World*, 25 October). The party also opposes immigration reform on grounds that the Simpson-Mazzoli bill abets racism and aids corporations that exploit workers. Its solution to illegal immigration is to eliminate the poverty in the Third World that leads its citizens to seek entry to America (ibid., 20 June).

Auxiliary Organizations. The CPUSA has a whole panoply of front organizations. The Young Communist League (YCL), founded in 1983, sees its main task to be extending the "all-people's front" against Reagan among students and youth. It was active in registering new voters. Led by James Steele, a member of the party's Politburo, the YCL publishes a monthly newspaper, *Dynamic*, with a claimed circulation of nearly 20,000. The YCL is preparing for a World Festival of Youths and Students to be held in Moscow in the summer of 1985. A National Preparatory Committee has been set up and endorsed by Jesse Jackson. It includes representatives from the Young Democrats of Connecticut and the offices of Congressmen Ronald Dellums and Walter Fauntroy. Representative George Crockett of Detroit spoke at one of the committee's meetings (ibid., 12 September, 14 November).

Other party auxiliaries include the National Alliance Against Racist and Political Repression (Frank Chapman, executive director, Angela Davis, cochair), the United States Peace Council (Michael Myerson, executive director), the Labor Research Association, National Congress of Unemployed Organizations, Trade Unionists for Action and Democracy, and the Benjamin Rush Society, an organization of Marxist-oriented health workers, particularly psychologists and psychiatrists, chaired by Dr. Irving Crain. Women for Racial and Economic Equality held its third conference in May. Among its leaders are Cheryl Allen Craig (national president), Vini Burrows, and Norma Spector.

International Views, Positions, and Activities. The CPUSA does not deviate from the Soviet line in foreign policy. It praises all aspects of the Soviet line and defends its actions. Nonetheless, Gus Hall insisted that on occasion there are disagreements with the USSR. He claimed that the CPUSA had taken a harder line on the Watergate affair and was an earlier opponent of China's Cultural Revolution. Hall also insisted that he had originally welcomed the Polish Solidarity movement as "a positive step" and had suggested that other socialist nations should learn from it the value of more independent unions (*NYT*, 2 November). Yuri Andropov's death elicited a warm tribute: "He left deep footprints along the path of human progress" (*Daily World*, 11 February). Throughout the year, the CPUSA denied that the Soviet Union represented any kind of threat to the United States. Those "third-campers" who blame both superpowers equally for the arms race ignore history and the consistent peace policy of the USSR. Their activities "put them on the side of the Reagan administration on the key ideological question of the day: the absurd idea that the Soviet Union is a military threat to the U.S." It is the United States, with its criminal deployment of Pershing missiles in Europe, that is the danger to world peace (ibid., 9 February, 3 July). Gus Hall defended the Soviet decision to boycott the Olympics, calling it a consequence of Reagan's "vicious, hysteria-building, anti-communist evil empire, big lie" (ibid., 9 May).

The CPUSA demanded that the American government should be forced to make a 180 degree turn in Central American policy. It called for "hands off Nicaragua" and was part of the Coalition Against US Intervention in Central America, which sponsored a big rally in June in New York. An estimated 20,000 people attended, and it was claimed that the party had one of the largest contingents (ibid., 11 May, 12 June). The party downplayed the threat of international terrorism. One commentator, while admitting that the murder of a British policewoman by gunmen inside the Libyan Embassy in London could not be condoned, denied that the Libyans were solely to blame; rather they had been provoked (ibid., 2 May). The party's prevailing line is that the United States is the source of much of the world's terrorism because of its deployment of missiles, support of Israel, and purported involvement in the assassination of Indira Gandhi by militant Sikhs (ibid., 1 November).

Biography. *Gus Hall.* The most seasoned candidate for president this year was CPUSA leader Gus Hall. This was his fourth campaign for the presidency. Hall has been general secretary of the CPUSA since 1959 and a party member since his boyhood. He was born in Iron, Minnesota, in 1910; his parents, Finnish immigrants, were both charter members of the communist movement, and Arvo Halberg (his given name) was a party member by the time he was sixteen years old. In the early 1930s he was sent to the Lenin School in Moscow for training. After returning to the United States in 1933, he worked for the YCL in the upper Midwest. Using the name Gus Hall, he became an organizer for the Steel Workers Organizing Committee in Ohio when the CIO began to organize in the middle of the decade. After pleading guilty to a misdemeanor (malicious destruction of property), arising out of violence during a 1937 strike, Hall returned to party activities and soon became state chairman for Ohio. He served in the navy during World War II. In 1950 he moved into the party leadership in New York as acting secretary while Gene Dennis was in jail. Hall was convicted of violating the Smith Act along with the rest of the party's Political Board; rather than surrender after his appeals were exhausted in 1951, he jumped bail and fled to Mexico. Captured and returned to prison, he resumed party work in 1959 and immediately challenged Dennis for the leadership of the CPUSA and won. During his 25 years at the helm, the party has recovered from the minuscule membership it was left with after the factionalism of the late 1950s; it has not, however, been able to reestablish itself as a key force in the labor movement or among intellectuals. Nor was it able to take advantage of the radical upsurge among the young in the 1960s. Nonetheless, in the last few years the CPUSA has once again been able to recruit some prominent individuals to join its front organizations and lend their names to its causes.

Socialist Workers Party. The largest of several Trotskyist parties in the United States is the Socialist Workers Party, founded in 1938. It is not formally affiliated with the Fourth International because of American laws, but cooperates with it. The SWP publishes the *Militant*.

The SWP has been severely shaken during the past year by a purge of its membership and extensive internal upheaval. Party membership, around 2,000 a few years ago, has now dropped to fewer than a thousand. A number of well-known, longtime leaders have either been expelled or have quit, including George Breitman, Frank Lovell, and Peter Camejo. One group of dissidents has organized a new group, Socialist Action, with several hundred members, and publishes a newspaper with the same name. Its members argue that the SWP has abandoned traditional Trotskyist views. They have found some support in the United Secretariat of the Fourth International, which has urged the SWP to readmit them. Another group, led by Peter Camejo, the party's presidential candidate in 1976, has formed the North Star Network, which is trying to promote dialogue among those with varying leftist orientations.

The cause of the internal conflict is the SWP's abandonment of several staples of Trotskyist ideology. Beginning in 1981, the party leadership under the direction of Jack Barnes, began to abandon the idea of permanent revolution, the idea of fighting for a direct socialist revolution in underdeveloped countries. It also muted its call for a revolutionary transformation of communist regimes, arguing that they could be reformed instead.

The SWP held its Thirty-second National Convention in August at Oberlin College with about a thousand people in attendance. Jack Barnes is national secretary; Barry Sheppard, Malik Miah, and Mary-Alice Waters are national cochairs. Craig Gannon is national organizational secretary. Reflecting the party's turn to the shops several years ago, 61 percent of its members are industrial workers. The party adopted a resolution asserting that American workers were finally coming to grips with the offensive of capitalists; it saw a growing polarization that would increase opportunities for Communists. Workers had to be taught that reformism was futile. (*Militant*, 7 September.) In line with this reasoning, the SWP opposes any cooperation with capitalist parties. It denounced the Jesse Jackson campaign as a delusion that made the formation of an independent workers' party more difficult (ibid., 17 February). The SWP supports the National Black Independent Political Party. The party's candidates for president, Mel Mason, and vice-president, Andrea Gonzalez, were on the ballot in 23 states and received 24,687 votes.

The SWP believes that American imperialism is moving toward war in Central America to counter the growth of socialism and at its convention discussed how to prepare to resist that war. The Political Committee instructed its union groups to make antiwar activity their central campaign (ibid., 31 August).

The SWP's youth group, the Young Socialist Alliance, held its Twenty-third National Convention in St. Louis in December 1983. Its leaders include Andrea Gonzalez, national chair, Stuart Crone, national organizer, and Peter Thierjung, national secretary. Two-thirds of its members are in industry, 22 percent are oppressed nationalities, and 52 percent are women (ibid., 20 January).

The SWP has become more pro-Soviet in recent years as it has abandoned traditional Trotskyism. The *Militant* has published articles extolling Soviet economic progress with mild criticisms of the political demoralization caused by its bureaucratic caste (ibid., 17 February). The attention given to the plight of Andrei Sakharov was part of an anti-Soviet, big-business campaign, it has claimed, and has nothing to do with human rights, although the Soviets should have allowed him to emigrate rather than give ammunition to their critics (ibid., 20 July). Charges of a plot against the life of the pope were "anticommunist slanders against Bulgaria and the Soviet Union" (ibid., 9 November). Barry Sheppard praised the achievements of Cuba and insisted that its revolution was the most important one since that of the Bolsheviks. The SWP fully supports Cuba, the guerrillas in El Salvador, and the Sandinistas and argues that the American intervention in Grenada was a serious defeat since it overthrew the first socialist regime in an English-speaking black country (ibid., 20 January).

Other Marxist Parties. The Revolutionary Communist Party (RCP) is a Maoist group founded in 1967 as the Bay Area Revolutionary Union. Around 1970 it became the Revolutionary Union; its present name was adopted in 1975. Its leader is Bob Avakian, now 40, a onetime student at Berkeley and son of a judge, and now in exile in France. In 1984 it set up a new Revolutionary Internationalist Movement (RIM) with a dozen or so foreign groups. The heated rhetoric and inflated sense of self-importance the group attaches to its own activities is indicated by the breathless report of RIM's emergence in its journal, *Revolutionary Worker* (4 May): on the eve of 1 May "as the clock ticked midnight, small groups of proletarians . . . waited for copies of the Declaration and studied them into the night in advance of May 1st actions the next day."

The RCP is critical of those radical groups that supported Jesse Jackson; it denounced his foreign policy as being pro-imperialist. The party denounced elections as meaningless and urged people not to vote: "We want to tear the whole system down! Elections are the wrong arena. It's going to come down to revolutionary war!" (Ibid., 13 July.)

The Workers World Party, founded in 1958 after a split within the SWP, is led by Sam Marcy. It supported Jesse Jackson in the presidential election before nominating its own candidate, Larry Holmes, who got 15,000 votes. The Communist Workers Party, which achieved notoriety when five of its members were killed in a shoot-out with Nazis and Klansmen in Greensboro, North Carolina, in 1980, is led by Jerry Tung. One of eight domestic groups under FBI surveillance, it also supported Jackson's candidacy. The Workers League's presidential ticket, Ed Winn and Helen Halyard, was on the ballot in six states and got 10,800 votes. There are a number of other small Marxist-Leninist groups. None of them has more than a few hundred members.

Harvey Klehr
Emory University

Uruguay

Population. 2,926,000
Party. Communist Party of Uruguay (PCU)
Founded. 1920
Membership. 7,500 (estimated)
Secretary General. Rodney Arismendi
Leading Bodies. No data
Status. Illegal, but permitted to run within Broad Front coalition
Last Congress. Twentieth, December 1970
Last Election. 25 November 1984, 6.0 percent, no representatives
Auxiliary Organizations. No data
Publications. No data

The year under review finally brought the end of Uruguay's eleven-year-old military dictatorship. A year that started with continued demonstrations against a united and stubborn military saw an agreement in August that permitted elections on 25 November, with the installation of a civilian government scheduled for 1 March 1985.

The military chose to exit in the face of its increased isolation both domestically and internationally. The return to democracy in Argentina and the promise of the same in Brazil would have left Uruguay's generals as the odd men out in the Rio de la Plata. At the same time, they were presiding over an economy that saw an unprecedented 20 percent drop in the gross domestic product from 1981 to 1983, with no recovery in sight. The generals' desire to turn power over to civilians was apparent, but there was one fly in the ointment—the possibility that exiled Senator Wilson Ferreira Aldunate, leader of the Blanco, or National, Party, would return and win the election. Wilson, as he is known, returned on 16 June and, as expected, was promptly arrested by the military. A charismatic populist, he was feared by the military more for his personal popularity and strong stand against the dictatorship than for his ideology or policies.

In preparation for their exit, the military began to release important political figures they had jailed for years. In March, Gen. Liber Seregni, presidential candidate for the leftist coalition known as the

Frente Amplio (Broad Front) in the 1971 elections, was released and permitted to represent his still banned coalition. At about the same time, Luis Massera, world-renowned mathematician and a leader of the PCU, was also released. In addition, the government began to allow the return of political exiles. In October, Enrique Rodríguez, a member of the PCU's Executive Committee, returned after eleven years in exile, and on 3 November Rodney Arismendi, longtime PCU secretary general, made a well-received return to Montevideo.

During August, the parties that constituted the Frente Amplio were relegalized with the exception of the PCU. Nevertheless, the Communists were permitted to run stand-in candidates under their own list (Democracia Avanzada) within the leftist coalition, with the understanding that the party would regain legal status under the new civilian government. Clearly, the military had decided that rehabilitating the left would split them from their antimilitary alliance with Ferreira Aldunate and make them amenable to an agreement on the elections. The military was right. The PCU supported the pact between the armed forces and the Colorado Party and the Frente Amplio, while rejecting the Blanco Party's position of refusing to negotiate while its leader, Wilson Ferreira Aldunate, was in jail.

The campaign ended with a not untypical burst of anticommunism. Julia María Sanguinetti, the soon to be victorious candidate of the Colorado Party, attacked the Frente Amplio in harsh terms:

> Behind that person who acts so calmly [Seregni] there are groups whose strength is well known. We have seen that the flag with the hammer and sickle which has been hidden for 20 years has started to appear. And there is no doubt that they are now determined to try to assert, within the Broad Front, their predominance in the working sectors. They are stating this. This is not a personal issue, it is a political fact. There is a philosophical battle, a battle of principles, regarding these ideas. A front which has totalitarian currents, to the detriment of those which are not totalitarian, undoubtedly represents a danger and a threat to the institutional stability of a country. [*FBIS*, 16 November.]

The elections themselves proved no great surprise. With General Seregni prohibited from running and with Wilson Ferreira Aldunate still in jail,

the odds favored the Colorados. The Colorado Party won with 39 percent of the vote. The Blanco Party got 33 percent, and the Frente Amplio, a relatively poor 21 percent. The Frente Amplio increased its share of the vote by some 3.5 percentage points compared with its 1971 totals. Many observers were surprised by the left's poor showing, expecting after eleven years of a brutal dictatorship, deteriorating economic conditions, and significant numbers of first-time voters, that the left would do better. However, given the large numbers of exiled activists, the prohibition of Seregni's candidacy, and the ban on known communist candidates, the relatively poor showing could have been expected.

The Communists and Socialists, the only self-defined Marxist-Leninist parties in the Frente Amplio, did poorly in the elections. The PCU received only 25 percent of the left's vote, some 6 percent of the total vote. Its relatively poor showing cost the Frente the mayoralty of Montevideo, considered the second most important political position in the country, by fewer than 15,000 votes. Within the leftist coalition, the social-democratic faction, led by Hugo Batalla (List 99) garnered almost 45 percent of the vote and emerged as the dominant electoral group within the Frente. Whether this result was merely a personal victory for Batalla or could be converted into organizational power remains to be seen.

The new government will have no choice but to seek the widest possible base for support. First, no party will command a majority in the Senate or in the Chamber of Deputies. Second, with real purchasing power down 50 percent since the early 1970s and with unemployment running around 14 percent, labor is desperate for an improvement in salaries and employment possibilities. A newly relegalized labor movement with important segments of PCU leadership is anxious to act responsibly, but fully intends to defend labor's interests. Third, Uruguay's foreign debt, which is now over $5 billion, must be renegotiated in a manner that will not have a negative impact on an already bleak economic situation.

Another major issue facing Sanguinetti is the hundreds of remaining political prisoners. The Blancos and the Frente Amplio have both called for a blanket amnesty. The Colorado position during the campaign was to favor the release of all prisoners arrested after the June 1973 coup, but not those arrested prior to the coup who had committed such crimes as bank robbery, kidnapping, or murder. In view of the horrible conditions and documented tortures these prisoners have endured, and given the fact that the electoral agreement virtually guarantees the military immunity from prosecution, public opinion overwhelmingly supports an amnesty that would wipe the slate clean for everyone.

Martin Weinstein
The William Paterson College of New Jersey

Venezuela

Population. 18,552,000
Party. Communist Party of Venezuela (Partido Comunista de Venezuela; PCV)
Founded. 1931
Membership. 4,000 (estimated)
Secretary General. Jesús Faría
Politburo. 18 members, including Héctor Mujica, Radamés Larrazábal, Eduardo Gallegos Mancera
Status. Legal
Last Congress. Sixth, 8–11 August 1980 (Seventh Congress scheduled for May 1985)
Last Election. 1983, 2.0 percent, 3 of 195 seats
Auxiliary Organizations. United Central of Venezuelan Workers (Central Unitaria de Trabajadores Venezolanos; CUTV); Communist Youth (Juventud Comunista; JC)
Publication. *Tribuna Popular* (weekly)

A year of severe economic crisis, with high unemployment and unpopular austerity measures, did not revive the languishing fortunes of the leftist parties but seemed rather to emphasize their diminishing relevance to the country's political life. Despite uncharacteristically high abstention in municipal elections in May, the governing Democratic Action Party (AD) confirmed its predominance, with the Social Christian Party (COPEI) following in a distant but still solid second place, far ahead of the left as a whole. Although plagued by serious desertions and dissension, the Movement to Socialism (Movimiento al Socialismo; MAS) eschewed alliances and kept its third place with a meager 4 percent of the vote. The United Left coalition (Unidad de la Izquierda; UI) did less well, even though it combined the votes of four parties and some local groups. Members included the PCV; the People's Electoral Movement (Movimiento Electoral del Pueblo; MEP); the Revolutionary Left Movement (Movimiento de Izquierda Revolucionario; MIR); and the New Alternative (Nueva Alternativa; NA). Following the resignation of its secretary general, Julio Escalona, the Socialist League (Liga Socialista; LS) presented separate slates with no success at all, but a regional labor-based movement, Radical Cause (Causa R), elected 5 of the 57 councilmen in the state of Bolívar.

The reverses suffered by the left in both the municipal contests and the preceding presidential election (see *YICA*, 1984, p. 179) raised some fears of a resurgence of armed struggle. Although no such trend is admitted by the parties, a disturbing increase in urban violence can be seen. Instigation is usually attributed to the Red Flag (Bandera Roja; BR) guerrillas or to the presumably disbanded

Committees of Popular Struggle (Comités de Lucha Popular; CLP). The BR remains active in the Venezuelan-Colombian border region.

Communist Party of Venezuela. Leftist unity, transcending ideological differences, has been a watchword of the Moscow-line PCV for many years. Secretary General Jesús Faría praised the strategy before the May elections: "We are in magnificent condition . . . the allied left will obtain a significant vote in important districts" (*El Nacional*, 11 May). Less than a month later, Deputy Radamés Larrazábal referred to such predictions as an "illusory expectation of miracles, a rare phenomenon in politics . . . the left must learn to work in revolutionary fashion, without whining or fainting" (ibid., 5 June). Larrazábal will apparently challenge Faría's 30-year leadership at the Seventh National Congress in May 1985. According to a statement released by a Committee for Internal Democracy, Faría's recent replacement of JC directors for "violation of the party line" was a move to block the challenge. With support from Lino Pérez, Faría named Deputy Pedro Ortega Díaz and Simón Rodríguez as caretakers of the JC prior to the congress (ibid., 11 December).

The small, PCV-dominated CUTV has gained some publicity by presenting itself as a combative organization in contrast to the major Confederation of Venezuelan Workers (CTV), which has become almost a branch of the AD government. A CUTV-sponsored "labor unity encounter" in September attracted the two other small labor confederations as well as COPEI and MEP directors from the CTV. AD labor leaders linked the meeting to a "resurgence of subversive activity" and said the attendance of a few "useful idiots" in no way compromised the CTV, which represents 90 percent of organized labor" (ibid., 25 September). Through its symbiotic relationship with the government, the CTV has obtained some cushions to offset the effect of austerity measures on workers, chiefly a CTV-sponsored bill on costs, prices, and wages. The CUTV was not satisfied and drafted its own compensation legislation. Permission for a march planned in conjunction with presentation of the bill was denied by Caracas authorities. Despite ideological differences, the AD labor bureau offered a small dinner honoring veteran labor leader Cruz Villegas, honorary president of the CUTV.

Together with all the leftist parties, the PCV criticizes the "disastrous social impact" of the economic adjustments required for refinancing of the foreign debt, the International Monetary Fund–inspired measures that benefit only the "monopolistic bourgeoisie and their political instruments, COPEI and AD" (ibid., 6 August; *FBIS*, 16 August). Larrazábal has no faith in the promised economic recovery because the 1985 budget—already "potentially destabilized" by the unpredictability of the petroleum market—reserves the greatest funds for unproductive spending and debt service, not to investment (*El Nacional*, 28 November). Praising the tentative steps of the Cartagena Group toward international cooperation on the debt issue, the PCV states that "all the continent's contradictions with U.S. imperialism are concentrated in the foreign debt problem. The position of the working class calls for the unification into one powerful stream of all the social strata that have been hit by the crisis." (*Tribuna Popular*, 26 June; *IB*, October.)

Jesús Faría headed a PCV delegation to Havana but did not speak with Fidel Castro. The two parties agreed only that "current U.S. policy endangers the region and international peace" (AFP, 3 October; *FBIS*, 15 October). On the "Day of Solidarity with Nicaragua" decreed by the World Peace Council, the PCV delivered a document to the Venezuelan Foreign Ministry demanding even greater government support for the Contadora peace plan, which, the PCV charged, was being "obstructed by the U.S. government" (*El Nacional*, 15 November). Faría praised President Jaime Lusinchi's courage in telling President Reagan that "the solution in Central America is not military" (ibid., 6 December). In the same vein, the PCV protested Venezuelan participation in U.S.-sponsored military maneuvers in the Caribbean, as well as the courtesy visit to Venezuela of the U.S. aircraft carrier *America*.

Eduardo Gallegos Mancera lamented the death of Indira Gandhi as a grave loss to India and the Nonaligned movement, adding, "There is no doubt that the CIA was behind the assassination" (ibid., 1 November). The Chamber of Deputies approved a PCV-proposed letter of condolence to the Soviet embassy on the death of Yuri Andropov (ibid., 17 February).

Movement to Socialism. The PCV's lack of internal democracy and intolerance of dissident opinion were major causes of the massive desertions it suffered in 1970. The dissident leaders founded the MAS in January 1971. Thirteen years later, the same leaders still control the party. In turn, Teodoro Petkoff, Pompeyo Márquez, Freddy

Muñoz, Germán Lairet, Eleazar Díaz Rangel, and other MAS leaders are considered intolerant Stalinists by many of the social democrats who abandoned the MAS this year (ibid., 25 and 27 January; 12 and 20 March). (Just to confuse matters, one small group resigned to protest the party's takeover by the social democrats.)

During the 1983 presidential campaign, polls predicted a 14 percent vote for MAS candidate Petkoff. Returns of less than half that led to a period of agonizing self-criticism that will continue through the Sixth National Convention in 1985. The two major problems that have emerged are the lack of democratic channels referred to above and the party's ideological ambiguity. In February, the entire 45-member National Directorate, including Secretary General Pompeyo Márquez and President Petkoff, was replaced by three committees: political; reorganization and convention; and a municipal electoral command. The changes may be purely cosmetic, as some critics claim, but they will remain in place throughout the convention, which will have two parts. January sessions will be devoted to revising the political platform, and the February session to electing new leaders.

The issue of ideological ambiguity refers not so much to MAS theory, which is fairly clear and democratic enough. Petkoff, for example, recognizes the limits of Marxism and places the party somewhere between the "communist left . . . the sociopolitical bloc that revolves around the Soviet Union in one way or another" and the so-called social democracy of AD, which has "carried out a savage, monopolistic capitalist development." He does not agree with his former Teodorista followers who would remove any mention of socialism from the program. (*Bohemia*, 16–22 January; *JPRS*, 29 February.) The heaviest criticism has focused rather on muddled MAS practices: membership in the Left Coordinator for two years, with the PCV and other Marxist-Leninist groups; electoral alliance in 1983 with the MIR; participation with the PCV in university elections; and undemocratic treatment of MAS minorities.

The old guard, or "apparatus," supports the candidacy of Freddy Muñoz for secretary general. In November, the Emergent Force tendency officially presented its candidate, Juvencio Pulgar, chief of the MAS fraction in congress. Pulgar said, "The movement should continue as a socialist party with clear democratic content" (*El Nacional*, 29 November). Pulgar has strong support from the MAS Youth, which is still an important force in the uni-

versities. A new Movement of Labor Union Opinion will present its own, strictly labor slates in the National Convention elections. The group is headed by Jesús Urbieta, MAS representative on the Executive Committee of the CTV.

United Left. The parties of the UI hoped—in vain—that the expected large abstention in the municipal elections (more than 50 percent, compared with 27 percent in 1979) would somehow favor them. Otherwise, the effort was aptly described by the LS as a bureaucratic pact: funds could be stretched, and promising candidates placed more effectively. Aside from the PCV, the parties involved are engaged in self-criticism similar to that of the MAS, if less dramatic.

The Revolutionary Left Movement. After a debilitating split in 1980, the Moisés Moleiro faction won the legal right to the MIR name because the court judged that it better represented the party's Marxist-Leninist position. MIR president Héctor Pérez Marcano started a polemic this year by suggesting the MIR drop that dogma and "open a way toward the construction of a revolutionary theory deeply rooted in Venezuelan reality, oriented toward achievement of an authentic social democracy" (ibid., 11 December). Deputies Macario González and Eduardo Semtei went further, proposing that the old leaders be scrapped along with the old ideology (ibid., 7 December). The MIR began as an AD splinter in 1960, engaged in guerrilla warfare for most of the decade, and made a very respectable comeback with the presidential campaign of Américo Martín in 1978. Martín's option for democratic socialism caused the split noted above, and his departure was a real loss to the party.

Moisés Moleiro intends to resign as secretary general of the MIR, believing that the post should rotate among all leaders, that it should be regarded neither as a lifetime post nor as the all-powerful body within political parties (*Bohemia*, 20–26 February; *JPRS*, 9 April). MIR leaders are also seriously considering the MEP proposal for a fusion of the two parties. Decisions on these issues will be reached at the National Conference in April 1985.

The People's Electoral Movement. Unlike the MAS and MIR, which are moving away from their revolutionary beginnings, the MEP has moved steadily to the left in the seventeen years since its nonideological split from the AD. It has followed the trend of the other parties, however, in changing its leadership. Jesús Angel Paz Galarraga, secretary general since the party was founded, announced his decision to resign early this year. At the party's December National Assembly, he was succeeded by acting secretary general Adelso González Urdaneta. It was González who first publicly discussed the subject of a MEP fusion with other parties of the left: "We have agreed to explore the degrees of proximity with other left forces in the understanding that this is a process that cannot be decreed from above nor imposed artificially... The objective is to facilitate and intensify leftist integration in view of the existing archipelago of parties." (*El Nacional*, 23 January.)

A MEP-COPEI pact is being planned to wrest control of the important Federation of Petroleum Workers (Fedepetrol) from the AD. None of the three parties won a majority in recent Fedepetrol elections, but the AD's plurality was largest. If the MEP-COPEI pact is carried through, the AD threatens to effect changes in the pluralistic structure of the CTV Executive Committee. The MEP has two seats on the committee. The CTV National Congress will probably be convened in April 1985. As of October, the AD had elected 553 delegates; COPEI, 198; MEP, 37; and MAS, 6. (Ibid., 2 October, 10–13 December.)

New Alternative. A fusion of Guillermo García Ponce's old United Vanguard (VUC) and the Américo Martín faction of the MIR, NA joined the rest of the left in the "to be or not to be Marxist" debate. García Ponce condemned both "left-wing extravagance and right-wing opportunism" (ibid., 9 February). Américo Martín defended his social-democratic theories for a short time but then opted out of the NA and all organized politics (*El Universal*, 10 February). He has formed a left-wing think tank that is working on social and economic development projects (*El Nacional*, 15 October).

Guerrillas. Troops were alerted frequently throughout 1984 along several stretches of the border with Colombia. The Colombian National Liberation Army (Ejército de Liberación Nacional; ELN) has made no more overt attacks across the border like that at Cutufí in 1983 (see *YICA*, 1984,

p. 181), but its clashes with the Colombian army are close enough to cause considerable nervousness. The Venezuelan and Colombian armies are also integrating border operations to better control narcotics traffic, cattle rustling, and ELN kidnapping of Venezuelan ranchers, who are held for ransom in Colombia. The kidnappings seem to be the work of the ELN alone, but ranchers on both sides of the border attributed the cattle rustling—30,000 head in five months—to both the ELN and the Venezuelan Red Flag group (BR) (ibid., 22 October). The Venezuelan interior minister denied opposition reports of BR links with Colombian and Peruvian guerrillas, admitting only "occasional contacts perhaps but no permanent and systematic connections" (ibid., 14 November). Colombian authorities have no doubt about guerrilla involvement with narcotics traffic, and Venezuelans may learn more about it if Lizardo Márquez Pérez is extradited. King of the Venezuelan cocaine connection, Márquez was arrested in Miami in October, but identified only in December (*Diario las Américas*, 20 December). Interestingly, Márquez was perhaps the first Venezuelan rancher kidnapped by Colombian guerrillas (1978); he was apparently not involved with narcotics at the time.

Much of the violence at the Central University in 1984 was provoked by police stupidity: asked in September to stop students from Maracay who had commandeered three buses to mount a protest in Caracas, they opened fire on the buses, wounding seventeen students. This had been preceded by a number of violent demonstrations, usually by a large group of students who had not been admitted to the university. In other cities, students burned buses to protest transportation hikes. The 23 de Enero public housing project and the schools nearby again became the scene of major battles between police and "masked agitators" (*encapuchados*). In all these cases, police reports were vague, sometimes referring to arrests of "subversives" or "ex-guerrillas," but most observers attributed the worst of the violence—shooting and explosives—to the BR and the CLP, an Albanian-line group that has reportedly disbanded.

Carole Merten
Miami, Florida

ASIA AND THE PACIFIC

Introduction

Communist activity in Asia and the Pacific region showed patterns similar to those of the recent past: Soviet military power in Afghanistan continued to support the communist People's Democratic Party (PDPA) in its attempt to extend its hegemony over the country; the Vietnamese Communist Party continued its efforts to build socialism in Vietnam, tighten its "special relations" with communist Laos, and extend its control over Kampuchea.

But communist activity in the Republic of the Philippines rapidly mushroomed as the party's New People's Army increased its military activities to control perhaps as much as 20 percent of the countryside's population in Mindanao and even more remote island areas.

Elsewhere in the region communist activities merely replicated those of recent years with minor variations that can be highlighted by classifying communist activity as follows: states with ruling communist parties, states with legal communist parties in opposition, and states with banned communist parties.

States with Ruling Communist Parties. As the war in Afghanistan enters its sixth year, the half-dozen major Mujahedeen groups have become increasingly unified. They are learning to use new weapons, including small ground-to-ground rockets. Even though Soviet forces carpet-bomb villages and assault the valleys with helicopter-borne troops, there are strong Mujahedeen bases less than ten miles from Kabul. Since the Soviet invasion and its reliance on the tactics of "migratory genocide," between 250,000 and 1 million people have died, more than 2.5 million others live as refugees in Pakistan, and another 1.5 million exist under similar conditions in Iran. But the Soviet Union appears dedicated to putting the PDPA regime in power, and it made a special effort to commemorate the twentieth anniversary of Afghanistan's communist party on 18 December (Moscow international service, 18 December).

In Communist China the Central Committee of the Chinese Communist Party (CCP) announced on 20 October its intention to press forward with urban economic reforms. Proclaiming the new "responsibility system" in the countryside an enormous success, the CCP pledged to carry reform into the cities. Toward that end, party cadres will be instructed to develop new "guidance" planning, make more effective use of price and tax levers, remove the government from management, and raise technological and managerial standards in all urban enterprises (*Beijing Review*, 29 October). Sino-Soviet talks were held 21–23 December, and the two sides concluded an economic agreement that will increase the volume of trade to around $6 billion over the next five years and provide new Soviet investment, technology, and economic advisers (*NYT*, 30 December). Deng Xiaoping and Margaret Thatcher signed a treaty on 21 December that will return Hong Kong to China in 1997 under the principle of "one country–two systems."

In North Korea Pyongyang announced a joint venture law on 8 September that signaled a major shift away from isolation to a new open-door economic policy. In the fall, the regime also expressed to South Korea its desire for economic cooperation and new discussions. Although the first round of talks were interrupted by the defection of a Soviet student at Panmunjom and again discontinued because of joint

South Korean and American military maneuvers in January 1985, the communist regime has made clear it wants further negotiations with South Korea. Kim Il-song reportedly visited Beijing 26–28 November to confer with Chinese leaders about Soviet requests for joint military exercises with North Korea and for military use of the ports of Wonsan and Chongjin in exchange for supplying MiG-23s, other weapons, and economic aid (*Seoul Sinmun*, 9 December). Kim Il-song also told visiting Japanese Diet members in early November that he had rejected a Soviet offer to deploy SS-20 medium-range nuclear missiles in North Korea.

September marked the fortieth anniversary of Ho Chi Minh's proclamation of Vietnam's independence from France. Vietnam has 160,000 troops occupying Kampuchea and in December launched an offensive against guerrilla bases along the Thai border. The Vietnam leadership underwent no change in 1984, and it still remains committed to extending collectivist control over Vietnam's economy and to integrating the communist party more deeply into routine economic affairs, especially agriculture. Toward this end the Vietnamese Communist Party aims to make the district the basic control unit for political indoctrination and control over villages, eventually transforming villages into farm-factory towns.

States with Legal Communist Party Opposition.   In the six states where communist parties are legal and in opposition, little had changed in party efforts to work through front organizations to criticize and destabilize the political regimes under which they enjoy the right of protest and criticism. But party factionalism existed.

In Australia the Socialist Party of Australia (SPA), a pro-Soviet communist party, had expelled party secretary and Building Workers Industrial Union leader Pat Clancy and other union leaders in 1983. This action undoubtedly cost the SPA considerable influence in the 47,000-member union. In New Zealand various communist party splinter groups in 1984 temporarily unified their efforts to help defeat the National Party and strongly supported the union-affiliated Labor Party at the polls.

In India the communist party endorsed the Gandhi government's "anti-imperialist" foreign policy yet attacked Gandhi's domestic policies by forging a "left and democratic" alternative at the polls. But that party stopped short of supporting right-wing opposition groups such as the Hindu revivalist Bharatiya Janata Party.

States with Banned Communist Parties.   Eight states in Asia and the Pacific currently ban communist parties. In 1984 the picture was very mixed. In Thailand a government official announced in October that the Communist Party of Thailand no longer posed an armed threat to the country. This announcement came after numerous defections of leading and middle-echelon cadres over the preceding eighteen months. Thai police also launched a series of effective raids that netted several Central Committee members in Bangkok, including Pirun Chatwanichkul and his wife, leading intellectuals in the party. But a new development in Thailand could pose a real threat to the government. A pro-Soviet Thai People's Revolutionary Movement now worries authorities. Formed in 1978 by a faction of the pro-Beijing party, this group has turned to Vietnam and the Soviet Union for support. This new movement, which refers to itself as the Pak Mai or New Party, perceives Thailand as a neocolony dominated by monopoly capitalists and feudalists. The Pak Mai looks to the rural population for its mass base, but places industrial workers in the vanguard of a front movement and calls for co-opting of students, intellectuals, and even Buddhist monks to support its cause (*FEER*, 6 December).

In Malaysia, Indonesia, Singapore, and Burma, the various communist parties have long been forced underground and do little more than circulate propaganda criticizing the respective governments.

But in the Philippines events took a dramatic turn in 1984 toward an upsurge of communist military activity. During the March elections more than 60 government troops were killed in ambushes set by the New People's Army (NPA), the armed wing of the Communist Party of the Philippines (CPP). During the year the NPA increasingly stepped up its military attacks, often to company strength. Army officers in Manila now claim that the NPA has embarked upon a strategy of "encircling the cities" and of expanding its activities on many fronts to stretch the government's military forces (ibid., 28 June). Some 2,000 civilians and military personnel were killed in NPA attacks (*NYT*, 10 January 1985). A key reason for the rapid growth of the communist insurgency is the public perception that the rebels offer justice, which the government troops do not (*New York Times Magazine*, 6 January 1985).

Soviet Activity in the Region. Soviet military and economic aid to Vietnam continued at the same rate as in the recent past. Soviet military offers of SS-20 missiles to North Korea clearly indicate a new thrust in Soviet military expansion. Meanwhile, the Soviet Union continues to negotiate with the People's Republic of China in an attempt to woo that communist power away from strengthening ties with Japan, the United States, and Western Europe.

Ramon H. Myers
Hoover Institution

Afghanistan

Population. Unknown; estimated 13–14 million (no census ever taken; refugee flow plus wartime casualties since the Soviet invasion have reduced significantly a population that in 1978 was thought to total 15–17 million) (*San Francisco Chronicle*, 30 December).

Party. People's Democratic Party of Afghanistan (Jamiyat-e-Demokrati Khalq-e-Afghanistan, literally Democratic Party of the Afghanistan Masses; PDPA). The party's two wings, Parcham (Banner) and Khalq (Masses), remain locked in fierce rivalry.

Founded. 1965

Membership. Officially more than 120,000 members and candidate members (*Kabul New Times* [*KNT*], 8 November; *Pravda*, 11 January 1985). In previous years, candidate members comprised about half the claimed total, a ratio that presumably remains unchanged. The number of claimed members is unquestionably inflated; one journalist put the figure at the end of 1983 at 50,000–80,000, of whom less than 15 percent were thought to be convinced Communists (*CSM*, 29 December 1983). In previous years Western estimates ranged from a half to an eighth the figures claimed by the party.

Secretary General. Babrak Karmal

Politburo. 9 members: Babrak Karmal, Sultan Ali Keshtmand (prime minister of the Democratic Republic of Afghanistan [DRA]), Dr. Najibullah (chief of the State Intelligence Service [KhAD]), Nur Ahmad Nur (Revolutionary Council Presidium member), Ghulam Dastigir Panjsheri, Maj. Gen. Mohammed Rafi (deputy prime minister), Dr. Anahita Ratebzad (Presidium member and head of the Peace, Solidarity, and Friendship Society and of the Democratic Women's Organization of Afghanistan [DWOA]), Lt. Col. Mohammed Aslam Watanjar (minister of communications), Dr. Saleh Mohammed Zeary (Presidium member and head of the National Fatherland Front); 4 alternate members: Mahmoud Baryalai (a leading party theoretician and half-brother of Babrak), Mohammed Ismail Danesh (minister of mines and industries), Abdul Zaher Razmjo (secretary, Kabul city committee), Gen. Abdul Qader (until December 1984 minister of defense and then first deputy prime minister)

Secretariat. 7 members: Babrak Karmal, Mamoud Baryalai, Dr. Niaz Mohammed Mohmand, Nur Ahmad Nur, Dr. Saleh Mohammed Zeary, Gen. Mohammed Yaseen Sadeqi (army chief of political affairs), Mir Saheb Karwal (administrator of Central Zone). (Of those listed above, only Danesh, Watanjar, and Zeary are believed to have been associated with the Khalq faction at one time or another, and none of the three is known to have taken part in the traditional heavy infighting with Parchamis; all other Secretariat and Politburo members and alternates are known or assumed to have been associated with Parcham. The present status of Nur, however, is not entirely certain [see below].)

Central Committee. As of 1983, 52 identified full members, 27 identified alternates (*YICA*, 1984, p. 186; *KNT*, 3 July 1983); there were no known appointments or dismissals in 1984. These figures may be high because the Afghan official press never reports assassinations of party members by the resistance. Thus, it is unknown how many newly reported members may just be replacements for the fallen.

Status. Ruling party

Last Congress. First, 1 January 1965, in Kabul; National Conference, 14–15 March 1982

Last Election. None ever held

Auxiliary Organizations. National Fatherland Front (NFF) (claims 55,000–650,000 members) (*KNT*, 25 April, 6 July), Saleh Mohammed Zeary, chairman; Central Council of Trade Unions (claims 170,000 members) (ibid., 8 September), Abdus Sattar Purdeli, president; Democratic Youth Organization of Afghanistan (DYOA; claims 120,000 members) (ibid.), Farid Mazdak, first secretary (ibid., 11 September); Peace, Solidarity, and Friendship Organization, Dr. Anahita Ratebzad, chair; Democratic Women's Organization of Afghanistan (DWOA; claims 25,000 members), Dr. Anahita Ratebzad, chair (ibid., 31 October); Pioneers (claims 85,000 members) (ibid., 29 October); Council of Religious Scholars and Clergy; Council of Tribal Elders; Economic Advisory Council; peasants cooperatives; "groups for the defense of the revolution." In all, "more than 15 social organizations [participate] in all revolutionary transformations" (ibid., 1 September). Like the statistics on party membership, the front figures are suspect, and they vary markedly, as illustrated by the disparate claims for the NFF. Where there are discrepancies, the lower figures can be taken as closer to the truth.

Publications. *Haqiqat-e-Enqelabe Saur* (The Saur Revolution's truth), Central Committee daily organ; *Haqiqat-e-Sarbaz* (The soldier's truth); *Dehqan* (Peasant); *Darafsh-e Diavanan* (The banner of youth), a daily in Pushtu and Dari; *Kar* (Labor); *Kabul New Times*, English-language daily; *Storai* (Story), DYOA monthly; *Peshahang* (Pioneer), Pioneer monthly. The DRA claims to have eleven national newspapers and periodicals, eighteen provincial newspapers of the party, and 42 periodicals "which cater to a diversity of audiences" (*WMR*, January). The official news agency is Bakhtar.

In 1967, two years after its founding, the PDPA split into opposing Parcham and Khalq wings. Both kept the PDPA name and both were loyal to Moscow, but each maintained a separate organization and recruitment program. Khalq, led by Nur Mohammed Taraki, the PDPA's founder, depended for support on the relatively poor rural intelligentsia and recruited almost solely among the Pushtuns, the dominant (55 percent) Afghan ethnic group. Parcham, less numerous but more broadly representative ethnically, was urban oriented and appealed to a wealthier group of educated Afghans. It was led by Babrak Karmal, son of an Afghan general. Both groups focused their initial recruitment efforts on intellectuals, media employees, and especially teachers. When Mohammed Daoud overthrew the Afghan monarchy in 1973, the Parchamis at first collaborated with him, but the Khalqis remained in opposition and began an intensive clandestine recruitment effort among the military in preparation for the PDPA coup that was to follow five years later.

Under Soviet pressure, Parcham and Khalq formally reunited in mid-1977, and their combined strength was enough to overthrow Daoud and inaugurate the DRA in April 1978. They almost immediately fissioned again, however, with Taraki sending the most prominent Parchamis into diplomatic exile as ambassadors and jailing or demoting most of those who remained in Afghanistan. When a Parchami plot to unseat Taraki was discovered in the summer of 1978, the ambassadors were recalled but disobeyed the order and fled into exile in Eastern Europe.

Meanwhile, popular resistance to Khalq's rigorous Marxist-Leninist rule grew rapidly and soon threatened to topple the new regime in spite of massive Soviet military aid. In September 1979, the Soviets attempted to force another artificial reconciliation between Parcham and Khalq, but their plan to place all the blame for the schism on Taraki's deputy, Hafizullah Amin, backfired when Amin himself seized power and murdered Taraki. Amin, however, could not pacify his rebellious people, and on 27 December 1979, Soviet troops invaded, shot Amin, and restored the Parchamis to power. Babrak (he affects the surname Karmal, "friend of labor" or "Kremlin," for political purposes) became the new leader and tried to heal the breach with the Khalqis on the one side and the Afghan population on the other. In neither effort was he successful, and the regime maintained a tenuous hold on power only in a few main Afghan towns during daylight hours, thanks to a Soviet presence that slowly swelled from 85,000 combat troops in 1980 to about 115,000–120,000 by the end of 1984 (*CSM*, 27 December).

Since the Soviet invasion, the PDPA technically has not been a communist or even a "socialist" (in the Soviet lexicon) party but the ruling—and only permissible—party in a country undergoing the "national democratic stage of revolution." Unlike the avowedly socialist PDPA ideologues of 1978–1979, party spokesmen since the invasion have gone through contortions to avoid using the terms "socialist" and "socialism" in referring to Afghanistan. Socialism has not even been held out as an eventual goal to domestic audiences. In late 1984 party theoretician Baryalai finally admitted to a Polish journalist that socialism was the PDPA's ultimate goal, but his comments were not replayed in the Afghan media (*Trybuna ludu*, Warsaw, 26 September; *FBIS*, 4 October). Nevertheless, the total dedication and subservience of the PDPA to Moscow's interpretation of Marxism-Leninism is unmistakable, and its belief in such principles as "proletarian internationalism" and "democratic centralism" show that the party is communist in all but name.

Party Developments. Although the PDPA and DRA continued to avoid socialist labels in 1984, they appeared to be cautiously laying the groundwork for eventual open incorporation into the socialist camp. An article hailing the sixty-third anniversary of the Mongolian People's Republic probably indicated the route that PDPA—and Soviet—theoreticians foresaw for Afghanistan. Noting that the "democratic stage of revolution" in Mongolia had lasted from 1921 to 1940, the article ascribed to this era the accomplishment of the following preconditions for socialism: "abolition of feudal serfdom; end of foreign capital and dependence on foreign capital; strengthened people's democratic order and state sovereignty; establishment of the foundations of a non-capitalist economy; abolition of feudalists and monks; establishment of dictatorship of the working class." After 1940 there ensued a "socialist development" stage that covered political as well as economic institutions and lasted to the 1960s, after which the country embarked on a new stage whose goal was the "completion of the building up of socialism." (*KNT*, 11 July.) Although the DRA already boasted of having accomplished many of the "democratic" stage's requirements and appeared to be pushing for completion of the rest, PDPA officials remained circumspect about predicting eventual socialism for Afghanistan. They ascribed the country's current difficulties in coping with "domestic and foreign counter-revolution" to the pre-invasion regime's mistake of "skipping over the stages of the revolution" (ibid., 6 November). A Soviet theoretician listed one of that regime's cardinal errors as voicing "rash slogans [that] the government's aim was to establish a socialist society" and thus frightening off indispensable supporters (ibid., 27 November).

Leadership and Party Organization. If there were any fundamental PDPA leadership changes during 1984, the party did not acknowledge them. Nur Ahmad Nur left abruptly with his family for Moscow on 18 January amid rumors that he had tried to overthrow Babrak or, alternatively, had been caught by the secret police in an attempt to defect to India (*Pakistan Times*, 2 February; *Afghanistan Forum*, March). His name was not noted in Afghan media during the balance of 1984, and his fate was unknown. A group picture of PDPA and DRA leaders published in May did not seem to include him (*KNT*, 2 May). The regime was less reticent about shifts within the DRA administration: Air Force commander Lt. Gen. Nazar Mohammed was made chief of staff in January, replacing the retiring Baba Jan, and was then promoted to minister of defense when Lt. Gen. Abdul Qader was dismissed from this post in December (U.K. Foreign and Commonwealth Office, *Background Brief*, July; *NYT*, 4 December). These and other shifts of ranking military officers were ascribed to the inability of Afghan troops to deal with the resistance. A new Ministry of Light Industry and Foodstuffs was established, and Engineer Mohammed Aziz was appointed minister (Bakhtar, 23 March; *FBIS*, 26 March). Finance Minister Abdul Wakil was quietly dropped from his post during the summer and dispatched as ambassador to Vietnam; he was replaced by Mohammed Kabir (Bakhtar, 7 July; *FBIS*, 10 July; *KNT*, 4 August).

The party organization also remained unchanged, although the number of units appears to have increased overall. With a reported membership growth from 90,000 in 1983 to 120,000 in 1984, there was an expansion of primary party cells from "over 2,000" in 1983 to "about 3,000" in 1984.

At the same time, however, city and superdistrict party committees fell from 70 to 61 units, whereas district and subdistrict committees increased from 114 to 207. (*KNT*, 24 April 1983, 5 May.) Given the total number of cities and superdistricts (89) and of districts and subdistricts (285) reported for the DRA in February, this would indicate party representation among them of only 72 percent overall and only 68 percent in the larger units (Radio Kabul, 12 February; *FBIS*, 17 February). There is also the suspicion that some of the alleged party committees may have been merely paper organizations; resistance control of the countryside would seem to preclude any significant rural strength. Such a conclusion is supported by Babrak's complaint in October that in Jauzjan province (a district he had singled out for praise for its party work the week before) 82 percent of the party cadres were concentrated in Shebarghan city; presumably other provinces have even higher concentrations in their relatively secure capitals. In the same speech Babrak called for a better quality of cadres and candidly observed that the necessary establishment of party cells in the villages required "bravery." (*KNT*, 2 October.)

Such complaints about the quality of the party's rank and file were not uncommon. As before, members of the armed forces, peasants, and workers required only six months' candidacy before becoming eligible for full membership, whereas others required a year. Fifty percent of the members were under 30 years old, 16.9 percent were workers, and 33.3 percent were peasants and artisans. (*Pravda*, 8 July; *FBIS*, 19 July.) It is somewhat suspicious that these percentages reflect exactly the percentages of the social origin of *new* party members reported in 1983 (*YICA*, 1984, p. 187). In 1984, 60 percent of the members were on duty with the army, the police security service (Sarandoy), or the State Information (secret intelligence) Service (KhAD). In turn, 60 percent of those three services were supposed to be party members (*KNT*, 5 May). Complaints about the low number of army officers who enlisted in the party (ibid., 7 July 1983) may indicate that the percentage of membership in the other security services was near 100. The relative weight of the two factions in the party was estimated at 40 percent Parcham and 60 percent Khalq, a continuing improvement in relative Parchami strength that in 1982 was believed to be roughly one-quarter the total and in 1983 one-third (*YICA*, 1983, p. 139; U.S. Department of State, *Afghani-stan: Five Years of Occupation*, Special Report no. 120, Washington, D.C., December).

The Parcham/Khalq feud remained a priority party concern throughout the year. There were repeated calls in official media for "iron discipline" and "consolidation of unity," indicating the continued inability of party leaders to cope with the problem. Babrak himself voiced the frankest official recognition of the dispute when he lectured officers of Sarandoy (a Khalqi stronghold) that "fist and sword do not have a place in the party . . . The equipment and military means given to you are not to be used in the party." (Radio Kabul, 11 October; *FBIS*, 15 October; *KNT*, 14 April.) Meanwhile, reports reaching the West contained mounting evidence that the casualties suffered among PDPA officials were only partly ascribable to the resistance; many of them resulted from the ongoing intraparty rivalry (*Washington Times*, 27 June; Radio Karachi, 7 October; *FBIS*, 10 October). During the summer, there were unconfirmed but persistent rumors that Babrak himself and his minister of communications, Watanjar, had both been wounded in an exchange of gunfire with then–Minister of Defense Qader, following an altercation between the two ministers in the Politburo. Babrak's extended trip to the USSR that followed immediately after the reported shooting did nothing to dispel such speculation, especially when his stay of "about a week" for "a general medical examination" stretched into nearly four weeks. (AFP, 17 July; *FBIS*, 17 July.) Interestingly, the Soviet press interpreted the Afghan calls for unity as pertaining to the various ethnic groups in the country, avoiding all reference to the party split (*Pravda*, 8 April).

Domestic Affairs. If a major weakness of the party lay in its continued internal disunity, an even greater menace threatened from without—the increasingly effective military activities and growing confidence of the resistance. During 1983, there had been a marked increase in urban operations, and this trend continued in 1984. Whereas in previous years major cities—especially Kabul—had been considered relatively safe at least by day, security for PDPA officials and their Soviet mentors now became uncertain at all times. A senior Soviet officer, probably military attaché Krakhmanov, was reported assassinated when getting out of his car in broad daylight on 18 January in Kabul, and killings of PDPA officials continued throughout the year (AFP, Hong Kong, 24 January; *FBIS*, 24 January;

NYT, 28 March). On 24 and 26 September, coordinated large-scale resistance attacks in and around Kabul killed some one hundred Afghan and Soviet soldiers and required tank reinforcements from outside the city to put down (*Times*, London, 3 October). As the year wore on, rocket and mortar attacks against Soviet and DRA targets in Kabul became more common (*NYT*, 5 November). Babrak roundly criticized Sarandoy (and by implication its Khalqi chief, Sayed Mohammed Gulabzoy) in a speech to the Politburo in November, urging "new tactics for dynamic fighting" and threatening the creation of a "new type of Sarandoy" (Radio Kabul, 24 November; *FBIS*, 26 November).

Regional centers were also unsafe. On the anniversary of the Saur (April) Revolution, parades in Ghazni and Charikar came under resistance attacks, and participants suffered heavy casualties. In Herat and Kandahar, no attempt was even made to hold parades. (*Background Brief*, July.) The governor of Kandahar province, who lived under Soviet protection at the Kandahar city airport, was unable to travel into town even in an armored personnel carrier; his rare visits were accomplished only by helicopter (Department of State, *Afghanistan*, no. 120, December).

The growing cooperation of the various resistance groups was an important factor in the success of their operations. In anticipation of the large-scale Soviet and Afghan army attack on the Panjshir Valley in April, the Panjshir leader, Ahmad Shah Massoud, was able to rally a number of disparate guerrilla groups to attack Soviet supply convoys coming over the Salang Pass, forcing a delay in the attack and requiring the Soviets to bring in their fuel supplies for the attack by air (*Times*, London, 2 June). In August, a well-planned resistance maneuver saw an entire Afghan tribe that had been entrusted with guarding the electric pylons leading into Kabul defect safely to Pakistan. Behind them, the *mujahideen* (holy warriors), who had been in touch with tribal leaders for months, blew up 150 of the pylons and left the capital dependent on two Soviet diesel generators for 80 percent of its power. (Ibid., 31 August.) Meanwhile, resistance groups were also organizing areas under their control economically and politically, as well as militarily. Schools, mosques, tax collection, a court system, and a functioning local government were set up in the Panjshir, for example, and in Parwan province mujahideen engineers took over maintenance, power distribution, and revenue collection for the

second-largest electric power station in the country. (*CSM*, 2 October; *Pakistan Times*, 3 January.) By contrast, the PDPA and DRA appeared to be ever less able to control the restive population.

The Thirteenth Plenum of the PDPA, held on 29 February, reflected the growing PDPA insecurity. Whereas the Twelfth Plenum (and most before it) had given top priority to the futile search for party unity, at the Thirteenth Babrak identified "the fight against armed counter-revolution" as "the main and determining factor of our life on which everything depends." Identifying party unity and party discipline as necessary preconditions for victory, Babrak said the PDPA would be purged of anyone who opposed these ideals. (*IB*, May.) Somewhat unwisely, in April he told party members from the various security services that this was the "decisive year" for defeating the counterrevolution and for achieving party unity, "without which the revolution will never succeed" (*Background Brief*, July). At year's end, however, defeat of the resistance and party unity appeared to be as unattainable as ever.

Attempts to transform the rhetoric into practice had met with spotty success at best. On 8 March, immediately after the Thirteenth Plenum, a new military service law extended the standard tour of duty from three to four years. Desertions promptly skyrocketed, and there was a mutiny in Kabul's 8th Division that had to be put down by tanks from other units. (BBC, 13 March; *FBIS*, 14 March; *WP*, 13 May.) The government then resorted to drafting PDPA members, a group that formerly had been exempt from military service (*NYT*, 1 April). In so doing, it probably removed one of the prime incentives for joining the party, thus cutting into another priority PDPA objective, the attraction of new members. In April, during the Soviet attack on the Panjshir Valley, some 400 of the 2,000 Afghan troops involved deserted on their way to the front (ibid., 2 May). In October, the regime modified its law on military duty, permitting those who had served in combat units to be discharged after three years. Those in support units, however, were still obliged to remain for four years. (Radio Kabul, 25 October; *FBIS*, 26 October.)

Exhortations by Babrak and others to improve the work of the security services also failed. Resistance leader Massoud found it "extraordinary" that neither the Soviets nor KhAD had any information on his plans for tactical retreat in the Panjshir during the Soviet spring offensive, whereas Massoud himself was fully informed on details of the offensive well before it occurred (*CSM*, 2 October). The rivalry between the Parchami-dominated KhAD and Khalqi-oriented Sarandoy undoubtedly played a role in the security services' inefficiency.

Attempting to put the best light on its activities, the regime continued a propaganda campaign of several years' standing that embodied a number of fundamental themes: the resistance was being "crushed"; arms were being seized; refugees were returning home from Pakistan; all who qualified were taking advantage of the government's generous amnesty; "deceived compatriots" were surrendering; the revolution was "irreversible"; and finally (all else having seemingly failed) time was on the side of the government (Radio Kabul, 15–17 July; *FBIS*, 18 July; *KNT*, 20 October).

In recognition of the resistance's popularity and in an effort to counteract it, the party late in the year launched a new and massive propaganda campaign to "immortalize the heroic martyrs of the Revolution." New badges and medals were authorized for army regulars and volunteer defense units, all state organs were ordered to publicize the "deeds of martyrs and heroes," and local authorities were told to arrange for mass visits by their citizens to cemeteries where heroes were buried. The issue of commemorative postage stamps, the staging of rallies, the permanent dedication of a fixed number of columns in every newspaper, and a host of other measures to popularize military service were also to be undertaken. (Radio Kabul, 19 November; *FBIS*, 23 November.) Given the average Afghan's view of the government, however, the prospects for this campaign to succeed in rousing enthusiastic support for the party and state were less than assured.

One possible reflection of insecurity could be found in an apparent rebirth of the cult of personality around Babrak. During his protracted absence in Moscow during the summer, there were few references to him in DRA media. On his return, however, there was a clearly discernible pattern of increased press attention to him, culminating at the end of the year in a use of the term "beloved leader" with increasing frequency (Radio Kabul, 24 November; *FBIS*, 26 November).

Since 1981, the regime has been talking of promulgating a law on local organs of state power. On several occasions it has been mentioned as if it were in effect, yet only in 1984 was it listed as having been approved by the Revolutionary Council. At year's end its implementation remained in abeyance. Taken at face value, the law appears to grant local autonomy to communities, an Afghan political tradition. Examined closely, however, it is designed to do just the reverse: all candidates for local office must be nominated by the PDPA-controlled NFF or one of its PDPA-controlled member-groups; the local government's major duties are to carry out Kabul's orders on land and water reform, tax collection, and military conscription; should local governments oppose a DRA order, they can be dissolved by order of the Revolutionary Council Presidium (Radio Kabul, 12 February; *FBIS*, 17 February). In short, the law is designed to ensure Kabul's centralized control over each rural community. The prolonged failure of the government to put the law in effect is doubtless a result of the DRA's inability to control even the capital, much less outlying districts. A necessary prelude to implementing the law is a series of local elections, most recently scheduled for March 1985 (Radio Kabul, 28 September; *FBIS*, 1 October).

The various frustrations of the party and state in dealing with the resistance were probably best illustrated by the order of "the most important tasks" presented at the Fourteenth Plenum, held on 19 September: "the further unity of the patriotic, revolutionary, and democratic forces in the country; coordinating the masses of the people and state power toward crushing the armed counterrevolution; consolidating revolutionary sovereignty [i.e., regaining administrative control over areas lost to the resistance]; maintaining peace and security in the country; accomplishing vital socio-economic and cultural tasks" (Radio Kabul, 22 September; *FBIS*, 4 October).

The low priority of "vital socio-economic and cultural tasks" was only relative. In fact, Afghanistan was beset with extremely serious economic problems as a result of five years' continuous warfare. Although the DRA in 1984 claimed to have reached the production levels of 1978, the measurement was made in units of the local currency (afghanis), which had fallen to a quarter or less of their 1978 value due to inflation. Inflation seemed bound to accelerate in the wake of a 1983 budget that anticipated expenditure of 3.2 billion afghanis and income of only 340 million. (*KNT*, 12 April 1983, 25 August.) Resistance control of the countryside and interception of convoys heading for the cities caused food and energy shortages that led to rationing, hoarding, and speculation (*Times*, London, 30 May).

Regarding agriculture, the PDPA pursued an

ambivalent policy. On the one hand Babrak asserted that the party was not at all opposed to private ownership of land "in the present phase," yet on the other the DRA continued to push hard for a disguised preliminary form of collectivization, the formation of state-run "peasant cooperatives." To induce farmers to join these proto-kolkhozes, the government promised to exempt them from all taxes for four years, from half their taxes for the subsequent six years, from registration fees and transportation taxes and charges, from 50 percent of both import and export duties, and from 25 percent of consumer good import duties. It also promised to give them easy loan terms from the state bank. (*KNT*, 14 July.) A Soviet claim that the Afghans had 236 cooperatives embracing 52,000 peasant holdings as of mid-1983 is suspect (Radio Moscow, 5 October; *FBIS*, 9 October). There were even indications that an old Soviet device for controlling the peasantry in the early stages of collectivization, the machine tractor station, was being revived as a concept for Afghanistan (Radio Kabul, 12 and 29 January; *FBIS*, 13 and 31 January). An agreement for Soviet participation in setting up such stations was signed in 1979, but implementation in four provinces (Kabul, Baghlan, Jowzjan, and Herat) appeared to have taken place only in 1984 (Radio Kabul, 10 December; *FBIS*, 11 December). The regime laid great emphasis on land and water reform, boasting of having distributed 697,567 hectares of land free of charge to 308,210 "landless families" since the 1978 coup (Radio Kabul, 29 November; *FBIS*, 3 December). Oddly, this was about 42,000 families short of the same claim made the previous year (*KNT*, 25 May 1983). Late in the year, Babrak stated that "democratic water and land reforms constitute the most fundamental task of the national and democratic revolution of the DRA" (ibid., 4 November). Nevertheless, whatever land reforms the regime might attempt to undertake, they could have little effect when practical control of the countryside lay in resistance hands. Moreover, as a result of war destruction there was little left to reform; overall agricultural production in 1984 was estimated at less than a quarter the 1978 level (*CSM*, 31 July).

Regarding other economic activity, there was similar ambivalence. Industrial production, never an important factor in the Afghan economy and largely concentrated in the food-processing industry, remained low. Babrak complained to the Fourteenth Plenum that "construction work on most ma-

jor projects has either stopped or is sluggishly proceeding" (Radio Kabul, 21 September; *FBIS*, 24 September). There were contradictory indications that the state was planning to take over distribution activities, thus eliminating private trade. Early in the year Babrak voiced the intention of eventually making the sale of all consumer items a government monopoly and meantime of setting up a system of price controls (*Background Brief*, September). By year's end price controls were still under discussion, but a government consumer goods–trading organization called KART had been set up and was in operation (Radio Kabul, 22 September, 4 October, 15 and 18 November; *FBIS*, 4 October, 19 and 29 November).

On the other hand, there were also signs of official encouragement for the nongovernment business community. Under the headline "Great Importance Attached to Private Sector," the official press pushed for private initiative in the fields of light and medium industry, transportation, and foreign trade, noting that 68 permits involving 1.245 billion afghanis of investment for such activity had been approved in 1983. The article gave other detailed statistics showing the profitability of such enterprises and claimed that control of 40 percent of exports and 59 percent of imports was still in private hands (*KNT*, 29 October). None of this was much comfort to the Afghan bazaar community, which was being squeezed by both the government and the resistance for tangible proofs of its allegiance. These pressures plus the increasing problem of resistance rocket and mortar attacks on Kabul (some of which inadvertently struck the bazaar) contributed to an exodus of small businessmen during the latter part of the year. (*Times*, London, 9 October.) It is not impossible that the disappearance of so many traders prompted the government's voicing of official support for private enterprise; Kabul would have trouble surviving without the stimulus of its colorful bazaars. Paradoxically, a Marxist-Leninist regime seemed to be stepping in to save a bourgeois middle class.

Although one of the regime's major propaganda efforts from the time of the invasion was to convince its citizens that it would respect religion, very few Afghans accepted its protestations. Apparently in recognition of its inability to appear to be anything but atheist, the government removed twenty mullahs in Kabul at year's end (U.S. Department of State, *Afghan Resistance and Soviet Occupation*, Special Report no. 118, December). The fact that the NFF had been charged with setting up secular commissions to regulate the activities of the "patriotic" clergy undoubtedly increased the people's distrust of the regime's religious policies (Radio Kabul, 13 December; *FBIS*, 17 December).

Auxiliary and Front Activities. The National Fatherland Front (NFF), the unifier of all subfronts that have been set up to smooth relations between the PDPA and various segments of the population, appeared to run into serious problems in the course of the year. At the NFF's fourth plenum, held on 7 April, Chairman Zeary spoke confidently of the impending defeat of enemies and the rallying of the people to the DRA standard, but he also said that the NFF's activities did not "match these possibilities" (*Background Brief*, July). Although membership was usually asserted to total over a half million, a 25 April *Kabul New Times* article claimed only 55,000 in "more than 1,000 committees." The same article included a precise figure for DWOA members (19,287) that was far lower and more realistic than the 50,000 more customarily claimed in previous years. The implication was that true figures had somehow found their way by accident into the paper.

In September, Babrak named some typical NFF member organizations for an Indian correspondent and also included some unusual subgroups: tribal representatives, jirgahs, the Afghan Olympic Committee, the Afghan Red Crescent Society, and the Centre for Social Activities of Kabul University (*KNT*, 12 September). In a long article devoted to the NFF in October, there was one column of generalized praise for the organization, but this was followed by two columns of harsh criticism that completely negated the positive preface. The NFF was characterized as aimless; growing too slowly; lacking chapters in many communities; internally uncoordinated; uncooperative with the PDPA and DRA authorities; lacking in "great plans"; weak in training and recruitment; slow in filling vacant leadership posts; poor on pro-Soviet, pro-PDPA, pro-DRA, pro-army, and anti-enemy propaganda; failing in its sociopolitical work; inadequate in its organization of meetings (rarely held on schedule); lacking in control and implementation of resolutions; poor in administration; and generally without order. The article concluded with seven brusque commands from the Politburo designed to correct these failings. (Ibid., 18 October.)

On the occasion of the NFF's fifth plenum, in December, it came in for renewed sharp criticism for its failure to establish councils in Wardak and Paktika provinces (Radio Kabul, 13 December; *FBIS*, 17 December). The intended key role of the NFF in administering the nomination machinery for local organs must have given added emphasis and urgency to demands for its reform. Although such critiques would normally herald the disgrace of the person in charge, there was no indication at year's end that Zeary, a remarkable survivor in the various internecine party battles since 1978, was in trouble.

Other fronts were viewed less negatively. The fourth plenum of the DWOA claimed a membership of 22,000 that included 130 graduates and 60 students of the Institute of Social Sciences, an enrollment of 13,500 women in 865 literacy courses, 1,200 armed women "defending the revolution," and connections with more than 80 regional, national, and international organizations (*KNT*, 31 October). Other DWOA activities included donating blood, caring for the families of those killed in battle, and helping 81 women find "work opportunities" (ibid., 12 September).

The DYOA also boasted of its contributions to the PDPA and DRA: running "work emulation" drives that involved "strike [i.e., speedup] brigades" in various industries; providing eight construction brigades totaling 10,000 students to state enterprises; providing over 12,000 persons to serve on "social order brigades"; making its own contribution to the literacy campaign; and establishing propaganda brigades in fifteen Afghan provinces (Radio Kabul, 30 September; *FBIS*, 3 October). According to a diplomat who served in Kabul until mid-1984, however, the DYOA was unable to attract many new members; of Kabul University students, allegedly only 16 percent belonged to the organization (statement at Middle East Conference, San Francisco, December). The unpopularity of the DYOA was indirectly confirmed by Babrak when he warned against forcing people into it against their will (*KNT*, 20 November).

The Institute of Social Sciences attached to the PDPA Central Committee is the central organ for training and retraining party cadres. Its importance is indicated by the fact that it was established on 31 December 1979, probably the first important organizational innovation after the Soviet invasion. (Radio Kabul, 28 September; *FBIS*, 1 October.)

So-called consensus headquarters were supposed to be set up in communities all over the country in 1983. Consisting of representatives of the PDPA, NFF, KhAD, Sarandoy, local army units, local elders, and virtually any other person willing to collaborate with the authorities, the head-quarters were endowed with "special powers" and were supposed to give legitimacy to any measure proposed by the government. The "weak leader-ship" of the headquarters and their failure to get established in most of the country's communities, however, were criticized sharply by Babrak at the Fourteenth Plenum (Radio Kabul, 21 September; *FBIS*, 24 September).

Efforts to establish various volunteer self-defense forces to counter the resistance have con-tinued for several years, but apparently without much success. Units such as "revolution defense groups, self-defense, revolution guards, and tribal units" are frequently mentioned in Afghan media (Radio Kabul, 19 March; *FBIS*, 27 March). They seem to cover various territorial militias as well as volunteer groups in government enterprises, both industrial and agricultural.

At least part of the reason the front groups have not been more successful is that the resistance has devoted some of its energies to eliminating those who join. Particularly embarrassing to the regime was an upsurge in urban operations in March, just when a Conference of Scholars and Clergy was being held in Kabul, with observers from India, South Yemen, and the Soviet Central Asian re-publics in attendance. Several mullahs lost their lives in these attacks (*Background Brief*, July). Similarly, the mujahideen claimed success in killing an undisclosed number of delegates (including seven Soviet citizens) during attacks on a December conference of the Afro-Asian Peoples' Solidarity Organization in Kabul (resistance radio "Voice of the Islamic Revolution," 11 December; *FBIS*, 12 December).

International Views, Positions, and Activi-ties. Because the PDPA is totally dependent on the Soviet military occupation for its continued exis-tence, the party has no independent voice. PDPA foreign policy is Soviet foreign policy, with Kabul faithfully projecting Moscow's views on all issues worldwide, many of them bearing no relation to Afghanistan or its national interests. Soviet pol-icies, strategies, and tactics toward Afghanistan, however, have changed subtly over time and deserve

closer examination because of their bearing on the PDPA and DRA, as well as on regional stability. Certainly in the short term, they appear to have met with little success in 1984.

The failure of the Afghan army and existing Soviet forces to cope with an ever more active and aggressive resistance led to yet another increment of Soviet occupation forces, from 105,000 in 1983 to at least 115,000–120,000 by the end of 1984 (*Economist*, London, 26 May; *NYT*, 1 November). Typical of Soviet efforts to wrest the initiative was their seventh major assault on the Panjshir Valley, which took place in April. The last previous major offensive, in 1982, had included 12,000 combat troops plus tactical aircraft, armor, and artillery. This time the attacking force numbered 20,000 (plus a limited and ineffective contingent of Afghan army troops), and for the first time there was carpet bombing by strategic aircraft (TU-16s) based in the USSR. Informed in advance of the attack, the re-sistance evacuated civilians and faded into side val-leys, which they had mined beforehand, and then launched brief raids on Soviet convoys and strong-points. In the first weeks the offensive cost the Soviet army 500 killed. In spite of the increased commitment, however, the outcome was the same as in previous years: eventual isolation of garrison forts, slow withdrawal of occupation forces from the upper valley, and an eventual bid for a truce from the Soviet side. (*NYT*, 23 and 27 May; *CSM*, 2 October.)

Nevertheless, attacks such as this throughout the country have wrought havoc on Afghanistan's agri-cultural infrastructure. Moreover, Soviet air and artillery bombardments of villages in the vicinity of any resistance activity have left the country sprin-kled with ghost towns, whose entire populations have moved either into exile or to the relative se-curity of regional centers. In this process of forced migration and genocide, the Soviet intention seemed to involve emptying the countryside of all who would support the mujahideen, reducing the population to the dead, the exiled, and the intimi-dated. (*CSM*, 26 September.) Estimates of the number of exiles vary widely (there is an incentive to inflate figures by those who receive aid for exiles in Pakistan, and Iran does not provide statistics), but probably a minimum of 2.5–3.0 million have been forced from the land. In spite of high civilian casualties, however, the Soviet policy has not yet succeeded in breaking Afghan morale, and mean-while costs of the war in men, matériel, and international prestige have continued to rise for both the PDPA and the USSR.

In the Islamic world, opinion has been overwhelmingly opposed to the Soviet occupation. Afghanistan was suspended from the Islamic Conference in 1980 because of it, and the Fourth Islamic Summit meeting, which took place 16–20 January in Morocco, closed with a resolution calling for all-out support to the people of Afghanistan in their struggle against occupation forces. (*Pakistan Times*, 21 January; *Afghanistan Forum*, March.) Opposition also continued in other international forums. On 15 March the U.N. Commission on Human Rights at Geneva voted 27 to 8 with six abstentions to recommend appointment of a special rapporteur to examine human rights in Afghanistan (*Background Brief*, July). In November, the annual U.N. vote on removal of all foreign troops from Afghanistan passed by the most lopsided vote yet: 119 to 20 with fourteen abstentions (*NYT*, 16 November).

Throughout the year there was a stream of publicity worldwide regarding the plight of the Afghan refugees in Pakistan. Aid from the United Nations, from governments, from both ad hoc and permanent organizations, and from individuals came in large and small donations—and received broad media coverage. The picture of a small, backward people fighting a neighboring military superpower to a standstill but suffering frightful casualties in the process received the world's attention and sympathy.

Soviet efforts to minimize embarrassment took several forms. The USSR voiced support for the effort by U.N. Secretary General Javier Pérez de Cuellar and his deputy for political affairs, Diego Cordovez, to arrange for a peaceful settlement and withdrawal of Soviet forces. The third session of talks to this end took place 24–30 August in Geneva, but there was no resolution of basic issues. The United Nation's goals remained (1) a fixed timetable for withdrawal of Soviet troops; (2) international guarantees against future interference in Afghanistan's internal affairs by any of its neighbors; (3) the gradual return of refugees; and (4) free choice by the Afghan people for their own form of government. The only two interests directly represented at the talks were the DRA and Pakistan, with Cordovez shuttling between the two sides' delegates, who were located in separate rooms because of Pakistan's refusal to recognize the Kabul regime. Little if any progress was registered, but a fourth session was set for February 1985. (*Los Angeles Times*, 1 September.) Representatives of the real contestants in the war—the USSR and the Afghan people—were not present, and even if some agreement had been reached in Geneva, there was no chance it could be implemented in Afghanistan without their consent.

The USSR periodically attempted to turn aside unfavorable publicity by presenting its own view of the war as an internal Afghan affair where the Soviet involvement was merely in response to American, Chinese, Pakistani, and right-wing Arab states' support of the resistance. This view, also echoed regularly in the Afghan press, found little credibility in the outside world. More subtly, the Soviets apparently were able to convince some Third World leaders, among them Mrs. Indira Gandhi, that "little [is] to be gained from repeated public condemnation of the Soviets" (*Pakistan Times*, 6 July; *Afghanistan Forum*, October). There was also what appeared to be an ongoing international campaign, using non-Soviet journalists who were allowed on a selective basis to visit Kabul, to project the image of a steadily improving security situation and consolidation of PDPA power in the country. According to accounts by such individuals, time was on the side of the DRA, and the resistance was progressively losing prestige and power. (*WP*, 13 May; *Le Monde diplomatique*, September 1983; *KNT*, 31 March, 1 April.) Their reporting, however, was at odds with the undeniably deteriorating security situation in the capital, which in the latter half of the year included a bomb explosion at the airport, progressively heavier rocket attacks, and even resistance assaults on Soviet convoys inside the city limits. The end of the year saw punctuation of the fifth anniversary of the Soviet invasion with five consecutive days of rocket attacks in the city. (*Financial Times*, London, 5 September; *Sunday Times*, London, 30 September; *Times*, London, 9 October; *CSM*, 31 December.)

In the course of its efforts to throttle or distort news from inside Afghanistan, the USSR provoked opposition from some of its nonruling communist party supporters. An Italian Communist Party (PCI) journalist, Giulietto Chiesa, visited Kabul at the PDPA's invitation and published his impressions in early January in *L'Unità*, the official PCI organ. His reporting, though generally slanted in favor of the PDPA, included allegations of violations of human rights, questioned a ridiculously low figure of Soviet advisers (1,000) provided by a Soviet source, and observed that the Afghan people had trouble understanding the new reforms. These were not at all the views expected by either Kabul or Moscow. The PDPA responded with an outraged open letter of protest to the PCI. The dispute was then replayed in Soviet international media, indicating full Soviet support (if not instigation) of the protest. (*Bakhtar*, 18 January; *FBIS*, 20 January; BBC, 9 February.)

Later, the Soviet party and the PDPA offended even the orthodox French Communist Party (PCF). To discourage unfavorable eyewitness accounts from Western newsmen who crossed into Afghanistan with the mujahideen, the USSR arranged an ambush of a French television reporter, Jacques Abouchar, who was captured on 17 September. After lengthy interrogation by his Soviet captors, he was turned over to DRA authorities, who threatened to try him for espionage but finally settled on illegal border crossing and purported association with "counterrevolutionaries." His sentencing by the DRA on 20 October to eighteen years in prison provoked a storm of protest in France and throughout the Western world. At first the DRA and USSR tried to brazen out the international reaction. The Soviet ambassador to Pakistan said that Abouchar had been lucky, and he warned that any future journalists caught with the mujahideen would be "eliminated." But when French parliamentarians threatened to boycott celebration of the sixtieth anniversary of Soviet-French diplomatic relations, and the PCF broke off relations with the PDPA, Moscow finally relented, and Abouchar was freed. The manner of his liberation, however, was almost as embarrassing for the USSR as his incarceration. The news was released in Moscow, not Kabul, thus provoking the PCF, which heretofore had steadfastly maintained the fiction of the DRA's national independence, into maintaining its own boycott of the anniversary celebrations, even though noncommunist deputies attended. (*CSM*, 23 October; *Economist*, 3 November.)

At the invitation of the PDPA Central Committee, the "general secretary" of the New Communist Party of Britain, Eric Trevett, and a member of that organization's Central Committee, Ian Mosley, paid an "official" visit to Kabul in October. The visit, which lasted for about a week, received prominent coverage in Afghan media. (Radio Kabul, 10 October; *FBIS*, 12 October; *KNT*, 10, 13, and 14 October.) Given the subservience of the PDPA to the Soviet party, the visit seemed to indicate official Moscow preference for the new British party over older and more independent factions.

Relations with ruling parties proceeded smoothly. There were ritual exchanges of congratulatory telegrams on anniversaries. The occasional state visits, such as that of Polish foreign minister Stefan Olszowski in June, were probably intended to confirm the PDPA's legitimacy (Radio Kabul, 11 June; *FBIS*, 12 June). The PDPA claimed relations with 52 "fraternal communist parties" and in December established relations with the People's Republic of Benin (Bakhtar, 25 November, 6 December; *Afghanistan Forum*, January 1985).

If the short-term view of Soviet involvement in Afghanistan seemed bleak, Moscow still appeared to be counting on long-term strategies for eventual victory. These included not only the military effort to grind the civilian population into eventual submission but a calculated program of sovietization, involving political, economic, and educational factors.

The political process has included not only organization of the PDPA and front groups along Soviet-approved lines but in many cases direct administration of the DRA state machinery. Soviet advisers have dominated the activities of Afghan ministries, with two or more assigned personally to each minister (*Central Asian Survey*, July 1983). In 1984 the process appeared if anything to accelerate. KGB officers, for example, began taking over direct interrogation of mujahideen captives instead of leaving this to their Afghan surrogates in KhAD or Sarandoy (Radio Karachi, 31 August; *FBIS*, 31 August). An amendment to army regulations gave the Soviet army freedom to operate anywhere in the country without prior consultation with the Afghan army, which was obliged to carry out orders issued at the last moment, with no voice in the planning (*Afghanistan Forum*, June).

Economically, Afghanistan fell more and more into the Soviet orbit. A five-year plan to be launched in 1985 was scheduled to coincide with that of the USSR (*KNT*, 14 September). In 1983–1984, countries belonging to the Soviet-dominated Council for Mutual Economic Assistance (CMEA) accounted for 93 percent of Afghanistan's foreign aid and 80 percent of its trade (70 percent with the USSR alone), compared with 39.5 percent in 1978 (*Background Brief*, July; State Department, *Afghanistan*, no. 120, December). The USSR had 170 aid projects in Afghanistan, of which 90 were complete. Enterprises built with Soviet aid yielded 60 percent of Afghan industrial output, 75 percent of the state-owned sector, and 40 percent of the country's budget. (Radio Kabul, 13 December; *FBIS*, 14 December.) Afghanistan was one of four countries that received 86 percent of all Soviet foreign aid (esti-mated to total $8 billion) in 1983 (*FEER*, 24 December 1982; *Afghanistan Forum Newsletter*, March 1983). Because of widespread war destruc-tion, the USSR was selling and donating an ever greater volume of staples, including wheat, flour, rice, edible oil, sugar, tea, soap, and petroleum products. Imports of wheat, for example, which had totaled 100,000 tons in 1978, had increased to 250,000 tons by 1982 and probably have continued to mount. Trade imports from the USSR in 1984 were to total $911 million ($800 million of it in barter trade), to which the USSR would add $112 million in grants in aid for food staples, vehicles, and household goods. (*KNT*, 23 and 27 October 1983; *Background Brief*, "The Afghan Economy," September; State Department, *Afghanistan*, no. 120, December.)

As in previous years, the USSR continued to be the major consumer (95 percent) and only foreign recipient of Afghanistan's natural gas reserves. Al-though after 1980 the USSR increased the rates paid to the Afghans per cubic meter, the price in 1984 still did not reach free-market levels, and in any case it was meaningless: all proceeds from natural gas sales were applied to Afghanistan's debt to the USSR (including an undisclosed portion of the costs of the occupation), which by 1983 had soared to $3 billion and would climb annually far faster than gas sales could compensate. (*Afghanistan Council Newsletter*, March 1983.)

Among the more menacing signs of Soviet en-croachment was the announcement in 1983 that "border trade" between Afghanistan and the Central Asian republics of Tajikistan, Turkmenistan, and Uzbekistan had amounted to over $1.2 million in a recent six-month period, a 250 percent increase over the same period the previous year. Four new border trading posts undertook agreements with Soviet cooperatives in 1983, with another planned for the near future. Such trade was described as barter, and a Soviet spokesman announced inten-tions to expand it further. (*KNT*, 11 November 1983, 4 April; Bakhtar, 16 September; *FBIS*, 17 September.) The implication is that such trans-actions are being handled as if they were an internal Soviet matter instead of an international exchange.

Soviet attempts to influence Afghan youth and students predate the invasion, but they intensified in 1984. Such standard Soviet course materials as dialectical materialism, historical materialism, and history of revolutionary movements were intro-duced into Kabul University some years ago. Soviet teachers were imported for these and many other courses, and their relative strength compared to the Afghan faculty has grown steadily, with 150 in the Kabul Polytechnic Institute alone. The Russian lan-guage has been made a standard requirement, with some 6,000 Afghan secondary school and college students enrolled in such courses. (Radio Karachi, 1 March; *Pravda*, 2 September; *FBIS*, 2 March, 28 September.)

In addition to domestic indoctrination, Afghan students have been sent to the USSR and its allies for political as well as substantive studies since before the 1978 coup. This has had the advantage of isolating the Afghans from their families and culture, and since 1978 some 20,000 to 25,000 have gone through the experience. Only 10,000 are esti-mated to have taken advantage of the scholarships offered since 1979, however; according to one re-port, only 200 out of 1,500 scholarships offered in 1982–1983 were taken up, with the poor turnout ascribed to parental objections. At the end of 1984 it was estimated that the rate was roughly 4,000 per year, but the results have not been entirely positive. There has been no noticeable upsurge in PDPA effectiveness, and some students returning from their Soviet schooling reported serious incidents of racial prejudice against them, even including murder. (*Central Asian Survey*, July 1983; *Afghan-istan Studies Association Newsletter*, Fall 1983; State Department, *Afghanistan*, no. 120, Decem-ber; *San Francisco Chronicle*, 29 November.)

Since 1980 Afghan schoolchildren have been sent off in large numbers to the USSR for a few weeks of summer camp. In 1984, 1,400 between the ages of ten and thirteen were supposed to make this trip. In the fall, a far more serious program got under way as some 870 children of seven–nine years of age were dispatched to the USSR for ten years of schooling. According to official Afghan sources, these children, accompanied by 35 Afghan teachers, were orphans of parents killed in the war, and it was anticipated that the program would con-tinue in years to come. Already the growing num-ber of orphans had prompted the authorities to set up a series of orphanages inside Afghanistan to look after them. Called *Watan* (homeland) and presided over by Mahbuba Karmal, wife of Babrak, they appeared to be patterned after similar institutions set up in the Soviet Union after the civil war by the first secret police chief, Felix Dzerzhinsky. The avowed goal in both the Soviet and Afghan cases was to indoctrinate the orphans in communism from the earliest age. (*KNT*, 18–20 November; Radio Kabul, 5 November; *FBIS*, 6 November.)

Clearly the ten-year education program will not bring any immediate benefits to the USSR or DRA, and meanwhile existing measures have failed to halt the deterioration of the internal security situation. To arrest this slide, the USSR began applying ever heavier pressure on Pakistan through the DRA. Afghan aircraft and artillery bombarded Pakistani border villages "several hundred times" during the summer months. Pakistani protests about the few of these acts it chose to acknowledge were either rejected or went unanswered. (*WSJ*, 12 September; *Financial Times*, 21 August.) Meanwhile, Afghan protests about alleged Pakistani border violations and bombardment of Afghan territory continued unabated, increasing sharply toward the end of the year. Stridently anti-Pakistan propaganda and veiled threats were featured in Afghan media, including one statement by Babrak that the Pakistanis should be grateful that "we so far have not used our legitimate right to pursue the counterrevolutionaries . . . who take refuge in Pakistan" (Bakhtar, 19 September; *FBIS*, 20 September). Equally defamatory but less immediately threatening declarations were made about Iran (Radio Kabul, 29 November; *FBIS*, 3 December). Although neither the Iranians nor the Pakistanis chose to complain to Moscow about the campaign, no one was under any illusion about its true instigator.

Instead of intimidating the targets, however, the vituperation seemed to have the opposite effect. For the Pakistanis, it seemed to stiffen their resolve and convince them that the Geneva talks held few prospects for success. Whereas in earlier years they felt they had to walk a delicate tightrope in order to limit outside support to the mujahideen so as not to infuriate the Soviets, now their concerns about Soviet sensitivities seemed to be lessened by the DRA's aggressiveness. (*WSJ*, 12 September.) The reported increase in covert U.S. aid to the resistance, supposed to total $280 million in 1985, may have been one outgrowth of this changed Pakistani outlook (*NYT*, 28 November).

In the sharpening conflict between the Soviet Union on the one side and the Afghan people and neighboring states on the other, the PDPA acquired more outward prominence during the year, but its real importance declined. As 1985 dawned, the party's significance as an independent factor in the complex regional and local equations that were developing had been reduced essentially to zero. Its sole remaining function seemed to be that of a polite screen between the USSR and its antagonists.

Ruth *and* Anthony Arnold
Novato, California

Australia

Population. 15,462,000

Parties. Communist Party of Australia (CPA); Socialist Party of Australia (SPA); Communist Party of Australia—Marxist-Leninist (CPA-ML); Socialist Workers Party (SWP); Socialist Labor League (SLL); Spartacist League of Australia and New Zealand (SLANZ)

Founded. CPA: 1920; CPA-ML: 1964; SPA: 1971; SLL: 1972

Membership. CPA: 1,500; SPA: 1,000; CPA-ML: 300–400; SWP: 400; SLL: 100; SLANZ: 50

Leadership. CPA: Judy Mundey (general secretary); SPA: Peter Dudley Symon (general secretary); CPA-ML, Edward Fowler Hill (chairman); SWP: Jim Percy (national secretary)

Status. Legal
Last Congress. CPA: Twenty-eighth, 4 November 1984; SPA: Fifth, September 1984
Last Election. 1 December 1984, negligible vote for communist parties, no representatives
Publications. CPA: *Tribune* (weekly); SPA: *Socialist* (fortnightly); CPA-ML: *Vanguard* (weekly), *Australian Communist*; SWP: *Direct Action* (weekly)

Over the past decade Australia's communist organizations have suffered from a lack of direction and strong leadership. Continued internal bickering coupled with Australia's gradual political shift to the right has resulted in declining membership and makes an upsurge in communist party influence unlikely in the next several years.

Australia's largest and most influential communist parties include the Communist Party of Australia, the Socialist Party of Australia, and to a lesser extent the Communist Party of Australia—Marxist-Leninist. The remainder of the communist parties—the Socialist Workers Party, the Socialist Labor League, and the Spartacist League of Australia and New Zealand—are Trotskyite and have little or no influence.

Communist Party of Australia. The Eurocommunist CPA, the largest communist party in Australia, was formed in the early 1920s. It has strong ties with several large trade unions—including Australia's largest, the Amalgamated Metal Workers and the Shipwrights Union. The CPA's influence in these unions, with their combined membership of over 400,000, enables it to have a limited voice in the union-dominated Australian Labor Party (ALP) (which assumed office in March 1983 and was returned to power in December 1984).

The CPA's influence on the Australian political scene has waned dramatically over the past 35 years. Membership in the CPA, for example, has fallen from a peak of about 25,000 in the late 1940s to fewer than 1,500 members today. Less than 180 of these reside outside the Sydney and Melbourne metropolitan areas. In addition, recent recruits from the "Vietnam generation" have weakened the party by polarizing the CPA between younger, college-educated recruits and older, blue-collar members. A further blow came in May 1984 when 23 members of the CPA's Victoria executive resigned. They had long suggested that they could contribute more to the movement by dissolving the CPA and adding their efforts to those of other parties—including the ALP (*The Bulletin*, 30 November 1982).

Socialist Party of Australia. The pro-Soviet SPA, boasting fewer than a thousand members, was organized in 1971 following a doctrinal dispute within the CPA over adherence to the Moscow line. In 1975, the Soviet Union publicly recognized the SPA as the only Marxist-Leninist party in Australia and was rewarded with SPA support for the imposition of martial law in Poland. In addition, the SPA serves as the most active proponent of the Soviet-front World Federation of Trade Unions' activities in the South Pacific.

Despite its reputation as the most effective communist voice in Australia, internal weaknesses have surfaced, highlighted by the expulsion of SPA secretary and Building Workers Industrial Union (BWIU) leader Pat Clancy and other union leaders in 1983. The expulsion followed a fallout between Clancy and party purists. For his part, Clancy believed that party leaders were seeking to impose too much control over union affairs and that their philosophical rigidity prevented any working relationship with the Labor government. SPA leaders, on the other hand, rejected Clancy's support for the ALP government's wage accord. They also denounced Clancy's efforts to promote a new coalition of the left—the Australian Marxist Forum (AMF). The Clancy expulsion has probably cost the SPA most of its influence within the 47,000-member BWIU. It continues to have ties, however, with several smaller unions, including the 12,000-member Australian Federated Union of Locomotive Enginemen.

Communist Party of Australia—Marxist-Leninist. With a national membership between 300 and 400, the CPA-ML exists largely on the fringe of Australia's political spectrum. The pro-Beijing CPA-ML is a highly doctrinaire group that split from the CPA in 1964 over its members' ideological support for the Chinese Communists. As such, it is not surprising that the party finds its strongest support among leftist university students. The CPA-ML, unlike the CPA, has denounced the ALP and its pragmatic leader, Bob Hawke, for his "conservative" policies on domestic and foreign affairs.

Unlike most leftist parties, the CPA-ML has only one primary union connection—the 24,000-member Building Laborers Federation (BLF) led by renegade union boss Norm Gallagher. The BLF—one of Australia's most militant unions—has attempted to undermine the Hawke government by bucking Labor's wage and price accord with business and unions—the centerpiece of Canberra's economic policy. The CPA-ML's influence may have been diminished by the highly publicized investigation of Norm Gallagher on charges of corruption and recent moves to deregister the BLF from the Australian Council of Trade Unions (ACTU—the Australian equivalent of the AFL-CIO).

Other Leftist Groups. Australia's other left-wing splinter groups—with less than 400 members each—include the SWP, SLL, and SLANZ. All are Trotskyite parties and espouse worldwide class revolution. These groups support the "revolutionary movement" in Central America and concentrate their domestic efforts on protests against uranium mining and exports and U.S.-Australian military ties. Although bent on attracting support from industrial workers, they have been only marginally successful in gaining influence in the trade union movement.

The Australian Political Scene. Overall, leftist influence in Australian politics is waning. Leftist goals—including radically redistributing income, banning the potentially lucrative mining and exporting of uranium, and dismantling the 33-year-old ANZUS alliance—are not representative of the mainstream of Australian society. For one thing, Australia's blue-collar workers—once the backbone of the left—increasingly identify themselves as "middle-class," with attendant values and voting preferences. Further, the Labor Party's recent re-election—despite its diminished parliamentary majority—under the helm of the charismatic Bob Hawke will likely further undercut the left's prospects in the next several years. Since assuming office, Hawke has made significant inroads against the left. He has exploited his long-standing union ties, resulting in the ACTU's retreat from its former antiuranium stance and the virtual absence of politically motivated strikes.

Christine A. Gould
Arlington, Virginia

Michael Morell
Vienna, Virginia

Bangladesh

Population. 99,585,000
Party. Communist Party of Bangladesh (CPB)
Founded. 1948 (as East Pakistan Communist Party, banned in 1954, re-emerged in 1971 following the establishment of Bangladesh)
Membership. 3,000
Secretary General. Muhammed Farhad
Secretariat. 10 members
Central Committee. 26 members
Status. Legal

Last Congress. Third, February 1980
Last Election. 1981 national election; CPB ran no candidates, though it did support candidates of other parties.
Auxiliary Organizations. Trade Union Centre, Cultural Front, Bangladesh Chatra Union, Khetmozdur Samiti
Publications. *Ekota* (in Bengali)

Twelve pro-Soviet parties, including the CPB, operate within a fifteen-party left-wing alliance (*Indian Express*, Bombay, 11 July). The Bangladesh Krishak–Sramik Awami League (BAKSAL) is a rabidly pro-Soviet splinter group that broke off from the Awami League (AL) in 1983. Abdur Razzak, the guiding hand behind BAKSAL, cooperates closely with the CPB and promotes Soviet foreign policy themes. On 3 February, Razzak told an interviewer from the pro-Soviet organ *Sangbad* that the regime of President Hussain Mohammed Ershad was following a "pro-American, imperialist-submissive foreign policy." He went on to repeat the Soviet-inspired canard that the United States was preparing to acquire a naval base in Bangladesh. (*FBIS*, 15 February.)

Another leftist constituent of the fifteen-party alliance is the Jatiya Samajtantrik Dal (JSD). In February, the once formidable JSD underwent another split when a pro-Chinese wing led by M. A. Jamil agreed to participate in government-sponsored local elections (Dhaka domestic service, 28 January; *FBIS*, 3 February). The JSD general secretary, A. S. M. Abdur Rab, who had supposedly tendered his resignation in August 1983, then attempted to regain control of the party. Rab led a band of supporters in a bid to take JSD headquarters in Dhaka by force. Police were called in to put down the melee (*Bangladesh Observer*, 8 February). The JSD rump that remains in the fifteen-party alliance is now headed by former member of parliament Shahjahan Siraj (*New Nation*, 8 February).

Other leftist factions within the alliance include the Samyabadi Dal (SD), the Workers Party (WP), and two factions of the National Awami Party (NAP). The SD is the personal political vehicle of Mohammed Toaha, a former Maoist whose guerrilla exploits during the 1971 liberation war are legendary. In 1983, Toaha performed a remarkable ideological reversal when he embraced the Soviet Union and threw his political support behind the fifteen-party alliance. The general secretary of the WP is Hyder Akbar Khan Rono, although the group's leading spokesman is Nasim Ali. The two pro-Moscow factions of the NAP are headed by Harun-ur Rashid and Muzaffar Ahmed. The remaining pro-Moscow splinter groups within the fifteen-party coalition include the Ekota Party, the Sramik-Krishak Samajbadi Dal, the Labour Party, and two factions of the Proletariat Party. None of these minor parties exercises political influence outside the coffeehouses and union halls of Dhaka.

The CPB itself has limited popular appeal and has never won a seat in parliament. The CPB student front, the Bangladesh Chatra Union, has a strong following at Dhaka University and some support on campuses at Mymensingh, Rajshahi, and Chittagong. The peasant front, the Khetmozdur Samiti, tried with little success to capitalize on the rural hardships caused by massive floods during the rainy season. Other fronts are the Trade Union Centre, the Cultural Front, and the Federation of Bangladesh Transport Workers. Although the last organization is not under exclusive CPB control, the party has a strong following among Dhaka's rickshaw pullers. Each time the CPB joins in an opposition-sponsored *hartal* (general strike), the walkoff by rickshaw pullers paralyzes transport in the capital city.

Muhammed Farhad, the CPB general secretary, was extremely active during the year in organizing and leading antiregime demonstrations. In foreign policy matters, Farhad adhered closely to Soviet policy lines (see, for instance, *Pravda*, 22 April). Moni Singh, the aging CPB president and theoretician, was reported to be seriously ill in February (*New Nation*, 29 February). Other party stalwarts include Abdur Salam (secretary, agricultural affairs), Saifuddin Ahmed Manik (secretary, labor and industry), and Central Committee activists Ajoy Roy, Matiur Rehman, and Manzuru Hasan Khan.

A number of small communist groupings operate on the political fringes. Revolutionary parties maintaining a position of ideological equidistance between Moscow and Beijing or tilting toward China include the Communist Party of Bangladesh (Marxist-Leninist), the Janamukti Party, and the Revolutionary Communist Party of Bangladesh. In addition, there are numerous pro-Chinese parties. Four small parties follow in the tradition of the pro-Chinese Islamic movement inspired by the revered peasant leader Maulana Bhashani. The pro-Chinese groups, which operate within a seven-party alliance led by the Bangladesh National Party, include the United People's Party, the Biplabi Communist League, the Ganatantrik Party, and a third faction of the National Awami Party. An ultra-leftist fringe, however, brands the current Chinese leadership "revisionist" and advocates a revolutionary line styled after the Albanian communist movement and the guerrilla doctrines of the Indian Maoist Charu Mazumdar. These underground, conspiratorial parties include the Purbo Banglar Communist Party (Marxist-Leninist) and two factions of the Purbo Banglar Sarbahara Party. Bangladeshi Maoists were largely inactive in 1984, though the movement retains an emotional appeal in some student circles.

Domestic Developments. The year's first test of strength occurred on 4 January when the combined opposition staged a half-day general strike timed to coincide with local elections for *upazilla*, or subdistrict seats. The election was intended as a preliminary step leading up to presidential elections on 27 May. Voter turnout was heavy, though the balloting was marred by sporadic incidents of violence in Dhaka (*NYT*, 1 January). In mid-January, a CPB Central Committee meeting adopted a six-phase program of demonstrations and civil disobedience designed to thwart a second round of upazilla elections scheduled for March. CPB president Moni Singh denounced Ershad's efforts to line up support among the opposition as a "waste of time" (*Sangbad*, 17 January). At the end of the month, both opposition alliances endorsed the militant protest strategy, vowed to block President Ershad's bid to secure a popular mandate, and reaffirmed their support of a five-point opposition program (an end to martial law, restoration of political rights, the holding of parliamentary elections before the presidential elections, release of political prisoners, and prosecution of those responsible for killing students during a protest march in February 1983).

On the eve of a nationwide general strike on 1 March, Ershad partially gave in to opposition demands when he announced that presidential and parliamentary elections would be held simultaneously in May. In addition, Ershad lifted some restrictions on political activities in an effort to induce moderate opposition parties to participate in the election. Undeterred, the opposition went ahead with the general strike and brought much of the country to a standstill. As many as 500 candidates for local office withdrew their nominations in response to the opposition's call for a boycott. On 18 March, one week before the scheduled election, Ershad bowed to opposition pressures and canceled the balloting. On 24 March, the combined opposition celebrated its victory at CPB headquarters in Dhaka by observing a "black day" to commemorate the second anniversary of the Ershad coup. Ershad's supporters countered by observing a "day of deliverance." (*Economist*, London, 12 March.)

The following month, Ershad tried to salvage his plans for national elections by engaging in a political dialogue with opposition leaders (Dhaka overseas service, 15 April; *FBIS*, 16 April). The opposition leaders demanded that a neutral, caretaker government be installed in advance of national elections in order to ensure that Ershad could not use his position to influence the election outcome. Ershad rejected the demand. On 23 April, the CPB staged a rally in support of the five-point formula—in effect signaling that the pro-Soviet wing of the alliance would brook no compromises with the regime (*Bangladesh Times*, 24 April). Ershad's efforts to woo the opposition proved unsuccessful, and on 12 May the national elections scheduled for two weeks later were canceled.

Starting in June, Ershad made a series of significant concessions by scheduling parliamentary elections in advance of the presidential contest, agreeing to broadcast opposition rallies, and disbanding military courts. A new polling date was set for 8 December. During a pro-government rally in October, Ershad went a step further and pledged to withdraw martial law in phases beginning on 1 November if the opposition agreed to participate in the election (*Calcutta Telegraph*, 16 October).

These tactical retreats failed to satisfy the opposition and ran the risk of undermining Ershad's support base within the army. Fearing that an election would split the opposition vote and thereby guarantee victory for Ershad's party vehicle, Janadal, the opposition alliances pressed ahead with the campaign to force the army leadership to step aside. On 14 October, the fifteen-party, seven-party, and Islamic fundamentalist alliances staged separate rallies in Dhaka during another general strike. Press reports estimated that as many as 2 million people attended the rallies (*NYT*, 15 October). The largest demonstration was held by the fifteen-party alliance, which promised a crescendo of protests leading up to an election boycott. At the end of the "resistance fortnight," Ershad yielded to opposition pressures once again and canceled the December elections.

Antiregime pressure, for the most part non-violent, was maintained throughout the remainder of the year. The combined opposition called general strikes on 8 and 22–23 December, as well as a large-scale demonstration in Dhaka on 27 December (Delhi domestic service, 25 December; *FBIS*, 26 December). In exasperation, Ershad announced yet another series of concessions to the opposition on 15 December. During a nationally broadcast address, Ershad conceded that "a country like ours cannot afford to have the curse of an atmosphere of conflict." Parliamentary elections were rescheduled for some time in April 1985. Ershad also announced the gradual replacement of martial law administrators with civilians and pledged that no serving ministers in his government would be eligible to run in the elections. (Dhaka domestic service, 15 December; *FBIS*, 17 December.) By year's end, the political struggle was deadlocked, with the opposition promising more demonstrations and the military regime determined to press ahead with its controversial election plans.

Foreign Affairs. Relations with the Soviet Union became outwardly strained in December 1983 when the Ershad government expelled fourteen Soviet diplomats and closed down the Soviet Cultural Center in Chittagong. Ershad took this dramatic step after Bangladeshi intelligence confirmed that Soviet personnel had financed and encouraged local Communists during violent anti-regime demonstrations in November. In an interview with the *Christian Science Monitor* on 1 March, Ershad accused the Kremlin of "attempting to bring me down" by installing a leader "who toes the Soviet line." AL leader Hasina Wajed scoffed at the charges, accused Ershad of fabricating the evidence against the Soviets, and blamed the regime for inciting the street violence (*Sangbad*, 24 January). CPB leader Moni Singh issued a similar statement and called the expulsion "unreasonable" (ibid., 17 January).

Predictably, the Soviets pleaded innocence in the affair and initiated diplomatic retaliation. To signal their displeasure with Ershad's "sinister campaign" (Radio Moscow, 15 December 1983; *FBIS*, 19 December 1983), the Soviets halted imports of Bangladeshi jute, postponed negotiations over the annual barter trade protocol, and stalled the confirmation of a new Bangladeshi envoy to Moscow.

After making their point, however, both sides stepped back, softened their rhetoric, and resumed cool but correct relations. In February, Rear Admiral Mahbub Ali Khan (the number-two figure in the martial law regime) conveyed a conciliatory message to the Kremlin while attending the funeral of Yuri Andropov. By midyear, jute exports were resumed, and a modest trade protocol was finalized. By the end of 1984, new ambassadors were posted in Moscow and Dhaka. Soviet encouragement of Bangladeshi Communists remains a serious source of concern for the military government.

Throughout the year, the CPB and other pro-Moscow constituents of the fifteen-party alliance were sharply critical of Ershad's pro-Western orientation. In November, the Soviet-front Bangladesh Peace Council advanced the Kremlin propaganda line that the CIA was linked to the assassinations of Indian prime minister Indira Gandhi; Sheikh Mujibur Rahman, the founder of Bangladesh; and a host of Third World leaders. At a hastily convened meeting to mourn Gandhi's death, CPB general secretary Farhad termed the assassination a "planned conspiracy to thwart the anti-imperialist progressive movement" (*New Nation*, 9 November). Another durable propaganda theme is the bogey of U.S. military bases in Bangladesh. During an opposition rally commemorating Martyrs' Day on 21 February, Hasina (who is Rahman's daughter) railed against Ershad's pursuit of an "imperialist war strategy by allowing the United States a naval base at Chittagong" (*Bangladesh Times*, 23 February).

Relations between Bangladesh and China remained warm. The strengthening of ties between the two countries is a direct consequence of Dhaka's mounting troubles in dealing with India and the Soviet Union, both of which maintain cool relations with Beijing. China is Bangladesh's primary supplier of military equipment. In January Air Vice-Marshal Sultan Mahmud conducted an extensive tour of Chinese air facilities. In July Zhang Tingfa, commander of the Chinese air force, traveled to Bangladesh (Xinhua, Beijing, 24 July; *FBIS*, 25 July). In May, President Ershad laid the foundation stone for a Chinese-constructed "friendship bridge" across the Buriganga river outside Dhaka (Xinhua, Beijing, 3 May; *FBIS*, 14 May).

Douglas C. Makeig
Library of Congress

Burma

Population. 36,196,000
Party. Burmese Communist Party (BCP)
Founded. 1939
Membership. 3,000 (1979); estimated armed strength 8,000–15,000
Chairman. Thakin Ba Thein Tin
Politburo. 8 members: Thakin Ba Thein Tin, Pe Tint, Khin Maung Gyi, Myo Myint, Tin Yee, Kya Mya, Kyin Maung, Yeba Taik Aung
Central Committee. At least 20 members
Status. Illegal
Last Congress. Second, July 1945; a major meeting, variously characterized as a "congress" was held in November 1979.
Last Election. N/a
Auxiliary Organizations. None identified
Publications. None identified; broadcasts over the Voice of the People of Burma (VOPB), located in Yunnan province in southern China

On 15 August the BCP celebrated its forty-fifth anniversary. Few communist parties have weathered a more tortuous course, few have faced such an uncertain and problematic future. The BCP was a leading part of the nationalist coalition that led the struggle for Burmese independence. At the end of World War II, many of Burma's nationalists thought of themselves as Communists or at least professed a belief in Marxism-Leninism. Attachment to the symbols of Marxism, however, masked considerable ideological debate within the "leftist" national front. Differences over "the road to power" and unresolved questions of cooperation with British colonial authorities split the nationalist front along "communist"/"socialist" lines. Further ideological schism plagued the BCP. A Trotskyite group broke with the party mainstream in 1947 and went into open rebellion against both the nationalist front and the colonial administration—the latter then committed to fashioning some form of Burmese independence within the year. In March 1948, three months after Burma gained independence, the BCP broke completely with the new Fabian-oriented, parliamentary socialist government and went un-

derground. Outlawed, the party has been in insurrection ever since. Periodic attempts, most recently in 1980, to bring the BCP into the government fold have been unsuccessful. Many of the BCP's ideological luminaries defected from the party. Several became influential figures in the military-socialist government that has ruled Burma since 1962. Their ideological imprint was everywhere apparent in the unfolding of the Burmese Way to Socialism, a blending of their Marxist-Leninist ideas with more deeply rooted notions of Buddhist social welfare as well as metaphysics. Most of these ex-BCP cadres, however, were purged from the government's Burma Socialist Programme Party (BSPP) when it jettisoned its more radical programs in the mid-1970s in favor of pragmatic (at least in the Burmese context) development initiatives.

Since the early 1960s, the BCP has been avowedly and unswervingly pro-Chinese, characterizing itself as a party guided by Marxism–Leninism–Mao Zedong thought. Pro-Soviet Communists, including some of the BCP founders, were purged from the party—in some cases killed—in a paroxysm of ideological conflict that nearly destroyed the BCP when the Sino-Soviet dispute erupted and the Chinese Great Proletarian Cultural Revolution spilled over into Burma in 1966–1967. Since then BCP propaganda organs have adapted to the shifts in Chinese communism, accepting Chinese enemies as the BCP's enemies, parroting Beijing's worldview, and subordinating Burma's problems to larger Chinese issues.

Leadership and Organization. The BCP lost most of its old-line leadership in the purges of the mid-1960s and in the successful Burmese army campaigns against BCP base areas in lower Burma in the early 1970s. For more than a decade, the party has been controlled by septuagenarian Central Committee chairman Thakin Ba Thein Tin. An early party member and veteran of the pre-independence struggles, Ba Thein Tin was one of a handful of BCP cadres who fled to Beijing in 1953. He remained in the background for ten years but returned to Burma in 1963 to participate in the Windemere peace conference. With the failure of that initiative to arrive at an accommodation with Rangoon, Ba Thein Tin returned to Beijing, where he has since resided except for brief visits to the BCP headquarters in Pang Hsang, a small Shan village on the Sino-Burmese border.

The BCP's Central Committee is believed to have at least twenty members, but few have been identified. A 1983 article (*FEER*, 14 April 1983; see *YICA*, 1984, p. 205) identified six key members of the Central Committee. A subsequent article (*FEER*, 13 December) reported that Ba Thein Tin is in need of continual medical care and has dropped out of active party work. The article noted that the BCP's "second strongman," Yeba Taik Aung, not previously identified as a Central Committee member, had been paralyzed by a stroke. According to this report, the BCP's day-to-day affairs were now in the hands of two party vice-chairmen: Khin Maung Gyi, at 44 probably the youngest of the party leadership, and Pe Tint, an old-guard communist organizer from Pyinmana, Burma, who had fled to Beijing with Ba Thein Tin in 1953. He operates from party headquarters in Pang Hsang. (Ibid.) Although Khin is Moscow-educated, there is no indication that he is other than committed to the BCP's pro-Beijing line. The article noted that Khin also appears to be the forward commander of the BCP's activities west of the Salween River, where he alternates between the party's 108 Military Region near Lawksawk and the Hsipaw headquarters of the BCP's ally, the Shan State Army.

BCP propaganda offered up few new insights on party organizational developments this year. Party activities, especially the conduct of the insurgency, are controlled within military-administrative regions. The devolution of party leadership to the two vice-chairmen and indications of growing independence of subordinate military commanders, particularly in eastern Shan State and in the area west of the Salween River, suggest a further weakening of the BCP's organization, an organization that has never had the rigid command and control of the Chinese Marxist-Leninist model it emulates. Ideological ambiguities at the center, decreased material support from China, continued poor communication between headquarters, and widely dispersed insurgent units have all continued to the decentralization, if not fragmentation, of the party.

Estimates of the size of the BCP's military strength vary between 8,000 and 15,000, but even this range is questionable. There were no large-scale (battalion-size) BCP military engagements this year either as a result of BCP initiatives or in response to Burmese army actions. This probably reflects the BCP's continued attachment to the military line laid down in 1979–1980, which discouraged large-unit actions and enjoined the insurgents to conduct guerrilla war. Nevertheless, it also may indicate the extent to which the party has been hobbled by ideological and logistical problems.

Party Internal Affairs. The most distinctive quality of party pronouncements during the year was the absence of anything but the most general references to the "armed, revolutionary struggle." While party propaganda organs continued their criticism of the Burmese government—albeit with less vitriol than in the past—and while they still held out the promise of negotiating a settlement with Rangoon, little of the BCP's argument seemed informed by Marxist-Leninist ideology. From statements offered up by VOPB during the year, one could almost conclude that the BCP had transformed itself into a "parliamentary, socialist" party. In a major article commemorating the thirty-ninth anniversary of the resistance against fascist Japan entitled "The Contradiction Between the People and the Military Government Is the Main Contradiction in Burma Today" (VOPB, 26 March; *FBIS*, 29 March), the party detailed its critique of the "military, one-party dictatorship" and endorsed the line that "people's freedom can only be won through armed struggle." Nevertheless, both this article and a subsequent series laying out demands for workers, peasants, students, and others seemed to call less for a dictatorship of the proletariat than for a plural society offering competing political parties, private ownership, free enterprise, and so forth. The government was criticized for state control of enterprises and for depriving the people of "the right to believe, to rally and speak, and to practice their religious faith." Furthermore, the government was chided for destroying creativity, for not promoting culture, and for publishing newspapers and magazines that were simply military propaganda. (Ibid.)

In cataloging demands for peasants and workers later in the year (see VOPB, 24 and 27 August; *FBIS*, 28 and 30 August), the BCP argued for widespread improvement in wages and working conditions, changes in wage policy, and extension of educational and social services. In the agricultural sector, cultivators must have the right to grow the crops they choose, taxes must be lowered, long-standing loans forgiven, production quotas dropped, agricultural pricing policies revised, and procurement targets lowered. The private sector should be expanded, government must reduce its control of marketing, owners must be compensated for activities nationalized since 1963, export and import controls must be liberalized in order to facilitate modernization. (VOPB, 5 September; *FBIS*, 19 September.)

In sum, the brief for change resembled far more recommendations the International Monetary Fund might present to Rangoon than the demands advanced by the BCP in the past. In fact, they incorporate many of the issues that surfaced a decade earlier when the government's BSPP began its own reform program to reverse the radicalism of its first ten years of socialism.

The new BCP "liberalism" undoubtedly owes its inspiration to the profound ideological changes under way in China, the BCP's mentor. The challenge to the BCP lies in minimizing the costs of mirroring China's modernization line. The Chinese Communist Party is a party in power, not one struggling to gain power. What might make sense for the former may not meet the needs of the latter.

The Insurgency. Apart from a growing involvement in the narcotics trade, the scope of the BCP insurgency has changed little from 1979 when the leadership adopted a guerrilla warfare strategy. The BCP maintains a base area east of the Salween River along the mountainous Shan State border with China. Small guerrilla units, sometimes in cooperation with allied ethnic rebels, harass government forces with raids and ambushes west of the Salween in the southern Kachin and central Shan states. The level of military activity fluctuates from year to year. Government drives against BCP enclaves in past years resulted in heavy casualties on both sides, yet made little headway. Obtaining a comprehensive picture of the insurgency is difficult, however, because both government and VOPB reports of the fighting are sporadic and offer few details.

The government did not mount a major dry-season offensive against the BCP in 1984, although some attacks occurred in various areas. This does not reflect a lessening of concern over the BCP threat but rather a decision to focus limited military resources on some of the other insurgencies. The army conducted a sustained campaign against the separatist Karen National Union (KNU), struck at narcotics warlord groups in central Shan State during the annual Mohein operation, and retaliated against several bold raids by the Kachin Independence Army (KIA) in northern Kachin State (*FEER*, 18 May, 4 October). The absence of a full-scale anti-BCP offensive contributed to an apparent decline in BCP military activity from 1983 levels. From January to April, guerrillas staged frequent small attacks in northern, central, and south-central Shan State, according to VOPB reports.

Several government soldiers were reported killed in each incident (VOPB, 10 March, 1 and 28 April; *FBIS*, 14 March, 5, 28, and 30 April). VOPB battle summaries for the remainder of the year were not carried by the *FBIS*, presumably because none was broadcast.

The BCP's efforts to expand its influence outside its base area in recent years have been aided by marriages of convenience with the 5,000-strong KIA and with several of the smaller ethnic insurgencies in the Shan and Kayah states. During 1984, the VOPB reported a few "small" joint operations by the BCP and units from the KIA, the Shan State Nationalities Liberation Organization (or "Red Pa-O"), the northern faction of the Shan State Army, and the Palaung Liberation Army (VOPB, 11 March; *FBIS*, 15 March). BCP-provided weapons, and not ideology, form the basis for these and other cooperative arrangements. Key insurgent groups such as the KNU and the Kayah New People's Party, however, so far have shunned collaboration with the BCP (*FEER*, 9 February; *Washington Times*, 17 August).

In the face of declining Chinese aid, the BCP has

turned increasingly to opium and narcotics trafficking. It controls many of the most productive opium-growing areas in Burma and is a major supplier of raw opium to heroin refineries on the Thai-Burma border. Government efforts to eradicate opium poppy fields and intercept opium caravans en route to refineries thus have an impact on the insurgency. The government has begun to highlight the BCP's narcotics activities to undercut the party's political credibility.

In late 1983 and early 1984, the BCP tried unsuccessfully to establish a base along the Thai border near Doi Lang, evidently to secure a direct outlet to the international narcotics market. Despite the attraction of increased revenues, the deepening involvement in narcotics may eventually pose ideological problems for the BCP. Moreover, it requires a significant diversion of resources to develop and protect the trade. Clashes occurred in early 1984 between the BCP and the Shan United Army (SUA), a warlord group that dominates heroin refining and trafficking at the Thai-Burma border (*Bangkok Post*, 6 January). There are indications that former Kuomintang groups may be interested in cooperation with BCP elements to counter the SUA, proving once again that the political economy of narcotics trafficking in the Golden Triangle can make strange bedfellows (ibid., 13 August).

International Views and Contacts. As noted above, historically the BCP has drawn its ideological inspiration from the Chinese Communist Party and the BCP's positions on international developments have mirrored those of Beijing. *FBIS* has carried very little VOPB commentary this year dealing with the BCP's international views. The party's 1984 New Year's Statement (see *YICA*, 1984, p. 208) predictably followed Chinese positions on Afghanistan, Kampuchea, and USSR-Vietnamese hegemonism. *FBIS* did not carry a 1985 New Year's statement, but it is unlikely that the BCP has taken positions independent of China.

The continued warming of Beijing's relations with Rangoon, however, must give pause to some of the BCP leaders. Burma reaffirmed its *Paukphaw* (a term variously rendered "kinship" or "younger brother/elder brother") relationship, with exchange visits of foreign ministers in February and a widely heralded ten-day "official friendly visit" by Burmese President U San Yu to China in late October and early November. San Yu met with all top Chinese leaders, and extensive press coverage by both Chinese and Burmese media hailed the close ties between the once-estranged countries. While neither side publicly commented on Chinese support for the BCP, the tenor of the exchanges suggested that China had further subordinated the BCP's interests to the larger goals of Chinese diplomacy. (Burmese commentary from both press and Rangoon domestic radio service as well as Chinese reporting were published at length in *FBIS* during the visit.)

Alice Straub
Jon A. Wiant
U.S. Department of State

Note: Views expressed in this article are the authors' own and do not necessarily reflect those of the U.S. Department of State.

China

Population. 1,034,907,000
Party. Chinese Communist Party (Zhongguo gongchan dang; CCP)
Founded. 1921

Membership. Over 40 million (Xinhua, 1 July; *FBIS*, 2 July)

General Secretary. Hu Yaobang

Standing Committee of the Politburo. 6 members: Hu Yaobang, Ye Jianying, Deng Xiaoping, Zhao Ziyang (premier), Li Xiannian (president, PRC; chairman, National People's Congress [NPC]), Chen Yun

Politburo. 24 full members (listed in order of number of strokes in their surname): Wan Li (vice-premier), Xi Zhongxun, Wang Zhen, Wei Guoqing (vice-chairman, NPC), Ulanfu (vice-president, PRC), Fang Yi (state councillor), Deng Xiaoping, Deng Yingchao, Ye Jianying, Li Xiannian, Li Desheng, Yang Shangkun, Yang Dezhi, Yu Qiuli (state councillor), Song Renqiong, Zhang Tingfa, Chen Yun, Zhao Ziyang, Hu Qiaomu, Hu Yaobang, Nie Rongzhen, Ni Zhifu, Xu Xiangqian, Peng Zhen (chairman, Standing Committee, NPC); 3 alternate members (listed in order of number of votes): Yao Yilin (vice-premier), Qin Jiwei, Chen Muhua (state councillor)

Secretariat. 9 full members: Wan Li, Xi Zhongxun, Deng Liqun, Yang Yong, Yu Qiuli, Gu Mu (state councillor), Chen Pixian, Hu Qili, Yao Yilin; 2 alternate members: Qiao Shi, Hao Jianxiu

Central Military Commission. Chairman: Deng Xiaoping; 4 vice-chairmen: Ye Jianying, Xu Xiangqian, Nie Rongzhen, Yang Shangkun (permanent vice-chairman)

Central Advisory Commission. Chairman: Deng Xiaoping; 4 vice-chairmen: Bo Yibo (state councillor), Xu Shiyou, Tan Zhenlin, Li Weihan

Central Commission for Discipline Inspection. First secretary: Chen Yun; second secretary: Huang Kecheng; permanent secretary: Wang Heshou; 5 secretaries: Wang Congwu, Han Guang, Li Chang, Ma Guorui, Han Tianshi

Central Committee. 348 full and alternate members

Status. Ruling party

Last Congress. Twelfth, 1–11 September 1982, in Beijing

Last Election. 1981, all 3,202 candidates CCP approved

Auxiliary Organizations. All-China Women's Federation, led by Kang Keqing; Communist Youth League of China (50 million members), led by Hu Jingtao (replacing Wang Zhaoguo on 14 December); All-China Federation of Trade Unions, led by Ni Zhifu

Publications. The official and most authoritative publication of the CCP is the newspaper *Renmin Ribao* (People's daily; *RMRB*), published in Beijing. The theoretical journal of the Central Committee, *Hongqi* (Red flag), is published approximately once a month. The daily paper of the People's Liberation Army (PLA) is *Jiefangjunbao* (Liberation Army daily). The weekly *Beijing Review* (*BR*), published in English and several other languages, carries translations of important articles, editorials, and documents from these three publications and from other sources. *China Daily*, the first English-language national newspaper in the PRC, began official publication in Beijing and Hong Kong on 1 June 1981. It began publishing an edition in New York in June 1983. The official news agency of the party and government is the New China News Agency (Xinhua; NCNA).

Leadership and Party Organization. According to the party constitution, the National Congress of the party is the "highest leading body" of the CCP. Normally, the National Congress is held once every five years. However, except for the most recent congress, the twelfth, which met in September 1982, all previous ones were convened early or postponed. The congress elects a Central Committee, which governs when the congress is not in session. The Central Committee elects the Political Bureau (Politburo), the Standing Committee of the Politburo, the Secretariat, and the general secretary of the Central Committee. The Politburo and its Standing Committee act for the Central Committee when it is not in session. The Secretariat handles the day-to-day work of the Central Committee under the direction of the Politburo and its Standing Committee. The general secretary of the Central Committee convenes the meetings of the Politburo and presides over the work of the Secretariat (in September 1982, the CCP abolished the post of chairman). The Central Committee also decides on the members of the Central Military Commission of the Central Committee, whose chairman is a member of the Standing Committee of the Politburo. There is also a Central Advisory Commission, created in September 1982, which "acts as political assistant and consultant to the Central Committee." Members of this commission must be party members of at least 40 years' standing who have rendered considerable service. Finally, there is a Central Commission for Discipline Inspection, which functions under the Central Committee.

The Twelfth Party Congress elected the Twelfth Central Committee in September 1982 with 348 full and alternate members. More than 60 percent of these were elected to the Central Committee for the first time, and two-thirds of these new members were under 60. More professional and technological cadres were included. The Second Plenary Session was held 11–12 October 1983. The Third Plenary Session was held 20 October.

Primary party organizations are found in factories, shops, schools, offices, city neighborhoods, people's communes, cooperatives, farms, townships, towns, companies of the People's Liberation Army (PLA), and other basic units where there are three or more party members. The PLA's General Political Department is the political-work organ of the Central Military Commission, and it directs party and political work in the armed forces. According to the latest revised party constitution (Article 23), the organizational system and organs of the party in the PLA are to be prescribed by the Central Military Commission.

The highest organ of state power in the PRC is the National People's Congress (NPC). The NPC is elected for a term of five years and holds one session each year, although both of these stipulations are subject to alteration. The first session of the Sixth NPC was held 6–21 June 1983; the second session was held 15–31 May 1984.

The NPC elects a Standing Committee composed of a chairman, vice-chairman, the secretary general, and other members. The officers and members of the Sixth NPC Standing Committee were elected on 18 June 1983.

The 1982 PRC constitution restored the post of president (previously translated as chairman) of the PRC. The president represents the state in its domestic affairs and in its relations with foreign states. A vice-president assists him in his tasks. Both are elected for five-year terms and may not serve more than two consecutive terms.

The State Council is the Central People's Government of the PRC and as such is the executive body of the NPC and the NPC's Standing Committee; it is the highest organ of state administration. The State Council was extensively reorganized in 1982. It consists of the premier, vice-premiers, the state councillors, the ministers in charge of ministries and of commissions, the auditor-general, and

the secretary general. (For a list of members, see *BR*, 27 June 1983.)

The Chinese People's Political Consultative Conference (CPPCC) is the official organization of the PRC's united front policy. The CPPCC is organized into a National Committee, which holds plenary sessions and elects the CPPCC's Standing Committee. At its first session in June 1983, the current Sixth National Committee had 2,039 members. Its second session was held 12–26 May. Deng Yingchao is chairperson of the CPPCC's National Committee. The CPPCC also has local committees at the provincial, autonomous region, municipal, and other levels.

The PLA includes the Chinese navy and air force. It numbers over 4 million men, but is cutting back. Its political influence has been reduced in recent years. The 1982 PRC constitution established a Central Military Commission, which directs the armed forces of the country. From 1978 to 1982, the chairman of the CCP (a post now abolished) was commander-in-chief of the armed forces. The constitution says little of the specific responsibilities of the state Central Military Commission or of its relationship to the Central Committee's Central Military Commission. Deng Xiaoping is chairman of both commissions.

Domestic Affairs. This was another banner year for Deng Xiaoping and his reform program. The rectification campaign launched in October 1983 seemed to falter at the beginning of the year, having been distracted by the ancillary "spiritual pollution" campaign, also begun late in 1983. However, following the decisive curtailment of the latter campaign, party rectification began to regain momentum, slowly for a time but with renewed vigor toward the end of the year. Rectification was seen as an essential complement to the rural economic reforms already successfully under way since 1979 and to the wide-ranging and important urban economic reforms introduced and formally sanctioned by the party this year. The economic reforms were the focus of attention at the two most important meetings of the year, the Second Session of the Sixth NPC in May and the Third Plenary Session of the Twelfth Central Committee in October. Also distinguishing this year was an agreement with Great Britain on the return of Hong Kong in 1997. Perhaps most intriguing of all, however, in this most interesting year were indications that the relevance to the present of Marxist ideology itself was being reassessed. However, the publication during the year of a report on China by Amnesty International served as a sober reminder of a less salutary aspect of China's political reality.

On 1 January, the Party Rectification Guidance Committee issued a circular calling for the punishment of corrupt party functionaries but did not specifically mention the leftists who are among the main targets of the campaign (Xinhua, Beijing, 2 January; *FBIS*, 3 January; *NYT*, 3 January). Indeed, subsequent reports revealed that a number of prominent officials and relatives were being exposed and prosecuted for misconduct, the most celebrated instance being the execution of the grandson of the late Marshal Zhu De (*Cheng Ming*, Hong Kong, February; *FBIS*, 9 February). But it was apparent that the ancillary "spiritual pollution" campaign was being manipulated by some to distract from the main purpose of the rectification program and to oppose changes brought about by economic reforms and the open-door policy. Intellectuals were being targeted in particular. Novelist Zhang Xiaotian, among others, made public self-criticism (*RMRB*, 9 January; *FBIS*, 17 January). In fact, the diatribes against "spiritual contamination" raised anxiety levels considerably and made many Chinese fear a return to a more xenophobic atmosphere in China and less willing to cooperate overtly in rectification work or even in the implementation of some of the new economic policies. The Deng Xiaoping leadership tried repeatedly to contain this dangerous drift from its ambitious program. A confidential directive circulated in early January sought in effect to cancel the spiritual pollution campaign by attaching a great many restrictions to it (*NYT*, 24 January). Even so, disagreement over the spiritual campaign and the effects of it continued to hamper Deng Xiaoping's main efforts for months.

Western press reports, however, that the dispute had forced Deng Liqun to resign as head of the party's Propaganda Department proved to be incorrect (ibid., 13 April). By March and April, the focus began to turn away from the distraction, although rather tentatively at first. Circular number seven of the Rectification Guidance Committee issued on 4 March still scarcely mentioned the leftists (Xinhua, Beijing, 4 March; *FBIS*, 5 March). A *People's Daily* editorial on 15 March admitted that "an obstruction in the middle" was preventing satisfactory implementation of the rectification (*FBIS*, 15 March). Articles began to appear that specifically stressed the party's policy on raising the status of intellectuals, including their induction into the party itself in greater numbers (e.g., *RMRB*, 10 July; *FBIS*, 13 July), and explicit attacks on leftists resurfaced and became increasingly bold. By midyear, demands to negate the Cultural Revolution appeared. An article in *Hongqi*, for example, argued the importance of "totally negating" the radical slogan "Politics in Command" that was prominent during the Cultural Revolution (Xinhua, Beijing, 15 July; *FBIS*, 16 July). By year's end, particularly following the Third Plenum (discussed below), the Rectification Campaign took on a more serious and determined tone.

The sixtieth anniversary of the First National Congress of the Kuomintang was commemorated at a forum in Beijing on 20 January, at which Deng Yingchao, chairman of the National Committee of the CPPCC, gave an address. Deng reviewed the history of earlier cooperation between the Communists and the Nationalists and proposed that the Nationalists enter yet a third round of cooperation in order to accomplish the reunification of China (*BR*, 30 January). This reiteration of a now familiar proposal fell on deaf ears in Taiwan. Nor did the successful negotiation during the year between London and Beijing of the return of Hong Kong in 1997 succeed in impressing Taiwan's political leadership.

On 6 April it was announced in Beijing that flexible economic policies currently being practiced in four special economic zones in south China would be extended to fourteen more coastal cities and to Hainan Island (ibid., 16 April).

The State Council promulgated tentative regulations on 6 April governing the identity of residents of the PRC and requiring that all adult Chinese citizens in residence apply for resident identity cards. Details on the implementation of these regulations were to be formulated by the Ministry of Public Security (Xinhua, Beijing, 6 May; *FBIS*, 11 May.)

The Second Session of the Sixth NPC, with over 2,700 deputies in attendance, was held in Beijing, 15–31 May. The session ended with a resolution calling on governments at all levels to implement economic reforms. The resolution also endorsed the government work report given by Premier Zhao Ziyang on 15 May. Peng Zhen, chairman of the NPC Standing Committee, gave the closing address. The meeting also passed a Law on Regional Autonomy for Minority Nationalities and a Conscription Law (which also restored military rank insignia). The session also adopted the 1984 economic and social development plan, the 1983 final state accounts, and the 1984 economic state budget and the work reports of the NPC Standing Committee, the Supreme People's Court, and the Supreme People's Procuratorate. It also approved a decision to establish the Hainan Administrative Region, under the leadership of the provincial government of Guangdong. (*BR*, 11 June.)

Premier Zhao, in his work report, could speak with some satisfaction regarding economic progress made in the preceding year. Following four consecutive years of increased agricultural output, 1983 brought yet another excellent harvest. Both urban and rural living standards were further improved. Gross industrial production increased by 10.5 percent, agricultural production by 9.5 percent. Zhao stressed that the various economic relations were yet to be straightened out and the price system, in particular, was irrational. Two major issues were to receive special attention: the restructuring of the economic system and the opening to the outside world. In this regard, the following points were to be emphasized: (1) overcoming, step by step, the defect of "everybody eating from the same big pot" in the urban economy so as to bring the initiative of the enterprises and workers and staff into fuller play; (2) restructuring the managerial systems of the building industry and capital construction and substantially increasing returns on investment (the building industry, it was acknowledged, has long been plagued with problems of low efficiency, a high rate of consumption, great waste, and technical stagnation—the key to the reform was said to lie in carrying out the investment responsibility and public bidding systems); (3) reform of the circulation system and improving circulation channels so as to ensure a smooth flow of goods; (4) striving to make the special economic zones a success, opening more coastal cities, and expanding economic and technological exchanges with other countries; and (5) giving full play to the role of the intellectuals in socialist construction and putting the talents of all trained personnel to rational use. (Highlights, Xinhua, Beijing, 15 May; *FBIS*, 16 May; full text, *BR*, 11 June.)

The Second Session of the Sixth CPPCC was held in Beijing, 12–26 May. Some 1,700 delegates met, partly in joint session with the NPC. The political resolution adopted by the CPPCC session supported the government's decision to pay special attention to the two major issues of economic re-

structuring and opening to the outside world. The *Beijing Review* (4 June) reported that the CPPCC delegates "spoke their minds on major state affairs, candidly criticized the work of the CPPCC and the NPC and submitted more than 1,000 motions in which they aired their opinions and suggestions." There was no mention regarding their views of the work of the CCP.

In May it was reported that a new 60-volume Chinese edition of the collected works of Lenin will be published in China. Based on the fifth Russian edition (with some pieces added from the Russian edition of the *Works of Lenin*), it will supplant the present 39-volume collection, which, based on the fourth Soviet edition and published two decades ago, is said to have "some faults and can no longer meet today's needs." The present collection neglects many of Lenin's works, especially those published after the October Revolution; its quality of translation is "not good enough"; and it includes too few references, some of which are either "too simple or inaccurate." The new edition includes more than 9,000 essays and has 6,000 more pieces than the previous edition. "A rather large proportion of the newly collected works," it is said, "which are more realistic and significant to China's present situation, were written after the October Revolution." These "will create more favourable conditions for the Chinese people to study Marxism-Leninism systematically." The first four volumes were to be published in 1984. Eight volumes containing the works written after 1917 were scheduled to be off the press in 1985. The whole collection will be available by 1990. (*BR*, 28 May.)

Regarding the effort to separate government administration from commune management, it was reported in June that as of the end of 1983, 22,897 townships had been set up throughout China. It was expected at that time that the process would be completed by the end of 1984. (Ibid., 4 June.) In October it was reported that more than 60,000 township cadres had been selected and employed on the basis of a contract system as part of an effort to recruit better educated and more professional cadres (*RMRB*, 15 October; *FBIS*, 19 October).

On 1 July, the Organization Department of the Central Committee announced that more than 4.8 million people had been admitted into the party over the preceding five years. There are now more than 40 million members, 2.5 million grass-roots party organizations, and about 9 million cadres. Of the 800,000 new members who joined in 1983, only 80,000 were peasants. About 150,000 specialists and professionals have been admitted in the preceding four years. In the central government organizations, 6,887 such people joined, comprising 53 percent of new recruits. It reported that almost 10,000 college students are being admitted every year. In Beijing in 1983, 2,000 students became members, while 7,000 others applied for membership. (Xinhua, Beijing, 1 July; *FBIS*, 2 July.) But later in the year reports indicated continuing dissatisfaction with the pace of this reform. Only 4 percent of the party members had a college education; only 17.8 percent had a secondary education. Many intellectuals were being blocked from entry into the party for fear that they would threaten the "iron seats" (the positions) of party functionaries. This opposition is a disguised one, with such functionaries practicing "formalism" or giving only lip-service to directives. (*FEER*, 20 December.)

On 21 July, it was announced that the Central Committee's Secretariat had recently decided to decentralize personnel and a relevant Organization Department circular stipulated that the change was to take effect as of 1 August. Under the new system cadres under the direct management of the Central Committee will mainly be senior officials at the level of vice-minister of ministries and provincial vice-governor and above, and leading cadres of big and influential enterprises, institutions of scientific research, and major institutions of higher education. The next lower level of cadres, formerly also managed by the Central Committee's Organizational Department, will henceforth be managed by the ministries, provinces, regions, municipalities, and other institutions of the same level. This change cuts the number of cadres managed directly by the Central Committee by two-thirds. (*China Daily*, Hong Kong edition, 22 July.)

The Chinese team did remarkably well at the Summer Olympics in Los Angeles in July and August. Although it was the first full-fledged appearance at the Olympics of a PRC team, the Chinese athletes won fifteen gold, eight silver, and nine bronze medals and ranked fourth in the overall standings at the close of competition (*BR*, 20 August). Most Soviet bloc countries did not participate.

Deng Xiaoping's daughter Mao Mao published an article in the *People's Daily* on 22 August on her father's experience for three years in Jiangxi province during the Cultural Revolution (*FBIS*, 23 August). The English translation of the *Selected Works of Deng Xiaoping* was placed on sale in China on 28 September.

On 15 August, the General Office of the Central Committee affirmed the achievements of Beijing municipality and the Anshan Iron and Steel Company "in making their leading bodies more revolutionary, younger in average age, better educated, and more professionally competent" (*RMRB*, 7 September; *FBIS*, 14 September). The Anshan Iron and Steel Company had previously been a prominent radical model (or at least its "charter" was) during the Cultural Revolution period.

On 5 September, the *China Daily* reported on the status of efforts to streamline the government structure by mid-1984. This program, intended to overcome bureaucracy and increase efficiency, was now completed at the central, provincial, prefectural, and municipal levels. Leading cadres at the provincial level were reduced in number by 34 percent, their average age lowered by seven years, those with a college education increased from 20 to 43 percent, and those below the age of 45 are now said to constitute 10 percent of the total. At the prefectural and municipal levels, the number of leading cadres had been cut by 36 percent, their average age reduced by eight years, those with a college education increased from 14 to 44 percent, and those below the age of 45 now constitute one-third of the total. The average age of leading county government cadres, already reorganized, is now 42–43 years. By 1985, all cadres below the rank of government minister and provincial governor are to retire at age 60. (*FBIS*, 5 September.)

After two years of intensive, secret negotiations, Beijing and London concluded a historic draft agreement on 26 September to return Hong Kong to China in 1997. The draft agreement was initialed in Beijing by British ambassador Richard Evans and Chinese assistant foreign minister Zhou Nan. The Chinese pledged to maintain Hong Kong's capitalist system and lifestyle for at least 50 years after 1997. Also affirmed was that Hong Kong will remain an international financial center (it is the world's third largest) and free port, hold on to its convertible currency, its gold, its securities and futures markets, and its free flow of capital. China will assume responsibility for foreign affairs and defense. (*NYT*, 27 September.) This will include the stationing of PLA forces in Hong Kong. Deng Xiaoping, earlier in the year had scolded two of his senior colleagues (Geng Biao and Huang Hua) who had been heard to say that the PLA would not be sent to Hong Kong (*FEER*, 7 June). On 19 December, Prime Minister Margaret Thatcher and Premier Zhao Ziyang signed the agreement in the Great Hall of the People, in front of Deng Xiaoping and more than a hundred dignitaries (AP, Beijing, 19 December; *Honolulu Star-Bulletin*, 19 December). A full text of the Joint Declaration can be found in the 1 October issue of the *Beijing Review*.

On 1 October, the PRC celebrated its thirty-fifth anniversary with an exceptional pageant in Tian An Men Square. Deng Xiaoping lionized the event. He reviewed the PLA formations before the parade commenced. He gave the only speech—twelve minutes long. More than 10,000 troops marched with various kinds of equipment and armament through the square, where over 100,000 people stood in colorful groupings. A flyover by 94 air force aircraft was largely obscured by haze. (*CSM*, 2 October.)

Following six days of preparatory meetings, the Third Plenary Session of the Twelfth Central Committee was held on 20 October in Beijing. It was a landmark meeting, rivaling in historic importance the famous Third Plenum of the Eleventh Central Committee in December 1978. Attending the plenum were 321 members and alternate members of the Central Committee. Nonvoting delegates who also attended were members of the Central Advisory Commission and of the Central Commission for Discipline Inspection and principal leading comrades from the relevant local and central departments, 297 in all. The plenum adopted a 39-page document entitled "Decision of the Central Committee of the Communist Party of China on Reform of the Economic Structure." The plenum also decided to convene in September 1985 a "national conference" of party delegates. Such a meeting would be distinct from a fourth plenary session of the present Central Committee or from a new party congress, the thirteenth. It was reported that the agenda of the national conference would include (1) discussion and adoption of the proposals on the essentials of the seventh five-year plan (1986–1990) for China's economic and social development; and (2) election of additional members of the Central Committee and other organizational matters. (Xinhua, Beijing, 20 October; *FBIS*, 22 October.)

In essence, the "Decision" extended the rural economic reforms initiated at the 1978 Third Plenum to the urban economy and throughout China. Moreover, although many of its specific measures have already been the subject of experiments, the "Decision" carries with it the full official sanction of the party, which is expected to provide fresh impetus to the reform movement. By implication it suggests the end of the road for the Soviet model in China. Greater independence is given to a million state-owned enterprises, compelling them to compete in order to survive. Government functions are to be separated from purely economic ones, the latter being left to plant managers, who will operate within guidelines. Central planning will be limited, many consumer subsidies will be phased out, and the prices of many products are to be determined by supply and demand. The present pricing system was termed "irrational." The document also pledged to expand foreign trade, promote younger technical experts in government service, and retire old managers in key industries in 1985. Increases in urban wages are to be based upon greater productivity. Deng Xiaoping reportedly told visiting Chancellor Helmut Kohl of West Germany that he regarded these changes as "a kind of revolution" for China. The "Decision" did declare that China would continue to adhere to communist principles, but it also conceded that so far they had not worked very well in China. The superiority of the socialist system, it said, "has not been brought into full play." (*NYT*, 21 October; full text of the "Decision" in *BR*, 29 October.)

The results of an interesting, unprecedented experiment that had taken place about three months earlier was revealed in November. Bai Jinian, the party secretary of Shaanxi province, was elected by secret ballot from among thirteen nominees (who were subsequently reduced to eleven, then six by ballot) at a meeting of more than 300 cadres at the level of county party secretary or above. It was reported that neither the central nor the provincial leadership intervened in the election; the candidates had not been put up by the higher authorities beforehand. Bai met the three conditions for eligibility: he was under 60 and highly educated, and he had not compromised himself during the Cultural Revolution. (*RMRB*, 13 November; *FBIS*, 14 November.) It has been suggested that such democratization within the party itself represents an extension of the current economic reforms into the political sphere (*Asiaweek*, 7 December).

In late November the party toughened its stance considerably regarding opponents of the economic reforms. The *People's Daily* declared that such opponents must be "cleared out" and prosecuted. "It is impossible to change their minds by the means of ideological education, so we must take effective measures to dismiss them from office," it said. (Combined News Services, Beijing, 30 November; *Honolulu Advertiser*, 30 November.) On 22 November the party announced that all party members would have to re-register over the next two years. All party members from the highest level of government to the grass roots would be reassessed. The re-registration process "will be completed generally within a month or so." (*BR*, 17 December.)

On 22 December, 40 senior PLA officers retired in the wake of Deng Xiaoping's campaign to promote younger, "more open-minded" officers to key military posts, according to the PLA's newspaper (Combined News Services, Beijing, 30 December; *Honolulu Sunday Star-Bulletin & Advertiser*, 30 December).

On 7 December, the *People's Daily* published a leading article that generated considerable reaction around the world. The article said: "We cannot expect the works of Marx and Lenin in their day to solve the problems of today." The newspaper subsequently printed a correction to this remarkable *faux pas* indicating that the word "all" had been inadvertently omitted. The sentence should have read: "We cannot expect the works of Marx and Lenin in their day to solve all the problems of today." Immediate speculation tended to be somewhat unrestrained in some quarters. However, even the corrected version is rather bold and subject to liberal interpretation, particularly since no heads rolled at the newspaper nor were any abject apologies rendered publicly. (See, e.g., *FEER*, 20 December.) About two weeks later, the *People's Daily* publicized an editorial that again challenged critics within the party and elsewhere by asserting that "Marxism is not a dogma but a guide to action." An accompanying commentary said that at present "there are many new things and new problems that have never been seen or heard, and that do not appear in books at all." It added: "More than ever before, we cannot cut our feet to fit our shoes." (*NYT* Service, Beijing, 25 December; *Honolulu Star-Bulletin*, 25 December.)

On 31 December, a new 72-page book of Deng Xiaoping's speeches went on sale. Entitled *Building Socialism with Chinese Characteristics*, it asserts that China will remain socialist despite the adoption of "some capitalism" in order to advance modernization. Its appearance seemed timed to rebut allegations that China may be gradually discarding socialism. (AP, Beijing, 31 December; *Honolulu Star-Bulletin*, 31 December.)

Much attention during the year continued to be given to legal reform. On 21 September Xinhua provided some relevant statistics. In the past five years China promulgated more than 850 laws, decrees, and legally effective regulations. Thirty-four of these and eighteen decisions on revisions and amendments of laws were issued by the NPC and its Standing Committee. The State Council and its ministries and commissions issued more than 260 regulations and decrees. More than 530 local regulations were enacted at the provincial level and below. In the past five years, some 300 economic laws and regulations have been promulgated, of which 107 are specially formulated for foreign economic activities or involve the latter. There are now nine law research institutes and 69 journals and newspapers devoted to the law. In addition to one university and four colleges of political science and law, there are 31 universities with law courses in their curriculum. More than 1 million officials are working in the field of political science and law, with more than 140,000 judges serving at the Supreme People's Court, 29 Higher People's Courts, some 300 Intermediate People's Courts, and nearly 3,000 Basic People's Courts. There are 16,000 lawyers and about 2,500 legal advisory offices. There are also more than 5 million mediators and 800,000 mediation committees. (*FBIS*, 4 October.)

The crime rate since August 1983 dropped noticeably, it was reported. The current crime rate, in September, was near the lowest historical record—3 per 10,000 people. Only about 5 percent of the country's prison inmates commit new offenses after their release. (Ibid.)

Another view was provided in a major new report published on 25 September by Amnesty International. The report cites evidence of mass executions, of political prisoners held for years without trial or convicted after summary proceedings, and of ill-treatment of prisoners. The report says nonviolent dissent has been suppressed by convicting political activists of "counter-revolutionary offenses" carrying sentences of ten to fifteen years in prison. Prisoners include workers and students active in the "democracy movement" that blossomed in 1978, Roman Catholic priests loyal to the Vatican, and Tibetan nationalists. Concern was expressed about the mass executions that began with the nationwide anticrime campaign in August 1983. The report indicates that 44 crimes are now punishable by death in the PRC, including "counter-revolutionary offenses, theft, embezzlement, the molestation of women and pimping." It called on China to end the death penalty, release political prisoners, and ensure fair trials. (Amnesty International, *China: Violations of Human Rights* [London: Amnesty International Publications, 1984].)

On 2 November, the Ministry of Public Security announced the removal of the designations of landlords, rich peasants, counterrevolutionaries, and bad elements from a final group of 79,000 people of a total of 20 million who were convicted in the 1950s in the above four categories. This completed a process that had begun in 1979. There still remained another 195 in jail or undergoing forced labor for actual offenses committed. (Xinhua, Beijing, 2 November; *FBIS*, 5 November.)

The Chinese government refused an opportunity to respond to Amnesty International's appeal, but later a spokesman for the Ministry of Public Security defended the execution of thousands of criminals during the preceding fifteen months. He noted that the crime rate had fallen by more than 30 percent because executions "educate" the public. He denied that the number of executions was as high as 10,000, but refused to give a figure. (AP, Beijing, 16 November; *Honolulu Star-Bulletin*, 16 November.)

On 31 December, it was announced that peasants would no longer be obliged to sell part of their harvest to the state. Instead, grain is to be purchased through contracts with the state or sold on the open market. This decision was made at a rural work conference attended by the premier and the party general secretary among others. It is designed to enable market demand to prevent surpluses, help diversify supplies, and promote animal husbandry, forestry, transport, and other services, it was said. China's state granaries were currently overflowing. A week earlier, it had been announced that the 1984 grain crop of more than 400 million metric tons was the first surplus in the history of the PRC, up 12.5 million tons from 1983 and 82 million tons from 1980. (AP, Beijing, 31 December; *Honolulu Star-Bulletin*, 31 December.)

Auxiliary and Front Organizations. This was not as important a year for the auxiliary organizations as was 1983 when the Communist Youth League, the Women's Federation, and the Federation of Trade Unions all held congresses, as did the eight democratic parties and the All-China Federation of Industry and Commerce. (The meetings of the latter organizations were reported upon in *BR*, 16 January.) The most important meeting in 1984 was that of the CPPCC, whose Sixth National Committee held its Second Session 12–26 May, as noted above. The CPPCC is the most important organizational expression of the party's united front policy.

On 19 March it was announced that the United Front Work Department of the Central Committee recently held ten forums in succession "to solicit the opinion of responsible persons of the democratic parties and nonparty friends on the work of the department and on party rectification." There were 65 participants, including leaders of the democratic parties, the All-China Federation of Industry and Commerce, the All-China Federation of Taiwan Compatriots, and other nonparty friends. Afterwards, members of the United Front Work Department called upon or met separately with sixteen leaders of the democratic parties and nonparty persons to solicit their opinions. (Xinhua, Beijing, 19 March; *FBIS*, 21 March.)

The All-China Federation of Returned Overseas Chinese held its Third National Conference 11–16 April in Beijing, with 694 delegates in attendance. This federation was founded in 1956 and held its last national conference in 1978. The federation revised its constitution and elected Ye Fei and Zhuang Xiquan as honorary chairmen and Zhang Guoji as chairman. It was reported that as of the end of 1983, 5,040 returned Chinese intellectuals and their relatives had joined the CCP. (*BR*, 23 April.)

In July, the Communist Youth League (CYL) held a national conference on educational activities in Harbin to study party rectification documents. At the end of the meeting, the CYL was called upon to lead all of China's youth to participate vigorously in economic reform, to serve as assistants for the party, and to play a vanguard role. (Heilongjiang provincial service, Harbin, 9 July; *FBIS*, 10 July.) The CYL held the third plenum of its Eleventh Youth Congress in December. On 14 December Hu Jingtao was elected first secretary, succeeding Wang Zhaoguo (*Asiaweek*, 4 January 1985).

In September, the Central Committee's Propaganda Department called a meeting of more than 50 important writers, artists, critics, and senior cadres in cultural departments. The participants agreed that reforms in finance and administration should take place without delay, and it was affirmed that the immediate central task was to promote creative writing in support of China's modernization program. The meeting reportedly agreed that much more confidence had been placed in writers and artists since late 1978 and that literature and art had thrived since then. Preparations were under way for a forthcoming fifth national congress of writers and artists. No date was set; the last such congress was held in 1979. (Xinhua, Beijing, 18 September; *FBIS*, 26 September.)

International Views and Positions. The PRC's foreign relations continued to be highly energetic in

1984, highlighted by the expressly "open-door" policy, which was resoundingly reaffirmed at the Third Plenum in October. Clearly, the trend was toward increased foreign involvement both domestically and abroad. The party's International Liaison Department in September announced that it had friendly ties with more than 150 political parties and organizations overseas (Xinhua, Beijing, 15 September; *FBIS*, 17 September) so that the brisk activity is on both a state-to-state and a party-to-party basis.

Premier Zhao Ziyang in midyear told U.S. sinologist A. Doak Barnett that two important groups, neither of which had previously been mentioned publicly by a top Chinese leader, are involved in the foreign policy decisionmaking process. One is a special foreign affairs group under the party's Secretariat, reportedly headed by President Li Xiannian. This group brings together most of China's leading foreign affairs specialists to discuss key policy issues. It may make some policy decisions. The other group is a coordinating body under the State Council, headed by State Councillor and former foreign affairs minister Ji Pengfei. Ji meets frequently to coordinate the foreign affairs work of government ministries with Foreign Minister Wu Xueqian and Minister for Foreign Economic Relations and Trade Chen Muhua. The interview additionally made it apparent that the main locus of day-to-day policymaking has shifted from the Politburo to the Secretariat and the State Council. (*NYT*, 13 August.)

The most comprehensive authoritative statements on Chinese foreign policy during the year were made by Premier Zhao in his "Report on the Work of the Government" to the Second Session of the NPC on 15 May (*BR*, 11 June for full text) and Foreign Minister Wu's speech to the U.N. General Assembly on 26 September (ibid., 8 October). Underscored in these presentations were the intended stability of the open-door policy, China's nonalignment with either superpower, and its orientation toward the Third World.

As noted above, on 19 December Premier Zhao and Prime Minister Margaret Thatcher signed the historic Sino-British Joint Declaration, which returns Hong Kong to China's sovereignty in 1997.

Trips abroad were made by President Li Xiannian, General Secretary Hu Yaobang, Premier Zhao Ziyang, and Foreign Economic Relations and Trade Minister Chen Muhua. President Li made two separate trips, the first, 5–12 March, to Pakistan, Jordan, Turkey, and Nepal; the second,

12–24 November to Spain, Portugal, and Malta. General Secretary Hu visited North Korea, 4–11 May. Premier Zhao made two trips. The first was to the United States, 9–17 January, and Canada, 17–23 January. The second was 29 May–16 June, to France, Belgium, Sweden, Norway, Denmark, Italy, and the headquarters of the European Community in Brussels. Foreign Minister Wu visited Burma and Malaysia, 22–28 February; Yugoslavia, Romania, Austria, France, Tunisia, and Kuwait, 29 March to 12 April; Mexico, Venezuela, Brazil, and Argentina, 1–15 August; Iran, 23–27 November; and accompanied Li Xiannian on the southern European trip in November and visits to the United States. Chen Muhua visited the United States in May and made two trips to Eastern Europe in June and September.

Among the prominent visitors to China were Australian prime minister Bob Hawke, Japanese prime minister Yasuhiro Nakasone, U.S. president Ronald Reagan, PLO chairman Yassir Arafat, Yugoslav president Dragoslav Marković, Brazilian president João Baptista Figueiredo, Mozambican president Samora Moisés Machel, North Korean premier Kang Song-san, Equatorial Guinean president Teodoro Obiang Nguema Mbasogo, Burmese president U San Yu, Norwegian prime minister Kaare Willock, and North Korean president Kim Il-song (an unofficial visit).

Illustrating China's commitment to the Third World, Xinhua (Beijing, 16 September) revealed in September that by the end of 1983, "New China had sent more than 400,000 technical personnel to help with 1,062 development schemes in the Third World" (*FBIS*, 17 September).

Relations with Japan were highlighted by Prime Minister Yasuhiro Nakasone's visit to China in October. During his visit, Nakasone indicated that "Japan was willing to give first priority to cooperating as much as possible with China in the fields of energy, transportation and communications" (Xinhua, Beijing, 12 October; *FBIS*, 15 October). Three thousand Japanese youth were invited for a fifteen-day visit to China in late September and early October (*RMRB*, 10 October; *FBIS*, 15 October). On 10 September, the first meeting was held in Tokyo of the new Committee for Sino-Japanese Friendship in the 21st Century; Nakasone attended (*RMRB*, 11 September; *FBIS*, 17 September). Of greater significance were reports of military consultations during the year, in response to Soviet military developments. This included overt mutual inspection of military facilities in China and Japan and also secret meetings to exchange military information and discuss strategy toward the USSR. (*Guardian*, London, 30 December; *Honolulu Sunday Star-Bulletin & Advertiser*, 30 December.)

Relations with India were warm, marked particularly by the fifth round of talks between officials of both countries in Beijing. The talks, concluded on 22 September, were conducted in "a cordial, friendly and frank atmosphere." It was decided to hold the next round in New Delhi. (Xinhua, Beijing, 22 September; *FBIS*, 24 September.)

Relations with Vietnam remained tense. On 6 April, Chinese soldiers struck a short distance into Vietnam in retaliation for a Vietnamese invasion into Thailand in pursuit of Khmer Rouge soldiers (*FEER*, 19 April). In July, China accused Vietnam of fomenting trouble along the border in order to sabotage efforts to normalize Sino-Soviet relations (*NYT*, 25 July).

Roman Catholic Cardinal Jaime Sin of the Philippines made a ten-day visit to China in October-November. Such a trip provided room for speculation, but there was no overt discussion of a reconciliation between Beijing and the Vatican. (*Economist*, London, 3 November.)

Great emphasis was placed on the open-door policy during the year. On 7 October, Deng Xiaoping told the chief responsible persons of dozens of the world's largest enterprises that "China's open-door policy will be carried out for at least 50 to 70 years." He added, "It is not an expedient measure for a period of time, but China's long-term developing strategy. Therefore, you should set your minds at ease." The business executives were attending a symposium on Chinese-foreign joint economic cooperation at the invitation of the China Trust and Investment Corporation. (*Wen Wei Po*, Hong Kong, 7 October; *FBIS*, 9 October.)

China's latest ventures toward a supplemental supply and demand economy with less government control was seen by some foreign businessmen and bankers as a mixed blessing as many came to be inundated by telephone calls and other approaches from many different directions and sources in China. One Canadian exclaimed, "It's like the Wild West" (*Asian Wall Street Journal* [*AWSJ*], 9–10 November). But the announcement by Wei Yuming, vice-minister of the Ministry for Foreign Economic Relations and Trade, that China plans to attract $30 billion in foreign funds during its Seventh Five-Year Plan (1986–1990) was encouraging. About $5–7 billion of this would be direct invest-

ment, it was hoped, with the remainder mainly in low-interest loans from foreign governments and financial institutions. The $30 billion target figure represents a significant increase over the achievement of the past five years. From early 1979 to June 1984, China attracted $15.8 billion in foreign funds, of which $12.5 billion was loans and $3.3 billion was direct investment. (Ibid., 16–17 November.)

In late November the *China Daily* said that over the next three years China will spend $14.2 billion in hard currency to buy foreign technology. China's foreign exchange reserves had grown to $16.48 billion by the end of June from $2.26 billion in 1980 and $14.34 billion at the end of 1983. China's investment priority in the next five years is to modernize industrial enterprises; hence about $20 billion in domestic funds is being earmarked to purchase domestic technology and to install foreign purchases. This will be an attempt to avoid earlier problems when China bought factories that it could not use because of the lack of electricity or equipment that it could not install properly in existing factories. (Ibid., 26 November.)

On 8 November, the Ministry of Foreign Economic Relations and Trade announced that, effective 1 January 1985, "a distinction will be made between government administration and enterprise management and the ministry will no longer intervene in the daily operations of its subordinate general corporations of various special professions and trades. Meanwhile, it will adopt a series of reform measures to push the development of foreign trade." (Xinhua, Beijing, 8 November; *FBIS*, 16 November.)

On 20 December, the *China Daily* announced that a new visa policy would go into effect that month. The new policy would enable some businessmen and tourists to fly into China and apply for visas on arrival at the Beijing airport. The precise details were not provided in the account, and while some problems are likely, the new policy appears to be much more liberal than entry procedures for any other socialist country. The purpose is to streamline the entry process "especially for those who wish to enter China as quickly as possible for business reasons." (*NYT* Service, Beijing, 25 December; *Honolulu Star-Bulletin*, 25 December.)

Relations with the USSR. The year saw a modest continuation of improvement in China's relations with the Soviet Union, albeit with some barbed exchanges traceable primarily to China's posture towards the United States and differences over Indochina. The Soviets remained doubtful about the Chinese economic reforms.

On 24 January, in an interview with French journalists, Hu Yaobang renewed China's call for rapprochement with the Soviet Union, suggesting that greater flexibility on the part of Soviet negotiators could help reduce the differences between the two countries (*WP*, 25 January).

On 14 February, Chinese vice-premier Wan Li led a delegation to Moscow to attend the funeral of the late Soviet president Yuri Andropov, who had died on 9 February (Xinhua, Moscow, 14 February; *FBIS*, 14 February). The Chinese weekly *Liaowang* (20 February) noted that Andropov had expressed "many times" his desire to improve Sino-Soviet relations, "and there was a certain degree of improvement in them; but no substantive progress was made in eliminating the 'three great obstacles'" (*FBIS*, 21 February). At the funeral, General Secretary Konstantin Chernenko did not meet with Wan Li, although Chernenko actively sought meetings with Western leaders (*Inside China Mainland*, 2 March).

Talks on the 1984 border trade between Heilongjiang province and its neighboring area in the Soviet Union were held in Nakhodka from 12 to 23 March. The two sides signed minutes of the talks and a contract on imports and exports, which included a greater variety of goods and a larger volume of trade than at present. (Xinhua, Harbin, 24 March; *FBIS*, 26 March.) On 21 April goods-exchange contracts were signed by the Trade Corporation of the Inner Mongolia Autonomous Region and the Far East Foreign Trade Corporation of the Soviet Union. These talks, lasting ten days, were also held in the port city of Nakhodka. The contracts "call for large increases over 1983 in the value and variety of goods traded." (Xinhua, Huhehot, 24 April; *FBIS*, 25 April.)

The fourth round of Sino-Soviet consultations took place in Moscow 12–26 March. They were held in a "frank and calm atmosphere" and were considered "useful." The next round was scheduled for Beijing in October. The principals were Chinese vice–foreign minister and special envoy Qian Qichen and Soviet vice–foreign minister and special envoy Leonid Ilyichev. (Xinhua, Beijing, 26 March; *FBIS*, 27 March.) While in Moscow, on 23 March, Qian Qichen met with Soviet first vice-chairman and foreign minister Andrei Gromyko (Xinhua, Moscow, 23 March; *FBIS*, 26 March).

Foreign Minister Wu Xueqian later made clear that "no substantive progress" was achieved in the fourth round of consultations (AFP, Beijing, 28 March; *FBIS*, 30 March).

On 16 April, the Chinese Ministry of Education and the USSR Ministry of Higher and Secondary Specialized Education signed a 1984–1985 protocol on student exchanges in Moscow. This year both sides will exchange 70 students who will study in each other's country for one or two years. The students from both sides will expand their specialized studies in the natural, technical, and social sciences, in addition to language study. (Xinhua, Moscow, 16 April; *FBIS*, 23 April.)

Both countries exchanged visits of friendship delegations. Y. V. Bernov led a delegation from the Union of Societies for Friendship and Cultural Relations with Foreign Countries to China in April, and Wang Bingnan led a delegation from the Chinese People's Association for Friendship with Foreign Countries to the Soviet Union in May (Xinhua, Beijing, 5 April, 5 June; *FBIS*, 5 April, 6 June). A Soviet archery team visited China in April (*FBIS*, 1 May), and a Chinese women's volleyball team won a four-nation women's volleyball invitational tournament in the USSR in May-June (Xinhua, Beijing, 5 June; *FBIS*, 6 June).

In mid-April more than 400 Soviet marines performed landing exercises along the Vietnamese coast south of Haiphong, the first such Soviet military game to be held in Vietnam (Xinhua, Tokyo, 18 April; *FBIS*, 25 April). Perhaps in response to this move or to the current Vietnamese campaign against Kampuchean resistance forces, the Chinese undertook two actions of their own within a few days. They mounted a series of attacks against Vietnam on 28 April (during President Reagan's visit to China), and then on 1 May, China's southern fleet sailed around the Spratley islands in the South China Sea and then held amphibious landing exercises on Hainan Island (*FEER*, 14 June).

In a surprising move, the Soviets suddenly postponed the visit to China of First Vice-Minister Ivan Arkhipov on the eve of his arrival in early May. The postponement was especially unexpected in that the intended visit had only been announced a few days earlier. The reason given in the announcement of the postponement released by the Chinese was that the Soviets "need more time to prepare." Special significance was being given to the visit because Arkhipov was the highest-level Soviet official to come to China since Premier Aleksei

Kosygin met Premier Zhou Enlai in 1969. (*AWSJ*, 10 May.) Announcement of China's invitation to Arkhipov had appeared in early February (KYODO, Beijing, 3 February; *FBIS*, 6 February).

There followed a period of several weeks highlighted by barbed public exchanges between the two countries. Chernenko reportedly assailed China twice in June, during meetings successively with Vietnamese leaders Le Duan and Pham Van Dong in Moscow and then with Laotian prime minister Kaysone Phomvihane (*Ta Kung Pao*, Hong Kong, 28 June; *FBIS*, 28 June). A *Guangming Daily* article on 29 June, according to Xinhua, "refuted the slanders and attacks lashed out at China by *Izvestiya* amid the escalating Soviet anti-China propaganda" (*FBIS*, 29 June). The charges and countercharges dealt primarily with differences over Vietnam.

In the midst of such relatively mild exchanges, Vice–Foreign Minister Qian accepted Vice–Foreign Minister Mikhail Kapitsa's invitation to Moscow. He arrived there on 30 June and subsequently met on 2 July with Andrei Gromyko "for an exchange of views on Sino-Soviet relations and some international issues" (Xinhua, Beijing, 3 July; *FBIS*, 3 July).

An article in the *Beijing Review* (9 July) argued that the problems in Sino-Soviet relations were "in essence, a struggle between control and anti-control." "The real problem," said the article, "lies in the fact that while the Soviets attempt to control us, we are opposed to being controlled. Or, in the Kremlin's logic, you are good and revolutionary if you toe its line, and you become a bad counter-revolutionary or a narrow-minded nationalist if you don't."

Another *Beijing Review* article (10 September) commented on Soviet foreign policy as expressed by Chernenko since he assumed power in February. "According to world press reports, the Soviet Union has shown inflexibility in its foreign relations and imperiousness in handling major international affairs." Various Soviet actions "give an impression of frustration and anger, obstinacy in the face of an adverse international environment."

However, relations began to warm again with talks between the Chinese and Soviet foreign ministers in New York in September. The Gromyko-Wu talks lasted for a total of six hours over two days and covered a wide range of issues. Both sides agreed to open high-level talks between the two countries. However, Gromyko reportedly was still noncommittal about the postponed Arkhipov visit, although it was still to take place. (KYODO, Beijing, 29 September; *FBIS*, 3 October.)

On 26 October, Chernenko said that the normalization of relations between the Soviet Union and the PRC would "contribute to improving the situation in the Asian Continent." This was particularly important since "the situation in the world has become tense and the danger of war is growing." Chernenko asserted that the Soviet Union had tried to improve relations with China and was "taking the necessary steps in that direction." "We always keep open the door to constructive talks with China," he added. The comments were made during Chernenko's banquet for his visiting Mongolian counterpart, Jambyn Batmonh. (Xinhua, Moscow, 26 October; *FBIS*, 29 October.)

The fifth round of Sino-Soviet consultations was held in Beijing, 18–26 October. The two chief negotiators, Qian Qichen and Leonid Ilyichev, had "friendly, businesslike and open discussions." Both sides continued to agree not to reveal to third parties what was discussed or what was agreed upon. No substantive breakthrough was made, but it was agreed to expand economic, scientific, cultural, and sports exchanges. (KYODO, Beijing, 27 October; *FBIS*, 29 October.)

In October, articles critical of China's decisions on economic reforms appeared in *Pravda*. In an article from Beijing, *Pravda* said that such measures would result in a "pluralistic economy." The paper also carried a Tass report from Washington listing the capitalistic ills to which the Chinese economy would presumably fall victim, such as disproportional development, inflation, unemployment, and rural-urban social disequality. (*CSM*, 26 October.)

In December, First Vice-Premier Ivan Arkhipov finally visited China. During the visit, Arkhipov and his Chinese counterpart, Vice-Premier Yao Yilin, agreed to sign a five-year trade pact by mid-1985. Expectations were that this accord would be signed during the sixth round of consultations in Moscow next April and seek to boost trade to $6 billion by 1990. Sino-Soviet trade is to increase from an estimated $1.2 billion in 1984 to $1.6 billion in 1985. (*Honolulu Sunday Star-Bulletin & Advertiser*, 23 December.) The nine-day visit was climaxed by the signing of three cooperation agreements calling for technological exchanges and scientific collaboration, including the sharing of research and the establishment of a joint committee to promote trade and other cooperation

(AP, Beijing, 28 December; *Honolulu Star-Bulletin*, 28 December).

Relations with the United States. This was a year of stable, warming relations between China and the United States, symbolized best by the exchange of visits by Premier Zhao Ziyang and President Ronald Reagan, following the very marked improvement of relations registered in 1983.

Premier Zhao visited the United States from 9 to 16 January. The highly successful trip included stops in Honolulu, San Francisco, Berkeley, New York, and Washington, D.C., where Zhao signed two agreements with President Reagan. One, the U.S.-China Science and Technology Co-operative Agreement, extended for five years a similar agreement signed in 1979. The other was the U.S.-China Industrial and Technological Co-operation Accord, a framework agreement to be implemented through the U.S.-China Commission on Commerce and Trade. (*BR*, 23 January.)

It was announced in January that American firms had been awarded 41 percent of the contracts signed in the first round of bidding for the exploration of China's offshore oil resources. Eleven of the 27 foreign oil companies sharing in the contracts were American. (*AWSJ*, 24 January.) However, after three years and the expenditure of an estimated $20 million, Mobil Oil Corporation decided to leave China without a contract (ibid., 17–18 February).

In February five men were arrested in the United States and charged with trying to ship to China a sophisticated piece of equipment that could be used in missile guidance (ibid., 13 February). Another person was charged in early February with attempting to ship computer components to China illegally. The Chinese government denied any involvement with such smuggling. (Ibid., 13 and 23 February.)

On 1 March, it was announced that a U.S. District Court judge, following intervention by the State Department had canceled a $43 million default judgment against the Chinese government in a case brought by American owners of Qing Dynasty railroad bonds (ibid., 1 March).

U.S. Treasury Secretary Donald Regan held three days of economic talks in Beijing in mid-March, in order to define certain issues before President Ronald Reagan's visit to China in April (ibid., 20 March).

In April it was reported that U.S. customs officials were investigating two Vermont companies suspected of illegal arms sales to China (ibid., 6–7 April).

President Ronald Reagan enjoyed a highly successful visit to China, 26 April to 1 May. Reagan's arrival in Beijing was greeted with a 21-gun salute, the first accorded a visitor since the practice was revived recently. The Chinese also chose the day of Reagan's arrival, however, to announce the forthcoming visit of Soviet first vice-premier Ivan Arkhipov. Another controversial incident during the visit was the Chinese decision to delete references to god, freedom, and the Soviet Union in a Chinese broadcast of the president's speech, after having undertaken to air it nationwide and uncensored. An invitation to General Secretary Hu Yaobang to visit the United States was immediately accepted (*FEER*, 10 May). A bilateral nuclear accord was initialed by Reagan following three years of difficult negotiations. This agreement was to run afoul of opponents in Congress in the months ahead (see William Proxmire, "The Risks in Selling China Nuclear Technology," *AWSJ*, 25–26 May; and Nayan Chanda and Robert Manning, *FEER*, 28 June).

Efforts to reach accords on the allotment of shipping business and on bilateral investments in time for the Reagan visit were unsuccessful (see *AWSJ*, 9 and 19 April).

While Reagan was still in China, the Chinese announced that an agreement had been reached with Occidental Petroleum Corporation to begin work on a $600 million coal mine in Shaanxi province. This is the largest joint venture ever between China and foreign interests. Foreign investment in the mine would be about $400 million; China would contribute $240 million. (Ibid., 30 April.)

It was announced in May that the Reagan administration was setting up bilateral "work programs" to accelerate the flow of American technology to China in the fields of telecommunications, electronics, and metallurgy. The Commerce Department set aside nearly $10 million in grants to finance feasibility studies on Chinese projects in which American vendors could participate. Secretary of Commerce Malcolm Baldrige identified four projects: the development of a heavy oil reservoir and of a natural gas field, a railway transportation project, and the processing of silicon materials for semiconductor manufacturing. Arrangements were also made for sale of a $10 million Landsat ground station to the Chinese Academy of Sciences to enable Chinese scientists to receive signals from the remote-sensing U.S. Landsat IV satellite. (Ibid., 10 May.)

In May Reynolds Tobacco International announced a $20 million joint venture with China, making it the first foreign cigarette company to gain access to China's huge domestic cigarette market. The company expects to produce about 2.5 billion cigarettes a year in China, with production of the yet unnamed brand to begin in late 1985. (Ibid., 30 May.)

Chinese defense minister Zhang Aiping led the highest-ranking Chinese military delegation ever to visit the United States for a twelve-day stay in June, marking a new step in U.S.-PRC ties. With the signing of an agreement in principle on arms sales (antitank and antiaircraft weapons), China became the second socialist country (after Yugoslavia) to be eligible for American military sales and credit. China was also promised advanced avionics for its jet interceptors and training for its flyers at American airbases. For its part, China sold half a squadron of its copy of the Soviet MiG-21, the F7, to the United States. (*FEER*, 28 June.)

On 25 July an American presidential trade mission signed an agreement with China to increase aerospace cooperation, purportedly opening the door for American aviation firms to a Chinese market worth billions of dollars. Under the terms of the agreement, the United States will sponsor an aviation seminar in Beijing in 1985 and an aircraft exhibit in 1986. This will be the first such display in a socialist country. The Chinese will send aviation delegations to the United States and will receive an American executive trade mission in 1986. (*South China Morning Post*, Hong Kong, 27 July.)

In late September, China announced it had signed a $140 million contract to purchase 24 helicopters from Sikorsky Aircraft of Stratford, Connecticut. The first three of these aircraft arrived near Beijing by early November. (*AWSJ*, 26 September, 5 November.)

IBM decided to increase its China staff more than sevenfold, to about 45 by the end of 1984, as well as form a new subsidiary unit in China rather than work through its Japanese subsidiary as in the past. This is in recognition of the fact that one of China's highest priorities is the acquisition and development of computer technology. Moreover, IBM has observed that Chinese ministries and factories were beginning to possess cash that had not been previously available. (Ibid., 12 November.)

Meanwhile, one of the largest U.S.-Chinese joint ventures, the Great Wall Hotel, appeared to be in trouble. The first installment on a $80 million loan, due last June, had not been fully paid by late November. Creditor banks were negotiating with American and Chinese owners of the hotel to reschedule the loan. (Ibid., 26 November.)

Evidence of increased military cooperation mounted by year's end. A high-level American military training delegation traveled through China in October, visiting PLA facilities in six cities, including Beijing and Shanghai. Another delegation specializing in military logistics, headed by the assistant secretary of defense for manpower, installations, and logistics toured four cities in November (*Honolulu Sunday Star-Bulletin & Advertiser*, 2 December). Beijing has invited the chairman of the Joint Chiefs of Staff, General John Vessey, to visit China in mid-January 1985. It was expected that Vessey's trip would be followed by the first visit of a U.S. naval ship to a Chinese port since 1949. (*FEER*, 13 December.)

U.S.-Chinese trade reached $4.94 billion in the first ten months of 1984, a 43 percent increase over the same period in 1983. The U.S. embassy in Beijing indicated that the figure could surpass $6 billion by the end of the year. (The two-way trade had fallen by 15 percent in 1983 to $4.41 billion.) The U.S. trade deficit reached $316.4 million in the January-October period, compared with a $298.1 million deficit in the same period in 1983. (*AWSJ*, 20 December.)

Stephen Uhalley, Jr.
University of Hawaii

India

Population. 746,388,000
Party. Communist Party of India (CPI); Communist Party of India–Marxist (CPM)
Membership. CPI: 478,500 (*Calcutta Telegraph*, 26 October); CPM: 271,500 (*Calcutta Statesman*, 3 November 1982)
Secretary General. CPI: C. Rajeswara Rao; CPM: E. M. S. Namboodiripad
Politburo. CPI: Central Executive Council, 11 members; CPM: 9 members
Central Committee. CPI: National Council, 124 members; CPM, 45 members
Status. Legal
Last Congress. CPI: Twelfth, 21–28 March 1982, at Varanasi; CPM: Eleventh, 26–31 January 1982, at Vijayawada
Last Election. 1984: CPI: 2.71 percent, 6 seats; CPM: 5.96 percent, 22 seats (out of 509 contested seats in 544-seat parliament)
Auxiliary Organizations. CPI: All-India Trade Union Congress, All-India Kisan Sabha, All-India Student Federation; CPM: Centre for Indian Trade Unions, All-India Kisan Sabha, Students Federation of India
Publications. CPI: *New Age*, *Party Life*, Indian-language dailies in Kerala, Andhra Pradesh, West Bengal, Punjab, and Manipur; CPM: *People's Democracy*, Indian-language dailies in Andhra Pradesh, Kerala, and West Bengal

India's communist parties were swept aside in the landslide victory of Rajiv Gandhi in the December elections. The strength of the Soviet-recognized CPI dropped from 12 to 6 seats in the 544-member Lok Sabha. Although the more powerful CPM continues to control state ministries in West Bengal and Tripura, the loss of 14 of its 36 seats reversed the electoral momentum that the party had been building for over a decade. The CPM's electoral drubbing confirmed that the party is a regional (albeit Marxist) political machine whose goal of becoming a national political force is still in the distant future. For the CPI, the electoral verdict will surely strengthen the hand of a sizable minority within the party who, with the encouragement of the Soviet party, urge support for Congress-I in common opposition to "reactionary" forces at home and "imperialist" forces abroad. With only 28 seats between them in the new parliament, India's Communists have joined a myriad of "bourgeois" parties in the political wilderness. Moreover, Rajiv's party secured an unprecedented 49.2 percent of the 238 million votes cast.

On the international front, the Communists actively promoted the Soviet-sponsored "peace offensive" directed against the West. Noisy, though usually peaceful, demonstrations were periodically staged around the country to protest the deployment of U.S. missiles in Europe, the U.S. invasion of Grenada, and the presence of the U.S. navy in the Indian Ocean. Another propaganda theme that was strongly encouraged by the Soviets accused Pakistan and the United States of underwriting Sikh terrorism in the Punjab as part of a concerted effort to destabilize India. A clear indication of the central position India occupies in Soviet foreign policy was the treatment the Soviets accorded Mrs. Gandhi during the funeral of Yuri Andropov in February. India was officially regarded for protocol purposes as a "friendly state," and Mrs. Gandhi was the first noncommunist delegation head to meet with the Soviet hierarchy. In March, Soviet defense minister

Dimitri Ustinov conducted a six-day barnstorming tour of India. The two sides finalized agreement over the transfer to India of a long list of military hardware for all three service branches, including an agreement to coproduce the advanced MiG-29 aircraft in India (*India Today*, 31 March). In April, an Indian air force officer became the first cosmonaut from a noncommunist Asian country to participate in a Soviet manned space flight. Lastly, the USSR surpassed the United States in 1984 as India's largest trading partner. The Communists looked favorably on all of these developments.

When Indira Gandhi was assassinated, Indian Communists lent credence to the Soviet media charge that the CIA had had a hand in the conspiracy (see, for instance, Moscow world service, 31 October; *FBIS*, 1 November). Rajiv's succession to power tempered the Communists' anti-Congress rhetoric, thereby bringing the parties closer in line with the Kremlin's more accommodating posture toward New Delhi. The Soviets and their Indian allies were genuinely concerned that the orgy of anti-Sikh violence that erupted after the assassination could threaten India's stability and usher in another period of emergency rule. Moreover, the Communists could not rule out the possibility of a foreign policy tilt toward the West. The CPI, CPM, and Kremlin each had a vital stake in ensuring that Rajiv carried on the tradition of close Indo-Soviet ties nourished under Mrs. Gandhi. The CPI is the only Indian communist group formally recognized by Moscow. Both the CPM and the Soviet party, however, have kept open the option of forging ties in the future. Moscow's preference is to facilitate the reunification of the CPI and the CPM, which parted company in 1964. The Indo-Soviet Cultural Society (ISCUS) is a "people-to-people" front operated jointly by the CPI and the Soviet Union. Another such front, the Friends of the Soviet Union, was formed under the auspices of the Congress-I in an attempt by Mrs. Gandhi to undercut the domestic influence of her CPI critics. Both fronts enjoy an equal measure of support from the Kremlin.

India's relations with China remained low-keyed as both sides moved to improve cultural and economic ties pending a settlement of the long-standing border dispute. In August, the two sides entered into the first bilateral trade agreement since the resumption of diplomatic ties in 1976. Sino-Indian trade remains stagnant, but efforts by both countries to liberalize their economies may spur modest increases in bilateral trade. The CPM renewed party-to-party links with the Chinese party in 1983.

Several CPM delegations went to Beijing in 1984 to follow up on the opening. Although CPM foreign policy attitudes generally follow a pro-Soviet line on bedrock issues such as Afghanistan and Kampuchea, the Marxists advocate a policy of "equidistance" between Moscow and Beijing. CPM leaders are careful to blame both communist superpowers for perpetuating the split in communist solidarity, though the Chinese party comes in for muted criticism for making accommodations with "U.S. imperialism." By contrast, the CPI adheres strictly to Moscow's foreign policy line and regards the Chinese party as heretical.

Communist Party of India. Throughout the year, the CPI pursued a complex and somewhat contradictory tactical line. On one hand, the party endorsed the Gandhi government's "anti-imperialist" foreign policy. As the leader of the Nonaligned movement, Mrs. Gandhi was trusted by the CPI to use her influence to promote close ties between the Soviet Union and the developing world. On the other hand, the CPI attacked Gandhi's domestic policies and sought to defeat her at the polls by forging a "left and democratic" alternative to Congress-I. This two-track approach narrowed the CPI's electoral options considerably since the party regarded the election of a government dominated by "communalist" and "reactionary" parties a worse alternative than Congress-I. Thus, while the CPI was reluctant to drop its anti-Gandhi line, it could not throw its support behind opposition groupings that included right-wing parties such as the Hindu revivalist Bharatiya Janata Party (BJP). The 1984 elections were thus the second test of the CPI electoral strategy at the national level. As the deadline for calling elections neared, however, two countervailing tendencies surfaced within the CPI: support for the Congress-I versus joint efforts with the CPM.

Even in states where the CPI and the CPM reached agreement over candidate selections, bitter squabbles broke out as each side tried to press its advantage. Outside of the communist strongholds of West Bengal and Kerala, where the CPI was a junior partner in CPM-led Left Front coalitions, competition between the two was intense. Since electoral competition was overlaid with ideological frictions, communist cooperation was, at best, strained. In January there were reports of physical clashes between CPI and CPM party workers in Kerala, where the CPM attempted to bypass the

CPI by taking control over the Soviet-sponsored "peace" campaign in the state (*Patriot*, 16 January).

Another continuing obstacle to communist unity is the "China factor." The CPI accuses its rival of promoting "anti-Sovietism" because of the CPM policy of ideological "equidistance." An eventual merger of the two organizations is heavily dependent on improvements in Sino-Soviet relations since the CPI is unlikely to oppose Moscow on a fundamental question of ideology. Lastly, the CPM determined that closer affiliation with the CPI would add little to the solid base of support the CPM enjoys in the three key states of West Bengal, Kerala, and Tripura. From the CPM perspective, a merger would inevitably compromise the party's vociferous opposition to Congress-I and dilute its more independent foreign policy line.

The dominant CPI faction advocated continued domestic opposition to Gandhi and limited cooperation with the CPM. Briefing the press after a three-day Central Executive Committee (CEC) session in January, CPI General Secretary C. Rajeswara Rao declared that the party's anti-Gandhi line "will not change. We have settled it in the party once and for all." Rao then leveled a blistering attack on Mrs. Gandhi for being "soft" on communalism, "pandering" to the Hindu vote, and pursuing "bankrupt political and economic policies." Asked to justify his harsh stance in view of Moscow's professed desire for the CPI to cooperate with Gandhi, Rao made it clear that the "tactical position of the Soviet Union and the CPI could not be identical on all issues and at all times . . . We have to fight Mrs. Gandhi here." (Ibid., 12 January.)

Other reports on the internal workings of the CPI suggested that the party line was far from settled. Three dissidents at the CEC meeting voiced criticism of the anti-Gandhi line, abstained on the final vote, and pleaded their case to the press. The dissidents included Mohit Sen, H. K. Vyas, and Yogendra Sharma. Vyas had already been censured by the party for publishing an article critical of CPI policy, and Sharma faced suspension from the party for pleading the "alternate line" directly to Soviet party officials in Moscow in June 1983. Although Rao managed to push through the anti-Gandhi plank without precipitating an open split in the party, his reluctance to take disciplinary measures against the dissenters indicated that the "alternate line" had considerable appeal among the rank and file. Observers speculated whether Rao could keep the party in line for long. (*Indian Express*, 24 January.)

In April, the CPI's highest policymaking body, the National Council, met in New Delhi to map out electoral strategy on the basis of the "left and democratic" line. In a lengthy public document, the council noted that the CPI had participated in opposition conclaves at Calcutta and Srinagar during the previous year. But the council found the "question of opposition unity in a fluid state" and determined that the CPI was "not for any kind of alternative but only a Left and democratic alternative which can meet the needs of the situation" (*The Hindu*, 30 April). The document branded the BJP a "pro-imperialist communal party" that the CPI would not cooperate with under any circumstances. By inference, this also hindered CPI cooperation with the landlord-dominated Lok Dal, which had joined with the BJP in 1983 to form the National Democratic Alliance. The CPI agreed to work selectively with the feeble United Front coalition led by the Janata party, though again the National Council document was silent on the thorny problem of cooperating with nonleftist parties working with the BJP. (Ibid., 7 May.) In October, a more promising opposition combination, Charan Singh's Dalit Mazdoor Kisan Party (DMKP), emerged. The CPI agreed to work with it on a selective basis, provided the BJP was excluded (*Calcutta Statesman*, 25 October). The CPI's reluctance to throw its full support behind an opposition alliance effectively meant that the CPI and CPM constituted a separate, though informal, opposition combine.

Probably because of pressure applied by the pro-Gandhi faction of the party, the CPI National Council formulation issued in April was relatively restrained in its denunciations of Mrs. Gandhi. Although critical of the government's "perilous drift" in the Punjab crisis and its "departures from a policy of economic self-reliance" (codewords for Indian dealings with international lending agencies), the document refrained from charging Gandhi with "authoritarianism." The council did, however, expel from the party G. K. Garg, a vocal advocate of the "alternate line." (*The Hindu*, 29 April.) On foreign policy issues, the document included approving references to Gandhi's commitment to "anti-imperialism," but criticized her for blaming *both* superpowers for aggravating international tensions. According to one source, the CPI planned to send a delegation to Moscow to iron out differences with the Soviet party over communist attitudes toward the Gandhi government. Rao publicly denied the rumor, saying defiantly that "we have our own brains to think [sic]" (ibid., 7 May). Romesh Chandra, the head of the Moscow-based

World Peace Council, made an appearance at the session. In an indirect criticism of the CPI itself, Chandra chastised the CPM for indiscriminately joining hands with "bourgeois" political parties solely on the basis of a common opposition to Gandhi (ibid., 30 April). This undoubtedly served as added reminder from Moscow that the main enemies of Indian Communists were "right reactionary forces," not the Congress-I. Moscow's tacit encouragement of pro-Gandhi dissidents within the CPI was a clear indication that the Kremlin's close ties with the Gandhi government took priority over the electoral machinations of the CPI.

In October, the internal debate over tactics resurfaced when another dissident party member, S. G. Sardesai, raised the "patriotic front" line during a National Council strategy session. Contained in a document the party leadership refused to distribute to the membership, the Sardesai thesis argued that CPI participation in "anti-Indira electoral alignments" failed to take into account the "class character" of opposition parties. Only by supporting Mrs. Gandhi, the document argued, would communist class interests be sufficiently protected. The council voted down the proposal, though this time at least fifteen of the hundred-odd members in attendance took the rare step of voting against the party line. (*Calcutta Telegraph*, 18 October.)

Events in the Punjab, Kashmir, and Andhra Pradesh presented the CPI with new dilemmas. In regard to the strife-torn Punjab, the party criticized Gandhi for failing to come to terms with moderate sections of the Akali Dal, the major Sikh political party. Simultaneously, the CPI lent circumspect support to Gandhi by vigorously condemning the terrorist activities of militant Sikhs. In April, the CPI and CPM joined forces in sponsoring a leftist opposition conference to formulate a political solution to the crisis. The conference was poorly attended and failed to have an impact. On 5 June, just two days after the CPI central secretariat had issued a statement critical of Gandhi's handling of the crisis, the Indian army stormed the Sikh's major shrine, the Golden Temple. The CPI quickly backtracked and reluctantly concluded that the massive deployment of the army had been necessary to curb terrorist violence (*Times of India*, 5 June). The two communist parties have pockets of support within the Punjab. In previous elections, the CPI and CPM polled an average 10 percent of the popular vote between them, though neither party had ever won a seat in the state. Elections in the Punjab, as well as in the northeastern state of Assam, were deferred

in 1984 because of the sharp deterioration in law and order.

When Gandhi toppled the opposition ministry in Kashmir in July, the CPI joined the entire spectrum of opposition parties in denouncing the move as unconstitutional (*Patriot*, 14 July). Prior to the ouster of Chief Minister Farooq Abdullah, however, the CPI secretary of the Kashmir state unit had called for central government intervention to halt "nefarious activities" in the state—an allusion to Abdullah's ties to Moslem communal parties (*The Hindu*, 30 April). Similarly, when Gandhi unsuccessfully attempted to unseat the opposition ministry of N. T. Rama Rao in Andhra Pradesh in August, the CPI was careful to condemn Gandhi's "authoritarianism" without coming to the defense of the conservative Telegu Desam ministry. The electoral alliance between Telegu Desam and the BJP prompted the CPI to deal with Rama Rao at arm's length in the early stages of the election campaign. Eventually, however, the CPI agreed to make seat adjustments with the Telegu Desam. Rama Rao's regionally based party emerged from the December elections as the single largest opposition bloc in parliament.

As was the case with all Indian political parties, the CPI was stunned by Gandhi's assassination and was uncertain how to react. Both the CPI and CPM probably feared (correctly) that the nation would rally behind Rajiv's leadership. Moreover, the crisis atmosphere after the assassination prevented the Communists from engaging in partisan attacks that could be construed by the voters as unpatriotic. Consequently, both parties shied away from making personal attacks on Rajiv and distanced themselves from opposition harping over the impropriety of "dynastic succession" (*Times of India*, 9 November). General Secretary Rao gave the CPI blessing to the succession by arguing that Rajiv's appointment was an internal Congress-I matter that was subject to the voters' approval. As the campaign wore on, Rao stepped up CPI criticism of the "anti-people policies" of the Congress-I, but pleaded that the "CPI does not want to prejudge Mr. Rajiv Gandhi" (*Calcutta Telegraph*, 23 November). Rao's moderate tones contrasted sharply with press statements he had made prior to Mrs. Gandhi's death. In January, he declared that "Congress-I has a one-point program of installing Rajiv on the throne" (*Patriot*, 12 January). Rao even hinted at one point in the campaign that the CPI "would have given the new Prime Minister . . . a chance, but unfortunately the elections were called unexpectedly and the party's electoral policy of defeating the Congress-I remains the same" (*Calcutta Telegraph*, 16 November). The CPI campaign, spelled out in a catchall 23-point manifesto, concentrated its attacks on the Congress-I and ignored Rajiv altogether (Delhi domestic service, 28 November; *FBIS*, 29 November).

In a last-ditch effort to reorient the party line on the eve of elections, CPI dissidents led by S. G. Sardesai argued in public that the main attack of the left should be aimed against the "BJP and the antinational forces gathering around it." In pursuance of this line, the CPI should lend "selective assistance to progressive candidates of other parties whom we consider seriously and sincerely progressive" (*Calcutta Telegraph*, 23 November). The CPI high command rejected the dissidents' pleas and categorically ruled out the possibility of supporting Congress-I candidates anywhere in the country (*Patriot*, 23 November). The Soviets left little doubt that they supported Rajiv's election. Although the Soviet media praised both communist parties for spearheading the fight against "imperialism" and "antinational elements," Moscow usually downplayed the fact that both of their fraternal allies in India were campaigning against the Rajiv Congress (see, for instance, *Pravda*, 18 December; *FBIS*, 26 December).

The CPI fielded 61 candidates in seventeen states and one union territory. More so than the regionally based CPM, CPI support is spread thinly across the country. Pockets of support are concentrated in the Hindi-speaking heartland of Bihar and Uttar Pradesh and in urban industrial areas of Maharashtra and Gujarat. Three of the six CPI candidates who managed to win Lok Sabha seats, however, were from constituencies in West Bengal, where the CPI had the advantage of contesting the election as a partner of the CPM. A fourth CPI candidate was elected on Rama Rao's coattails in Andhra Pradesh. The remaining two seats won in Bihar were the only races in which CPI candidates outpolled the Congress-I and a full slate of opposition candidates. Rajiv's party came very close to making a clean sweep of the CPI at the polls, even though the Congress-I campaign directed the bulk of its resources against centrist and right-wing parties and largely ignored the Communists outside of West Bengal. An even more telling indication of CPI decline was the percentage of the popular vote garnered by the party. When it was allied with Mrs. Gandhi in the early 1970s, the CPI entered parliament with 4.7 percent of the popular vote. Its share

of the vote dropped to 2.8 percent when the electorate swept Gandhi out of office after the Emergency was lifted in 1977. When Gandhi returned to office in 1980—this time with the CPI in the opposition—the party's share of the vote dropped to 2.6 percent. In the 1984 polls, the CPI share was 2.71 percent of total votes cast. Surveying the wreckage of the CPI electoral disaster, an editorial in the pro-Soviet newspaper *Patriot* (31 December) concluded that the "so-called Left and Democratic Front was more an illusion than a reality . . . It will be a greater disaster if the two main Left parties persevere in the wrong policies they have chosen."

Despite its poor showing at the polls, the CPI took solace in the even worse defeats of the centrist and right-wing parties (except in the limited cases of Andhra Pradesh and Jammu and Kashmir). The hated BJP secured only two seats, and its party leader, A. B. Vajpayee, went down to defeat. The Lok Dal, Janata, and DMKP coalitions suffered roughly similar fates. It remains to be seen whether the CPI strategy of opposing Congress-I will be reversed by the party leadership. In any event, Rajeswara Rao's grip over the party will be severely tested as dissidents continue their attempts to move the CPI in the direction of an accommodation with the Rajiv government. The CPI, unlike the CPM in West Bengal, cannot retreat to a regional stronghold to lick its wounds and prepare for the next electoral fight. As long as India's relations with the Soviet Union remain cordial, the CPI leadership will come under intense pressure to abandon the party's opposition role. Another possibility is that the elections will accelerate the process of communist unity since both organizations may have to rely more heavily on each other for support in the aftermath of the Congress-I landslide. This is particularly true for the CPI, whose performance in the 1984 polls showed that the party cannnot rely on its own resources to win elections, even with Soviet backing. Indian communist unity would please the Soviets, who are anxious to rein in domestic criticism of Rajiv as long as New Delhi's foreign policy is kept on an "anti-imperialist" track.

While the 1984 elections have put the CPI in a quandary, the party remains a political force to reckon with outside of parliament. With a party membership approaching 500,000, an extensive cadre-based organization, and the backing of the Soviet party, the CPI will continue to exert political influence in India.

The major CPI front organizations are the All-India Kisan Sabha (the peasant arm of the party) and the All-India Student Federation. The CPI labor arm, the All-India Trade Union Congress, encompasses over 3,000 union affiliates with workers in most nationalized industries. On the propaganda front, the party publishes a number of organs in English and in Indian languages with the help of generous Soviet subsidies. The People's Publishing House in New Delhi propagates Soviet and CPI views through a wide variety of educational and propaganda materials.

Communist Party of India–Marxist. In the months leading up to elections, the CPM was in the forefront of attempts to forge a semblance of opposition unity against the Congress-I government. Although the CPM yearned to create a left and democratic front, the Marxists were less adamant than the CPI over the question of treating the BJP as a political untouchable. In an August interview, CPM General Secretary E. M. S. Namboodiripad stated that the party's electoral strategy rested on three objectives: (1) the defeat of the Congress-I; (2) the isolation of "divisive forces" such as the BJP and the Muslim League; and (3) an increase in the number of parliamentary seats for the "Left, democratic, and secular forces in general and the Left parties in particular." While Namboodiripad conceded that Mrs. Gandhi had demonstrated "limited resistance to imperialism," he cautioned that leftist parties should not be lulled into supporting the government since Gandhi was guilty of "backsliding" on certain foreign policy issues. Namboodiripad envisioned a bright future for the opposition. He labeled the Congress-I a "party of the Indian ruling class—the bourgeoisie and landlords . . . I have no doubt that the possibility of a rapid erosion in the mass base of Congress-I is great." (*Patriot*, 3 August.)

In order to protect its position as the dominant force in the ruling coalitions of West Bengal and Tripura, the CPM gave full support to the handful of opposition ministries in other states, irrespective of the parties in power. Ever since Gandhi returned to power in 1980, the Left Front government in West Bengal had maintained that Mrs. Gandhi was preparing to engineer a crisis in the state in order to pave the way for the imposition of central government rule. When Gandhi dismissed the opposition ministries in Kashmir and Andhra Pradesh under highly suspicious circumstances, the CPM led the opposition chorus against "authoritarianism." With respect to the Punjab, the CPM urged the Akali Dal leadership to denounce the activities of Sikh ter-

rorists and accept the conditions of an opposition-sponsored political settlement to the crisis. When the army cracked down on the state in June, the CPM Politburo placed the blame for the breakdown in negotiations squarely on the Gandhi government. According to news reports, however, the Politburo was deeply divided over the issue (*Calcutta Statesman*, 12 June). As in the case of the Punjab debate within the CPI, some CPM members were hesitant to come down heavily on New Delhi for acting decisively against "reactionary" elements that, according to the Communists, were supported by Pakistan and the CIA. The debate over linking the party (however indirectly) with "undesirable elements" also surfaced when militant sections of the CPM rank and file protested the party's slogan "Red salute to Rama Rao" because of the chief minister's close links with the BJP (ibid., 14 February). In the final analysis, however, ideological purity gave way to political pragmatism. Both the CPM and CPI agreed to seat adjustments with Rama Rao.

Another issue preoccupying the CPM in 1984 was in the area of center-state relations. As a ruling party in the two states, the CPM had a vital stake in enhancing the powers of individual states in their dealings with New Delhi. In May, the CPM proposed a sweeping series of constitutional reforms and administrative changes intended to correct what the party saw as the growing imbalance of power in New Delhi's favor. The proposals were part of the CPM's testimony before the Sarkaria Commission, a panel formed in 1983 to look into the question. Reforms recommended by the CPM included the abolition of state governorships, more state control over central administrative cadres, exclusive state control over local security matters, a system of proportional representation in state and national legislatures, and a requirement that New Delhi remit 75 percent of all central government revenues to the states (*The Hindu*, 1 June). The West Bengal government was particularly incensed over New Delhi's parsimonious distribution of revenues to non-Congress states. Jyoti Basu, the chief minister of West Bengal and a leading figure on the CPM Politburo, charged repeatedly that the Gandhi government was starving his state of funds as part of a concerted effort to paralyze the Left Front ministry in advance of the elections.

In the tiny northeastern state of Tripura, the CPM-led Left Front government had similar anxieties about being dismissed from office by Mrs. Gandhi. In September, New Delhi dispatched a team of army commanders to the state to assess the security situation on the borders with Bangladesh. The army was asked to recommend ways to quell the tribal insurgency that had been festering in remote areas of the state for years. The team reported that rebel tribesmen fighting under the banner of the Tripura National Volunteers (TNV) posed a significant threat to the security of the region and urged New Delhi to declare several outlying districts "disturbed areas." Under this provision, control over the affected areas would revert to the central government, giving the army a free hand in putting down the insurgent menace. Chief Minister Nripen Chakravarty agreed that TNV activists were a problem, but vehemently rejected any role for New Delhi in administering the state or conducting counterinsurgency operations. The national CPM organization rallied to the defense of the embattled chief minister and accused Gandhi of meddling in the affairs of yet another opposition-controlled state. (*Economic and Political Weekly*, 20 October.) At the end of October, the Congress-I state unit in Tripura staged a general strike to protest the Left Front's inability to put down the insurgency. The strikers' call for Gandhi to intervene in the state led to street fights between Congress-I and CPM party workers (*NYT*, 28 October). The CPM ministry in Tripura managed to survive the year in office, in part because Congress-I has a shallow base of support in the state. A move to topple the ministry would have complicated Mrs. Gandhi's campaign strategy by providing the opposition with another *cause célèbre*. Moreover, Gandhi probably did not want to make martyrs of the CPM, which was steadily losing ground to Congress-I in the pivotal state of West Bengal.

The well-oiled CPM electoral machine was put into high gear well in advance of the call for elections. The party hoped to capitalize on the public outrage stirred up by Gandhi's heavy-handed maneuvers in opposition-ruled states. Gandhi's death dealt a heavy blow to CPM's electoral prospects. Lacking a cohesive electoral strategy in the absence of Mrs. Gandhi, the CPM was on the defensive throughout the campaign. Immediately after the shooting, the party high command ordered communist flags to fly at half-mast—a mark of respect never extended to CPM or Soviet leaders.

The 1984 electoral verdict was a stinging rebuke for the CPM. In West Bengal, the party suffered reverses in urban, suburban, industrial, and rural areas—all at the hands of Congress-I. Particularly galling was the loss of CPM seats in industrial strongholds around Calcutta (Jadavpur, Dum Dum,

Howrah) and outlying "red belt" districts (24-Parganas, Burdwan, Hooghli). Not only did fourteen sitting members lose their seats in the Congress-I onslaught, but the 22 CPM winners were returned with majorities that fell far short of the 1980 results. Most of the CPM losers were veteran party leaders such as Samar Mukherjee. Conversely, many of the successful Congress-I candidates were young, inexperienced politicians who were recruited into the party by Rajiv at the eleventh hour. This "youth wave" in West Bengal politics does not bode well for the CPM because the party is dominated by a geriatric leadership and is sorely in need of new blood. Although the party has openly acknowledged the problem since the 1978 Howrah plenum, the recruitment and promotion of a new generation of leaders into the higher party ranks has been extremely slow. The only major leadership change announced during the year was the appointment of 78-year-old Nripen Chakravarty to the Politburo to look after party affairs in the northeastern states (*Calcutta Statesman*, 19 July). The CPM's three coalition partners in West Bengal (Forward Bloc, Revolutionary Socialist Party, and CPI) managed to lose only two seats, leaving a total of eight seats between them. Consequently, the Left Front still maintains an edge over Congress-I in Lok Sabha seats in the state (26 to 16), though the Congress-I gain of 12 seats over the 1980 election marks a significant shift in voter preference away from the Left Front. It remains to be seen, however, whether Congress-I inroads in West Bengal will translate into a loosening of the CPM's grip over seats in the state assembly, municipal boards, and *panchayats* (tiers of local governing bodies extending to the village level). Although signs of a CPM decline were evident in elections for the latter two bodies in 1982–1983, the party apparatus runs deep in the state and will be difficult to dislodge.

Samar Mukherjee, the former head of the CPM parliamentary delegation, attributed the poor showing to factors beyond the party's control, most notably to the "sympathy wave for Indira Gandhi." Spokesmen for the other Left Front parties disagreed with this assessment and blamed the "nonperformance of the CPM-led ministry." (*Calcutta Statesman*, 30 December.) Jubilant Congress-I workers demanded that the Left Front ministry follow the example of the Janata ministry in Karnataka by dissolving the state assembly and calling fresh elections. CPM state leaders, fearing that the Congress-I momentum might carry over into state contests, were reluctant to call a snap poll. On the other hand, retaining power in a state where the voters had rejected the Left Front at the national level was an equally distasteful prospect.

The CPM also fared poorly elsewhere in India. In Kerala, a state ruled by a CPM-led coalition as recently as 1981, the party managed to hang on to only one seat. The once solid CPM following in the state was reduced to the Ezhava caste group. The CPM also bagged solitary seats in Andhra Pradesh and Tamil Nadu because of arrangements with non-leftist opposition parties. The only state where CPM candidates bucked the national trend was in Tripura, where the party retained its two seats with comfortable margins. The remaining 29 CPM candidates who ran for seats in other states were all swamped. Clearly, the CPM has become an island of opposition in a Congress-I sea.

In international affairs, the CPM lived up to its reputation as a maverick communist party. In May, West Bengal chief minister Jyoti Basu traveled to Beijing to hold high-level discussions with Chinese party officials. CPM sources noted that the timing of the trip was particularly delicate since another round of Sino-Indian border talks was scheduled for the end of the summer. The CPM Politburo instructed Basu to tread warily on the border issue since the Congress-I would surely dredge up the visit during the upcoming election campaign if the Chinese used their influence with the CPM to push for a favorable settlement (*Patriot*, 2 May). Upon his return home, Basu offered an upbeat appraisal of the prospects for Sino-Soviet rapprochement and China's economic modernization strategy. Basu claimed the two sides did not dwell on obvious differences of opinion over issues such as Afghanistan and Kampuchea. (*Calcutta Statesman*, 31 May). The pro-Soviet lobby in India criticized the CPM for its "unmistakable softness" toward the Chinese party and took Basu to task for "condoning the Chinese crimes against Vietnam," among other charges (*Patriot*, 7 May). Other CPM delegations

traveling to China were headed by former CPM general secretary P. Sundarayya (Xinhua, Beijing, 15 October; *FBIS*, 16 October) and a CPM Central Committee member from Andhra Pradesh, Hanumantha Rao (Xinhua, Beijing, 19 September; *FBIS*, 20 September). In March, the Chinese demonstrated their own flexibility in dealing with foreign Communists when a Chinese trade union delegation headed by Ni Zhifu met in New Delhi with Indrajit Gupta, the general secretary of the CPI trade union front. The two sides signaled a willingness to work together in noncontroversial areas, although Gupta reportedly pressed his Chinese counterparts to join the Soviet-sponsored World Federation of Trade Unions (*Calcutta Statesman*, 19 March).

In July, Jyoti Basu raised eyebrows in Indian communist circles when he spent nearly a month traveling in the West, including a lengthy visit to the United States. Basu's mission was to attract American private investment (including multinational corporations) to his home state. Taking a page from the Chinese economic model, Basu promised tax holidays and liberal repatriation of profits to potential American investors. Basu saw no conflict between Marxist ideology and the encouragement of private sector growth, at least as long as the CPM was not in power in New Delhi. Furthermore, Basu argued that Mrs. Gandhi's strategy of denying funds to West Bengal compelled the Left Front to look abroad for new investments. Once again, the pro-Soviet lobby ridiculed the CPM for pursuing an aberrant foreign policy line. "The parties and people who claim to be staunch anti-imperialists and uncompromising enemies of neo-colonialism and monopolists," wrote one critic, "change their stand once they come to power" (Girish Mishra, in *Patriot*, 16 August).

Douglas C. Makeig
Library of Congress

Indonesia

Population. 169,442,000
Party. Indonesian Communist Party (Partai Komunis Indonesia; PKI)
Founded. 1920
Membership. 100–300, in exile
Secretary General. Pro-Moscow: Satiadjaya Sudiman; pro-Beijing: Jusuf Adjitorop
Leading Bodies. No data
Status. Illegal
Last Congress. Seventh Extraordinary, April 1962
Last Election. N/a
Front Organizations. None identifiable in Indonesia
Publications. None known in Indonesia

The PKI, which with its mass organizations once claimed to have some 20 million members, has, since its abortive coup of 30 September 1965, been reduced to a few hundred members living abroad, split between pro-Moscow and pro-Beijing factions. There is no hard evidence that any actual remnant of the party exists in Indonesia, but the government has increasingly expressed suspicion that the PKI is behind some of the unrest in the country.

Leadership and Party Organization. The PKI remains a shadow party with no known organization inside Indonesia, and information about its adherents abroad is extremely limited. Jusuf Adjitorop is still believed to be the leader of the pro-Beijing faction. Satiadjaya Sudiman probably remains head of the Moscow-based faction, although an Indonesian newspaper identified Tomas Sinuraya, previously known as secretary of the Overseas Committee of the PKI, as leader of the Moscow wing (*Kompas*, 6 August). Little was heard from either wing of the party in 1984. The delegation of the PKI Central Committee that sent a message of greeting to the Chinese Central Committee on the thirty-fifth anniversary of the founding of the PRC can be assumed to have been the Beijing faction (BBC, 2 October). The PKI, presumably the

Moscow branch, was among the 91 delegations represented at the Conference of Representatives of the Communist and Workers Parties on the Activity of the Periodical *Problems of Peace and Socialism* held in Prague from 4 to 6 December.

The Beijing wing of the party appears to have more opportunity for impact on events in Indonesia through contact with the numerous Indonesian visitors to China. However, although the Indonesian government remains suspicious of PRC assistance to Communists in Indonesia, nothing is heard of the PKI leadership in Beijing.

Domestic Party Affairs. It is difficult to determine what if any role the PKI played in the various manifestations of public unrest in Indonesia during 1984, but government officials spoke repeatedly of resurgent communist activity. In February, the commander of the Indonesian armed forces, Gen. Benny Murdani, called for increased vigilance against communist subversion, warning that although banned, the PKI would never give up its struggle. Communism, General Murdani said, had contributed nothing but suffering and tragedy to Indonesia. He urged that history books be rewritten to correct the impression that the uprising of 1926 and 1927 had been communist-inspired; the revolts had not indicated approval of communism but hatred of Dutch colonial subjugation. General Murdani's statement came just days after the weekly magazine *Topik* was banned for an editorial that the Information Ministry said showed Marxist tendencies. The ban remained in effect for two months. (Reuters, 27 February; Jakarta domestic service, 23 April; *FBIS*, 1 May.)

Almost at the same time as General Murdani's statement on resurgent communism, the army chief of staff, General Rudini, called for an "intensive cleaning-up" of communist remnants within the Indonesian army. There was press speculation that this announcement might be related to the recent discovery of a major corruption case involving the alleged embezzlement of some 20 billion rupiah ($20 million) over an unknown period of time by an army lieutenant colonel said to have had ties to the Communists before the September 1965 coup. The authorities were concerned about where the money had gone. (AFP, 2 March; *FBIS*, 2 March.)

Other signs of unrest included the continued mysterious killings of suspected criminals. Although they apparently diminished during the year, the problem nevertheless persisted. The government denied any involvement in the death squad killings, attributing a number of the deaths to gang warfare and noting that some criminals had been killed but only because they were resisting the authorities. There is no way of judging whether any of the targets of these killings had communist connections. Meanwhile, the government continued its drive, begun in mid-1983, to re-register all former prisoners charged with involvement in the 1965 coup. The drive was started after the discovery that some alleged hard-core communist ex-prisoners had been found outside their hometowns without proper papers. The 1.6 million former communist prisoners are required to report their every move, whether on a trip or to resettle elsewhere, to their ward and village chiefs (AFP, 2 March; *FBIS*, 2 March).

State prosecutor's offices throughout East Java were instructed to seize clandestine leaflets and pamphlets circulating in the province and arrest those distributing them. The publications were described as discrediting the present government and the *Pancasila* (Five Principles of the Nation), but their political genesis is not clear. It may be coincidental that they were cited in a newspaper article that reported on the impending execution of two former members of a PKI regional committee in East Java. The two men who had been sentenced in 1976 for political crimes involving subversive activity had just lost their appeal to the president and the Supreme Court for clemency. The men were identified as the chief of the propaganda section of the PKI in the Gaya Baru area of Blitar Regency and a member of the plenum and of the Daily Affairs Council of the PKI in Blitar, but how long before their 1976 conviction their subversive activities took place was not specified. (*Surabaya Post*, 8 October.)

There was sporadic unrest in Irian Jaya during the year, but neither the political demonstrations nor the occasional terrorist activities there appeared to be in any way related to communist efforts, although different factions accused each other of being Marxist. As for the separatist movement in East Timor, despite government suspicions that there were some ties to communist-affiliated organizations in other former Portuguese colonies, there was no evidence of PKI involvement there.

There were many ambiguities about the political antecedents of a series of incidents that began in mid-September with major riots in Tanjung Priok, Jakarta's port. The original demonstration supposedly centered on Moslem objections to the government's proposal to make Pancasila the guiding principle for all the country's social and religious organizations, a draft law that Moslems, Protestants, and Catholics opposed. However, before and after the Tanjung Priok riots, pamphlets had reportedly been circulated warning the armed forces not to side with the country's ethnic Chinese, who are widely perceived as exorbitantly wealthy, elitist, and closely tied to the government. The rioters attacked Chinese families and businesses as well as the local police and military outposts, along with a Protestant church and other targets at hand. Estimates of the numbers killed and wounded varied widely, but all reports agreed that this was the most serious outbreak of violence in a number of years. There were arrests of riot leaders as well as of antigovernment activists not involved in the riots.

The Priok riots were followed in three weeks by a series of bomb blasts in the Chinese section of Jakarta. Then in early November a fire caused a major explosion at the ammunition depot at the Jakarta Marine base. Next came an outbreak of fires in several of Jakarta's leading department stores. Whether these events were part of a terrorist campaign or isolated incidents, some government officials spoke of a "rain" of subversive pamphlets in Jogjakarta, Surabaya, and Jakarta that allegedly gave a distorted account of the Tanjung Priok riots and the subsequent bombings. General Rudini warned that the Communists might try to take advantage of the Priok riots to incite Moslems against the government and the armed forces. The military chief of Surabaya said that responsibility for the unrest lay with the Communists. However, most of those arrested in the wake of the riots and the bombings were identified as fundamentalist Moslems. (Reuters, 20 September; *FEER*, 29 November, p. 13; *Asiaweek*, 14 December, p. 31.)

International Views, Positions, and Activities. Virtually nothing was heard from either faction of the PKI in 1984 beyond the nominal listing of the party as a participant in the routine meetings and exchanges of greetings noted above. Both factions presumably have encountered difficulties in formulating positions appropriate to a revolutionary opposition ranged against an Indonesian government that has increasingly cordial relations with the PKI's host countries.

The first official visit to Moscow in ten years by an Indonesian foreign minister was one of a series of Indonesian-Soviet exchanges at the cabinet level. These seemed to be unaffected by the highly publicized trial and conviction of an Indonesian naval officer found guilty of spying for the Soviets. Indonesia also vigorously pursued trade agreements with the USSR, East Germany, and other bloc members.

Indonesian relations with Vietnam improved markedly during the year. General Murdani made his third, but first official, visit to Hanoi in February, in the course of which he said that the Indonesian people and armed forces did not consider Vietnam a threat to Southeast Asia. Rather, he said, Indonesia tended to believe that the main danger to Southeast Asia would come from the PRC. Shortly thereafter, an Indonesian delegation that included some government officials participated in a seminar in Hanoi on Southeast Asian relations. Indonesia had already concluded a trade agreement with Vietnam, and the Indonesian press speculated about possible cooperation between the two countries' armed forces. (*Merdeka*, 12 March; *FBIS*, 27 March.)

Official Indonesian attitudes toward the PRC conveyed somewhat mixed signals. The military retained its suspicions of PRC machinations and of the ethnic Chinese minority. Foreign Ministry officials, on the other hand, speak periodically of resuming ties with China, frozen since 1967. Nevertheless, the foreign minister continues to insist on a formal renunciation by Beijing of ties to Commu-

nists in Southeast Asia as a prelude to the resumption of official ties. (*FBIS*, 12 March; *Financial Times*, London, 30 April.)

Biography. *Tomas Sinuraya.* (The following information comes from a newspaper article by Yusuf Abdullah Puar, who had been active with Sinuraya in the early days of Indonesian independence.) Tomas Sinuraya, a leader of the pro-Moscow wing of the PKI, was born on 12 September 1939 in the town of Kuta Buluh, Tiga Nderket subdistrict, in the Kabupaten of Tanah Karo, North Sumatra. The town was the center of activities associated with seeking the dissolution of the East Sumatra state, a chapter in the history of the early days of the republic, and reportedly Sinuraya's first political activity, as a boy of twelve, was participation in the series of demonstrations held for that purpose in 1950.

As a member of the Indonesian Youth and Student Organization (IPPI), Sinuraya was one of those given government support to continue their studies in Java in the Student Army (TP) group. In Jogjakarta, he and his fellows finished their senior high school studies, and most continued their education at Gadjah Mada University there. In 1959 he was one of the Indonesian students given a scholarship to study abroad. He studied at Lumumba University and spent three years at Lomosonov University in Moscow, from which he graduated with a master's degree in economics. While there, he became a member of Komsomol, joined Soviet delegations visiting other socialist countries, and was sent to Western Europe, Africa, Latin America, Laos, Kampuchea, and Vietnam.

Sinuraya became a *Pravda* correspondent and covered events in Spain, Portugal, Cuba, Nicaragua, El Salvador, Guatemala, Ethiopia, Uganda, Angola, Mozambique, Egypt, the Philippines, Kampuchea, India, Vietnam, and Sri Lanka. As a *Pravda* war correspondent, he covered the Falklands war, the Vietnamese invasion of Kampuchea, the Soviet invasion of Afghanistan, and the Syrian army's move into Lebanon. He spent the longest time in Vietnam, participating in military training in that country. Sinuraya subsequently became secretary of the Central Committee of the Soviet branch of the PKI. (*Kompas*, 6 August.)

No information is available about Sinuraya's views or his actual role as a PKI leader beyond the positions he had held. Interestingly, the newspaper article from which the above information is drawn contains the comment that Sinuraya is little known because he was never mentioned in PKI publications in the past and did not play an important role in the attempted PKI coup. Attention was drawn to Sinuraya when Rosihan Anwar of *Kompas* came across Sinuraya's name in the checklist of communist parties in the March–April 1984 issue of *Problems of Communism*. Anwar asked in the columns of *Kompas* for information about this hitherto unknown figure, and the article by Puar, cited above, was the only response.

Jeanne S. Mintz
Washington, D.C.

Japan

Population. 118,896,000
Party. Japan Communist Party (Nihon Kyosanto; JCP)
Founded. 1922
Membership. 480,000 (*KDK Information*, February)
Central Committee Chairman. Kenji Miyamoto
Presidium Chairman. Tetsuzo Fuwa
Central Committee. 189 regular and 22 candidate members
Status. Legal
Last Congress. Sixteenth, 27–31 July 1982
Last Election. December 1983, 9.43 percent, 14 of 252 in House of Councillors, 26 of 511 in House of Representatives
Auxiliary Organizations. All-Japan Student Federation, New Japan Women's Association, All-Japan Merchants Federation. Democratic Foundation of Doctors, Japan Council of Students, Japan Peace Committee, Japan Council Against Hydrogen and Atomic Bombs
Publications. *Akahata* (Red banner), daily circulation 620,000, Sunday circulation 2,480,000, total readership, 3,100,000; *Zen'ei* (Vanguard), monthly theoretical journal; *Gekkan gakushu* (Education monthly), education and propaganda magazine; *Gikai to jichitai* (Parliament and self-government), monthly; *Bunka hyoron* (Culture review); *Sekai seiji shiryo* (International politics); *Gakusei shimbun* (Students' gazette), weekly

Leadership and Organization. Kenji Miyamoto remained chairman of the party's Central Committee and the top leader of the JCP. Tetsuzo Fuwa retained the position of chairman of the Presidium and ran party business on a day-to-day basis, while Miyamoto announced most policies. Central Committee Chairman Emeritus Sanzo Nosaka, at age 93, was still active during the year and continued to represent the party.

Domestic Issues and Activities. The Seventh Plenum of the Sixteenth Central Committee met from 24 to 27 January. Miyamoto reported that the readership of *Akahata* had declined and was below the 1980 level in terms of the ratio of readers to eligible voters. He set a goal of 4 million readers. Miyamoto stressed party-building efforts and called for efforts to increase membership to 500,000. The decline in the number of younger party members is especially worrisome. (*JCP Central Committee Bulletin*, March.)

Miyamoto recommended a decentralization of party authority, particularly of the youth movements and their activities. He also called on local party leaders to work harder and to fulfill party goals before the upcoming Tokyo metropolitan elections in 1985. Recruiting should emphasize youth, and Miyamoto suggested more work at colleges and universities and at factories. Miyamoto spoke optimistically of JCP efforts in the antinuclear area and mentioned that he had sent letters to Andropov and Reagan asking for the total abolition of nuclear weapons. He reported that the Conference on Trade Unions for a United Front was growing, as was the number of local JCP organizations. The party was also forging closer links with the masses.

The plenum passed a resolution against U.S. plans to equip U.S. Pacific Fleet ships with Tomahawk cruise missiles that can carry nuclear warheads. The resolution contended that this increased the probability of nuclear war.

The JCP held its first national conference (a meeting between party congresses to consult with all party organizations for discussion on a national scale) from 10 to 14 April—the first such meeting under the present party constitution. At the meeting it was decided to establish a committee to be chaired by Eizo Kobayashi to fight anticommunism. This action was a response to the efforts of other parties to form coalitions without the JCP and to anti-JCP comments and criticisms from the other parties.

The meeting also discussed a "comprehensive program," *Akahata* subscriptions, party building, decentralization of the party's authority and decisionmaking systems, and the next party congress. The delegates decided that the next congress would convene in the fall of 1985 following the Tokyo elections, even though this violated the party constitution's stipulation that congresses must be held at least every three years. (Ibid., October.)

The Ninth Plenum met from 16 to 19 October. A party report given at the meeting noted that fees were up 8 percent since the Seventh Plenum, but subscription receipts from *Akahata* remained down 30–40 percent. Membership and the distribution of party literature were also down. The plenum appealed to members to work harder in these areas and to bring the numbers up to the levels of the last party congress.

Other issues discussed included party building, the ideological struggle, international questions,

the Tokyo (antinuclear) Declaration, a coming summit meeting with the Communist Party of the Soviet Union, the Nakasone government (which the JCP regards as the worst in recent years), and the expiration of a ten-year agreement with the Sokagakkai (a Buddhist organization affiliated with the Komei Party). In regard to the last, Miyamoto said that the agreement had long since been given a "dishonorable death." (Ibid., November.)

Throughout the year, the JCP remained highly critical of the Nakasone government. The party continued to hammer at Nakasone's connection with former prime minister Kakuei Tanaka and called for Tanaka's resignation from the Diet because of his conviction in the Lockheed bribery case. The JCP argued that the case did not end because Tanaka had been returned to the Diet in the last election by a huge majority. JCP Diet members presented a resolution calling for Tanaka to step down and called on the Japan Socialist Party (which has also been critical of Tanaka) to support the JCP's efforts. (*FBIS*, 23 June.) The party also publicly criticized and opposed the appointment by Nakasone of Susumu Nikaido as vice-president of the Liberal Democratic Party (LDP) because of his involvement in the Lockheed scandal.

The JCP solidly opposed the LDP's efforts to pass a political party law dealing with party ethics, which it likened to Japan's "fascist" policies before and during World War II. The party law would restrict political party activities (which would hurt the JCP) and was undemocratic, according to party spokesmen. (*Japan Times*, 7 December.) Similarly the JCP opposed an "administrative reform" law that would reduce the size of the Diet and local government assemblies in order to make debate and business in these organs more efficient; the JCP charged that the proposed law was an LDP effort to hurt the smaller opposition parties.

The JCP also assailed the so-called realistic policies of the other opposition parties in seeking an alignment with the LDP or a "center coalition" that might wrest political leadership from the LDP. JCP leaders argued that it was unrealistic to expect the LDP to split and that the other parties were, in fact, trying to join the LDP and were in the process of abandoning their own party ideals and goals. The JCP contended that it was the only real opposition party. Its response was the same to efforts by the other parties to form coalition-type agreements— all of which excluded cooperation with the JCP and were often anticommunist in tenor.

On economic issues, the JCP continued to oppose the government's favoritism toward big business and policies that discriminated against small businesses, workers, and the unemployed. JCP leaders tried to make an issue of the record number of bankruptcies and high unemployment during 1984. Party officials continued to call for safer working conditions, higher minimum wages, and more and better welfare benefits—noting correctly that Japan was way behind European nations and the United States in these areas. The JCP also attacked the massive use of robots by Japanese companies, saying that they were not necessarily used to reduce the burden of labor or because there was a labor shortage and that the number of robots was being increased at a time of high unemployment, exacerbating that problem. (*JCP Central Committee Bulletin*, June.)

The JCP's statements on economics seemed to be less effective than in the past because of the public's realization of more serious economic problems in other countries, especially in the United States and Europe, and because of foreign criticism of Japan for its trade surplus and foreign charges that Japan was exporting its unemployment. Third World countries have been publicizing their plight and their need for aid in Japan, and this may have weakened the JCP's case.

On specific economic legislation, the JCP joined with the Japan Socialist Party in trying to block a bill in the House of Councillors to turn Nippon Telegraph and Telephone into a private enterprise (*Japan Times*, 14 December). These efforts, however, failed.

In the military realm, the JCP continued to oppose the U.S.-Japan Security Pact. In fact, the JCP was the only party to unequivocally oppose the defense relationship. Similarly the JCP sought to prevent the Nakasone government from increasing defense spending and at every opportunity criticized "militarism" and defense spending and the resulting cuts in welfare, pensions, and other social programs. JCP leaders contended that the government was ignoring public opinion, which according to the polls, favored a more neutral foreign policy.

JCP activities outside the Diet and the government, however, were more effective. In November the party organized demonstrations against the emplacement of Tomahawk cruise missiles and on one occasion got 3,800 people to form a "human chain" at a park near Yokata Airbase, which is used by the United States. (*FBIS*, 13 November.)

The JCP's antinuclear efforts were even more successful in terms of attracting followers and get-

ting press coverage. The party sponsored the Tokyo Declaration early in the year, drawing 120 foreign delegates and 11 from international organizations. The JCP also organized meetings attended by 20,000 people at Hiroshima and Nagasaki to protest the use of nuclear weapons. The JCP's Japan Council Against Hydrogen and Atomic Bombs provided much of the impetus for the growing antinuclear movement in Japan. (*Akahata*, 11 August.) In the process, this organization seemed to engineer a successful reconciliation with Japan's other large antinuclear organization, the Japan Congress Against Hydrogen and Atomic Bombs, which is affiliated with the Japan Socialist Party. The two groups have been at odds for twenty years.

In December JCP leaders announced that in 1985 the party would sponsor an international conference on nuclear arms to commemorate the fortieth anniversary of the bombing of Nagasaki and Hiroshima. Representatives of ten communist parties would attend, including the Communist Party of the Soviet Union but not the Chinese Communist Party or the (North) Korean Workers' (communist) Party. (*Japan Times*, 31 December.)

In another military-related matter, in the fall the JCP opposed a state visit by President Chun Doo-Hwan of South Korea, seeing it as an effort to cement U.S.–Japan–South Korean military ties. Party leaders called the Chun government "reactionary, anti-democratic, and military backed" and led demonstrations while Chun was in Tokyo. (*FEER*, 13 September.)

The party's defeat in the December 1983 elections (when the JCP received less than 10 percent of the vote for the first time in a number of years) loomed large in party deliberations. The JCP had to reassess its electoral strategy and try to deal with the problems the defeat caused. However, it was unable to deal constructively with the efforts of the other opposition parties to form a coalition that excluded the JCP. Party leaders also found it difficult to cope with the continuing hostility of the other parties and the negative impact on the party of poor relations between Japan and the USSR and of such incidents as the Soviet downing of a South Korean civilian airliner and the North Korean assassination of a number of South Korean leaders in Rangoon. The party has been critical of Soviet and North Korean behavior as well as of events in Afghanistan and Kampuchea, but these incidents have damaged the JCP's image.

The JCP fared rather poorly in local elections in 1984 with the exception of the local assembly elections in Okinawa. Party leaders were not optimistic about the party's chances in a major election. JCP leaders looked ahead to the Tokyo metropolitan elections in 1985 and a House of Councillors election in 1986, but had to think in terms of successful work efforts before gains could be expected in the elections.

International Views, Positions, and Activities. The JCP continues to regard itself as a Eurocommunist party and maintains good relations with a number of European parties. Its relations with the Communist Party of the Soviet Union, which have been strained in recent years, improved during the year—perhaps indicating a permanent thaw and amicable relations in the future. Relations with the communist parties of Vietnam and Kampuchea also improved, but relations with the Chinese party continued to be bad.

Early in the year Miyamoto sent a letter to Yuri Andropov calling for the prevention of nuclear war and the abolition of nuclear weapons. Andropov answered the letter just before he died, agreeing with the JCP position. This was followed in April by two days of talks in Tokyo with Soviet representatives on a total ban on nuclear weapons (*FBIS*, 27 April). It was agreed that Miyamoto would visit Moscow for talks with Chernenko late in the year.

In mid-December Miyamoto arrived in Moscow at the head of a delegation of high-ranking JCP officials for an eight-day visit. The JCP and the Soviet party issued a joint communiqué at the end of the visit pledging to persuade other countries not to use nuclear weapons in a pre-emptive strike. The communiqué also promised efforts against weapons in space and for nuclear-free zones in Asia. The meeting was important because of the communiqué and because Miyamoto was the first Japanese politician to meet Chernenko as leader of the Soviet Union. It was the first high-level meeting between the JCP and the Soviet party since 1979. As agreed by the JCP in advance, however, the talks did not touch on Afghanistan or the "Northern Territories" issue. (*Japan Times*, 18 December.)

Relations with the Chinese Communist Party did not improve during the year. A number of Chinese leaders visited Japan, but none made any effort to contact JCP officials or Diet representatives. One Chinese visitor in April pointed out that China was "not in a hurry to improve relations with the JCP" (*FBIS*, 2 April).

The same was true of relations with the North Korean party. The JCP was critical of North Korea's attack on a Japanese fishing vessel in August. North Korea characterized the JCP's remarks as interference in its internal affairs. The JCP replied with an argument based on international law (*Akahata*, 27 September).

A JCP delegation visited Vietnam and Kampuchea in the fall for meetings with the leaders of both countries. Public statements by all parties condemned the U.S.-Japan Security Treaty, U.S. imperialism, and nuclear weapons. The JCP made concessions on some issues, for example, Vietnam's invasion of Kampuchea and Pol Pot's crimes, although it did stop short of supporting Vietnam's continued military occupation of Kampuchea. The JCP announced that it favored Japanese aid to both countries. No joint statements were issued at the end of the visit, but Kampuchean leader Heng Samrin agreed to send a delegation to Japan in the future. (*Japan Times*, 29 September.)

In June Tetsuzo Fuwa visited Italy for the funeral of Italian Communist Party leader Enrico Berlinguer and after the funeral visited Romania and Finland. In both places he discussed Japan's role as a Eurocommunist party and areas of common interests. In November Fuwa led a JCP delegation to Mexico, Cuba, and Nicaragua, where he was critical of U.S. policy and praised the governments of Cuba and Nicaragua (ibid., 4 December). In May a delegation from the League of Yugoslav Communists visited with JCP leaders in Tokyo and discussed party relations and international issues (*FBIS*, 31 May).

John F. Copper
Rhodes College

Kampuchea

Population. 6,118,000
Party. Kampuchean People's Revolutionary Party (KPRP); Kampuchean Communist Party (KCP)
Membership. KPRP: 700 (estimated); KCP: no data
Founded. KPRP: 1951; KCP: 1960
Secretary General. KPRP: Heng Samrin; KCP: Pol Pot
Politburo. KPRP: 7 members—Heng Samrin, Hun Sen, Chea Soth, Bou Thang, Chea Sim, Say Phutang, Chan Si (died in December 1984); KCP: no data—leading figures are believed to include Pol Pot, Ieng Sary, Son Sen, Ta Mok, and Nuon Chea.
Secretariat. KPRP: 8 members—Heng Samrin, Chea Soth, Khang Sarin, Chan Phin, Say Phutang, Bou Thang, Hun Sen, Chan Si (died in December 1984)
Central Committee. KPRP: 25 full and 2 alternate members
Status. KPRP: ruling, recognized as legitimate party by the Soviet bloc and Albania; KCP: illegal from the perspective of the Vietnamese-installed government in Phnom Penh, recognized by China, North Korea, and Yugoslavia, formally dissolved in June 1982 in accordance with the united front strategy that included formation of the Coalition Government of Democratic Kampuchea, in conjunction with noncommunist political organizations led by Prince Sihanouk and Son Sann
Last Congress. KPRP: Fourth, May 1981
Last Election. N/a
Auxiliary Organizations. KPRP: Kampuchean Federation of Trade Unions, Association of Revolutionary Youth of Kampuchea
Publications. KPRP: *Kampuchea*

Party Internal Affairs and Organization. Kampuchea is the only country in the world that has had two communist parties competing for legitimacy as the ruling communist party. Both the KPRP, led by Heng Samrin, and the KCP, led by Pol Pot, can be traced back to the party formed by Vietnamese Communists in June 1951. However, the KCP has since 1977 refused to accept such a genealogy and claims it was formed in September 1960.

When the Vietnamese army invaded Kampuchea in December 1978, it installed in Phnom Penh a regime—the People's Republic of Kampuchea (PRK)—controlled by a recreated KPRP, led by KPRP Secretary General Pen Sovan and chief of state Heng Samrin. The former was one of the

"Khmer Vietminh" who had been kept behind in Hanoi and thereby escaped execution at the hands of Pol Pot. The latter was a former Pol Pot functionary and defector from the KCP, who fled to Vietnam in 1978 in order to avoid execution in the Pol Pot–Ieng Sary–Ta Mok purges. In early 1982 Pen Sovan was replaced as party secretary general by Heng Samrin, who thereby became the single most powerful of the KPRP leaders.

Today the leadership of the KPRP reflects these two basic tendencies: the Khmer Vietminh remnants and the ex–Khmer Rouge. At least three of the seven-man Politburo—Heng Samrin, Hun Sen, and Chea Sim—are former Khmer Rouge (*FEER*, 16 February).

The KPRP and Vietnamese Communists

proudly speak of the KPRP as a "brother party" of the Vietnamese Communist Party, both "born in the Indochinese Communist Party of past years" (*Tap Chi Cong San*, June 1981). The Vietnamese and the KPRP commonly refer to the KCP as the "Pol Pot–Ieng Sary–Khieu Samphan genocidal clique" that usurped power from the "Kampuchean revolution" on 20 May 1975—only one month after the victory against "U.S. imperialism." According to the Hanoi and Phnom Penh party leaders, the usurpation took place after a visit to Beijing by Pol Pot and came at the instigation of the "Beijing expansionists." The twentieth of May is now the official National Day of Hatred, directed against "the genocidal Pol Pot–Ieng Sary–Khieu Samphan gang and the Beijing hegemonist-expansionists" (*FBIS*, 22 May).

The KPRP officially announced its existence after its Fourth Congress, held in late May 1981. The KPRP Central Committee's Eighth Plenum met from 28 to 30 March.

The KCP leaders speak of the KPRP as a puppet of the Vietnamese, whose purpose is to drag Kampuchea into an Indochinese federation and to assist Vietnam in its objective of "swallowing" Kampuchea and exterminating the Khmer race and culture. The Vietnamese Communists are usually described by the radio of Democratic Kampuchea as "the Le Duan Vietnamese aggressors."

The KCP was, from its inception, a Maoist party, inspired by the most radical phase of communism in China—particularly Mao's Great Leap Forward and the Great Proletarian Cultural Revolution. Its domestic policies in power from 1975 to 1978 can best be understood as the carrying of Maoist policies to a further extreme than did their originator.

In 1982 the KCP was formally dissolved, and the state organization it controlled—Democratic Kampuchea—was formally integrated with the noncommunist political forces of Prince Sihanouk and Son Sann into the Coalition Government of Democratic Kampuchea (CGDK). Each of the three parties to the CGDK has its own independent political and military organization. The statement of dissolution of the KCP was in accordance with the strategy of the united front, which also included a profession of commitment to freedom of religion, freedom of speech, a capitalist economy, and a democratic, liberal regime. But Democratic Kampuchea remains the political entity that expresses the views of the anti-Vietnamese Kampuchean Communists. Although the areas under the control of Democratic

Kampuchea are not today run on liberal, democratic lines, nevertheless there has been some relaxation by the regime. Religion is tolerated, as is a form of free enterprise via the black market. The ban on music and dancing appears to have been lifted. Nothing is known of the activities of the KCP today.

Political, Economic, and Military Issues. The KPRP faces three fundamental problems in attempting to establish its authority in Kampuchea: (1) the military challenge posed by the insurgent guerrilla forces grouped in the CGDK; (2) the political challenge posed by the nonrecognition by most of the world's governments of the People's Republic of Kampuchea, which the KPRP controls; (3) the inability of the PRK to survive without Vietnamese military forces or to function independently of Vietnamese advisers.

During 1984 the CGDK insurgent forces struck deep inside Kampuchea, including areas around the Tonle Sap (Great Lake). The National Army of Democratic Kampuchea (NADK)—the armed forces of the Khmer Rouge—attacked the cities of Battambang and Siem Reap, the latter being the site of the headquarters for the main Vietnamese military operations against the resistance.

In contrast, the armed forces of the PRK continued to suffer from defections and poor morale. The most important cause of this continues to be the popular perception of the PRK as an instrument of Vietnamese colonial domination. But another factor appears to be the lack of political controls within the army, particularly a lack of party cadres.

A national meeting of KPRP party cadres was held in Phnom Penh from 2 to 9 November. The meeting elected eight more members to the party Central Committee (ibid., 15 November). The KPRP suffers from a severe shortage of members. Half of the KPRP Central Committee consists of former Khmer Rouge and half are Khmer Vietminh returnees. Equally important is its inability to establish an identity independent of the Vietnamese—the hereditary enemy of the Khmer. In April Sek Yen, 39, deputy director of the Department of Education and Political Theory within the Propaganda and Education Commission of the Central Committee, defected to Thailand. He claimed that "Vietnam was practicing real colonialism in Cambodia" (ibid., 13 April).

In spite of the violence of the KCP in power, its new "united front" policy, which has attempted to moderate its image, and its nationalist credentials, has given it the edge over the KPRP in recruitment of those Khmer who would still want to become Communists.

KPRP Politburo member Chan Si died in Moscow in December of heart disease. He was replaced as premier by Foreign Minister Hun Sen.

International Views, Positions, and Activities. KPRP foreign policy is identical with that of the Vietnamese Communist Party. So close are the ties between the two parties that major Vietnamese political holidays, such as the birthday of Ho Chi Minh and the Victory Day at Dien Bien Phu, are celebrated in Kampuchea. Identity with the Vietnamese foreign policy means that KPRP foreign policy is aligned with that of the Soviet Union.

During a visit to the Soviet Union in February to attend the funeral of Yuri Andropov, KPRP Secretary General Heng Samrin stated:

> The PRK has always been supported in all international forums by its Soviet friends, working for the heightening of the PRK's prestige and international position in world arena. The whole party and people regard the Soviet Union as their firm bastion in national defense and reconstruction in its gradual advance through the period of transition toward socialism.
>
> The relations between the KPRP and the CPSU and between our mass organizations have grown and developed most satisfactorily. [Ibid., 21 February.]

In June a delegation from the KPRP Central Committee Propaganda and Education Department, headed by Men Samon, visited the Soviet Union. According to *Pravda*, "The delegation's members familiarized themselves with the activity of party organizations in the ideological-political education of working people and the life and labor of Soviet people in Moscow, Moscow oblast and Leningrad" (*FBIS*, 18 June).

The Soviet Union and its allies are the principal suppliers of economic aid to the PRK.

The KPRP has extremely close ties with the Cuban Communist Party and with the Sandinista National Liberation Front of Nicaragua. In May a delegation of the Sandinista Youth, led by María Fonseca, secretary of the Central Committee, arrived in Phnom Penh for a friendship visit (ibid., 31 May).

The KPRP has cordial ties with other Soviet client parties. In April Khang Sarin, member of the Secretariat of the KPRP Central Committee received a delegation of the Yemen Socialist Party headed by Salih Hasan Muhammad, member of the Central Committee and director of the Institute of Marxism-Leninism (ibid., 23 April).

The KPRP also has good relations with the Albanian Party of Labor. Heng Samrin sent birthday greetings to Enver Hoxha on the latter's seventy-sixth birthday (ibid., 22 October). Albania, which is independent of the Soviet Union, supports Vietnam in its conflict with China.

The KCP has had the unswerving support of the Chinese Communist Party over the years. Its state organization continues to be supported by the ruling parties of Yugoslavia and North Korea. However, since the KCP was officially dissolved in 1982, there are no published reports of interparty relations.

Stephen J. Morris
University of California, Berkeley

Korea: Democratic People's Republic of Korea

Population. 19,630,000
Party. Korean Workers' Party (Choson Nodong-dang; KWP)
Founded. 1949
Membership. 3 million
General Secretary. Kim Il-song
Presidium of the Politburo. 3 members: Kim Il-song (DPRK president), Kim Chong-il (Kim Il-song's son and designated successor), O Chin-u (minister of People's Armed Forces)
Politburo. 17 full members: Kim Il-song, Kim Chong-il, O Chin-u, Kang Song-san (DPRK premier), Pak Song-chol (DPRK vice-president), Yim Chun-chu (DPRK vice-president), Yi Chong-ok (DPRK vice-president), So Chol, Kim Yong-nam (DPRK deputy premier and foreign affairs minister), Ho Tam, Yon Hyong-muk, Chon Mun-sop, Choe Yong-nim (first deputy premier), O Kuk-yol, Kim Hwan (deputy premier), Paek Hak-im, So Yun-sok; 18 alternate members: Hyon Mu-kwang, An Sung-hak, Chon Pyong-ho, Kong Chin-tae (deputy premier and chairman of the Trade Commission), Hong Song-yong (deputy premier and chairman of the State Planning Commission), Cho Se-ung (deputy premier), Choe Kwang (deputy premier and chairman of the Fisheries Commission), Kim Pok-sin (deputy premier and light industry minister), Chong Chun-ki (deputy premier), Kim Tu-nam, Kye Ung-tae, Yi Kun-mo, Kang Hui-won, Chong Kyong-hui, Kim Kwang-hwan, Yi Song-sil, Hong Song-nam, Kim Chung-nin
Secretariat. 12 members: Kim Il-song, Kim Chong-il, Ho Tam, Yon Hyong-muk, Hyon Mu-kwang, An Sung-hak, Hwang Chang-yop, Ho Chong-suk, Chae Hui-chong, So Kwang-hui, Kim Yong-sun, Pak Nam-ki
Central Committee. 145 full and 103 alternate members
Status. Ruling party
Last Congress. Sixth, 10–15 October 1980, in Pyongyang
Last Election. 1982, 100 percent, all 615 candidates for the Supreme People's Assembly approved by the KWP beforehand
Subordinate and Auxiliary Organizations. Korean Social Democratic Party, Young Friends' Party of the Chondogyo Sect, General Federation of Trade Unions of Korea (2 million members), League of Socialist Working Youth of Korea (2.7 million members), Union of Agricultural Working People of Korea, Korean Democratic Women's Union, General Federation of the Unions of Literature and Arts of Korea, General Federation of Korean Workers in Industry and Technology, Korean Committee for Solidarity with the World People, Committee for the Peaceful Reunification of the Fatherland, United Democratic Fatherland Front (united front organization), Korean Writers' Union
Publications. *Nodong Sinmun* (Workers' daily), KWP daily; *Kulloja* (Workers), KWP monthly; *Minchu Choson* (Democratic Korea), organ of the Supreme People's Assembly and cabinet; *Choson Inminkun Sinmun* (Korean People's Army news). English-language publications are the *Pyongyang Times*, *People's Korea*, and *Korea Today*, all weeklies. The Korean Central News Agency (KCNA) is the official news agency.

Leadership and Organization. The cult of Kim Il-song and his family members (especially his son and heir-designate, Chong-il) continued unabated in 1984. DPRK mass media constantly stressed that loyalty to the North Korean dictator and his ideology of *chuch'e* ("self-identity" or "national identity") should continue from generation to generation, and the Pyongyang regime continually waged an intensive campaign to solidify the younger Kim's position. On 15 April the senior Kim's seventy-second birthday was celebrated throughout the country with great fanfare. The DPRK government decided to step up the overseas publicity of Kim Il-song's works in foreign languages through the Foreign Literature Publishing House in Pyongyang.

In the summer of 1984, Kim Chong-il was promised all-round support from the country's armed forces. Paek Hak-im, Pyongyang's vice–defense minister, wrote in the 26 July issue of the KWP organ *Nodong Sinmun* that it was the "resolute creed" of the DPRK People's Armed Forces to unconditionally and strictly adhere to the junior Kim's "orders and directives" on top of his "lines and policies."

The KWP has successfully resolved the question of political succession by upholding "our dear leader Kim Chong-il as the sole successor to great leader Kim Il-song," according to Radio Pyongyang on 9 August. It also indicated that one of the primary aims of Kim Il-song's East European tour in May–June 1984 was to persuade the leaders of the host countries of the succession plan. The radio said: "The leaders of the Soviet Union and other socialist countries have evaluated the achievements by the great leader [Kim Il-song] and our dear leader [Kim Chong-il]." It was the first time, meanwhile, that the ruling KWP apparatus described the junior Kim by name as the heir.

In its annual report released in London on 24 October, Amnesty International revealed that during the period from January to April 1983, 1,096 people had been purged for objecting to the planned hereditary succession from Kim Il-song to his son. The report also said that several prominent figures purged a few years ago could not be located.

During 1984 Kim Chong-il appeared in all important events in North Korea, in place of his father or in company with the senior Kim, accompanied by key party-government officials to conduct "on-the-spot guidance" at various sites. And his remarks were quoted more frequently than ever.

Pyongyang media escalated their campaign to further consolidate Kim Chong-il's position as a new ruler of the country. For example, on 11 March the North Korean Central Broadcasting Station aired a special commentary entitled "The Center of the Party Unity Is the Leader," urging that everyone should follow the example of the junior Kim in inheriting the revolutionary tradition of "great leader Kim Il-song."

Kim Chong-il in 1984 began to function as the real powerholder, in place of his father, even in the diplomatic field. Every indication was that his role in foreign policy would increase as time went by. North Korea watchers in Seoul noted that Kim Il-song was reported to have told Bulgarian president Todor Zhivkov, when he met with him in Sofia in June, that the junior Kim would begin to receive foreign heads of states as their counterpart when they visited North Korea in the near future.

Meanwhile, Soviet deputy foreign minister Mikhail Kapitsa met with Kim Il-song on 20 November and with Kim Chong-il on 23 November. The junior Kim held a welcoming banquet for Kapitsa on the same day. Kapitsa's meeting with Kim Chong-il may be interpreted as the Kremlin's positive response to Pyongyang's hereditary succession plan, considering the fact that Kapitsa was the first high-ranking Soviet official to be officially received by the junior Kim other than the Soviet ambassador to Pyongyang, who met with Kim on 24 September.

On 28 December 1983 Kim Yong-nam was named deputy premier and foreign affairs minister of the Administrative Council, replacing Ho Tam, who had held the office for thirteen years. (Kim was elected Politburo member and secretary of the KWP Central Committee at the Sixth Party Congress of October 1980.)

Former deputy premier and foreign affairs minister Ho Tam was appointed chairman of the Committee for the Peaceful Reunification of the Fatherland.

On 27 January, the third session of the seventh Supreme People's Assembly (SPA) named Kang Song-san, who had been deputy premier of the Administrative Council since August 1982, premier in place of Yi Chong-ok, and elected Yi vice-president. Yi's selection to the post brought the number of vice-presidents to four. The other three were Kim Il, Pak Song-chol, and Yim Chun-chu. (Kim Il died on 9 March.)

The session also replaced Secretary General Yi Yong-ik of the Central People's Committee (CPC) with Kim I-hun, who had been a secretary of the

Presidium of the SPA since February 1982, and elected Kim and Kang Song-san members of the CPC.

In the SPA, Kim Pong-chu, who was chairman of the General Federation of Trade Unions, was appointed secretary of the SPA's Standing Committee. Kim Man-kum (former chairman of the Pyongyang Municipal People's Committee), Chu Chang-chun (former ambassador to Yugoslavia), Pak Su-dong (chairman of the South Hwanghae Provincial People's Committee), and Chi Chang-ik (president of Kim Il-song University) were elected members of the Standing Committee. The assembly also elected An Sung-hak (party secretary in charge of light industry) and Chae Hi-chong (party secretary in charge of planning and finance), chairmen of the Budget Consultation Committee and Bills Consultation Committee of the SPA, respectively.

On 25 January the DPRK regime appointed Sin In-ha, former ambassador to Romania, ambassador to China.

On 8 February Kim Yong-sun, deputy director of the International Affairs Department in the Sixth KWP Central Committee, was appointed party secretary, replacing Kim Yong-nam, who was named deputy premier and foreign affairs minister of the Administrative Council in December 1983.

On 14 February Politburo member Choe Yong-nim was appointed deputy premier of the Administrative Council.

In mid-July Politburo member Chon Mun-sop was appointed chairman of the State Censorship Committee in the CPC. (Chon made his first public appearance in February after a seventeen-month hiatus.)

On 10 September the Pyongyang government reappointed Choe Kwang deputy premier of the Administrative Council, thereby bringing the number of the deputy premiers to ten. The other nine deputy premiers were Choe Yong-nim (first deputy premier), Kim Yong-nam, Kim Kwan, Kim Pok-sin, Cho Se-ung, Kong Chin-tae, Chong Chun-ki, Hong Song-yong, and Kim Chang-su.

On 2 October Pak Sung-il replaced Yun Ki-pok as chairman of the Pyongyang Municipal People's Committee (mayor of the DPRK capital).

The tenth plenary meeting of the Sixth KWP Central Committee on 4 to 10 December elected Pak Nam-ki secretary of the Central Committee and Kang Sun-hui, Kim Won-chon, and Chon Chin-su as members of the Central Committee to fill vacancies. It also elected Kim Kwang-hak, Chon Ho-kyun, Nam Sang-nak, Kim Song-ku, Choe Pong-

man, and Kim Chol-myong as alternate members of the Central Committee to fill vacancies.

The Central Auditing Commission of the KWP elected Kim Chae-yol and Pak Sung-il as members to fill vacancies.

On 14 February Kim Chung-nin, party secretary in charge of anti-Seoul activities since 1969, was removed from the Secretariat and demoted to candidate Politburo member from regular member. (Ho Tam replaced Kim as party secretary.) Kim Chung-nin's demotion came after the Pyongyang-plotted Rangoon terrorist bombing attack of 9 October 1983, which killed 21 people, including seventeen visiting South Korean government officials.

On 16 June Public Security Minister Yi Chin-su, who had been in the post since March 1973, was replaced by Yi Chol-pong. (The DPRK Public Security Ministry and the People's Armed Forces Ministry are separated from the Administrative Council [the North Korean cabinet] and under the direct control of the KWP Central Committee.)

During 1984 the following high-ranking party-government figures died: Tong Min-kwang (60), alternate member of the Sixth KWP Central Committee and minister of forestry of the Administrative Council; Ko Tae-un (55), alternate member of the Sixth KWP Central Committee and manager of the Pukchang thermal power plant; Vice-President Kim Il (75), who was concurrently a member of the Presidium of the Sixth KWP Politburo; party Politburo member O Paek-yong (71), who was concurrently vice-chairman of the National Defense Committee in the Central People's Committee; Yi Ki-yong (89), chairman of the Central Committee of the General Federation of the Unions of Literature and Arts and member of the Central Committee of the Democratic Front for the Reunification of the Fatherland; Kim Man-kum (73), member of the Sixth KWP Central Committee, member of the SPA Standing Committee, and member of the Presidium of the Central Committee of the Democratic Front for the Reunification of the Fatherland; and Choe Il-pong (51), alternate member of the Sixth KWP Central Committee and major general of the (North) Korean People's Army.

Domestic Attitudes and Activities. President Kim Il-song's New Year's address, like those of previous years, concentrated on economic problems, urging more production of coal, power, steel, synthetic fibers, and marine food to complete the seven-year economic plan (1978–1984). In mid-1984 Pyongyang again stepped up its drive to attain the targets of the current economic plan, especially in mining, metal industries, and railway transportation.

In mid-October the DPRK regime intensified its drive to increase the production of export materials, urging that this year's export goal must be attained at all costs and by any means. The 16 October issue of *Nodong Sinmun* carried an editorial stressing the importance of exports. The paper said that the success of the current economic plan depended greatly on the attainment of the export goal. (North Korea's exports and imports in 1983 reportedly amounted to U.S. $1.38 billion and $1.55 billion, respectively.)

According to the December 1984 issue of *Gunji Kenkyū* (Military research) magazine published in Tokyo, the DPRK government adopted plans to set up 24 general colleges, six factory colleges, and four technical high schools by the 1985 school year in accordance with an urgent directive from Kim Il-song, who reportedly was dismayed to discover, during his tour of Eastern Europe in May and June, that his country lagged behind in science and technology.

On 26 January the DPRK fixed its budget for fiscal 1984 at 26.2 billion won (U.S. $11.9 billion). The budgetary action came during the three-day third session of the Seventh SPA, which opened on 25 January in Pyongyang. The 1984 budget showed an increase of 7.6 percent in revenues over the previous year and a 9.2 percent rise in spending. Military spending for fiscal 1984 constituted 14.6 percent of the total budget; 63.4 percent was allocated for the people's economy sector, 20.1 percent for social welfare and culture, and 1.9 percent for administration and management. (The actual defense expenditure is no doubt higher because Pyongyang hides military expenditures in other sectors.) According to the breakdown, military spending amounted to 3.8 billion won (U.S. $1.7 billion). This represented an increase of 8.5 percent over the previous year.

The third session adopted a resolution calling for further strengthening of "south-south" cooperation and promotion of trade with capitalist countries. On 26 January Deputy Premier Kang Song-san, who was to be named premier the next day, mentioned that North Korea had so far constructed more than 30 factories and a number of irrigation facilities in 22 Third World countries and dispatched 5,000 technicians to more than 50 nonaligned countries to promote "south-south" cooperation.

According to Kang, North Korea would like to promote technical cooperation and joint venture projects with socialist countries and develop trade relations and technical exchanges with "friendly" capitalist nations in the coming years. Pyongyang would like to import more materials and fuel as well as machinery from socialist countries and increase the trade volume by ten times in five or six years. He said that North Korea's main export items to earn foreign exchange from capitalist countries would include nonferrous metals, cement, and steel products, but he did not mention what items his government would import from those countries.

To implement the economic resolution, North Korea established an Economic Policy Committee in the CPC, the top policymaking body in the DPRK government.

On 8 September the government enacted a joint venture law to attract foreign investment and expand trade with capitalist countries. On 10 September the North Korean Central Broadcasting Station reported that the law was adopted by the Standing Committee of the SPA in order to "expand economic and technological exchanges and cooperation with foreign countries." The law, consisting of five chapters and 26 articles, defined the following areas as suitable for joint ventures: industry, construction, transportation, science and technology, and tourism. The law guaranteed that the assets invested and earned by foreign partners would be protected and that joint ventures would be conducted on "principles of equity and mutual benefit." Pyongyang will also guarantee the property and profits of foreign partners in all joint ventures. Raw materials and partially assembled products purchased in North Korea would be valued at international market prices, and no tariffs would be imposed on materials imported by joint venture partners.

The 13 October issue of *Nodong Sinmun* denied that there was any chance of modifying Pyongyang's existing external economic policy and said that North Korea was considering promotion of economic relations with socialist countries before it tried to develop any trade relations with capitalist countries. The paper also noted Pyongyang's "persistent" economic policy, but stated that economic relations between the socialist countries did "not necessarily mean that these socialist countries should not conduct trade with capitalist nations."

Relations with South Korea. Relations between North and South Korea remained basically hostile during 1984. The DPRK stepped up its harsh propaganda and other attacks on the Seoul government under President Chun Doo-Hwan, calling him the head of a "mangy fascist clique."

The two Koreas began a particularly tense period in their relationship immediately after the Pyongyang-hatched terrorist bombing of 9 October 1983, which killed seventeen South Korean government officials making a state visit to Burma. Seoul kept demanding the DPRK's official apology for the Rangoon bombing incident, but Pyongyang continued to refuse to acknowledge its responsibility.

Kim Il-song on 4 February ordered "combat readiness" for all members of the People's Armed Forces, the Security Guard, the Worker and Peasant Red Guard, and the Red Youth Guard to guard against a U.S.–South Korea joint military exercise, "Team Spirit '84," which had been launched in the South on 1 February.

North Korea on 10 January proposed three-way talks involving Washington, Seoul, and Pyongyang to discuss peace and reunification of the divided Korean peninsula. Seoul turned down the proposal and renewed its standing call for direct intra-Korean dialogue. South Korea insisted that larger forums to include "those countries concerned with the Korean problem" could be held only after direct North-South negotiations.

On 9 April Pyongyang's delegation unilaterally walked out of the North-South conference discussing formation of a single, united team to represent Korea in the Summer Olympics in Los Angeles in July 1984. (The DPRK also decided to boycott the 1984 Olympics.)

In early May North Korea issued acrid remarks about Pope John Paul II's visit to South Korea, alleging that the papal visit was "designed to slander us and heighten the sense of confrontation" between the two Koreas. It claimed that the canonization of 103 Korean Catholic martyrs and the papal visit were "part of South Korea's disguised peace offensive."

In September, the two Koreas returned to a mood of détente when Pyongyang on 8 September proposed to offer rice, cement, and other commodities to South Korean flood victims. Seoul accepted the DPRK proposal on 14 September. (In accepting the North Korean offer, the Seoul government said: "We do not need the supplies from the North but we accepted the North Korean offer in the hope of breaking the impasse in intra-Korean relations and thus reduce tension on the Korean peninsula.") An intra-Korean Red Cross meeting took place in Panmunjom on 18 September to discuss delivery procedures. Pyongyang delivered 50,000 *sok* (roughly 7,200 tons) of rice, 500,000 meters of cloth, 100,000 tons of cement, and fourteen kinds of medical supplies to Panmunjom and two South Korean ports. (The Seoul side sent north truckloads of gifts—800 suitcases that South Korean officials said contained transistor radios, wristwatches, cosmetics, clothing, and household items.)

On 15 November in the truce village of Panmunjom, the two Koreas held the first intra-Korean economic talks. They ended with an agreement to hold the next meeting on 5 December at the same site. Among the suggestions made by both sides were the establishment of a joint economic committee, the relinkage of the railroad between the South and the North, and the opening of ports in both sides for trade. Actual agreement on these matters, however, was yet to be made.

As for possible trade items, chief South Korean delegate Kim Ki-hwan suggested that Seoul would like to export steel and copper products, sewing machines, pianos, electronic and household commodities and to import from the North such materials as iron ore, lead and zinc ingots, coal, pollacks (a type of codfish), silk cocoons, and red beans.

North Korean chief delegate Yi Song-nok said that North Korea would like to sell some mineral and agricultural products to the South and buy from Seoul steel products, naphtha, textile products, and agricultural products such as mandarin oranges.

The main difference between the two sides emerged when Seoul insisted that trade should precede economic cooperation programs such as joint ventures, while Pyongyang argued that "collaboration" was more important than trade. The North Koreans explained that collaboration meant the development of joint venture programs in such fields as mining, fishing, tideland construction, and so forth. The South Koreans, however, were reluctant to accept this terminology as genuine because the word smacked of the communist concept of "united front tactics."

On 20 November delegates from the two sides' Red Cross societies met in Panmunjom and agreed to restart negotiations suspended in 1973 toward reuniting families separated by the Korean War. To facilitate cooperation, they agreed to open a liaison office in Panmunjom, establish two direct telephone lines, and meet again in Seoul within two months.

Seoul and Pyongyang also agreed in late December to resume intra-Korean economic talks in Panmunjom on 17 January 1985 and full-dress Red Cross talks in Seoul on 22–25 January 1985. (The economic talks scheduled for 5 December were postponed by the North after a firefight at Panmunjom on 23 November when 20 to 30 North Korean guards intruded into the southern zone and fired at a Russian defector. Three North Korean soldiers and one South Korean guard were killed in the shooting; the Russian escaped unharmed.)

International Views and Positions. During 1984, Pyongyang mounted an intensive diplomatic offensive against South Korea to undermine the international position of the Seoul regime and to develop world support for its own reunification policy. Parliamentary, trade, and goodwill missions were dispatched abroad or invited to North Korea. Pyongyang made numerous friendly diplomatic gestures and offers of economic, military, and technical aid, especially to Third World countries, which increasingly dominate the United Nations. In particular, the DPRK sought to prevent recognition of the "two Koreas" concept by the world community; to isolate South Korea from the Third World, the communist bloc, and even the Western world; and to drum up diplomatic support for its demand to remove U.S. forces from South Korea.

On 18 January the DPRK recognized the Sultanate of Brunei, which won its independence from the United Kingdom in 1983.

Diplomatic relations between the DPRK and the Socialist Republic of Vietnam were normalized after a five-year hiatus on 24 June when Kim Chong-chun, the new North Korean ambassador to Hanoi, presented his credentials. (This action came after President Kim Il-song's visit to the Soviet Union in late May. Meanwhile, Prince Norodom Sihanouk, head of the anti-Vietnamese Kampuchean United Front, visited Pyongyang in December 1983 and April 1984 as Kim Il-song's special guest.)

In a bid to boost its standing in the Nonaligned movement and win friends in Third World countries, North Korea on 7 March gave strong support to Syria over the Lebanon situation. (Chairman Yassir Arafat of the Palestine Liberation Organization made a three-day visit to North Korea in May.)

On 20 March the DPRK severely denounced the United States for "undermining the interest of the Nicaraguan people." A Nicaraguan military mission, led by Defense Minister Humberto Ortega flew into Pyongyang on 2 April. On 11 July O Kuk-yol, chief of the general staff of the People's Armed Forces, left Pyongyang on a visit to Nicaragua as the head of a DPRK military mission.

O Kuk-yol also made a seven-day visit to Libya from 6 to 12 August to enhance military cooperation between the two countries. Since 1978, North Korea has exported some $430 million worth of arms to Libya, including mortars, antiaircraft guns, artillery pieces, and tanks. Pyongyang currently maintains about 240 servicemen in Libya.

In mid-1984 the Pyongyang regime boasted that it maintained about 1,500 pro–North Korean organizations such as "solidarity committees," "*chuch'e* idea study groups," and "friendship associations" in more than a hundred countries, most of which were in the Third World.

United Press International in Kinshasa reported on 25 September that more than a thousand North Korean soldiers had entered Angola over the preceding few months to help Angolan troops fight against antigovernment guerrillas. On 10 October the DPRK denied any military involvement in Angola's internal war.

The Soviet Union and China. During 1984, Pyongyang continued to maintain its middle-of-the-road position in the Sino-Soviet rift. Moscow and Beijing competed with verbal assurances and material support for North Korea's friendship. Both countries urged the prompt withdrawal of U.S. troops from South Korea and supported Pyongyang's formula for reunification and its demand for direct U.S.-DPRK contacts to settle the Korean problem.

North Korea declared 13 and 14 February days of national mourning for Yuri Andropov. Kim Il-song sent a message of condolence to the Central Committee of the Soviet party (CPSU) as well as the Soviet government. Vice-President Pak Song-chol headed for Moscow on 13 February, leading a party-government mission to attend the funeral the next day.

Radio Moscow reported on 29 February that Korean-Soviet trade would be increased by 30 percent over the previous year. The radio, however, did not disclose the volume of trade in 1983 between the two countries. (In 1981 North Korea's trade with the Soviet Union totaled $730.2 million, and its trade deficit with Moscow increased to $39.4 million that year, from $5.8 million in 1980.)

Radio Moscow on 13 June said that a combined nuclear research center near Moscow, the Dubna Nuclear Institute, had trained some 150 North Korean physicists since it was established; 25 of them had received the degree of doctor or associate doctor. One of the main fields of research had been on the technique of directional explosion to produce atomic power. (North Korea imported its first reactor from the USSR in 1962. Now the DPRK runs an atomic energy research center in Nyongpyon in North Pyongan province.)

On 16 May, Kim Il-song left Chongjin by train, leading a party-government mission on an official visit to Moscow, his first visit in 23 years. (Kim's Moscow visit came shortly after Chinese communist leader Hu Yaobang's visit to Pyongyang in early May.) Kim's last visit to Moscow was in October 1961 when he attended the Twenty-second Congress of the CPSU.

Kim Il-song stayed in Moscow from 23 to 25 May. According to diplomatic observers, he tried to secure Soviet support for his son as successor and more economic and military aid.

Kim Il-song and Soviet party leader Konstantin U. Chernenko held three rounds of talks, and the premiers and defense and foreign affairs ministers of both sides discussed military, political, and economic relations in separate meetings. The Soviet news agency, Tass, reported both sides had taken practical measures aimed at strengthening cooperation, suggesting Moscow had agreed to increase its aid to Pyongyang.

As for the Korean question, Chernenko said in the joint statement that the Soviet Union would "support Pyongyang's call for replacing the current Armistice Agreement with a peace pact and a declaration of nonaggression by South and North Korea." However, he did not directly refer to the Pyongyang-proposed three-way talks among Washington, Seoul, and Pyongyang. Kim Il-song, in his reply, stressed that "the Soviet Union and other countries" strongly supported the proposal. Moscow also said it supported North Korea's struggle to achieve reunification through peaceful, democratic means, "without any foreign interference."

A DPRK military mission, led by Deputy Director of the General Political Bureau of the People's Armed Forces Lt. Gen. Yun Chi-ho, left Pyongyang on 20 June for a visit to the Soviet Union. The mission's Moscow visit was probably designed to carry out a working-level discussion of Soviet military aid to North Korea, which was reported to have been discussed during Kim Il-song's Moscow visit in May. Speculations were that the Kremlin assured Kim that it would provide Pyongyang with 20 to 30 MiG-23 fighters and an unspecified number of T-72 tanks and newly developed combat helicopters. Zbigniew Brzezinski, former U.S. national security adviser, disclosed in a keynote address to a two-day conference in Japan in late November that the Soviet Union had supplied North Korea with an unspecified number of Scud missiles. He also implied that Pyongyang may have been given significant discretionary power in the use of the weapons.

A North Korean economic mission led by Kim Kwang-chin, first economic affairs director of the Sixth KWP Central Committee, visited Moscow around 18 June, possibly to discuss in detail the question of Soviet economic aid to Pyongyang. Pyongyang media did not report the mission's departure for the Soviet Union or its activity in Moscow.

North Korea and the Soviet Union held talks on border problems from 12 to 19 November in Pyongyang for the first time since 1957, when the two countries signed a border agreement. A Soviet delegation led by Deputy Foreign Affairs Minister Mikhail Kapitsa arrived in Pyongyang on 12 November for the talks and was given a welcoming banquet by his North Korean counterpart, Yi Chong-mok.

The border talks came unexpectedly. There had been no sign of any controversy between the two countries. The Soviet–North Korean border runs along the Tumen River estuary where seven islets are located. This river may have become a subject of dispute in connection with the cargo traffic between the two countries. On 26 November, North Korea and the Soviet Union concluded a treaty in Pyongyang concerning the border. Neither side gave details of the treaty, except to say that "the treaty deals with passage across the border."

On 21 November, Kapitsa and his North Korean counterpart signed the "plan of exchange for 1985–1986" to expand and develop bilateral relations between Moscow and Pyongyang during the next two years.

North Korean deputy premier and foreign affairs minister Kim Yong-nam visited China on 7–14 February at the invitation of Chinese foreign affairs minister Wu Xueqian. They discussed bilateral relations between Beijing and Pyongyang and international problems of mutual concern, according to Radio Beijing (14 February).

In a meeting with a visiting North Korean newspaper delegation on 27 March, General Secretary Hu Yaobang of the Chinese Communist Party reaffirmed Chinese support of the DPRK's proposal for three-way talks among Seoul, Pyongyang, and Washington and also of President Kim and Secretary Kim Chong-il's idea to reunify the Korean peninsula under their formula, the "Confederal Republic of Koryo." Hu was quoted as saying, "China will come to the rescue of North Korea at any time, as it did in the past, if the DPRK is invaded by any foreign aggressor."

General Secretary Hu Yaobang arrived in Pyongyang on 4 May by train for a one-week visit to exchange views with Kim Il-song on the Korean question and the current situation in Asia. During his stay in North Korea, Hu was reported to have had three rounds of talks with Kim, among many other activities. The three meetings reportedly concentrated on the Korean issue in connection with recent developments in the region, such as the visits to China by Japanese prime minister Yasuhiro Nakasone on 23–26 March and by U.S. President Reagan on 26 April–1 May.

No details were revealed, however. Both Pyongyang and Beijing media simply reported that the two sides had agreed on ways of resolving the Korea problem. In four speeches at mass rallies and banquets held in Pyongyang and Chongjin, Hu endorsed North Korea's call for three-way talks, withdrawal of American troops from South Korea, and Pyongyang's reunification formula, the Confederal Republic of Koryo. Hu was quoted as saying that China would continue to support North Korea's stand as far as the Korean question was concerned. He did not reveal the details of the agreement reached with Kim, but he said that the only way to resolve the Korean question was to hold talks among the concerned parties. He went on to say, "If the talks cannot be held immediately, an alternative solution will be to maintain contact among them because contact is better than confrontation." As for enhancing economic relations between Beijing and Pyongyang, Hu said, "We have not talked much about the economic question."

Trade between China and Japan through the port of Chongjin had increased sharply, according to Radio Beijing (11 May). Volume through the port was expected to reach some 200,000 tons by the end of 1984 compared with only 34,000 tons in 1983.

Premier Kang Song-san visited Beijing on 5–10 August at the invitation of Zhao Ziyang. The purpose of Kang's visit was not made known, but he was expected to confer with Chinese leaders on economic matters during his six-day stay in China.

According to the 18 August issue of *Yomiuri Shimbun* (Tokyo), Premier Kang protested the ongoing exchanges of personnel between South Korea and China by way of Hong Kong. Premier Zhao was quoted as telling Kang that Beijing had allowed only some South Koreans who had relatives in its northeastern region to visit China. Zhao made it clear that no South Korean government officials had visited China.

On 23 November North Korea and China concluded in Pyongyang the thirty-seventh conference protocol of the Council for the (North) Korea–China Yalu River Hydroelectric Power Company, apparently after some intense negotiations between the two countries.

Kim Il-song made an unofficial three-day visit (26–28 November) to China at the invitation of General Secretary Hu Yaobang of the Chinese Communist Party, the North Korean Central Broadcasting Station reported on 30 November. During his stay in Beijing, Kim met with Deng Xiaoping (26 November) and had two rounds of talks with Hu (26 and 27 November).

The purpose of Kim's sudden visit to China was not disclosed. (Noteworthy in this connection is the closeness of Kim's visit to China following Soviet deputy foreign minister Mikhail Kapitsa's visit to North Korea on 12–27 November and the firefight that broke out at Panmunjom over a Russian defector on 23 November.) Both North Korean and Chinese radio broadcasts merely reported on 30 November that the two countries' leaders had reached complete agreement on matters of mutual concern and on the strengthening of relations between the two countries.

After Kim Il-song's return from China, the North Korean Central Broadcasting Station cited Kim's visit to China as greatly promoting relations between the two capitals and added that China had always supported North Korea's struggle to achieve socialist construction and reunify the divided Korean peninsula.

Europe. In May and June Kim Il-song continued his train journey from Moscow to visit Poland, East Germany, Czechoslovakia, Hungary, Bulgaria, Yugoslavia, and Romania.

DPRK premier Kang Song-san made a five-day visit to Bucharest beginning 20 August, leading a North Korean party-government delegation to join the fortieth anniversary celebration of Romania's communist government.

KYODO News Service in Tokyo reported on 22 November that the KWP had recently decided to create a special liaison division to promote contacts with noncommunist political parties. The division, which would come under the KWP Central Committee, was to liaise with political parties in Japan, the United States, and other Western bloc nations.

The team was to be headed by Ho Tam, a veteran Politburo member and party secretary.

The Korean Central Broadcasting Station reported on 18 October that North Korea and France had signed an agreement on cultural exchange in Pyongyang, but the radio neither indicated the date it was signed nor gave any details of the agreement. On 19 October the French Ministry of External Relations denied the report. A ministry spokesman explained that the director-general of culture, science, and technology in the Ministry of External Relations had discussed the matter when he visited Pyongyang in early October, but no agreement had been signed. Discussions had been made on a *procès-verbal* basis and not for a diplomatic agreement, the spokesman said.

National Secretary Marcel Debarge of France's ruling Socialist Party visited Pyongyang on 2–7 November. Though the purpose of this visit was not made public, North Korea watchers in Seoul believed that Debarge might have discussed the possibility of promoting ties between North Korea and France. (As of this writing, Paris and Pyongyang have no diplomatic relations.)

Francis Gutmann, secretary general of the French Foreign Ministry, told reporters on 23 November that France had decided six months before to allow North Korea to upgrade its trade mission in Paris to the status of "general delegation"—a quasi-diplomatic representative.

The French Campenon Bernard Construction Company in Paris entered into a joint venture to build a high-rise hotel in Pyongyang. Campenon Bernard became the first foreign company to set up a joint venture firm in Pyongyang.

Japan. Relations between the DPRK and Japan have never been cordial. In Pyongyang's view, Japan is excessively partial to Seoul, pursues a policy of "two Koreas," and is hostile toward North Korea, as exemplified by the Japanese government's strong opposition to a drastic reduction of U.S. ground forces in South Korea. North Korea media continued to denounce growing Japanese "imperialism" in South Korea and the alleged collusion between Tokyo and Washington to preserve their mutual "colonial interest" in the Korean peninsula.

The Japanese government has never had political or diplomatic ties with the DPRK regime, limiting itself to low-level cultural and economic exchanges to maintain a pipeline into North Korea. Due to combined pressures from Japanese business and trading interests and left-wing political and labor

groups, nongovernmental contacts are expected to continue to increase during the 1980s, although official exchanges between Pyongyang and Tokyo appear unlikely. Officially the expanding nongovernmental contacts with the DPRK are presented as Japan's contribution to easing tensions between the two Koreas.

The North Korean government–run *Minchu Choson* (Democratic Korea) said on 24 March that the "U.S.–Japan–South Korea tripartite military alliance scheme" was aimed at dispatching Japanese armed forces to Korea in case of war. The paper went on to say that the "American and Japanese warmongers have developed a joint plan to provoke a war on the Korean peninsula" and called on them to accept without delay the Pyongyang-proposed three-way talks to end the tension.

The North Korean navy captured Japanese fishing boats on four occasions (16, 26, and 28 July and 16 August) on the grounds that they had violated the DPRK's economic or military sea zones. (In the 28 July incident, North Korea fired on a Japanese fishing boat, killing its captain.)

In mid-1984 Tokyo permitted a group of four North Korean social scientists to visit some fifteen Japanese universities, including Tokyo University, and attend a philosophy seminar in Kyoto in a month-long tour, which began on 17 May. They were the first North Koreans allowed to visit Japan since the Tokyo government restricted personnel exchanges with North Korea in response to the 13 October 1983 bombing attack in Rangoon. This entry of North Korea's "cultural delegation" into Japan was an indication of the easing of the restriction on personnel exchanges.

In late October Japan notified the Seoul government of its decision to lift Rangoon-related sanctions against North Korea in January 1985. The Tokyo government felt it appropriate to end the sanctions soon because of increasing contacts between the two Koreas during the second half of 1984.

The Nakasone cabinet allowed entry into Japan of a goodwill mission from Pyongyang during 8–22 November—the first such mission to visit since Japan imposed restrictions on North Koreans a year ago. This four-member mission was led by Pyon Sung-tok, director general of the (North) Korean Society for Cultural Relations with Foreign Countries, an organization dealing with countries with which Pyongyang has no diplomatic ties.

Masashi Ishibashi, chairman of the Japan Socialist Party, led a ten-member party delegation on a five-day visit to Pyongyang 22–26 September at the invitation of the KWP. Ishibashi held four rounds of talks with Kim Il-song, including a private meeting. Although details of the talks were not disclosed, Pyongyang media noted that the Kim-Ishibashi talks concentrated on matters of mutual concern between North Korea and Japan, especially the Japan–North Korea fishing accord.

On 15 October Pyongyang and Tokyo agreed to extend for two years their nongovernmental fishing agreement, which allows Japanese fishermen to operate in North Korean waters directly outside of its "50-mile military security zone." (An earlier agreement had expired in June 1982.)

Nodong Sinmun (6 August) strongly denounced the Japan Communist Party (JCP) for "trying to drive a wedge between the North Korean and Japanese people." This was Pyongyang's response to the JCP's severe criticism on 4 August of North Korea's firing on a Japanese fishing boat off the North Korean coast on 28 July. Relations between the DPRK and the JCP have been estranged since October 1983 after the latter blamed the former for the Rangoon bombing incident.

The United States. During 1984, the DPRK increased its hostility toward the United States. Pyongyang condemned the United States for supporting Chun Doo-Hwan's "fascist" regime in Seoul and repeatedly urged Washington to withdraw all U.S. troops and lethal weapons from South Korea. It renewed its call for direct talks with the United States to replace the 31-year-old Korean armistice with a peace agreement.

On 10 January the Pyongyang regime put forward a proposal of three-way talks among Washington, Seoul, and Pyongyang. It said that the agenda for the talks should first include a peace agreement between the United States and North Korea to prepare for a pullout of U.S. forces and that the question of concluding a nonaggression accord between South and North Korea would come next.

In an exclusive interview with Tokyo NHK Television Network on 1 April, DPRK deputy premier and foreign affairs minister Kim Yong-nam disclosed for the first time that since September 1983 the United States and North Korea had been secretly sounding out each other through China on the issue of holding a three-way dialogue.

The Reagan administration's position on the DPRK proposal has been that there should first be talks between the two Koreas. But it has also made clear that it would accept expanded discussions that include both the United States and China. (That is to say, the United States has backed the South Korean position on the North Korean idea of four-way talks.)

During a discussion with Chinese premier Zhao Ziyang on international issues during a visit to China in late April, U.S. president Reagan said that Washington supported direct talks between Pyongyang and Seoul to find a settlement and also proposed holding four-way discussions involving Washington and Beijing. Zhao restated support for North Korea's position on three-way talks.

Following its 10 January proposal for three-way talks, Pyongyang heightened its allegation that the Korean peninsula was on the brink of war due to the provocative schemes of the United States and South Korea. Radio Pyongyang (17 January) said, in a special commentary, that the United States had strengthened its offensive capability by deploying 1,000 nuclear weapons in South Korea.

On 28 February *Nodong Sinmun* attacked President Reagan for "attempting to liquidate all the anti-imperialist potentials" in Asia and called him a "warmonger." North Korea escalated its personal attacks on Mr. Reagan over his trip to China. *Nodong Sinmun* said, in a series of commentaries denouncing Reagan on 24–25 April (on the eve of his Beijing visit), "Reagan now poses as a peacemaker only to win in the coming U.S. presidential election."

North Korea's annual Month for Anti-U.S. Joint Struggle, which stretches from 25 June, the day when the Korean War broke out in 1950, to 27 July, when the Armistice Agreement was signed in 1953, was celebrated with mass rallies and demonstrations throughout the country.

The DPRK decided on 2 June to boycott the Los Angeles Olympics in accord with the Soviet Union's 8 May decision to boycott the games.

A Communist Party USA delegation arrived in Pyongyang on 31 August for a friendly visit.

United Nations. As in preceding years, the Korean question was absent from the agenda of the annual session of the U.N. General Assembly.

Diego Cordovez, U.N. undersecretary general for political affairs, flew to Pyongyang from Moscow on 16 July to probe ways for easing tension on the Korean peninsula. (Cordovez was the second high-ranking U.N. official to visit both Seoul and Pyongyang since 1979.) A diplomatic source speculated that Cordovez probably proposed a Seoul-

Pyongyang conference with U.N. mediation. But DPRK officials repeated their desire for three-way talks.

In a news conference on 17 September, U.N. Secretary General Javier Pérez de Cuellar said that he and the United Nations would continue an intermediary role in an attempt to ease tensions on the divided Korean peninsula.

In a report submitted to a committee of the United Nations General Assembly on 2 October, the Burmese government reconfirmed that the terrorist bombing attack in Rangoon in October 1983 was the work of three North Korean army officers acting on orders of Pyongyang. North Korea also submitted a report to the committee repeating its previous allegation that the incident was fabricated jointly by South Korea and Burma. More than twenty foreign delegates took the floor to denounce North Korea over the incident.

Tai Sung An
Washington College

Laos

Population. 3,732,000
Party. Lao People's Revolutionary Party (Phak Pasason Pativat Lao; LPRP)
Founded. 22 March 1955
Membership. 35,000 (estimated)
General Secretary. Kaysone Phomvihane (premier)
Politburo. 7 members: Kaysone Phomvihane, Nouhak Phoumsavan, Souphanouvong (president), Phoumi Vongvichit, Khamtai Siphandon, Phoun Sipaseut, Sisomphon Lovansai
Secretariat. 9 members: Kaysone Phomvihane, Nouhak Phoumsavan, Khamtai Siphandon, Phoun Sipaseut, Sisomphon Lovansai, Sali Vongkhamsao, Sisavat Keobounphan, Samon Vi-gnaket, Maichantan Sengmani
Central Committee. 47 full members, 6 alternate members (for names, see *FBIS*, 30 April 1982)
Status. Ruling and only legal party
Last Congress. Third, 27–30 April 1982, in Vientiane
Last Election. 1975, all 46 candidates LPRP approved
Auxiliary Organizations. Lao Front for National Construction (LFNC)
Publications. *Pasason* (The people), LPRP central organ, published in Vientiane (daily). The official news agency is Khaosan Pathet Lao (Pathet Lao News Agency; KPL), established 6 January 1967; the KPL is "a national-level organization which acts as the official voice of our party and state," with 12 branch offices located in 12 provinces, and publishing daily 355 copies of the KPL news bulletin in Lao, 682 copies of the KPL news bulletin in French, and 296 copies of analytical news items. (Radio Vientiane, 6 January; *FBIS*, 12 January.)

The year 1984 was marked in Laos by the continued primacy of the LPRP in all the decisionmaking processes of the Lao People's Democratic Republic (LPDR), continued tightening of the "special rela-tion" with Vietnam, and strict adherence to the Vietnamese line on all major foreign policy issues. The principal unforeseen event during the year was the eruption of a serious border dispute between the

LPDR and Thailand over three villages located near the border between Sayaboury and Uttaradit provinces of these two countries.

Leadership and Party Organization. The only change in the party's top leadership was the death of Central Committee member Sanan Sout-thichak (64) on 4 February in a Vientiane hospital. Death was attributed to cirrhosis of the liver. He was a member of the Propaganda Commission, one of five central commissions of the party, and played an active role during the party's seizure of power from within in 1975, especially in southern Laos.

Domestic Party Affairs. The LPRP held two plenums during 1984: the fifth plenum of the third session in early January and the sixth plenum of the third session from 10 to 27 August. Both were chaired by Kaysone.

The fifth plenum reviewed results achieved in 1983 and set goals for 1984, particularly insofar as "the two strategic tasks of defending the country and building socialism" were concerned (Radio Vientiane, 11 January; *FBIS*, 12 January). The plenum criticized production development for being slow, circulation and distribution work for encountering difficulties, and management work as still lacking firmness and organization. Generally speaking, the report on the plenum said, movements in numerous fields in many localities were not yet smooth.

As for goals for 1984, the fourth year of the First Five-year Plan, the plenum set a target of producing 1.4 million tons of foodstuffs (including 1.3 million tons of rice) and of increasing the number of cattle to 1.45 million head and of pigs to 1.3 million. Other goals were to mobilize and organize farmers to follow the path of collectivization; to restore and reorganize industrial and forestry production; to exploit farm and forest products for export; to control supplies, currency reserves, and imports and exports; and to use international aid effectively (Radio Vientiane, 19 January; *FBIS*, 19 January).

The sixth plenum devoted considerable attention to economic matters, as well as to possibly alarming developments on the international scene. "The plenum studied and tried to appreciate more profoundly the socialist revolutionary line, especially the economic line. At the same time, it also outlined a direction for transforming the economic management mechanism, stepping up the party leadership aimed at fulfilling the 1984 plan, and making preparations for the 1985 plan and for the second five-

year state plan from 1986–90." According to the plenum, "the party's economic line has not yet been implemented due to a lack of a complete set of management mechanisms and because the spirit of responsibility and a sense of vigilance toward organization, discipline, and socialist coordination and cooperation among the branches of work and among the various levels are not yet high, and because the level of organization, direction, and supervision as well as the capabilities of cadres are still limited." (Radio Vientiane, 28 August; *FBIS*, 29 August.)

An LPRP Central Committee Secretariat instruction dated 19 June and broadcast on 1 August detailed procedures for the first national population census, scheduled for 1–7 March 1985. The census was clearly needed, the instruction noted, "to establish a firm foundation for economic and social development plans, to reorganize and reclassify production forces of society, to reorganize the national defense forces and security forces, to organize educational, cultural, public health, and administrative work, to improve the material and spiritual life of the people, and to implement the policy of solidarity and equality among all ethnic tribes throughout the country" (Radio Vientiane, 1 August; *FBIS*, 3 August).

Auxiliary Organizations. The LFNC Central Committee held its annual enlarged session in Vientiane from 18 to 21 February under the chairmanship of President Souphanouvong. The session adopted a number of resolutions on domestic and foreign affairs (KPL, 22 February; *FBIS*, 23 February). The LFNC has been the principal mass-mobilization organ of the party since 1979, when it superseded the Lao Patriotic Front.

International Views, Positions, and Activities. A significant portion of the deliberations of both party plenums was taken up by matters connected with foreign relations. The border dispute with Thailand, in particular, became a focus of attention at the August plenum. By that time, the conflict had escalated to gunfire exchanges across the border lines claimed by each side, and two rounds of attempted negotiations (21–23 July and 6–15 August) had failed to resolve the issue. Prior to the outbreak of the armed conflict in the contested area in early June, the LPDR had been attempting to steer a course of improving relations with Thailand, with which it shares a 1,090-mile border. At the same time, Vietnam, by virtue of its special relationship with the LPDR, was an interested party to the conflict. Vietnamese positions on the Kampuchea issue needed to be taken into account in any moves initiated by the LPDR towards Bangkok.

Accordingly, the plenum adopted relatively strong language in its August communiqué, speaking of "an open and arrogant act" on the part of the "ultrarightist reactionaries in the Thai ruling circles, supported and assisted by the Beijing reactionaries." The communiqué said further that the action "runs counter to the just aspirations of the Thai people, who want to live in peace and friendship with the Lao people." It said that "our entire party, masses, and army" must clearly see the nature of the "struggle between our side and the enemies" and the need it imposed of consolidating further the "special solidarity, militant alliance, and all-round cooperation" with Vietnam. (Radio Vientiane, 28 August; *FBIS*, 29 August.)

The eighth regular conference of foreign ministers of the three Indochina countries was held in Vientiane on 28–29 January and the ninth, also in Vientiane, on 2 July. The communiqués adopted at these meetings reflected Hanoi's view of the world situation (Radio Vientiane, 29 January; Radio Hanoi, 3 July; *FBIS*, 30 January, 6 July).

Souphanouvong attended the funeral of Yuri Andropov in Moscow in February (Radio Vientiane, 11 and 14–17 February; *FBIS*, 13, 15, and 17 February). Kaysone, in Moscow for the June summit of the Council for Mutual Economic Assistance, met with Konstantin Chernenko on 26 June (Radio Vientiane, 27 June; Radio Hanoi, 27 June; *FBIS*, 28 June). Souphanouvong attended the funeral of Indira Gandhi in New Delhi in November.

On several occasions LPRP statements mentioned the strengthening of the special relationship with Vietnam and with the Vietnamese Communist Party (VCP). In what may have been a move in this connection, a VCP delegation headed by Politburo member Nguyen Duc Tam paid an eight-day visit to Vientiane in April (KPL, 11 and 13 April; *FBIS*, 17 April). On 18 July the seventh anniversary of the Treaty of Friendship and Cooperation between the LPDR and Vietnam was commemorated, with a listing of results achieved in state-state relations (Radio Vientiane, 18 July; *FBIS*, 19 July).

The LPRP and VCP appear to be cooperating closely in aiding the establishment and development of the Pak Mai, a party formed in 1978 and centered in the northeastern region of Thailand, which has ethnic and historical ties to Indochina. The Pak Mai is reported to have more than 1,100 members and armed supporters and to use 25 bases and fifteen training centers in Laos (*Nation Review*, Bangkok, 5 September; *FBIS*, 6 September). The Pak Mai is reported to be headquartered at Paksane on the Mekong. (See profile on Thailand for further details.)

Biographies. *Prince Souvanna Phouma.* Although not a member of the LPRP, Prince Souvanna Phouma assumed the title of adviser to the government on the establishment of the LPDR in December 1975. Therefore, his death in Vientiane at the age of 82 on 10 January and his funeral were prominently reported in LPRP organs. The obituary in *Pasason* called him "a great patriot, a senior politician, an experienced technician and a beloved son of the nation, the party" (KPL, 12 January; *FBIS*, 13 January). Souvanna Phouma became prime minister for the first time in 1951 when Laos was still under French rule and was prime minister in the three coalition governments between 1956 and 1975.

Kaysone Phomvihane. The general secretary of the LPRP since its formation, Kaysone Phomvihane was born in Savannakhet on 13 December 1920. His father was a Tonkinese member of the Indochinese civil service, and his mother was a Lao. His original name appears to have been Nguyen Tri Muu. Nevertheless, Phomvihane is an invented name, like Ho Chi Minh; it is the Lao transliteration of the Pali *Brahma-vihara*, meaning the four sublime states of mind to be achieved by the Buddhist monk (loving kindness, compassion, sympathetic joy, and equanimity). He was known by the party rank and file as Comrade Kaysone.

Kaysone was educated in Hanoi, where he attended *lycée* and then the law faculty at the University of Hanoi. He took part in nationalist activities of the students' union. According to his official biography, Kaysone joined the Indochinese Communist Party in 1949, but it seems at least possible that he was already a member by 1945, when he was entrusted with a special mission in his homeland by Ho Chi Minh. He returned to Savannakhet to monitor and possibly infiltrate the guerrillas of the noncommunist Free Lao, who had seized control in the wake of the Japanese surrender, taking advantage of the continuing imprisonment of all French administrators. He crossed paths at this time with Souphanouvong, who also returned to Laos from Vietnam, but assumed no role in the Lao

Issara government formed in Vientiane, of which Souphanouvong was a member. There is no record of his having participated directly in the Lao Issara resistance to the French forces that reoccupied Laos in 1946.

Kaysone reappeared in 1949 in the strategic border area of Laos adjoining northern Vietnam, which was Ho's base area. He is credited with having set up the first unit, called the Latsavong unit, on 20 January of that year, of what was to become the People's Liberation Army of Laos. This was at a time when Souphanouvong was organizing anti-French guerrilla raids across the Mekong from the Lao Issara base in Thailand.

At the Vietnamese-sponsored First Congress of People's Representatives of Laos (13–15 August 1950), Kaysone was elected to the Central Committee of the Lao Liberation Front and became minister of defense in the government of national resistance, a position he held until this government was dissolved in November 1957 by the terms of the Vientiane agreements with the royal government. In the supplementary elections of May 1958, Kaysone was an unsuccessful candidate for the National Assembly from Attopeu province. Since he was not a deputy, he escaped being arrested in 1959 with

Souphanouvong and a number of other LPRP Politburo members living in Vientiane. His ascendancy to the top position in the LPRP was apparently consolidated during this period.

During the years of heaviest fighting between the U.S.-supported royalist forces and the Vietnamese-supported Pathet Lao forces of the LPRP (1961–1975), Kaysone remained in the secure Pathet Lao base area of Sam Neua province, within easy traveling distance of the Pathet Lao's mentors in Hanoi. He did not re-emerge in public, so far as the non-communist population of Laos was concerned, until the LPRP completed its seizure of power in December 1975 with the proclamation of the LPDR, of which he became premier.

Kaysone's travels abroad have included attendance at the 1955 World Peace Congress in Helsinki and visits to Moscow at the head of LPRP delegations to the twenty-second through twenty-sixth congresses of the Soviet party and the fiftieth and sixtieth anniversary celebrations of the Great October Socialist Revolution.

Arthur J. Dommen
Bethesda, Maryland

Malaysia and Singapore

Population. Malaysia: 15,330,000; Singapore: 2,531,000
Party. Communist Party of Malaya (CPM); Communist Party of Malaysia (MCP)
Founded. CPM: 1930; MCP: 1983
Membership. CPM: estimated 3,000 insurgents on Thai side of border, estimated 350 fulltime in Peninsular Malaysia, 125 in Sarawak, 200–500 in Singapore; MCP: estimated 800 insurgents
Secretary General. CPM: Chin Peng; MCP: Ah Leng
Politburo. No data
Central Committee. CPM: no data; MCP: Chang Chun (chairman), San Cheng Ming, San Sen, rest unknown
Status. Illegal
Last Congress. CPM: 1965 (last known)

Last Election. N/a

Auxiliary Organizations. CPM: Malayan People's Army (MPA), Malay Nationalist Revolutionary Party of Malaya (MNRPM), Islamic Brotherhood Party (Paperi), Malayan People's Liberation Front (MPLF), Barisan Sosialis, People's Liberation Organization (the last two based in Singapore); MCP: Malaysian People's Liberation League (MPLL)

Publications. No regular periodicals known; CPM: Voice of Malayan Democracy (VOMD), clandestine radio station broadcasting from southern China; MCP: Voice of the People of Malaysia (VOPM), clandestine radio station, location unknown

The Communist Party of Malaya (CPM), its guerrilla bases along the Thai border increasingly under attack by combined Thai-Malaysian government forces in 1984, was further challenged when two of its breakaway factions combined in December 1983 to form a rival Communist Party of Malaysia (MCP).

Leadership and Party Organization. There was no visible change in CPM leadership or organization in 1984. (For background, see *YICA*, 1984, pp. 251–52.) Chin Peng, secretary general of the party since 1947, is still referred to in that capacity. The likelihood that he is still in command of the CPM is underscored by his being the principal target of spokesmen of the rival MCP. The CPM, while seeking to broaden its appeal to all segments of the Malaysian population, is still essentially composed of ethnic Chinese, and its orientation in the communist world remains unabashedly pro-Beijing. The one apparent change in recent months has been the degree to which the CPM has intensified its efforts to identify itself with Moslem interests and specifically the fundamentalist Moslem groups currently at odds with the principal Malay party in the country's governing coalition, the United Malays National Organization (UMNO).

The new party, the MCP, dates its founding from 5 December 1983, the occasion of the first session of the party's Central Committee, which adopted a general program and constitution. The MCP is a merger of two factional offshoots of the CPM, the Communist Party of Malaya–Marxist-Leninist (CPM/M-L) and the Communist Party of Malaya–Revolutionary Faction (CPM/RF). (For background on both factions, see ibid., p. 252.) From its first communiqué, the MCP made clear its intention to seek more than ethnic Chinese support, stating that the party "represents the interests of people of various nationalities in Malaysia." The party's use of *Malaysia* in its name is clearly intended to distinguish it from the CPM, which retains the word *Malaya* because of its refusal to accept the existence of Malaysia and Singapore as two separate entities.

Not so the MCP, which referred in its initial statement to the merger of Peninsular Malaysia and North Kalimantan into one country, with a common foe, the Kuala Lumpur regime, and sharing the common aim of liberating the people of both regions. Singapore, on the other hand, is described as having been made into "a new country with unique social conditions . . . the Singapore people must combine the general truth of Marxism-Leninism with the concrete conditions of the Singapore revolution to promote revolutionary struggle in Singapore," a struggle to which the MCP "will pay great attention and extend strong support," a pledge reiterated as the last item in the party's ten-point program (VOPM, 31 December 1983; *FBIS*, 9 January). The MCP clearly intends to avoid the mistakes of the CPM, which, insisting upon a classic Maoist peasant-based party, has failed to attract broad support from the largely Moslem Malay peasantry and has also been unable to attract significant Chinese support in urban communities of Malaysia or in economically booming Singapore. Malaysia, the MCP communiqué pointed out, "is a multinational country, but there has been serious alienation among the people of various nationalities due to the divide-and-conquer policy" of the imperialists and the reactionaries. "Under no circumstances, should the struggle rely upon a single nationality." (Ibid.)

In a communiqué issued in Chinese shortly after its founding, the MCP announced that it was fighting under the leadership of 60-year-old Ah Leng, head of the CPM/M-L, with Huang Chen, leader of the CPM/RF, as his deputy (*Bangkok Post*, 3 January; *FBIS*, 5 January). Other leaders of the MCP are Chang Chun, identified as chairman of the Central Committee, San Cheng Ming, and San Sen, in whose names the party issued its New Year's greetings (VOPM, 1 January, 6 December; *FBIS*, 4 January, 14 December).

On the first anniversary of its founding, the MCP still referred to the masses in the CPM/M-L and the CPM/RF revolutionary bases, leaving the impression that despite the year-old merger, the rank and file and possibly the leaders of the new party still saw themselves as members of the two factions in a coalition, not a unified party (VOPM, 4 December; *FBIS*, 14 December).

The rival communist parties engaged in bitter exchanges, each professing to be the true standard bearer of Marxism-Leninism–Mao Zedong thought and accusing the other of being unwilling to negotiate to resolve their differences. The MCP attacked Chin Peng and his henchmen for having pursued both leftist and rightist opportunistic policies at various periods of history and for being unwilling to accept responsibility for the schism in the party and its army (VOPM, 31 December 1983; *FBIS*, 9 January). They appealed to "those deceived and influenced by Chin Peng and his ilk" to join the new party (VOPM, 1 January; *FBIS*, 4 January).

Initially, the CPM only obliquely acknowledged the existence of the new party, stepping up the pace of its appeals to "brothers and sisters of all nationalities" (VOMD, 2 January; *FBIS*, 10 January). The party soon became more explicit in its attacks on the MCP, charging that the "Kuala Lumpur ruling clique" was behind its establishment, using it to consolidate its power in Malaysia because Brunei's independence was intensifying the trend toward separating Sabah and Sarawak from Malaysia. The CPM fearing that the MCP would concentrate most of its efforts on destroying the old party's influence, recalled in detail a series of earlier betrayals allegedly carried out by government agents with the connivance of the two breakaway factions. In a plaintive account of more recent misdeeds, the party statement said, "We always maintain our own bases and never cross over their areas. However, the Marxist-Leninist faction has repeatedly sent its soldiers to invade our bases, blatantly conduct armed provocations, threaten the public, forcefully collect taxes, disseminate poisonous brochures, hold ill-intentioned rallies, and deliberately destroy our bases and public life. Not surprisingly, armed clashes have broken out." (VOMD, 7 May; *FBIS*, 10 May.)

Recounting the history of the CPM, the party stressed its positive contributions to the international communist movement, noting that "the party receives valuable support from fellow Marxist-Leninist parties and the people of various countries." In its turn, the CPM called upon "all cadres and members who are willing to carry out the revolution but who are still deceived and trapped in the antiparty cliques" to free themselves "from the grip of the enemy's agents, courageously choose their

own correct path and return to the revolutionary fold." (Ibid.)

Little is known about communist activities in Sarawak other than the fact of the continued existence of some hundred-odd guerrillas.

There is no visible communist activity in Singapore, although periodically the government warns against possible subversive elements. For Singaporeans, what either communist party has to offer is essentially irrelevant. For the Chinese, with Singapore's economic boom, communist attacks on capitalist compradors are meaningless. For the Malays, even though they are a minority and at the bottom of the economic ladder, their situation is improving. In any case they are aware that they are in far better shape than their fellow Moslems in Malaysia. The left-of-center Workers' Party, which in 1981 won a seat in the legislature, breaking the fifteen-year monopoly of the People's Action Party, is careful to avoid any statements that could be construed as Marxist. (*FEER*, 28 June, 18 October. For background on the CPM and Singapore, see *YICA*, 1980, p. 295, 1984, pp. 251–52.)

Domestic Party Activities. Evidence of actual communist activity in the domestic political arena is necessarily drawn by inference, largely from government statements. The overall level of communist terrorism reportedly continued to decline in 1984. As of late November, only 52 people had been detained in the previous twelve months under the Internal Security Act aimed at subversive and communist militant elements (Kuala Lumpur domestic service, 23 November; *FBIS*, 27 November).

Where the Communists may have had greater success was in exploiting the opportunities provided by the increasing internal dissension within and between Malaysia's legal political parties. The level of debate between UMNO and the fundamentalist Moslem opposition Parti Islam (PAS) mounted sharply, with PAS charging repeatedly that UMNO leaders were infidels. On 9 November, the government published a White Paper, *The Threat to Muslim Unity and National Security*, which named more than a dozen members of PAS as members of extremist groups and charged that the CPM was exploiting rifts in the Moslem community (*FEER*, 22 November). The White Paper said that "directly or indirectly, [PAS] activities have helped the CPM gain support from among the Malay/Muslim community, which it has been unable to do for a long time" and that several of the Islamic organizations named as disruptive influences were in fact nothing more than communist puppet organizations (*CSM*, 26 November; *Asia Research Bulletin*, 30 November, p. 1128).

There were increasing official reports of CPM efforts to influence religious extremists through programs aimed at attracting the interest and sympathy of the Islamic community. Among communist activities cited were the circulation of religious brochures and the broadcasting of religious programs on the Voice of Malayan Democracy, the clandestine radio station of the CPM. (Kuala Lumpur domestic service, 9 November; *FBIS*, 16 November, 11 December.) An interesting sidelight on the role of modern technology was the report that the CPM was exploiting religious confusion by issuing videotapes and other propaganda portraying its members as true Moslems. The tapes are said to show party members at prayer and celebrating the Ramadan fast. Military intelligence sources believe that members of the CPM's 10th Regiment, based along the Malaysian-Thai border, are responsible for producing the cassettes. (Kuala Lumpur domestic service, 10 November; *FEER*, 6 December.)

The CPM marked its fifty-fourth anniversary with the adoption of a new ten-point rural policy calling for the free distribution of land to landless peasants. The program called for resisting government violation of traditional Malay land, respecting the power of the sultans over the management of state land, and protecting the land belonging to landlords supportive of or neutral to the establishment of a democratic coalition government. Estates, mines, industrial complexes, and commerce belonging to medium and small national capitalists were also to be protected. Reacting to government charges that the CPM is an enemy of religion and opposes the sultans and aristocrats, the party cited its rural program as proof of the CPM's concern for religious, cultural, and welfare organizations and for the sultans and aristocrats. (VOMD, 14 June; *FBIS*, 19 June.)

Auxiliary and Front Organizations. For each communist party, the principal auxiliary is its military arm. The CPM's Malayan People's Army (MPA), with most of its bases reportedly on the Thai side of the Malaysian-Thai border, apparently continued to function at a relatively low level of activity, although there were reports that they were extorting as much as 10 million baht annually in protection money from Thai rubber planters (Bang-

kok domestic service, 3 August; *FBIS*, 6 August). On the thirty-fifth anniversary of its establishment, the MPA took special pains to cite its role as "a revolutionary armed force which genuinely wages war for the interests of the people of all Malaysian nationalities" (VOMD, 31 January; *FBIS*, 7 February).

At the time of its founding, the MCP announced the merging of the revolutionary armed forces of its two factions into a single Malaysian People's Liberation Army (MPLA), under a single leadership. It was then estimated that the breakaway factions making up the MCP had a combined armed force of about 800 and the CPM proper commanded some 1,000 insurgents in adjacent areas (*Bangkok Post*, 3 January; *FBIS*, 5 January).

At the beginning of the year, the Thai-Malaysian combined task force reported that its previous year's operations had disrupted the communist terrorists' logistics and that the whole of the previous year had been almost incursion free. The military chief of Sarawak said that only 96 communist terrorists remained active there. (AFP, 31 January; Kuala Lumpur domestic service, 28 February; *FBIS*, 2 and 29 February.) Nevertheless, there were continued reports of armed CPM attacks. In September the chief of the Malaysian Intelligence Staff estimated that there were still some 350 terrorists carrying on their armed struggle in the country, about 260 in Peninsular Malaysia, and another 90 in Sarawak (Kuala Lumpur domestic service, 8 September; *FBIS*, 11 September). In mid-December, it was estimated that a total of 2,180 communist terrorists were still operating actively along the Thai border, recruiting new members among both Thai and Malaysian citizens. Estimated communist strength in Sarawak remained at about 100. (Kuala Lumpur domestic service, 8 November, 19 December; *FBIS*, 21 December.)

Communist reports predictably painted a somewhat different picture of military activities during the year. Among the "glowing victories" cited by the MCP in commemorating the first anniversary of its founding, the MPLA claimed to have inflicted a hundred casualties on government troops while suffering not a single casualty itself, though several of its jungle bases were overrun and destroyed. Despite these "victories," listeners to this broadcast were exhorted to strengthen the base areas as well as to increase the unity between the MPLA and the people since "the regions will sooner or later fall to counterrevolutionary or other destructive forces if they are not occupied by the revolutionary forces."

(VOPM, 4 and 6 December; *FBIS*, 14 December.)

The Malay Nationalist Revolutionary Party of Malaya (MNRPM) remained the CPM's principal front organization, aimed at winning Moslem Malay adherents. During the debate over the government's proposed constitutional amendments designed to limit the powers of the king, the MNRPM vigorously supported the positions of the sultans and the opposition parties against UMNO, attempting to bring its arguments to UMNO members through a series of open letters while attacking the leaders of that party for slandering PAS and arresting three key PAS leaders. (VOMD, 2 January, 6 February; *FBIS*, 10 January, 9 and 10 February.)

In a speech on the occasion of the Moslem holiday, Id al-Adha, the chairman of the MNRPM Central Committee announced the official adoption of a constitution on 1 February, an action taken because "more and more patriotic people in our country have expressed the desire to join the MNRPM." He also announced a new manifesto issued in May spelling out a twelve-point program of struggle that included a rural program in line with the CPM's, aimed at eradicating the poverty of rural people in general and Moslems in particular. (VOMD, 5 September; *FBIS*, 13 September.)

The Central Committee of the CPM's other major front organization, the Islamic Brotherhood Party (Paperi), in its Id al-Adha greetings, reaffirmed its adherence to the principle of a broadly based united front and its willingness to work shoulder to shoulder with any democratic and patriotic party regardless of nationality or religion. Paperi, aiming to establish a democratic coalition government under the system of constitutional monarchy, expressed dismay at widespread instances of behavior incompatible with Islam and asked why, with Islam the official religion, crimes rare during the colonial era were rampant after many years of independence. The Central Committee took government leaders to task, quoting passages from the Koran about those who use religion for self-esteem and for their own benefit.

An earlier CPM front organization, the Malayan National Liberation Front (MNLF), founded in 1968 under the auspices of the CPM, enjoyed a curious resurrection in midyear. In a 1 July statement, the MNLF described itself as a revolutionary mass underground group armed with Marxism-Leninism and Mao Zedong thought and led by the CPM. The organization reviewed its years of contribution to the revolution, including its strong support for the MPA, to which it had sent some of its best youths; its armed action in the towns; its publications and circulars; and such activities as planting red flags. However, the statement then turned to self-criticism, saying that the MNLF suffers from overemphasis in its struggle on the aspect of fighting valiantly per se without regard for how to fight competently. The organization lacked fighting experience, the statement continued, had not mastered the rules of underground struggle, and had made several mistakes in strategy and operations, especially due to impatience and extremism. Thus, the MNLF had been subjected to sabotage and suffered losses, not only as a result of various counterrevolutionary plots but because of the subjective weakness of the organization itself. The statement's salutes to fallen and imprisoned comrades reinforced the impression of major defeats. The statement included vigorous attacks on the MCP and that party's front organization, which the MNLF claimed had to be a creature of the enemy since it had never been sabotaged, while those who sought to leave it were immediately arrested. The MNLF declared its commitment to a two-pronged effort, armed struggle and underground activities, appealing to the masses of all nationalities in the country, especially the Malay, Chinese, and Indian nationalities since "under no circumstances can they afford to depend on the forces of any one of the nationalities only." The emphasis of mass movement and united front tactics was now to be on the urban areas, the factories, and the mines. Finally, the Central Committee of the MNLF announced that in response to the changing situation in the country, it had decided to change the organization's name to Malayan People's Liberation Front (MPLF). (VOMD, 30 July; *FBIS*, 3 August.)

The MPLF announced its change of name as effective from the date of its statement in July. The MCP's principal front organization had been rechristened more than six months earlier. In a statement of 15 December 1983, the Central Committee of the Malayan People's Liberation Union announced that, in order to adjust to the development of history, the Malayan People's Liberation Union was changing its name to Malayan People's Liberation League (MPLL). Like the CPM front organization, the MPLL endorsed a united front directed at the establishment of a democratic and free society. However, the MPLL laid particular stress on its independent view in following both domestic and international problems. (VOPM, 7 January; BBC, *Summary of World Broadcasts*, 14 January; *FBIS*, 18 January.)

International Views, Relations, and Activities. Both the CPM and the MCP are pro-Beijing parties, albeit to different degrees, and both are vigorous critics of Soviet and Vietnamese hegemonism. This was a difficult year for pro-Chinese communist parties in Southeast Asia, given the PRC's increasing ties to the governments of the Association of Southeast Asian Nations (ASEAN). During a visit to Malaysia in February, marking ten years of official diplomatic relations between the two countries, Chinese foreign minister Wu Xueqian said the question of China's relations with the communist parties of Southeast Asian nations had basically been solved through consultations with the governments of the countries concerned. The activities of communist guerrilla movements in those countries are the business of those governments. "It is an internal matter in which China will not interfere." The Chinese Communist Party (CPC), Wu said, "maintains only a moral relationship with the Malaysian [sic] Communist Party." (*Financial Times*, London, 2 March; *Beijing Review*, 12 March.)

Although to some observers, the CPC's influence over nonruling foreign communist parties had reached a low point because of China's pursuit of official economic relationships, the government of Malaysia still had its misgivings. Citing foreign aid to political parties in Malaysia and continued underground communist activities, Kuala Lumpur refused to permit people-to-people relations with the PRC, allowing only government-to-government relations. It also raised the question of the PRC's allegedly issuing special overseas Chinese entry permits to Malaysians of Chinese origin. (*Sekai Nippo*, Tokyo, 20 November; Central News Agency, 20 November; Kuala Lumpur home service, 9 July; BBC, 12 July; Kuala Lumpur international service, 27 February; *FBIS*, 27 February.)

The CPM continued to reaffirm its ties to Beijing, citing the PRC as the main pillar of world peace and progress for mankind in its message to the CPC Central Committee on the thirty-fifth anniversary of the founding of the People's Republic of China (VOMD, 1 October; *FBIS*, 3 October; Xinhua, 30 September; BBC, *Summary of World Broadcasts*, 2 October.) (References to the "Communist Party of Malaysia" in reports emanating from Beijing probably do not indicate an intentional reference to the MCP rather than the CPM. In the case of the anniversary greetings to the CPC, for example, the evidence is that this was from the CPM and not the MCP.)

Initially the MCP did not appear to be markedly pro-Beijing, though it never failed to mention the correctness of Mao Zedong thought along with Marxist-Leninist teachings. It was believed that the new party might be more Maoist but less pro-PRC than its rival, but in time it came to sound more like the CPM in this regard. The MCP's constitution had stressed the party's opposition to external interference and advocated internationalist assistance that is cordial and unselfish. However, as the government's refusal to permit more direct ties between the people of Malaysia and the PRC became clearer, the MCP took up the argument on behalf of the PRC. Reviewing PRC ties to local communist parties, the MCP said that PRC leaders had repeatedly stressed that the social system of a country can be chosen only by the people of that country. Thus the PRC had established friendly relations with numerous countries that have different social systems, while never interfering in the internal affairs of those countries, thereby winning the friendship of many Third World countries. (VOPM, 31 January; *FBIS*, 9 January; Michael Williams, "A New Communist Party in Malaysia," *Communist Affairs*, 1984, p. 281; VOPM, 22 August; BBC, *Summary of World News*, 28 August.)

The MCP referred frequently to the importance of revolutionary principles and guidelines being determined independently and freely by the Marxist-Leninist party of a given country, based on the concrete conditions of the country itself. The objective of friendly relations with fraternal parties in other countries, the MCP said, is to support each other and advance revolutions in the respective countries, but isolation from the revolution in one's own country for a long period of time "is not a healthy symptom" (VOPM, 22 August; BBC, *Summary of World News*, 28 August). The MCP extended cordial greetings to the Communist Party of the Philippines on the anniversary of its founding (*FBIS*, 16 March). On the first anniversary of its own establishment, the MCP noted the congratulatory letters its Central Committee had received from "revolutionary comrades and patriotic brothers abroad" (VOPM, 4 December; *FBIS*, 14 December).

Jeanne S. Mintz
Washington, D.C.

Mongolia

Population. 1,860,000
Party. Mongolian People's Revolutionary Party (MPRP)
Founded. 1921
Membership. 76,240 (claimed)
Secretary General. Jambyn Batmonh
Politburo. 8 members: Jambyn Batmonh (chairman, Presidium of People's Great Hural), Bat-Ochirym Altangerel (chairman, People's Great Hural), Dumaagiyn Sodnom (premier), Tumenbayaryn Ragchaa (first deputy premier), Damdiny Gombojab, Demchigiyn Molomjamts, Bujyn Dejid, Tserendashiyn Namsray; 2 candidate members: Nyamin Jagbaral, Sonomyn Lubsangombo
Secretariat. 7 members: Jambyn Batmonh, Damdiny Gombojab, Demchigiyn Molomjamts, Tserendashiyn Namsray, Paavangiyn Damdin, M. Dash, Tserenpilyn Balhaajab
Central Committee. 91 full and 71 candidate members
Status. Ruling party
Last Congress. Eighteenth, 26–31 May 1981, in Ulan Bator
Last Election. 1981, 99 percent, all 370 seats in MPRP approved
Auxiliary Organizations. Mongolian Revolutionary Youth League (over 200,000 members), T. Narangerel, first secretary; Central Council of Mongolian Trade Unions (400,000 members), B. Lubsantseren, chairman; Committee of Mongolian Women, L. Pagmadula, chairwoman
Publications. *Unen* (Truth), MPRP daily organ, published Tuesday–Sunday. Montsame is the official news agency.

Leadership and Organization. In 1984 a major power transfer took place in Mongolia's foremost position of leadership. Yumjaagiyn Tsedenbal was removed as MPRP general secretary and chairman of the Presidium of the Great People's Hural, "with regard for the state of his health and with his consent," as reported by Montsame. It was suggested, however, that this was a reflection of his increasingly authoritarian style (*FEER*, 6 September). Nevertheless, his departure was marked by eulogies focusing on his 40-odd years of service to the party and to the state. Tsedenbal was replaced by Jambyn Batmonh, heir apparent and prime minister, who was unanimously elected at a special plenary meeting of the Central Committee. In an address to the plenum, Batmonh stressed continued dedication to the general party line and to the implementation of policies developed by the Eighteenth MPRP Congress, which emphasized the need to

utilize established economic potential (Montsame, 23 August; *FBIS*, 24 August).

Other significant changes in MPRP leadership include the election of Dumaagiyn Sodnom and Tserendashiyn Namsray to the Politburo and Tserenpilyn Balhaajab to the Secretariat. Damdinjabyn Maydar and Gelegiyn Adiyaa were relieved of their duties as Central Committee Politburo member and secretary, respectively. Namsray's election is especially noteworthy in that he skipped the traditional candidate membership (*FEER*, 6 September). A. Jamsjanjab was appointed minister of public safety, replacing S. Lubsangombo, who became deputy chairman of the Council of Ministers and chairman of the State Committee for Construction, Architecture, and Technical Control, after the removal of C. Suren from that position. T. Gurbadam was named ambassador to the Soviet Union, replacing D. Gotob, and P. Jasray was designated chairman of the State Planning Commission.

Domestic Affairs. Nineteen eighty-four was a year of special anniversaries and celebrations for Mongolia. A ceremonial meeting of Mongolian and Soviet officials on 20 August honored the forty-fifth anniversary of their countries' united victory over Japanese aggression. The Soviets were hailed for their valiant assistance. Party officials also lauded the socialist community for its persistent efforts to preserve peace over the past four decades.

Three noteworthy gala meetings were held in November: the sixty-seventh anniversary of the Great October Socialist Revolution on 6 November, the sixtieth anniversary of the naming of Ulan Bator as Mongolia's capital on 10 November, and on 26 November the sixtieth anniversary of both the Third MPRP Congress, which specified the party's general line of developing the country along a socialist path, and the proclamation of Mongolia's first constitution, which transferred political power to the people. On this festive occasion, speeches were given by Batmonh, and Viktor Grishin, Soviet Politburo member and leader of the Soviet delegation. The "fraternal and indestructible friendship" between Lenin and D. Suhe-Baatar, the founder of the MPRP, was reaffirmed. Each leader discussed the importance of further broadening Soviet-Mongolian ties.

During this visit an assistance agreement was signed by the Intergovernmental Commissions for Economic, Scientific, and Technical Cooperation, providing for construction of three school and three hospital complexes, 50,000 square meters of housing, including all cultural and consumer amenities, and hundreds of radio relay lines to be built in Mongolia with Soviet aid (*Izvestiia*, 28 November; *FBIS*, 29 November).

Currently, the USSR accounts for about 80 percent of Mongolian trade, with the remainder generated mainly through the Council for Mutual Economic Assistance (CMEA). Mongolia participated in a number of CMEA conferences in 1984, including the economic summit held in Moscow on 14 June, the regular session of the Executive Committee in Moscow on 23 September, and the session held in Havana on 29 October. On 7 June Ulan Bator hosted a session of the CMEA Standing Commission on Cooperation in the food industry. The discussion covered food supply and transportation (Montsame, 8 June; *FBIS*, 11 June). Mongolia benefits immensely from CMEA membership because

of the economic, scientific, and technical cooperation it facilities. For example, the Havana meeting approved long-term measures on cooperation in the spheres of energy, fuel, and raw materials, for the period through 1990 (Montsame, 7 November; *FBIS*, 8 November). During the past five years, 9,600 thoroughbred cattle, 3,500 sheep, and nearly 400 goats have been brought to Mongolia from the USSR in order to improve livestock. Hot houses built with Bulgarian aid in Ulan Bator now provide vegetables year around. Assistance from East Germany increased potato, vegetable, milk, and fodder production at the Bornuur State Farm in northern Mongolia, and Poland supplied up-to-date equipment for diagnostic and laboratory work. (Montsame, 13 April; *FBIS*, 24 April.)

At the close of the year, the Ninth Plenum of the MPRP Central Committee adopted a resolution approving the drafts of the 1985 state plan and budget, accepted the report of Batmonh on mobilizing workers and developing their political and labor activity in order to fulfill plan tasks, and expressed confidence in the ability of the people to meet the 1985 goals and thus the targets of the Seventh Five-Year Plan (Montsame, 11 December; *FBIS*, 12 December).

Auxiliary Organizations. The Third Plenum of the Mongolian Revolutionary Youth League elected T. Narangerel first secretary and bureau member, replacing L. Tudeb, who was relieved of his duties for other work (Montsame, 23 October; *FBIS*, 2 November). In December Narangerel made two important speeches. At a meeting of the international preparatory committee for the Twelfth World Festival of Youth and Students, he called for strengthening solidarity among progressive youths of the world in an anti-imperialistic struggle for peace (Montsame, 6 December; *FBIS*, 11 December). At the Fourth Plenum of the Mongolian Revolutionary Youth Union, he praised the members for carrying out planned tasks through active organizational and ideological work (Montsame, 17 December; *FBIS*, 19 December).

A plenary meeting of the Central Council of the Mongolian Trade Union was held on 17 December. Chairman B. Lubsantseren discussed the need for economizing on work time and resources. Politburo member and secretary of the MPRP Central Committee T. Namsray directed attention to the important role of the trade unions in achieving planned targets. (Montsame, 18 December; *FBIS*, 20 December.)

The Committee of Mongolian Women, chaired by L. Pagmadula, received Nguyen Thi Dinh, chairwoman of the Union of Vietnamese Women and a member of a Vietnamese delegation to Mongolia on 17 July. The women exchanged information regarding the activities of their respective organizations (Montsame, 18 July; *FBIS*, 20 July).

International Affairs. In August Batmonh succinctly described Mongolia's approach to international affairs: "The cornerstone of our party's foreign policy is an all-round strengthening of friendship and cooperation with the Soviet Union and other Socialist community countries and development of fraternal ties with Communist and workers' parties. Our Communists view the further strengthening of the unity and cohesion of the Socialist community as their primary internationalist task." (Montsame, 27 August; *FBIS*, 28 August.) In light of this, it is evident that the USSR's oldest ally does not deviate from the Soviet path in foreign affairs. It, in fact, reiterates most of the accepted views of the Soviet Union in its assessments of international events.

The United States is blamed for imperialistic aggression worldwide and is accused of escalating construction of armaments, thereby threatening global security. The Washington-Tokyo-Seoul political-military axis is observed with trepidation. The peaceloving initiatives of Vietnam, Kampuchea, and Laos directed at transforming Southeast Asia into a zone of stability are encouraged. The people and government of Afghanistan are supported in their constructive revolutionary accomplishments. North Korea has Mongolian approval for its plans to reunify the Korean peninsula in the absence of American troops. Israel is condemned for its hostile behavior in the Middle East. Opposition to the United States' overt and covert activities in Latin America is strongly voiced. China is urged to engage in meaningful dialogue with the Soviets and to abandon its demand for the removal of Soviet troops in Mongolia (Montsame, 17 June; *FBIS*, 21 June). Chinese-American intentions to expand military and technological trade are viewed with disfavor. Nevertheless, Mongolia wishes to continue good relations with China, as was evidenced by the signing of the border demarcation agreement in July.

The death of Andropov and subsequent rise of Chernenko seems to have had little effect on Mongolian-Soviet relations. Mongolia stood firmly in the Soviet camp on the issue of boycotting the Olympic Games in Los Angeles. In October, Batmonh went to Moscow for a working visit, at the invitation of the Soviet Central Committee. Discussions were structured to entail the continued development of political, economic, and cultural cooperation. At this time, Batmonh bestowed the Mongolian government's highest awards for outstanding service in the struggle for peace, democracy, and social progress on Konstantin Chernenko, Viktor Grishin, and Andrei Gromyko (Montsame, 26 October; *FBIS*, 29 October).

Throughout 1984 Mongolia pursued an active policy of promoting international peace. Addressing the Geneva Conference on Disarmament in July, a Mongolian representative expressed the view of CMEA members that the preservation of peace was the most important task of the international community. The prevention of the militarization of space is, he said, becoming ever more important. (Montsame, 18 July; *FBIS*, 20 July.) On 12 November the U.N. General Assembly adopted a Mongolian proposal on "the right of peoples to peace." The declaration confirmed the universal, sacred right to peace, the safeguarding of which is considered to be one of the principal obligations of each state (Montsame, 17 July; *FBIS*, 18 July). This pacific orientation was further propounded by leaders in speeches given throughout the year. Specific mention was made of a Mongolian proposal for a convention on mutual nonaggression and nonuse of force in Asia and the Pacific.

Numerous cultural pacts were signed during the year, with an eye to sustaining propitious foreign relations beyond the CMEA, in the areas of science and education. Such agreements were concluded with Finland, France, India, Ethiopia, and Yemen. Two prominent treaties were counted among 1984's diplomatic achievements. The first was a new treaty of friendship with Hungary, heralding a consolidation of mutual interests. The second was a treaty of friendship and cooperation with Cuba. Batmonh and Fidel Castro planned the establishment of an intergovernmental commission on economic, scientific, and technical integration in order to implement the treaty.

Biography. *Jambyn Batmonh.* Batmonh was born into a herdsman's family in Hyargas Somon, Uvs Symag, on 10 March 1926. He graduated from the Mongolian State University and the Soviet Central Committee's Academy of Social Sciences. In 1948 he became an MPRP member, in 1971 a Central Committee candidate member, and in 1974 a Central Committee member and MPRP Central Committee Politburo member. During 1951–1973, he taught at and was prorector of the MPRP Central Committee Higher Party School and rector of the Mongolian State University. In 1973, he was promoted to work in the MPRP Central Committee apparatus, where he headed the science and education departments. In May 1974 he became deputy chairman and in June 1974 chairman of the Mongolian Council of Ministers. He was elected general secretary of the MPRP Central Committee by the Eighth Plenum of the MPRP Central Committee on 23 August 1984, replacing Y. Tsedenbal.

On 12 December 1984 he was elected chairman of the Presidium of the Great People's Hural. Batmonh has been praised as an eminent party figure who has shown great organizational abilities, distinguished high party principles, and loyalty to Marxism-Leninism and proletarian internationalism. He has contributed to enhancing of Mongolian-Soviet friendship and Mongolia's other fraternal socialist friendships, while strengthening the cause of peace and security. Batmonh's services have been marked by many orders and medals of Mongolia as well as of the Soviet Union and other socialist countries. (*Pravda*, 25 October; *FBIS*, 26 October.)

Colleen E. Foraker
Fremont, California

Nepal

Population. 16,578,000

Party. Nepal Communist Party, 2 neutralist factions (NCP); Nepal Communist Party (Marxist-Leninist)/ pro-Beijing, 3 factions (NCP[M-L]/B, NCP/B); Nepal Communist Party/pro-Moscow, 3 factions (NCP/M)

Founded. NCP: 1949; NCP(M-L): 1978

Membership. 5,000 (estimated), with pro-Chinese and neutralist factions accounting for almost 75 percent

Leadership. NCP/neutralist factions: Man Mohan Adhikary and Mrs. Sahana Pradhan (Pushpa Lal's widow); NCP(M-L)/B: Radha Krishna Mainali and Mohan Chandra Adhikary; NCP (Fourth Congress)/B: Mohan Bikram Gharti; NCP (Mashal)/B: Nirmal Lama; NCP (Rayamajhi faction)/M: Dr. Keshar Jung Rayamajhi; NCP (Manandhar faction)/M: Bishnu Bahadur Manandhar; NCP (Tulsi Lal faction)/M: Tulsi Lal Amatya

Politburo. No data

Secretariat. No data

Central Committee. 35 members in the NCP (Rayamajhi faction)/M; no data on other factions

Status. Proscribed

Last Congress. 1961 (last pre-split congress)

Last Election. 1959, 7.5 percent, 4 of 109 seats

Auxiliary Organizations. NCP/neutralist: Nepal Progressive Student Union; NCP/B: All Nepal National Free Student Union, All Nepal National Teachers Organization; NCP/M: Nepal Student Federation. In addition, pro-Beijing and neutralist factions have shadow organizations within the government-sponsored labor and peasant organizations.

Publications. NCP/neutralist: *Naya Janabad* (New democracy) and *Nepal Patra*; NCP(M-L)/B: *Barga Sangharsha* (Class struggle); NCP/B: *Mashal* (Torch); NCP/M: *Samikshya Weekly* (reflects views of all pro-Soviet factions)

In 1984 Nepalese politics was dominated by confusion and a lack of direction in nearly every sphere of national activity. Popular discontent against the Panchayat system continued to grow, and the rift between hard-line and liberal Panchas widened. Pancha politics was characterized by muscle flexing by the ruling Panchas, led by Prime Minister Lokendra Bahadur Chand, and opposition Panchas, led by former prime minister Surya Bahadur Thapa, resulting in the latter's face being smeared with soot (*FBIS*, 10 April; *Nepal Press Digest* [*NPD*], 16 April). The banned Nepali Congress (NC) continued to promote "national reconciliation." In an effort to consolidate the organization, NC leaders toured many parts of the country, notwithstanding the harassment of the regime. The banned NCP, fragmented into as many as eight different groups, made several attempts to forge unity.

Relations with India remained cool in the early part of the year following India's disenchantment over the United States' endorsement of Nepal's "peace zone" proposal during King Birendra's visit to Washington in early December 1983. Relations with China were further strengthened when Chinese president Li Xiannian visited Nepal and agreed that China would undertake the construction of the Pokhara-Baglung sector of the proposed Pokhara-Mustang road as a token of good will, friendship, and close understanding (*FBIS*, 26 March). Earlier, a visiting Romanian trade delegation had signed an agreement on trade and payment with the Nepalese government (ibid., 13 January). In the regional sphere, Nepal has remained an active and enthusiastic supporter of the South Asian Regional Cooperation (SARC).

Leadership and Organization. The history of the NCP is a history of factionalism. Despite the existence of several factional groups and the organizational weakness of the NCP, these groups remain capable of attracting increasing numbers of Nepalese to their ranks, thus making it possible to portray themselves as a powerful alternative to the present order if and only if they can form a single unified party. So far, however, party unification is unimpressive.

The year 1984 began with a split in the pro-Moscow NCP. Dr. Keshar Jung Rayamajhi was expelled from the chairmanship of the party by a 25 to 2 vote. K. R. Varma and B. B. Manandhar, sponsors of the expulsion motion, accused Dr. Rayamajhi of acting as a Pancha, of advocating socialism within the Panchayat system, and of preventing the union of different communist groups (*NPD*, 2 January). Dr. Rayamajhi, however, maintained that "no one has expelled anyone" and that Varma and Manandhar had left the party on their own accord because of differences with the party's line (ibid.). Dr. Rayamajhi's group convened its sixth conference at Patan, attended by 167 delegates from 57 districts, in late March. The conference re-elected Dr. Rayamajhi president of the party for a fifth term and also formed a 75-member National Assembly and a 35-member Central Committee (ibid., 2 April). Another pro-Soviet group, led by a former communist member of the 1959–1960 parliament, Tulsi Lal Amatya, occasionally issues statements against the government.

Meanwhile, the Man Mohan Adhikary group, formerly a pro-Beijing faction, changed its political and ideological line at a meeting held at Gorakhpur, India, attended by about 65 delegates from different parts of Nepal. The meeting elected a Central Committee with Mr. Adhikary as president. The party platform dropped the term "Mao Zedong Thought" and decided to remain neutral in the ideological conflict between the Chinese and the Soviet communist parties. Similarly, a former Maoist group led by the late Pushpa Lal (now led by his widow, Mrs. Sahana Pradhan), known as the PL group, has avoided embracing either Beijing or Moscow. This group seeks close relations with the Communist Party of India–Marxist (CPM) in order to extend its contact with both the Chinese and the Soviet parties. So far, neither the Chinese nor the Soviet party has responded.

The Fourth Congress group led by Mohan Bikram Gharti suffered a setback when two of its leaders, Nirmal Lama and Jaya Govinda Shah, broke away from the group and convened a conference of their own in India. The split was apparently caused by Gharti's claim that China has abandoned fundamental principles of communism after Mao and that true communism does not exist anywhere in the world. Gharti and his group still believe in the ideology and activities of China's disgraced Gang of Four. Lama and Shah's group, however, decided to continue the struggle against the anti-China line. Thus, a former pro-Chinese extremist group has now divided into Maoists and Dengists, with Gharti leading the former and Lama the latter.

The NCP(M-L), an offspring of the Indian Naxalite movement, has been particularly active in eastern Nepal since the early 1970s, when it launched a "class annihilation" movement against the alleged "exploiting class." Its leaders—Mohan Chandra Adhikary and Radha Krishna Mainali—are serving sentences of life imprisonment (twenty years in jail according to Nepalese law) for their terrorist activities. At present this group seems divided into three subfactions, headed by Prakash Chandra Mainali, Mod Nath Prasrit, and Durga Bahadur Singh. Their ideological line is a mix of Maoism, Lin Biaoism, and the ideas of the Gang of Four. The leadership of this group is considered immature by other communist factions. Nevertheless, it is influential among radical university students.

Domestic Party Affairs. The main issue dividing Communists since the mid-1950s has been the problem of identifying the main enemy and creating a united front against that enemy. The Sino-Soviet dispute came to be the issue after the mid-1960s. The Maoists belonging to the Fourth Congress and the Mashal groups both regard the king and the Nepali Congress as enemies of equal importance and hence reject the idea of any form of united front with the NC. The NCP(M-L), also known as the Naxalites, regards the monarchy as enemy number one but rules out the possibility of any united front with the NC, believing it to be a puppet of both comprador capitalism and the reactionary Indian government. Among the neutralist factions, Mr. Adhikary's activities seem guided more by the ideology of radical socialism than by Marxism-Leninism. His program envisages the replacement of the Panchayat system by a democratic system rather than overthrowing the monarchy. Another neutralist faction, the PL group, advocates the overthrow of the monarchy by a broad-based united front of all progressive and democratic elements,

including the NC. The pro-Soviets, on the other hand, see different roads to democracy and hence advocate both covert and overt strategy.

The unity talks between these factions continued throughout the year. The two pro-Moscow groups and the two neutralist groups were partially united in a Leftist Unity Front. Whether the orthodox pro-Soviet group of Dr. Rayamajhi and the dogmatic Maoist groups chose not to participate in the Unity Front or if they were excluded by their moderate counterparts is not known. According to the moderate pro-Moscow leader, K. R. Varma, Adhikary's changing political stand has helped both groups to unite. He further said that his group does not view the Maoists as they once did, and they have reviewed their position vis-à-vis the Chinese party and other leftists of Nepal (ibid., 30 April). The moderate pro-Soviets and the neutralists have constantly appealed to the NC and other democratic forces to unite and fight against the Panchayat system. The NC's response, however, has remained largely negative.

On the fifth anniversary of the NCP(M-L)'s formation, it called on all leftist revolutionary forces and all democratic and militant groups to unite in a concerted struggle against the common enemy, meaning the king and his Panchayat system. Radha Krishna Mainali's petition for a writ of habeas corpus was dismissed by the supreme court (ibid., 2 January). On 15 January police fired over a gathering of approximately 3,000 people in Piskar village (about 30 miles east of Kathmandu), describing the gathering as "illegal activities of extremist elements." The "extremist elements" and their "illegal activities," however, were never identified or disclosed by the government. The death toll in this incident ranged from the official figure of two to unofficial figures as high as eleven (ibid., 23 January). According to unofficial accounts, a crowd had gathered for a cultural show organized by activists of NCP(M-L). Former prime minister Thapa, NC leader K. P. Bhattarai, and all prominent communist leaders condemned the police shooting and demanded a judicial inquiry (ibid., 30 January, 6 February).

The neutralist communist leaders, M. M. Adhikary and Mrs. Sahana Pradhan, were prevented from speaking at a meeting in Biratnagar marking the centenary of Karl Marx's death on 26 December 1983 (ibid., 9 January). The Adhikary faction's Politburo meeting expressed concern over the worsening economic situation and the growing restrictions on fundamental rights. It called for a political change to overcome the crisis and appealed for a joint front of all leftists and the NC to struggle for the restoration of democracy (ibid., 27 February). Meanwhile, King Birendra made it clear in addressing a mammoth rally at Nepalgunj that there would be no changes in Nepal's present governmental system since the majority of the people had already expressed themselves in favor of the Panchayat in the May 1980 referendum. The king also warned political leaders to be "alert while discharging their responsibilities," thus giving the go-ahead to the government of Prime Minister Chand, which had been accused of failing to check administrative malpractices or to control market prices, and of performing poorly (*FBIS*, 23 February). While Maoists and neutralists did not participate in the Panchayati elections, the pro-Soviets actively campaigned for their candidate in a by-election in Chitwon district to fill a vacancy. Pro-Moscow leader K. R. Varma maintained that there are various ways to democracy; hence his group would participate in the Panchayat elections (ibid., 30 April).

International Views, Positions, and Activities. M. M. Adhikary's Politburo meeting condemned President Reagan's decision to deploy Pershing II missiles in Europe and called for the destruction of all nuclear missiles (ibid., 27 February); it remained silent on Soviet intervention in Afghanistan. Although all pro-Soviets continued to support the Soviet intervention in Afghanistan, the Maoists continued to condemn it. The pro-Moscow faction of Dr. Rayamajhi seems to have been abandoned by the Soviet party, for there are rumors in Nepal that the Soviet party has shifted its support to the B. B. Manandhar and K. R. Varma faction. There is no indication of any covert or overt Chinese support for the divided Maoist groups.

Chitra Krishna Tiwari
Arlington, Virginia

New Zealand

Population. 3,238,000
Parties. Communist Party of New Zealand (CPNZ); Socialist Unity Party (SUP); Workers Communist League (WCL); Socialist Action League (SAL)
Founded. CPNZ: 1921; SUP: 1966; WCL: 1980; SAL: 1969
Membership. CPNZ: circa 50; SUP: 100; no data on others
Leadership. CPNZ: Richard C. Wolfe; SUP: G. H. "Bill" Andersen (national president), George Jackson (national secretary)
Status. Legal
Last Congress. CPNZ: 26–28 January 1979 (first since 1966); SUP, Sixth, 22–24 October 1982
Last Election. July 1984, no representatives elected
Auxiliary Organizations. SUP: New Zealand–USSR Friendship Society, New Zealand Council for World Peace, Union of New Zealand Women, Young Workers' Alliance; SAL: Young Socialists
Publications. CPNZ: *People's Voice* (weekly); SUP: *New Zealand Tribune* (bimonthly), *Socialist Politics* (quarterly); WCL: *Unity* (monthly news sheet); SAL: *Socialist Action* (bimonthly)

With a national total of fewer than 500 members, New Zealand's communist parties have little influence in the primarily agricultural, middle-class country. Some of these groups, nevertheless, find a disproportionate voice through their ties to trade unions and other auxiliary organizations, such as the Young Socialists. Recent developments, such as the support of some communist groups for the Labour Party in the June elections, suggest communist leaders may be adopting a more pragmatic approach to politics.

The Communist Party of New Zealand. The CPNZ, originally a pro-Soviet party, broke with Moscow in the mid-1960s and adopted a pro-Beijing line. After the fall of the Gang of Four, however, the CPNZ changed its ideological orientation once again and aligned itself with Albania. As the result of several decades of factional splitting, the CPNZ has been reduced to approximately 50 members, almost exclusively based around its Auckland headquarters. As such, the CPNZ exerts almost no influence on New Zealand's political life and is considered—by fellow Communists—an impotent arm of the communist movement.

The Socialist Unity Party. The SUP was organized in 1966, the result of the CPNZ's break with Moscow. It has retained its Soviet ties and is the only communist party in New Zealand recognized by Moscow. In May 1984, the SUP sent a delegation to the Soviet Union at the invitation of the Central Committee to study organizational and party activities (Tass, 20 May). The SUP's pro-Moscow line has, in recent years, included endorsement of the Soviet invasion of Afghanistan and support for Soviet proposals on disarmament.

Most New Zealanders view the SUP as the country's leading communist party, probably because of its higher public profile. The SUP boasts extensive trade union connections. For example, SUP leader Ken Douglas is secretary-treasurer of New Zealand's 450,000-member Federation of Labor (FOL) and is generally considered one of the trade union movement's best tacticians. In addition, SUP National President Bill Andersen serves as a member of the FOL's national executive and as president of the Auckland Trades Council, the largest in the country.

The Workers Communist League. The WCL was formed in 1980, the result of a merger of two pro-Beijing groups that had split from the CPNZ. It is composed primarily of young college graduates, factory laborers, and the unemployed in the Wellington area. Though legal, the WCL keeps its membership and organizational goals secret. It is generally considered one of the most radical communist groups in New Zealand, and a government security report released several years ago called the WCL "a revolutionary communist party dedicated to the violent overthrow of the state." Still, no evidence exists linking the WCL to violence. The WCL's known activities center around the trade union movement, primarily in the Wellington Trades Council and the Wellington Unemployed Workers' Union. The party has also lent its support to a number of political causes, including organizing protests against apartheid in South Africa.

Socialist Action League. The SAL is a pro-Cuban, Trotskyite group formed on New Zealand's campuses during the student uprisings of 1969. As such, the SAL differs from most other communist groups because of its heavy emphasis on Latin American issues, such as human rights in Chile and the current "revolutionary movement" in Central America. It has maintained its university ties through its affiliations with the Young Socialists.

The Political Scene. Overall, communist groups in New Zealand exert little influence on the dominant political players—the National Party, the Labour Party, and the Social Credit Party. In the past, communist groups have refused to recognize the unwillingness of most New Zealanders—including industrial workers—to risk their relatively comfortable living standards for militant strike action or ideological causes. The Communists' position in the labor movement, for example, has recently been threatened by the rise of a group of young, moderate trade union leaders who appeal to workers' more pragmatic interests. The Communists are also hurt by their own failure to articulate a coherent, long-term program of national goals.

During the past year, however, some signs have emerged that indicate communist leaders recognize these shortcomings and are adopting a slightly less doctrinaire approach to politics. For example, several communist groups—including the SAL and the Young Socialists—campaigned for the Labour Party in last July's national elections. According to press reports, these groups felt that after nine years of "conservative" rule under Robert Muldoon's National Party, the union-affiliated Labour Party offered a more realistic choice for voters (*Intercontinental Press*, 6 August).

Although David Lange's Labour government has proven less expansionary on economic policy than its predecessor, Communists have been clearly encouraged by several of Wellington's foreign policy initiatives. The most important of these is Labour's ban on port visits by nuclear-armed and nuclear-powered ships—a long-standing communist goal. In addition, Communists almost certainly were pleased by the Labour government's call for South Africa to close its consulate in Wellington immediately following its election victory.

Michael Morell
Vienna, Virginia

Christine A. Gould
Arlington, Virginia

Pakistan

Population. 96,628,000
Party. Communist Party of Pakistan (CPP)
Founded. 1948
Membership. Under 200 (estimated)
Secretary General. Ali Nazish
Leading Bodies. No data
Status. Illegal
Last Congress. First, 1976 (clandestine)
Last Election. N/a
Auxiliary Organizations. No data
Publications. None

Domestic Developments. Communists operating outside the CPP exercise political influence in Pakistan through trade unions, student organizations, and established political parties. Leftists do not currently pose a major threat to the government, although the regime of President Mohammad Zia-ul Haq recognizes the potential of the left to exploit signs of unrest by mounting street demonstrations and indulging in political violence. A more pressing cause of concern to the regime is the subversive activities of Pakistani leftists based in Kabul and London. Zia has charged the Soviet Union, Afghanistan, and India with assisting radical Pakistanis living abroad in a campaign to overthrow his regime.

During the year, the main opposition to the regime centered on the eleven-party alliance known as the Movement for the Restoration of Democracy (MRD). The MRD is a center-left coalition that coalesced in 1981 to press the fight against martial law. The makeshift alliance is dominated by the Pakistan People's Party (PPP), probably the only political organization that enjoys a degree of support in all regions of the country. The PPP is headed by Benazir Bhutto, the daughter of the executed former prime minister whom Zia overthrew. Benazir is a political novice who took over the party's leadership after her mother, Begum Nusrat Bhutto, stepped down for reasons of ill-health. Benazir was released from house arrest in January in order to receive medical treatment abroad. While traveling in Western Europe and the United States, Benazir displayed considerable oratorical skills and argued passionately against the continuation of Western support for the Zia regime (*India Today*, Bombay, 15 February).

The MRD platform calls for an immediate end to martial law, the holding of free and fair elections open to all political parties, and the restoration of the 1973 constitution. In foreign affairs, the influence of the militant wing of the PPP and the small leftist parties is clearly visible in the MRD program. Pronouncements issued by the alliance are critical of U.S. efforts to enlist Pakistan as a "frontline state" against the Soviet Union. The MRD urges direct negotiations between Pakistan and the Soviet-installed regime in Kabul and denounces the Zia government for compromising Pakistan's nonaligned status.

In August 1983, President Zia announced his intention to hold elections some time before March 1985. Throughout 1984, Zia reaffirmed his commitment to carry out these elections in the face of vehement objections on the part of the MRD. Under Zia's plan, elections will be contested on a nonparty basis. Candidates will be carefully screened to ensure that leftists and other undesirable elements do not win office. Zia termed his proposed system of government a "shooracracy"—that is, one based on Islamic law and traditions. According to this hybrid experiment in Islamic statehood, Pakistan will be a guided democracy headed by a pious *amir* (religiously sanctioned leader) advised by a *shoora* (consultative assembly). (*Dawn*, Karachi, 9 October.) The MRD condemned the scheme as a thinly veiled attempt by Zia to legitimize his rule, destroy the PPP, and consolidate the power of the army.

By December, Zia apparently calculated that MRD plans to boycott the election might render the polls meaningless and trigger widespread disturbances. In order to keep the opposition off balance, Zia appealed directly to the Pakistani public for support by calling a national referendum on 19 December. Voters were asked whether they supported the transfer of power to elected representatives as envisioned under Zia's shooracracy scheme. During a nationally broadcast address on 1 December, Zia told the nation: "The future of Pakistan and Islamization is in your hands. Come forward and stabilize this future through your votes." (Karachi domestic service, 1 December; *FBIS*, 3 December.) Voters were given the option to vote yes or no. Zia maintained that a positive response to the referendum would be interpreted as a mandate for him to retain the presidency for another five years.

Virtually the entire Pakistani political spectrum denounced the referendum as a fraud since few Pakistanis could be expected to cast a vote against Islam. Zia silenced the opposition when he decreed that advocating an election boycott would be a crime punishable by three years in prison (*NYT*, 9 December). The opposition was also hobbled by a decree issued in May that prevented the press from reporting its views (ibid., 20 May).

To no one's surprise, the referendum passed by a huge majority. Spokesmen for the government and the MRD differed, however, over the effectiveness of the boycott. According to the government election commissioner, over 60 percent of eligible voters cast ballots, with 97.7 percent voting yes (Karachi domestic service, 21 December; *FBIS*, 21 December). According to the opposition, voter turnout was considerably lower than the government claimed, with as few as 10 percent of eligible voters going to polls in Sind. Independent observers were unanimous in the belief that incidents of vote rigging and ballot stuffing had taken place on a massive scale. (AFP, Hong Kong, 20 December; *FBIS*, 21 December.) On 25 December (a national holiday marking the birth of Pakistani founding father Mohammad Ali Jinnah), the MRD staged an angry demonstration in Karachi to protest the referendum verdict. Police broke up the march and arrested several prominent MRD figures. (AFP, Hong Kong, 25 December; *FBIS*, 26 December.)

Opposition to Zia's political program runs deep, particularly among Pakistani leftists and in the minority provinces. Within the MRD, the most intransigent elements are the PPP and three leftist parties with strong ties to the former Bhutto regime. The PPP maintains a solid following among the urban middle class, bureaucrats and lawyers, and landowners in Punjab and Sind. Seven years of martial law, however, have frustrated the PPP and transformed the party's political program into a personal vendetta against President Zia. The ineffectiveness of PPP moderates such as the Bhutto women has strengthened the hand of militants who have pushed the party to adopt an increasingly confrontationalist strategy toward the regime.

The other leftist constituents of the MRD include the Qaumi Mahaz Azadi (QMA), the Pakistan Socialist Party (PSP), and the Pakistan Progressive Party. The general secretary of the QMA is Iqbal Haider, who also serves as an associate secretary of the MRD. The leading personality in the QMA is Meraj Mohammad Khan, a longtime political activist with a reputation for fiery oratory. Meraj was one of a handful of opposition leaders who remained in jail after Zia ordered the gradual release of leading political prisoners in advance of national elections (*FEER*, 29 November). The party's main constituency consists of *muhajir* (Moslem immigrants from India) students in Karachi and a sprinkling of urban supporters in the Punjab. The PSP is led by veteran organizer C. R. Aslam. The party appeals to parlor revolutionaries whose involvement in opposition activities goes little beyond sloganeering. The Pakistan Progressive Party, led by Azaz Nasir, is a Soviet-sponsored front with a rigidly pro-Moscow orientation.

Grass-roots opposition to the regime is strongest in the minority provinces, where an array of nationalist parties has exploited long-standing grievances against the Punjabi-*muhajir* alliance that has dominated Pakistani politics since independence. Although many of the regional parties pursue moderate programs aimed at enhancing the power of the provinces within the federal system, some parties advocate secession from Pakistan.

In Sind, the rural-based Sindhi Awami Tehrik (SAT) has built a well-knit party apparatus with a large number of ideologically motivated cadres. The party directed the antiregime agitation that rocked the province in 1983. Although the agitation had played itself out by the beginning of 1984 because of the massive deployment of the army throughout the province, it is clear that the SAT has displaced the landlord-dominated PPP as the leading opposition party in the province. SAT ideology is an eclectic blend of Sindhi nationalism and Marxism. The party is headed by Rasool Bux Palejo, a die-hard Sindhi nationalist with Maoist leanings. Palejo has spent the past four years in prison. Because of a heart attack in January and his continuing detention, Palejo's grip over the party appears in doubt. The SAT supports an impressive network of auxiliary organizations catering to students, women, and intellectuals, although the party's main strength is among the peasantry. News reports allege the SAT is stockpiling arms purchased from Afghan guerrillas (*Indian Express*, Bombay, 27 October). Other parties in the forefront of the MRD-sponsored agitation in Sind include Jaiy Sind and its student front, the Jaiy Sind Student Federation. Jaiy Sind is headed by octogenarian nationalist G. M. Sayed.

In the Northwest Frontier province (NWFP),

Pushtun opposition to the regime finds expression in the Mazdoor Kisan Party (Workers and Peasants Party; MKP), led by Sardar Shaukat Ali and Fatehyab Ali Khan. Direction of the MKP is provided by Afzal Bangash, an expatriate Pakistani who divides his time between Kabul and Moscow. As the party's name suggests, the MKP attracts the support of militant trade unionists and a section of the peasantry. The MKP maintains links with the pro-Soviet regime in Kabul and actively works to sow discord among Afghan resistance forces based in the NWFP.

In the sprawling province of Baluchistan, separatist discontent poses a serious challenge to Pakistan's national integrity. The Zia regime has skillfully defused tension in the province by buying off tribal leaders with promises of political patronage and an increased stake in the province's economic development. When persuasion has not worked, the presence of the army and rigorous enforcement of martial law restrictions have effectively prevented radical Baluch leaders from renewing the guerrilla insurgency that raged in the province between 1973 and 1977.

The leading figures in the Baluch nationalist movement are Ghaus Bux Bizenjo, Khair Bux Marri, and Ataullah Mengal. All are hereditary tribal *sardars* (chieftains) who advocate either Baluch autonomy or outright independence. Bizenjo heads the Pakistan National Party (PNP), the successor organization of the National Awami Party, which formed a short-lived provincial ministry during the Bhutto era. Bizenjo, who is kept under tight police surveillance in Quetta, is a bitter opponent of the Zia regime. His public pronouncements, however, fall short of endorsing Baluch independence. Marri, the leader of the Baluch tribe that was in the forefront of the insurgency in the 1970s, resides in Soviet-occupied Afghanistan, while Mengal operates from exile in Great Britain. Both Marri and Mengal promote the cause of Baluch independence and actively solicit Soviet support. Marri and Mengal assert their leadership claims through traditional tribal networks, whereas Bizenjo operates within the conventional framework of opposition politics. There are unconfirmed reports that the PNP has forged a tactical alliance with the Pakistan Progressive Party, the MKP in the Northwest Frontier, and the SAT in Sind (*Economic and Political Weekly*, Bombay, 29 October 1983).

The Baluch Students' Organization (BSO), founded in 1967, also advocates Baluch independence, with the help of the Soviet Union if necessary. Under the leadership of a "professional student," Razik Bakti, the BSO enjoys a wide following among students in the province. Although Baluch militants were relatively inactive during 1984, the BSO has the capacity to mobilize large crowds on short notice for use in demonstrations and strikes. A hard-core BSO element is reportedly receiving Soviet-style political indoctrination at Kabul University (*WSJ*, 1 October). Although it has a strong appeal on Baluchistan campuses, BSO activists have no standing within the feudal *sardari* system of tribal leadership.

In 1983, the Marxist-dominated National Student Federation (NSF) suffered setbacks in campus elections. The main beneficiary of the NSF decline was the Islami Jamiat-e Tulaba, a generally progovernment student organization composed of religious fundamentalists. The NSF, however, expected to recoup its losses during student elections scheduled for early 1984. The ideological rivalry between the two groups erupted in violence as both sides organized attacks on each other. In February, the government banned student organizations altogether in a move designed to curb the violence of the right as well as the left (*Pakistan Times*, Lahore, 10 February). Even though Pakistan has formally agreed to conduct student exchanges with the Soviet Union, the Zia regime allows very few Pakistanis to study in the USSR because of the disruptive potential that returned students could pose.

Foreign Affairs. Relations between Pakistan and the Soviet Union showed no marked improvements in 1984, although both sides were anxious to maintain a semblance of normal relations in noncontroversial areas such as trade, economic aid, and scientific exchanges. The Soviets agreed to supply economic and technical aid for Pakistan's five-year plan (1983–1988), most notably for showcase projects such as the Karachi steel complex and the Multan thermal power project (*WP*, 27 January). The Soviets, however, wield little economic leverage over Pakistan, and ties with Moscow are carefully circumscribed. The only major Soviet presence in Pakistan is at the Karachi steel complex, where almost 800 Soviet technicians are employed (*Muslim*, Islamabad, 5 October).

On the central issue of Afghanistan, the two sides remained far apart. The Red Army's occupation of Afghanistan is now in its fifth year, with no end in sight. The Kremlin continues to insist that Pakistan, the United States, and China are waging an "undeclared war" against the "legitimate" pro-Soviet government in Kabul (see, for instance, Tass, 30 November; *FBIS*, 3 December). Moscow demands that Pakistan stop providing arms and sanctuary to Afghan guerrillas. The Soviets urge direct talks between Pakistan and the Afghan government. To ensure the survival of the Kabul regime, Moscow maintains that international guarantees prohibiting external aggression against Afghanistan must be in place before Soviet troops are withdrawn.

Vitali Smirnov, the highly visible Soviet ambassador to Pakistan, publicly outlined the elements of Soviet policy toward Pakistan on several occasions during the year. In a highly controversial address in Karachi in February, Smirnov urged Pakistan to "practice political realism" (*Dawn*, 3 February)—an implicit reference to Leonid Brezhnev's 1980 statement that the Afghan revolution was "irreversible." Smirnov also broadly hinted at Soviet "hot-pursuit" raids against Afghan guerrilla encampments within Pakistan (*WP*, 27 January). In December, Smirnov told a Karachi newspaper that there were three hurdles standing in the way of closer relations. These included Pakistan's involvement in the "undeclared war against Afghanistan," preferential treatment accorded to all diplomatic missions in Pakistan except the Soviet Union, and Pakistan's "hostile propaganda" against the USSR. (*Jang*, 9 December; *FBIS*, 18 December.)

Soviet and Afghan security forces committed over 60 violations of Pakistani territory during the year as part of an orchestrated Kremlin campaign to pressure Pakistan into making concessions on Afghanistan. All reported violations were shallow air and ground probes along ill-defined boundaries in Baluchistan and the NWFP. Fearing that an aggressive military response to the violations might provoke a large-scale Soviet incursion into Pakistan, the Zia regime relied exclusively on diplomatic means to deter the Soviets. To complement the Kremlin's campaign of intimidation, Soviet media churned out a steady barrage of disinformation and propaganda attacks against Pakistan. For example, a Moscow radio broadcast on 10 January insinuated that the Zia regime was laying plans to deploy U.S.-supplied Pershing II missiles on Pakistani soil (*FBIS*, 11 January).

From Islamabad's perspective, the Soviet occupation of Afghanistan and the presence of 3 million Afghan refugees in Pakistan pose serious, long-term security threats. Ever since Soviet troops arrived in Afghanistan in 1979, Zia has sought to rally international opinion behind Pakistan's four-point negotiating formula (withdrawal of foreign troops; restoration of Afghanistan's nonaligned, Islamic status; installation of a representative government in Kabul; and repatriation of refugees under honorable circumstances).

In February, Zia traveled to Moscow to attend the funeral of Yuri Andropov and to sound out the new Soviet leadership on Afghanistan. Upon his return home, Zia reaffirmed Pakistan's commitment to a diplomatic settlement of the Afghan crisis, although he reported no change in Soviet thinking on the subject (*Baluchistan Times*, 16 February). In August, Pakistani and Afghan negotiators convened a fourth round of indirect talks in Geneva. Progress toward a negotiated settlement of the Afghan conflict has been slow, but both sides are reluctant to bear the onus for breaking off the U.N.-sponsored talks. Unlike previous sessions, however, this round was deadlocked from the start. The Soviets refused to advance a timetable for a troop withdrawal or discuss the composition of the Kabul government. Another round of talks is tentatively scheduled for February 1985.

In sharp contrast to the suspicions and mutual recriminations that characterize Pakistan-Soviet relations, Islamabad's ties with China remain a cornerstone of Pakistani foreign policy. Pakistan views China as a reliable ally that has stood by Pakistan since the 1960s. Moreover, Pakistan regards Chinese economic, military, and diplomatic support as a counter to Soviet pressures and an attractive alternative to overreliance on the West. China, for its part, extends full support for the Zia regime's handling of domestic affairs and foreign relations.

Sino-Pakistani relations continued to prosper and expand during the year. In March, Chinese president Li Xiannian conducted a state visit to Pakistan. At the conclusion of the visit, Zia reported that the two countries shared a "complete identity of views on all international issues," particularly regarding Afghanistan (Karachi domestic service, 6 March; *FBIS*, 6 March). In June, Chinese prime minister Zhao Ziyang stopped in Karachi while en route to Europe. During a press conference, Zhao pledged Chinese support for Pakistan "no matter what happens" (AFP, Hong Kong, 17 June; *FBIS*, 18 June). Although no new defense agreements or military transfers were announced during the year, military contacts between the two countries are extensive and extremely close. There were numerous exchanges during the year of Chinese and Pakistani military delegations representing all three service branches. Both sides denied persistent allegations that China has assisted Pakistan in its covert nuclear weapons program (see, for instance, Karachi domestic service, 18 January; *FBIS*, 18 January).

Douglas C. Makeig
Library of Congress

Philippines

Population. 55,528,000
Parties. Communist Party of the Philippines, Marxist-Leninist (CPP-ML); Philippine Communist Party (PKP)
Founded. CPP-ML: 1968; PKP: 1930
Membership. CPP-ML: 7,500; PKP: 400 (both estimated)
Secretary General. CPP-ML: Rafael Baylosis; PKP: Felicismo C. Macapagal
Leading Members. CPP-ML: Rodolfo Salas (chairman), Juanito Rivera (vice-chairman and leader of

National People's Army [NPA]), Benito Tiamzon (Politburo member), Benjamin De Vera (Politburo member), Ignacio Capegsan (Politburo member); PKP: Alejandro Briones (Politburo member), Jose Lava (Politburo member), Merlin Magallona (Central Committee member), Jesus Lava (Central Committee member)

Status. Illegal, but the PKP, because of its moderate stance, enjoys a semilegal status.

Last Congress. PCC-ML: no data; PKP: Eighth, 1980

Last Election. N/a

Auxiliary Organizations: PCC-ML: National Democratic Front (NDF), May First Movement, Nationalist Youth, League of Filipino Students, Youth for Nationalism and Democracy, Christians for National Liberation, Nationalist Health Association, Nationalist Teachers' Association, Union of Democratic Filipinos, Justice for Aquino for All, August 21 Movement, Task Force Detainees, Association of Concerned Teachers, Ecumenical Movement for Justice and Peace, Movement of Attorneys for Brotherhood, Integrity and Nationalism, Parliament in the Streets; PKP: National Association of Workers (Katipunan), Democratic Youth Council of the Philippines, Philippine Committee for Development, Peace, and Solidarity, Association of Philippine Women Workers, Philippine Printers Union, Agricultural Workers Union

Publications. CPP-ML: *Ang Bayan*; NDF: *Liberation*, *NDF-Update*, *Ang Katipunan*; PKP: *Ang Kommunista*

Two communist parties operate in the Philippines: the dominant, nominally independent CPP-ML and the much smaller PKP. The semilegal PKP flirts with the government of Ferdinand Marcos while gently criticizing its excesses. The PKP stresses peaceful change and eschews violent revolution. The CPP-ML supports both political and military struggle against the Marcos government. Its military arm is the NPA, and its political arm the NDF. Together they are an increasing threat, not only to the Marcos government but ultimately to the hopes any noncommunist Filipino might have for a restoration of democracy.

The NDF was formed in 1980–1981. In August 1980, the Seventh Plenum of the CPP-ML Central Committee discussed moving from the preparatory stage to the creation of a front to challenge Marcos politically. The CPP-ML formally describes itself as a member of the NDF, which is portrayed as a radical umbrella organization. Also in 1980, the CPP-ML announced that it would resume the armed struggle. Over the next three years, the NDF and NPA made impressive gains. The NPA has extended itself geographically from its original base in the mountains north of Baguio in Luzon and the rugged Samar region to the Bicol region of southern Luzon, the northern part of the central Luzon province of Nueva Ecija, the mountainous regions of northern and southern Mindanao, and the West Visayan islands of Negros and Panay (*FEER*, 28 June).

According to CPP-ML figures, between 1980 and December 1983 party membership grew from 10,000 to 30,000, CPP-ML regional organizations increased from twelve to seventeen, the number of guerrilla fronts jumped from 28 to 45, and full- and part-time NPA members increased from 8,000 to 20,000 (excluding village militia members) (ibid.).

Organization and Leadership. *Philippine Communist Party.* Both Felicismo Macapagal, PKP secretary general, and ranking Politburo member Jose Lava are in their seventies. Prominent members of the Central Committee include University of the Philippines law professors Merlin Magallona and Jesus Lava, who was released from prison recently. Magallona is the PKP secretary for political affairs. In this capacity, he is believed to share the duty of leading party theoretician with fellow University of the Philippines law professor Haydee Yorac. Magallona is often mentioned as the heir apparent to Macapagal.

Communist Party of the Philippines, Marxist-Leninist. There are believed to be between a dozen and two dozen Central Committee members. Although most have been members for many years, the Central Committee is a surprisingly young group, with most members in their mid-thirties. Prominent members include Chairman Rodolfo Salas (alias Commander Bilog), who heads the Central Committee's rural branch; Secretary General Rafael Baylosis, head of the urban branch; chief propagandist Antonio Zumel, and Vice-Chairman Juanito Rivera (alias Commander Juaning), who leads the NPA and is chairman of the CPP-ML's Military Commission.

Effective control of the party theoretically rests with the Central Committee, but it rarely meets, and the regional party organizations enjoy de facto autonomy. This has helped the party take advantage of local opportunities to expand. The party is now active in all 72 provinces. This expansion—and the archipelagic nature of the Philippines—has made it harder for the Tagalog-speaking leadership to maintain effective control of the local organizations. Decentralization has also made it harder for the government to mount an effective counterinsurgency campaign.

Domestic Activities. During the first half of 1984, President Marcos continued to belittle the NPA's effectiveness and was critical of those who claimed that its influence was widespread. Government officials estimated that there were only 5,000 active NPA guerrillas, mostly in rural areas. On 22 March Defense Minister Juan Ponce Enrile noted that the NPA had changed tactics from small-group operations to larger attacks on secluded military or police detachments. However, he rejected the idea that this was an indication that the NPA was growing stronger, claiming instead that it was the NPA's way of "creating the impression" that NPA fighters existed throughout the country (*FBIS*, 26 March).

However, it was not long before the government had to begin taking the NPA seriously. At the beginning of the year, the CPP-ML vowed to increase ambushes by company-strength units significantly. Heightened liaison between rural NPA units and urban front organizations was also expected, with occasional NPA-initiated terrorism in the cities. (*FEER*, 28 June.)

By April, the NPA was so successful that it felt it could abandon its emphasis on hit-and-run tactics and adopt more conventional military warfare. Instead of operating only in small groups of three to nine guerrillas, it began to field groups of 200 in some areas. (*CSM*, 27 September.)

In addition a well-organized urban insurgency was rapidly becoming a serious problem. The CPP-ML is trying to expand its influence via urban front organizations, and the NPA has developed "sparrow units" consisting of three or four urban terrorists. These sparrow units began attacking local police in Davao in southern Mindanao—the Philippines' third-largest city—in early 1984 and by the end of April had killed 22 policemen (*FEER*, 28 June). In May, the CPP-ML took credit for the assassination of northern Manila commander Brig. Gen. Thomas Karingal. The CPP-ML Central Committee indicated it planned to increase the frequency of such terrorism during the rest of 1984 (ibid.).

By May, Marcos was taking the NPA more seriously. He admitted that the insurgency was growing despite the counterinsurgency drive launched in 1983 by the army. He also stated that intelligence estimates placed the armed strength of the NPA at 6,810, 25 percent higher than the previous year's estimate (*FBIS*, 4 May). That same month the NPA more credibly claimed 20,000 trained fighters, of whom half were armed.

Also in May, the NPA began to inflict extensive property damage. It destroyed a multimillion-dollar coconut and cocoa plantation in the south and in northern Luzon attacked projects run by the Cagayan Valley Development Authority, which is closely associated with Defense Minister Enrile.

During the May parliamentary elections, the NPA attempted to disrupt the elections. For example, in Samar it snatched 427 ballot boxes and on election day alone killed more than 60 soldiers.

In June the NPA stated that it was especially proud of its success at assassination operations. During the first six months of 1984, the NPA claimed responsibility for 56 assassinations of political or military leaders (*FEER*, 28 June).

Despite some successes in the counterinsurgency campaign, by July even Enrile was changing his cavalier attitude. He called the NPA insurgency a "sensitive matter" and stated that the situation had "deteriorated. The building of the NPA was quite dramatic." (*FBIS*, 16 July.)

By August it was clear that the NPA guerrillas and cadres had penetrated metropolitan Manila. They are the core of what the CPP-ML calls "composite units," militant and well-disciplined students, workers, and urban poor, who appear to be at the forefront of recent demonstrations. These units demonstrated their discipline and precision at a rally on 17 August (*CSM*, 27 September).

In October, the government revealed that the NPA had killed approximately 6,000 soldiers and civilians, 1,600 of these in the first nine months of 1984 (*San Francisco Examiner*, 14 October). The report of the commission investigating the murder of Benigno Aquino, which implicated 25 senior military officers, including the chief of staff, was a shot in the arm to the NPA's efforts to win the loyalties of Filipinos. With new confidence the NPA showed increasing willingness to sustain losses and engage the Philippine army in conventional battles. The NPA began stepping up its activity, enlarging its attack units to battalions of about 300 guerrillas and bringing the insurgency into towns and cities.

These activities prompted the military to be more candid about the NPA. In November, the army revealed that in the first ten months of 1984, the NPA had killed 2,650 persons, including 800 soldiers and 65 civilian officials, and caused an estimated $10 million worth of property damage in about 3,500 ambushes, raids, and other incidents. The official estimate of NPA strength was put at 10,000–12,000.

The serious upsurge in NPA-initiated violence, especially in Mindanao, led Marcos to convene cabinet meetings on 8 and 11 December to discuss the situation. Following these meetings, Marcos met with military leaders in an effort to devise counterinsurgency techniques that would more effectively arrest the terrorism (ibid., 27 December 1984, 3 January 1985). At a December press conference, an army spokesman stated that more than a hundred casualties had occurred in recent weeks in Mindanao alone. Ambushes of military patrols and urban shootings were almost daily occurrences. (Ibid.)

In mid-January 1985, Manila admitted that the insurgency was out of control, and it could no longer cope with it without increased U.S. aid, including U.S. military advisers (*WP*, 19 January 1985).

The CPP-ML is discussing with urban guerrillas in Manila a possible new alliance. One of the largest groups, the April 6 Movement, turned down the offer, but tried to persuade the CPP-ML to concentrate on urban violence, arguing that the party was much better equipped and organized for urban warfare than it was.

The CPP-ML plans to intensify its political and military activities throughout the Philippines, culminating in 1987 in what it calls a "first-quarter storm." At this point, the CPP-ML and the NPA expect to have armed urban partisans operational in Manila on a regular basis. Moreover by 1987, the CPP-ML expects to be strong enough to meet the Philippine army in conventional clashes throughout the Philippines, and NPA units plan to be operating in company-size units, something it is now capable of only in Mindanao. NPA guerrillas also plan to launch "local uprisings" in smaller urban areas. (*CSM*, 27 September.)

Front Groups and Affiliated Organizations.
The new threat posed by the NDF is largely the result of a shift in CPP-ML strategy. "Up to now our concentration has been on the armed struggle," says an NDF supporter in Manila who often meets with traditional political opposition figures. "But the political struggle is gaining more and more importance. It is no longer just an auxiliary to our battles in the countryside. We are organizing in the white [urban] areas, forming alliances with all sectors and organizing them." (*San Francisco Examiner*, 11 November.)

The NDF essentially coordinates the activities of most of the CPP-ML's fronts. The NDF has been more successful than any other group—communist or noncommunist—in exploiting anti-Marcos sentiment since the Aquino assassination. It has infiltrated its leaders and organizers into every aspect of the protest movement, including labor, religious, and student groups and organizations of the urban poor. The NDF is also making inroads among the middle and upper-middle classes, newly awakened by the Aquino murder. In particular, the CPP-ML/NDF appeals to businessmen who want a smaller role for U.S. and other foreign business. Another key ally of the NDF has been the Catholic church. In fact, the rapid growth of the NDF owes much to the work of radical clergy and lay people.

In addition, CPP-ML/NPA links to the Moro National Liberation Front (MNLF)—Moslem separatists centered in Mindanao—appear to be continuing. The MNLF's expertise in weapons smuggling made it most attractive to the NPA, which needed increased amounts of weapons in 1984 in order to exploit the instability in the Philippines. Reports of CPP-ML/MNLF links are not new. In fact, the first time the Marcos government noted that the NPA had joined with the MNLF in seeking independence for Mindanao occurred in October 1977. But the reports became more credible in the early 1980s.

The greatest triumph for the NDF in 1984 was its ability to alter significantly the nature of the moderate opposition. And it did so despite a setback during the May elections. The NDF, allied with a radical minority faction in moderate ranks, pushed for an election boycott; the majority of the moderate camp supported the elections and wanted to keep its distance from the CPP-ML. At first, it seemed that the 59 seats the majority faction won vindicated it and strengthened the forces of democracy in the Philippines. But although the victory demonstrated the unpopularity of the Marcos government, it soon became apparent that the opposition would have no impact on the Marcos government. Once the moderates realized that their electoral successes were ephemeral and provided little leverage with Marcos, a new polarization began to develop. Many moderates began to see the logic in a "parliament in the streets" approach to ousting Marcos. These newly radicalized moderates found nothing wrong in alliances with the CPP-ML. Those who want to avoid working with the CPP-ML are now in the minority.

By the end of the year, the NDF had become virtually indispensable to the moderates' attempt to end Marcos's rule. NDF strategists point out that this dependency makes the moderates "much easier" for the NDF to exploit (ibid.). The NDF is now advancing its aggressive and increasingly successful political offensive in Manila and other major cities. During 1984, it became a major partner in opposition activities.

International Views and Activities. For years the PKP has been almost totally controlled by the Communist Party of the Soviet Union (CPSU). This continued to be the case in 1984, as the PKP dutifully attended CPSU-sponsored meetings around the world.

A more interesting and significant development, however, has been the gradual evolution of the CPP-ML from a Maoist, pro-Chinese party into one that, while still formally independent, has increasing links with the CPSU. To be sure, the CPSU and the CPP-ML assiduously perpetuate the myth that they have no links. It is, for example, almost impossible to find Soviet statements about the NPA insurgency, and the CPP-ML rarely discusses Soviet activities in the Philippines. Evidence of material Soviet support for the insurgency would severely damage the independent image of the CPP-ML. The Soviet hand became apparent in 1982 when a defector from the KGB testified before the U.S. Congress of his involvement in channeling funds to the CPP-ML. Evidence of another link was uncovered when military intelligence arrested an East German in Davao. Confiscated documents revealed that the CPP-ML maintained links with Soviet-sponsored solidarity groups in foreign countries through its International Liaison Committee. (*Manila Today Bulletin*, 3 April 1983.)

Philippine military authorities believe that the CPP-ML receives about 80 percent of its agitation and propaganda funds from international funding institutions, many of which are Soviet sponsored. The *Manila Times Journal* (29 March 1983), citing captured documents, noted that the humanitarian organizations in the Netherlands and West Germany were being used to channel funds to CPP-ML front organizations.

The CPP-ML also supports many Soviet foreign policy initiatives. Although the Chinese, for example, label the Nicaraguan revolution a victory for Soviet "social-imperialism," the CPP-ML supports the Soviet position (*Intercontinental Press*, 28 February 1983).

The Soviets, for their part, have moved quickly to exploit the growing anti-Marcos, anti-American sentiment since the Aquino assassination. The Kremlin sharply increased the size of the Soviet mission and changed its character in late 1983 and early 1984. Energetic Soviet operatives replaced tired old diplomats. One of the finest KGB officials, Boris Smirnov, was assigned to Manila on 12 April as the "first secretary" of the embassy. Smirnov is a superb disinformation expert. In 1976, he successfully passed off the "last will of the Zhou Enlai" in Tokyo, sowing confusion among Chinese leaders. (*Business Times*, Kuala Lumpur, 5 December.) A few weeks after Smirnov's arrival, a bogus questionnaire "from the U.S. Information Service" was distributed among leading Filipinos seeking sensitive information on subjects such as their political leanings and military experience. The anti-American operation was deemed successful, as many of the recipients were reportedly outraged by this "American impertinence."

During the last ten months of the year, there was a notable increase in the number of Soviet cultural, sports, and economic missions, themselves often a cover for covert activities.

Soviet involvement in arms transfers to the NPA is more difficult to detect. The number of islands in the Philippines makes smuggling almost impossible to detect. The Soviets were evidently involved in at least one shipment of arms from Eastern Europe through South Yemen to the NPA (*Foreign Policy*, Fall).

From 30 November to 4 December, the Soviet-controlled World Peace Council and its Philippine affiliate, the Philippine Peace and Solidarity Council, cosponsored the first International Conference on Peace and Security in East Asia and the Pacific. The conference was held at the University of the Philippines, a central location for NDF activity. The conference coincided with a wave of protests and demonstrations throughout the Philippines, duly noted by *Pravda* (4 December).

Leif Rosenberger
Defense Intelligence Agency

Sri Lanka

Population. 15,925,000
Party. Communist Party of Sri Lanka (CPSL)
Founded. 1943
Membership. 6,000 (estimated)
Secretary General. Kattorge P. Silva
Politburo. 11 members, including K. P. Silva (secretary general) and Pieter Keuneman (president)
Central Committee. 50 members
Status. Legal
Last Congress. Twelfth, 27–29 January 1984, in Colombo
Last Election. 1977, 1.9 percent, 1 of 168 representatives
Auxiliary Organizations. Ceylon Federation of Trade Unions, Youth League, Women's Organization
Publications. *Aththa*, *Mawbima*, *Deshabimani*, *Forward* (journal)

Ethnic conflict continued to be the overriding concern in Sri Lanka. The Twelfth Congress of the pro-Moscow CPSL met in January, after being delayed by the July 1983 communal violence and consequent banning of three leftist parties, including the CPSL. Charges against the CPSL, however, were dropped three months later.

The congress produced no major changes in senior leadership or policies. A presidium consisting of K. P. Silva, Pieter Keuneman, M. G. Mendis (a trade union leader), A. Vaidyalingam (a member of Sri Lanka's minority Tamil community), and Sarath Muttetuwegama (member of parliament) conducted the proceedings. The congress elected a new Central Committee, Control Commission, and Auditing Commission. (The new eleven-member Political Bureau was elected in February [*Pravda*, 6 February].) A new party constitution was adopted that upgraded and consolidated previous provisions and provided for new levels of party organization, according to K. P. Silva (*WMR*, August).

On party matters the congress recognized the continuing disarray within the leftist movement and the "relatively weak position of the working class movement," according to Silva's review. It also concluded that "the fight to build greater cohesion and unity of the left movement will be . . . protracted," but the CPSL should lead the struggle "to unite the left and democratic forces." United action with former prime minister Sirimavo Bandaranaike's Sri Lanka Freedom Party (SLFP) was "possible and necessary" but complicated by a split in the SLFP. A priority task for the CPSL itself will be "strengthening the party politically, organisationally and ideologically so that its capacity will correspond . . . to its political influence." The party will concentrate on building its influence among the working class, but will also expand efforts among the peasantry. (Ibid.)

In an appeal to the people of Sri Lanka, the congress declared that the country faced "the biggest threat to its political independence, its sovereignty, its territorial integrity, and the unity of its multiracial people" since independence (*New Age*, 19 February). The CPSL saw the conservative United National Party (UNP) government and the United States as the sources of the threat and strongly attacked them in various reports and resolutions.

In assessing domestic developments, the CPSL charged the UNP with abuse of emergency powers and feared the possibility of a military government. The UNP's free-market economic policies and cooperation with international aid organizations, such as the International Bank for Reconstruction and Development, were termed a "disaster." The party asserted there had been no real economic growth in key areas like the plantation sector, although tourism and the service trades had developed. A special resolution on "national harmony" was passed on the continuing crisis between the Sinhalese majority and Tamil minority, which had erupted during 1983 in the most severe communal violence in decades. Citing the government's failure to resolve Tamil grievances, the congress, in fact, accused the UNP of "fanning" ethnic strife. The CPSL decided to campaign for (1) reduction of the armed forces in the predominantly Tamil northern and eastern regions, (2) withdrawal of certain emergency regulations, (3) repeal of the Prevention of Terrorism Act, and (4) amnesty for Tamil militants. (Ibid.)

Early in the year Pieter Keuneman also commented on this issue. The CPSL approach, he stated, has been based on both the recognition of Sri Lanka's territorial unity and the Tamils' right to self-determination. The solution should be a united country with regional autonomy for the Tamils. Keuneman said the demand for a separate state enjoys only limited support among the Tamils. He also ridiculed the government's "clumsy" attempt to blame the Communists for the July 1983 riots. (*WMR*, February.)

The communal crisis has clearly been the major preoccupation in Sri Lanka this year. Although political talks sponsored by President J. R. Jayewardene and encouraged by Indian mediation began in January, young Tamil extremists have stepped up their guerrilla campaign for a separate state in northern Sri Lanka. Little progress toward a solution was apparent by the end of the year.

The All-Party Conference to seek a solution to the ethnic conflict convened on 10 January in Colombo. Several political parties and religious delegations participated in meetings of the conference during the year, including the UNP; the Tamil United Liberation Front (TULF), the leading Tamil party; the CPSL; and the Trotskyist Lanka Sama Samaja Party (LSSP). Pieter Keuneman was elected to the committee responsible for the conference's communiqués. (*FBIS*, 10 January.) Mrs. Bandaranaike's SLFP, however, has boycotted the conference and demanded restoration of her civil rights, which were taken away for alleged abuse of power.

President Jayewardene told a meeting of the conference on 30 September that he would draft legislation based on proposals presented. The UNP offered a second chamber of parliament and a stronger system of local government. This was being considered by the TULF in November, although its leader had earlier described the conference as "an exercise in futility." (*FEER*, 18 October; *Economist*, London, 1 December.)

The political negotiations, however, were overshadowed, by the increased activity of the militant Tamil separatists. These militant forces are divided into a number of guerrilla groups, several of whom have operational headquarters in Madras, on India's southeastern coast and within India's own Tamil region. All profess socialism and advocate armed struggle to achieve a separate Tamil state, but differ on strategy. The government estimates the number of Tamil guerrillas in Sri Lanka at 300–500; other estimates of the number range upward to 2,000. Overseas Tamil communities in Europe, the United States, Canada, and Australia provide financial support. Some of the leading Tamil groups have links with the Palestine Liberation Organization, and North Korea has reportedly given aid. (*FEER*, 26 April, 20 September.)

The largest group is the Liberation Tigers of Tamil Eelam, whose official spokesman, A. S. Balasingham, commented in Madras: "We have taken up arms after 35 years in which all peaceful, democratic processes have been exhausted," he said, and "have to launch an armed revolutionary struggle." (Tamils generally believe they are treated as second-class citizens and face discrimination in language, education, and jobs.) This would show the government, he added, that it could not solve the problem through "military repression." Balasingham claimed that they wanted a united state, but their "basic demands" had been rejected by Sinhalese-dominated governments. (Ibid., 20 September.)

In the UNP government's view this is not a conflict between Sinhalese and Tamils, but a threat to the country's unity and sovereignty. President Jayewardene declared on 9 April that terrorists were attempting to effect "a communist revolution" and were supported by "international agencies" (*FBIS*, 10 April). The government, with its large parliamentary majority, periodically extended the state of emergency over the objections of the small group of opposition representatives, including the sole CPSL member. The UNP set up a surveillance zone in the narrow waters between Sri Lanka and India, and its air and naval forces worked to interdict movements between the two countries by the militants.

The most frequent guerrilla targets were banks and police and security forces. In May, however, an American couple was kidnapped in northern Sri Lanka. They were released a few days later, due largely to Indian government pressure on the Tamil extremists using India as a sanctuary (*CSM*, 22 May). Later in the year the guerrilla attacks escalated, and in November, 24 policemen were killed in a bombing, the largest single government loss since the separatist campaign was launched. Within the next two weeks, four civilian settlements were attacked and nearly a hundred Sinhalese killed, raising fears of another Sinhalese backlash like the 1983 riots (*FEER*, 6 and 13 December).

In the international sphere, the Sri Lanka government's relations with the Soviet Union remained correct in spite of suspicions of communist involvement in the Tamil conflict. Jayewardene sent a representative to Yuri Andropov's funeral in February, and a protocol on scientific and cultural exchanges was signed in April. Relations with the United States continued to be very good and were marked by an official visit by Jayewardene in June. He had earlier agreed to allow the United States to upgrade its Voice of America transmission facility. He was also planning a state visit during the year to China to underline the good relations between the two states.

The pro-Moscow CPSL, for its part, continued to express strong support for Soviet policies and "appreciated highly [Soviet efforts] towards curbing the nuclear arms race." The congress received messages from the Soviet, Bulgarian, and 60 other "fraternal parties." (*WMR*, August.) In April Silva traveled to Moscow to receive an award, the Order of Friendship of the Peoples.

The congress, on the other hand, harshly criticized the United States on various issues. A special resolution on the nuclear threat laid the blame on "US imperialism." The congress also supported mass campaigns against U.S. "nuclearisation of the Indian Ocean." The party condemned U.S. actions in Grenada, Lebanon, and Central America as well as the Voice of America agreement. (Ibid.)

Barbara Reid
Charlottesville, Virginia

Thailand

Population. 51,724,000
Party. Communist Party of Thailand (CPT)
Founded. 1942
Membership. 1,200–1,500
Secretary General. No data (Virat Angkhathavorn, active leader)
Leading Bodies. No data
Status. Illegal
Last Congress. Fifth, February 1984, clandestine (reported only by Thai government, no announcement by party [*FBIS*, 17 February])
Last Election. N/a
Auxiliary Organizations. No data
Publications. None

The numerous defections of communist insurgents in Thailand during the past five years have led the Thai government to proclaim total victory over the Communist Party of Thailand (CPT). In 1984 Supreme Commander and Army Commander-in-Chief Gen. Arthit Kamlang-ek and Deputy Army Chief of Staff Lt. Gen. Chawalit Yongchaiyut both announced the collapse of the insurgent group. In October, Chawalit stated that the CPT will never again be able to pose an armed threat to the country.

General Chawalit reported that the largest remnants of the CPT are now in the south, with about 1,200 to 1,500 armed insurgents. In the north he estimated that only between 50 and 80 insurgents are left and in the northeast only 30 to 40 insurgents are active. Lt. Gen. Chuthai Saengthawip, chief of staff for information attached to the Internal Security Operations Command, said in March that only about 1,200 armed insurgents were left in the country. He said that there were 100–200 insurgents left in the central region, 200 in the northeast, another 200 in the north, and between 300 and 400 in the south. These divergent numbers are consistent with government proclamations of the past two years about the demise of the CPT.

The general decline of CPT in 1983 has continued through 1984, with the collapse of the united front, the defection of cadres and leaders, the loss of guerrilla bases, and the reduction of support from outside powers. The reasons for the loss of support for the CPT are both internal and external. The government has continued its counterinsurgency strategy of "politics over military," the central theme of Order No. 65/2525 decreed by Prime Minister Prem Tinsulanond in 1982. The strategy emphasizes improved effectiveness of government officials, a large-scale development program for the impoverished areas of the nation, and an amnesty program that has persuaded thousands of insurgents to defect. The loss of material support from both China and Vietnam has also contributed to the demise of the CPT. Kampuchea and Laos were increasingly inaccessible, cutting Thai insurgents off from former sanctuaries and supply sources.

In 1984 a series of raids by government authorities undermined the party's strength. On 2 July Internal Security Operations Command and Special Branch police agents arrested several CPT Central Committee members in Bangkok and charged them with plotting to overthrow the government with foreign support. The raid produced evidence that the CPT had been requesting aid from Irish Republican Army sources in England for urban terrorist operations.

The most famous persons arrested were Pirun Chatwanichkul (37) and his wife, Chontira (37), both Central Committee members and leading intellectuals. Pirun disclosed that he had remained in the jungle because of his admiration for CPT Politburo member Virat Angkhathavorn, who reportedly controls the party's finances. Virat had put Pirun and Chontira in charge of improving the image of the CPT by producing propaganda materials, establishing contacts with CPT fronts, and formulating a new CPT foreign policy.

On 11 July a second raid resulted in the arrest of university lecturer Dr. Preecha Piempongsarn and journalist Chatcharin Chaiwat on charges of assisting a communist organization. On 17 July the arrest of alleged CPT member Lert Chaichamorn brought to nineteen the number of CPT members detained in just one month. These arrests were controversial because they seemed to contradict the government's policy of amnesty. Government spokesmen argued that the arrests were justified because there was evidence that the Bangkok CPT cell had been seeking new means of support from Vietnam, Moscow, and the Irish Republican Army.

The arrests were made, according to Special Branch police investigators, to prevent the CPT from switching its strategy to urban activities. General Arthit and Prime Minister Prem announced that the raids were limited and did not represent a change in the overall counterinsurgency policy of politics over military, but were necessary to prevent stepped-up subversion that could have led to an outbreak of urban terrorism.

The arrest of Kasetsart University Professor Preecha caused the most controversy because he is the son of former deputy prime minister Sawet Piempongsarn. Preecha was granted freedom from prosecution under Article 17 of the Anticommunist Act by agreeing to undergo reindoctrination. Preecha had been arrested following surveillance of Pirun and Chontira, who were found to have been in contact with Preecha. Investigators determined that Preecha had had CPT contacts in southern Thailand while working for the National Economic and Social Development Board. (*FEER*, 15 November.)

Shortly before his arrest in July, Pirun gave an interview to the Thai weekly magazine *Arthit*, which was reprinted in *TIC News* (July). Pirun admitted that in the past the CPT had made mistakes in its political strategy and operational procedures.

Pirun reported that a new system had been introduced to correct these mistakes by assuring that leading party positions would be filled through elections rather than by seniority. He stated that the age range of the Central Committee members had changed. Now 20 percent of the committee was composed of former leading members who were 60 years and older, 20 percent were newcomers who were 30–40 years, and 60 percent were in the 40–60 year range. Special Branch commander Maj. Gen. Kasem Saengmit responded to Pirun's analysis by stating that the party remained in the hands of the old guard and that it is wishful thinking for party "progressives" to expect the old-guard leadership to change its basic approach. The general noted that the old-guard Maoists were so indoctrinated with Chinese revolutionary thinking that they have never deviated from it. (*FEER*, 19 July.)

Pirun noted that the CPT members had wrongly evaluated Thailand's internal stability following the 6 October 1976 military coup. Then most members had believed the nation was ripe for revolution. The government's strategy of politics over military, however, had caught the party by surprise and undermined its propaganda message of oppression of the people.

Pirun stated that the former CPT foreign policy based on China's Three World Theory had been refuted at the Fourth Party Congress in 1982. Instead, the United States had been singled out as the international enemy, and the Soviet Union and Vietnam were accepted as allies despite some differences over theory and policy. Pirun specifically referred to the party's disagreement with Vietnam's invasion of Kampuchea and the severing of relations between the Lao government and the CPT.

The Insurgency. Insurgency activity in the south decreased markedly in 1984. The Moslem separatist movement consists of several groups that have not yet created a common front. The degree of communist involvement in the separatist groups differs. The movement in Pattani, Yala, Narathiwat, and Satun, the four southernmost provinces (where 75–80 percent of the population is Moslem), received a blow in November when about a hundred separatists defected to the government. Armed attacks by insurgents were reduced to defensive operations with fighting occurring only when army troops attacked guerrilla bases first.

Much of the decrease in insurgency activity in the south had been attributed to the policies and

leadership of Gen. Harn Linanond, the former commander of the southern-based Thai Fourth Army, who left his post in October 1983 to enter politics. His popular program of *tai rom yen* (peaceful south) had galvanized the population to struggle against communist and Moslem insurgents. Harn was popular with southern Thais but not with Malaysian authorities, who resented his criticism of the Malaysians' lack of support for Thai moves against Moslem separatists. Harn's successor, Lt. Gen. Wanchai Chitchamnong, established smoother relations with the Malaysians, although it is not yet clear how the closer ties will affect insurgent activity. There were no joint operations by Malaysian and Thai troops in 1984 as there had been before Harn took over.

The insurgency situation in the northeast is complicated by the rise of a faction of the CPT known as Pak Mai (New Party). Pak Mai is a pro-Soviet movement formed in 1978 and now supported by Lao and Vietnamese forces. Laos is the operating base and training center for the movement, according to Maj. Gen. Michai Nakunkit, commander of the Region Two Border Patrol Police. Officially known as the Thai People's Revolutionary Movement, it has been active in the areas of Loei, Nong Khai, Mukdahan, and Ubon Ratchathani. General Michai reported that Laos is supporting the movement by helping operate 25 bases and fifteen training centers for Pak Mai members. Soviet and Vietnamese military instructors were reported to have been training recruits in the Tha Kaek area of Laos.

The Pak Mai movement ostensibly provides a base for Soviet involvement in Thai insurgency and Thai communism. Heretofore, the major foreign influence on the CPT was China, and there was little Soviet involvement. With Soviet financial help through Vietnam and Laos, Pak Mai is in the recruitment stage. It is not yet well organized, lacks a mass following, and is capable of infiltrating no more than 200 insurgents into Thailand's northeast.

According to Pak Mai leaders, Thailand is under the domination of monopoly capitalists. This interpretation parallels that reached at the CPT Fourth Congress, which changed the definition of Thai society from semifeudal, semicolonialist to semicolonial, semicapitalist. The movement attempts to recruit intellectuals, disaffected ethnic Lao and Vietnamese populations in the northeast, and urban laborers as well as peasants. (Ibid., 6 December.)

Counterinsurgency specialists in Bangkok believe that former Thai national assemblyman Bunyen Worthong, a former member of the Socialist Party of Thailand, heads the Pak Mai. He is a graduate of Thammasat University and the University of Indiana, where he received a master's degree. Although there is little information on the group, Thai analysts speculate that the party structure will be made up of a nine-person politburo and a larger central committee.

Foreign Relations. In 1984 Thailand's relations with Vietnam continued to be strained. A series of conflicts on the Kampuchean border centering on Khmer rebel camps exacerbated Thai-Vietnamese relations. Vietnam claimed that the incursions were aimed at knocking out Khmer Rouge complexes that served as bases for guerrilla forays into Kampuchea. On 26 December Vietnamese troops overran the largest rebel camp in Kampuchea, causing hundreds of casualties and sending an estimated 63,000 civilians into Thailand. The attacks focused on the anticommunist Khmer People's National Liberation Front.

Relations with Laos were also contentious in 1984 because of a dispute over three villages on the Thai-Laotian border claimed by both nations. The Thais claim that the villages of Ban Mai, Ban Savang, and Ban Klang are in Thailand's Uttaradit province; Laos claims these villages have been part of its Sayaboury province for almost 80 years.

Thailand charged that Vietnam was behind the conflict to "divert world attention from its military occupation of Kampuchea." The ruling Lao People's Revolutionary Party accused Thailand of destroying the friendship between the two countries and said that Bangkok's attitude was dominated by an "ultra-rightist military gang who were manipulated by the Chinese hegemonists and expansionists and the US imperialists" (ibid., 16 October). By the end of the year, the dispute between Thailand and Laos had not been settled, although a threat to Thailand's candidacy for membership on the U.N. Security Council on the part of Laos's communist allies fell through when Thailand was elected to the position.

Thailand and the United States have supported the policies of the Association of Southeast Asian Nations to isolate Vietnam, to support the Kampuchean rebels against the Heng Samrin regime in Phnom Penh, and to bring world opinion to denounce Soviet-Vietnamese aggression. These policies have strengthened Thailand's relationship with the government of the People's Republic of China, which also opposes the Vietnamese-dominated regime of Heng Samrin. The Thai military no longer see China as the principal security threat.

Clark D. Neher
Northern Illinois University

Vietnam

Population. 59,030,000
Party. Vietnamese Communist Party (Dang Cong San Viet Nam; VCP)
Founded. 1930 (as Indochinese Communist Party)
Membership. 1,730,214 (claimed)
Chairman. Vacant since death of Ho Chi Minh
Secretary General. Le Duan
Politburo. 13 full members: Le Duan, Truong Chinh (president, Council of State), Pham Van Dong (chairman, Council of Ministers), Pham Hung, Le Duc Tho, Sen. Gen. Van Tien Dung (defense minister), Sen. Gen. Chu Huy Man (vice-president, Council of State), To Huu, Vo Chi Cong, Vo Van

Kiet, Do Muoi, Le Duc Anh, Nguyen Duc Tam; 2 alternate members: Nguyen Co Thach (foreign minister), Dong Sy Nguyen

Secretariat. 10 members: Le Duan, Le Duc Tho, Vo Chi Cong, Nguyen Duc Tam, Nguyen Lam, Le Quang Dao, Hoang Tung, Nguyen Thanh Binh, Tran Kien, Tran Xuan Bach

Central Committee. 116 full and 36 alternate members

Status. Ruling party

Last Congress. Fifth, 27–31 March 1982, in Hanoi

Last Election. 1981, for Seventh National Assembly, 97.96 percent, 496 of 614, with all candidates VCP endorsed

Auxiliary Organizations. Fatherland Front (Huynh Tan Phat, president); Ho Chi Minh Communist Youth Union (Vu Mao, secretary general)

Publications. *Nhan Dan* (The people), VCP daily; *Tap Chi Cong San* (Communist review), VCP theoretical monthly; *Quan Doi Nhan Dan* (People's army), army newspaper

Party Internal Affairs and Leadership. The VCP's aged Politburo-level leadership underwent no change in 1984, nor was there any appreciable change at the Central Committee level just below it. This meant that government by gerontocracy in Vietnam remained unchanged. And that, in turn, meant further perpetuation of the long inadequate party-state ruling apparat: institutions that are over-organized, excessively centralized, full of cross-purposes smothering initiative and militating against innovation or flexibility in solving the country's many social, economic, and external problems.

There were, as in years past, rumors that the party's top leadership would address the central issue, generational transfer of leadership. Beginning in September, a persistent rumor in Hanoi was that the next (sixth) party congress would be held in advance of its scheduled date of 1978 (every five years according to party bylaws), possibly as early as spring of 1985, for the purpose, the rumors continued, to announce the retirement of many overaged leaders and to introduce their younger replacements. The Politburo twice has been on the verge of such a move—in late 1976 and again in 1982—only to pull back at the last moment with the argument that the time was not propitious for such a move, which would come as soon as conditions in the country improved.

The average age of the fifteen men on the Politburo is 70 (that of the Central Committee is about 65). There must eventually be a handing over of the reins of power to the next generation. If this is not done in a deliberate and orderly manner, no one can be sure of the sort of government that will follow, but inexorable as is the onset of change, little is being done to prepare for it. Transitional leaders are not being developed. No young men are seen being groomed for eventual top leadership. Vietnam will

have to stumble across the generational gap to new leadership.

The VCP Politburo has a greater concentration of power than perhaps any other ruling body in the world, communist or noncommunist. There is no significant outside challenge to its authority, either institutional, as in the USSR, or geographic, as in China. The men of the Politburo reign supreme. This is not to say they are free agents whose every wish is an automatic command to the rest of the Vietnamese. On the contrary, politics, a very high order of politics, marks their decisionmaking. Generally, it is accepted that the Politburo works under an operational code of collective leadership, with the rule that no decision is taken that is not tolerable to all members. A decision may be strongly disliked by a single member, but it may not be a total anathema to him. Collective leadership is practiced, not out of consideration for individual ego, but as an expression of the internal politics within each of the constituencies of the thirteen members. Le Duan, for example, speaks for the party cadre administrative apparat; Pham Van Dong for the bureaucracy; Gen. Van Tien Dung for the Armed Forces; Truong Chinh for the mass organizations and the National Assembly; Pham Hung for the security apparatus; Le Duc Tho for the technocrat cadres. Thus the Politburo is seen not as a small group of leaders debating personal position, but a factionalized arena where the chief representatives of the country's major institutions battle out and ultimately determine the most important policies for the state and the society. Each Politburo member has a constituency that he runs, but that also constrains him and fixes the policy positions he must take on any given issue before the Politburo.

Pressure on these men, and in the past decade it has been extraordinary, could be a centrifugal force. But to date pressure has united them, partly because of the natural tendency to close ranks under fire, partly because of close lifelong relationships and overlapping interests, and partly because of the leadership's overriding interest in maintaining political equilibrium. An altered Politburo membership would be a different matter. Should one or several key members die or become incapacitated, a new dynamic would go into effect, with unpredictable developments. The result could be an extreme, even bloody, struggle for power among the surviving members, or between young Turk challengers and the Politburo survivors.

Domestic Affairs. The backdrop against which party political infighting was conducted during 1984 included (1) a somewhat improved general economic condition, particularly in the all-important agricultural sector—food production increased, possibly enough to make the country self-sufficient for the first time in modern history; (2) the war in Kampuchea, which the resistance has managed to turn into a protracted conflict, continued indecisively but at a level that did not appear to place excessive strain on Vietnam; (3) continued social fragmentation in Vietnam as the party chose to serve contradictory economic and ideological interests with respect to its former southern enemy; and (4) isolation in the region—Vietnam faced undiminished Chinese hostility and opposition from the Association of Southeast Asian Nations (ASEAN).

The party's Sixth Plenum (of the Fifth Congress) met 3–10 July, with the sessions devoted chiefly to two economic matters: better management of the economic sector ("promoting the people's right of collective mastership over society, their creativeness and all possibilities of production establishments to reorganize production so as gradually to set up a new structure of economic management") and improvement of domestic trade by gaining better control over commodity/money flow ("to resolve a number of urgent problems related to goods circulation and distribution, especially markets, prices, and monetary, so as to correctly handle the problem of distribution in the national economy"). These guidelines were in the direction of the thinking of the pragmatist faction but probably did not represent a political victory over the ideologues so much as a mandatory response by the society to the pressing economic matters of the moment. (*FBIS*, 19 July.)

Do Muoi, considered to be the tsar of the Vietnamese economic rectification drive, made a lengthy speech at the Sixth Plenum on "rearranging production and renewing the industrial management apparatus." His thesis was the need for "decentralized management," the issue that has plagued Marxist economic systems everywhere—namely, the trade-off between planning and control at the center and incentive and latitude for production management at the farm or factory level. Recent moves to allocate authority down the line threaten the center's control, particularly in the domestic trade sector. Vietnam has in effect two trading systems operating simultaneously, the socialist trade system of the state or "organized" market and the nonsocialist trade system, which is of two types, the free market (indirect state controls or shared authority) and the black market (which is illegal but tolerated). The fear of many party influentials in Hanoi continued to be that the center would lose out in the competition fought on the "hot battlefront of distribution and circulation," as it is termed. The center's chief weapon in enforcing its decisions has been what is called the quota system, a form of subsidy. Do Muoi indicated it has not worked well. The Do Muoi address was published by *Nhan Dan* on 15 August (*JPRS*, 84–132; *FBIS*, 20 and 23 August).

Post–Sixth Plenum party activity took on the character of renewed determination by the party to exert itself as the central and most dynamic force in the drive to lift the country by its economic bootstraps. This was no easy matter since the thrust of policy was to approach problems pragmatically rather than ideologically, to "allow the logic of the situation" to determine, for example, how much more rice might be grown. But the party's intent clearly was to maintain direct and firm leadership of the economic sector. Its main high-level instrument for this was the Central Economic Organs Bloc, formed in late 1983, which came into its own in 1984—in effect an economic task force composed of representatives of party organizations in fifteen central state economic organs. Chaired by Nguyen Lam, head of the Central Committee's Economic Department, the block set up its own secretariat and scheduled a "congress" to be held each July. Officially, it is defined as a coordination instrument, but it does economic trouble-shooting and also appears to be charged with certain defense tasks, for instance, ensuring that the army's needs in Kampuchea are promptly met.

An important directive was issued in October (*FBIS*, 19 October) governing basic-level party cadre work and designed to "raise the combativeness and the quality of leadership" at the grass-roots party organization in state-run economic units. It reflected what was a clear trend throughout the year, the drive to renovate and reinvigorate basic-level party organizations. The focus is on the young and on weeding out deadwood among party members and cadres.

As the directive suggested, a good deal of the day-to-day activity of party cadres during the year was given over to efforts to integrate the party more deeply into routine economic activity, which in Vietnam chiefly means agricultural activity since this is where about 85 percent of the country's work force is found.

The code word here is "control," and the institution involved is the party's Control Committee system. This is a vast mechanism—comprising nearly 100,000 party "control cadres" (or one out of every seventeen party members), organized into some 400 control committees that operate at the urban ward and district levels and are charged with monitoring basic-level economic activity to ensure adherence to policy directives sent down from Hanoi (such activity is supervised by Tran Kien and the Central Committee's Party Control Committee). This is all on the party side; a similar apparat, an inspection system (directed by Bui Quang Tao), operates on the state side.

Asserting party centrality in the economic system at the rice-roots level in the name of control thus was one of the clearly identifiable trends within the party in Vietnam during the year. It was made in the name of higher agricultural productivity and greater efficiency in domestic trade and to establish that the party cadre can contribute to the desired goal of greater efficiency of the economic sector. This claim served the interests of the pragmatic factions of the party; the ideological factions also were served with the contention that emphasis on party control has simply been redefined, from the once exclusive control by the center in Hanoi to a more decentralized system.

A second major trend in party organization concerned the concept of the district as the central or all-important operational element for both party and state. This idea was unveiled first in 1976 in the flush of wartime victory, but after a year or so of experiment it came to be considered as overly ambitious and was scaled down to the more manageable New Economic Zone (NEZ) program. It was an idea that both ideologue and pragmatist could embrace, although for different reasons. Now, apparently because of factional infighting within the party, it is being revived.

The "district concept" is that the rural demographic structure of Vietnam must be basically altered by simultaneously redistributing and concentrating the rural population—hence the seeming oxymoron "rural urbanization." It calls for villagers now living in some 160,000 Vietnamese hamlets to be "rearranged" into some 20,000 new or existing district-sized "agricultural" towns or "centralized" villages. By the year 2000—when the planners say Vietnam's population will be at least 100 million—the population density is to be equalized in terms of productive farmland, averaging about nine persons per hectare in the north and seven per hectare in the south. The idea stems from the ideological principle of "mass concept," sometimes described by outsiders as the Red Ant syndrome. In industry, as well as in agriculture, the Hanoi leaders are driven by the idea of large-scale production, of consolidation and amalgamation, of combining the many small into the few large. Their fundamental assumption is that bigger is better, that the larger a factory or state farm the more efficient it will be, and the better off society will be for having created it.

The official grand dream is to eliminate the village and replace it with farm-factory towns. This means that most Vietnamese eventually will be relocated. If this program is pressed to completion, as the leadership is now again indicating, it is a safe estimate that 40 million people eventually will be moved to a new home. City dwellers would be moved to rural areas, villagers to agricultural towns, and the party elite would remain in place. On a per capita basis there has never been anything so ambitious in Vietnam. The program would have a more profound effect on Vietnam than anything that has ever happened in its long history.

Party and state personnel changes during the year were few. Nguyen Huu Thu, a Central Committee member and state minister, was relieved as secretary general of the Council of Ministers and as director of the Council of Ministers Office on 29 May. He was also stripped of his ministerial rank. No reason was given for the action. His replacement is Doan Trong Truyen, previously chairman of the State Pricing Commission.

Deaths during the year included Bui Thanh Khiet, 60, Central Committee member and senior colonel in the People's Army of Vietnam (PAVN), on 7 January; Dang Van Dinh (pen name Dan Hong), editor of the PAVN newspaper *Quan Doi Nhan Dan*, on 16 February; Nguyen Dang (party name Nam Trung), 56, Central Committee member from Cuu Long province, on 7 April; and Maj. Gen. Luong Van Nho, 69, deputy commander, 7th PAVN Military Region, on 11 August.

Front Organizations. The Fatherland Front remained the major "umbrella" of sociopolitical organizations in Vietnam, implemented through the mechanism of the National Assembly and always under close party supervision.

One of the major elements of the Fatherland Front, the Vietnam Confederation of Trade Unions (VCTU), came in for high-level attention. A Politburo order in July fixed 28 July 1929 as the VCTU's official formation date. That was the date the Bac Ky Confederation of Red Trade Unions was founded in Hanoi, with Nguyen Duc Khanh as its first president; later it operated under the leadership of the Indochinese Communist Party.

International Views, Positions, and Activities. Vietnam remained largely isolated from most of the world during 1984, with few true or reliable friends—the USSR and Cuba being the most dependable—and surrounded locally by enemies.

Vietnam's key foreign ally remains the USSR. Relations here, both state-to-state and party-to-party, continued to deepen during the year. The most important developments along the Hanoi-Moscow axis seemed to relate to military or security affairs.

Defense Minister Sen. Gen. Van Tien Dung traveled at least twice to Moscow during the year to confer with Soviet defense minister Marshal Dimitri Ustinov (now deceased). The visits were linked to the Vietnam-China border war and to PAVN logistical needs in the protracted Kampuchea campaign. Soviet military aid in the 1980s has been running at an estimated U.S. $1 billion per year (about three times the yearly average of Soviet aid to North Vietnam during the Vietnam war) and is of the costly item type—MiG fighter planes, helicopters, naval vessels, and missiles. At least nine Badger bombers are now believed to be stationed at Camranh Bay and about 30 Soviet war vessels now operate out of its port.

In mid-April, as part of a Pacific-wide Soviet naval exercise, some 400 Soviet naval-infantry troops (similar to U.S. Marines) equipped with 50 armored personnel carriers staged, together with PAVN forces, amphibious landing maneuvers along the central Vietnam coast a hundred miles south of Haiphong. Nine Soviet warships were employed in the exercise, including a Kiev-class aircraft carrier. The exercise was denounced by Beijing and protested by Bangkok as a threat to Thailand and the region. Visiting Vietnam at the same time was a Soviet military delegation headed by Lt. Gen. A. N. Agafonov.

In August the Western press reported that the USSR had offered Vietnam access to its main technical information–processing center in Moscow through a satellite communications link with a ground station in Hanoi. Earlier, in February, the USSR conferred the Order of the Red Star on five PAVN generals "as an expression of respect" for their victories in the Viet Minh and Vietnam wars.

Secretary General Le Duan and Premier Pham Van Dong went to Moscow in early June to attend the socialist world's economic summit, the ten-nation conference of the Council for Mutual Economic Assistance (CMEA). Earlier, in January, at a session of the CMEA Executive Committee in Moscow (Tran Quynh representing Vietnam), a "package" aid agreement designed to improve food production in Vietnam and elsewhere was discussed. In August Hanoi reported that the CMEA had approved a proposal to increase assistance in the economic development of Vietnam. CMEA factories built in the past several years now account for 82 percent of Vietnam's die-cutting work, 35 percent of its electricity, and 20 percent of its superphosphate production. Some 60,000 Vietnamese technicians were in work-study programs in CMEA countries (USSR, Bulgaria, East Germany, and Czechoslovakia) during the year. The Hanoi press reported in midyear that Vietnam and the USSR were carrying out long-range planning for the period "between now and the year 2000." Some 200 Soviet-aided projects were reported under way or recently completed. Trade between the two countries trebled under the present five-year plan (from 1980 to 1985), and a team of Soviet-Vietnamese petroleum technicians reported striking oil on the "southern continental shelf" (presumably off Vung Tau). Hanoi announced that a number of wells will be drilled to determine the size of the find.

During the Summer Olympics in Los Angeles, the Hanoi press devoted considerable space and time to negative coverage, with themes that the games were exploitive, dangerous to health, and, because of absentees, "not genuine." A team of twenty Vietnamese athletes led by Nguyen Van Trong (General Department for Physical Culture) went to Moscow in August to participate in the Friendship '84 Games, competing in sharpshooting, swimming, and track and field events.

Three days of official mourning were ordered throughout Vietnam to observe the death in February of Yuri Andropov; Truong Chinh led the party-state funeral delegation to Moscow. The previous month a delegation of VCP officials headed by Le Duc Binh, chief of the Central Committee Organizational Party Work section, had spent ten days in Moscow conferring with counterparts on cadre recruitment, training, and assignment.

Vietnamese-Chinese relations remained frozen at the cold war level throughout 1984. The border war continued unabated during the year, although it was marked by swings in military action and rhetoric. Each side steadily denounced the provocations and "crimes" of the other, made and denied charges, and presented inventories of shells fired, incursions launched, psychological warfare actions taken, and POWs captured (with "confessions"). China would accuse Vietnam of using "beguiling rhetoric"; Vietnam would accuse China of sophistry.

The Commission for Investigation of War Crimes Committed by Chinese Expansionists and Hegemonists released a lengthy communiqué in Hanoi in February that summarized Vietnam's chief grievances against China: (1) war preparations and permanent tension at borders and at sea; (2) a land-nibbling war on the northern border; (3) economic sabotage; (4) ideological sabotage and incitement to sedition; and (5) isolation of Vietnam internationally and refusal to resume negotiations. The Chinese reply spoke of Vietnamese "crimes" in Kampuchea and accused Vietnam's leaders of engaging in "anti-Chinese hysterics" chiefly to divert attention from their many policy failures.

Such military rationale as did seem to exist in the border war was designed to take the high ground. Artillery battles were most intense in two stretches of border, the Vi Zuyen and Yen Minh districts of Ha Tuyen province (50 percent of all Chinese shells fired, Vietnam said) and the Trang Dinh district of Lang Son province (25 percent). Shelling averaged 2,000 rounds per day through the summer, Hanoi said, some days reaching a total of 10,000. In an early August claim, Hanoi said it had inflicted 7,500 casualties on China ("enemy put out of action") in the previous five months.

Both sides identified the border war with larger issues, Hanoi saying the Chinese assault was part of

U.S.-Beijing strategy to stem the spread of communism, and China charging that Vietnamese action was a surrogate's contribution to the USSR's imperial ambitions in Asia. China also accused Vietnam of prolonging the festering border war as a means of poisoning Sino-Soviet relations. Hanoi repeatedly and stridently asserted that Moscow was fully behind Vietnam, implying the USSR could do nothing else but take this "principled stand."

On 10 May the Hanoi press noted briefly and without comment Moscow's abrupt postponement of a trip to Beijing by Soviet first deputy vice-premier Ivan Arkhipov. Elsewhere the action was interpreted as indicating, among other things, worsening Sino-Soviet relations aggravated by the Sino-Vietnamese border clashes. Moscow's handling of border actions was what might be called minimally correct. It duly reported various Vietnamese statements of grievance and criticized the Chinese. In what was probably its most authoritative statement (Tass, May 4), the USSR indicated it was confident Vietnam could handle the matter. Vietnamese spokesman Hoang Tung brought up the subject of the USSR-Vietnam treaty, which calls for consultations in event either party is under threat, while talking to foreign journalists on 5 May, by saying Hanoi has no intention of invoking the treaty.

Vietnam returned to what might be called a two-front war during the year—one with Thailand along the Thai-Kampuchean border and the other, noted above, along the China border.

The festering Thai border war exploded into major combat in northern Preah Vihear province in Kampuchea, then into Sisaket province (Thailand) in late March and continued sporadically during the rest of the year. It was marked by vitriolic verbal exchanges, diplomatic maneuvers among all countries of the region, and by a war of nerves between the two contenders and their associates, as well as by military action that left several hundred dead.

For the most part, military initiatives were by Vietnamese, with the Thais reacting and attempting to contain them. PAVN generals appear to believe that a seemingly endless border war will eventually pressure Bangkok into changing its policies with respect to Kampuchea and the refugees it is harboring. Vietnam's foreign minister, Nguyen Co Thach, was busy in the region and at the United Nations during the year, apparently dealing with the issues of a negotiated settlement in Kampuchea, but at year's end this had come to nothing, which may have been his intention. Meanwhile, the protracted conflict in Kampuchea continued with no foreseeable hope of settlement.

Biography. *Le Duc Tho.* Le Duc Tho is one of the five members of the "inner circle" of the ruling Politburo in Hanoi and is considered by many outsiders to be the cleverest (the other four are Le Duan, Truong Chinh, Pham Van Dong, and Pham Hung). Tho is highly adept at the *bung di* (faction-bashing) style of political infighting in Vietnam, influenced as it is by the Sinic political tradition.

Much of Tho's skill, and the reason for his political durability, comes from his long experience working with party cadres. As the chief figure in recruiting, training, and assigning the party's organizational or infrastructure cadres (who are more technicians than ideologues), he has for decades been in a unique position to build a constituency within the party able to withstand the challenges of more formidable opposing factions. As a result he has developed the reputation of a specialist on party organization, "infrastructure expert," theorist on organizational and agitprop work, and ideological watchdog.

Le Duc Tho (which is his revolutionary name) was born Phan Dinh Khai on 14 October 1910, in Dong Mac village, Nam Ha province, some 60 miles south of Hanoi, the son of a poor rural family. This is according to his official biography. French and other sources fix his birthday as 1911 or 1912, his birthplace as Thai Binh province, and his family's status as rural gentry, with his father serving the French colonial administration. The latter is more probable in view of the fact that Tho received a *baccalauréat* from a French *lycée*, unlikely at the time for a rural Vietnamese youth without French connections.

His official biography says he became a licensed electrician in 1928 and immediately became active in the Hanoi trade union movement. He joined the Indochinese Communist Party when it was founded in 1930.

In the party's first decade, Tho did covert organizational work as assistant to Truong Chinh and was jailed twice for his efforts. Apparently he was at Pac Bo for the formation of the Viet Minh in 1940 and with Ho Chi Minh when the provisional government was established in Hanoi in August 1945, the same year he became a member of the Central Committee.

During the Viet Minh war, Tho served in the south, where most party activity was organizational and involved agitprop work rather than combat. He was, at first, deputy to Le Duan, then succeeded him when Le Duan was recalled to Hanoi. Reportedly the two did not work well together then and have been political rivals ever since.

At the end of the Viet Minh war, Tho returned to Hanoi and to the party's senior training school, eventually becoming its director. He first appeared as a major party figure in 1960 when he authored the new party bylaws, which were approved at the Third Party Congress. In the 25 years since, Tho has been seen as the main mover and shaker in matters involving the all-important party administrative cadres. He held no state position during most of this period, the major exception being his assignment to Paris in 1968 as special adviser to the North Vietnamese delegation to the Paris talks, which were headed by his protégé Xuan Thuy.

Since the end of the Vietnam war, Tho has gone abroad frequently on goodwill missions. His current substantive work is believed to be developing the party apparat in the south and assisting in the rebuilding of the communist party in Kampuchea. Speculation in Hanoi in 1984 suggested he might eventually succeed Le Duan as party secretary general.

Tho is a stocky, wirehaired man who exudes supreme confidence, an articulate speaker, and an austere, brusque, and imperious person. He has been married at least twice and has two, possibly three, brothers in key party positions and at least one son, a mechanical engineer at a machine tool factory in Hanoi.

Douglas Pike
University of California, Berkeley

EASTERN EUROPE AND THE SOVIET UNION

Introduction

The year 1984 was, like 1983, one of uneasy transition in Soviet politics. The deaths of General Secretary Yuri Andropov in February and of Defense Minister Dimitri Ustinov in December underscored that the "old guard" that has ruled the Soviet Union for so many years will not be in power much longer. To Western observers it was apparent that the process of change initiated by the deaths of Mikhail Suslov and Leonid Brezhnev in 1982 was both deepening and expanding. Until a new, long-term leader takes power, however, Soviet politics and, of necessity, world politics will be in a state of uncertainty and flux.

Soviet Union. A Soviet joke has it that Konstantin Chernenko was chosen by his peers to succeed Yuri Andropov for two reasons: his advanced age and poor health. Chernenko swiftly accumulated the trappings of power, but, in light of his inevitable interim status, Western analysts began to concentrate their attention on his possible successors. While there remained a chance that yet another gerontocrat would be selected to replace Chernenko—perhaps Moscow party boss Viktor Grishin, age 70—one was inclined to agree with the opinion of former U.S. national security adviser Brent Scowcroft: "However long he [Chernenko] stays, the odds are now that the leadership will go to a younger generation" (*WSJ*, 24 September).

Following Andropov's death and throughout 1984, there were only two "younger" Soviet leaders with the necessary credentials—full membership in the Politburo and membership in the Secretariat—to succeed Chernenko: Mikhail Gorbachev, 53, and Grigori Romanov, 61. As the front-runner and "heir apparent," Gorbachev attracted considerable attention from Western analysts, though they cautioned that only one heir apparent, Brezhnev, had succeeded previously and then under unusual circumstances. Gorbachev's unquestionable status as a reformer, at least in the agricultural and economic spheres, added to his interest and allure. After a month-long visit to the Soviet Union, former Moscow correspondent Robert Kaiser reported: "Gorbachev has asked economists for briefings on the reforms designed by Pyotr Stolypin, Czar Nicholas II's enlightened prime minister, who encouraged entrepreneurship among the peasants, and on Lenin's New Economic Policy, or NEP . . . According to some reports, Gorbachev has overseen drafting a new variant on the NEP that he would like to implement now, making room for much more private enterprise in the private sector and in agriculture." (*WP*, 23 September.) During the year, Gorbachev unambiguously allied himself with the cause of economic and agricultural reform, something that may have almost cost him his job.

The order of speeches by the leadership preceding the elections to the Supreme Soviet, held on 4 March, showed that Gorbachev ranked third in the Kremlin hierarchy, behind only Chernenko and the chairman of the Council of Ministers, Nikolai Tikhonov. At Defense Minister Ustinov's funeral in late December, Gorbachev again was third in the pecking order. In between these events, however—especially during the period September-November—Gorbachev's fortunes dimmed, and it has been suggested that his position was endangered.

In July, Chernenko left Moscow for seven weeks of vacation and recuperation, during which his name seldom appeared in the Soviet press. Gorbachev, by contrast, remained visibly active during the time Chernenko was out of the public eye. In early September, Chernenko returned to Moscow, and a flurry of unusual events began to occur. First, and most dramatically, there was the removal of Nikolai Ogarkov as armed forces chief of staff. Then there took place an incomprehensibly lavish funeral for an obscure deputy minister, Leonid Kostandov. In late October, a long-awaited Central Committee plenum devoted to agriculture was held. Surprisingly, the central address was given not by Gorbachev, who was in charge of agriculture, but by Tikhonov; Chernenko also spoke on the occasion. The policy adopted at the plenum— an expansion of land reclamation—directly contradicted the "intensive agriculture" advocated by Gorbachev and represented a setback for his policies.

In mid-November, Gorbachev was reportedly absent from a Politburo meeting that endorsed the economic plan and budget for 1985; the meeting was addressed by Chernenko. During this period, Romanov temporarily surged past Gorbachev in Kremlin lineups (see, for example, the 19 October issue of *Pravda*). Foreign observers even speculated that Gorbachev had lost the agricultural portfolio.

The seemingly emphatic rejection of Gorbachev's policies coincided with a crackdown on Soviet economists, spearheaded by articles in *Kommunist*, the arbiter and touchstone of Marxist-Leninist orthodoxy. In September and November, *Kommunist* assailed the ideas of economist Evgeni Ambartsumov, contained in an article in the April issue of *Voprosy istorii* (Problems of history), in which the author had called for an extension of the role of private enterprise in the Soviet economy and cited the NEP as a model. In October, the prestigious journal *Voprosy filosofii* (Problems of philosophy) was forced to admit "serious errors" in its editorial policy. Earlier it had published a controversial piece by Anatoli Butenko, head of a sector of the Institute of the Economics of the World Socialist System of the USSR Academy of Sciences, in which the author warned that "antagonistic contradictions" could arise if the Soviet Union did not modernize its economy. Events in Poland were explicitly cited as a warning. Two important articles advocating maximum economic decentralization, by Academician Abel Aganbegyan, director of the Institute of Economics and Organization of Industrial Production of the Siberian department of the Academy of Sciences, appeared in late August in the newspaper *Trud* (Labor).

The clash between reformers and dogmatists seemed to have ended in a clear-cut victory for the dogmatists. But in December, Gorbachev rebounded with perhaps his most important speech to date. The occasion for this address was a Moscow conference devoted to ideology, intended as a follow-up to the "benchmark" conference of June 1983 at which Chernenko, then the secretary for ideology, gave the keynote address. It should be noted that Chernenko and Gorbachev engaged throughout much of 1984 in a tug-of-war over the position of ideological secretary. In March, *Pravda* editor Viktor Afanasyev told a Swedish reporter that Chernenko, rather than second secretary Gorbachev, was seeing to ideology (*FBIS*, 22 March). But the evidence suggests a more complex situation. In April, for example, Gorbachev assumed Suslov's old post of chairman of the Commission of Foreign Affairs of the Council of Union of the Supreme Soviet. The tussle over the post of secretary for ideology was reflected in the somewhat schizoid signals emanating from Moscow in the months following Andropov's death.

Chernenko's ideology can quite accurately be described as neo-Stalinism. In his frequent pronouncements on Soviet literature and the arts, he invariably hearkens back to socialist realism in the Stalin mold. "Milkmaid meets collective farmer" is how the London *Times* (7 May) summarized Chernenko's view of the arts. During the year, one noted a growth in the cult of Stalin. Writing in late November, Dusko Doder observed: "During the past few months, Joseph Stalin's image and name have been reappearing with a frequency and regularity to suggest more than the pendulum swing of time" (*WP*, 26 November). Vyacheslav Molotov, Stalin's foreign minister and longtime associate, was readmitted to the party in July; Stalin's restless daughter, Svetlana Alliluyeva, was enticed back to the Soviet Union. The resurrection of Stalin's prestige seemed close to complete.

But other, contradictory developments were also occurring. Russian nationalist writers, particularly adherents of the so-called "village prose" tendency, who had been vilified under Andropov, were awarded major literary prizes. Vladimir Soloukhin, who had been assailed in *Kommunist* for allegedly preaching the existence of god, became the recipient of the Red Banner of Labor award. Chernenko had repeatedly underlined his distaste for this group and their ideas—for example, for their strong criticism of collectivization and their religious proclivities—yet they managed to regain the ground they had lost under Andropov. One wondered whether this could be due in part to Gorbachev's influence.

Gorbachev's December address on ideological issues demonstrated the gulf separating him from Chernenko. It is instructive to compare this speech, which was published in the 11 December issue of *Pravda*, with Chernenko's June 1983 address, which appeared in the 15 June 1983 number of *Pravda*. In domestic matters, Gorbachev stressed that it was the economy that mattered. He was contemptuous of "dogmatic ideas that sometimes do a disservice to our theory and practice." He advocated decentralization and intensification of the economy and articulated a personalistic concern for the Soviet citizenry. "Lenin," he warned, "never counterposed Soviet state power to self-government by the people." And he added: "No references to objective circumstances can serve to justify a lack of attention to people's needs." "Socialist self-government by the people" was Gorbachev's motto. Despite the apparent rejection of his ideas by the party leadership between September and November, it was clear that Gorbachev intended to stick to his guns. (His comments on foreign affairs, on the other hand, were entirely conventional; ideology, it appeared, was for foreign rather than domestic consumption.)

Grigori Romanov apparently did not benefit more from Gorbachev's obvious differences with Chernenko over the economy and the appropriate application of ideology to Soviet life because he and Chernenko are not close. Chernenko's patron, Brezhnev, kept the hubristic and hard-driving Romanov in Leningrad for thirteen years; it was Andropov who brought Romanov to Moscow after Brezhnev's death, almost certainly as a counterweight to Gorbachev. Analysts have noted Romanov's warm praise for Andropov and the tepidness of his references to Chernenko. Romanov's "program" would appear to be similar to Andropov's—police methods, discipline, military-industrial expansion. Like Andropov, Romanov prefers a stick to a carrot in dealing with the Soviet populace.

Soviet foreign policy reflected the leadership struggles during 1984. Both Chernenko and Gorbachev, though for perhaps different reasons, appear to favor the resumption of something like the détente practiced under Brezhnev. Andropov, on the other hand, did not shrink from confrontation, and during his brief reign Soviet-American relations entered a period of deep freeze. Ronald Reagan was even compared by Soviet spokesmen to Adolf Hitler, a degree of vituperation unusual for a major Western leader. The Reagan administration's toning-down of its anti-Soviet rhetoric in preparation for the 1984 elections undoubtedly influenced the Soviets (as did their growing certitude that Reagan would, in fact, win re-election), but it may also have been that pro-détente Soviet leaders gained the upper hand against those advocating a tougher policy. Gorbachev's visit to Britain was a success, and Margaret Thatcher's oft-cited comment, "I like Mr. Gorbachev. We can do business together" (*NYT*, 23 December) can hardly have hurt his standing in the Kremlin. The visit of Ivan Arkhipov, first deputy chairman of the Council of Ministers, to China during the same month was similarly irenic. Negotiation and diplomacy rather than saber rattling seemed to have become the order of the day, if only temporarily.

As 1985 dawned, one was mindful of a comment by former national security adviser Zbigniew Brzezinski: "The longer the struggle [for the succession] goes on, the less likely Gorbachev is to win. Romanov is more brutal, less likely to rock the boat." (*WSJ*, 24 September.) The deepening Soviet succession crisis was being watched attentively by the entire world.

Eastern Europe. In contrast to his immediate predecessors, Konstantin Chernenko has made himself more available to other bloc leaders. He met all of them briefly during Andropov's funeral in February 1984. Prior to a midyear economic summit, the individual meetings were longer and interspersed with Soviet awards to faithful "allies." Among the bloc members, only Romania refused to join the USSR's boycott of the Summer Olympics in Los Angeles.

Warsaw Pact. Apart from providing lines of communication and logistic support in Central Europe, the subordinate members of the Warsaw Treaty Organization (WTO) also are expected to fight on the Soviet side in case of a war against NATO. To prepare them for such an eventuality, WTO has conducted annual maneuvers. During 1984, the southern tier (Bulgaria, Hungary, Romania) and the USSR held joint command post exercises covering land as well as the Black Sea. These took place on maps, testing command and control, because the Romanians refuse to allow any foreign troops on their territory.

The largest war games (160,000 troops) covered parts of Czechoslovakia, East Germany, Poland, and the Baltic Sea under Defense Minister Ustinov. Soviet armed forces alone held maneuvers near the border between the two Germanys, with a strike force of 60,000 men. Other smaller exercises took place throughout the year.

Economic Relations. In early April, the chairman of the USSR State Economic Planning Committee suggested that East European countries make greater use of natural gas since the Soviet Union would not be able to provide them with as much petroleum as heretofore.

The midyear Council for Mutual Economic Assistance (CMEA) summit in Moscow registered some opposition to closer ties within the bloc by those member-governments that want greater access to Western markets. Overall national income throughout Eastern Europe has experienced a sustained decline over the past fifteen years, from an average of 7.6 percent (1971–1975) down to a projected 2 percent for the most recent five-year plan (1981–1985). Including the USSR, the bloc owes the West more than $100 billion, which complicates trade with hard currency areas of the world.

Albania is the only East European state without membership in either the WTO or the CMEA. Only recently did it complete a railroad line to the Yugoslav border and open a road crossing into Greece. Unwilling to accept even short-term credits, Tirana's foreign trade is conducted on a barter basis. Approximately a hundred Albanian students have been permitted to enroll at West European universities. During 1984, most of the foreign contacts took place with that part of the world and not with the Soviet bloc.

Domestically, the top echelons in the Albanian Party of Labor are being rebuilt after the most recent purge swept out the prime minister (an alleged suicide), about sixteen cabinet members, and hundreds of his followers. The cult of Enver Hoxha (76), party head since 1941, continues in an effort to project an image of a world leader and statesman. A third development appears to be directed at "cleansing" the lower party levels of unreliable elements, which will continue probably until the next congress is held.

Bulgaria also has an older leader, Todor Zhivkov (73), who in 1984 celebrated 30 years in power. Two new members of the Politburo filled vacancies caused by an expulsion and a retirement. Four candidates for membership on this decisionmaking ruling body also are of the younger generation, which suggests that Zhivkov may be preparing for an orderly succession.

On the eve of the fortieth anniversary of communist rule, fourteen retired party leaders received decorations. Most of them had been removed during the de-Stalinization period. Prior to the celebration, explosions occurred at Varna airport and the Plovdiv railroad station, presumably the work of dissidents. The Soviet party sent heir apparent Gorbachev to the festivities in Sofia.

More than three-quarters of Bulgaria's foreign trade is within the CMEA; some 57 percent of this is with the Soviet Union. Arms sales to the Third World accounted for almost one-tenth of all export earnings during 1982 and may have increased since then. However, a national party conference heard blunt criticism of the low quality of many Bulgarian products, which adversely affects hard currency earnings. Local initiative will be encouraged as one possible remedy.

Czechoslovakia's party leader Gustáv Husák (72) celebrated his fifteenth year in office, having been placed there by the USSR, which had invaded the country. The date was marked by a warning in *Pravda* against tolerating "internal reactionary forces" throughout Eastern Europe. A generation gap exists in the Czechoslovak party, in that one-fourth of its functionaries will retire by 1988.

The fortieth anniversary of the Slovak national uprising was attended by Soviet defense minister Ustinov, among other foreign guests. He heard about the "brotherly help of the Soviet Union," which in fact had given no assistance and stood aside while the Germans killed the Slovak insurgents. Husák advocated an independent "Soviet Slovakia" at the time, but this was not mentioned.

Except for neighboring Hungary, the economy of Czechoslovakia compares favorably with that of other bloc countries. However, consumer price increases during the fall and continuing inflation eroded purchasing power. Basic commodities are in short supply; innovation is absent; and the average citizen seems to have little interest in working hard for shrinking rewards.

East Germany seems to be preparing for a leadership transition, with four high-ranking officials named to the ruling party's Politburo in late May, all in their early fifties. They seem to be more pragmatic than the older, hard-line generation. An even younger man, Egon Krenz (47), appears to be the unofficial heir apparent to Erich Honecker (73).

Fifty-five East German citizens entered the Federal Republic's mission in East Berlin and remained there until permitted to leave for West Germany. The latter reportedly paid the equivalent of $1.8 million to the communist regime, which amounts to $33,000 per head. West Germany continues to purchase the freedom of approximately 5,000 political prisoners from East Germany every year. It has been reported that Bonn paid an average of $2,700 for each of the first 25,000 East Germans allowed to emigrate during 1984.

Local elections were held in early May, and candidates representing the communist-dominated National Front won 99 percent of the vote. About 260,000 handpicked individuals vied for some 203,000 positions at district, county, and commune council levels. Leaflets reportedly were distributed by dissidents who urged voters to stay away from the polls.

Hungary has scheduled its thirteenth party congress for March 1985 and will stress continuity in leadership as well as policy, under János Kádár (71). There is evidence of a slackening in discipline and a need to reinvigorate the ruling movement. Attempts have been made to broaden popular participation in the electoral process and the trade unions while preserving the communist party's leading role.

Since national income rose by only 0.4 percent during the year, about three-fourths of the population now derives some benefit from the "second economy." A small group of millionaires (private entrepreneur farmers, doctors, artisans) are the envy of the general public. On the other hand, more than a hundred government-operated enterprises are insolvent and over 100,000 workers fill unneeded positions.

With a 2 per 1,000 decline in the population, the birthrate has reached a historical low. Hungary also holds the world record of 43.5 per 1,000 in suicides. The growing number of retired adds to economic problems, which already include a shortage of skilled labor. The attitude of the young towards the system manifests strong nationalism, avoidance of membership in official organizations, and a growing involvement with religion.

A small group of the Hungarian "democratic opposition" endorsed a joint Czechoslovak-Polish appeal by human rights activists. Underground publications have appeared, questioning regime policies. The Politburo response took the form of a directive that "administrative [that is, police] measures must be employed against all who question the . . . policy of our party and government."

Poland also celebrated the fortieth anniversary of its "liberation" by the Red Army. The former chief ideologist, Adam Schaff, published a book in Vienna exile that states that the system had been imposed from the outside and degenerated into a "dictatorship of the apparatus." The Roman Catholic church is involved with the search for a new political system that gives support to the nonviolent means used by the democratic opposition.

The ruling Polish United Workers' (communist) Party, headed by a career military officer, would seem to be anathema to the Kremlin. However, Gen. Wojciech Jaruzelski (62) has maintained order if not law inside the country. Since 1980, the party has lost 1 million members, which is one reason for the governing military junta in Poland.

The brutal murder of Father Jerzy Popieluszko by the security police resulted in a trial of several officers, with the public prosecutor demanding the death penalty for the captain who issued the orders and participated in the killing itself. A colonel attempted to mislead the investigation. The proceedings are unprecedented for a Soviet bloc state. By mid-1984, there were 72 documented cases of mysterious deaths that involved Solidarity activists, probably murdered by the secret police.

Local elections on 17 June returned only official candidates. There were two communist-approved individuals running for each council seat, again something unique in Eastern Europe: a choice between participation and boycott. The regime claimed a 75 percent turnout. The underground Solidarity movement monitored selected voting places and concluded that the government had inflated its figures by at least one-fifth. In Warsaw, for example, the turnout reached only 57.4, not the claimed 71 percent.

Romania still has proportionally to its population the largest communist party throughout the bloc. A congress in November reconfirmed Nicolae Ceauşescu (67) as party/government leader. His wife is the unofficial deputy, and their son heads the Union of Communist Youth. The policymaking Political Bureau was reduced from thirteen to eight members. About half of the county-level party leaders were rotated out.

Ceauşescu has admitted that a food crisis exists and has instituted more deliveries to the state from private peasant plots without any compensatory increase in prices or other government assistance. Completely unrealistic growth targets were announced, and investments will remain the highest in the bloc.

Although he did not cancel his visit to Bonn, like Honecker and Zhivkov, the Romanian party/government leader brought back few benefits in October. The presidents of mainland China and North Korea came to Bucharest. By far the most interesting were the high-level contacts with Moscow. Ceauşescu made his first state visit to the USSR in more than a decade. He also attended Andropov's funeral and the CMEA summit. Apparently, the Soviets are delivering more natural gas and petroleum to Romania.

Yugoslavia, although only an associate member of CMEA, has become more heavily involved with trade in the bloc. The country had a 62 percent rate of inflation and 950,000 unemployed. Productivity declined, and real income fell by 11 percent. Foreign debts to the West totaled $19.2 billion, with $5.3 billion due for repayment during 1984.

In a desperate attempt to remedy the deteriorating situation, authorities imposed a six-month price freeze and subsequently more than half of the prices on the internal market were set free. The International Monetary Fund and Western banks rescheduled their loans and made arrangements for a standing credit to Yugoslavia.

The ruling League of Communists has deteriorated over the years into a "loose coalition of republic and province parties." Even the principle of democratic centralism has become a "voluntary obligation." Opportunism, lack of unity, passivity, misuse of party rank for personal gain are other weaknesses openly admitted.

Unrest among the Albanian minority continues, evident in December when two "illegal and hostile organizations" with 152 members were discovered. They wanted a Kosovo republic within the federal system. Neighboring Albania was denounced for encouraging irredentists and nationalists inside Yugoslavia.

John B. Dunlop
Richard F. Staar
Hoover Institution

Albania

Population. 2,906,000
Party. Albanian Party of Labor (Partia e Punës e Shqipërisë; APL)
Founded. 8 November 1941
Membership. (Approximate) 122,000 full members and 24,363 candidate members; workers and peasants 66 percent; office workers and "intellectuals" 34 percent; women 30 percent full and 40 percent of candidate members
First Secretary. Enver Hoxha
Politburo. 12 full members: Enver Hoxha (chairman of Democratic Front, commander-in-chief of armed forces), Ramiz Alia (president of the republic), Adil Çarçani (premier), Hajredin Çeliku (minister of

mines and industry), Lenka Çuko, Hekuran Isai, Rita Marko, Pali Mishka, Manush Myftiu (deputy premier), Simon Stefani, 2 positions vacant; 5 alternate members: Besnik Bekteshi (deputy premier), Foto Çami (party chief of Tirana District), Vangjel Çerava, Llambi Gjegprifti, Qirjako Mihali (deputy premier)

Secretariat. 6 members: Enver Hoxha, Ramiz Alia, Vangjel Çerava, Lenka Çuko, Hekuran Isai, Simon Stefani

Central Committee. 80 full and 38 alternate members. Currently there are 10 vacancies resulting from purges of Shehu followers.

Status. Ruling party.

Last Congress. Eighth, 1–8 November 1981, in Tirana

Last Election. 1982, all 250 candidates Democratic Front. Only one voter cast a ballot against Front candidates.

Auxiliary Organizations. Trade Union Federation of Albania (UTUA), 610,000 members, Sotir Koçallari, chairman; Union of Labor Youth of Albania (ULYA), Mehmet Elezi, first secretary; Women's Union of Albania (WUA), Lumturi Rexha, chairman; Albanian War Veterans, Shefqet Peçi, chairman; Albanian Defense of Peace Committee, Musaraj Shefqet, acting chairman

Main State Organs. Council of Ministers (20 members). The People's Assembly (250 members) is constitutionally the leading body of state, but in reality it rubber-stamps decisions reached at the party Politburo and Central Committee levels.

Publications. *Zeri i Popullit*, daily organ of the APL Central Committee; *Rruga e Partisë* (theoretical journal), organ of the Central Committee of the APL, monthly; *Bashkimi*, organ of the Democratic Front; *Zeri i Rinisë*, organ of ULYA; *Puna*, weekly organ of UTUA; *10 Korik* and *Luftetari*, biweekly organs of the Ministry of Defense; *Nendori* (literary), monthly organ of the Albanian Writers and Artists League; *Laiko Vema*, organ of the Greek minority. The Albanian Telegraphic Agency (ATA) is the official news agency.

The Albanian Communist Party was founded in Tirana on 8 November 1941 on instructions from the Comintern, carried out by two emissaries of Josip Broz Tito. A total of fifteen individuals, claiming to represent established party organizations of Korçë, Shkodër, and Tirana assembled in a private home in the old part of Tirana under the supervision of Dušan Mungoša and Miladin Popović, Tito's representatives, and united the three groups under a national leadership with Enver Hoxha as the provisional first secretary.

The dominant segment of the Albanian communist movement was the Korçë group, which traces its origins to 1931 and was organized by two tinsmiths, Pilo Peristeri and Koçi Xoxe. Peristeri was one of the sponsors of Enver Hoxha for admission to the Korçë party cell, which had close links with the Greek Communist Party. The second group, bearing the same name as that of Korçë (*Puna*, or "work"), was located at the Gheg city of Shkodër and had close ties with the Yugoslav and Austrian communist parties. It was led by a prominent Albanian intellectual, Zejfula Maleshova, who has the distinction of being one of Hoxha's first victims. Elements of the Korçë and Shkodër groups, along with representatives of the Tirana youth group, which had come under Hoxha's influence as of 1936 and under his total control by 1941, formed the Albanian Communist Party, which was immediately instructed by its Yugoslav mentors to prepare for armed resistance against the foreign enemy. At the party's First Congress (1 November 1948), its name was changed to Albanian Party of Labor, and Enver Hoxha was elected first secretary, a post he still holds. It was this congress that legitimized the break with Yugoslavia (on the advice of Moscow) and purged Koçi Xoxe and several of his followers "as Titoite revisionists." Xoxe was executed in 1949, and hundreds of his followers were given long prison terms.

A permanent characteristic of the APL is its instability at the highest ranks, manifested in sweeping purges. Since 1941, five major purges have been undertaken and carefully managed by Hoxha and his ephemerally close associates. A total of 47 party leaders, all of whom had reached the rank of Central Committee member and two-thirds of whom were full or alternate members of the Politburo have been purged since 1941. The latest purge, which seems to continue, affected Mehmet Shehu, prime minister for 28 years, sixteen members of his cabinet, and hundreds of his "followers."

Historically, the Albanian purges followed the Stalinist pattern of purging the purgers, as soon as the situation permitted. Since 1948 all leaders of two of the country's most powerful institutions, the police and the armed forces, have been the targets of Hoxha's "cleansing" of the party and state apparatus. Thus, with the exception of himself, all Albanian defense ministers and ministers of interior who served between 1948 and 1982 were purged.

Three major trends characterized party life in Albania during 1984. First, a continuing attempt to "normalize" life at the top and to reconstruct the hierarchy, following the convulsions of the anti-Shehu purges, which still continue at lower levels. In this direction, Qirjako Mihali, a promising member of the younger generation, regained the ground that he lost following the government shake-up after the November 1982 elections. On the recommendation of Prime Minister Adil Çarçani, Mihali was elevated to the post of deputy premier (*Gazeta Zyrtare*, 16 February). A relatively unknown quantity, Niko Gjizari, assumed the post of finance minister, previously occupied by Mihali (ATA, 16 February; *FBIS*, 17 February).

The second trend involved a massive effort on the part of party organs, press, and major leaders to repolish the cult of Enver Hoxha and cast him in the role of the "most important" leader of the Albanian nation, a "father-like figure" comparable to other national heroes, who is at the same time, a major world "thinker" (Radio Free Europe–Radio Liberty, *RAD Background Report*, 13 January). Spearheading this effort was the Albanian Writers and Artists League, which held its Third Congress in Tirana on 23–25 April (*Zeri i Popullit*, 26 April). Dritero Agolli, the chairman of the Albanian Writers and Artists League, devoted a substantial part of his address to the congress to stressing the literary qualities of Hoxha (ibid.), and the theoretical journal of the party devoted substantial amounts of space and effort to stressing the "contributions" of Enver Hoxha to the science of Marxism-Leninism (*Rruga e Partisë*, October). Furthermore, Ramiz Alia, in a major address on the occasion of the fortieth anniversary of the country's liberation, staked a claim for Hoxha as a source of the "pure science of Marxism-Leninism" and for Albania as a center toward which "the revolutionary movements of the world look for guidance" (*Zeri i Popullit*, 28 November). For good measure Alia linked Hoxha's name to the "old man of Vlore" (Ismail Qemal, founder of the first Albanian state) and to other national heroes. Similarly, Vangjel Çerava, secretary to the Central Committee and alternate Politburo member, stressed the same theme in his May Day address (ATA, 1 May; *FBIS*, 2 May). Hoxha, as well as his wife, contribute to this broad effort to put the final touches on the "new Hoxha image." In his greetings to the Albanian people on the occasion of the fortieth anniversary of communist rule, the Albanian leader, rather immodestly, claimed that "the world proletariat looked and looks to you, Albania, with hope and trust because in your course and determination it sees the great ideals of Marxism-Leninism" (*Zeri i Popullit*, 29 November).

Finally, an intense campaign critical of party cadres for insufficient attention to the tasks laid out by the Eighth Party Congress and the government and for failing in several key economic areas characterized party life during 1984. Criticism of insufficient party work in the military (ibid., 16 March, 1 August), the internal security forces (*JPRS*, 84–247, 12 April; ATA, 15 May; *Rruga e Partisë*, December 1983), the trade unions (*Zeri i Popullit*, 13 January), and the oil industry was voiced repeatedly during the year, suggesting that the hierarchy is eager to cleanse the lower party ranks of unreliable elements. In fact, suggestions for "new criteria" in party admissions have been made, and the imbalance of party versus nonparty members in several ministries has been pointed out (ibid., 17 January). It would be safe to say that a turnover in party membership has continued since Shehu's demise, and it will probably continue until the Ninth Party Congress, for which a date has yet to be set.

Internal Party Affairs. An apparent degree of normalcy has returned to the upper echelons of the APL. No significant changes have occurred in its hierarchy or the government, with the exception of the return of Qirjako Mihali to the post that he held until November 1982, deputy premier. Mihali's return may very well signal the beginning of the inevitable power struggle between a Gheg, Ramiz Alia, and a Tosk, Adil Çarçani, to succeed Hoxha, who is reported to be very ill and suffering from diabetes and an advanced case of Parkinson's disease (KYODO, 9 September; *FBIS*, 10 September; *WP*, 17 September).

As expected, the "purification" of the lower ranks of the party, after the massive purges of the top during the 1981–1983 period (*YICA*, 1984, pp. 294–97), seems to have received high-level attention during the past year. There are at least three problems manifested in the cadre ranks that drew the attention of the Central Committee during its Ninth Plenum: alien manifestations among its younger members; an unusually high number of party members in certain ministries and enterprises, suggesting carelessness in selection or nepotism; and the failure of some party organizations to rejuvenate themselves (*Zeri i Popullit*, 28 July).

The theoretical journal dealt extensively with the need for "further deepening of the ideological struggle against alien manifestations and influence" (*Rruga e Partisë*, April, p. 26). One of the problems created by these phenomena, according to the authors of several major articles, is negative attitudes toward work, particularly among the younger people sent to perform manual tasks during the summer months. Some of them, according to party spokesmen, "instead of performing the assigned duties, are eagerly searching for a cozy corner" (ibid., p. 28).

Ramiz Alia took the issue of "alien manifestations" and emergence of negative values before the students of the University of Tirana in a special meeting organized by its president, Dr. Osman Kraja (ATA, 31 May; *FBIS*, 1 June). At this gathering, Alia stressed emphatically the need for a "greater spirit of militancy" and underscored the role of the party cadres in all aspects of university life and higher education.

Party "purification" at the lower levels commenced with the elimination of Kadri Hazbiu and Feçor Shehu (see *YICA*, 1984, pp. 294, 298) and aimed at the administrative apparatus of the state. The need for "party leadership in the internal organs of security, particularly since the discovery of the Shehu plot" has been pointed out repeatedly (*JPRS*, 84–247, 12 April; *Rruga e Partisë*, 1983). There was direct criticism of party members in the various ministries for "not speaking up when the plots were obvious." Failure of party work in administrative organs suggests a probability of membership turnover and disruption on the production line. There were indications that as a result of confusion emanating from above, regional party organizations were reluctant to admit new members for fear of repercussions over their choices. The districts of Elbasan, Dibër, and Korçë were singled out for failing to replenish their ranks. In their case, they "have not had any admissions to the party, some of the districts for two to three years in a row."

The excuse given by some districts for not admitting new members was that "there were no suitable elements." (*Zeri i Popullit*, 28 July.)

The confusion that prevails at the lower party ranks is compounded by the constant criticism of party organizations in certain ministries for failure to be vigilant against actual or potential putschists. Three areas have been particularly singled out for criticism of party work: the Ministry of the Interior, the security forces, and some trade unions.

Foto Çami, alternate Politburo member and Tirana party chief, attacked the practice of certain ministries of "holding closed-door meetings" and at the same time criticized the lowest-level organizations for not blowing the whistle on such practices. "The APL Central Committee has made clear to us," Çami stated, "the harm caused and the consequences of the closed-door meetings carried out by the party organizations of the Ministry of Internal Affairs and its various organs, which, supposedly for the sake of preserving secrecy, was stimulated and cultivated for their own purposes by Kadri Hazbiu, Feçor Shehu and others." (Ibid., 30 July; *FBIS*, 14 August.)

Party organs in trade unions came under criticism on several occasions for failing "to educate the workers to respect the law." Apparently the party seems to have some problems with the working class, particularly in the district of Vlorë, where "50 percent of trade union committee decisions concerning workers' rights were overruled by courts." (*Zeri i Popullit*, 4 April.)

Problems with the lower party structures did not prevent the hierarchy from roaming the country to celebrate the fortieth anniversary of the establishment of the communist regime. Ramiz Alia, as in the previous year, made the most appearances in various activities related to the country's liberation from the Germans, with Çarçani following close behind. On the other hand, Enver Hoxha missed most of the opportunities to participate in the commemoration of historical events marking the anti-German and antinationalist struggle. Instead, members of the Politburo and the Central Committee, often in groups, presided over major celebrations, routinely read Hoxha's messages, and proclaimed their total faith in his ideas. Although Ramiz Alia actively "promoted" his own career and received top billing in key events, there are some indications that Hoxha is distancing himself from Alia. For example, in numerous commemorations of the formation of "shock brigades," Alia and Carcani were equally projected as "messengers" of Hoxha. In a total of eighteen such commemorations, Alia acted as Hoxha's and the Central Committee's representative in two, the same number as Çarçani. (ATA, 22 January, 29 April; *FBIS*, 23 January, 30 April.) In commemorating the formation of the Seventh Shock Brigade of Shkrapar, in which both Alia and Çarçani served as political commissars, Hoxha praised both of them in almost identical terms (ATA, 18 March; *FBIS*, 19 March). At least four other high-level party officials were active in various parts of the country in connection with the fortieth anniversary celebrations: Hekuran Isai, Manush Myftiu, Prokop Mura, and even the nationalist-turned-communist Shefqet Peçi. They were all given top billing in several regional festivities.

Hoxha missed several major opportunities to make public statements, reinforcing persistent rumors that he is seriously ill (*NYT*, 11 November). He made a shaky appearance on the occasion of May Day, and according to viewers of Albanian television, he had to be assisted to the dais (*San Francisco Examiner*, 12 August). On that occasion, Vangjel Çerava gave the keynote speech, which by communist standards was short: it lasted only five minutes, perhaps in deference to Hoxha's condition (ATA, 1 May; *FBIS*, 2 May). But the first secretary was absent from the ceremonies at Përmet, where on 24 May 1944 the Anti-Fascist National Liberation Committee (de facto government) was established, and from the celebrations in Berat, where this committee was declared the provisional government (20 October 1944). In both instances Alia and Çarçani attended, with the first giving the major address. Hoxha also missed, for the first time, the opening of the legislative session of the Albanian parliament, which commenced on 18 June. (*RAD Background Report*, 10 July.)

Instead of personal appearances, the first secretary published what the Albanian press called "major works" to coincide with the major events that he missed. Thus, on the eve of the ceremonies at Permët, Hoxha's theory *On the People's Power* (ATA, 22 May; *FBIS*, 23 May) and on the occasion of the Berat meeting the forty-first volume of his memoirs and *Reflections on the Middle East* were published. On national liberation day, Hoxha issued a highly emotional "congratulatory" message to his "people and country," which was instantly published as a pamphlet and translated in all major languages (*Zeri i Popullit*, 29 November).

During 1984 Hoxha made only four public appearances. It is claimed that he also attended the Central Committee's Ninth Plenum, but there is no public confirmation of this. In addition to his May Day appearance, he attended a concert in Tirana. (ATA, 22 May; *FBIS*, 23 May.) He opened a sports rally (ATA, 20 October; *FBIS*, 22 October), in the Qemal Stafa stadium of Tirana, and the following month presided over the festivities in commemoration of the fortieth anniversary of communist rule (ATA, 29 November; *FBIS*, 3 December). On this occasion, Alia gave a major address at a closed meeting held in the parliament hall, from which Hoxha was absent (*Zeri i Popullit*, 28 November). Defense Minister Prokop Mura gave the customary speech on 29 November and issued the order of the day to his troops (ATA, 29 November; *FBIS*, 3 December).

However, all high-level party officials made a concerted effort to mythologize Hoxha and to put the final touches to a political portrait that is intended to reflect his nationalism and his contributions to the science of Marxism-Leninism. Towards this end, a major gathering was organized by the Presidium of the People's Assembly and the Council of Ministers to "discuss" the inner meaning of Hoxha's book, *On the People's Power* (ATA, 28 July; *FBIS*, 30 July). Manush Myftiu, considered to be a "moderate," gave the main address, which contained a suggestion for a greater role for the parliament. Myftiu, quoting from Hoxha's "thoughts," pointed to the need "for a strict observation of the correct ratios between the representative organs and the executive ones" in all tasks. (Ibid.) Two other vice-presidents of the People's Assembly, Rita Marko and Xhafer Spahiu, echoed Myftiu's views. Several other "events" were organized during the year for the purpose of redefining Hoxha's personality, including a symposium on "revisionism" presided over by his wife, Nexhmije (ATA, 15 May; *FBIS*, 16 May).

In retrospect, one can say that 1984 was a "relatively calm year" in the turbulent life of the Albanian Party of Labor. Yet beneath the calm, one senses the ongoing power struggle to succeed Hoxha. Alia still remains in the forefront, but it is questionable whether he will, finally, succeed the aging chief. Alia has two problems that he must overcome: his past and his origin. As a young man, he flirted with fascism and for a brief period in 1939 was a member of the Black Shirts (*Washington Times*, 2 January). No doubt, at the appropriate time his opponents will bring up this youthful indiscretion. Second, Alia is a Gheg with Yugoslav

(Kosovo) roots, living among a Tosk majority. If the past is any guide, Ghegs do not fare well in communist Albania.

Party Control of the Military. As in the previous year, there is some evidence that the party authorities are not satisfied with the overall state of the relationship between the armed forces and civilian authorities. Several escapees to Greece (a total of 23 young Albanians reached Greece during 1984), among whom were several military men, have confirmed reports of low morale in the armed forces (*Acropolis*, 15 September).

In ceremonies celebrating the forty-first anniversary of the founding of the Albanian army, Defense Minister Prokop Mura repeated last year's theme on the "need for greater party work" in the military. Deputy Defense Minister Bajram Mane, who is apparently a newcomer to that post, was more emphatic on this matter as well as on the need "to better integrate the people's militia into the country's defense doctrine." (ATA, 10 July.)

The organ of the APL Central Committee dealt twice in a relatively short time with the problem of poor relations between the "professionals" and the so-called "free military schools" (*Zeri i Popullit*, 16 March, 1 August). There are some problems, the party organ points out, related to "effectiveness of weapons, perfecting the communications system, revision of combat readiness norms; prolongation of the life of weapons, increase of military equipment, ammunition, clothing," which are more pronounced in the "civilian training schools" (ibid., 1 August). These problems, according to a previous analysis, are the result of failure by the center to occupy itself with the training of cadres in the paramilitary schools: "The small-scale training is left up to the volunteer schools while the commands and staffs of the volunteer units do not always show an interest in them (ibid., 16 March). The debate on this subject suggests tensions between the professional military men and the "armed people."

A more direct approach to the need for "party control over the military" was revealed by Deputy Defense Minister Simon Balabani, who comes from the Political Directorate of the Defense Department. He reminded the defense establishment of the importance of the "political commissars" who were reinstated on Hoxha's orders by his "open letter to the Central Committee of 1966." (*Rruga e Partisë*, July.) It is apparent that the "commissars" were sidestepped by the former defense ministers Kadri Hazbiu and Beqir Baluku, as well as by

professional soldiers like Veli Lekaj (former chief of the defense staff), who reportedly was executed along with Hazbiu and Feçor Shehu (*JPRS*, 84–931, 13 July; *Neue Zürcher Zeitung*, 6–7 November 1983).

Auxiliary and Mass Organizations. All auxiliary organizations were mobilized to meet production goals, which apparently have been set at a high level "as a concrete way of celebrating the fortieth anniversary" of the establishment of the communist regime.

The Democratic Front's general council held what was termed an "important meeting" to "lay the tasks and main activities of the organization" for the fortieth anniversary of the liberation. Ramiz Alia, vice-chairman of the Front, opened the proceedings and listed in detail all "branches of the economy in which great efforts are needed" (ATA, 3 April). The keynote address, however, was given by an old stalwart of the party, Pilo Peristeri, who lost his Politburo position in 1981, but who was quite active in party affairs in 1984. Sheqet Peçi, another member of the old generation who was in eclipse during the Shehu years, also spoke during the proceedings.

A significant change in the top leadership of the Front occurred in February with the death of Muslim Peza, the fervent Albanian nationalist and Gheg warrior who was among the first to be co-opted by the communist party and who, under pressure from the British intelligence mission, joined the communist "united front" following a conference (16 September 1942) in the northern city that still bears his name. Peza died on 7 February and was given a hero's funeral with all major party leaders in attendance. (*Zeri i Popullit*, 8 February.) Peza, an illiterate chieftain, was a legendary figure among the Ghegs, a kind of Robin Hood, who contributed immensely to the legitimization of the communist-controlled Fronti Naçionale Clirimtarë (National Liberation Front) as a *national* force. Apparently, Sheqet Peçi, a man with similar background, seems to have replaced Peza as the "old man" of the Front.

The ULYA followed the same general pattern in its activities as the Democratic Front. It, too, called a special meeting of representatives from all district organizations to discuss "objectives and goals to be fulfilled" in honor of the national holiday and the fortieth anniversary of the "liberation." The two goals set out to be achieved were "raising productivity in all sectors of the economy" and "raising ideological standards and militancy." (Ibid., 17 April.) In addition to the April conference, which had broad regional participation, the ULYA Central Committee also held its annual plenum in Tirana with participation by all regional youth secretaries (ATA, 12 May). This plenum was attended by Ramiz Alia, who gave a brief speech. But ULYA Secretary General Mehmet Elezi used the opportunity to launch a severe attack against "modern revisionism and the capitalist encirclement" (*Zeri i Popullit*, 12 May). On 8 August, the ULYA held a mass meeting in Tirana commemorating the fortieth anniversary of its first congress. Alia attended this gathering, accompanied by Foto Çami. The latter was selected to read Hoxha's message and to convey the greetings of the Central Committee of the party.

The WUA was also mobilized by the party organizations and their leadership to intensify its efforts in all directions in honor of the fortieth anniversary of the country's liberation from the Nazis. In addition, the WUA played host to several foreign women's delegations, including a large one from Vietnam. Underscoring the close relations that exist between the two countries, the Vietnamese guests were received by Premier Çarçani and were given a grand tour of cultural and industrial centers. (ATA, 27 April, 8 May.)

On 20 January, the UTUA held a plenum of its Central Council in Tirana. The proceedings were attended by Premier Çarçani, who took the organization to task for not dealing with those who fail in the goals set by the five-year plan, which in his words "is the law and must be executed." The premier pointed to specific problems in the economy and the difficulties faced by the country due to the "bourgeois-revisionist blockade." Çarçani singled out the district of Vlorë as a problem area and pointed to the deviations of "unilateralism, globalism, departmentalism, and localism, which are manifested to some degree in the management activity of some administrators." He criticized labor unions for not playing their role properly and for causing problems through loss of time and nonfulfillment of quotas. (*Puna*, 10 January.)

Sotir Koçallari, chairman of the UTUA's General Council, delivered the keynote address to the plenum and was equally critical of the Vlorë district, "where there has been violation of discipline, low-quality work in the maintenance of machinery and equipment, low qualification standards, and a lack of a sense of responsibility." As a result of poor management and low productivity, according to Koçallari, "norms had to be revised for 57,000 work processes." (Ibid.) The campaign against the

unions was carried a step further when the party newspaper deplored the superficial way in which union committees deal with workers' grievances in the district of Vlorë: "50 percent of the trade union committee decisions dealing with material responsibilities were baseless and were overruled by the courts" (*Zeri i Popullit*, 4 April). The tone of criticism by the authorities against the trade unions seems to suggest that the Albanian workers are restless or that the quotas set for the five-year plan are simply too high.

The Albanian Writers and Artists League held its Third Congress in Tirana from 23 to 25 April under the chairmanship of Dritero Agolli, who delivered a major address. This influential organization participated during the year in the overall process of redefining the role of Enver Hoxha and placing Albanian literature on a broader international scale. The intelligentsia has been subjected to severe shocks during the experimentation with an Albanian version of a "cultural revolution" and has often been the object of party criticism for avoiding manual labor. As a result, fifteen years had lapsed since the league's Second Congress.

Deputy Premier Manush Myftiu addressed the congress and implored the participants to persist in the themes of class struggle and revolution and to avoid the notions of "ideological noninvolvement," "nonengagement," "class neutrality," "ideological convergence" (ibid., 24 April). Agolli, who was reelected chairman of the league, merged the themes of "national spirit" and the "struggle against all manifestations of bourgeois-revisionist decadence and modernism" (ATA, 24 April). Although the speakers at the congress concentrated on the known themes of Albanian cultural life, their self-assurance was obvious, and they were willing to have their achievements examined by a broader group of peers. Delegations from Greece, Syria, Egypt, Denmark, France, and Arberesh Albanians (Italy) participated. Numerous speakers decried the Yugoslav government's decision not to permit Kosovo Albanians to participate in the congress.

Domestic Affairs. The Albanian state apparatus and mass organizations showed excessive preoccupation with persistent social problems that affect relations between "party and people." Social disorientation, negative attitudes toward work, the large number of citizens' complaints against the bureaucracy, and, more important, work absenteeism dominated the domestic agenda of Albanian political leaders.

In a special report to the judiciary committee of the parliament, Rrapo Mino, the procurator general of Albania, pointed out to that body the problems created by a lack of adequate attention by the "prosecuting organs against those who expropriate socialist property." The committee, whose proceedings were followed by the deputy chairman of the parliament, Rita Marko, criticized the shortcomings of the prosecuting organs and stressed "the need to raise the quality of their work and to further elevate internal control." (*Zeri i Popullit*, 15 May.) This is the first piece of evidence suggesting that Alia, who in the previous year took the Office of Public Investigator under his direct control (*YICA*, 1984, p. 297), is making use of it to advance his control of the state apparatus. However, despite increased police activity, social problems persist in all fields, as evidenced by citizen boldness in complaining about the state machinery and enterprise managers.

The party newspaper took to task the state organs that deal with such complaints in a routine, bureaucratic manner—"you complain, I respond"—rather than "delve deeply into the nature of these complaints." The implication of the criticism is that there are hidden ideological causes in citizen grievances and a definite failure of lower party and state organs to detect the origins of social discontent. "Is it right," the paper asked, "that the central organs of Tirana should receive about 4,000 complaints in a year?" (*Zeri i Popullit*, 13 April.)

In another attempt to deal with "social problems" that have resulted in alien manifestations, the party organ ran a front-page, boldfaced editorial in which the complaints of citizens were indirectly linked to "bourgeois" influences. Three categories of problems were singled out by party authorities as deserving close attention. The first is petit-bourgeois psychology, "which is reflected in demands for selected work, violation of discipline, unjustified absenteeism, nonfulfillment of norms, poor-quality work, defects, increased sick leave, and so forth." The second is excessive nepotism in all spheres of social activity, "a malady that has affected even Communists." According to party spokesmen, "there are people who approach officials to ensure that their children are established in privileged jobs; there are those who try to put pressure on teachers to give their children undeserved grades; and there are those who try to secure unlawful privileges through favoritism." These problems are attributed to manifestations of "bureaucratism, intellectualism, and technocratism." These "negative phenomena" even have external manifestations in "the way that some young people dress, wanting to be in with the times." The third problem is the persistence of religious practices, with which the basic organizations and cadres fail to deal. (Ibid., 14 June.)

These "outdated" social attitudes were the subject of numerous articles in 1984. Thus, "old practices" are blamed for the young people's current attitude toward work and socialist property. According to the theoretical review, young people pay little attention to work and abstain for frivolous reasons such as "watching a soccer game." Cadres casually ignore favoritism and "unhealthy friendships" among the young and the "re-emergence of religious practices" among the old. As a result, "people, particularly old people, have returned to celebrating some religious festivities and rites, such as circumcising their sons, visiting former religious shrines, prohibiting marriages between young people of different religious backgrounds." (*Rruga e Partisë*, April.)

Negative social attitudes had a harmful impact on the economy, according to major party officials. Foto Çami, alternate Politburo member and Tirana party chief, criticized the lack of party militancy in some areas and linked it to the failure in some critical sectors of the economy such as coal and oil production. Laziness and "unsteady fulfillment of plans" have resulted from excessive loss of work, according to Çami. (Ibid., July.) Some specific examples of problems caused by nonsocialist attitudes were revealed. During 1983, about 770,000 work days were lost through temporary incapacity. In the first six months of 1984, the total was 340,000. This problem, according to official spokesmen, is the result of "poor party work" and inadequate educational activity on the part of trade unions. (*Zeri i Popullit*, 9 September.)

Human Rights Violations. While Albania continues to seek to draw international attention to "human rights violations" of ethnic Albanians in Kosovo by the Yugoslav authorities, it itself has again been the target of broad international criticism for "gross violations" of the human and political rights of its own citizens. A well-documented record of human rights violations by the Albanian authorities, as a "matter of policy," was published by Amnesty International in London (*Albania: Political Imprisonment and the Law, 1984*). Criticism of the Tirana regime voiced by spokesmen of expatriate Greek ethnics in Greece and the United

States and concern for the "well-being of the Greek minority in Albania" were expressed by Greek prime minister Andreas Papandreou (*Vradnyi*, 22 February). Tirana's response to the latter's concern came rather swiftly in an editorial in the party organ that accused Papandreou of "interference in the internal affairs of a neighboring state" (*Zeri i Popullit*, 29 February). Nevertheless, there is a growing body of evidence that the Albanian government has engaged in harsh policies against the Greek minority as well as against Catholics (Amnesty International, *Albania*, p. 40; *Paris Match*, 12 October; *Guardian*, London, 30 December).

Tirana dismisses such criticism as being the work of "enemies of Albania" and charges that the strings that put into motion "this anti-Albanian triangle—Great Serbian chauvinism, Northern Epirotic societies, and Greek 'reactionaries'—are certainly pulled by Washington" (*Zeri i Popullit*, 1 March). Albanian leaders, however, found it necessary to respond to such criticism and claimed that the Greek minority has "rights equal to those of the rest of the Albanian people" and that it "needs no protectors." Ramiz Alia reiterated that theme in his speech in connection with the festivities at Përmët (ATA, 25 May), as did other leaders whenever they appeared before Greek minority audiences (ibid., 3 September). Apparently, Albanian authorities seem concerned about their international image. In order to counter adverse publicity, they opened a press office in Geneva and activated a press section in the permanent Albanian mission to the United Nations. The latter disseminates information to newspapers, academics, and some ethnic Albanian organizations.

The Economy. The Albanian economy continued its uneven pace of development, judging from the contradictory analyses and projections made by economic officials and party spokesmen. The proposed budget for fiscal year 1984 envisaged an overall increase of 9.8 percent over the previous year, with the growth to be covered by "reductions in the cost of production" and "increased productivity in all spheres" (ibid., 27 December 1983; *FBIS*, 3 January). Overall industrial production was to increase by 8.5 percent, agricultural production by 14.7 percent, and the volume of investment by 3.5 percent. Exports were to grow by 21.4 percent and labor productivity by 5.1 percent. (*Zeri i Popullit*, 28 December 1983.) Defense was allocated 11 percent of total expenditures (1.01 billion lek), out of total outlays of 9.2 billion. According to the initial

state plan for 1984, about 280 major projects were under way, half of which were expected to be completed by the end of the calendar year. (Ibid., 4 January.) Toward the end of the year, however, the number of projects mentioned as "being under way" was cut in half, and 83 percent of the total planned investment had already been absorbed by the end of the third quarter (ATA, 7 September). Reports from 17 out of 26 districts, often addressed directly to Enver Hoxha, showed fulfillment of the state plan by modest margins above expectations. However, from persistent and often unusually frank criticism voiced by major party and state figures during the year, it becomes obvious that the Albanian economy faced serious problems during 1984. The Seventh Five-Year Plan either may have to be revised downwards or remain unfulfilled in some key areas. The sectors most affected by problems have been the oil and extractive industries, which constitute the bulk of Albania's exports as well as light food and consumer products, which are perennial problems. The authorities blamed "nonfulfillment of plans" on "breakdowns" (which are not always mechanical), discipline problems, and "internal and external enemies."

A major analysis at the beginning of the year, entitled "After Breakdown at Work, Let Us Examine the Attitude and Responsibility of People Toward Work," blamed the managerial elite and "technocrats" for failing to meet production quotas (*Zeri i Popullit*, 13 January). These "failures," according to the article, caused deficits in production and reduced revenues from exports. Oil enterprises, geological work, and mining, as well as construction, were mentioned as having problems.

Hajredin Çeliku, minister of mines and industry (and perhaps responsible for the failures), accused internal enemies who seek "to undermine, sabotage, and reverse our progress on the road to socialism" (*Bashkimi*, 2 August). Reflecting the opinions of powerful figures, the party daily blamed the failure on a lack of discipline on the part of managers and workers (*Zeri i Popullit*, 13 September, 3 October). The net result of "wrong attitudes" and "poor maintenance of machinery," according to the party paper "is that a considerable deficit was created in exports, involving oil, chrome, and light industry products." As far as light industry was concerned, it was reported that "it delivered only 50 percent of the commodities earmarked for export during the last week of August" (ibid., 13 September). Problems are indicated in other areas, including exports of agricultural products. It was reported that the state treasury "lost 5.8 million lek just as a result of nonadherence to schedule in exporting tomatoes" (ibid., 23 June).

Foto Çami had a slightly different explanation of the problem in fulfilling export quotas. He called it unsteady "fulfillment of enterprise goals": "There are calm periods during the first ten days of the month, and then periods of attack during the last ten days of the month, or the third month of the quarter." Yet he had to confess that "fulfillment of production plans under all headings remains a worrisome problem." (*Rruga e Partisë*, July.)

A share of the blame for reduced productivity, nonfulfillment of quotas, and breakdown in work discipline, as we have seen, was laid on the doorstep of the labor unions, which apparently have been playing a more active role than originally thought (*Puna*, 10 January). Yet, the openness in discussing economic shortcomings suggests cleavages in the top leadership. Two areas, mines and industry, as well as the light food industry, in the region of Vlorë have been singled out for specific criticism. The ministers of these two agencies, Hajredin Çeliku and Vito Kapo (widow of the late theoretician, Hysni Kapo), known anti-Soviets, draw their support from the Vlorë district.

Foreign Affairs. Albanian foreign policy continued on the cautious path of an opening to the West, without a letup in anti-American and anti-Soviet rhetoric. Indicative of the Tirana regime's wish to reach out to the noncommunist world is a grudging willingness to permit increased foreign group travel to Albania and an increase in the number of students abroad, mostly in France and the Scandinavian countries (*Die Presse*, 1 August; *FBIS*, 8 August). Approximately a hundred Albanian students are studying at West European universities, and during 1984, 3,000 tourists were allowed to enter the country (*NYT*, 11 November). Although the Tirana regime stayed away from such international gatherings as the Stockholm Conference on Security and Disarmament, it did send a nine-member delegation to the Fifth International Congress of the International Association of Southeast European Studies held in Belgrade. The delegation was led by Aleks Buda, chairman of the Albanian Academy of Sciences and a Central Committee member. Large delegations from the United States and the Soviet Union also participated. (ATA, 9 September; *FBIS*, 11 September.)

Indicative of the "new era" in Albanian foreign policy is the fact that the bulk of exchanges and formal contacts during the past year was not with the communist bloc but with West European and NATO member-countries. Officials and groups from Italy, Turkey, Greece, and Denmark were among the most frequent visitors to Albania. Ironically, Italy, which annexed Albania in 1939, has broadened relations with Albania. During 1984, major transportation, cultural, and communications agreements were signed, and for the first time since 1939 the Italian language is to be taught in Albanian high schools. (ANSA, 4 April; *FBIS*, 5 April.) Relations with West Germany took a turn for the better after the surprise "unofficial visit" by Bavarian prime minister Franz-Josef Strauss, who during three days had a lengthy meeting with Deputy Premier Manush Myftiu (*Economist*, London, 25 August). Although the Bavarian politician called his visit "private," Albania and West Germany have since been engaged in delicate negotiations for the establishment of diplomatic relations (*NYT*, 25 November). The stumbling block in this process remains Albania's claim of war reparations, a claim that has been rejected.

The rhetoric of all major figures, however, remains intensely anti-bourgeois and anti-American. In a major interview granted to the president of the Italian news agency ANSA, Myftiu stated that Albania does not "want relations with the Soviet Union or the United States because both of them have sought to overthrow the Albanian regime" (ANSA, 4 April; *FBIS*, 5 April). Relations with China were the same as previously, with only occasional "theoretical attacks" against the revisionism of Mao Zedong (*Zeri i Popullit*, 29 November). A trade protocol with Beijing is in effect and high-level officials, including Deputy Foreign Minister Sokrat Pliaka, attended a formal reception at the Chinese Embassy on the occasion of China's national day (ATA, 10 October). Thus, contrary to press perceptions of "isolationism," the practice of Albanian foreign policy during 1984 was one of extended contacts with the Third World, West European, and neighboring countries, coupled with intensified controls and repression.

Yugoslavia. There was no noticeable improvement in Yugoslav-Albanian relations during the year. Tirana and Belgrade continued their polemics against each other over the treatment of the Albanian minority in Kosovo. The Albanian press, often quoting Yugoslav sources, reported all trials of its nationals in Kosovo and accused Belgrade of attempts to undermine Albanian culture and identity (*Zeri i Popullit*, 13 October).

The Third Congress of the League of Albanian Writers and Artists became a forum of intense criticism of Yugoslavia for refusing to permit Albanian writers from Kosovo to attend its proceedings (ibid., 27 April). Tirana also maintained the offensive against what it called the "abortive policy of Yugoslav leaders" against Albania and highlighted Yugoslavia's economic problems and its slippage into the bourgeois camp (ibid., 13 October; ATA, 29 September). Belgrade in turn accused Tirana of fostering the idea of a Greater Albania. Despite the rhetoric, however, both countries held talks on a new cultural agreement, which remained inconclusive due to the Yugoslav demand that the "cultural rights" of the Macedonian minority in Albania be protected (ATA, 19 June, 7 October; *FBIS*, 20 June, 10 October). Nevertheless, the two countries signed a trade protocol (ATA, 10 October; *FBIS*, 11 October), and an Albanian delegation visited Yugoslavia in pursuit of a "cultural agreement" (*Zeri i Popullit*, 23 June).

Greece. In response to Greek prime minister Andreas Papandreou's criticisms of Albania's treatment of the Greek minority (*Kathimerini*, 22 February), which Tirana labeled "interference in the internal affairs of a neighboring country," Albania launched an unprecedented attack against "Greek reactionaries, the pope of Rome, and the Yugoslav revisionists" for forming an unholy triangle aimed at smearing the reputation of Albania (*Zeri i Popullit*, 29 February; *NYT*, 2 March).

Despite this inauspicious beginning, Greek-Albanian relations in 1984 included several high-level contacts between the two countries (*Daily Telegraph*, London, 23 August). On 15 May, Greek deputy foreign minister Karolos Papoulias held talks with the Albanian ambassador in Athens to "seek ways to expand relations in trade, culture, science, technology, and transportation" (ATA, 17 May; *Vradnyi*, 16 May). On 28 June, at the invitation of Papoulias, Deputy Foreign Minister Muhamed Kaplani visited Athens, where several agreements were concluded involving the above areas. On 29 August, a high-level meeting, held in the Greek Foreign Ministry and presided over by Papoulias and attended by the archbishop of Athens and all Greece, discussed in depth the minister's planned visit to Albania. It was agreed during the meeting that contacts with Albania should be ex-panded, but the question of ending the state of war, since it involves prewar treaties, should be negotiated at a later time. (*Kathimerini*, 10 September.) Two incidents, however, complicated the process of normalization.

First, on 16 September border guards shot and killed a Greek forester (*WP*, 9 December). A few weeks earlier, the Greek government had uncovered an Albanian spy network in the city of Ioannina near the Albanian border, engaged in gathering information on military deployments and activities of Northern Epirotans in that city (*Apogevmatini*, Athens, 12 December). Two Albanian diplomats were quietly expelled, and a Greek national was arrested for espionage. The incident was revealed only two weeks before the Papoulias visit to Tirana. Perhaps in response and to set the stage for that visit, Enver Hoxha, in a message to the Albanian people, launched an attack against "the chauvinist" Eleftherios Venizelos, a liberal politician revered by Greeks (*Zeri i Popullit*, 29 November). The Papoulias visit, however, did take place as scheduled (3–5 December), and all public pronouncements about it indicated that negotiations were carried out in a cordial atmosphere. The visitor was received by Prime Minister Çarçani, to whom Papoulias delivered a warm message from Papandreou. (ATA, 4 December; *FBIS*, 6 December; Athens News Agency, 10 December.) At least publicly neither side raised the two touchy issues that have hampered development of relations: the Albanians did not raise the issue of the state of war, and the Greeks remained silent about human rights violations against the Greek minority. Both subjects were discussed in private, however.

Eastern Europe. Relations with East European countries showed no appreciable improvement at the ideological level, but in government-to-government contacts, there appears to be a new pragmatism. Enver Hoxha included the "Soviet revisionists and those of the countries of Eastern Europe" among those who "had ulterior, hostile, enslaving aims" against Albania (*Zeri i Popullit*, 29 November).

Trade protocols, almost identical in form and with similar products bartered, were signed with Bulgaria (ATA, 10 November; *FBIS*, 13 November), Czechoslovakia (ATA, 17 November; *FBIS*, 19 November), the German Democratic Republic (ATA, 3 October; *FBIS*, 4 October), and Cuba (ATA, 17 November; *FBIS*, 19 November). There is no information available on economic exchange with Poland, whose regime Tirana often criticized for slipping back into a bourgeois status.

The Albanian government seems to have developed closer relations with Asian communist regimes than with East European ones. Several delegations from Hanoi visited during the year. A trade protocol with the Socialist Republic of Vietnam was signed early in 1984 (ATA, 17 January; *FBIS*, 18 January), and another Vietnamese delegation visited Tirana for the purpose of negotiating a science and technology agreement (ATA, 1 August; *FBIS*, 3 August). Similarly, several groups from North Korea came to Albania. A joint Commission on Technical and Scientific Cooperation has been activated, and it processes all economic agreements (ATA, 22 November; *FBIS*, 3 December). North Korea seems to be the only country with which Tirana maintains such a joint commission.

Western World. Relations with the West witnessed a dramatic improvement in all spheres, except those with the United States. A minor setback with France occurred in the summer when Albanian border guards shot a French swimmer who had come too close to the coast. In this incident, the Albanian government claimed that "its guards did not know whether the violators were French, Greek, Russian, or persons sent by the son of the former King Zog" (*Zeri i Popullit*, 7 July). Paris responded by recalling its ambassador "for consultations" (*NYT*, 28 June).

The most dramatic improvement in relations, as previously indicated, involved Italy. At least eight high-level official visits were undertaken during 1984. On 27 January, a protocol for cultural and scientific exchanges was signed in Rome (ATA, 28 January; *FBIS*, 3 February). Subsequently, Italian foreign trade minister Nicola Capria arrived in Tirana to sign a commercial protocol (ATA, 18 March; *FBIS*, 19 March). Provisions for cultural ties include a chair of Italian literature at the University of Tirana, student exchanges, and, more surprisingly, the teaching of the Italian language in Albanian high schools (ATA, 4 April; *FBIS*, 5 April). These agreements were followed by formal links between the Italian and Albanian news agencies for the exchange of news, several visits by members of the Italian Chamber of Commerce, and an Italian film week in Tirana (*Radio Free Europe–Radio Liberty*, no. 141–1, August). Albanian health minister Ajli Alushani paid an official visit to

Rome, where he met with his counterpart and was received by Prime Minister Bettino Craxi (ATA, 3 October; *FBIS*, 4 October). Finally, an agreement on scientific cooperation is in effect between the University of Tirana and La Sapienza University of Rome (ATA, 30 April; *FBIS*, 5 May). Relations with Italy have reached such a level of improvement that Yugoslavia—mindful of the 1939–1940 experience when Italy used Albania as a stepping-stone into the Balkans—considers their growth as a "new element" with long-range implications. Total exports from Albania to Italy reached 850 billion lira, and imports 250 billion lira. (*Borba*, 22 March; *FBIS*, 26 March.)

The surprise development in Albania's quest for links with the West was the arrival in that country of the veteran Bavarian politician Franz-Josef Strauss, who traveled by car for a three-day stay and was received by Deputy Premier Manush Myftiu (*NYT*, 21 August; *CSM*, 22 August). Following the Strauss visit, speculations were revived that the two countries might soon establish diplomatic relations. West Germany is one of only three West European countries with which Tirana has no formal relations. The other two are Spain and Great Britain, both of which have shown a willingness to "resolve" outstanding issues and establish ties. (*Die Welt*, 8 May; *FBIS*, 9 May; *NYT*, 25 November.) Talks between the Spanish and Albanian ambassadors have been under way in Belgrade (Madrid radio, 21 August; *FBIS*, 22 August).

A further development of Albanian-Turkish relations was also noticeable during the year. Next to Italy, Turkey was the most "conspicuously present" NATO member with which Albania developed contacts in all areas and signed several important agreements, including one on air transportation (ATA, 8 February; *FBIS*, 9 February). Four high-level visits, involving government officials of the two countries, were undertaken during 1984. Deputy Foreign Minister Sokrat Pliaka went to Ankara, in what appears to be an annual affair (ATA, 1 February; *FBIS*, 3 February); Albanian foreign trade minister Shane Korbeci followed soon thereafter (ATA, 19 February; *FBIS*, 24 February); Turkish agriculture minister Hosnu Dogan paid a visit to Albania for talks on agricultural cooperation (ATA, 8 May; *FBIS*, 14 May); and the mayor of Istanbul came to Tirana and was given a tour of the country (ATA, 9 October; *FBIS*, 11 October). In addition, a week of Turkish films was organized (*RAD Background Report*, 1 August).

With Sweden, a long-standing commercial partner to which chrome is exported, Albania concluded an unusual four-year trade agreement (ATA, 7 December; *FBIS*, 11 December). A trade protocol was also signed with the Netherlands (ATA, 11 April; *FBIS*, 16 April) and a transportation agreement with Switzerland (ATA, 10 May; *FBIS*, 15 May). Finally, diplomatic relations with Australia were established (ATA, 14 September; *FBIS*, 17 September), and continued close contacts with Iran were maintained. The Albanian minister of foreign trade visited Tehran; earlier in the year a radio and television crew had been there (ATA, 22 February, 30 November; *FBIS*, 24 February, 3 December). Thus, "Albanian isolationism" may no longer be an appropriate term in light of the growing contacts with the noncommunist world. A more appropriate term may be "Ramanization": that is, while Albania expands relations with the rest of the world, it also intensifies its Stalinist domestic controls.

China. Relations with China continued uneventful. A trade protocol signed in 1983 is still in effect, and there has been an appreciable reduction in the anti-Beijing rhetoric emanating from Tirana. Enver Hoxha, in a "congratulatory message" to his people on the occasion of the fortieth anniversary of the communist regime, attacked with his usual fervor "Mao Zedong's revisionism" (*Zeri i Popullit*, 29 November). However, Ramiz Alia, in his capacity as president of the republic, sent a congratulatory message to China. Sokrat Pliaka, along with a number of other second-level Albanian officials, attended the reception on China's national day (ATA, 1 October; *FBIS*, 2 October). Tirana attacks only the "opening to Western capitalist investment" (ATA, 18 May; *FBIS*, 21 May), but lengthy articles written by lower-echelon functionaries are often critical of Mao's revisionism (e.g., *Rruga e Partisë*, May).

USSR. There was no significant change in Tirana's position vis-à-vis Moscow. Anti-Soviet rhetoric continued unabated. In a wide-ranging interview with the president of the Italian news agency, Deputy Prime Minister Manush Myftiu unequivocally stated that Albania does not want relations with the two superpowers (ANSA, 4 April; *FBIS*, 5 April). However, so far Albanians have not editorialized against Chernenko personally. His assumption of the post as general secretary was simply announced in a two-line bulletin by the Albanian Telegraphic Agency (ATA, 11 April; *FBIS*, 16

April). The same source reported factually on the lengthy interview given by Chernenko to NBC (ATA, 17 November; *FBIS*, 19 November). Although Tirana remains negative toward the Soviets, there have been several initiatives on the part of Moscow to resolve differences. In a commentary by Radio Moscow (30 May) in Albanian, the Soviets claimed that they "are making consistent efforts to normalize relations with the People's Socialist Republic of Albania" (*FBIS*, 1 June). More important, while on a visit to Sofia for Bulgaria's fortieth anniversary of communist rule, current Soviet heir apparent Mikhail Gorbachev declared the Soviet Union to be "in favor of normalization of relations with Albania" (*RAD Background Report*, 26 October). Characteristic of this attitude is the fact that Moscow reactivated the Soviet-Albanian Friendship Society soon after Brezhnev's death in December 1982, and Moscow unexpectedly marked the anniversary of the Berat Conference (22 October 1944) during which Hoxha formed the provisional government (ibid., 6 November). So far, Albanian party officials have responded negatively to all Soviet overtures. Nevertheless, a pro-Soviet group does exist in the higher echelon of the Albanian party and could become active after Hoxha's departure (*Washington Times*, 2 January).

United States. There was no let-up in the anti-American rhetoric coming from Tirana. Albania's quest for links with the Western world does not include the United States. Washington seems satisfied that relations have improved with some of its close allies, that is, Italy, France, and Turkey (*NYT*, 25 November). Yet, there are some signs that Tirana is showing an interest in American affairs. Albania's mission to the United Nations is active in broadening its ties with ethnic Albanians and with "friends of Albania." A press office has been activated for the purpose of disseminating "information," and bulletins of the Albanian Telegraphic Agency are now routinely mailed to editors of American news organizations. Finally, Foreign Minister Reiz Malile held his traditional October reception at U.N. headquarters for a select group of pro-Tirana Albanians living in the United States, some of whom were also permitted to travel to their former homeland (ATA, 8 October; *FBIS*, 9 October).

International Party Congresses. Several Third World and European Marxist-Leninist party delegations visited Albania on the occasion of the fortieth anniversary of communist rule. Among them were delegations from Spain, Denmark, Brazil, Ecuador, Portugal, Greece, and Algeria (ATA, 27 November; *FBIS*, 29 November). Of the ruling communist parties, only Vietnam and North Korea were represented. A Greek Communist, resistance hero Manolis Glezon, timed his visit to Albania to coincide with that of Deputy Foreign Minister Karolos Papoulias and was received by Ramiz Alia (ATA, 27 November; *FBIS*, 29 November). Earlier in the year, Marxist-Leninist delegations were invited from Great Britain and West Germany (ATA, 22 June, 9 October; *FBIS*, 26 June, 12 October). Enver Hoxha privately received João Amazonas, first secretary of the Brazilian (Marxist-Leninist) Communist Party, and Professor Paul Milez, chairman of the French-Albanian Friendship Society (ATA, 27 November, 1 December; *FBIS*, 29 November, 3 December).

Nikolaos A. Stavrou
Howard University

Bulgaria

Population. 8,969,000

Party. Bulgarian Communist Party (Bulgarska komunisticheska partiya; BCP)

Founded. Bulgarian Social Democratic Party founded in 1891; split into Broad and Narrow factions in 1903; the Narrow Socialists became the BCP and joined the Comintern in 1919.

Membership. 825,876; 42.7 percent industrial workers (*Otchet na Tsentralniya komitet na BKP pred XII kongres*, Sofia, 1981, pp. 112–13)

Secretary General. Todor Khristov Zhivkov

Politburo. 11 full members: Todor Zhivkov (chairman, State Council), Chudomir Alexandrov (first deputy prime minister), Milko Balev (member, State Council), Todor Bozhinov (deputy prime minister; minister of energy and raw material resources), Ognyan Doynov (minister of machine building and electronics), Dobri Dzhurov (minister of national defense), Grisha Filipov (prime minister), Pencho Kubadinski (member, State Council; chairman, Fatherland Front), Petur Mladenov (minister of foreign affairs), Stanko Todorov (chairman, National Assembly), Yordan Yotov (editor-in-chief, *Rabotnichesko delo*); 7 candidate members: Georgi Atanasov, Stanish Bonev (deputy prime minister; chairman, State Planning Committee), Petur Dyulgerov (chairman, Central Council of Trade Unions), Andrey Lukanov (deputy prime minister), Grigor Stoichkov (deputy prime minister; minister of construction, territorial structure, and architecture), Dimitur Stoyanov (minister of internal affairs), Georgi Yordanov (chairman, Committee on Culture)

Secretariat. 8 members: Georgi Atanasov, Milko Balev, Ognyan Doynov, Emil Khristov (member, State Council), Stoyan Mikhailov, Dimitur Stanishev, Vasil Tsanov, Kiril Zarev

Central Committee. 191 full and 138 candidate members

Status. Ruling party

Last Congress. Twelfth, 31 March–4 April 1981, in Sofia; next congress scheduled for 1986

Last Election. 7 June 1981. All candidates run on ticket of Fatherland Front, an umbrella organization (4.4 million members) comprising most mass organizations. Fatherland Front candidates received 99.9 percent of votes cast. Of the National Assembly's 400 members, 271 belong to the BCP and 99 to the

Agrarian Union; 30 are unaffiliated (some 20 of these are Komsomols). The Bulgarian Agrarian National Union (BANU, 120,000 members) formally shares power with the BCP, holds 4 of the 29 places on the State Council, the ministries of justice, public health, communications, and forestry, and about one-sixth of local people's council seats. BANU leader Petur Tanchev's post as first deputy chairman of the State Council makes him Todor Zhivkov's nominal successor as head of state.

Auxiliary Organizations. Central Council of Trade Unions (CCTU, about 4 million members), led by Petur Dyulgerov; Dimitrov Communist Youth League (Komsomol, 1.5 million members), led by Stanka Shopova; Civil Defense Organization (750,000 members), led by Col. Gen. Tencho Papazov, provides training in paramilitary tactics and disaster relief; Committee on Bulgarian Women (30,000 members), led by Elena Lagadinova, no real significance

Publications. *Rabotnichesko delo* (*RD*; Workers' cause), BCP daily; *Partien zhivot* (Party life), BCP monthly; *Novo vreme* (New time), BCP theoretical journal; *Otechestven front* (Fatherland front), front daily; *Durzhaven vestnik* (State newspaper), contains texts of laws and decrees. Bulgarska telegrafna agentsiya (BTA) is the official news agency.

Although little official attention was paid either to Todor Zhivkov's seventy-third birthday or the thirtieth anniversary of his becoming head of the BCP, there was no indication that the Bulgarian leader suffered from any political or physical problems. Zhivkov supervised organizational and personnel changes in the party and government, launched a major campaign to raise the quality of industrial production, and maintained a vigorous schedule of public appearances and travel. The celebration of the fortieth anniversary of the 9 September 1944 uprising was marred by news of mysterious bombings, whose cause and extent could not be fully determined. On the international scene, Bulgaria continued to try to refute the charges of a "Bulgarian connection" in the attempted assassination of Pope John Paul II.

Leadership and Party Organization. On 3 January a Central Committee plenum accepted the retirement of Tsola Dragoycheva from the Politburo. Born in 1898, Dragoycheva joined the BCP in 1919, became a member of the Central Committee in 1937, and played a major role in the leadership during World War II and the communist takeover that followed. She was relegated to minor positions during the Vulko Chervernkov era (1950–1953) but made a comeback under Zhivkov and had held a seat on the Politburo since 1966. She gave as the reason for her retirement her advanced age and the desire to devote her remaining strength to the completion of her memoirs.

Dragoycheva's retirement and the purge of Alexander Lilov in 1983 (see *YICA*, 1984, p. 303) left two openings on the Politburo, and the plenum named Chudomir Alexandrov and Yordan Yotov to fill them. Alexandrov, born in 1936, has been rising rapidly in recent years, having been appointed first

secretary of the Sofia city party committee in 1979 and a Central Committee secretary in 1981. He was relieved of the latter post by the plenum and resigned the former in March. Immediately after the plenum the National Assembly elected him a first deputy prime minister, an indication that he will have a large part to play in dealing with the management of the economy. Yotov is an older man, born in 1920. He is a professor of party history and has edited the party daily, *Rabotnichesko delo*, since 1977. Additional qualifications include his birthplace, Zhivkov's own Botevgrad region, and his WWII service with the Chavdar partisan brigade, in which Zhivkov was also active.

The January plenum also named four new candidate members of the Politburo: Grigor Stoichkov, Stanish Bonev, Georgi Atanasov, and Dimitur Stoyanov. Stoichkov, born in 1926, has held many party positions and posts in the economic ministries and was most recently in charge of territorial development. Following the plenum, the National Assembly appointed him minister of construction, territorial structure, and architecture. Bonev, an economic specialist, was born in 1931. He has been chairman of the State Planning Commission since 1982. Atanasov, born in 1933, is a former head of the Komsomol and has been a Central Committee secretary since 1977. Stoyanov, born in 1928, is minister of internal affairs. (Sofia domestic service, 3 January; *FBIS*, 4 January; *RFE Situation Report*, 16 January, item 2.)

The plenum also added a new Central Committee secretary, Emil Khristov. Khristov, on the faculty of the Central Committee's Academy for Social Management is believed to be a specialist in the legal aspects of social and economic administration. (Sofia domestic service, 3 January; *FBIS*, 4 January; *RFE Situation Report*, 16 January, item

2.) Misho Mishev, a Central Committee secretary since 1979, died on 3 February (Sofia domestic service, 3 February; *FBIS*, 6 February). It became apparent during the year that the BCP had reorganized and renamed several of its Central Committee departments. Details of this reorganization were not made public, but references to new departments began to appear in the press in May. An Ideological Policy Department was created by merging the old departments of Propaganda and Agitation, Mass Information and Media, and Culture, and possibly also the Informational-Sociological Center. Central Committee secretary Stoyan Mikhailov heads the new department (*Le Monde*, Paris, 14 December; *FBIS*, 20 December). The departments of Economic Planning, Industry, Transport and Communications, and Construction and Public Works seem to have been combined into a new department of Economic, Scientific, and Technical Policy. The head of this new department is not known with certainty, but Central Committee secretary Kiril Zarev, former head of the State Planning Committee, would seem to be the most likely candidate. The old Military-Administrative Department was renamed the Social and National Security Department. Colonel General Velko Palin remains its head. There was also some indication that the Organizational Department and the Department of People's Councils and Mass Organizations were merged (they had been one department before their separation in 1980). As a result of this reorganization, the number of Central Committee departments has been reduced from fifteen or sixteen to about ten. (*RFE Situation Report*, 18 July, item 1.)

Petko Rusev, a member of the Central Committee and the editor-in-chief of the party journal *Partien zhivot*, died in October. The name of the new editor was not immediately announced. (Sofia domestic service, 15 October; *FBIS*, 16 October.)

Accountability-election conferences in February brought few changes in party leadership at the provincial level. In Mikhailovgrad, Petur Nikolov, a secretary on the provincial party committee was elected chairman, replacing Anastas Purvanov. In Kiustendil, Stanko Dimitrov was replaced by Georgi Grigorov, who had formerly been head of the Central Committee's Organizational Department. No reason was given for these changes other than that the incumbents were "transferred to other work." (BTA, 10 January; *FBIS*, 11 January.) In Vidin, however, Zhivkov and Mladenov attended the conference, which heard criticism of the party's

efforts to improve the goal of production quality. Khristofor Ivanov was replaced as first secretary by Khristo Bonin, who was brought in from Sofia, where he had been a district party secretary. (Sofia domestic service, 23 February; *FBIS*, 24 and 25 February.) Other shifts in provincial party leadership were clearly the result of promotions. Vladimir Sandev, first secretary of the Blagoevgrad party organization, was named deputy chairman of the BCP's Central Control and Auditing Commission. He was replaced by Lazar Prichkapov, who had headed the Central Committee's Propaganda and Education Department until the reorganization described above. (BTA, 9 and 10 January; *FBIS*, 10 and 11 January.) Following Chudomir Alexandrov's resignation in March, Georgi Georgiev took Alexandrov's position as first secretary of the Sofia party committee, a post that has often been the springboard to rapid advancement. Georgiev carried out a purge of the Varna party organization in 1981 and had been named first secretary in Stara Zagora the preceding October. (See *YICA*, 1984, pp. 303–4; Sofia domestic service, 14 March; *FBIS*, 15 March.) Georgiev was replaced in Stara Zagora by Mincho Yovchev (Sofia domestic service, 16 March; *FBIS*, 19 March).

A degree of rehabilitation was extended to several party figures who had been victims of past purges. Former prime minister Anton Yugov, a nonperson since his ouster by Zhivkov in 1962, was awarded the decoration Hero of Socialist Labor on the occasion of his eightieth birthday. A published biographical sketch emphasized his contributions to the wartime resistance, but passed over his role in the postwar government and his downfall. The same award was given to thirteen other former party leaders on the eve of the fortieth anniversary of 9 September. The majority of them had been accused of some form of Stalinism. (*RFE Situation Report*, 10 September, item 2.) Venelin Kotsev, a former Central Committee secretary and candidate member of the Politburo until he was dropped from these positions in the early 1970s and consigned to a series of diplomatic posts, made a minor comeback with his appointment as deputy minister of machine building in Ognyan Doynov's ministry (ibid., 17 July, item 2). Posthumous rehabilitation was given to Dobri Terpeshev on the centenary of his birth. Terpeshev, who died in 1967, was the military commander of the wartime resistance, but never made a successful transition from fighter to bureaucrat. He held a number of positions in the communist government, but was expelled from the party in 1957, reportedly for persistent criticism of the leadership. In a long article published in *Rabotnichesko delo* (15 May), he was praised as a champion of the communist cause and a major contributor to the overthrow of capitalism. No mention was made of his purge. (*RFE Situation Report*, 17 July, item 3.)

Domestic Affairs. As the Bulgarian regime prepared to celebrate the fortieth anniversary of the 9 September seizure of power, news of a series of bombing incidents created disquieting rumors. According to reports in the foreign press, on 30 August explosions occurred at the Varna airport and the railroad station in Plovdiv. Reports followed of other bombings in a number of different cities, and foreign observers noted a sharp increase in security measures in the capital. The Bulgarian press agency confirmed only the explosion in Plovdiv, but described it as an incident of a purely criminal nature and denied that it had any political significance. Rumors circulated, however, that one bomb had been found with an explicitly political message: "Forty years—forty bombs." As far as could be determined no group or individual claimed responsibility for the bombings, and speculation centered on political dissidents, who have not been visible in the recent past, and the country's Turkish minority. Perhaps to quell the rumors, the Bulgarian press gave unusual publicity to two bombing incidents, one involving an attempt to send a letter bomb in an act of personal revenge, the other involving a bank robbery. In both cases the culprits were arrested, tried, and executed. (*Economist*, London, 29 September; *Frankfurter Allgemeine Zeitung*, 21 September; BTA, 21 September; *FBIS*, 24 September; *RFE Situation Report*, 23 October, item 1.)

The bombing incidents, whatever their extent and motivation, did not interfere with any of the official events celebrating the anniversary. Zhivkov made a rousing speech, boasting that Bulgaria has made great contributions to proving the viability and attractiveness of socialism and paying tribute to the immense help received from the Soviet Union. The Soviet delegate to the celebration was Politburo member Mikhail Gorbachev, who praised Zhivkov's and Bulgaria's efforts to create a nuclear-free zone in the Balkans. (Sofia domestic service, 8 September; *FBIS*, 10 September; *RFE Situation Report*, 24 September, item 1.)

Government Changes. Immediately after the Central Committee plenum in January, the National Assembly held a special session to approve a series of changes in government structure and personnel. The purpose seems to have been to streamline administration by consolidating some of the economic ministries into "superministries" headed by high-ranking party leaders. A Ministry of Production and Trade in Consumer Goods was created by merging the Ministries of Light Industry and of Internal Trade and Services. Georgi Karamanev, who had headed the latter, was appointed to lead the new ministry. Two other ministries, Metallurgy and Mineral Resources, and Energy, were combined into a Ministry of Energy and Raw Material Resources. Politburo member Todor Bozhinov was appointed to head this ministry, having been minister of metallurgy and mineral resources since 1982. At the same time he was demoted from the position of first deputy prime minister to deputy prime minister, the former position going to Chudomir Alexandrov. Politburo member and Central Committee secretary Ognyan Doynov was appointed minister of machine building and electronics. His predecessor, Toncho Chakarov, became the first deputy minister. Two other ministers who lost their posts in the government restructuring received new positions that indicated little change in their duties. Ivan Sakarev, the former minister of construction, became first deputy minister of construction and territorial structure, and Rumen Serbezov, former minister of light industry, became first deputy minister of production and trade in consumer goods. Both men retained their ministerial rank. (*RFE Situation Report*, 16 January, item 2, 1 February, item 3.)

The National Assembly also released Nacho Papazov from his post as chairman of the State Committee on Science and Technical Progress, replacing him with former energy minister Nikola Todoriev. Both Papazov and Politburo member Miko Balev were elected to the State Council. Kiril Zarev was released from his post of deputy prime minister, a move that had been expected since he became a Central Committee secretary in 1982. (Ibid., 1 February, item 3.)

Rumors circulated during the year of discontent and shake-ups in the military, but there was little that could be confirmed. Colonel Alexander Nikolov, the editor-in-chief of the army newspaper, *Narodna armiia*, was apparently removed late in 1983 and has not appeared in public since that time. According to some reports, he was confined to a psychiatric clinic for persistently criticizing the party leadership. (Ibid., 24 September, item 2.) Colonel General Kiril Kosev (age 65), chief of the

Main Political Directorate of the Army since 1971, was released from the army in February in connection with "his transfer to another position." Although no direct criticism of Kosev appeared in the press, shortcomings in ideological education in the military and the need to overcome them were heavily emphasized during the year. (Ibid.; *Narodna armiia*, 4 February, 12 December; *FBIS*, 30 March, 17 December.)

Economy. Economic issues, particularly the problem of raising the quality of Bulgarian products, provided the main focus of attention in domestic life. According to the report of Stanish Bonev, chairman of the State Planning Committee, economic performance during 1983 fell short of plan targets in several categories. Domestic net material product increased by 3.0 percent over 1982 against a target of 3.8 percent. Labor productivity was said to have improved by 5.0 percent, but only in the nonagricultural sector; the target was 3.9 percent growth in the total economy. Industrial production grew 4.6 percent, close to the 4.8 percent target, but agricultural production, scheduled to grow by 2.7 percent, fell below the 1982 level. No precise figure for agriculture was given. Bad weather, including a prolonged drought and then heavy rainfall during the harvest period, was primarily responsible for the setback in this sector. Real per capita income rose 2.8 percent, as called for by the plan. The growth in the volume of foreign trade exceeded the plan target, but reflected a trend toward increased dependence on the Council for Mutual Economic Assistance (CMEA) and the Soviet Union. "More than three-quarters" of Bulgaria's trade was with the CMEA in 1983, 57 percent with the USSR alone. Corresponding figures for 1981 were 72.3 percent and 51.6 percent and for 1982, 74.8 percent and 54.0 percent. In the late 1970s Bulgarian trade with the noncommunist world expanded significantly, but in more recent years Western markets for Bulgarian goods have been contracting. This was one of the factors stressed by Zhivkov in opening the campaign for improved quality in production. (BTA, 16 January; *FBIS*, 18 January; *RFE Situation Report*, 15 February, item 1.) A report issued by Wharton Econometrics pointed to the importance of arms sales to Third World countries as a major element in Bulgaria's exports to the noncommunist world. Based on "official unpublished Bulgarian foreign trade statistics," the report concluded that in 1982 arms exports amounted to 990 million devisa leva or 9.1 percent of Bulgaria's total export earnings (*WP*, 10 August).

The National Party Conference, held on 22–23 March and attended by 2,944 delegates, was devoted to the theme of raising production quality. The work of the conference had been defined previously by Zhivkov in a speech given in May 1983 that was bluntly critical of the low quality of many Bulgarian products and in six lectures delivered to the students and faculty of the BCP Central Committee Academy of Social Sciences and Social Management. The lectures were published separately and provided the guidelines for the policies endorsed by the conference. In his speech opening the conference, Zhivkov stated that the quality of industrial goods had been neglected in the past, when the country was in a more primitive stage of development, but it was now the "key problem." He stressed the need to make Bulgarian products more competitive with those of the advanced capitalist states. To meet the goal expressed in the party's slogan "High quality everywhere and in everything," Zhivkov emphasized the contributions of science and technology, industrial reorganization and modernization, and further reforms in the New Economic Mechanism. According to the summary that appeared in the press, the following principles were described as "the heart" of the policies adopted at the conference: (1) production relationships should rest on an economic, not administrative, foundation; (2) the Bulgarian National Bank should give priority to financing projects based on a high level of technology; (3) wages and salaries should be tied more closely to improvements in quality; (4) small and medium-sized enterprises with advanced technology should be given priority over massive projects; (5) 70 percent of the funds allocated to an enterprise for renovation must go to "real modernizations"; and (6) the educational system should be improved and the educational requirements for positions in the economy should be raised. (BTA, 2 April; *FBIS*, 4 April; *RFE Situation Report*, 30 March, item 3.)

In an interview with the Yugoslav newspaper *Borba* (2 August), Central Committee secretary Emil Khristov stated that Bulgaria's new policies were based on the recognition that it was no longer possible to direct the entire economy from the center and that local initiative would have to be encouraged. He cited as one example a new measure that allows some exporters to retain their foreign exchange earnings provided that they use them to finance the production of exportable goods. He also stated that wage ceilings for brigades have been removed, so that workers may keep the full fruits of their improved efficiency. (*FBIS*, 6 August.)

Alexander Petkov, chairman of Bulgaria's National Agro-Industrial Complex, reported that the administration of agriculture underwent a significant reform. A 22 percent reduction in the administrative apparatus was achieved by eliminating the middle level in the old administrative structure (agro-industrial complexes—local branch farms—agricultural brigades) and by consolidating the country's 8,850 brigades into 3,560 "brigades of a new type." (BTA, 6 February; *FBIS*, 7 February.) On the negative side, heavy rains in February and March delayed the preparation of the fields for sowing (Sofia domestic service, 21 March; *FBIS*, 22 March). Delays in the delivery of farm machinery and fertilizer were also reported. Later in the year poor management in the use of "voluntary" student labor during the summer months led to serious delays in the harvesting of summer crops (*RFE Situation Report*, 24 September, item 4).

In connection with the celebration of the fortieth anniversary of the Fatherland Front's seizure of power, the government issued a decree on the standard of living that raised minimum wages in several categories of employment. As of 1 September the basic minimum wage was raised from 100 to 110 leva monthly and will be raised again to 120 leva in 1986; the minimum salary for specialists with higher education will rise from 155 to 170 leva; and minimum pensions will be raised from 40 to 50 leva. Holders of high state awards will also have their pensions increased. A precise amount was not given, but these pensions are believed to be far higher than the minimum. (Sofia domestic service, 24 April; *FBIS*, 25 April; *RFE Situation Report*, 12 May, item 1.)

The economic plan for 1985 was adopted by the National Assembly on 30 November. It called for a 4.1 percent increase in net material product; a 4.3 percent increase in labor productivity; a 3.2 percent increase in agricultural production; a 4.5 percent increase in foreign trade; and an increase in real income per capita of 3.0 percent. It also called for the construction of 78,900 new apartments. (Sofia domestic service, 30 November; *FBIS*, 3 December.)

Demography. The low birthrate of ethnic Bulgarians has been the subject of increasing concern by state leaders (see *YICA*, 1983, pp. 254–55; 1984, p. 304). A survey of the population of Stara Zagora province found few people in favor of large families. The main reasons given were the heavy pressure on women created by the combination of work and child-rearing responsibilities and inadequate housing conditions (BTA, 13 January; *FBIS*, 18 January). The decree on the standard of living contained several measures aimed at creating improved conditions for large families. As of 1 July 1985 the monthly child allowance for a second child will be increased from 15 to 30 leva. When a second child is born, the allowance for the first child will also double from 15 to 30 leva. And the monthly allowance for a third child will rise from 45 to 50 leva. The time of paid maternity leave will be extended from eight months until the child's second birthday. Moreover, fathers and grandparents will be eligible for paid leave if they are providing childcare. The housing construction industry was encouraged to take into greater account the needs of large families. Of greater significance was the provision that entitles newly wed couples to low-interest loans of up to 15,000 leva for purchasing homes. These loans are to be paid back over a 30-year period; upon the birth of the family's second child 3,000 leva of the debt will be canceled, and an additional 4,000 leva will be canceled on the birth of a third child. At the same time the decree announced that income taxes for childless couples will be raised. (*RD*, 25 April; *FBIS*, 1 May; *RFE Situation Report*, 12 May, item 1.) During August it was announced that 25 percent of the stock of new housing will be reserved for newly wed couples and for families with three or more children (Sofia domestic service, 9 August; *FBIS*, 10 August).

In August the draft of a new family code was published for public discussion. The principal changes from the previous code, adopted in 1968, include provisions making more explicit the obligations of adult children to aged parents and making divorce more expensive and difficult to obtain. (*RFE Situation Report*, 10 September, item 3.)

Culture and Education. The national party conference called for changes in the educational system as part of the effort to upgrade the quality of Bulgarian products. In September a plenum of the Central Committee of the Dimitrov Communist Youth League was devoted to the problem of introducing computer training in education. Politburo member Chudomir Alexandrov, who addressed the plenum, stated that the computerization of the entire economy was necessary if the country was to continue on the road to communism. The plenum decided that during the 1984–85 academic year schools be equipped with approximately 3,500 microcomputers. This number will rise to 30,000 in 1990. Komsomol organizers were also directed to organize and promote "computer clubs" and training classes outside the classroom. (Ibid., 10 October, item 2.)

The regime began to implement the expansion of vocational training for students in nonvocational high schools that had been called for by a BCP plenum in 1979. According to the system now going into effect, academic training will be concentrated in the ninth and tenth grades, with the eleventh spent in "educational-professional complexes," that is, training workshops in factories and enterprises. These enterprises are encouraged to offer employment to the graduates. (Ibid., 12 May, item 3.)

Party leaders in the cultural field launched an intense campaign against "alien influence" in Bulgaria's "musical environment." Directed primarily against Western popular music, seen as a form of cultural imperialism, the campaign included stronger party controls over Bulgarian musical organizations, greater time devoted to Bulgarian popular and folk music on radio and television, and propaganda directed against Western music. During 1982 Komsomol leader Stanka Shopova criticized discotheques and called for them to offer "current political and cultural information" as well as dancing (see *YICA*, 1983, p. 253). As a result, it was reported this year, attendance at Bulgarian discotheques has fallen in half (*RFE Situation Report*, 30 March, item 5).

A nationalist reaction to the influx of foreign words into the Bulgarian language was also apparent at a meeting of the National Assembly's Standing Commission on Spiritual Values of Society, headed by writer-politician Georgi Dzhagarov. It called for the establishment of a specialized state agency, analogous to the French Academy, to work for the purification of the Bulgarian tongue. (Ibid., 18 July, item 4.)

Numerous indications appeared in the press that the party has become seriously concerned by the spread of video recorders in the country. Apparently many citizens have turned their homes into theaters where audiences view films "lacking in moral or ideological value." It was reported that several people had been prosecuted, under laws prohibiting the possession of "unearned income," for having charged admission to video performances. In August a Bulgarian Video Association

was set up under the Committee on Culture to exercise control over the marketing of video tapes and equipment. According to a decree of the Council of Ministers, all privately owned video cameras and recorders must be registered with the association. (Ibid., 15 February, item 2; 10 October, item 1.)

Bulgaria's two most prominent violinists, Emil Kamilarov and his Soviet-born wife, Dina Schneidermann, left Bulgaria to seek asylum in Sweden. They expressed gratitude for the training and facilities they had received in Bulgaria, but objected to the absence of artistic and creative freedom. (Ibid., 10 September, item 4.)

Auxiliary Organizations. In early September BANU hosted an International Peace Meeting attended by 76 left-wing parties from 45 countries. The opening speech was given by BANU leader Petur Tanchev, who saw U.S. imperialism as the main threat to world peace (BTA, 5 September; *FBIS*, 6 September). Dimitur Karamukov, a secretary of the BANU's Permanent Board and a member of the National Council of the Fatherland Front, died in March (Sofia domestic service, 16 March; *FBIS*, 21 March).

The CCTU hosted the thirty-sixth session of the World Federation of Trade Unions. It was attended by representatives of 90 organizations from 82 countries (BTA, 16 October; *FBIS*, 17 October). After the session ended, the CCTU held its sixth plenum and made substantial organizational changes to adapt to the country's shift in economic policies. According to Petur Dyulgerov, head of the CCTU and a candidate member of the Politburo, the increasing responsibilities given to brigades and labor collectives had created confusion over the rights and responsibilities of these units vis-à-vis the trade unions. According to Dyulgerov, the preparation of the counterplan, allocation of wages, and proposals for improving production must rest with the collective rather than the trade unions. The role of the unions should be to inspire the work of the labor collectives, providing them with organizational advice and making sure that the new rules are followed correctly. Changes were made in the CCTU's structure to link it more closely with the organization of industry. At the brigade, labor collective (enterprise), and corporation levels, corresponding trade union units (elementary, basic, and trade union council) will be created. This structure will largely replace the old, regionally based one. Changes in the CCTU leadership approved by the plenum also indicated that the organization will emphasize ideological and educational work. Three of the seven CCTU secretaries were released and two new ones were elected. The new secretaries were Ivan Angelov, who was also the first deputy minister of finance, and Rusi Kararusinov, who had been director of the Institute for Contemporary Social Theories and deputy head of the BCP Central Committee's Department for Mass Media. (Sofia domestic service, 24 October; *FBIS*, 25 October; *RFE Situation Report*, 7 November, item 1.)

Foreign Affairs. World attention continued to be focused on the Italian investigation of the "Bulgarian connection," the alleged complicity of Bulgarian agents in the 1981 attempt on the life of Pope John Paul II. In November 1982 Italian authorities arrested Sergei Ivanov Antonov, head of Bulgaria's Balkan Airline office in Rome and allegedly a State Security agent. The Italian prosecutor also sought the arrest of two embassy officials, Todor Aivazov and Maj. Zhelyo Vasilev, who had previously returned to Bulgaria (see *YICA*, 1983, p. 256; 1984, pp. 306–7). At the end of 1983 Ilario Martella, the magistrate in charge of the investigation, submitted his report to the Italian state prosecutor, who filed his own summary of the case with the court in May. A copy of this report was leaked to American journalist Claire Sterling, who was among the first to call attention to the alleged "Bulgarian connection." She published a summary of the prosecutor's report in the *New York Times* (10 June), emphasizing those elements that pointed to Bulgarian complicity. As more information became available, however, it appeared that the case against Antonov and the other two Bulgarians still rested heavily on the testimony of would-be assassin Mehmet Ali Agca and that conclusive corroborating evidence was still lacking (*WP*, 8 and 22 July). In October formal indictments were at last handed down. Martella recommended that Antonov, Aivazov, and Vasilev along with four Turkish nationals be tried for conspiracy to assassinate a head of state. At the same time, the report of Martella's investigation, more than 1,200 pages long, was made available to the public. Different analyses of the report appeared in the Western press, with some journalists and political figures arguing that the case against the Bulgarians was decisively proven, while others remained skeptical (*CSM*, 30 October; *WP*, 14–17 October). The trial of Antonov is expected to begin early in 1985.

Bulgaria vigorously denied the charges against Antonov and the others, portraying them as part of a broad CIA campaign to discredit socialism (BTA, 26 October, released by the Bulgarian embassy in Washington). At the end of the year, BTA director Boyan Traykov, who has been the principal Bulgarian spokesman on this issue, wrote a series of open letters to Judge Martella attempting a point-by-point rebuttal of the case made in the indictment. In them he accused Martella of acting as Agca's defense counsel and of singing with Agca in a "duet of calumny." (BTA, 4 and 8 December, released by the Bulgarian embassy in Washington.)

In February Bulgaria set up a National Front for Peace and Solidarity to give financial support "to people, groups, and organizations struggling against militarism and imperialism." It will be funded by donations from Bulgarian citizens, public organizations, and economic enterprises, and is led by Politburo member Pencho Kubadinski, who is also head of the Fatherland Front's National Council. (Sofia domestic service, 8 February; *FBIS*, 9 February.)

The Soviet Union. As in the past, Bulgarian leaders continued to emphasize their loyalty to the Soviet Union and to support Soviet positions on all major international issues. The question of a possible rift between Zhivkov and Yuri Andropov (see *YICA*, 1984, p. 307) became moot with the death of the Soviet leader in February. Zhivkov was believed to have always favored Konstantin Chernenko, with whom he had previously established a close relationship, as Brezhnev's successor and appeared quite pleased at Chernenko's election to the post of party general secretary (*RFE Situation Report*, 1 March, item 1). Bulgaria was the first country to join the Soviet Union's boycott of the Olympics, in spite of earlier expressions of eagerness to attend (BTA, 9 May; *FBIS*, 10 May; *Bulgaria at the Olympics*, Sofia Press Agency, December 1983). Zhivkov also yielded to obvious Soviet pressure by canceling a scheduled visit to West Germany in September (*WP*, 10 September).

Bulgaria signed a trade protocol with the USSR in January providing for a 12.6 percent increase in trade during 1984. According to the terms that were made public, Bulgaria would import 33,000 automobiles, 36,000 color TV sets, and other consumer goods, along with heavy equipment for machine building and nuclear power. (Sofia domestic service, 27 January; *FBIS*, 30 January.)

Zhivkov visited the Soviet Union three times: for Andropov's funeral in February; to open a Bulgarian exhibition in Moscow in June; and later that same month to head the Bulgarian delegation to a CMEA summit meeting (BTA, 10 February, 30 May, 11 June; *FBIS*, 13 February, 1 and 12 June). The highest-ranking Soviet visitors to Bulgaria were Mikhail Gorbachev, who represented the USSR at the celebration of the 9 September revolution, and Marshal Viktor Kulikov, the Warsaw Pact commander, who came for the celebration of the fortieth anniverary of the Bulgarian People's Army (Sofia domestic service, 7 September; BTA, 21 September; *FBIS*, 7 and 24 September).

Other East European and Balkan Countries. In October 1982, shortly after Andreas Papandreou's electoral victory in Greece, Zhivkov revived the concept of making the Balkan peninsula a nuclear-free zone. Since that time all the Balkan states, with the exception of Albania, have given the idea lukewarm to enthusiastic approval. In January and February Athens hosted a meeting of experts from Bulgaria, Romania, Greece, Turkey, and Yugoslavia to discuss that and other issues of Balkan cooperation. Bulgaria welcomed this step, but wanted the meeting confined to the nuclear problem; other participants, particularly Turkey and Yugoslavia, sought to broaden its focus. The meeting issued the usual proclamations in favor of peace, but resulted in little real progress. (*RFE Situation Report*, 16 January, item 5; *Sofia News*, 15 February.) Shortly afterward, stories appeared in the Western press that Soviet nuclear missiles were already deployed on Bulgarian soil. The Bulgarian press denied these rumors categorically (BTA, 20 April, released by the Bulgarian embassy in Washington).

Milka Planinc, Yugoslavia's prime minister, visited Bulgaria 17–19 July. Except for Zhivkov's attendance at Tito's funeral in 1980, this was the highest level of direct contact between Yugoslavia and Bulgaria since the 1960s. During her visit, Planinc pressed the Bulgarians to recognize the existence of a distinct Macedonian people, including a Macedonian minority inside Bulgaria. Zhivkov and Prime Minister Filipov declined to do this, but also avoided asserting the Bulgarian position that Macedonians are ethnic Bulgarians living in the territory of Macedonia. The Bulgarians preferred to concentrate on economic issues. The final communiqué called for expanded cooperation in education, science, culture, communications, sports, and tourism. (BTA, 19 June; *FBIS*, 20 June; *RFE Situation Report*, 14 August, item 1.) Po-

lemics on the Macedonian question, which had become very intense in Bulgaria in 1983, were almost nonexistent in 1984. In the summer thousands of Bulgarians and Yugoslavs participated in a friendship rally in Blagoevgrad, capital of the Bulgarian portion of Macedonia (*RD*, 4 June; *FBIS*, 11 June).

Although Bulgaria's relations with Albania have not been close, the two countries did sign a trade protocol. Details were not reported, but the Bulgarian press stated that the potential for a much larger volume of trade exists, and sent warm congratulations on the fortieth anniversary of the Albanian revolution (*RD*, 29 November; *FBIS*, 5 December).

Despite Romania's more independent foreign policy, Romanian-Bulgarian relations have for some years been very cordial. Zhivkov and Nicolae Ceauşescu exchanged visits, the Romanian leader visiting Zhivkov's birthplace, Pravets, in March, and Zhivkov going to Romania in late December. The two leaders endorsed the concept of a Balkan nuclear-free zone and called on both the United States and the USSR to take steps to reduce international tension. They also agreed to develop a program for long-term economic cooperation through 1990 and in some areas through 2000. (Sofia domestic service, 29 March, 20 December; *FBIS*, 29 March, 24 December; *RFE Situation Report*, 11 April, item 1.)

Relations between Bulgaria and Turkey remained good. A meeting of the Bulgarian-Turkish Joint Economic and Technical Cooperation Commission called for the current level of trade between the two countries to rise from its present $200 million level to $500 million "in coming years" (Ankara domestic service, 11 September; *FBIS*, 12 September).

Foreign Minister Mladenov visited Greece in May. Prime Minister Papandreou used the occasion to describe Bulgarian-Greek relations as a "model for states with differing social systems" (BTA, 7 May; *FBIS*, 10 May).

Bulgaria has always stressed its loyal and active participation in the Warsaw Pact and the CMEA. At the end of the year it was announced that Sofia would be the site of a Warsaw Pact summit in January 1985 (*WP*, 28 December). Zhivkov made a state visit to Poland 4–5 April. At a Bulgarian-Polish friendship rally in Warsaw, he allowed himself to speak as the "doyen" of socialist leaders, and he warned "the imperialists" that Poland was surrounded by friends and allies who would never desert it. During his visit agreements were signed on long-term economic, scientific, and technological cooperation (Warsaw domestic service, 4 April; *FBIS*, 5 April). The prime ministers of Hungary and Czechoslovakia visited Bulgaria during the year; both were concerned with expanding economic cooperation (*RD*, 17 and 31 May; *FBIS*, 21 May, 6 June).

The Third World. Libya is the largest of Bulgaria's Third World trading partners. It was revealed this year that approximately 9,000 Bulgarian specialists are working in Libya. Bulgarians were credited with building the international airport at Tripoli and were said to be at work on many other projects in agriculture, public health, transport, and construction. Zhivkov visited Libya 6–8 March, his third visit there in the last eight years. His meetings with Libyan head of state Maommar Khadafy reflected "a spirit of unanimity and mutual understanding." The two leaders exchanged ratification papers of a friendship treaty that had been negotiated during Khadafy's visit to Sofia in January 1983 and signed agreements that seemed to focus on clarifying the legal status of Bulgarians working in Libya. (BTA, 6 March; *FBIS*, 7 March; *RFE Situation Report*, 30 March, item 2.) One month later Bulgarian defense minister Dobri Dzhurov visited Libya to sign an agreement on cooperation "in all areas of life, including the military" (BTA, 8 April; *FBIS*, 9 April).

Ali Nasir Muhammad al-Hasani of the People's Democratic Republic of Yemen visited Zhivkov in Sofia for what was described as an "unofficial and friendly" meeting (BTA, 30 September, 1 October; *FBIS*, 2 October). Bulgaria is believed to be one of Yemen's major arms suppliers. Diplomatic relations between Bulgaria and Egypt, broken off since December 1978, were quietly restored in September (*al-Wafd*, Cairo, 22 August; *FBIS*, 31 August). Earlier in the year the Bulgarian-Egyptian Economic and Technical-Scientific Committee, dormant since 1978, held a meeting in Cairo that resulted in the signing of a trade protocol (BTA, 15 and 20 January; *FBIS*, 16 and 24 January).

Bulgaria continued its efforts to strengthen relations with several African states. Samora Moisés Machel, president of Mozambique, paid an official visit to Bulgaria 25–27 August. He and Zhivkov jointly condemned South Africa, Zionist aggression, and U.S. imperialism. Several agreements were signed, but nothing of substance about them was reported (Sofia domestic service, 25 August;

RD, 26 August; *FBIS*, 27 and 30 August). Ethiopian head of state Mengistu Haile Mariam met with Zhivkov in Sofia 20–24 December. The two leaders condemned American-sponsored neocolonialism in Africa. Mariam thanked Bulgaria for the aid it has extended to the Ethiopian revolution and expressed the hope that it would continue. (BTA, 22–24 December; *RD*, 22 December; *FBIS*, 27 and 28 December.)

Politburo member and Prime Minister Grisha Filipov made an extensive tour of Africa during the summer, visiting Ghana, Angola, the Congo, Zimbabwe, Mozambique, Tanzania, and Ethiopia. At each stop agreements were signed on economic, scientific, and cultural cooperation. While the details were not always clear, most of these agreements seemed to provide for the assignment of Bulgarian specialists to the African countries. (BTA, 29 and 30 June, 4, 7, 11, and 15 July; *RD*, 10 July; *FBIS*, 2, 3, 5, 9, 12, 16, and 19 July.) Defense Minister Dobri Dzhurov was also active in Africa, leading military delegations to Ethiopia in April and Angola in May (BTA, 8 April, 5 May; *FBIS*, 9 April, 8 May). Politburo candidate member Grigor Stoichkov led a Bulgarian delegation to Nigeria, where agreements were arrived at on cooperation in agriculture, construction, electrification, and water supply, and on increasing the number of Nigerian students in Bulgaria and Bulgarian teachers in Nigeria (BTA, 30 May; *FBIS*, 1 June). Three Bulgarian specialists, described as two teachers and a pediatrician, working in Angola were captured by the forces of the National Union for the Total Liberation of Angola and held for eight months before their release was arranged by the International Red Cross (BTA, 31 March, 22 November; *FBIS*, 3 April, 23 November). The Bulgarian press reported that there were about 200 Bulgarians working in Angola (*Pogled*, 9 April; *FBIS*, 10 April). Bulgaria extended recognition to the new state of Brunei at the beginning of the year (BTA, 19 January; *FBIS*, 20 January).

Kim Il-song, North Korean head of state, visited Bulgaria 15–17 June. He and Zhivkov signed a treaty of friendship and cooperation to remain in force for twenty years (BTA, 17 June; *FBIS*, 18 June). Later in the summer Chan Si, premier of Kampuchea, visited Bulgaria to sign agreements on trade, cultural exchanges, and Bulgarian technical assistance in the fields of tobacco and rubber production (BTA, 26 July; *FBIS*, 27 July). An official in the Bulgarian embassy in Tokyo was expelled from Japan for attempting to obtain classified information in the field of genetic engineering from Japanese firms (Kyodo, Tokyo, 15 July; *FBIS*, 16 July).

Bulgaria has long pursued good relations with India. Zhivkov declared a day of mourning for Indira Gandhi after her assassination and was the first foreign head of state to arrive for her funeral. Afterward he met with her successor, Rajiv Gandhi, to express his condolences and desire for continued good relations (Sofia domestic service, 2 November; BTA, 4 November; *FBIS*, 2 and 5 November). At the end of the year the two countries signed a protocol providing for the volume of trade in 1985 to increase by 40 percent over the 1984 level. Bulgaria will import Indian iron ore, manganese, and textiles and will export to India urea and other chemicals and industrial goods. (BTA, 17 December; *FBIS*, 18 December.)

A Bulgarian Committee for Solidarity with the Peoples of Latin America was established in November (BTA, 14 November; *FBIS*, 15 November). Its functions were not immediately apparent. A trade protocol signed with Cuba called for a 14.5 percent increase in turnover. Cuba will send Bulgaria sugar, molasses, citrus fruit and juice, and nickel; Bulgaria will supply Cuba with machine-building equipment and metallurgical and chemical products (BTA, 29 January; *FBIS*, 30 January). Forbes Burnham, president of Guyana, met with Zhivkov in Sofia in June. The two leaders condemned U.S. aggression in Central America and signed agreements on economic, cultural, and scientific-technological cooperation (BTA, 6, 9, and 10 June; *FBIS*, 7, 11, and 13 June). During the year Bulgaria was also accused of being a major arms supplier to Nicaragua, a charge that was not denied (*Washington Times*, 4 July).

Western Europe and the United States. Although the investigation of the "Bulgarian connection" in the attempted assassination of the pope has caused traditionally good relations between Bulgaria and Italy to be strained, there were a few signs of improvement. Investigations of Bulgarian involvement in contraband weapons and drugs, although they received considerable attention in the Western press, did not lead to any clear result, and some were dropped altogether (*WP*, 17 October). Diplomatic relations were normalized with the appointment of new ambassadors; both the Bulgarian ambassador to Italy and his Italian counterpart had been recalled for "consultations" in December 1982 following the arrest of Sergei Antonov (*RFE Situa-*

tion Report, 30 March, item 4). Bulgaria amnestied two Italian citizens convicted in 1983 of espionage (BTA, 5 September; *FBIS*, 6 September; see *YICA*, 1984, p. 310).

Dr. Fred Sinowatz, federal chancellor of Austria, paid an official visit to Bulgaria 27–29 September. He pronounced himself "extremely satisfied" with the results of his discussions with Zhivkov and described Bulgarian-Austrian relations as "very good." He invited Zhivkov and Prime Minister Filipov to visit Austria in 1985. (BTA, 27 and 29 September; *FBIS*, 28 September, 1 October.)

Foreign Minister Mladenov met with President François Mitterrand and Foreign Minister Claude Cheysson in Paris on 12–13 April. Both sides agreed that an expansion of bilateral relations was possible. They mentioned cooperation in the fields of automobile production, telecommunications, and metallurgy as likely possibilities. (BTA, 12 and 13 April; *FBIS*, 12 and 16 April.) Mladenov also visited Finland, where he called for the establishment of nuclear-free zones in both northern and southern Europe (BTA, 15 February; *FBIS*, 16 February).

West Germany is Bulgaria's largest trading partner among the Western nations. On 9 September Zhivkov canceled a planned visit to Bonn ten days before it was scheduled to begin. Official reasons included heightened tensions due to the deployment of new American missiles in West Germany in 1983 and due to NATO maneuvers under way with West German participation. The cancellation of Zhivkov's visit followed within days the cancellation of a visit to Bonn by East German head of state Erich Honecker. This in turn was the product of an intense Soviet campaign against West German "revanchism." There was no open Soviet pressure on Zhivkov as there had been on Honecker, but the Bulgarian leader's decision coincided with the presence in Sofia of Soviet Politburo member Mikhail Gorbachev. (*WP*, 10 September; *CSM*, 11 and 12 September.) The Bulgarian press did not echo Soviet criticism of West Germany, and there were expressions of hope that conditions would soon revert to normal. Social Democratic leader Willy Brandt was welcomed in Sofia in early December (BTA, 1 and 2 December; *FBIS*, 3 December). Later in the month the two countries signed a trade protocol that focused on expanding tourism and cooperation in the transportation of West German goods to the Middle East. Shipments will be sent by container train to Dimitrovgrad, where they will be loaded onto Bulgarian trucks for the final stage of their journey (BTA, 3 December; *FBIS*, 5 December).

Relations between Bulgaria and the United States, normally cool but correct, became more openly hostile. Bulgarian leaders and the Bulgarian press accused the United States in more violent terms than usual of seeking to orchestrate a worldwide campaign against the countries of "mature socialism." The Bulgarian press also accused the United States of provocative acts and "gross violations" of the Olympic Charter when it announced Bulgaria's adherence to the Soviet-led boycott of the Los Angeles Summer Olympics (*Sofia Press*, 26 May, released by the Bulgarian embassy in Washington). Bulgaria also complained that the construction of a new military airport by NATO at Corlu in European Turkey, 86 miles from the Bulgarian border, was an act of provocation aimed at disrupting friendly relations between Bulgaria and Turkey (*Otechestven front*, 5 January; *FBIS*, 8 January). On 28 June the U.S. Senate overwhelmingly passed an amendment offered by Senator Jesse Helms to the State, Justice, and Commerce departments appropriations bill that called for cutting off all funds for encouraging U.S. trade with Bulgaria for the reason that Bulgaria engages in "state-sponsored terrorism." In the Senate debate the backers of the amendment stated that there was no doubt that Bulgaria was responsible for the attempt on Pope John Paul II's life or that Bulgaria was heavily involved in international arms and drug smuggling (*WP*, 29 June). Shortly afterward the State Department banned "nonessential" travel to Bulgaria as an "expression of displeasure" (ibid., 10 July). The Bulgarian press vehemently denied the accusations, calling them "fabrications" and the work of "professional anticommunists." It also accused the United States of attempting to pressure Italian authorities to find Sergei Antonov guilty (*RD*, 30 June; *FBIS*, 3 July; BTA, 27 July, released by the Bulgarian embassy in Washington). Relations improved when the Helms amendment failed to pass a joint House-Senate conference committee. The arrival of a new American ambassador in Sofia in November received unusually heavy attention, and Zhivkov took the opportunity to express his wish for a dialogue with the United States (*RD*, 14 November; *FBIS*, 16 November). Zhivkov also met in Sofia with a group of congressmen to discuss cooperation in efforts against drug smuggling (BTA, 15 December; *FBIS*, 17 December). An agreement extending cultural, scientific, and educational exchanges for the period 1985–1986 was signed in Washington at the end of the year (Sofia domestic service, 17 December; *FBIS*, 18 December).

International Party Contacts. In January the BCP hosted a conference of the chief editors of the Central Committee organs from fraternal socialist countries. The meeting adopted a resolution stressing the importance of peace and condemning the deployment of new American missiles by NATO (Sofia domestic service, 6 January; *FBIS*, 9 January).

For several years Zhivkov has invited party leaders to vacation at Bulgaria's Black Sea resorts. This year's summer visitors included Peter Symon of Australia, Franz Muhri of Austria, George Hawi of Lebanon, Ezekias Papaioannou of Cyprus, Álvaro Cunhal of Portugal, Jan Debrouwere of Belgium, and James Mortimer of the British Labour Party. Zhivkov met with most of these leaders, and the usual statements on solidarity and friendship were issued. Other communist party leaders who visited Bulgaria during the year and met with Zhivkov were Max van den Berg of the Netherlands, Hans Kleven of Norway, Moses Mabhida of the Republic of South Africa, Kharilaos Florakis of Greece, and Meir Vilner of Israel.

During the year, the BCP sent delegations to participate in congresses, celebrations, or other events sponsored by communist or leftist parties in the USSR, Austria, the German Democratic Republic, Romania, Norway, Finland, Greece, the Congo, and Ethiopia. Bulgaria was visited by communist party delegations from the USSR, Poland, Syria, Angola, Guyana, and the Dominican Republic.

This year's recipients of Bulgaria's highest award, the Order of Georgi Dimitrov, included Nikolai Tikhonov, Andrei Gromyko, Viktor Grishin, Mikhail Zimianin, and Viktor Kulikov of the USSR; György Lázár, prime minister of Hungary; Lubomír Štrougal, prime minister of Czechoslovakia; Wojciech Jaruzelski, first secretary of the Polish United Workers' Party; Álvaro Cunhal, secretary general of the Portuguese Communist Party; Carlos Rafael Rodríguez, member of the Communist Party of Cuba's Politburo; and C. Rajeswara Rao, secretary general of the Communist Party of India.

John D. Bell
University of Maryland Baltimore County

Czechoslovakia

Population. 15,420,000
Party. Communist Party of Czechoslovakia (Komunistická strana Československa; KSČ)
Founded. 1921
Membership. 1,623,000 (*WMR*, June)
Secretary General. Gustáv Husák
Presidium 11 full members: Vasil Bil'ák, Petr Colotka (deputy prime minister), Karel Hoffman (chairman, Revolutionary Trade Union Movement), Gustáv Husák (president of the republic), Alois Indra (chairman, Federal Assembly), Miloš Jakeš, Antonín Kapek, Josef Kempný, Josef Korčák (deputy prime minister), Jozef Lenárt, Lubomír Štrougal (federal prime minister); 3 candidate members: Jan Fojtík, Josef Haman, Miloslav Hruškovič
Secretariat. 10 full members: Gustáv Husák, Mikula Beno, Vasil Bil'ák, Jan Fojtík, Josef Haman, Josef Havlín, Miloš Jakeš, Josef Kempný, František Pitra, Jindřich Poledník; 2 members-at-large: Zdeněk Hoření, Marie Kabrhelová
Control and Auditing Commission. Jaroslav Hajn, chairman
Central Committee. 123 full and 55 candidate members
Status. Ruling party
Last Congress. Sixteenth, 6–10 April 1981, in Prague; next scheduled for 1986
Slovak Party. Communist Party of Slovakia (Komunistická strana Slovenska; KSS); membership: 400,000 full and candidate members; Josef Lenárt, first secretary; Presidium: 11 members; Central Committee: 91 full and 31 candidate members
Last Election. 1981, 99.0 percent, all 350 National Front candidates; 66 percent of seats reserved for KSČ candidates
Auxiliary Organizations. Revolutionary Trade Union Movement (Tenth Congress, April 1982), Cooperative Farmers' Union, Socialist Youth Union (Third Congress, October 1982), Union for Collaboration with the Army, Czechoslovak Union of Women, Union of Fighters for Peace
Main State Organs. The executive body is the federal government, which is subordinate to the 350-member Federal Assembly, composed of the Chamber of the People (200 members) and the Chamber of the Nations (150 members). The assembly, however, merely rubber-stamps all decisions made by the KSČ Presidium and Central Committee.
Publications. *Rudé právo*, KSČ daily; *Pravda* (Bratislava), KSS daily; *Tribuna*, Czech-language ideological weekly; *Predvoj*, Slovak-language ideological weekly; *Život strany*, fortnightly journal devoted to administrative and organizational questions; *Práce* (Czech) and *Práca* (Slovak), Trade Union Movement dailies; *Mladá fronta* (Czech) and *Smena* (Slovak) Socialist Youth Union dailies; *Tvorba*, weekly devoted to domestic and international politics; *Nová mysl*, theoretical monthly. Československá tisková kancelář (ČETEKA) is the official news agency.

The KSČ developed from the left wing of the Czechoslovak Social Democratic Party, having co-opted several radical socialist and leftist groups. It was constituted in Prague and admitted to the Com-munist International the same year. Its membership in the Comintern, however, was an uneasy one until in 1929 the so-called bolshevization process was completed and a leadership of unqualified obedience to the Soviet Union assumed control. During the First Czechoslovak Republic (1918–1939), the KSČ enjoyed legal status, but it was banned after the Munich Agreement. After the war, it emerged as the strongest party in the postwar elections of 1946, although it did not poll a majority of votes. In February 1948, the KSČ seized all power in a coup d'etat and transformed Czechoslovakia into a communist party-state of the Soviet type. The departure from Stalinist practices started later in Czechoslovakia than in other countries of Central and Eastern Europe, but it led to a daring liberalization experiment known as the Prague Spring of 1968. A Soviet-led military intervention by five Warsaw Pact countries in August of the same year ended the democratization course and imposed on Czechoslovakia the policies of so-called normalization—a return to unreserved subordination to the will of the Soviet Union and the emulation of the Soviet example in all areas of social life.

Party Internal Affairs. On 17 April Gustáv Husák celebrated his fifteenth anniversary as secretary general of the party. This date is historically important because only then, some eight months after the Soviet-led military intervention of August 1968, was Alexander Dubček's reformist team removed from the KSČ leadership, and the so-called normalization process gained its full momentum in Czechoslovakia. The event was remembered by an editorial in *Rudé právo* (17 April). Significantly enough, the organ of the Soviet communist party, *Pravda*, carried on the same date an article recalling the change in KSČ governance fifteen years earlier and containing a stern warning to all communist parties in Central and Eastern Europe not to yield to "internal reactionary forces." The rest of 1984 brought little change in the composition of the party executive bodies. Of the three posts in the Presidium and the Secretariat made vacant by the deaths of incumbents in 1983, only one was filled. On 3 October the Central Committee elected Zdeněk Hoření, editor-in-chief of *Rudé právo*, a member of the Secretariat (Radio Prague, 3 October). The Central Committee held two plenary sessions during the year. The Tenth Plenum took place 17 and 18 April; it dealt mainly with "the tasks and development of engineering, electrical engineering, and metallurgy after the Sixteenth Party Congress in 1981" and with "furthering directions of development of initiative and activity of the working people" (ibid., 18 April). The Eleventh Plenum met 2 and 3 October; the most important point on the agenda was the state of agriculture. The Central Committee found that agricultural production finally exceeded the level attained before collectivization, 35 years ago, but that the 1984 harvest ran three weeks behind schedule and that chronic problems of bad management, waste, shortage of feed grains and bulk fodder, outdated machinery, and lack of manpower persisted (*Rudé právo*, 4 October). Throughout the year, too, the party press complained about the possible decline of KSČ influence due to the insufficient proportion of members with a true working-class background. Although currently 45 percent of party cardholders claim working-class origin, only 31 percent can be really considered to be "active workers." Among the newly recruited members and candidates to membership, only 20 percent come from working-class families. Also, there exists a generation gap in the party; while a good half of the membership are younger people in their thirties and forties admitted after the great purge of 1971, the average age of the party officials is 50 years and rising; 25 percent of all functionaries will go into retirement by 1988 (*Život strany*, no. 5, 27 February, no. 21, 10 October; *Rudé právo*, 15 May; *Tribuna*, no. 29, 20 July).

Domestic Affairs. The fortieth anniversary of the Slovak National Uprising of 1944 was celebrated with great pomp. Secretary General Gustáv Husák was the main speaker at the commemoration ceremony in Banská Bystrica on 28 August. Among the foreign guests and speakers were Soviet Marshal and Politburo member Dimitri Ustinov, who died later in the year. Not surprisingly, the historical event commemorated in Banská Bystrica was presented to the public as having occurred by the exclusive merit and on the initiative of the communist party; Moscow's indifference in 1944, which doomed the uprising, was called an example of "brotherly help of the Soviet Union to the Slovak people." Husák's hostility during World War II to the reconstitution of the Czechoslovak republic, the actual goal of the uprising (Husák then advocated a "Soviet Slovakia"), was passed over in silence (Prague television, 28 August; Tass release in English, 27 August).

Relations among the various ethnic groups in Czechoslovakia remained a problem in 1984. Dissatisfaction with the prevailing state of things was especially voiced by spokesmen of the Hungarian minority (see below). It even became a topic of discussion between Gustáv Husák and his Hungarian counterpart, János Kádár, in Budapest in the fall (*Népszabadság*, 28 November).

It was not the only domestic problem with international repercussions, however; the environmental impact of economic development, systematically ignored for several decades, caused some apprehensions in Czechoslovakia's southeastern neighbor. A group of Hungarian scientists and concerned citizens expressed misgivings about the possible effect on the ecology of the joint Czechoslovak-Hungarian hydroelectrical project under construction on the Danube between Gabčíkovo and Nagymaros (*Die Welt*, Hamburg, 23 November). Political decisionmakers in Czechoslovakia faced other ecological dilemmas, such as a water shortage. The latter became serious enough in early 1984 to prompt the authorities to regulate water supplies in the East Bohemian, North Moravian, and Central Slovak regions; water was rationed in 630 towns and villages (Radio Hvězda, 3 February).

Another domestic problem appears to be the long-term population trend. After improving in the late 1970s and early 1980s, population growth slowed down again during 1983 and 1984. Statisticians anticipate a negligible increase, or even a decrease, in the Czech provinces until the end of the century. The total population figure is expected to reach 16 million by the year 2000, but the growth is likely to come almost exclusively in Slovakia. Demographic experts also worry about the imbalance between the economically active population and the aged, whose number will increase dramatically during the remaining years of the century (*Rudé právo*, 31 January). This segment of the population will require a far better performance from the health service system, which at present leaves much to be desired. According to Minister of Health of the Czech Republic Jaroslav Prokopec, "It is not in the country's power to meet world standards of scientific and technical development in health care" (ibid., 27 June).

The health of the population does not seem to be helped by its food and beverage consumption habits. Czechs and Slovaks, according to official statistics, annually consume 9.2 kilograms per capita less milk and dairy produce than is desirable from the point of view of a balanced diet; fruit consumption is 12 percent and vegetable consumption 30 percent below the desirable levels; people eat too much pork and too little poultry; and the consumption of fats is more than 20 percent above the dietetic optimum (ibid., 3 August). The drinking habit has spread: Czechoslovaks spend about 24 billion Kčs ($3 billion) per year for alcoholic beverages. In terms of pure alcohol, per capita consumption rose from five liters in 1960 to ten liters in 1984 and now ranks among the highest in the world (*Lidová demokracie*, 9 July).

A serious social problem is seen in the continuing rise of economic crimes (theft or misuse of public funds or property). Since 1980 the number of persons convicted for such violations increased by 19 percent (*Hospodářské noviny*, no. 42, 19 October). The difficulty of the problem is compounded by a peculiar notion entertained by the public about state property and characteristic of all communist-governed societies. Misappropriation of what belongs to the state is perceived not as dishonest, but as inevitable ("Whoever does not steal from the state, steals from his own family!").

The Economy. The general economic situation of Czechoslovakia in 1984 compared favorably with that of the majority of communist-governed nations in Eastern Europe except for Hungary, but it continued to show signs of strain. Some of the economic problems were due to the crisis in the world economy: energy costs, recession, and unemployment in the West reduced the demand for certain goods or limited it to areas where Czechoslovakia cannot successfully compete. Some, however, were specifically Czechoslovak, of an old date, and only aggravated by the present crisis: low labor productivity, obsolescence of industrial equipment, inordinate delays in the completion of new plants and projects, low agriculture yields, and the unresponsiveness of the centrally planned and managed production to real consumer needs, which caused oversupplies of less demanded goods and shortages of important commodities. The number of citizens' complaints, for example, concerning unsatisfactory supplies of merchandise and services as well as their low quality, increased by more than 10 percent over 1983 (*Pravda*, Bratislava, 31 May; *Hospodářské noviny*, no. 26, 29 June). The present economic system, basically of a Stalinist type, appears unable to adjust easily to structural changes in production technology, such as the diminishing importance of coal and steel. In 1984 the production targets in these two areas were increased for the years until the end of the decade.

Czechoslovakia signed an important agreement with the Soviet Union, the German Democratic Republic, and Hungary concerning intensive exploitation of iron ore deposits in the Ukraine.

Czechoslovak investment in this project will amount to 365 million rubles ($475 million) (*Země-dělské noviny*, 22 December 1983).

The 1984 budget, adopted by the Federal Assembly, foresaw a total expenditure of 324.3 billion Kčs (ca. $54 billion). The balance between revenues and outlays was to be achieved mainly by cutting direct investment and investment subsidies. On the other hand, the allocation of funds for research and development was raised by 5.9 percent over the figure spent in 1983, indicating an awareness among planners of the need to modernize. Nominal wages and social subsidies were to grow only by 1.1 percent and 2.9 percent respectively, a growth that could be more than offset by even modest inflation (*Rudé právo*, 15 and 16 December 1983).

A matter of serious concern for Czechoslovak economists was the possible impact of the Soviet-American arms race and of the deployment of Soviet missiles on Czechoslovak territory. Party leaders did not conceal that this would heavily burden the economy (ibid., 24 November 1983). As economic activity gradually unfolded during the year, some of the budget assumptions had to be revised. Fuel consumption quotas had to be cut by 1.5 percent in addition to the 2 percent reduction contained in the original plan (ibid., 29 March). Finding that the average wage increased by 5.7 percent between 1981 and 1983, although an increase of only 4.1 percent had been planned, the government took special measures in early spring to limit further wage growth (*Hospodářské noviny*, no. 10, 16 March).

The labor shortage that has long plagued Czechoslovakia was partly mitigated by the employment of a foreign work force, especially in Slovakia. The authorities hope, nevertheless, that the need for guest workers will subside by 1990 (*Práca*, Bratislava, 13 March).

In 1984, too, the adjustment of Soviet oil prices to the level of world prices was widely felt in Czechoslovakia. Another price increase for crude, early in the year, translated into higher gasoline costs that severely affected Czechoslovak car owners and drivers. Their problem can hardly be minimized, considering that presently there are 2.5 million passenger cars in Czechoslovakia, or one car per every two households (*Socialistický obchod*, no. 10, October). As a consequence of oil price increases, economists admitted, "the terms of foreign trade radically worsened." Economists also warned that the USSR had already reached "economically

tenable limits" of oil deliveries to other Soviet bloc countries and that new supply sources had to be sought, especially in the Third World (*Československý zahraniční obchod*, no. 3, March; Reuters, Prague, 29 May). Oil shortages were further aggravated by slow development of alternative sources of energy, notably nuclear energy (Radio Prague, 13 September).

Serious nonfulfillment of plan targets hampered other vital areas of life, such as housing. Of the plan figure of 90,000 dwelling units set for 1984, in itself considerably lower than construction performance in the 1970s (144,678 units in 1977), only 49,638 units, or 55.2 percent, had been built by the end of October (Radio Hvězda, 6 November). This may further worsen the already dramatic shortage of apartments, which forced some 580,000 married couples with children—about 15 percent of the total population—to live with parents or friends (AFP, Prague, 13 September; *Politická ekonomie*, no. 10, October).

The consumer prices policy implemented by the party in 1984 brought some disagreeable surprises. Popular beverages, especially beer, became as much as 65 percent more expensive on 15 October. The price increases were explained as a necessary step to reduce or eliminate government production subsidies and to discourage excessive consumption of beer; regime spokesmen, however, denied that these or any prior price increases would have inflationary effects (*Rudé právo*, 13 October).

Nevertheless, continuing inflation, although not so pronounced as in the West, has eroded part of the purchasing power of salaries and wages. Consumer goods, regardless of quality, became less available to the average wage-earner. This was clearly reflected in reduced consumer spending since 1980. The situation in the retail market was the subject of an extensive comment by the Federal Prime Minister Lubomír Štrougal in a speech to the Federal Assembly in March. He deplored the shortages of basic commodities, absence of innovation in production, and the resulting loss of interest on the part of the consumer (ibid., 22 March).

Armed Forces. In 1984 the armies of the Warsaw Pact conducted military exercises, named Shield '84, in Czechoslovakia. It was one of the largest concentrations of Soviet bloc troops since the military intervention against the Dubček leadership in August 1968. Sixty thousand men took part in the operations. The participation of Romania, however, was probably limited to members of the general staff only, with no regular troops involved (Radio Bucharest, 16 August). The extraordinary size of the total contingent may have been a symbol with political message, in response to the tense atmosphere between the USSR and the United States. The exercises were carried out under the command of Czechoslovak defense minister Martin Dzúr, and according to the media they were held "throughout the entire territory of Czechoslovakia" (Radio Hvězda, 31 August). The USSR's supreme command was represented by Marshal Viktor Kulikov, current commander-in-chief of the Warsaw Pact troops, and Anatoli Gribkov, chief of staff of the Joint Armed Forces. Western observers were somewhat surprised by an unexpected postponement of the actual exercises by three weeks, ordered when the troops were already in place (*Rudé právo*, 25 August).

In October, Col. Gen. Grigori Borisov, commander of the Soviet troops stationed in Czechoslovakia, was replaced by Lt. Gen. Viktor Yermakov. Both officers were received by Gustáv Husák, who emphasized the contribution of the Soviet army to the preparedness of the Czechoslovak People's Army (Radio Prague, 9 October).

Regime sources indicated that the Czechoslovak army suffered from lack of officers and commanders of all ranks. Special skills needed by the army, such as rocketry, microelectronics, electrical engineering, road and railroad construction, also seemed to be in short supply. Nor was there a sufficient number of pilots, physicians, and rear-echelon service personnel (*Práca*, Bratislava, 25 January). The causes of this problem are complex: on the one hand, an officer's career has never carried much social prestige in Czechoslovakia; on the other hand, the demanding training at the military academies and the harsh conditions of military life make for a high dropout rate among the cadets (Radio Prague, 1 February).

Mass Movements. Despite several decades of regime propaganda attempting to equate the cause of world peace with the triumph of the Soviet Union, the issue of peace and war has become somewhat more ambivalent and delicate in Czechoslovakia. Czechoslovaks are apprehensive of the danger of a nuclear conflict and condemn the deployment of missiles on or near Czechoslovak territory. As a consequence of this popular mood, two peace movements were active in 1984. The official one blames world tensions on the United States and the West and presents the Soviet warheads in Czechoslovakia as "instruments of peace." The unofficial but more genuine one desires a ban on all nuclear weapons, regardless of their origin. This opinion also recognizes Soviet responsibility for the threat of war and thus parallels the more general dissidence movement, which rejects the model of "real socialism" imposed upon Czechoslovakia in the course of the post-invasion "normalization" (see below).

The regime-sponsored peace organization held an international meeting in Prague, attended by thirteen organizations and institutions, on 26 and 27 February. Among these were the International Organization of Journalists, which coordinated the meeting, the Women's International Democratic Federation, and the International Union of Students, all communist front organizations. The final resolution of the conference took an unqualified pro-Soviet stand on the issue of nuclear missiles in Europe, putting all the blame for the danger of war on the United States (*Rudé právo*, 27 February).

The Czechoslovak chapter of the Women's International Democratic Federation, the Union of Czechoslovak Women, held a national congress in Prague in June. It praised the sociopolitical system in Czechoslovakia for having brought women "full equality—political, economic, and social" and adopted the same position on the question of war and peace as had the international body with which it is affiliated (Radio Prague, 18 June).

The International Union of Students, the secretariat of which is located in Prague, supported the communist peace campaign by an "Open Letter to the Students of the United States," adopted at its Fourteenth World Congress in Sofia in April. This letter restated the official Soviet thesis about American responsibility for international tensions, and exhorted U.S. students not to vote for Ronald Reagan in the forthcoming presidential elections (*Mladá fronta*, 13 April).

As part of the post-invasion program of "normalization," the Czechoslovak National Student Union has been fully integrated into the central youth body, the Young Socialist League. Students constitute 51 percent of the 1.7 million members of the league (*WMR*, July).

Another mass organization active in 1984 was the Central Trade Union Council. The council held a plenary session in Prague in March. The plenum's opening message focused on the international role of trade unions and reiterated the regime's position on the causes of international conflicts (*Rudé právo*, 28 March).

Culture, Youth, and Religion. The most important event in the world of Czechoslovak culture in 1984 was undoubtedly the award of the Nobel Prize for Literature to poet Jaroslav Seifert. Although Seifert's major contribution to modern Czech poetry is indisputable, the award put the regime into a somewhat delicate political situation. Seifert has an unbroken record of courageous support for the freedom of art and thought, as well as for the democratic traditions of his country. As a member and official of the Czechoslovak Writers' Union, Seifert called, as early as the brief "thaw" of 1956, for an end to the party's interference in intellectual life. His voice was again heard during the Prague Spring of 1968 and later in protest against the Soviet military intervention and the "normalization" that considerably curtailed the independence that artists had acquired during the previous years. There can be little doubt that Seifert is an opponent of the now prevailing "real socialism."

After some hesitation, the regime nevertheless decided to accept the fact of Seifert's international distinction and recognition with more grace than, for example, the Soviets had done in the case of Boris Pasternak. Although complaining that "his work as a poet and a citizen was not easy, was even controversial," the party press acknowledged Seifert's true stature. It compensated by vigorously attacking Western commentators and critics, accusing them of "attempts to use the laureate's name in the psychological war against the countries of socialism," a reference to the frequent mentions in Western media to Seifert's various conflicts with party ideological watchdogs (ibid., 13 October).

Czechoslovak literature and art continued their uneven struggle for more freedom from political supervision. Despite systematic official pressure, a few good-quality works were nonetheless published during the year. In most cases, their themes were either historical or timeless and thus escaped the requirements of socialist realism. This was particularly true of Czech and Slovak children's books, many of which were translated and reproduced in the West (Radio Free Europe–Radio Liberty, *Background Report*, no. 120, 29 June). As often in recent years, semiclandestine samizdat book production contributed to Czechoslovak literary output in 1984. One distinct aspect of samizdat publications has been an ever more pronounced religious inspiration of a number of them (Radio Free Europe–Radio Liberty, *Situation Report on Czechoslovakia*, no. 16, 7 September).

Czechoslovakia under communist rule faced many problems with youth similar to those elsewhere. The media recorded growing drug abuse, alcoholism, and promiscuity. "The passion for alcohol," according to some official commentators, "is immune to all measures." (Since 1965 alcohol consumption per capita has risen by 43 percent in the Czech lands and by 46.5 percent in Slovakia [*Nové slovo*, no. 21, 24 May].) Drug addiction among the teenagers, according to media reports, affects "tens of thousands of people" and was considered serious enough to prompt a conference of experts on drug abuse in Prague in November 1983. The regime allows no statistics to be published about the extent of drug consumption, but the dissident group Charter '77, in a letter to the Federal Assembly, drew attention to the increases in drug-related crimes and deaths caused by drug overdoses (Charter Document no. 42; AFP, Prague, 2 January). Starting in February, Radio Prague introduced a regular monthly panel discussion on the topic of drugs in order "to inform the public, particularly young people, of the dangers inherent in the drug plague" (Radio Prague, 6 February). Concern about drug abuse, however, was not the regime's only worry relative to the behavior of the young. "Overall demoralization," believed to be caused by the bad example of the generations now in control, who commit "unsocialist offenses" such as graft, misuse of power, nepotism, and nonobservance of work discipline on a large scale, was deplored by party spokesmen on several occasions during the year (e.g., *Haló sobota*, 29 April).

A reform of the school system, phased in with the start of the 1984–85 academic year, could, among other objectives, be seen as an attempt by the regime to gain better control of youth. The reform, thus far, has produced only confusion and severe criticism from the public. The criticism was articulated in a paper issued by the dissident group, Charter '77 (Charter document no. 7, 2 April). The new law extends compulsory school attendance to ten years, but specialization begins only in the ninth year when the students are to be distributed among three types of high schools: vocational, specialized (scientific and technological), and academic (called gymnasiums). Heavy emphasis on mathematics and practical skills in the lower grades considerably reduces the room for general education. On the other hand, ideological indoctrination is to begin as early as kindergarten. Regime media reported strong opposition to this aspect of the reform, both from parents and teachers (*Učitelské noviny*, Bratislava, 29 March). It remains to be seen whether the intended changes will bring the expected results.

The party also appeared to be alarmed by signs of increasing religiosity among the young. Unofficial religious discussion groups have recently been meeting in private, masses have been served in private houses, and the number of seminarians and students in the theological faculties of the universities has increased (*WP*, 3 May, quoting the Czechoslovak Catholic primate, František Cardinal Tomášek). Private exercise of religion is prohibited by law, and many young people have already been imprisoned on this account. But the trend has not been reversed. Religiosity on the whole is still very strong in the country. According to a recent, officially sponsored survey, no less than 36 percent of the adult population are religious believers of some kind. Broken down by the two main ethnic groups, the figures are 30 percent for the Czech lands and 51 percent for Slovakia (*Sociológia*, no. 1, January).

The voice of the Catholic church was heard louder than ever in 1984. Cardinal Tomášek officially protested against the persecution of believers for their activities outside the church (BBC, London, 17 January). He also rejected, in an open letter distributed to foreign embassies and journalists, an attack by the party review *Tribuna* on Pope John Paul II (*Tribuna* called him "the most reactionary pope of modern history") as "unobjective demagogy" (Radio Vatican, 16 April).

One action of Tomášek's that could complicate relations between the church and the communist state was his invitation to the pope to visit Czechoslovakia in 1986 to participate in the commemoration of the 1100th anniversary of the death of St. Methodius, the first missionary and archbishop on the territory of what is now Czechoslovakia. Tomášek's initiative was enthusiastically endorsed by all Catholic believers, more than 10,000 of whom signed a petition to this effect (Kathpress, Vienna, 11 April).

Tomášek officially informed the authorities about the invitation, and their reaction was predictable. Party Presidium member Vasil Bil'ák, a well-known hard-liner, declared that Tomášek should have invited the Moscow patriarch of the Russian Orthodox church (Radio Vatican, 7 July). It was even rumored that Bil'ák had suggested Czechoslovak Catholics seek a new orientation towards Orthodox Christianity and away from Rome. Bil'ák's alleged statement was vehemently disclaimed by the party press as "a lie on short legs, fabricated in Vienna and spread further by infamous Western media" (*Rudé právo*, 7 July). The regime-sponsored Catholic organization, Pacem in Terris, rejected the rumors in even stronger terms as "naive lies—false, un-Christian, and inhuman" (*Katolícke noviny*, no. 29, 22 July).

The apparent strain in relations between the regime and the Catholic church, however, did not prevent isolated positive moves on the part of the latter, such as the intercession of John Paul II for the liberation of Czechoslovak technicians taken hostage by the antigovernment partisan forces in Angola (*La Libre Belgique*, Brussels, 25 July).

Czechoslovak Protestants were present in Budapest at the Seventh Assembly of the Lutheran World Federation, 22 July–5 August (MTI, Budapest, 23 July).

Dissidence. The best-known human rights defense group in Czechoslovakia, Charter '77, remained active throughout 1984. According to the records of another dissident group, the Committee for the Defense of Unjustly Persecuted Persons (VONS), in January 1984 there were 91 individuals sentenced by courts or serving prison terms for political crimes (*Background Report*, no. 5, 9 January).

The regime's failure to silence the dissenters may have led it to resort to the practice of "protective supervision," made possible by special legislation during the post-invasion period. Under this practice (which strongly resembles the famous Nazi institution of *Schutzhaft* or "protective custody"), individuals who have already served their sentence in jail are confined to a certain place, their residence is regularly searched without court warrant, all sources of income must be reported to the police, and all contact with certain individuals or groups of individuals is forbidden. In 1984, Chartists Václav Benda, Jan Litomiský, and Ladislav Lis became the most prominent objects of this "protective supervision" and of all possible police chicanery (*NYT*, 9 April). In an open letter addressed to Gustáv Husák, Charter '77 protested against this treatment, reminding Husák that he himself had been a victim of the same abuse of power during the Stalinist terror period (AFP, Prague, 14 March; Reuters, Prague, 23 March).

The 1983 Annual Report of Amnesty International also charged violation of human rights in dealing with dissidents in Czechoslovakia. The report singled out, among others, the outrageous conditions in which prisoners in the Bory prison at Pilsen had to live (Amnesty International report,

New York, 4 April). The regime responded by a venomous campaign against Amnesty International, claiming that it was an anticommunist organization supported by the CIA (*Tribuna*, no. 13, 28 March; *Život strany*, no. 10, 7 May; *Rudé právo*, 29 June).

Documents published by Charter '77 during 1984 addressed all major issues of domestic and international politics: the economic situation of the country, which it characterized as stagnating (Charter document no. 6, 12 March); the inconsistencies and the perils of the new school system reform (ibid., no. 7, 2 April); the anniversary of the Soviet invasion of Czechoslovakia on 21 August (Charter statement of 19 August); and the problem of peace and arms control (message to the Third International Peace Conference in Perugia, Italy, signed by Jiři Hájek, Václav Havel, and eleven other Charter members, 17 July).

The unofficial peace movement, which refuses to support the cause of the Soviet Union, found an important mouthpiece in Charter '77. In its peace-promoting efforts, the Charter group was supported by activists from other communist countries of the Soviet orbit. In February, 22 Charter members and 24 members of the Polish Committee for Social Self-Defense (KOR) released a joint peace appeal in Prague and Warsaw (*Situation Report on Czechoslovakia*, no. 4, 7 March). On 22 November the first anniversary of the deployment of long-range Soviet missiles in Central Europe, Charter '77 and the East German chapter of Peace Initiative East-West issued in Prague the "Joint Statement of the Independent Defenders of Peace" (*Frankfurter Rundschau*, 26 November). All these documents linked the cause of international peace to the need to respect human rights ("governments desiring peace abroad must live in peace with their own citizens"). The international solidarity of the peace movement visibly alarmed the authorities, who on several occasions arrested and deported Western peace workers who tried to contact their Czechoslovak counterparts (Austrian radio and television, 5 March).

Links among human rights groups and dissidents in 1984 reached not only over the national border but also across ethnic boundaries within Czechoslovakia. Czech and Slovak dissidents formally endorsed the cause of the Hungarian minority. Miklos Duray, the most prominent spokesman of this minority, was arrested in May on charges of "having caused harm to the country's interests abroad." A member of Charter '77 since 1983, Duray received outspoken support in 1984 from a group of Slovak intellectuals who in their public statements emphasized that "legal persecution can under no circumstances establish whether an analysis of an ethnic problem is correct or not" (letter from Milan Simecka, a Czech philosopher living in Slovakia and author of the novel *Restoring Law and Order*, which was recently published in English translation in the West, to Petr Colotka, prime minister of the Slovak republic government, 27 June). The dissident movement's international and multiethnic scope promises a continuing moral challenge to the communist establishment in the future.

Foreign Affairs. As always, the KSČ toed the Soviet line on foreign policy. Unqualified support of the Soviet position on nuclear arms was the most obvious, although not the only, example of the party's stand. The latter was formally summed up in a foreign policy resolution submitted to, and endorsed by, the Federal Assembly in the fall (*Pravda*, Bratislava, 13 November). Media coverage of international events reflected the regime's loyalty to its Soviet big brother. The U.S. presidential elections were a case in point. On the other hand, in a rather unprecedented move, the party daily published a letter from U.S. ambassador to Czechoslovakia W. H. Luers, who reminded readers of the active role U.S. officers and soldiers had played in the Slovak National Uprising of August 1944 (*Rudé právo*, 18 August). Czechoslovak radio and television audiences learned for the first time from official communist sources of the relentless, bloody war in Afghanistan, which involves hundreds of thousands of Soviet troops. Previously nothing of the kind had ever been mentioned in reports from that country. (Reports by Zdeněk Kropáč, ČETEKA reporter, from Kabul; in *Rudé právo*, 27 and 28 April, 3, 4, and 10 May.)

Relations with Western nations were, on the whole, not very warm in 1984. The regime was offended, for example, by the French media's treatment of the Nobel Prize award to Jaroslav Seifert and lodged a protest with the French government (Radio Prague, 19 October). The climate between Czechoslovakia and its southern neighbor, Austria, was also severely strained. Party Presidium member Karel Hoffman, chairman of the Central Council of the Revolutionary Trade Union Movement, paid a visit to Austrian president Rudolf Kirchschläger, "to discuss the possibility of further deepening economic and political contacts between the two countries" (ibid., 5 September), but a serious border incident shortly afterwards clearly showed the limits of such possibilities. Czechoslovak border guards shot and mortally wounded a defector who was already on Austrian territory and let him die without notifying Austrian authorities. The Austrian government strongly protested this violation of international law and human rights, and the Austrian parliament unanimously condemned it (AP, Vienna, 7 November; UPI, Vienna, 8 November). The Prague regime reacted with a campaign of violent attacks in the media on "some circles who want to unleash a campaign of hate against Czechoslovakia" (Radio Prague, 9 November). Eventually, it recalled the Czechoslovak envoy from Vienna for an indefinite period. Several joint cultural projects had to be canceled or postponed as a consequence of this incident (Radio Hvězda, 13 November; Reuters, Vienna, 13 November).

Other diplomatic contacts reported by official sources in 1984 were either formal or routine. Minister of Foreign Affairs Bohuslav Chňoupek met the foreign minister of the Republic of Germany, Hans-Dietrich Genscher, in New York, on the occasion of a U.N. session (ČETEKA, 1 October). Belgian foreign minister Leo Tindemans came for a short visit to Prague in the same month (Radio Prague, 15 October). In July, Greek prime minister Andreas Papandreou visited Czechoslovakia. The media gave extensive coverage to this event, partly because of the hopes Soviet foreign policy had been entertaining about the possibility of Greece's either quitting or restricting its cooperation with NATO. The final communiqué did not mention this issue, but instead stressed "the development of the two countries' relations in all spheres" (ibid., 5 July). A Greek Cypriot parliamentary delegation visited Prague in July (ČETEKA, 10 July). A delegation of the Czechoslovak Federal Assembly visited Yugoslavia in October (Rudé právo, 1 October). Federal Assembly Chairman Lubomír Štrougal paid a three-day state visit to Libya, on the occasion of which "identity of views" with the government of Moammar Khadafy was emphasized (ibid., 8 May). In February, Federal Deputy Prime Minister Rudolf Rohlíček toured Venezuela (ČETEKA, 14 February). Minister Chňoupek received in Prague the foreign minister of Yemen (Radio Prague, 1 August) and the Syrian premier (Rudé právo, 24 October). The foreign minister of Zimbabwe arrived in Czechoslovakia in November (ČETEKA, 8 November). Czechoslovakia established diplomatic relations with the Ivory Coast in September (Radio Prague, 6 September).

Foreign Trade and Foreign Debt. Czechoslovak party economists appeared to have expected important decisions at the meeting of foreign trade ministers of the member-states of the Council for Mutual Economic Assistance (CMEA) in Moscow in June. The meeting, however, accomplished little in the way of closer economic integration and of a true international division of labor. Both had been favorite ideas of the Soviets since the beginning of the 1960s. On the other hand, it endorsed further expansion of economic exchanges with nonsocialist nations and encouraged direct cooperation among the enterprises of the member-countries, without the intermediary of the central planning authorities (Tass, 15 June). Since Czechoslovak economic planners have frowned on both these options, the KSČ could hardly see its trade policies vindicated in Moscow. This may have been the reason why at the subsequent session of the CMEA in Havana, Federal Premier Lubomír Štrougal voiced dissatisfaction with CMEA performance, especially in the fields of joint scientific-technical development and coordination of the national economic plans for the five-year period 1986–1990 (Radio Hvězda, 29 October). Czechoslovakia's economic ties with the CMEA countries have been the closest and the most important.

Economic ties with the USSR are to expand further, following an agreement reached during a special visit by Premier Štrougal to Moscow (Rudé právo, 10 July). However, this orientation of Czechoslovak foreign trade is not without problems. Since 1975, the balance of payments with the Soviet Union has been increasingly unfavorable to Czechoslovakia, and the deficit has now reached the level of about 5 billion Kčs ($425 million) (Statistické přehledy, no. 3, March).

Among the highlights of trade with non-European communist countries in 1984 were a contract to deliver diesel engines to Vietnam (Radio Prague, 28 March) and an agreement with the People's Republic of China on a car assembly line to be set up there in 1985 (ČETEKA, 27 July).

Trade with the West amounted to some 16.5 percent of the total volume (Statistické přehledy, no. 6, June). An eventual broadening of exchanges in this area has been hampered by a number of factors, among which the hard currency foreign debt has played an important role (trade with the West and other noncommunist countries does not run at a deficit; on the contrary, here Czechoslovakia has even accumulated a surplus). Czechoslovakia's debt in convertible currencies is not staggering by general standards and compares well with the much more serious indebtedness of countries like Poland or Romania. In 1984 it amounted to less than $3 billion (*Handelsblatt*, Frankfurt, 19 September). It is believed that the government's goal is to reduce it substantially, if not entirely eliminate it, which rules out any appreciable growth of imports or credits from the West in the near future.

Reaction to Polish Events. Since the beginning of the Solidarity movement in 1980, both the party and the population at large have followed developments in Poland very closely. Early in the year, Jerzy Urban, press spokesman for the cabinet of General Jaruzelski, came on a special mission to Prague to brief Czechoslovak journalists about the internal Polish situation. He claimed that 1984 would be the first year of "normalization" since the opposition symbolized by Lech Walesa and the forces behind him "has collapsed totally" (Radio Prague, 10 February). The meeting between representatives of the Polish regime-sponsored Catholic organization, PAX, and the Federal Deputy Premier Rudolf Rohlíček in Prague the following month was obviously meant to give full support to the Polish experiment of restoring "normalcy" (ibid., 6 March).

Assurances of this kind were taken with a pinch of salt by public opinion, however, which was shocked by the assassination of Polish priest Jerzy Popieluszko. While the regime media only very reluctantly and incompletely reported this event (*Rudé právo*, 31 October, 8 November), the civil rights group Charter '77 condemned the act. In an "Open Letter to Our Polish Friends," Charter spokesmen said that Popieluszko had become a martyr for his beliefs on freedom, justice, and social solidarity, which were extraordinarily close to Charter's own goals (Charter document no. 19, 2 November).

International Party Contacts. In 1984 the KSČ participated actively in the ideological disputes within the world communist movement, invariably taking the side of the Soviet Union against all possible "deviations." The Moscow center obviously appreciated the efforts of the Czechoslovak comrades because it more than once opened the pages of its own periodicals to their views and comments. In early spring, the KSČ daily published a long article in which "tendencies towards particu-

larism" in some fraternal parties were criticized. Such parties allegedly fall into a trap set for them by Western imperialists wishing to drive a wedge between the countries of the socialist bloc. The authors of the article argued that a bias had developed among certain Communists, who always praise those who pursue reforms and take new departures and condemn those who are more circumspect. This, the article went on to say, is nothing but an imperialist ploy (*Rudé právo*, 30 March). No parties were mentioned by name, but it was not difficult to guess that the target of the criticism might be the Hungarian, the Romanian, and, possibly, the East German parties. It was characteristic of the agreement between these views and those entertained by Soviet party ideologists that the article was translated and reprinted in eight different language editions of the Soviet ideological weekly *Novoe vremya* (17 April).

The need to preserve the solidarity of the world communist system under the leadership of the Soviet Union was also the topic of an article that Gustáv Husák wrote for the July issue of *World Marxist Review*. The Central Committee weekly *Tribuna* (no. 16, 18 April) carried an attack on the Yugoslav party in the spring. On 11 May, *Rudé právo* again went on the offensive, this time against what the Czechoslovak Communists consider a deviation in theoretical Marxism. The article recalled the seventy-fifth anniversary of the publication of Lenin's *Marxism and Empiriocriticism* and, in a manner similar to Lenin's vitriolic polemic against the Russian Social Democrats of 1909, condemned all currents known under the rubric of "creative Marxism," East and West, as an attempt "to improve Marxism even at the price of its destruction."

Exchanging roles, the ideologists of the Soviet party sometimes used the pages of Czechoslovak party periodicals to air their own views on the purity of Marxist teachings and on the need of internal discipline within the Moscow-dominated communist movement. Thus, Vadim Zagladin, first deputy chairman of the Soviet Central Committee's International Department, published an article about the increasing diversity among the communist parties and party-states. According to Zagladin, diversity is not a sign of weakness but rather of strength; in this he seems to differ from many Czechoslovak commentators (*Rudé právo*, 18 August).

Ideological unity nevertheless seemed to preoccupy party bosses in Central and Eastern Europe in

1984. A visible sign of this concern was the conference of Central Committee secretaries for international and ideological affairs of eleven communist parties held in Prague in July. It was the third meeting of its kind within one year. The closing communiqué was very explicit on the issue of nuclear arms and peace, but did not address the usual purpose of such gatherings, the resolution or at least clear articulation of ideological differences among the various communist movements of the Soviet bloc (ibid., 14 July).

Zdeněk Suda
University of Pittsburgh

Germany: German Democratic Republic

Population. 16,717,000
Party. Socialist Unity Party of Germany (Sozialistische Einheitspartei Deutschlands; SED)
Founded. 1918 (SED, 1946)
Membership. 2,202,277
General Secretary. Erich Honecker
Politburo. 21 full members: Erich Honecker (chairman, State Council), Hermann Axen, Horst Dohlus, Herbert Häber, Kurt Hager (member, State Council), Joachim Herrmann, Werner Felfe (member, State Council), Heinz Hoffmann (minister of defense), Günther Kleiber (deputy chairman [deputy premier], Council of Ministers), Werner Jarowinsky, Egon Krenz (deputy chairman, State Council), Werner Krolikowski (first deputy chairman [first deputy premier], Council of Ministers), Erich Mielke (minister of state security), Günter Mittag (deputy chairman, State Council), Erich Mückenberger (member, Presidium of People's Chamber), Konrad Naumann (first secretary, Berlin regional party executive; member, State Council), Alfred Neumann (deputy chairman [deputy premier], Council of Ministers), Günter Schabowski (editor-in-chief, *Neues Deutschland*), Horst Sindermann (member, State Council; member, Presidium of People's Chamber), Willi Stoph (chairman [premier], Council of Ministers; deputy chairman, State Council), Harry Tisch (member, State Council; chairman, Free German Trade Union Federation); 4 candidate members: Ingeborg Lange, Margarete Müller (member, State Council), Gerhard Schürer (chairman, State Planning Commission), Werner Walde (first secretary, Cottbus regional party executive)
Secretariat. 12 members: Erich Honecker, Hermann Axen (international relations), Horst Dohlus (publications), Werner Felfe (agriculture), Herbert Häber (intra-German relations), Kurt Hager (ideology, culture, and science), Joachim Herrmann (agitprop), Werner Jarowinsky (commerce and welfare), Egon Krenz, Ingeborg Lange (women's affairs), Günter Mittag (economic affairs), Konrad Naumann
Central Committee. 156 full and 51 candidate members
Status. Ruling party
Last Congress. Tenth, 11–16 April 1981
Auxiliary Organizations. Free German Trade Union Federation (FDGB), 9.1 million members, led by Harry Tisch; Free German Youth (FDJ), 2.3 million members, led by Eberhard Aurich; Democratic

Women's League (DFB), 1.4 million members, led by Ilse Thiele; Society for German-Soviet Friendship (DSF), 3.5 million members

Main State Organs. State Council, chaired by Erich Honecker; Council of Ministers (45 members, all but 4 belong to SED), chaired by Willi Stoph; both constitutionally answer to People's Chamber

Parliament and Elections. 1981, 99.9 percent, all 500 seats. All candidates run on ticket of National Front, an umbrella organization comprising the SED, the Democratic Peasants Party of Germany (DBD, 103,000 members), the Christian Democratic Union (CDU, 115,000 members), the Liberal Democratic Party of Germany (LDPD, 82,000 members), the National Democratic Party of Germany (NDPD, 91,000 members), and other groups. The 500 seats in the People's Chamber are distributed as follows: SED 127, 52 each to the DBD, CDU, LDPD, and NDPD, FDGB 68, FDJ 40, DFB 35, Cultural League (KB) 22.

Publications. *Neues Deutschland*, official SED daily; *Einheit*, SED theoretical monthly; *Neuer Weg*, SED organizational monthly; *Junge Welt*, FDJ daily; *Tribüne*, FDGB daily; *Horizont*, foreign policy monthly. The official news agency is the Allgemeiner Deutscher Nachrichtendienst (ADN).

In 1984 the German Democratic Republic (GDR) stepped into the forefront of East-West relations as the result of the persistent efforts of Erich Honecker and the SED leadership to maintain a positive working relationship with the Federal Republic of Germany (FRG) in spite of the Soviet Union's growing hostility to Helmut Kohl's government in Bonn. For several years, Honecker had played a prominent role in the Soviet propaganda campaign aimed at pressuring West Germany into canceling the deployment of Pershing II and cruise missiles by the United States in conformity with NATO's "two-track" decision of December 1979. Honecker had warned the West Germans of a new "ice age" in intra-German relations in the event that the missiles were deployed, and in 1981 he personally told then-chancellor Helmut Schmidt that favorable relations between the two German states could not endure "in the shadow of the missiles." Once the first missiles arrived in West Germany on schedule at the end of 1983, however, Honecker began to back off from this intransigent position. As early as November 1983 he spoke of the need to "limit the damage" to intra-German relations that might result from the missile issue, and he even went so far as to assert that new Soviet missiles scheduled for deployment in the GDR as part of the "countermeasures" threatened by Moscow were "no cause for jubilation" in the GDR.

These departures from the prevailing Soviet position on policy towards West Germany grew somewhat bolder in 1984. Throughout the year, Honecker made it clear that the GDR had a strong interest in keeping détente with the FRG alive, largely for economic reasons. For their part, the Soviets were assuming an increasingly antagonistic posture towards Bonn and in late spring launched a rhetorical offensive against "revanchism" in the

Federal Republic. The increasingly evident conflict between the East German and Soviet positions on policy towards West Germany culminated in early September, when Honecker dramatically postponed the official visit he was scheduled to make to West Germany later in the month. The hastily announced postponement was universally regarded in the West as the outcome of Soviet pressures on the East German government. In the months that followed, Honecker and other SED leaders repeatedly reaffirmed the unity of the GDR and the Soviet Union and adopted more critical tones in their characterizations of West German policies. At the same time, however, they continued to make known their hope for a return to "reason" in East-West relations and proceeded with negotiations on a wide range of topics with the West Germans.

It was around these two major developments—the desire of the SED for détente with the FRG and the conflict with the Soviet Union that ensued as a result—that many of the principal events occurring in the GDR in 1984 revolved.

Internal Party Affairs. On 24 May, a reshuffling of assignments in the SED leadership significantly strengthened Honecker's position as undisputed leader of the party. Four high-ranking officials were named full members of the Politburo. Three of them were already candidate members of that body: Günther Kleiber (deputy chairman of the Council of Ministers and an expert on agriculture and occasional emissary to the Middle East); Werner Jarowinsky (deputy minister for trade and supply); and Günter Schabowski (editor of *Neues Deutschland*). The fourth person to be inducted into the Politburo as a full member was Herbert Häber, for two decades one of the GDR's leading specialists on relations with West Germany. Häber was also named to the Secretariat of the Central Committee, thus confirming his sudden ascent to the role of Honecker's chief adviser on intra-German affairs within the highest echelons of the SED hierarchy. Also named to the Secretariat was Konrad Naumann, a full member of the Politburo and head of the SED's East Berlin party organization. It was also announced that Paul Verner, veteran member of both the Politburo and Secretariat, was relinquishing his positions due to illness. (*FBIS*, 25 May.)

Three weeks later, Egon Krenz and Günter Mittag, both full Politburo members, were made deputy chairmen of the Council of State, the GDR's collective presidency chaired by Honecker. Naumann was also added to the Council of State. (BBC, 18 June.)

These new assignments seemed to be intended to reinforce Honecker's commitment to pursuing détente with the FRG. All four of the newly appointed full members of the Politburo were younger personalities (in their early fifties) with rather pragmatic orientations to the problems facing the GDR. In both age and outlook, they contrasted markedly with the older generation of SED leaders like Verner, Hermann Axen (responsible for relations with foreign communist parties), Kurt Hager (ideology), Erich Mielke (minister of state security), and Gen. Heinz Hoffmann (minister of defense). In the past these more senior figures had tended to take a more hard-line approach to relations with West Germany. (Recent reports circulating in the West suggested that Verner, Hoffmann, and Mielke were opposed to Honecker's West German policy and to his planned visit to the FRG in September [ibid., 25 May; *FBIS*, 7 August].) Naumann also has a reputation as a hard-liner, and his dual appointment to the Secretariat and the Council of State may have been an indication of Honecker's sensitivity to more hard-line elements within both the SED and the USSR.

Meanwhile, Egon Krenz, at 47 the youngest member of the Politburo, continued his steady rise within the upper levels of the SED, replacing Verner as the unofficial number-two man in the party leadership. Like Honecker, Krenz had risen to prominence as head of the SED's youth organization, the FDJ. Since his induction into the Politburo and Secretariat in 1983, Krenz has become increasingly visible at Honecker's side, fueling speculation that the SED chief has already designated him as the party's "crown prince." (*Radio Free Europe/Radio Liberty* [*RFE/RL*], 28 March.) For his part, Mittag, the SED's leading economics specialist, is probably a supporter of Honecker's foreign policy approach. Both he and Krenz accompanied Honecker and Premier Willi Stoph to Yuri Andropov's funeral in February.

Domestic Affairs. *Political and Social Affairs.* East Germany's unofficial peace movement, which had been active since 1981, was somewhat more quiescent in 1984 than in previous years. To some extent this relative inactivity reflected a sense of disillusionment among many peace activists following their failure to stop either the deployment of the new American missiles in West Germany or the installation of new Soviet missiles in the GDR as "countermeasures" to the NATO missiles (ibid., 13 July). It also reflected a decision by leading members of the Lutheran and Catholic church hierarchies to be realistic about the limited prospects for successfully challenging the authorities in East Germany (*NYT*, 9 October). To be sure, the SED leadership continued to demonstrate its determination to prevent public opposition to its policies. In January, for example, four young peace activists were arrested in Weimar (*FBIS*, 8 February), and in April three individuals associated with the peace movement were tried and sentenced to prison terms ranging from eighteen months to two years (BBC, 25 April).

A new form of citizen disaffection with the communist regime made its appearance in 1984, however. On 20 January six East Germans entered the U.S. Embassy in East Berlin and refused to leave until granted asylum in the West. Apparently anxious to avoid adverse publicity over the event, the East German government raised no strenuous objections as the six were taken to West Berlin two days later. On 24 January a similar incident occurred as twelve GDR citizens installed themselves in the West German mission in East Berlin. They, too, were quickly transferred to West Berlin. (*NYT*, 1 February.) The most sensational of what was to become an epidemic of such cases came in late February, when five relatives of Premier Stoph took refuge in the West German Embassy in Prague. The incident was an embarrassment to both German governments, as both were actively searching for ways to keep their relationship outside the widening sphere of East-West tensions as much as possible. The five Stoph relatives were finally persuaded to leave the embassy after East German authorities assured them that they would be allowed to emigrate to the West (which they subsequently did).

(Ibid., 26 February; *CSM*, 23 March.) The ample publicity given to these cases by the West German broadcast media seemed to engender a desire on the part of a number of East German citizens to emulate the tactic. In early summer, 55 East Germans entered the West German mission in East Berlin with the intention of emigrating to West Germany. They were later allowed to leave for the West amid reports (which, perhaps for political reasons, were denied by West German authorities) that the FRG had paid the GDR $1.8 million for them (*Economist*, London, 7 July; *CSM*, 12 July). Finally, in October, more than 40 East German citizens ensconced themselves in the West German Embassy in Prague. The FRG decided to close the embassy the next day, but as many as 160 East Germans occupied the building over the next three months. By December, some of them, after breaking a hunger strike, agreed to go back to the GDR in hopes of gaining permission to emigrate legally (*Der Spiegel*, 31 December). The rest did not leave until January 1985 (*WP*, 16 January 1985). The use of the West German Embassy in Czechoslovakia as a means to leave the GDR was a matter of considerable concern to the East German leaders, inasmuch as over 450,000 East German tourists visit Prague annually (*NYT*, 4 October). In an effort to discourage further incidents of this kind, East German police intensified their watch outside the FRG mission in East Berlin in the spring and jailed a Lutheran pastor as he came out of the mission following an attempt to emigrate (*CSM*, 31 May).

Just as noteworthy as these occurrences was the Honecker government's decision to increase massively the number of East Germans allowed to leave the country officially. In recent years, approximately 9,000–12,000 GDR residents had been allowed to emigrate to the West annually (ibid., 21 May). (The figure for 1983 was 11,343 [*RFE/RL*, 21 April].) In the first four months of 1984, however, some 23,000 people emigrated to West Germany from the GDR; by August the number had risen to 33,000 (ibid., 31 May; *WP*, 18 August). The unprecedented legal exodus from the GDR was due in large measure to a conscious decision by the Honecker administration to demonstrate its willingness to meet at least some of the Kohl government's demands for concessions in the domain of human rights, concessions West German officials claimed they had asked for in the summer of 1983, when the FRG agreed to back a credit of nearly $400 million to the East German government. There may also have been economic considera-

tions. Although no hard evidence is available, it was reported that Bonn may have paid the GDR an average of $2,700 for each of the first 25,000 East Germans to leave for West Germany in 1984 (*CSM*, 12 July). Finally, it is possible that as many as 25 percent of the new emigrants may have been political dissidents of one kind or another whom the SED authorities may have been quite willing to expel (*RFE/RL*, 28 March). In another goodwill gesture apparently aimed at Bonn, the GDR released two founding members of the illegal organization "Women for Peace" who had been earlier imprisoned for their activities (*NYT*, 1 February).

At the same time that the East German leadership was cultivating Bonn's favor through increased emigration, however, it was also tightening restrictions on the ability of East Germans to have Western contacts or to engage in antiregime activity. New regulations made it more difficult for many East German citizens to have direct contacts with their relatives in the West or to communicate with Westerners by mail or telephone (*WP*, 21 February). The authorities apparently increased the number of people in positions considered too sensitive for Western contacts from 2 million to 3 million (*RFE/RL*, 21 April). On 16 May, new police regulations were announced that increased the fines imposed on those guilty of offenses against "public order" and banned meetings that "abuse the interests of society." It was also now forbidden to write petitions against government policy or to display symbols considered offensive to the regime, such as the patches worn by the peace group known as "Swords into Ploughshares," or the letter *A* placed on windows of those who wished to emigrate (*ausreisen*). The new laws made it more difficult for peace activists to use church property for their demonstrations. (BBC, 17 May; *CSM*, 31 May.) These actions, together with the continuing arrests of peace activists and the efforts made to block the further use of West German embassies for purposes of gaining political asylum, all clearly demonstrated that the East German government still had both the resolve and the capability to keep all forms of dissent within bounds in the GDR and to maintain the supreme authority of the party irrespective of the generally favorable climate of East-West relations the party leadership now sought.

Together with these repressive measures, the Honecker administration seemed to be heading in the direction of a more vigilant cultural policy. In September, Honecker delivered an address to cultural officials that placed great emphasis on the need to establish a separate "socialist national culture" for the GDR. The speech seemed to reflect the leadership's decision to insist on strict adherence to socialist values in the GDR and to accelerate efforts to distinguish East German culture from that of the "other" Germany. (*RFE/RL*, 28 September.) This reaffirmation of ideological *Abgrenzung* (delimitation) vis-à-vis West Germany appeared to be particularly appropriate in view of mounting evidence that East German youth were taking their cues from the West in their adaptations of punk styles and dropout mentalities (*Der Spiegel*, 18 June).

Honecker's call for a distinctive GDR cultural identity was not new. It represented the latest in a long series of attempts by the East German authorities going back to the era of Walter Ulbricht (1960–1971) not only to assert the distinctiveness of "socialist" German culture as opposed to "bourgeois" culture in West Germany, but also to stake the GDR's claim of constituting the true repository of the positive elements in German history (with the FRG cast in the role of the inheritor of the more sordid aspects of the German tradition, such as fascism, militarism, and the like). In a recent variation on these themes, the GDR since 1983 has even reappraised religious and political figures in Germany's past whom it had earlier defamed in keeping with a more strict Marxist-Leninist characterization of bourgeois class enemies. By 1983, figures such as Martin Luther, Frederick the Great, and even Otto von Bismarck merited re-evaluation for their positive contributions to certain "progressive" tendencies in their activities. In commemoration of the 500th anniversary of Luther, 1983 was proclaimed Martin Luther Year in the GDR, and the highest political authorities presided over memorial events that drew large groups of Western visitors. In 1984, this reassessment of erstwhile standard-bearers of German nationalism continued, as the GDR promoted efforts to fuse its own brand of Soviet-style socialism with a more pronounced emphasis on national traditions and sentiments. (*RFE/RL*, 24 July, 29 October.) Interestingly, one of the individuals singled out for praise was Count Claus von Stauffenberg, one of the organizers of the abortive attempt on Hitler's life in 1944. In their own appraisal of Stauffenberg some forty years after the event, several Soviet commentators took precisely the opposite approach, denouncing him as a staunch German chauvinist and anticommunist.

Another political occurrence in the GDR in 1984 was the election held for *Bezirk* (region), *Kreis* (district), and communal councils on 6 May. Over 260,000 handpicked candidates vied for approximately 203,000 posts. As expected, candidates representing the SED-dominated National Front parties received more than 99 percent of the vote. (*FBIS*, 7 May.) During the tightly controlled election campaign, dissidents distributed leaflets urging citizens to stay away from the polls (*Der Spiegel*, 9 April).

The Economy. In many respects, 1984 was a banner year for the East German economy. By midyear net material product in the GDR had grown 5.1 percent over the previous year, marking the highest growth rate in the GDR in several years. On 18 January 1985, the official news agency announced that in 1984 the GDR had achieved the highest absolute growth to date. National income rose 11.7 billion marks, or 5.5 percent, over 1983. Ninety percent of this growth resulted from a 5 percent increase in labor productivity in the economy. Labor productivity rose by 7.7 percent. Industrial production increased by 4.5 percent in the sphere of the industrial ministries and by 4.2 percent in the economy as a whole. Approximately 56 billion marks were expended for investment and the continuation of social policy. In construction net production rose by 7.7 percent and labor productivity by 7.6 percent. Home construction reached its highest annual level to date with 207,034 newly built or modernized homes. Agriculture gathered in the biggest cereal harvest in the history of the GDR, over 30 million metric tons. Foreign trade turnover increased by 8 percent, including an increase of 10 percent with the USSR and a 6 percent increase with the nonsocialist area. The net money income of the population increased by 3.9 percent and per capita real income by over 4 percent. (ADN, East Berlin, 18 January 1985; *FBIS*, 23 January 1985.) State subsidies for foodstuffs registered a 50 percent increase over 1983, rising to 33 billion East German marks. Prices for agricultural produce also rose 50 percent, as the government moved to implement a realignment of food prices designed to increase incentives for producers while guaranteeing low prices for consumers through subsidies. (BBC, 23 August.)

On the down side, investment continued to decline, falling to a growth rate of only 3 percent in the first half of the year. The GDR still lagged considerably behind the West in industrial productivity, and Honecker himself admitted that East Germany was 30 percent behind the FRG in this category. (*CSM*, 3 October.)

All in all, however, the East German regime had reason to congratulate itself on maintaining its position as the strongest and most successful economy in the Warsaw Pact.

Foreign Policy. *Intra-German Affairs.* As already noted, the main thrust of the GDR's policy towards the West in 1984 centered on Honecker's express intent, first articulated at the end of the previous year, to limit the damage to GDR-FRG ties expected to result from the installation of the new American missiles in the Federal Republic. As already pointed out, up to this time, Honecker himself had warned of dire consequences in intra-German relations should the missiles be installed. As it happened, East German foreign policy specialists as well as key decisionmakers appeared to be divided over the proper way to deal with West Germany in the event of Bonn's acceptance of the Pershing II and cruise missiles. Two leading schools of thought emerged on the issue. One argued that the West German governments under both Helmut Schmidt and his successor, Helmut Kohl, bore a large share of the responsibility for the global deterioration in East-West relations in general and for the NATO two-track decision in particular. The clear implication of this logic was that Bonn would have to be punished in some way or other for the missile deployments. The other line of argument contended that it was primarily the United States that was at fault for both the decline of détente and for the NATO missile decision. Proponents of this view strongly hinted that good neighborly relations between the two German states could continue in spite of the deployment of the American intermediate-range weapons. After appearing to support the first view until the end of 1983, Honecker opted for the second set of opinions about the time the deployments actually began. He reinforced this position throughout the first eight months of 1984 and retreated from it (albeit only partially) under apparently intense Soviet pressure in the final four months of the year. Throughout this period, Honecker evidently succeeded in gaining at least tacit support for his policies from those members of the SED Politburo who might have been less favorably disposed towards Bonn.

Accordingly, Honecker struck a positive note in his early estimations of the effect of the deployments on the future of arms talks concerning intermediate-range nuclear forces (INF) in Europe. Although the Soviets had walked out of the INF

talks at Geneva at the end of 1983, Honecker stressed at the beginning of 1984 that the talks would be resumed "sooner or later," a position that contrasted sharply with Soviet expressions of intransigence. (*RFE/RL*, 9 January.) In February the SED chief once again called for a revival of détente (*Neues Deutschland*, 13 February; *FBIS*, 17 February). Moreover, in most of his speeches, Honecker reserved his harshest criticisms for the Reagan administration but usually spared the Kohl government from direct attack (see, for example, *Neues Deutschland*, 7 May; *JPRS*, 4 June). At the funeral of Yuri Andropov in February, Honecker met personally with Kohl, and the two leaders issued a statement calling for efforts to avoid war and to use "common sense" to keep "the course of international affairs from getting out of hand" (*CSM*, 22 February).

In March, the biannual Leipzig trade fair provided the forum for a host of meetings between East German officials and their West German guests. The latter included Finance Minister Otto Lambsdorff and the conservative chief of the Christian Social Union, Franz-Josef Strauss. Strauss had broken away from his traditionally hostile attitudes towards the GDR in the summer of 1983, when he was instrumental in arranging the large credit agreement worked out that summer between the GDR and a consortium of West German banks. Strauss attributed the recent wave of officially sanctioned emigration of East Germans to the FRG to promises he claimed to have obtained from the GDR during his first visit to East Germany that same summer (*FBIS*, 13 March). Over the course of the first four months of 1984, the East Germans played host to over 140 West German government officials, an extraordinary number (*RFE/RL*, 30 April). The visitors included high-level personalities from the Social Democratic Party of Germany (SPD) as well as from the ruling Christian Democratic and Free Democratic parties (*FBIS*, 6, 14, and 16 March). In December, leaders of the SPD and SED joined in talks aimed at proposing agreements on the reduction of chemical weapons in Europe (ibid., 6 December).

Meanwhile, the East German leadership manifested its interest in maintaining a favorable relationship with Bonn not only through the unprecedented increase in emigration, but through such additional actions as the gradual dismantling of deadly automatic weapons at the border (ibid., 19 April).

One of Honecker's chief aims (perhaps his leading aim) in his pursuit of détente with the West Germans was to secure continuing West German economic assistance for the GDR. West Germany already contributes about 2.5 billion Deutschemarks to the GDR annually through a variety of mechanisms, including transit tolls, visas, currency exchanges by tourists, and other payments (*RFE/RL*, 12 January). (Approximately 6 million West Germans and West Berliners visit the GDR each year [*CSM*, 22 February].) Of this amount, about 700 million DM is given to East German citizens by private contacts in the West (*RFE/RL*, 12 October). In addition, the GDR's gross debt to Western banks in 1984 was estimated to be in the neighborhood of $10 billion, most of it owed to banks in the FRG. Between 20 and 40 percent of this debt was repayable within a year. Finally, the GDR's trade with the Federal Republic and West Berlin, although down 5 percent from the 1983 level, was still important for the East German economy, and it was estimated that it would total approximately 15 billion DM at year's end. Thanks to these and other economic benefits received from West Germany, the GDR by 1984 had amassed nearly $4 billion in hard currency deposits, a sizable figure for a Soviet-bloc country. (Ibid.)

A particularly vivid example of the GDR's specific economic relationship with the FRG occurred in February, with the announcement by the Volkswagen company that it had reached an agreement with the East German government to build facilities in the GDR capable of turning out 290,000 cars a year by 1988, in addition to furnishing East Germany with 15,000 ready-made vehicles by 1993 (*Der Spiegel*, 13 February).

In short, the GDR had acquired over the years a healthy economic stake in détente with Bonn. The economic importance of this relationship was underscored on 25 July, when the West German government disclosed that it had approved a new credit to the GDR of approximately $333 million, to be provided by several West German banks. The West Germans also announced that the GDR had agreed to lower the minimum currency exchange requirement for elderly persons from 25 to 15 DM, together with ten additional measures intended to ease travel restrictions on selected categories of West and East German travelers, to promote further emigration of East Germans, and the like. West German spokesmen officially denied that these East German measures constituted a quid pro quo for the new credits. (*NYT*, 26 July.) Coming in the midst of the mounting Soviet invective against West German revanchism, the credit agreement provided a dramatic demonstration of the determination of both German governments to shield their relationship from the fallout of broader East-West tensions.

Following the announcement of the agreement, the Soviets intensified their pressure on the leaders to rein in their blossoming relationship with Bonn (see below). This pressure resulted in the postponement of Honecker's September visit, as already noted. In announcing the postponement, however, East German officials stated that the "date" for the planned trip was "no longer realistic," in view of allegedly inappropriate statements by West German officials in recent months on various questions relating to the legal status of Germany's borders (*FBIS*, 5 September). This implied that the trip could be rescheduled at a later date, a possibility confirmed by Honecker himself (ibid.). For their part, the West Germans regretted the postponement, but noted that the two German states were proceeding with negotiations on some seventeen separate issues (*CSM*, 6 September).

In the weeks following the announcement of the postponement, Honecker and other GDR leaders shifted their rhetoric somewhat to reflect the prevailing anti-Bonn line emanating from Moscow. Like the Soviets, the East Germans placed the onus of the blame for the failure of the trip on the FRG, suggesting that Bonn needed to be more forthcoming with concessions on issues relating to the status of Germany (*NYT*, 11 September). Apparently the GDR leadership was looking for some signs of movement towards the resolution of four demands Honecker had posited in a speech in Gera several years earlier. These included West Germany's recognition of a separate GDR citizenship; the elevation of the two countries' permanent representatives to the status of ambassadors; the final delineation of the intra-German border as the middle of the Elbe River; and the closing of the Salzgitter center that monitors "crimes against the people" allegedly committed by the East German government. The East Germans also joined the Soviets in condemning recent affirmations by Kohl and other West German officials of the continuing de jure validity of Germany's 1937 borders (*FBIS*, 9 October). They also aligned themselves more unequivocally than before behind Moscow's position that no reversal of the recent "countermeasures" taken by the Warsaw Pact in response to the Pershing II and cruise missile deployments in the FRG could take place until all the new American weapons were removed (ibid., 10 October). (Earlier, Honecker had said that a "reduction" in the number of the new

U.S. intermediate-range weapons could create the conditions for a reversal of the countermeasures [*RFE/RL*, 6 June].)

In another display of pique at the West German government, the East German leaders made overtures to West German opposition parties, particularly the Greens. On 26 September, Honecker personally apologized to Green leader Petra Kelly for the refusal of East German authorities to admit her to the GDR in late July. Honecker wrote her that from now on, Greens who are members of the Bundestag would be allowed the same rights of entry to the GDR as other West German parliamentarians. (*FBIS*, 27 September.)

Despite the GDR's rhetorical realignment with the Kremlin's position on West Germany in the last four months of the year, distinct nuances in the GDR's positions could be detected that signaled the GDR's continuing interest in cooperation with the West Germans. For example, Honecker and other SED officials continued to blame the Reagan administration more than the FRG when distributing the blame for the collapse of détente. When attacking revanchism in the Federal Republic, they also tended to refrain from mentioning Helmut Kohl by name in these attacks, unlike many Soviet commentators. Finally, they made explicit references to the continuing need for "dialogue," "reason" and a return to détente in East-West relations. (Ibid., 12 September; *RFE/RL*, 29 October.) At the end of the year, the intra-German dialogue was still moving forward, as Häber and Foreign Minister Oskar Fischer met with West German officials responsible for relations with the GDR (*FBIS*, 6 and 7 December).

The East Germans also showed that they regarded the Greens with a measure of suspicion, possibly fearing their influence on the East German peace movement. In October several Green party officials were denied entry to East Germany (ibid., 15 and 23 October).

Relations with Other Western States. The GDR buttressed its interest in East-West dialogue with important overtures to other Western states. Although the United States was the chief target of East Germany's criticism of Western foreign policy throughout the year, several high-level meetings with American officials took place in 1984. In February, as the GDR's position on the need for détente was becoming increasingly differentiated from that of the Soviet Union, Assistant Secretary of State Richard Burt went to East Berlin for consultations

with East German officials (*WP*, 21 February; *CSM*, 22 February). In September, Undersecretary of State Michael Armacost, the State Department's number-three official, attended a luncheon at the GDR Embassy in Washington, and the U.S. ambassador to the GDR hosted Armacost's East German counterpart (*WP*, 9 September). In October, Foreign Minister Fischer conferred with Secretary of State George Shultz during the opening sessions of the U.N. General Assembly. Shultz described the meeting as "warm and cordial" and indicated that the topics discussed included trade, scientific, technical, cultural, and humanitarian issues (ibid., 5 October).

Several prominent Western leaders made visits to the GDR in 1984. At the end of January, Canadian prime minister Pierre Trudeau was received in East Berlin (*FBIS*, 2 and 7 February). In early summer, the GDR played host to three Western heads of government. Swedish prime minister Olof Palme began a two-day visit on 29 June, Greek premier Andreas Papandreou visited the GDR from 5 to 7 July, and Italy's Bettino Craxi went there from 9 to 10 July. Palme and Papandreou were on record as opposed to the installation of new American missiles in Europe, while Craxi, whose government had accepted cruise missiles, had earlier called for a moratorium on INF deployments. These visits not only enhanced the GDR's prestige in international diplomacy, but served the GDR's dual purpose of promoting both the Warsaw Pact's antimissile campaign and the GDR's own interest in East-West cooperation (*RFE/RL*, 30 July). In October, Honecker journeyed to Finland (*FBIS*, 19 October). Consultations with other Western states took place at various times throughout the year at the Foreign Ministry and other levels.

Relations with the Third World. The GDR's burgeoning relations with selected Third World countries and revolutionary groups have also served to enhance the GDR's prestige, both internationally and within the Warsaw Pact, over the past dozen years. By the 1980s, the GDR was the Soviet Union's most important ally in Third World activity. The Honecker government continued to cultivate its Third World ties in 1984. Honecker himself traveled to Ethiopia in September, less than a week after postponing his scheduled trip to West Germany (ibid., 11, 12, and 14 September). As one of the Soviet Union's most important client states in Africa, Ethiopia received considerable attention from East German officials (ibid., 8 March, 1 June, 21 and 27 December). Honecker also stopped in Djibouti on his way back from Addis Ababa (ibid., 14 September). In December, the SED general secretary journeyed to Algeria (ibid., 17 and 20 December). Another of the GDR's African clients, Mozambique, figured prominently when it was disclosed that seven East Germans (presumably on an official mission) had been murdered by "counter-revolutionary groups" operating in the country (ibid., 11 December).

The GDR's Middle East diplomacy included a visit to Syria by Schabowski (ibid., 21 June), and a trip to Iraq by Kleiber (ibid., 26 June). Honecker met with the chief of South Yemen's Socialist Party in East Berlin in November (ibid., 13 and 15 November). The Honecker government's growing interest in Latin America was highlighted by Foreign Minister Fischer's trip to Mexico (ibid., 1 June) and by Honecker's meeting in Berlin with Nicaraguan Sandinista leader Daniel Ortega (ibid., 21 June).

In addition to these and other diplomatic forays, the GDR continued to pursue economic agreements with Third World countries and to provide educational opportunities to students from certain Third World countries. According to official figures, the GDR in 1984 had economic agreements with 63 less-developed countries, including joint economic commissions with 15 of them. Over 200,000 East German experts were working in the Third World, and nearly 30,000 students from the developing world were studying in the GDR. (*Horizont*, no. 17; *JPRS*, 20 August.)

International Party Relations. As noted above, a serious debate took place among East German foreign policy experts and policymakers concerning policy towards West Germany in the context of the INF controversy. Significantly, the same debate along much the same lines was also taking place in the Soviet Union. A close scrutiny of the writings and statements of prominent foreign policy specialists in the Soviet Union, many of whom enjoyed influential political positions or connections, reveals that just beneath the surface of the Politburo, a lively discussion was being conducted in public over precisely the same sorts of questions concerning policy towards West Germany that were under consideration in East Germany. The absence of strong one-man leadership in the Kremlin, however, made the Soviet leadership's position somewhat ambiguous.

Honecker reportedly welcomed Chernenko's accession to the highest Soviet leadership position following Andropov's death in February. The SED chief apparently obtained the new Soviet leader's approval for the September trip to West Germany as early as February and perhaps as late as June (*NYT*, 15 February, 11 September.) General Heinz Hoffmann, the GDR's defense minister and a full member of the SED Politburo, met with Chernenko in Moscow and "reached full agreement" with him on European issues, according to official accounts (*Neues Deutschland*, 21 March). Nevertheless, the Soviet media began intensifying their attacks on the West German government in May (*CSM*, 31 May). These attacks on the reputed revanchism of the West Germans, some of which were directed squarely at Chancellor Kohl and other cabinet ministers by name, grew even more acerbic in late July, following the conclusion of the new intra-German credit deal (*Der Spiegel*, 13 August). Strikingly, several Soviet commentators were unmistakably addressing their criticisms at the GDR leadership. On 27 July, a *Pravda* article by Lev Bezymenski, provocatively entitled "In the Shadow of the Missiles" as a reminder of Honecker's earlier warnings to West Germany about the detrimental consequences of the imminent American missile deployments, sharply denounced the FRG and offered repeated citations from Honecker and *Neues Deutschland* critical of Bonn's positions on a variety of intra-German issues (*FBIS*, 2 August). On 2 August, *Pravda* carried an editorial stating explicitly that the FRG was using an "economic lever" to "disturb the stability of the GDR" and to "gradually erode the foundations of the socialist system there" (ibid., 2 August). This was without question the most hostile anti-FRG propaganda to emanate from authoritative Soviet sources since the period prior to the onset of détente in the 1960s.

Nevertheless, there were other signs that various influential people in the Soviet foreign policy establishment did not share this negative attitude towards West (or, for that matter, East) Germany. *Izvestiia*, for example, printed an article at the end of July that clearly implied approval of the recent GDR-FRG credit arrangement, which *Neues Deutschland* (31 July) quickly reprinted. In addition, a significant number of articles appearing in such Soviet journals as *World Economy and International Relations* and *International Affairs* echoed the more openly pro-détente positions articulated by Honecker and his supporters in the SED. Precisely where the various Soviet Politburo members stood on these questions was difficult to ascertain, in view of Chernenko's withdrawal from the political limelight during the summer, apparently for reasons of ill health, and the relative paucity of clear expressions of opinion by other Soviet leaders.

Meanwhile, the discussion over policy towards Bonn fanned out from the GDR and the Soviet Union to embrace other Warsaw Pact states. Hungary and Romania were clearly taking the GDR's side in the controversy, while Czechoslovakia lined up behind the Soviets. On 21 February, *Neues Deutschland* reprinted an article from the Hungarian party daily, *Népszabadság*, praising the "useful dialogue" taking place between the two German states (*RFE/RL*, 30 April). In April, the SED daily published statements by Hungarian party chief János Kádár and by Mátyás Szürös (the Hungarian party Secretariat official responsible for foreign policy) supporting the notions that each socialist state had its own national interests and that the small and medium-sized states of Europe had an important role to play in promoting détente (*Neues Deutschland*, 12 and 17 April). Certain Soviet commentators, however, explicitly contradicted these views (see, for example, *RFE/RL*, 30 April). Similarly, the Czech party daily *Rudé právo* (30 March) expressed the view that certain Warsaw Pact states were seeking "one-sided advantages from capitalist governments," a barbed allusion to the GDR and Hungary. The Soviet weekly *New Times* reprinted the Czech article (*WP*, 19 April; *RFE/RL*, 4 May).

Until the announcement of the cancellation of Honecker's West German visit in early September, the East Germans held their own in this dispute among the socialist countries (*WP*, 2 August). The East Germans tended to avoid utilizing the revanchism theme in their commentary on West Germany during the summer. (When Krenz referred to "great German expansionism" in remarks made in Poland, this phrase was deleted from the *Neues Deutschland* account [*CSM*, 27 July].) As late as August, the GDR foreign policy weekly, *Horizont*, insisted that socialist countries could have different positions on certain questions (*Los Angeles Times*, 8 August). On 10 August, Häber renewed the GDR's appeals for détente (*WP*, 11 August). And at the end of the month, Honecker was the only Warsaw Pact party chief to attend the celebrations in Romania commemorating the fortieth anniversary of that country's liberation from the Germans (*NYT*, 25 August).

The GDR also sought, and apparently obtained, the support of the Italian, French, and Spanish communist parties for its viewpoints. Several meetings were held with Italian party leaders (*RFE/RL*, 4 September); French party chief Georges Marchais visited East Berlin (*FBIS*, 27 and 28 February); and an SED delegation went to Spain for talks with Spanish party leaders (ibid., 5 December).

Soviet pressure against independent East German overtures towards the Federal Republic proved overwhelming, however, as the anti-Bonn orientation became dominant within the Soviet leadership by late summer. As indicated earlier, the GDR moved closer to this orientation after the postponement of Honecker's trip to West Germany, but persisted in uttering hopes for a return to a less confrontationist stance in relations with the FRG. To be sure, there was little chance that Honecker would challenge the Soviets over this issue; he was fully aware that the GDR's room for independent foreign policy maneuvering was narrowly circumscribed by Moscow. Moreover, Honecker also recognized (and probably welcomed) the fact that the Soviet Union was the ultimate guarantor of the GDR's existence on a continent divided into two opposed political blocs. Honecker had neither the opportunity nor the inclination to chart as autonomous a foreign policy course as Romania's Nicolae Ceauşescu. It was therefore a foregone conclusion that the GDR would accept Soviet SS-21 missiles in retaliation for West Germany's acceptance of the new U.S. intermediate-range missiles; the first of the launchers for these Soviet rockets reportedly arrived in the GDR in July (ibid., 16 July). Similarly, the GDR backed the Soviet boycott of the Los Angeles Olympics.

Hence the magnitude of the divergence between the Soviet and East German positions on policy towards West Germany should not be exaggerated. As indicated above, conflicting viewpoints on how to deal with the FRG were to be found in both the GDR and the Soviet Union. Foremost in the Kremlin's considerations, it appeared, was the basic principle that the USSR, not East Germany, had the final authority to determine policy on West Germany. Moreover, both the Soviets and the East Germans agreed that relations with Bonn involved a mixture of rewards and risks. In 1984, the East Germans tended to stress the rewards while the Soviets emphasized the risks. Not even the Kremlin, however, was interested in an irreparable breach in relations with Bonn. Accordingly, *Pravda* (7 September) indicated that the Honecker trip had been "postponed" and not "canceled." (Honecker had postponed a trip to West Germany once before, in 1983, as Moscow intensified its antimissile campaign against the West German government.) More tellingly, the Soviets themselves concluded three credit agreements totaling $541 million with the FRG in 1984 (*WP*, 20 September). Ultimately, the controversy between the GDR and the Soviet Union in 1984 centered mainly on the tactics and timing of relations with Bonn rather than on the fundamental questions of grand political strategy towards the West.

The GDR kept up the usual round of contacts with other communist parties, both ruling and nonruling, in 1984. Poland's Gen. Wojciech Jaruzelski visited East Berlin in November (*FBIS*, 19 November); Mittag led one of the SED delegations to Cuba (ibid., 21 September); and North Korean party chief Kim Il-song came to the GDR in the spring to sign a treaty of friendship and cooperation (ibid.,

1 and 5 June). On the state level, the GDR pursued trade agreements with China (ibid., 19 April, 21 September). Among the nonruling parties of Western Europe (other than those already mentioned), the GDR leadership had contacts with the parties of Austria (ibid., 13 January), Belgium (ibid., 10 January), and Finland (ibid., 22 October). Among the Third World parties, East German leaders met delegations from the Palestine Communist Party (ibid., 10 February) and from the communist parties of Israel (ibid., 8 June), El Salvador (ibid., 31 August), and Uruguay (ibid., 20 June).

Michael J. Sodaro
George Washington University

Hungary

Population. 10,681,000
Party. Hungarian Socialist Workers' Party (Magyar Szocialista Munkáspárt; HSWP)
Founded. 1918 (HSWP, 1956)
Membership. 852,000 (1983); workers and farmworkers 44.6 percent; women 28.3 percent; average age 45.5; 74 percent joined after 1956 (1980 statistics)
First Secretary. János Kádár
Politburo. 13 full members: János Kádár, György Aczél, Valéria Benke, Sándor Gáspár, Ferenc Havasi, Mihály Korom, György Lázár, Pál Losonczi, László Maróthy, Lajos Méhes, Károly Németh, Miklós Óvari, István Sarlós
Secretariat. 7 members: János Kádár, György Aczél (culture and ideology), Ferenc Havasi (economic policy), Mihály Korom (party, mass organizations, and military), Károly Németh (youth and party building), Miklós Óvari (agitprop and cultural policy), Mátyás Szürös (foreign and intraparty affairs)
Central Committee. 127 full members
Status. Ruling party
Last Congress. Twelfth, 24–27 March 1980, in Budapest; next congress scheduled for March 1985
Auxiliary Organizations. National Council of Trade Unions (NCTU, 4.5 million members), led by Lajos Méhes; Communist Youth League (874,000 nominal members), led by György Fejti
Main State Organs. Presidential Council, chairman, Pál Losonczi; Council of Ministers, chairman, György Lázár; both constitutionally responsible to the National Assembly (352 deputies)
Last Elections. Elections are administered by the Patriotic People's Front (PPF). In 1980, PPF candidates received 99.3 percent of the vote. Next election scheduled for 1985.

Publications. *Népszabadság* (People's freedom), HSWP daily; *Társadalmi Szemle* (Social review), HSWP theoretical monthly; *Pártélet* (Party life), HSWP organizational monthly; *Magyar Hírlap*, government daily; *Magyar Nemzet*, PPF daily; *Népszava*, NCTU daily. The official news agency is Magyar Távirati Iroda (MTI).

The Hungarian Section of the Russian Communist Party (Bolshevik) was founded in Moscow in March 1918 by Béla Kun (1886–1939) and a few other Hungarian prisoners of war. The Communist Party of Hungary came into being in Budapest in November 1918. Kun was the dominant figure in the communist–left socialist coalition that proclaimed the Hungarian Soviet Republic on the collapse of Mihály Károlyi's liberal-democratic regime. The red dictatorship lasted from March to August 1919.

During the interwar period, the party functioned as a faction-ridden movement in domestic illegality and in exile. The underground membership numbered in the hundreds. With the Soviet occupation at the end of World War II, the Hungarian Communist Party (HCP) re-emerged as a member of the provisional government. Kun had lost his life in Stalin's purges, and the party was led by Mátyás Rákosi (1892–1971). Although the HCP won no more than 17 percent of the vote in the relatively free 1945 elections, it continued to exercise a disproportionate influence in the coalition government. Thanks largely to Soviet-backed coercive tactics, the HCP gained effective control of the country in 1947. In 1948, it absorbed left-wing social democrats into the newly named Hungarian Workers' Party.

Rákosi's Stalinist zeal was exemplified by the show trial of József Cardinal Mindszenty and the liquidation of alleged Titoist László Rajk. The New Course of 1954–1955 offered some relief from economic mismanagement and totalitarian terror; inspired by some of Stalin's successors, it was led in Hungary by the moderate communist Imre Nagy (1896–1958). De-Stalinization undermined the party's authority and unity, and the replacement of Rákosi by Ernö Gerö (1898–1980) could not halt the rising tide of popular opposition. Following the outbreak of revolution on 23 October 1956, Imre Nagy became prime minister for the second time and eventually headed a multiparty government that withdrew Hungary from the Warsaw Pact. On 25 October, János Kádár (1912–) became leader of the renamed party, the HSWP. The Nagy government was overthrown by the armed intervention of the Soviet Union on 4 November.

Since the end of the revolution, the HSWP has ruled unchallenged as the sole political party, firmly aligned with the Soviet Union. After an initial phase of repression that culminated in the final collectivization of agriculture (1959–1960), Kádár's rule came to be marked by his conciliatory "alliance policy" and by pragmatic reforms, most notably the New Economic Mechanism launched in 1968.

Party and Government. Low-key preparations are in progress for the HSWP's Thirteenth Congress, scheduled for 25 March 1985. The task of the congress, technically the party's top legislative body, is to elect the leadership and to map out policy guidelines for the next quinquennium. All party units have therefore been mobilized to elect delegates, to analyze the record of the past five years, and to develop proposals for the future. It is expected that the congress will stress continuity in leadership and policy. Congressional issues highlighted by the party's theoretical monthly (*Társadalmi Szemle*, July–August) include maintenance of the standard of living amidst adverse economic conditions; the preservation of social and political stability at a time of growing domestic debate; and the reconciliation of the party's leading role, exercised through persuasion rather than authoritarian intervention, with the ongoing administrative decentralization and the expansion of "socialist democracy." There is evidence of a slackening in party discipline, and the need to reinvigorate party life as well as the principle of centralism is stressed: "It has not been easy to be a communist in the past, but it will be even less easy in the future."

In a speech at a Budapest factory anticipating the work of the congress, the 72-year-old Kádár observed that "if we do not want to preserve our system by force and the use of arms—which we do not wish to do—then we must prove by other means that our social system is superior," i.e., by economic reforms. He called for understanding for the principle that "he who produces more should get more, and he who produces less should get less" and for the corollary that "we should subsidize from budgetary funds only the basic essentials." (Radio Budapest, 25 July; *FBIS*, 26 July.)

The drive against corruption in party ranks resulted in the dismissal in November 1983 of a deputy minister of justice and longtime member of the Central Committee apparatus, Ádám Bonifert. *Pártélet* (December 1983) noted that he had exploited his office for illegal financial gain, in gross violation of party standards, and he therefore had been expelled from the HSWP. An accompanying article called for strict observance of party rules and deplored the prevalence of "incorrect political and ideological views" in basic party units in Budapest. Proceedings against party members for abuse of authority are frequent. In 1982, in Budapest alone, discipinary action was taken against some 1,500 members, 154 of them in leading positions.

A Yugoslav commentator reflected on the difficulty of promoting economic reform with a ruling party enjoying monopoly power and noted the Hungarian leadership's attempts to broaden popular participation—in the trade unions as well as in the electoral system—while preserving the party's ultimate leading role (*Start*, Zagreb, 21 April; *RFE Research*, 17 May). Indeed, the HSWP has stimulated much debate and promoted a few palliative reforms to achieve this objective. At its April session, the National Assembly passed a bill creating a Constitutional Law Council designed to "oversee the constitutionality of statutory regulations and legal directives." Its members are to be elected by the National Assembly from its deputies and from nominees of the PPF. Cases may be submitted by "authorized entities" or selected by the council itself. Another constitutional amendment, passed by parliament at its December 1983 session, entailed a revision of the electoral law (see *YICA*, 1984, p. 336). The amendment provides for compulsory multiple candidacies in all parliamentary and local council electoral districts as well as for an additional, national list of candidates for election to the assembly. This national ticket will be equal to about 10 percent of the number of National Assembly electoral districts and will consist of candidates nominated by the National Council of the PPF on the basis of recommendations submitted by its constituent organizations. Dissatisfaction with the role of parliament was aired in *Népszava* (22 May). The two or three sessions of the National Assembly each year last only two days, and this severely curtails the deputies' nominal right to participate actively in debate and take initiatives. There is generally no detailed discussion of proposed legislation, bills are put to the vote as a whole, and committee scrutiny is perfunctory. It can be anticipated that the regime will take some steps to make parliament more active.

In the wake of the Polish crisis, the party has devoted much attention to the role of trade unions. On the occasion of a visit to Poland in October 1983, Kádár declared that "socialism has a need for independent trade unions" (*RFE Research*, 21 December 1983), but his definition of independence was necessarily inspired by the Hungarian model. In a lecture to the HSWP's Political Academy in December 1983, the outgoing secretary general of the NCTU, Sándor Gáspár, observed that trade union independence was "one of the most complicated problems in the operation of our political system"; full independence, however, would mean "opposition to the socialist state and the communist party," which was unthinkable (*Népszava*, 15 December). The Central Committee reviewed the status of trade unions at its 12 October 1983 meeting. Károly Németh's report called for "renewal," meaning a more active exercise of existing rights tempered by realism and "political sensitivity" (*Pártélet*, November 1983). The unions are expected to promote productivity and efficiency through a participatory process that safeguards the welfare and economic interests of the workers. One sanction the trade unions possess is the right of veto over management decisions, a right exercised some 170 times in 1982, mostly, it was said, with justification. In theory, the unions work independently under the political direction of the party, a course that lies between the "dogmatic" Stalinist concept of a unidirectional transmission belt and the "revisionist" demands for full autonomy. This course, according to the HSWP, is correct and remains unaltered. The party has officially deplored unjustified and petty intervention by party representatives in the activities of trade unions.

At its December 1983 meeting, the Central Committee approved the appointment of Lajos Méhes (56) as the new secretary general of the NCTU. He joined the party as a young worker, served as first secretary of the Communist Youth League in 1964–1970, and had been minister of industry since 1980. His predecessor, Sándor Gáspár (66), was promoted to the largely honorary post of NCTU president; Gáspár remains head of the World Federation of Trade Unions. Gáspár's deputy, Sándor Jakab (55), also retired. The new minister of industry is László Kápolyi (51), who has a solid engineering and academic background.

The HSWP's desire to distance itself from its Stalinist antecedents was displayed in media coverage commemorating the purge of two leading party members in 1949, Tibor Szönyi and László Rajk. Numerous books and films dealing with the horrors of the Rákosi era have appeared in recent times, prompting some concern in party circles that the positive achievements of that period may be overlooked (ibid., March).

Economic Affairs. The Hungarian economy continues to suffer from its own structural weaknesses as well as from unfavorable shifts in the terms of trade. Industrial production in 1983 failed to meet the modest targeted increase of 1–2 percent. Agriculture, hit by drought, suffered a 3.2 percent shortfall in output, and this in turn reduced hard currency export earnings. Price increases held real incomes below the planned level. The foreign trade surplus reached only half the planned level, even though exports to the West grew by 11 percent while imports from the same sector were cut by 9 percent. (Hungary's largest Western trade partners are the Federal Republic of Germany, Austria, Italy, and the United States; trade with the United States increased 20 percent in 1983.) Overall, it was reported that the national income rose by only 0.4 percent (MTI, 27 April).

The economic plan for 1984 anticipated an increase of 1.5–2.0 percent in domestic net material product and of the same range in industrial production; a decrease of 1.0–1.5 percent in domestic expenditures and of 2.0–3.0 percent in construction; an increase of up to 1.0 percent over 1982 in agricultural production; and no change in per capita income. The 1984 state budget provided for a substantial drop in enterprise and price subsidies, their share falling from 29.8 to 25.0 percent of the budget. (*RFE Research*, 25 February.) The aggregate price index was expected to rise by 7–8 percent, and wages by 4–5 percent. The net foreign debt was reduced in 1983 by $148 million to approximately $5.2 billion. By juggling repayments and new borrowings, Hungary has managed so far to preserve its creditworthiness in international capital markets. The trade balance in the first half of 1984 showed a convertible currency surplus of $263 million, the twelve-month target being in the range of $700–800 million. The emergency import restrictions introduced in September 1982 were relaxed in April and lifted effective 1 January 1985. This measure and the cuts in central subsidies are necessitated in part by Hungary's recently acquired membership in the International Monetary Fund. Expectations in mid-1984 were that the plan would

be fulfilled in most respects, with agricultural production exceeding the planned rate of growth.

The first round of price increases occurred in January, including meat (by an average of 21 percent) as well as building materials and energy. The increases were only partly offset by compensatory adjustments in state-funded social benefits. The reasons given were the reduction in state subsidies and the need to reduce domestic consumption to free goods for export. Further selective price increases were announced in March and June, bringing the cumulative rise in consumer prices to over 8 percent. A monthly minimum wage of 2,000 forints came into effect on 1 January, and consultations with the NCTU produced agreement on other modifications to the wage system in certain employment sectors. Teachers received a special pay raise on 1 September, in an overdue response to the problem of low morale and low pay in the educational sector. Amid a multitude of similar demands, the regime is arguing that economic rationality requires greater wage differentiation but no general increase in wage levels.

Prime Minister Lázár visited Moscow on 12 November to discuss the coordination of economic plans for 1986–1990. Close to 30 percent of Hungary's trade is conducted with the Soviet Union, and this trade is expected to rise by 7 percent in 1984. Hungary has been compelled to boost its export deliveries to pay for Soviet raw materials and energy, prices for which have risen to near world-market levels (*Népszabadság*, 13 November).

As prospects dim for further improvement in the standard of living, the issue of income differentiation is receiving much attention in political as well as academic circles. In recent years the standard of living of some two-thirds of the population has declined, the impact being the greatest on the aged and large families. One survey indicated that one-tenth of the population has to survive on barely half of the average monthly income of 3,600 forints (*Magyar Hirlap*, 20 April 1983). These "multiple disadvantaged" groups, observed sociologist Zsuzsa Ferge, are also the least likely to be among the three-quarters of the population deriving some benefit from the "second economy" (Radio Budapest, 2 November 1983; *RFE Research*, 20 December 1983). At the other end of the income scale, the existence of "forint millionaires" and the conspicuous consumption habits of the relatively wealthy (notably farmers, doctors, and private artisans) have drawn public envy and criticism of the evolving economic mechanism. In defense of the reforms that allow for this differentiation, leading economist Iván T. Berend argued that they promoted general prosperity better than the former command model with its equality of poverty and claimed that they were consistent with socialist values (*Magyar Nemzet*, 24 December 1983). The editor-in-chief of *Népszabadság*, János Berecz, also defended the government's policies against "pseudo-radical" critics (7 April), but the latter, including maverick economist Tamás Bauer, are allowed to air their views even in *Társadalmi Szemle* (March). The government daily, *Magyar Hirlap* (15 September), stressed that the differentiation of individual and enterprise incomes is economically rational and that taxation and anticorruption laws serve to curb excesses. However, many people find ways to earn "invisible income," and the controversy is not likely to subside as long as the economy remains in the doldrums.

The regime, meanwhile, is pursuing its efforts to spur productivity and improve the economic balance with a wide variety of modifications to the mechanism introduced in 1968. Regulations for enterprises were altered in January to raise their social insurance contributions (because the central social insurance fund is in deficit) and to provide tax incentives for a more rational use of labor. Cooperative and state farms were also given incentives to make them more sensitive to costs and profits. At its 17 April meeting, the Central Committee approved proposals presented by Secretary Havasi for improving the economic management system, proposals that essentially preserved the current orientation in favor of decentralization and economic rationality (*Népszabadság*, 19 April). State subsidies would have to be trimmed, productivity improved by new incentives, including wage differentiation (although "unjustified" social inequalities had to be eliminated), and the cooperation of workers enhanced by the democratization of management. Enterprises would have some limited freedom in choosing among alternate managerial models. Public utility and other social service enterprises, covering some 20–25 percent of all enterprises and 35 percent of workers, will remain under state administration. Other large enterprises, accounting for half of the total, will be permitted to opt for management by enterprise councils, to which partial ownership rights will be transferred. These councils will consist in part of workers' elected representatives, will meet two or three times a year, and will elect the enterprise's managers. In the third model, encompassing smaller en-

terprises, the management may be directly elected by the employees. The new models are to be phased in over the next two years (*Pártélet*, October). The first election of an enterprise manager, by secret ballot by the shop stewards' committee, took place at a glove-knitting factory in Győr in September. Election of managers is also planned for the agricultural sector (*Népszabadság*, 27 October).

Other measures are planned to improve the competitiveness of Hungarian industry. According to Béla Csikós-Nagy, chairman of the National Material and Price Office, market prices for capital goods will be phased in over the next few years, so that by 1987 much of industry will belong to a "price club" whose members can set prices freely as long as they do not exceed those of actual or potential imports (*Economist*, London, 14 April). Deputy Premier Lajos Faluvégi, who is also chairman of the National Planning Office, announced that new measures governing industrial wage policy will come into effect 1 January 1985. These will provide variously for relaxed controls over upward and downward adjustment ("income regulation"), for restriction on the rate of wage increases in monopolistic industries ("wage-rise regulation"), and for central wage regulation, with some choice among these alternatives being left up to the individual enterprises. At the same time, enterprises will be given greater discretion in financing modernization and expansion and less protection against insolvency. Faluvégi stressed that these provisions must be interpreted realistically and not with exaggerated anticipation of a fully free market since Hungary's international competitiveness was limited; moreover, the "planned nature of our relations" with the countries of the Council for Mutual Economic Assistance (CMEA) and "certain social barriers that affect price and employment policy" had to be taken into account. He warned that inflationary pressures could not be quickly overcome. (*Népszabadság*, 18 October.)

The device of raising investment capital by bonds, introduced two years ago, has stimulated some thirty bond issues, a few of which are available for individual purchase. Experience has shown that there is a demand among individuals for such bonds, and on 1 September the State Development Bank established a special office to aid and organize the operation of the market. The government plans to expand the banking system to create a more competitive lending market.

The government's impatience with loss-making enterprises became manifest when in August the business-machine manufacturer IGV was declared bankrupt and closed by the minister of industry. The defunct enterprise's 1,300 workers were promised new jobs. An even larger enterprise, Tungsram Electrical, announced substantial cuts in its work force, including managers, in order to improve efficiency and profitability (ibid., 25 August). Official sources report that over a hundred enterprises are chronically insolvent and that over 100,000 workers hold redundant jobs (*Heti Világgazdaság*, 8 September; *Népszabadság*, 8 September). Another measure to improve business practices is a law on "dishonest economic competition," which took effect 1 January 1985.

Since 1982 the number of "economic work associations," a new entrepreneurial variant of contract work, has rapidly grown. Some of them consist of groups of workers who contract with their factory to produce certain goods after regular working hours at the same plant where they are employed. This has contributed in no small way to the concern over income differentiation. In Budapest alone, there existed by the end of 1983 some 7,504 contractual work units, including leased retail outlets, employing 70,424 people. Reportedly results have been generally positive, although in some cases "conflicts have emerged and . . . the incomes are not proportional to the achievements" (*Népszabadság*, 2 August). The regime's purpose is "legalization and harmonization of as great a part of the 'second economy' as possible with the activity of the first economy," with the expectation that the economic work associations will indirectly stimulate reform of the managerial and wage systems (*Társadalmi Szemle*, June 1983). An ideologically more orthodox technique is that of "socialist work competition," in which enterprises or groups of workers such as "socialist brigades" set themselves ambitious production targets. Projects of this type have proliferated in celebration of the upcoming party congress and the fortieth anniversary of Hungary's liberation by the Red Army.

Social Issues and Dissent. In 1984 demographic trends continued to cause concern. In 1983 Hungary's population declined by 21,240 to 10,697,000. The rate of decrease has risen from 0.2 per thousand inhabitants in 1981 to 2 per thousand in 1983, in which year the birthrate reached a historical low of 11.9 per thousand. The causes cited are the overall aging of the population, abortions, working women, and the housing shortage. Hungary has the highest suicide rate in the world, at

43.5 per 100,000 in 1982. (*Figyelö*, 21 June.) The low birthrate and the growing proportion of pensioners adds to the problems of an economy already said to be suffering from a shortage of labor. In 1983 the labor force numbered some 5 million. Of these, 56 percent were workers in state industries and state farms, 14 percent were cooperative farmers, 26 percent were professionals and white-collar workers, and just under 4 percent were small producers and merchants.

Of more immediate concern to the ruling party is the attitude of young people, particularly students, toward socialism. Surveys show that many young people express antisocialist views, are dissatisfied with the system's economic achievements and degree of democracy, and compare these unfavorably with the Western model. They note the hypocrisy of adults who merely pay lip service to socialism; they exhibit strong nationalism, avoid the official mass organizations, and show a growing interest in religion. (*Népszabadság*, 19 May; *Társadalmi Szemle*, July–August.) Ferenc Pölöskei, dean of the Faculty of Humanities of Budapest University, observed in an interview that students yearn for change, that many adopt an oppositional attitude while others remain politically passive, and that their avid curiosity is not satisfied by the official treatment of certain historical periods, notably the interwar years and the Rákosi era (*Népszabadság*, 25 February). After hearing Károly Németh's report on youth policy, the Central Committee at its 9 October meeting called on the Communist Youth League and the army to improve their socializing work among young people and promised to improve housing and other benefits of interest to young families (ibid., 11 October).

Interest in religion is growing, notably among young people. The head of the State Office for Church Affairs, Imre Miklós, said in a lecture to the trade union shop stewards' academy that this was the "fault" not of the churches but rather of those who fail to popularize socialism. Religiousness does not necessarily mean antisocialism, for the churches are allies of the Hungarian socialist state, and therefore believers must not be discriminated against (*Népszava*, 30 November 1983). In a subsequent interview, Miklós noted that although there were disagreements between church and state on religious education and the shortage of priests, the state continued to give the churches financial aid. He denied that graduates of the ten remaining church schools were handicapped in gaining admission to institutions of higher education (*Magyar*

Nemzet, 29 April). Both the regime and the church hierarchy are hostile to the several thousand–strong "basic communities" of Roman Catholics, which represent a pacifist and autonomist orientation. In December 1983 the police seized unauthorized religious printed matter from two such activists and imposed heavy fines. Meanwhile, a group of Jewish dissidents calling themselves Shalom wrote an open letter protesting the signing by the Jewish community's leaders of a statement denouncing the United States and unreservedly supporting the Soviet Union's policies (*RFE Research*, 6 February). The Hungarian Jewish community numbers some 80,000. The official media commemorated the fortieth anniversary of the Holocaust, and the renovated Jewish museum was reopened in Budapest. Delegates from East and West attended the Seventh Assembly of the Lutheran World Federation in Budapest 22 July–5 August. Hungarian Bishop Zoltán Káldy was elected president of the federation over the protest of some Hungarian Lutherans who disapprove of the excessive political collaboration inherent in his "theology of service." An international conference of Marxist and Christian philosophers and theologians was held in Budapest 28 February–1 March.

Political dissent remains in evidence, and the regime has taken steps to silence the most embarrassing spokesmen. The purge in September 1983 of the editorial board of *Mozgó Világ*, a young writers' periodical, aroused much debate and unrest, partly thanks to the publicity given to the affair by Radio Free Europe. The dismissed editors' letter of protest at official distortions of their case was published in *Új Tükör* (8 January). They issued a call for a "new intellectual popular front." The selection of György Konrád, a prominent writer who has criticized the regime and the Soviet Union in Western interviews, as the winner of the West German Herder Prize, was violently denounced in the party press (*Népszabadság*, 18 February). In March, nineteen members of the "democratic opposition" made public their endorsement of a joint appeal by Polish and Czechoslovak human rights activists for the release of political activists in their countries and for national independence (*RFE Research*, 20 March). The Hungarian statement also addressed "the most burning concern of every Hungarian," the difficulties faced by the Hungarian minorities in Czechoslovakia and Romania.

A new underground publication, *Hírmondó* (Messenger), appeared in November 1983, professing dedication to Eastern Europe's "democratic renewal" and to the dissemination of information withheld by the official media, notably regarding the Hungarian minorities. A similar, older publication reappeared in June. *Beszélö* (9) contained articles criticizing the Gabcikovo dam project (see below) and the dissolution of the independent peace movement Dialogue. In connection with the latter, reference was made to a leaked Politburo resolution of 29 March 1983 to the effect that "administrative measures must be employed against all those who question the validity of the peace policy of our party and government" (ibid., 30 August).

A conference of European peace activists in Milan in November 1983 was attended by two prominent critics of the regime, András Hegedüs and László Rajk. The latter reported in an interview that there was growing represssion of dissident activity in Hungary. The dissident sociologist and samizdat publisher Gábor Demszky, who had been searched and beaten by the police in September 1983, was found guilty on 21 December 1983 of assaulting two policemen; he was given a six-month suspended sentence and was put on probation, with restricted freedom for three years. Some 200 supporters staged a demonstration at the courtroom. A protest by 179 signatories, including well-known dissident intellectuals and students and workers, was made public when it was rejected by the minister of justice. In October and November, heavy fines were imposed on other dissidents for the possession and distribution of illegal publications. One of them, the economist György Krassó, who had written about the party's responsibility for the trial and execution of Imre Nagy in 1958, was put under police surveillance and a form of house arrest. On 3 November, a group of dissidents sent a letter of sympathy to the parish of the murdered Polish priest, Father Jerzy Popieluszko. On 19 November, the authorities denied the Club of Young Artists permission to hold a round-table conference on income differentiation in Hungary planned to coincide with the Budapest Cultural Forum in October 1985.

Foreign Affairs. Against a background of tense East-West relations, the Hungarian regime has been maintaining its traditional stance of solidarity with all Soviet policies, notably on disarmament, while pursuing normal diplomatic and commercial relations with the West.

Intensive contacts are maintained with the Federal Republic of Germany, which is Hungary's second-largest trading partner after the Soviet

Union and which has supported Hungary's bilateral negotiations with the European Community. (These talks have been temporarily suspended, largely because of Soviet and CMEA reservations.) The Hungarian and West German foreign ministers have met annually since 1977, and Péter Várkonyi visited Bonn in December 1983 for talks with his counterpart. Várkonyi stressed that Hungary remained committed to détente in Europe (*Népszabadság*, 22 December 1983). West German foreign minister Hans-Dietrich Genscher noted that the over 200,000-strong German ethnic minority in Hungary was well treated. The joint Hungarian–West German economic commission met in Bonn in January, and a Bundestag delegation visited Budapest in March. The major meeting of the year was the visit to Budapest 21–23 June of Chancellor Helmut Kohl, who was hailed by *Népszabadság* (21 June) as a "promoter of improved East-West relations." His talks with Kádár were described as open and cordial.

The same words were used to describe the meeting between Kádár and British prime minister Margaret Thatcher, who was in Budapest 2–4 February. The two sides praised bilateral cooperation while stressing their own ideological values and versions of disarmament and alliance commitments. The Hungarian media termed the visit a success. The visit of Italian prime minister Bettino Craxi 11–13 April generated similar positive commentaries despite disagreement on the deployment of Euromissiles. General agreement on the need for détente and economic relations mixed with differing views on the missile question also marked the meeting between Kádár and French president François Mitterrand in Paris 15–16 October. U.S. assistant secretary of state Richard Burt paid a quick visit to Budapest in February; in December the State Department made known its concern over the Hungarian regime's repressive measures against Krassó and other dissidents.

The Hungarian press loses no opportunity to hail the special and cordial relationship with Austria. The new Austrian chancellor, Fred Sinowatz, visited Budapest 15 November 1983 to review the close economic and cultural relations between the two countries. Trade has more than doubled over the past ten years, and there are numerous cooperative ventures in effect between Austrian and Hungarian firms. Austrian credits and enterprises figure prominently in the modernization of Hungary's tourist facilities, including hotels and the expansion of Budapest Airport. In June, a three-year bilateral agreement was signed on environmental protection, the first such East-West pact.

Hungary is busily preparing for the European Cultural Forum, an offspring of the Madrid review of the European Security Conference, which will be held in Budapest in October 1985.

Communist Relations. The HSWP persists in efforts to define and refine a foreign policy that encompasses both the sovereignty of Hungarian national interests and the requisites of membership in the Soviet bloc. This question was addressed in particular by the secretary in charge of international relations, Mátyás Szürös, during the course of the year. Without a central organ such as the Comintern, he noted, the reconciliation of diverse national interests has proven more difficult. The ruling parties must now show patience in reaching a "mutually acceptable consensus based on voluntarism," and the smaller members, such as Hungary, should work toward rational compromises within the limits of their alliance obligations. The relative favor that Hungary enjoyed in the West should not be regarded as a flaw of its foreign policy, argued Szürös. (*Társadalmi Szemle*, January.) In an interview with the newspaper *Tokyo Shimbun* (7 April; *RFE Research*, 8 May), *Népszabadság* editor János Berecz stressed the continuity in Soviet-Hungarian relations and rejected the possibility of Soviet "interference"; he said, "It is natural for socialism to vary according to national features, and domestic reform in Hungary will be carried out as before." He also stressed the importance of the presence of Mikhail Gorbachev in the new collective leadership under Chernenko.

There were, as usual, frequent contacts between Hungarian and Soviet officials in the course of the year. On 19–20 April in Budapest, the Warsaw Pact foreign ministers held their semiannual meeting, the first since Chernenko's accession to the leadership. The communiqué addressed the issue of nuclear weapons and made no mention of intrabloc differences. (Soviet, Czechoslovak, and Hungarian forces held joint military exercises in Hungary in June under the codename Danube '84.) The visit to Budapest of Foreign Minister Andrei Gromyko 17–18 April yielded a tough and uncompromising statement, but it coincided with the release of an HSWP Central Committee pronouncement calling for dialogue to reduce East-West tensions (Radio Budapest, 18 April; *RFE Research*, 8 May). Visits to Moscow included that of Minister of Culture and Education Béla Köpeczi on 20 April; of Politburo member Miklós Óvári on 24–28 April for talks with Soviet Central Committee secretaries Mikhail Gorbachev and Mikhail Zimianin; and of Peter Varga, head of the HSWP Central Committee's Public Administration Department, 23–27 April for talks with Grigori Romanov. János Kádár led the Hungarian delegation to the CMEA summit in Moscow 12–14 June and met with his Soviet counterpart, Konstantin Chernenko. Szürös held talks in Moscow 28–29 June on mainly international topics.

The nature and technique of Soviet influence on Hungarian foreign and domestic policies varies with the issue. The Hungarians may request guidelines, may engage in less formal consultation before a decision is taken, or in some cases may inform their Soviet partner after the fact. The intrabloc differences on the East Berlin–Bonn détente (see below) offered a useful insight into this complex relationship, but less critical issues are equally revealing. Early in the year the government was apparently prepared to restore to its original place in Budapest a statue to Raoul Wallenberg, the Swedish diplomat who saved many Hungarian Jews from deportation to Nazi Germany and who disappeared into Soviet captivity in January 1945; it later changed its mind, reportedly under Soviet pressure (*CSM*, 8 May). It was also rumored that the HSWP Politburo had been divided on the merits of participation in the Olympics before finally acceding to Moscow's wishes.

A certain commonality of interest materialized early in 1984 between East Berlin and Budapest. Kádár's meeting with Erich Honecker on 30 November 1983 had resulted in a joint statement calling for East-West dialogue even in the face of adverse conditions (*Népszabadság*, 1 December). On the occasion of the visit of East German prime minister Willi Stoph 21–22 March, the Hungarian media stressed the two countries' common interest in reviving détente (*Magyar Hirlap*, 21 March). The Czechoslovak party daily, *Rudé právo* (30 March), thereupon voiced criticism of deviations in the foreign policies of unnamed Warsaw Pact allies, clearly aiming at Hungary and East Germany; the article was reprinted in the Soviet foreign affairs weekly, *Novoe vremya* (13 April). This veiled criticism prompted another defense by Szürös of independent initiatives designed to promote peaceful coexistence. He claimed that Hungary was both a reliable ally and a constructive partner in East-West contacts, that détente remained an "objective necessity," and that Hungarian-Soviet relations would

continue to develop with greater cooperation and mutual counsel (*Magyar Hirlap*, 4 April). The East German party daily, *Neues Deutschland* (12 and 17 April), proceeded to reprint this interview as well as another defense of Hungarian foreign policy by Kádár, who opined that "small and medium-sized countries" can help to preserve the East-West dialogue. The weekly *Magyarország* (2 August) praised the rapprochement between the two Germanys, and *Neues Deutschland* (30 July) reprinted a similar piece from *Népszava* (28 July). A speech by Szürös denying the existence of an "irreparable breach" in East-West relations and endorsing intra-German cooperation was similarly carried by *Neues Deutschland* (22 August). In the end, the concern voiced in Moscow, Prague, and Warsaw prevailed, and on 4 September Honecker called off his proposed visit to Bonn, putting an end to this unprecedented display of East Berlin–Budapest solidarity.

Hungary's relations with Romania remain cool at best, and Szürös conceded in a 31 January radio interview that apart from the economic realm these relations were "stagnating and even regressing" (*RFE Research*, 25 February). At issue is the welfare of the Hungarian minority, whose treatment arouses intense dissatisfaction in Hungary. Reports of limitations on the number of Hungarian students at the University of Cluj-Napoca, of the requirement that geography and history teachers be ethnic Romanians, of the firing of Hungarian theater directors, and of the arrest of a Hungarian priest (who died in prison) all incense public opinion (*Times*, London, 6 June).

Celebrations of the sixty-fifth anniversary of the creation of the modern Romanian state, which involved the incorporation of former Hungarian territories of Transylvania and the Banat, gave rise to scarcely veiled disagreements in the media of the two countries regarding interpretations of history as well as the current status of national minorities (*RFE Research*, 30 December 1983). Nicolae Ceauşescu's grandiose project for new government buildings in Bucharest drew caustic comment from *Népszabadság* (19 June). At a rally on 23 August, Romania's national day, Deputy Prime Minister Lajos Faluvégi invoked Lenin's views on the need to accommodate the cultural and other interests of national minorities and cited past evidence of the mutual cultural enrichment of the two countries. Hungary's official greeting to Romanian leaders on the same occasion called for improved bilateral relations in the spirit of proletarian internationalism

(*Népszava*, 23 August). On 2 September a high-level Romanian delegation met with Hungarian leaders, but the meeting produced no evidence that relations are mending.

Hungarian-Czechoslovak relations have also been marked by some discord apart from the issue of East-West détente. The Slovakian-Hungarian dissident Miklós Duray was once again placed in pretrial detention on 10 May and charged with "harming state interests abroad." His previous trial for "subversion" had been adjourned without verdict, possibly thanks in part to pressure from Budapest. Duray had joined the Charter 77 group in August 1983 and had been making protests at proposed educational reforms that would reduce Hungarian-language education for the 600,000-strong minority in Slovakia. Objections from the minority as well as from Budapest led the Slovakian government to shelve the project for the time being (*RFE Research*, 8 May).

Meanwhile, a major popular protest movement materialized in Hungary over the proposed Gabcikovo-Nagymaros hydroelectric power dam project on the Danube, a joint undertaking based on a 1977 agreement between Hungary and Czechoslovakia. Hundreds of prominent Hungarian intellectuals signed a petition objecting to the foreseeable environmental and human drawbacks of the project, part of which has already been built. Although the Austrian government has offered financial credits, the Budapest regime is pleading a shortage of funds for the project, and lengthy delays are likely to ensue.

The Polish crisis continues to generate intensive consultation between Warsaw and Budapest. Szürös led a delegation to Poland 24–25 October to conclude a long-term cooperation pact. Prime Minister Wojciech Jaruzelski paid a brief "working visit" to Budapest on 9 November, possibly to seek support in the wake of the murder of Father Jerzy Popieluszko. Hungarian commentators referred to Jaruzelski's "two-front struggle" against dogmatists and revisionists, reminiscent of Kádár's dilemma in the post-1956 period, and termed the assassination a dangerous provocation (*Magyarország*, 11 November).

The Yugoslav media comment frequently and generally positively on the Hungarian economic model, and on the occasion of his visit on 7–9 March Kádár was praised for his realistic brand of socialism. For his part, Kádár was generous in his praise for the Yugoslav party and once again described the Hungarian minority in Yugoslavia as a useful bridge between the two countries. Recent political tensions regarding that minority appeared to recede after Kádár's visit.

In keeping with Soviet policy, there are still no interparty relations between Budapest and Beijing, but a certain normalization of relations is in progress, and numerous specialized governmental delegations have exchanged visits. Deputy Prime Minister József Marjai visited China 20 August–1 September for trade talks.

The HSWP's contacts with parties outside the Soviet bloc are frequent and largely ritualistic. Notable among the many such foreign visitors was North Korea's Kim Il-song, who had last visited 28 years ago and who came in June; and Kharilaos Florakis at the head of a Greek party delegation in March. Óvári headed an HSWP delegation to the Finnish Communist Party's congress in May, following a visit by Aczél the month before; Szürös led a group to Spain at the invitation of that country's party in April; and Korom represented the HSWP at the Ethiopian party's congress in September.

Bennett Kovrig
University of Toronto

Poland

Population. 36,887,000
Party. Polish United Workers' Party (Polska Zjednoczona Partia Robotnicza; PZPR)
Founded. 1948
Membership. 2,327,349 (claimed); workers, 40 percent (*Nowe drogi*, May)
First Secretary. Army Gen. Wojciech Jaruzelski
Politburo. 15 full members: Wojciech Jaruzelski, Kazimierz Barcikowski, Tadeusz Czechowicz, Jozef Czyrek, Zofia Grzyb, Stanislaw Kalkus, Hieronim Kubiak, Zbigniew Messner, Miroslaw Milewski, Stefan Olszowski, Stanislaw Opalko, Tadeusz Porebski, Jerzy Romanik, Albin Siwak, Marian Wozniak; 6 candidate members: Stanislaw Bejger, Jan Glowczyk, Czeslaw Kiszczak, Wlodzimierz Mokrzyszczak, Marian Orzechowski, Florian Siwicki
Secretariat. 9 members: Kazimierz Barcikowsi, Jozef Czyrek, Jan Glowczyk, Manfred Gorywoda, Zbigniew Michalek, Miroslaw Milewski, Wlodzimierz Mokrzyszczak, Marian Orzechowski, Waldemar Swirgon
Central Committee. 200 full and 70 candidate members
Status. Ruling party
Last Congress. Extraordinary Ninth, 14–20 July 1981, in Warsaw
Last Election. 1980, 99.5 percent (Fatherland Front), all 460 seats, next elections scheduled for 1985
Publications. *Trybuna ludu* (*TL*), party daily; *Nowe drogi* and *Ideologia i polityka*, party monthlies; *Zycie partii*, fortnightly party organ; *Zolnierz wolnosci*, army daily. Polska Agencja Prasowa (PAP) is the official news agency.

Search for a Model. The fortieth anniversary of Poland's "liberation" by the Red Army was celebrated on 22 July. It had been expected that the new system would accelerate economic development, eliminate social tensions, create an abundance of goods, and, above all, provide security from both Germany and the USSR. However, the balance sheet of the past four decades does not reflect that optimism. According to the official view, half of this period is considered a time of either "dogmatic-sectarian" mistakes (1948–1956 and 1964–1970) or "extensive voluntaristic inclination" (1975–1980). The many crises have been attributed to Poland's difficulties in "harmonizing universal principles with national characteristics" (*TL*, 15 September 1983), implying that the Soviet version of socialism and the national characteristics of the Poles are not compatible.

A particularly sharp attack on the political system in Poland was recently delivered by Adam Schaff, who during the 1950s and 1960s had been considered the chief ideologist in Warsaw. He published a book, entitled *The Communist Movement at a Crossroads* (Vienna, 1982), explaining why the regime in Poland deviates from classic Marxist philosophy. The "original sin" of the Polish system is that because it was imposed from the outside, it has degenerated into a "bureaucratic socialism" or "dictatorship of the apparatus," enslaving individuals and frustrating economic progress. This imposition, a product of the 1945 Yalta decision to divide Europe into spheres of influence, disrupted sociopolitical continuity in Poland and became the ever-present source of instability.

Following Marxist dialectics, Schaff argues that real socialism, in addition to being a product of internal developments, can be achieved only in highly industrialized societies. So far, there has been no successful shortcut. At this point, Schaff questioned the Leninist theory that any society guided by a communist party can successfully bypass capitalism. (*Rzeczpospolita*, 22 July.)

It is not surprising that this attack on the ideological legitimacy of the regime produced a violent reaction within the ruling elite in Warsaw. Schaff was accused of neo-Trotskyism in advancing the idea that the revolution in Poland had been "betrayed." His argument, however, is difficult to challenge because of its Marxist foundation and substantial evidence that points to the failure of communism. Consequently, Schaff's book became one of the many reasons for public discussion of the socioeconomic situation in Poland and the search for solutions.

The reaction of "hard-liners" in Warsaw to the failures of the Polish system and to criticism of it shows how little they have learned from the past forty years and how blind they are to the existing socioeconomic reality. They follow the old primitive Leninist view that every social disorder is a manifestation of the class struggle and a result of Western ideological aggression. The source of domestic instability is outside the country, a product of "perfidiously playing the so-called Polish card" by the new advocates of the "rollback" and "liberation" doctrines (*Tu i teraz*, 2 November 1983).

This school of thought assumes that the major reason for the continuous crises lies in the constancy of the basic model of government since 1948. Universal principles of socialism should be adapted to local conditions in the same way as during the 1956 crisis, whose solution legitimated the "Polish road to socialism." The only form of socialism that can produce stability is one that is distinctly Polish. Despite frequent accusations of chauvinism and preference for petty-bourgeois socialism and despite fear that a pluralistic political system would leave no room for the communist party, the idea of "Polish socialism" founded on liberal-democratic values, the rule of law, sovereignty, and a strong sense of national identity has been frequently discussed in the press (*Argumenty*, 15 January).

The Roman Catholic church also has become involved in the search for a new political system. The political philosophy of the church has its foundation in the assumption that Poland's affairs have to be seen in the broad context of an international system, which has not changed significantly since 1945. The key factor is not what the Poles would like to have, but what is feasible under existing

international conditions. In such circumstances, the church sides with the nation, and this approach is a source of its remarkable political flexibility. Although the party is constrained by its permanent ally, the Soviet Union, the church has a permanent interest and is willing to get along with the ruling party or any other organization, as long as it can be justified by the interest of the nation. (*Tygodnik powszechny*, 11 March.)

To the Poles, the church is the repository of national identity. To the party, it is a welcome ally whose support, limited and highly conditional as it may be, is indispensable for internal stability. Atheism, therefore, is not a prerequisite for party membership, and active recruitment among believers is considered fully compatible with Marxism-Leninism. It has become a well-established practice for the political authorities to actively seek the support of the church, especially in times of crisis.

Finally, the so-called democratic opposition is gradually perfecting nonviolent means of struggle against communist totalitarianism. Its program calls for emancipation from Marxist-Leninist phraseology and doctrine, which narrow the focus of attention to the working class, and for the development of a comprehensive national strategy designed to achieve independence from the Soviet Union. The democratic opposition assumes that the perpetuation of crisis would force the ruling elite to make concessions and a "democratization of the base that would eventually alter the political superstructure" (*Kultura*, January–February).

This program is based on the conclusion, actually identical to that reached by communist hardliners, that in 1984 Poland was back where it had been in 1944. Since another ice age of Stalinism is unlikely, the regime, facing determined social and economic pressure, must retreat step by step until a new ideological and political framework for the state becomes possible. It is a reversal of priorities—instead of approaching political issues first by asking for immediate free elections, the political framework would not be questioned until a fundamental restructuring of the economic system and social relations has been completed. In Marxist terms, this is an appeal for a social revolution that in its last stage would culminate in political change.

The method of opposing communism outlined above appears to be realistic. It avoids hopeless head-on confrontation with a ruthless regime, and it takes full advantage of the communist inability to stimulate a pluralistic society and to administer a highly industrialized economy. Last but not least, this program has its roots in the philosophy of positivism, with its ideas of "organic work" and a "long march" strategy. It assumes that via education and emphasis on cultural tradition and economic growth, it will be possible to withstand sovietization. Also, this political program has a well-established tradition in Polish history and is credited with saving Poland from russification after the unsuccessful 1863 uprising.

The Party. During 1984, the PZPR, under Gen. Wojciech Jaruzelski, did not undergo any significant change. It remains divided into three factions: the liberals, who advocate pluralism; the centrists, who are trying to preserve a political monopoly but are willing to pursue a "policy of accord" with the nation; and the dogmatic hard-liners, who advocate a "policy of combat" founded on police methods and administrative measures (*WP*, 2 April). These ideological differences are unlikely to be resolved in the foreseeable future.

The party is quite open about its numerous and serious problems. First of all, the ideas of Marxism-Leninism have lost their inspiration and appeal, particularly to the working class. "Socialism is losing its ideological legitimacy," admitted a member of the Institute on Basic Problems of Marxism-Leninism in Warsaw. Another ideologist stated frankly that "Polish society is clearly indifferent" to official ideology. The labor movement and the Roman Catholic church are the real and authentic sociopolitical forces in Poland. The teachings of John Paul II affect believers and nonbelievers, including PZPR members "who were good comrades years ago, but were moved by the visit of the Pope," concludes that Polish official. (*WSJ*, 1 February.)

The party is no longer a mobilizing or innovative force in society. It has become preoccupied with one issue only—staying in power despite compelling social pressure to introduce a pluralistic political order in Poland. In a highly dogmatic way, the official philosophy of the PZPR is blind to the facts that society is made up of a multiplicity of groups and that open debate on social and political issues is beneficial to the well-being of the nation. The PZPR is stubbornly opposed to the idea of "socialist pluralism," and it is rapidly becoming intellectually sterile, isolated from society and reality, and parochial and nationalistic.

This situation is reflected in the declining popularity of the party. In the summer of 1980, just before the emergence of Solidarity, the PZPR had attained a claimed strength of 3,149,000 members

and candidates. In the next two years, the official figure dropped by almost 800,000, and by 31 December 1983, there were only 2,186,000 members and candidates. The numerical decline of the party is one of its most serious problems. (*Nowe drogi*, May.)

Reluctance to confront reality was evident in the decision to expel from PZPR ranks former first secretary Edward Gierek and former premier Piotr Jaroszewicz, both accused of political crimes during the 1970s. These accusations became a substitute for a public trial of the top leadership, whose "voluntarism" triggered the 1980–1981 revolt. General Jaruzelski and his colleagues apparently have concluded that it would be impossible to separate the system from individuals who represent it (*CSM*, 23 February). However, the party expelled Adam Schaff from its ranks on the grounds that his interpretation of Marxism-Leninism was incompatible with active membership in this organization. Schaff, who is 71 years old, has lived in Vienna since 1968. He joined the party in 1931 and was among its earliest members. (*NYT*, 30 June.)

Still the PZPR continues to be a shield against a Soviet invasion, and it is careful to avoid large-scale violence, which might provoke an anticommunist uprising. The ruling group of centrists demonstrates remarkable self-restraint because everyone understands that a civil war in Poland, by providing Moscow with an excuse to invade, would be suicidal.

PZPR activities in 1984 reflected a desire to revitalize the organization. The fifteenth Central Committee plenum, meeting in Warsaw on 18 February, discussed the dilemma of one-party rule and democracy, that is, how to ensure the "workers' party's leading role—indispensable if the primacy of the interests of the working class and the stability of the socialist system are to be guaranteed—[and how] to satisfy the needs of democratization in society as a whole" (*Nowe drogi*, February).

In more concrete terms, the PZPR looked into the question of decentralization since the excessive concentration of authority over the economy was identified as a crisis-producing factor. The desirability of decentralization received endorsement in principle, providing that it does not lead to anarchy that "undermines the uniformity of goals and strategies."

Consequently, the fifteenth plenum failed to institutionalize any internal checks and balances, essential for an organization with democratic attributes. Instead, it was in favor of the so-called accountability-election campaign at all levels of the party organization. This is a form of self-criticism, allegedly stemming from ideological commitment and conducted via a five-way test: (1) Where does this evil come from? (2) Does it occur in my activity? (3) What are the causes of this evil? (4) Who will bear responsibility for it? and (5) How should the situation be improved? (*Zolnierz wolnosci*, 20 February.) This metaphysical soul-searching method of combating Poland's socioeconomic problems demonstrates the regime's fear of any realistic policy that would inhibit the authority of the PZPR leadership to make arbitrary decisions.

The plenum also recognized the necessity of recruiting youth into the party. The struggle for the young generation, which is decisively Catholic and anticommunist, is viewed as a struggle for the fate of socialism and the country. However, the only concrete measure that was recommended involved revitalization of the youth organizations "to create the basis and forms of social life that will guarantee and activate the socialist, creative character of the transformation" (Jaruzelski, quoted in *IB*, May). It seems fair to conclude that this summit meeting produced only empty rhetoric.

The same emphasis on democratic centralism and an "unambiguously class-based" approach to every question dominated the party's national conference of delegates, held in Warsaw from 16 to 18 March. General Jaruzelski condemned "so-called horizontal structures which are defeatist and easily affected by ideologically alien forces." Moreover, he repeatedly warned against "counterrevolutionary dangers" and stressed the necessity of faithful adherence to the "universal principles of socialism." (*TL*, 17 March.) In effect, the conference rejected the idea of democratization within the PZPR in favor of the old centralism, even though the latter was identified as the principal cause of the party's basic lack of pragmatism and of its ineffectiveness. As noted before, the paramount concern of the PZPR is how to stay in power. For this reason, it is making no effort to provide a channel through which society's interests might be expressed, offers no constructive program, and is again leading the nation toward another disaster. The "socialist renewal" has become a renewal of all the communist wrongdoing that has plagued the society since 1944.

The sixteenth Central Committee plenum, which met in Lodz from 2 to 4 June, provided further evidence that the party, particularly its top leadership, is living in a fantasy world. Instead of searching for concrete and pragmatic ways to halt the continuing sociopolitical decline, the PZPR chose a theoretical issue—"the role and significance of the working class in our party and in our state"—as the topic for the plenum proceedings (Warsaw radio, 2 June; *FBIS*, 6 June).

It appears that the sole purpose of this plenum (open to selected members of the public among its 800 participants) was to conclude that although socialism had been created from working-class wisdom, "history proves that it is not possible to construct socialism unless a Marxist-Leninist party" plays the leading role. It went on to say that "attacks on the party's leading role are in the final analysis attacks against the working class, against our system." General Jaruzelski concluded that the entire plenum should be viewed as a "great consultation" with the working class and that "this is how our party imagines a conversation with the workers today and tomorrow. This was no window dressing plenum." (Ibid.)

The sixteenth plenum, officially labeled a "workers' plenum" (Warsaw radio, 3 June; *FBIS*, 4 June), was to demonstrate that party and nonparty workers have only one single concern—namely, the strengthening of the leading role of the PZPR. One must wonder, therefore, whether the ruling clique of party, military, and security forces, in the roughly three years since a coup brought it to power, has lost all sense of reality.

The same motive, a desire to fabricate legitimacy behind the continuing effort to centralize as much power as possible in the hands of the top leadership, was evident at the seventeenth Central Committee plenum, which met in Warsaw on 26 and 27 October. The plenum was devoted to problems concerning consolidation of the state. On that occasion, General Jaruzelski identified "socialist renewal" and "progress" in general with the consolidation of authority by the party-state apparatus (Warsaw radio, 26 October; *FBIS*, 29 October). It sounded like a revival of the Stalinist "vanguard of the vanguard" doctrine, the ideological mechanism that had led to a personal dictatorship in Soviet Russia.

A resolution entitled "The Party's Tasks in Strengthening the State; Developing Socialist Democracy; and Perpetuating Law, Order, and Social Discipline" concluded the seventeenth plenum. The party formally recognized the need for greater freedom for state authorities, the desirability of territorial self-management, an increase in the activities of all state bodies, and the drawing up of a new law for the 1985 elections to the Sejm (the Polish parliament). This appeal to enhance the authority of law and discipline contrasted sharply with the daily practices of Polish security forces. As has been the case so many times in the past, calls for the democratization of political life carefully avoided any reference to institutional changes indispensable for securing popular influence on government authorities. (*TL*, 31 October.)

Despite those hard-line demands for more authority, the PZPR, entangled in its own internal affairs, has been gradually losing control of society and is playing an ever smaller role in shaping reality in Poland. It has become a status quo force in Polish politics.

The Church. The power struggle, publicly referred to as a dialogue, between the church and the communist regime is now forty years old. It began with a decision by the new rulers of Poland to eliminate the influence of religion on society. Religion was viewed as a relic of feudalism and the Roman Catholic hierarchy as the stronghold of anticommunism. A final campaign against the church was considered only a matter of time.

It was soon discovered that a frontal attack on the church would produce mass revolt, especially in the countryside. The regime, therefore, adopted a policy of leaving the institution of the church intact but limiting its freedom and access to society. This approach was founded on the ideological view that religion would lose its social relevance, once full industrialization had been achieved. In order to make elimination of religion as easy as possible, the short-term goal of the authorities was to subordinate the church to the state.

In 1950, when the hierarchy agreed to a compromise with the government, the authorities were deprived of an excuse to launch an all-out campaign against it. At the price of recognizing the communist regime, the church survived the most dangerous years of Stalinism. With the emergence of national communism in the post-1956 era, church-state rivalry in Poland entered a new stage. No longer on the defensive and primarily concerned with its own survival, the church began to compete actively with the regime for popularity among the Poles, a contest that the church dominated from the start. Now, the government became interested in reconciliation with the church and in finding a model for partnership, defined by the church as "coexistence amid contradictions" (*CSM*, 3 April).

Achievement of full understanding, however, has so far been impossible because neither the church nor the PZPR is willing to endorse the political aspirations of the other. In order to compensate for its lack of popularity, the party would like to have a full and unconditional mandate from the church to rule Poland. The church, on the other hand, despite its tremendous popular support, has no constitutional status. Also, full diplomatic relations between the Polish government and the Vatican are yet to be established. It is a *sui generis* paradox that the status of much smaller churches in Poland is recognized by law, while the Roman Catholic church, which represents more than 90 percent of the population, legally does not exist.

Until recently, church-state relations in Poland were relatively easy to manage because of the highly centralized structure of both organizations. In the post-Solidarity period, however, the relationship is no longer between two monolithic groups, since additional factors have come into the picture. The communist party's "fundamentalists" use relations with the church as an instrument to undermine Jaruzelski's leadership. Jozef Cardinal Glemp also must cope with powerful internal opposition from a group, consisting mostly of young radicals, which openly favors a policy of confrontation with the authorities. Events in 1984 exemplified this pattern of confrontation and coexistence in church-state relations.

Never in a thousand years has the church been as influential as it is under communism. During four decades of People's Poland, the church has completed about 1,200 investment projects, and more than 600 places of worship are currently under construction. As of 31 December 1983, Poland had more than 14,000 churches and chapels, that is, an average of 2,500 faithful per church. There are now twice as many churches and twice as many people in cassocks as there were before the war (Warsaw radio, 9 September; *FBIS*, 10 September).

The second papal pilgrimage to Poland in the summer of 1983 brought hope for considerable improvement in church-state relations. At the end of 1983, General Jaruzelski and Cardinal Glemp issued a joint communiqué that contained several elements of compromise. Cardinal Glemp condemned the escalation of the nuclear arms race without, however, blaming NATO or the United States for it. General Jaruzelski agreed to "further development of contacts between Polish authorities and the Holy See." (*Los Angeles Times*, 28 December 1983.)

The prospect of improvement in church-state

relations was soon frustrated by factional groups in both organizations. When Cardinal Glemp transferred Reverend Mieczyslaw Nowak, a highly vocal supporter of Solidarity who headed a parish in one of the largest industrial centers, some 2,000 believers staged a demonstration. A delegation came to church authorities demanding a reversal of Glemp's decision. (*NYT*, 21 February.) Father Nowak was transferred, but not without public embarrassment to the cardinal.

The next incident, the "crucifix affair," was more serious. Despite a compromise solution, it precipitated considerable deterioration in church-state relations. Party hard-liners raised the question of whether a crucifix, the highest symbol of the church, could be displayed in secular educational institutions. It all began as a local dispute when school authorities in Mietno, southeast of Warsaw, attempted to enforce a 1961 law banning religious symbols from secular buildings. In response, students occupied the school, and the local bishop, Jan Mazur, promptly declared a "war of the cross." (*CSM*, 2 April.)

For a while there was a fear of escalation into a nationwide confrontation between church and state, between General Jaruzelski and Cardinal Glemp. The government imposed a strict ban on crosses and called in the riot police. The principal demanded that returning students sign a declaration of obedience to the school administration. The bishop, on the other hand, pledged to his congregation that "as long as you are in trouble, my daily meal will consist of bread and water." His example was soon followed by more than 450 clergymen across Poland as well as by many students. (*WP*, 28 March; *NYT*, 7 April.)

A compromise solution to the crisis was reached through direct negotiations between the episcopate and the government. The church, represented by Archbishop Bronislaw Dabrowski of Warsaw, continued to insist on the right of the people to display crosses in school buildings and other public institutions. In practice, however, they would appear only in reading rooms and dormitories. The government, represented by Internal Affairs Minister Czeslaw Kiszczak, had saved face since the principle of separation between church and state had been upheld. The authorities promised to take no reprisals against students and dropped their original demand that re-entry to school be conditional on signing a declaration in support of strict separation between state and church (*TL*, 7 April).

The final impact of the second major clash,

namely the savage murder by security officers of Father Jerzy Popieluszko, an outspoken critic of the communist regime, was yet to be fully determined at year's end. Especially significant was the timing since the killing took place at the same time as Italian officials were publishing the details of the Bulgarian involvement in the attempted assassination of the pope and only one day before another meeting between General Jaruzelski and Cardinal Glemp. For a while, it was speculated, therefore, that Moscow might be directly involved in a plot to eliminate a charismatic individual accused of conducting "hate sessions," otherwise known as "Masses for the Motherland," against the communist regime and that the decision to kill the priest was made by the Russians and even implemented without General Jaruzelski's knowledge. (*Newsweek*, 12 November.)

Jaruzelski and Kiszczak's protestations of innocence created the impression that the plot had been designed to undermine and possibly bring down the regime. This hypothesis is supported by the reaction of the regime and the church, both of which advocated calm and by the arrest and trial of four suspects involved in the murder. The truth may not be known for some time, but this incident has frustrated already exceedingly difficult church-state relations, embarrassed Jaruzelski's regime, slowed improvement of Poland's relations with the West, and, most important perhaps, undermined Jaruzelski's legitimacy as the "lesser evil."

Another undesirable aspect is the impression this event gives that the regime has adopted terroristic practices in dealing with its opponents, whereas it has carefully avoided terrorism for fear it might strengthen the hard-liners. This threat of terror led to a Central Committee statement to the effect that "provocation and terror" have always been alien to the "morality of our party" and to the "centuries-old Polish tradition of political tolerance." Also, the Central Committee characterized the murder of Father Popieluszko as an act against the policy of social renewal adopted by the PZPR and of the understanding between state and church. Finally, the Politburo reviewed the question of political supervision over internal security forces. (*Rzeczpospolita*, 27–28 October.) For this reason, the entire affair is unprecedented in a Soviet bloc state.

Under such circumstances, the Roman Catholic hierarchy has more openly assumed the role of representative of the Polish nation. This relative hardening of the church's position, known as "political neutralization," took place at the end of 1984. In a statement, prepared in 1971 but only recently published, the hierarchy had presented in order of priority a set of principles to guide the church's loyalties. They include, first of all, the fact that the church in Poland is a part of the universal church subordinate to the Holy See. Second, for a thousand years the church has served the Polish nation. Third, the Polish nation, despite the efforts of the regime, is Catholic. And, finally, in its relations with the state, the church would be guided by strict neutrality that precludes support for any political party or group, and the church will never relinquish its mandate to challenge materialistic doctrine. (*Powsciagliwosc i praca*, July–August.)

Domestic Affairs. In order to comprehend the situation in Poland, it is necessary to borrow from the jargon of Marxism-Leninism. A general and constantly deepening crisis in the Soviet-like system is clearly evident, even though apathy in both social and economic affairs gives a semblance of stability. Four decades of communism have left Poland in a situation that contrasts sharply with the stability and economic prosperity of West European countries, notably the Federal Republic of Germany, where democratic political institutions and a free market have provided what the party promised but was never able to deliver.

Moreover, the political confrontation in Poland has become increasingly violent. By June 1984, there were 72 documented cases of mysterious killings of Solidarity activists or sympathizers. In the majority of these cases, government authorities made no effort to identify the assailants. In those few cases where official investigations started, all but one were promptly discontinued. Among the latter were the killings of three workers in the copper mines of Lublin and two other workers in Wroclaw. (*Committee in Support of Solidarity Reports*, 13 July.)

Because a public outcry had been raised, the authorities investigated and issued an indictment in the case of a high school student, Grzegorz Przemyk, who was beaten and over a two-day period denied medical treatment by the Warsaw police. On 12 May 1983, the boy died on the operating table. After waiting for six months, the authorities indicted two police officers and two ambulance drivers on charges of indirectly causing the death of Przemyk. They also charged two doctors with failure to provide the youth medical care. However, the policemen and doctors were found innocent,

while the ambulance drivers were sentenced to two and two and a half years in prison, respectively. (*Prawo i zycie*, 21 July.)

Meanwhile, the authorities were busy intimidating Przemyk's mother, Barbara Sadowska, a known Solidarity activist and an organizer of aid to political prisoners. Her attorney has been arrested and charged with aiding a police deserter and encouraging him to engage in illegal activities. (*Committee in Support of Solidarity Reports*, 13 July.)

Political prisoners in Poland are also subjected to increased harassment, which includes being placed in "starvation" cells with no food or light or in five-square-meter "thermes" cells, where up to three prisoners are kept for as long as three days. Symptoms of suffocation and heart attack were common among the prisoners. The police also use straitjackets, handcuffs, and isolation cells and frequently hose down the most aggressive political prisoners outdoors in freezing temperatures (ibid., 6 June). The lawlessness and the techniques of torture closely resemble the Soviet practices described in detail by Alexander Solzhenitsyn in *Gulag Archipelago*. For this reason, the current political system in Poland is frequently called "Red fascism."

For the sake of internal détente, however, the regime of General Jaruzelski offered a sweeping amnesty for political prisoners on the occasion of the fortieth anniversary of People's Poland, celebrated on 22 July 1984. This move was to complete the process of normalization, the first step of which involved the suspension of martial law on 20 December 1982, when more than 700 prisoners were released. Next, on 22 July 1983, martial law was lifted, and another 660 were freed, including thousands suspected of common crimes. More than 61,000 people benefited from the amnesty, including two former leading politicians, Piotr Jaroszewicz and Edward Gierek (*Zycie Warszawy*, 31 July).

Of the greatest importance, however, was the release of the Solidarity Seven and the KOR (Committee for the Defense of Workers) Four, all of whom had been jailed for plotting against the state. For a while the government contemplated banishing them from Poland (*Rzeczpospolita*, 21 September). Then it decided to put them on trial, unless they were willing to emigrate to the West. However, all refused to emigrate, forcing the government to proceed with a controversial judicial procedure that would further aggravate social tensions and signify a political victory for the communist hard-liners.

The amnesty had been designed to build national accord, as well as to signal the continuation of a moderate political program. (*Zycie Warszawy*, 31 July.)

The released Solidarity leaders and those who are still in hiding condemned the amnesty as a "new act of injustice" because they had not been proven guilty and because their freedom was to be conditional on abstention from antiregime activities. The government warned that the freed dissidents would be rearrested if they continued to engage in antigovernment activities. For this reason, Jan Rulewski, one of the leading officials of the banned Solidarity, summarized the amnesty as the exchange of a "barred cell for a larger one" (AFP, Paris, 11 August; *FBIS*, 13 August). The government's view is, however, that the amnesty constitutes a conciliatory gesture toward the political opposition and concludes the regime's victory over Solidarity.

The same political purpose was behind the 17 June local and district elections. These elections, which had been delayed for two years, were proclaimed by the official press as a "yes to socialism" or at least a "step toward limited democracy" since voters had a choice between two candidates for every seat, an unprecedented freedom of choice in any Soviet bloc state (*NYT*, 17 June; *WSJ*, 18 June). These so-called free elections were aimed at uniting the Poles behind the regime, as well as humiliating Solidarity, whose underground Temporary Coordinating Commission (TKK) called for a boycott of the elections on the ground that society was still denied "its right to make meaningful decisions on issues concerning its own country" (AFL-CIO, *Free Trade Union News* 39, no. 5, May, p. 7).

Consequently, voter turnout became the most critical issue of the elections, a test of the regime's strength and popular confidence in it. Although under Poland's new election law two candidates competed for each seat, it was obvious that both were equally acceptable to the party. The only meaningful choice left to the voters was that of participating in or boycotting the elections.

Hand in hand with encouraging the people to go to the polls, the government made it clear that refusal to vote would have negative repercussions, including loss of jobs, rejection of applications for passports, and all the numerous other forms of pressure that the regime has exercised since the first communist election in January 1947. The elections were preceded by a wave of arrests of politically suspect individuals and by the opening of the trial

against eleven Solidarity leaders (UP, 14 June). These proceedings were later brought to a halt by the amnesty, but they had served the purpose of political intimidation.

Both the regime and Solidarity produced estimates of how many people had cast ballots. The authorities claimed a nationwide turnout of 75 percent (ibid., 24 June). That was a relatively modest percentage for a communist regime to claim. Soviet bloc countries usually report at least a 90 percent turnout. Even in communist Poland the lowest ever recorded was in the range of 95 percent (*NYT*, 19 June). In the previous Polish elections, held in early 1980, just before the emergence of Solidarity, a 98.87 percent participation was officially claimed (ibid., 18 June). The figure of 75 percent was designed by the authorities to lend credibility to the claim that they had received a mandate from the majority. They implied that more than two-thirds of the people supported the socialist order in Poland and compared the turnout favorably with those in Western democracies.

Solidarity conducted its own tabulation by monitoring selected voting places and accused the authorities of inflating the turnout figure by as much as 20 percent. For example, the government indicated a 71 percent voter participation in Warsaw, but Solidarity's analysis showed only 57.4 percent (*CSM*, 21 June; *WP*, 24 June). The latter's goal had been to keep 10 million people—the union's memberships in 1980–1981—away from the polls, which would have made a turnout of about 60 percent. This objective was most likely achieved.

The Roman Catholic church adopted a completely neutral position on the elections. It was concerned more with the fate of political prisoners than with a political contest, whose outcome was known in advance and where the only open question, voter turnout, was of more than academic significance. Nonetheless, a government spokesman informed the public that 30 percent of the Roman Catholic clergy had voted, including 5 of the 86 bishops (*NYT*, 20 June).

Instead of the free elections that Solidarity had demanded in December 1981, Poland experienced elections in 1984 that offered no real choice. The ruling elite continues to be unaccountable to the public, and none of the fundamental socioeconomic problems that triggered the emergence of Solidarity have been rectified. It is probably only a matter of time before Poland experiences another internal shock, for which the communist authorities again will blame counterrevolutionary and imperialistic forces in the West. Despite rather unusual flexibility, the regime must still fabricate popularity. The authorities are fully aware that they are not popular, but they have gained confidence in the ability of the police to control and manipulate the people. This confidence prompted the regime to conduct elections and grant an amnesty, acts that symbolize the end of the Solidarity era.

The fact is, however, that the Solidarity era is not over despite the political defeat of that free and independent trade union. It is estimated that a million Poles continue to pay dues to the outlawed organization; the "flying universities" so instrumental in bringing intellectuals and workers together are flourishing; and underground theaters, radio stations, and publications are more active than ever. Since 1981, more than 80 titles (in press runs of 1,000 to 10,000 copies each) have been printed. It is predicted that Poland has now reached an apex of liberalization and that from now on there will be a gradual tightening of political control. As the vice-president of the Polish Academy of Science and an adviser to General Jaruzelski stated, "The tragedy of previous Polish crises is that the leadership proved incapable of learning from history. What I now fear is that some in the state and party apparatus didn't learn enough." (*WSJ*, 14 August.) Another outbreak of mass demonstrations is certain; the only uncertainty is the date.

The regime has violated every single provision of the 1980 agreement with Solidarity. "General Jaruzelski betrays the trust of the Polish people when the Gdansk accords are only honored in articles and speeches published by the state-run press. What about union pluralism? What about freedom of speech? Freedom of the press? What about lifting repressions on matters of conscience? Where are the prisons without political prisoners? What about wage adjustments and prices? Where is the selection of managers on the principle of qualifications rather than party membership? Where is the reduction in the waiting period for an apartment?" asked Lech Walesa, former Solidarity leader.

Official policy on Solidarity is that it does not exist any more, and consequently the former union representing more than 10 million people and its leader, the recipient of the 1983 Nobel Peace Prize, are irrelevant to the process of normalization. This is the clearest evidence that the regime is unwilling to enter into a meaningful dialogue with society and believes that tanks and water cannons can always bring a solution.

The new unions established by the authorities to replace Solidarity, despite their claimed numerical strength of 4.9 million (Warsaw radio, 15 November; *FBIS*, 16 November) are, by and large, ineffective organizations unable to represent the interests of the workers. They have assumed the function envisioned by Lenin; that is, they serve as transmission belts between the party and the working class. Genuine union pluralism is rejected because it "divides the work force and presents the danger of conflict," according to the executive committee chairman of the National Trade Union Accord (Warsaw radio, 3 December; *FBIS*, 4 December). These developments demonstrate that 1984 has been another year wasted by the authorities on erecting a facade of unity, reconciliation, and renewal, while the old communist theory of politics based on monolithic unity and totalitarian control continues. Elimination of political pluralism is the ultimate goal of Jaruzelski's normalization, and in this respect his policies are surprisingly similar to those in post-1968 Czechoslovakia.

The Economy. Reforms intended to overcome the economic crisis that devastated Poland in 1980 have now been in force for two years. Their purpose is to inject some degree of flexibility into the highly centralized economic system. Measures introduced include deregulation of prices, fiscal accountability, and more self-management of large government-owned economic enterprises. The regime has also given the green light to development of both private firms and genuine cooperatives. Although the economy has reacted positively thus far, several domestic and international developments have had adverse effects on the economic system.

Internal hurdles are unquestionably the most difficult to overcome, primarily because of their political nature. Public enterprises, now entitled to bargain over the prices of goods purchased by the government, are in no position to oppose the regime, which keeps tight control over the distribution of raw materials and hard currency. Thus, the principal objective of the reform, development of a realistic system of prices, has yet to be achieved. Other serious obstacles include the outflow of hard currency to pay off the foreign debt, excessive investments in nonproductive or long-term economic ventures, and the budget deficit. Among external factors hampering economic recovery are the continuing economic sanctions imposed by the West and the low ratio of exports to GNP.

Considering political and economic conditions, the performance of the economy in 1984 was satisfactory. It is estimated that the value of goods manufactured and sold by socialized industry rose by 2.4 percent and the output of the mining industries increased by 6 percent. However, the production of fuel other than coal fell by 3.6 percent, and the food industry, despite a good harvest, declined by 2.4 percent. In remaining branches of industry, production rose by 6.7 percent; overall productivity increased 2.6 percent. (*TL*, 18 April; *WSJ*, 6 August.)

At the same time, runaway inflation continues. The estimated rate for 1984 is 30 percent, twice as high as the government anticipated (*Glos wybrzeza*, 7–8 April). Blame for this situation is being placed on the public sector of the national economy, despite continuing reduction of its share in the total GNP (*Przeglad Tygodniowy*, 18 March). Increases in the purchasing power of the public were soon "neutralized" by higher prices for coal, gasoline, electricity, and transportation. This is another example of the government's policy of fighting inflation in "small steps" by allowing prices to increase more rapidly than wages (*Zycie partii*, 1 August). Consequently, the standard of living has declined again by approximately 5 to 10 percent since the average income had risen by only some 20 percent (*Los Angeles Times*, 24 November).

Other adverse influences are the continuing global overproduction of fuel, including coal, which accounts for 17 percent of total export earnings (*Rzeczpospolita*, 7–8 January) and the fact that Poland's per capita rate of exports is the lowest in Europe. Political pressure forced the government to reverse its decision to increase food prices by 10 percent at the beginning of 1984, but a "moderate" increase is planned for early 1985 (*NYT*, 24 November). During the past year, Poland exported $162 per capita while Hungary, for example, exceeded $600 (*Rzeczpospolita*, 8 October). At best, the Polish economy is not export-oriented, and the economic reforms that have been introduced have not helped to make it so.

American economic sanctions imposed to protest martial law continue to hamper economic progress. However, in 1984 the United States reacted positively to the amnesty by first lifting the suspension of landing rights for the Polish national airline and then authorizing the resumption of full-scale scientific exchanges (U.S. Department of State, Bureau of Public Affairs, *Current Policy*, no. 621, 11 October). At the end of the year, the American government withdrew its opposition to Poland's membership in the International Monetary Fund.

As of 1 January 1985 suspension of the most-favored-nation status and a freeze on U.S. credits were the only sanctions that remained. Poland currently owes $13.5 billion to American creditors, and since 1982 loan guarantee arrangements have forced the U.S. Treasury Department to pay American banks close to $1 billion (*NYT*, 6 August).

The Polish government, on the other hand, estimates that American economic sanctions have cost Poland up to $13 billion or more than $350 per capita (*TL*, 30 July, 3 August). By the end of 1984, the total amount of Poland's foreign debt had reached $29.3 billion, an increase of more than $2 billion since 1983 (*NYT*, 16 March). However, with those of its Western creditors who belong to the so-called Club of Paris, the regime reached agreement to reschedule part of the debt on which payments fall due between 1984 and 1987 (*TL*, 17 May; *Zycie gospodarcze*, 13 May).

Poland's recovery has also been slowed by a 2 percent reduction in investment (*WSJ*, 6 August), generally believed to be the result of increased investment in so-called joint economic ventures with the USSR. Most of these involve long-term capital investment in production facilities and mining industries located deep in the Soviet Union and being developed with capital provided by the East European dependencies. This policy of "coordinating" national economic plans (*Rzeczpospolita*, 17 September) not only provides the USSR with a source of funding but also serves to strengthen the political control that has been developing since the early 1970s. In recent years, Moscow has stressed the desirability of harmonizing economic policies within the Soviet bloc. This new phase of the Soviet economic offensive directed against East European states has resulted in Poland's becoming more dependent than it need be on Soviet oil (ca. 80 percent), natural gas, iron ore, chrome, and manganese (ca. 75 percent). Taking quality into account, the prices of Soviet commodities sold to Poland are believed to be as much as twice those on the world market, while the prices for goods purchased from Poland are 30 percent below those on the world market (interview with Polish economist). A fifteen-year economic agreement between the two countries, signed by Chernenko and Jaruzelski (*NYT*, 5 May) perpetuates the disparity and is generally regarded as the most submissive political step taken by the Warsaw regime.

In order to gain the upper hand in its balance of payments, Poland imposed additional restrictions on imports. Consequently, it achieved an $805 million trade surplus in the first half of the year (*WSJ*, 26 July) and announced a 10.6 percent devaluation of the Polish zloty against the dollar. The official exchange rate is now 123 zlotys to one dollar (*NYT*, 4 September), but the black market exchange rate fluctuates between 500 and 650 to one. Still, the entire year's earnings, which are expected to amount to about $2 billion, will be spent on paying the interest on Western debts. At the same time, Poland also owes Soviet bloc nations some 3.8 billion transferrable rubles (Warsaw radio, 17 May; *FBIS*, 18 May).

When the regime rewrote regulations governing foreign-owned *Polonia* companies (see *YICA*, 1984, pp. 354–55), it took a self-defeating step. The new law increased the tax on income by 85 percent, thereby severely inhibiting the development of these prosperous businesses (*WP*, 23 May). Investment in these privately owned firms brings a 77 percent return compared with no more than a 10 percent return expected from publicly owned enterprises (*Tygodnik powszechny*, 26 February). It is expected that this experiment in free enterprise will inhibit the government's ability to earn hard currency and will undermine the credibility of the regime's economic policy.

This development, which is designed to restrict private business, has thus far not affected the program to modernize Polish agriculture with the help of Western funds administered by the Roman Catholic church. After a two-year delay, the regime finally enacted legislation authorizing the endowment, which should modernize Polish agriculture (*Odrodzenie*, 6 March). The church hopes that the program will become operational in 1986, at the latest. In five years, it will channel more than $2 billion directly to private farmers and private craftsmen. It is expected that the program will "self-multiply"—that is, funds paid back by farmers will be reinvested in the economy (*Glos niedzielny*, 29 January).

Foreign Policy. Diplomatic activities were moderately successful in overcoming the international situation that followed imposition of martial law in December 1981. Maintenance of good relations with the Kremlin has always had top priority in Warsaw. This is no easy task, considering the well-known hostility of the Polish people toward Russia and communism as well as Soviet mistrust of Polish leaders, who appear to have adopted the political philosophy of Wallenrodism. (Konrad Wallenrod, in the version popularized by the

nineteenth-century Polish national poet Adam Mickiewicz, was a Lithuanian kidnapped as a child by Teutonic knights and raised by them. He eventually became their leader, although he secretly remained a Lithuanian patriot. Wallenrod deliberately sabotaged an attack by the knights on the Polish-Lithuanian commonwealth in order to save his country from conquest.) For these reasons, Polish-Soviet relations receive special attention in the press, which is responsible for making the public aware that it is not a question of choice but of necessity without any national alternative. Socialism, it is argued, provides the only common denominator between Poland and the USSR. And, as was the case 200 years ago at the time of the partitions, the future of the Polish state will be determined not by the likes and dislikes of the Polish people, but by the regime's relations with its neighbors and, above all, within the Soviet–East German–West German triangle. (*Rzeczpospolita*, 4–5 August.)

Polish foreign minister Stefan Olszowski recently summarized this credo of foreign policy:

A new conception for Polish foreign policy was born out of the experiences of the September [1939] calamity, the terror of the occupation, the threat of biological extermination, and out of thoughts on the course of events. It was formed by the socialist left wing, together with all the other democratic forces of the nation. Three fundamental thoughts lie at the roots of the programmatic reorientation of Poland's foreign policy.

First: The above conception was a program for the return of Poland to historical Polish territory situated on the Odra and Nysa rivers and on the Baltic. The implementation and perpetuation of this program was one of the basic national tasks of foreign policy during the postwar period.

Second: It was a program of permanently establishing friendly Polish-Soviet relations. This reorientation has been achieved.

Third: It was a program whose implementation in accordance with the Yalta Conference declaration [1945] was meant to guarantee that Germany will never again be able to disturb world peace. [Report on speech at a meeting of the Foreign Affairs Committee in Wroclaw, *TL*, 12 July.]

As always, when East-West tensions are high, Polish dependence on Moscow increases. Jaruzelski's talks in Moscow during May appear to have produced a compromise: in exchange for Poland's closer integration with the Soviet economy, the So-viet leadership endorsed his moderate domestic course. It is interesting to note that the joint com-muniqué, issued at the end of the visit, charac-terized the views on international relations as "iden-tical," whereas in the area of domestic affairs the parties were said to have reached "complete mutual understanding." When translated from communist jargon, the latter statement "simply means that they understood why they had differing views," ex-plained *Le Figaro*'s correspondent in Warsaw (*FBIS*, 9 May). Nonetheless, Chernenko officially accepted an invitation to visit Poland (*TL*, 22 May).

Perhaps the most unpopular foreign policy deci-sion during 1984 was the decision not to participate in the Summer Olympics in Los Angeles. This move was presented by Warsaw as an independent action, in response to an alleged American vio-lation of the Olympic charter, rather than man-datory support for the Soviet boycott. U.S. vio-lations cited by the Polish Olympic Committee included organizational work by private individuals and "lack of the necessary guarantees for the peace and serenity of the teams from socialist countries" (ibid., 30 July). Facing determined Soviet pressure, Jaruzelski had no choice but to refrain from sending a Polish team to Los Angeles. This action caused disappointment among Poles inside and outside the country, particularly because émigré organizations in the United States had contributed funds toward the expenses of the representatives who never ar-rived from Warsaw.

Poland's most significant diplomatic achieve-ment within the Soviet bloc was preventing a visit by East German leader Erich Honecker to the Federal Republic of Germany at the end of the year. As *Trybuna ludu* (6 September) phrased it, can-cellation of the visit indicated that the "calculations of the 'great German' mythomaniacs in Bonn have ended in failure." One of the essential conditions for Polish international security is the continued divi-sion of Germany and antagonistic relations between the two German states. Any indication of a détente between Bonn and East Berlin would immediately trigger a barrage of anti-German propaganda in Poland and, most likely, strong Polish pressure on Moscow to cut the intra-German dialogue. In War-saw, relations between the two German states are interpreted as an erosion of the international order established in Yalta forty years ago (*Argumenty*, 26 February). Poland is vehemently opposed to so-called German politics, which are seen in Warsaw as synonymous with the long-term German aspira-tion for unification. As far as the Poles are con-cerned, the only issue involved in the "German problem" is perpetuating the division of Germany and preventing any resurgence of German re-vanchism (*Sztandar mlodych*, 24 May).

Poland's policy has its roots in history as well as in anticipation of possible future developments. Germany is the only state in Europe that would be able to assume regional leadership in the event the United States and the Soviet Union were simul-taneously to decline in power or lose interest in European politics. A statement of Edmund Os-manczyk, journalist and member of the Polish par-liament, reflects Polish fears: despite their division into two states the Germans "among themselves . . . still communicate in German" as they await the opportunity to dominate Europe again. Even di-vided, Germany "is still in a position to bring about a revision of the frontiers that might even result in a renewed partition of Poland—but this time of so-cialist Poland by two socialist neighbors" (*Die Zeit*, 10 August), meaning East Germany and the USSR!

Therefore, Warsaw with great satisfaction re-ceived a statement by Italian foreign minister Giulio Andreotti to the effect that the existence of two German states benefits all of Europe. Warsaw im-mediately pointed out that Andreotti is not only a member of a Christian Democratic party, as is West German chancellor Helmut Kohl, but is also chair-man of the European Christian Democratic Union (Warsaw radio, 17 September; *FBIS*, 20 Sep-tember). The defeat of pan-Germanism, therefore, is viewed in Warsaw as a guarantee of peace in Europe.

Poland's relations with West Germany continue to be tense, and a previously announced visit of West German foreign minister Hans-Dietrich Gen-scher to Warsaw was postponed. On numerous oc-casions in 1984, the Polish press attacked the Federal Republic of Germany, the "Teutonic Knights of today" (*TL*, 23 September). In particu-lar, Warsaw has denied the claim, officially sup-ported in West Germany, that more than a million Germans still live in Poland. The Poles are particu-larly sensitive to such assertions because the alleged desire to protect German nationals living in Poland served as an excuse for several invasions of Poland in the past. The Polish position is that the great majority of Germans living within the post–World War II borders left immediately after the war, and the remaining 120,000 emigrated in the 1970s. Bonn, however, suddenly announced that some 1.2 million Germans still live in Poland. This appears threatening to the Poles, particularly in the context of West German insistence that all Germans have the right to live in one political community. (*Zycie Warszawy*, 2 September; *TL*, 8 September.)

There has been little visible improvement in Polish-American relations. Warsaw's foreign policy follows a hard anti-U.S. line. It accuses the Reagan administration of an anticommunist crusade, promotion of West German imperialism, attempts to destabilize Poland's internal conditions, and "unceremonial and notorious" interference in Poland's domestic affairs (*TL*, 29–30 September). The partial lifting of sanctions following the amnesty was defined in Warsaw as an insignificant "softening of the course" since economically crucial restrictions remain in force (ibid., 5 November). Furthermore, Polish authorities labeled as discriminatory a new U.S. regulation that requires employees of Polish foreign trade agencies who apply for an American visa to answer a question regarding membership in the communist party, apart from questions concerning drug addiction, criminal record, tuberculosis, and racist activities (Warsaw television service, 13 September; *FBIS*, 14 September). Despite a few encouraging developments in Polish-American economic relations, the overall atmosphere is far from cordial, and the Polish press continues to be saturated with anti-U.S. propaganda.

In sum, the attempt made during 1984 to revive Poland's *Westpolitik* had disappointing results: three major Western countries (the United States, France, and West Germany) refused, in one way or another, to resume normal relations with Warsaw. The only positive events included the visit in October by Austrian foreign minister Leopold Gratz, proclaimed in Warsaw as having an "ice-breaking" effect (*TL*, 16 October), and the visit of Greek prime minister Andreas Papandreou, who later described Jaruzelski as a Polish patriot (ibid., 25 October). That comment, made by the prime minister of a NATO member-country, became a propaganda watershed for Warsaw. In addition to a rather vaguely phrased joint communiqué, the two leaders announced an agreement on economic cooperation, which included a contract for skilled Greek workers to build freighters for Poland in Polish shipyards. This contract is valued at more than $100 million. (Ibid., 25 October; Warsaw radio, 23 October; *FBIS*, 24 October.)

Poland's relations with the rest of the world consisted of visits by Egypt's deputy foreign minister, the president of Angola, the Vietnamese defense minister, and a Nicaraguan delegation headed by Daniel Ortega (*TL*, 11 and 20 April, 30 May, 11 June). Polish foreign minister Stefan Olszowski visited several countries including Afghanistan, where he expressed support for the pro-Soviet regime (ibid., 10 June). The only significant achievements of Polish diplomacy vis-à-vis the Third World involved the conclusion of a consular convention and development of new economic contacts with the People's Republic of China (*Rzeczpospolita*, 1 October). Relations with China have very special political meaning in Warsaw, where they are seen as a measure of independence from Moscow. Although *Westpolitik* has failed, Poland did play its "China card."

Arthur R. Rachwald
U.S. Naval Academy

Romania

Population. 22,683,000
Party. Romanian Communist Party (Partidul Comunist Român; PCR)
Founded. 1921
Membership. 3,440,000 (*FBIS*, 21 November)
General Secretary. Nicolae Ceauşescu
Political Executive Committee (PEC). 23 full members; 8 of whom belong to the Permanent Bureau: Nicolae Ceauşescu (president of the republic), Emil Bobu (chairman, Council on Problems of Economic and Social Organization), Elena Ceauşescu (first deputy prime minister), Constantin Dăscălescu (prime minister), Manea Mănescu (vice-president), Gheorghe Oprea (first deputy prime minister), Gheorghe Rădulescu (vice-president), Ilie Verdeţ (chairman, Central Council of Workers' Control and Economic and Social Activities); other full members: Iosif Banc, Virgil Cazacu, Lina Ciobanu (chairwoman, Central Council of the General Union of Romanian Trade Unions), Ion Coman, Nicolae Constantin, Ion Dincă (first deputy prime minister), Miu Dobrescu (chairman, RCP Central Collegium), Ludovic Fazekas (deputy prime minister), Alexandrina Găinuşe (deputy prime minister), Paul Niculescu, Constantin Olteanu (minister of national defense), Gheorghe Pană, Ion Păţan (minister of light industry), Dumitru Popescu, Ştefan Voitec (deceased, 8 December); 25 alternate members: Ştefan Andrei (foreign minister), Ştefan Bîrlea (chairman, State Planning Committee), Nicu Ceauşescu, Leonard Constantin, Gheorghe David (minister of agriculture and the food industry), Marin Enache (deputy prime minister), Petru Enache (vice-president), Mihai Gere, Maria Ghiţulică, Nicolae Giosan (chairman, Grand National Assembly), Suzana Gâdea (chairwoman, Council of Socialist Culture and Education), Nicolae Mihalache, Ioachim Moga, Ana Mureşan (minister of internal trade), Elena Nae, Marin Nedelcu (counselor to the president), Cornel Pacoste, Tudor Postelnicu (chief of secret police), Ion Radu, Ion Stoian, Gheorghe Stoica, Iosif Szasz (vice-chairman, Grand National Assembly), Ion Totu, Ion Ursu (first vice-chairman, National Council of Science and Technology), Richard Winter (minister of technical-material supply and control of fixed assets)
Secretariat. 10 members: Nicolae Ceauşescu, Iosif Banc, Emil Bobu, Ion Coman, Silviu Curticeanu, Petru Enache, Constantin Radu, Ion Radu, Ion Stoian, Ilie Verdeţ
Central Committee. 265 full and 181 alternate members
Last Congress. Thirteenth, 19–22 November 1984 in Bucharest; next congress scheduled for 1989
Last Election. 1980, 98.5 percent of votes, all 369 seats in the Grand National Assembly won by the Front of Socialist Democracy and Unity. Next elections scheduled for 17 March 1985.
Auxiliary Organizations. Union of Communist Youth (UTC, 3.2 million members), Nicu Ceauşescu, first secretary; General Union of Romanian Trade Unions (7 million members), Lina Ciobanu, chairwoman of the Central Council; National Council of Women, Ana Mureşan, chairwoman; Councils of Workers of Hungarian and German Nationalities, Mihai Gere and Eduard Eisenburger, respective presidents
Publications. *Scînteia*, Ion Mitran, editor-in-chief, PCR daily (except Monday); *Era Socialistă*, PCR theoretical and political biweekly; *Munca de Partid*, PCR monthly for party activists; *România Liberă*, electoral bloc daily (except Sunday); *Lumea*, foreign affairs weekly; *Revista Economică*, economic weekly. Agerpress is the official news agency.

Founded as the result of a split in the Romanian socialist movement in May 1921, the PCR was outlawed in 1924. Completely subservient to the Comintern, its leadership factious and dominated by ethnic minorities, and its policies inimical to the territorial integrity of the Romanian nation-state, the PCR was numerically weak, if sporadically disruptive, during the interwar period. Having played a subordinate and relatively minor role in the antifascist uprising of August 1944, the PCR, supported by the occupying Soviet army, engineered the assumption of power by fellow traveler Petru Groza in March 1945. In December 1947, a people's republic was established. The PCR merged with the rump Social Democratic Party in 1948, forming the Romanian Workers' Party (Partidul Muncitoresc Român; PMR). Overcoming leadership challenges from alleged Titoists (1948), Muscovite elements (1952), and intellectual Khrushchevites (1957), Gheorghe Gheorghiu-Dej directed party and state affairs until his death in March 1965. Nicolae Ceauşescu succeeded to the PMR leadership and in 1974 became president of the Socialist Republic of Romania, a name change effected in 1965 when the party reclaimed its original designation.

As a consequence of its commitment to the Stalinist model of economic development, in the early 1960s the party rejected Soviet plans for bloc economic integration, embarking on an assertively national course that has often conflicted with Soviet priorities. The PCR's autonomy has been most stridently expressed in state foreign and interparty relations. Domestically, however, the PCR has maintained a rigidly orthodox Stalinist regime. Fueled by Western credits and draconian rates of capital accumulation and investments, the Romanian economy was among Europe's fastest growing between 1965 and 1975. As much a result of unfavorable international economic conditions as of administrative overcentralization and imprudent planning, the economy stagnated in the late 1970s and early 1980s. Instead of implementing genuine economic reforms, the PCR re-emphasized its Stalinist economic priorities, provoking widespread consumer privation and worker apathy.

The major event of 1984 was the Thirteenth PCR Congress, convened in November. Some economic recovery, the result of stringent austerity measures, can be documented. Romanian-Soviet bilateral relations improved during 1984, causing some speculation that economic distress was forcing Bucharest to moderate its autonomous policies.

Leadership and Organization. PCR membership continued to grow in 1983, reaching 3,370,343 by 31 December of that year. Representing 15 percent of the total population, 21.6 percent of the adult population, and 32.2 percent of the work force, the PCR remains proportionally the largest party in the bloc. The membership is reportedly 55.76 percent workers, 15.76 percent peasants, 20.63 percent intellectuals and clerical workers, and 7.85 percent other categories. At the end of 1983, 31.61 percent of PCR members were women, as opposed to 30.59 percent in 1982. (*Scînteia*, 27 March.)

In his report to the Thirteenth PCR Congress, General Secretary Ceauşescu said the party had more than 3.4 million members, of whom ethnic Romanians made up more than 90 percent, Hungarians 7 percent, Germans 0.75 percent, and other nationalities the remainder. Ceauşescu said the PCR had 600,000 activists and employed 11,300 cadres in the apparat (7,000 in the party and 4,300 in the auxiliary organizations). (Ibid., 20 November.)

The personality cult surrounding Ceauşescu and his wife, Elena, continued unabated during the year, with particular stridency in January, the month of the presidential couple's birthdays (Radio Free Europe, *Romanian Situation Report* [*RFE SR*], 14 February), from June to November during the "campaign" for Ceauşescu's re-election as PCR general secretary (*Economist*, London, 3 November), and in July and August between the nineteenth anniversary of the Ninth PCR Congress, the beginning of the "Ceauşescu epoch," and the fortieth anniversary of the coup d'etat that overthrew the wartime regime on 23 August 1944. In 1984 the cult began to showcase the monuments of the Ceauşescu epoch, including the Bucharest subway, the Danube–Black Sea Canal, the House of the Republic, and the Boulevard of the Victory of Socialism in Bucharest. These grandiose constructions of questionable economic utility are supposed to remind Romanian citizens of their country's great achievements under the general secretary's guidance. The propaganda campaign to disassociate Ceauşescu from the country's economic problems has not been entirely successful. When John P. Wallach of the Hearst newspapers asked the general secretary about the cult in a July interview, Ceauşescu answered that it was a reflection of the nation's approval of his policies.

Elena Ceauşescu remained the regime's second most powerful person. She was described as an "eminent politician and scientist of global renown" during the observation of her birthday (*Scînteia*, 7 January), and Romanian newspapers have featured her scientific works, which have been translated into a number of languages. Evidence of her influence on her husband was particularly pronounced during the Thirteenth Congress. In his speech to the congress, the general secretary stressed the importance of science and technology, his wife's special areas of oversight, in fulfilling the party's program for increasing productivity and economic efficiency. Elena Ceauşescu is generally believed to be the driving force behind the increase in women in the party membership and in higher party bodies. Three full and four alternate members of the new PEC are women, as are 57 full and 73 alternate members of the Central Committee (ibid., 23 November). The percentage of women in higher party organs is the highest in the bloc. The number in the party apparat is close to 21 percent, up nearly 4 percentage points in only two years (*FBIS*, 9 April). Elena Ceauşescu also controls PCR cadre policies.

The dramatic rise of Nicu Ceauşescu, Nicolae and Elena's son, is usually interpreted as another proof of his mother's power. In December 1983 Nicu Ceauşescu, then 33, became first secretary of the UTC and de facto minister of youth affairs. His activities, both as UTC secretary and as chairman of the United Nations Commission for the International Year of Youth, were meticulously chronicled by the media. In the latter capacity he traveled extensively. As UTC secretary he hosted Chinese and North Korean youth delegations and visited the Soviet Union and Yugoslavia. Nicu Ceauşescu was reported to have married Poliana Cristescu, chairwoman of the National Council of the Young Pioneers (RFE *Background Report* [*RFE BR*], 27 July). At the Thirteenth Congress Nicu Ceauşescu gave a featured address and was elected an alternate member of the PEC. Poliana Cristescu was elected to full membership in the Central Committee.

Though rumors persist that Elena Ceauşescu is grooming her son to succeed his father, Nicu Ceauşescu is not yet a full-fledged beneficiary of his parents' personality cult. Some light was shed upon the dynastic question when Nicolae Ceauşescu gave his implicit benediction to the succession of Kim Chong-il, son of North Korean leader Kim Il-song. The parallels between the North Korean and Romanian regimes are obvious and Ceauşescu's endorsement of dynastic socialism in Korea is widely interpreted as an aspiration for a similar succession in Romania (*RFE SR*, 20 September). Nicu Ceau-

şescu's international activities, including both visits and speeches, might indicate that his next post will be in foreign affairs.

Other alleged Ceauşescu clan members were also prominent in 1984. Foremost among these was Manea Mănescu, whose political resurrection since 1982 has been spectacular (*YICA*, 1983, p. 327, 1984, p. 363). A respected former prime minister, Mănescu led a high-level economic delegation to France in January (*RFE SR*, 2 March). Perhaps because he is so well liked by apparently all actors in the system, he was given the distinct honor of renominating Nicolae Ceauşescu for the PCR general secretaryship at a June Central Committee plenum (*Scînteia*, 28 June) and again at the congress (ibid., 23 November). He was the only nonmember of the PEC Permanent Bureau to be elevated to it during its December reconfiguration (*Le Monde*, Paris, 11 December). Ilie Verdeţ, another rumored clan member and survivor of the 1982 scandals (*YICA*, 1983, pp. 326, 330–31), retained his Central Committee secretaryship for economic affairs as well as his membership in the Permanent Bureau of the PEC (*RFE SR*, 14 December). Lieutenant General Ilie Ceauşescu, the general secretary's brother, remains deputy minister of national defense and secretary of the Higher Political Council of the Armed Forces. In October he led a military delegation to the USSR, which was hosted by Gen. Aleksei A. Yepishev, chief of the Main Political Administration of the Soviet armed forces (*Scînteia*, 6 October). Ilie Ceauşescu was elected a full member of the PCR Central Committee at the Thirteenth Congress (*Le Monde*, 25–26 November).

Even though the policy of "cadre rotation" is a practice of long standing, the number and unpredictability of high-level changes in the PCR during 1984 was unusual. The example of Lina Ciobanu, a protégée of Elena Ceauşescu's, is enlightening and not particularly atypical. In January it was announced that she had been relieved of her duties as minister of light industry (*Scînteia*, 29 January). In March she was made a Central Committee secretary (ibid., 22 March). In October she relinquished her secretaryship to become chairwoman of the Central Council of the General Union of Romanian Trade Unions (*FBIS*, 23 October). In March five new Central Committee secretaries (Ciobanu, Constantin Radu, Ion Radu, Ion Stoian, and Silviu Curticeanu) were added to the seven who were retained, bringing the number to a record twelve, while Miu Dobrescu lost his secretaryship to become chairman of the PCR Central Collegium (*RFE SR*, 4 April). In October Ciobanu departed for the trade unions and Gheorghe Stoica was sent to Dolj county as first secretary to remedy its disastrous economic situation. This left a Secretariat of ten members (ibid., 2 November, 14 December). In December, two weeks after the close of the congress, the PEC Permanent Bureau was reduced from thirteen to eight members. Manea Mănescu gained a seat. However, longtime Central Committee secretary Iosif Banc, the only ethnic minority member of the former Permanent Bureau (ibid., 14 December); Virgil Cazacu, earlier reprimanded for lax safety standards at the Teleajen petrochemical plant in Prahova (*Scînteia*, 8 February); Nicolae Constantin, who had lost his trade union job to Ciobanu in October (*RFE SR*, 2 November); Ion Pățan, whose Ministry of Technical-Material Supply and Control of Fixed Assets was a constant target of sharp criticism; Ștefan Andrei, the foreign minister; and Petru Enache, whose fortunes had been sliding for some time (*YICA*, 1984, p. 363), lost their seats. Seventeen of the 40 county first secretaries were removed in the first ten months of 1984 (*RFE SR*, 17 November). Among the rising stars who emerged during 1984 were Nicolae Mihalache, who took over the troubled Constanța first secretaryship in May; Gheorghe David, who was given the unenviable position of minister of agriculture in March; and Maria Ghițulică, first secretary of the Vrancea PCR organization. All three were elected PEC alternate members at the Thirteenth Congress (ibid., 14 December). The only new full member of the PEC was Miu Dobrescu, who, presumably, had been demoted in March (ibid., 4 April, 14 December).

The net effect of all these changes was to solidify the Ceaușescus' complete control of the party. Although cadre rotation prevents any potential challenger from establishing a bureaucratic base of support, the efficiency lost to inexperience is a high price to pay for dynastic security.

Domestic Affairs. One cannot easily distinguish the Romanian government from the PCR. Unification of some party and state offices is legally mandated, and administrative cadres regularly come and go from those that are not. In addition, there are a number of mixed party-state bodies (e.g., the Central Council of Workers Control and Economic and Social Activities) that coordinate PCR plans with government legislation. All 369 members of the Grand National Assembly elected

in March 1980 were candidates of the PCR's electoral front, the Front of Democracy and Socialist Unity, of which Nicolae Ceaușescu is president. Elections for the Grand National Assembly are scheduled for 17 March 1985. This unicameral parliament meets infrequently (three times in 1984), serving as a sounding board and rubber stamp for PCR policies. Its most important session occurs in December of each year, when it adopts the following year's economic plan and state budget. A more important legislative body is the 27-member State Council, over which Ceaușescu presides, which meets frequently and issues decrees. As president of Romania, Nicolae Ceaușescu also exercises decree power. The cabinet has 26 ministers.

Economy. The troubled economy continued to dominate domestic affairs in 1984. The report on 1983 plan fulfillment was mixed. The only disastrous results were in agricultural production (see below). Depending upon the source, industrial output was 2.9 to 4.8 percent greater than in 1982 (a 6.6 percent increase had been planned), capital investment was up 2.9 percent (0.7 percent planned), and foreign trade turnover grew by 1.4 percent (14 percent planned), but agricultural production decreased by 2 percent (5.1–5.6 percent growth was planned). Domestic net material product, the closest one can come to an inclusive aggregate, given Romania's arcane system of reporting economic statistics, rose 3.4 percent (5.0 percent planned). (Ibid., 14 February; The Economist Intelligence Unit, *Quarterly Economic Review of Rumania, Bulgaria, Albania* [EIU], no. 1, 1984, and *Annual Supplement*, 1984; *Scînteia*, 29 January.)

The dismal performance of the agricultural sector, which had been a bright spot in 1982, drew quite a bit of national attention in 1984. No less than four times (January, May, September, December), General Secretary Ceaușescu delivered major policy pronouncements on agricultural matters. In January a national conference on increasing the marketable produce of privately cultivated land was held at Sinaia. The result was a law, passed in March, stipulating that the 15 percent of Romania's agricultural land in that category had to produce more food. Compulsory state deliveries were to be replaced by contracts with local people's councils in which production quotas would be stipulated according to plot size and land quality. Failure to fulfill the quotas would result in loss of the land. Monetary bonuses, production inputs, and low-interest loans were offered in return for quota fulfillment (*FBIS*, 26 January; *RFE SR*, 30 January). In May Ceauşescu addressed a meeting of the National Council of Agriculture, Food Industry, Forestry, and Water Management. While he praised the success of the livestock sector, which had dramatically increased herds in 1983, he vented his frustration on the late spring sowing by criticizing agricultural specialists who had instructed peasants to delay planting until after the ground had dried up and temperatures had moderated (*Scînteia*, 20 May). Ceauşescu again targeted experts in a speech to a Central Committee meeting on 1 September. He said that blaming bad crops on the weather was an unacceptable excuse (ibid., 2 September). At the Thirteenth Congress he projected grain harvests of 30 million metric tons by 1990 (as opposed to 20 million harvested in 1983) but did not stipulate any corresponding increase in agricultural investments (ibid., 20 November). In his December address, the general secretary did promise a 12.8 percent increase in investment during 1985 (ibid., 14 and 15 December). However, the 1985 plan's projected 29.7 million metric tons of grain seems to be unattainable, given the expected small increase in the 1984 crop.

The aggregate industrial growth rate for 1983 concealed a number of significant failures. Steel production, for example, is reported to have totaled 12.6 million tons, less than the planned 14.85 million tons, and less than the 13.06 million tons produced in 1982 (EIU, *Annual Supplement*; *Scînteia*, 16 December 1983). Part of the steel industry's difficulties may be attributed to continuing problems in the energy sector. Electric power generation fell 8.6 percent, coal production 14.8 percent, and oil production 14.1 percent below plan (EIU, no. 2). Ceauşescu's approach to solving these persistent deficiencies has been twofold: increase energy supplies and decrease energy consumption. Unlike in 1983, when he paid particular attention to coal production and to decreasing consumer demand for electrical power (*YICA*, 1984, p. 364), he did not propose specific programs of either sort during 1984. He did fire the minister of electric power, whose major failure was that hydroelectric production had been stymied by the prolonged drought. His replacement, Aneta Spornic, a protégée of Elena Ceauşescu's, had been a principal victim of the 1982 Transcendental Meditation scandal (*Economist*, 31 March; *YICA*, 1983, p. 330).

One of the most intriguing developments in 1984 was the political fallout from a serious industrial accident that apparently occurred at the Teleajen petrochemical plant in Prahova county on 6 December 1983. Work hazards at Romanian industrial sites are notorious and cause serious demoralization. The explosion at this relatively modern plant in which a substantial sum had been invested was disastrous not only in human terms—perhaps more than a hundred workers died—but also in economic terms since it was supposed to supply much of the domestic demand for industrial lubricants (*RFE SR*, 18 July). The fact that chemical production in 1983 was 13 percent below plan (ibid., 14 February) coupled with the need for a scapegoat cost the minister of the chemical industry his post. His deputy was also fired; the Prahova PCR first secretary and a deputy prime minister were publicly reprimanded. Furthermore, in a speech to PCR economic specialists, Ceauşescu laid the blame for the tragedy on managerial shortcomings (*Scînteia*, 8 and 9 February.) The irony in this series of events is that the accident itself was never reported, but was generally known through the Romanian rumor network. Safety technology is expensive, and the cost-conscious Romanians often do without it. Chemist Doctor Engineer Academician Elena Ceauşescu is held to have considerable influence over the chemical industry.

The Romanian consumer continued to be hardpressed in 1983 and 1984. According to figures supplied to the International Monetary Fund, real individual income fell by 2.5 percent in 1983 and a total of 9.5 percent overall from 1980 to 1983 (EIU, no. 3). This verification of the plight of the average Romanian was obscured by an announced 5.1 percent increase in money incomes in 1983 (ibid., no. 2). Application of the new wage law (*YICA*, 1984, p. 364) was gradually implemented during the year even though its provisions were sometimes circumvented (*RFE SR*, 26 July). In theory the law gives a 5 percent increase to Romanian workers who meet their plan targets and whose enterprises meet theirs (EIU, no. 3). Although it remains to be seen whether consumer prices would stabilize as Ceauşescu promised in May (ibid.), real income might still be flat in 1984 since increased taxes on individuals were built into the 1984 state budget (*RFE SR*, 2 March). Average net monthly wages were said to have increased from 2,601 to 2,925 lei in the first nine months of 1985 (EIU, no. 2; *Scînteia*, 11 September). Even if the average worker had more disposable income, however, there was little to buy with it, a fact that might partially account for increased savings.

Work discipline continued to be a problem in

1984. Crusades against absenteeism and alcoholism (EIU, no. 1; *RFE SR*, 17 May) were coupled with the general secretary's frequent condemnations of corruption and exhortations for greater worker commitment to the plan (e.g., *Scînteia*, 9 February). There is little positive incentive for workers, who must shoulder most of the burden of the austerity program. Ceauşescu's emphasis on raising labor productivity to well above its modest 2.7 percent gain in 1983 was bolstered by a nebulous but encouraging PEC report in August (*FBIS*, 30 August), but the planned 8 percent increase for 1984 (*Scînteia*, 16 December 1983) was probably not met. The 14.7 percent increase planned for 1985 (ibid., 14 December) and the 60 percent increase announced for the 1986–1990 five-year plan (ibid., 20 November) are fantasies.

This same aura of unreality pervades the rest of the 1985 plan. It calls for a 13.5 percent increase in industrial output (ibid., 14 December), whereas an overly optimistic Ceauşescu had prognosticated a 7 percent increase in 1984 during the PCR congress (ibid., 20 November), and a 9 to 10 percent increase in agricultural production. Similarly impractical goals are set for investment growth (8.3 percent), reductions in production costs (6.7 percent), and increased volume of foreign trade (15 percent) (ibid., 14 December). In the Eighth Five-year Plan (1986–1990), increases in aggregate growth are supposed to average 8 percent and in industrial product 6 percent a year. By 1990 Romania hopes to harvest a grain crop of at least 30 million metric tons. Some 1,500 new production facilities should come into operation. Quality is to increase so that 95 percent of Romanian manufactures will be internationally competitive by 1990. The price for these and other equally imaginative achievements was made clear by what the general secretary did not say in his speech to the congress. He made no commitment to improve the Romanian standard of living (ibid., 20 November; *RFE SR*, 17 October).

Ceauşescu's speech to the congress was not, however, without its interesting points. He quite clearly indicated that investment priorities and development strategy would change: "In the future, we will no longer concentrate on extensively developing production capacities: our emphasis will shift to modernizing and raising the technical level of existing capacities" (*FBIS*, 20 November). This shift from an extensive to an intensive strategy is to be achieved through science and technology, Elena Ceauşescu's purview. In his entire speech, which occupied nearly six pages of *Scînteia*, the general secretary uttered the pat phrase "multilaterally developed" only a handful of times. Ceauşescu's turn from the extensive growth model was foreshadowed earlier in the year by his willingness to discuss production specialization within the Council for Mutual Economic Assistance (CMEA; see below) and by an article criticizing the model that appeared in the externally distributed *Revue roumanine d'études internationales* (*RFE SR*, 5 October). However, Ceauşescu firmly rejected decentralization of the economy or any other type of structural reform (*Scînteia*, 20 November).

Demographic Problems. In March, Ceauşescu addressed a meeting of the Higher Health Council after the PEC had debated the worrisome decline in the nation's birthrate (ibid., 25 February). Live births had fallen to a little over 14 per 1,000, whereas a rate of 20 per 1,000 was necessary to reach the goal of a population of 25 million by 1990. In 1983, Ceauşescu told the council, there were 1.5 pregnancy terminations for every live birth. Only 9 percent of these 420,000 abortions were medically justifiable. Firm actions had to be taken to ensure the future of the nation. (Ibid., 8 March.) The programs implemented were, appropriately for 1984, Orwellian. Severe punishments were to be imposed on physicians performing unjustifiable abortions (ibid.). Agitation for larger families began to appear in the press (e.g., ibid., 9 March). Factory health officials were to keep careful track of fertile women's health. *Le Monde* (2 June) reported that one Bucharest factory required all women employees to be checked monthly to determine if they were pregnant. A 5 percent tax was imposed on childless couples as well as on single men and women over the age of 25. The legal marriage age was lowered to fifteen (EIU, no. 2). It remains to be seen whether these measures will reverse current demographic trends. It is generally difficult to convince adults to have children during economically hard times, and modernized, materialistic young people are often not as willing to have large families as were their village-bound elders. Moreover, Romania has the highest infant mortality rate in Eastern Europe (ibid.). Under these circumstances the renewed pronatalist policies may not yield positive results.

Public Works. On 26 May President Ceauşescu cut a ceremonial ribbon to open the Danube–Black Sea Navigation Canal, a 62-kilometer-long waterway that reduces the distance between Cernavoda on the Danube and the Black Sea port of Constanța by 336 kilometers (*Scînteia*, 27 May; *Le Monde*, 29 May; *FBIS*, 31 May). Reported to have cost at least $2 billion, some of which came from the World Bank, the canal was hailed as "a grandiose achievement of the Ceaușescu epoch" (*RFE SR*, 14 June). Originally started with slave labor in 1949, the construction was not pursued between 1954 and the mid-1970s, when armies of workers, soldiers, students, and more prisoners were set to the task (*RFE BR*, 31 August). Its multiple economic benefits appear to be dubious, especially before the completion of the Rhine-Danube Canal in West Germany in 1992. However, its political benefits are patent. Unlike the main Danube channel and the Black Sea estuary, the canal is under complete Romanian sovereignty (*Romania: Documents-Events*, no. 11, March). It is thus clearly part of Ceaușescu's attempt to capitalize on Romanian nationalism, specifically its anti-Russian component. Apparently impressed by the canal's grandeur and its alleged economic benefits, in July the PEC announced its approval of two similarly monumental constructions: the 30-kilometer-long Poarta Alba–Midia–Navodari Canal and the 72-kilometer-long Danube-Bucharest Canal (*RFE SR*, 5 October; *Scînteia*, 22 July).

Another such project was officially inaugurated on 25 June by the presidential couple (*Scînteia*, 26 June). During the preceding year, one of the most pleasant sectors of Bucharest, the historic Rahova-Antim-Uranus district, had been bulldozed to the ground, displacing 40,000 people and destroying a number of irreplaceable architectural masterpieces and old churches. In their place a "civic center," with a huge House of the Republic as its centerpiece, is to be built. Mock-ups of the building reveal a mammoth neoclassical construction of questionable taste. The main thoroughfare of the center will be the Boulevard of the Victory of Socialism, lined with statues of Romanian heroes and the now commonplace shoebox-like apartment buildings (*Le Monde*, 31 August; *RFE SR*, 26 July). Popular resistance to the project, first announced in 1979, has been significant, especially among Bucharest intellectuals, who have dubbed the project "Ceaushima" (*New Republic*, 17 December).

Culture. Culture has never been one of the Ceaușescu family's top priorities. The 1984 state budget called for a 37 percent reduction in government funding for culture (*RFE SR*, 2 March). The daily press was full of stories extolling the virtues

of socialist realism, a theme to which Ceaușescu returned in his speech at the PCR congress (*Scînteia*, 20 November). Since Ceaușescu's blistering attack on the cultural community in August 1983 (*YICA*, 1984, p. 365), artistic creativity has been further stifled, and the influence of sycophants has increased. In August the Western press reported that two Romanian artists had turned in their party cards to protest limitations on their creativity (*Le Monde*, 29 August). The desperation of this act underscores the present demoralization of Romanian intellectuals (ibid.; *RFE SR*, 2 November).

Religion. In his speech to the Thirteenth Congress, Nicolae Ceaușescu devoted a paragraph to the need to combat religious ("mystical and obscurantist") beliefs (*Scînteia*, 20 November). Two incidents in 1984 touched upon such issues. The first involved replacement of the chairman of the Department of Religious Affairs, which is usually viewed as an arm of the secret police and supervises the fourteen officially recognized denominations. In recent years a religious revival of sorts has occurred in Romania. Second, relations between Bucharest and the Vatican improved during the year. In late September the apostolic nuncio for special assignments arrived in Bucharest for a ten-day visit. The Roman Catholic church has no legal status in Romania. The Vatican gave the apostolic administrator of the Bucharest diocese the personal title of bishop. Acceptance of this indicates the regime's desire not to further alienate Romania's 1.7 million Roman Catholics.

Minorities. In another part of his speech to the congress, Ceaușescu said: "It is necessary to resolutely combat any manifestations of nationalism, chauvinism, anti-Semitism, and other forms of humiliation of man" (*FBIS*, 20 November). The condemnation of anti-Semitism was in striking contrast to the regime's earlier silence when the Romanian Jewish community, which is said to number about 30,000, protested the officially sanctioned publication of a volume containing anti-Semitic poetry by a member of the pro-Ceaușescu dogmatic-nationalist literary clique. Poems attacked not only Jews in general but also Romania's chief rabbi. A protest meeting was held in Bucharest, and the community's concern was relayed to the U.S. government, which warned Bucharest about the consequences of anti-Semitism on U.S.-Romanian relations (*RFE SR*, 14 June; *Le Monde*, 7 April). Apparently the hint was taken. In 1984 Ceaușescu received the president of B'nai B'rith and the president of the World Jewish Congress. Both conversations were reportedly "cordial" (*Scînteia*, 5 May, 2 August).

On 27 December, before the Councils of Workers of Hungarian and German Nationalities, President Ceauşescu delivered a polemical and spirited defense of the government's nationalities policies. According to the speakers at the meeting, Romania had completely resolved the national problem on the basis of full equality of rights for all citizens (ibid., 28 December). The first signs of renewed international concern about treatment of the sizable Hungarian minority (ca. 2 million) surfaced in June with reports that a number of artists had lost their posts in Transylvania and that admissions of Hungarians to Babeş-Bolyai University in Cluj-Napoca would be cut from 20 to 5 percent (BBC, 7 June).

Hungarian deputy prime minister Lajos Faluvégi raised the minority issue in reiterating the Kádár regime's position that national minorities should serve as bridges between socialist countries. He urged a freer flow of family visitors across the border. Faluvégi's remarks were reproduced in the party daily *Népszabadság* and cited in other newspapers. At the same time the Hungarian media disputed Ceauşescu's version of the overthrow of Romania's WWII regime and the ensuing liberation of Transylvania and Hungary. On 2 September a Romanian delegation, including three PCR secretaries, arrived in Budapest. Their discussions, which probably included the minority issue, were termed "frank" by the Hungarian media. *Scînteia* (5 September) termed the talks "warm" and "comradely."

Ceauşescu's response to these issues, which prompted a hurried trip to Bucharest by the Hungarian foreign minister (*Economist*, 26 January 1985), was a masterpiece of innuendo and esoteric meaning. He defended the admissions policies at Babeş-Bolyai University by asserting the logic of sending students (read, Hungarians) to those institutions where they could receive the best education in their specialty. He denied any cultural persecution and alluded to atrocities during the wartime Hungarian occupation of Transylvania. More interesting, he identified those who spread anti-Romanian disinformation with reactionary organizations in the West; with Horthyite elements; and, with "revanchists" seeking to overturn the postwar territorial settlement (*Scînteia*, 28 December).

Foreign Affairs. Foreign Minister Andrei's speech to the U.N. General Assembly in September outlined Romania's foreign policy goals and priorities: first are East-West issues, foremost of which is the Euromissile problem; second the two major conflicts in the Middle East; third, Korean unification; fourth, Namibia; fifth, strengthening (i.e., democratizing) the United Nations; sixth, the gamut of North-South issues, especially the debt problem; and finally, the U.N. Year of Youth, Nicu Ceauşescu's special concern (ibid., 29 September).

President Ceauşescu is no longer the world traveler he was at the height of his international prestige in the mid-1970s. Perhaps as a consequence of his declining international standing or perhaps of his advancing age, he no longer undertakes the long multiple-stop trips for which he was once famous. In 1984 he used his aides for diplomatic missions that he might have undertaken himself a decade ago. Prime Minister Dăscălescu, Foreign Minister Andrei, Vice-Presidents Mănescu and Rădulescu, Deputy Prime Minister Dincă, and Grand National Assembly Chairman Nicolae Giosan were all used in such a manner in 1984. Presidential counsellor Constantin Mitea emerged as President Ceauşescu's constant companion during diplomatic meetings in 1984.

Indebtedness. Although precise figures for Romania's hard currency indebtedness are difficult to obtain, the actual figure is probably a bit higher than the $8 billion that President Ceauşescu gave in his July interview with John Wallach (*RFE SR*, 19 April). However, even pessimistic sources concede that Romania managed to pay back 20 percent of this indebtedness between 1982 and 1984. When pressed to explain how this phenomenal feat was accomplished, Ceauşescu was uncharacteristically blunt: "Practically speaking, we have reduced imports by 50 percent . . . we decided not to apply for any more external loans from foreign institutions." Western estimates of Romania's trade balance and payments bear out Ceauşescu's contentions. Exports have remained relatively stable over the past five years, but imports have fallen 25 percent overall and nearly 65 percent with Western countries (1981–1983). Current account balances for the first three quarters of 1984 showed a surplus of $902 million, making the goal for 1984 of $1 billion not only within reach but surpassable (EIU, no. 3; *Economist*, 20 October).

These achievements have come at a cost to the individual consumer, to the original objectives of the 1981–1985 plan, and to Romania's previously held policy of market diffusion (*CSM*, 25 January,

3 October). In 1984, however, in contrast to the recent trend in which the entire surplus could be accounted for in terms of import reductions, imports increased while exports grew even faster (*Economist*, 20 October). Furthermore, the government felt encouraged enough by the excellent 1983 results and annoyed enough by the International Monetary Fund's conditions for further loans that Romania unilaterally abrogated its agreement with the IMF, forgoing the last $285 million it was entitled to draw.

In his speech to the PCR congress Ceauşescu reiterated his call for a new international economic order as well as a restructuring—amounting to a partial forgiving—of Third World debts. He bitterly denounced high Western interest rates and the IMF's policy of dictating austerity to debtor nations. He also promised that Romania would pay back its remaining foreign debt in the first years of the new five-year plan. (*Scînteia*, 20 November.)

Trade. One of the consequences of Romania's debt repayment strategy has been a dramatic increase in non–hard currency trade. In 1980 Romania's trade with its CMEA partners amounted to only 38.8 percent of the total. In 1983 it reached 53 percent. From its CMEA partners Romania hopes to receive the technology it can no longer afford to buy from the West, raw materials paid for in soft currencies, petroleum for its underutilized petrochemical industry, and natural gas and coal for its energy-starved industry and agriculture. In return, Romania is willing to enter into specialization agreements, joint ventures, investment programs, and plan cooperation and coordination. Romania was not and is not willing to accept plan integration or a supranationally planned "socialist division of labor." CMEA cooperation must aim at gradually equalizing the levels of development of member-states while rejecting any diminution of each member's sovereign authority politically or economically (ibid., 23 March). To this end Romania, after several years of delay caused by sharply diverging Soviet and Romanian views, agreed to participate in the CMEA summit held in Moscow on 12–14 June. Ceauşescu's state visit to the USSR in early June (see below) presumably focused on working out a mutually agreeable summit agenda and outcome. Romanian press accounts of the summit emphasized the Romanian agenda, omitting any reference to the standard Soviet code words for integration (*RFE SR*, 18 July). The promise of the summit was not, in the Romanian view, fulfilled, a fact clearly stated by Prime Minister Dăscălescu in his address to the Havana CMEA meeting some five months later (*Scînteia*, 2 November). At the end of 1984 it remained clear that renewed cooperation with the rest of the CMEA was the peculiar product of Romania's economic crisis, not of a basic shift in its policy of autonomy.

The West. In 1984 improved relations with the West were imperiled by continuing economic problems, by Romania's drawing closer to the USSR, and by a number of spy scandals involving Romanian diplomats. Romanian relations with the United States began with the second Romanian-American roundtable on human rights, held in Washington on 27–29 February. Assistant Secretary of State Elliott Abrams, the head of the U.S. team, noted that, with Czechoslovakia, Romania had the worst human rights record in the bloc, but emigration had shown marked improvement (*RFE SR*, 4 April). The Romanian regime bristles at the not-too-subtle American attempts to persuade it to live up to the obligations stipulated in the Helsinki Accords. Ceauşescu himself defended the regime against the accusations of elected officials in the United States who, during the annual review of Jackson-Vanik waivers (ibid., 26 July), had raised questions concerning the treatment of national minorities and religious believers (*Scînteia*, 28 December). His annoyance with the annual most-favored-nation renewal procedures was clear in his interview with John Wallach. He correctly identified the uncertainty associated with the yearly renewal as a disincentive for increased American business interest in Romania, but held out the hope that bilateral trade would once again top $1 billion in 1984. He vigorously denied the belief of some U.S. officials that American technology transferred to Romania was made available to the USSR. In June reports had circulated that Pentagon officials were blocking the sale of a Landsat remote sensing station to Romania because of such fears (AP, 10 June).

Relations benefited significantly from Romania's decision to send its Olympic team to Los Angeles, despite pressure from the Soviet Union for Romania to join the rest of the bloc in a boycott. When the Romanian team entered the Los Angeles Coliseum during the opening ceremonies, it was greeted by an ovation second only to that of the U.S. team, and the team's second-place finish in total medals was a propaganda coup of considerable importance for a country that in the past had been the victim of a bad press in the West (*RFE SR*, 4 September). The release of a dissident priest shortly after the games added to Romania's improved public image. Still, Romania's increasingly pro-Soviet line on the Euromissile issue continued to sour bilateral relations with the United States.

Relations with France, which have deteriorated in recent years, did not recover significantly in 1984. In January Manea Mănescu paid a ten-day visit to Paris aimed at increasing bilateral trade. Although the mission was depicted as a smashing success in the Romanian press, French accounts of Mănescu's mission were more restrained. France remains Romania's largest creditor. Romanian joint ventures with France have been unqualified disasters of late, and France and its European Community partners have accused Romania of dumping products, especially steel, on a number of occasions (*RFE SR*, 2 March; EIU, no. 3). In addition a number of political issues divide the two states, including their divergent views on the Euromissile controversy and on the crisis in Lebanon (*RFE SR*, 2 March). However, the most thorny issues of the past few years have involved the activities of Romanian intelligence agents in France (see *YICA*, 1983, p. 333). A popular French weekly published an interview with secret police defector Ion Pacepa, who detailed the industrial, political, and military aspects of Romanian intelligence operations in Western Europe (*L'Express*, Paris, 6 July). Later, Ceaușescu told *Le Figaro* that President Mitterrand would probably visit Romania during the autumn (*FBIS*, 21 August). He did not come. Foreign Minister Andrei visited France (ibid., 16 November) immediately before a new spy scandal came to light over French television. In prime time Matei Haiducu of "Tanase affair" infamy (*YICA*, 1983, p. 333) identified several diplomats at the Romanian embassy in Paris as secret police agents (*Le Monde*, 22 November). Coming as it did during the PCR congress, the revelation was not well received in Bucharest, where the French ambassador was summoned to the Foreign Ministry for a protest (ibid., 30 November). The cooling of Franco-Romanian relations of late is annoying for the Romanians, who have long perceived themselves as France's "special friends" in Eastern Europe. Particularly frustrating is the fact that Hungary seems to have replaced Romania as France's most valued Eastern contact. Mitterrand visited Budapest in 1982, the same year he canceled a visit to Romania, and János Kádár visited Paris in October 1984.

The latter visit coincided with Ceaușescu's most important contact with the West, a three-day visit to West Germany on 15–17 October. The visit, which contrasts with the cancellations of scheduled trips to Bonn by Erich Honecker and Todor Zhivkov, was the result of calculated efforts to accelerate the diplomatic momentum of the second half of 1983 (*YICA*, 1984, p. 367). In early March Foreign Minister Andrei was the guest of his West German counterpart, who had played an important role in the denouement of the emigration crisis of 1983 (ibid.). Andrei asked for, and later received, the resumption of government-guaranteed credits suspended in 1982. Bonn, apparently impressed by Romania's timely payments to Western banks in 1983 and the first half of 1984, overlooked huge unpaid debts to West German firms and, in June, extended the 300 million mark credit line for exports to Romania (EIU, no. 2; *RFE SR*, 4 April, 20 September, 17 October). Furthermore, Bonn was pleased by the record number of ethnic Germans allowed to emigrate during the first nine months of the year, by Bucharest's steadfast refusal to participate in Moscow's orchestrated campaign to label the Kohl government as "revanchist," and by Ceaușescu's rhetorical differences with the Soviets on the Euromissile issue (*RFE SR*, 17 October; *NYT*, 16 and 17 October). Although the visit was a partial public relations success for Ceaușescu, there were difficulties caused by the differing agendas of the two governments. Chancellor Kohl did not meet Ceaușescu at the airport (*Le Monde*, 30 September–1 October). The visit was cut from five days to three. No final communiqué was issued because, it seemed, the Romanian side declined to include an endorsement of the right of emigration by Romanians of German origin and because the German side would not budge from its position on the Euromissile controversy (ibid., 19 October; *RFE SR*, 17 October; *FBIS*, 18 October). The Soviet coverage of the visit was terse (*Pravda*, 16 and 18 October), although some satisfaction was apparent in a Tass item reporting the failure of the two sides to agree on a communiqué (ibid., 19 October). Both sides benefited from the visit: Bonn was able to refute Moscow's charges of revanchism and to expose a rift within the Soviet bloc, of which the Romanian visit was only the most obvious manifestation; Ceaușescu was able to polish his badly tarnished image in the West and to regain some nationalistic support at home.

Unfortunately for both Bonn and Bucharest, the mutual advantages of the Ceaușescu visit were almost immediately shrouded by still another spy scandal. A defecting diplomat had accused five of his former colleagues in the Bonn embassy of being employees of the secret police charged with violently disrupting the activities of Romanian exiles in West Germany. The five were asked to leave the country immediately (*Die Welt*, 10–11 November; *WP*, 10 November). The Romanian government denied the allegations but agreed to the departure. In retaliation, four West German diplomats were expelled from Bucharest, and ethnic German emigration was substantially reduced (*RFE SR*, 14 December). Two facets of this exchange are of particular interest. First, both sides seemed anxious to avoid a serious crisis, and neither declared the expelled diplomats persona non grata. Second, as a result of the French revelations, coupled with the West German and Austrian press allegations, the headquarters of the Romanian secret police operations in the West was identified as the economic section of the embassy in Vienna, headed by Nicolae Ceauşescu's eldest brother, Marin Ceauşescu (ibid.).

Other 1984 contacts with the West were of lesser significance. In February then Canadian prime minister Pierre Trudeau visited Romania and found in Ceauşescu a sympathetic supporter of his unique views on current East-West issues (*Scînteia*, 2 February; *FBIS*, 7 February). A week later Foreign Minister Andrei continued the exchange of views in Ottawa (*Scînteia*, 8 February). Both the Dutch and Belgian foreign ministers visited Bucharest during the year, but Ceauşescu was unable to convince either of the efficacy of halting deployment of U.S. cruise missiles in Western Europe (ibid., 17 April, 31 July). Keeping up the campaign for a Balkan nuclear-free zone, Ceauşescu received Greek president Constantin Karamanlis in November (ibid., 27 and 28 November) and dispatched Prime Minister Dăscălescu to Turkey in July (ibid., 5–7 July). As usual, Ceauşescu played host to a number of lesser figures from Western governments and political parties.

The Middle East. In comparison with recent years, Romanian activity in the Middle East was subdued in 1984 (see *YICA*, 1984, pp. 367–68). In May Nicolae and Elena Ceauşescu paid official visits to Pakistan and Syria. Judging from the communiqués, economic issues were the primary topics of discussion (*Scînteia*, 11 and 12 May), especially Romanian assistance in petroleum exploration and exploitation in return, one would assume, for oil (EIU, no. 3). Curiously, the subject of Afghanistan was not mentioned or even hinted at in the Roma-

nian press coverage of Ceauşescu's talks with Pakistan's Zia-ul Haq (*Scînteia*, 8–11 May). The latter attended the 23 August festivities in Bucharest (*FBIS*, 24 August). In Damascus Ceauşescu repeated Romania's well-known stand on the Arab-Israeli conflict (*Scînteia*, 11 and 12 May).

Romania's need for oil may also have motivated high-level exchanges with both parties in the Persian Gulf conflict. In February Iranian foreign minister Ali Akbar Velayati visited Bucharest (*RFE SR*, 19 April) and in April Prime Minister Dăscălescu visited Iraq (ibid., 17 May). Ceauşescu continues to encourage a settlement of the Gulf War that would facilitate a freer flow of the region's oil to Romania's underutilized refining industry.

Palestine Liberation Organization chief Yassir Arafat twice visited Bucharest (ibid., 4 September; *Scînteia*, 29 January). A number of Israeli officials also came. The most interesting of these was the visit of the Israeli communications minister, who reportedly again raised the possibility of a resumption of Israeli-Soviet diplomatic relations, presumably with the mediation of Romania (*FBIS*, 25 June). Prime Minister Dăscălescu visited Egypt in July (*Scînteia*, 17–20 July), and high-ranking Libyan and Sudanese delegations came to Bucharest during the year (ibid., 26 July, 22 and 25 August).

Africa. The most intensive Romanian–Third World contacts during 1984 were with Angola. Support of the Angolan party predates Angolan independence and has included military and economic assistance. In March Angolan Foreign Minister Paulo Teixeira Jorge arrived in Bucharest to explain the cease-fire that his government had reached with South Africa (*Scînteia*, 17 March). He was followed by Angolan leader José Eduardo dos Santos in April. Although both sides reiterated their support for the South-West African People's Organization, the Romanian media, in contrast to those of the rest of the bloc, praised the agreement, even appreciating the positive role played by the United States (ibid., 7–10 April; *RFE SR*, 17 May). The presence of the Angolan defense minister (*Scînteia*, 4 May) served to underscore that, regardless of the Angolan–South African arrangement, Romania would continue to assist Angola militarily.

Other African leaders who came to Bucharest during 1984 included the Togolese president (ibid., 22–26 May), the president of the National Revolutionary Council of Bourkina Fasso (Upper Volta) (ibid., 25–28 July), the Guinean prime minister (ibid., 11–12 July), and the presidents of Zimbabwe and Mozambique (*RFE SR*, 4 September). African countries are among the only markets that welcome Romanian manufactured goods, and high on the agenda of all of the visits was bilateral trade. In addition, Ceauşescu courts African political support for his pursuit of autonomous policies in forums such as the Group of 77, the Nonaligned movement, and the United Nations.

Bloc Relations. Soviet-Romanian bilateral contacts were more frequent and at a higher level during 1984 than any year's exchanges in recent memory. Soviet Foreign Minister Gromyko visited Bucharest (*Scînteia*, 30 January–1 February); General Secretary Ceauşescu paid his first *official* visit to the USSR in fourteen years (ibid., 5 June) and attended the CMEA summit there only a week later; Soviet Politburo members Vitali Vorotnikov, Boris Ponomarev, and Vladimir Shcherbitsky came to Bucharest (ibid., 22 August, 14 November; *FBIS*, 23 November); many other high-ranking visits were exchanged. Time and again Ceauşescu publicly affirmed that Romania placed a high priority on strengthening relations with all socialist states, especially the USSR (e.g., *Scînteia*, 23 March). It was within the context of these exchanges that the three levels of conflict were reflected.

An article by Dumitru Popescu, rector of the PCR's Ştefan Gheorghiu Academy, reiterated that solidarity among communist parties did not preclude the existence of contradictions (read, conflicts) between parties. Indeed, it was in serving a nation's specific needs and aspirations that such conflicts could arise. (*Era Socialistă*, 10 March.) On the exact anniversary of the 1964 "declaration of independence," another publication repeated the assertion that each nation had the inherent sovereign right to determine its own destiny free from any external interference (*România Libera*, 26 April). Following Ceauşescu's June visit to Moscow, it was again stressed that strengthening ties among socialist countries had to be achieved within the context of the principles of "equality, respect for national sovereignty and independence, noninterference in internal affairs, mutual benefit, and friendly mutual aid" (*Era Socialistă*, 25 June). The same points were emphasized on the fourteenth anniversary of the signing of the Romanian-Soviet Treaty of Friendship, Collaboration, and Mutual Assistance (*Scînteia*, 7 July). Again, in his speech to the PCR congress, Ceauşescu returned to the same themes.

A second terrain on which the Romanians have contested the Soviets on fundamental issues is history, specifically the overthrow of the Ion Antonescu regime on 23 August 1944. The standard Soviet version is that the Red Army "liberated" Romania with the timely assistance of a PCR-organized coup (e.g., *International Affairs*, Moscow, September; *New Times*, Moscow, no. 46, November). The Romanian version, most authoritatively articulated by Nicolae Ceauşescu, concedes the USSR's contribution in creating the objective conditions for the coup but assigns the primary credit for the liberation to the PCR and other national forces (*Scînteia*, 23 August). Indeed, sometimes the Soviets are not even mentioned, as in Lt. Gen. Ilie Ceauşescu's rendition of the events (ibid., 14 July). In fact, neither account is entirely accurate because neither acknowledges the leading roles of the king, the Romanian army, and the democratic parties.

On the bloc institutional level, the Romanian-Soviet conflict is the result of the two divergent perspectives. The USSR, while paying lip service to the functional objectives of the CMEA and the Warsaw Treaty Organization (WTO), views the other members as clients or dependencies and sees in the two organizations vehicles for perpetuating political control. Romania sees the CMEA in almost strictly economic terms and as a vehicle for equalizing the developmental levels of its member-states through coordination and cooperation, not integration (*Era Socialistă*, 25 June).

Romania's membership in the WTO has, since the mid-1960s, been a case of "partial alignment." While vigorously participating in the pact's political functions, often bedeviling Moscow's intentions, Bucharest has hosted only map exercises, advocates structural reform of the pact, consistently refuses to increase military expenditures, and has adopted a military doctrine not only incompatible with those of other pact members but also implicitly directed to impede a Soviet military intervention in Romania (*RFE SR*, 19 April).

At the policy level, Soviet-Romanian conflicts continued, but, with the exceptions of the Stockholm conference on confidence- and security-building measures, the Olympics boycott, and relations with West Germany, they were more muted and fewer than in recent years. The reduction in intensity of policy conflicts may in large part be explained by Romania's economic problems.

At the Stockholm conference, Foreign Minister Ştefan Andrei introduced a detailed package of confidence-building measures, in contrast to the positions taken by Gromyko and the loyalist bloc delegations. The package contained some standard WTO proposals, some of Western or neutral origin, and some purely Romanian suggestions (*RFE BR*, 30 April). Significantly, Bucharest submitted a WTO proposal on the freezing of military budgets to the NATO countries on 5 March (*RFE SR*, 4 April). In all these actions involving East-West issues, it was not clear if Romania's proposals were its own or if they were trial balloons for other parties to gauge both Soviet and Western reactions. In official American circles it was widely believed that Romania may have been speaking on behalf of the East Germans, Hungarians, and Bulgarians, for whom deviations from Moscow's line would have been more difficult. Other Western analysts could find no substantial difference between Romania's proposals and those of the USSR.

The motivation for Romania's muting of its policy differences with the USSR was clearly economic. The information released about high-level contacts and the personnel involved are evidence to this effect. In January Soviet foreign minister Gromyko arrived in Bucharest. Included in the delegation were Central Committee secretary Konstantin Rusakov, who is in charge of relations with ruling parties, and Deputy Prime Minister Nikolai Talyzin, who oversees CMEA affairs and Soviet-Romanian bilateral economic affairs. While the intent of Gromyko's mission was probably to obtain Romanian support for Moscow's position on a number of East-West issues, the presence of Talyzin, who had twice visited Bucharest in 1983, indicated that the Soviets were willing to offer economic rewards for Romanian political support (ibid., 14 February). Indeed, the visit came only a month after the signing of the annual bilateral trade protocol, which envisioned a 15 percent increase over 1983 (EIU, no. 1). During the visit Soviet diplomats spread disinformation to the effect that the USSR would provide Romania at preferential prices an additional 1.5 million metric tons of oil above and beyond contracted amounts (*FBIS*, 2 February; *RFE SR*, 2 March). In fact, the Soviet delegation made no economic concessions to Ceausescu, and the latter made few, if any, political concessions to the USSR. The communiqué was vaguely worded. It did, however, allude to both sides' commitments to deepening CMEA cooperation and to the 1983 Prague WTO proposals (*Scînteia*, 2 February).

Nicolae Ceausescu led the PCR delegation to Yuri Andropov's funeral. Romania observed a single day of official mourning in contrast to the rest of the bloc's four days. Ceausescu's relations with Andropov were rumored to have been bad, whereas he was said to have an excellent personal relationship with Chernenko (*RFE SR*, 14 March, 2 April).

In April and May Soviet ambassador Yevgeny Tyazhelnikov had four meetings with Nicolae Ceausescu (*Scînteia*, 1 and 23 April, 5 and 15 May). They were probably in connection with the Soviet effort to line up bloc support for the Olympics boycott, which was announced on 8 May. The press had absolutely nothing to say about the Soviet bloc boycott (*RFE SR*, 14 June). Romania's decision to send a team to Los Angeles, despite Soviet objections, was a relatively low-risk defiance that yielded substantial domestic and foreign benefits.

Ceausescu's one-day official visit to Moscow on 4 June again gave some indication of the two sides' differing priorities. Romania seemed to come away with more than it had to give up. Although Ceausescu did agree to be cooperative during the CMEA meeting, the record of his public comments and the communiqué revealed that he did not align Romania any more closely with the USSR on crucial East-West or interparty issues (*FBIS*, 6 June). On the other hand, the Soviets agreed to enter into long-term agreements on exchanges of goods, production-sharing, technology transfers, and coordination of national plans (*Scînteia*, 6 June; *Izvestiia*, 6 June). They represent significant concessions to the Romanians, who are seeking to replace Western markets and technology imports with those that do not require as high a quality or payment in hard currency. The matter of raw materials and energy supplies from the Soviet Union was left to the imagination of the observer in the immediate aftermath of the visit. However, in the Wallach interview, Ceausescu said, "We even agreed to cooperate to ensure some raw materials for Romania" and went on to specify that hundreds of Romanian engineers would be sent to help the Soviets construct a natural gas pipeline. In its September issue, *International Affairs* (Moscow) confirmed the agreement. Nikolai Baibakov, chairman of the USSR's central planning agency, visited Bucharest (*Scînteia*, 22 December), and Foreign Minister Andrei and PCR secretary Bobu exchanged views with state planning officials in Moscow (ibid., 29 December).

Still, the Soviet leadership manifested its displeasure with Ceausescu's intransigence and independence by symbolically snubbing both Romania and the PCR at important events during the second half of the year. Of all East European delegations to the CMEA summit, the Romanian was met by the lowest-ranking welcoming committee (*FBIS*, 12 June). The Soviet delegation to the 23 August celebrations was led by Vorotnikov, and the Soviet telegram of congratulations insisted upon the Red Army's role in the "liberation" of Romania (*RFE SR*, 4 September). Just prior to the PCR Congress, Ceauşescu received Ponomarev, Soviet Politburo candidate member and chief of the Central Committee's International Department, for what was most likely a preview of the congress proceedings (*Scînteia*, 14 November). The Soviet delegation to the Congress was led by Ukrainian party boss Vladimir Shcherbitsky, who delivered an address in Piteşti that implicitly outlined the difference between the two parties (*Pravda*, 21 November). The speech was not covered in the Romanian press. And, just before the congress another Soviet article pointedly criticized Ceauşescu's economic policies (*New Times*, November).

In sum, while Bucharest drew rhetorically closer to Soviet positions on a number of policy issues and appeared to be willing to assume a slightly less divergent posture in regard to bloc institutions, the PCR neither gave in nor toned down its stance on fundamental issues that continue to inhibit closer Soviet-Romanian relations.

Relations with other bloc governments and parties reflected the interplay of Soviet-Romanian relations with contemporary issues. The most interesting bloc visitor was East German leader Erich Honecker. The highest-ranking bloc leader to attend the 23 August festivities, his visit came at a time when Soviet pressure on him to cancel his visit to West Germany was at its height (*RFE SR*, 4 September). Coverage of the cordial Ceauşescu-Honecker meetings stressed economic relations (*Scînteia*, 25 August). However, political issues, such as intra-German relations, were most likely discussed. Shortly after Honecker's departure, Ceauşescu's visit to West Germany was announced, a full month and a half in advance (ibid., 28 August). Such advance notice of a foreign visit is highly unusual and may have been meant to support Honecker's resistance to Soviet demands to cool East Berlin–Bonn relations.

Quite a different aura surrounded Ceauşescu's stop in Poland on his way back from his official visit to Moscow. General Wojciech Jaruzelski had paid a brief visit to Romania in June 1982 (*YICA*, 1983, p. 334). The 1984 communiqué stressed economic relations but also touched upon political issues.

Both sides assigned the blame for the new stage in the arms race to the United States and NATO, but they also agreed that states in which the new missiles were sited had a special responsibility in the process leading to their removal. The bilateral talks were said to have taken place in "an atmosphere of sincere friendship, trust, and mutual understanding" (*Scînteia*, 9 June). This contrasts with the Ceauşescu-Chernenko talks, which were characterized as having taken place "in a warm atmosphere of friendship and frankness" (*Pravda*, 6 June).

As is their habit, Nicolae Ceauşescu and Todor Zhivkov also exchanged visits: Nicolae and Elena Ceauşescu traveled to Sofia in March, and Zhivkov reciprocated by visiting Bucharest in December. The latter also inspected the Danube–Black Sea Canal in July (*Scînteia*, 31 July). The communiqué, while mentioning the usual themes of economic cooperation and a Balkan nuclear-free zone, also reflected Romania's drift toward Moscow. The worsening European situation was the fault of the United States, which should halt deployment of its Euromissiles and withdraw those that had been deployed. The USSR would reciprocate, and the Geneva negotiations could be resumed (ibid., 31 March). The second communiqué reiterated U.S. culpability but welcomed the recently announced potential resumption of Soviet-American talks on a number of issues. The most interesting passage read: "The parties emphasized the danger to peace and security represented by conceptions that call into question European interstate frontiers, their social-political order, and the other territorial-political realities stabilized after World War II" (ibid., 21 December). To the bloc loyalist, this statement might refer to President Reagan's comments on Yalta, but coming as it did at the height of new Romanian-Hungarian polemics with irredentist overtones, its inherent antirevisionism was probably directed at Budapest.

Romanian relations with Hungary deteriorated during the year, and relations with Czechoslovakia, whose media often berated certain parties' flirtations with autonomy, were also poor. Neither side sent high-ranking delegations to either the 23 August celebrations or the PCR congress.

Romanian relations with Yugoslavia have been excellent since the mid-1960s and have yielded important mutual economic and political benefits. In 1984, however, relations appeared to sour. Ceauşescu paid a visit to Yugoslavia, at his own request according to Yugoslav sources (*RFE SR*, 19

April). Bilateral trade has declined in recent years, as both countries have adopted austerity measures. The composition of the Romanian delegation and the final communiqué indicate that mutual economic problems were high on the agenda (*Scînteia*, 14 April). Although no mention of the Euromissile issue was made in the communiqué, Ceauşescu's toast at the state dinner hosted by Yugoslav president Mika Špiljak was far more evenhanded in its assessment of blame than were his comments in Bulgaria two weeks earlier (ibid., 13 April). At the time of the PCR congress, to which the Yugoslav party sent a relatively low ranking delegation, Radio Belgrade dwelt upon minority issues and the difficulties arising because of Romania's drift toward Moscow (*RFE SR*, 14 December).

Asia. The level and frequency of high-level Romanian-Chinese exchanges during 1984 rivals that only of the Soviet exchanges. Chinese foreign minister Wu Xueqian was his Romanian counterpart's guest from 31 March to 2 April. While the Romanian media were particularly uninformative about the substance of the discussions between Wu and Foreign Minister Andrei, Prime Minister Dăscălescu, and President Ceauşescu, the subdued coverage of the visit came at a time when Romania was edging closer to the USSR on a number of issues. Deputy Prime Minister Dincă later traveled to Beijing (*FBIS*, 5 June), and in July a Chinese military delegation led by army chief of staff Yang Dezhi stayed nine days in Romania (*Scînteia*, 18 July; *Pravda*, 20 July). The foremost event of 1984 was President Li Xiannian's state visit on 27–29 August. Li had arrived in Romania for the 23 August celebrations and then had three days of intensive talks with Romanian leaders. While primarily a visit of mutual symbolic support, Li went out of his way to stress favorite Romanian themes, such as the continuing relevance of the nation and the dangers of superpower hegemony (*RFE SR*, 20 September). The Chinese party sent a relatively high level delegation to the PCR congress, and it was accorded special treatment almost on a par with that given to Soviet representatives (ibid., 14 December). One curious development involved the unusual prominence of security officials in the exchange of visits. Romanian Minister of Internal Affairs George Homoştean was received by Hu Yaobang in Beijing (ibid., 20 September), and the deputy minister of public security was among the officials accompanying Li Xiannian to Romania in August. Chinese minister of public security Liu Fuzhi also visited Romania (*Scînteia*, 2 December). One could speculate that the presence of the usually shadowy figures in diplomatic exchanges might indicate a higher stage of Romanian-Chinese cooperation in the intelligence field.

North Korea's Kim Il-song called on his close friend and fellow dynast, Nicolae Ceauşescu. As is their habit, the two leaders ran out of superlatives in their public admiration for one another (ibid., 17–22 June). What caught Western analysts' attention, however, was Ceauşescu's explicit endorsement of Kim Chong-il as his father's designated successor. Indeed, the Ceauşescu benediction may have motivated the previously unannounced visit (*RFE SR*, 20 September).

The significance of the Chinese and Korean visits in a year when other former Ceauşescu supporters were critically assessing the Romanian rapprochement with the rest of the Soviet bloc is clear. Regardless of policy and institutional readjustments brought on by changing domestic and international circumstances, Ceauşescu's Romania was still following an autonomous and national course worthy of nonbloc support.

Latin America. Sandinista leader Daniel Ortega Saavedra slipped in and out of Bucharest almost unnoticed. The Romanian press naturally supports Nicaragua (*Scînteia*, 27 June), but just prior to the most-favored-nation hearings in the U.S. Congress caution was indicated. Prime Minister Dăscălescu met with Castro at the time of the CMEA meeting in Havana (ibid., 1 November).

International Party Contacts. The PCR's relations with nonruling European communist parties followed a predictable course. Ceauşescu and *Scînteia* sharply criticized the founding of a parallel (read, pro-Soviet) Spanish communist party (ibid., 27 and 28 January), which the Soviet and the bloc loyalist parties supported (*RFE SR*, 2 March; *RFE BR*, 27 January). As if to underscore the CPR's support of the Spanish Communist Party (PCE), Ceauşescu hosted Gerardo Iglesias, PCE secretary general, in May. A joint communiqué, an unusual display of mutual respect, stressed the identity of views between the two parties and the need for unity among workers' parties (*Scînteia*, 19 May). As is her custom, Dolores Ibárruri, PCE president, spent her summer holidays in Romania (*FBIS*, 27 July). Romania mourned the passing of Italian party leader Enrico Berlinguer (*Scînteia*, 12 June) but, perhaps because of the PCR leadership's attendance at the Moscow CMEA summit, sent a relatively low level delegation to the funeral (ibid., 13 June). French party leader Georges Marchais spent two weeks in Romania, and in a joint communiqué (ibid., 28 July) he and Ceauşescu expressed identity of views on pressing international problems. Portuguese communist leader Álvaro Cunhal visited Bucharest but, in keeping with his pro-Soviet posture, was not accorded the same degree of publicity (ibid., 4 February) as his Spanish and French comrades. None of the West European parties sent impressive delegations to the PCR congress. Miu Dobrescu, an old hand at such things, represented the PCR at the founding congress of the Ethiopian Workers' Party (ibid., 11 September).

In 1984, faced with severe economic problems and intensive Soviet pressure, the PCR and its leader retreated somewhat from the forceful assertion of party and state independence that had guaranteed the regime a certain degree of popular legitimacy in the past. Ceauşescu and his entourage seem to have no new ideas, only excuses and scapegoats for failed policies. As long as the PCR is disinclined to reform itself or the Romanian economy, however, a degree of highly publicized divergence from the Soviet Union is essential in keeping a long-suffering population acquiescent.

Walter M. Bacon, Jr.
University of Nebraska at Omaha

Union of Soviet Socialist Republics

Population. 274,860,000 (June 30; Tass, 21 July)
Party. Communist Party of the Soviet Union (Kommunisticheskaia Partiia Sovetskogo Soiuza; CPSU)
Founded. 1898 (CPSU, 1952)
Membership. 18.5 million (*Pravda*, 4 June 1984); 44.1 percent workers; 12.4 percent peasants; 43.5 percent technical intelligentsia, professionals, administrators, and servicemen; women, 27.6 percent of all party members, 33 percent of candidates; estimated total membership of 1 January 1985, 18.7 million
General Secretary. Konstantin U. Chernenko
Politburo. (Unless otherwise indicated, nationality is Russian) 11 full members: Konstantin U. Chernenko (b. 1911, president), Geidar A. Aliev (b. 1923, Azerbaijani, first deputy chairman [first deputy prime minister], Council of Ministers), Mikhail S. Gorbachev (b. 1931), Viktor V. Grishin (b. 1914, first secretary, Moscow city party committee), Andrei A. Gromyko (b. 1909, first deputy chairman, Council of Ministers, and foreign minister), Dinmukhamed A. Kunaev (b. 1912, Kazakh, first secretary, Kazakh Central Committee), Grigori V. Romanov (b. 1923), Vladimir V. Shcherbitsky (b. 1918, Ukrainian, first secretary, Ukrainian Central Committee), Mikhail S. Solomentsev (b. 1913, chairman, Party Control Committee), Nikolai A. Tikhonov (b. 1905, Ukrainian, chairman [prime minister], Council of Ministers), Vitali I. Vorotnikov (b. 1926, chairman, Russian Soviet Federated Socialist Republic [RSFSR] Council of Ministers); 6 candidate members: Viktor M. Chebrikov (b. 1923, Ukrainian, chairman, Committee of State Security [KGB]), Piotr N. Demichev (b. 1918, minister of culture), Vladimir I. Dolgikh (b. 1924), Vasili V. Kuznetsov (b. 1901, first deputy

chairman, Presidium of the USSR Supreme Soviet), Boris N. Ponomarev (b. 1905), Eduard A. Shevardnadze (b. 1928, Georgian, first secretary, Georgian Central Committee)

Secretariat. 10 members: *Konstantin U. Chernenko (general secretary), *Mikhail S. Gorbachev (party organization, foreign affairs, and agriculture), *Grigori V. Romanov (defense industry, bloc affairs, and internal security), *Vladimir I. Dolgikh (heavy industry), *Boris N. Ponomarev (international affairs), Egor K. Ligachev (b. 1920, cadres), Ivan V. Kapitonov (b. 1915, light industry), Konstantin V. Rusakov (b. 1909, ruling communist parties), Nikolai I. Ryzhkov (b. 1929, economic planning), Mikhail V. Zimianin (b. 1914, Belorussian, culture) (*member of Politburo)

Central Committee. 319 full and candidate members elected at Twenty-sixth CPSU Congress; approximately 285 active full members as of 1 November 1984. Central Committee apparatus is organized under 24 departments; key department heads include Boris N. Ponomarev (international), Nikolai I. Savinkin (b. 1913, administrative organs), Vladimir A. Karlov (b. 1914, agriculture), Nikolai E. Kruchina (b. 1928, administration of affairs), Nikolai I. Ryzhkov (economics), Klavdii M. Bogolyubov (b. 1909, general), Egor K. Ligachev (party organizational work [cadres]).

Status. Ruling and only legal party

Last Congress. Twenty-sixth, 23 February–4 March 1981, in Moscow; next congress scheduled for 1986

Last Election. Supreme Soviet, 4 March 1984; more than 99.9 percent of vote for CPSU-backed candidates, all 1,500 of whom were elected; 71.4 percent of elected candidates were CPSU members.

Defense Council. The inner circle of the leadership concerned with national security affairs; only the chairman is publicly identified. Chairman: Konstantin U. Chernenko; probable members, as of 1 January 1985: Andrei A. Gromyko, Nikolai A. Tikhonov, Marshal Sergei L. Sokolov (b. 1911), minister of defense; possible members: Mikhail S. Gorbachev, Grigori V. Romanov; probable associates: Viktor M. Chebrikov, Marshal Sergei F. Akhromeyev (b. 1923), chief of staff and first deputy minister of defense

Government. 115 members of Council of Ministers, confirmed by Supreme Soviet April 1984, including three first deputy chairmen (first deputy prime ministers), ten deputy chairmen (deputy prime ministers), 63 ministers, and 22 chairmen of state committees. Key members of government not identified above: Ivan V. Arkhipov (b. 1907, first deputy chairman), Nikolai K. Baibakov (b. 1911, deputy chairman and head of Gosplan, the state planning commission), Guri I. Marchuk (b. 1925, Ukrainian, deputy chairman for science and technology), Ziya N. Nuriev (b. 1915, Bashkir, deputy chairman for the agroindustrial complex), Leonid V. Smirnov (b. 1916, deputy chairman for the military-industrial complex), Nikolai V. Talyzin (b. 1919, deputy chairman for CMEA affairs), Pavel V. Finogenov (b. 1919, minister of the defense industry), Vitali V. Fedorchuk (b. 1918, Ukrainian, minister of internal affairs), Vasili F. Garbuzov (b. 1911, minister of finance), Valentin K. Mesyats (b. 1928, minister of agriculture), Yakov P. Ryabov (b. 1928, deputy chairman, Council of Ministers), Mikhail S. Smirtyukov (b. 1909, administrator of affairs)

Auxiliary Organizations. Communist Youth League (Kommunisticheskii Soyuz Molodezhi; Komsomol), 42 million members (Moscow domestic service, 6 July; *FBIS*, 9 July), led by Viktor M. Mishin (b. 1943); All-Union Central Council of Trade Unions (AUCCTU), 130 million members, led by Stepan A. Shalayev (b. 1929); Voluntary Society for the Promotion of the Army, Air Force, and Navy (DOSAAF), led by Georgi M. Yegorov, more than 65 million members; Union of Soviet Societies for Friendship and Cultural Relations with Foreign Countries

Publications. Main CPSU organs are the daily newspaper *Pravda* (circulation more than 11 million), the theoretical and ideological journal *Kommunist* (appearing 18 times a year, with a circulation over 1 million), and the semimonthly *Partinaia zhizn*, a journal of internal party affairs and organizational matters (circulation more than 1.16 million). *Kommunist vooruzhennikh sil* is the party theoretical journal for the armed forces, and *Agitator* is the same for party propagandists; both appear twice a month. The Komsomol has a newspaper, *Komsomolskaia pravda* (6 days a week), and a monthly theoretical journal, *Molodaia gvardia*. Each USSR republic prints similar party newspapers in local languages and usually also in Russian. Specialized publications issued under supervision of the CPSU Central Committee include the newspapers *Sovetskaia Rossiia, Selskaia zhizn, Sotsialisticheskaia industriia, Sovetskaia kultura,* and *Ekonomicheskaia gazeta* and the journal *Politicheskoie samoobrazovaniie*. Tass is the official news agency.

During the 1960s and 1970s the CPSU experienced a period of exceptional leadership stability. Four senior members of the "collective leadership" that had assumed power in October 1964 retained office at the outset of the 1980s. However, the deterioration in the health of General Secretary Leonid Brezhnev in the spring of 1979 signaled the beginning of an extended "succession crisis" that had not run its course by the end of 1984. The Brezhnev era had been marked by the rise of the USSR to unquestioned superpower status, but, in its waning years, stability had eroded into stagnation. Brezhnev's successor, Yuri Andropov, sought to reinvigorate the system and come to grips with an accumulation of unresolved problems, such as corruption, economic inefficiency, and impediments to party leadership renewal. Andropov emphasized reimposition of discipline in the economy and carried out a substantial turnover of personnel in party and government. But Andropov's precarious health and the brevity of his tenure precluded the general overhaul of the Soviet system that he obviously desired. Upon his death in February 1984, he was succeeded by the most prominent representative of the "old guard" in the party secretariat, Konstantin Chernenko. The new general secretary also appeared to have serious health problems and seemed destined to provide only a relatively weak interim leadership. During 1984, the party proceeded to implement certain of Andropov's initiatives, such as reform of the educational system, and in October set in motion a major land reclamation project, promising some long-run relief for the serious food problem. It seemed clear that more fundamental reforms would have to await the coming to power of a younger leadership. Meanwhile, the renewed cold war continued, although couched in less strident rhetoric than in 1983. No real progress was evident in the resolution of outstanding international issues, but the meeting of Foreign Minister Gromyko with U.S. president Reagan in September and the visit of party secretary Gorbachev to London in December indicated a Soviet willingness to resume dialogue with the West. While Gorbachev was in London, the passing of the old guard resumed in Moscow: the death of longtime leadership stalwart Dimitri F. Ustinov left a major gap in the Soviet hierarchy.

Leadership and Party Organization. At the beginning of the year, the physical condition of General Secretary Yuri Andropov was the subject of much speculation among Western observers. Andropov had not been seen in public since the previous 18 August and had missed the anniversary celebrations of the 1917 Revolution on 6–7 November and the meetings of the Supreme Soviet and CPSU Central Committee in December. Nevertheless, the December Central Committee plenum had seemed to confirm Andropov's political leadership, as three of his clients had been elected to full or candidate membership on the Politburo.

During January, Soviet sources leaked to the Western media reports that Andropov's health was improving and that he would soon fully resume his duties. But the attempted cover-up of the true state of the leader's health, evidently orchestrated by Central Committee International Information Department head Leonid M. Zamyatin, was not very successful; the announcement of Andropov's death on 9 February (Tass, 10 February) occasioned little surprise at home or abroad. In contrast to the secretiveness surrounding Andropov's long illness, Soviet officialdom now provided a detailed account of his ailments. His personal physician revealed that Andropov had suffered from nephritis, nephrosclerosis, hypertension, and diabetes (ibid., 11 February).

Under these circumstances, the passing of Andropov could hardly have surprised the Kremlin leadership, but the Politburo had evidently not settled the succession in advance. Party secretary Konstantin Chernenko had returned to the limelight during Andropov's illness, presiding over the important meetings and ceremonies during November and December. But party secretary Mikhail Gorbachev was thought the favorite by some Western observers. During 1983, he had evidently assumed responsibility for personnel matters and had also been given a role in foreign affairs; moreover, he appeared to be in charge of party committee elections in December and January and the Supreme Soviet election campaign. When Chernenko was appointed to head the Andropov funeral commission (*NYT*, 11 February), he appeared to be the probable successor. However, in contrast to the previous succession, when Andropov had emerged as the nominee one day after Brezhnev's death, more than 72 hours elapsed between the announcement of the leader's demise and the confirmatory meeting of the Central Committee. During this period, there were indications that the Politburo was in virtually continuous session, probably engaged in some very hard bargaining (ibid., 14 February). Finally, on the eve of Andropov's funeral, Chernenko was "unanimously" elected by the Central Committee as Andropov's successor (*Pravda*, 14 February).

Although the deliberations of the Politburo were, of course, shrouded in secrecy, there seemed no doubt that factional conflict, apparently suppressed under Andropov, had instantly reappeared when the ruling body confronted the succession decision. Andropov's vigorous campaign for party renewal had resulted in a considerable shake-up in the ranks of regional and district party secretaries, particularly in Moscow, the Ukraine, and Kazakhstan (see below), and Politburo members Grishin, Shcherbitsky, and Kunaev, together with Prime Minister Tikhonov, were reportedly Chernenko's strongest supporters. But absence of enthusiasm for Chernenko was strikingly evident in other quarters. Foreign Minister Gromyko's Supreme Soviet election speech virtually ignored the new leader (*Sovetskaia Belorussia*, 28 February), and an editorial in the principal military newspaper on Armed Forces Day dealing with the Central Committee plenum made no mention of Chernenko (*Krasnaia zvezda*, 23 February).

Whatever support Gorbachev or other candidates may have received within the Politburo, Chernenko enjoyed one crucial advantage. An anti-Chernenko group in the Politburo could scarcely entertain an appeal to the Central Committee. Virtually all the members of that body had been elected under Brezhnev, and it was heavily populated with elderly party and government officials threatened by Andropov's reversal of the "stability of cadres" policy. But Chernenko's acceptance speech reflected awareness of the lack of a clear mandate from power brokers. The new leader emphasized "collectivity," praised the work of his predecessor, and assured the military that "we will further see to it that our country's defense capacity is strengthened." On the other hand, Chernenko declared that "the most important source of the party's strength has been, is, and will be its contact with the masses," indicating that he would emphasize citizen involvement over a rigorous enforcement of discipline in attempting to cope with the system's sluggish performance in various areas. (*Pravda*, 14 February.)

The Politburo. Although Chernenko was widely regarded as a stopgap interim leader, he accumulated the formal trappings of power much more rapidly than had Andropov. Two weeks after his election as general secretary, it was disclosed that he had been named chairman of the Defense Council, the inner circle of the leadership that apparently constitutes the main decisionmaking body

on security policy and world affairs (BBC, 28 February). When the new Supreme Soviet met in April, he added the position of head of state, being elected as Andropov's successor as chairman (president) of the Presidium of the USSR's nominal parliament (see below).

Western observers tended to discount these additional titles as a matter of convenience for the leadership; "collective leadership" appeared to be much more than a slogan, with Chernenko's authority severely limited. Moreover, concern for the leader's health again emerged as a possibly destabilizing factor. Chernenko reportedly suffered from emphysema and possibly other ailments, and these reports were given credence by his usually frail appearance on public occasions. Never an effective speaker, he also appeared bumbling and uncertain; an embarrassing incident occurred during his televised Supreme Soviet election speech when he lost his place, causing a 30-second pause in the speech (*NYT*, 3 March). However, later in the year Chernenko appeared stronger both physically and politically. Following an impressive interview with an American correspondent, he chaired the October Central Committee plenum with reasonable vigor. Chernenko and Prime Minister Tikhonov introduced a new land reclamation project (*Pravda*, 24 October). Since this was a key addition to the "food program," it was noteworthy that Mikhail Gorbachev, party secretary for agriculture since 1978, was not listed as a speaker at the plenum. Gorbachev had previously spoken out against such a scheme, and it seemed likely that he had been overruled, sustaining a major political defeat.

Although Gorbachev retained the aura of heir apparent, his year was marked by political ups and downs. His role in Andropov's personnel shuffles surely made entrenched bureaucrats in both party and state wary of his ambitions. Further, his relative youth (at 53, the youngest Politburo member) may not have been an immediate advantage; the septuagenarian hierarchs were apparently unwilling to share power voluntarily with the next generation. Gorbachev's protocol position varied in the ceremonies connected with Andropov's funeral, yielding no clear clues as to his rank. He delivered the closing speech at the plenum that elected Chernenko, but this was not immediately reported in the central press, an omission that seemed calculated to undercut Gorbachev. Subsequently, the brief speech was released in pamphlet form and was reprinted in the party's theoretical journal (*Kommunist*, no. 3, February). The order of Supreme Soviet election speeches, usually considered a very authoritative protocol ranking, provided a more substantial indicator. Gorbachev was followed only by Tikhonov and Chernenko (*Pravda*, 28 February), giving him the apparent designation of number-two man in the party.

The first session of the new Supreme Soviet further enhanced Gorbachev's image by electing him chairman of the Foreign Affairs Commission of the Council of the Union (*Izvestiia*, 12 April), a position formerly held by the late Mikhail A. Suslov. Although there were some reports that Chernenko had retained responsibility for ideology, the weight of evidence seemed to point to Gorbachev's assumption of Suslov's old portfolio for ideology and international affairs; in any case, he had emerged as the party's de facto second secretary. The October Central Committee plenum brought an apparent downturn in Gorbachev's political fortunes (see above). Although the land reclamation scheme seemed something of a direct slap at Gorbachev, it was recalled by some observers that his apparent lack of enthusiasm for the 1982 food program had had no adverse effects upon his subsequent career. Whatever the power constellation at the October plenum, the dramatic announcement two weeks later of his forthcoming visit to Britain (Tass, 6 November) clearly reaffirmed his high standing in the leadership. In the line-up for the anniversary parade on Red Square, he occupied the same position as in the previous year, behind Grishin and ahead of Romanov (*NYT*, 8 November).

Party secretary Grigori Romanov also was upgraded in the transitional political jockeying. His visits to East Europe signaled his responsibility for bloc affairs, and he reportedly was assigned as the Secretariat's overseer of the police apparatuses. Further, his appearances at ceremonial military affairs (*Pravda*, 23 February, 10 March) indicated a broadened role in supervision of the armed forces, probably including oversight of the Main Political Administration. This latter role may have brought him into conflict with Defense Minister Ustinov. The ouster of Chief of Staff Nikolai V. Ogarkov (see below) occurred while Romanov was absent from Moscow. Notably, Ogarkov's reappearance at an important meeting in East Berlin in October (AP, 14 October) coincided with Ustinov's absence from public view in Moscow, reportedly due to illness.

First Deputy Prime Minister Geidar Aliev also expanded his portfolio. For a first deputy premier he assumed an unusually prominent role in foreign affairs, most notably with a highly publicized visit to Syria (*Pravda*, 12 March). As the Politburo's point man on educational reform, he delivered the major speech on the subject at the opening session of the new Supreme Soviet (*Izvestiia*, 14 April). He was reportedly also playing a major role in consumer affairs.

While these younger Politburo members exercised greater weight in the party councils, Foreign Minister Gromyko and Defense Minister Ustinov appeared the most powerful figures in the transitional leadership. In the months following Chernenko's accession, Gromyko seemed to hold near total control over the regime's foreign policy, and his status was confirmed when he delivered the major address at the November anniversary celebration in the Kremlin (*NYT*, 7 November). Ustinov's powerful position was further enhanced by the September ouster of Marshal Ogarkov, whose frictions with the defense minister had surfaced publicly in recent years. However, Ustinov vanished from public view after 27 September and missed the 7 November parade in Red Square, a ceremony at which the defense minister normally plays a prominent role. The official explanation was that Ustinov was ill; privately Moscow sources identified his illness as flu. First Deputy Defense Minister Marshal Sergei Sokolov substituted for Ustinov as reviewer of the troops (ibid., 8 November). Later unofficial reports suggested that Ustinov had suffered a stroke (ibid., 16 November). As usual, the Soviets had attempted to conceal the seriousness of the illness of a member of the hierarchy; six weeks after the 7 November parade, Ustinov died (Tass, 21 December), reportedly due to heart failure. He was succeeded by Marshal Sokolov (*Pravda*, 23 December; *Izvestiia*, 23 December).

Two candidate members of the Politburo attained greater prominence during the year. KGB head Viktor Chebrikov was named a marshal of the Soviet Union, the first police chief so honored since Lavrenty Beria (*Los Angeles Times*, 20 April). Party secretary for heavy industry Vladimir Dolgikh was assigned the prestigious role of Lenin anniversary speaker (*Pravda*, 23 April), indicating that his career, on hold during Andropov's tenure, was on the upturn.

While these developments marked some changes in the Politburo's pecking order, the most impressive feature of inner party politics following Chernenko's election was the total absence of change in composition of the leadership. Three

Central Committee meetings during the year yielded no alteration whatever in the three highest party levels—full and candidate Politburo members and the Secretariat. At least at the top, party renewal had come to a grinding halt, and the delicate balance on the post-Andropov Politburo seemed more productive of stalemate than of stability. Events in the latter part of the year, particularly the sidelining and subsequent demise of Ustinov, seemed likely to enhance the position of Chernenko, and he did display a more assertive leadership. However, Chernenko appeared frail at Kremlin ceremonies honoring Ustinov and missed the funeral (*NYT*, 23 and 25 December), reviving doubts about his stamina and his potential to emerge as something more than a weak interim leader.

Party Organization and Personnel. The brief Andropov era was marked by the most vigorous shake-up of party personnel in more than two decades, with particular emphasis upon the key regional secretaries. Thirty-two of the 157 regional secretaries were replaced, including 18 of the 120 considered automatically qualified for the Central Committee by virtue of their posts (AP, 2 February). A few regional secretaries were dismissed due to blatant corruption or incompetence, but the major thrust of the campaign was the introduction of younger men into positions of responsibility, in line with Andropov's August 1983 call for generational turnover. Available data on the replacements indicated that the newcomers may have been, on average, as much as twenty years younger than their predecessors. But some of the openings occurred due to promotion of incumbents to positions in Moscow.

Some of the new appointees had been second secretaries in their regions; some were shifted from lower-ranking posts in other regions; others were transferred from Moscow to the provinces. In general, the new men tended to have more experience, either direct or supervisory, related to the economy than had their predecessors at the time of appointment. This reflected Andropov's overriding interest in recharging the economy; the party leader evidently aimed to create, virtually from scratch, an organizational tail, based largely on technocratic qualifications, to buttress his leadership. Regular party committee elections in late 1983 and early 1984 provided a special opportunity for replacements, and the turnovers almost assumed purge proportions in the last weeks of Andropov's life.

The election of Chernenko was interpreted by many Western observers as a reaction of frightened officeholders to this rigorous process of party renewal, with the leadership of the Moscow city, the Ukraine, and Kazakhstan organizations especially affected. Although party renewal slowed to a crawl under Chernenko, the Andropov appointees remained in place, and substantial revitalization and realignment of power relationships at the party's middle levels were carried out. But the full impact of these personnel changes would perhaps not be felt until the reconstitution of the Central Committee at the Twenty-seventh CPSU Congress in 1986.

Clientelism, diminished but certainly not eliminated under Brezhnev's "stability of cadres" policy, was evident in some of the appointments. Principal beneficiary among the successors was party secretary Mikhail Gorbachev. With his clients already ensconced in his native Stavropol and in Krasnodar, he added the key regions of Volgograd and Chelyabinsk to his patronage network. Vladimir Kalashnikov, RSFSR minister of land reclamation and water resources and a former Gorbachev subordinate in Stavropol, was named first secretary of Volgograd *obkom* (*Pravda*, 25 January). Gennadi Vedernikov, an official in the Central Committee apparat and another former subordinate of Gorbachev's in Stavropol, was assigned to Chelyabinsk (ibid., 8 January). The important Rostov province organization apparently remained in friendly hands. Longtime *obkom* first secretary Ivan Bondarenko, a Suslov client, retired "for reasons of health" and was replaced by Aleksandr Vlasov, former first secretary in Chechen-Ingush province (ibid., 26 July).

Gorbachev's influence was also evident elsewhere. He gained a foothold in Tadzhikistan, where Yuri Belov, an official in the Central Committee Agriculture Department, assumed the post of union-republic party second secretary (*Kommunist Tadzhikistana*, 31 January). Earlier, a Gorbachev client had been installed as head of the Central Committee's chancellery. Nikolai E. Kruchina, deputy head of the Central Committee Agriculture Department, had been promoted to head of the Central Committee Administration of Affairs Department (*Pravda*, 3 December 1983).

When Mikhail Ponomarev, 65, first secretary of Vladimir *obkom*, moved up to a deputy chairmanship of the Party Control Committee, party secretary Grigori Romanov managed to replace Ponomarev with one of his clients. Ratmir Bobovikov, 57, formerly chairman of the Leningrad *oblast* Soviet Executive Committee, was Ponomarev's successor in Vladimir (ibid., 17 December 1983). Another former Romanov subordinate in Leningrad, Vadim A. Medvedev, had been appointed in the summer of 1983 to head the Central Committee Department of Science and Educational Institutions.

Party Control Committee chairman Mikhail S. Solomentsev solidified his dominance of the party watchdog agency with the appointment of a longtime associate, Chelyabinsk *obkom* first secretary Mikhail Voropaev, 64, as one of its deputy chairmen (ibid., 8 January). Mikhail Ponomarev was also named a deputy head of the Party Control Committee (ibid., 17 December 1983). Nikolai Konovalov, 76, first secretary of Kaliningrad *obkom*, was granted membership on the Party Control Committee, opening his former post to the province's second secretary, Dimitri Romanin (Tass, 14 January).

Latvia's party leader was also kicked upstairs to an honorific post. Avgust E. Voss, 67, was elected chairman of the USSR Supreme Soviet of Nationalities. His replacement as Latvian Communist Party first secretary was Boris Pugo, 46, head of the union-republic KGB since 1980 (*Sovetskaia Latvia*, 15 April; *FBIS*, 1 May).

East Kazakhstan province first secretary Aleksandr Protozanov, 69, retired and was replaced by Anatoli Malkin, chairman of the Kazakh Republic People's Control Committee (*Pravda*, 20 December 1983). Ivan Skiba, successor to Nikolai Kruchina as deputy head of the Central Committee Agriculture Department, was succeeded as first secretary of Ivano-Frankovsk *obkom* by the second secretary, I. A. Lyakhov (ibid., 23 December 1983). Grigori Pavlov, 70, first secretary of Lipetsk *obkom*, retired and was replaced by Y. A. Manayenkov, second secretary of the Tambov province party committee (ibid., 15 January).

Evgeny Sizenko, 52, first secretary in Bryansk province, was named USSR minister of the meat and dairy industry. His post in Bryansk was filled by A. F. Voistrichenko, who had been serving as second secretary (ibid., 29 January). In the Ukraine, the Vinnitsa first secretaryship, left vacant by the appointment of Vasili Taratuta as ambassador to Algeria, was filled by L. L. Krivoruchko (ibid., 13 January). Boris Nikolsky, a secretary of the Moscow city party committee, was appointed second secretary of the Georgian Communist Party (*Izvestiia*, 7 January).

An interesting and symbolic event was the readmission to party membership of Vyacheslav Molotov, 94, Stalin's longtime deputy, 22 years after his expulsion (*WP*, 6 July).

Amid the flurry of personnel changes, the usual calls for improved party organizational performance were repeated. A front-page editorial in *Pravda* on 12 March called for closer linkage "with the masses," a favorite theme of party leader Chernenko, and noted "omissions and errors in the style and methods of leadership." The editorial pointed to the continuation of the practice, severely condemned for many years by the central leadership, of proliferating committees and resolutions. The Alagirsky *raikom* in the North Ossetian province was cited as an especially egregious example. Two weeks earlier, another front-page editorial had called for party leadership in the campaigns for "enhancing discipline and organization in all spheres of society's life" (*Pravda*, 25 February). However, the practice of *podmena*, direct party interference in the regular functioning of state agencies, was also frequently criticized. Another front-page *Pravda* editorial (5 July) said that party committees should allow soviets and economic organizations "independence and initiative in resolving all questions under their jurisdiction." Two party organizations in Kazakhstan were cited for violations, the Volodarsky *raikom* in Kokchetav *oblast* and the Talgarsky *raikom* in Alma Ata province.

The Komsomol, headed by Andropov appointee Viktor Mishin, drew considerable criticism following Chernenko's accession. A front-page *Krasnaia zvezda* editorial on 9 June noted criticisms of the Komsomol's work in communist education of the armed forces. A report on a June Politburo meeting concerned with the youth organization warned that "there must be no acceptance of the shortcomings that exist in the leadership of the Komsomol and in the activity of Komsomol organizations" (*Krasnaia zvezda*, 29 June). A Central Committee resolution in July charged that "the Komsomol Central Committee and the local Komsomol organs are only slowly restructuring the style and work of their activity and are allowing substantial shortcomings to occur in work with Komsomol cadres" (*Pravda*, 8 July).

Meanwhile, work continued on the new party program, scheduled for adoption at the Twenty-seventh CPSU Congress, to replace the 1961 document, which Andropov had admitted was outdated.

An article by academician P. Lopata noted that in the program's formulation "the party assigns the central, decisive place to economic tasks" (*Krasnaia zvezda*, 24 May).

The Moldavian Communist Party, long a political preserve of first Brezhnev and then Chernenko, had its image refurbished under the new leadership. A December 1983 Central Committee resolution had sharply criticized the Moldavian party for "bureaucratic methods of leadership." At the beginning of March, the press reported a speech by Moldavia's first secretary, Semyon Grossu, that referred to the December resolution but pointed to the republic's success in meeting industrial plans (*Pravda*, 1 March). Later in the month, Grossu was awarded the Order of Lenin on the occasion of his fiftieth birthday (BBC, 19 March). Chernenko's hold on the rehabilitated Moldavian organization evidently remained strong. Nikolai Merenishchev, 65, second secretary of the Moldavian party, was relieved of his post and replaced by V. I. Smirnov, an official of the CPSU Central Committee Cadres Department (*Sovetskaia Moldavia*, 15 August).

Government. The year's most spectacular personnel change occurred in the Defense Ministry. Marshal Nikolai Ogarkov, 67, first deputy minister of defense and chief of staff of the armed forces, was abruptly dismissed and replaced in both posts by his deputy, Marshal Sergei Akhromeyev, 61 (*Krasnaia zvezda*, 7 September). The suddenness of the shift was underscored by the appearance of a press report on Ogarkov's ceremonial farewell to Finland's top soldier (*Izvestiia*, 6 September) almost simultaneously with the announcement of his ouster. The dramatic move came less than 48 hours after General Secretary Chernenko's return from his summer vacation. Prime Minister Tikhonov and party secretary for military affairs Romanov were not in Moscow when the change was announced (*NYT*, 8 September). Romanov's absence led to speculation that Ogarkov might have been involved in a Politburo power struggle. The official announcement said that he was being transferred to another post, but his new assignment was unspecified, suggesting the possibility of a humiliating demotion. However, in October Ogarkov resurfaced in East Berlin, where he met East German leader Erich Honecker (AP, 13 October); it seemed likely that he had been given an important job in the Warsaw Treaty Organization.

Ogarkov had served in his high posts since 1977, gaining an unusually high level of public attention for a professional soldier. He had participated in the SALT II negotiations in 1978–1979 and served as principal spokesman for the Soviet government on the 1983 downing of a South Korean airliner, hosting an almost unprecedented press conference for Western and Soviet correspondents. Rather outspoken and independent, he had appeared at times to be at odds with the political leadership but was widely regarded as the probable successor to Dimitri Ustinov as defense minister. Ogarkov's successor, Marshal Akhromeyev, had followed a steady if unspectacular route to the top, moving from field commands to the General Staff, where he served over the past decade as deputy chief and then first deputy chief, attaining marshal's rank along the way and gaining admission to full membership in the CPSU Central Committee in 1983.

Some early Western speculation on Ogarkov's ouster pointed to the possibility that he was belatedly made the scapegoat for the Korean airliner incident in 1983. However, an unnamed "senior Soviet diplomat" was quoted by U.S. officials as saying that Ogarkov was dismissed because he was showing "unpartylike tendencies" (*NYT*, 13 September). Western analysts viewed a May interview with Ogarkov as possible evidence of a policy conflict. In the interview, Ogarkov had described a "qualitative leap in the development of conventional means of destruction," implying the need for significant allocation of resources to the manufacture of such arms. He quoted an April statement by Chernenko that "the present situation requires us to make constant, all-round efforts to safeguard the country's security," bluntly adding, "This demand must be unconditionally fulfilled" (*Krasnaia zvezda*, 9 May).

Some significant personnel changes also occurred in governmental sectors not directly related to the military. Barely noticed amid the publicity surrounding "party renewal" was a substantial overhaul of the governmental bureaucracy under Andropov. As of the new Supreme Soviet's first session in April, 25 newcomers had taken a seat on the Council of Ministers since Andropov's accession in November 1982, accounting for more than one-fourth of the positions with ministerial rank. However, reflecting the stabilization associated with the Chernenko leadership, only minor changes were announced at the April meeting of the Supreme Soviet, where 115 members of the Council of Ministers were confirmed in their posts, including 63 ministers, 22 heads of state committees, the first deputy and deputy prime ministers, and the chairmen of the 15 union-republic Councils of Ministers (*Radio Liberty Research*, 16 April).

Boris Shcherbina, 64, was promoted to a deputy chairmanship of the Council of Ministers (*Izvestiia*, 15 January). Shcherbina had served as USSR minister for construction of petroleum and gas industry enterprises since 1973, following eleven years as first secretary of Tyumen *obkom*. His important ministerial post was filled by the appointment of Vladimir Chirskov, 48 (ibid., 23 February).

A veteran member of the Council of Ministers Presidium, Deputy Premier Leonid Kostandov, 68, died of a heart attack in September while on an official visit to East Germany (Tass, 5 September; AP, 5 September). Kostandov had served as a deputy prime minister since November 1980 and, prior to that appointment, had been minister of the chemical industry for fifteen years. Kostandov was replaced by Yakov P. Ryabov, chairman of the State Committee on Foreign Economic Relations; his appointment as deputy prime minister was confirmed by the Supreme Soviet in November (*Izvestiia*, 30 November).

Evgeny Sizenko, 52, first secretary of the Bryansk province party committee, was named in January as USSR minister of the meat and dairy industry (*Pravda*, 29 January).

Boris Kravtsov, chief prosecutor of the Russian Republic, moved up to the position of USSR minister of justice, succeeding Vladimir Terebilov, who had been justice minister since 1970. Terebilov was named chairman of the USSR Supreme Court, replacing Lev Smirnov, who retired. (*NYT*, 23 April.)

Ivan Laptev, 50, deputy editor of *Pravda* since 1982, was appointed chief editor of *Izvestiia*, succeeding Lev Tolkunov, 65, who was elected chairman of the Supreme Soviet's Council of the Union (*Radio Liberty Research*, 19 June).

Two union-republics added momentum to the general process of generational transfer by selecting younger prime ministers. Valter Klauson, 70, chairman of the Estonian Republic Council of Ministers since 1961, retired and was replaced by Boris Saul, 51, a secretary of the Estonian Communist Party Central Committee (*Pravda*, 19 January). In Kazakhstan, the new prime minister was Nursultan Nazarbaev, 44, promoted from a secretaryship in the Kazakh Communist Party Central Committee (*Kazakhstanskaia pravda*, 28 April). Nazarbaev succeeded Sattar N. Imashev, who died in February at age 58 (*Radio Liberty Research*, 2 April).

Supreme Soviet. Elections for the USSR Supreme Soviet were held on 4 March. The single slate of candidates endorsed by officially approved "public organizations" rolled to the usual landslide. The election commission reported that 184,006,373 voters, 99.99 percent of those eligible, took part; the official slate won 99.94 percent of votes cast for the Council of the Union and 99.92 percent in the various political subdivisions for the Council of Nationalities (*Izvestiia*, 9 March).

The usual balance between party and nonparty members was maintained, with 71.4 percent of the deputies being either full or candidate members of the CPSU. Workers accounted for 35.2 percent and collective farmers for 16.1 percent of the deputies; 32.8 percent of those elected were women. Holdover deputies made up nearly 60 percent of the total, and according to Electoral Commission Chairman Georgi Markov, more than 60 nationalities were represented. (Tass, 6 March; *FBIS*, 7 March.)

The first session of the Eleventh Supreme Soviet was held in Moscow, 11–13 April. On the recommendation of the CPSU Central Committee, General Secretary Chernenko was unanimously elected chairman of the Presidium of the Supreme Soviet, thus becoming head of state two months after his selection as party leader (*Izvestiia*, 12 April). The nominating speech was delivered by party secretary Gorbachev, a clear indication of his upgraded status in the governing hierarchy. Gorbachev praised Chernenko as a "tested leader of the Leninist type" but stressed the convenience of having the general secretary as head of state. This double officeholding, Gorbachev said, "is of tremendous significance to the execution of the Soviet Union's foreign policy" (ibid.; *NYT*, 12 April). In his brief acceptance speech, Chernenko called for setting in motion the "many untapped reserves of the soviets" and hailed recent initiatives "in the field of the economy and ideological and political education" (Tass, 11 March; *FBIS*, 12 March). After a formal vote on the composition of the USSR Council of Ministers, the assembled Supreme Soviet deputies heard a major speech by First Deputy Prime Minister Geidar Aliev on school reform (*Izvestiia*, 14 April) and adopted a resolution "on the main avenues of the reform of general education and vocational schools."

The first meeting of the newly constituted Supreme Soviet Presidium featured a speech by General Secretary Chernenko calling for an expansion of the role of the soviets "in economic and social construction and the intensification of their responsibility for the solution of social questions and fuller satisfaction of the working people's requirements" (Moscow domestic service, 13 April; *FBIS*, 13 April). The speech accorded with Chernenko's oft-repeated insistence on closer contact with "the masses," but such talk had frequently been heard before, and it was not clear that the soviets would gain any increment of real power.

Lev Tolkunov, 65, moved from the editorship of *Izvestiia* to the chairmanship of the Council of the Union, replacing Aleksei Shitikov, 72. Avgust Voss, 67, first secretary of the Latvian party since 1966, succeeded Vitalijs Rubenis, 70, as chairman of the Supreme Soviet of Nationalities. (*Radio Liberty Research*, 16 April.)

Among the standing commissions, the most significant appointment was that of Mikhail Gorbachev as chairman of the Council of the Union's Commission on Foreign Affairs. This post was held for many years by Mikhail Suslov, and the assignment was indicative of Gorbachev's expanded responsibilities in the CPSU Central Committee Secretariat. Boris Ponomarev was re-elected to the corresponding chairmanship in the Council of Nationalities.

Egor Ligachev, party cadres secretary, was elected to the important chairmanship of the Council of the Union Legislative Proposals Commission; the corresponding post in the Council of Nationalities was filled by Vladimir Mironov, recently installed first secretary of Donetsk *obkom*. Other key selectees for chairmanships included Plan and Budget Commission: (Union) Vitali Masol, Gosplan chairman of the Ukrainian Republic; (Nationalities) Nikolai Maslennikov, Gosplan chairman of the Russian Republic; Agro-Industrial Complex Commission: (Union) Georgi Razumovsky, first secretary of Krasnodar *obkom*; (Nationalities) Ivan Mozvogoi, Ukrainian Communist Party secretary for agriculture; Youth Affairs Commission: (Union) Anatoli Logunov, rector of Moscow State University; (Nationalities) Kenes Aukhadiev, first secretary of Alma Ata *obkom*; Commission on Nature Conservation and Natural Resources: (Union) Semyon Grossu, first secretary of the Moldavian Communist Party; (Nationalities) Vasili Grebenyuk, first deputy chairman of the Kazakh Republic Council of Ministers (*Izvestiia*, 12 April).

Domestic Affairs. The condition of the economy attracted most attention during the year, as evidence of intractable problems mounted. Labor productivity remained a major concern, and the limited reforms in management introduced under Andropov were continued, with uncertain results. Agriculture remained the biggest problem area, and the farms recorded another massive shortfall in grain production. An ambitious program for the draining of swampland was announced, apparently as an alternative to fundamental reform in the agricultural sector. An extensive long-range school reform program was adopted, designed in part to alleviate the shortage of skilled labor. Meanwhile, the anticorruption drive launched by Andropov continued, albeit with less urgency. Dissidence, now reduced to a minor irritant, remained a target, and the regime displayed a renewed determination to enforce cultural conformity. Against the pragmatic emphasis of the brief Andropov era, the new leadership seemed committed to a more ideological orientation in the organization and control of society.

Economy. The limited economic experiment adopted in the summer of 1983 got under way at the beginning of the year as the usual retrospectives on annual performance emphasized continuing shortcomings. Labor productivity had reportedly risen by 4.0 percent in 1983, against only 2.8 percent in 1982, but much of this gain had occurred during the first quarter, evidently induced by the shock of Andropov's discipline drive, which lost steam in the course of the year. A discreet silence was maintained concerning the grain crop; clearly, another poor harvest had been registered. And a Council of Ministers statement in the last week of January warned that several ministries would have to "drastically improve" the organization of their work and stated that "substantial shortcomings and bottlenecks" still afflicted many areas of the economy (BBC, 30 January).

New party leader Chernenko, in his Supreme Soviet campaign speech, set the figure for the 1983 harvest at 190 million tons, a result achieved, he said, despite the fact that "we were unlucky with the weather." Chernenko endorsed the economic experiment, stressing the party's emphasis upon "a large-scale improvement of economic management and restructuring of the economic mechanism." Further, he said that forms of management "should correspond to present-day demands. This will be, undoubtedly, facilitated by the current economic experiments." At the same time, Chernenko called for a strengthening of centralized management and planning but said that "national-level economic bodies" should direct "all their resources at resolving the questions of really key importance to the country." (*Pravda*, 3 March.)

The economic experiment, which aimed at increased labor productivity via incentives and rationalization of production through the granting of limited autonomy to enterprises, seemed initially to have engendered confusion by rendering economic management even more complex. And the cautious limitation of the reform to selected enterprises naturally produced frictions between the target firms and the vast majority of unreformed ones. It seemed quite likely that, like economic reforms of the past, the experiment would finally result in even more centralized control (*Radio Liberty Research*, 16 April). One particular problem concerned the provision that selected enterprises could temporarily fix prices on new consumer goods; this rationalization of market activity was undercut by the absence of any reform in the system of material supply (*Ekonomicheskaia gazeta*, no. 10). And a *Pravda* editorial (10 March) admitted that, not unexpectedly, many organizations involved in the experiment were playing it safe, unwilling to take the risks necessary for the success of the innovations.

The midyear economic report showed mixed results. Industrial output reportedly rose by 4.5 percent, with productivity in industry up by 4.2 percent. However, labor productivity in industry was below average in Turkmenistan, Tadzhikistan, Moldavia, and Uzbekistan, and shortfalls in plan fulfillment were recorded in the timber and paper industries and in fruits and vegetable farming. The report noted that "there are many unreliable suppliers among the enterprises producing fertilizers, construction materials, and consumer goods." (*Pravda*, 23 July.)

There were, however, some bright spots in the generally dismal economic picture. The Soviets appeared to have made substantial strides in technological adaptation, with the machine-tool industry, supplier of military hardware and consumer durables, a major beneficiary. Tightened Western controls had not appreciably slowed the illegal Soviet acquisition of technology from advanced capitalist countries. Technological advance was spearheaded by the recently bolstered State Committee for Science and Technology, under Deputy Prime Minister Guri Marchuk (*WSJ*, 24 July).

In November, the government reported that industrial output rose 4.4 percent in the first ten months of 1984 over the corresponding period in 1983; labor productivity was reportedly up 4.1 percent (AP, 14 November).

Another bright spot was the projected completion of track laying for the Baikal-Amur Mainline (BAM) railway by early November. However, even if the important rail line were completed ahead of schedule, as indicated in a March Central Committee resolution, there would probably still be a delay of at least a year in the opening of the line for fulltime operation (BBC, 27 March).

Oil production was a source of growing concern for Soviet planners during the year. Gosplan head Nikolai Baibakov, in Budapest for a meeting of Council for Mutual Economic Assistance (CMEA) planners, said that East European countries could not expect future increases in Soviet oil deliveries. "The shifting of oil production to the North has implied serious problems," Baibakov said. "We are to increase production but at a slower pace and with extra costs." (Ibid., 3 April.) In the same week, a continuing shortfall in production at the vast Tyumen oilfield was reported (*Pravda*, 4 April). The poor performance was blamed on the method of extraction, production of poor-quality equipment, late deliveries, and poor living conditions of the workers. Earlier, "inadequate organizational work" had been cited as the principal reason for a shortfall of 3 million tons in the oilfield's production in 1983, the first time that Tyumen province had failed to meet its production goal (*Sotsialicheskaia industriia*, 28 February).

However depressing the performance in some other areas of the economy, the most pressing problem area remained agriculture. Over the five-year period 1979–1983, grain production reportedly increased by only 4 percent, compared with 18 percent in general economic growth (*Vestnik statistiki*, no. 2; *Current History*, October). Private plot production has declined from 35 to 25 percent of foodstuffs over the past quarter-century (BBC, 9 April), apparently due largely to lack of logistical support. The prevalence of drought conditions in many areas has been a growing problem. And long-standing evidence of waste and inefficiency, absence of incentives, poor transportation and storage facilities, and the stultifying effects of bureaucratic centralization are still apparent. The Soviet agricultural crisis has obviously intensified during the six-year tenure of Mikhail Gorbachev as overseer of the farm sector, although results might have been quite different had the party secretary been given a free hand to carry out fundamental reforms. Apparently successful reform experiments in Georgia,

Azerbaijan, and Moldavia have not been generalized, probably due to opposition from the entrenched central bureaucracy.

Gorbachev's favored alternatives have evidently centered on the decentralization of management and the promotion of additional incentives. A major element in this approach has been the *zveno* system of organization of farm labor. Prospects for expansion of this incentive-oriented experiment seemed promising during the first half of 1984. A Central Committee resolution in January praised the Glazunovka *raion* in Oryol province for putting all its arable farming on the basis of collective contracts (ibid., 30 January). Gorbachev's speech to an all-union conference on problems of the agro-industrial complex in March seemed to give a major boost to expansion of the zveno system (*Pravda*, 27 March).

A very different approach was adopted at the October Central Committee plenum. The discouraging outlook for the grain harvest, expected to reach no more than 170 million tons, probably inspired the special session of the party body. General Secretary Chernenko said that the 1984 grain crop would fall substantially short of plan and that the supply of feed grains would be tight. The reclamation program adopted at the plenum envisages a 60 percent expansion in the combined area of irrigation and drained swamps by the year 2000. According to Chernenko, implementation of the plan will enable the Soviet Union to count regularly on nearly one-half of its agricultural output regardless of weather (*NYT*, 24 October). Although the plan appeared to be an extension of the food program adopted in 1982 and followed a Politburo decision earlier in the year calling for an expansion of agricultural land through irrigation or swamp drainage, it clearly gave priority to the pouring of more investment into agriculture over the organizational reform of that sector apparently favored by Gorbachev. Notably, twelve officials in addition to Chernenko and Tikhonov spoke on the reclamation plan at the October plenum, but Gorbachev was not listed as a speaker (*Pravda*, 24 October).

Faced with bleak harvest prospects, the Soviet Union had already pushed its purchases from the United States to near record levels. By mid-August, the Soviets had purchased 13.7 million metric tons of corn and wheat for 1983–1984 and 7 million metric tons for the second-year of the five-year sales agreement, beginning 1 October (*WP*, 18 August).

For the foreseeable future, the overall prospect was for more tinkering with economic mechanisms; bureaucratic resistance and the lopsided structure of the economy seemed inimical to fundamental reform. Given the pervasive inefficiency of nonmilitary sectors of the economy, the extremely high levels of investment devoted to both armaments and agriculture, and the marked slowing of growth rates, the general prospects for Soviet consumers over the remaining years of the 1980s were bleak indeed.

School Reform. A major reform of the Soviet school system was adopted, and the first phase of its implementation began with the fall term of the 1984–85 academic year. The idea of school reform had been introduced at the June 1983 Central Committee plenum dealing with ideology; the subsequent formulation and publicizing of the plan proceeded under the general direction of First Deputy Prime Minister Geidar Aliev. At the outset of the year, the Central Committee issued a draft entitled "Basic Guidelines for the Reform of General Educational and Vocational Schools" (*Pravda*, 4 January). After some revisions, mostly minor, the final draft was approved by the USSR Supreme Soviet at its April session (ibid., 13 April).

Major aims of the reform plan were the revival of ideological awareness among young people and reduction in the deficit of skilled labor. Years of required schooling are to be increased from ten to eleven, with entry at six years of age instead of seven. Special attention will be devoted in the tenth and eleventh years of schooling to "mastering mass trades required for material production" (BBC, 5 January), and most secondary school graduates will spend at least a year in a special vocational school. In recent years, Soviet officials have bemoaned both the shortage of skilled labor and an oversupply of intelligentsia; lack of the proper "psychological mind-set" has been blamed for the failure to develop and use new technology (*CSM*, 4 January). With this in mind, a revision of textbooks is slated to upgrade ideological and vocational training.

The new vocational curriculum was to be introduced during the 1984–85 schoolyear, and in the following year, new rules for pupils are to be introduced, together with a new system of norms and marks for behavior and for diligence in studying and carrying out socially useful labor (*Radio Liberty Research*, 8 June). The reform plan also contains a new emphasis upon the teaching of written and spoken Russian in non-Russian areas. Years of required training for teachers are to be increased from four to five, and teacher salaries are to be raised as much as 35 percent (*NYT*, 13 April).

The first two years are envisioned as essentially preparatory to full implementation of the program, and much room has been left for revision as the plan is implemented. It is anticipated that the full effects of the initiative will not be felt before the mid-1990s. The school plan reflects Yuri Andropov's drive for the revitalization of Soviet society, but the momentum for this reform was not slowed by the accession of a less aggressive leader, perhaps in large part because the hard-driving Aliev was in charge. Whether the momentum can be maintained to achieve a genuine overhaul of the school system depends, of course, upon those variables that render problematic all Soviet reform efforts.

Environment. During the year the Soviet press displayed heightened concern for ecological problems; this was apparently also a carryover from the Andropov era. A major focus of attention was the 1983 Dniester River disaster. In September 1983 a dike that held back saline wastes from a potassium factory burst, pouring polluted water into the Dniester basin, causing the loss of 2,000 tons of fish, destruction to plant life, and water shortages for some cities, including Odessa. In April, Water Resources Minister Nikolai Vasiliev reported that as a result of cleanup efforts, the waters of the Dniester were now "nearly as pure as before" (*Izvestiia*, 18 April). There were persistent reports of a cover-up in the aftermath of the Dniester disaster, and a wide-ranging investigation looked into the activities of several prominent officials in the Ukraine (ibid., 1 July).

Considerable publicity was also accorded industrial pollution in the Leningrad, Chelyabinsk, and Zaporozhye areas, and it was reported that a coordinating center had been opened in Tallinn to promote a campaign against pollution of the Baltic (BBC, 19 April). Continuation of the open discussion of such problems, given impetus by Andropov, was notable, but in the absence of a punitive drive by the political leadership, few industrial managers were expected to give priority to environmental concerns over plan fulfillment.

Anticorruption Campaign. The early months of Chernenko's leadership gave little indication of a letup in the anticorruption campaign that had been one of the hallmarks of Andropov's tenure, perhaps because the drive had been widely popular with the Soviet masses. Indeed, the promise of correction of flagrant abuses had been crucial to the general expectation of systemic revitalization, a legacy from Andropov that the less than charismatic Chernenko could ignore only at his own political peril (*NYT*, 21 November). The new party leader gave no encouragement to members of the "old guard" who might have hoped for a return to the free and easy ways of the late Brezhnev era. The vigorous Mikhail Solomentsev had restored the Party Control Committee to its assigned function as the CPSU's watchdog against official misconduct after years of lethargy and ineffectiveness under the late Arvid Pelshe, and the agency took a major role in the campaign, alongside the KGB and the uniformed police (MVD).

During the first two months following Chernenko's election, a mixed array of officials in the Bashkir Autonomous Republic, Khabarovsk, and Kiev and a former deputy minister of agricultural machine building were ensnared in the anticorruption drive. In early May, Bella Borodkina, former director of the restaurant and canteen trust in the Black Sea resort of Gelendzhik, was sentenced to death for giving and receiving bribes (BBC, 3 May). Gelendzhik is in Krasnodar *krai*, notorious for corruption under its former first secretary Sergei F. Medunov, a Brezhnev favorite; this territory had been singled out as the first target of Andropov's cleanup campaign in June 1982, five months before his election as general secretary.

At the beginning of the summer, the media directed heavy fire at party officials in two union republics. It was charged that Uzbekistan had failed to meet its plan targets due to favoritism in appointments and protection of incompetent and corrupt officials. In Latvia, over 250 people had been charged with embezzlement, and more than 100 officials expelled from the party for abuse of position (ibid., 29 June).

Events in July indicated a fresh impetus for the drive, amid speculation that certain elements of the leadership were forcing the pace and overriding Chernenko on the issue. The execution of Yuri Sokolov, former manager of Moscow's Gastronom No. 1, was announced (*Vechernaia Moskva*, 13 July). Sokolov had been sentenced to death for black-market dealings in November 1983. The food store official had reputedly been close to the Brezhnev family, particularly the late leader's daughter Galina Churbanova, and it was believed that Chernenko had been responsible for the unusual delay in carrying out the court's sentence. In the same week, a scandal involving Roskontsert, the agency responsible for orchestras and concert bookings in the Russian Republic, was revealed. Ten orchestras had been reorganized, and six officials of the Irkutsk Philharmonic had received sentences of three to thirteen years for corruption (BBC, 18 July).

Two days after the announcement about Sokolov, a major scandal in Rostov was disclosed. Seventy-six people, including officials of the RSFSR Ministry of Trade, had been arrested for black-market activities (*Izvestiia*, 15 July). A *Pravda* leader on the following day reaffirmed the party's commitment to the anticorruption campaign, calling for "an uncompromising struggle" against "abuse of power and conceit, bureaucracy and overcautiousness, and other vices."

The drive seemed to lose some of its steam in the latter part of the year and certainly was no longer borne along by the sense of urgency that had characterized Andropov's tenure and the first months under Chernenko. Although there had been no official announcement on the matter, it was reported that criminal proceedings against two of Brezhnev's close associates, former Krasnodar first secretary Medunov and former minister of internal affairs Nikolai A. Shchelokov, had been quietly dropped (*Radio Free Europe Research*, 21 September).

Despite such indications that Chernenko maintained some reservations about the "restoration of discipline," at the October People's Control Conference, he publicly identified himself with the campaign and endorsed the measures taken:

> In recent years, we have really gotten down to putting our house in order, so to speak. The task is precisely formulated: to put an end to bribetaking and speculation, to the squandering and theft of socialist property, to abuse of office. We have sharply stepped up the struggle for strengthening law and order, for improving the work of our law enforcement agencies, for raising the responsibility of leading workers for the overall state of organization and discipline. In this direction, the central bodies of the party and state have taken quite a few practical measures, in some cases quite severe ones, as for example in the case of a number of workers in Krasnodar *krai*, Uzbekistan, and Rostov *oblast*. Our people approve this line and support it. [*Pravda*, 6 October; *FBIS*, 9 October.]

An interesting development on the "law and order" front was a new departure in the practice of denunciation. Cards for the reporting of offenses

and antisocial behavior had reportedly been distributed in Kiev in 1981 and in Krasnodar in 1983. In April, a Russian émigré newspaper published a photocopy of a card that has been distributed by the police in Lithuania. The card provides a checklist of crimes and "other violations of public order and the rules of socialist communal life," making it unnecessary for the anonymous informer to write out a denunciation (*Russkaia mysl*, 5 April; *Radio Liberty Research*, 11 April).

Dissent. Although organized dissidence had been reduced to negligible proportions by KGB-led repression over the previous eighteen years, regime leaders seemed more determined than ever to stamp out any expression of unorthodox opinion. While the "administrative organs" maintained relentless pressure upon less prominent dissidents, the attention of the world outside the USSR was riveted upon the fate of Andrei Sakharov.

Chief spokesman for the dissidents throughout the 1970s, Sakharov had been seized by the KGB in January 1980 and exiled to Gorky, a "closed" city, and has been in effect under house arrest since that time. A Sakharov article in the journal *Foreign Affairs* critical of the regime's international policies had evoked severe condemnation of him by the Soviet media in late 1983. Faced with official refusal to let his wife, Elena Bonner, go abroad for medical treatment, Sakharov began a hunger strike 2 May. Meanwhile, it was disclosed in Moscow that Bonner had been charged with anti-Soviet slander and might face a treason charge as well (BBC, 9 May). On 7 May, Sakharov was removed from his home in Gorky (AP, 21 May), and two weeks later a government spokesman issued a virulent personal attack on Bonner (*Izvestiia*, 20 May), who had also threatened to go on a hunger strike.

A Tass statement at the end of May implied that Sakharov had given up his hunger strike and suggested that he was carrying on his normal daily routine in good spirits but gave no indication of where Sakharov and Bonner were being held (*Los Angeles Times*, 31 May). Friends believed that they were confined in a psychiatric hospital near Gorky; sources in Moscow subsequently reported that Sakharov had been subjected to force-feeding and the administration of psychotropic drugs. Both Sakharov and his wife were known to be in precarious health, and Western supporters feared that their lives were endangered.

In July, a videotape, reportedly furnished by Victor Louis, a correspondent with alleged ties to the KGB, was shown on West German and American television, apparently demonstrating that both Sakharov and Bonner were alive and active. Some skepticism was expressed in the West about the videotape, but a letter from Bonner to friends in Moscow, in early August, stating that Sakharov was "well" and had ended his hunger strike, appeared genuine (BBC, 7 August). However, it seemed likely that Sakharov was still under confinement, probably in a KGB-supervised "psychiatric hospital." On 23 August, the U.S. State Department issued, without confirmation, a report that Bonner had been convicted of slandering the Soviet state and sentenced to five years of internal exile (*NYT*, 24 August). Robert Van Vooren of the Bukovsky Foundation reported in December that Sakharov had been released from the hospital on 7 September and that Sakharov and Bonner had since been allowed limited freedom of movement in Gorky (AP, 3 December).

A former fellow member with Bonner in the Helsinki Accords monitoring group, Yuri Orlov, was sent into internal exile in the harshest and most remote region of Siberia, upon completion of a term in a strict-regime camp (BBC, 16 February). Authorities had confirmed to Orlov's wife that he was receiving treatment for skull and brain injuries; apparently these had been sustained in a severe beating by camp guards.

A new law, introduced in October 1983, allowed the authorities to lengthen sentences of prisoners for "malicious disobedience" in the camps. In January, it was reported that Valeri Senderov, an Orthodox believer and member of the unofficial trade union organization SMOT, had had five years added to his sentence. It was also learned that several "unregistered" Baptists had been "rearrested" in the camps under provisions of the new law. (Ibid., 27 January.)

The West German news agency DPA reported in March that the Ukrainian dissident translator and writer Valeri Marchenko had been sentenced to fifteen years in camps and exile for "anti-Soviet" slander (ibid., 22 March). And in Lithuania, Father Sigitas Tamkevicius became the second Catholic priest sentenced within a year's time to a long term for religious activities. A protest declaration signed by 123,000 believers was taken to Moscow (ibid., 14 February).

Nationalities. Religious-oriented nationalism in Lithuania, highlighted by the Tamkevicius case, has been one of the more troublesome internal problems for the regime in recent years. Events during 1984 pointed toward concern with the persistence of nationalism and resistance to "russification" in all of the Baltic republics.

The CPSU Central Committee warned the Estonian Communist Party in August concerning "shortcomings and omissions" in its political education work, particularly a failure to create an "international consciousness." The resolution also noted the adverse effects of "anti-Soviet centers abroad" and "the subversion of foreign television" (ibid., 2 August). Earlier, "ethnic tours" of the Baltic republics had been reportedly subject to official harassment, and in June an American tour operator was briefly detained in Tallinn (*CSM*, 12 June).

The long and fruitless efforts of the Crimean Tatars for restoration of their rights was spotlighted again by the punishment of a leading activist. Mustafa Dzhemilyev was sentenced to his sixth term in prison or internal exile (BBC, 13 March).

Despite much evidence of national tensions over the past decade, the authorities have continued to affirm the "drawing together" of the hundred-odd nationalities in the USSR as part of the general process of the "homogenization" of Soviet society. A *Pravda* editorial (28 August) asserted that "the strong vital force of the Leninist principles of the multinational state" was being demonstrated "at the stage of mature socialism" and called the soviets a "powerful instrument" for the "harmonious development of the union state."

Ideology. Much ideological discussion during the year revolved around the concept of "mature socialism." Advanced during the Brezhnev era as an idea summarizing the advanced level of social and economic development in the Soviet Union, it had meshed poorly with the utopian projections of the party program adopted at the Twenty-second CPSU Congress in 1961, particularly in the late 1970s and early 1980s, when the stark reality of economic stagnation could not be denied. Moreover, the concept seemed out of joint with the existing disparities in economic, social, and political power in the USSR. These discrepancies had been papered over with an emphasis upon the "scientific-technological revolution" and the proposition, argued most strongly by Anatoli Yegorov, head of the Institute of Marxism-Leninism, that the division of labor intensifies with the movement toward communism. That proposition, at least implicitly, justified the continuation of social and political stratification.

Yuri Andropov had adopted a more realistic approach to such theoretical matters. His early speeches strongly suggested that the Soviet Union had attained a level of development somewhat lower than that claimed under his predecessor, and he set in motion the revision of the party program to eliminate its unfounded claims and disproved projections. But during his tenure there was considerable disagreement on the question of what level of development the Soviet Union had actually attained. This debate continued following Chernenko's accession, shadowed by the necessity for an early resolution of all disputed theoretical questions to meet the deadline for adoption of a new party program at the upcoming congress in February 1986. Not surprisingly, the debate became entwined with practical matters of economic reform, as both proponents and opponents of economic decentralization grasped for ideological legitimation to support their views.

In April, when addressing the Central Committee commission for preparation of the new party program, Chernenko strongly endorsed Andropov's position on "developed socialism." Notably, he indicated that Soviet society is merely at the "start" of a "historically protracted period—the stage of developed socialism." He called for overcoming "the simplified ideas that have become current for a certain period of time on the ways and the time for transition to the higher phase of communism." (*Pravda*, 25 April.)

Chernenko had spoken of "improving developed socialism," and this became a standard touchstone for subsequent theoretical discussions. Just what precisely needed to be "improved" was spelled out bluntly by economist V. Kulikov in an August article. Kulikov said that "problems left over from yesterday and phenomena which should not appear at the stage of developed socialism still remain." These included "above all the negative processes which came to light at the end of the seventies and the start of the eighties in a reduction of the growth rates of labor productivity and production and its efficiency, and the presence of levels of imbalance, including a number of consumer goods and services." (*Krasnaia zvezda*, 8 August; *FBIS*, 10 August.)

Kulikov's lengthy August article emphasized the need for the comprehensive development of economic regions and regional specialization and for greater independence at every level of management, but his rhetoric was considerably toned down

from that of an earlier article, perhaps because his views had been attacked in *Pravda* two weeks earlier. In a June article, Kulikov had argued in favor of using the "contradictions" in a socialist society as a positive force for change and improvement. Often, he said, the concept of "unity" was used to stifle a healthy competition between various interest groups. Significantly, Kulikov used extensive quotations from both Lenin and Andropov to support his call for reform in the direction of a market economy. (*Kommunist*, no. 9, June.)

The journal *Voprosi istorii* appeared to be the main outlet for reformist views, publishing several articles of this genre, most notably one in February by Anatoli Butenko of the Institute of Economics of the World Socialist System (IEMSS). Here and elsewhere, Butenko advocated a return to the New Economic Policy introduced by Lenin in the early 1920s (BBC, 27 July).

Without mentioning Kulikov and Butenko by name, Richard I. Kosolapov, editor of *Kommunist*, clearly attacked their views in a featured article in *Pravda* (20 July). He acknowledged that there were competing interests in socialist society but these were "nonantagonistic." If individual factories and farms were to be independent and compete with one another in a free market, this would inevitably lead to "antagonistic contradictions," Kosolapov argued, since the enterprises would be free of the mediating influence of central planning.

There were two curious aspects of Kosolapov's major intervention in the reform debate. First, Kulikov's earlier controversial article had appeared in *Kommunist*. Second, Kosolapov has supposedly been a close associate of Mikhail Gorbachev since they were fellow Komsomol activists at Moscow State University in the early 1950s; while Gorbachev has been publicly a cautious reformer, his views are obviously far removed from those expressed by Kosolapov.

An interesting contribution to the debate was made in a June article entitled "The Growth of the CPSU's Leading Role." During the 1970s, the expansion of the CPSU's "leading role" had been mainly attributed to the growing technological complexity of society; the article explicitly tied it to the clash of competing interests under "mature socialism": "It has been proved through the practice of socialist building that there is no other force in our society that would be able to combine and coordinate the interests and needs of all classes and social groups, of all nations and ethnic groups, and of all generations of people so fully and so consistently as is done by the communist party" (*Krasnaia zvezda*, 19 June).

A lengthy, authoritative article by Vadim V. Zagladin, deputy head of the CPSU Central Committee International Department, on the world communist movement reaffirmed the traditional conception of the party's organization in carrying out its "leading role." Zagladin emphasized "democratic centralism" and ideological commitment and implicitly castigated experimentation in certain European communist parties:

> It is true that in some countries recently there has been quite frequent expression of the view that the term "party of the new [Leninist] type" has become obsolete. At times people say that what is needed now is no longer a party of the Leninist type but some kind of "new party" "broadly open to the masses." Essentially, however, all these concepts boil down to one thing: to advise the rejection of precise class criteria and approaches, the Marxist-Leninist ideological foundation, and proletarian internationalism. [*Pravda*, 5 June.]

The general ideological tightening of the cultural scene, already apparent under Andropov, was intensified, evidently reflecting the predilections of the new leader. In May a joint resolution of the Central Committee and the Council of Ministers made it binding on responsible figures in the film industry to implement party decisions on the cinema and called for films that "meet the demands of the contemporary stage in building communism and propagandize the Leninist foreign policy of the Soviet Union, actively exposing the aggressive course of imperialism, heightening the vigilance of the armed forces, and assisting military-patriotic education" (ibid., 8 May).

Yuri Lyubimov, noted director of Moscow's Taganka theater, was fired; his dismissal was apparently related to an interview given to the *Times* (London) in September 1983. Lyubimov had complained of his treatment by Soviet officials over the years and had said that although he had been a CPSU member for 30 years, he also considered himself to be a Christian (BBC, 7 March). The Taganka had established a reputation as one of Moscow's most avant-garde theaters, a reputation won while Lyubimov constantly warred with Ministry of Culture officials. His successor, Anatoli Efros, issued a statement warning actors that he would not tolerate dissension (*Literaturnaia gazeta*, 28 March). Some of the Taganka actors claimed that Efros had betrayed Lyubimov (*CSM*, 29 March).

Auxiliary and Front Organizations. Two major auxiliary organizations, one headed by an Andropov appointee, the other by a Chernenko protégé, were both called to task for failure to perform up to the leadership's expectations.

The Komsomol, led since December 1982 by Viktor Mishin, was severely criticized on several occasions for shortcomings in its work (see above), and in July a Central Committee resolution criticized both the leadership and local organs of the youth organization for slowness in "restructuring the style and work of their activity." The resolution further charged that Komsomol organizations do not always make effective use of the opportunities for influencing young people, attempt to resolve new tasks using "tired," hackneyed ways and means, and frequently are late to react to new interests among young people and fail to give them the necessary direction (*Pravda*, 8 July).

The trade unions were subjected to a major purge of officials. The All-Union Council of Trade Unions (AUCCTU) has been headed by Stepan Shalayev since March 1982, when Chernenko personally supervised his installation. But the Chernenko connection brought no slowing down in the purge after the party leadership change. By midsummer, 289 officials had been dismissed from the Geological Workers Union alone. Many of the organizational shortcomings in the unions were attributed to the practice of co-opting "exemplary workers" instead of appointing career professionals (*Sovetskaia Rossiia*, 24 July).

The Soviet Academy of Sciences invited U.S. Senator William S. Cohen (R., Maine) to Moscow. E. P. Velikhov, vice-president of the academy and chairman of the Committee of Soviet Scientists in Defense of Peace, accompanied him for a discussion of U.S.-Soviet relations with Soviet vice-president Kuznetsov (*Pravda*, 21 February).

The Soviet Union of Journalists signed an agreement with the New England Society of Newspaper Editors for an exchange of reporters, scheduled to begin in mid-1984 (*NYT*, 29 January).

Pravda editor Viktor G. Afanasyev was the chief Soviet representative at a March conference on security and disarmament in Europe sponsored by the front group, the International Forum of Peace-Loving Forces (*Pravda*, 13 March).

At a February meeting in Havana, the preparatory committee for the Twelfth World Festival of Youth and Students announced that the meeting will be held in Moscow in the summer of 1985 (Tass, 12 February).

International Views, Positions, and Activities. Soviet performance in international affairs during the year evoked serious questions about the planning, execution, and results of the USSR's world policy. The general outlook for Moscow seemed less favorable at the end of the year than at the beginning. This was partially traceable to the linkage between domestic politics and external events, especially the uncertainties engendered by a continuing succession crisis and leadership instability. There were indications that the Soviet leadership had been thrown off balance by the flurry of negative developments in the final months of 1983—the Korean airliner incident, the American invasion of Grenada, and the beginning of deployment of new NATO missiles in Western Europe— and had never really recovered. Nevertheless, at the beginning of the year, there were some grounds for optimism in the Kremlin. Prospects were favorable for at least a limited rapprochement with China, the cohesion of the Western alliance was most uncertain amid continuing controversy on the missile issue, and the United States faced an election that promised to test severely the Reagan administration's policy stance toward the USSR. Apparently marking time, the Soviets bluntly made known their unwillingness to negotiate further with the incumbent administration in Washington.

The advent of Chernenko's leadership in February aroused hopes in the West for a revival of détente since the new general secretary had been closely identified with the policy. Chernenko proceeded to issue conflicting statements about Soviet policy, apparently reflecting his precarious political position and absence of a mandate from the Politburo. Most Western observers soon concluded that Foreign Minister Gromyko had attained virtually total dominance over the formation of the USSR's external policies. The apparent ascendancy of Gromyko coincided with the most virulently anti-American propaganda heard in Moscow since Stalin's time. Moreover, the Soviets seemed to have withdrawn into a general isolationism vis-à-vis the outside world reminiscent of the "class against class" period (1928–1934). Just as in the earlier era,

this international posture was paralleled by an ideological toughening at home. The most extreme "isolationist" action was the sudden cancellation of First Deputy Prime Minister Ivan Arkhipov's planned visit to Beijing in May, in response to the Chinese reception of President Reagan.

The strategic balance between the United States and the USSR remained the paramount Soviet concern. From an adamant position of no negotiations until the new NATO missiles were withdrawn, the Soviets moved, by fits and starts, toward greater flexibility. One major reason may have been the serious disadvantages faced by the ailing Soviet economy in the threatened "star wars" competition with the United States. Continuing refusal to negotiate also posed the possibility of yielding the "peace" issue to the United States. Further, détente was reviving in spite of the Soviets as the East European allies, even Bulgaria, reached out to the West for the advanced technology that Moscow could not provide. The Soviets were obliged, in September, to face down the East Germans on the issue of growing contacts with Bonn, demonstrating clearly the absence of the bloc cohesion absolutely essential to the maintenance of hard-line isolationism.

The turning point came in September. In the week following the sacking of Chief of Staff Ogarkov, it was announced that Gromyko would confer with Reagan while in the United States for the annual U.N. meeting. At the United Nations, Gromyko hurled more harsh rhetoric at the Americans, but his meetings with Reagan and U.S. secretary of state George Shultz laid the groundwork for an important subsequent development. In late November, it was agreed that Gromyko and Shultz would meet in Geneva in January 1985 to discuss resumption of talks on arms control.

As the two sides approached the January talks, it was obvious that the USSR's relative weight in the world "correlation of forces" had eroded during the six years or so that had elapsed since the onset of Moscow's extended succession crisis. The vaunted "restructuring of international relations" had lost most of its momentum as the Soviets confronted reverses or deadlocks in virtually every theater. Even the fiasco of American involvement in Lebanon had not appreciably bolstered the USSR's position in the Middle East, where the Soviets were caught in cross-pressures between their volatile and mutually hostile allies. Yet the Soviets' awesome military machine still commanded respect, and as Gromyko's maneuvers demonstrated, the USSR retained the capacity to seize the initiative in super-power politics by diplomatic gestures. No fundamental alteration of Soviet policies was in prospect. Circumstances had dictated a tactical shift, a partial return to the *razriadka* (relaxation of tensions) approach that had served Moscow so well in the early 1970s.

U.S.-Soviet Relations. At the outset of the new year, the renewed cold war seemed to be intensifying. The Soviets' tactics of bluff, bluster, and encouragement of "peace" groups having failed to prevent or delay the scheduled installation of NATO missiles, Moscow settled into a belligerent, uncompromising attitude. Several statements emanating from the Kremlin voiced Moscow's demand for a return to what was perceived by the Soviets as the strategic status quo in Europe and indicated unwillingness to negotiate with the Reagan administration. Some Western observers viewed the Soviet stall as a holding tactic pending the outcome of the American elections; clearly, the Kremlin leadership did not wish to assist Reagan's re-election. On the other hand, Reagan was under pressure at home to demonstrate that he was a "man of peace" since rising superpower tensions seemed likely to figure prominently in the U.S. election campaign. But a return to the negotiating table by the Soviets could be presented by the incumbent administration in Washington as the payoff and validation of Reagan's strategy of confronting the Soviets from a position of strength. This was clearly a trap that the Kremlin intended to avoid.

In a generally conciliatory January speech, Reagan urged the Soviets to resume the aborted Geneva talks on limiting nuclear weapons. Shortly thereafter he dispatched Secretary of State George Shultz to Stockholm for a meeting of the European disarmament conference. Addressing the conference, Soviet foreign minister Gromyko delivered a blistering attack on the United States, dismissed Reagan's latest proposal, and depicted the U.S. administration as motivated by "militarism, enmity, and war hysteria." A three-hour private talk between Shultz and Gromyko "made no headway," according to Shultz, on the question of resuming nuclear arms talks. (*NYT*, 20–22 and 25 January.)

The accession of Konstantin Chernenko in February raised hopes in the West for a thaw in U.S.-Soviet relations; unlike Andropov, the new leader was not personally involved in the existing stalemate and had been a vocal advocate of détente in the 1970s. Vice-President George Bush represented the United States at Andropov's funeral and carried a letter from President Reagan to Chernenko. Bush met privately with Chernenko in the Kremlin; afterwards, the vice-president said that the general secretary had agreed on the need to resume talks on serious U.S.-Soviet disputes and "to place our relationship upon a more constructive basis" (AP, 14 February).

Chernenko followed this favorable signal with a statement that the USSR was prepared to enter negotiations with the United States "provided they are honest negotiations, on the basis of equality and "equal security" (*Pravda*, 19 February), omitting the usual precondition of "a return to the situation existing prior to the deployment of the Pershing II and cruise missiles." However, an official statement two days later reaffirmed that the condition was still in force (Tass, 21 February), and Chernenko reverted to the formulation in an interview published in early April (*Pravda*, 9 April).

In his March Supreme Soviet campaign speech, Chernenko accused the United States of militarism and of seeking world domination but said that reaching an agreement on important issues could "signal the start of a very drastic change in Soviet–American relations" (ibid., 3 April). However, the effect was somewhat spoiled by the gap in Chernenko's speech, when he lost his place for some 30 seconds; when he recovered from his stumble, he inadvertently omitted discussion of the substantive issues on which progress might be made, mostly involving nuclear weapons, and 200 words had to be inserted in the subsequently released official text (*NYT*, 3 March; *CSM*, 5 March).

Chernenko seemed, however erratically, to be trying to get U.S.-Soviet negotiations back on track. However, there was considerable doubt in the West that he was really in charge. Foreign Minister Gromyko appeared to hold the reins of foreign policy; in meetings with foreign leaders such as Canadian premier Pierre Trudeau and West German foreign minister Hans-Dietrich Genscher, Gromyko dominated the discussions, and Chernenko mostly remained silent (*Newsweek*, 4 June). And Gromyko presented a consistent scowl to the world, reflecting a Kremlin intransigence that covered all fronts.

The Soviets continued to maintain that negotiations with the Reagan administration were useless. Aleksandr Bovin, *Izvestiia's* influential political commentator, was quoted as saying that serious negotiations with the Americans "under the present leadership [have] hardly any serious prospects"

(*Sunday Telegraph*, London, 18 March). Meanwhile, the Soviet media escalated the propaganda offensive against Washington to a decibel level unmatched in decades. The United States was accused of "preparing for nuclear war" (*Pravda*, 18 and 23 March), and the Reagan administration was said to be "worse than Hitler and Eichmann" (*Komsomolskaia pravda*, 14 March).

The Soviets' practical response to installation of the Euromissiles was the announced stationing of an unspecified number of additional missile-equipped submarines off the American coast, which evoked no perturbation in Washington, and the deployment of new missiles in East Germany and Czechoslovakia, which produced consternation in the bloc countries affected (see below).

The approaching Summer Olympics afforded the Soviets the opportunity to return the slap dealt them by Washington in 1980. After playing cat and mouse with the Olympic organizing committee for several months, the Soviets withdrew from the games, citing security problems in Los Angeles (Tass, 8 May). Again, the cohesion of the bloc was put in question; only the countries subservient to Moscow followed its lead and only after considerable grumbling. The substitute bloc games held in Moscow in late summer were to prove something less than a smashing success.

More serious were several incidents at sea in early spring, notably an explosion involving the Soviet tanker *Lugansk* near Puerto Sandino in Nicaragua caused by a rebel mine and a collision between the U.S. carrier *Kitty Hawk* and a shadowing Viktor I submarine in the Pacific (*Newsweek*, 2 April). These events precipitated another round of name-calling and drew attention to the precarious state of U.S.-Soviet relations, which at the diplomatic level soon approached the vanishing point. By midsummer, virtually the only formal contact remaining between the superpowers was the regular talks between Soviet ambassador Anatoli Dobrynin and U.S. secretary of state Shultz in Washington.

The blatant Soviet belligerence toward the United States was starkly apparent in a series of incidents in Leningrad. In late summer, a Western diplomat described the atmosphere in Moscow as one of "anti-American fanaticism," and in Leningrad, according to the U.S. State Department, there had been "approximately a dozen cases of flagrant harassment" of Americans in recent months, notably an assault on Vice-Consul Ronald Harms in April and the beating of Marine Sgt. Ronald Camp-

bell in August. The State Department accused the Soviets of violating the consular agreement between the two countries and issued an unprecedented advisory against travel by Americans to Leningrad. (Ibid., 20 August.)

The atmosphere changed abruptly in early September with Chernenko as the main signal sender on the Soviet side. In a *Pravda* interview (2 September), Chernenko said that if the United States would accept a moratorium on space weapons, the USSR might be willing to talk not only about the demilitarization of space but also about "limiting and reducing other strategic armaments." On the following day, the Soviet Foreign Ministry issued a "clarification" to the effect that the demand for prior removal of the Euromissiles was still in effect, but in addressing an award ceremony on 5 September, Chernenko again failed to mention the precondition when he noted that an agreement on space weapons "could infuse Soviet-American relations with the elements of mutual trust they so badly need" (Tass, 5 September).

It was hardly coincidental that Chernenko's rather conciliatory statements were followed successively by the dismissal of Marshal Ogarkov (see above) and the announcement that Foreign Minister Gromyko would meet with President Reagan during his visit to the United States in late September for a session of the U.N. General Assembly. While in the United States, Gromyko met with Secretary Shultz on 26 September and with President Reagan on 28 September; between these two talks, he conferred with Democratic presidential candidate Walter Mondale and addressed the U.N. General Assembly (*NYT*, 27–29 September). The meetings with Shultz and Reagan reportedly focused on arms control and regional and bilateral issues (ibid.; *Radio Liberty Research*, 5 October). The talks led to no immediate breakthroughs but clearly laid the foundation for the November agreement on resumption of negotiations.

Gromyko's U.N. speech was a mixture of hardline belligerence and calls for a resumption of negotiations. In a lengthy survey of world problems, he soundly denounced the United States as the source of all of them and termed Reagan's earlier speech to the General Assembly an "empty vessel." Gromyko called for talks on arms control but said that the United States must "remove the obstacles it has put in the way." On space weapons, he expressed the hope that the United States would "refrain from actions that would make irreversible the process of turning outer space into an area of military rivalry and that it would be willing to engage in talks with a view to reaching an agreement" (*NYT*, 27 September). Secretary Shultz deplored the "distortions" in Gromyko's speech (UPI, 27 September), but U.S. spokesmen emphasized the private talks, conveying a generally favorable impression (*NYT*, 29 September).

A Chernenko interview with *Washington Post* reporter Dusko Doder in October seemed to confirm the impression of a mellower mood in Moscow and conveyed an image of a Soviet leader reasonably fit and articulate. Chernenko suggested to Doder that U.S.-Soviet relations could be improved if Washington showed interest in reaching agreement on at least one of four Soviet arms control proposals. These included a ban on the militarization of outer space, a mutual freeze on nuclear weapons, U.S. ratification of test-ban treaties, and a pledge by the United States not to be the first to use nuclear weapons (*WP*, 17 October). The Reagan administration reaffirmed its opposition to the Soviet proposals but expressed satisfaction "with the positive tone" of Chernenko's remarks. A White House spokesman said that "when the Soviet Union is prepared to move from public exchanges to private negotiations and concrete agreements, they will find us ready" (*CSM*, 18 October).

President Reagan was congratulated on his reelection by the USSR Supreme Soviet Presidium in a telegram expressing the Soviet Union's willingness to work jointly "to rectify Soviet-American relations on the basis of equity and respect for the legitimate interests of each other." In his reply, Reagan said that he shared the hope "that the coming years would be marked by improved relations" (AP, 14 November). Relations remained tense, however, reflected in Soviet charges of U.S. responsibility for the assassination of Indian prime minister Indira Gandhi and in Washington's nervous reaction to reports, not subsequently substantiated, of the shipment of Soviet MiGs to Nicaragua (*NYT*, 7 November). Meanwhile, the United States carried out its second test of an antisatellite weapon, accompanying it with an offer about limiting weapons in space, while at the same time rejecting calls for a halt in the American program (AP, 14 November).

The September talks in Washington bore fruit in late November with the announcement that Gromyko and Shultz would meet in Geneva, 7–8 January, to discuss resumption of nuclear arms talks and other issues (*NYT*, 23 November). *Pravda* (25 November) echoed an earlier statement by Chernenko

characterizing the forthcoming talks as a follow-up to the détente of the 1970s but carefully avoiding suggesting that Moscow had abandoned previous positions on disarmament. Chernenko followed the *Pravda* commentary with a statement saying that U.S.-Soviet arms talks should combine the "interconnected questions" of space weapons and both medium-range and strategic missiles (Tass, 26 November). Earlier, Chernenko had pledged in a speech to the Politburo "to work vigorously" to limit and reduce nuclear weapons; at the same time, he had called for a "strengthening of the country's defense capability" as a response to the "growing aggressiveness of imperialism" (*Pravda*, 16 November). When the Supreme Soviet met in late November, it ratified a 12 percent increase in the official Soviet defense budget (*Izvestiia*, 29 November), which reportedly accounts for about one-third of the USSR's total defense expenditure.

A letter from Chernenko in early December to the International Physicians for the Prevention of Nuclear War expressed Soviet willingness "to go for the most radical solutions in arms control" (Tass, 5 December; AP, 5 December). However, the letter implied that Soviet agreement on other arms control issues would be contingent upon U.S. willingness to agree not to deploy space weapons. Similar views were expressed by party secretary Gorbachev during his December visit to Britain (*NYT*, 18 December), but Western diplomats seemed highly uncertain about the Soviet strategy for negotiations in the forthcoming talks.

A minor, if somewhat dubious, propaganda coup was scored by the Soviets when Stalin's daughter, Svetlana Alliluyeva, who had defected to the United States in 1967, returned to the USSR. Upon her return, Soviet officials announced that her USSR citizenship had been restored (ibid., 5 November). On the day of the announcement, the Komsomol's newspaper printed a story concerning the difficulties of Soviet defectors in the West and affirmed the Soviet government's willingness to "receive back the straying person" (*Komsomolskaia pravda*, 2 November).

Western Europe. Heads of government of three major West European states attended the Andropov funeral and met with Chernenko and other Soviet leaders. Even the most committed of the U.S. allies, British prime minister Margaret Thatcher and West German chancellor Helmut Kohl, obviously hoped that the encounter would presage a thaw in East-West relations, and French premier Pierre

Mauroy expressed confidence in the improvement of Franco-Soviet relations. Much of the continuous optimism centered on the assumed attitudes of Chernenko, regarded as a supporter of détente. Soviet media accounts of the meetings were considerably more restrained than the Western reports (Tass, 12 February; *NYT*, 13 and 14 February).

The expected thaw was slow in developing. In general, Soviet influence on the West European states appeared to diminish during the year, in part because Moscow's refusal to negotiate on nuclear arms took much of the remaining steam out of the Western "peace" movements. Further, Moscow was compelled to concentrate upon the cohesion of its East European bloc, and efforts to curb contacts between the satellites and the West worked against a general "normalization," particularly straining relations with West Germany.

There were also particular irritants in relations between the USSR and the West European states. One such matter was the continuing public revelations concerning the massive Soviet industrial and military espionage in the advanced capitalist countries. Soviet diplomatic personnel had been expelled from Britain and France for spying in 1983 (see *YICA*, 1984, p. 391); several incidents in 1984 indicated no slowdown in Soviet illegal activities abroad. On 1 February, Norway expelled five Soviet diplomats for spying (Reuters, 2 February; *FBIS*, 3 February). In May, Britain expelled a Soviet envoy named in a recent spy trial, Embassy First Secretary Arkady V. Gouk, and Moscow responded by ordering the first secretary of the British embassy in Moscow, John Burnett, to leave the USSR. The government of Belgium also expelled a Soviet trade official for allegedly trying to steal NATO secrets (AP, 22 May). In July, West German authorities seized a sealed Soviet truck at the Helmstedt border crossing to East Germany. The Soviets claimed the truck's nine tons of cargo were diplomatic materials; the West Germans believed that it was contraband Western technology (AP, 20 July).

Another source of friction was the Soviet treatment of dissident Andrei Sakharov. The Sakharov matter was raised by West German foreign minister Hans-Dietrich Genscher on his May visit to Moscow, by the European Community, and by French president François Mitterrand in Moscow in June.

The Genscher visit coincided with a Soviet media campaign against the alleged appearance of neo-Nazi and fascist tendencies within the Federal Republic. The campaign denounced so-called re-

vanchist and militaristic circles in West Germany, including "elements" within the Bonn coalition (*Radio Free Europe Research*, 5 June). The propaganda barrage was evidently designed for East German consumption; Moscow's subsequent efforts to contain a developing détente between East and West Germany would further strain relations with Bonn (see below).

Mitterrand created something of a sensation during his June visit to Moscow when he publicly criticized the treatment of Sakharov and questioned Soviet military policies at a Kremlin banquet. In their media coverage of the event, the Soviets censored out the offending remarks. The French leader met twice with Chernenko and had a private session with Gromyko. Following the talks, Mitterrand said that the Russians had demonstrated an ultimate "desire to move forward" in reducing East-West tensions (*WP*, 23 June). A Soviet press commentary noted that the talks between Chernenko and Mitterrand had "attracted worldwide attention" and spoke of "the useful nature of this dialogue" (*Izvestiia*, 26 June). Nevertheless, it was clear that relations between Moscow and Paris still fell far short of the ties maintained during the tenure of President Valéry Giscard d'Estaing, and the meetings showed no substantive results.

Meetings with other Western leaders, such as Foreign Minister Giulio Andreotti of Italy and King Juan Carlos of Spain were similarly inconclusive (*Newsweek*, 28 May), but showed Moscow's desire to maintain at least minimal contacts with the West during a period of general diplomatic retrenchment and relative isolationism.

One Western country continued to hold promise for the expansion of Soviet influence, and Moscow moved to exploit these possibilities. A delegation of the Greek General Confederation of Labor, led by its chairman and general secretary, visited Moscow and Azerbaijan in April and was welcomed· by AUCCTU head Stepan Shalayev and other officials (*Trud*, 6 April; *FBIS*, 10 April). The importance attached by Moscow to the new, closer relationship with Greece was manifested in the following month when a strong Soviet delegation, led by Politburo candidate member and party secretary Vladimir Dolgikh, attended the congress of the ruling Socialist Party (PASOK) in Athens. Comments by both Greeks and Soviets at this conference suggested a close and ever improving friendship between the two countries (BBC, 11 May).

Despite the failure of earlier Soviet efforts to undercut the cohesion of the Western alliance through encouragement of opposition groups in Western Europe, a November visit to Moscow indicated that the Kremlin had not entirely written off the tactic. British Labour Party leader Neil Kinnock and veteran party bigwig Dennis Healey were received with much fanfare by Chernenko and Tikhonov (Tass, 26 November; *Pravda*, 27 November). The Soviet leaders suggested that Britain would be removed from the USSR's nuclear targeting list if that country renounced installation of the Euromissiles (*NYT*, 27 November).

Britain was again a diplomatic and propaganda target in December, when Central Committee secretary and Politburo member Mikhail Gorbachev led a Supreme Soviet delegation on a visit at the invitation of the British Parliament. Despite one rough exchange on Soviet domestic human rights policy and heckling by protesters, the visit appeared to be a resounding success for the Soviets. Accompanied by his wife, Raisa, Gorbachev captivated his hosts just as he had done on his 1983 visit to Canada, drawing high praise from British leaders, including Prime Minister Margaret Thatcher. Gorbachev pledged that the USSR would not "start any new round in the arms race" and reaffirmed Moscow's position on the militarization of space. Following talks at Chequers, Gorbachev and Thatcher expressed agreement on the need for nuclear weapons reductions and avoidance of an arms race in space. (Ibid., 16–19 December.)

Eastern Europe. Yuri Andropov's tenure had aroused expectations in Eastern Europe of more flexibility in Moscow's dealings with the communist regimes of the region. A particularly favorable gesture was the 1983 replacement of Piotr A. Abrasimov, Moscow's ambassador to East Germany, by Vyacheslav Kochemasov, a friend of GDR leader Erich Honecker.

East European hopes for a modified relationship with the USSR concentrated on three goals: freedom to carry out domestic economic experimentation along the lines successfully pursued in Hungary, a course so popular in the region that even the ultraorthodox Bulgarians were moving toward it; increased trade with Western Europe, especially in areas of technological deficit, an objective pursued by all of the allies, including Bulgaria; and greater political autonomy vis-à-vis Moscow, particularly in decisions relating to consumer satisfaction in the bloc states.

Under Chernenko, the Soviets displayed a stubborn unwillingness to accommodate their allies' desires for greater independence. But at the outset of the year, a more immediate problem confronted the Soviet leaders. The decision to install new missiles in East Germany and Czechoslovakia triggered protest movements in both countries and evidence of resistance by the governments concerned. Faced with this fresh indication of bloc incohesion, the growing pressures for a measure of autonomy, and the continuing troubles in Poland, Moscow displayed a hard line on all key bloc matters but concentrated its efforts on the strategically most important satellite, East Germany.

Soviet ire was aroused by two initiatives: a $330 million bank credit to East Germany announced by Bonn in July and the planned September visit of Honecker to Bonn and Essen (ibid., 6 September). During July and August, the Soviet media reverted to harsh attacks on Bonn's alleged "revanchism," supposedly displayed by West German attempts to weaken East Germany's ties with the bloc. But the quarrel was really with the satrap in East Berlin, and the conflict escalated into a messy public dispute between Moscow and the German Democratic Republic (GDR).

The Soviets, in a late July official commentary, sharply criticized Bonn's, and by implication East Berlin's, policy on intra-German relations (*Pravda*, 27 July). The East Germans responded with an editorial defending GDR policy as enhancing détente and "limiting the damage" to East-West relations. Further, the editorial stressed, in bilateral relations, both East and West Germany "are independent in their domestic and foreign affairs" (*Neues Deutschland*, East Berlin, 1 August; *CSM*, 2 August). Moscow followed with an editorial sharply criticizing the loan agreement, which had provided as a quid pro quo East German relaxation of travel and emigration restrictions. West Germany was accused of trying to "undermine" East Germany and of using "an economic lever" to "break the postwar peaceful setup in Europe" (*Pravda*, 2 August).

The East Germans continued to resist Moscow's pressure and, on 10 August, published a top-level defense of the détente with Bonn. Herbert Häber, East Germany's senior expert on relations with West Germany, was quoted by *Neues Deutschland* as calling for a return to "peaceful economic and political relations through dialogue" (*NYT*, 12 August). On the following day, Moscow returned to the attack, accusing the Federal Republic of Germany (FRG) of turning away from the key principle of the 1970 USSR-FRG treaty on the renunciation of force, "the inviolability of the postwar European borders" (Tass, 11 August). A separate Tass commentary on the same day lashed out at Foreign Minister Genscher as the architect of the West German policy of "revanchism" (*NYT*, 12 August). The propaganda drumbeat rose to a crescendo at the beginning of September. Moscow charged that West Germany had not abandoned hope "for an end to the socialist system" and that Kohl was trying to "tranquilize" public opinion by presenting East-West relations as good despite the deployment of the Euromissiles (*Pravda*, 1 September).

On 3 September, *Pravda* reported favorably on Honecker's appearance at the Leipzig trade fair, suggesting that Moscow had won its test of wills with the East German leader. On the following day, the announcement was made that Honecker had postponed his visit to West Germany (*NYT*, 5 September).

The Soviets had won the round, at considerable cost, as the public washing of dirty linen clearly demonstrated the underlying incohesion of the bloc. The East Germans evidently intended to continue détente with the FRG but, in deference to Moscow's pressure, at a slower pace. Soviet pressure evidently also caused postponement of Bulgarian leader Todor Zhivkov's scheduled November visit to Bonn.

A much less dramatic event affecting Soviet-Yugoslav relations may have been related to general "isolationist" trends in Soviet policy through much of the year. In June, Intourist advised all Yugoslav tourist agencies that it would not send Soviet citizens to spend vacations in Yugoslavia from 1 August to the end of the year. Yugoslav tourists in the Soviet Union were not affected. Soviet officials denied that there was any special significance in the move and cited lack of reciprocity (Yugoslav tourists in the USSR outnumber Soviet visitors to Yugoslavia by more than six to one) and expensive travel arrangements as the reasons for the decision (*Borba*, Belgrade, 20 June; *FBIS*, 25 June).

Afghanistan. The war in Afghanistan entered its sixth year in the last week of December, with no prospects of an early peace. The war escalated in savagery during the year, the massive Soviet assaults against the rural population assuming genocidal proportions. Carpet bombing and strafing depopulated vast areas in eastern Kazakhstan, and Western sources estimated that the country's population had been reduced by one-fourth during the

war, with more than 4 million refugees and about 1 million killed.

Western diplomats in India and Pakistan reported in February that Soviet forces had carried out a massacre of guerrillas and women and children in the town of Istalef, 25 miles north of Kabul, in one of a series of offensives in the southern Shomali Valley (*Los Angeles Times*, 8 February). Meanwhile, the Soviet media increased coverage of the war, playing up stories of heroes returning from the fighting.

Yuri Andropov had given some indications of hoping for a truce under the aegis of the United Nations; the new leadership in the Kremlin seemed determined to deal with the guerrilla problem by the overwhelming application of firepower. In April, the Soviets launched a major offensive in the Panjshir Valley, supporting thousands of troops with high-level saturation bombing. It was reportedly the first time that the Soviets had used heavy bombers in the war (*CSM*, 25 April). After two weeks of the offensive, the Soviets had consolidated their positions in the southern half of the Panjshir Valley but still faced hit-and-run resistance from Afghan guerrillas (*WP*, 9 May). In early May, Soviet helicopter gunships caught a rebel force in the valley, killing 200 guerrillas (ibid.).

Sporadic fighting continued in the valley throughout the year, featuring high-altitude bombing by TU-16 Badger bombers and attacks by heavily armored SU-24 and SU-25 aircraft. In August, the Soviets reported successes against rebels operating in Ghazni province, in southwest Afghanistan (Moscow television service, 19 August; *FBIS*, 21 August).

A new tactic in the long-range struggle was disclosed in November when Radio Kabul announced that hundreds of Afghan children were being taken from their parents and shipped to the USSR for years of political indoctrination (*Newsweek*, 3 December).

U.S. officials said in late November that $280 million had been earmarked in covert military aid for the Afghan insurgents during the current fiscal year, more than doubling the aid in fiscal year 1984, bringing total American aid to $625 million since the war began in December 1979 (*NYT*, 28 November). U.S. officials reported that the Soviets had been "largely successful" in their strategy of controlling urban areas and major transport routes but that control of cities and roads was not yet secure. CIA and State Department sources said that the Soviets had suffered 40,000 casualties during the war, with 6,000–7,000 killed; Soviet forces in Afghanistan were said to total 110,000, with 40,000 others making occasional forays from Soviet territory (ibid.).

China. After 1981, with the United States and the USSR in direct opposition, China had moved toward a more independent foreign policy and a partial rapprochement with the Soviet Union. Andropov's more conciliatory approach, particularly on the issue of Afghanistan, had helped; since October 1982, three rounds of normalization talks had been held, cultural exchanges had been revived, and trade increased (*Inside China Mainland*, Taipei, March). A trade agreement signed on 10 February set the expected trade total for 1984 at 1 billion rubles, about 60 percent more than in 1983 (*NYT*, 11 February).

The fourth round of normalization talks was held in Moscow, 12–16 March, with Soviet deputy foreign minister Leonid F. Ilyichev and PRC deputy foreign minister Qian Qichen as the chief representatives for the two sides. A Soviet communiqué termed the talks "useful"; another round of talks was set for October in Beijing (Tass, 26 March; *FBIS*, 27 March).

There were, however, some storm clouds on the horizon. PRC deputy premier Wan Li attended Andropov's funeral; although Chernenko held private conversations with Western leaders, he did not meet with Wan Li (*NYT*, 15 February). Central Committee secretary for relations with ruling communist parties Konstantin Rusakov, in a Supreme Soviet election campaign talk on 10 February, said that "we hope to establish good relations with China." However, he added, "we cannot allow bilateral relations to violate the interests of third countries" (Moscow radio, 11 February; *FBIS*, 11 February), presumably meaning Afghanistan and Vietnam. And a lengthy article by historian V. Yasenev in April contained a detailed refutation of PRC territorial claims against the USSR and accused the Chinese of "falsification of historical facts" (*New Times*, Moscow, April; *FBIS*, 23 April).

Although serious obstacles remained, the scheduled visit of USSR first deputy prime minister Ivan Arkhipov was an indicator of serious intent since this would upgrade the Sino-Soviet talks to a new protocol level. Chinese officials said that talks during the visit, the first by a high-ranking Soviet official in fifteen years, would focus on trade (AP, 25 April). A special major topic was expected to be Moscow's offer of nuclear power generation equipment to China (KYODO, Tokyo, 5 May; *FBIS*, 7 May). However, at the last moment, Moscow called off the Arkhipov visit, apparently in reaction to improved PRC-U.S. relations, reflected in Premier Zhao Ziyang's visit to Washington in January and the friendly reception accorded President Reagan when he visited China in April.

At this point, Moscow's self-isolation was virtually complete, with only India among the world's major countries having reasonably friendly relations with the USSR. While Moscow did modify somewhat its general isolationist stance later in the year, there was little indication of Soviet interest in pursuing an early rapprochement with the PRC.

In response to several articles critical of Soviet policies, *Pravda* (19 July) accused the Chinese media of directing "coarse invective" and "base insinuations" against the Soviet Union. A low-level delegation from the PRC embassy attended a Moscow soiree in August honoring Chinese writer Ye Shengtao (Moscow radio, 15 August; *FBIS*, 16 August), and Soviet deputy foreign minister Ilyichev arrived in Beijing as scheduled in October for the next round of normalization talks (*CSM*, 17 October).

Major breakthroughs were not expected. It seemed highly unlikely that Moscow would yield on the three major Chinese demands: reduction of Soviet forces along the two countries' borders; Soviet withdrawal from Afghanistan; and cessation of Soviet support for Vietnamese "expansionism."

These expectations concerning Soviet policy were given some confirmation by First Deputy Prime Minister Arkhipov's visit to Beijing in December. In line with Moscow's general recovery from stark isolationism in the autumn, the visit had been rescheduled, but Arkhipov was not accompanied by any senior Foreign Ministry officials, indicating an absence of plans to discuss substantive issues. Instead, the talks in Beijing were limited to trade, science, and technology, culminating in four treaties on these matters (*NYT*, 24 and 29 December). PRC vice-president Yao Yilin pointedly observed that "differences between the two countries on how to normalize relations have yet to be overcome" (AP, 21 December).

India. One major exception to the general isolationist trend in Soviet policy was relations with India. Moscow and New Delhi upgraded ties on several fronts, especially in matters of arms supply, but there was doubt that this closer relationship could be maintained after the assassination of Prime Minister Indira Gandhi.

Defense Minister Ustinov, whose scheduled visit in early February had been postponed due to Andropov's final illness, arrived in New Delhi on 5 March (*Pravda*, 6 March) for talks with Prime Minister Gandhi and Defense Minister Ramaswamy Venkataraman. At the outset of the talks, the two sides pledged to strengthen defense cooperation, and both Ustinov and Gandhi expressed concern over the United States' $3.2 billion arms package for Pakistan and the American military presence in the Indian Ocean (UPI, 5 March). Subsequently, the two countries confirmed their first major arms deal since 1981, as the USSR agreed to sell India top-of-the-line fighter jets, warships, missiles, army hardware, and electronic surveillance systems (AP, 9 March).

A dramatic event in space provided an occasion for the Soviet media to emphasize the growing special relationship with India. The first Indian cosmonaut, Rakesh Sharma, participated in the docking of a Soyuz T-11 spacecraft with an orbiting Salyut 7 space station. The event was followed by a round of congratulatory messages among Chernenko, Gandhi, and the cosmonauts (ibid., 4 April).

Closer Soviet-Indian military ties were indicated by the visit of India's air chief, Marshal D. Singh, to the USSR in June. Singh conferred with Defense Minister Ustinov and other military leaders and toured Soviet air force installations (*Krasnaia zvezda*, 22 and 23 June). An Indian parliamentary delegation led by House of the People Speaker Balram Jakhar also visited the USSR in June and was welcomed by Supreme Soviet Presidium Vice-Chairman Kuznetsov (Tass, 25 June; *FBIS*, 26 June). Rakesh Sharma and a fellow Indian cosmonaut received an exceptionally warm welcome when they visited Moscow, Leningrad, Kiev, and Alma Ata in August (Tass, 14 August; *FBIS*, 15 August). In the same month, a symposium on Soviet-Indian trade was held in Moscow under the auspices of the two countries' chambers of commerce, in conjunction with an Indian exhibition in the Soviet capital (Tass, 16 August; *FBIS*, 21 August).

The assassination of Prime Minister Gandhi was a severe blow to the special relationship between Moscow and New Delhi; there were indications that Mrs. Gandhi's successor, her son Rajiv, would follow a more independent course and seek to improve relations with the United States. Prime Minister Tikhonov led the Soviet delegation at Mrs. Gandhi's funeral (*NYT*, 5 November). Earlier in the year, the Soviets had charged that the United States was training Sikh separatists in Pakistan for terrorist activities (Tass, 15 August; *FBIS*, 15 August). In the aftermath of the assassination, the Soviet media repeated the accusation, specifically naming the CIA, implying U.S. responsibility for Mrs. Gandhi's murder. The United States responded with a vehement protest, while Secretary of State Shultz, leading the American delegation to the funeral, met in New Delhi with Indian leaders (*NYT*, 4–6 November).

North Korea. Kim Il-song, the North Korean dictator, made his first visit to the Soviet Union since 1964. He met three times with Chernenko, who also hosted a banquet in the Kremlin in Kim's honor (*Pravda*, 25 and 26 May). The visit followed by two weeks the cancellation of First Deputy Prime Minister Arkhipov's trip to Beijing, and the two events were not unrelated. In his speech at the banquet Chernenko used the term "hegemonism" to describe Chinese policy, the first such reference in some time, and said that the United States had made Asia "another Eastern front of struggle" against the Soviet Union and its allies (*NYT*, 26 May).

The visit was a plus for a USSR confronted with an increasingly unfavorable political balance on its eastern frontiers since it served notice on the PRC that Kim would return to the policy of equidistance he had pursued between Moscow and Beijing before 1975. However, Soviet wariness was evident in the cautious communiqué, which described the atmosphere of the talks as "warm and friendly" (Tass, 25 May). Chernenko made it clear that the USSR wanted no revival of hostilities on the Korean peninsula. The two sides agreed to an expansion of trade and other economic links, and it was believed that Kim had obtained a promise of new fighters to replace aging Soviet-built MiGs.

The two communist party-states had been brought closer together by strategic developments adversely affecting both countries, including the bolstering of American forces in South Korea, growing military cooperation between the United States and Japan, and the improvement in relations between Washington and Beijing (*NYT*, 26 May).

Japan. Soviet-Japanese relations, strained for years over fishing rights, territorial questions, and other issues, had plummeted to new depths in the wake of the Korean jetliner incident in September 1983. Thereafter, despite nuclear jitters that affected Japan as well as Western countries, the government of Prime Minister Yasuhiro Nakasone moved toward closer relations with the United States. At the turn of the new year, the Soviet media issued two commentaries sharply critical of Japanese policy.

The Soviets denounced "Japanese ruling circles" for more actively joining Reagan's "adventurist strategy" (Tass, 31 December 1983; *FBIS*, 3 January) despite "the fact that the recent parliamentary elections clearly demonstrated strong public opposition in Japan to the policy aimed at making the country a base of militarism and to the plans for drawing Japan closer to NATO" (Tass, 1 January; *FBIS*, 3 January). The 1 January release noted that when Nakasone had recently said that Japan should "maintain a dialogue" with the USSR, he had mentioned "Tokyo's groundless territorial claims to several islands belonging to the Soviet Union." This question, the commentary continued conclusively, "had been settled."

No progress was recorded on long-standing issues; in addition, the Soviets displayed concern over Japanese policy regarding the Soviet intervention in Afghanistan. But the main Soviet worry was strategic, the fear of an "encirclement" rounded out in the east by a Beijing-Tokyo-Washington axis, a specter largely conjured up by the Soviets' own policy, classified at various times by statesmen of the other three states under the rubric "hegemonism." Moscow's fears along these lines were reflected in two press commentaries at the beginning of October.

Proposals for the upgrading of the role and status of the Japanese Self-Defense Forces were denounced as part of a policy of turning Japan into an "unsinkable aircraft carrier" of the United States (Tass, 1 October; *FBIS*, 3 October). The Soviet press also reported unfavorably on consultations in Bonn between the head of the Japanese Defense Agency and West European NATO military leaders. The main point of these talks, according to the Soviets, was the "establishment of an anti-Soviet espionage network with the participation of intelligence services of Japan, the United States, and Western European NATO member countries" (ibid.).

Despite the frosty attitude displayed by Moscow, Nakasone sought to achieve some measure of "normalization" in relations with the USSR. Foreign Minister Shintaro Abe, in Moscow for Andropov's funeral, invited Gromyko to visit Japan and repeated the invitation at the United Nations in September; on both occasions, he was rebuffed by the

Soviet foreign minister, who described such a visit as "inappropriate" (*Radio Liberty Research*, 25 October).

As in other areas, Moscow suddenly emerged from its isolationist cocoon in early fall. The turning point was a statement by First Deputy Prime Minister Aliev, who expressed the USSR's readiness for improved relations, provided that a "similar readiness" was displayed by Japan and supported by "practical deeds" (ibid.; Tass, 12 October). Two weeks later, the highest-level Soviet-Japanese meeting since 1976 took place when Kazakh Communist Party first secretary and CPSU Politburo member Dinmukhamed Kunaev led a Supreme Soviet delegation on a visit to Japan (Tass, 25 October; *FBIS*, 25 October). Kunaev conferred with Prime Minister Nakasone and toured several Japanese cities. As expected, the visit led to no breakthroughs on major problems. Kunaev's public comments emphasized "reciprocal trade and economic cooperation" (Moscow radio, 30 October; *FBIS*, 1 November).

Southeast Asia. Renewed border fighting between North Vietnam and the PRC complicated Soviet-Chinese relations but Moscow evidently had more compelling reasons for dampening rapprochement with Beijing. In any case, the Soviets were not about to squander one of their main assets in the East Asian regional "correlation of forces" and continued their strong support for Hanoi and its allies. North Vietnam's defense minister, Gen. Van Tien Dung, conferred with Marshal Ustinov in Moscow during a June visit to the USSR (Moscow domestic service, 26 June; *FBIS*, 27 June). A *Pravda* commentary by Y. Fadeyev on Kampuchea (2 August) emphasized "proletarian internationalism and Vietnamese, Lao, and Kampuchean militant solidarity with the Soviet Union and the other socialist community states."

Moscow backed Laos in its border dispute with Thailand. Chernenko held talks with Kaysone Phomvihane, general secretary of the Lao People's Revolutionary Party, in Moscow in June. The official communiqué said that the two leaders "strongly condemned the hostile actions of the Chinese authorities against Vietnam, Laos, and Kampuchea as well as the recent armed provocations of Thai reactionary quarters" against Laos (Tass, 26 June; *FBIS*, 27 June). But evidently not wishing to close all doors to the Bangkok regime, the Soviet welcomed a National Assembly of Thailand delegation on a visit to the Soviet Union. In Moscow, the Thai parliamentarians were received in the Kremlin by Supreme Soviet Presidium Vice-Chairman Kuznetsov (Moscow domestic service, 3 August; *FBIS*, 6 August).

Middle East. The region providing the best news for the Soviets during the year was the Middle East. The U.S. withdrawal from Lebanon left a power vacuum that the Soviets moved to fill, with Syria assigned the role of proxy; full diplomatic relations with Egypt were restored after a long break; the Soviet foothold on the Arabian peninsula was bolstered by successful initiatives toward both Yemens; Moscow's influence was also felt in Jordan, Iraq, and Kuwait. Nevertheless, Soviet clout in the region was still less than that attained in the halcyon years of 1967 to 1972 and the complexities of Middle East politics tended to confound Moscow's searches for a consistent and successful policy.

A scheduled February trip to Syria having been postponed due to Andropov's funeral, First Deputy Prime Minister Geidar Aliev finally arrived in Damascus, 11 March, on a much-heralded mission (*CSM*, 12 March). There he conferred with President Hafiz al-Asad and other Syrian officials and conveyed a message of strong support from Moscow. The joint communiqué issued at the end of the visit expressed "satisfaction at the steady development and expansion of all-round relations between the Soviet Union and Syria" and the determination of both countries "to continue the joint struggle for the attainment of a comprehensive and just Near East settlement." The communiqué also pointedly stressed the need to "overcome as speedily as possible" the disagreements within the Palestine Liberation Organization (PLO) and for the "close cooperation by the PLO with Syria" (*Pravda*, 14 March).

Soviet-Syrian cooperation steadily deepened following the Aliev visit. Karen Brutents, deputy head of the CPSU Central Committee's International Department, led a Soviet delegation that was received by President Asad in April; the two countries reaffirmed their April commitment to work together in the region (Tass, 18 April; *FBIS*, 19 April). The Soviet press lent strong verbal support to Asad and vehemently opposed U.S. and Israeli actions in Lebanon (*Pravda*, 17 April; *Izvestiia*, 27 April), alongside reportedly accelerated delivery of military hardware to Damascus. In May, the eighth session of the Permanent Intergovernmental Commission on Economic, Scientific, and Technical

Cooperation between the Soviet Union and the Syrian Arab Republic met in Moscow. The chief Soviet spokesman, Yakov P. Ryabov, chairman of the State Committee on Foreign Economic Relations, hailed Soviet-Syrian economic cooperation, especially current projects, including a dam, power plant and transmission lines, railways, and bridges (Tass, 23 May; *FBIS*, 25 May). In the following week, Syrian vice-president Rif'at al-Asad journeyed to Moscow, where he was warmly received by Chernenko and Kuznetsov (*Pravda*, 31 May, 1 June).

The withdrawal of American and other Western forces from Lebanon and Lebanon's denunciation of the 17 May 1983 agreement with Israel were trumpeted in the Soviet press as military and political defeats for the United States (ibid., 26 June).

President Asad visited Moscow in October. The Syrians reported that the Soviets had promised more military aid but the general atmosphere was characterized by a Western observer as "lukewarm, bordering on cool." An unusual feature of the visit was the Soviets' failure to publish the speeches of Chernenko and Asad and the Kremlin's pointed pledge to give "all-round assistance" to Syria and "the other Arab peoples." Moscow was obviously unwilling to tie itself too closely to Damascus, a major reason being the continuing bitter dispute between Asad and another Moscow ally, PLO leader Yassir Arafat. Soviet pressure on both sides had apparently failed to heal the rift. (*CSM*, 19 October.)

A more unmixed, if less impressive, gain was the resumption of full diplomatic relations between the USSR and Egypt; the two countries had not maintained ambassadorial ties since 1981. Moscow named Aleksandr Belonogov, 53, as ambassador to Egypt (AFP, Paris, 29 June; *FBIS*, 29 June); Cairo designated senior career diplomat Salah Bassiouni as envoy to the USSR (BBC, 4 July). The Soviets obviously hoped to utilize this diplomatic link to recover lost influence in the region, but the main immediate benefit was indirect, the downgrading of the American impact on Middle Eastern politics. Egypt had chosen to adopt a balanced position between the superpowers in order to underscore its independence from the United States and emerge from its long isolation within the Arab world.

The very active Yakov Ryabov represented the USSR in March at ceremonies in Baghdad marking the twenty-fifth anniversary of the signing of the first Soviet-Iraqi agreement on economic and technical cooperation (*Pravda*, 19 March). Ryabov also headed the Soviet delegation at the fourteenth session of the Soviet-Iraqi Commission on Economic Cooperation and met President Saddam Husayn of Iraq. The communiqué on their meeting stressed the "mutual desire of the USSR and Iraq to strengthen and develop friendly relations and economic ties" (Moscow domestic service, 20 March). One sour note was sounded by Moscow's denunciation of the "unwarranted persecution" by the Husayn regime of the Iraqi Communist Party (*Pravda*, 31 March). As Soviet relations with Iran continued to deteriorate, the Kremlin leadership evidently hoped to obtain greater leverage in Baghdad and the fate of the Iraqi Communist Party was surely a minor hurdle. But any such hopes were considerably dampened in November when the United States and Iraq resumed diplomatic relations.

An unexpected bonanza came with new inroads in the Persian Gulf area. After being rebuffed by the United States on a similar proposed deal, Kuwait agreed to buy Soviet antiair defenses and other military matériel worth $325 million. Kuwati defense minister Salim Sabah al-Salim al-Sabah was warmly received on a July visit to the USSR at the invitation of Defense Minister Ustinov (*Krasnaia zvezda*, 15 July).

The growing military role in Soviet diplomacy in the region was emphasized in August when, on successive days, Ustinov welcomed to Moscow Lt. Gen. Sharif Zayd ibn-Shakir, commander of the armed forces of Jordan (Tass, 6 August; *FBIS*, 7 August) and Brig. Gen. Salih Muslih Qasim, defense minister of the People's Democratic Republic of Yemen (PDRY) (Moscow domestic service, 7 August; *FBIS*, 8 August).

President Ali Nasir Muhammad al-Hasani of the PDRY visited Moscow in October and met with Chernenko (*Pravda*, 9 October). One day after his departure, the leader of North Yemen, President Ali Abdullah Salih, arrived in Moscow and also conferred with Chernenko. During his visit, the USSR and the Yemen Arab Republic signed a twenty-year treaty of friendship (*NYT*, 10 October).

Africa. Aside from Egypt, Soviet influence on the continent evidently continued to diminish, especially south of the Sahara. The dream of Soviet penetration of Africa under the banner of "national liberation" that appeared so close to realization via the effective use of Cuban proxies in the 1970s seemed to be fading.

Alternate Politburo member Eduard Shevardnadze, first secretary of the Georgian Communist Party, made an apparently successful trip to Algeria

in May. Shevardnadze headed the Soviet delegation at the Sixth Congress of the Afro-Asian Peoples' Solidarity Organization (AAPSO) and met with Algerian president Chadli Benjedid and other officials. The joint communiqué expressed "satisfaction with the state of bilateral Algerian-Soviet friendly relations" (Tass, 31 May; *FBIS*, 1 June). Zambia's president, Kenneth Kaunda, "assessed highly the relations between the USSR and Zambia" in March when he received a Soviet delegation headed by Oleg S. Miroshkin, second secretary of the Kazakh Communist Party (*Pravda*, 14 March).

Major problems developed in Moscow's relations with its two closest allies in sub-Saharan Africa. In March, South Africa concluded a nonaggression pact with Mozambique and signed a cease-fire agreement with Angola. Moscow reacted sharply to the news. Foreign Minister Gromyko summoned U.S. ambassador Arthur A. Hartman for talks on southern Africa, and General Secretary Chernenko issued a statement charging that Washington and Pretoria were seeking to draw African states "into their own far-reaching militarist plans" (*NYT*, 8 April).

Subsequent efforts by Moscow appeared to have no major impact on the course of events in the region. Talks between Angola's deputy foreign minister V. Moura and USSR deputy foreign minister Leonid Ilyichev in Moscow in August resulted only in a terse communiqué reporting a "businesslike and friendly atmosphere" (*Izvestiia*, 29 August). At the same time, a Soviet delegation led by Antanas S. Barkauskas, chairman of the Presidium of the Lithuanian Supreme Soviet and deputy chairman of the USSR Supreme Soviet, was in Angola. This visit did produce a statement rejecting linkage of Namibia's decolonization with the withdrawal of Cuban forces from Angola (ibid.). From Luanda, the Barkauskas delegation went on to Mozambique, where it was received by a relatively low-level group of parliamentarians. The official communiqué on the visit affirmed Soviet-Mozambican support "for the liberation struggle of the peoples of Namibia and South Africa" (ibid., 30 August). Earlier in the month, the USSR and Mozambique had concluded an agreement on cooperation in fishing (Moscow radio, 13 August; *FBIS*, 14 August).

Discussions on the strengthening of trade links between the USSR and the Democratic Republic of Madagascar (DRM) were held in Moscow in August between G. K. Zhuravlev, first deputy minister of foreign trade, and R. T. Andrianarivo, DRM minister of industry (*Izvestiia*, 10 August).

The relationship between Moscow and the Marxist regime in Ethiopia retained elements of tension, a situation not helped by the USSR's slow response to the disastrous famine in the East African country, which was understandable in view of the Soviets' own agricultural problems. However, major diplomatic efforts were devoted to the somewhat uncertain ally. Ethiopia's leader, Mengistu Haile Mariam, visited Moscow in March (*Pravda*, 31 March) and in December (ibid., 20 December); he was received by Chernenko on both occasions. In October, a high-level Soviet delegation, headed by Politburo member Grigori Romanov and including Deputy Prime Minister Guri I. Marchuk, visited Ethiopia (ibid., 6 October). The Soviet media played up a July statement by Ethiopian defense minister Tesfaye Gebre Kidan lauding the USSR's support to the country "in defending its revolutionary gains, freedom, and territorial integrity" (ibid., 20 July).

Latin America. The major focus of attention continued to be the conflicts in Central America. In the aftermath of the successful American invasion of Grenada, Cuba appared to be more wary about taking risks in Central America, but the Soviets continued to pour armaments into Nicaragua. In March, the Soviet tanker *Lugansk* was damaged off Nicaragua by a rebel mine allegedly laid with CIA support, leading to vociferous Soviet protests (*Newsweek*, 2 April). In the fall, it was Washington's turn to protest. Unnerved by a report of a Soviet shipment of late-model MiG fighters to Nicaragua, U.S. secretary of state Shultz held urgent consultations with Soviet ambassador Dobrynin (*NYT*, 7 and 9 November). The report was not subsequently confirmed, but American authorities stated emphatically that such shipments would drastically upset the existing military balance in Central America and would not be tolerated.

Several visits by Nicaraguan officials to Moscow reaffirmed the Soviets' strong support for the Sandinistas. In March Nicaraguan minister of planning Henry Ruiz Hernández met with Yakov P. Ryabov, chairman of the USSR State Committee for Foreign Economic Relations, to discuss petroleum deliveries, cooperation in the textile industry, and other economic matters (*Pravda*, 24 March). Junta leader Daniel Ortega Saavedra visited Moscow in June for wide-ranging talks with Soviet officials (ibid., 21 June), and in April Nicaraguan defense minister Humberto Ortega Saavedra stopped in

Moscow for talks on his return from a trip to North Korea (*Krasnaia zvezda*, 15 April).

The cozy relationship established with Argentina through grain sales to the USSR during the U.S. embargo and Moscow's verbal support for the Argentines in the Falklands war seemed unlikely to survive the fall of the military junta and reestablishment of democratic government in Buenos Aires. Elsewhere, minimal contacts were maintained with South American regimes.

A Soviet delegation led by Kurban A. Khalilov, chairman of the Azerbaijan Supreme Soviet and deputy chairman of the Presidium of the USSR Supreme Soviet, met with the leadership of the ruling Democratic Action Party during a February visit to Venezuela (*Izvestiia*, 9 February). Mikhail Zimianin, Central Committee secretary for culture, headed a Supreme Soviet delegation on an official visit to Brazil in May (ibid., 6 May). During the visit, Zimianin addressed the Brazilian National Congress and denounced American "aggression" against Grenada and "undeclared war" against Nicaragua (Tass, 8 May; *FBIS*, 9 May).

The USSR and Uruguay signed an agreement on the resumption of Soviet oil exports in July. Under the agreement, the Soviets agreed to provide 5,000 barrels of oil daily to Uruguay (EFE, Madrid, 17 July; *FBIS*, 23 July). Gaibnazar Pallayev, chairman of the Tadzhik Republic Supreme Soviet and a deputy chairman of the USSR Supreme Soviet, represented the USSR at the inauguration of Ecuador's new president, León Febres Cordero (*Izvestiia*, 12 August; *FBIS*, 14 August). Yuri Y. Fokin, general secretary of the USSR Foreign Ministry, met with senior officials of Colombia's Foreign Ministry in Bogotá in August to discuss the upcoming session of the U.N. General Assembly and questions of bilateral relations (ibid.).

International Party Contacts. The passing of the torch of leadership and the continuing succession crisis did not slow the pace of contacts with other communist parties; indeed, the pressures upon the new team of leaders may have tended to accelerate such activity, particularly in regard to the nonruling parties in Europe. Relations with nonruling communist parties seemed to be carried out with more consistency than was Soviet foreign policy in general, perhaps due to the continuity provided by Boris Ponomarev, longtime head of the Central Committee International Department and party secretary for liaison with parties outside the bloc. There were three major thrusts of CPSU interaction with the other parties: a continuing effort to capitalize on the "peace" issue and inhibit NATO's nuclear rearmament; pursuit of a militant anti-Americanism on all fronts; the promotion of cohesion of the international movement under Moscow's leadership and the banner of "proletarian internationalism" and encouragement of pro-Moscow factions where they existed. Given the diversity of the world movement, the third tactic could be promoted only selectively and, where necessary, was sacrificed to the other two. Relations with other communist parties also figured symbolically in the jockeying for position among Andropov's heirs, providing rising Politburo stars Grigori Romanov and Mikhail Gorbachev the opportunity to showcase their talents in foreign affairs.

In Eastern Europe, interparty contacts were directed toward the holding together of an increasingly fractious bloc and generating support for Soviet policy toward NATO. East Germany, where opposition to installation of new Soviet missiles had appeared, was the number-one problem. Minister of Defense and Politburo member Dimitri Ustinov was in Berlin in June in conjunction with Soviet army staff exercises and met Socialist Unity Party (SED) leader Erich Honecker and other officials (Tass, 29 June; *FBIS*, 29 June). In the same week, N. A. Stashenkov, deputy chief of the CPSU Trade and Consumer Services Section, was in the GDR to study East German experience in his areas of work and met with Werner Jarowinsky, candidate member of the SED Politburo and secretary of the Central Committee (*Pravda*, 24 June). Over the following two months, tremendous Soviet media and diplomatic pressure was brought to bear on East Berlin to check the developing détente with Bonn, culminating in the September postponement of Honecker's scheduled visit to the FRG (see above).

Relations between Mosow and Warsaw were relatively quiet during the year. Poland was not directly involved in the missile controversy, but the Polish party gave verbal support to Soviet policy and the situation within the country had stabilized sufficiently that Moscow was able to turn its attention elsewhere. A highlight of interparty relations was the May visit to Moscow by Polish prime minister and party leader Wojciech Jaruzelski and party secretary Jozef Czyrek (ibid., 6 May). They met with CPSU Politburo members Tikhonov, Ustinov, and Gromyko, and with CPSU Central Committee secretary for bloc affairs Konstantin Rusakov. Jaruzelski pledged that Poland would be "a faithful ally of the USSR, a permanent link of the

Warsaw Treaty, and an active member of COMECON" (PAP, Warsaw, 5 May; *FBIS*, 8 May).

As usual, Romania performed a balancing act in its relations with Moscow. Nicolae Ceauşescu welcomed Nicaraguan leader Daniel Ortega to Bucharest with much fanfare and endorsed Soviet policy on Central America (*Pravda*, 28 June). But on issues of more concern to Romania, the Romanian party declined to follow Moscow's lead, refusing to join the boycott of the Olympics or the Soviet propaganda campaign against the FRG, which Ceauşescu visited as scheduled in November. Gromyko, Rusakov, and Deputy Premier and Central Committee member Nikolai Talyzin visited Bucharest in January for talks with Ceauşescu and other officials (ibid., 2 February), apparently with no major impact upon Romanian policies. In June, a delegation of CPSU party workers headed by Y. N. Altunin, a secretary of the Tyumen *obkom*, visited Romania to study economic experience and was received by Ilie Verdeţ, secretary of the Romanian Central Committee and member of the Political Executive Committee (ibid., 29 June). Boris Ponomarev journeyed to Bucharest in November and conferred with Ceauşescu and with Ion Stoian, candidate member of the Political Executive Committee and Central Committee secretary (Bucharest domestic service, 13 November; *FBIS*, 14 November).

Czechoslovakia was another country where the "peace" movement turned sour for the CPSU. Moscow was sufficiently concerned to dispatch party secretary and Politburo member Grigori Romanov to Prague, where he conferred with Gustáv Husák and other Czech leaders. During the visit, Husák presented Romanov with the Order of Victorious February (Prague domestic service, 18 May; *FBIS*, 21 May). Also in May, Anatoli Yegorov, head of the CPSU's Institute of Marxism-Leninism, visited Prague for a conference with Czech party secretary Josef Havlin on ideological matters (Bratislava domestic service, 22 May; *FBIS*, 23 May).

The Bulgarian Communist Party continued to profess its loyalty to Moscow. In September, the Bulgarian State Council awarded Moscow city first secretary and CPSU Politburo member Viktor Grishin the Order of Georgi Dimitrov on the occasion of his seventieth birthday, and Bulgarian leader Todor Zhivkov led the celebration of the fiftieth anniversary of the founding of the Bulgarian-Soviet Friendship Society (Moscow domestic service, 18 September; *FBIS*, 19 September). However, such public manifestations of a close relationship could not conceal the growing rift over détente with Bonn. In November, Zhivkov's scheduled visit to the FRG was called off, evidently as a result of Soviet pressure (see above).

Relations between Moscow and Belgrade remained cool but correct. A delegation of CPSU party workers led by G. G. Bartoshevich, second secretary of the Belorussian Communist Party, visited Yugoslavia, 27 March–3 April, to discuss questions of party organizational work (*Pravda*, 5 April).

The regular conference of bloc party secretaries for international and ideological questions was held in Prague in July; Ponomarev and Rusakov represented the CPSU. As expected, the conference produced a statement condemning the NATO position on Euromissiles (ibid., 13 July; *FBIS*, 16 July).

Contacts with ruling communist parties in Asia were aimed at forging closer links with the CPSU and coordinating policy positions, particularly vis-à-vis China. Interparty contacts with the Chinese Communist Party (CPC) remained at a low level, and intergovernmental contacts did not rise above the first deputy prime minister level. The visit of First Deputy Prime Minister Arkhipov to Beijing in December indicated a slight mellowing in Moscow's attitude toward the PRC (see above), but acute differences between the CPSU and the CPC remained unresolved.

USSR deputy prime minister and Central Committee member Ziya Nuriev visited Kabul in September for talks with Babrak Karmal and other Afghan officials on economic cooperation (*Pravda*, 11 September).

North Korean leader Kim Il-song made his first visit to the Soviet Union in twenty years and met in Moscow with Chernenko and other Politburo members (ibid., 25 and 26 May).

Representatives of all of the USSR's Southeast Asian allies visited Moscow during the year. Vietnamese defense minister and Politburo member Van Tien Dung met with Defense Minister Ustinov in June (Moscow domestic service, 26 June; *FBIS*, 27 June). Kaysone Phomvihane, general secretary of the Lao People's Democratic Party and Laotian premier, was received in the Kremlin by Chernenko (ibid.). Kampuchean premier and Kampuchean People's Revolutionary Party (KPRP) Politburo member Chan Si met with Tikhonov (*Izvestiia*, 25 July).

Meir Vilner, general secretary of the Israeli party, and three other officials of that party's Central Committee met in Moscow in January with Ponomarev and Karen Brutents, deputy head of the CPSU International Department. The conferees issued a statement denouncing the "aggressive" policies of the United States and "Israeli ruling circles" (*Pravda*, 22 January).

A delegation of the Communist Party of India led by Politburo member Harkishan Singh Surjetan visited Uzbekistan in September (Tashkent international service; 4 September; *FBIS*, 6 September).

CPSU ideologists made two visits to Tokyo for talks with their Japanese party counterparts. Piotr Fedoseyev, vice-president of the USSR Academy of Sciences, and Ivan Kovalenko, deputy head of the International Department, were guests of the Japanese Central Committee in April (Tass, 25 April; *FBIS*, 26 April). Kovalenko made another visit in September, accompanied by Anatoli Yegorov, head of the Institute of Marxism-Leninism (Tass, 11 September; *FBIS*, 12 September). International Department deputy head Vadim Zagladin, a member of the USSR Supreme Soviet delegation that visited Japan in October, met with Mitsuhiro Kaneko, chairman of the Central Committee Secretariat, and other Japanese party leaders (Tass, 30 October; *FBIS*, 1 November).

Mengistu Haile Mariam, chairman of the Commission to Organize the Party of the Working People of Ethiopia (COPWE) and Ethiopian head of state, visited Moscow in March for talks with Chernenko and other officials (*Pravda*, 31 March). The visit was returned in October when the Soviets dispatched a full Politburo member to Africa, a rare event in recent years. Party secretary and Politburo member Grigori Romanov led the delegation to Addis Ababa, which also included USSR deputy prime minister and Central Committee member Guri I. Marchuk (ibid., 6 October). Mengistu visited Moscow again in December for further meetings with Chernenko (ibid., 20 December).

Daniel Ortega Saavedra, head of the ruling junta in Nicaragua and member of the National Directorate of the Sandinista Front of National Liberation, visited Moscow in June and met with Ponomarev and other officials (ibid., 21 June).

Ivan S. Gustov, first deputy chairman of the Party Control Committee, represented the CPSU at the Eighth Congress of the Guadeloupe Communist Party (ibid., 26 April).

The area of most intensive activity by the CPSU during the year was Western Europe, and virtually all contacts with the nonruling parties played up the Euromissile issue. The crucial importance of Germany in Soviet strategic concerns was emphasized in January when party secretary Romanov led the CPSU delegation to the congress of the German Communist Party (DKP) in Nuremberg. Since the DKP has fewer than 50,000 members, it would ordinarily rate only a secondary CPSU representative (BBC, 5 January). Another CPSU delegation visited West Germany in May at the invitation of the DKP and was led by R. G. Yanovsky, rector of the Academy of Social Sciences (*Pravda*, 7 May).

A delegation of the Socialist Unity Party (SED) of West Berlin, led by party chairman Horst Schmitt, visited Moscow in February and declared its firm support for the Soviet position on the missile issue. Schmitt met with Chernenko and Ponomarev and with Vadim Zagladin, first deputy head of the International Department (Tass, 1 February; *FBIS*, 3 February). Gennadi F. Sizov, chairman of the Central Auditing Commission, led the CPSU delegation to the Seventh Congress of the West Berlin SED in May (Moscow television service, 26 May; *FBIS*, 29 May).

Vasili I. Konotop, first secretary of Moscow *obkom*, led a CPSU delegation to the Netherlands, 16–21 April, and met with Communist Party of the Netherlands (CPN) chairman Elli Izeboud and other party figures. Representatives of the two parties declared their firm opposition to deployment of NATO cruise missiles in the Netherlands (Tass, 21 April; *FBIS*, 24 April).

A CPSU delegation led by International Department deputy head Zagladin visited Brussels in May at the invitation of the Belgian Communist Party (Tass, 18 April; *FBIS*, 20 April). In July, Belgian party president Louis van Geyt met in Moscow with Gorbachev (Tass, 19 July; *FBIS*, 23 July).

A delegation of the Communist Party of Denmark visited the USSR, 26 June–5 July, and expressed "full support for the peace initiatives of the CPSU and the Soviet government." The group was led by Poul Emanuel, member of the party's Executive Committee and secretary of the Central Committee (*Pravda*, 7 July).

Viktor Afanasyev, editor-in-chief of *Pravda* and member of the CPSU Central Committee, conferred with Rolf Hagel, chairman of Sweden's Communist Workers' Party, while in Stockholm for an international conference on problems of security and disarmament in Europe (Tass, 14 March; *FBIS*, 16 March).

The split in the Finnish Communist Party (FCP) over questions related to the issue of Eurocommunism aroused considerable concern in Moscow.

Pravda (28 March) repeated earlier criticism in the weekly *Za rubezhom* directed at General Secretary Arvo Aalto and former party chairman Aarne Saarinen, and in April, the CPSU dispatched a high-level delegation led by Lev N. Zaikov, first secretary of Leningrad *obkom*, to Helsinki (Tass, 30 April; *FBIS*, 30 April). Still concerned, the CPSU sent an even weightier group to Helsinki in the following month. The delegation, led by Party Control Committee chairman Mikhail S. Solomentsev and including Karl G. Vaino, first secretary of the Estonian Communist Party, met with Aalto and other leaders of the Finnish party (*Pravda*, 30 May).

A message from the CPSU to the Eighteenth Congress of the Norwegian Communist Party, in March, stressed the missile issue, denouncing the "senseless and adventurist" actions of U.S. imperialism and affirming support for a nuclear-free zone in northern Europe (ibid., 30 March). The Euromissile issue also dominated the May meeting in Geneva between Boris I. Stukalin, head of the CPSU Propaganda Department, and Armand Magnin, secretary general of the Swiss Labor Party (Tass, 26 March; *FBIS*, 2 April).

The small Communist Party of Austria (KPO) has for years attracted CPSU attention far out of proportion to its size due to its vigorous support of "proletarian internationalism" and submission to Moscow. This high level of recognition for the KPO was displayed again when Central Committee secretary Nikolai I. Ryzhkov, accompanied by Kharkov *obkom* first secretary Vladislav P. Mysnichenko, attended the Twenty-fifth KPO Congress in Vienna (Tass, 12 January).

Anatoli Chernyayev, deputy head of the Central Committee International Department, led the CPSU delegation at the Twenty-fourth Congress of the Communist Party of Luxembourg (*Pravda*, 4 February). As expected, the congress gave a resounding endorsement to Moscow's position on the Euromissile issue (Tass, 4 February; *FBIS*, 8 February). An extraordinary congress of the Communist Party of the Netherlands held at the same time expressed similar views on "peace" and the "nuclear arms race" (*Pravda*, 5 February).

A low-level French Communist Party (PCF) delegation visited the USSR in July at the invitation of the CPSU. The delegation was received by officials of the Heavy Industry Department of the Central Committee and visited nuclear and other industrial installations in Voronezh (ibid., 11 July).

Much favorable publicity was accorded the new

Communist Party of Spain, organized in January, and its leader, Ignacio Gallego (*Pravda*, 6 March; *Za rubezhom*, no. 10, March). In May, Gallego led a delegation to Moscow, where it was received by Zagladin (Tass, 22 May; *FBIS*, 24 May).

A delegation of the Portuguese Communist Party visited the USSR in July at the invitation of the CPSU Central Committee to study development of the Soviet power industry (*Pravda*, 11 July).

Stepan V. Chervonenko, head of the Central Committee's Cadres Abroad Department, led a CPSU delegation to Rome in May for meetings with officials of the Italian Communist Party (PCI) (Moscow television service, 2 May; *FBIS*, 3 May). In the following month, Gorbachev led the Soviet mourners at the funeral of the PCI leader Enrico Berlinguer (Moscow domestic service, 13 June; *FBIS*, 14 June). While in Rome, Gorbachev and Zagladin met with PCI leaders (Tass, 13 June; *FBIS*, 14 June), evidently hoping to overcome past frictions in the interest of cooperation on the urgent questions of nuclear arms in Europe.

Biographies. *Konstantin Ustinovich Chernenko.* Born 24 September 1911 in the village of Bolshaia Tes in south-central Siberia, Chernenko was of peasant origins. He was listed in all official Soviet sources as an ethnic Russian, but it is believed that his ancestry was Ukrainian and that his family was part of the vast outmigration from the Ukraine to Siberia around the turn of the century.

While still in his teens, Chernenko served in the Border Guards in Central Asia and joined the party in 1931. A decade later, he was named a party secretary in his native Krasnoyarsk *krai*. One of the few party officials of his generation who did not see active service in World War II, he spent most of that period at the Higher Party School in Moscow, from which he graduated in 1945. He also holds a diploma from the Kishinev Pedagogical Institute, awarded in 1953.

Chernenko was posted to Moldavia in 1948, and while serving there as head of the agitation and propaganda section of that republic's party central committee, he began his long association with Leonid Brezhnev, who was the Moldavian Communist Party's first secretary (1950–1952). When Brezhnev was named to the CPSU Central Committee Secretariat in 1956, he arranged for Chernenko's transfer to Moscow, where the latter served in the Central Committee and, from 1960, in the Secretariat of the Supreme Soviet.

Shortly after Brezhnev's election as first secre-

tary of the CPSU, Chernenko was appointed, in 1965, to head the Central Committee's General Department, in charge of liaison between the Politburo and the Central Committee and security arrangements for Politburo members. He was elected a candidate member of the Central Committee in 1966 and a full member in 1971 and has served continuously as a deputy of the USSR Supreme Soviet since 1966.

Elected a secretary of the Central Committee at the Twenty-fifth CPSU Congress in 1976, he was named a candidate member of the Politburo in October 1977 and was promoted to full member in November 1978. Following his election to full membership, he was recognized as Brezhnev's closest associate and a leading candidate for the succession. After the death of Mikhail Suslov in January 1982, Chernenko assumed an even more prominent role and directed the March 1982 reorganization of the trade union leadership. Passed over for the party leadership following Brezhnev's death in November 1982, he served under Andropov as secretary for ideology and was the major speaker at the June 1983 Central Committee plenum dealing with ideological questions. Otherwise thrust into the background during the first ten months of Andropov's tenure, he re-emerged into prominence during the party leader's final disabling illness and presided over the Bolshevik Revolution anniversary celebrations in November 1982.

Following Andropov's death and unusually lengthy consultations on the succession, Chernenko was elected 13 February 1984 general secretary of the CPSU Central Committee.

Chernenko accompanied Brezhnev on several trips abroad, including Ghana in 1961, Helsinki in July 1975 for the signing of the Final Act of the Conference on Security and Cooperation in Europe, and Vienna in July 1979 for the SALT II summit. He visited Washington in 1974 and in February 1982 represented the CPSU at the French Communist Party congress. He has been awarded the Red Banner of Labor and three Orders of Lenin. He received his third Order of Lenin at a Kremlin ceremony on 27 September 1984; the presentation was made by Defense Minister Dimitri Ustinov. Following a long illness, Chernenko died on 10 March 1985. (Sources: *Bolshaia sovetskaia entsiklopediia*, 3rd ed., Moscow, 1978, 29:84; Borys Lewytzkyi and Juliusz Stroynowski, eds., *Who's Who in the Socialist Countries*, Munich, 1978, p. 102; *Time*, 27 February; *Pravda*, 4 February 1982; 14 February, 28 September.)

Sergei Leonidovich Sokolov. Born 1911, Sokolov is the son of a clerk. He joined the Soviet army in 1937 and was admitted to membership in the communist party in 1937. During World War II, he commanded a tank battalion. Sokolov graduated from the Military Academy for Armored and Mechanized Troops in 1947 and the General Staff Military Academy in 1951. Between 1945 and 1965, he held various command and staff positions, rising in the latter year to the post of commander of the Leningrad Military District.

Appointed first deputy minister of defense in 1967, Sokolov subsequently played a key role on the general staff, particularly in regard to Soviet operations in Ethiopia in the late 1970s, and is believed to have been the chief planner of the invasion of Afghanistan. When Defense Minister Dimitri Ustinov was disabled in September 1984, Sokolov apparently assumed most of his duties. Filling in for Ustinov at the Bolshevik Revolution anniversary parade on 7 November, Sokolov reviewed the troops and delivered the main address, a hard-line speech blaming the "ruling circles of the United States and of the NATO bloc" for increasing world tensions. Sokolov was appointed defense minister on 22 December 1984, succeeding Ustinov, who had died two days earlier.

Sokolov was a candidate member of the CPSU Central Committee, 1966–1968, and has been a full member since the April 1968 plenum. He has also served as a deputy to the USSR Supreme Soviet since 1966. He has been awarded the Order of the Red Banner, two Orders of the Red Star, and other decorations. (Sources: Borys Lewytzkyi and Juliusz Stroynowski, eds., *Who's Who in the Socialist Countries*, Munich, 1978, p. 575; *Radio Liberty Research*, 30 May 1982; *Pravda*, 8 November; *NYT*, 23 December.)

R. Judson Mitchell
University of New Orleans

Yugoslavia

Population. 22,997,000

Party. League of Communists of Yugoslavia (Savez komunista Jugoslavije; LCY). As the only political party in the Socialist Federative Republic of Yugoslavia (SFRY), the LCY exercises much of its power through its leading role in the Socialist Alliance of the Working People of Yugoslavia (Socijalistički savez radnog naroda Jugoslavije; SAWPY), a mass organization that includes all major political and social organizations as well as individuals representing various social groups.

Founded. 1920

Membership. 2,500,000 (*Danas*, 18 December)

President of Presidium. Ali Šukrija (elected at the end of June for a 1-year term)

Secretary of Presidium. Dimče Belovski (serving the first half of his 2-year term)

Presidium. 23 members, 3 from each republic, 2 from each of the autonomous provinces, and 1 from the army. Slovenia, Mitja Ribičič, Milan Kučan, Andrej Marinc; Croatia, Jure Bilić, Dušan Dragosavac, Josip Vrhovec; Bosnia-Hercegovina, Nikola Stojanović, Franjo Herljević, Hamdija Pozderac; Montenegro, Veljko Milatović (resigned in August 1984), Miljan Radović, Dobroslav Ćulafić; Serbia, Dragoslav Marković, Dobrivoje Vidić, Dušan Čkrebić; Macedonia, Dimče Belovski, Kiro Hadži-Vasilev, Krste Markovski; Kosovo, Ali Šukrija, Ilijaz Kurteši; Vojvodina, Petar Matić, Slavko Veselinov; Army, Dane Duić

Central Committee. 165 members

Status. Ruling party

Last Congress. Twelfth, 26–29 June 1982, in Belgrade; next congress scheduled for 1986

Auxiliary Organizations. Confederation of Trade Unions of Yugoslavia, League of Socialist Youth of Yugoslavia

Main State Organs. The president and vice-president of the 8-member State Presidency serve 1-year terms, and positions rotate among members. The current president, Veselin Djuranović (Montenegro), assumed the duty of president in the middle of May 1984; the vice-president is Radovan Vlajković (Vojvodina). Other members are Stane Dolanc (Slovenia), Sinan Hasani (Kosovo), Nikola Ljubičić (Serbia), Branko Mikulić (Bosnia-Hercegovina), Lazar Mojsov (Macedonia), Josip Vrhovec (Croatia), and Ali Šukrija, an ex-officio member in his capacity as president of the LCY Presidium of the Central Committee. Under the 1974 constitution the main administrative organ is the 29-member Federal Executive Council (FEC) chosen by and responsible to the Yugoslav Federal Assembly. FEC members serve 4-year terms. Major figures include Milka Planinc (premier); Borislav Srebrić, Mijat Šuković, and Janez Zemljarič (vice-premiers); the most important among the fourteen federal secretaries and chairmen of federal committees are Raif Dizdarević (foreign affairs), Branko Mamula (defense), Dobroslav Ćulafić (internal affairs), and Vlado Klemenčič (finance); 11 members of the FEC are ministers without portfolio.

Parliament and Elections. 1982; all candidates to the 220-seat Federal Chamber and the 88-seat Chamber of Republics and Provinces run on the ticket of SAWPY. All delegates are chosen indirectly through a multilayer process closely supervised by the LCY.

Publications. The main publications of the LCY are *Komunist* (weekly) and *Socijalizam* (monthly). The major dailies are *Borba*, with Belgrade and Zagreb editions, *Vjesnik* (Zagreb), *Delo* (Ljubljana), *Nova Makedonija* (Skoplje). The most important weeklies are *NIN* (*Nedeljne informativne novine*, Belgrade), *Ekonomska politika* (Belgrade), and *Danas* (Zagreb). Tanjug is the official news agency.

1983

(Editor's note: the 1984 edition of the *Yearbook* did not contain a profile for Yugoslavia. The following is a summary of events in Yugoslavia in 1983. For a listing of party and government officials in 1983, see *YICA*, 1984, pp. 403–4.)

Domestic Affairs. Economic conditions continued to deteriorate in 1983 despite a bountiful harvest (Tanjug, 29 September), an increase in industrial production of 1.3 percent, and a surplus of $300 million in Yugoslavia's current account balance with the convertible currency area. Productivity declined by 3.5 percent (*Socijalizam*, no. 6, 1984), unemployment reached 915,000, and the rate of inflation, which was 32.7 percent in 1982 (Tanjug, 13 January 1983), reached "50 percent" at the end of 1983, according to the Yugoslav prime minister (ibid., 27 December 1983). Food shortages forced the introduction of rationing in some urban areas, while the drought and lack of fuel oil imposed power cuts in factories and cities. The dinar continued to depreciate in relation to hard currencies.

At the end of July 1983 the Central Committee of the LCY and the National Assembly adopted the Long-term Stabilization Program following a lengthy debate in the course of which differences of opinion among top leaders were apparent. The program, the result of a compromise between republic and provincial party organizations, involved austerity measures, the encouragement of exports, and attempts to increase the profitability of Yugoslav enterprises.

The sponsors of the economic reforms insisted that quick results were not to be expected. Their warnings added to the existing malaise in the LCY, which, as Dimče Belovski, a member of the LCY Central Committee Presidium, pointed out, is "blamed for everything that is happening in our country and for everything that is bad" (*Borba*, 1 December).

The abrupt end to three political careers illustrates the tensions within the Yugoslav political system. On 13 December 1983 Tanjug confirmed that Jože Florijančič had resigned as federal secretary for finance. "Health reasons" were originally given for the resignation of Pavle Gaži, secretary for the interior in Croatia, in September 1983. On

27 January 1984, however, *Borba* announced his expulsion from the LCY and accused him of "attacking and slandering" unspecified members of the party leadership in Zagreb. Mahmut Bakalli, ex-chairman of the Kosovo provincial party committee, was the most prominent Albanian expelled from the LCY (Tanjug, 12 April 1983).

The eleventh session of the LCY Central Committee, held on 20 December 1983, discussed the question of the "realization of the Political Platform of Action by the LCY in Developing Socialist Self-Management, Brotherhood and Unity and Togetherness in Kosovo." The official statement admitted that the exodus of Serbs and Montenegrins from Kosovo "still continues under pressure," claimed that the "real objectives of the Albanian leadership" in Tirana "towards Yugoslavia are to undermine and destabilize the situation in Kosovo, in Yugoslavia and even on a larger scale," and maintained that the "situation in the Province of Kosovo has undergone positive changes" (*Socialist Thought and Practice*, Belgrade, January 1984).

In the meantime the inhabitants of Kosovo headed the list of those charged with "political crimes" in 1983. They provided 32.1 percent of that category, with Croatia coming second and Serbia (without Kosovo and Vojvodina) third (*Komunist*, 8 June 1984). As Vidoje Žarković, vice-president of the State Presidency, explained, "Manifestations of nationalism are more intensive when economic problems are aggravated" (Tanjug, 24 May 1983).

Foreign Affairs. The collective leadership in Belgrade pursued the policy of nonalignment associated with Tito after the expulsion of the Communist Party of Yugoslavia from the Cominform in 1948. No major controversies disturbed Yugoslav relations with the superpowers and neighboring countries except for periodic press polemics with Sofia over Macedonia and with Tirana over Albanians in Kosovo.

The three most prominent visitors to Yugoslavia were Nikolai Tikhonov, the Soviet prime minister (21–25 March 1983), U.S. vice-president George Bush (16–18 September 1983), and French president François Mitterrand in December 1983. A North Korean delegation representing the Democratic Front for the Unification of the Fatherland also came to Yugoslavia.

Yugoslav prime minister Milka Planinc met with Margaret Thatcher during a stay in Great Britain (15–18 November 1983), and Lazar Mojsov, the federal secretary for foreign affairs, visited Tripoli in September.

In 1983, a total of 2,082 individuals from seven Warsaw Pact countries and Albania were granted U.N. refugee status in Yugoslavia and were later resettled in the West. They included 965 Romanians, 900 Czechoslovaks, and 21 Soviet citizens (*Los Angeles Times*, 18 February 1984).

International Party Contacts. During the year the LCY maintained contacts "with senior representatives of progressive and democratic parties and movements in practically the entire world" (*Komunist*, 16 March 1984). Representatives of the Dutch, French, Greek, and Lebanese communist parties visited Yugoslavia as guests of the LCY, and Sam Nujoma, leader of the South-West Africa People's Organization (SWAPO) came at the invitation of the Socialist Alliance.

Relations with the Chinese Communist Party were closer than those with the Soviet party, which in September hosted a study group of the LCY Central Committee led by Frane Popit. Boško Krunić, a member of the LCY Central Committee, made a trip to Beijing in February, and the secretary general of the Chinese Communist Party, Hu Yaobang, came to Yugoslavia in May. He was followed in September by a study group led by He Jingzhi, deputy director of the Propaganda Department of the Central Committee.

Mitja Ribičič led an LCY delegation to the Sixteenth Congress of the Italian Communist Party.

1984

Party Affairs. A debate over the economy (see below) was often intertwined with that over the performance of the LCY, its role, and its future. *Borba* (29–30 September) maintained that the LCY had been reduced over the years "to a loose coalition of republic and provincial parties" and acknowledged that "the principle of democratic centralism has been watered down almost to the end and for many has become a sort of 'voluntary obligation.'" Nikola Stojanović, secretary of the LCY Central Committee Presidium in 1983–1984, claimed that "opportunism" in communist ranks was one of the "greatest and deepest problems" (*Oslobodjenje*, 21 April). Ivica Račan, a member of the Central Committee of the LCY and director of the Josip Broz Tito Political School, referred to "dissatisfaction over lack of unity in the leadership of the League of Communists" and "the traditional passive waiting for the leadership to 'agree' and send the directive or guidance on what is to be done" (*Danas*, 18 December). The misuse of party rank for private gain led Josip Vrhovec to exclaim: "Comrades, we should not allow the League of Communists to become a league of thieves" (*Verčernji list*, 13 September).

The solutions offered to these problems ranged far and wide. A group of former members of the International Brigades in the Spanish Civil War urged the convocation of an extraordinary party congress. The proposal to replace the single slate of candidates with a genuine choice in elections to party bodies received some support. A few favored the revitalization of the Socialist Alliance, which Kiro Grličkov, a veteran Communist, admitted was an "anemic transmission belt" (*Danas*, 24 January). More frequent were the appeals to the top leaders to display leadership. One of the latter, Dragoslav Marković, tried to explain the situation by pointing out that "there is not enough responsibility, not enough consistency in carrying out what has been agreed on and decided upon . . . the problem is not that we lack answers . . . The problem is that we do not have the forces to carry them out in practice faster than we are doing now." (Ibid., 1 May.)

Domestic Affairs. *The Economy.* Although in the first ten months of 1984 production increased by 5.3 percent and exports by 7.0 percent compared with the same period in 1983 (*Politika*, 28–30 November), the economic situation remained very difficult. The rate of inflation reached 62 percent (*NIN*, 12 August), the number of unemployed 950,000 (*Politika*, 28–30 November), and productivity continued to decline and real incomes fell by 11 percent in the first quarter of 1984 compared with the same period in 1983 (*Ekonomska politika*, 16 July). Low wages caused work stoppages here and there. Steelworkers at Nikšić abandoned work for 24 hours (*Borba*, 3 August); at the Idnina factory at Kratovo a strike lasted 45 days (*Komunist*, 28 September); in Zemun 400 workers at the Galenika plant went on strike and invited journalists and municipal officials to come and hear their complaints (*NIN*, 16 December).

Foreign debts amounting to $19.2 billion (*Ekonomska politika*, 19 November) compounded the economic problems because $5.3 billion had to be repaid in 1984 (*Politika*, 1 April). Josip Vrhovec, a member of the LCY Central Committee

Presidium before his election to the membership of the State Presidency in May, warned: "The repayment of debts will take place under extraordinarily difficult circumstances" (*Vjesnik*, 30 April).

The FEC took a number of steps to cope with the deteriorating economic situation. At the very end of 1983 the authorities imposed a six-month price freeze (Tanjug, 23 December 1983). In May 55 percent of the prices on the internal market were set free (*Ekonomska politika*, 17 September). Ad hoc arrangements for the use of Yugoslavia's scarce hard currency resources provoked complaints when exceptions were made in favor of some enterprises (*NIN*, 16 December). The International Monetary Fund and banks in the West helped by rescheduling loans and by granting a standing credit to Yugoslavia.

The sorry state of the economy was the subject of frank debate in the press, in particular in *Ekonomska politika*, and at sessions of the Central Committee of the LCY at which there was "much criticism and self-criticism" (ibid., 8 July). Academics, government leaders, and senior party officials were unable to agree on the causes of the poor performance of the Yugoslav economy. Professor Jovan Mirić of Zagreb University and author of *Sistem i kriza*, put forward the view that the 1974 constitution "generates and reproduces the entire crisis in Yugoslavia" (ibid., 16 December). Hence the need for a return to the constitutional arrangements proclaimed during World War II. Professor Ljubomir Madjar saw in the communist hostility to the peasantry since 1945 a source of Yugoslavia's ills (ibid.). Others laid the blame on unwise investment decisions and on the zeal with which Yugoslav firms and banks sought loans in the West, loans that now they cannot repay. The secretary of the LCY Central Committee Presidium, Dimče Belovski, mused that what they missed was "the historic mission and role of Comrade Tito and of Edvard Kardelj" (*Borba*, 12 September). Dragoslav Marković, president of the LCY Central Committee Presidium in 1983–1984, drew attention to the "inadequate integration and inappropriate functioning of the unified Yugoslav market and the manifestation of autarchy and encapsulation of their republic-provincial economies" (*Danas*, 1 May).

Dissent. Debate in communist ranks did not exclude the need to fight "nationalism," which the Communists claimed the three leading churches, the Catholic, the Serb Orthodox, and the Islamic, were using to strengthen their hold. Religious organizations were warned not to step outside their functions and were reminded that "extra-curricular activities" were not permitted. Dušan Dragosavac, a key member of the League of Communists in Croatia, insisted that "secularization must be more thoroughly spread" (*Socialist Thought and Practice*, March).

Although no serious incidents marred the Catholic pilgrimage to Marija Bistrica in September, party leaders and the press criticized some of the statements that the cardinals and bishops made at the time (Tanjug, 4 October).

The authorities acted against the growing dissent movement among Belgrade intellectuals and students. Books and nonconformist plays were banned before and after the police raided a meeting of the "free university" that Milovan Djilas addressed in a private apartment on 20 April. He and his audience were soon released, although one of them, Radomir Radović, died under suspicious circumstances after his liberation.

Six of the 28 arrested in April were charged with "illegal" activities in July. Periodic postponements of their trial were attributed to differences of opinion among the LCY leaders on how to cope with this type of nonconformists. When the trial finally took place on 6 December, the accused denied the charges against them and called for the removal of the presiding judge because of his LCY membership. The defiant attitude of one of the accused led to his removal from the courtroom on the ground that he was "disturbing the functioning of the court" (*Politika*, 8 December).

The six accused enjoyed considerable support among intellectuals in Belgrade, Ljubljana, and Zagreb. Petitions with several hundred names asked the authorities to abandon their policy of harassment and persecution, drew attention to the harm that the treatment of dissidents was causing to Yugoslavia's reputation abroad, and warned against a return to Stalinist practices. In the middle of November a dozen intellectuals, including several members of the Serb Academy of Sciences and Arts, formed the Committee for the Defense of Thought and Expression (Belgrade radio, 15 November).

Some of the petitions dealt with the persecution of Vojislav Šešelj, a young sociologist at Sarajevo University and a former member of the LCY. At the request of two editors of the Belgrade edition of *Borba*, Šešelj wrote a paper dealing with the problems facing Yugoslavia and offering his own, somewhat unorthodox solutions. His unpublished critique provided a pretext for his arrest and for the imposition of an eight-year sentence (subsequently reduced to four years).

Unrest in the Albanian community remained a major source of concern to the rulers of Yugoslavia. In 1984 the authorities uncovered "two illegal hostile organizations, the Front of National Liberation and the Kosovo Party of Struggle, and eleven illegal hostile groups" embracing 152 individuals. Their demand for the creation of a Kosovo republic within the Yugoslav federal system was dismissed as a smokescreen for an ethnically pure Kosovo that would seek unification with Albania. In addition, the arrested Albanians and their sponsors were accused of "spreading hatred between Albanians and Serbs" (*Politika*, 4 December).

Poor relations between Albanians and South Slavs living in Kosovo continued to plague the political situation in that highly explosive part of Yugoslavia. Albanian opponents of the status quo attacked "pan-Serb oppression," and Serbs drew attention to their plight at the hands of Albanians. The Yugoslav press reported cases of rape and arson, the desecration of tombs, and economic and administrative moves and measures designed to speed up the exodus of Serbs and Montenegrins from Kosovo. The conditions under which they were forced to leave induced a prominent Communist in Kosovo to state that "this is really the greatest moral degradation of our revolution" (*Komunist*, 18 May).

Although the authorities claimed to have the situation under control except insofar as the exodus of Serbs was concerned, there was no end of arrests, trials, and minor cases of sabotage in Kosovo. The activist elements among the young Albanians enjoyed considerable sympathy among their elders. Belgrade newspapers complained that some Moslem religious leaders and some of the Albanian teaching staff at Priština University were either silent or merely paying lip service to the struggle against "nationalists" and "irredentists" (ibid., 22 June; *NIN*, 5 August).

Accounts in Belgrade and Priština newspapers also showed that Albanians prominent in the government and party apparatus in Kosovo tried to avoid too close an identification with the League of Communists of Serbia, of which the Kosovo party organization is formally a part. They displayed the same sentiments in the debate over the channel through which federal funds are to be allocated for the purpose of improving the Kosovo economy (*Politika*, 24 November; *Rilindja*, 3 April).

Foreign Affairs. As in previous years, Yugoslavia maintained its policy of nonalignment and its opposition to the arms race, to military blocs, and to various forms of neocolonialism. Hostile to the interference of the superpowers in the domestic affairs of other countries, Yugoslavia supported in the U.N. debate on Afghanistan the resolution of 56 nonaligned states calling for the withdrawal of foreign troops from that country (Tanjug, 15 November).

As in 1983, two of Yugoslavia's neighbors came under particular criticism. The Albanian government was denounced for its interference in Yugoslavia's domestic affairs by encouraging "irredentists" and "nationalists" among the Albanian community in Yugoslavia. *Komunist* (27 January) claimed that "anti-Yugoslavism" was the only unchanged thread in Enver Hoxha's foreign policy. Tirana's complaints about the treatment of Albanians in Yugoslavia were countered with those about the fate of South Slav minorities in Albania.

The Yugoslav press also condemned Bulgaria's ambivalent attitude towards Macedonia. The same treatment was reserved for a Bulgarian film depicting life in wartime Macedonia and Bulgarian accounts of the contribution of the Bulgarian army in the struggle against the Wehrmacht on Yugoslav soil in 1944–1945 (*Politika*, 27 November). (The Yugoslav media reacted in the same way when Moscow failed to provide suitable acknowledgment of the contribution of Tito's Partisans in World War II [I. Orlik, in *Kommunist*, Moscow, December, pp. 72–83].)

After meeting Mika Špiljak, the president of the State Presidency, in Washington on 1 February, President Reagan reaffirmed U.S. support for Yugoslav independence and territorial integrity. Prime Minister Planinc went to Bulgaria in July, and Nikola Ljubičić, a member of the State Presidency, called on Libyan leader Moammar Khadafy in November.

Visitors to Yugoslavia included the presidents of Angola and of the People's Republic of China, the Australian minister for foreign affairs, and the deputy chairman of the Council of Ministers of the German Democratic Republic.

An associate member of the Council for Mutual Economic Assistance (CMEA), Yugoslavia sent an observer to the CMEA summit in Moscow (12–14 June). The CMEA states remained Yugoslavia's leading trading partners (Tanjug, 13 September). In the first ten months of 1984 trade with socialist countries rose by 5 percent (*Politika*, 28–30 November). Some of the 6,500 Yugoslavs employed by Yugoslav firms on construction sites in the USSR struck for higher wages.

During a visit to the Soviet Union in February, Lazar Mojsov, the federal secretary for foreign affairs, and Vidoje Žarković, the vice-president of the State Presidency, had a "warm and friendly" meeting with Chernenko.

In June the Soviet tourist agency, Intourist, canceled agreements on the stay of 24,000 Soviet tourists in Yugoslavia from 1 August to the end of the year (*Borba*, 20 June).

Prince Sihanouk, president of the Kampuchean government in exile, accepted the credentials of the Yugoslav ambassador in January.

Morocco broke off diplomatic relations with Yugoslavia after the Yugoslav government recognized the Saharan Arab Democratic Republic (*Politika*, 1 December).

International Party Contacts. The LCY is not represented on the editorial board of the Prague-based *Problems of Peace and Socialism* (*World Marxist Review*) and did not attend the meeting of Central Committee secretaries of fraternal parties in Prague on 11–12 July (*WMR*, September). The LCY was also absent from the meeting of communist parties held under the auspices of *Problems of Peace and Socialism* in December. Yugoslav publications came out against such international gatherings on the ground that they are not representative of the communist movement as a whole, that the struggle for peace can be carried on without such "consultations," and that the "exchange of views" at such meetings precedes the "passing of sentences" (*Danas*, 18 December).

This outlook did not prevent the LCY from holding bilateral talks with a fair number of communist parties and representatives of "anti-imperialist" forces. Ali Šukrija, the newly elected president of the LCY Central Committee Presidium, met leaders of the Italian party, and other LCY delegates attended the congresses of the Romanian party and of the Congolese Labor Party, and the founding congress of the Workers' Party of Ethiopia. Andrej Marinc, a member of the Central Committee Presidium, visited China, North Korea, and Japan early in 1984. Dragoslav Marković followed him to Beijing in May. Another LCY delegation visited Ecuador, Mexico, Nicaragua, Panama, Peru, and Venezuela at the "invitation of progressive and democratic parties" (*Socialist Thought and Practice*, June).

The LCY acted as host to Álvaro Cunhal of the Portuguese party and to Hermann Axen, a secretary of the Central Committee of the Socialist Unity Party of East Germany. On 7–9 July the LCY and the Socialist Alliance hosted in Belgrade the Conference of Progressive Parties and Movements of the Mediterranean. It was attended by representatives of 28 parties (including the French, Greek, and Italian communist parties) and movements from fourteen Mediterranean countries, two na-

tional liberation movements, the Palestine Liberation Organization and the Polisario Front, and the Standing Secretariat of the Progressive Socialist Organization of the Mediterranean (Tripoli). The conference came out in favor of "turning the Mediterranean into a zone of peace, security and cooperation" (ibid., September).

Ivan Avakumovic
University of British Columbia

Council for
Mutual Economic Assistance

This was the year of the summit. After fifteen years the top leaders, with one exception, of the ten-member Council for Mutual Economic Assistance (CMEA) came to Moscow and issued two joint policy statements. This in itself was an achievement, for the gathering had been delayed by significant differences among the members on important economic as well as political issues and by the problems of leadership succession in the Soviet Union. But the summit and other key meetings of the CMEA, including the thirty-ninth session of the CMEA Executive Committee, did not lead to radical changes or suggest profound solutions. Rather, they all illustrated the fundamental difficulties faced by the member-states. These ranged from the need for structural internal reforms to subsequent logical alterations of the CMEA integrative mechanisms to the question of economic and political relations with the West.

There was considerable evidence, as in previous years, of increasing dissatisfaction on the part of both the Soviet Union and the East European states with previous arrangements for the sale of manufactured goods and energy supplies and with the nonconvertibility of the ruble. In Moscow's case there were stronger indications that the Kremlin

was far less willing to provide further subsidies for its CMEA partners. Yet at the same time, it wished to push forward with its integrative plans for the organization. This could only increase tension with the East European states in particular, but Moscow appeared determined to further enhance its control. If Moscow, however, were to provide fewer economic benefits to Eastern Europe, then those economic levers of control might possibly be weakened. But the Kremlin seems determined to make more efficient use of whatever subsidies it provides. Consequently, perhaps the most important question emerging from developments during the year is whether the Soviet Union will be able to do more in Eastern Europe with less.

Background and Function. Created in 1949, the CMEA has members on three continents. It comprises the Soviet Union, Bulgaria, Czechoslovakia, the German Democratic Republic (GDR), Hungary, Poland, Romania, and the non-European states of Cuba, Mongolia, and Vietnam. Furthermore, it has special agreements with Yugoslavia, Finland, Iraq, and Mexico, while Laos, Angola, Mozambique, North Korea, Ethiopia, and Nicaragua attend meetings as observers. Although

Western scholars continue to dispute the reasons why the Soviet Union decided to create this organization, officially at least the CMEA rejects the notion of supranationality and appears to conform to the oft-declared principles of national sovereignty and equality of member-states. Unlike the European Community, it does not have an international legal personality.

Although the principles of equality are reiterated every year, the CMEA has been since its inception a Soviet-controlled organization. Since World War II Moscow has sought to impose general conformity in domestic and foreign policies in Eastern Europe. The Kremlin favored integration, and this was stated in very broad terms. At first the motivation was largely political, and Moscow itself may have had an inadequate understanding of the ramifications of integration. Western-style economic integration would not have been compatible with the Soviet and East European system of "command economies" revolving around a central plan. Genuine socialist integration would involve the creation of a single command economy encompassing all member-states.

The Thirty-eighth CMEA Session. This was the first meeting of the highest representatives of the member-countries of the CMEA to deal primarily with economic matters since April 1969. Such a "special" or "extraordinary" session, as it was officially characterized, had been proposed four years before by the USSR but had to be postponed because of Soviet succession problems and due to difficulties in resolving issues among the member-states. Moreover, although the uncertainties in the Kremlin, as one old and ill leader succeeded another, may have been the prime factor in the delay, differences among the member-states appear to have played a significant role. For instance, whereas the Czechoslovaks favored a "new economic order" in the CMEA, the Hungarians wanted to strengthen their national interest within the international interest. The Romanians called for a new and different policy of development and distribution of energy and other resources. On the other hand, Moscow insisted on more "integrational policies and community cohesion." (Tanjug, 30 May; *FBIS*, 31 May.)

Tensions between Romania and the USSR failed to ease completely even before the summit. Talks between Soviet leader Konstantin Chernenko and Nicolae Ceauşescu one week before the summit were characterized by the Moscow press not only as

comradely but also as "business-like and frank," which in communist parlance means that there had been disagreement (*Times*, London, 6 June).

Yet when the 12–14 June summit ended in Moscow, all ten members expressed at least some satisfaction with the outcome. Every party leader, with the exception of Fidel Castro of Cuba (who sent Carlos Rodríguez, the deputy chairman of both the State Council and the Council of Ministers), came. Apparently there was some tough bargaining. The meeting approved two documents: "Statement on the Guidelines for the Further Development and Deepening of the CMEA Member-States' Economic, Scientific, and Technical Cooperation" and a political declaration entitled "Preservation of Peace and International Economic Cooperation" (*IB*, August, pp. 6–11). The second document, which harshly condemned the United States, was evidence both of Moscow's insistence on linkages between economic and political issues and of the Kremlin's ability to induce Romania to join the East European chorus in supporting the Soviet position. The most important document, however, was the first, which dealt with a broad range of key CMEA issues.

In general terms, the summit participants agreed to develop collective ways of resolving major national economic problems of mutual interest. As Moscow put it, these included the all-round intensification and improvement of efficiency and quality in all spheres of the economy, supplying the CMEA countries with fuel, power, raw materials, foodstuffs, industrial goods, and modern machines, and equipment, and reaching the forefront of technological progress (*Izvestiia*, 21 June).

In more specific terms, as part of the effort to strengthen integration among the CMEA states, the participants agreed to draft, on the basis of national programs, a fifteen-to-twenty-year comprehensive program of scientific and technological progress. This, it was contended, would be the basis for a coordinated and, in some areas, a uniform scientific and technical policy that would seek solutions through joint effort to the most important questions in the fields of science and technology. It was further agreed that the member-states would hold regular meetings at the highest party and state levels to coordinate the fundamental directions of the member-states' long-term economic development and "the deepening of the international division of labor." Measures were to be taken to ensure that coordination of plans was implemented before the start of the new planning period and that there would be an increase in mutual delivery of the most important goods. The Statement declared that the participants in the meeting believed that mobilization of "their *own* resources and intensification of mutual cooperation can resolve the raw material and fuel-and-energy problems of all CMEA member-countries" (emphasis added). But, to achieve this, it was agreed to take measures to economize on the consumption of energy and raw materials.

As far as deliveries of fuel and raw materials from the USSR itself, the Statement was rather specific in declaring that this would be implemented as part of an agreement with the other CMEA states to "gradually and consistently develop their production and export structure and carry out the necessary measures for this in the area of capital investments, and in the construction and rationalization of their industry so as to supply the Soviet Union with the products it needs, notably foodstuffs and manufactured goods, some types of construction materials, machines and high quality and world class equipment." In the realm of energy it was also stated that there would be increased cooperation and development of atomic power generation and of new, nontraditional sources of energy. Other important aspects dealt with the need to strengthen cooperation in the area of planning, with better utilization of commodity-monetary relations. Hence, the pricing system in operation would be further developed and the collective currency—the transfer ruble—would be strengthened.

In addition, the participants agreed that in the process of coordinating national economic development plans, there would be input where necessary from branch management and economic organizations as well. Furthermore, East European states undertook to continue to help the non-European CMEA members to accelerate their rate of development as part of a gradual process to even out economic development levels within the organization. And lastly, among the more important measures, the members agreed to continue to develop mutually advantageous trade, economic, scientific, and technical ties with developed capitalist countries. (Ibid.)

It would seem, then, from the first document that all the participants received something. But as in the past, the gains at these meetings tend to be rather uneven. One of the main tasks of the summit had been to work out methods for further integrating CMEA member economies. And Moscow did make progress in that area. The Kremlin expressed its satisfaction that the conference had resulted in

growth "in the cohesiveness of the fraternal socialist countries and the development of a unified approach to key economic and political issues" (Tass, 26 September; *FBIS*, 27 September). And this was more than just a declaratory position, for a closer examination of the Statement shows that Moscow did make considerable gains. It is also true that the USSR appears to have made significant concessions as well. The door to trade with the West was left open, the member-states would continue to receive Soviet energy supplies, there would be further development of the collective currency, and there was an affirmation of the trend to establish direct ties between enterprises and organizations. These were matters of great concern to the East European states, and even limited concessions were important to them.

On the other hand, if one places these measures in the context of overall relations, it is rather difficult to avoid the conclusion that the summit moved far more in the direction that Moscow had desired and that it resulted in the creation of closer ties and a further turning inwards by the CMEA. The general thrust toward deeper integration was reflected, for instance, in the fifteen-to-twenty-year scientific and technical program, which is to cover the use of robots, electronics, and atomic energy. Progress was also made in another area of Soviet interest, namely plan coordination, and a decision to hold regular summit meetings was a further step in ensuring Soviet goals of integration and international socialist division of labor. The decision to work out "on a collective basis" solutions to major problems of mutual interest is part of the integrative process.

In the areas where the Soviet Union appeared to have made significant concessions, the conditions laid down by Moscow for implementation are such that they raise grave doubts whether the East European states would receive many benefits. Since the latter are heavily dependent on the USSR for fuel and raw materials, they have long sought to ensure the security of supplies. Moscow's assurances on continuation of supplies were conditional. One assumption was that the CMEA would be able to satisfy its needs by relying on its *own* resources. This means mutual participation, which, in the past, entailed East European investment in Soviet exploration and delivery systems. The East European states would also have to agree to economize on their use of energy and raw materials. But more than conservation and investment, the USSR also made supplies conditional on the other CMEA states' restructuring their exports so as to provide it with "hard" goods. These are products that the non-Soviet CMEA states had been able to sell on the world market for hard currency. They include foodstuffs and high-quality, "world-class" products.

These conditions for the supply of fuel and raw materials, therefore, cannot be separated from the other "concession" the Soviet Union made to such members as Romania and Hungary; namely, to allow for the continuation of significant trade with the Western states. The East European countries, in order to maintain their supplies of Soviet raw materials and fuel (and, given their dependence on Moscow for these supplies, they have little choice) will have to redirect some of their exports from the West to the Soviet Union. In effect, the Statement called on the other CMEA states to restructure their exports to provide Moscow with food and world-class equipment in exchange for energy and raw materials. Academician Oleg T. Bogomolov, the director of the Institute of Economics of the World Socialist System, which is attached to the USSR Academy of Sciences, complained that the USSR sometimes imported machines, for instance, from Bulgaria and Czechoslovakia that could not be sold on the world market because of their inferior quality. On the other hand, he contended that energy and raw materials Moscow supplied to these countries would have brought hard currency returns that could have been used to buy first-quality machines from West Germany (*Borba*, Belgrade, 26 July; *FBIS*, 31 July).

Several East European countries, though, wanted to receive higher prices for their agricultural exports (particularly Hungary). Although the Statement mentioned that "monetary-financial instruments of cooperation" are to be developed, there is virtually nothing in it that reveals much about future pricing policy. Given the leverage that the USSR has and the East European dependence on Soviet raw materials, it is unlikely that the East Europeans will obtain significantly higher prices for their products. In a related area, the summit's promise that the collective currency—the transfer ruble—would be strengthened, is not really meaningful. Some of the smallest states (particularly Hungary, which has an advanced economy but has incurred huge trade deficits with the Soviet Union) would have liked to see the ruble given an independent exchange rate to allow its free use among member-states. Since the member-states have no hard currency, except what they receive from exports, this would appear to be an essential develop-

ment. Unfortunately for the smaller states, the kind of domestic reforms that a truly convertible currency would necessitate throughout the CMEA, particularly in the Soviet Union, so far have proven to be unacceptable to Kremlin leaders.

Furthermore, even though the Statement announced that measures would be introduced to create suitable conditions for direct ties between enterprises and organizations in various states and for the creation of joint firms, this falls far short of what the Hungarians have been seeking for years. Given Moscow's insistence on strong centralized control in the Soviet Union, which produces the bulk of the organization's economic output, the scope for decisionmaking of enterprises engaged in transnational relations is bound to be extremely restricted.

The participants, though, tried to put the best face on the outcome. Bucharest emphasized the aspects of the summit that interested it the most. Various Romanian publications stressed the agreement on the energy question. The communist daily, *Scînteia* (17 June), reported that great importance was given to expanding cooperation in production and mutual deliveries of energy and raw materials together with more economical use of energy and the introduction of new technology. *Lumea* (21 June), the foreign policy weekly, put it even more strongly by contending that the summit recognized that solution of the issue of raw materials, energy, and fuels is a sine qua non for progress in the contemporary world for all states (Agerpres, 22 June). The Romanians also downplayed the integrative measures that the summit had suggested and argued that the proposed meaures would be carried out by the planning and economic bodies in *each* country (*Scînteia*, 17 June).

Budapest also tried to put the best face on the summit results. For instance, it emphasized the importance assigned to cooperation in agriculture, which it believed meant that exporters (Hungary) would be guaranteed incentives for deliveries both on a bilateral and on a multilateral basis. The Kádár government also seemed pleased at promises to strengthen the transfer ruble. (Budapest domestic service, 15 June; *FBIS*, 18 June.) Omissions in the Hungarian assessment tend to indicate some of the areas of disappointment. Budapest favored free association between individual enterprises across national boundaries, without any interference from national authorities. But, as noted, this stance, which would require a far greater use of price levers, market mechanisms, and other free-market forces, has never been acceptable to the Soviet Union.

The Polish approach, as expressed by Politburo member and Deputy Premier Zbigniew Messner, was one of satisfaction that together with further cooperation in the technological sphere, the session had dealt with key issues relating to fuel, raw materials, and the provision of food supplies. The last, of course, is of particular concern to Poland. Messner added that the projected qualitative change in future cooperation within the CMEA was another vital development. (Warsaw television service, 14 June; *FBIS*, 15 June.) A qualitative change would be helpful, naturally enough, in assuring better provision of food and consumer goods from the CMEA states to the Polish people. The price though, of course, would be even closer Polish adherence to Soviet policies and greater integration with the CMEA. For ultimately, as noted, the session did point toward greater Soviet control. As Nikolai Ryzhkov, secretary of the CPSU Central Committee and a member of the delegation to the summit, stated, "The main economic result was the elaboration of a common course towards further deepening socialist integration and determining the strategy of national economic collaboration to the end of this century" (*Pravda*, 30 July).

The Thirty-ninth CMEA Session. Following the thirty-eighth session (extraordinary) of top leaders in June, the thirty-ninth, held between 29 and 31 October in Havana, was almost anticlimactic. In addition to the heads of government from the ten member-states, observer-delegations were present from Yugoslavia, Angola, Afghanistan, South Yemen, Laos, Mozambique, Ethiopia and, for the first time, Mexico and Nicaragua. The direction was clearly laid out by the thirty-eighth session. As part of the seventh coordination of national economic plans, the CMEA states assigned importance to cooperation in science and technology, with the intention to ensure, for instance, that by 1990 the total robot pool in the organization reached the planned 200,000-unit level.

Moreover the USSR reiterated in rather unequivocal terms that in order for it to continue what it called high levels of deliveries of crude oil and other materials in short supply, compensation from the recipient states for the high level of Soviet expenditures had to be adequate. That is, the USSR would have to receive in return large amounts of commodities, such as foodstuffs and consumer goods and engineering products of "world standard." (Nikolai Inozemtsev, deputy chairman of the USSR's State Planning Committee, in *Rudé právo*, Prague, 18 October; *FBIS*, 24 October.) Furthermore, the USSR proposed to build jointly with the East European states a new natural gas pipeline from western Siberia. This would be the largest integrated facility during the next five-year plan (1986–1990). It would carry gas from the northern Piumenskaia oblast over a distance of 4,605 kilometers (slightly longer than the pipeline from Urengoi to Uzhgorod), and it would be used to deliver 20 to 22 billion cubic meters of natural gas annually once it goes into operation in 1989–1990. In addition, Moscow indicated that the development of nuclear power and expansion of electrical power grids of the CMEA states would be stressed. (Ibid.)

At the Havana session, these trends were reemphasized, particularly in the area of energy and energy-related fields. As usual, there was a blending of political and economic statements on the part of most leaders but particularly in the case of Soviet prime minister Nikolai Tikhonov. He used the opportunity to denounce the United States and its allies over such issues as arms control (Tass, 29 October; *FBIS*, 30 October). But the main concerns appeared to be very similar to those expressed at the thirty-eighth session. In that sense, this meeting summed up the decisions of the previous summit and elaborated on their implementation. Cooperation was to increase in the scientific-technical fields as part of a fifteen-to-twenty-year plan, and general agreements on cooperation were signed in the areas of electronics, microprocessing, and robot engineering. Even more important, long-term comprehensive measures were approved for cooperation in energy, fuel, and raw materials. This, in turn, envisioned joint construction of major economic projects and increased specialization in the production of energy and machinery for the extraction and conservation of fuel. Included among these projects would be the Krivoi Rog ore-dressing complex and the natural gas pipeline between Yamburg (western Siberia) and the USSR's western frontier. (Tass, 31 October; *FBIS*, 1 November.) The total investment for all joint energy-related projects might add up to $65 billion (*FPI International Report*, 7 November).

Furthermore, Moscow again made it clear that it wanted improvements in the quality of goods it imported from the CMEA states in barter deals.

Tikhonov declared at Havana that "all the goods that are traded must reach comparable quality to the best available in the world" (ibid.). Although he left the door open to continued trade with Western states by declaring that "economic self-isolation is alien to us" (Tass, 29 October; *FBIS*, 30 October), Tikhonov's insistence that the USSR would have to be paid with first-quality goods for its energy exports, while the process of diversifying energy sources continued, means that the East European states, in particular, would have considerable difficulty in avoiding a restructuring of their economies toward closer links with the Soviet Union.

Growth and Development. The problem is not one of a complete halt in the economic growth rate of the CMEA states; rather, it involves the question of whether the current rate of development is adequate to sustain politically defined goals. At least a partial fulfillment of these objectives is necessary to ensure stability and legitimacy in the East European states and the Soviet Union. Therefore, the sharp slowdown in growth rates over the past several years, particularly in the USSR, which possesses the bulk of CMEA productive capacity, may have yet-to-be-understood repercussions. According to a CIA study, the USSR, with an extra 40 million people, produces only slightly more than half as much as the United States and stopped catching up with the latter in 1975 (*Toronto Globe and Mail*, 15 October). But the situation is even grimmer than that. Many of the USSR's gains in industry, in the production of raw materials, and in agriculture have been squandered. Additional output is often employed inefficiently, Soviet industry uses far too much fuel, and it turns out machines that are too heavy. Furthermore, Soviet feed conversion ratios (that is, the amount of grain it takes to produce a pound of pork, beef, or chicken) are almost double those of efficient Western farms. In addition, the Soviet system has failed to produce sufficient incentives for the rapid and efficient introduction of new technology, as have Japan and other capitalist states.

If the Soviet Union does not significantly narrow the gap in productivity with the industrialized states, then its relations with the West and with Eastern Europe are likely to be affected. The technological gap would widen, and in order to compete militarily with the United States, the USSR would have to then so heavily drain the civilian economy that downward pressures on the living standard for its citizens would create significant political risks.

In the case of the East European states, the Soviet Union, if current trends continue, will be less and less able to provide subsidies.

Even the more optimistic projections of the Soviet growth rate do not suggest that the Soviet Union will catch up. Wharton Econometrics has suggested that growth of the Soviet gross domestic product could average 2.5 to 3.0 percent a year to the end of the decade (ibid., 15 October). This would not narrow the gap. The U.N. Economic Commission for Europe projected that the USSR would attain its 1984 goal of a 3.6 percent increase in "net material product" (which differs from the Western measure of the gross national product by excluding services). This would compare with the previous year's figure of 4 percent. (*Financial Times*, London, 2 April).

Yet the USSR may be in considerably better shape than its East European allies. There are significant differences among the East European economies, and some have performed considerably better than others. But overall, given their far smaller size and the fewer natural resources available to them, they have proved to have more fragile economies. East European economic slowdowns have been forecast for some time now (see Jan Vanous, "East European Economic Slowdown," *Problems of Communism*, July–August 1982, pp. 1–19). More recently, structural economic flaws combined with political expediency have multiplied problems in Eastern Europe. Most of these states have reduced investment too much and consumption too little because of the political priority they have placed on preventing Polish-style unrest, according to Jan Vanous, research director on East bloc economies at Wharton Econometrics (*Toronto Globe and Mail*, 7 May). In a sense, therefore, they have mortgaged the future of their economies and, in Vanous's words, are "dooming" themselves to increasing relative technological backwardness and declining competitiveness on the world market because political considerations do not permit further reduction in the level of the growth of living standards and low growth rates of output necessitate even slower growth of net capital formation. Only Bulgaria has shown an increase in investment spending, but Vanous believes that the rate is seriously overstated because of hidden military spending, low depreciation rates, and inflation.

Hungary seems to be something of an exception, though, because it has made relatively better use of its investments, but even its progress has been somewhat limited. Although worker productivity has improved, this has been accompanied by significant inflation. Of the non-European CMEA members, Cuba projected a 7.4 percent growth in 1984, which is not as impressive when viewed in the context of the low starting base, but even here the country's planning chief admitted that there were significant shortfalls in the production of sugar, nickel, and citrus fruits (ibid., 1 January 1985). Thus the Third World CMEA states would need even more help from Moscow in the future in order to maintain existing standards of living. And, as the U.N. Economic Commission for Europe stated, they would be less well placed than the Soviet Union to reach the year's growth targets (ibid., 2 April).

In contrast to the difficulties that the Soviet bloc states encountered in their trade with the West, intra-CMEA exchanges have been increasing at a healthy pace over the past several years. Total trade among CMEA member-countries rose to 58.6 percent in 1983 (*Rabotnichesko delo*, Sofia, 30 May; *FBIS*, 7 June; *Izvestiia*, 2 November). Furthermore, as the June summit indicated, the bloc states fully intend to increase trade among themselves faster than total external exchanges. One sees evidence of this trend even in the case of Romania, the one East European state that traditionally has viewed trade with other socialist states, particularly the USSR, with less than total equanimity since it feared the economic levers that Moscow might develop. But in the past few years Bucharest increased its exchanges with the CMEA sharply, from 33.8 percent in 1980 to 53 percent in 1983 (*Times*, London, 27 August).

A breakdown of the trade figures further highlights the strong linkages among the CMEA states. For instance, the Soviet Union provides 90 percent of the group's oil and about half of its total energy needs (*WSJ*, 11 June). In the case of East Germany, that country exports to the USSR more than half of the total volume of major machine-building products (*Sotsialisticheskaia industriia*, 6 October). Hungary sells a large portion of its bus production to the Soviet Union and most of its agricultural exports are shipped to the CMEA states (*New Times*, no. 40, October, pp. 6–9; *FBIS*, 11 October). Even in the case of Romania, imports of raw materials from other CMEA partners have continued to grow substantially. Bucharest now buys a third of its imported coke and copper and half of its cotton from bloc states and 45 percent of its iron ore imports and 20 percent of its phosphorus comes from the USSR itself (*Trybuna ludu*, Warsaw, 17 August; *FBIS*, 24 August).

Over the past several years, Moscow has achieved a substantial trade surplus in exchanges with its CMEA partners. In large part this has been due to increases in the price of Soviet oil and gas. Edward Hewett of the Brookings Institution has calculated that Soviet terms of trade with its bloc partners have improved substantially. In 1983, for instance, the USSR ran a trade surplus of 3.7 billion rubles ($4.62 billion). Moreover, Hewett contends, if the Soviet Union had calculated the five-year world average price for oil exactly, then its terms of trade might have increased even more over a ten-year period. (*Financial Times*, 28 May.) Moscow, as was apparent at the summit in June, has been more and more reluctant to provide credits or hidden subsidies, although in the past it has been willing to make economic concessions in order to achieve political gains.

Trade figures, however, should be treated somewhat cautiously in any analysis of bloc integration. In the CMEA, trade flows are a function of the central plan, and they tend to operate as limited catalysts for integration. Bloc integration, as opposed to absorption or annexation, is more difficult than integration in the West, where market forces are allowed free play. The Soviet Union itself has begun to take a more sophisticated approach to integration. Soviet leaders have called for a "qualitatively new level" of integration, and Soviet economists have formulated more comprehensive integration theories. The Soviet direction, however, is toward a centralized form of integration that would result in a unified plan that Moscow would invariably wind up controlling. Even the most sophisticated economists, like Oleg Bogomolov, have spoken of extending economic integration through greater international specialization and cooperation and by supplementing the coordination of the CMEA countries' five-year national economic plans "with coordination of their economic policy as a whole" (*Argumenty i fakty*, Moscow, no. 4, January 1983, p. 326). This comes quite close to the vision of a supranational entity.

Moscow's views of integration, though, are not shared by the other CMEA member-states. Romania, in particular, has been for a long time a vocal opponent of any trend toward supranational integration. It has insisted that all cooperative agreements must fully respect the national sovereignty of each state and must ensure noninterference in internal affairs (Nicolae Ionescu, *Revista economica*, Bucharest, no. 33, 12 August 1983, pp. 18–19). Nevertheless, the Romanians have participated in all five special programs for long-term collaboration adopted at earlier CMEA meetings (these resulted in over 200 contracts) and have pushed enthusiastically for more integration in the limited area of energy production. Given its dire economic straits, Bucharest has had to exhibit some flexibility, although it continues to insist on preserving the prerogatives of sovereignty.

Perhaps an even more potent challenge to integration has come from Hungary. Mátyás Szürös, the Central Committee secretary responsible for international policy, declared that "national interest can be subordinated to the common [logically, Soviet] interest only in exceptional circumstances. The only kind of cooperation which could be profitable is one based on a freely chosen common program of action. This could be gradually achieved within the framework of a new kind of relationship amongst socialist countries." (*Guardian*, London, 22 July.) This subtle rejection of supranationality and of Soviet control has in fact been a part of Hungarian reform efforts for quite some time. One of the architects of the New Economic Mechanism (NEM), Rezsö Nyers, called for an outward-looking strategy whereby CMEA cooperation is viewed as a complement to expansion of economic relations with the developed market economies and with the developing countries. This, in turn, involves the relationship between foreign and domestic prices and intrabloc monetary relations. For integration to proceed successfully, there would have to be reform both of the CMEA and of the economic mechanisms of its member-countries in a direction similar to the Hungarian NEM. Such profound reforms do not appear acceptable to the Soviet Union, as noted. Therefore, Nyers is rather pessimistic and finds systemic, size-related, and developmental barriers to progress in CMEA integration. At the summit, it appeared that Hungary was willing to go along with Soviet suggestions of integration in certain fields, including science and technology, as long as this did not impose barriers to Western economic markets and vital imports.

Recognizing these difficulties in multilaterality, Moscow has reached a thousand or so bilateral agreements with the CMEA states. The greater manageability of bilateral agreements has acted as an incentive for the USSR to follow this road to integration. But as the June summit indicated, it is not about to abandon the multilateral approach to integration. To a considerable extent, though, Moscow's success in pushing for greater integration, whether on the multilateral or on the bilateral level, will depend on its ability to use a key set of commodities, particularly energy, to induce the other CMEA states to follow its directions.

Energy. As the primary source of energy supplies, the Soviet Union has provided massive subsidies to the other CMEA member-states (*YICA*, 1984, pp. 413–14). The subsidies increased more sharply as the price of oil rose. Although the USSR devised a five-year averaging plan that stabilized prices, Moscow continued to provide a subsidy that, given its own domestic constraints, it found more and more difficult to afford, even when the price of oil fell on the spot markets. The subsidy has been provided in two ways. First, Soviet oil prices, in particular, have been below world market levels, and second, the USSR has been willing to accept payment in the form of commodities (with the exception of Romania) that were not of world market quality. The Kremlin indicated at the June summit that it wanted substantial changes in this arrangement, particularly in terms of what the other CMEA states have to provide in order to continue to receive energy supplies. It would appear, therefore, that Moscow was significantly reducing its subsidies to the other bloc countries.

Nevertheless, the Kremlin has had to be careful that its demands on the East European states did not create the kind of economic crisis that would result in economic and political instability. An *Izvestiia* editorial (4 September) declared, "It is now perfectly clear that the days of cheap raw materials and fuel are gone for all countries, including the socialist community countries. This applies to exporters of primary resources as well as importers." But at the summit, Moscow appeared to opt for gradual changes, although these would have profound implications. It pressed for conservation of energy to lower demand in Eastern Europe. It gave hints of a change in prices, and after the summit Boris Gotsev, deputy head of the CPSU Economic Department, said that the Soviet Union was changing the oil-pricing system so that it would be more closely based on current prices on the world market (*NYT*, 15 June). This could result in lower oil prices for the CMEA states. Furthermore, Moscow pushed for the development of other sources of energy, particularly nuclear, but also natural gas. As noted, the Soviet Union formulated plans for a major joint undertaking to construct a pipeline from gas fields in Siberia to Eastern Europe. The USSR also suggested to its bloc partners that they should also seek some of their energy supplies from Third World states. According to the Organization of Petroleum Exporting Countries, East Germany agreed to buy 20,000 barrels of oil a day from Iran in 1985. And prior to the June summit, the USSR even agreed to supply a small amount of oil (1.5 million tons) to Romania for goods in kind and nonconvertible cash (*Times*, London, 7 June).

Moscow's package of carrots and sticks is based on previous developments and earlier linkages that included cooperation in the areas of energy exploration and in the production of atomic energy in the joint electrical grid systems, all of which will be strengthened. An incremental process such as this, if pursued with some sophistication, is likely to produce no more than controllable resentment on the part of the East Europeans. And gradually the integrative web is likely to thicken, even though the Soviet Union may provide vastly fewer subsidies and decrease the amount of energy supplied. Thus, in terms of the energy lever, the USSR might be able to do more with less in the future.

Indebtedness and Trade with the West. Although some of the East European states, particularly Hungary, must have been quite distressed by the further turning inward that the June summit indicated, this was a trend that had developed some years ago, as a reaction both to the huge debts that some of the East European states acquired and to the disappointed hopes that a great leap forward could be achieved through the infusion of Western technology bought on easy Western credit terms. There was, therefore, great concern in the bloc over the CMEA states' huge hard currency debts and immense servicing costs. These burdens are not evenly spread. Bulgaria and Czechoslovakia owe very small sums in comparison with Romania or Poland. Furthermore, East Germany's special relationship with West Germany has allowed it privileged access to Western funds. Still, at the East Berlin conference in October 1983, the bloc agreed to reduce capitalist imports to the minimum "as a temporary necessity" in order to reduce the debt (ibid., 11 June).

There has been a recognition throughout the bloc that it cannot cut itself off completely from the West. Soviet leaders themselves have repeated that they did not wish to embark on an autarkic form of development. And during the year, there was some slight easing on imports. Trade trends, nevertheless, appear to be moving in the other direction. Whereas the USSR's two-way trade with the CMEA rose by 6.9 billion rubles in 1983, it increased by less than 1 billion rubles with the West (*Financial Times*, 2 April). Nevertheless, the Soviet Union continues to rely on certain important imports from the West. For the past six years one poor grain harvest has followed another. It appears that the 1984 Soviet harvest fell far short of expectations as well. The International Wheat Council estimated that Soviet grain imports in 1984–1985 would reach a record 48 million tons (*Toronto Globe and Mail*, 26 October). Much of this grain has to come from the United States. Moscow also has gone to Western banks for loans. Furthermore, the Kremlin has continued to buy or at least to try to buy the latest in Western technology. Thus it is not that Moscow has opposed trade per se but rather that it wants it conducted within controllable limits, especially in the case of Eastern Europe.

As the USSR attempts to push the latter toward greater integration and diminished reliance on trade with the West, there are bound to be significant strains. Despite the reduction in Soviet subsidies, it does not necessarily follow that the Kremlin's economic leverage will diminish. On the contrary, as Moscow gradually increases its mechanisms of control by effecting a turning inward of the CMEA states, through greater integration in the areas of science and technology and energy production, it may eventually be able to induce conformity more smoothly and with less need to employ political and military tools. The East European states are aware of this danger, particularly Hungary and Romania, and they will work hard to counter it. Developments during the year, though, would tend to indicate that the odds are in Moscow's favor.

Aurel Braun
University of Toronto

Warsaw Treaty Organization

Moscow founded the WTO on 14 May 1955 with the declared aim of preventing the remilitarization of West Germany and its integration into NATO. The Kremlin also offered to disband the WTO in exchange for the liquidation of NATO, an offer it has repeated every year since. In addition to the multilateral WTO, the Soviet Union also created a network of bilateral treaties in Eastern Europe after 1945, but a multilateral treaty provides it with political, military, and juridical benefits that bilateral treaties might not have. Moreover, in certain limited ways, a multilateral forum is useful for conflict resolution among the member-states and as a safety valve for nationalistic frustrations.

Military Developments. Structural changes and doctrinal developments have continued the integrative trend of the WTO under Soviet command. Details are emerging of significant organizational changes within the Soviet defense structure since 1983 (International Institute for Strategic Studies, *The Military Balance, 1984–85*, London, 1984, pp. 13–15; hereafter *Military Balance*). Moscow has divided its forces into three main "theaters"—Western, Southern, and Far Eastern—with a central strategic reserve area comprising the Moscow, Volga, and Ural military districts (MD). The Western theater is the strongest, with the most modern equipment, and it includes the non-Soviet WTO member-states. Apparently it is further subdivided into three Theaters of Military Operations (TVD), which provide strategic planning and operational control for continental as well as oceanic and intercontinental forces placed under their command. (Ibid., p. 13.)

It has been known now for some time that the East European WTO divisions would be incorporated within the Soviet force structure in wartime. This would allow for integrated commands for the three TVDs (Northwestern, Western, and South-western) of the Western Theater. The Western TVD apparently incorporates Polish, Czech, and GDR tanks and motor-rifle divisions. The Northwestern TVD would incorporate the Polish naval infantry brigade together with Soviet forces. The Southwestern TVD covers the territories of Hungary, Romania, and Bulgaria in addition to parts of the USSR. Even though Soviet troops are not stationed in the last two East European countries, they (with the possible exception of Romania) are expected to contribute several tank and motor-rifle divisions to the overall Soviet command. (Ibid., p. 14.) The Kremlin's apparent decision in September to demote its chief of staff, Marshal Nikolai Ogarkov, and place him in charge of the Western Theater forces may thus indicate not only displeasure with that officer, but also a possible desire to reinforce Soviet control over the East European military.

Indeed, these structural changes appear to be part of a shift in Soviet military doctrine toward even greater emphasis on highly mobile surprise attack. In June Soviet defense minister Dimitri Ustinov stated that military technology was becoming so advanced that Moscow was revising its combat tactics to surprise the enemy. Innovations in nuclear and conventional weapons derived from microelectronics and computers, necessitated "revisions of tactics, troop control and the art of warfare as a whole . . . it is important to display initiative in preparation for combat and in actual combat operations and to find tactical decisions that would come as a surprise to the enemy." (*Toronto Globe and Mail*, 28 June.) This is not a fundamental change but rather represents further refinement of the standard doctrine of mass firepower, rapid movement, and surprise. Defectors and émigrés from the USSR and Eastern Europe have confirmed that war plans include the stationing of Soviet officers with East European forces down to the divisional level (*WSJ*, 4 June).

Psychologically, it is important for the USSR to convey to the East European forces that they are on the winning side. A doctrine that involved rapid forward movement and surprise attack would tend to reinforce the image of military invincibility. WTO leadership manuals assure East European officers that they will be on the winning side not only because the WTO is politically and morally superior but also because they have more equipment and men, enjoy geostrategic advantages of rapid reinforcement, have standardized weapons, and can count on many West Germans taking part in sabotage missions once fighting began. (Ibid.)

Little consideration is given to defensive operations; the emphasis is on offensive movement. Even in the rare situation where the WTO, according to its leaders, might find itself in defensive tactical situations, emphasis is placed on practicing "reconnaissance through combat." Such missions can be ordered only by the commander of an army group or higher and would involve heavy losses in men and materiel. Reconnaissance through combat could be conducted while on the defensive, but preferably as part of the preparation for an attack. In offensive operations it would force the enemy to fight while on the defensive. If the WTO units were on the defensive, among the objectives of "reconnaissance through combat would be to achieve a timely recognition of the approach of enemy units and to ascertain intended enemy offensive operations. East German sources also assert that these types of operations present opportunities for WTO ground forces to form joint combat teams that are effective in such complex missions." (*Truppenpraxis*, August, pp. 590–93; *JPRS*, 9 October.)

The East European states have introduced more modest qualitative improvements in their forces than has the USSR. The Polish and Romanian navies received a small number of new vessels. All the WTO allies received from Moscow limited numbers of new MiG-23 aircraft and T-72 tanks. Manpower levels in Bulgaria decreased by 15,000 and in Poland by 16,750, whereas those of Czechoslovakia and East Germany increased by 2,750 and 5,000, respectively. Overall, then, there has been relatively little change in East European forces. (*Military Balance, 1984–85*, pp. 23–28.)

Since the modernization programs of the East European states have been rather modest, Moscow has continued to pressure them to increase defense spending. But as their economies suffer from increased structural problems and drastically slower growth rates than in the past, there has been a good

deal of resentment against the USSR. Yet over the past few years, only Romania has been able to resist Soviet desires successfully. Consequently, the other East European allies have had to invest in expensive new Soviet equipment that they were reluctant to purchase. Furthermore, there is evidence to suggest that there is considerable East European unhappiness over the Soviet Union's near monopoly over military production. Even when East European states managed to design some of the military equipment they wished to use themselves (with the exception of Romania), the Soviet Union often took over production. (*WSJ*, 13 June.)

Perhaps some of the best indicators of the direction of development in the WTO military is to be found in the large-scale military maneuvers that are held each year. General of the Army Anatoli I. Gribkov, WTO chief of staff, called joint maneuvers the supreme form for comprehensive training of troops, commanding officers, and staffs. He asserted that during exercises the troops dealt with various questions of efficiency regarding combat deployment, evaluated operations and combat plans, and resolved questions of coordination of various units and subunits of the allied armies (*Sovetskaia Belorossiia*, Minsk, 14 May 1983; *FBIS*, 27 May 1983). This is a usual function of joint maneuvers in all allied systems. Such exercises are essential in raising the effectiveness of military cooperation.

Between 6 and 11 February, units of the Czechoslovak, Soviet, and Hungarian armies held joint winter exercises in Czechoslovakia (*Rudé právo*, Prague, 13 February; *FBIS*, 15 February). The maneuvers involved rapid offensive operations that included coordinated action by motorized infantry and tank units from the three armies, as well as fighter bombers and assault helicopters. The Czechoslovak communist party daily, *Rudé právo* (11 February), expressed its satisfaction at the result—not only in military terms, but also because the exercises "provided an opportunity to test the effectiveness of party-political work under exacting conditions" (*FBIS*, 14 February).

New joint maneuvers in late February and early March, code-named "Druzhba '84," in western and northwestern Poland included Soviet, Polish, and East German forces under the nominal command of Poland's deputy minister of national defense, Gen. Eugeniusz Molczyk. The official objective of the exercise was to improve the operations of the WTO command and units under winter conditions. (Warsaw television service, 24 February; *FBIS*, 27 February.) As usual the exercises involved offensive operations. Although the military operations were rather standard, Polish participation and the satisfaction at the outcome expressed by the head of the political directorate of the Northern Group of Soviet Armed Forces, Lt. Gen. Nikolai Lushnichenko (*Neues Deutschland*, East Berlin, 9 March; *FBIS*, 15 March), indicate that the effective reintegration of Polish forces might also have been a key consideration.

On 22 February the Soviet Union announced that joint WTO maneuvers, code-named "Soyuz '84" (Union '84), would be held in March on the territories of Bulgaria, Hungary, Romania, and the southwestern region of the Soviet Union and on the Black Sea (*Pravda*, 22 February). In actual fact, these were map exercises only (Bucharest domestic service, 21 February, 20 March; *FBIS*, 22 February, 21 March), without troops on Romanian soil. The rest of the exercise ranged over a huge geographic area under the command of Marshal of the Soviet Union V. G. Kulikov, commander-in-chief of the WTO.

Yet these maneuvers also had considerable political significance. They indicated that the USSR may have begun to place greater emphasis on the somewhat neglected southern tier of the WTO. At the very least, the Soviet Union was trying hard to convey the impression that the Romanians were cooperating routinely in WTO exercises. Lastly, these maneuvers may also have been designed in part to exert pressure on one of NATO's allies, Turkey, and to demonstrate to the Western alliance as a whole the WTO's ability to project tremendous force southwards and not only westwards.

Soyuz '84 was closely followed by another set of war games code-named Yug '84 (South '84). The exercises were held in the southern part of East Germany on 26–31 March with participation of staffs and troops from the Polish army, the group of Soviet forces in Germany, and the East German National People's Army (ADN, 26 March; *FBIS*, 27 March). From a military point of view, the operations were rather standard, involving scenarios in which bloc forces stopped "enemy aggression." They were commanded by Gen. Horst Stechbarth, deputy minister of national defense and chief of the East German ground forces. But the political aspect of the maneuvers was also emphasized. The participation of the Polish army gave implicit proof of the successful rebuilding of Poland's forces and of their now effective participation in the WTO (*Krasnaia zvezda*, Moscow, 19 April).

Hungary conducted major military exercises, called "Sopron '84," between 18 May and 7 June involving air, land, and amphibious operations that tested the call-up of reservists (Budapest domestic service, 7 June). Joint WTO maneuvers resumed at the end of May. Code-named "Summer '84," these war games were held in the northwestern region of Poland under the command of the Polish minister of national defense. The maneuvers involved field communications as well as the training and organization of capabilities of the higher commands and staffs of the allied forces. They were designed to improve the combat efficiency of the Polish army. (Warsaw television service, 31 May; *FBIS*, 1 June.)

WTO exercises in Hungary's Trans-Danubian region included 16,000 Soviet, Czechoslovak, and Hungarian troops. Held between 22 and 30 June, they were code-named "Danube '84" and were designed to improve the operational-tactical training of officers, perfect the military training of personnel, and consolidate the "comradeship-in-arms among the armies of the socialist community countries" (Moscow domestic service, 2 July; *FBIS*, 2 July). These large combined-arms exercises involved a wide range of scenarios. They included commando operations by Soviet soldiers carried on dozens of large helicopters (*Népszabadság*, Budapest, 30 June), movements by hundreds of tanks and army personnel carriers, supported by Soviet fighters, and major river crossings. In one part of the exercise WTO troops were reported to have built a 400-meter-long bridge across the Danube in only 28 minutes (Budapest television service, 29 June; *FBIS*, 2 July).

The Soviet Union alone held very large-scale exercises involving its land, air, and naval forces between 20 June and 5 July on the frontiers of East Germany, Poland, Czechoslovakia, and in the southern part of the Baltic Sea. Under the command of the Soviet minister of defense, Marshal Ustinov, they were designed to improve combat skills and command and control of troops and naval forces. (*Pravda*, 28 June.) East European military leaders were invited to observe the exercises. According to Western sources, about 60,000 Soviet troops practiced new tactics designed for a swift, deep strike westward into West German territory (*NYT*, 14 July). The signal was not too subtle—namely, that the West German decision to deploy American missiles had led to heightened tensions, as Moscow had threatened it would.

In September, in Czechoslovakia, the Warsaw Pact held one of the year's largest joint maneuvers, code-named "Shield '84." As required by the Helsinki agreement, the WTO notified NATO that 60,000 of its air and ground troops would be participating in maneuvers lasting through September (*CSM*, 5 September). As in the case of Soyuz '84, the USSR and its allies again tried to create the impression of full Romanian participation along with that of all other WTO states. The Romanians, however, informed Western sources that they had sent only staff officers (Vienna television service, 6 September; *FBIS*, 7 September). Nevertheless, the exercises gave an impressive demonstration of Soviet and WTO power. Huge numbers of tanks and armored vehicles moved in close cooperation with fighter bombers and with tank-killing Mi-24 combat helicopters. According to Soviet reports, there was also further demonstration of the high level of integration in combat operations of the allied forces, which were under the nominal command of the Czechoslovak minister of defense Army General Martin Dzúr since the operations were held in Czechoslovakia (*Krasnaia zvezda*, 16 September). The declared military purpose of the maneuvers was to improve the interaction of the staffs and troops of the allied armies during joint combat operations. But there was another clearly stated purpose. WTO commander-in-chief Marshal of the Soviet Union V. G. Kulikov contended that "the exercise also had great political significance. The conduct of it was a further graphic example of the growing military cooperation among the fraternal armies, our countries' unity, and their unswerving desire to strengthen our defensive alliance." (Ibid.)

Just as it is difficult to distinguish at times between political and military motivations in the case of maneuvers, so it is often virtually impossible to distinguish between military and political concerns in some of the other activities of the Warsaw Pact. Moscow itself cultivates the linkages among political, military, and even economic factors. Sessions of the WTO Council, the Committee of Defense Ministers (CDM), and the Committee of Foreign Ministers (CFM) usually tend to emphasize military issues. Meetings of the Military Council during the year were routine. The one held in Prague during 24–26 April and chaired by Marshal Kulikov reviewed the implementing of decisions made at meetings of the Political Consultative Committee and CDM. Moscow reported that the meeting was held in a "business-like atmosphere and in the spirit of friendship and mutual understanding" (Tass, 6 April; *FBIS*, 27 April).

The next Military Council session, held 17–19

October in Sofia, was also routine. Soviet reportage characterized it as "constructive and businesslike" and as demonstrating "fellowship in arms and friendship and *complete mutual understanding and unity*" (Moscow television service, 19 October; *FBIS*, 22 October; emphasis added). Romania attended both sessions, and the stress on complete unity in the latter meeting at least tried to create the impression that all the WTO states were in agreement with Moscow's policies.

The most important meeting of the CFM was designed both to give an impression of unity among the WTO states and to increase pressure on NATO countries that had allowed deployment of American intermediate-range missiles. It was a regular meeting held in Budapest with the foreign ministers of all seven WTO states in attendance (Tass, 20 April; *FBIS*, 23 April). The communiqué not only underlined bloc unity but also took a rather hard line on resumption of arms control negotiations. It drew attention again to the Prague political declaration of 5 January 1983, which, among other things, had suggested a treaty on nonuse of military force (i.e., a nonaggression pact between East and West) and to the Moscow joint statement of 28 June 1983 (*YICA*, 1984, pp. 423–24), thus reconfirming previous positions and proposals for a mutual freeze on military spending, a chemical weapons ban, a pledge by all nuclear powers not to be the first to use nuclear weapons, and the creation of nuclear-free zones.

Perhaps the most important part of the communiqué declared that "the Warsaw Pact countries demand the halting of the deployment of the U.S. medium-range nuclear weapons in Western Europe and declared that should such measures be adopted that lead to removal of the missiles that have already been deployed, then at the same time steps would be taken for lifting the retaliatory measures" (ČETEKA, 20 April; *FBIS*, 23 April). Even though this blamed the West for the breakdown of talks and conditions for resumption appeared harsh, there was a very small opening at least. The possibility of resuming talks now hinged on the initiation of measures to dismantle the Western missiles, and this differed from previous Soviet demands that the prerequisite for talks would be the return to the status quo ante. During an October visit to Bonn, Ceauşescu suggested to West German chancellor Helmut Kohl that the two countries issue a joint statement calling for withdrawal of all medium-range nuclear missiles from Europe, but this was unacceptable to the West German government. (*Facts on File*, 2 November, p. 807.)

Other members of the WTO had already made their decision to follow Soviet policy lines. *Krasnaia zvezda* disclosed on 18 January that new missiles of an "enhanced range" were now positioned in East Germany, and on the following day it stated that such missiles were already stationed in Czechoslovakia. These were part of the so-called retaliatory measures instituted by the Soviet Union and included SS-21s, SS-22s, or SS-23s. Moscow also managed to coerce the East German leader, Erich Honecker, to cancel a scheduled fall visit to West Germany. Bulgaria's Todor Zhivkov did the same.

Political Developments. In order to maximize the pressures that it wanted to exert on the West European members of NATO (and somewhat more indirectly on the United States), Moscow carefully nurtured the image of a noncommunicative superpower that froze channels on important arms talks as a retaliatory measure for the deployment of intermediate-range missiles in Western Europe. As advantageous as this stance might have been from a practical point of view and as effective as the Soviet propaganda machine might have been in helping to whip up new fears of an East-West confrontation in Europe, the impression of a total freeze hardly corresponded with reality. Although Moscow refused to return to the Intermediate-Range Nuclear Force talks (INF) or the Strategic Arms Reduction Talks (START) in Geneva, it continued to discuss armaments in various other forums, including the Conference on Confidence and Security-Building Measures and European Disarmament in Stockholm and at the Mutual and Balanced Force Reduction (MBFR) talks in Vienna.

Little progress was made at the European Disarmament Conference, which commenced on 17 January in Stockholm. No new confidence- and security-building measures were agreed upon at the meeting. The Soviet Union and its allies reiterated their previous positions, including proposals for a spending freeze (which was first put forth by the Romanians), but in large part these were designed to boost the Soviet bloc's "peace image." Nevertheless, the U.S. chief delegate, James Goodby, and his Soviet counterpart, Oleg Grinevsky, had the opportunity to meet face-to-face, and the former suggested that there were at least some signs of a common ground (*Toronto Star*, 9 May).

The MBFR talks, which had recessed in December 1983, did not resume until 16 March, but the eleven-year-old negotiations yielded few results except in terms of maintaining top-level communications on armaments between East and West. Two of the key problems blocking agreement were the numbers of Soviet and East European troops and verification. The WTO states showed some limited flexibility on verification procedures. But even though West Germany apparently wanted to pursue this further, the concession was considered insufficient by the United States (*Times*, London, 17 March). On the other hand, Western proposals that would allow for greater flexibility in counting the number of Soviet/WTO troops were not acceptable to the East. NATO has contended that the East has almost 170,000 more ground troops than the Western alliance. Under the new plan NATO offered to accept WTO figures on force levels if they fell within an acceptable range of Western estimates. This would lie between 5 and 10 percent. Moreover, NATO proposed counting only ground combat troops and combat support units, thereby leaving out service support forces that may have accounted for much of the imbalance in troop strength assessment charged by NATO. (*Facts on File*, 27 April, p. 294.) The WTO also rejected NATO's proposal for initial reductions of 13,000 U.S. and 30,000 Soviet troops, as part of a five-year plan of phased withdrawals that would leave both sides with the same overall troop ceiling (ibid.). Moscow, moreover, criticized these proposals harshly (*Pravda*, 21 April) but remained willing to continue discussions with the NATO countries.

The WTO continued to perform most of its traditional functions for Moscow. It acted as a forum that supported Soviet views, and on substantive issues this, by and large, applied to Romania as well. It was also a useful instrument in demonstrating Soviet might as part of the Kremlin campaign that was designed to force concessions from the West on the deployment of intermediate-range missiles. Eastern Europe functioned as a convenient geographic glacis for the USSR to institute what it called retaliatory measures when it deployed new medium-range missiles in East Germany and Czechoslovakia. And the increased frequency of maneuvers performed three interlinked roles. First, it helped increase integration of the WTO military forces under Soviet command and enhanced their efficiency in line with the development of bloc military doctrine. Second, it helped the USSR maintain its political control over Eastern Europe. Third, it helped convey to the West Europeans anger over their decision to proceed with the deployment of cruise and Pershing II missiles. But Moscow decided to return to the negotiating table after it had failed to drive a wedge between the United States and its allies and because the United States was moving ahead with the Strategic Defense Initiative. As Zbigniew Brzezinski put it, "The campaign of propaganda did not work. The U.S. did not listen to the panicky advice from Europe and to some extent from Canada . . . as a result the Soviets lost a year."

(*Toronto Globe and Mail*, 4 January.) And consequently, even though the East Europeans may be relieved at Moscow's decision to resume talks, they can take very little credit for it. The Kremlin continues to make all the important decisions in the WTO.

Aurel Braun
University of Toronto

International Communist Organizations

WORLD MARXIST REVIEW

(See *YICA*, 1984, pp. 426–27 for a full treatment of this subject, but also note the following.) The February 1982 issue of *Party Life*—the "for members only" theoretical publication of the communist Workers' Party of Jamaica—had the following to say about the *Review* in connection with the November 1981 conference on its work:

> Why was the Conference at such a high level? To understand this, we need to understand that there is presently no formal centre of the International Communist Movement. Due to the opposition of the Euro-communists, the Chinese CP and their supporters in the movement (e.g., Romania), it is difficult to hold even meetings of C[ommunist] and WP [workers' parties]. The last was held in 1969. The Journal and its regular Conferences, therefore, play an important role of providing for contact, exchange of views and formulation of international policy. Through their representatives in the Journal at Prague (very often CC members) and in these conferences now being held every four years, important international questions can be tackled. This has to be done, unfortunately, without any formal acknowledgement of its role, which would intensify the charges that the WMR is acting as a "centre" of the movement.

The above was found in the New Jewel Movement archives after the Grenadian invasion and appears to have been in error in only one detail: the next conference on the work of the *Review* occurred only a little over three years later, in December 1984.

FRONT ORGANIZATIONS

Control and Coordination. The international Soviet-line communist fronts operating since World War II are counterparts of organizations established by the Comintern after World War I. Their function today is the same as that of the interwar organizations: to unite Communists with persons of other political persuasions to support, and thereby lend strength and respectability to, Soviet foreign policy objectives. Moscow's control over the fronts is evidenced by their faithful adherence to the Soviet policy line as well as by the withdrawal patterns of member-organizations (certain pro-Western groups after the cold war began, Yugoslav affiliates following the Stalin-Tito break, and Chinese and Albanian representatives as the Sino-Soviet split developed).

The Communist Party of the Soviet Union is said to control the fronts through its International Department (ID), presumably through the Soviets serving as fulltime Secretariat members at front headquarters (U.S. Congress, *The CIA and the Media*, 1981, p. 574). This is the case in eight fronts: the World Peace Council (WPC), the World Federation of Trade Unions (WFTU), the Women's International Democratic Front (WIDF), the Afro-Asian Peoples' Solidarity Organization (AAPSO), the International Organization of Journalists (IOJ), the Christian Peace Conference (CPC), the International Association of Democratic Lawyers (IADL), and, most recently, the International Union of Students (IUS). Past experience indicates that it may be the Soviet vice-presidents who exercise this function in the two other major front organizations: the World Federation of Democratic Youth (WFDY) and the World Federation of Scientific Workers (WFSW).

In addition to Soviet control of each front through the ID and headquarters personnel, coordination of front activity appears to be effected by the WPC. This makes sense because the Soviets consider the "peace movement" the most important joint action by the "anti-imperialist" forces and the most important of the movements "based on common specific objectives of professional interests"— that is, the front organizations (*Kommunist*, no. 17, November 1972, p. 103, no. 3, February 1974, p. 101; see also J. A. Amerson Fermaat, "Moscow Fronts and the European Peace Movement," *Problems of Communism*, November–December, pp. 43–56). A glance at the nearly 200 positions on the WPC Presidential Committee reveals that they include, in addition to ID Deputy Chief Vitali S. Shaposhnikov, slots for one or two of the top leaders of each of the ten fronts discussed here except for the IADL. The IADL president is, however, one of the 1,500-plus members of the WPC proper (WPC, *List of Members, 1980–1983*).

Still another method of coordination consists of consultative meetings among representatives of the various fronts themselves, which in recent years have taken place on an annual basis. That of 1984, held in Prague in February and hosted by the IOJ, apparently had participation from each of the ten major fronts noted above, except for the IADL (Radio Prague, 26 February). The IADL had missed similar meetings in 1982 and 1983 (*Flashes from the Trade Unions*, Prague, 23 March 1982, 21 October 1983), but there is evidence of resurgence of that organization's activity later in 1984 (see below). Three minor fronts apparently striving to project a separate identity by attending all three of these annual meetings were the World Federation of Teachers' Unions (FISE), a trade union interna-

tional of the WFTU; the International Institute of Peace (IIP), the WPC's research body; and the Organization of Solidarity with the Peoples of Africa, Asia, and Latin America (AALAPSO or OSPAAL) (see *YICA*, 1984, pp. 429, 431). The latter appears to be an extension of the AAPSO into Latin America. It is also linked to other fronts in that its president, Susumo Ozaki (Japan), is a vice-president of the IADL (*Barricada*, Managua, 18 July) and its secretary general, Melba Hernández (Cuba), is a presidential committee member of the WPC (*New Perspectives*, Helsinki, no. 4, p. 2).

Policies and Emphases. The peace theme remained paramount for the fronts throughout 1984. The stage had more or less been set by the end of 1983, when WIDF Secretary General Mirjam Vire-Touminen declared that her organization's activity during the following year would be totally devoted to the struggle for peace and against nuclear war (ADN, East Berlin, 30 December 1983); this was followed by a WIDF Consultative Meeting on Disarmament in East Berlin in late January. *The 1984 Programs of Action* of both the WPC and WFDY as well as their largest gatherings during the year, the January West Berlin Presidential Committee and the April New Delhi Bureau meetings of the former and the February Havana Executive Committee meeting of the latter, also had this emphasis (WPC, *1984 Objectives of the Program of Action*, Helsinki, pp. 5–6, 17–18; *Neues Deutschland*, East Berlin, 23–25 January, 9–10 February; *Pravda*, 10 April). Two other fronts also emphasized this subject at their largest meetings of the year: both the Fourteenth IUS Congress (Sofia, April) and the Thirty-sixth WFTU General Council session (Sofia, October) had special sessions devoted solely to this subject. It was also listed as the number-one subject for consideration at the Twelfth IADL Congress (Athens, October), at least in the publicity *Pravda* (22 October) gave this meeting, and seems to have dominated the forty-seventh session of the WFSW Executive Council (Varna, April) (BTA, Sofia, 10 April).

The specific approach here was to present the American deployment of intermediate-range nuclear missiles in Western Europe as the most immediate danger (see below) but then to go on to a point-by-point program that appears to treat both the American and Soviet sides equally (see *YICA*, 1984, pp. 434–35, for a description of an apparent change in emphasis from a one-sided to a more "equal" approach during 1983; during 1984, the two lines appeared to have been more intertwined, perhaps reflective of a more indecisive Soviet leadership). In any case, both the WPC's *1984 Objectives of the Program of Action*, coming out early in the year (pp. 5, 17–18), and the WFTU General Council resolution, "Fortieth Anniversary of the Victory over Hitlerite Fascism," coming out late in the year (*World Trade Union Movement*, Prague, no. 12, p. 19), do just that.

In contrasting emphasis to this was the following statement that came out of the April WPC Bureau meeting in New Delhi: "The WPC considers that under prevailing conditions, the struggle to end the deployment of the new U.S. nuclear missile weapons and to dismantle or withdraw those already deployed is the main task for the planet's peace movement" (*Pravda*, 10 April). This was certainly one of the stronger statements on this subject by any front organization, but similar sentiments were expressed by the January WPC Presidential Committee meeting in West Berlin (*Flashes from the Trade Unions*, 10 February), the March–April WFDY Youth Peace Meeting in Copenhagen (*Berlingske Tidende*, Copenhagen, 2 April), the April WFTU Bureau meeting in Paris (*Flashes from the Trade Unions*, 27 April), and the June CPC Presidential Board meeting in Warsaw (*CPC Information*, Prague, 11 June). It was also the emphasis in the WPC's call for an early December "week of action" involving demonstrations before U.S. diplomatic and military installations abroad, the implementation of which in such irrelevant (to the issue at hand) places as Kabul, gave ample evidence of the contrived nature of the campaign (see Tass, Moscow, 12 December; *FBIS*, 13 December; *Pacific Tribune*, Vancouver, 21 November). Finally, the row between official delegations from the USSR and Eastern Europe, on the one hand, and the representatives of more truly neutral "equal responsibility" peace groups, on the other, at the July European Nuclear Disarmament (END) meeting in Perugia over 59 East bloc dissidents who were not able to attend the gathering is illustrative (*La Stampa*, Rome, 19 July; *Corriere della Sera*, Milan, 19 July; see also *YICA*, 1984, p. 434, for a similar disagreement surrounding the END meeting of May 1983, which, however, had not been attended by official Soviet bloc peace movements). These dissidents could certainly have approved the "equal" propositions enumerated in the WPC *Objectives* and WFTU resolution cited above, and their linkage of these to the human and civil rights issues is ironically mirrored in the former, point 12 of which

is "to defend human rights and the rights of the people to struggle against racism, racial discrimination, and the political practices of repressive regimes" (WPC, *Objectives*, p. 19).

Development in and of the Third World was an important secondary emphasis during the year. This could be especially seen in the October WFTU General Council meeting, where "the role of trade unions in solving economic problems of developing countries" was the first item on the agenda and appeared to be the most publicized theme (*World Trade Union Movement*, no. 12, p. 4). The "right to development" was just behind the "right of peace and security" as an emphasis at the Twelfth IADL Congress, also in October (*Flashes from the Trade Unions*, 9 November). The sixth AAPSO Congress (Algiers, May) related the arms race to economic backwardness (Tass, Moscow, 31 May; *FBIS*, 1 June) just as the aforementioned WPC *Objectives* (p. 18) cites the arms race and the threat of nuclear war as hindrances to a New International Economic Order (NIEO). An NIEO, in which the unequal relationships between the developed and the underdeveloped worlds in general would be replaced by ones of "equality and mutual benefit" as specifically manifested in "socialist" Third World relationships, is in fact the stated objective of the fronts here (*Flashes from the Trade Unions*, 9 November). Culprits here are said to be transnational corporations, who are engaged in "plunder," and the World Bank and International Monetary Fund, who impose "draconian conditions" on their loans (*World Trade Union Movement*, no. 12, pp. 4–5). Incidentally, a seminar specifically focused on an NIEO was cosponsored by the WPC and held in Kathmandu in April.

There was also much activity focused on youth during the year, in preparation for the WFDY-IUS cosponsored World Youth Festival, to be held in Moscow in the summer of 1985 (the United Nations' International Youth Year). Three large preparatory committee meetings were held for the festival: Havana in February, Sofia in April, and Moscow in November. The last, attended by 517 delegates from 117 countries, was addressed by Konstantin Chernenko as well as by Boris Ponomarev, a secretary and alternate Politburo member of the CPSU and de facto chief of its International Department (Moscow television, 5 November; *FBIS*, 6 November; *People's Democracy*, New Delhi, 18 November)—illustrative of the importance with which the Russians regard the effort. The November meeting also saw the establishment of a Permanent Commission of 43 representatives to act as a coordinating body between the Soviet preparatory committee and others that had been set up in 87 countries by that time (ibid.). Related to this youth emphasis was a series of sketches of various WFDY affiliates carried in the *World Marxist Review*, beginning with the April issue, which described the Soviet and French organizations.

After some years of relative inactivity, the IADL seemed to have sprung to life in 1984. Its Twelfth Congress in October, attended by some 600 delegates, appears to have been the largest front meeting of the year (*Flashes from the Trade Unions*, 9 November). It—along with the WPC, WFTU, WIDF, WFDY, AAPSO, and IUS, but not the three other major fronts—participated in the sponsorship of the International Conference of Solidarity with Nicaragua and for Peace in Central America, held in Lisbon in May (ibid., 16 March). This grouping of fronts, minus the WIDF and IUS, had earlier participated in staging a conference on Korean unification held in Paris in March (*Peace Courier*, special issue, April).

Other topics treated by the fronts in a significant manner during the year were meetings devoted to South Africa (attack on the "apartheid regime"—Harare, May, WFTU cosponsored; solidarity with the "liberation struggle" in South Africa and Namibia—Cologne, October, WPC/AAPSO International Committee on Southern Africa); Cyprus (support of Greek Cypriots against the Turks—Nicosia, November, WPC supported); and a New International Information Order (to give the Third World "fair treatment" in the media—Kabul, November–December, AAPSO sponsored). The Middle East and the traditional attacks on Israel appear to have been slighted in 1984; but the AAPSO at its 6 May congress was able to get Palestine Liberation Organization leader Yassir Arafat to address its opening session, and the IOJ's International Committee on Defense of Journalists (Varna, August) appears to have concentrated on Palestine (BTA, Sofia, 9 August).

Personnel. The most noteworthy personnel changes in the major international fronts during 1984 occurred in the WFDY and IUS, which obtained new secretaries general, and in the AAPSO, which was to receive a new president. Vilmos Cserveny (Hungary) and Georgios Michaelides (Cyprus) got the new WFDY and IUS jobs, respectively. The former took over in February when his predecessor, Miklos Barabas, became secretary

general of the Hungarian National Peace Movement (Radio Budapest, 29 February; *FBIS*, 1 March). The latter succeeded Srinivasan Kunalan (India) as a result of the Fourteenth IUS Congress in April, which retained Miroslav Stepan (Czechoslovakia) as president (ČETEKA, Prague, 16 April; BTA, Sofia, 11–16 April). In late December, it was announced that Ahmad Hamrush had been nominated to succeed the ailing Abd-al-Rahman Sharqawi as AAPSO's president, a job slotted for an Egyptian (*al-Jumhurriya*, Cairo, 30 December).

It is also interesting that WFTU President Sandor Gaspar had been replaced as secretary general of the Hungarian National Council of Trade Unions by Lajos Mehes and given the presidency of that body instead (*Hungarian Trade Union News*, Budapest, March, p. 2). Such a career pattern is generally regarded as a "kick upstairs" and may be related to Gaspar's previously noted liberal tendencies (see *YICA*, 1983, p. 397). Consistent with this, Gaspar also lost his position as Hungarian representative on the WFTU General Council to Mehes (*Népszabadság*, 10 April), the job apparently going with the secretary generalship of the national organization.

There were also a number of changes at the vice-presidential level during the year. Rodolfo Mechini had replaced the deceased Amerigo Terenzi as Italian vice-president of the WPC by December (*L'Unità*, 3 December), but it is not known who, if anyone yet, has replaced the other WPC vice-president who died during the year, the Argentinian Alfredo Varela. The Syrian A. al-Asad was noted as an AAPSO vice-president in April (*Pravda*, 24 April), which brought the pre–Sixth Congress total to nine. The latter meeting—held in May and re-electing Egyptian Abd-al-Rahman Sharqawi as president (see above) and Iraqi Nuri Abd-al-Razzaq Husayn as secretary general—provided slots for seventeen vice-presidents: four from "liberation movements," seven from African countries, and six from Asian ones (*FBIS*, 1 June), an apparent expansion almost entirely in the African sphere. New WFDY vice-presidents noted during the year were Nguyen Van Ky from Vietnam, Li Jong-gun from North Korea, and Binoy Viswam from India (*WFDY News*, nos. 3, 6, 7).

Secretariat changes included, most notably, Miguel Gonzáles Regas's replacement of fellow-Colombian Óscar Gonzáles as one of the two deputy secretaries general of the WFDY (ibid., no. 6) and Dev Kumar Ganguli's replacement of fellow-Indian K. G. Srivastava as one of the WFTU's five secretaries (*Flashes from the Trade Unions*, 2 November). Other new WFDY secretaries noted during the year were Andre Gerhardt from Poland, Joe Sims from the United States, Jackie Selibi from South Africa, Konstantin Stathis from Greece, Mihai Botorog from Romania, and Freddy Fernández from Venezuela (*WFDY News*, nos. 1/2, 3, 6, 7, and 12). Also, one Elson Concepción (nationality unknown) was noted as the new IOJ secretary for Latin America (*IOJ Newsletter*, no. 8), possibly replacing either Miguel Arteaga from Cuba or Leopoldo Fernández Vargas from Colombia in this position (see *YICA*, 1984, p. 432). Similarly, Phil Spillman (nationality unknown) and Paivi Aarotainen from Finland apparently joined the WPC Secretariat during the year, and Denmark's Carl Rosschou left that body (*New Perspectives*, no. 2, p. 2, no. 4, p. 2, no. 11, p. 3). Finally, it was revealed that Archpriest Georgi Goncharov was the "representative of the Russian Orthodox Church at the CPC Central Office in Prague" (*CPC Information*, 11 June); this suggests that Russian CPC Deputy Secretary General (Archmandrite) Sergei Fomin may not actually be resident at the organization's headquarters and that Goncharov gives on-the-spot Soviet guidance there.

No more new information on top front personalities emerged during the year except that the IADL's 14 October congress re-elected Joe Nordmann from France as president; and Amar Bentoumi from Algeria as secretary general (*Flashes from the Trade Unions*, 9 November); and added a South African vice-presidential slot, filled by Archie Gumede (*Johannesburg Star*, 1 November).

Wallace H. Spaulding
McLean, Virginia

Soviet Propaganda Themes

Propaganda is an important instrument of Soviet (and other communist) foreign policy, no less a factor than political and cultural diplomacy or the armed forces. Political propaganda is designed to spread Marxism-Leninism and to fight against bourgeois and revisionist ideology. It is, therefore, the most important component of the ideological activity of the party.

The communist propaganda orchestra utilizes all modern instruments—television, radio, films, newspapers, journals, books, posters, party and government officials, delegations, cultural exchanges, foreign aid, and trade—in pursuit of long-held objectives. The Central Committee of the Communist Party of the Soviet Union (CPSU) has characterized the press, radio, TV, and films as the "shock forces on the ideological front." These media, therefore, are designed not for entertainment but to propagate Marxism-Leninism and Soviet foreign policies and to oppose enemy propaganda.

The great importance that Moscow assigns to overt propaganda is reflected in its annual budget, estimated at $4 billion (U.S. Congress, House, Permanent Select Committee on Intelligence, *Soviet Active Measures*, 1982). If KGB covert action activities—for example, forgeries, planted press articles, disinformation, and controlled media—are included, the financial expenditures would be substantially higher. This enormous outlay enables the USSR to conduct propaganda and disinformation campaigns unprecedented in history.

A CIA study asserts that "the Soviet leadership regards propaganda and covert action as indispensable adjuncts to the conduct of foreign policy by traditional diplomatic, military and other means" (U.S. Congress, House, Permanent Select Committee on Intelligence, *Soviet Covert Action*, 1980, p. 59). A recent book on the subject concludes that "propaganda and political influence techniques do in fact constitute significant instruments of Soviet foreign policy and strategy" (Richard H. Shultz and Roy Godson, *Dezinformatsia: Active Measures in Soviet Strategy*, 1984, p. 1).

Major Propaganda Agencies. Although the Ministry of Foreign Affairs, the KGB, the Ministry of Defense, and several committees under the Council of Ministers all have propaganda roles, the CPSU Central Committee's International Information (IID) and the International (ID) departments are assigned the major responsibility. The IID was established in 1978, the successor of the Department of Agitation and Propaganda (Agitprop), itself later renamed the Department of Information.

The head of IID is Leonid Zamyatin, who had previously served as chief of the press department in the Ministry of Foreign Affairs and subsequently as director of the official Soviet news agency, Tass. The IID's jurisdiction encompasses the most important propaganda instruments: both Tass and the Novosti news agency, international broadcasting, major newspapers (for example, *Pravda* and *Izvestiia*), periodicals (for example, the weekly *New Times*, which is published in nine languages), books, and the information sections of Soviet embassies.

The ID has been directed by candidate Politburo member Boris Ponomarev since its establishment in 1957 and is responsible for relations with nonruling communist parties. However, some experts consider it pre-eminent in Soviet foreign policy. Stanislav Levchenko, a KGB agent who had worked in the ID and defected to the United States, adds the substantial weight of his testimony to other evidence that the ID, under Politburo direction, sets the propaganda line and has a more substantial staff than the IID (ibid., p. 27). Among its responsibilities, the ID is charged with maintaining contact with the numerous organizations through which Soviet propaganda is disseminated.

The third major propaganda agency is the Committee of State Security (KGB), formally a government organization, but characterized accurately as the "sword and shield" of the party. In addition to its better-known functions of internal security and intelligence, the KGB contributes to the total Soviet propaganda effort by covert or nonattributable techniques. These include disinformation, planted press articles and rumors, and controlled informa-

tion media. A frequently used technique is placement in foreign publications of selected pro-Soviet or anti-American propaganda themes to be replayed for audiences in a targeted third country. Forgeries, always a staple, have proliferated in recent years. Well-known, respected personalities and leading publications are especially sought for placement to achieve credibility (U.S. Congress, House, Permanent Select Committee on Intelligence, *The CIA and the Media*, 1978, pp. 19–21).

An English-language edition of the monthly *World Marxist Review* (*Problems of Peace and Socialism* [*PPS*]) is published in Ontario. Described as the "theoretical and information journal of communist and workers' parties," the *Review* appears in 35 languages. Its control by Moscow is clear. At the December 1981 *PPS* conference, the Japanese Communist Party, supported by others, criticized Soviet control. It called for dissolution of the journal, charging that it "has tended to become a propaganda publication justifying hegemonism of a particular party" (Wallace Spaulding, *Problems of Communism*, November–December 1982, p. 62).

The first *PPS* editor was A. M. Rumiantsev, an ideologue and former editor-in-chief of *Kommunist*, the CPSU theoretical journal. Over the years, the *PPS* has been Moscow's organ to further the international communist movement and the current Soviet policy line and a source of ideological inspiration. Claimed *PPS* circulation is over 500,000, with nearly half in the "nonsocialist" world; it is distributed in 145 countries. It serves as a major communications channel between the CPSU and communist parties and left-wing organizations throughout the world through its 65-member editorial council and "various forums." The fourth and current editor-in-chief is Yuri A. Shkliarov, who came from the equivalent position at *Pravda*.

The agendas of conferences held in Prague to discuss *PPS* and other matters include the work of the journal and issues such as "the struggle for peace," "the struggle against imperialism," and the "hidden political, ideological, and class significance of the concept of the strategic balance of forces" (Radio Free Europe Research, *Czechoslovakia*, no. 22, 20 December). At a meeting in December, 91 parties were represented. However, the French, Spanish, Yugoslavs, Chinese, Albanians, and Nicaraguans did not come. The Soviet delegation, led by Boris Ponomarev, included Vadim Zagladin, first deputy chief of the ID.

In his address, Ponomarev stressed the special

significance of "the close cooperation and further cohesion of the socialist countries, their coordinated actions in international politics, and their joint opposition to the subversive activity of imperialism, which is doing everything possible to bring contradictions into our community and to split it." He also "concentrated on the unprecedented, intensive, anticommunist activity of imperialistic propaganda, recalling at the same time imperialism's frantic and reckless psychological warfare." (Radio Prague, 6 December.)

In an interview, Shkliarov revealed plans for future contents of the journal: "We anticipate that the subject of the struggle for peace, exposing the aggressive plans of imperialism, and the aggravation of the international situation will occupy a prime position on the pages of the journal in the future." And "as always, an important place on the pages of the journal will belong to articles on the activity of the communist and workers' parties in countries which are waging national liberation struggles." (Ibid., 8 December.)

International Broadcasting. The Committee on Radio and Television is the Soviet government body responsible for the organizational structure of domestic and external broadcasting. The USSR is the leading international broadcaster, with 2,176 hours weekly in 81 languages, compared to 986 hours in 42 languages by the Voice of America. Radio Free Europe (626 hours and 9 languages) and Radio Liberty (422 hours and 12 languages) broadcasts to Eastern Europe (RFE) and the Soviet Union (RL) totaled 1,048 hours weekly (Office of the Director, VOA, 3 January 1985; *RFE-RL Research*, 4 January 1985). Radio Moscow surpasses VOA in external broadcasts to all areas and possesses a more powerful signal and more high-powered shortwave transmitters.

The ID is responsible for clandestine radio stations, originating from Soviet or East European locations, identified as, for example, the National Voice of Iran (NVOI), which transmits from the Baku area, or the Voice of the Turkish Communist Party, which comes from Eastern Europe. NVOI has been a constant source of mendacious, inflammatory anti-U.S. propaganda and pro-Moscow commentary. It continues inciting the Iranian people to action against the United States. (*Soviet Covert Action*, p. 78.)

In November 1964, the USSR established Radio Peace and Progress (RPP), purportedly the voice of Soviet public opinion, but in reality an extension of Radio Moscow, whose facilities it uses. The claim that it determines the content of its own broadcasts is designed to absolve Moscow from responsibility for the RPP's strident tone, which is even more inflammatory than that of Radio Moscow.

Propaganda Objectives and Themes. According to the CIA's *Report on Soviet Propaganda Operations*, Moscow's external propaganda extols Soviet achievements and policies, praises pro-Soviet governments and organizations, condemns the enemies of those governments and organizations, and attacks adversaries, especially China and the United States. Most Soviet propaganda is aimed against the United States, NATO member-states, and other pro-American countries.

While the content of Soviet propaganda may fluctuate to reflect current policy changes, the CIA report listed the following continuing objectives:

1. to influence both world and American public opinion against U.S. military and political programs that are perceived as threatening the Soviet Union;

2. to demonstrate that the United States is an aggressive, "colonialist," and "imperialist" power;

3. to isolate the United States from its allies and friends;

4. to discredit those who cooperate with the United States;

5. to demonstrate that the policies and goals of the United States are incompatible with the ambitions of the underdeveloped world;

6. to discredit and weaken Western intelligence services and expose their personnel;

7. to confuse world public opinion regarding the aggressive nature of certain Soviet policies; and

8. to create a favorable environment for the execution of Soviet foreign policy.

The USSR employs various propaganda themes, communicated and reflected around the world, in pursuit of its objectives. A major target of this propaganda is the Third World, whose cause Moscow seeks to be perceived as championing. Fundamentally the themes are strongly pro-Soviet and vehemently anti-American. The USSR projects itself as the vanguard of the world's proletariat, with a scientific ideology (Marxism-Leninism) that is freedom-loving, and as the builder of "socialism," the champion of peace and disarmament, and an undaunted fighter against "imperialism."

The Soviet Union's struggle is chiefly against the United States, pictured as the strongest "imperialistic" and a militarily aggressive power that seeks to dominate the world. The United States is portrayed as dominated by the industrial-military complex, which controls the government; an exploitative capitalistic society of the domineering rich and the starving, downtrodden millions; a colonial power with a huge military budget and vast arms sales that seeks military superiority and is bent on conquest; and an enemy of the USSR, the other "socialist countries," and all progressive people of the world, which not only slanders the communist system but intends to destroy it.

Over the years, certain themes have been constant, although varying in intensity. These can be described as follows: Marxism-Leninism versus capitalism; peace versus militarism and war; communist unity versus imperialist rift; communist progress versus capitalist decay; détente versus cold war; negotiation versus procrastination; altruism versus profiteering.

Propaganda Techniques. Lenin's dictum on morality continues to guide Soviet officials and propagandists: "We repudiate all morality that is taken outside of human, class concepts. We say that this is deception, a fraud . . . our morality is entirely subordinated to the interests of the class struggle." (Lenin, *Selected Works*, New York, 1943, 9:475.)

Unconstrained, Soviet officials at all levels, commentators, specialists, and others appearing publicly, as well as professional propagandists, employ a variety of techniques, legal or illegal, utilizing truths or lies, half-truths, deception, innuendo, distortion, indirection, selection, disinformation, diversion, and forgery. A frequently used technique has been to attribute questionable or false motives to the United States, its government, or President Reagan personally. The latter is often maligned, and there is no reluctance to resort to pejorative references.

For decades Moscow has arrogated for itself a lexicon of words and phrases intended to devolve righteousness and legitimacy upon the Soviet Union and communism and cast aspersions upon its perceived enemies, especially the United States. Soviet and bloc terms to portray themselves include "socialist" (rather than "communist"), "democracy" (instead of "dictatorship"), "freedom" (not "slavery"), "peace-loving" (not "militaristic"), "détente," and "peaceful coexistence." Among the words employed against the West are "capitalism," "imperialism," "militarism," "military-industrial complex," and "ruling class."

This kind of vocabulary is used as a conditioned reflex by Soviet officials from the highest to the lowest, by commentators and specialists, as well as by professional propagandists. They speak with a harmonious voice in a lulling drumbeat that ultimately makes an impact on some in the West through usage of that specialized language. For example, normally no one challenges the Soviet use of "socialism," a term that is not only accepted but even repeated by Westerners. Nor do Western listeners generally appear upset, even when maligned by pejorative expressions.

U.S.-Soviet Relations. The United States generally, and President Reagan in particular, have been the major targets of Soviet propaganda during past few years, and 1984 witnessed no fundamental change. Soviet propagandists blamed the United States for the "acute deterioration" of relations. Charges of militarism, aggression, policy of strength, anti-Sovietism, propaganda tricks, perfidy, lies, and slander were favorite Moscow invectives. As the year began, Soviet officials and media were still recalling the president's "evil empire" description of the USSR. The president was contradicted on his "peace-loving" statements by his support of mass production of nuclear weapons and the huge defense budget to achieve military superiority over the USSR. Thus, his overtures were simply "peacemaking cosmetics" to improve his image and calm the antiwar, antinuclear movements in Western Europe, Japan, and the United States. The president, *Pravda* (4 January) charged, bases his policy "on force and nothing but force."

President Reagan's 16 January speech on U.S.-USSR relations, despite its positive features, was attacked nevertheless for containing "nothing essentially new" since it reaffirmed his "bankrupt" policy of dealing from a "position of strength." The speech was "propaganda," Tass (16 January) said, adding that "no peaceful rhetoric coming out of Washington" can conceal the Pentagon budget, the U.S. role in the "undeclared war against sovereign Afghanistan," and American military actions against Lebanon, Grenada, and Nicaragua. Soviet media joined Foreign Minister Andrei Gromyko in assailing the United States at the opening of the Stockholm Disarmament Conference, which *Pravda* (18 January) charged Washington with trying to undermine by "preaching the possibility of a nuclear war limited to the confines of Europe."

The State of the Union message was also attacked. Tass (26 January) charged that President

Reagan's "three-year rule" had been marked by "extreme aggressiveness" internationally and "total disregard for the needs of the common people" domestically; his foreign policy section "was notable for demagoguery and hypocrisy" for claiming that the United States and the world were more secure in 1984. The contrary is true, "the threat to general security, including the security of the U.S. itself, has increased," and America is responsible. The president's comment that "we occupy no countries" was called a "lie." These and other invectives were to be frequently repeated throughout the year.

Following the death of Yuri Andropov (9 February), Soviet propaganda projected a more moderate tone toward the United States, but criticism of U.S. policies continued. However, after a slight lull, the anti-American stridency became even harsher under the new leader, Konstantin Chernenko. Continuity of Soviet policy was emphasized, as were familiar themes, such as a policy of peace, peaceful coexistence and opposition to the "aggressive forces of imperialism." The media reflected Chernenko's call for peace and military balance. Radio Moscow (15 February) said the USSR "does not seek military superiority and does not intend to dictate to others, but it will not permit anyone to upset the achieved balance of armed strength," adding that the Soviet Union is ready for "serious and equitable talks, honest and constructive talks."

At the same time, however, Chernenko in a Central Committee plenum speech referred to the "threat created today to humankind by the reckless, adventurist action of imperialism's aggressive forces," and Gromyko talked about "a policy of militarism, the mad arms race, and interference in the internal affairs of other countries" (*Pravda*, 14 and 15 February). Harshness was to prevail. According to Defense Minister Ustinov, "The American 'imperialists' in the grip of class hatred have proclaimed the Soviet Union to be the 'focus of evil' and have declared a 'crusade' against the USSR and world socialism" (ibid., 23 February).

Any reasonableness detected in the Soviet posture during the days following Andropov's death appeared to be shattered by Gromyko's 27 February election speech. Although not as blustering as his Stockholm tirade, Gromyko accused the Reagan administration of "recklessness and irresponsibility" and of disrupting or destroying much of what had been achieved by its predecessors in improving U.S.-Soviet relations (*Sovetskaia Belorossiia*, 28 February). Chernenko, also in an election speech, charged that "the past few years have seen a dra-

matic intensification of the policy of the more aggressive forces of U.S. imperialism, a policy of blatant militarism" (*Pravda*, 3 March). A Tass commentator went further on 20 March, alleging that "Washington has made militarist plans for 'limited' nuclear war." Political observer Valentin Falin depicted the U.S. position on arms talks as a "ruse" or a "sham" and that "everything is as prescribed in psychological warfare" (*Nedelia*, no. 13, 28 March). At a 29 March dinner for Ethiopian leader Mengistu Haile Mariam, Chernenko accused the Reagan administration of conducting a policy of "state terrorism and intervention" (*Pravda*, 30 March).

A comparison of the United States with Hitler's Germany was not beneath Soviet propagandists. According to a Tass commentator (5 April), "like Nazi Germany's leaders at their time, the White House leaders nowadays accompany preparations for war by stirring up hatred for the Soviet Union." The following day, reporting on the president's press conference, Tass stated that "since the times of Hitler's Reich no government has openly set the task of liquidating lawful regimes in other sovereign states and so cynically declared its intention to use the force of arms, armed intervention and blockade for subversive purposes." These accusations were echoed by the director general of Tass a week later (*Ogonek*, 14 April).

In an interview, CPSU leader Chernenko said that while "peace-loving rhetoric is heard in Washington," he discerns "no signs of readiness to back up these words with practical deeds" (*Pravda*, 9 April). Moscow consistently attempted to place the onus for its own walkout at Geneva and for lack of movement in arms control on the United States. For example, in reporting on President Reagan's press conference at which he allegedly presented Congress with an "ultimatum" for additional MX missiles, Tass (15 May) charged that "the president again hypocritically appealed to the Soviet Union to return to the negotiating table of the Geneva talks, although they had been scuttled by the deployment."

The media continued to blame President Reagan for lack of improvement in U.S.-Soviet relations, dismissing his statements as "camouflage" for nuclear missiles targeted at the USSR (*Pravda*, 7 July). Ten days later, Radio Moscow went so far as to say that his policies would lead the United States to war.

President Reagan's 24 September address to the United Nations was conciliatory, inviting the Soviet

Union to join the United States in "constructive negotiations" on arms control under a "bigger umbrella" and to institutionalize regular high-level meetings. In sharp contrast to this presentation, three days later Foreign Minister Gromyko gave a devastating critique of U.S. policies. He again alleged U.S. militarism and military superiority and accused American officials at the "highest" level of demanding the "right" to start a nuclear war. He concluded that "concrete deeds rather than verbal assurances" are necessary for improved relations. Blaming the United States for its "deliberate" intention to wreck the Intermediate-Range Nuclear Forces (INF) and Strategic Arms Reduction (START) talks, his speech gave no indication of Soviet willingness to resume those negotiations, but he reflected interest in holding talks on space weapons "as soon as possible" (Tass, 27 September).

Expectations for a breakthrough were higher in the West than was justified by previous Soviet propaganda, and there was no visible evidence of substantive change during or immediately after Gromyko's visit to Washington, D.C., for discussions with President Reagan and other U.S. officials.

Only a week later, political observer Falin castigated the president for advocating arms discussions, then "cynically killing time devising options that sought to make, and succeeded in making, any constructive discussion and progress towards accords unthinkable." He labeled negotiation from a position of strength "the most fraudulent option." (Izvestiia, 4 October.) Subsequently, Falin alleged that the United States is "jeopardizing all arms control accords" (ibid., 12 October). Politburo member Grigori Romanov, speaking at Helsinki, said that the danger of war is increasing. He charged that the United States is "escalating the arms race and is preparing to move it to outer space"; however, he added that the Soviet Union "is preparing to negotiate with the United States" (Moscow radio, 14 October).

The tone of Chernenko's interview with the Washington Post (16 October), obviously addressing the U.S. audience, differed from Gromyko's bombastic assertions at the United Nations and his own earlier Pravda interview of 2 June. He indicated possible interest in improving relations with Washington. Coming as it did on the eve of the presidential elections, the Kremlin perhaps sought to extract concessions from the Reagan administration, whose chance of winning appeared bright. In addition to the customary written questions and answers, the interview included a rare face-to-face

format. Chernenko counted on creating a favorable impression for himself and the USSR's position and placing the burden for improving U.S.-Soviet relations on Washington.

The party leader accused the U.S. administration of lacking in "real deeds" for a dialogue and chided the United States for continuing the deployment; he stressed the Soviet desire for improved bilateral relations. The perception was positive as Chernenko said that "the Soviet Union will not be found wanting" if the president's expression of a desire for dialogue was "not merely a tactical move." He repeated his earlier position that progress in "at least some" areas of arms control could alter U.S.-Soviet relations: space weaponry, a nuclear freeze, nuclear weapons tests, and no first use of nuclear weapons.

Post-election rhetoric in Moscow resembled the standard propaganda portrayal of the United States, rather than that anticipated after the Washington Post interview. Gromyko's speech on the occasion of the sixty-seventh anniversary of the October Revolution came as another broadside. He referred to the customary formulation about the Soviet desire for negotiations and improved relations, but accused the United States of "not only blocking the path to new accords but also undermining all the accords that have been concluded previously." He demanded that Washington "abandon" its "hegemonist ambitions" and called for "practical deeds." Chernenko also reverted to form. In addressing an international youth meeting, he accused the United States and its allies of trying to achieve the "insane goal of military superiority" (Tass, 5 November).

In written questions submitted to Chernenko through the U.S. embassy two days later by NBC correspondent Marvin Kalb, who reported the answers on 16 November, the secretary general said a return to détente would open the way to "broad possibilities for cooperation," including arms control.

On 22 November Washington and Moscow announced that the two countries had "agreed to enter into new negotiations . . . on the whole range of questions concerning nuclear and outer space arms." Secretary of State George Shultz and Foreign Minister Gromyko would meet in Geneva from 7 to 8 January 1985 to reach a common understanding as to the subject and objectives of such negotiations. There were exceptions, however. Chernenko criticized "aggressive U.S. circles" (ibid., 17 December). Commentators were less reserved. For example, Tass (22 and 24 December) accused the

U.S. administration of using "deception" to win the space arms race. Secretary of Defense Caspar Weinberger and his aides were attacked harshly for their "political hypocrisy" regarding the Geneva talks by claiming "readiness" for them, while actually working "to block any mutually acceptable agreement." Perhaps the mildest expression was that of a Soviet correspondent in Washington who wrote that "a constructive realistic approach" toward the Geneva talks had not yet appeared in the administration (*Pravda*, 31 December).

Chemical Weapons. A standard Soviet theme on chemical weapons has been that the USSR is "waging a struggle to ban chemical weapons" and that the United States is seeking "chemical rearmament." Following President Reagan's announcement at a news conference of a "bold, American initiative for a comprehensive worldwide ban on chemical weapons," to be submitted in Geneva by Vice-President George Bush, Tass immediately called the offer "nothing more than a propaganda trick," and *Pravda* (6 April) charged that the White House will use it "to camouflage and justify a program for the rapid buildup of its chemical arms arsenal."

Following submission of the proposal to the U.N. Committee on Disarmament in Geneva, Moscow's propagandists continued their assault on the U.S. administration's offer, dismissing it as "deliberately unacceptable." An editorial, after praising Soviet proposals, attacked the United States as follows: "Having made extensive use of toxins in the Vietnam war, the United States continues even today to allocate this means of mass destruction an important place in its aggressive military plans" (ibid., 21 and 27 April). The U.S. Arms Control and Disarmament Agency director's remarks before the Senate Foreign Relations Committee presented another occasion for Soviet propaganda attacks. Only "verbally" is the U.S. administration "allegedly in favor of a total ban on chemical weapons" (*Krasnaia zvezda*, 19 July).

At the United Nations, Gromyko ignored the U.S. treaty proposal, leveling criticism at "some states" for pretending interest in an agreement "to control their plans for a chemical weapons buildup" (Tass, 27 September). A report by a panel of experts on chemical weapons became a peg for criticism of the United States. Moscow charged that in 1982 the administration had announced plans for "nuclear rearmament" and at present the United States has enough chemical weapons "to eliminate

the world's population 50 times over" (Radio Moscow, 23 November).

After NATO Commander Gen. Bernard Rogers referred to chemical weapons in Western Europe, the Soviets alleged that his statements "are further evidence that the U.S. military-industrial complex is not suspending for a single day its preparations for waging a wide-scale chemical war" (*Krasnaia zvezda*, 22 November).

Afghanistan. The Soviet invasion and occupation of Afghanistan at the end of December 1979 is a dramatic illustration of Moscow's control of the instruments of propaganda, censorship, Marxist-Leninist ideology, and its aggressive foreign and military policy. Propagandists have sought to portray the Soviet role in Afghanistan as one of assisting a legitimate government struggling against "counterrevolutionaries," aided and abetted by the U.S. government, especially the CIA. Thus, American "imperialism" is accused of opposing a national liberation struggle in Afghanistan, as it does in other Third World countries.

In the frugal reports on the fighting, the Soviet media nevertheless give its readers a glimpse of a war zone, including the killing of Soviet troops. For example, a dispatch from Kabul reported "another bloody crime staged by the Afghan counterrevolution," in citing a bomb explosion in a mosque. It charged the United States with complicity: "The crime was committed the day after President of the United States Reagan proclaimed support for the Afghan counterrevolution." (Tass, 22 March.)

Anti-American criticism continued, including the citation of foreign sources out of context. Noting that Senator Paul Tsongas of Massachusetts did not run for re-election, *Izvestiia* (1 December) charged that a Senate resolution "perpetuates" his name. "Thus, the senator is gone, but his resolution lives on. It lives in order to kill." The government organ cited a *Congressional Quarterly* (August) report alleging U.S. financing of "rebels" as far back as mid-1979 and the *New York Times*, *Time*, and *Harper's* for additional "evidence."

The fifth anniversary (27 December) of the Soviet invasion evoked Western condemnation but relatively little Soviet coverage. The Soviet media did not mention the date itself: *Pravda* (27 December) carried a piece about the twentieth anniversary of the Afghan communist movement but on that same day *Komsomolskaia pravda*, although repeating the customary phrase about "international duty," reported on military service in Afghanistan, including soldiers' accounts of atrocities.

Gandhi Assassination. The 31 October assassination of Prime Minister Indira Gandhi revealed an aspect of Soviet propaganda that put in question any Soviet desire for genuine improvement of relations with the United States. On 21 November the Department of State issued the following statement about the disinformation campaign regarding alleged American involvement in the assassination: "The United States Government has previously made clear its concern over groundless Soviet accusations of U.S. complicity in the assassination of Prime Minister Gandhi. Despite our denials, those allegations have continued. In fact, they provide a case study of how Soviets attempt to manipulate public opinion through an active campaign of disinformation."

The Soviet attempt to manipulate public opinion, the State Department pointed out, began on 31 October, the day of the assassination: "The Soviet Union and its allies actively promulgated and encouraged reports accusing the U.S. Government of complicity in that crime." These charges were picked up in third countries and reported in many cases as credible. Certain papers are known as Soviet disinfomation outlets. The Soviet-generated accusations received particularly heavy coverage in India. Of the legitimate media, some questioned the veracity of the charges and identified the source as Moscow.

Radio Moscow's world service in English asserted on 31 October that the responsible people "received their ideological inspirations" from the CIA and charged that U.S. policy toward independent states consists of "state terrorism." The same day Tass reported a World Peace Council statement calling the assassination a result of "a heinous conspiracy of reactionary forces, internal and external." A *Moskovskaia pravda* (31 October) article accused the CIA of responsibility, charging that "there can be no doubt that Washington is prepared to pay any price to remove the Indian Congress Party."

John J. Karch
USIA, Vienna

(Note: Views expressed in this article are the author's own and do not necessarily reflect those of the U.S. Information Agency or any other agency of the U.S. government.)

THE MIDDLE EAST

Introduction

In general the parties of the Middle East remained bystanders to the major events of the region during 1984. The principal exceptions were the ruling Yemen Socialist Party of the People's Democratic Republic of Yemen and the Lebanese Communist Party and its allied Organization of Communist Action. The combined effects of the continuing war between Iran and Iraq, the related ideological shockwaves of Iran's revolution, and the turmoil in Lebanon increased the mood of defensiveness in many Arab countries. Such a mood, for the most part, reduced opportunities for communist and other revolutionary parties.

The Khomeini regime continued its siege of the Tudeh Party, once the largest pro-Soviet party in the region. After ten of Tudeh's military leaders were executed following trials in February, the planned November trial of its aging political leadership provoked a campaign by Tudeh exiles, Soviet bloc governments, and communist parties abroad ostensibly sufficient to cause an indefinite postponement of the proceedings. With presumably significant covert membership extant in Iran and many members in exile, however, the Tudeh is hardly defunct. Historically it has survived its suppressors and can be expected to rebuild. Although the party may find sympathizers among various disaffected political elements in Iran, its rigidly pro-Soviet stance will be a limiting factor. Iranian media focus harshly on Soviet atrocities in Afghanistan and on Soviet military assistance to Iraq, particularly on weapons used against Iranian towns. Iranian media also criticized Soviet pressure for Khomeini to negotiate with Iraq to end the war, citing Iran's status as the injured party.

The continuing war also meant siege status for Iraq's communist party, which celebrated its fiftieth anniversary isolated in northern Iraq's mountains with Kurdish guerrillas allied against Baghdad in the National Democratic Front. An almost wistful *Pravda* article (31 March; *FBIS*, 5 April) contrasted the party's position in the early 1970s—two ministers in the cabinet, a legal publishing program, and the glowing prospects of the party's front—to its current plight.

The Gulf war and Iran's revolution have also reduced opportunities for revolutionary party activity. Moderate leaders of the Arabian peninsula most fear subversion from religious extremists deployed from or inspired by Tehran. As a result, the Gulf Cooperation Council, which consists of the six moderate Gulf states, has evolved over the past four years from chiefly rhetorical capabilities to impressive levels of cooperation in security matters. Far more exacting screening of travelers, including pilgrims to Mecca, and other measures have reduced the already slim opportunities available to revolutionaries of either the left or the right for overt activity. Tehran's strident and inflammatory radio and television, on the other hand, beam continuously to the Gulf populations. Though anti-Soviet, the theme of revolution and hatred of the United States works to undermine stability and security cooperation with the West.

The largely expatriate Bahrain National Liberation Front is defined as "revolutionary democratic" rather than communist by the Soviets (*WMR*, May). In cooperation with the equally elusive Popular Front for the Liberation of Bahrain and through its auxiliary National Union of Bahraini Students, appearances are made at occasional conferences abroad. Bahrain's large Shia population and Khomeini's revival of Iran's ancient territorial claim to the island make Bahraini authorities particularly alert for dissident activity. Similarly, the Communist Party of Saudi Arabia was visible during its second year of existence almost solely through references in Soviet or bloc publications. Rigidly pro-Soviet in its statements, the Saudi party surfaced for its Second Congress in Aden during August and at the Prague conference on the *World Marxist Review* in December. Without more detailed knowledge, it is impossible to judge whether the Bahraini and the Saudi parties are merely convenient propaganda tools for the Soviets in cooperation with a handful of expatriate dissidents or genuine national parties with effective underground cells. The USSR's seemingly major priority of widening its diplomatic representation in the Gulf beyond Kuwait poses limits on Moscow's willingness to provide overt support for the two parties.

The ruling Yemen Socialist Party, Moscow's most successful investment in the area, celebrated the fifth anniversary of the signing of the Treaty of Friendship and Cooperation with the USSR with an apparently major increase in Soviet military and economic aid. Party leader Ali Nasir Muhammad al-Hasani visited Moscow for the occasion. Divisions in the party and with its allies represent important concerns for Moscow. Although four members of the party's militant wing were added to the cabinet in May, strong currents of disunity plague the Aden leadership. Moscow's dependence on air and naval facilities in Aden alone justify the substantial aid investment. Certainly, Aden's isolation and weakness of voice in the Arab world offer scant diplomatic returns for the USSR. Aden's support for Marxist Ethiopia vis-à-vis Arab Somalia and the Eritrean liberation struggle put the tiny nation at cross-purposes with most Arab states. Although achievement of the long-sought unity with North Yemen would open a theoretical path of far greater influence for Aden, such unity remains a receding horizon as rhetoric and preparatory institutional exercises nonetheless continue. Dominant conservative tribal factions in North Yemen, heavily subsidized by Saudi Arabia, preclude the kind of unity sought by Aden's present leaders. North Yemen displayed its long-established ability to obtain substantial aid from both East and West by signing a treaty of friendship and cooperation with the USSR. Although this might appear to favor movement toward unification of the two Yemens on terms favorable to the USSR, Moscow remains extremely cautious on the unification issue. Given the volatile and factional characteristics of Aden's and Sana's ruling groups, the unknowns to be faced in the event of unification must surely appear threatening to the reasonably secure Soviet position in Aden.

Moscow's influence during 1984 was badly hurt in the region by Afghanistan's and Ethiopia's inability to control their populations or feed them despite heavy Soviet involvement in both countries. On the other hand, Soviet military assistance to Iraq has once again demonstrated Soviet preparedness to rescue a treaty-allied Arab state seemingly in danger of losing to a non-Arab enemy. Whatever the war's outcome, a scenario that would markedly improve the fortunes of the region's communist parties is difficult to imagine.

Egypt's national elections in May excluded Communists altogether, reflecting the Mubarak government's strategy of trying to contain and co-opt the energies of religious fundamentalists while actively suppressing the Communists and their allies. Egypt's leftist groups are tremendously splintered. They are allowed reasonable media expression, but as a political force, even with full freedom, would not compare in political significance with the country's non-Marxist militant religious groups on the right. Many Egyptian Communist Party members are jailed or are repeatedly arrested and retried. Of greater political significance than the Egyptian party is the leftist opposition front, a legal grouping of parties called the National Progressive Unionist Party (NPUP), headed by longtime Marxist Khalid Muhyi al-Din. The NPUP includes Nasserites and other non-Marxists; its weekly, *al-Ahali*, is influential and widely circulated. Egypt's cautious rapprochement with the USSR, evidenced by an exchange of ambassadors as well as upgraded trade and aid agreements, is designed to promote a nonaligned image and offset opposition charges of Egyptian subservience to the United States.

In North Africa, the only legal Marxist party, the Party of Progress and Socialism in Morocco, increased its representation from one to two in the September parliamentary elections, but its total percentage of the vote remained at 2.3 percent. But with 360 seats in the legislature, the influence of this pro-Soviet party remains small. King Hassan blamed Marxist-Leninists, Zionist agents, and Khomeini followers for serious food riots in early 1984. The party's daily, *Al Bayane*, was suspended for nearly two months; most of the Moroccan press was suspended for a few days. Algeria's Socialist Vanguard Party maintained a very low profile during the year, eschewing public positions on either domestic or international affairs. Tunisia's communist party, though legal, is unrepresented in parliament and acts as part of the loyal opposition to the government.

The Lebanese Communist Party continued to benefit from the civil war, in which its relatively small numbers can be joined with other radical factions in both military and political actions. The party has benefited from the radicalization of southern Lebanon's large Shia community as a response to the Israeli invasion. Together with the Organization of Communist Unity (OCAL), the party has involved itself successfully in patriotic resistance in the south, reportedly in the first guerrilla actions against Israel by an Arab communist party. Although the party and the OCAL have apparently both increased their overall political influence as a result, the politics of Lebanon remain too confused to permit longer-term judgments. Soviet and Eastern bloc officials have visited Lebanon frequently for meetings with cabinet ministers and other leaders. Syria, however, remains highly possessive of its political influence in Lebanon, and it is doubtful that Damascus would allow Soviet meddling in Lebanon at more than a token level. The Lebanese party held its sixtieth anniversary celebrations in Beirut in October with representatives from Moscow, Syria, and many foreign communist parties present.

The Syrian Communist Party, headed by veteran Marxist Khalid Bakhdash, continued in its role as a member of the ruling National Progressive Front, where it functions as a docile fixture in the facade over President Hafiz al-Asad's military dictatorship. The USSR's position in Syria was weakening seriously until Israel's invasion of Lebanon during 1982 brought the destruction of important elements of Syria's military forces. The Soviets remain generally unpopular there, however, and the relationship is not without differences over Syrian support for Iran in its war with Iraq, Damascus's support for dissident elements of the Palestine Liberation Organization (PLO) against Soviet support for Yassir Arafat and the Fatah mainstream, and Syria's unrelenting enmity toward Iraq. Asad's control of Syrian Communists is precise, and the Soviets can be under no illusion that he will permit wide freedom for party activists.

The tiny Communist Party of Israel, together with its allies in the Democratic Front for Peace and Equality, won 3.4 percent of the vote and four seats in the 120-member parliament in national elections in July. Neither of the two major parties possesses a majority, however, and circumstances could create a possibility of communist participation in the government. Essentially, however, the Communists, with their pro-Soviet, pro-PLO, and anti-U.S. posture, remain outside the mainstream of Israeli politics.

In its second year of activity, the Palestine Communist Party remains tolerated in the occupied territories of the West Bank and the Gaza Strip. The party became caught up in the debilitating quarrels within the PLO during the year and risked its status with Israeli authorities by, according to one report, organizing a 150-man military force in eastern Lebanon near the Syrian border (*NYT*, 19 November). The party is almost entirely preoccupied with Palestinian problems per se and, apart from rhetorical associations, seems isolated from communist parties elsewhere.

Although the Communist Party of Jordan enjoyed somewhat greater freedom during the year, following improvements in Jordanian-Soviet relations, it is still illegal and was prohibited from participating in national elections in January. The Jordanian government has permitted life to be breathed into the Jordanian-USSR Friendship Society, for example, as part of a general effort to pressure the United States and obtain Soviet military equipment in place of weapons denied by Washington. Jordan had other grievances with the United States—over Camp David and Washington's attitude toward continued Israeli settlement of the West Bank—but there is little prospect that the Soviets will develop major influence in Jordan during King Hussein's lifetime or that of his heir.

James H. Noyes
Hoover Institution

Algeria

Population. 21,351,000
Party. Socialist Vanguard Party (Parti de l'avant-garde socialiste; PAGS)
Founded. 1920 (PAGS, 1966)
Membership. 450 (estimated)
First Secretary. Sadiq Hadjeres
Leading Bodies. No data
Status. Proscribed since 1962
Last Congress. Sixth, February 1952
Last Election. N/a
Auxiliary Organizations. No data
Publications. *Sawt al-Sha'b* (Voice of the people), issued clandestinely at infrequent intervals

The Algerian Communist Party (Parti communiste algérien; PCA) was founded in 1920 as an extension of the French Communist Party. It has existed independently since October 1936. Although the PCA participated in the nationalist struggle against France, it was proscribed in November 1962, only four months after Algerian independence. In 1964, dissident left-wing elements of the legal National Liberation Front (FLN) joined with Communists from the outlawed PCA to form the Popular Resistance Organization. In January 1966, this group was renamed the Socialist Vanguard Party. The party has not held a congress since 1952. Barely tolerated by the Algerian government, the PAGS is recognized in the communist world as the official Algerian communist party.

Leadership and Party Organization. Sadiq Hadjeres is first secretary of the party. Although the precise membership of the PAGS Politburo and Secretariat is not known publicly, other prominent members of the party in recent years are believed to include Larbi Bukhali, a former party secretary general, Bashir Hadj 'Ali, Ahmad Karim, and 'Ali Malki. Both Hadjeres and Malki have contributed to the *World Marxist Review* and the *Information Bulletin* on behalf of the PAGS.

Party Views, Positions, and Activities. The PAGS generally has viewed the regime of President Chadli Benjedid, which has ruled Algeria since early 1979, as opportunist and reformist compared with the more militant regime of Houari Boumediene (1965–1978) (see *YICA*, 1983, p. 5). Operating in a hostile political climate and without legal standing, the PAGS prudently opted to maintain a low profile during 1984. The party did not take any public positions of note on either domestic or international issues. Instead, the PAGS continued to focus its energies on the mass organizations of the ruling FLN. PAGS members worked to gain influence among the leadership of the National Union of Algerian Youth, and the party maintained its efforts to place cells in factories to compete with the units of the General Union of Algerian Workers, the government-sanctioned labor union.

State Relations with the Soviet Union. In 1984, Algeria continued its pattern of receiving official visits of Soviet dignitaries. The year's highlight in this regard was a five-day official visit, from 4 to 9 October, of a four-member Soviet delegation headed by Boris N. Ponomarev, candidate member of the Politburo and secretary of the CPSU Central Committee. The visit was at the invitation of the

FLN. During the visit, the members of the Soviet delegation held talks with senior Algerian officials, including President Benjedid, Prime Minister Abdelhamid Brahimi, and Foreign Minister Ahmad Taleb Ibrahimi, plus a number of FLN delegations. The talks focused on the consolidation and expansion of Soviet-Algerian relations and an exchange of views on the current international situation. The joint communiqué issued at the conclusion of the talks stressed, among other things, that a just and lasting settlement of the Arab-Israeli conflict must be based on satisfying the legitimate national rights of the Palestinian people, including the right to create their own state, and on the total and unconditional withdrawal of Israeli troops from all Arab territories occupied since the 1967 war. (*Pravda*, 11 October; *FBIS*, 12 October.) In November, Algeria once again abstained on the U.N. General Assembly resolution calling for the withdrawal of foreign (Soviet) troops from Afghanistan. In December, however, at a meeting in Sana in North Yemen of the Organization of Islamic Conference, Algeria voted for a resolution condemning the Soviet Union and calling for the withdrawal of Soviet troops from Afghanistan.

In addition to Algeria's relations with the Soviet Union, the Benjedid regime also received visits during 1984 from high officials and party delegations of a number of other communist countries, including Hungary, Cuba, Yugoslavia, the German Democratic Republic, Bulgaria, Czechoslovakia, and the People's Republic of China.

John Damis
Portland State University

Bahrain

Population. 409,000
Party. Bahrain National Liberation Front (NLF/B)
Founded. 1955
Membership. Unknown, but believed to be negligible
Chairman. Yusuf al-Hassan al-Ajajai
Executive Committee. (Not necessarily complete) Aziz Ahmad Mudhawi, Jasim Muhammad, Abdallah 'Ali al-Rashid, Ahmad Ibrahim Muhammad al-Thawadi
Status. Illegal
Last Congress. Unknown
Last Election. N/a
Auxiliary Organizations. Bahrain Democratic Youth Union, National Union of Bahraini Students, Women's Organization of the NLF/B, Bahrain Workers' Union (?)
Publications. No data

An article by NLF/B spokesman Abdallah al-Rashid in the May issue of the *World Marxist Review* perpetuated the implication that the party is composed of Communists. The Popular Front for the Liberation of Bahrain was again noted favorably, this time as a formal ally. The article stressed the evolutionary rather than the revolutionary posture of the party and called for "an end of repressions, full compliance with the Constitution, and the restoration of the parliament." Rashid further proposed the removal of U.S. military forces from Bahrain and the Gulf region; an end to foreign (especially American and West European) economic domination of the region; and countering of the Gulf Cooperation Council and establishment of diplomatic relations with the USSR and other communist states.

As in the 1981–1983 period (see *YICA*, 1983, p. 10, 1984, p. 13), the NLF/B again took part in an Arab party conference, where it was the only group not officially characterized as communist—the eleven communist and workers' parties of the Arab East apparently met in Damascus in early June (Radio Damascus, 3 June; *FBIS*, 5 June). The NLF/B also participated in a conference on the work of the *World Marxist Review* held in Prague in December (*Rudé právo*, Prague, 7 December).

The Fifth Congress of the NLF/B's student organization, the National Union of Bahraini Students, met in Damascus in February. The organization reportedly has branches in nine countries (*World Student News*, Prague, no. 4, p. 12), illustrating the expatriate nature of much, if not most, of the pro-Soviet Bahraini left.

Wallace H. Spaulding
McLean, Virginia

Egypt

Population. 47,049,000 (*NYT*, 20 June)
Party. Egyptian Communist Party (al-Hizb al-Shuyu'i al-Misri; ECP)
Founded. 1921; revived in 1975
Membership. 500 (estimated)
Secretary General. (Apparently) Farid Mujahid
Politburo. Michel Kamil (chief of foreign relations), Najib Kamil (representative to the *WMR*); other names unknown
Central Committee. Farid Mujahid, Yusuf Darwish; other names unknown
Status. Proscribed
Last Congress. First, 10 April 1980 (National Progressive Unionist Party)
Last Election. N/a
Auxiliary Organizations. No data
Publications. Circulars under the heading *al-Wa'i* (Consciousness) and leaflets; *al-Yasar al-Arabi* (published by Egyptian Communists in Paris)

The communist movement in Egypt dates back to the formation in 1921 in Alexandria of the Egyptian Socialist Party (al-Hizb al-Ishtiraki al-Misri) by Joseph Rosenthal and some former members of a more diverse group founded in Cairo the year before. With its name soon changed to the Egyptian Communist Party, it was admitted to the Comintern in 1923. Suppression by the authorities started almost immediately and has continued sporadically ever since.

The movement has also been beset by factionalism. It virtually disappeared during the late 1920s and 1930s. Numerous communist factions emerged during the early 1940s, and the two largest groups combined to form the Mouvement démocratique de libération nationale (MDLN) in 1947. This group also splintered with the formation of a Unified Egyptian Communist Party in 1958. Soon, additional splintering meant that no one faction was important enough to be singled out for international recognition. At least two groups heeded Soviet instructions to cooperate with "progressive" single-party regimes by dissolving themselves in return for a commitment by the Egyptian government to tolerate individual Communists. Many of the latter occupied important positions in the Arab Socialist Union (ASU) and the mass media. But with President Anwar al-Sadat's shift to the right during the 1970s, a new ECP emerged, officially in 1975.

The Egyptian communist movement remains as splintered as ever. Besides the ECP, several groups—including the Revolutionary Current, the Egyptian Communist Party–8 January, the Egyptian Communist Workers' Party, the Popular Movement, and the Armed Communist Movement—have allegedly surfaced during recent years. The existence of "an extremist communist group consisting of nine leftist elements" (al-Sharq al-Awsat, London, 16 October; FBIS, 18 October) was reported during 1984. All indications point to the relative insignificance of such groups in comparison with the threat to the regime potentially posed by non-Marxist, particularly militant religious, movements.

Leadership and Party Organization. Little is known about the ECP's leadership and organization. Few party officials have been mentioned in available publications; official statements by ECP leaders published abroad are mostly anonymous. The name most often mentioned is Politburo member Michel Kamil, obviously because of his position as the party's chief of foreign relations. All indications point to the typical pattern of "democratic centralism," but in a rudimentary form resulting from the group's small membership and clandestine character.

Domestic Party Affairs. The Central Committee of the ECP met during January "to examine developments in the world, the Middle East and Egypt since its meeting in May 1982" (IB, May). No other meetings of party organs were reported during the year.

Perhaps with some ECP involvement, violent riots occurred in the Delta industrial town of Kafr al-Dawar at the end of September as a result of the government's attempt to raise the price of bread and to increase social security deductions from workers' pay (NYT, 2 and 7 October). In any case, the riots were followed by the arrest of members of an alleged communist group that included members of the ECP on charges of "trying to incite the masses . . . and of preparing a plan of action . . . by exploiting" the riots and "printing leaflets and other materials . . . which were ready for distribution." The typewriter allegedly used by the ECP to produce the leaflets (al-Wa'i) was seized. (Al-Sharq al-Awsat, 16 October; FBIS, 18 October.)

The trial of sixteen people accused of being members of the Armed Communist Movement (whose relationship with the ECP, if any, is unknown) began 1 February and was continued, following an initial postponement, on 1 April. Witnesses alleged that the accused individuals had weapons and leaflets in their possession at the time of their arrest (August 1983), but defense attorneys claimed that the whole affair had been fabricated by the regime to provide an excuse for continuing the state of emergency in existence since 1981. (AFP, Paris, 1 February; MENA, Cairo, 1 April; FBIS, 2 February, 2 April.)

Many members of the ECP are in prison or are repeatedly arrested and retried. (For cases cited in a recent Amnesty International report, see YICA, 1984, p. 19.)

In a book review published in the August issue of the World Marxist Review, Yusuf Darwish (identified elsewhere as a member of the ECP Central Committee) criticized the author of the work under review for ignoring President Sadat's expression of "the interests of the reactionary compradore bourgeoisie closely linked with foreign capital and fearing every progressive trend in the country or the region like death" and concluded that Sadat's "legacy still largely determines the policy of the present regime."

An article by Politburo member Michel Kamil published in the March issue of the World Marxist Review and entitled "What Has Changed in Egypt" argued against the "wishful thinking" of many people that "the more 'enlightened' sections of the capitalist class" could rectify the policies of the section of "the ruling bloc . . . dominated by the 'Sadat group' . . . made up of businessmen virtually unconnected with the productive sphere" and engaged in "speculation in foreign exchange and real estate, smuggling, brokerage and import operations" and in "the black market and" as "agents of foreign companies." Kamil expressed "concern" over increased military spending under President Mohammed Husni Mubarak and characterized the policy of *infitah* (open door) since 1974 as having brought about the domination of "political and economic decision-making" by "big foreign, mixed and domestic private capital." He further deplored the emergence of a rentier economy, the outflow of capital, increased foreign debt, "dependence on imported necessities," and the "monopolistic trend" of "domestic capital," as well as the continuing "use of police terror," the restriction of opposition groups, and "meddling and intrigue" in trade union elections.

A communiqué issued by the Central Committee in January predicted that the year would see "spontaneous actions and strikes" as a result of the failure of "parasitical capitalism" to allow democracy and "the pent-up anger of the working class," as well as "the influence of our party" and "that of some officially recognized patriotic and democratic organizations" (an apparent reference to the National Progressive Unionist Party, see below). Citing "the lessons" of the January 1977 revolt, the statement warned that such movements must not be left "to chance" lest increased repression succeed and called on party cadres to "maintain close ties with the masses, with the working classes, with the workers, peasants and students" and to be "in the forefront of their movement." (For another version of the same document, see *African Communist*, no. 98, pp. 84–88.)

In regard to the upcoming general elections in May, the Central Committee called for efforts to repeal the new election law, which provides for a system of proportional representation but with political parties getting under 8 percent of the vote denied seats in the People's Assembly (parliament). It predicted that "a minimum of neutrality, legality and freedom" in the conduct of the elections would deprive "the ruling party and the parasitical bourgeoisie" of its present "spurious parliamentary majority." While criticizing some parties for hastily participating "on the terms imposed by the government," the Central Committee called for the nomination of "some members of our party." (*IB*, May.) In light of the ECP's clandestine character, the last proposal presumably related to candidates that would run under the banner of another group, the National Progressive Unionist Party.

Auxiliary and Front Organizations. Little information has come to light about any auxiliary organizations of the ECP. Under present condi-

tions, it seems safe to assume that children's and youth organizations and the like do not exist. In light of the party's longtime stress on working with students (and workers), it seems likely that official allegations that communist groups (presumably including the ECP) have "tried to set up committees of supporters, primarily among the students" (Ami Ayalon, "The Arab Republic of Egypt," in Colin Legum, ed., *Middle East Contemporary Survey, 1981–82*, New York: Holmes and Meier, 1984, p. 457) appear accurate.

Much more important than the ECP is the broad, legal leftist opposition front, the National Progressive Unionist Party (NPUP), whose secretary general is longtime Marxist Khalid Muhyi al-Din. (For a biography of Muhyi al-Din, see *YICA*, 1984, pp. 20–21.) Its deputy secretary general is Rif'at al-Sa'id. Some of the members of the NPUP (organized in 1976 when President Sadat first permitted the formation of leftist and rightist opposition groups) are Marxists, while others are Nasserites or other opponents of the nonsocialist, pro-Western direction of the regime. The NPUP publishes the weekly newspaper *al-Ahali* (edited by Muhyi al-Din), which has a large circulation. The party at one time had three seats in the People's Assembly but lost them in the 1980 elections. While some contacts with the ECP have been reported, the NPUP is not a front group for any organization per se.

The NPUP gained a seat in the People's Assembly as the result of the surprise victory of its candidate in a by-election in Alexandria in January (*NYT*, 8 January).

In the 27 May general elections, the NPUP received 3.8 percent of the total vote, but application of the 8 percent rule prevented it from winning any seats. The governing National Democratic Party (NDP) got 73 percent of the votes and 391 of the 448 seats in the assembly; of the four opposition parties, only the New Wafd Party (which had been banned by Sadat in 1978 but re-emerged following a high court decision in its favor in January), with 12.7 percent of the votes, won any seats (57). President Husni Mubarak pledged to make this the freest election Egypt had seen in 60 years (ibid., 29 April), but opposition party leaders charged coercion and fraud. Khalid Muhyi al-Din, in reference to the killing of one opposition candidate and the alleged barring of opposition observers from the polls in some places, maintained that nothing but "violence and forgery" could have enabled the NDP to win (*CSM*, 29 May). Rif'at al-Sa'id claimed that

NDP supporters stabbed twelve supporters of the NPUP in one village and forcibly closed polling stations or stuffed ballot boxes in other places (*NYT*, 28 May). However, *Pravda* (31 May; *FBIS*, 12 June) admitted that "opposition circles were not subject to repression as they were previously and enjoyed much greater freedom of action." The president later appointed ten additional members of the assembly, including four from the opposition Socialist Labor Party (non-Marxist), but none from the NPUP (*NYT*, 20 June).

The seventh plenary session of the NPUP Central Committee met on 19–20 October. A statement at the end of the meeting stressed that "the session was of particular importance" since "it came following the biggest battle of the masses fought by the Egyptian left in its contemporary history" (apparently in reference to the recent riots in Kafr al-Dawar) and also because of the task of preparing for the party's Second Congress. Some members of the Central Committee and others were unable to attend since they had been jailed on accusations of "supporting the aspirations and urgent demands of the working people, of defending the rights of Kafr al-Dawar workers" and proclaimed a "dream" of "achieving . . . a homeland enjoying freedom, socialism, and unity." The statement deplored the "viciousness of U.S. imperialism and its frenzied efforts," particularly its increased attempt to dominate the Middle East "with the help of Israel and many Arab rulers," and hailed the "escalation of popular movements and the victories they achieve" in Central America, Africa, and Lebanon. (*Al-Ahali*, Cairo, 24 October; *FBIS*, 15 November.)

Al-Ahali criticized the Egyptian-Israeli peace treaty, which was said to have led to the Israeli invasion of Lebanon and to have reduced chances for real peace (*Pravda*, 20 April; *FBIS*, 25 April). It had strong praise for the USSR and welcomed normalization of Soviet-Egyptian relations (Moscow international service, 13 July; *FBIS*, 17 July). (This statement was in response to an announcement earlier in July that Soviet-Egyptian relations were being restored at the ambassadorial level for the first time since 1981.) *Al-Ahali* accused the United States and Israel of laying mines in the Red Sea in order to provide an excuse for a Western naval buildup in the area (*NYT*, 23 August).

ECP statements call for "a national front led by the working class" and point to the failure of the (presumably Nasserite) "petty and middle bourgeoisie" (*WMR*, March). Previous efforts to establish a "National Salvation Front" including "those in and outside the regime who advocated 'rationalization' of the official policy" are regarded as unpromising (ibid.).

The document adopted by the ECP plenary session in January refers to the existence of a Committee of Patriotic Parties and Forces for the Defense of Democracy and reiterates some of the committee's demands, particularly with regard to the electoral law, the denial of political rights, and the right to strike (*IB*, May). No further information about the committee is available.

The same document presents the party's evaluation of three other forces. The New Wafd is characterized as representing "the national bourgeoisie (its parasitical and industrial sections), members of the free professions, and some other groups of intellectuals," and as being "somewhat more democratic and less susceptible to corruption" than the NDP, but tied to the United States and "hostile to the communist and popular movement." Still, the possibility of future cooperation with the New Wafd seems to be left open by a reference to "the need to have an idea of the struggle going on inside" it and to a current within it that may counter the party's present direction. The Nasserites are declared to be essential partners "in terms of assuring the unity of patriotic and progressive opposition forces." Neither the Nasserites nor the Moslem Brothers are analyzed in terms of class. The latter are dismissed as having "permanent contacts with the government" but with the caveat that "some of them declare for joint action with the progressive opposition," particularly the NPUP. (Ibid.)

International Views, Positions, and Activities. Representatives of the ECP joined six other communist and workers' parties of the Arab East in a joint statement in October 1983 (*Sawt al-Watan*, mid-October 1983; *IB*, January). Also, a meeting was held in Prague in November 1983 of representatives of the ECP and eight other Arab communist parties (*IB*, January). Another meeting of nine communist and workers' parties of Arab countries—including the ECP—was reported in *Sawt al-Watan* in June (ibid., September). In October, Politburo member Michel Kamil met with the assistant secretary general of the (Syrian) Arab Ba'th Party in Damascus (Syrian Arab News Agency, Damascus, 20 October; *FBIS*, 22 October).

Michel Kamil described Egypt's present foreign policy as "conforming to . . . Sadat's capitulationist policy . . . on the basis of Camp David and subservience to the United States." He called the "restoration of Jordanian-Egyptian diplomatic relations . . . the second link in the Camp David plot." (Damascus domestic service, 20 October; *FBIS*, 22 October.) Pointing to joint military exercises and reports of a U.S. military base in Egypt, he said that "the armed forces of Egypt" were being harnessed "to the implementation of the Pentagon and NATO plans aimed at bringing our region under their sway" (*WMR*, March). A Central Committee statement dealt with the "negative consequences" of Palestine Liberation Organization leader Yassir Arafat's meeting with Mubarak (*IB*, May).

On broader world issues, a statement by communist parties of nine Arab countries, including the ECP, blamed the United States and its allies for rejecting "constructive proposals . . . made by the Soviet Union" relating to reduction of tension and arms control and for creating "new seats of tension" in such areas as Central America. The nine parties declared their approval for "the Soviet Union's principled peace-loving policy" and "for all the defensive counter-measures" it had found necessary to take (*IB*, September).

Glenn E. Perry
Indiana State University

Iran

Population. 43,820,000
Party. Communist Party of Iran (Tudeh Party)
Founded. 1941 (dissolved May 1983)
Membership. 2,000 (early 1983 estimate)
Secretary General. Nurredin Kianouri (imprisoned), Ali Khavari (provisional party leader in exile)
Leading Bodies. No data
Status. Illegal
Last Congress. 1965
Last Election. 1980, 3 percent, no representation
Auxiliary Organizations. No data
Publications. *Rahe Tudeh* (Tudeh path), *Mardom*; both published in Europe; party statements are broadcast over the National Voice of Iran, thought to be located in the USSR, and the Voice of the Toilers of Iran, thought to be located in Kabul or Aden.

In 1984, attempts to destroy the Tudeh Party inside Iran continued unabated. The repression of the party was closely intertwined with the Iran-Iraq war, creating a triangular crisis among the Islamic Republic, the Soviet Union, and Iraq. Partly as a result, the new regime proved much more systematic and comprehensive in its persecution of the Tudeh Party than had predecessor governments.

The deterioration of Soviet-Iranian relations was both a cause and an effect of the Tudeh's catastrophe. Moscow's formal condemnation of Iran's refusal to negotiate with Iraq expectedly provoked Iranian steps against the Soviets. On public occasions, most notably at Friday prayers, Islamic government spokesmen frequently criticized the Soviet Union for supplying Iraq with modern weapons, especially the long-range surface-to-surface missiles wreaking havoc on civilians in towns and cities adjacent to the Iran-Iraq frontier (Tehran radio, 17 January; *FBIS*, 18 January; Islamic Republic

News Agency, quoted in *FBIS*, 26 November). The regime's hostility to the Tudeh Party stemmed from its disaffection with Moscow over the war, the conviction that any political organization not fully integrated with the Islamic Republic would ultimately turn against it, and concern that Tudeh infiltration of the military and the *Pasdaran* (Islamic Revolutionary Guards Corps) was perilous.

The outlawing of the Tudeh, however, neither ended pro-Soviet activity in Iran nor achieved the goal of total public discrediting of the party. Indeed, the party may eventually benefit from its official abolition, for it has usually flourished in opposition to government and could again become a credible (though outlawed) dissident group. In anticipation of that, the Tudeh has resumed activity in many foreign countries with significant Iranian populations. The Tudeh Party inside Iran has likely resumed clandestine activity. The tendency of sympathizing with the underdog may influence many Iranians in its favor; the party may thus acquire more status among current opposition forces than when it functioned as an unappreciated ally of a progressively more repressive theocratic regime.

Domestic Activities. In early 1984 when indictments against the Tudeh Party's leading cadres were made public and the trials of its military network concluded, members who had escaped Iran joined their comrades in Europe and called the party's Eighteenth Plenum, in East Germany (see *Rahe Tudeh*, 10 January, for the resolutions of this plenum; and *IB*, March, for English versions). The plenum passed resolutions characterizing the 1979 revolution as anti-imperialistic and popular, but one that allowed the state apparatus to remain almost intact despite some measures to destroy the foundation of the previous monarchical regime. The plenum accused the ruling clergy of representing a combination of big landlords, big capitalists, and middle bourgeoisie, who favored a dependent capitalist system. "These groups ruled Iran in the name of the *Moslem Unmat* [Islamic community] and have led the country back into the most archaic form of existence. Despite the valiant efforts of the Tudeh Party, the clergy prevented the transformation of the political revolution into a social one. Instead, it established a medieval, theocratic despotism to revive the system of dependent capitalism."

Reiterating the party's pro-Soviet stance, the plenum maintained that Iran's anti-imperialist struggle was not possible without recognizing the fighters for freedom, independence, and social progress led by the Soviet Union.

The plenum resolved that the revival of its organization inside Iran, based on decentralization, integration of overt and clandestine work, maintenance of autonomy of smaller cells, and observance of absolute discipline, constituted the party's main tasks. It also supported the unity of all revolutionary, democratic, anti-imperialistic forces, particularly the People's Mojahedin.

Communist and other leftist parties around the world intensified their defense of the Tudeh. At the height of the "tanker war" in the Persian Gulf in May-June 1984 when both sides attacked oil tankers and freighters using the upper and middle Persian Gulf, some effort was made by Iran and the Soviet Union to reach a measure of accommodation. The Soviet Union reportedly offered to terminate hostile propaganda against the Islamic regime for its persecution of Tudeh Party leaders in return for a joint declaration of the inadmissibility of military intervention of extra-regional powers in the Persian Gulf crisis.

The Iranian government sent Mohammad Sadr, head of the European Department of the Ministry of Foreign Affairs, to Moscow. Sadr, known for his radical anti-Americanism and involvement in the capture and holding of American hostages, tried to persuade the Soviets to scale down the level of their military support for Iraq. Met by Foreign Minister Andrei Gromyko and other Soviet officials, the Iranian envoy gave assurances that the imprisoned civilian Tudeh leaders, notably Dr. Kianouri and Ehsan Tabari, would not be executed. (Tehran radio, 3 and 7 June.) On Sadr's return to Iran, government officials, including Hashemi Rafsanjani (the speaker of the Majlis), described Soviet-Iranian relations as rather tense but disclaimed the intention of either government to cause further deterioration (Islamic Republic News Agency, 1 June).

In February, ten members of the military organization of the Tudeh were executed at the height of a new Iranian offensive in the southern sector of the Iran-Iraq war zone. The Islamic government, however, appears indecisive about the fate of the civilian leaders, particularly Dr. Kianouri (the 73-year-old party secretary) and Ehsan Tabari (the 75-year-old party ideologue). According to reports from Iran, the prosecutor of the Islamic military tribunal completed the indictment against the two men on eleven specific charges and has asked for the death sentence, urging prompt trial and conviction.

On 7 November the prosecutor announced that

the trial of nonmilitary leaders of the party would begin 12 November (ibid., 10 November; *FBIS*, 13 November). That declaration prompted a renewed campaign by the party in exile and many foreign communist parties and governments around the world to persuade the Iranian government to call off the trial and release the imprisoned party leaders lest they too be executed. In a message to the U.N. secretary general on 10 November, the party's Central Committee accused Iran of violating the most elementary judicial principles and appealed for prompt and effective intervention (*Pravda*, 16 November).

In another message, to the Association of Democratic Lawyers, the Central Committee asked for similar assistance on behalf of "a number of leaders and members of the central cadre of the Iranian Tudeh Party . . . a group of the best sons of our country" (*Namehe Mardom*, November).

Four days before the start of the trial, the government postponed it indefinitely. Some government sources maintained that the interests of the Islamic Republic did not allow for a public trial of Tudeh leaders at that moment lest it inopportunely reveal the scope of activity of Soviet agents in Iran (*Iran Va Jahan*, Paris, 21 November). The party and its supporters interpreted the indefinite postponement of the trial differently.

The National Voice of Iran (NVOI; 13 November), for example, contended that the postponement was due to the government's fear that a public trial might disclose the crimes and atrocities committed against the Tudeh prisoners. According to the NVOI, "If the Islamic regime attached the slightest credence to its claims of treating the Tudeh prisoners fairly, it would agree to hold a completely open and free trial in the presence of domestic and foreign media and neutral international legal and medical experts."

Noncommunist exile groups such as the Paris-based Front for Iran Liberation accused the regime of bowing to the Soviets by postponing the trial of the best-known Tudeh leaders, by then imprisoned for nearly 21 months on charges of espionage for the Soviet Union (Radio Nejate Iran, 11 November; *FBIS*, 14 November).

The Eighteenth Plenum of the Tudeh Party's Central Committee, whose resolution was noted above, also named Ali Khavari as the provisional party leader pending convocation of a party congress. Since that time he has been so mentioned in the communist media, including those of the Soviet Union. Iranian exile publications such as *Keyhan*

(London) also confirmed Khavari's appointment in early July 1984. The Soviet party's reference to Khavari, as well as his own writings in a variety of communist media around the world leave little doubt that in 1984 he served as the Tudeh Party leader-in-exile.

If and when the better-known members of the party are released from prison or manage to flee Iran, as many did in December 1950 after the first banning of the party a year earlier, they will most likely be reinstated. While Kianouri's health or safety has never been doubted, Ehsan Tabari's has been a source of much concern. To discredit the latter and dispel a communist-sponsored rumor of his death in prison, the government staged a television appearance in which Tabari denounced Marxism and embraced the goals and ideals of the Islamic Revolution (Islamic Republic News Agency, 8 May; *FBIS*, 9 May).

Foreign Relations. Regarding relations with the Soviet Union and other communist states, in early summer 1984 the Islamic media gave extended coverage to a written message from Foreign Minister Ali Akbar Velayati to the Soviet foreign minister in which the Islamic government declared its intention to establish friendly relations with the Soviets. Gromyko's alleged reciprocation was also noted (*FBIS*, 26 June). At the end of June the first deputy minister of the Soviet Ministry of Power and Electrification visited Tehran with a large delegation of technical experts. After viewing a number of power stations in the country, including the renowned Ramin plant in Ahwaz, the Soviet delegation was told by Iran's acting minister of commerce that relations between Iran and other countries depended on mutual respect and international relations among Moslem and non-Islamic countries. Prime Minister Mir Hossein Musavi told a Tehran radio reporter that "as far as possible, we wish to live in peace and security with our neighbors and expand relations with them on the basis of the principle of neither East nor West" (Tehran radio, 27 June; *FBIS*, 28 June).

These and similar visits by East European delegations did not, however, augur a genuine accommodation. The U.N. General Assembly in September and October witnessed renewed Soviet efforts to end the Iran-Iraq war, and the Iranian media sharply criticized Moscow for equating the two belligerents. Tabriz radio on 6 November, for example, responded to Radio Moscow's commentary about the absence of any major obstacle to ending the war by accusing the Soviets of neither understanding nor supporting Iran's nonalignment or its defensive posture in that imposed war (*FBIS*, 14 November).

In a commentary entitled "A Senseless War" broadcast on 30 October, the Soviets reiterated opposition to Iran's reluctance to terminate the war (ibid.). On 13 November, the failure to improve state-to-state relations through commercial and technical cooperation became evident in a Moscow radio broadcast entitled "Who Does Not Favor Soviet-Iranian Cooperation in the Field of Energy?" It was obvious that tension in the Iranian-Soviet-Iraqi triangle had not perceptibly changed by the end of 1984.

Equally obvious was that efforts by both the People's Republic of China (PRC) and the Islamic Republic to exploit tension in this triangular arena had fallen short of their goals. On 25 November PRC foreign minister Wu Xueqian told his Iranian counterpart that the prospect of better relations between the two countries was promising. In another meeting between the two, bilateral commercial relations were discussed, and the Iranian foreign minister and the president made similar statements. A common theme stressed by both officials was the need for cooperation among all Third World countries and implicit criticism of both superpowers. (*Keyhan*, London, 26 November.)

But global political realities beyond Iran's control prevented the ploy of improving ties with the PRC to serve as a counterweight to the Soviets and as a source of arms. President Reagan, in a visit to China in early fall 1983, reportedly dissuaded PRC leaders from supplying Iran with military hardware. The U.S. intent was to pressure the Iranians into peace negotiations and to enhance U.S.-PRC relations overall.

A by-product of the tension in relations with communist governments was the intense propaganda warfare by public and clandestine broadcasting stations. Not only did the official media of communist governments or parties across the world engage in this type of verbal warfare, but did so in over ten different opposition-managed, clandestine radios from both inside and outside Iran.

The Tudeh Party in September moved its headquarters from East Germany to Stockholm. Its clandestine radio is called the Voice of the Toilers of Iran and reportedly is located in either Kabul or Aden. Since the official banishment of the party in May 1983, the Iraqi Communists, and to a lesser extent the government in Baghdad, have aided and abetted the Tudeh in its antigovernmental campaign. At the end of December 1984, another communist clandestine station, Moje Sorkh (Red wave), began broadcasting to Iran; its tone was even more radical than that of the NVOI.

At the end of 1984 the party returned to a rigid Stalinist interpretation of post–World War II developments in Soviet-Iranian relations. On 12 December Tudeh media commemorated the 1945–1946 Azarbayjan and Kurdistan separatist Soviet republics in terms reminiscent of the Soviet position during the Stalin era. Similarly, the Tudeh returned to its traditional Stalinist interpretation of the Mossadegh era despite more moderate, and even self-incriminatory, accounts of these events in the initial stage of the 1979 Revolution.

To summarize, 1984 was another turbulent year for what was once the largest pro-Soviet communist party in the Middle East. Likewise, uncertainty in relations with the Soviet Union and communist world persisted. What is clear, however, is the emergence of a pattern among the main actors in the unfolding political drama marked by prudent and measured Soviet reaction to the Islamic government as well as by sustained criticism of its repression of the Tudeh Party.

Similar caution marked Soviet policy toward the Iran-Iraq war. Resumed Soviet support for Iraq seemed basically a means of terminating, or at least containing, the war. The Soviet debacle in Afghanistan continued to cloud Moscow's relations with the Islamic world as a whole and could loom as a mounting factor of discord with both Iran and Iraq in the event of settlement of the Gulf conflict.

Sepher Zabih
Hoover Institution

Iraq

Population. 15,000,000
Party. Iraqi Communist Party (ICP)
Founded. 1934
Membership. No data
First Secretary. Aziz Muhammad
Leading Bodies. No data
Status. Illegal
Last Congress. Third, 4–6 May 1976
Last Election. N/a
Auxiliary Organizations. No data
Publications. *Tariq al-Sha'b* (People's road), clandestine

The ICP celebrated its fiftieth anniversary in 1984, and First Secretary Aziz Muhammad received congratulations from the Central Committee of the Soviet party on the occasion of his sixtieth birthday. There was little else for the party to celebrate. Heavy government repression continues, and the ICP's center of operations is in the mountainous north, where, with its Kurdish allies of the National Democratic Front, it conducts guerrilla warfare. Party leaders are in exile, and the ICP has no visible effect on affairs in the Arab heartland of the country.

On the ICP's anniversary, a brief congratulatory message from the Soviet Central Committee and a longer article in *Pravda* (31 March; *FBIS*, 5 April) dwelt on the great contributions that the ICP had made to Iraq's liberation and to the struggle against imperialism. The *Pravda* article recalled the time in the early 1970s when the "Communists had two ministers in the government," could publish openly, and had hopes for transforming the National Patriotic Front into a mass movement. It regretted that changing circumstances—i.e., the hostility of the current government—had forced the ICP to go underground and contented itself with praising the ICP for having trodden a "difficult but glorious path."

Leadership and Organization. A Central Committee meeting in late June instituted some changes in the ICP. According to press reports, three members were dismissed from the Central Committee and a fourth, Baqir Ibrahim Musawi, a Shia Arab, was dropped from the Politburo. Aziz Muhammad and his fellow Kurds continued to dominate the leadership of the ICP (*al-Siyasah*, Kuwait, 26 September; *FBIS*, 28 September). The Soviet party underlined its support for Muhammad by front-page treatment for its sixtieth birthday message to this "eminent figure of the Arab communist and national liberation movement" (*Pravda*, 1 July). The Presidium of the USSR Supreme Soviet awarded him the Order of Lenin (Moscow domestic service, 30 June; *FBIS*, 2 July).

Differences within the ICP Central Committee have led to a split in the party. Baha al-Din Nuri, who rebuilt the party in the early 1950s after the execution of its founder and who has been a member of the Central Committee for the past twenty years, is reported to have left the party (*al-Siyasah*, 26 September; *FBIS*, 28 September). The circumstances of this event are unclear; so is the number of those who may have followed him and the specific issues that led to the rupture. The break either had occurred or was anticipated early in the year, however, for an article on the party's history in the April issue of the *World Marxist Review* made no mention of him.

Domestic Affairs. The increasingly Kurdish focus of the ICP's activity is in no small measure forced by the vigor and efficiency of the Iraqi regime's repression of opposition in Baghdad and throughout most of the country. Rugged terrain and the preoccupation of the military with the Iranian war have reduced Baghdad's ability to enforce order in all of Iraqi Kurdistan. But it is not surprising that the heavily Kurdish ICP leadership emphasizes Kurdish issues. Politburo member Fakhri Karim pointed out that Kurdistan is "the most suitable geographical, political, and popular field to counter the violence of the fascist dictatorship with revolutionary violence." Karim admitted that "popular unrest is latent" but that did "not mean that it is nonexistent." He insisted that "the struggle is . . . in every part" of the country. (*Tishrin*, Damascus, 1 December; *FBIS*, 7 December.)

Concentration of forces and efforts in Kurdistan has involved the ICP in purely Kurdish squabbles. There are six Kurdish organizations functioning in Iraq, and efforts to keep them together have foundered in the absence of a strong leader. The ICP is closely connected with the Kurdish Democratic Party/Iraq (KDP/I) and the United Socialist Party of Kurdistan in the Democratic National Front (DNF). Efforts to establish a broad national front have not succeeded. The ICP was one of eighteen groups that in 1983 signed a statement of intent to do so. Only three of them have joined the DNF (ibid.). Baghdad's efforts to play on the divisions among the Kurds by offering a separate deal to the Patriotic Union of Kurdistan (PUK) continue. However, the government has grown more confident since it withstood a major Iranian assault in February and March. In consequence, it has not made the concessions the PUK wants.

These developments affect the ICP in two ways. First, the Kurdish groups with which it is formally associated appear, on the basis of incomplete evidence, to be weaker than the PUK. Second, the ICP, which condemned Iraq's 1980 invasion of Iran as an aggressive war, "demand[s] that an end be put to the fratricidal war" on the basis of nonannexation of territory, respect for international borders as of mid-1980, and the right of each people to choose their own political and social system (ICP and Tudeh Party joint communiqué, *Pravda*, 14 November; *FBIS*, 14 November). Although it is linked to Iran through its Iranian-supported KDP/I ally, the ICP has not supported Iran's insistence on the ouster of the Iraqi president as a condition for a cease-fire.

Outside the Kurdish area, the Iraqi government's ability to control the country persisted. Elections for the People's Assembly were held in October. Communists were not allowed to run, and the 250-person body is safely pro-Ba'th. The Iraqi-Soviet Friendship Society, headed by a Ba'thist militant, took the lead in celebrating both the twenty-fifth anniversary of the first economic aid agreement between Iraq and the USSR and the twelfth anniversary of the Treaty of Friendship and Cooperation (Iraqi News Agency, Baghdad, 17 March; Radio Baghdad, 9 April; *FBIS*, 20 March, 10 April). The Iraqi national Council for Peace and Solidarity is controlled by the Ba'thist regime, as are all professional and people's organizations.

Foreign Relations. In the region, the ICP is closely associated with Syria, which supports forces opposing the Baghdad regime. The party held a rally in Syria at the end of March that drew high-level attendance from the Syrian Ba'th party and from Arab communist parties (Syrian Arab News Agency, Damascus, 30 March; *FBIS*, 4 April). Its representatives participated in a meeting of Arab communist and workers' parties of the Arab East in June (*Pravda*, 19 June), probably in Damascus (Syrian Arab News Agency, Damascus, 21 July; *FBIS*, 23 July). Syrian president Hafiz al-Asad received Politburo member Fakhri Karim late in the year (Radio Damascus, 25 October, 6 November; *FBIS*, 26 October, 6 November).

The confrontational attitude between the ICP and Baghdad contrasted sharply with the good and improving relations between Moscow and Baghdad during the year. The USSR continues to supply a large percentage of Iraq's military requirements. A visit by the chairman of the Soviet State Committee for Foreign Economic Relations served to point up the importance of the joint Iraqi-Soviet Economic Committee. Iraqi foreign minister Tareq Aziz summarized the good state of relations between the countries in midyear by mentioning a $2 billion loan, assistance in development projects, and supply of large quantities of sophisticated weapons

(Radio Monte Carlo, Paris, 14 July; *FBIS*, 16 July). *Izvestiia* (10 September) devoted space to a run-down of Iraqi-Soviet ties and the benefits to Iraq over the forty years since diplomatic relations be-gan (*FBIS*, 13 September). The ICP was not mentioned.

John F. Devlin
Swarthmore, Pennsylvania

Israel

Population. 4,235,000 (end of 1984, Israeli Central Bureau of Statistics [*Jerusalem Post*, international edition, 13–20 May]), apparently including East Jerusalem

Party. Communist Party of Israel (CPI); also called New Communist List (Rashima Kommunistit Hadasha; RAKAH)

Founded. 1922 (CPI, 1948)

Membership. 1,500 (estimated)

Secretary General. Meir Vilner (member of the Knesset [parliament])

Politburo. 9 members: David (Uzi) Burnstein, Benjamin Gonen, Wolf Erlich, Emile Habibi, David Khenin, Ruth Lublitz, Emile Tu'ma, Tawfiq Tubi (deputy secretary general and member of the Knesset), Meir Vilner; 4 alternates

Secretariat. 7 members: Zahi Kharkabi, Saliba Khamis, David Khenin, Jamal Musa, Tawfiq Tubi, Meir Vilner; name of replacement for a member who died in 1983 unknown

Central Committee. 31 members, 5 candidates

Status. Legal

Last Congress. Nineteenth, 11–14 February 1981, in Haifa

Last Election. 23 July 1984, 3.4 percent of the vote (with Democratic Front for Peace and Equality allies), 4 seats (3 for the CPI and one for a Front partner, the Black Panthers); no change from previous parliament

Auxiliary Organizations. Young Communist League (Banki), Young Pioneers

Publications. *Al-Ittihad* (now a daily), *Zo Ha-Derekh*, *al-Jadid*

The communist movement in Palestine began in 1920. Two years later, a Palestine Communist Party (Palestinische kommunistische Partei; PKP) was established; it joined the Comintern in 1924. Following the periodic appearance of factional divisions, the PKP split along ethnic lines in 1943, with the Arab breakaway faction called the League for National Liberation. In October 1948, with the new state of Israel gaining control of most of Palestine, the two groups reunited to form the Israeli Communist Party (Miflaga Kommunistit Isra'elit; MAKI).

The movement split again in 1965, partly along ethnic lines. The RAKAH—pro-Moscow, strongly anti-Zionist, and primarily Arab in membership, though with many Jewish leaders—soon eclipsed the almost completely Jewish and increasingly moderate MAKI. The latter's disappearance by the late 1970s left RAKAH (a name that is still used) as the undisputed communist party in Israel and internationally recognized successor to the pre-1965 communist organizations. With Arab nationalist parties not permitted, it has served mainly as an outlet for the grievances of the Arab (Palestinian) minority. Almost all of the party's vote comes from the Arab population (the CPI-dominated Democratic Front for Peace and Equality [DFPE] got about 50 percent of the Arab vote in 1977 and 37 percent in 1981). The DFPE has dominated most Arab town councils since the 1970s.

Leadership and Party Organization. The organization of the CPI is typical of communist parties in general. The Congress normally meets at four-year intervals and chooses members of the Central Committee and the Central Control Commission, as well as the Presidium and the Secretariat. There are also regional committees, local branches, and cells (the latter based both on residence and place of work).

Although at least 75 percent of the members of the party are Arabs, Jews predominate in the top party organs. In recent years, the Jewish secretary general has been balanced by an Arab deputy secretary general. (Though partially dated, a still-useful analysis of the party's Arab leadership and a relatively detailed description of its organizational structure may be found in Ori Stendel, "The Rise of New Political Currents in the Arab Sector in Israel, 1948–1974," in Moshe Ma'oz, ed., *Palestinian Arab Politics*, Jerusalem: Academic Press, 1975, pp. 119–24.)

Domestic Party Affairs. The nineteenth plenary session of the Central Committee met on 30 December 1983. Other plenary sessions in April and August were reported.

Two motions of no confidence citing a report that an increasing number of Israelis live under the poverty line were introduced jointly by DFPE members of the Knesset and the Likud government's main opposition, the Labor Alignment, in January and were defeated (*NYT*, 25 January; *Jerusalem Post*, international edition, 29 January–4 April). A bill introduced by the DFPE members of the Knesset in March calling for early elections was adopted (*NYT*, 23 March).

When President Chaim Herzog visited Nazareth in September, he was greeted by the DFPE-dominated city administration headed by communist Mayor Tawfiq al-Zayyad. But the visit was boycotted by representatives of the central government on the grounds that it would encourage Nazareth's Communists (*Jerusalem Post*, international edition, 16–22 September).

A resolution of the plenary session of the Central Committee in December 1983 declared that the "government is launching an attack on the working people's wages and living standard" and that it "serves the interests of the big bourgeoisie and state monopoly capital." The "colossal growth in military spending" was blamed for "taking Israel to the brink of bankruptcy." The Histadrut (Israel Federation of Labor) was accused of "only paying lip service to the struggle for working people's wages and rights," and a demand that its leadership "call a national protest strike" was issued. (*IB*, April.)

As usual, CPI spokesmen devoted much attention to the conditions of the Arab minority, which Politburo member Emile Tu'ma described as "very harsh," resulting from "national discrimination and racial discrimination . . . policies of the government" (interview in *Journal of Palestine Studies*, Fall 1983, p. 16). He spoke specifically of the obstruction of the formation of local councils, of discrimination in providing government services, and of "expropriating Arab land" (ibid., pp. 16–17). CPI leaders again participated in the annual Day of the Land celebrations on 30 March in Arab towns and villages. Unlike in some previous years, there was no major violence (*Jerusalem Post*, international edition, 1–7 April). But members of the more nationalistic (but non-Marxist) Arab movement, the Sons of the Village, tried to disrupt communist speakers, including Knesset member Tawfiq Tubi at the main rally in the village of Arraba (Jerusalem domestic service, 30 March; *FBIS*, 2 April).

The CPI Central Committee—referring to Rabbi Meir Kahane's election to the Knesset and to the growth of terrorism against Arabs—protested against "the growth of the right-wing extremist forces, racist, fascist organizations" (Tass, 12 August; *FBIS*, 14 August). At a large meeting in Nazareth on 28 January in which Jews and Arabs joined together to protest against recent manifestations of racism, Mayor Zayyad stressed that "Arabs are part of Israel, part of her future" (*New Outlook*, Tel-Aviv, March/April, p. 36). The three CPI Knesset members participated in a demonstration of an estimated 30,000 Arabs and Jews in the Arab village of Umm al-Fahm on 4 August to protest Kahane's plans to enter the community and demand the mass emigration of Arabs. Zayyad compared the demonstration's significance with that of the original Day of the Land in 1976 (*Middle East*, London, September, p. 7). (For the text of the resolutions adopted at the protest meeting, see *Journal of Palestine Studies*, Fall, p. 209, or *New Outlook*, August/September, p. 15.)

A new factor in the 23 July election was the

appearance of an electoral list rivaling the DFPE as an expression of Arab discontent. The Progressive List for Peace (PLP) was headed by an Arab lawyer, Muhammad Mi'ari, who had formerly belonged to the proscribed al-Ard (the Land) Arab nationalist movement, while Dr. Mattityahu Peled of the Alternativa faction, formerly part of the now-defunct dovish Sheli Party, was in second place. The Central Elections Committee banned the new list for allegedly being sympathetic to the Palestine Liberation Organization (PLO), but this was overruled by the Supreme Court. (*Jerusalem Post*, international edition, 20–27 May, 10–17 June, 24 June–1 July, 2–8 July.) The PLP took much the same position as the DFPE on issues relating to Palestine and to the Arabs in Israel in particular but had the added appeal to many Arabs of being noncommunist and nonsubservient to Moscow; also, while the DFPE list was headed by a Jew (CPI leader Meir Vilner), the PLP had the additional advantage of having an Arab in first place (Yosef Goell, "Multiple Identities," *Jerusalem Post*, international edition, 15–21 July). (For the text of the PLP platform, see *Journal of Palestine Studies*, Fall, p. 209, or *New Outlook*, June/July, p. 27.)

Much of the DFPE's attention was focused on this new rival. Although the Communists condemned the initial ban on the PLP (*Jerusalem Post*, international edition, 3–10 July), the DFPE refused a PLP proposal for an arrangement to share surplus votes—that is, votes for each party insufficient to provide an additional seat. Tu'ma gave three reasons for this refusal: "First, because the PLP submits itself as an alternative bloc to the DFPE; second, because of its campaign against communism and the Soviet Union and the historic struggle of the DFPE; and third, we did not like to give the PLP legitimacy" (*al-Fajr*, Jerusalem, 27 July). The DFPE campaign against the PLP emphasized that the latter's leaders had been favorable to the Camp David agreements and that it was threatening to divide the Arab vote (ibid., 6 July). On the other hand, Mi'ari argued that his list complemented the DFPE by appealing to Arabs who had previously voted for Zionist parties or else had stayed at home and that in fact the PLP diverted few votes from the DFPE (Muhammad Mi'ari, "The Making of a Political Movement" [interview], *Journal of Palestine Studies*, Fall).

CPI Knesset member (and candidate) Tawfiq Tubi pointed to PLP candidate Uri Avnery's past as "a member of the Irgun Zvai Leumi together with Begin" and ridiculed Mi'ari and others for calling themselves "proud Arabs" while running on such a list (*Jerusalem Post*, international edition, 8–14 July). Arguing that "without Rakah, we would be refugees," he pointed out that "the famous [Israeli Arab] poets of our generation . . . grew on the soil of the party" (ibid.).

The DFPE and the PLP rivaled each other with claims of being favored by the PLO. Actually, some elements of the PLO favored one or the other, with one argument for the DFPE being that it had preserved the Palestinian cause inside Israel for so long, but DFPE appeals to Moscow to pressure Yassir Arafat to oppose the PLP were to no avail (Stephen Harrison, "Where the Arab Vote Went," *Journal of Palestine Studies*, Fall, p. 187).

In final election results, the DFPE received 69,815 votes (as opposed to 64,452 in 1981) or 3.4 percent of the total vote, giving it four seats in the Knesset, the same as before. The PLP got 1.8 percent of the vote and two seats. (*Jerusalem Post*, international edition, 5–11 August.) All four incumbent DFPE members of the Knesset were returned: Vilner, Tubi, and Zayyad of the CPI and Charlie Biton of the Black Panthers. Vilner explained that his party, unlike others, was not "so unsuccessful" as to need "new faces" (ibid., 27 May–3 June). The DFPE was able to maintain its four seats despite a reduction of its percentage of the Arab vote from 38 to 34 (and still getting no significant number of Jewish votes) by virtue of an increase in the Arab turnout to 73 percent (compared with 68 percent four years before and a 79 percent Jewish turnout, about the same as before) (*New Outlook*, August/September, p. 29; *Jerusalem Post*, international edition, 22–28 July). DFPE acceptance of the earlier PLP proposal for a vote-sharing arrangement apparently would have enabled the former to pick up a fifth seat (Mi'ari, in *Journal of Palestine Studies*, Fall, p. 43).

Both mainly Arab-backed parties are thus peripheral in a Knesset of 120 members in which the two main constellations of parties are led by the Labor Alignment and the Likud Bloc respectively. While no communist party has ever participated in an Israeli government, the failure of either the Labor Alignment or the Likud Bloc to win a clear majority raised the possibility of a government led by the former that would be dependent on DFPE and PLP support without participation, although other potential members of a Labor-led coalition objected to such an arrangement (*Jerusalem Post*, international edition, 12–18 August). (The formation of a coalition including both Labor and Likud ended whatever possibility had existed of such a role for the DFPE and the PLP.)

The inability of the two largely Arab-backed parties to get representation in the Knesset proportionate to the 17 percent Arab population of the state that is usually cited (particularly in an electoral system based on proportional representation) results from several factors in addition to the lower turnout of this sector. First of all, the 17 percent figure is misleading in that it includes the population of East Jerusalem, which was unilaterally annexed but whose Arab population did not obtain Israeli citizenship and voting rights in national elections. Second, some Arabs apparently choose to vote for the Labor Alignment as the only alternative to the Likud. Third, a disproportionate percentage of the Arab population is not of voting age. Other Arabs reject even the DFPE and PLP as too moderate in that both accept the existence of the state of Israel. (Yosef Goell in ibid., 15–21 July.) In addition, various kinds of patronage secure Arab support for Zionist parties, which also co-opt a few Arab members into their electoral lists.

Auxiliary and Front Organizations. The CPI dominates the DFPE, which includes two noncommunist partners, the Black Panthers (an Afro-Asian, or Oriental, Jewish group protesting discrimination by Jews of European origin) and the Arab Local Council Heads. Aside from the one member of the Black Panthers included in the DFPE delegation in the Knesset, there was formerly (1977–1981) a representative of the Arab Local Council Heads. The fifth member of the list in the 1984 election was Hashim Muhammad, chairman of the Umm al-Fahm local council (ibid.). The DFPE is also organized on the local level, particularly in Arab towns and villages.

The CPI sponsors the active Young Pioneers and Young Communist League and the Israeli Committee Against the War in Lebanon and participates in the Democratic Women's Movement, the Israeli-USSR Friendship Movement, and the Israeli Association of Anti-Fascist Fighters and Victims of Nazism.

Spokesmen for the CPI continue to emphasize the importance of popular front tactics. Tu'ma affirmed that the Communists are in fact the power behind the DFPE and that it may be "an attraction for future forces, something which you can put everyone in." He cited the DFPE's ability to form the Committee Against the War in Lebanon in 1982 with a "very wide base" and to organize a 20,000-

strong demonstration in contrast to communist isolation in 1967. (*Journal of Palestine Studies*, Fall, p. 19.) Politburo member Wolf Erlich explained his party's willingness to cooperate with moderate Zionists and said that the DFPE seeks "to bring more and more people of different ideological opinions into common work" (*IB*, February).

International Views, Positions, and Activities. In January, a CPI delegation headed by Vilner visited Moscow and was received by Soviet leaders, including Konstantin Chernenko (*Pravda*, 22 January; *FBIS*, 24 January). In March, Dr. Yuri Barabash, chief editor of *Sovetskaia kultura* and head of the Soviet Committee for Friendship and Solidarity with the Palestinian People, headed a delegation to Israel on the invitation of sixteen members of the Knesset; although this was not a visit to any political party in particular, Tubi met the delegation at the airport (Jerusalem domestic service, 16 March; *Ha'aretz*, Tel-Aviv, 28 March; *FBIS*, 16 and 29 March).

In April, a delegation led by Tubi visited Czechoslovakia on the invitation of the Czechoslovak Central Committee and signed an agreement on cooperation between the two parties (*Rudé právo*, Prague, 7 April; *FBIS*, 11 April). A Bulgarian Communist Party delegation visited Israel in May "in implementation of the protocol for cooperation" with the CPI and was received by Vilner (BTA, Sofia, 26 May; *FBIS*, 29 May). Vilner was interviewed by telephone in *Sovetskaia Rossiia* on 10 June (*The Soviet Union and the Middle East*, Jerusalem, 9, no. 6, p. 7). Also in June, Tubi visited East Berlin and was received by Hermann Axen of the GDR Politburo (ADN, East Berlin, 7 June; *FBIS*, 8 June). In July, Politburo member Emile Habibi visited Hungary and was interviewed on television (Budapest television service, 12 July; *FBIS*, 13 July). He also visited Bulgaria and was met by Dimitur Stanishev of the Bulgarian Politburo (Sofia domestic service, 29 August; *FBIS*, 30 August). Vilner met Arafat in Geneva in July, and the two issued a joint statement supporting simultaneous mutual recognition by Israel and Palestine (Jerusalem domestic service, 12 June; *FBIS*, 13 July).

Also in August, the CPI Central Committee sent "fraternal greetings" to Romanian leader Nicolae Ceauşescu on the fortieth anniversary of his country's "liberation from the fascist yoke" (*Scînteia*, Bucharest, 31 August; *FBIS*, 7 September).

A CPI delegation headed by Politburo member

David Khenin visited the Armenian Soviet Socialist Republic in August and was briefed by party officials there (*Sovetakan Ayastan*, Yerevan, 29 August; *FBIS*, 18 September). In September, a delegation led by a CPI Central Committee candidate member went to Tashkent to study Uzbekistan's achievements in the area of nationality (Tashkent international service, 10 September; *FBIS*, 13 September) and also visited Moscow and Leningrad (*Pravda*, 19 September; *FBIS*, 1 October).

Vilner visited Bulgaria in October and met with Secretary General Todor Zhivkov (BTA, Sofia, 11 October; *FBIS*, 12 October).

DFPE member of the Knesset Charlie Biton was listed as one of several plaintiffs in a lawsuit filed in the United States to end the tax-exempt status of the United Jewish Appeal and related organizations (*Jerusalem Post*, international edition, 12–18 February). Biton visited Morocco early in the year on a mission related to an Israeli submarine that disappeared several years ago (ibid., 15–21 April).

As usual, statements on foreign affairs were mainly restricted to the immediate region, particularly to matters relating to Palestine. The platform adopted for the election campaign blamed "all of the other factions" in the country for having "supported the aggressive war" in Lebanon, condemned the Camp David accords, and attributed "the root of the problem" to the policies of "the Likud, the Alignment, and the other parties of the 'national consensus.'" The consensus was summarized as rejection of withdrawing from the territories conquered in 1967, of Palestinian self-determination and "the establishment of an independent state alongside Israel," of canceling the annexation of Jerusalem, of recognizing the PLO, of "unconditional withdrawal from Lebanon," and "the cessation of global strategic services to a foreign power—the US—against the true interests of Israel." (Text in *New Outlook*, June/July, p. 28, and *Journal of Palestine Studies*, Fall, pp. 210–11.)

CPI spokesmen described Soviet policies as "principled and invariably peace-loving" (*Pravda*, 22 January; *FBIS*, 24 January). The United States was said to be "blatantly flouting the norms of international law" in such places as Grenada and Central America, as well as in Lebanon and against Syria (ibid.). Several joint statements in foreign capitals praised Soviet initiatives to end the arms race.

Other Marxist Groups. For information on the Israeli Socialist Organization and other breakaway groups, including the Revolutionary Communist League, see *YICA*, 1982, p. 29, and 1984, p. 33.

PALESTINE COMMUNIST PARTY

Population. East Jerusalem: 127,000; the rest of the West Bank: 771,000; Gaza Strip: 497,000 (Meron Benvenisti, *The West Bank Data Project: A Survey of Israel's Policies*, Washington: American Enterprise Institute, 1984, figures projected to the end of 1984); total number of Palestinians: at least 4.5 million (estimate), including 1.2 million in Jordan (estimate) and nearly 600,000 in Israel, excluding East Jerusalem (calculated from figures in *Jerusalem Post*, international edition, 13–20 May)

Party. Palestine Communist Party (al-Hizb al-Shuyu'i al-Filastini; PCP)
Founded. 1982
Membership. 200 (estimated)
Secretary General. (Presumably) Bashir al-Barghuti (described as the PCP "leader" in some sources)
Politburo. Sulayman al-Najjab, Na'im Abbas al-Ashhab, others not known
Secretariat. No data
Central Committee. Dhamin Awdah, Mahir al-Sharif, Sulayman al-Nashshab, Ali Ahmad, Mahmud al-Rawwaq, Na'im Abbas al-Ashhab, Mahmud Abu-Shamas, others not known
Status. Illegal, but tolerated to a large degree in Israeli-occupied areas
Last Congress. First, 1984
Last Election. N/a
Auxiliary Organizations. Unknown
Publications. *Al-Tali'ah* (The Vanguard)

The roots of the communist movement among Palestinians in the Israeli-occupied West Bank and Gaza Strip and among those in diaspora may be traced to the pre-1948 Palestine Communist Party (see the profile on Israel) and particularly to the post-1943 breakaway faction, the League for National Liberation, as well as to the Communist Party of Jordan (CPJ). According to Na'im Abbas al-Ashhab, a member of the PCP Politburo, one remnant of the League for National Liberation evolved into the Gaza Strip Palestinian Communist Party in 1953. Other Palestinians joined communist parties in the various Arab countries in which they resided, particularly the CPJ. In 1974, the section of the CPJ in the West Bank became the West Bank Communist Organization; with the addition of members from the Gaza Strip, the group became the West Bank and Gaza Strip Palestinian Communist Organization (PCO). Also, members of the CPJ in Lebanon became the Palestinian Communist Organization (PCO) in Lebanon. (*WMR*, February 1983.) Formation of a separate PCP was long delayed by Soviet opposition (Meir Litvak and Elie Rekhess, "The West Bank and the Gaza Strip," in Colin Legum, ed., *Middle East Contemporary Survey, 1981–82*, New York: Holmes and Meier, 1984, p. 373), although the PCO in the occupied areas was said to be "relatively independent" (*Middle East Intelligence Survey*, Tel-Aviv, 16–30 March 1980), while a breakaway faction calling itself the PCP was reported during the late 1970s (ibid., 16–31 May 1978). A faction described as "the organization of Palestinian Communists in the Gaza Strip" (Naim Ashhab, "With a Sense of Responsibility for the Country's Future: The Results of the Palestinian Communists' First Congress," *WMR*, September) apparently was not united with the PCP until 1984.

With the approval of the CPJ, the PCP was organized in February 1982. The party was to include Communists in the Gaza Strip and the West Bank, members of the PCO in Lebanon, and all Palestinian members of the CPJ except for those living in Jordan, i.e., the East Bank.

Leadership and Party Organization. Relatively little is known about the organization of the PCP. Politburo member Ashhab related that the "First (constituent) Congress" was announced two years after the party's founding, which presumably means during 1984 (*WMR*, September). Earlier reports that a founding congress was held in 1982 and chose a secretary general possibly referred to an unofficial meeting. The congress adopted a program and rules for the party and "elected its governing bodies" (ibid.), presumably the Politburo, Secretariat, and Central Committee. Several non-PCP sources (including *al-Hamishmar*, Tel-Aviv, 4 September; *FBIS*, 7 September) refer to Bashir al-Barghuti as the party's "leader" (he had previously

been described the same way in relationship to the West Bank and Gaza Strip PCO), but there is no evidence that he is necessarily secretary general.

Ashhab made several claims about the composition and procedures of the First Congress and the makeup of the party. The debate on "material put up for discussion" was "serious and responsible, and the atmosphere was "genuine democratic." Also, "most of the delegates were young," a "natural reflection" of the fact that the PCP's "members' average age is about 24 years," and "a high proportion of the Congress participants were of proletarian origin . . . due to the fact that many of the Communists are workers—almost 50 percent." The "established norms of representation" required that "one delegate [be] elected from 30 working class party members, and one from 50 members from other social strata." (*WMR*, September.)

Domestic Party and Intra-Palestinian Affairs. Ashhab wrote of the "extremely difficult situation" resulting from involvement in activities "both in the occupied territories and in the numerous countries of the Palestinian diaspora" and from having "to act in the underground, all of which make the maintenance of inner-party ties an extremely formidable problem" (ibid.).

A major part of the party's activities is in the occupied territories. The party is illegal there, but while concern for security sometimes leads to crackdowns (and there have been reports of individuals arrested at times for possessing communist literature), it in fact is generally tolerated. It has been described as "one of the curiosities of the Israeli occupation that [it is] the party which appears to function most openly"; Barghuti, who was jailed for eight years under Jordanian rule, now edits the weekly party newspaper, *al-Tali'ah*, in East Jerusalem (*Manchester Guardian Weekly*, 12 February). There were reports in the past of another PCP newspaper, *al-Watan* (The homeland), presumably published outside the occupied territories. PCP statements are also disseminated by the Communist Party of Israel (CPI) press, particularly by *al-Ittihad*.

A leading Communist, George Hazboun, who was dismissed from his position as deputy mayor of Bethlehem in 1983, was subjected to an order from the occupation authorities in September banning him from any movement out of the town for six months and requiring daily reports to the police station (Jerusalem domestic service, 10 September; *FBIS*, 11 September). This action allegedly was related to PCP "willingness to join the PLO leadership and take part in hostile activities" (ibid.).

According to one report, the PCP has organized a 150-man military force in eastern Lebanon, close to the Syrian border (*NYT*, 19 November).

As summarized by Ashhab, the PCP political program adopted by the First Congress provides an "internationalist approach" to the Palestine question that is not found in other Palestinian organizations' approaches. Defining the first stage as one of "national liberation," its tasks are listed as (1) defeating the Israeli occupation and securing the liberation of the Arab lands occupied in 1967; (2) ensuring the Palestinian people's right to self-determination through establishment of their own state on the West Bank, the Arab part of Jerusalem, and the Gaza Strip; (3) enabling the refugees to return home; and (4) frustrating all plans of imperialism, Zionism, and reaction to liquidate the Palestinian problem and destroy the Palestinians' national identity (*WMR*, September). While Ashhab emphasizes the need to delay proposals "unattainable at this stage" that would divide the Palestinian national movement, he quotes the party program's last section ("The Party's Long-Term Goal: Socialism") as calling for "pursuit of a policy of socialist transformations so that it be a component part of the front of the anti-imperialist forces in the region and throughout the world, all the way to the establishment of socialism" (ibid.).

Although the PCP is not represented in the Palestine National Council (PNC) and other organs of the PLO, which is an umbrella group for various groups in the Palestinian national movement, it was active during the year in intra-Palestinian quarrels that threatened to destroy the movement's unity. The Palestinians found themselves divided into two opposing camps—the National Alliance (dissident, Syrian-backed elements in Yassir Arafat's Fatah; Syrian-supported al-Sa'iqah; and the Popular Front for the Liberation of Palestine–General Command [PFLP-GC]) and Arafat's supporters (mainly the majority faction in Fatah but also the Iraqi-backed Arab Liberation Front). The PCP was aligned with the Popular Front for the Liberation of Palestine (PFLP), the Democratic Front for the Liberation of Palestine (DFLP), and the smaller Palestine Liberation Front in the Democratic Alliance, which adopted an intermediate position and tried to mediate between the two extremes. The PCP and its allies in the Democratic Alliance opposed Arafat's overtures to Egypt and Jordan but also opposed the Syrian-backed attempt to overthrow him by force.

The Democratic Alliance was closely associated with the governments of Algeria and South Yemen.

Following earlier rounds of talks in Algiers, representatives of the Democratic Alliance (including the PCP, represented by Politburo member Sulayman al-Najjab) met with representatives of the pro-Arafat faction in Aden in June. (The National Alliance refused to participate in the meetings.) An agreement between the two groups was reached on 27 June in the hope of making way for convening the PNC. The agreement rejected Arafat's rapprochement with Cairo and any option, such as the Reagan Plan, that prejudices the attainment of Palestinian independence under PLO leadership. Forcible attempts to overthrow the PLO's leadership, however, were rejected, and the "legitimacy of its institutions" was affirmed. While Arafat, according to the agreement, would thus continue to hold his leadership position (at least until voted out by the PNC), his powers would be limited by a proposed group of deputies to the chairman and a "collective working leadership." The agreement, however, was rejected by the National Alliance. (For the texts of the Aden agreement and the statement of the National Alliance, see *Journal of Palestine Studies*, Fall, pp. 200–207; for an analysis of the split, see *NYT*, 18 November.)

The Democratic Alliance (including the PCP) subsequently announced that it would not attend a PNC meeting unless it were held in either South Yemen or Algeria (*NYT*, 12 November) and that it continued to oppose Syria's forcible attempts to remove Arafat (*CSM*, 16 November). With Syrian pressures on South Yemen and Algeria not to allow the meeting to be held in either of those countries, the PNC met in Amman in November without the participation of the representatives of either the National Alliance or the Democratic Alliance— presumably including the PCP, although, according to one report, "some party members in the [occupied] territories [and not necessarily as representatives of the party] . . . had been accepted as members" (*all-Hamishmar*, 4 September; *FBIS*, 7 September).

Ashhab argued that "the mainsprings and causes" of the present PLO crisis—the "most severe crisis since its formation"—can be explained only in terms of class analysis. He noted the existence of "two dangerous trends"—rejectionism and capitulationism—and concluded that the latter now is the more dangerous of the two because it represents the interests of "the big bourgeoisie," which can be salvaged by embracing the Jordanian option at the expense of national goals and to which "the PLO leadership...has begun to succumb." (*WMR*, March.) Despite such criticism of the PLO leadership, including a condemnation by Ashhab of Arafat's meeting with the Egyptian president (see *The Soviet Union and the Middle East*, 9, no. 5), several PCP statements and statements issued jointly with other Arab communist parties (see particularly *IB*, January) abhorred intra-Palestinian violence and implicitly condemned the Syrian-backed rebellion.

Auxiliary and Front Organizations. There is little information on auxiliary organizations, but PCO or PCP involvement with labor, student, and professional groups has been reported in the past (*Middle East Intelligence Survey*, 16–30 March 1980). Before his "town arrest" (see above), Hazboun was said to have been "active in organizing the workers in the territories where the Communists are in control" (Jerusalem domestic service, 10 September; *FBIS*, 11 September).

In effect, the PLO is a government-in-exile. Its supporters and its leadership span the political spectrum. Its dominant component, Fatah (headed by Arafat) might in a sense be called a "united front" since it avoids ideology in favor of pursuing a national cause. It contains some Marxists, but is dominated by centrists (or even conservatives) like Arafat. It "represents some 80% of the Fedayeen and probably a like percentage of the Palestinian population" (*Foreign Affairs*, Fall 1983). The Syrian-backed dissidents also include both Marxists and rightists. The Israeli coordinator of activities in the occupied territories admitted that "almost all the inhabitants" of the West Bank backed Arafat (*Davar*, Tel-Aviv, 22 January; *FBIS*, 24 January). The PFLP, the PFLP-GC, and the DFLP—small organizations with minimal representation on PLO organs—are Marxist but are not considered to be "communist."

The Palestine National Front (PNF) was organized in 1973 as an alliance of Communists and others in the occupied territories. It gained representation in the PLO and thus provided a small component of the organization that was partially communist. Its candidates won victories in the local elections in the West Bank in 1976, but a rift between Communists and Fatah supporters thereafter "rendered...it virtually impotent" (Helena Cobban, *The Palestinian Liberation Organization*, London: Cambridge University Press, 1984, p. 179; see also Galia Golan, *The Soviet Union and*

the Palestine Liberation Organization, New York: Praeger, 1980, pp. 169–72; on the PNF and some other attempts to organize communist Palestinian organizations, see John W. Amos II, *Palestinian Resistance: Organization of a Nationalist Movement*, New York: Pergamon Press, 1980, pp. 113–28). Presumably reflecting the concerns of the PCP, the Aden agreement (see above) called for reviving the PNF (*Journal of Palestine Studies*, Fall, p. 201).

The PCP recognizes the PLO as "the sole legitimate representative" of the Palestinian people and seeks representation in the organization in order to make it a national front. Ashhab, relating the party congress's demand for representation in PLO organs, declared that "it is time to put an end to the discrimination against the Communists and their party" (*WMR*, September).

International Views, Positions, and Activities. The PCP participated in joint statements by Arab communist parties in October and November 1983, as well as in June 1984 (see *IB*, January, September). PCP Politburo member Sulayman al-Najjab headed a delegation visiting East Berlin in February and talked with members of the East German Central Committee (*Neues Deutschland*, East Berlin, 8 February; *FBIS*, 10 February). Later in the same month, a commentary by him was broadcast in Moscow (Moscow radio, 15 February; *FBIS*, 17 February); no mention was made of his presence in the USSR but it was implied by his reference to "attendance by representatives of all the progressive and revolutionary forces in the world" at Andropov's funeral. The PCP sent congratulations to Konstantin Chernenko on his election as general secretary of the Soviet Central Committee (*Pravda*, 21 February; *FBIS*, 2 March). In June, Politburo member Ashhab visited East Berlin and met with German party officials to sign an agreement of cooperation (*Neues Deutschland*, 6 June; *FBIS*, 11 June). He also visited Hungary in April (MTI, Budapest, 12 April; *FBIS*, 19 April). Sulayman al-Najjab and two Central Committee members met with East German Politburo member Günter Schabowski in Damascus in June (*Neues Deutschland*, 23–24 June; *FBIS*, 27 June). A PCP delegation that included Ashhab visited Portugal in July and issued a joint communiqué with the Portuguese Communist Party (*Avante!* Lisbon, 26 July; *FBIS*, 27 August). Najjab met with Bulgarian Communist Party officials in Sofia in August (BTA, Sofia, 6 August; *FBIS*, 15 August). He also visited the USSR (*Pravda*, 15 August; *FBIS*, 17 August). Another PCP delegation headed by Ashhab met with Vietnamese party officials in Hanoi in August (VNA, Hanoi, 17 August; *FBIS*, 24 August). Najjab led a delegation that visited Poland in October and held talks with Polish officials (*Trybuna luda*, Warsaw, 15 October; *FBIS*, 19 October). The delegation then visited Czechoslovakia at the invitation of the Czechoslovak Central Committee (ČETEKA, Prague, 19 October; *FBIS*, 22 October).

Party statements mostly dealt with the Palestine question (see above). Fewer statements covered broader aspects of the Arab world; in one example of the latter, Ashhab stated that "the revolutionary potential" of some regimes had "sometimes" been "exaggerated" and that a "bureaucratic bourgeoisie" had emerged. "Petrodollars" were given much of the blame. Only South Yemen was singled out as demonstrating positive achievements by the "petty bourgeoisie." (*WMR*, March.) Particularly in joint statements with other Arab communist parties, the PCP hailed the "fresh blow...dealt at the United States' plans to occupy Lebanon" and condemned the "U.S.-Israeli strategic alliance" and U.S. "cooperation with reactionary Arab regimes" (*IB*, September).

A few statements touched on broader international matters, mainly those by PCP leaders on visits to socialist countries or in joint statements with other communist parties. These generally reflected a pro-Soviet line. Thus, "the most aggressive forces of the United States and its allies" were blamed for "endangering world peace," while "full support for the détente and disarmament proposals of the USSR" was affirmed (*Neues Deutschland*, 8 February; *FBIS*, 10 February). The PCP–Portuguese Communist Party communiqué declared the two parties' "solidarity with Cuba, Nicaragua and the people of El Salvador, as well as the people of Grenada, who are the victims of criminal invasion and occupation," and also with Angola, Mozambique, the Namibian people, and the people of South Africa (*Avante!* 26 July; *FBIS*, 27 August). In a rare reference to China, Ashhab "exalted the historic victory of the Vietnamese people in their resistance war against U.S. aggression" and proclaimed "full support...for the three Indochinese peoples' struggle against the expansionist and hegemonist policy of the reactionaries in the Beijing leadership" (VNA, Hanoi, 22 August; *FBIS*, 24 August).

Glenn E. Perry
Indiana State University

Jordan

Population. 2,689,000
Party. Communist Party of Jordan (al-Hizb al-Shuyu'i al-Urduni; CPJ)
Founded. 1951
Membership. Accurate estimate not available
Secretary General. Fa'ik (Fa'iq) Warrad
Leading Bodies. No data
Status. Proscribed
Last Congress. Second, December 1983

Last Election. N/a
Auxiliary Organizations. None
Publications. *Al-Jamahir, al-Haqiqa*

After the partition of Palestine, the League for National Liberation (the communist party of undivided Palestine since 1943) reorganized its followers on the West Bank and decided in June 1951 to change the party's name to the Communist Party of Jordan. The Central Committee headed by Fu'ad Nassar opposed Jordan's annexation of eastern Palestine (renamed the West Bank) and called for the establishment of an independent Palestinian state in accordance with U.N. General Assembly Resolution 181 (II) of 29 November 1947.

Because it was subject to legal restriction, the party operated in the 1950s under the guise of several front organizations, entering the parliamentary campaign of 1951 under the name Popular Front. Three candidates were elected. The party abandoned its earlier dogmatic posture and took a more practical view of politics, campaigning on a platform calling for legalizing political parties and trade unions, land reform, and industrialization in order to provide employment.

The government countered the party's activities by sentencing its secretary general, Fu'ad Nassar, to ten years' rigorous imprisonment in December 1951, and two years later by amending the Law to Combat Communism to make any association with party activities punishable by a jail sentence of three to fifteen years. Despite these restrictions, the CPJ entered the 1954 parliamentary campaign under the name National Front, organized mass demonstrations against the Baghdad Pact, and together with nationalist parties helped create the atmosphere in which Jordan terminated the 1948 Anglo-Jordanian Treaty in 1956. The party polled an impressive 13 percent of the vote in the 1956 elections and was the first communist party in the Arab East to be represented in a cabinet. A subsequent all-out offensive by King Hussein's army, backed by the Eisenhower administration, led to the ouster of the cabinet, imposition of martial law, dissolution of the parliament, and imprisonment of CPJ deputies and hundreds of Communists, most of whom remained in prison until the general amnesty of April 1965.

The CPJ embraced the political outlook advocated by Egypt and Syria in the 1960s, a position consistent with the prevailing Soviet policy of cooperation with national bourgeois regimes in the Third World. The party benefited from the decision of the Jordanian government to establish full diplomatic relations with the Soviet Union in August 1963, but it continued to function clandestinely.

The party's 1964 program called for rapid industrialization, social welfare legislation, and a nonaligned foreign policy for Jordan. It endorsed the first Arab Summit meeting of January 1964 and the creation of the Palestine Liberation Organization (PLO). But when its new official organ, *al-Taqaddum* (Progress), published a front-page article that considered Arab solidarity a positive trend and regarded Jordan as progressive, an internal party rift ensued. Elements responsible were purged as right-wing deviationists.

Party Internal Affairs. Following the 1970 CPJ congress, an internal rift in the party produced a faction led by Fahmi Salfiti and Rushdi Shahin. This left-wing faction operates under the name of the Communist Party of Jordan–Leninist Cadre. It publishes the newspaper *al-Haqiqa* (Truth—not to be confused with the journal of the same name published by the CPJ).

The CPJ became entrenched in PLO politics after the 1967 Israeli occupation, and until the formation of the Palestine Communist Party (PCP) in 1982, its work centered on the West Bank.

A party congress, held in Amman in 1970, established the Ansar militia to contribute to the armed Palestinian resistance against the Israeli occupation. Two years later Secretary General Fu'ad Nassar was elected to the Palestine National Council (PNC), and in 1974, the CPJ published a transitional plan, which influenced the posture of the Democratic Front for the Liberation of Palestine (DFLP) and ultimately the PNC decision to struggle for the establishment of an independent Palestinian state.

In late December 1981, the CPJ's Central Committee decided to authorize the Palestine Communist Organization, the leading component of the PNF in the West Bank and Gaza, to prepare for the establishment of an independent Palestinian communist party (*IB*, March 1982). The PCP, which continued the work of PNF underground, was established on 10 February 1982 (*WMR*, February).

Domestic Attitudes and Activities. CPJ leaders have consistently denounced the "antidemocratic regime" of Jordan for having followed a policy of "divide and rule" ever since the annexation of the West Bank in 1950. Politburo member and theoretician Izhaq al-Khatib analyzes this policy in the context of the socioeconomic differences between Palestine and Jordan and describes modern Jordan as a consumerist society suffering from a "neo-classical dependence" (ibid., October 1983). The economy of Jordan is portrayed as being dominated by a parasitical bourgeoisie, which enriches itself on consumerism spurred by remittances from the Gulf, and a bureaucratic bourgeoisie, which creates state enterprises. The tensions between the two, as well as the growing number of indigenous and foreign laborers deprived of the benefits of social legislation and trade unionism, provide the CPJ with the opportunity to mobilize support among workers, students, women, and youth. Jordanian Communists are represented in the General Secretariat of the Alignment of Popular and Trade Union Forces as well as in the newly established Committee of Political Parties and Organizations. The program of the CPJ's Second Congress (December 1983) called on party members to work for the formation of a "broad national democratic front of workers, peasants, members of the petty and national bourgeoisie and revolutionary intellectuals in order to bring about national democratic rule" (ibid., July). Al-Khatib asserts that a Middle East settlement based on the Camp David scenario can be defeated by emphasizing the "revolutionary unity" of the Palestinian and Jordanian peoples as well as the struggle against the socioeconomic base of the regime, whose interests are linked to those of imperialism and Israel. This "unity of struggle and organization" was also emphasized in the program of the congress as a phenomenon that "does not contradict the Palestinian people's right and obligation to fight for the recovery of their rights flouted by Israel, anymore than the struggle for national democratic rule in Jordan." Warrad warns that the existence of any organization based on "region or commune would undermine the class and national struggle in Jordan." And in apparent contradiction of the perspective of the PCP leadership, on matters of priority, he maintains that "the Palestinian struggle serves the solution of the Jordanian problem, which consists in establishing national democratic rule and putting an end to Jordan's dependence on imperialism, while the Jordanians' struggle serves the solution of the Palestinian problems . . . those two problems . . . merge into one problem having

two aspects." (Ibid.) Al-Khatib views the establishment of a Palestinian state as a "bastion of unity" of the two people and "a dependable barrier to Israeli expansion into Jordan." This view, he implies, was vindicated by a PNC declaration in February 1983 in favor of a confederative relationship between Jordan and a future Palestinian state.

Auxiliary and Mass Organizations. Jordan's all-out offensive against the PLO in September 1970 and Israel's creeping annexation of the West Bank and Gaza spawned the indigenous nonviolent resistance that was organized under the banner of the Palestine National Front (PNF) *inside* the West Bank. Organized in August 1973, the PNF attracted a broad nationalist coalition reminiscent of the 1950s. The PNF organized against land expropriation and publicized Israeli violations of the 1949 Geneva Conventions in the Knesset through the Communist Party of Israel. The PNF urged Arab businessmen not to pay taxes to the occupation authorities and organized mass demonstrations against Israeli expulsion of Palestinian leaders from the occupied territories. Israel clamped down on the PNF in April 1974 and placed many of its leaders under administrative detention.

International Activities and Attitudes. In his October 1983 article, al-Khatib describes the CPJ goal of bringing about national democratic rule as meaning the establishment of a "new system, breaking with imperialism, and opting explicitly for a policy of close relations with the Arab national liberation movement, the Palestinian revolution, and of course the world revolutionary movement and the Soviet Union." The program of the 1983 congress recognized serious difficulties facing the Arab national liberation movement, which it attributed to the "abandonment of radical positions by the majority of patriotic Arab regimes," and the inability of the petty-bourgeois regimes to preserve gains made in the 1960s. The congress concluded that the Arab national liberation movement had entered a "new stage . . . characterized by the manifestly inadequate ability of the petty bourgeoisie to continue leading" that movement and that a new leadership is taking shape in the form of "an alliance between the parties of the working class and revolutionary democrats." The fulfillment of the task now requires a movement with a "socialist perspective." A resolution entitled "National Liberation and Universal Peace Are Indivisible," called on the Arab national liberation movement to intensify the struggle against "the U.S. ploys, Israeli aggression, the policy of military blocs and bases, the U.S. rapid deployment force, the military presence of the U.S. and other NATO powers, and the U.S. Israeli strategic cooperation," and considered that struggle as "inseparably linked with the struggle for universal peace." Thus the Arab people's battle for freedom is dialectically connected with the worldwide struggle for peace manifested in the "campaign against the U.S. nuclear missile deployment and against imperialism's militant provocations and adventures." (*IB*, May.) Warrad asserts that the Arab people's real contribution to world peace consists in resisting a transformation of their region "into a bridgehead for aggression against the Soviet Union" and struggling against the "arms race, the deployment of U.S. nuclear first-strike weapons in Western Europe, and attempts to go back on the Helsinki Accords and revert to the cold war."

Restrictions on the CPJ have been relaxed lately in view of the government's improved relations with the USSR. A Jordanian-USSR Friendship Society sponsors an annual cultural event celebrating Jordanian-USSR Friendship Week (*FBIS*, 18 April), and the society's chairman, Bahjat Talhouni,

a former prime minister and presently a senator, visited Moscow on 29 August and praised the Soviet position on the Middle East as "identical with the Arab positions, with the U.N. resolutions, and with the other international organizations' resolutions" (ibid., 29 August). The Jordanian commander-in-chief held talks with Soviet defense minister Dimitri Ustinov on 6 August (ibid., 7 August), and Jordanian prime minister Ahmad 'Ubaydat visited the Soviet Union on 2 August (ibid., 27 August).

The CPJ concern about the split in the PLO was expressed in an appeal signed by nine communist and workers' parties of the Arab East on 7 November 1983 at the height of the Tripoli battles between Arafat loyalists and the Fatah dissidents supported by Syria. Without fixing blame on any faction, the appeal warned that the fighting had eroded the "alliance of the Palestinian revolution, Syria, and the Lebanese patriotic national forces" and called on them to "end the strife between the brothers-in-arms now" (*IB*, January).

Naseer H. Aruri
Southeastern Massachusetts University

Lebanon

Population. 2,601,000
Party. Lebanese Communist Party (al-Hizb al-Shuyu'i al-Lubnani; LCP); Organization of Communist Action in Lebanon (OCAL)
Founded. LCP: 1924; OCAL: 1970
Membership. LCP: 14,000–16,000 (claimed); LCP: 5,000, OCAL: 2,000 (author's estimates)
Secretary General. LCP: George Hawi; OCAL: Muhsin Ibrahim
Politburo. LCP, 11 members
Central Committee. LCP, 24 members
Status. Legal
Last Congress. LCP: Fourth, 1979; OCAL: First, 1971

Last Elections. 1972, no representation
Auxiliary Organizations. LCP: Communist Labor Organization; World Peace Council in Lebanon; and
a number of labor and student unions and movements
Publications. *Al-Nida* (The call) daily; *al-Akhbar* (The news) weekly; *al-Tariq* (The road) quarterly

The LCP was established in October 1924 as the Lebanese People's Party (al-Hizb al-Sha'b al-Lubnani). During the French mandate over Syria and Lebanon (1920–1946), the LCP recruited members in both of these countries, but the Syrian element dominated the party despite its name.

The LCP was banned from 1939 to 1970, when, along with several other organizations, it was granted legal status by the Lebanese government. Despite the LCP's lack of legal recognition prior to 1970, it was tolerated and enjoyed some measure of freedom of action. On the eve of Lebanon's civil war of 1975–1976, the LCP entered the leftist, Moslem-dominated Front for Progressive Parties and National Forces, later known as the Lebanese National Movement (LNM).

Both the LCP and the OCAL have participated actively in Lebanon's civil war and continue to play active roles in the country's political affairs. Traditionally, the communist appeal in Lebanon was largely confined to Orthodox Christians, particularly the Greek Orthodox community, which provided the bulk of the LCP's leaders and followers. The factional character of the LCP hindered communist efforts to attract a following among other Lebanese religious groups. Since the party's legalization, however, Shia Moslems have become increasingly visible in the LCP.

Leadership and Organization. George Hawi has been the LCP's secretary general since 1979, and Muhsin Ibrahim has led the OCAL since its foundation in 1970.

The Congress, theoretically the highest organ of the LCP, is supposed to convene every four years; however, the LCP has held only four congresses since 1924. Authority is vested in the 24-member Central Committee, which in turn elects the 11-member Politburo. (For a listing of Central Committee members, see *YICA*, 1981, p. 14.)

The LCP is believed to have a well-organized and highly controlled network of local cells, which are, in turn, organized into districts and regions. Both the LCP and OCAL maintain well-armed "self-defense" paramilitary units that participate actively in street battles and other "military operations," mainly aginst the Christian/rightist Lebanese Forces.

Domestic Views and Activities. The LCP continued to hold "U.S. imperialists," "Israeli occupationists," and "Phalangist fascists" responsible for the increasing political instability and factional warfare in Lebanon. An enlarged plenary meeting of the LCP Central Committee in February put forward the following six principles for "the struggle to ensure the triumph of our people's national liberation revolution": the affirmation of Lebanon's Arab character; the complete removal of confessionalism from Lebanese politics; the radical reform of the parliamentary system through the introduction of proportional representation; the reform of Lebanon's constitution so as to redistribute authority among the executive, legislative, and legal branches; the close cooperation of the executive authority, including the army, with "fraternal Syria first and foremost"; and radical socioeconomic transformation "to lessen dependence on international monopolies" and "to prevent the ruin of the working class and rural workers" (*IB*, May).

The LCP affirmed the communist "alliance" with the Progressive Socialist Party (PSP) and its "solidarity" with other "progressive and patriotic forces," presumably within the LNM.

In its circulars and public statements, the LCP continued to condemn Israel's presence in southern Lebanon and its "atrocities against the population" and demanded the "full and unconditional" withdrawal of Israeli troops. LCP leaders lauded party members for their active participation "in the national armed resistance" against Israel and underscored the importance of stepping up "the struggle for liberating the south" through armed popular uprising and "the isolation of the fascist forces who would like to continue to rely on the Israelis" (Radio Budapest interview with Hawi, 4 July; *FBIS*, 6 July).

In a statement issued on 23 June by the LCP Politburo, the party reaffirmed its "alliance" with the Popular Front for the Liberation of Palestine (PFLP) and reiterated its support for the Palestinian people's "lawful national rights." The LCP also called upon the Palestine Liberation Organization (PLO) to "return to the vanguard positions in the struggle against imperialism, Zionism and Arab reaction"; the same statement also urged the strengthening of the PLO's relations "above all with

Syria, and the Lebanese progressive and patriotic forces, and with forces of national liberation, progress, peace and socialism throughout the world, with the Soviet Union in the first place" (*IB*, September).

Although both the LCP and the OCAL remained unswerving in their public support of the LNM during the year, persistent problems continued to mark "fraternal" ties between the Communists and other "progressive" forces. In April street clashes occurred between LCP gunmen and members of the Shia Amal Movement who had attacked LCP strongholds in West Beirut (Radio Free Lebanon, 20 April; *FBIS*, 25 April). Armed clashes were also reported between the Communists and the Islamic Unification Movement in Tripoli in May (*FBIS*, 26 October), and again with the Amal Movement in Beirut in June (ibid., 6 June). Amal leader Nabih Birri admitted in an interview that "our relations with the LCP have passed through periods of ebb and flow to the point that at one stage clashes and problems occurred between us" (*al-Hawadith*, London, 24 August; *FBIS*, 28 August). During 1984 Amal and various other Islamic groups effectively overpowered the voices of both the LCP and the OCAL in West Beirut. Some of the public statements of these two communist organizations, however, continued to be broadcast by the clandestine Voice of the Mountain radio station of the PSP. The LCP maintained its contacts with various Palestinian groups, including al-Fatah, "to protect Palestinian refugee camps in Lebanon and to coordinate military operations against the Israeli enemy" (*al-Dastur*, Amman, 14 July; *FBIS*, 17 July).

International Views and Contacts. The LCP has been a strong and consistent supporter of the Soviet Union. The party considers the United States, NATO, Israel, and their regional Arab and local Lebanese "lackeys" as implacable enemies of the Lebanese people and the LCP itself. The LCP believes that the Lebanese people can rely with confidence on the USSR in the political, economic, and other spheres (Tass, Moscow, 6 August; *FBIS*, 7 August). The LCP condemns the Camp David "deal" and subsequent American proposals to settle the Arab-Israeli conflict peacefully and maintains that the achievement of a lasting and just settlement of the Arab-Israeli conflict requires the withdrawal of Israeli troops from all Arab territories occupied since 1967. The legal right of the Palestinian people to establish an independent state must be assured. The LCP calls for an international peace conference, including representatives from the USSR, to settle the Middle East crisis. The LCP expresses strong support for "the anti-imperialist struggle of Syria" and advocates the strengthening of "the unity of progressive forces" throughout the Middle East (MTI, Budapest, 5 July; *FBIS*, 6 July). The party also supports all Soviet "peace initiatives."

During the year the LCP maintained extensive official contacts with communist party officials from the USSR, Eastern Europe, and other areas. Hawi visited Sofia in early January and held extensive discussions with Todor Zhivkov, secretary general of the Bulgarian Communist Party, on the arms race, American and Israeli policies in the Middle East, and Lebanon's domestic situation. They noted the unanimity of views between the two parties and confirmed their resolve "to further develop and intensify mutual relations of friendship, cooperation, and fraternal solidarity" (*Rabotnichesko delo*, Sofia, 5 January; *FBIS*, 10 January). Nabil Abd al-Samad, an LCP Politburo member, visited South Yemen on 28 January and held talks with Yemeni party and state leaders on Lebanese developments, bilateral ties, and the political situation in the Arab world. In a statement to the Aden News Agency, al-Samad praised South Yemen's solid support for the LNM in its struggle against foreign interference (Aden domestic service, 1 February; *FBIS*, 2 February). On 15 February Hawi met Boris Ponomarev and Karen Brutents of the CPSU Central Committee's International Department in Moscow and exchanged views on the situation in the Near East and the continuing "Israeli aggression and the imperialist intervention" in Lebanon (Moscow television service, 15 February; *FBIS*, 16 February). In late February and early March Nadim Abd al-Samad visited Bulgaria, Poland, Hungary, and Czechoslovakia and joined with high-ranking communist leaders in each country in expressing mutual support and solidarity on international and communist issues. Special attention was given to the Middle East and developments in the Lebanese crisis. In an interview with the Czechoslovak party daily *Rudé právo* (5 March; *FBIS*, 9 March), Abd al-Samad reiterated the LCP's solidarity with the USSR and asserted that the departure of U.S. forces from Lebanon had dealt a serious blow to U.S. efforts "to destroy the LNM," to launch "a new offensive against the Palestinian people, against Syria, and to establish rule over the entire region"; Abd al-Samad also noted that the American debacle in Lebanon "does not constitute a definitive victory" for the LCP. "For us it is only one stage in the struggle against American imperialism," he added. Hawi, accompanied by Joseph Abu Akl, a member of the LCP Politburo, visited Hungary on 1–5 July, meeting with János Kádár and other high-ranking Hungarian officials. The two sides discussed international, regional Middle Eastern, and local Lebanese developments and expressed their solidarity and "their readiness to comprehensively develop inter-party relations and strengthen cooperation" between the two parties (MTI, Budapest, 5 July; *FBIS*, 6 July). Similar views were expressed when Hawi met Bulgarian leader Todor Zhivkov in Sofia on 26 July (BTA, Sofia, 26 July; *FBIS*, 31 July). George Hawi, accompanied by George Habr, an LCP Politburo member, visited Cyprus on 7 June and met with high-ranking officials of the communist party of Cyprus (*Kharavyi*, Nicosia, 9 June; *FBIS*, 12 June).

A Soviet delegation headed by Karen Brutents visited Beirut and held talks with LCP leaders on 31 March–2 April. The participants expressed support for Soviet peace initiatives to strengthen world peace and end the arms race. They also noted with satisfaction Lebanon's annulment of the May 1983 agreement with Israel and asserted their desire to strengthen relations of friendship and cooperation between the Soviet party and the LCP (*Pravda*, 4 April; *FBIS*, 5 April). Brutents also met with Lebanese premier Rashid Karami and Lebanese minister of foreign affairs Elie Salim, while Sergei Kozmin, the deputy head of the Soviet delegation, met with various LNM members, including the OCAL (Voice of the Mountain, 2 April; *FBIS*, 3 April). On 18–21 September Gyula Horn, the head of the Hungarian Central Committee's Foreign Affairs Department, visited Beirut on the invitation of the LCP and met Hawi, LCP Politburo members Karim Murawah and Joseph Abu Akl, and other Lebanese communist leaders. The two parties discussed further strengthening of contacts (MTI, Budapest, 21 September; *FBIS*, 25 September).

During the year, the LCP celebrated the sixtieth anniversary of its foundation, highlighted by a 21 October public meeting in Beirut, attended by representatives of various local Lebanese organizations, Syria, and foreign communist parties. Many of these conveyed "comradely greetings" and expressed solidarity with the LCP (Voice of the Mountain, 21 October; *FBIS*, 22 October). Karen Brutents represented the Soviet Union in the celebrations and read the text of the Soviet Central Committee greetings (Moscow domestic service, 21 October; *FBIS*, 22 October).

Publications. The principal LCP publications are the Arabic-language daily newspaper *al-Nida*, the weekly *al-Akhbar*, and the quarterly *al-Tariq*. The party also publishes the weekly *Kanch* (The call) in the Armenian language. They contain articles dealing with Lebanese political and socioeconomic issues, international and Arab politics, and Marxist-Leninist ideology. These organs often disseminate the news of illegal communist parties in the Middle East, although in recent years their publication or distribution has been disrupted because of insecurity in Beirut. Both the LCP and the OCAL also publish a number of booklets and pamphlets.

The Organization of Communist Action in Lebanon. The precursor of the OCAL was the now-defunct Arab Nationalist Movement (ANM), founded by George Habash in 1954. When the ANM split into various groups after the 1967 Arab-Israeli war, Muhsin Ibrahim and his colleagues established the Organization of Lebanese Socialists (OLS) in 1969. In May 1970 the OLS merged with the smaller Organization of Socialist Lebanon and a few dissident Communists to form the OCAL. The First Congress of this newly established "revolutionary" organization met in 1971, elected a Politburo, and designated Ibrahim its secretary general. At present Fawwaz Tarabulsi acts as the assistant secretary general (Aden domestic service, 8 February; *FBIS*, 9 February).

Like the LCP, the OCAL is an active member of the LNM. Ibrahim is also the secretary general of the LNM, a position that gives the OCAL a weight far beyond the numerical strength of its members, who are mostly students, ex-students, and other young working-class people. Shia Moslems are heavily represented in the ranks of the OCAL.

During the Lebanese civil war and its aftermath, the OCAL played an important role in frontal activities against the Lebanese Forces, fighting alongside the PSP and other leftists within the LNM. Its membership in the LNM, however, has not prevented the OCAL, and many other leftist groups, including the LCP, from engaging in periodic street battles against the Amal Movement. Sporadic clashes between the two intensified in late March when Amal gunmen stormed OCAL strongholds in West Beirut (*FBIS*, 23 March). The OCAL has maintained close ties with the Democratic Front for the Liberation of Palestine and other leftist Palestinian commando groups. Aside from West Beirut and other Shia-populated areas where OCAL activity has been visible, the organization also maintains a presence in the northern Lebanese city of Tripoli and elsewhere (ibid., 26 October).

Initially, the OCAL was critical of the LCP, charging that it had become rigid and was not genuinely Marxist (*Arab World Weekly*, 15 May 1971). It also sided with China in the Sino-Soviet conflict. Since the Lebanese civil war, however, the OCAL has moderated its original views and adopted an independent position vis-à-vis both the USSR and the PRC. In recent years the OCAL and LCP have drawn closer. Interviewed in August 1977, Fawwaz Tarabulsi asserted that "our policies have been very close, at times even identical" (*MERIP Reports*, no. 61, October 1977). During the year the OCAL maintained ties with both the USSR and the LCP (Voice of the Mountain, 2 April; *FBIS*, 3 April). Several meetings, reportedly urged by the Soviet Union, took place between George Hawi and Muhsin Ibrahim to further coordinate LCP and OCAL activities. Agreement was reached "to intensify the communist military presence through the two organizations and to set up additional positions along the contact lines" (Radio Free Lebanon, 28 May; *FBIS*, 1 June). The OCAL also maintained close contacts with party and state officials in South Yemen. On 28 January Muhsin Ibrahim arrived in Aden to discuss the domestic situation in Lebanon and matters of bilateral cooperation between the OCAL and the ruling Yemen Socialist Party (YSP). It was significant that George Hawi also arrived in Aden the same day for a similar purpose (Aden domestic service, 28 January; *FBIS*, 30 January). Ibrahim thanked Yemeni leader Ali Nasir Muhammad al-Hasani for South Yemen's "principled and firm stance" in support of the "struggle of the Lebanese people" and called for further develop-ment of "the firm alliance" between the YSP and the OCAL (Aden domestic service, 29 January; *FBIS*, 30 January). OCAL Politburo member Tarabulsi also paid a visit to South Yemen in early February (*FBIS*, 9 February).

Like the LCP, the OCAL denounces the "Zionist-imperialist-reactionary alliance" in Lebanon and elsewhere and focuses on the imperative of ending the Israeli occupation of southern Lebanon through armed struggle (ibid., 21 May 1982). The organization believes it has adapted Marxist teachings to the peculiarities of Lebanon's sociopolitical life. It gives particularly close attention to members' military training, preparation for "armed struggle," "mass political action," and party work in labor unions and student organizations. During the year the OCAL reportedly was preparing to launch its own radio station (*Monday Morning*, 13–19 August; *FBIS*, 17 August).

Other Organizations. A number of other Lebanese communist and communist-dominated organizations have been mentioned in the news media from time to time; among these, the more significant seem to be the Communist Labor Organization, the Organization of Arab Communists, the Revolutionary Communist Party (Trotskyite), the Lebanese Communist Union, and the World Peace Council in Lebanon.

Nikola B. Schahgaldian
The Rand Corporation

(Note: Views expressed in this article are those of the author and should not be construed to represent the position of the Rand Corporation or its research sponsors.)

Morocco

Population. 23,565,000
Party. Party of Progress and Socialism (Parti du progrès et du socialisme; PPS)
Founded. 1943
Membership. 2,000 (estimated)
Secretary General. 'Ali Yata
Politburo. 12 members: 'Ali Yata, Ismail Alaoui, Mohamed Ben Bella, Abdeslem Bourquia, Mohamed Rifi Chouaib, Abdelmajid Douieb, Omar El Fassi, Thami Khyari, Abdallah Layachi, Simon Lévy, Mohamed Moucharik, Abdelwahed Souhail
Secretariat. 4 members: 'Ali Yata, Mohamed Rifi Chouaib, Omar El Fassi, Mohamed Moucharik
Central Committee. 65 members
Status. Legal
Last Congress. Third, 25–27 March 1983, in Casablanca
Last Election. 14 September 1984, 2.3 percent, 2 of 306 seats
Auxiliary Organizations. No data
Publications. *Al Bayane* (daily), French and Arabic editions

The Moroccan Communist Party (Parti communiste marocain), founded in 1943 as a branch of the French Communist Party, was banned by the French protectorate in 1952. After three years of open operations in independent Morocco, it was again banned in 1959. Renamed the Party of Progress and Socialism, it was granted legal status in 1974. In the 1976 municipal elections, the party won thirteen seats on the city council of Casablanca. The PPS participated in the Moroccan national elections in the spring of 1977 and won one seat in parliament. In the last municipal elections, held in June 1983, the PPS won only two seats on the Casablanca city council. In Morocco's recent parliamentary elections, held 14 September, the PPS won two seats in parliament.

Leadership and Party Organization. The PPS's Third National Congress, held in March 1983, re-elected 'Ali Yata secretary general of the party. The congress re-elected 50 of the 57 members of the Central Committee elected by the party's Second National Congress in 1979 and elected fifteen new members. The 1983 congress elected a twelve-man Politburo, all of whose members were on the thirteen-man Politburo elected in 1979. At the conclusion of the Third National Congress, the Central Committee reduced the party Secretariat from seven to four members. (For details of the Third Congress, see *YICA*, 1984, pp. 45–46.)

Domestic Party Affairs. Morocco experienced a series of violent riots in mid-January that constituted the worst outbreak of urban unrest since the bloody Casablanca riots in mid-1981. When army and security forces moved in to quell the "bread riots," bloody clashes ensued in which at least 100–200 Moroccans were killed. The violence continued until 22 January, when King Hassan announced the cancellation of price increases for bread, sugar, and cooking oil. Hassan blamed the violence on "a multifaceted conspiracy perpetrated by Marxists-Leninists, Zionist agents, and Khomeinists" (*NYT*, 23 January). Although other Moroccan newspapers were suspended only a few days during the riots, both editions of the PPS daily, *Al Bayane*, were suspended for nearly two months, from 21 January to 16 March.

The PPS refuted the charge that the party had incited the confrontation with the government. It pointed out that party members or sympathizers who had joined the rioters did so because of the severe economic conditions imposed on most Moroccans by the regime's policies. (*African Communist*, Third Quarter.) In a detailed analysis presented to the sixth plenary session of the Central Committee on 1 April and published in the 28 April edition of *Al Bayane*, PPS leader 'Ali Yata attributed the January riots to a combination of underlying economic, social, and political causes. On the economic level, Yata cited a variety of internal factors, including a stagnant economy, inadequate investment in the industrial sector, a large deficit in the current accounts balance, and a decline in agricultural production. On the social level, the PPS secretary general argued that basic social services like health and education were grossly inadequate and that growing social problems—begging, crime, prostitution, drugs, and corruption—were contributing to the resentment of the masses. As for political causes, Yata stated that the regime had fradulently rigged the municipal elections of June 1983 and, by postponing parliamentary elections, had left the country in a political void. In short, the government had failed to provide adequate policies to deal with the growing crisis in Morocco and thus the regime bore the essential responsibility for the outbreak of violence.

When Morocco's parliamentary elections were held in September, the PPS waged a vigorous campaign and fielded candidates in 160 electoral districts. This organizational strength derived from two factors. First, unlike members of the major opposition party, the Socialist Union of Popular Forces (USFP), PPS militants were not imprisoned by the government following the Casablanca riots of June 1981. Second, the PPS has more followers among students and intellectuals than among the working class. (*Le Monde*, 15 September.)

PPS candidates received 102,314 votes in the parliamentary elections, 2.3 percent of all votes cast. Although this percentage was virtually identical to that received by the PPS in the previous parliamentary election in 1977, the party increased its seats in parliament from one to two because of the distribution of the votes. At the conclusion of the electoral campaign, 'Ali Yata commented on the campaign's "healthy climate" and "administrative neutrality" (ibid.). After the balloting, however, the PPS joined the Istiqlal Party and the USFP in denouncing fraudulent measures employed by the regime to ensure the parliamentary predominance of pro-government parties. And in the weeks following the elections, the PPS voiced its fear that the new government would merely be an "alternation" of officials pursuing the same old policies, rather than a genuine "alternative" that could radically change economic and social policies (*Lamalif*, Casablanca, October).

International Views, Positions, and Activities. The PPS continued to back the Moroccan government's international efforts to "recover" the Western Sahara. On 5 August, for example, *Al Bayane* supported the position of Libyan leader Moammar Khadafy, who declared that the Western Sahara issue is an Arab problem that should be settled in an Arab framework, and it denounced Algeria's efforts to keep the Sahara issue before the Organization of African Unity (OAU) (Maghreb Arabe Presse, Rabat, 6 August; *FBIS*, 7 August). The PPS fully supported the Treaty of the Union of States signed by Morocco and Libya on 13 August, declaring: "Anything that improves prospects for the reinforcement of ties of unity among the Maghreb and Arab nations should be regarded as positive, in that it serves to reinforce the combat undertaken by the Arab nation against Zionist imperialism" (*Al Bayane*, 15 August). Like all Moroccan political parties, the PPS strongly denounced the admission of the Polisario Front's government-in-exile, the Saharan Arab Democratic Republic, to the OAU on 12 November. The party declared: "It is a defiance of good sense and reason to admit a phantom state into the OAU, which possesses neither a territory, a people, institutions, laws, or traditions" (ibid., 13 November).

The PPS reaffirmed its pro-Soviet orientation in an article by party leader 'Ali Yata in the June issue of the *World Marxist Review*. In this article Yata warned of the danger posed by U.S. efforts to gain military-strategic superiority and accused the United States of torpedoing the negotiations in Geneva on medium-range missiles. Yata argued that the Reagan administration's massive arms buildup showed that the White House was planning and preparing for a "limited" nuclear war in Europe.

John Damis
Portland State University

Saudi Arabia

Population. 10,794,000
Party. Communist Party of Saudi Arabia (CPSA)
Founded. 1975
Membership. Unknown but believed negligible
Secretary General. Ahmad Musa
Spokesmen. (Positions not identified) Abdallah Muhammad, Abd-al-Rahman Salih, Salim Hamid, Hamad Mubarak, Abu Abdallah
Status. Illegal
Last Congress. Second, August 1984
Last Election. N/a
Auxiliary Organizations. Saudi Peace and Solidarity Committee, Saudi Democratic Youth
Publications. Apparently exist, but titles unknown (see *YICA*, 1984, p. 55)

The Second Congress of the CPSA was held in August, according to a Tass dispatch from Aden on 17 September. The origin of the dispatch (published in *Pravda* the following day) suggests that the congress may have been held in that city. The dispatch itself speaks of the "increased strength of the party" and of its "viability," just as pre-congress greetings sent by the Australian Socialist Party noted the "successes in your work and victories scored" (*The Socialist*, Sydney, 6 June), and a post-congress broadcast of the Communist Party of Turkey's message to the meeting spoke of the CPSA's "increased political influence" (Our Radio, 27 September; *FBIS*, 27 September). The nature of the CPSA "successes" remains a mystery, but an abridged reprint of the Second Congress's "Final Communiqué" toward the end of the year strongly suggested that they were connected with ability of the party to survive at all in the oppressive environment in which it operates (*IB*, no. 23). The congress was said to have approved a Central Committee report, a party program, and a party charter and to have elected a new Central Committee, Politburo, and secretary general (*Pravda*, 18 September).

The CPSA was said to have participated in a meeting of eleven Arab communist parties apparently held in Damascus in early June (Radio Damascus, 3 June; *FBIS*, 5 June). Just afterwards, Moscow's Radio Peace and Progress broadcast a statement that strongly implied Saudi government subservience to the United States (see *Soviet Analysis*, 25 July). Such Soviet support is consistent with the strongly pro-Soviet stand taken by the CPSA's Second Congress, which condemned the "American-Israeli-NATO aggressive policy in the Middle East" and noted "the importance of strengthening the bond of friendship and solidarity" with the Soviet party (*Pravda*, 18 September).

The CPSA's continued shadowy existence is revealed in a listing of its delegation among the 90 other communist and "revolutionary democratic" parties attending a December conference in Prague on the work of the *World Marxist Review* (*Rudé právo*, Prague, 7 December). Further evidence of party activity surfaced when Kabul Radio (8 January 1985) announced that a CPSA delegation led by Ahmad Musa, CPSA secretary general, had arrived for the twentieth anniversary celebrations of the founding of the Afghan party (*FBIS*, 9 January 1985).

Wallace H. Spaulding
McLean, Virginia

Syria

Population. 10,075,000
Party. Syrian Communist Party (al-Hizb al-Shuyu'i al-Suri; SCP)
Founded. 1924 (as a separate party in 1944)
Membership. 5,000 (estimated)
Secretary General. Khalid Bakhdash (deputy secretary general: Yusuf Faysal)
Politburo. Khalid Bakhdash, Ibrahim Bakri, Khalid Hammami, Maurice Salibi, Umar Siba'i, Daniel Ni'mah, Zuhayr Abd al-Sammad, Ramu Farkha (not necessarily complete or up-to-date)
Secretariat. No data
Central Committee. Nabih Rushaydat, Muhammad Khabbad, Issa Khuri, other names unknown
Status. Component of the ruling National Progressive Front
Last Congress. Fifth, May 1980
Last Election. 1981, 0.78 percent, no representation
Auxiliary Organizations. No data
Publications. *Nidal al-Sha'b*

The Party of the Lebanese People, founded in 1924, was one of several Marxist or quasi-Marxist groups that appeared in Syria and Lebanon during the early 1920s. It united with two other factions in 1925 to form the Communist Party of Syria and Lebanon (CPSL). The Syrian and Lebanese parties separated in 1944, soon after the two countries were officially declared independent, but maintained close ties with each other. The CPSL and the subsequent Syrian Communist Party (SCP) underwent alternate periods of toleration or legality and of suppression. The SCP often emphasized nationalism and reform and played down revolutionary ideology. It gained a considerable following and a membership that may have reached 10,000 by 1945. The party became quite influential during 1954–1958 but suffered a serious blow with the creation of the United Arab Republic and the subsequent suppression. Seemingly no longer a serious threat and following a foreign policy that often paralleled that of the Ba'thist regime, it gained a quasi-legal status after 1966 and finally joined the Ba'th-dominated National Progressive Front (NPF) in 1972.

The Syrian communist movement has undergone several schisms in recent years. Riyad al-Turk was chosen as secretary general of one breakaway group in 1974. Yusuf Murad, a former member of the SCP Central Committee, formed another group, the Base Organization, in 1980. There is no recent information on these groups.

Leadership and Party Organization. Little is known about the dynamics of the SCP's leadership except for the fact that Secretary General Khalid Bakhdash has long been the dominant figure. There have been some divisions among the top leadership; for example, Politburo member Daniel Ni'mah (now a representative of the SCP on the Central Command of the NPF) broke with the party for a while during the early 1970s.

The SCP is organized like other communist parties. The Fifth Congress met in 1980. It has a Central Committee (a plenary session was reported in February), a Secretariat, and a Politburo.

Domestic Party Affairs. There were few available reports on domestic party affairs during 1984. Secretary General Bakhdash apparently made few public appearances during 1984. There was one reference to his "convalescence" (ADN, East Berlin, 21 June; *FBIS*, 22 June). He reappeared in September and on 26 October gave a long speech to a "mass meeting" in Damascus celebrating the SCP's sixtieth anniversary. The gathering included "eminent representatives of the country's political and public organizations and SCP activists" (*Pravda*, 28 October; *FBIS*, 9 November).

Several statements of top SCP officials indicated dissatisfaction with the government's domestic policies. Writing in the *World Marxist Review* (June), Politburo member Khalid Hammami referred to the "discrepancy, as in Syria, between the anti-imperialist trend of foreign policy and an inner political trend toward curbing social progress" and declared that "Syrian communists are not shutting our eyes to the negative aspects of the socio-economic policy of our state." He cited "unemployment, a high cost of living and a shortage of housing" as problems confronting "numerous working people, whose pressing requirements are often ignored," while "the parasitic bourgeoisie is growing and corruption is rife" and the "ruling quarters are suspicious and fearful" of "the masses" and "curtail democratic freedoms." At one point in this most extensive criticism of the regime's policies, he bluntly concluded that "Syria has abandoned its progressive socio-economic policy," but gave "influential forces in the political leadership" credit for realizing the dangers involved. He prescribed greater "democracy" as the "chief instrument" for "exposing and frustrating plots hatched by home reaction and of defending and furthering the working people's gains." In another article, he declared that "Syria's social progress will demand removal of this bourgeoisie from participation in political and economic affairs" (*WMR*, October).

In the same vein, at the sixtieth anniversary celebration, Bakhdash asserted that the SCP "is struggling to maintain and consolidate economic transformations such as the agrarian reform, nationalization, and the establishment of the state sector in the economy" (*Pravda*, 28 October; *FBIS*, 9 November). Deputy Secretary General Yusuf Faysal spoke in Bulgaria about his party's "activities against the negative influence of the parasitic and bureaucratic bourgeoisie" (*Rabotnichesko delo*, Sofia, 2 July; *FBIS*, 11 July).

A Syrian woman who has been imprisoned in Damascus since 1981 for distributing material critical of the regime's treatment of women was named by Amnesty International as a "prisoner of conscience." She was described as belonging to the "Communist Party," but it was unclear whether the reference was to the official SCP or to a breakaway group. (*Middle East and Mediterranean Outlook Memo*, London, December.)

Auxiliary and Front Organizations. Little information on auxiliary organizations is available. The SCP probably participates in such groups as the Arab-Soviet Friendship Society, the Syrian Committee for Solidarity with Asian and African Countries, the National Council of Peace Partisans in Syria, and the Syrian-Bulgarian Friendship Society.

The present Syrian regime is officially based on the NPF, which includes the SCP, the Arab Socialist Union, the Socialist Union, and the Arab Socialist Party, in addition to the dominant Ba'th Party (non-Marxist). This does not mean that the SCP has any significant influence but rather that it has at least for the time being more or less abandoned revolutionism in favor of the comforts of a largely formal role in the personalistic dictatorship, which is garbed as a party regime. This quiet role as the regime's partner also conforms to the wishes of the USSR, whose foreign policy Syria tends to parallel in many respects. Exceptions are recent Syrian support for dissident elements in the Palestine Liberation Organization (PLO), Damascus's conflict with Iraq, and its support for Iran in the Iraqi-Iranian war.

Hammami defined the question of justifying the alliance with the regime as one of "vast importance" and argued that the struggle "against colonialism and imperialism and their schemes" (a phrase quoted from the statement of the Fifth SCP Congress) provides "the fundamental criterion." But he also stressed the continuing "political, organizational and ideological independence" of his party and its battle "for the return of the country to the road of social progress." (*WMR*, June.) He described the SCP as being "active in its work at different levels, including the government level, as well as in public organizations . . . work[ing] to ensure a greater and more profound role for the Front" (ibid., October). It was reported that "representatives of the Ba'th Party" were included in the SCP's sixtieth anniversary celebration, where Bakhdash called for "strengthening the front" (*Pravda*, 28 October; *FBIS*, 9 November).

Despite their disagreements, the USSR and Syria continued to cooperate with each other against U.S. influence in the Middle East and against Israel. (For basic facts on Soviet military assistance to Syria during 1983, see *YICA*, 1984,

p. 67.) In addition to the massive quantities of up-to-date Soviet weapons now provided to Syria, an estimated 6,000 Soviet advisers were involved with the Syrian military (Jerusalem radio, 1 April; *FBIS*, 2 April). Syrian defense minister Gen. Mustafa Talas confirmed plans for two Soviet airborne divisions to reach Damascus in eight hours in case of a new conflict with Israel but added that his country "does not need the assistance of these USSR troops" (*El País*, Madrid, 19 May; *FBIS*, 24 May). Spokesmen for each country generally praised the other, but Soviet stress on "the need to maintain the unity of the Palestinian resistance movement" (*Izvestiia*, 27 April; *FBIS*, 1 May) implied criticism of Syria.

Several important official visits occurred during the year. A Syrian delegation headed by Defense Minister Talas attended the funeral of Yuri Andropov in Moscow in February amid signs that the Syrians were then worried about their future relationship with the Soviets. A Soviet delegation headed by First Deputy Chairman of the Council of Ministers Geidar Aliev visited Damascus in March, allegedly in part to urge that Syria's internal power struggle be resolved. Karen Brutents, deputy chief of the International Department of the Soviet Central Committee, visited Damascus in April for talks with Syrian leaders, including President Hafiz al-Asad. Syrian vice-president Rif'at al-Asad visited the USSR in May and held talks with Konstantin Chernenko. In October, President Asad visited Moscow for talks with Soviet leaders, the first publicly acknowledged visit since 1980 (at the time of the signing of the twenty-year Treaty of Friendship), although there were hints that two other, unpublicized visits occurred during Andropov's presidency. Despite signs of disagreement between the two countries on the Iraqi-Iranian war, divisions in the PLO, and Syrian concern over recent Soviet overtures to Egypt and other "moderate" Arab regimes (*NYT*, 16 October), the Syrian media stressed the "strategic nature" of the visit (Damascus domestic service, 18 October; *FBIS*, 18 October).

Syrian-Soviet cooperation is hardly the result of the official existence of a "national front" government in Damascus. Its basis is purely pragmatic, not ideological, and President Asad is said to be basically hostile to the USSR (David Price-Jones, "Assad the Terrible," *New Republic*, 30 January, p. 25). Asked by a Western journalist whether Syria might "change superpowers," Defense Minister Talas answered, "Why not?" (*CSM*, 11 June).

International Views, Positions, and Activities. The SCP joined in statements of seven Arab communist and workers' parties in mid-October 1983 (*IB*, January), of nine Arab communist and workers' parties on 7 November 1983 (in Prague) (ibid.), and of eleven Arab communist parties at a meeting in an undisclosed place in June (ibid., September).

Several contacts between the SCP and socialist countries were reported during the year. A talk by Khalid Bakhdash was broadcast by Moscow television service on 16 February (*FBIS*, 17 February); it was unclear whether he was visiting the USSR at the time. During his visit to Damascus in March, Aliev met with Deputy Secretary General Faysal and other representatives of the SCP, as well as with Lebanese Communist Party leader George Hawi (*World Affairs Report*, 14, no. 2, 1984, column 492). During his visit to Syria in April, Brutents met with Faysal and other SCP leaders (*Pravda*, 22 April; *FBIS*, 26 April). SCP Politburo member Ibrahim Bakri (who is also chairman of the Trade Union Commission of the Central Committee) led an SCP "study delegation" to Prague in June "to discuss experiences in the activities of the trade union movement" and met with Czechoslovak party leaders (ČETEKA, Prague, 4 June; *FBIS*, 5 June). East German Politburo member Günter Schabowski (chief editor of *Neues Deutschland*) met with Faysal and other SCP officials in Damascus in June (ADN, East Berlin, 21 June; *FBIS*, 22 June). Faysal led an SCP delegation to Bulgaria from 24 June to 1 July as guests of the Bulgarian Central Committee (*Rabotnichesko delo*, Sofia, 2 July; *FBIS*, 11 July). Bakhdash visited Prague in September and gave an interview to *Rudé právo* (*The Soviet Union and the Middle East*, Jerusalem, 10, no. 1, 1984, p. 15).

The celebration of the SCP's sixtieth anniversary had its international aspects. A "public meeting" was held at the Soviet Central Committee's Marxism-Leninism Institute on 30 October in honor of the occasion. Representatives of the SCP and the Lebanese Communist Party (whose sixtieth anniversary was simultaneously being celebrated) were present as the director and the deputy director of the institute hailed the "heroic path" of the two parties (*Pravda*, 31 October; *FBIS*, 9 November). Delegates from several "communist and workers' parties" attended the anniversary celebration in Damascus. Soviet representative Karen Brutents gave a speech and read the greetings of the Soviet Central Committee (*Pravda*, 28 October; *FBIS*,

9 November). Brutents later held a meeting with Bakhdash and other SCP leaders (*Pravda*, 30 October; *FBIS*, 13 November). The Bulgarian Central Committee also sent a long laudatory telegram to the SCP on the occasion (text in *Rabotnichesko delo*, 28 October; *FBIS*, 31 October).

Also in October, SCP Politburo member (and member of the NPF central leadership) Daniel Ni'mah was one of several Syrians traveling to Moscow with President Asad (Damascus domestic service, 15 October; *FBIS*, 16 October). Bakhdash was interviewed by Tass on 15 October (*World Affairs Report*, 14, no. 1, 1984, column 215). Greetings were also received from the Central Committee of the Korean Workers' Party (Korean Central News Agency, Pyongyang, 28 October; *FBIS*, 29 October).

No deviation from the Soviet line appears in SCP statements. Bakhdash declared the USSR to be "the vanguard of all progressive mankind" (Moscow television service, 16 February; *FBIS*, 17 February). He said that the "cornerstone" of the SCP's "national and international policy since its inception . . . has been friendship, cooperation, and alliance" with the Soviet party (*Pravda*, 28 October; *FBIS*, 9 November). A joint statement of the SCP and the Bulgarian Communist Party lauded "the creative proposals of the USSR . . . aimed at halting the arms race, of bringing about disarmament, especially nuclear disarmament, and at creating an atmosphere of confidence and cooperation." The "serious exacerbation of the situation in the world" was blamed on "the most reactionary imperialistic circles in the United States and in some other NATO countries." (*Rabotnichesko delo*, 2 July; *FBIS*, 11 July). Faysal spoke of "the attempts of U.S. imperialists to establish a direct military presence in this region with the help of its Israeli allies" (ADN, East Berlin, 21 June; *FBIS*, 22 June). Hammami labeled "the U.S. armed intervention in Lebanon . . . a plain backslide to gunboat diplomacy" (*WMR*, June). The SCP Politburo issued a statement lauding "the great victories for the Lebanese nationalist forces, the steadfast Syrian nationalist policy, and the whole Arab liberation movement" as "a major blow to the U.S. imperialist policy in the area" (*Tishrin*, Damascus, 6 March; *FBIS*, 13 March).

The joint statement of eleven Arab communist parties supported the right of Palestinians "to return to their native land, attain self-determination and create an independent national state" and reaffirmed the PLO's "right to act as the sole legitimate representative of the Palestinian people" (*IB*, September). While calling for "solidarity with Syria" (Hammami, in *WMR*, June) and avoiding any outright criticism of its foreign policy (*The Soviet Union and the Middle East*, 10, no. 1, 1984, p. 15), the SCP and other Arab communist parties seemed to be critical of both PLO leader Yassir Arafat and Syrian interference in PLO affairs when they called for the preservation of "the unity" of the organization "on the basis of an anti-imperialist national patriotic course" (*IB*, September). Hammami also treaded gently on the subject by declaring the SCP's "regret" over "less than normal" PLO-Syrian relations (*WMR*, June).

SCP condemnations of "the terror unleashed by the Iranian authorities against Iran's [communist] Tudeh Party" (*Krasnaia zvezda*, Moscow, 4 March; *FBIS*, 7 March) provide a clearer example of differences in the attitudes of the SCP and the Syrian regime, which is aligned with Iran.

Glenn E. Perry
Indiana State University

Tunisia

Population. 7,202,000
Party. Tunisian Communist Party (Parti communiste tunisien; PCT)
Founded. 1934
Membership. 2,000 (estimated; PCT claims 4,000)
Secretary General. Muhammad Harmel
Politburo. 6 members: Muhammad Harmel, Muhammad al-Nafa'a, 'Abd al-Hamid ben Mustafa, Hisham Sakik, 'Abd al-Majid Tariki, Salah al-Hajji
Secretariat. 3 members: Muhammad Harmel, Muhammad al-Nafa'a, 'Abd al-Hamid ben Mustafa
Central Committee. 12 members
Status. Legal
Last Congress. Eighth, February 1981, in Tunis
Last Election. 1981, 0.78 percent (official figure), 15–20 percent (PCT claim), 5 percent (estimated), no representation
Auxiliary Organizations. Tunisian Communist Youth
Publications. *Al-Tarik al-Jadid* (The new path), weekly

The Tunisian Communist Party was founded in 1920 as a branch of the French Communist Party and became independent in 1934. The banning of the PCT in 1963 formalized a single-party state under the direction of the Destourian Socialist Party (PSD). In July 1981, the government lifted the ban on the PCT, ending the party's eighteen-year period of clandestine existence. The PCT was the only opposition party allowed to operate openly from July 1981 to November 1983, when President Habib Bourguiba legalized two other opposition parties (see *YICA*, 1984, p. 70).

Leadership and Party Organization. The PCT's Eighth Congress (February 1981) re-elected Muhammad Harmel as secretary general and elected a three-member Secretariat, a six-member Politburo, and a twelve-member Central Committee.

Domestic Party Affairs. Tunisia suffered a serious outbreak of domestic violence at the end of 1983 when a cabinet decision to double the price of bread and flour touched off riots throughout the country. The resultant clashes between angry demonstrators and the army and police left about 70 dead and hundreds injured during eight days of food riots that ended only in the first week of January when President Bourguiba announced the cancellation of the price increases. There are no indications that the PCT was involved in either fomenting the riots or contributing to the subsequent violence. In an interview following the riots and Bourguiba's dismissal of the minister of interior, PCT leader Muhammad Harmel called for a new national dialogue "to find a democratic convergence of all forces, both from the government and the opposition, to resolve the problems now facing the country's development." Harmel warned that the necessary sacrifices of an austerity policy must not be borne solely by Tunisia's low-income groups and added that political pluralism "must be given a new impetus in order to enable it to fulfill all its potential." (*L'Unità*, Milan, 12 January; *FBIS*, 19 January.)

Enjoying the status of a legal party, the PCT continued to operate in 1984 as a loyal opposition. The legalization of two other opposition parties in late 1983 spurred the PCT to be more active during 1984. The party signed several joint declarations with the other two parties about such national issues as the wage and price policy, the government's responsibility in the bread riots, and the political freedoms that the government should guarantee to the opposition parties, including the fundamentalist Islamic Tendency Movement. This greater activity, however, did not increase either the PCT's membership or its influence. The party remains quite weak among Tunisian youth, which may explain why a congress of Tunisian Communist Youth was held in Tunis during the summer (Moscow international service, 17 September; *FBIS*, 19 September). On 14 April, the PCT newspaper, *Al-Tarik al-Jadid*, resumed publication after being banned by the government for six months. The Arabic-language weekly was banned in October 1983 for allegedly publishing what the government termed "false information." (AFP, Paris, 14 April; *FBIS*, 16 April.)

International Views, Positions, and Activities. In March, PCT leader Muhammad Harmel visited Czechoslovakia, where he met on 8 March with Czechoslovak Politburo member and Central Committee secretary Vasil Bil'ák. The meeting involved an exchange of views on the activities of the two parties, the present international situation, and the international communist movement. The two representatives also discussed possibilities of expanding relations between the two parties. (ČETEKA, Prague, 8 March; *FBIS*, 9 March.)

In June, a PCT delegation that included Harmel, Politburo and Secretariat member Muhammad al-Nafa'a, and Central Committee member Bu Jama'a Ramili visited the Soviet Union. On 21 June, the PCT delegation met in Moscow with Boris Ponomarev, candidate member of the Politburo and secretary of the Central Committee, and Karen Brutents, deputy head of the International Department of the Central Committee. The two sides affirmed their two parties' solidarity with Syrian, Lebanese, and Palestinian victims of "U.S.-Israeli aggression" and their support for efforts to strengthen the cohesion of the Palestinian resistance movement, led by the Palestine Liberation Organization (PLO). They also supported an international conference to reach a just and durable settlement of the Arab-Israeli conflict. Finally, the two sides condemned the "aggressive strategic alliance" between the United States and Israel. (Moscow international service, 21 June; *FBIS*, 22 June.)

John Damis
Portland State University

Yemen: People's Democratic Republic of Yemen

Population. 2,147,000
Party. Yemen Socialist Party (YSP)
Founded. 1978
Membership. 26,000 (claim)
Secretary General. Ali Nasir Muhammad al-Hasani
Politburo. 10 members
Central Committee. 47 members

Status. Ruling party
Last Congress. Second Extraordinary, 12–14 October 1980
Last Election. 1978; all candidates YSP approved

Upon its independence in 1967 South Yemen, now the People's Democratic Republic of Yemen (PDRY), was ruled by the National Liberation Front, which, as a result of successive reorganizations, emerged in 1978 as a full-blown Marxist governing party, the Yemen Socialist Party, deliberately structured after the Soviet model. The People's Democratic Union, a small communist party founded in the early 1960s with membership in both North and South Yemen, still exists and enjoys official status in the PDRY, although its insignificant membership of a few hundred precludes any rivalry with the far larger YSP. Ideological differences between the two organizations are minimal.

At the grass-roots level the YSP provides guidance and indoctrination through trade unions and cooperatives, unions of youth, peasants, and women, and the Popular Defense Committees, all of which have legitimate standing under the PDRY Constitution. Coordination of policy between the party and the government apparatus is ensured at all levels by overlap of personnel. Thus, YSP leader Ali Nasir Muhammad is chairman of the People's Supreme Council (PSC: the 111-member elected legislature) and of the Presidium (the PSC's permanent standing committee) as well as chairman of the Council of Ministers. Most cabinet ministers sit at the same time on the YSP's 47-member Central Committee, of which the Politburo, enlarged in May 1984 from five to ten seats, is a key policymaking organ.

Major national decisions are decided within the party leadership, at times with the threat or use of armed force. From its inception the YSP has been divided between a "hard-line" radical wing and a relatively "moderate" pragmatic faction—a rivalry encompassing both personal ambition and ideological conviction (within the bounds of Marxist doctrine). An important point at issue is the PDRY's posture toward dissident movements in the Yemen Arab Republic (YAR: North Yemen) and Oman. Ali Nasir Muhammad has withheld material support from the rebellious National Democratic Front in the YAR and from the Dhofar insurgents in Oman. He has established something approaching normal relations with the Sultanate of Oman. This flexible policy has produced some benefits in the form of economic assistance from Saudi Arabia and other

members of the Gulf Cooperation Council (GCC); it is, however, opposed by other senior YSP figures who would prefer to lend all possible support to revolutionary elements throughout the Arabian peninsula and beyond. Four cabinet ministers, appointed to the Politburo in May, including Defense Minister Salih Muslih Qasim, reputedly belong to the militant wing. Moreover, Abd al-Fattah Ismail, the rigidly doctrinaire former chief of state, was rumored at the end of the year to be returning from exile in Moscow. These developments suggest that the internecine struggle, and inherent instability, will continue. Disunity among the party leaders may furthermore explain the absence of elections for a new PSC. The present council, elected in October 1978, held its second session in February, having already passed its term of five years set by the constitution.

Despite reports of deteriorating relations between the YAR and PDRY leaders, the Yemeni Supreme Council, established at the chief-of-state level under the unity agreement signed between the two Yemens in 1979, held its second meeting in February in Aden, and a third in Sana in December. In concluding the earlier session, the two chiefs of state expressed satisfaction with progress in issuing identity cards to citizens on both sides of the border. This permits free passage from one Yemen to the other. They also noted progress in forming the joint commercial ventures previously agreed upon. They promised to begin cooperation in the fields of scientific research and technology. The two leaders also praised the work of the joint committee set up to unify school curricula—a quite sensitive task, as the YAR continues to invoke religion as the criterion of government. The foreign affairs section of the communiqué issued at the close of the December meeting quoted Ali Nasir as calling upon all Arab states to cultivate close and friendly relations with the Soviet Union, whereas Ali Abdullah Salih, the YAR chief of state, studiously avoided any mention of this subject.

While the process of laying the institutional bases for the merger of North and South Yemen thus appeared to be progressing, the political obstacles remain very substantial. The PDRY is firmly committed to Marxist forms of government, and possible alternatives to the YSP as the locus of political leadership have been totally liquidated. On the other hand, the traditional elites in the YAR are largely intact, and important sectors of the population. notably the Zaidi tribes, could and would use armed force to forestall revolutionary change. The PDRY is oriented toward world revolution and alignment with the USSR, at some sacrifice of potential sources of economic aid. In the YAR, by contrast, there is little dissatisfaction with the neutralist posture, maintained with fair consistency since the days of the imams, which permits the country to work both sides of the global economic aid street and preserve flexibility in its external relations. The YAR is furthermore dependent for financial support upon Saudi Arabia and, to a lesser extent, the smaller GCC states, as well as upon the still considerable remittances from North Yemeni migrant workers in those countries. These are assets that no foreseeable YAR regime would jettison, however deep the sentiment that there should be a single Yemen. The PDRY constitution forthrightly asserts the YSP's claim to leadership of the entire Yemeni people, north and south. Although the YSP has some sympathizers in the North, and although some of its prominent leaders are of North Yemeni origin, the fundamental incompatibility of political outlook makes the prospect for genuine unity dim. The USSR has maintained a circumspect attitude toward the Yemeni unity movement. Obviously, its access to strategic air and naval facilities in the PDRY could be jeopardized if Yemen were unified under a regime motivated by the YAR's predilection for true nonalignment, free economic enterprise, and a relatively open society. The Soviet Union, as the YAR's principal source of arms, is well established in the South, and doubtless is reasonably content with the continuing division.

PDRY relations with the other peninsula countries remained correct, if tinged with suspicion heightened by escalation of the Iran-Iraq conflict. The GCC states found unconvincing the South Yemenis' insistence that there is no Soviet military presence on their territory (aside from instructors and technicians) and lent some discreet cooperation to American strategic preparations in the Indian Ocean region. PDRY leaders had to resort to some nimble rationalization in defending themselves against the charge that they were abandoning Arab solidarity by supporting communist Ethiopia against Arab Somalia and by joining Libya and Syria in a tilt toward the Iranian side in the Gulf war. Ali Nasir addressed these accusations in an interview published by the Kuwaiti paper *al-Siyasah* on 25 April. The Somali invasion of Ethiopia constituted aggression in international law, as confirmed by the Organization of African Unity, he said, and the PDRY's position is a "civilized" one affirming that the Arabs do not have expansionist ambitions; it furthermore serves the Arab peoples, who will not profit by being hostile to the Ethiopian revolution. Ali Nasir flatly denied any PDRY partiality in the Iraq-Iran dispute, insisting that it should be resolved by peaceful means and accusing the United States of fomenting the conflict in order to justify the introduction of its armed forces into the region. Noting that the existing differences in concepts of Arab unity constitute an obstacle to solidarity, he continued: "We favor an Arab solidarity that is based on the protection of the Arab peoples' interests and defense of their security and stability and on the restoration of their usurped rights. This means we must stand against all the hostile and capitulatory plans which the imperialist and the Zionist circles are trying to impose on our Arab peoples."

The PDRY resumed its efforts, begun the year before, to restore unity within the Palestine Liberation Organization (PLO). In February, representatives of the small left-wing components of the PLO—the Popular Front for the Liberation of Palestine, the Democratic Front for the Liberation of Palestine, and the Palestine Communist Party— were invited to Aden for discussions toward this end, along with leaders of the Lebanese and Syrian communist parties. These talks were followed by a meeting with senior leaders of Fatah. It appears likely that this initiative contributed to the successful convening of the Palestine National Council in Algiers in April. Several hundred PLO guerrillas remained in South Yemen, with full freedom to engage in military training (forbidden by some other host countries).

At midyear the USSR formally announced a set of proposals for the settlement of the Arab-Israeli dispute: evacuation of all Arab territory seized by Israel in the 1967 war and since, including East Jerusalem; the establishment of a Palestinian state under the PLO's leadership; the right to security and independence of all states in the area; peace between Israel and its Arab neighbors; and the convening of a conference under U.N. auspices to achieve these objectives, to include Israel, the Arab states contiguous to Israel, the USSR, the United States, and other participants as agreed upon. Ali Nasir promptly endorsed these proposals, adding a warning to the imperialists against using the mining of shipping lanes in the Red Sea, then occurring, as a pretext for interference in the internal affairs of the peoples of the region and for justifying the American military presence.

On the broader international scene the PDRY continued its assiduous cultivation of relations with the Soviet Union and other socialist countries in a variety of fields, including interparty cooperation, technology, economic development, propaganda, and military and cultural affairs.

In March a Soviet trade delegation visited Aden to negotiate the annual renewal of the USSR-PDRY agreement on the exchange of commodities. In May the PDRY followed the Soviet lead by joining the boycott of the Los Angeles Olympics; its announcement referred to the United States' hostile campaign against Soviet and other athletes, thus endangering their safety, and to the commercialization of the games. In August Defense Minister Salih Muslih visited Moscow, conferred with Defense Minister Dimitri Ustinov, and signed an agreement for the USSR to augment the PDRY's naval capability with torpedoes, minesweepers, and shore-to-sea radar. In the same month the Soviets agreed to conduct a geological survey of goldfields in Hadramawt province. In November a delegation of the Soviet-Yemeni Friendship Association in the USSR arrived in Aden to participate in the celebration of Soviet-Yemeni Friendship Week.

The major event of the year, however, was the state visit of Ali Nasir Muhammad to Moscow beginning 1 October, near the fifth anniversary of the signing of the Treaty of Friendship and Cooperation between the USSR and the PDRY. Aden Radio set the scene with a detailed review of Soviet-Yemeni cooperation, expressions of appreciation for the marked increase in the scale of Soviet aid to the PDRY in 1984, and shrill diatribes against American "terrorism, blackmail, plots, and aggres-sion." Ali Nasir met with Konstantin Chernenko and other senior Soviet figures. The Standing Committee on Economic and Technical Cooperation between the USSR and the PDRY convened during the visit to complete its discussion of the 1985 Soviet contribution to South Yemen's development program, and a protocol was signed on the subject.

Ali Nasir's Moscow visit was preceded by an official visit to Bulgaria and followed by similar trips to North Korea and the Mongolian People's Republic. In November he visited Poland and the German Democratic Republic. In all of these capitals bilateral agreements were announced providing for expanded mutual cooperation, including development assistance to the PDRY, trade, and the strengthening of party ties. The joint communiqué issued at the conclusion of each visit faithfully reflected the Soviet Union's current preoccupations in world affairs: the expansion of the United States' nuclear arms capability and the resultant endangering of world peace; the stationing of U.S. missiles in Western Europe; the continuing Israeli occupation of Lebanon, with American acquiescence; the proper approach to an Arab-Israeli settlement; and the American military buildup in the Indian Ocean–Persian Gulf region.

A novel feature of the visit to Mongolia was a call issued by the PDRY leader for a summit conference of the states of the Arabian peninsula, the Persian Gulf, the Horn of Africa, and "other interested parties" to coordinate the struggle against imperialism, Zionism, and racism; liquidate imperialist military bases; and promote nonintervention in the internal affairs of the region's states and respect for their independence.

Robert W. Stookey
The University of Texas at Austin

WESTERN EUROPE

Introduction

Since the electoral victory of the French Socialists and the French Communists in France in 1981, political observers have been asking, "Where is Western Europe going?" In November 1982 the *World Marxist Review* concluded that "the ideas advanced by Europe's communists meet the innermost interests of peoples."

Throughout 1983 and 1984, however, it became clearer that the ideas of Western Europe's communist parties were not meeting "innermost interests." Indeed, by the end of 1984 Western Europe's communist parties not only found themselves in disorder, but those of France, Italy, and Spain—the leaders of the Eurocommunist movement—all experienced upheaval. In France the communist party resigned from the French cabinet and officially became an opponent of François Mitterrand's Socialist Party. In Italy the party leadership changed hands for the first time since 1972 as a result of the death of Enrico Berlinguer; the party has been without a new program since it left the Italian government in 1979. In Spain party factionalism continued, a second Spanish communist party was established, and the communist movement in Spain became an inconsequential force.

These developments sent a clear message during the year: that the countries of Western Europe are not choosing to follow communist ideology, whether of a traditional or of a Eurocommunist vintage. This point was illustrated most dramatically in the June elections to the European Parliament. In 1979 communist parties had garnered 48 seats, but five years later they won only 42 seats (a decline of 12.5 percent). Indeed, only four of Western Europe's communist parties are represented at all (Italy, 27 seats; France, 10 seats; Greece, 4 seats; Denmark, 1 seat).

The obvious question, in view of these developments, is Where are Western Europe's communist parties going? The answer may be found in the events that have transpired since the communist parties of France, Italy, and Spain first jointly espoused an independent path from the Communist Party of the Soviet Union (CPSU) in 1977 and embarked on the road toward socialism in nationalist and independent colors.

When the parties of France, Italy, and Spain selected Eurocommunism as the vehicle to travel paths independent of doctrinaire Marxism-Leninism, they also obligated themselves to redefine their goals; in other words, something had to be substituted for adherence to the direction provided by the CPSU. In the course of the past several years, they have been unable to do so in a systematic fashion. The consequence, in 1984, was electoral weakness, party factionalism, and in some cases—and very possibly in more cases in the future—a return to allegiance to the primary role of the CPSU and, thus, a return to the very dogmatism and ideological rigidity rejected as incommensurate with the goal of serving as a legitimate actor in the parliamentary life of Western Europe.

Western Europe's communist parties have been unable to present viable solutions for the myriad of economic problems confronting the continent. Thus, while the concept of Eurocommunism successfully challenged the monolithic approach presented by the CPSU and rejected the interference of one country in the internal affairs of another, it required more than simply rejection of the CPSU's leadership role. It required the development of new leadership. This has not taken place. What has occurred is that a concept devoid of positive substance has yielded to pragmatism.

Western Europe's socialists, who embraced the spirit of Eurocommunism, are returning to "a revival of nationalism or at least a sense of national dignity, which calls out for a more assertive role in world affairs" (see John Darnton, "Ideology Yields to Pragmatism for Socialists," *NYT*, 20 Novevmber 1983). What this means in practice is the introduction of economic principles that work in reality, as well as on paper, such as government policies that encourage free enterprise, limit government spending, endorse market competition, counter trade deficits, curb inflation, reduce unemployment, and lead to the conclusion that to build socialism means building a strong economy (see Paul Lewis, "Socialists Forced to Use Economics of the Right," *NYT*, 1 December 1983). In other words, the "class struggle" has become a question of what constitutes sound economic policy as opposed to the promises of a better life through ideology.

In 1984 Western Europe as a whole faced economic problems of major importance. They received primary attention. Solutions to them did not lend themselves to self-serving rhetoric consisting of communist party assertions that the future of Western Europe would depend on "the cohesion of the working class, unity of action of the political parties representing it, and joint efforts to bar reaction, defend democratic achievements and open new prospects for social progress" (*WMR*, November 1982). Communist party programs failed to achieve the "unity of action" necessary to provide solutions to economic questions; if, indeed, "unity of action" could provide any kind of solution to real problems. As a result 1984 was witness to further erosion of communist party influence in Western Europe, as had been the case during 1983.

Emphasis on "peace," "disarmament," and "détente," as well as on the establishment of socialism in nationalist colors, was appealing. Demonstrations against the deployment of new nuclear missiles in the NATO defense force in Western Europe were well attended. But while the "peace movement" did represent a laudable goal, which could be shared by all peoples, the "peace movement" could not explain why the Soviet government was developing the most powerful military arsenal in its history. Nor could it explain why the Soviet government had left the negotiating table in Geneva in early 1984, only to return at the beginning of 1985, following the re-election of Ronald Reagan as president of the United States of America. Thus, the inability to transform political slogans into political reality, also contributed to the general disarray in which Western Europe's communist parties found themselves at the end of 1984.

During 1984, as had been the case during 1982 and 1983, diminishing popularity and party strife within Western Europe's communist parties produced the conclusion that their decline "seems irreversible" because of "their incapacity to propose solutions acceptable to the societies in which they operate" (Alberto Jacoviello, *WSJ*, 24 March 1982). What this meant, in 1982, and what it has continued to mean in 1983 and 1984, is that the traditional Marxist-Leninist "ideology" has not provided solutions for difficulties confronting the continent's industrialized countries.

During the late 1970s the communist parties sought to convince voters in Western Europe that they did endorse pluralism, that they respected the autonomy and independence of each political party participating in the democratic process, that they rejected the authoritarian ideology of Marxist-Leninist doctrine, and that each country must follow its own individual path to socialism. Yet, in the mid-1980s there are indications, in France and in Spain, for example, that strong elements within the communist parties in these two countries favor a return to the very Marxist-Leninist, pro-Soviet views that they espoused prior to the introduction of Eurocommunism. If this is the case, the future of Western Europe's communist parties is a dismal one.

This latter development does not reflect a "crisis of communist ideology" nearly as much as it illustrates a strategy that has failed to give Western Europe's communist parties significant influence over the domestic and foreign affairs of their respective countries. There is one notable exception to this conclusion, and that is the Italian Communist Party (PCI). The PCI still has the loyalty of almost one-third of the Italian electorate. How the PCI conducts itself and how it formulates its policies in the future under new leadership may well foreshadow the decline or ascendancy of Western Europe's communist parties for the remainder of this decade.

Communist party activity elsewhere in Western Europe, as in West Germany, in Denmark, or in Scandinavia, for example, continues to warrant careful observation. But the key to communist party success in the future remains vested with the parties of France, Italy, and Spain. In the past these three parties have been much more successful in their attempts to reaffirm their respective independence in the face of Soviet attempts to assert the CPSU's authority in the international communist movement than they have in their efforts to adapt their party structures to political competition in a democratic society. The remainder of this decade will witness their success or failure.

In 1984, 14 of Western Europe's 23 parties were represented in their respective parliaments: those of Belgium, Cyprus, Finland, France, Greece, Iceland, Italy, Luxembourg, the Netherlands, Portugal, San Marino, Spain, Sweden, and Switzerland (the communist party is not represented in the legislatures of Austria, Denmark, Great Britain, Ireland, Malta, Norway, Turkey, West Berlin, and West Germany). In 1984, party members no longer held cabinet posts in Iceland, Finland, or France.

National elections were held during the year in one Western European country (ten held elections in 1983). That country was Denmark, and the communist party received 0.7 percent of the vote (1983: 1.1 percent). The Italian Communist Party remains the strongest in Western Europe, and the party holds slightly less than one-third of the parliamentary seats (198 of 630). Of the parties with legislative representation, Cyprus had the highest percentage of seats (34.29 percent), followed by Italy (31.43 percent), San Marino (25 percent), Portugal (17.6 percent), Iceland (16.66 percent), France (13.5 percent), and Finland (13.5 percent). The remaining parties held between 5.73 percent (Sweden) and 0.5 percent (Switzerland) of their respective parliamentary seats.

The views and positions of the French Communist Party (PCF) provide the best illustration of the problems confronting the communist parties of Western Europe. In 1981, the French national elections established François Mitterrand's Socialist Party (PS) as the most powerful political party in the country. As a result of an electoral coalition, the PCF was given four ministerial posts in the cabinet: Transport, Civil Service and Administrative Reform, Health, and Vocational Training (in 1983 the Ministries of Health and of Civil Service and Administrative Reform were reduced to sub-cabinet-level positions, but were still occupied by members of the PCF). These appointments were made on the basis of an agreement between both parties that required the PCF to pledge "entire solidarity" at all levels of government. In 1981, the CPSU endorsed this development as "an historic event for France and all Western Europe (*Guardian*, London, 5 July 1981). The results of the French election meant, according to French political analyst Jean-François Revel, that "Marxism had won" and that "government by ideology" had returned to France (*Public Opinion*, August/September 1981).

The electoral victory of 1981, however, did not turn into political success. On the contrary, the French government's domestic policies of the past three years have been marked by growing inflation, devaluation of the French franc, nationalization of major French banks and industries, and changes in tax policy aimed at a small minority, based on a rationale that is punitive by design and has proved to be economically unsound. In addition, the continuing growth of Soviet military power has elicited a response from the French government that is highly critical of Soviet foreign policy and very supportive of American foreign policy initiatives.

Since 1981 the PCF, as a participant in the Mitterrand government, has faced an increasingly frustrating political dilemma: that of remaining a loyal member of the PS-led government while maintaining sufficient independence from that party to preserve its own position as a separate and viable force on the left. During 1983 the PCF shared massive electoral losses with the PS in French municipal elections. At the same time, however, the party continued to assert its own views on a variety of controversial issues, even if these positions conflicted with official government policy.

The inevitable consequence was increasing uncertainty among PCF members concerning the party's actual positions. By the end of 1983 this had led to a decrease in membership, to a decline in the readership of *L'Humanité* (the party daily), and to a general malaise in the party as a whole. The defeat in the municipal elections of 1983, unprecedented since 1945, resulted in the loss of control of fifteen cities with populations in excess of 100,000 persons, including such long-held mayoralties as St.-Etienne and Nîmes.

At the beginning of 1984, the PCF faced a quandary, but it made a decision that may well mark a turning point in the history of the PCF. The year was marked by the party's worst electoral defeat in 60 years. The PCF obtained only 11.28 percent of the vote in the elections to the European Parliament in June. This disastrous result demonstrated the magnitude of the PCF's continuing slippage in popular support (in the early years of the Fourth Republic the PCF had been the largest party in France, with over 25 percent of the vote; in the national elections of 1981 the party received 15.5 percent of the vote).

The electoral defeat, however, served as a catalyst in the party's attempt to resolve the dilemma with which it had been living since 1981. The PCF was reluctant to return to a self-imposed political isolation that would leave the PS as the only large governing force on the left and perhaps erode even further the PCF's narrowing base of popularity. At the same time, the PCF did not wish to be held accountable in the eyes of its constituents for the failure of the PS/PCF coalition to fulfill the promises made in 1981. The party's dilemma was compounded by its lack of policymaking influence even though it had four members in cabinet or subcabinet posts under Prime Minister Pierre Mauroy.

Thus, when President Mitterrand dismissed the Mauroy cabinet and appointed Laurent Fabius as the new prime minister in July, the PCF took this opportunity to withdraw from the cabinet, enter the opposition, and in effect terminate the Union of the Left, thus ending the electoral coalition of 1981. These events initiated new controversies within the party, with serious debates taking place at all levels of the party hierarchy concerning the PCF's basic domestic and foreign policy orientation. In the months that followed, the party leadership emphasized that it would continue to endorse socialism in French colors, independent of the CPSU. But, as the year ended, questions arose concerning the ability of Georges Marchais, the PCF secretary general, to maintain his leadership position. Future control of the PCF would be of concern at the party's Twenty-fifth Congress, scheduled for 6–10 February 1985, as would the question of the party's future direction.

The Italian Communist Party (PCI), although not represented in the Italian government, holds 198 of 630 parliamentary seats (the PCI won 29.9 percent of the vote in the national elections of 1983). This electoral strength was demonstrated once again in 1984 in the election for the European Parliament, in which the PCI garnered 33.3 percent of the vote to win 27 seats.

The year was marked by the death of Secretary General Enrico Berlinguer in June. Berlinguer, who succeeded Luigi Longo as secretary general in 1972, played the principal role in developing the Italian form of Eurocommunism. It was under his leadership that the PCI gradually asserted its autonomy vis-à-vis the Soviet Union and re-established relations with the Chinese Communist Party. In rejecting the dictates of the CPSU as inappropriate for Italian communism, Berlinguer made the position of the PCI very clear at the Twenty-fifth Congress of the CPSU in 1976: "Socialist society must be built through the contribution of different parties in a pluralistic and democratic system" (*WSJ*, 14 June).

Berlinguer's direction resulted in the "historic compromise," which allowed the development of a coalition with the Christian Democratic Party (DC) and other political groups. This policy led the PCI to support the DC cabinet from 1976 until 1979, even though the party held no cabinet posts. Following the dissolution of the historic compromise, Berlinguer endorsed a policy of the "democratic alternative," which embraced alliance with the Socialists and other groups of the center-left, but which no longer endorsed participation in the Italian government.

Alessandro Natta, the 66-year-old chairman of the Central Control Commission of the PCI, was elected Berlinguer's successor as secretary general (he has been a member of the Italian parliament continuously since 1948). Whether his election is permanent will undoubtedly be a matter on the agenda of the next party congress, which will presumably be held sometime in 1985. The next congress will also address the issue of the future direction of the PCI. The importance of this direction for the future of the PCI and of Italian politics is self-evident. It is also of importance to the Soviet Union, which was well illustrated by the seniority of the Soviet delegation attending Berlinguer's funeral. The delegation was headed by M. S. Gorbachev, member of the Politburo and secretary of the Central Committee of the CPSU.

During 1984 the party remained in opposition at the national level, while sharing governmental responsibility in many regions, large cities, and municipalities. The PCI was generally critical of the Italian government's economic and social policies. Two internal developments were of significance. The PCI continues to be plagued by a cumulative deficit of almost 23 billion lire (equal to approximately one-fourth of the party's income for the year) and by a serious decline in membership in the Communist Youth Federation (FGCI). (In the early 1970s the FGCI had almost 500,000 members. By 1977 membership had declined to approximately 127,000, and in 1984 that number was less than 50,000.)

Throughout the year, major attention was devoted to the "peace movement," but the PCI endorsed the positions neither of the Soviet Union nor of the United States. The PCI urged both countries not to deploy nuclear weapons in Europe and to resume arms control negotiations. With respect to the deployment of U.S. missiles in Sicily, the PCI called for a national referendum on "the escalation of nuclear missiles in Italy" (ANSA, 27 March). Views and positions on other foreign policy issues concerned condemnation of the Soviet presence in Afghanistan, support for withdrawal of Italian troops stationed in Lebanon, support for Andrei Sakharov and criticism of the conditions under which he was being forced to live: "Anyone can agree or disagree with Sakharov's ideas . . . but one cannot fail to protest certain methods that constitute a violation not only of the most basic human freedoms but of common sense" (*L'Unità*, 22 May).

What emphasis the PCI will give domestic and foreign policies in 1985 is not evident at this time and will probably remain vague until it is absolutely clear that the party's leadership is stable. It is a logical conclusion that the PCI will continue to follow its own path toward socialism; the question is what direction that path will take in the future.

The Spanish Communist Party (PCE) was legalized in 1977 and during the succeeding four years became a principal advocate of Eurocommunism under the leadership of Santiago Carrillo. The resignation of Carrillo in 1982 was followed by the election of Gerardo Iglesias (then 37 years old) as secretary general. His first priority during 1983 was to heal the rifts within the party and to re-establish its influence in Spanish politics; he was re-elected head of the party for the three-year period 1984–1986 at the party's Eleventh Congress in December 1983.

As 1984 began, the PCE required a major rebuilding effort. It faced the formidable task of regaining the support of the Spanish electorate at a time when Spain, despite continued terrorist activity, was remarkably stable and was ruled by a socialist government. In addition, the PCE continued to hold only 4 seats in the Spanish Cortes, having lost 19 of its 23 seats in the 1982 national election. Thus, the party was not in a strong position at the beginning of the year.

The views and positions of the PCE reflected the party's weak position in Spain and did not serve to increase significantly the party's popularity or membership (party membership was estimated at 80,000 in 1984, a decline from 240,000 in 1977). Party strife continued, focusing on two rival factions within the PCE who supported Iglesias and Carrillo respectively. In addition, in January pro-Soviet dissidents who had earlier resigned or who had been expelled from the PCE formed the rival Communist Party (PC). It is led by Ignacio Gallego, a member of the PCE Executive Committee for nearly three decades.

Throughout the year the PCE criticized Spain's socialists for allegedly abandoning their goal of "real change," but at the same time declared that the real enemy was the "right" and not the ruling Spanish Socialist Workers' Party. Indeed, Iglesias called for a "wide electoral front" for the next general elections (1986). It was left unclear whether the PCE would seek an electoral coalition with the Socialist Workers' Party, but this possibility was not rejected. The PCE did stress, however, its intention to pursue domestic and foreign policy positions independent of any foreign interference. In this regard, the creation of the rival PC in January 1984 plagued the PCE throughout the year, not only because the PC received clear support from the CPSU but also because this split perpetuated and intensified the divisions of opinion among the left. It ensured that the Spanish left would continue to exert minimal impact on the country's political life and also that the internecine dissension of 1984 would continue.

The Portuguese Communist Party (PCP), led by Álvaro Cunhal, is pro-Soviet in orientation. The party dominates the communist movement in Portugal and, while considerably less influential than it was at the time of the aborted coup of 1976, still exercises significant influence over Portuguese political affairs. In recent years the majority of the radical-left groups, which thrived following 1974, have dissolved, while membership in the PCP has grown from approximately 115,000 in 1976 to an estimated 200,000 in 1984. The PCP, in addition to exercising significant control over the nation's labor movement, also occupies 44 of the 250 seats in the Portuguese parliament.

Following the 1983 national elections, the Socialist Party of Prime Minister Mário Soares rejected the PCP's offer to form a coalition government. During 1984 the PCP abandoned any effort to engage in "dialogue" with the Socialist government and called instead for its replacement by a "government of national salvation." Party leader Cunhal rejected claims that economic problems were the consequence of the impact of nationalization, land reform, and labor legislation implemented following the 1974 revolution and charged that the real cause lay in the systematic dismantling of those "advances," attempts to impose a totalitarian state, and Portugal's increasing "dependence" on American imperialism.

In Cyprus, Greece, Malta, San Marino, and Turkey, communist party strength did not result in significant influence on the domestic and foreign policies of these countries. In San Marino the communist party occupies 15 of 60 parliamentary seats and participates in that country's coalition government. The Communist Party of Malta (CPM) was established in 1969 and exerts minimal impact on that country's political life. The CPM did not participate in the most recent national elections held in 1981. CPM members attended numerous communist party congresses in Europe and elsewhere and also received an unusually large number of representatives from fraternal parties throughout Europe, which may suggest an increasing interest in Maltese affairs within the international communist movement. In Turkey, the communist party remains proscribed. The communist party of Cyprus (AKEL) finds its strongest representation among the Greek Cypriot majority, which comprises approximately 80 percent of the island's estimated population of 662,000. The AKEL has enjoyed legal status since the formal creation of the Republic of Cyprus in 1960 and claims a party membership of approximately 14,000. It is the island's strongest political party, although the AKEL is proscribed in the "Turkish Republic of Cyprus."

Since the last national election (1981), in which the AKEL received 12 of the 35 Greek Cypriot seats in the island's parliament, the party has followed a policy of cooperation with the Cypriot government. As a result of disputes with President Spyros Kyprianou concerning the future of the island, this policy was terminated in December. The issue that engendered the greatest controversy concerned an eventual federal union of the Greek and Turkish parts of the island. Discussions to be held under the auspices of the United Nations were scheduled for 1985, and the AKEL indicated clearly that it would continue to oppose the "partitioning of our island."

In Greece, the party remains split into pro-Soviet and Eurocommunist factions. In the Greek parliament, the pro-Soviet faction of the party (KKE) holds 13 of 300 seats (1981); KKE membership is estimated at 42,000. The KKE, originally established in 1921, was proscribed from 1947 until 1974. During the military government in Greece (1967–1974), the KKE split into two factions. The Eurocommunist faction, known as KKE-Interior, has maintained policy positions much more independent of the CPSU.

The KKE's views and positions on questions of domestic and foreign policy often parallel those of the ruling Panhellenic Socialist Movement (PASOK), established by Andreas Papandreou in 1974. The KKE-Interior failed to win a seat in the national elections held in 1981, while PASOK received 48 percent of the vote, elected 166 deputies, and formed the first socialist government in Greek history. In the June elections to the European Parliament, PASOK received 41.6 percent of the vote, the KKE 11.6 percent, and KKE-Interior 3.4 percent. While these elections were not to the Greek parliament, they nevertheless reflected growing support for the KKE-Interior. How the two factions will fare in 1985 is uncertain, but it is very clear that Papandreou's government is declining in popularity. This development (and the Greek elections in 1985) may explain, in part, PASOK's condemnation of the United States as "an imperialist power" and its praise of the Soviet Union as "a force against imperialism and capitalism" (see *NYT*, 12 May).

In Ireland the party (CPI) maintains a low profile and does not exert a significant political influence. The CPI advocates a united and socialist Ireland and views the government of the United Kingdom as responsible for the division. The Communist Party of Great Britain (CPGB) has not been represented in the House of Commons since 1950; Lord Milford is the sole CPGB member of the House of Lords. Party membership, at approximately 16,000, is at its lowest point since World War II, but CPGB influence in Great Britain's trade union movement is significant. There are two members of the CPGB on the 38-member General Council of the Trades Union Congress (Mick McGahey of the National Union of Mineworkers and Ken Gill of the Technical and Supervisory Section of the Amalgamated Union of Engineering Workers). Throughout the year a rift within the party continued between the Eurocommunist-inclined leadership and a pro-Stalinist faction. The dispute centered on the party's program, "The British Road to Socialism." In early 1985 the pro-Stalinist editor of the party newspaper was removed from his position by the Executive Committee of the CPGB. It is unclear how this dispute will be resolved; but a major step will undoubtedly be taken at the next party congress, scheduled for 18–20 May 1985.

Developments of major significance were not recorded in the activities of the communist parties of Belgium, Denmark, the Netherlands, and Luxembourg. The party in Luxembourg (CPL) played a minor role in political affairs, and its organizational structure remains in the hands of the Urbany family. The party's Twenty-fourth Congress, held in February, did not produce dramatic changes, but did stress the party's position of "social equality" in a "peaceful and democratic Luxembourg."

The internal dissension that plagued the Communist Party of Denmark (DKP) during 1982 and 1983 continued during 1984. Throughout 1984 the DKP played an insignificant role in Danish politics, while the country was governed by a four-party coalition enjoying a one-vote majority in parliament. For the past 25 years the DKP has competed with other Marxist parties to the left of the Social Democratic Party in Denmark. Since the beginning of the 1970s these leftist parties have normally captured an eighth of the national vote. In January 1984, they collectively polled 14.9 percent, but the DKP's popularity, with 0.7 percent (its worst showing in postwar history), continued to plummet. As a consequence of declining influence, the party has announced its intention to focus its efforts during 1985 on recruitment of new members and on strengthening the party's financial base.

The Communist Party of the Netherlands (CPN) holds 3 of 150 seats in parliament and plays a minor role in the politics of the Netherlands. During the year the CPN adopted its first new program since the end of World War II at an extraordinary congress held in February. The initial significance of this program reflects the result of a compromise between party factions endorsing an independent path to socialism and the traditional Marxist-Leninist position. As a consequence, a split within the CPN has been avoided, for the present. A small group of orthodox Marxist-Leninists did form the Alliance of Communists in the Netherlands at the end of February; however, it remains doubtful whether this group will be able to challenge the CPN successfully.

During 1985 the future direction of the CPN will be intensely debated within the party. The outcome of this debate is fundamental to the future of the party. It is also significant in another respect, for in many ways, it mirrors similar debates occurring within other communist parties of Western Europe. The lines of struggle are clear. They separate those members of the party who adhere to the direction provided by the CPSU, are pro-Soviet in orientation, and reject the idea of independent paths to socialism and those members who assert that the CPN will be unable to occupy a legitimate and viable role in a democratic society unless it subscribes to the rules of parliamentary democracy.

In Belgium, the communist party (PCB) holds 2 of 212 parliamentary seats, but does not play a significant role in Belgian political affairs. National elections are scheduled to be held in 1985, and the PCB will participate in the electoral process. At the party's Twenty-fourth Congress in 1982 the PCB sought to redefine its program to give the party an image of greater independence from the CPSU. Since that time, the PCB has been critical of the Soviet presence in Afghanistan and of martial law in Poland and has re-established contact with the government of the People's Republic of China.

In the Nordic countries of Iceland, Norway, Sweden, and Finland, no developments of political significance were registered. The factional strife that characterizes the Finnish Communist Party (SKP) and between the SKP and its electoral front, the Finnish People's Democratic League (SKDL), continues unabated. The SKDL experienced its worst electoral defeat in its history in 1983; the year 1984 did not bring improvement. The factional strife within the SKP produced a major split at the party's Twentieth Congress in May. Significant ideological differences within the party developed in the 1960s and became more pronounced in the following decade. The more moderate, majority wing of the SKP was part of the governing coalition in Finland between 1975 and 1982, while the Stalinist minority was in opposition. The tensions between the two wings of the party sharpened further when the veteran moderate leader of the SKP, Aarne Saarinen, gave up the party leadership in 1982 and was succeeded as chairman by Juoko Kajonoja. The latter promised to unify the two wings of the party, but his rigid adherence to the CPSU had the opposite effect.

In preparation for the party's congress, the chairman of the SKDL announced that the group would organize itself into an independent party if the SKP remained in the hands of the Stalinists. In addition, representatives of the CPSU indicated that the SKP should take every step to avoid a major division. In the end, Arvo Aalto, representing the moderate faction of the party, was elected the new chairman, and no pro-Soviet members would agree to serve on the Politburo and on the Central Committee. An extraordinary party congress has been scheduled for March 1985, but it appears unlikely that the "unity" the party seeks can be achieved.

The communist party of Iceland (AB) remains the third largest of six parties represented in the parliament, holding 10 of 60 seats. Following its loss of three cabinet posts in 1983 (social and health affairs; finance; industry), the AB became the largest opposition party in Iceland in 1984. The recent electoral decline of the AB can be explained, in part, by its participation in a coalition government forced to take unpopular economic measures in an economy experiencing an inflation rate of 159 percent at its peak in 1983. By the beginning of 1984, however, that rate had been reduced to 9 percent as a consequence of the economic policies of the nonsocialist government of Progressive Party leader Steingrimur Hermansson. In the area of foreign affairs, the party continues its opposition to membership in NATO and to modernization of the NATO military bases at Keflavik. In view of Iceland's economic problems, however, as well as the AB's declining popularity, it is not expected that the party will play an active role in Icelandic political affairs in 1985.

In Norway, the communist party (NKP) is not represented in the country's parliament and continues to play a minimal role in Norwegian politics. The internal disputes that plagued the NKP since 1975 continued to affect adversely the party's strength through 1983. During 1984, however, the NKP leadership endorsed efforts to form a broad united front of leftist parties in Norway. While parliamentary elections have not been held since 1981, the establishment of "unity of action" within the Norwegian labor movement could affect Norwegian electoral politics in the future. The NKP continues to be, however, one of the weakest communist parties in Western Europe, and any resurgence in popularity is likely to take a long period of time. The year concluded with a major split within the party concerning its leadership. It is likely that this rift will continue in 1985, and it may result in an extraordinary NKP congress in the spring of 1985.

In Sweden, the Left Party Communists (VPK) holds 20 of 349 parliamentary seats, but is not represented in the Swedish government. The party projects a Marxist image, even though it has disassociated itself from Moscow and is generally regarded as one of the more moderate Western European communist parties. According to a Swedish public opinion poll taken in April, the combined support for the ruling Social Democratic Party and the VKP is slightly larger than that for the nonsocialist parties (49 to 48.5 percent); however, it is unclear how well the VPK will fare in the national elections scheduled for 1985. (In the most recent national election, held in 1982, the VPK received 5.6 percent of the vote.)

The communist parties of Austria (KPO) and Switzerland (PdAS) exerted negligible influence on political affairs during the year. In the most recent national elections (1983) the KPO received only 0.66 percent of the vote and no representation in parliament. The most significant event of the year was the Twenty-fifth Congress in January, at which the principal subject of discussion was the weakness of the party in Austrian political life. The party's leader, as a consequence, urged his comrades to recall that the KPO originated "because the working class needed it" and to rededicate themselves to serving the needs of the workers. As in Austria, the communist party in Switzerland suffered an electoral defeat in 1983; it holds only 1 of the 200 Swiss parliamentary seats. In both countries the strength of the so-called Green parties outweighs that of the traditional communist parties. During 1985 it is unlikely that either party will experience significant increases in party strength or influence. As in the past both parties may be expected to endorse the "peace movement" and extol the policies of the Soviet government as major contributions toward the maintenance of peace.

The communist party of West Berlin (SEW) does not exert any significant influence on the political and economic life of that city. It enjoys no representation in the West Berlin parliament (the SEW received 0.7 percent of the vote in 1981). The party is pro-Soviet in orientation and reflects the views and positions of its counterpart in the German Democratic Republic. No leadership changes were reported during the year. The party competes with a number of leftist groups in the city, but the SEW's activities attract little support from a population living in a city isolated by the Berlin Wall and by the minefields dividing the Western sectors of the city from East Germany. Despite the SEW's efforts to form a "coalition against the right" for the city's municipal election in March 1985, the party's electoral performance is unlikely to improve.

The German Communist Party (DKP) is pro-Soviet and operates within a highly structured organizational framework. It is not represented in the West German parliament and received 0.2 percent of the vote in the national elections held in 1983. In January the DKP held its Seventh Congress, with the theme:

"Peace must win. Jobs, not missiles!" Endorsement of the "peace movement" and opposition to the deployment of nuclear missiles were recurring themes throughout the year, as was the necessity to achieve "unity of action" among the "working class." In addition, a new campaign for the recruitment of new party members was announced. It is estimated that the DKP receives an annual subvention of 60 million marks from the East German communist party (SED), and it is important to note in this connection that no other communist party in Western Europe is as strictly controlled by a foreign party as the DKP is by the SED. This control is unlikely to alter significantly during 1985, and the views and positions of the DKP should continue to mirror those of the SED.

Dennis L. Bark
Hoover Institution

Austria

Population. 7,579,000
Party. Communist Party of Austria (Kommunistische Partei Österreichs; KPO)
Founded. 3 November 1918
Membership. 12,000 (reported by *Profil*, Vienna, 7 November 1983)
Party Chairman. Franz Muhri (b. 1924; previously reported, in error, as 1921)
Politburo. 12 members: Michael Graber (editor of *Volksstimme*), Franz Hager, Anton Hofer, Hans Kalt (secretary of Central Committee), Gustav Loistl, Franz Muhri, Otto Podolsky (Vienna party secretary), Karl Reiter, Erwin Scharf (editor of *Weg und Ziel*), Irma Schwager, Walter Silbermayr, Ernst Wimmer
Secretariat. 3 members: Hans Kalt, Karl Reiter, Walter Silbermayr
Central Committee. 64 members
Status. Legal
Last Congress. Twenty-fifth, 13–15 January 1984, in Vienna
Last Election. Federal, 24 April 1984, 0.66 percent, no representation
Publications. *Volksstimme* (People's voice), KPO daily organ, Vienna; *Weg und Ziel* (Path and goal), KPO theoretical monthly, Vienna

Five elections took place in 1984: provincial elections in Salzburg, Tirol, Carinthia, and Vorarlberg, and elections to the governing body of the Chamber of Labor (labor's official representative body, with compulsory membership; *not* the Trade Union Congress). Results in Salzburg (*Arbeiter-Zeitung*, 25 March) and Tirol (*Presse*, 17 June) were similar. In both provinces, the conservative People's Party gained at the expense of the Socialist and Freedom parties, who form the federal coalition, with the Green groups doing rather poorly. While the KPO's vote share rose from 0.6 to 0.7 percent in the city of Salzburg, its share in Tirol remained at 0.4 percent (*Arbeiter-Zeitung*, 26 March; *Presse*, 18 June; *Wiener Zeitung*, 19 June). Results in Carinthia (*Wiener Zeitung*, 30 September) were different. Here, only the third-place Freedom Party gained, while the KPO vote decreased from 1.0 to 0.8

percent (ibid., 2 October). The Vorarlberg election of 21 October brought a sensational success for the Greens (13 percent) at the expense of all parties. The KPO vote decreased from 1.0 to 0.9 percent, with sharper declines in three of the four major cities (*Arbeiter-Zeitung*, 22 October).

Of greatest interest to the KPO were the elections to the Chamber of Labor, held on several days in early April. While in general the Socialists lost massively (ca. 6 percent) to the Catholic trade union group, in the case of the transport workers some of these losses benefited the KPO. Overall, the KPO vote share increased from 1.2 to 1.4 percent, giving its Left Bloc 5 of the 840 seats, an increase of one. The Left Bloc's vote share among workers remained at 1.3 percent; among white-collar employees at 0.9 percent. Among transport workers, the communist vote share doubled, from 1.5 to 3.1 percent, the first more or less spectacular KPO success in many years. (Ibid., 7 April.)

Leadership and Party Organization. The central event of 1984 for the KPO was its Twenty-fifth Congress, held in Vienna on 13–15 January. The congress was attended by 369 delegates and twelve foreign delegations with a total of 24 members. Twelve additional parties sent fraternal greetings. The senior guest was Nikolai I. Ryzhkov, secretary of the Soviet Central Committee. The other eleven delegations came from Bulgaria, Poland, Hungary, Romania, France, East Germany, Yugoslavia, Czechoslovakia, Italy, West Germany, and Switzerland.

The main organizational change was the replacement of one member of the Politburo (much of the information about party organization is derived from confidential Austrian sources). Otto Podolsky (47 years old), the Viennese party secretary, replaced Franz Karger (66). This brought the Politburo's average age down from 57 to 56 years (versus 54 years at the Twenty-fourth Congress in 1980). In a party used to an elderly leadership, the average ages for the Control Commission (72), the Arbitration Commission (67), and the Finance Committee (61) are hardly surprising. What is surprising is the average age of 50 years for the Secretariat and for the 54 of the 64 members of the Central Committee whose age was reported. No member of the Central Committee is above 69 years. Only six of the members are women (one each on the Politburo and the Arbitration Commission). Franz Muhri, now 59, was unanimously re-elected party chairman. Interesting is the age breakdown of the new Central

Committee: 60–69, 22 percent; 50–59, 27 percent; 40–49, 13 percent; 30–39, 22 percent; 20–29, 2 percent; and unknown, 14 percent. A younger leadership generation, born since the *Anschluss*, is developing. This is an interesting development in a party known hitherto for a leadership of near-Soviet age. Two members of the younger generation are on the Politburo: Michael Graber, editor-in-chief of *Volksstimme*, and Walter Silbermayr, one of the party secretaries.

Prior to the congress, there were some indications of trouble within the party's close-knit organization. The sensational-analytical weekly *Profil* (7 November 1983) reported a wild scene in the office of the *Volksstimme* on 20 October. Podolsky, the up-and-coming Vienna secretary, and Ernst Wimmer, the KPO's chief ideologist, read the riot act to the *Volksstimme* staff for being too independent, especially vis-à-vis the party's attitude on Poland and Austria's Green and Alternative movements. An altercation arose over benefits owing to resigning staff members, and the chief troublemaker called the party—in front of Podolsky, Wimmer, and Michael Graber, the young editor-in-chief—a "pile of s--t." Two months later, Vienna's *Presse* (3 January) reported a number of intraparty discussions, all prompted by uneasy feelings that the party had done so poorly in 1983 because protest voters preferred the new Green and Alternative organizations.

The general condition of the KPO was one of the main topics at the Twenty-fifth Congress (*Volksstimme*, 14 January). Muhri's report to the congress contained much soul-searching about the 1983 election and especially the relatively better showing of the Green and Alternative parties, which, according to Muhri, are nurtured by the media. The party was exhorted to emphasize elections where it had something to defend, especially shop steward elections. The exhortation also extended to the generation of more party influence in general interest matters, from rent control to the Austrian "social partnership." Communists were urged to compare the right to work in East bloc countries with Western unemployment. More use of *Volksstimme* and more information flow within the party were urged. Cell organization was proposed for more effective party work. Muhri claimed that half of the new members were young and that party work had to be strengthened in the workplace and the university. Youth needs to be acquainted with Leninist norms. All members, men and women, were urged to fight for the liberation of women. Finally, the party was reminded of the following point: "The KPÖ does not exist for its own sake. It originated because the working class needed it. It is more necessary than ever for the Austrian people, for Austria's working class."

Much of the preamble of the congress resolution (*Volksstimme*, 21 January) dealt with organizational matters. Not surprisingly, it sounded much like Muhri's report and the intervening discussion. Again, the party's dispirited stance vis-à-vis the new parties on the left was referred to. A reorganization at the top of the party was talked about: a new organization section was proposed to take the place of the Secretariat. It and the Politburo were to make sure that the members of the Central Committee did their work at the basic level of the organization. The new organization section is to become part of the party constitution at the Twenty-sixth Congress. Further loss of members was conceded, and a long-term renewal policy among party cadres was adumbrated. Youth was to be made acquainted with the peculiarities of communist politics. Women were urged to do effective work, when necessary at the side of Catholic and Socialist women. Finally, the party was reminded that twelve years of Socialist majority government have not changed the capitalist profit system. More critical politics, the KPÖ congress claimed, will lead to more Marxist-Leninist politics.

Domestic Affairs. The Twenty-fifth Congress passed two major domestic resolutions (ibid.). The economic one was entitled "Secure work! Protect the environment! Thwart the dismantling of social programs!" It opposes the increased taxation of working people, increased exploitation through new technology, and the continuing worsening of the situation of the working class, accompanied by corruption within the "social partnership" of the Economic Chamber and Trade Union Congress. Meanwhile, the destruction of the environment goes on. The immediate demand is the 35-hour week at full pay. Beyond this, the KPÖ demands a change in foreign economic policy, tax reform, environmental policies paid for by environment destroyers, *real* equal rights for women, and an educational system that prepares young people for a meaningful occupational life. The other domestic resolution was entitled "No more fascism! No more wars!" Fascism, the resolution claimed, is rearing its head once more and must be nipped in the bud. Communists proudly claim their part in the defeat of nazism and the rebirth of an independent Aus-

tria. The KPÖ demands the vigorous pursuit of the struggle against neo-fascism.

In his annual contribution to *World Marxist Review* (April), Muhri warned of the consequences of mass unemployment in Austria. It will lead to a more thorough exploitation of the working class, all under the aegis of the "social partnership." Muhri demanded a 35-hour week with no reduction in pay, increased purchasing power for the people, higher production of finished products, new housing and urban renewal, and a shift of economic relations from the European Community to socialist and developing countries. Communists must fight for a cleaner environment and against the "social partnership." They must do this by invigorating politico-ideological work, creating a more effective party organization, and intensifying work with young people.

International Affairs. The main international resolutions of the Twenty-fifth Congress were "Defend peace—secure life!" and "Long live international solidarity!" (*Volksstimme*, 21 January). The first resolution warned that the American deployment of Pershing II and cruise missiles has created an unprecedented danger of nuclear war. For this reason, the KPÖ will support the international peace movement. The second resolution was directed against U.S. imperialism in Lebanon, Chile, Turkey, South Africa, Pakistan, and South Korea and against U.S. efforts to undermine Cuba and Nicaragua.

Much of Muhri's *World Marxist Review* article was directed against Reagan's aggressive policy. He supported the international peace movement, this "new major phenomenon in international life," and reiterated some of the demands of the congress: prevent the use of Austrian broadcasting for imperialist propaganda and reduce Austria's military expenditures.

On 9 September, *Volksstimme* attacked a Vienna-born U.S. diplomat at the United Nations, Richard Schifter, who had come to defend American reservations vis-à-vis the United Nations. The KPÖ wondered why the United States is sending missionaries to Austria to criticize Austria's neutral behavior in the United Nations. Conversely, the KPÖ Politburo wondered (*Volksstimme*, 30 September) why Austria's neutrality had become so pro-American. In response, the Socialist *Arbeiter-Zeitung* (5 October) pointed out that Leopold Gratz, Austria's new foreign minister, had been criticized by the KPÖ and *not* by the USSR.

International Party Contacts. The KPO used its congress for numerous international contacts. The Soviet delegation, headed by Central Committee secretary Ryzhkov, was met at Vienna's airport by Muhri and Johann Steiner, the KPO's international secretary (Tass, 12 January). On 12 January the Soviet delegation met with Muhri, Steiner, Erwin Scharf, and Hans Kalt (*Volksstimme*, 17 January). On the same day, Muhri, Scharf, Kalt, Steiner, and Karl Reiter met with the East German party delegation headed by Central Committee secretary Horst Dohlus (ibid.). On 16 January, Muhri had a meeting with the heads of the delegations from Hungary, Poland, Bulgaria, Romania, and Yugoslavia (ibid.). While this meeting included Budimir Vukasinović of the League of Communists of Yugoslavia, there was no indication that President Mika Špiljak of Yugoslavia visited the KPO on the occasion of his state visit to Austria in March (Tanjug, 15 March).

On 20 March, Boris I. Stukalin, chief of the Soviet Central Committee propaganda section, visited Vienna and met with Muhri, Scharf, and Steiner (*Pravda*, 21 March). One week later, Vadim V. Zagladin, another member of the Soviet Central Committee, met in Vienna with the same KPO leaders (Moscow domestic service, 28 March).

In late June, Karl Reiter led a KPO delegation to the GDR and met Horst Dohlus in East Berlin (ADN, East Berlin, 28 June). Muhri visited Sofia in July and was received by Bulgarian leader Todor Zhivkov (BTA, Sofia, 26 July).

Frederick C. Engelmann
University of Alabama

Belgium

Population. 9,872,000
Party. Belgian Communist Party (PCB/KPB)
Founded. 1921
Membership. 10,000 (estimated)
Leadership. President: Louis van Geyt; vice-president and president of the French-speaking council: Claude Renard; vice-president and president of the Dutch-speaking council: Jef Turf
Politburo. 14 members: Pierre Beauvois, Marcel Couteau, Jan Debrouwere, Filip Delmotte, Robert Dussart, Roel Jacobs, Ludo Loose, Jacques Moins, Jacques Nagels, Claude Renard, Jef Turf, Louis van Geyt, Jules Vercaigne, Jack Withages
Central Committee. 72 full members: 37 in the French-language wing; 35 in the Dutch-language wing
Status. Legal
Last Congress. Twenty-fourth, March and December 1982 (two stages)
Last Election. 1981, 2.3 percent, 2 of 212 seats
Auxiliary Organizations. Communist Youth of Belgium, Union of Belgian Pioneers, National Union of Communist Students
Publications. *Le Drapeau rouge*, daily party organ in French; *De Rode Vann*, Dutch-language weekly (circulation 14,500 and 11,000, respectively); *Les Cahiers communistes*, PCB monthly ideological review; *Vlaams Marxistisch Tijdschrift*, KBP quarterly

The PCB/KPB was the last of Belgium's "traditional" parties to accommodate to the formal and actual separation of the country into three partly autonomous regions (Flanders, Wallonia, and Brussels-Capital) nesting in two cultural communities (Dutch-speaking in the north and for a minority—20–25 percent of the population of the city—of the Brussels-Capital region; French-speaking for the Walloon south and for the majority of the residents of Brussels). The de facto federalization of governmental and political institutions since 1970 was in large part legitimized by the concomitant division of the major, formerly national parties into Flemish, Walloon, and Brussels-based entities and by the emergence of newer parties with exclusively regional constituencies. The PCB/KPB sought to maintain a unitary, "national" party structure for fifteen years after others had begun to adjust their organizations and electoral profiles to progressive federalization. This lag was at once a symptom of the PCB/KPB's loss of touch with political reality and an important cause of the continuing decline of its appeal to the electorate. (The party lost more than 30 percent of its electoral support between the last two national elections, falling from 3.3 percent of the vote in 1978 to less than 2.3 percent in 1981. The next election is scheduled for late 1985.) Doctrinal adherence to the position that salient political issues continue to be class-based rather than ethnic or regional in scope underlay the national strategy, and that stance contributed to a loss of contact with a substantial minority of the party's small electoral constituency, which, like most other Belgians, had come to redefine its priorities in ethnic or regional terms in large measure—most particularly in terms of intercommunal and interregional relations.

At its Twenty-fourth Congress in 1982 (the regular congress in March and an extraordinary session in December), the PCB/KPB belatedly conceded the necessity to adjust to the realities of regionalized government and party politics. It "federalized, to be more united" at those congresses, and from late 1983 to date much of its internal activity entailed organization of the Flemish and French-language sections.

But neither such structural adaptation nor the continued effort to hone a Eurocommunist image by such steps as condemning the Soviet presence in Afghanistan and martial law in Poland, nor the reestablishment of contact with the People's Republic of China (undertaken in 1983), nor, most important from the perspective of the party's membership, the steadfast opposition to nuclear weapons in Europe (on both sides) and the general championing of the European peace movement helped its fortunes. Membership continues to shrink from an already small base; divisions among leaders and members alike along several doctrinal and issue-related dimensions are exacerbated by the formalization of regionally based ideological and policy differences. A series of terrorist bomb attacks against NATO and other "Atlanticist" installations that began in the fall of 1984 and for which responsibility has been claimed by a group calling itself Communist Combatant Cells—while probably not associated with the PCB/KPB—is hardly likely to help the party's quest for votes or the image of reasonableness it has long sought to foster.

Party Leadership and Organization. The organization of the PCB at the communitarian level (i.e., for Wallonia and the French-speaking majority of Brussels) began to take form at the regional party's first congress, 10–11 December 1983 (*Cahiers marxistes*, January), on the basis of the Federal Agreement concluded in June of that year at the national level (and in line with the decisions reached at the two sessions of the party's Twenty-fourth Congress in 1982). Claude Renard, one of the vice-presidents of the national party and a longtime member of its Politburo, was chosen president of the PCB.

The francophone segment of the party has always comprised a substantial majority of the total membership (presently estimated at approximately 65–70 percent). It is more traditional in ideological orientation—less open to either the Eurocommunist demarches of the Flemish wing or to associating with and attempting to capitalize on newer, single-issue movements, such as those revolving around the environment, the European peace movement, or homosexual rights (*De Waarheid*, 23 February). At the December 1983 congress, held in Tournai, the PCB defined its agenda principally in terms of classic socioeconomic concerns. It criticized the right-of-center coalition government of Wilfried Martens for the rigorous austerity policies it has followed since 1982, for its inclinations to privatize important segments of economic activity and for unemployment levels of around 15 percent. Renard, following his election as president, stressed the divergence of viewpoints between the francophone and Flemish populations in general and the Communists in particular. He suggested that the long-term structural divergence between the economies of the two ethnic communities (and the Flemish northern region and Walloon southern region) underlay in large part the different perspectives and priorities of Communists in the two parts of the country (*Le Soir*, 13 December 1983).

The Flemish wing of the party (KPB) held its first regional congress on 18–19 February. The party elected Jef Turf—who, like Renard, has been a vice-president of the national party for some time and a member of its Politburo—as its president. The KPB has, during the past several years, provided the balance of support for the PCB/KPB's shift in the direction of Eurocommunism. It is also considerably more open to association with both other elements of the left (in particular, the left wing of the Flemish Socialist Party) and with such newer political actors as the environmental and peace movements. The KPB has presented joint lists of candidates with such noncommunist elements in local elections of late (*De Waarheid*, 23 February). In general, it has sought to compensate for its very small membership and electoral share (the KPB has fewer than 3,000 members and tends to poll less than 2 percent of the vote in the Flemish region) by de-emphasizing classic class rhetoric and stressing the cross-party and cross-class convergence of interests on issues such as the environment and nuclear weapons, as well as the economy.

While accommodating itself to the federalization of the governmental and political structures of the country, the PCB/KPB is striving to retain a more extensive and visible "national organization." Both Turf and Renard made note of the need for maintaining a national communist party as long as a common class enemy controls the machinery of the state and the economy. It will take several years of practice before the extent and nature of the division of political resources and authority between the regional and central party organizations is stabilized and before the feasibility of maintaining the latter's effectiveness in the face of institutional change and the increasing influence of the regional organizations can be determined. At the beginning of 1985 it appeared that the relative positions of the PCB and the KPB in their respective regions will militate against maintaining substantial coherence at the national level, notwithstanding protestations of the regional parties' presidents. The fiscal and labor market–related issues that help to mobilize support in Wallonia fuel the traditional communist orientation long predominant in the PCB, and fruitful association with either the francophone Socialists or the newer, single-issue movements in that region appears less promising. In contrast, the KPB's strategy of fostering such associations and embracing both established and newer Eurocommunist positions may prove both effective and necessary in keeping the party from vanishing in Flanders. Furthermore, inasmuch as the Flemish region's economy has been far more dynamic in the past 25 to 30 years than that of Wallonia, more traditional labor market–related issues are relatively less effective vehicles for mobilizing electoral support or gaining new members in the north. These and other differences in regional conditions may contribute to a widening of the perspectives of party leaders and to diverging strategies, thus making the task of the national organization more problematic. It is noteworthy that soon after the larger parties began to federalize in the 1960s and 1970s, their national organizations began to atrophy.

Domestic Affairs. The Martens V government (so termed because it is the fifth coalition organized under the prime ministership of Wilfried Martens, a Flemish Christian Democrat) is a right-of-center coalition that is one of the longest-lived, most stable governments Belgium has had in decades. While it is likely to serve out its parliamentary term (the next elections are scheduled for late 1985), its dual strategy of stringent austerity and private sector stimulation for coping with the country's economic malaise has led to limitations on wage increases, a partial de-indexing of social security and other transfer payments, and high levels of unemployment. The PCB/KPB has made these issues its chief targets in the domestic arena. Since 1982, the PCB in particular has argued that the government's approach has increased already high degrees of income inequality in the society, and it has indicted the coalition's policies as "antilabor." While generally sharing with its francophone counterpart a critical view of the government's austerity and incomes policies, the KPB has stressed environmental and social concerns nearly as much as labor market and economic issues in the domestic arena.

Neither wing of the party is well situated in its region for emerging as the leading voice of opposition to the governing coalition on such domestic issues (or, for that matter, on foreign policy issues). The major labor union federations in both portions of the country are associated with the Socialist and the Christian Democratic parties, and the Socialists, as the major opposition party in both Flanders and Wallonia, are more credible critics. Furthermore, the KPB and particularly the PCB have been markedly unsuccessful in mobilizing support on environmental and other noneconomic domestic issues. (This explains in part the KPB's recent inclination to seek collaboration with noncommunist parties and groups in Flanders. The aggressiveness of the leaders of the Walloon Socialists, that party's extensive and historically widely respected political position in the south, and the more traditionally doctrinaire stance of the PCB—particularly in the major industrial region of Liège—has made Walloon Communists both less inclined and less successful in constructing such ties.) In sum, Belgian Communists are not well positioned to lead or even to play prominent parts in the opposition to the government's domestic policies. They lack crucial organizational resources—particularly in organized labor—and their electoral support is so scant that they are at or near the bottom of the roster of parties and other groups opposing the government. They are one of the smallest voices in opposition, in contrast to such major, traditional forces as the Socialists and the labor unions, as well as the new environmental parties and other single-issue groups.

Foreign Positions and Activities. Until recently, the PCB/KPB's claim of being in the forefront of the Belgian peace movement and of the opposition to the deployment of NATO cruise missiles in the country (deployment of 48 such missiles was scheduled to begin in March 1985), while an exaggeration of the importance of the party's role, was an arguable and modestly effective rallying point. But the broadening and growth of both the movement and the opposition to deployment in 1984 virtually eclipsed the communist position. By late 1984 even traditionally and vocally pro-NATO politicians in the leadership of the senior party of the governing coalition (the Flemish Christian Democrats) were expressing reservations or a strong interest in postponing—if not canceling—the deployment, pending Soviet moves and arms control negotiations (*CSM*, 6 December; *NYT*, 13 December, 13 January 1985). The principal opposition parties—the Flemish and Walloon Socialists—had, by mid-1984, contributed substantial support to the Belgian peace movement and had moved to the head of an emerging majority of public opinion opposed to emplacement of nuclear weapons.

When, in the early 1980s, the PCB/KPB had begun to call for mutual nuclear weapons reductions in Europe, it succeeded in establishing a visible and relatively respectable position on an increasingly important issue. The call for mutual rather than unilateral nuclear restraint placed it in the company of Eurocommunist parties in Europe. This marked an intraparty victory for the moderate elements, principally among the Flemish wing's leadership.

By mid-1984, with a substantially more catholic peace movement and growing reluctance to deploy cruise missiles among the leaders of the major—including some of the governing—parties, the PCB/KPB's position on this cluster of issues had become marginal. The party confronts a dilemma. If it continues to pursue a seemingly moderate course in opposing the installation of NATO nuclear weapons in Belgium while calling for the dismantling of at least some Soviet theater nuclear weapons, it becomes virtually indistinguishable from many other, larger political actors and loses its position on these issues as a rallying point. But if it chooses a more radical, unilateralist course (advocated by some in the Liège organization of the PCB), it returns to the margin of the political spectrum in this area. In either case—and it is likely that the party will continue to follow the more moderate, Eurocommunist course—it will make itself marginal on what is currently the most important foreign policy issue.

The concern with the deployment of cruise missiles overshadowed all other foreign policy matters for the PCB/KPB in 1984. The issue is likely to continue to remain salient until the parliamentary elections late in 1985. While the remarginalization of the party's position on this issue neutralizes what many of its leaders hoped would be an important mobilizing vehicle, the gains for the PCB/KPB's credibility as a reasonable opposition voice in foreign affairs that followed from its firm stands against the Soviet occupation of Afghanistan and events in Poland and its reopening of relations with the Chinese Communist Party in the early 1980s have not been dissipated.

Martin O. Heisler
University of Maryland

Cyprus

Population. 662,000 (80 percent Greek; 18 percent Turkish)
Party. Progressive Party of the Working People (Anorthotikon Komma Ergazomenou Laou; AKEL)
Founded. 1922 (AKEL, 1941)
Membership. 14,000 (*WMR*, October 1982); 67 percent industrial workers and employees, 20 percent peasants and middle class, 24 percent women, 30 percent under 30 years old; 80 percent from Greek Cypriot community
General Secretary. Ezekias Papaioannou
Politburo. 13 members: Ezekias Papaioannou, Andreas Fandis, Dinos Konstantinou, G. Katsouridhis, Khambis Mikhailidhis, Andreas Ziartidhis, Khristos Petas, Kiriakos Khristou, Mikhail Poumbouris, G. Khristodoulidhis, A. Mikhailidhis, G. Sophokles, Dhonis Kristofinis
Secretariat. 3 members: Ezekias Papaioannou, Andreas Fandis (deputy general secretary), Dinos Konstantinou (organizing secretary)
Status. Legal
Last Congress. Fifteenth, 13–15 May 1982
Last Election. 1981, 32.8 percent, 12 of 35 seats
Auxiliary Organizations. Pan-Cypriot Workers' Federation (PEO), 45,000 members, Andreas Ziartidhis, general secretary; United Democratic Youth Organization (EDON), 14,000 members; Confederation of Women's Organizations; Pan-Cyprian Peace Council; Pan-Cyprian Federation of Students and Young Professionals; Union of Greek Cypriots in England, 1,200 members (considered London branch of AKEL); Pan-Cypriot National Organization of Secondary Students; Cypriot Farmers' Union
Publications. *Kharavyi* (Dawn), AKEL daily and largest newspaper in Cyprus; *Demokratia*, AKEL weekly; *Neo Kairoi* (New times), AKEL magazine; *Ergatiko Vima* (Workers' stride), PEO weekly; *Neolaia* (Youth), EDON weekly

The original Communist Party of Cyprus (Kommonistikon Komma Kiprou) was secretly founded in 1922 by Greek Cypriot cadres trained in mainland Greece. Four years later the party openly held its first congress, after the island had become a British crown colony. Outlawed in 1933, the party thrived as an underground movement until 1944, when it resurfaced as the AKEL. All political parties were proscribed in 1955 during the insurgency against the British led by the paramilitary group known as EOKA. AKEL leaders chose not to take up arms in that anticolonial campaign and later rationalized their inaction as "a nonviolent alternative to EOKA terrorism in the independence struggle." This peaceful tactic may have been a

serious miscalculation because the AKEL is still criticized for its inaction by disaffected leftists. Since the establishment of the Republic of Cyprus in 1960, the AKEL has enjoyed legal status and has always been the island's strongest, best-organized political party.

The AKEL claims it is "a people's party of Greek and Turkish working people" (*WMR*, September 1979). While the AKEL is officially banned in the northern party of the island, which has been called the Turkish Republic of Cyprus since November 1983, the Communists have not stopped entreating the Turkish Cypriot minority population. One goal of the AKEL is to have "the patriotic front... include, as is done in the free territory, Turkish

Cypriots (Marxists and members of progressive, democratic groups living in the occupied areas)" (ibid., October 1982). Communist fronts do exist in the Turkish Cypriot part of the island, and representatives attended the World Conference on Peace and Life, Against Nuclear War held in Prague in 1983 (*Kharavyi*, 22 June 1983). The AKEL has offered an olive branch to "the entire Turkish Cypriot community, with whom we want to build a happy life for all and to live with them in peace and harmony" (ibid., 23 February).

Leadership and Organization. The AKEL is reputed to be a tightly controlled apparatus, structured along the principle of democratic centralism. Its highest body is the Congress, convened once every four years. The three-member Secretariat runs day-to-day operations, and few disagreements between AKEL members are ever aired in public. There was reportedly a "split" in the AKEL leadership in connection with the party's attitude toward President Spyros Kyprianou and the "democratic cooperation" with the ruling Democratic Party (DIKO). The controversy arose over whether the 30-month-old Minimum Program between AKEL and DIKO should be renounced (*O Agon*, Nicosia, 11 November). This dispute was apparently settled when Kyprianou himself terminated the alliance in December. As a result, the AKEL will lose such benefits as the appointment of party members to government posts and the promotion of leftists in the government machinery.

Replacement of the gerontocracy that now rules the party will be a concern for the AKEL as the present leaders grow older in their secure career positions. Today the AKEL attaches special importance to recruiting and educating younger people. Thus, "the party sees to it that comrades receive proper Marxist-Leninist training" (*WMR*, October 1982). The important youth front, EDON, has a membership of "factory workers, peasants, white-collar workers and higher school graduates between the ages of 14 and 30 . . . and it works in close cooperation with AKEL" (ibid., April). At the Fifteenth Congress in May 1982, the leadership hailed its "great success in the organizational sector" and in recruitment of "new members from all strata of the people of Cyprus." Since the previous congress, party membership "increased by 2,479" to its present strength of "nearly 14,000 members" (*Kharavyi*, 30 May 1982). What is more encouraging to

AKEL leaders is that some 96,000 Cypriots voted for the party in the 1981 parliamentary elections, which "is an indication of the potentialities of increasing the party's numerical strength." The AKEL also emphasizes its propaganda work "among the masses" so as "to take the offensive on the ideological and political fronts and expose imperialist and reactionary schemes more effectively." (*WMR*, October 1982.)

Each September, the AKEL holds a "fund-raising drive to provide money for the party's normal activity" and to demonstrate "a symbolic expression of mass support." Additional operating capital is generated "from activities under the indirect but tight control of the party in . . . branches of . . . production and distribution of goods (cooperatives, retail stores, financial enterprises, tourist agencies, export/import businesses)." As a consequence of these commercial endeavors, the AKEL has "probably become the major employer on the island." (*Andi*, Athens, 16 January 1981.) The two best-known communist-controlled enterprises are the Popular Distiller's Company of Limassol, which produces wines and brandies for the domestic market and export, and the People's Coffee Grinding Company in Nicosia. The communist-controlled labor union, PEO, is the strongest in Cyprus, and its members work in every phase of the island's economy.

Domestic Affairs. Domestic events in Cyprus are usually inextricably intertwined with international overtones and concerns. The Turkish Cypriots' unilateral declaration of independence in November 1983 and the exchange of ambassadors between the Turkish Republic of North Cyprus (TRNC) and Turkey in April is a case in point. Papaioannou criticized the creation of the TRNC, saying that "the act by itself represents the culmination of the imperialistic conspiracy against Cyprus" (*Pravda*, 24 February). On the occasion of the tenth anniversary of the Turkish invasion in July, the AKEL held a rally in Nicosia. The general secretary stated "that a way for rapprochement and understanding with the Turkish Cypriots must be found," which is an old communist slogan. He also added "that the Cyprus issue will not be resolved militarily but politically." (*Kharavyi*, 13 July.) Later he accused the forces of "U.S.-NATO imperialism" of securing three bases (air, naval, and missile) "in the areas of Cyprus that are occupied by Turkish troops . . . and all that is left for them now is to achieve the eradication of Cyprus's independence and nonalignment" (ibid., 14 October). The AKEL Central Committee's statement on the first anniversary of the TRNC noted that this is a calculated step "for the consolidation of the faits accomplis that have resulted from the invasion and occupation and for the definite partitioning of our island" (ibid., 11 November).

Attempts to bring the two communities in Cyprus together to negotiate the future of the island were also characterized by the international involvement of U.N. Secretary General Javier Pérez de Cuellar. In August, he held separate meetings with both sides in Vienna, where he presented "working points" prior to proximity talks between Turkish Cypriot leader Rauf Denktash and President Kyprianou in New York. The AKEL Political Office praised the U.N. initiatives, claiming that only "through a positive reply to them can the fatal dangers hanging over Cyprus be averted" (Nicosia domestic service, 27 August; *FBIS*, 28 August). Kyprianou criticized AKEL's enthusiasm by warning "that neither AKEL nor anyone else has the right to interpret our positions or my own stand . . . prior to completing the consultations which we have scheduled" (*FBIS*, 28 August). This difference of opinion was the opening wedge in the breakup of the Minimum Program alliance between DIKO and AKEL, which was announced by Kyprianou on 22 December.

The first round of the proximity talks began as scheduled in September, with the U.N. secretary general having "to plod patiently between" the two Cypriot leaders as they "sat in separate rooms" (*Economist*, London, 20 October). The first two rounds of the proximity talks ended without substantial progress, but a breakthrough was reached during the third round in November. Denktash finally agreed to the U.N. agenda paper for a summit meeting in January 1985 and offered to settle for less than 30 percent of Cypriot territory in an eventual federal union of the two communities. While the AKEL leadership complained that they "were not fully briefed," they were pleased that the talks spawned "some agreement in principle enabling a summit meeting to be held that would lead to an agreed solution" (*Cyprus Mail*, 11 November).

In May, there were elections to local administrative bodies in which "AKEL and all other left-wing forces won a major victory." The *World Marxist Review* (August) claimed this was "eloquent

evidence of the people's support for the party's patriotic political line." This article said that AKEL and other unnamed left-wing organizations "polled an absolute majority of votes in 57 communities and 11 suburban administrative councils and now have a minimum of one representative in the administrative bodies of all of the country's 70 communities." Reportedly more Cypriots voted for AKEL than ever before, with the second largest city, Limassol, producing 10.9 percent more votes than AKEL received in the previous national election of 1981. Expressing its gratitude, the AKEL Central Committee declared that "it would continue the fight for the country's liberation, the working people's interests, the modernisation of towns and villages, and a higher living standard and cultural level of the Cypriot people" (ibid.).

Foreign Positions and Activities. In its New Year's message, the AKEL Central Committee saw "mankind closer than ever to the verge of destruction because of the warmongering NATO circles headed by the Reagan administration." NATO, in intensifying its "aggressive activities," is using Cyprus "as a transit station" for a so-called multinational peacekeeping force in Lebanon that is "waging open aggression against the Palestinian people and the patriotic Lebanese forces" (*Kharavyi*, 1 January). The NATO countries "see Cyprus as an unsinkable aircraft carrier from which their planes, ships and missiles can be launched against the progressive regimes in the Eastern Mediterranean and mainly against the Soviet Union and other socialist countries" (Moscow radio, 4 January; *FBIS*, 5 January). In order to thwart those forces that want to partition the island, the AKEL general secretary insists "that Cyprus will remain in the Nonaligned movement, of which it is a founding member" (*Kharavyi*, 29 January).

During an AKEL plenary session, Papaioannou charged that "U.S. imperialism has been implementing a global anti-Soviet aggressive policy that is developing into an anticommunist crusade for worldwide domination." In contrast, the Soviet Union is the country that "shows the way to preserve and consolidate peace by means of deeds, not words." The Soviet Union "threatens no one, but it does not condone threat from any country or military bloc." Papaioannou praised the Soviet Union as "a socialist superpower that is now building a higher and most perfect society, the communist society." (Ibid., 23 February.)

In midyear, Papaioannou criticized Greece for wanting to send an army division to Cyprus. He further warned those who continue to support an "active involvement" of Greece in Cyprus that it would lead to "catastrophic consequences" (*O Agon*, 4 June). The AKEL, traditionally dedicated to nonmilitary approaches to problem solving, predicts that any confrontation between Greece and Turkey over Cyprus would result in defeat for Greece, ruin for Cyprus, and a Turkish occupation of the entire island. Thus, the AKEL is "against such an adventuristic war for Greece and Cyprus, as it does not serve their interests and would not solve the Cyprus problem as some might hope or believe" (ibid.). Despite the grim scenario spelled out by the AKEL leader, the Greek government has made it clear that a Cypriot request for troops would be honored.

After the unintentional worldwide airing of President Reagan's "bombing joke" in August, the AKEL Central Committee expressed indignation and outrage. Despite White House efforts to downplay the unfortunate incident, the AKEL said that the statement "reveals the U.S. administration's innermost thoughts in support of crime and war." The Central Committee concluded that "the disappearance of our civilization in a nuclear war is no joke" and denounced President Reagan as "an arsonist of a thermonuclear war." (Ibid.). According to AKEL leaders, the only way to save mankind is through "détente, substantive dialogue, removal of nuclear missiles from Europe, the demilitarization of outer space, respect for independence and territorial integrity, and gradual and complete disarmament." That is the way the Soviet Union recommends, along with "all liberal and pacifist people in the world." (*Kharavyi*, 19 August.)

International Party Contacts. The AKEL is known to maintain extensive relations with both ruling and nonruling communist parties, such as the (West) German Communist Party, which invited an AKEL representative to its Seventh Congress (ibid., 8 January). Later in the year, the AKEL sent greetings to East German leader Erich Honecker on the occasion of the thirty-fifth anniversary of the German Democratic Republic (ibid., 9 October). Closer to home, Papaioannou denied reports early in the year that he had serious differences with Communist Party of Greece leader Kharilaos Florakis over the Cyprus issue. During a visit to

Athens, where the AKEL leader spoke to Premier Andreas Papandreou and to Florakis, the two fraternal parties ended up "in full agreement" (*Cyprus Mail*, 8 January). Despite this testimony, it is well known that the Greek and Cypriot Communists have not always shared "monolithic unity."

A three-member AKEL delegation attended the funeral of Yuri Andropov, as did the Cypriot president, during February. In June, Papaioannou led a delegation to Moscow "to exchange views on questions of mutual interest." The Soviets took the opportunity to reaffirm their old suggestion that a Cypriot settlement "could be facilitated by the convocation of a representative international conference on Cyprus in the U.N. framework." The meeting ended with a pledge to "further consolidate the fraternal links that have formed between the two parties." (Tass, 2 June; *FBIS*, 4 June.) A Soviet delegation returned the visit in October. The discussions confirmed the "identity of positions on international issues and particularly on the preservation of world peace" (*Kharavyi*, 10 October).

At the invitation of the Bulgarian government, an AKEL delegation visited Sofia in June. During the "cordial and friendly talks," a mutual desire was expressed "for further strengthening and expanding friendship and cooperation" (Sofia domestic service, 23 June; *FBIS*, 25 June). During a vacation in Bulgaria in August, Papaioannou met with Todor Zhivkov, who presented the AKEL leader with the Order of Georgi Dimitrov "for his great contribution to the development of fraternal relations between the peoples of Bulgaria and Cyprus" (Sofia domestic service, 3 August; *FBIS*, 6 August). *Kharavyi*'s coverage of the meeting (5 August) highlighted the "full identity of the two parties' positions on all issues discussed." Relations between the governments of the Republic of Cyprus and Bulgaria have always been very friendly. President Kyprianou authorized a delegation of DIKO party members to accept an invitation of the National Council of the Fatherland Front to visit Sofia in July. The chairman of the Council, Pencho Kubadinski, received the delegation and reaffirmed his determination "to expand and intensify relations between the Fatherland Front and the Democratic Party of Cyprus" (Sofia domestic service, 23 July; *FBIS*, 25 July). Later in the year, the Bulgarian radio observed Cyprus Week. A message from the acting president of the Republic of Cyprus stressed "that such activities strengthen the existing relations between our two peoples and their governments"

(Nicosia domestic service, 5 October; *FBIS*, 10 October).

The AKEL usually exchanges greetings with other communist countries on national holidays and various other celebrations. One such went to Babrak Karmal, leader of the Democratic People's Republic of Afghanistan, and wished "further suc-

cesses in the struggle against imperialist intervention and the counterrevolutionary mercenaries and in the building of a new society in democratic Afghanistan" (*Kharavyi*, 27 April).

T. W. Adams
Washington, D.C.

Denmark

Population. 5,112,000
Party. Communist Party of Denmark (Danmarks Kommunistiske Parti; DKP)
Founded. 1919
Membership. 10,000 (estimated, actual number probably lower)
Chairman. Jørgen Jensen
Secretary General. Poul Emanuel
Executive Committee. 16 members: Jørgen Jensen, Ib Norlund (vice-chairman), Poul Emanuel, Jan Andersen, Villy Fulgsang, Margit Hansen, Bernard Jeune, Gunnar Kanstrup (editor of *Land og Folk*), Kurt Kristensen, Dan Lundstrup, Freddy Madsen, Jørgen Madsen, Anette Nielsen, Bo Rosschou, Ole Sohn, Ingmar Wagner
Central Committee. 51 members, 15 candidate members
Status. Legal
Last Congress. Twenty-seventh, 12–15 May 1983; next congress scheduled for 1986
Last Election. 10 January 1984, 0.7 percent, no representation
Auxiliary Organizations. Communist Youth of Denmark (Danmarks Kommunistiske Ungdom; DKU), Ole Sorensen, chairman; Communist Students of Denmark (Danmarks Kommunistiske Studenter; KOMM.S.), Mette Gjerløv, chair
Publications. *Land og Folk* (Nation and people), daily, circulation 13,000 weekdays and 16,000 weekends; *Tiden-Verden Rund* (Times around the world), theoretical monthly; *Fremad* (Forward), monthly

Nineteen eighty-four was another year in the political wilderness for the DKP. It began with a dismal electoral performance in the sudden parliamentary elections of 10 January. The party received a scant 23,085 votes, its worst showing since World War II. The DKP lost all its parliamentary seats in October 1979, when its vote fell below the 2 percent minimum required for proportional representation in

the Folketing (parliament). Such political losses since 1977 have encouraged internal strife, and the aging DKP leadership was attacked by prominent former members.

The January elections, Denmark's seventh parliamentary elections in less than thirteen years, reflect the continuing tenuous parliamentary balance of the past decade. Since the destabilizing election of December 1973, parties of the extreme left and right have controlled between a quarter and a third of the parliamentary seats, making it difficult for the more moderate parties to govern effectively. The current four-party coalition led by conservative Poul Schlüter consolidated its position following narrow gains in the elections. A last-minute recount gave the coalition an additional seat; in combination with the Radical Liberals (a reformist center party) and nonsocialist representatives from the Faeroe Islands and Greenland, this gave the government a one-vote majority. Against this parliamentary majority, the leading opposition, the reformist Social Democratic Party (SDP), as well as two leftist parties, could rarely prevail on domestic political issues. The Radical Liberals are opposed to aspects of Danish security and NATO policies, and on such questions the government has lacked full parliamentary backing. The government has chosen not to make foreign and security policy issues matters of confidence.

For 25 years the DKP has had to compete with other Marxist parties to the left of the SDP. In the past ten to fifteen years, these various leftist parties have typically captured an eighth of the national vote. In January, they collectively polled 14.9 percent, but the DKP share continued to plummet. These parties compete for the same voters, and whenever one moves ahead, another declines. Since 1981, the SDP has also apparently been losing votes to the leftist parties. The principal gainer has been the independent Marxist Socialist People's Party (Socialistisk Folkeparti; SF), which doubled its strength in the 1981 parliamentary elections. It held on to these gains in the 1984 elections. The third leftist party with significant support is the Left Socialist Party (Venstresocialisterne; VS), a contentious assembly of student radicals (from the late 1960s) that continues to enjoy substantial support from students and public employees (as does the SF). The VS retained its five Folketing seats.

Less important are three small sects: the Communist Workers' Party (Kommunistisk Arbejderparti; KAP), a "Maoist" group that has unsuccessfully sought a closer relationship with the VS and did not run in the January elections; the International Socialist Workers' Party (Internationalen Socialistisk Arbejderparti; SAP), the Danish branch of the Trotskyist Fourth International, which received 2,200 votes; and a newly formed group, the Marxist-Leninist Party (Marxistisk-Leninistisk Parti; MLP), whose pro-Albania line attracted fewer than 1,000 votes in the January elections.

Leadership and Organization. Through good times and bad, the DKP internal organization and leadership changes little. Despite the party's decline since his succession to the leadership, Jørgen Jensen was reconfirmed as chairman at the DKP's Twenty-seventh Congress in May 1983. Jensen, an activist in the Metalworkers' Union, succeeded to the party chairmanship in 1977 and is a veteran of more than 30 years in the DKP. Ib Nørlund, the party's number-two man and chief theoretician, has been in his post for decades. The same is true for the party's secretary (administrative director) Poul Emanuel. There have been periodic challenges to the party leadership from within, and such attacks were both public and vociferous in 1983. Such efforts at change are inevitably in vain, as the challengers are forced to leave the party by exclusion or resignation, usually accompanied by a barrage of calumny.

The party's highest authority is the triennial congress. The Central Committee is elected at the congress, and it, in turn, elects the party's Executive Committee (politburo), chairman, secretary, and other posts. Despite the attendance of some 453 delegates at the 1983 congress, the DKP functions fully in the Leninist model of a self-perpetuating elite. In recent years the Central Committee has met from four to six times annually. During noncongress years, the party holds an annual meeting. In mid-September such a meeting assembled in Nørresundby, Jutland, attended by some 313 delegates. Such meetings reaffirm the general party goals as set at the congress and are occasions for the party to use media coverage to make known its views on domestic and foreign affairs.

Not only has the DKP been concerned about its electoral fate, but in 1984 leaders expressed a determination to stimulate party membership. Although the party is secretive about membership information, Poul Emanuel admitted that during 1983 the party had lost members (*Berlingske Tidende*, 17 November 1983; *JPRS*, 5 January). At the September meeting, Emanuel designated 1985 as a "party year." This means that the party will make an energetic effort to raise funds for its "guarantee [endowment] fund" and to recruit party members. On the same occasion Emanuel reminded the party faithful that Communists held 3,000 elected positions in the trade union movement and that party members are active and influential in numerous tenants' and grass-roots organizations. Finally he noted the prominence of Communists in the peace and anti–European Economic Community (EEC) movements. (*Politiken Weekly*, 20 September.) Chairman Jensen also stressed the "common front" approach for communist influence in various political causes (*Weekendavisen*, 27 September).

The DKU is the DKP's largest affiliate; at the Twenty-seventh Congress in 1983 its leadership stressed two areas of activity: support for radical trade union factions appealing to apprentices and young workers and mobilization and influence over young participants in the various peace organizations. The DKU has not been successful in either area. The KOMM.S. overlaps the DKU, but concentrates its efforts on university students. Periodically Communists have held high posts in the Danish National Students' Council (Danske Studerendes Faellesraad; DSF), but the DSF's strength has been uncertain in recent years. KOMM.S. maintains some organizational autonomy and has its own publications, *Roed Blade* (Red leaves) and *Spartakus*, and its own meetings (Sixth Congress, October 1982).

Although the DKP has policies regarding the self-governing territories of Greenland and the Faeroe Islands, it does not have organizations in either. There was an attempt to form an autonomous Faeroe Communist Party in 1975 and later years, but it apparently failed. Neither of the leftist parties active in Greenland has ties to the DKP.

Domestic Affairs. Although the Danish economy is still struggling with economic problems, 1984 brought definite signs of improvement. National income, fueled by rapid export growth, was expected to rise by 3 percent in 1984, and inflation and the governmental deficit continue to decline. A large balance of payments deficit and high unemployment (averaging just over 10 percent) were dark spots on the economic horizon. As part of its opposition to the nonsocialist coalition, the DKP stressed these latter aspects. In its public statements (principally *Land og Folk*) the DKP divided its time between attacking the policies of the Schlüter government and attacking the SDP for ineffective opposition, but had ample quantities of vitriol remaining for the Radical Liberals, whose support on domestic issues was crucial to the government.

The DKP's domestic program is spelled out in the manifesto adopted at the Twenty-seventh Congress, "The Denmark We Want" and the action program "Our Answer." These were reaffirmed at the DKP annual assembly in September: establishment of new public enterprises; nationalization of all banks and financial institutions; close state supervision of investment, the cooperative movement, agriculture, and fisheries; increases in collective housing construction; and, finally, the famous DKP proposal to reduce the workweek to 35 hours, restrict overtime, extend various leaves, and other measures, with no reduction in real wages. These final goals are common to all of the socialist parties, although the SDP sees them as the gradual fruits of free collective bargaining.

After years of dithering, the government is easing the state monopoly on radio and television broadcasting in favor of local and even private stations. The issue has revived controversy over whether advertising should be permitted. The socialist parties, including the DKP, are opposed to direct commercial advertising.

The DKP has little influence over major trade unions, most of which are affiliated with the SDP. Communists are active in union locals, however, and the DKP has long been stronger in the labor movement than in electoral politics. Communist strength has been especially visible in the metalworkers', typographers', and maritime unions. Efforts to organize radical union shop stewards have not been particularly successful in recent years, and the DKP-dominated Greater Copenhagen Association of Shop Stewards was rejected by the SF-led local at the large B & W shipyards because of undemocratic procedures (*Politiken Weekly*, 20 December). The DKP supported but did not organize a massive wildcat strike that paralyzed public transport and some other public services in the Copenhagen region in May. The strike was caused by seven bus drivers who quit their union over union funding of socialist political parties. The drivers were dismissed by the Greater Copenhagen Council by a vote of the council's socialist majority, including a DKP member (*Nordisk Kontakt*, no. 10).

Foreign Affairs. The international political situation has always had a direct impact on the political fate of the DKP, often in uncertain ways. Increased East-West tensions, such as the cold war of the late 1940s and the waning of détente in the late 1970s, capped by the Soviet invasion of Afghanistan in 1979, spelled domestic disaster for the DKP. Few West European communist parties have been more steadfastly loyal to the foreign policy line of the Soviet Union than the DKP. On the other hand, the DKP has cleverly exploited international issues such as the growing unpopularity of Danish membership in the EEC and the strong revival of the peace movement over the issue of intermediate-range nuclear missiles in Europe. Through front organizations, the DKP has been able to promote positions that would attract little attention under the DKP label.

Thus despite a rigid foreign policy line, the DKP's ability to control foreign policy organizations through dedicated individuals has been notable. Central Committee member Jens Peter Bonde is a leading figure in the broadly based Popular Movement Against the EEC (Folkebevaegelsen imod EF), sits as one of its four members in the European Parliament, and edits its weekly paper, *Det ny Notat* (The new notice). The Folkebevaegelsen held on to its four seats in the June European Parliament elections. Anker Schjerning has similarly been prominent in the peace movement. The DKP has sought to deflect efforts to place at least some of the blame for world tensions on the foreign policies of the Soviet Union (*WMR*, October 1983).

Security policy issues were again prominent in Danish politics during 1984. Although the opposition SDP claims to be committed to continued NATO membership, it has forced a parliamentary motion (with the votes of VS, SF, and the Radical Liberals) prohibiting Danish financial contributions to NATO infrastructural programs that support U.S. missiles in Western Europe. Ib Nørlund stressed NATO's hostile intentions in a long article in the *World Marxist Review* (February). There can be little doubt of the effectiveness of the opposition on this issue, though DKP support has not been crucial.

Less popular have been DKP positions on other controversial international issues, such as Afghanistan. Chairman Jensen's visit to Soviet-held areas of Afghanistan in April were accompanied by articles and statements fully supporting Soviet policies (*Land og Folk*, 18 April; *JPRS*, 31 May).

Despite strong public support for the peace movement and related demands, such as the fuzzy concept of a "nuclear weapons–free Nordic zone," only the DKP defends Soviet foreign policies uncritically.

International Party Contacts. The DKP leadership maintains close ties with other pro-Moscow communist parties, especially those in Eastern Europe. Delegations from all of the Warsaw Pact countries regularly attend DKP congresses. DKP leaders are also ardent travelers to foreign communist meetings and countries. In addition to Chairman Jensen's visit to Afghanistan in April, Secretary Emanuel led a DKP delegation to the USSR in late June. After a stay in Moscow, the Danes visited Murmansk and Leningrad and were favorably impressed by all they saw (*Pravda*, 7 July; *JPRS*, 11 July). Chairman Jensen visited North Korea in September. After meeting with North Korean leader Kim Il-song and other leaders, the Danish leader again expressed his favorable impression (Korean Central News Agency, 21 September; *JPRS*, 25 September).

Other Marxist/Leftist Groups. The DKP is only one of several left-wing parties currently active in Danish politics. The SF is by far the most powerful of these groups. Originally a splinter from the DKP (in 1958), the SF has grown significantly despite internal splits and electoral setbacks. Ever since it won its first parliamentary representation in 1960, its primary political goal has been to push the SDP leftward. In 1966–1967 and 1971–1973, SF votes kept the Social Democrats in power. The first experiment in formal SF-SDP collaboration (the so-called Red Cabinet) ended when the SF's left wing split off to form the VS party. In 1973, several right-wing Social Democrats abandoned their party to form the Center Democrats. Following the SF's advance in December 1981, it appeared that another effort would be made at collaboration. However, the SF and SDP did not have sufficient votes to pass legislation without additional support. The VS rejected any cooperation with the SDP, and the Radical Liberals, another possible support party, would agree only on an issue-by-issue basis. SDP leader and Premier Anker Jorgensen found it increasingly difficult to satisfy these two parties on domestic issues, and he resigned in favor of the current nonsocialist coalition in September 1982. Although the SF has kept its high level of support, its influence on the new government is minimal.

The SF program is decidedly socialist and Marxian, but it emphasizes Danish origins and rejects foreign socialist models. The SF is explicitly non-Leninist in both its internal party governance and its attitudes toward Danish parliamentary democracy. As noted, it has had its share of feuds and schisms, but under the experienced leadership of its veteran chairman, Gert Petersen, the party has become a natural alternative to dissatisfied SDP and other leftist voters.

At the annual SF party meeting in Copenhagen (18 and 20 May), Petersen stressed the party's two goals: first to defeat the current nonsocialist government and second to form a "workers' majority" government (presumably in coalition with the SDP). The SDP leadership has been icily silent about future cooperation with the SF. The SF's foreign policy views reflect its strong antimilitarism, opposition to NATO and the EEC, and criticism of Soviet foreign policies, which "reflect the same superpower logic" as those of the United States (*Nordisk Kontakt*, no. 10).

The SF has increased its position in the trade union movement despite an "academic" image that has plagued its efforts to win working-class support. The SF has informal but close ties to analogous parties in Norway and Sweden and looser ties to the Italian Communist Party and other independent leftist groups. The SF is more than a protest party, although dissatisfaction with the DKP and the SDP have accounted for some of its support. It is a haven for activists and voters committed to Danish Marxist and democratic-socialist solutions without reference or apologies for less fortunate experiments elsewhere.

The VS is much weaker, but it kept its five Folketing seats in the January elections and holds several local government seats. It is a native party without significant foreign ties, but despite positive references to parliament and civil liberties, it is ambiguous about their applicability to a "revolutionary situation." Such matters as intraparty democracy and political tactics have occasioned periodic struggles within the VS. The party's extremist faction, the Union Common List (Faglig Faellesliste), which is also often referred to as the "Leninists," broke with the party for failing to work for a cadre party oriented toward revolutionary action. The Leninists themselves are not of one mind, but VS leader and founder (with others) Preben Wilhjelm has long sought to isolate the extremist faction (*Jyllands-Posten*, 31 July). In typical Danish fashion, the schismatics announced their intention to form a new party.

There are at least three or more tiny leftist groups that have obtained the required number of signatures to appear on the electoral ballot. The SAP appeared on the ballot in the January elections, but, as noted, its vote was minimal. Its newspaper,

Klassekampen (Class struggle), keeps Danes informed of developments in the international Trotskyist movement.

The Albanian perspective dominates the minuscule Marxist-Leninist Party, which sought registration as the Communist Party of Denmark–Marxist-Leninist but was denied this confusing name by the Interior Ministry. The MLP publishes a newspaper, *Arbejderen* (Worker) and a theoretical journal, *Partiets Vej* (The party's way).

The KAP is the oldest of the extreme leftist sects, dating back to 1968. Under its perennial leader, Copenhagen University lecturer Benito Scocozza, it has undertaken to keep alive a "Maoist" tradition even as China's own policies have changed dramatically in the past decade. More recently the KAP leadership has suggested closer ties to VS, but nothing has come of it yet. The party chose not to run in the January elections (Ib Garodkin, *Haandbog i Dansk Politik, 1983–84*, 6th ed., Praestoe: Mjoelner, 1984).

Danish electoral laws make it possible to run nationally for parliament with only about 20,000 signatures. Danes sign such petitions willingly. A major incentive to undertake even a hopeless parliamentary campaign is the free and generous radio and television time allowed all parties. Most such media access is in the form of rigorous questioning by professional journalists. Inexperienced party spokesmen can find the procedure devastating. Among the nascent political groups likely to make their electoral debut are the Greens (*De Groenne*), an eclectic ecology party modeled on the West German example, though less committed to a Marxian ideology than some other West European ecology parties. Finally former DKP activist (until his exclusion in 1982) Preben Moeller Hansen, chairman of the powerful Seamen's Union, has threatened to turn his personal political club, the Common Course Club (Falles Kurs Klub) into a proper political party. Hansen claims 1,500 members for the club (*Politiken Weekly*, 28 June).

Eric S. Einhorn
University of Massachusetts at Amherst

Finland

Population. 4,873,000
Party. Finnish Communist Party (Suomen Kommunistinen Puolue; SKP); runs as the Finnish People's
Democratic League (Suomen Kansan Demokraattinen Liitto; SKDL) in parliamentary elections
Founded. 1918
Membership. 50,000 (claimed)
Chairman. Arvo Aalto
Secretary General. Aarno Aitamurto
Politburo. 9 members: Arvo Aalto, Aarno Aitamurto, Helja Tammisola (deputy chairman), Erkki
Kauppila, Arvo Kamppainen, Mirja Ylitalo, Timo Laaksonen, Olavi Haeninen, Esko Vainionpaeae
Central Committee. 50 full and 15 alternate members
Status. Legal
Last Congress. Twentieth, 24–26 May 1984 in Helsinki
Last Election. 1983, 14 percent, 27 of 200 seats
Auxiliary Organizations. Finnish Democratic Youth League; Women's Organization
Publications. *Kansan Uuitset* (daily); *Tiedonantaja* (daily), Stalinist; *Folktidningen* (Swedish-language
weekly); all three published in Helsinki

The SKP became Finland's largest party after World War II. Unlike other European communist parties, the SKP has been part of the government coalition for some lengthy periods, from 1944 to 1948 and, with some interruptions, from 1966 to 1982. The party continued to win over 20 percent of the vote, but significant ideological differences surfaced within the party while it was in the ranks of the opposition in the 1960s. The differences became hardened during the 1970s, to the extent that the more moderate, majority wing of the party was part of the governing coalition between 1975 and 1982, while the Stalinist, pro-Soviet minority was in opposition. The tensions between the two wings of the party sharpened further when the veteran moderate leader of the SKP, Aarne Saarinen, gave up the party leadership in 1982 and was succeeded as chairman by Juoko Kajonoja. The latter promised to unify the two wings of the party, but his rigid adherence to the Kremlin line had the opposite effect.

In 1983, the SKP (and its electoral front, the SKDL) suffered the sharpest electoral defeat in its history. In 1958, the SKP had the largest group in the parliament—50 deputies—in 1983, the number was reduced from 35 to 27, the fourth largest parliamentary group. Its percentage of the vote fell to 14 percent, also the lowest ever (the high point was 23.5 percent in 1948). This was partly due to the increasing appeal of the Social Democrats and, to a lesser extent, the new Green Party to onetime communist voters. Also, many voters were alienated by the sharp, open differences between the two wings of the party and the perceived heavy-handed interference of the Soviets in SKP affairs.

Leadership and Organization. The Twentieth Congress on 25 to 27 May and the events surrounding it were by far the dominant news in Finnish communist politics in 1984.

A considerable amount of posturing took place before the congress. Kalevi Kivisto, chairman of the SKDL, said six weeks before the congress that the SKDL would organize itself into an independent party if the SKP remained in the hands of the Stalinists (*Helsingin Sanomat*, 9 April). There were a number of instances of none-too-subtle pressure from the Soviets to re-elect Kajonoja and others sympathetic to the Moscow line. For example, Stefan Smirnov, an official of the International Department of the Soviet party, said in a speech in Finland: "The Finnish Communist Party has reached a dangerous point at which its path is threatened with division . . . The Communist Party of the Soviet Union has no intention whatever of getting involved in the internal affairs of the SKP. Judgments have, however, always been given when asked for by the SKP leadership." (*Hufvudstadsbladet*, 30 April.) The contenders for the leadership were Kajonoja and the moderate secretary general, Arvo Aalto. One datum that gave support to the moderates' claim that a change was needed to recapture support for the party was a Gallup Poll taken in May that showed that the SKP had slipped to 12.6 percent, 1.4 points below its previous low ebb—the 14 percent showing in the 1983 parliamentary election.

On the opening day of the congress, even more Soviet pressure was forthcoming. A *Pravda* (25 May) article warned the SKP against splitting or weakening its ideological position. In the crucial vote, the moderates beat the Stalinists by 183 votes to 163. The hard-liners and their leader, Taisto Sinisalo, were offered three of the eleven places on the Politburo and 15 of the 50 seats on the Central Committee, but they turned down the offer. Aalto was elected chairman, and Aalto's previous position of secretary general was taken by a trade union leader with a reputation for toughness with the hard-liners, Aarno Aitamurto. Helja Tammisola became deputy chairman. Because of the Stalinists' refusal to accept leading positions in the party structure, the entire Politburo and Central Committee were composed of moderates. Nevertheless, the deeply split SKP emerged from the congress even more divided.

The minority still controls eight of the fifteen party district organizations and publishes its own hard-line paper (*Tiedonantaja*). It and its Soviet allies continued a drumbeat of demands to convene an extraordinary congress. Aalto and the moderates resisted that demand, but toward the end of 1984 the SKP decided to hold an extraordinary congress by the end of March 1985 (Finnish domestic radio, 27 October). The hard-liners said that the congress was necessary to forge "unity," but the majority's answer was that the Stalinists interpreted "unity" as strict adherence to the Moscow line. Thus, the often acrimonious internal struggle, which has been

going on for nearly twenty years, seems destined to continue.

One of the continuing points of conflict is that the moderates are attempting to set up parallel organizations or, at least, are trying to support moderate Communists in those districts that the Stalinists control.

Domestic Activities. In mid-April the SKDL urged the Finnish Foreign Ministry to participate, together with France, in removing American-laid mines from Nicaraguan waters (*Helsingin Sanomat*, 12 April). In early May, the SKDL Central Council voted 24–9 to take a stand against the building of new nuclear plants in Finland (ibid., 7 May). In late August, the SKP Central Committee demanded an increase in the foreign value of the Finnish mark and a reduction of the interest rate tied to it. The SKP also asked for a more active employment policy, further development of social security, and an increase in the construction of rental housing. The party's list of objectives also included lowering the retirement age to 55. The SKP proposed to fund its proposals, if enacted, by higher taxes on banks and insurance companies and by eliminating tax relief for economic incentive purposes (ibid., 26 August).

International Party Contacts and Positions. The Bulgarian media reported that a delegation headed by Bulgarian Politburo member Milko Balev attended the SKP congress in late May and read the standard message of "comradely greetings" (*Rabotnichesko delo*, Sofia, 27 May). At the same congress, Miklós Óvari, a leader of the Hungarian communist party, stated that his party and the SKP agreed that there "is no kind of reasonable alternative to the peaceful coexistence of states with different social systems and to détente" (Budapest domestic service, 27 May).

Petar Matić, a member of the collective leadership of the Yugoslav League of Communists, also addressed the congress, but took a slightly different tone. He spoke of "the irreplaceable role" of nonalignment and underlined the significance of the relations between communist parties "on the basis of consistent respect for the principles of autonomy, independence, equality, and noninterference" (Tanjug, 26 May).

An SKP delegation led by Aalto visited East Berlin on 5 October to participate in the celebration of the thirty-fifth anniversary of the German Democratic Republic. Also in the delegation was Anneli

Hoikka, Central Committee member and chairwoman of the Women's Commission. (ADN, East Berlin, 5 October.)

Throughout the year, there was a series of visits by Soviet leaders and delegations, some being government-to-government and others being party-related. The visits relating to party matters were widely seen as Soviet attempts to affect the internal politics of the SKP. For example, on 30 April a Soviet delegation led by Central Committee member Lev Zaikov, met with then-chairman Kajonoja and other party members and issued a statement stressing "the need to cherish Soviet-Finnish friendship as a great achievement of the two peoples' meeting their vital interests and strongly to repulse any attempt to subvert that friendship" (Tass, 30 April). This was seen as a thinly veiled attempt to convey a message to the moderate wing of the SKP.

The Soviet Union sent a high-level delegation, headed by Politburo member Grigori Romanov, to the "gala" at Helsinki's Cultural Palace to mark the fortieth anniversary of the Soviet-Finnish armistice and the Finland-USSR Society. There was considerable publicity in both the Finnish and Soviet press about this event. (Finnish international service, 13 October.)

Peter Grothe
Monterey Institute of International Studies

France

Population. 55,600,000
Party. French Communist Party (Parti communiste français; PCF)
Founded. 1920
Membership. 610,000 (*L'Humanité*, 2 November)
General Secretary. Georges Marchais
Politburo. 22 full members: Georges Marchais, Gustave Ansart (chairman of the Central Commission on Political Control), Mireille Bertrand (health), Jean Colpin (assistance with the advancement of members), Charles Fiterman (minister of transport until July 1984), Jean-Claude Gayssot (party activity in businesses), Maxime Gremetz (foreign policy), Guy Hermier (editor of *Révolution*), Philippe Herzog (economics), Pierre Juquin (propaganda and party spokesman), Henri Krasucki (secretary of the General Confederation of Labor), André Lajoinie (chairman of the PCF group in the National Assembly), Paul Laurent (party organization), Francette Lazard (director of the Institute of Marxist Studies), René Le Guen (science and technology), Roland Leroy (editor of *L'Humanité*), Gisele Moreau (party activity among women), René Piquet (chairman of the PCF delegation in the European Parliament), Gaston Plissonier (coordination of work by the Politburo and Secretariat), Claude Poperen (liaison with party federations), Louis Viannet (Mail Workers Federation), Madeleine Vincent (local communities, elections)
Secretariat. 7 members: Georges Marchais, Charles Fiterman, Maxime Gremetz, André Lajoinie, Paul Laurent, Gisele Moreau, Gaston Plissonier
Central Committee. 145 members
Status. Legal
Last Congress. Twenty-fourth, 3–7 February 1982; next congress planned for 6–10 February 1985

Last Election. 1981, 16.2 percent, 44 of 491 seats

Auxiliary Organizations. General Confederation of Labor (CGT), World Peace Council, Movement of Communist Youth of France (MCJF), Committee for the Defense of Freedom in France and the World, Association of Communist and Republican Representatives

Publications. *L'Humanité*, Paris, daily national organ; *L'Echo du centre*, Limoges, daily; *Liberté*, Lille, daily; *La Marseillaise*, Marseille, daily; *L'Humanité-dimanche*, Paris, weekly; *Révolution*, weekly publication of the Central Committee; *La Terre*, weekly; *Cahiers du communisme*, monthly theoretical journal; *Europe*, literary journal; *Economie et politique*, economic journal; 5 journals published by the Marxist Research Institute; 4 monthly magazines; other periodicals on sports, for children, etc., and books on political, economic, and social topics published by Editions sociales, the PCF publishing house, Paris

Party Internal Affairs. For the French Communist Party (PCF), 1984 may well come to be regarded as a turning point. The year was marked by the party's worst electoral defeat in 60 years, followed by the leadership's decision to withdraw its ministers from participation in the French government and to declare the formal termination of the Union of the Left, thus ending twelve years of off-again, on-again partnership with President François Mitterrand's Socialist Party (PS). These events sparked new controversies within the party itself, with serious debates taking place at the very highest levels of the party hierarchy concerning the PCF's basic domestic and foreign policy orientations. As the year drew to a close, questions arose concerning the ability of General Secretary Georges Marchais to maintain his leadership position, an issue that would surely be of concern at the PCF's Twenty-fifth Congress on 6–10 February 1985.

The chief catalyst to these developments was the PCF's poor showing in the 17 June elections to the European Parliament. The Communists obtained only 11.28 percent of the vote, a disastrous figure that demonstrated the magnitude of the PCF's continuing slippage in popular support. Once the largest party in postwar France, with over 25 percent of the vote in the early years of the Fourth Republic, the PCF had grown accustomed to garnering the support of about 20 percent of the electorate in the 1960s and 1970s. When one-fourth of these constituents abandoned the party in May 1981 as Marchais received 15.5 percent of the ballots in his first-round bid for the presidency, it was evident that many communist voters were punishing PCF leaders for their unwillingness at that time to close ranks with the Socialists and unite the forces of the left squarely behind Mitterrand. As it happened, Mitterrand went on to win the presidential election in the second round, with grudging PCF support, and

the PS won an absolute majority of the seats in the National Assembly several weeks later. Faced with the choice of either retreating into the opposition or of accepting Mitterrand's offer of four cabinet ministries, the Communists opted for participation in the government as the junior partner of the Socialists.

With the elections of 1984, it appeared that a growing number of erstwhile PCF supporters were expressing their discontent with the party after three years of PCF participation in the Socialist-dominated cabinet. For the party leaders, the dilemma facing them appeared to be virtually intractable. On the one hand, they were reluctant to return to a self-imposed political isolation that would leave the Socialist Party as the only large governing force on the left and perhaps erode even further the PCF's narrowing base of popularity. On the other hand, they did not wish to be held accountable in the eyes of their constituents for the failure of the leftist government to fulfill the promises made in 1981, notably with respect to reducing unemployment and transferring wealth from the upper classes to the lower. By mid-1984 these promises lay in tatters, with unemployment climbing well above the 2 million mark and the government increasingly turning away from its initial reformist impulses and moving toward stiff austerity measures. The PCF's dilemma was compounded by its lack of policymaking influence even though it had four members in the cabinets headed by Prime Minister Pierre Mauroy. Mitterrand and the Socialists, with their command of the National Assembly, had effectively relegated the PCF to the outer margins of the policymaking process.

Pressures from inside the PCF to quit the government were building up even before the 17 June election. In April two communist mayors urged the leadership to pull out of the cabinet rather than risk being identified with Mitterrand's policies (*Le Monde*, 7 April; *FBIS*, 10 April). After the electoral debacle, however, other voices were raised calling on the PCF to remain in the government, with some party figures suggesting that the roots of the PCF's electoral decline were to be found in its excessively pro-Soviet foreign policies and its undemocratic internal procedures. One of the most prominent exponents of this latter view was Marcel Rigout, then serving as minister for vocational training. Rigout reportedly told journalists that he was distressed that the PCF had acquired only 6 percent of the youth vote, and he noted that many young voters today equated communism with the USSR and prison camps. According to these reports (which Rigout subsequently denied), he called for a "cultural revolution" within the PCF and for efforts to distance the party from the Soviet Union. The PCF minister was also quoted by several journalists as appealing for more open debate at party congresses and as describing Marchais as a failure. (*NYT*, 5 July; *Economist*, London, 7 July.) Another high-level advocate of more open discussion in party forums at this time was Pierre Juquin, the PCF's official spokesman (*Le Monde*, 25 June). In a related incident, Daniel Karlin, a PCF intellectual, disclosed that the editor of *L'Humanité* had informed him that Marchais himself had rejected an article Karlin had coauthored criticizing the lack of internal democracy in the PCF and calling on the leadership to reverse its positions on such matters as the Soviet invasion of Afghanistan, the martial law regime in Poland, and the treatment of Soviet dissident Andrei Sakharov (*NYT*, 5 July).

These discussions intensified in July, as President Mitterrand abruptly dismissed the Mauroy cabinet and appointed Laurent Fabius prime minister. This move was accompanied by an announcement of a more pronounced shift to the right in economic policy, with a clear priority to be given to the fight against inflation as opposed to unemployment. Marchais interrupted a holiday visit to Romania to join in an all-night meeting of the PCF Central Committee on 19 July. After efforts to obtain policy clarifications and concessions from Fabius proved unsatisfactory, the PCF leader announced the withdrawal of the PCF ministers from the government. Party leaders added, however, that the PCF would continue to support the Socialist government in the National Assembly.

According to press reports, opinions were divided within the Central Committee on the wisdom of this step (ibid., 20 July; *CSM*, 25 July). Rigout and another PCF cabinet official, Anicet Le Pors, were reportedly among those arguing for remaining in the government, while Charles Fiterman, the number-two man in the PCF leadership and minister of transport in the last Mauroy cabinet, and Henri Krasucki, the head of the CGT, joined those in favor of withdrawal (*Le Monde*, 20 July). (Gaston Plissonier, an acknowledged hard-liner in favor of withdrawal, later maintained that the Central Committee decision was taken "unanimously" [*L'Humanité*, 26 July].) Meanwhile, PCF dissidents such as Henri Fiszbin opposed the leadership's decision (*Rencontres communistes hebdo*, 24 July).

The debates continued in two subsequent Central Committee meetings, with Marchais himself increasingly the target of criticism. Backed by hard-line party leaders such as Plissonier, Roland Leroy (editor of *L'Humanité*), and André Lajoinie (the PCF's parliamentary leader), Marchais asserted on 8 September that the PCF would no longer be bound by its earlier decision to vote with the governing majority in the National Assembly. He defended this position in a lengthy speech at the Central Committee plenum of 17 September. (*L'Humanité*, 21 September; *Radio Free Europe/Radio Liberty* [*RFE/RL*], 24 September.) Although edited summaries of Central Committee deliberations were now being published in the party press, it appeared that criticism of the PCF's recent decisions—and, to some extent, of Marchais himself—was more extensive than the veiled accounts released by the party had indicated (*Le Monde*, 24 September). Indeed, Marchais explicitly acknowledged his disagreements with Juquin on the question of democratic centralism (*L'Humanité*, 27 September; *FBIS*, 5 October).

These disagreements surfaced again at the Central Committee meetings of 29–30 October, which concluded with the publication of a draft resolution to be considered for adoption at the Twenty-fifth Congress. *L'Humanité* (1 November) acknowledged that six Central Committee members had abstained from voting on the resolution and noted that well over a hundred changes were made in the original text of the draft on the basis of the Central Committee discussions (*FBIS*, 7 November). *Le Monde* (1 November) reported that Juquin and Rigout were among the six who had abstained and that several Central Committee members who eventually voted for the revised draft had attacked the first version written by the Marchais leadership. One of the changes incorporated into the second draft suggested that Central Committee members who had views opposed to the leadership's decisions could not only "maintain" their viewpoints but could even "defend" them in the discussions that would precede the party congress.

In spite of these challenges to his leadership, Marchais appeared to be firmly ensconced as general secretary and gave every indication of his determination to remain at the helm. Even Fiterman, a man considered to be a possible successor to Marchais, rallied to the general secretary's defense on more than one occasion, stating in October that Marchais was "the best man" for the top job (*L'Humanité*, 16 October; *FBIS*, 26 October). It was perhaps a measure of Marchais's self-confidence that he assured an interviewer that the leadership issue would be the second item on the agenda of the congress (following an in-depth discussion of party strategy), while adding that the congress would be "an extension, an enrichment" of the three previous party congresses (*FBIS*, 10 September). This last statement suggested that Marchais had already decided that there would be no clean break from the leadership he had presided over since the early 1970s.

Domestic Issues. Political events in France in 1984 tended to be dominated by the country's worsening economic situation and its social ramifications. Although Mitterrand had declared upon taking office that he would endeavor to hold unemployment below 2 million, by the middle of the year over 2.4 million were unemployed, more than 10 percent of the work force. In February Marchais met with Mitterrand and urged the adoption of an industrial policy designed above all to combat unemployment (ibid., 22 February). Mitterrand, however, was committed to an economic modernization program and to a reduction in state expenditures, both of which would exacerbate unemployment, at least in the short run. By March the government foresaw the elimination of 5,000 jobs in the shipbuilding industry, 30,000 jobs in the coal industry, and 6,000 jobs at Citroën motors. There were additional warnings that as many as 200,000 steelworkers could lose their jobs in 1984. (*NYT*, 8 March, 18 April.) When the government announced plans to eliminate as many as 27,000 jobs in the state-supported steel sector, Marchais and other PCF leaders joined in demonstrations held to protest these plans (*Los Angeles Times*, 14 April).

This prompted the Socialists to schedule a vote of confidence in the National Assembly on 19 April to force the PCF's hand on the question of whether it still regarded itself as part of the governing coalition. Although the Communists voted to stay in the cabinet at this time, Marchais continued to criticize the Socialists for failing to keep the political and economic pledges they had made in 1981 (*WSJ*, 7 May). On the labor front, members of the communist-led trade union organization occupied all six Citroën plants in May to protest the planned layoffs (*U.S. News & World Report*, 19 June).

The elections to the European Parliament of 17 June took place in the context of these growing frictions between the PCF and the Mitterrand administration. The results of the elections constituted a major setback not just for the PCF, but for the left in general. The PS vote share fell to 20.8 percent. The two main parties of the center-right, the UDF (the party of former president Valéry Giscard d'Estaing) and the RPR (the neo-Gaullist party led by Jacques Chirac) together polled 42.9 percent. Most astounding was the figure of 11 percent compiled by the National Front (FN), an extreme right-wing party with an avowedly anti-immigrant orientation. The FN had done remarkably well against the PCF in municipal elections held in 1983; now it received almost as many votes (2.2 million) for the European Parliament as PCF candidates. Voter dissatisfaction was also apparent in the high abstention rate (43 percent). (*NYT*, 19 June.)

Communist officials readily admitted the enormity of the electoral setback the party had suffered. In their analysis of the elections, they blamed their losses primarily on the exceptionally high level of abstentions among communist voters, a fact they attributed to working-class discontent at the performance of the leftist government (*L'Humanité*, 28 June; *FBIS*, 13 July; *JPRS*, 28 August). Once Mitterrand announced the appointment of Fabius as prime minister in July and confirmed his intention to pursue austerity policies (including an across-the-board 5 percent tax cut and additional tax breaks for business), the PCF leadership concluded that the party would probably experience a further deterioration of its electoral base by remaining in the government. Party strategy was now aimed at recouping its recent losses by casting blame on the Socialists for the country's economic hardships.

Accordingly, PCF leaders stepped up their attacks on Mitterrand and the PS in the second half of the year. Following the Communists' decision to vote against the government in the National Assembly, the PS canceled a meeting with the PCF leadership scheduled for 12 September to discuss PCF-PS cooperation in the 1985 cantonal elections (*Le Monde*, 13 September). On 16 September, PS leader Lionel Jospin declared an end to the Union of the Left (*FBIS*, 19 September). At the end of October the PCF issued a lengthy pre-congress document strongly critical of the Socialists. The document implied that the PCF had erred in participating in the Mauroy cabinets in the first place and suggested that the party should have fielded its own candidate for president in 1974 instead of backing Mitterrand from the outset (*L'Humanité*, 1 November; *Le Monde*, 3 November). In the following month Marchais called for finalizing the breakup of the Union of the Left and condemned Mitterrand's "cult of personality" (*FBIS*, 9 November). The PCF chief even suggested that the PCF had inadvertently "contributed to creating illusions" about improving the standard of living of its supporters during the period of leftist unity, thus supplying further evidence of the party leadership's determination to press its attack on the Socialists in the months to come. Finally, the PCF voted against the Fabius government's 1985 budget in the National Assembly, with one communist deputy stating unequivocally, "We are in the opposition" (*Le Monde*, 20 December).

The extent to which the PCF may succeed in regaining its former levels of electoral support will not become clear until the cantonal elections of 1985. However, a partial glimpse of what may lie ahead in these elections could be gained from the results of cantonal elections held in the second half of 1984. Of the four cantons already controlled by the PCF, the party retained two and lost the other two to the center-right. The Communists won an additional canton from the center-right parties. Although the left's vote generally receded somewhat from the levels obtained in 1979 and 1982, the PCF's losses were not quite as great as those suffered by the PS. The Socialists lost three of the four cantons they held prior to the elections. In eight cantons that voted in 1982, the PCF's share of the vote fell by a total of 1.13 percent, whereas the PS lost 6.2 percent of its former constituency (ibid., 27 December).

Foreign Views and Activities. As it has in the past, foreign policy constituted another major area of contention between the PCF and the PS. The two parties differed on virtually every major issue of East-West relations, with the PCF adopting pro-Soviet positions on such issues as the European missile balance, the Soviet invasion of Afghanistan, and the imposition of martial law in Poland (ibid., 20 April; *FBIS*, 25 April). Curiously, the PCF supported Mitterrand's decision to send French troops to Chad, comparing the action favorably with the "request" of the government of Afghanistan for Soviet intervention in 1979 (*Rouge*, 17–23 February). (In September, the PCF approved the withdrawal of French forces from Chad [*FBIS*, 18 September].)

In its defense policy, the PCF reaffirmed its approval of the government's decision to construct France's seventh nuclear missile–carrying submarine, but opposed the development of neutron weapons and objected to the establishment of a French Rapid Action Force for use outside the European theater (ibid., 14 and 23 February). Party leaders also opposed Mitterrand's plans to increase French conventional military strength (*JPRS*, 16 April) and criticized Chirac's proposal for the creation of a European defense system.

PCF spokesmen were highly critical of U.S. foreign policy, particularly with respect to Central America and the deployment of new U.S. intermediate-range missiles in Western Europe. Party leaders such as Marchais and Maxime Gremetz conferred with Sandinista officials from Nicaragua (*FBIS*, 24 April) and with members of Salvadoran revolutionary organizations (ibid., 10 February, 26 March, 27 June). The PCF denounced U.S. ambassador Evan Galbraith for remarks critical of the party (*NYT*, 3 February) and implied that the United States had played a role in the assassination of Indira Gandhi (*L'Humanité*, 2 November; *FBIS*, 6 November).

On European issues, the PCF continued to voice misgivings about the projected enlargement of the European Communities (*L'Humanité*, 15 May; *FBIS*, 23 May) and called for the expulsion of Turkey from the Council of Europe for executing political prisoners (*L'Humanité*, 1 November; *FBIS*, 14 November).

In May, PCF Central Committee member Jacques Roux was elected president of the World Health Organization (*L'Humanité*, 23 May).

International Party Relations. The PCF's attitude toward the Communist Party of the Soviet Union (CPSU) in 1984 continued to be largely supportive of Soviet policies, with occasional criticisms of selected Soviet actions and reaffirmations of the PCF's independence from Moscow. Typical of this approach was Marchais's admission that Stalinism had been a tragic error and that there were "too many" political prisoners in the USSR today, statements that he counterbalanced with assurances that the Soviet Union now was much different from that of the Stalinist period, that *gulag* was simply the Soviet term for prison, and that the number of American prisoners on death row exceeded the known number of Soviet political prisoners. (*FBIS*, 24 January.) Marchais described the USSR as "neither a paradise nor a gulag" (ibid., 31 January).

Marchais adopted a guarded position on Konstantin Chernenko. The PCF chief did not send a congratulatory telegram to the new Soviet leader upon his accession and was not given a private audience with Chernenko following Yuri Andropov's funeral in February (*Le Monde*, 22 February). Marchais's reluctance to praise Chernenko contrasted with his continuing expressions of admiration for Andropov and Nikita Khrushchev, both of whom the PCF leader apparently esteemed as reformers of the Soviet system (ibid., 17 March; *FBIS*, 26 March).

Meanwhile, Marchais and other party leaders continued to stress their commitment to a French brand of socialism, which the general secretary described as "a self-managing, pluralist socialism, developing French patriotism, human freedoms and rights." "The days of models are over," Marchais insisted. (*Le Monde*, 17 March; *FBIS*, 26 March.) Demonstrating the party's willingness to criticize the Soviets, the PCF opposed the Soviet decision to boycott the Olympic games (*FBIS*, 11 May). Subsequently, Marchais addressed a letter to the Soviet leadership inquiring into the health of Andrei Sakharov and his wife at a time when rumors suggested that Sakharov had died as the result of a hunger strike (ibid., 21 May). Upon receiving assurances from Soviet authorities that the Sakharovs were in good health, Marchais warned of a possible "rupture" between the PCF and the CPSU if the Soviets were found to be lying (ibid., 4 and 8 June). Marchais also sent a letter to the CPSU Central Committee protesting the contention of a Soviet demographer that only 82 percent of the population of France was ethnically French. Marchais insisted that "all men and women of French nationality are French" (*L'Humanité*, 29 February; *FBIS*, 7 March). In another incident having a bearing on PCF-CPSU relations, the French Communists strongly protested the arrest and sentencing of a French journalist by the government of Afghanistan and suspended their ties with the People's Democratic Party of Afghanistan until the journalist was released and repatriated to France (*FBIS*, 24 and 29 October).

For their part, the Soviets seemed to approve of the PCF's decision to leave the French government (*Pravda*, 24 September).

PCF officials held meetings with high-ranking leaders of several of the ruling communist parties of Eastern Europe in 1984. In January, Marchais received a delegation from the Socialist Unity Party of Germany (SED) headed by Günter Mittag (*FBIS*, 12 January) and another SED delegation in September (*RFE/RL*, 11 September). Marchais journeyed to East Berlin in February, and joined with SED leader Erich Honecker in stressing the need for arms reductions (*FBIS*, 7 February). Marchais also traveled to Romania in the summer for an extended visit (ibid., 2 July). In September, Marchais met in Paris with Mátyás Szürös, the Hungarian party secretary responsible for foreign policy (ibid., 21 September), and welcomed János Kádár while the latter was on a state visit to France in October (*L'Humanité*, 16 October; *FBIS*, 22 October). In all of these meetings, Marchais seemed to be giving support to those Warsaw Pact countries on record as favoring a reinvigoration of détente in Europe in spite of the installation of new American and Soviet missiles in the European theater. The more hard-line Czech party sent a Central Committee delegation to Paris in October (*FBIS*, 22 October).

The PCF also cultivated its relationships with other ruling parties. Marchais visited Cuba in January (*FBIS*, 6 January), and Gremetz met with Chinese premier Zhao Ziyang in Paris in June (*JPRS*, 6 September). Gremetz also met with the president of the League of Communists of Yugoslavia, Dragoslav Marković, while in Yugoslavia (*FBIS*, 24 May) and conferred in Paris with Vietnam's foreign minister (*L'Humanité*, 27 October) and with a delegation from South Yemen's ruling Socialist Party (*FBIS*, 7 March).

Among the nonruling parties, the PCF accorded special attention to its relations with other West European parties. Marchais greeted Spanish Communist Party chief Gerardo Iglesias in Paris on 7 March (ibid., 20 March) and sent a personal message of condolence to the Italian Communist Party upon the death of Enrico Berlinguer (ibid., 18 June). The PCF chief also met with Kharilaos Florakis, head of the Greek Communist Party (Exterior), in Paris (ibid., 23 May). In addition, PCF officials also conferred with representatives of the communist parties of Austria, Belgium, Great Britain, and Luxembourg. The PCF also maintained contacts with a number of communist and revolutionary groups from the Middle East, Africa, and Latin America. (*JPRS*, 8 June, 6 September.)

Michael J. Sodaro
George Washington University

Germany:
Federal Republic of Germany

Population. 59,387,000
Party. German Communist Party (Deutsche Kommunistische Partei; DKP)
Founded. 1968
Membership. 50,482 (claimed)
Chairman. Herbert Mies
Presidium. 15 members: Herbert Mies, Hermann Gautier, Jupp Angenfort, Kurt Bachmann, Irmgard Bobrzik, Martha Buschmann, Werner Cieslak, Gerd Deumlich, Kurt Fritsch, Willi Gerns, Georg Polikeit, Rolf Priemer, Karl-Heinz Schröder, Werner Sturmann, Ellen Weber
Secretariat. 11 members: Herbert Mies, Hermann Gautier, Vera Achenbach, Jupp Angenfort, Werner Cieslak, Gerd Deumlich, Kurt Fritsch, Willi Gerns, Josef Mayer, Karl-Heinz Schröder, Wilhelm Spengler
Executive. 91 members
Status. Legal
Last Congress. Seventh, 6–8 January 1984, in Nuremberg
Last Election. 1983, 0.2 percent, no representation
Auxiliary Organizations. Socialist German Workers Youth (Sozialistische Deutsche Arbeiter Jugend; SDAJ), ca. 15,000 members, Brigit Radow, chairperson; Marxist Student Union–Spartakus (Marxistischer Studentenbund; MSB-Spartakus), ca. 6,000 members (MSB-Spartakus claim: 6,500), Bernd Gäbler, chairman; Young Pioneers (Junge Pioniere; JP), ca. 4,000 members
Publications. *Unsere Zeit* (Our time), Düsseldorf, DKP daily organ, circulation ca. 25,000, Friday edition ca. 50,000, Monday edition discontinued; *elan—Das Jugendmagazin*, SDAJ monthly organ, circulation ca. 35,000; *rote blätter* (Red pages), MSB-Spartakus monthly organ, circulation ca. 18,000; *pionier* (Pioneer), JP monthly organ

The pro-Soviet DKP is the successor organization of the Communist Party of German (Kommunistische Partei Deutschlands; KPD), which was founded on 31 December 1918. The KPD was the third-largest political party in the Weimar Republic. During the Hitler regime, the party was outlawed and became an ineffective underground party with most of its leaders either in exile or imprisoned. Following World War II, the KPD was reactivated in the Allied occupation zones. In the Soviet-occupied zone, the Soviet Military Administration forced the merger of the KPD and the Social

Democratic Party of Germany (Sozialdemo-kratische Partei Deutschlands; SPD). The "new" party adopted the name Socialist Unity Party of Germany (Sozialistische Einheitspartei Deutschlands; SED). In the first national elections in the Federal Republic of Germany (FRG) in 1949, the KPD received 5.7 percent of the vote and fifteen seats in the Bundestag. In the next elections in 1953, the KPD vote decreased to 2.2 percent, below the 5 percent required by German law for representation in the federal legislature. In August 1956, the Federal Constitutional Court outlawed the KPD for pursuing unconstitutional objectives. The KPD continued its activities as an underground party, led by Max Reimann, who resided in East Berlin. Substantial financial and operational support from the SED did not prevent the underground KPD from losing most of its members.

In September 1968, the DKP was founded as a concession from Chancellor Willy Brandt to Leonid Brezhnev. Most of the "new" party's leaders had been officials in the illegal KPD, which at that time had shrunk to about 7,000 members. In 1971, the Federal Security Service (BVS) stated that the DKP, which openly emphasizes it is part of the international communist movement and the only legitimate heir to the KPD, was the successor of the outlawed party.

According to the annual report of the BVS, there were two orthodox communist organizations (membership 44,500) at the end of 1983, with 13 affiliated organizations (27,600) and 52 organizations influenced by Communists (70,000). In addition there were 20 basic organizations of the dogmatic New Left (3,400) with 12 affiliated organizations (1,100) and 17 organizations in which these groups exerted some influence (4,500), as well as 50 undogmatic organizations of the New Left (4,900). After deducting for membership in more than one organization and children's groups, the BVS concluded that membership in these left-extremist organizations totaled 61,000, and membership in organizations influenced by these groups 56,000. (Bundesministerium des Innern, *Verfassungsschutzbericht, 1983*, Bonn, June 1984, p. 20.)

Leadership and Organization. The Seventh Congress of the DKP (6–8 January) was held in Nuremberg under the slogan "Peace must win. Jobs not missiles!" The congress was attended by 778 delegates and guests from affiliated and communist-influenced organizations and by representatives of more than 40 fraternal communist and workers' parties and national liberation movements (*IB*, March). The Soviet delegation was led by Grigori Romanov, member of the Politburo and secretary of the Central Committee (Tass, 9 January; *FBIS*, 10 January). Egon Krenz, member of the SED Politburo and secretary of the Central Committee, led the East German delegation, which also included the chief of the West Department of the SED Central Committee, Prof. Herbert Häber (*Deutscher Informations Dienst* [*DID*], November, p. 3). The congress confirmed Herbert Mies as DKP chairman and Hermann Gautier as vice-chairman and elected the 91-member Executive, which in turn elected the 15-member Presidium and the 11-member Secretariat. Ninety-five percent of the 778 delegates were active members of trade unions, and 347 were members of various "peace initiatives." Women accounted for more than one-third of the delegates. (*Frankfurter Allgemeine Zeitung* [*FAZ*], 9 January; *DID*, November, p. 1; Tass, 7 January; *FBIS*, 9 January.)

The congress unanimously adopted an "Action Program for Peace and Jobs." The program condemned the deployment of new "first-strike" U.S. nuclear missiles, applauded the SPD's rejection of the stationing of Pershing II and cruise missiles, and pledged continuing communist support for the actions of the "peace movement" (*Unsere Zeit* [*UZ*], 10 January). The delegates stressed the DKP's responsibility for explaining to West Germans the peaceful foreign policy of the Soviet state and of the other countries of the socialist community (Tass, 8 January; *FBIS*, 9 January). The congress further stressed the intensification of the "alliance policy" and the active participation of DKP members in the peace movement and in the various "citizens' initiatives" (*DID*, November, p. 9).

The financial report stated the party's income in 1982 as 16.5 million marks, excluding services party members rendered free of charge (ibid., p. 2). This amount would not be enough to pay for the 800 fulltime party workers and staff members at party headquarters in Düsseldorf and the over 200 local offices, whose salaries cost at least 30 million marks. The DKP annually receives 60 million marks from the SED by way of a net of about 30 communist economic enterprises in the FRG, such as import-export firms, freight companies, and travel and advertising agencies. The employment rolls of these firms contain many professional DKP officials. The financial support of the SED covers the DKP's costs for personnel, its intensive ideological schooling programs, propaganda material, mass rallies, election campaigns, and the financing of DLP-affiliated and communist-influenced organizations. (*Verfassungsschutz*, p. 37; *FAZ*, 21 May.)

The party also maintains several training schools and has a costly publications program. Not included in the 60 million marks received from the SED is the cost of schooling DKP functionaries in East Berlin and Moscow (*Verfassungsschutz*, p. 36) and an ambitious delegation program, sponsored by the SED. Several hundred delegations, in addition to a children's holiday program, visit East Germany every year. No other communist party in a Western country is as dependent and as strictly controlled by a foreign party as the DKP is by the SED. The Western Department of the SED Central Committee is charged with the direction and control of the DKP, and SED regional organizations are assigned the task of assisting specific DKP county organizations.

The DKP and the party organ *Unsere Zeit* held the Sixth "*UZ* Press Festival—DKP People's Festival," 25–27 May in Duisburg-Wedau. It was attended by about 330,000 people (the DKP claimed over 400,000). Among the official guests from more than 40 countries was a Soviet delegation led by Aleksandr Vlasov, a member of the Soviet Central Committee. Speeches stressed the solidarity of the workers' movement and the common cause of the workers' and peace movements. The DKP declared its total solidarity with striking metal and printing shop workers, who were demanding a 35-hour workweek at the same pay. The "non-partisan" Metalworkers' Union sent a goodwill telegram to the festival. The DKP claims that in the course of the festival, 739 new members joined the party. (Bundesministerium des Innern, *Innere Sicherheit*, no. 73, Bonn, 29 June, p. 5.)

The SDAJ is the largest of the DKP-affiliated organizations, with about 15,000 members organized in about 900 groups. Its chairperson is Brigit Radow. The majority of the SDAJ functionaries and about 40 percent of the members belong to the party. The Eighth Federal Congress of the SDAJ (15–16 December) was held in Bottrop (*FAZ*, 17 December). Ideological schooling in Marxism-Leninism takes place in "educational evenings" of SDAJ group organizations and in mostly one-week courses at the Youth Educational Center Burg Wahrburg. The official SDAJ organs are the monthly *elan—Das Jugendmagazin* (about 35,000 copies) and the monthly *Jugendpolitische Blätter* (Youth political pages). The SDAJ also publishes about 400 local papers for apprentices and students. *Elan* publishes the *Informationsdienst für Soldaten* (Information service for soldiers) and the soldier newspaper *"Rührt Euch"* (At ease) in three regional editions. (*Verfassungsschutz*, p. 41.)

The Young Pioneers–Socialist Children's Organization (JP) has a membership of about 4,000. Its chairman, Achim Kroos, is a member of the DKP and of the Executive of the SDAJ. Many other JP-functionaries are members of the DKP and SDAJ. Pioneer leaders attend courses offered by the communist Youth Education Center Burg Wahrburg. The JP Executive publishes the monthly *Pioneer-Info* and the children's newspaper *pionier* (ibid., p. 42). On 20 September, the U.N. Children's Day, JP groups organized several demonstrations under the slogan "We defend ourselves against everything hostile to children [such as] poor playing facilities, unsafe traffic, hostilities toward foreigners, and other measures of the right-wing government hostile to children" (*DID*, October, p. 2).

Another DKP-affiliated organization is the MSB-Spartakus, with 6,000 members (MSB-Spartakus claims 6,500). Its chairman, Bernd Gäbler, was elected a member of the DKP Executive at the Seventh DKP Congress. MSB members attend courses and seminars at the Youth Education Center Burg Wahrburg. In October, the MSB held a group leader conference in Dortmund, which was attended by about 300 participants. The MSB Executive declared that President Reagan's planned visit to Bonn in 1985, for an economic summit, is a "challenge to the peace movement." The MSB monthly publication *rote blätter* (Red pages) has an edition of about 18,000. (Ibid., p. 2; *Verfassungsschutz*, p. 42.)

In order to mobilize as many citizens as possible for DKP objectives, such as the fight against implementation of the NATO dual-track decision, the party has the support of about 50 organizations and initiatives (action groups) that outwardly appear to be independent organizations but in fact are strongly influenced by the Communists. The majority of the members of these organizations are not DKP members. However, key positions, especially in the organizational sector (secretariats), are held by Communists, some of whom are not openly members of the DKP. The less the target groups recognize communist influence, the more effective are these organizations. Almost all of the larger organizations belong to Soviet-directed front organizations and maintain close contact with the Peace Council of the GDR. Among the more important organizations are the Association of Victims of the Nazi Regime/League of Antifascists (13,000 members), the German Peace Union (1,000 members), the Committee for Peace, Disarmament, and Cooperation, the German Peace Society/United War Service Resisters (20,000 members), the Democratic Women's Initiative, the Association of Democratic Jurists, the League of Democratic Scientists, and various solidarity committees and friendship societies (*Verfassungsschutz*, pp. 43–48). The DKP also utilizes left-extremists among foreign workers. The Federal Security Service reported that at the end of 1983, about 114,300 of the 4,534,000 foreigners in the FRG belonged to extremist groups.

Ideological education of party members remained a high priority of party work and was strongly endorsed by the Seventh DKP Congress. The DKP "educational year 1983/84" added the topic "unemployment and the DKP" to those dealing with various aspects of the "alliance policy" (*DID*, January, p. 4). The role of the party in alliances was the subject of the educational evenings of the primary party organizations (*Verfassungsschutz*, p. 36). In an indoctrination letter to its members, the DKP asked them to establish contacts with Social Democrats, especially in factories. The letter described Communists and Social Democrats as the two main trends of the labor movement and as united in their concern for peace. (*FAZ*, 12 May.) Communist factory workers attended evening courses on Marxism-Leninism offered by Marxist factory workers' schools at party district levels. In 1983, close to 900 party members completed about 40 one- and two-week basic and special courses at the Karl Liebknecht School in Leverkusen. The DKP also sent almost 300 members to courses lasting one, three, and twelve months in East Berlin and Moscow. (Ibid.)

Domestic Attitudes and Activities. *Land* elections were held in Baden-Württemberg on 25 March. The DKP received 13,608 votes (0.3 percent) compared with 11,738 (0.3 percent) in 1980 (*FAZ*, 27 March). The DKP obtained 0.6 percent (1979: 1.3 percent) in elections for district administrations and 0.5 percent (1979: 0.9 percent) in community elections in the Saarland on 17 June. In local elections on the same day in Rhineland-Palatinate, the DKP received 0.1 percent (1979: 0.3 percent). (*Union in Deutschland*, Bonn, no. 20, 20 June, p. 14.) In local elections in Baden-Württemberg on 30 September, the DKP retained four seats and gained two seats on alliance lists

(*DID*, November, p. 8). Local elections were also held on 30 September in North Rhine–Westphalia. The DKP received 36,045 votes (0.4 percent) compared with 55,571 (0.7 percent) in 1979 (*Union in Deutschland*, no. 30/31, 5 October, p. 34).

The DKP attempted to utilize the elections to the European Parliament on 17 June to overcome its extremely low vote by combining forces with other left-wing groups and individuals from the peace movement. A so-called "peace list" of 90 candidates (45 of them were replacements) contained ten members of the DKP Executive in addition to several members of communist-controlled front organizations, peace initiatives, and coordinating and solidarity committees (*FAZ*, 31 March). The "peace list" received 312,756 votes (1.3 percent) (ibid., 1 July). It was the first time since 1965 that a communist-led alliance obtained more than 0.6 percent in nationwide elections. On 6 October the Second Membership Conference of the "peace list" decided to continue the work and possibly form a new party. However, the DKP has no interest in being absorbed into the alliance; for their part, the 500-odd members of the "peace list" group cannot carry on an election campaign without the support of the DKP apparatus (ibid., 8 October).

The party's "alliance policy" continued to be highly successful and was able to increase the influence of the DKP far beyond its electoral potential. The main techniques are "citizens' initiatives" and "democratic movements for peace and disarmament, for the defense of democratic rights, for social and cultural affairs, for womens' rights, and for the protection of the environment" (*Verfassungsschutz*, p. 49). Collaboration with Social Democrats has further improved. Individual Social Democrats and SPD organizations have participated in communist-initiated actions or signed communist-sponsored appeals. The attitude of the DKP toward the SPD leadership has changed dramatically since the SPD became an opposition party and officially rejected the implementation of the NATO dual-track decision. DKP Chairman Herbert Mies applauded the SPD's consistent work for a security partnership between East and West (ADN, East Berlin, 6 January; *FBIS*, 9 January).

A typical example of a "unity of action" was the congress "Peace for Southern Africa—Solidarity with the Liberation Struggle of the Peoples of South Africa and Namibia!—Solidarity with the Front States," held 12–14 October in Cologne. Among the speakers were members of the DKP Presidium, representatives from the SDAJ, Democratic Socialists, SPD, Green Party, and several communist-influenced groups (*DID*, September, pp. 2–3).

The most important objective of communist action remained the fight against the deployment of new U.S. missiles in the FRG. In order to conceal the DKP influence in numerous actions against the deployment, the DKP used various communist-controlled organizations. With their help, the DKP succeeded in forming coordination committees throughout the FRG and in securing for itself the decisive voice in planning. One of the most influential coordination committees held its Fifth Action Conference, on 11–12 February in Cologne. Thirty organizations and initiatives planned "peace actions" for 1984. The conference achieved a consensus among the participating groups on all peace issues promoted by the DKP and postponed a debate on the Soviet nuclear arms buildup. The deployment of Soviet SS-20s was not mentioned. It also rejected a resolution supporting twenty imprisoned members of an independent peace movement in the GDR. The conference decided to organize a "people's plebiscite" on the stationing of the new U.S. nuclear missiles on 17 June, the day of the elections for the European Parliament, and initiated another campaign to refuse "war service" or any other military service. (*FAZ*, 13 February; *radical info*, no. 1, pp. 2–3.)

The Sixth Action Conference of the peace movement was held on 5–6 May in Cologne. It was attended by about 700 persons (about half as many as the two previous conferences). The conference planned further strategy and actions for 1984. The participants were less representative of the overall peace movement than the previous conferences. DKP-influenced organizations supplied more than half of the participants. The DKP achieved an 80–90 percent majority of votes on various issues with the support of the nonextremists from traditional peace groups and from "anti-imperialist" forces from the "independent/autonomous" organizations.

At a meeting of the organization's Coordination Committee on 26 November in Bonn, several participating organizations questioned the continuation of the work of the committee. A representative of an environmental group demanded that the Coordination Committee for the FRG and the Coordination Bureau in Bonn should be retained. The movement set as its main efforts for 1985 the economic summit in Bonn, the fortieth anniversary of World War II, and actions in October when the Netherlands and Belgium will decide on the deployment of cruise missiles. (*FAZ*, 27 November.) DKP Chair-

man Herbert Mies officially endorsed the "Peace Autumn–1984" campaign and declared that the struggle for peace and the demand to withdraw U.S. nuclear "first-strike"weapons should be combined (ADN, East Berlin, 26 August; *FBIS*, 27 August). As in previous years, the DKP supported the "Easter March 1984" and utilized German Peace Union offices as organizational headquarters (*radical info*, no. 2, p. 6).

Trade unions remain a priority target for communist infiltration. Despite great efforts, the DKP was unable to increase substantially the number of its factory units or "factory action groups." In 1983, there were about 330 factory units, half of them were in the metal industry and over 40 in the public service sector. The DKP decided against running its own candidates in elections for workers' representatives in the factories and asked its members to support the candidates of the German Trade Unions (DGB). (*DID*, January, p. 2.) The aim of the DKP was to politicize the labor struggle. DKP members succeeded in occupying influential positions in some trade unions, especially in the printers' trade unions and in the trade union of employees of trading, banking, and insurance enterprises. (*FAZ*, 7 June; *Union in Deutschland*, no. 25, p. 12.)

The First Central DKP Shop Stewards' Conference was held on 21 February in Cologne. About 450 participants exchanged experiences and discussed with DKP leaders the "role of the working class in the struggle against the arms buildup and reactionary social changes." The conference unanimously approved an appeal for a Congress for Peace and Work, to be held on 27 October in the Ruhr industrial region to deal with resistance against the new U.S. nuclear missiles and reactionary developments. The congress also endorsed the "peace list" for the 17 June elections for the European Parliament. (*DID*, March, pp. 3–4, June, p. 4, August, p. 10.)

The SDAJ also assisted the DKP's efforts to strengthen its influence in the trade unions. For example, the SDAJ-controlled League of Representatives of Pupils organized a nationwide "action week" (26 November–1 December) under the heading "For the Right of Work and Education—Common Cause Against [the political] Right." The project was supported by various regional youth organizations of the DGB and by a broad alliance of other youth groups. (Ibid., November, p. 15.)

International Views and Party Contacts. The foreign policy statements of DKP functionaries are substantially identical with those made by Moscow and East Berlin. At the Seventh Party Congress, DKP Chairman Herbert Mies called for a new security policy for the FRG that is antimilitaristic and includes policies for the prevention of war and in favor of disarmament. He demanded the termination of the deployment of new U.S. nuclear missiles and the removal of those already stationed in the FRG. He declared that "all forces of peace and reason must resolutely oppose the aggressive U.S. military doctrine which provides for a war of aggression and for a nuclear first strike." (ADN, East Berlin, 6 January; *FBIS*, 9 January.) In an article in *Unsere Zeit* (4 April), Mies stated his party's strong opposition to NATO. According to him, the objectives of NATO are the destruction through war of the socialist community of nations, the submission of Western Europe to U.S. military and political hegemony, and the creation of a new instrument for the suppression of democratic and revolutionary forces. DKP Presidium member Ellen Weber confirmed the fact of the existence of "revanchism," which "flourishes in the FRG under the protection of the U.S. first-strike nuclear missiles." She accused Bonn of tolerating the activities of "neo-Nazi thugs." (Tass, 8 August; *FBIS*, 9 August.) The DKP welcomed the "new peace initiative" launched by the Soviet Union at this year's fall session of the U.N. General Assembly (Tass, 2 October; *FBIS*, 3 October).

According to the DKP, improvement of relations between East and West Germany must be based on the recognition of the inviolability of the boundaries that resulted from World War II. Bonn must abjure any kind of revanchism, respect GDR citizenship, and exchange ambassadors (Voice of the GDR, East Berlin, 3 October; *FBIS*, 3 October).

Contacts were maintained with many fraternal communist parties, especially with those of the Soviet Union and GDR. At the occasion of the thirty-fifth anniversary of the founding of the GDR, the DKP, in cooperation with the SED, organized 76 meetings from 19 November to 1 December throughout the FRG. All of the events were dedicated to the "achievements" of socialism in the GDR. (*DID*, November, pp. 16–20.) DKP Chairman Herbert Mies was received by Mikhail Gorbachev, member of the Soviet Politburo and Secretariat, and Boris Ponomarev, candidate member of the Politburo and a member of the Secretariat. The Soviet officials stressed the unchanging solidarity of Soviet Communists with the struggle of the DKP.

(Tass, 26 July; *FBIS*, 27 July.) A DKP delegation participated in a conference in Copenhagen entitled "Symposium About the Struggle of the Communist Parties of the Capitalist Industrialized States" with representatives of other communist parties from Western Europe and North America (*DID*, June, p. 5). The SDAJ organized a Western European meeting of communist youth organizations, held in September, to discuss preparations for the Twelfth World Festival of Youth and Students in Moscow in 1985. The main emphasis of this forthcoming event will be the struggle for peace and anti-imperialist solidarity. (Ibid., October, p. 2.) A delegation of the Coordination Committee of the German peace movement visited the Soviet Union (1–7 April). The group was received by Georgi A. Arbatov, member of the Soviet Central Committee and director of the Institute for the Study of the U.S. and Canada, Vadim V. Zagladin, deputy chief of the International Department of the Soviet Central Committee, and other high-ranking party and military officials. (Ibid., April, p. 11.)

Other Leftist Groups. Numerous associations, parties, initiatives (action groups), and revolutionary organizations of the New Left remained active during 1984. Many of these groups openly advocated the use of violence to overthrow and destroy the existing state, and some attempted to come closer to their revolutionary objective by engaging in "armed struggle." The ever-changing organizations and splinter groups pursued different revolutionary concepts but shared a rejection of pro-Soviet othodox communism. The New Left comprises various dogmatic Marxist-Leninists and Trotskyists, anarchists, "autonomists," and antidogmatic social revolutionaries. The dogmatic Marxist-Leninist organizations (K-groups) continued to decline and presently have about 3,400 members in their basic organizations. Membership in the antidogmatic groups (about 59 groups were identified) continued to increase (from 3,700 to 4,900). (*Verfassungsschutz*, p. 20.) The "autonomous" and anarchist groups were mainly responsible for violence against the state. They were frequently responsible for violent fights and formed the militant core of the protest movement directed against the United States, NATO, and the "imperialist preparations for war." They provoked open confrontation at street demonstrations, advocated sabotage, and committed numerous acts of arson and bombing.

The dogmatic New Left includes four Marxist-Leninist parties (K-groups), of which only two claim to have organizations nationwide. Once the strongest of the K-groups, the Communist League of Germany (Kommunistischer Bund Westdeutschlands; KBW) is no longer active. The Marxist-Leninist Party of Germany (Marxistisch-Leninistiche Partei Deutschlands; MLPD) is presently the strongest and most active K-group. It has about 1,000 members and an additional 600 to 800 members in affiliated youth and student organizations. The party regards itself as the "political avant-garde of the working class in the FRG and West Berlin." The aim of the MLPD is "the revolutionary overthrow of the dictatorship of monopoly capitalists" and "the establishment of the dictatorship of the proletariat." The party weekly, *Rote Fahne*, increased its press run from 8,000 to 10,000 copies. The MLPD also published more than 80 factory newspapers, indicating the party's emphasis upon work in the factories and trade unions. The chairman of the MLPD is Stefan Engel.

The pro-Albanian Communist Party of Germany (Marxist-Leninist) (Kommunistische Partei Deutschlands [Marxisten-Leninisten]; KPD) (formerly known as KPD-ML) has a membership of about 400, representing a loss of about 100. Its new chairman, Horst-Dieter Koch, a longtime member of the Central Committee of the KPD, was elected at the Fifth Party Congress (November 1983). Former chairman Ernst Aust did not seek re-election but was elected to the Central Committee. About 6,000 copies of the KPD's weekly organ *Roter Morgen*, are printed. Its affiliated organizations include youth, student, labor, and peace groups. The KPD intensified its collaboration with the Maoist League of West German Communists (Bund Westdeutscher Kommunisten; BWK). In January, the central committees of both organizations met in Cologne and decided to publish a joint supplement to their respective organs, *Roter Morgen* and *Politische Berichte* (*DID*, March, p. 17). The BWK has about 450 followers. Its biweekly organ, *Politische Berichte*, is printed in an edition of 1,500 copies, and its biweekly *Nachrichtenheft* in an edition of 1,200. The Working Groups for Revolutionary University Politics, founded by the BWK university groups, also contains representatives from the KPD and the anarchist Free Workers' Union (FAU) (*Verfassungsschutz*, p. 86).

The Communist League (Kommunistischer Bund; KB) retained its membership of about 500 (300 of them in Hamburg). It publishes *Arbeiterkampf*. The main activity of the KB was collaboration with local and regional peace initiatives, in "anti-imperialist alliances," and in the Green-Alternative List (GAL) in Hamburg. Former leading functionaries of the Center Faction, a group that split from the KB at the end of 1979, occupy influential positions in the Green Party at the federal and *Land* levels, in the Hamburg GAL, and in the editorial office of the socialist magazine *Moderne Zeiten* (Modern times). (Ibid.) The Workers' League for the Reconstruction of the KPD (AB) retained its membership of about 300. Its affiliated student organizations were active only in Bavarian cities (ibid., p. 87).

The thirteen Trotskyist groups, some of them with only regional organizations, have a total membership of about 700. They advocate "permanent revolution" and "dictatorship of the proletariat" and oppose the "decadent bureaucracy" in the socialist states. The Group of International Marxists (GIM) is the German section of the Fourth International in Brussels and has about 250 members. Its biweekly, *Was tun*, increased its edition to 2,300. During the metalworkers' strike it appeared weekly. (*DID*, May, p. 19.) At the end of February, the GIM held its National Conference in Frankfurt, attended by about 70 delegates. Two-thirds of them voted in favor of supporting the SPD and the Green Party in forthcoming elections. (Ibid., March, pp. 16–17.) The International Socialists of Germany (ISD), a Trotskyist splinter group with headquarters in Cologne, publishes *Sozialistische Rundshau* and distributes the paper at demonstrations and other political events. The ISD supported the struggle for the 35-hour workweek and demanded that the DGB, SPD, and Green Party form a united front. (*DID*, April/May, p. 19.)

The Marxist Group (MG) is a Marxist-Leninist cadre party marked by secrecy, a hierarchical structure, strict discipline, and intensive indoctrination. Its membership is about 1,300, mostly students and academics. It has several thousand sympathizers. The MG publishes the monthly *Marxistische Zeitung*, the *Marxistische Arbeiterzeitung*, the *Marxistische Hochschulzeitung* (14,000 copies), and the *Marxistische Schulzeitung*. MG followers participated in many demonstrations, interrupted university lectures and political events of other political organizations, and held numerous, usually well-attended puublic discussions.

The Socialist Buro (SB) with a membership

of about 700, publishes the monthly *links—Sozialistische Zeitung* (6,000 copies), the quarterly *Widersprüche*, a magazine dealing with education, health, and social affairs, and the monthly *express* (3,000 copies). The objective of the SB is to provide initiatives for the revolutionary change of society. (*Verfassungsschutz*, pp. 88–89.)

The anarcho-syndicalist group stagnated. The Initiative Free Workers' Union (I.FAU) with nineteen local groups and support bases and the Free Workers' Union (FAU) with sixteen local groups espouse a state of anarchy and a worldwide socialist council republic. The most active FAU organization, in Hamburg, broke up as a result of ideological differences. It reconstituted itself as Free Workers' Union/Council Communists (FAU/K). The FAU as a whole dissolved, and the I.FAU assumed the name FAU. A number of anarcho-syndicalist groups under the name Free Workers' Union/Students (FAUST) operated at several universities in northern Germany. (Ibid., p. 89.)

On the other hand, the Violence-free Action Groups–Grass-roots Movement increased to 85 groups and collectives at the end of 1983 as compared with about 50 in the previous year. It has a total of about 1,000 followers. The spokesorgan for the violence-free anarchists is the Federation of Violence-free Action Groups (FoGA). Its monthly organ is *Graswurzelrevolution* (4,500–7,000 copies). The FoGA propagates civil disobedience, boycotts, blockages, and occupations as means to change society. (Ibid., p. 90.)

The "autonomous" scene, comprising groups with different anarchistic concepts, totals several thousand followers, mostly among the young. As a rule, the groups are small, loosely organized, and short-lived. They fight against the state, its "preparation for war," nuclear power plants, NATO, and "U.S. and West German imperialism." Some of the "autonomous anti-imperialists" have declared themselves for militancy and have crossed the borderline into terrorism, sabotage, and arson. (Ibid., pp. 90–92.)

Most of the bombing attacks and arson cases in the FRG were the work of the Revolutionary Cells (RZ) and were directed against military and industrial installations and public buildings. The terrorist actions of the RZ and its women's group, Rote Zora, are a part of their "anti-imperialist" struggle, directed against the NATO alliance partners. The *Tageszeitung* (West Berlin) published excerpts in January of a 27-page-long strategy study paper of the RZ. The study pointed out that the terrorist groups wish to cut their dependence on the peace movement and to form their own fronts. They accused the peace movement of being concerned more with its own survival than with class issues. (*FAZ*, 17 January.) (For details of these organizations, see *YICA*, 1984, pp. 474–76.)

The Jusos and other youth, student, and women's organizations affiliated with the SPD, are usually not perceived as left-radical organizations. However, they share many objectives with the extreme left and have increasingly participated in unity actions with Communists and other leftists. Their anti-NATO and anti-U.S. policy and their support of Moscow's "peace plans" provide the basis for cooperation.

WEST BERLIN

Population. 2,000,000

Party. Socialist Unity Party of West Berlin (Sozialistische Einheitspartei Westberlins; SEW)

Membership. 4,500

Chairman. Horst Schmitt

Buro. 17 members: Dietmar Ahrens, Uwe Doering, Helga Dolinski, Detlef Fendt, Klaus Feske, Harry Flichtbeil, Margot Granowski, Heinz Grünberg, Klaus-Dieter Heiser, Volker June, Inge Kopp, Jörg Kuhle, Hans Mahle, Margot Mrozinski, Monika Sieveking, Erich Ziegler, Horst Schmitt

Secretariat. 7 members: Dietmar Ahrens, Klaus Feske, Harry Flichtbeil, Margot Granowski, Inge Kopp, Herwig Kurzendorfer, Horst Schmitt

Executive. 65 members

Status. Legal

Last Congress. Seventh, 25–27 May 1984, in West Berlin

Last Election. 1981, 0.7 percent, no representation

Auxiliary Organizations. Socialist Youth League Karl Liebknecht (Sozialistischer Jugendverband Karl Liebknecht; SJ Karl Liebknecht), ca. 500 members; Young Pioneers (Junge Pioniere; JP), ca. 250 members; SEW–University Groups, ca. 400 members

West Berlin is still under "Allied occupation" by the forces of the United States, Britain, and France. The 1971 Quadripartite Agreement concerning Berlin confirmed its "special status," based on previous agreements in 1944 and 1945, declaring that the former German capital is not part of the FRG. Even though the 1971 agreement was meant to cover the area of Greater Berlin, the Soviet-occupied eastern sector of the city has been declared the capital of the GDR. The Western allies have encouraged the FRG to maintain close ties with West Berlin, and West Berlin is represented in the federal parliament by nonvoting deputies.

Berlin's special status made it possible for the SED to set up a subsidiary in West Berlin. In 1959, an "independent" organizational structure was introduced for the West Berlin section of the SED. In 1962, the party was renamed the Socialist Unity Party of Germany–West Berlin; in 1969, the present designation was introduced in order to make the party appear a genuine, indigenous political party.

The SEW, like the DKP, is a pro-Soviet party and depends financially on the SED. Its statements are identical with the ideological and political views of the East German and Soviet parties. SEW membership is about 4,500. In the last elections (1981) for the city's House of Representatives, the SEW obtained 8,216 votes, or 0.7 percent, compared with 1.1 percent in 1979.

The SEW held its Seventh Party Congress in West Berlin (25–27 May). It was attended by 587 delegates. Twenty-five "fraternal parties" were represented. The Soviet delegation was led by Gennadi F. Sizov, chairman of the Soviet party's Central Auditing Commission. The SED delegation was headed by Egon Krenz, member of the Politburo and Secretariat of the SED. The delegates elected a 65-member Executive. Chairman Horst Schmitt and vice-chairpersons Dietmar Ahrens and Inge Kopp were also re-elected. The congress adopted a declaration "For a City of Peace and Labor—For a Safe Future," which demands that West Berlin neither politically nor materially support NATO's intensive armament. (*Neues Deutschland*, East Berlin, 26/27 May.) It also voted in favor of a resolution confirming the SEW as a firm component of the international communist movement. The West Berlin Communists unreservedly supported the just fight of the metalworkers and printers. The congress called for solidarity with the people of Nicaragua and with the just struggle of the peoples of Latin America against American aggression directed by the Reagan administration. (*Rudé právo*, Prague, 28 May; *FBIS*, 30 May.) The congress showed the SEW's unity and cohesion and its indestructible loyalty to the principles of Marxism-Leninism and proletarian internationalism (*Pravda*, 28 May; *FBIS*, 1 June).

The SEW asserted that the increased participation of West Berlin Communists in the peace movement made it into a genuine "people's movement." The core of the "unity of action," however, remains the collaboration of the SEW and SPD. The SEW suggested to the SPD and the Alternative List (AL) that for the forthcoming elections in March 1985, they form a "coalition against the right." (Bundesminister des Innern, *Innere Sicherheit*, no. 73, 29 June, p. 6.)

Among the affiliated organizations of the SEW are the Socialist Youth League Karl Liebknecht (Sozialistischer Jugendverband Karl Liebknecht), with about 300 members, 250 of them children in the Young Pioneers (JP). The SEW–University Groups have about 400 members and the SEW-influenced Action Group of Democrats and Socialists about 500 members. Other SEW-led organizations include the Democratic Women's League Berlin (about 600 members), the Society for German-Soviet Friendship (about 500 members), and the West Berlin organization of the Victims of the Nazi Regime/League of Antifascists (about 300 members).

The SEW maintained contacts in 1984 with the international communist movement by means of mutual visits, especially with the SED.

Many New Left and left-extremist groups and organizations operate in West Berlin. The problem posed by house occupations was successfully handled by the city's government and therefore no longer provided opportunities for militant elements. However, they turned many demonstrations and rallies into violent confrontations with the authorities. Terrorists were also active in West Berlin.

Eric Waldman
University of Calgary

Great Britain

Population. 56,023,000
Party. Communist Party of Great Britain (CPGB)
Founded. 1920
Membership. Under 16,000
General Secretary. Gordon McLennan
Political Committee. 16 members: George Bolton (chairperson), Philippa Langton (vice-chairperson), Gordon McLennan (general secretary), Ian McKay (national organizer), Pete Carter (national industrial organizer), Gerry Pocock (head of International Department), Nina Temple (head of Press and Publicity Department), Maggie Bowden (national women's organizer), Martin Jacques (editor of *Marxism Today*), John Peck (national election agent), Margaret Woddis (secretary to Executive Committee), Jack Ashton, Tricia Davis, Bill Dunn, Ron Halverson, Kevin Halpin, Chris Myant, Dave Priscott, Vishnu Sharma (list includes all officers)
Executive Committee. 42 members
Status. Legal
Last Congress. Thirty-eighth, 12–15 November 1983
Last Election. June 1983, 0.03 percent, no representation
Auxiliary Organizations. Young Communist League (YCL); Liaison Committee for the Defence of Trade Unions (LCDTU)
Publications. *Morning Star*, *Marxism Today*, *Communist Focus*, *Challenge*, *Spark*, *Our History Journal*, *Economic Bulletin*, *Medicine in Society*, *Education Today and Tomorrow*

The CPGB is a recognized political party and contests both local and national elections. It does not, however, operate in Northern Ireland, which it does not recognize as British territory. The party has had no members in the House of Commons since 1950, but has one member, Lord Milford, in the non-elected House of Lords.

Leadership and Party Organization. The CPGB is divided into four divisions: the National Congress, the Executive Committee and its departments, districts, and local and factory branches. Constitutionally, opposition is rare and the biennial National Congress, the party's supreme authority, usually rubber-stamps the decisions of the Political Committee. Responsibility for overseeing the party's activities rests with the 42-member Executive Committee, elected by the National Congress, and meeting every two months. The Executive Committee comprises members of special committees, fulltime departmental heads, and the sixteen members of the Political Committee, the party's innermost controlling conclave.

Party leaders remain deeply preoccupied by the continuing decline in support for the party. Electorally the party is so battered that it does not now even contest as many seats as formerly. Membership is at its lowest point since World War II and is little over 15,000. Only some 50 percent of these have actually paid their fees. The YCL with only about 500 members is close to collapse. The decline in electoral support was most graphically illustrated in Britain's last general elections, those of June 1983, when the party's 35 candidates polled only 11,598 votes.

However, the poor showing of the CPGB at the polls belies the party's strength in the trade union movement and in influencing opinion. Although the party does not control any individual trade union, it is represented on most union executives and has played a major role in most government-union confrontations of recent years. The CPGB's success is partly attributable to low turnouts in most union elections, to the fact that it is the only party seeking to control the outcome of these elections, and to its close interest in industrial affairs, which ensures support from workers who might not support other aspects of the party's program. There are 2 members of the CPGB on the 38-member General Council of the Trades Union Congress: Mick McGahey of the National Union of Mineworkers and Ken Gill of the Technical and Supervisory Section of the Amalgamated Union of Engineering Workers. In addition CPGB ideas exercise a considerable influence on other trade union executives and on several Labour Party members of parliament.

Domestic Affairs. In 1984 the row between the Eurocommunist-inclined leadership and the Stalinist hard left intensified. The conflict centered on the dispute between the party's Executive Committee and its chief theoretical journal, *Marxism Today*, on the one hand, and the *Morning Star* on the other. The *Morning Star*, although nationally recognized as the party's daily newspaper, is technically owned by the communist but separate People's Press Printing Society (PPPS). Throughout 1984 and early 1985 the PPPS continued to be in the hands of Stalinist opponents of the Executive Committee's Eurocommunist policies. The *Morning Star* group was bitterly opposed to the leadership's criticisms, muted though they were, of the Soviet Union and to the transformation of *Marxism Today* into a popular but broad-based magazine.

The dispute simmered throughout the year but reached a new peak toward the end of December. Then, two of the party's most distinguished senior members, Andrew Rothstein and Page Arnot, laid out a classic defense of the policies of fidelity to the Soviet Union. The article carried weight as Rothstein and Arnot were founding members of the CPGB and had been friendly with early Bolshevik leaders. The *Morning Star* then allowed a reply from the Executive Committee to appear. An indication of the gravity of the issue was to be found in the Executive Committee's choice of respondents: Mick McGahey, vice-president of the National

Union of Mineworkers, and Ron Halverson, a senior lay official of the Amalgamated Union of Engineering Workers. Both were former party chairmen. The reply strongly rejected the charge of "opportunism and revisionism" in the adoption by the leadership of the Eurocommunist road and argued that the leadership's critics were in reality attacking the party's long-established program, "The British Road to Socialism." McGahey and Halverson said that Rothstein in particular had "never agreed with the party's position on socialist democracy and its criticism of the Soviet Union on such questions as the interventions in Czechoslovakia and Afghanistan. For him working class internationalism means that because of the threat from imperialism there should be no criticism of any Soviet leadership—until it is replaced by another leadership which criticises its predecessors." It was this attitude, the Executive Committee's spokesmen alleged, that "led us to defend what later proved to be indefensible" during the Stalin years.

The dispute came to a crisis on 13 January 1985 when a special Executive Committee meeting expelled hard-line Stalinists including Tony Chater and David Whitfield, respectively editor and assistant editor of the *Morning Star*. The final struggle for power will probably not occur, however, until 18–20 May during a specially convened party congress. On that occasion the hard-liners can be expected to mount a vigorous counterattack. The *Morning Star* itself can be expected to resume its propaganda offensive against the party leadership, especially in the time up to the congress. However, the Executive Committee countered with a new party weekly called *Focus* that was to go out to every party member in tabloid form. It would be the first time for over a year that CPGB members had received the views of the party leadership on a regular basis because the *Morning Star* has frequently refused to print them. The party leadership's victory was by no means certain. Under party rules the entire 42-member Executive Committee has to come up for election at every congress. The hard-liners can be expected to make a maximum effort to get their members elected. They have already regained some support in Liverpool and London since 1983. However the dispute is settled, it seems certain to result in a significant split in what is already a marginal party in British politics.

Domestically, the CPGB's main efforts centered on the strike by the nation's coal miners. The strike by the National Union of Mineworkers (NUM) began at the beginning of March 1984 after a long period of a ban on overtime. The NUM called the strike in opposition to the National Coal Board's intention to close uneconomic mines. The strike caused deep divisions within the mining communities, which were never asked to vote on the issue. Mass picketing and violence further inflamed the issue but the Coal Board, strongly backed by the government, showed no sign of giving way. By January 1985 the strike was showing serious signs of breaking as growing numbers of miners drifted back to work. The Communists vigorously supported the strike. Mick McGahey and George Bolton were prominent in the NUM leadership during the strike, and many other CPGB members were active at all levels of the union. In addition the party organization was diligent in its propaganda, in encouraging other unions in acts of solidarity, and in collecting food and money to help miners' families, who felt the economic pressures of the strike increasingly as the year wore on.

The unions in general remained the Communists' main area of activity. They urged strong opposition to the government's trade union legislation, which they regarded as being essentially antiunion legislation. Accordingly, the party backed mass demonstrations, strikes, and open defiance of the law.

The CPGB supported a series of demonstrations objecting to most aspects of government policy, including the proposed abolition of the larger metropolitan councils, rate capping of big spending councils, and continuing cuts in government spending. The party also urged the creation of new jobs and encouraged protests against the rising level of unemployment in the country. The party was an active supporter of the Committee for Nuclear Disarmament and supported anti-U.S. demonstrations at the Greenham Common airbase, site of U.S. cruise missiles in Britain. The CPGB also supports unilateral nuclear disarmament by the United Kingdom.

Local council elections held on 3 May involved 14 million electors. In Scotland every district council was due for re-election. In England, borough councils in the six metropolitan areas had elections as did about a third of the other district councils. In Wales five councils had elections. In all, 74 Communists ran, a sharp decrease from the comparable elections in 1980 when 144 communist candidates competed. Thirty of the candidates ran in Scotland, where they won 4,424 votes, or 5.9 percent of the total. Two Communists were elected. There were 43 communist candidates in England and one in Wales. None was elected, although their total vote was 3,797 or 2.1 percent of those voting. The Communists' best recorded vote was 19 percent of those voting in Rossington ward of Doncaster Council.

Auxiliary Organizations. CPGB activity in industry centers on its approximately 200 workplace branches. Its umbrella organization is the LCDTU. Although the CPGB is riven by internal dispute, its trade union structure can still command considerable support from prominent trade union leaders. A meeting of the LCDTU held in January was attended by several prominent union leaders.

The YCL is the youth wing of the party but has only about 500 members. The party retains a number of financial interests including Central Books, Lawrence and Wishart Publishers, Farleigh Press, London Caledonian Printers, Rodell Properties, the Labour Research Department, and the Marx Memorial Library.

International Views and Activities. Although the CPGB leadership is regarded as revisionist by its own dissident hard-line faction, there are in fact few areas where the CPGB is anything less than unstinting in its support of the Soviet Union. The party is still critical of the Soviet invasions of Afghanistan and Czechoslovakia. However, on most issues the party is staunchly pro-Soviet. The CPGB favors arms reduction talks with the USSR, opposes the deployment of cruise and Pershing missiles in Europe, and the development of U.S. space weapons. The party campaigns for British withdrawal from NATO and the European Economic Community. The party is critical of Israel and seeks to promote the recognition of the Palestine Liberation Organization.

A high-level CPGB delegation visited Moscow in September. It was led by Gordon McLennan, general secretary, and included Jerry Pocock, head of the international section, George Bolton, the Executive Committee chairperson, and Philippa Langton, deputy chairman of the Executive Committee. It was met by leading Soviet officials, including Mikhail Gorbachev and Boris Ponomarev. In October McLennan also visited Budapest, where he was met by Hungarian leader János Kádár. Earlier in July Werner Felfe, a member of the ruling East German Politburo, visited London and held talks with the CPGB general secretary.

Other Marxist Groups. Besides the CPGB, several small, mainly Trotskyist, groups are also active. Although some of these groups were growing swiftly in the 1970s, their memberships are now waning. This, however, is probably partly attributable to the adoption by the Labour Party of hard-line left policies, which has encouraged extremists to join the Labour Party itself rather than some of the fringe revolutionary groups.

Probably the most important of the Trotskyist groups is Militant, which derives its name from its paper of the same name. Militant claims to be merely a loose tendency of opinion within the Labour Party, but there is no doubt that Militant possesses its own distinctive organization and for some years has been pursuing a policy of entryism (the tactic of penetrating the larger, more moderate Labour Party). Militant controls about 50 Labour Party constituencies.

The other significant Trotskyist organizations are the Socialist Workers' Party (SWP) and the Workers' Revolutionary Party (WRP). The SWP has been particularly active in single-issue campaigns, notably the antiunemployment campaign. It also actively gave support to striking miners' families but in fact enjoys little support in the coal-mining industry. The WRP's activities are more secretive but are known to center in the engineering, mining, theater, and auto industries. It focuses much attention on the young and has set up six centers around the country named Youth Training Centres, which are in fact more concerned with recruitment.

Richard Sim
London

Greece

Population. 9,984,000
Party. Communist Party of Greece (Kommunistikon Komma Ellados; KKE)
Founded. 1921
Membership. 42,000 (estimated)
Secretary General. Kharilaos Florakis
Politburo. 9 full members: Kharilaos Florakis, Nikos Kaloudhis, Grigoris Farakos, Kostas Tsolakis, Roula Kourkoulou, Loula Logara, Dimitris Gondikas, Andonis Ambatielos, Dimitris Sarlis; 2 candidate members: Takis Mamatsis, Orestis Kolozov
Status. Legal
Last Congress. Eleventh, December 1982, in Athens
Last Election. 1981, 10.9 percent, 13 of 300
Auxiliary Organization. Communist Youth of Greece (KNE)
Publications. *Rizospastis*, daily; *Kommunistiki Epitheorisi* (*KOMEP*), monthly theoretical review

During the military dictatorship (1967–1974), the KKE split into two factions. The pro-Moscow faction, initially known as KKE-Exterior, eventually emerged as the official KKE. The other faction, still known as KKE-Interior, shifted gradually to an increasingly independent and moderate line and has now become the representative of Eurocommunism in Greece. Its influence remains limited mostly to intellectuals. Much of its modest success in the 1984 elections to the European Parliament was due to the personality of one of its leaders, Leonidas Kyrkos.

In the October 1981 parliamentary elections, the KKE and KKE-Interior received a total 12.2 percent of the popular vote (10.9 and 1.3 respectively). The KKE made a more impressive showing in the 1982 municipal elections, when KKE-sponsored candidates received approximately 20 percent of the total vote. This, however, did not signify a permanent shift. The apparent rise in popular support was due in part to the appeal of local candidates or to the support given KKE candidates by Panhellenic Socialist Movement (PASOK) supporters or KKE-Interior followers. This is shown by the totals received by the Marxist-oriented parties—the PASOK, the KKE, and the KKE-Interior. These parties received 60.2 percent of the popular vote, exactly the percentage received in the 1981 parliamentary election. In the 17 June elections for 24 Greek deputies to the European Parliament, support for the three Marxist parties declined to 56.6 percent (PASOK 41.6, KKE 11.6, KKE-Interior 3.4). The decline was due to the losses suffered by PASOK (down from 48.1 percent in 1981), not to any losses of the two communist parties, which actually increased their electoral strength by 2.8 points, receiving almost half of the votes lost by PASOK. The major beneficiary was the KKE-Interior; its success reflected the disappointment of left and left-of-center voters with the policies of the PASOK government. The next parliamentary election will show if Eurocommunism is taking a hold in Greece.

Leadership and Organization. The KKE is well financed and very active throughout Greece. The party is organized along traditional communist party lines with party "cells" and groups in factories and other places of work and local organizations in neighborhoods and villages. The party has local offices and organized groups in most Greek cities and towns. Major cities such as Athens have city party organizations and communist base organizations that coordinate the activities of the neighborhood party organizations and the local cells and aktivs. The KKE also has very strong and influential branch organizations in the labor unions and in many professional organizations. The party congress is statutorily convened every four years, but this requirement has not always been observed. A Central Committee elected by the congress usually

convenes every six months. The actual power, however, resides with the Politburo, which currently has nine full and two alternate members. In addition to Secretary General Kharilaos Florakis, the most influential members in the Politburo are Andonis Ambatielos, Nikos Kaloudhis, and Grigoris Farakos. The party's active youth organization (KNE) has considerable influence in the student movement. The propaganda efforts of the KKE and KNE are facilitated by the leftist orientation of many programs and newscasts on the state-run television.

Views and Positions. KKE leaders started the year with a drive for "a democratic government based on all the progressive forces and the working-class movement." With PASOK having a comfortable majority (166 out of 300 seats) in the national legislature, the KKE had no leverage to bring about a government change. In fact, it is doubtful that the KKE would have accepted any ministerial posts even if offered by PASOK. The actual objective was to promote cooperation at the grass-roots level and expand opportunities for the KKE's propaganda and infiltration efforts. This was made evident at the 8 April plenary session of the KKE Central Committee, which called for a united front of "all supporters of change at the grass-roots level, irrespective of ideological differences." (Note: "Change" is the term used by all three Marxist-oriented parties in lieu of "socialist transformation.") PASOK countered the KKE efforts by giving a more leftist orientation to the proceedings of its party congress in May. In a major address to the party congress, Premier and PASOK Chairman Andreas Papandreou spoke of the United States as being imperialist because of its capitalist system but portrayed the Soviet Union in much more benign terms. Another telling sign of the leftward orientation of the congress was the tumultuous reception accorded Markos Vafiades, the erstwhile commander-in-chief of the Democratic Army, the communist-led guerrilla force of 1946–1949.

All this maneuvering was related to the major electoral event of 1984, the election of 24 Greek deputies to the European Parliament. The PASOK leadership was trying to prevent any serious defection of leftist voters. The electoral campaign turned into a popularity contest among the parties, with matters relating to the European Economic Community (EEC) obscured by the domestic issues. The KKE continued its opposition to Greek membership in the EEC and vowed "to free the country from the EEC," yet it actively campaigned to increase its share of the popular vote. In this the KKE was unsuccessful. It increased its share of votes by only 0.7 point, and its number of Eurodeputies remained at three. KKE-Interior adopted a positive view of Greece's participation in the EEC and criticized PASOK for its domestic policies. In the election KKE-Interior increased its share of the popular vote from 1.3 to 3.4 percent. However, it gained only one seat.

Following the Euroelection, the KKE hardened its attitude toward PASOK (and KKE-Interior), declaring in July that "there cannot be cooperation, not even discussion of cooperation, with the government as it exists at present." Largely through communist instigation, the number of strikes increased during the summer and fall. For the remainder of the year, the KKE kept its distance from PASOK in anticipation of the next parliamentary election, expected to take place either in March 1985 or in the fall. The KKE strategy is to attract any dissatisfied voters from PASOK's left-wing and increase its leverage in the next parliament. Unless there is a dramatic shift in favor of PASOK prior to the parliamentary election (or widespread fraud), the governing party is unlikely to gain an absolute majority of seats, in which case it will have to rely on the support of KKE deputies in the legislature to stay in power. This will provide the KKE with inordinate influence. To improve its chances for winning an absolute majority of seats, PASOK may revise the electoral system to give a premium to whichever party comes "first," hoping that PASOK will be that party.

In the area of foreign policy, the KKE continued its opposition to Greece's membership in NATO, the presence of four American bases on Greek soil, and membership in the EEC, all staple positions. In late summer, the KKE declared its full support for the initiative of U.N. Secretary General Javier Pérez de Cuellar on Cyprus. This position reflected the views of the Soviet government, which favors a nonaligned, demilitarized Cyprus. The existence of the "independent" Turkish state on the Turkish-occupied part of the island republic is a cause of concern for the Soviet Union. Information regarding the construction of an airport at Lefkoniko, within the Turkish area, has given rise to speculation that the airport is being built to serve American strategic interests.

In February the KKE Politburo criticized Premier Papandreou for a harsh statement on Albania. The Greek premier had spoken out against the violation of the rights of ethnic Greeks living in Albania. The KKE called for closer relations with Greece's northern neighbor as the best way to improve the lot of these Greeks.

Domestic Activities. During the year the KKE continued to be very active both in its organizational and propaganda work and in its parliamentary participation. Its parliamentary representatives were generally supportive of the legislative measures presented by PASOK. A major event during the year was the Tenth Festival of Greek Communist Youth (KNE) in September. The festival was well attended by foreign delegations and was given prominence on Greek television. Speaking to the participants, KKE Secretary General Kharilaos Florakis criticized PASOK, saying that "for the past three years the government has not implemented the program it has promised." He added that "the interests of the monopolies and the structures of dependence that feed the right and every rightist policy remain untouched." The speech was in line with the current KKE tactic of keeping its distance from PASOK in the hope of reaping whatever electoral benefits may accrue from PASOK's "failure to pursue a genuine change." On 18 September in Moscow Florakis was presented the Order of Lenin by Konstantin Chernenko. The occasion was Florakis's seventieth birthday. When the award was announced earlier in the summer, there was speculation that Florakis might be on the way out. Up to this moment there is no indication that his position is being challenged.

International Contacts. During the year, KKE intensified its contacts with other communist parties. In late February a delegation headed by Vasil Bil'ák, secretary of the Czechoslovak party, visited Athens at the invitation of the KKE leadership. Bil'ák was also received by Premier Papandreou, who praised Czechoslovakia as "a progressive, vibrant country." On 5 March KKE representatives met in Athens with a delegation of the Iraqi Communist Party. On 12–14 March Florakis visited Hungary and held talks with Hungarian leader János Kádár. On 10 April Florakis, accompanied by Politburo member Nikos Kaloudhis, visited Sofia. Two days later the KKE delegation went to Belgrade, where it had talks with leading members of the League of Communists of Yugoslavia (LCY). Coincidentally, an LCY delegation visited Athens and had talks with a leading member of PASOK. On 26–28 April, Florakis visited Moscow, where he was received by Chernenko. On 12 May Florakis met in Athens with Günter Schabowski, candidate member of the East German Politburo. Two days later Florakis flew to Paris for a meeting with Georges Marchais, leader of the French Communist Party. In early June a delegation of the Vietnamese Communist Party visited Athens at the invitation of the KKE. On the occasion, the KKE leadership restated its opposition to the Chinese leadership of Deng Xiaoping. On 8 August Florakis met in Athens with Andrey Lukanov, candidate member of the Bulgarian Central Committee. In mid-September Florakis again flew to Moscow to receive the Order of Lenin.

Lacking the financial resources of the KKE, the KKE-Interior was much less active on the international stage. One recorded foreign contact took place on 26 April when Yiannis Banias, accompanied by two members of the party's Executive Bureau, visited Bucharest. Romania is the only country in the Eastern bloc that continues to have contacts with KKE-Interior. The KKE is, however, improving its relations with Bucharest; on 30 August, the KKE sent a telegram of congratulations to the Romanian Communist Party on the occasion of the fortieth anniversary of Romania's liberation.

PASOK was also active both at the party and the government level. In June Premier Papandreou visited Czechoslovakia and the German Democratic Republic. Upon his return he met in Athens with a delegation of the Sandinista Liberation Front from Nicaragua. On 20–30 July the president of the legislature, Yiannis Alevras—a major PASOK figure—visited Moscow at the head of a parliamentary delegation and held talks with Soviet premier Nikolai Tikhonov and candidate Politburo member Vasili Kuznetsov. In September and October, Papandreou visited Libya, Poland, Syria, and Jordan. In November, PASOK, the KKE, and the KKE-Interior took the lead in organizing the annual celebration of the Polytekhnion Uprising, the student revolt that in November 1973 led to the overthrow of the dictatorship. PASOK tried to give the festivities and demonstrations a less partisan character, but communist activists succeeded in giving most activities a very leftist coloring.

Other Marxist-Leninist Organizations. The Revolutionary Communist Party of Greece and the Marxist-Leninist Communist Party of Greece continue to be active and to advocate more extremist views, but their following remains extremely small, as shown by the number of votes their candidates received during the 17 June Euroelections (0.2 percent).

D. G. Kousoulas
Howard University

Iceland

Population. 239,000
Party. People's Alliance (Althydubandalagid; AB)
Founded. 1968
Membership. 3,000 (estimated)
Chairman. Svavar Gestsson
Executive Committee. 10 member: Svavar Gestsson, Vilborg Hardardottir (deputy chair), Helgi Gudmundsson (secretary), Margret Frimannsdottir (treasurer), Bjarnfridur Leosdottir, Ludvik Josephsson, Olafur Gudmundsson, Olof Rikhardsdottir, Margret Bjornsdottir, Soffia Gudmundsdottir

Central Committee. 70 members, 20 deputies
Status. Legal
Last Congress. November 1983
Last Election. 1983, 17.3 percent, 10 of 60 seats
Auxiliary Organization. Organization of Base Opponents (OBO—organizer of peace demonstrations against U.S.-NATO bases)
Publications. *Thjodviljinn* (daily), Reykjavik; *Verkamadhurinn* (weekly), Akureyri; *Mjolnir* (weekly), Siglufjördhur

The AB is the successor to a line of leftist parties dating back to 1930, when the Icelandic Communist Party (Kommunistaflokkur Islands) was established by a left-wing splinter from the Labor Party. In 1938, the Social Democratic Party (SDP) splintered from the Labor Party and joined with the Communists to create a new party, the United People's Party–Socialist Party (Sameiningar flokkur althydu–Socialista flokkurinn; UPP-SP). Although basing its ideology on "scientific socialism–Marxism," the UPP-SP had no organizational ties to Moscow. At first its main political goal was to complete the political independence of the country. Denmark had granted home rule in 1918, but Iceland did not achieve complete independence until 1944. By this time, the other political parties had accepted the UPP-SP as a responsible democratic party, and it had participated in governing coalitions. In 1956, the UPP-SP formed an electoral alliance with still another group of left-wing social democrats and the small isolationist National Preservation Party. This coalition assumed the name People's Alliance. In 1968, the UPP-SP dissolved itself into the AB, which then formed itself into the present national Marxist party. It has participated regularly in coalition governments, most recently joining the Progressive (agrarian-liberal) Party in a coalition headed by the late maverick Gunnar Thoroddsen, formerly of the Independence (moderate-conservative) Party. The Thoroddsen government resigned in April 1983 following severe electoral reverses suffered by the constituent parties in the parliamentary elections of 23 April 1983. The AB held three cabinet posts: social and health affairs (Svavar Gestsson), finance (Ragnar Arnalds), and industry (Hjorleifur Guttormsson). It is now the largest opposition party.

Participation in the government during a severe economic recession hurt the AB. Its share of the vote fell to 17.3 percent, down considerably from the 22.9 percent and 19.7 percent it had received in the 1978 and 1979 elections. Falling fish catches, stagnation in international trade, and soaring inflation (which reached an unprecedented 159 percent

annual rate at the time of the elections) had already forced austerity measures on the Thoroddsen government. In May 1983 a new majority coalition government was formed under Progressive Steingrimur Hermansson by the Progressives and the Independence Party. Although Hermansson had hoped to include the moderate SDP, he was unwilling to relax the austerity measures. The new government enjoys a substantial majority: 37 out of 60 seats in the Althing (parliament). (John Madeley, "The Politics of Hyperinflation: Iceland's Election," *Western European Politics*, 7, no. 1, pp. 124–27.)

The austerity measures were successful in reducing the inflation rate to about 9 percent by the beginning of 1984. This occurred at the cost of significant declines in national income: −1.5 percent in 1982, −5.5 percent in 1983, and an expected −2.0 percent in 1984 (Economic Research Reports, *Nordic Economic Outlook*, Stockholm, July 1984). Unemployment reached 3.4 percent in January, a fifteen-year high, but this is modest in comparison with rates in most of Western Europe (*Nordisk Kontakt*, no. 3). The new government was also very concerned about the soaring foreign debt, which nearly doubled from 32 percent of GNP to 60 percent between 1981 and 1983 (ibid., no. 1).

Leadership and Organization. Increased party unity was reflected at the AB's 1983 congress. The inevitable compromises and pragmatism accompanying governmental responsibility were difficult for the AB's more rigid ideologues. The harmony was reflected in the uncontested re-election of Svavar Gestsson as chairman and the uncontested elections of Vilborg Hardardottir as deputy chair and Helgi Gudmundsson as secretary. Margret Frimannsdottir faced only minor opposition as treasurer. New party rules have sought to divide party posts equally between men and women. Not all of the candidates proposed by the internal nominating committee were elected. The newly expanded Central Committee (from 46 to 70, plus the party officers ex officio) is elected by a complex preference system. Observers conclude that it establishes pluralist rather than Leninist party governance (*Morgunbladid*, 22 November 1983; *JPRS*, 5 January).

Domestic Affairs. Icelandic politics remain turbulent in the wake of the severe economic problems confronting the country. The nonsocialist Hermansson government continued the austerity measures commenced by the Thoroddsen coalition in which the AB participated. Most controversial was the abandonment of the complex Icelandic wage-indexing system, which had accelerated the inflationary spiral. As noted, the austerity measures coincided with other economic difficulties, especially disappointing developments in the crucial fishing industry. A slight improvement in the expected supply of cod allowed the government to raise the fisheries quota by 10 percent in April, but the AB remained critical of the severe limits while admitting that continued conservation controls were necessary (*Nordisk Kontakt*, nos. 1 and 7). In recent years maritime products accounted for more than 75 percent of the country's exports.

The AB's recent electoral decline can in part be explained by its participation in a government forced to take unpopular economic measures. It has also faced increased competition for its traditional left-of-center voters. The reformist SDP lost six seats when some of its younger members broke off to form the Social Democratic Federation (Bandalag jafnadarmanna), which won four seats. The new socialist party remained reformist and committed to continued Icelandic membership in NATO. The untimely death of Vilmundur Gylfasson, the party's popular and charismatic leader, last winter has clouded the party's prospects (*News from Iceland*, February). Finally a left-centrist Women's Party (Samtök um kvennalista), which won three seats in parliament, has performed well in the judgment of seasoned observers. Given the AB's traditional pursuit of a broad spectrum of voters, this competition is a serious challenge.

Public opinion polls in July indicated that of those voters polled and expressing a party preference, the AB could count on 14.9 percent, a further drop in support since the 1983 elections. The Social Democratic Federation was preferred by 6.2 percent, a decline from 7.3 percent in the elections. The Women's Party attracted 8.1 percent, an increase from the 5.5 percent polled fifteen months earlier. The old SDP continued its decline—to 6.4 percent from 11.7 percent. The governing parties still attracted nearly two-thirds of those giving a

party preference (48.8 for the Independence Party and 14.7 percent for the Progressives). (Ibid., September.) Such polls suggest, however, that voter preferences are very volatile.

The government continued to tighten the austerity measures through the spring. AB leader Gestsson claimed during the budget debate that the measures were causing hardship for wage earners while failing to solve the fiscal dilemmas. Inflation remained at about 15 percent, while personal income was expected to fall by an additional 6.5 percent during 1984. Shortly after the government announced its next round of fiscal measures, the public sector union (BSRB) warned of forthcoming labor action. On 4 October most of the public sector employees struck, closing government offices, harbors, airports, television, radio, and all but essential public services. Newspapers had been closed by strikes in September. Private sector workers canceled their collective bargaining agreement of the previous spring. Iceland was approaching general strike conditions. BSRB demanded wage increases of 30 percent, while the government offered only 18 percent. In early November an agreement for the public sector was reached, which will raise wages by 20 percent over a fourteen-month period (through 1985). Premier Hermansson regretted the choice of inflation rather than wage moderation coupled with tax cuts. Nevertheless, the four-week strike cost the government about a billion kronor, and the settlement was expected to accelerate inflation again, to a 20–30 percent annual rate. In the private sector new wage agreements were also agreed on in early November, and their terms were very close to the public sector agreements (*Nordisk Kontakt*, nos. 1, 9, 12–15).

As the government contemplated a proper response to the wage explosion, including currency devaluation, tax increases, and postponement of public spending, AB leader Gestsson announced his party's support of all measures seeking to maintain the purchasing power of the new wage agreements. He suggested that middleman costs could be cut to avoid price increases. (Ibid., no. 15.) The AB is quite influential in most sectors of the labor movement, including the umbrella national labor federation, ASI. Interestingly, its principal competition for influence comes not from the weak SDP, as in other Nordic countries, but from the center-right Independence Party.

In other domestic developments, long discussions with the Swiss-owned aluminum works (Alusuisse) at Straumsvik were finally concluded, with the price of electrical power supplied to the works raised significantly and tied to the world price of aluminum. The AB had been aggressive in its negotiations with Alusuisse in the previous government, and former industry minister Hjorleifur Guttormsson criticized the government in parliament for not keeping the opposition parties adequately informed of the negotiations. Finally the new fishing quotas were debated in November, with AB spokesman Skuli Alexandersson again critical of excessive governmental control. (Ibid., no. 14.)

The AB's tactic seems to have been to criticize the government generally throughout the year without proposing detailed alternatives. Perhaps its recent experience in government has made it less sanguine about new departures at a time of severe economic difficulties (*Economist*, London, 13 October).

Foreign Views and Activities. Three issues consistently comprise the Icelandic foreign policy agenda: the NATO bases at Keflavik and elsewhere on the island, trade relations with its principal export markets, and national economic control of resources on shore and in adjacent waters. The first issue has traditionally been the main source of controversy. It would be only a slight exaggeration to suggest that without the related issues of the Keflavik bases and NATO membership, the AB would scarcely be the force it has been in Icelandic politics during the past 35 years. The AB's willingness to participate in several coalitions during the past decade has left a pattern of the party's evolving attitudes toward the country's security and foreign policy. Gradually and reluctantly the AB has come to realize that an immediate end to the American-manned base is not likely and that the issue should not keep the party in the political wilderness indefinitely. Second, through participation in government, the AB has sought to maintain and strengthen restrictions on NATO activities in Iceland. During the Thoroddsen government, the AB succeeded in delaying plans for modernization of both civilian and military facilities at Keflavik. Governmental participation gives the AB a veto right on all foreign and security policy matters. In opposition the AB reverted to its strong antibase policy.

Iceland maintains no armed forces as such (its coast guard is lightly armed), and the American forces at Keflavik provide the country's defense force (confusingly referred to as the "Icelandic Defense Force"). As a member of NATO, however, Iceland does participate in the alliance's political

processes. For the first time in more than 30 years, Icelanders were present at the May meeting of the NATO Military Committee in Brussels. The Icelanders have observer status similar to that of the French. The modernization of military facilities in Iceland was on the committee's agenda. The leader of the Icelandic delegation indicated that the new government intended to take a more active role in alliance affairs (*News from Iceland*, June).

The AB's position on foreign affairs has tended to separate NATO membership from the bases issue. Some party commentators have suggested that NATO provides a European balance of power and a mechanism to assure balanced force reductions. The bases, however, remain unacceptable to the AB, especially as the purposes of NATO installations in the country have changed in recent years. This nuance may reflect public opinion, as indicated by a recently published study of Icelandic attitudes toward defense. The study, based on surveys taken shortly after the 1983 elections, found that 53 percent favored Icelandic membership in NATO, 13 percent were opposed, and 34 percent expressed no opinion. Of AB voters, 56 percent were opposed, but a surprising 17 percent were in favor of NATO membership. Asked whether there should be a U.S. military presence at Keflavik, 54 percent were in favor, 30 percent were opposed, and 15 percent had no opinion. Asked whether Iceland should ask the United States to pay for its bases and forces (beyond current purchases of goods and services), 63 percent favored such payments, and 29 percent were opposed. Voters of the two parties opposed to the bases, the AB and the Women's Party, were opposed to payment for the bases, presumably so that the country would have no economic disincentives to closing the bases. With more than 5,000 American personnel and their families, maintenance purchases at Keflavik of over $11 million annually, and $9.3 million worth of construction under way, the NATO bases ironically represent a significant Icelandic "military-industrial complex." (Ibid., August; *Nordisk Kontakt*, no. 10.) More than a thousand Icelanders work directly for the defense forces at Keflavik and the radar station at Stokksnes.

These economic facts were made public by Foreign Minister Geir Hallgrimsson in a foreign policy report to the parliament on 16 May. In addition, he announced that the twelve F-4 jets would be replaced by eighteen F-15 fighters. This modernization was required by increased Soviet military activity near Iceland. Inspection and reconnaissance missions were important. Hallgrimsson justified the new radar stations in the western fjords and the northeastern regions on the same grounds. The radar stations would be manned by Icelanders.

AB leader Gestsson regretted the government's approval of various military projects. The AB leader despaired of the bases ever being removed, now that the country had become so economically dependent upon them. He accused the foreign minister of being more pro-American than the American government.

Icelandic parties do not dwell extensively on world politics, but at its last congress the AB had vehement internal debate on the proper phrasing of its concern over events in Afghanistan. A direct condemnation of Soviet policies in Afghanistan was softened after Gestsson objected (*Morgunbladid*, 22 November 1983).

Iceland continues to maintain extensive trade relations with the Soviet Union. Iceland exports fish and wool products and receives Soviet petroleum at world market prices in return. About 7.5 percent of Icelandic export earnings continue to come from Soviet purchases, but the United States remains Iceland's largest customer. Iceland tightened its ties with the United States by signing an agreement allowing Icelandic fishing craft to operate within the American 200-mile zone (*Nordisk Kontakt*, nos. 1 and 13).

International Party Contacts. The AB has remained aloof from the international communist movement. It has tended to identify more closely with democratic socialist parties, particularly those with strong leftist and pacifist positions. It interacts informally but regularly with the Socialist Left Party of Norway and the Socialist People's Party of Denmark. A discussion at the last AB congress indicated that such foreign ties are not entirely uncontroversial. Some delegates called for more regular relationships with similar parties, at least in the other Nordic countries. Gestsson claimed that such ties were not prohibited by current party rules, but he had no objection to adding explicit provisions allowing such ties. Delegates claimed that AB participation in a meeting of a leftist party in Norway had been prohibited by the AB Executive Committee. One member claimed that such xenophobia hurt the party in such efforts as the antinuclear movement. After a passionate discussion of this and several other controversial issues, former party leader Olafur Grimsson sent the issue of ties to foreign parties to the Central Committee for further discussion (*Morgunbladid*, 22 November 1983).

In sum, the AB continues to reflect the very personal and passionate style of Icelandic politics. Radical in program, but often pragmatic in practice, xenophobic by habit, but cosmopolitan in spirit, the AB remains a colorful but not currently influential element. The party's strength has eroded seriously in the past decade, and the rise of two new nontraditional parties suggests that the old slogans and patterns will no longer do. Elements in the AB are anxious to pursue a "common front" of all left-of-center parties. AB policies have been modified to encourage such developments. Political alliances in Iceland are often imaginative, but rarely predictable.

Eric S. Einhorn
University of Massachusetts at Amherst

Ireland

Population. 3,575,000
Party. Communist Party of Ireland (CPI)
Founded. 1933
Membership. 500 (estimated)
Secretary General. James Stewart
National Political Committee. Includes Michael O'Riordan, Andrew Barr, Sean Nolan, Tom Redmond, Edwina Stewart, Eddie Glackin
Status. Legal
Last Congress. Eighteenth, 14–16 May 1982, in Dublin
Last Election. 1982, no representation
Auxiliary Organization. Connolly Youth Movement
Publications. *Irish Socialist*, *Irish Workers' Voice*, *Unity*, *Irish Bulletin*

The CPI was founded in 1921, when the Socialist Party of Ireland expelled moderates and decided to join the Comintern. During the Civil War the party became largely irrelevant and virtually disappeared, although very small communist cells remained intact. The CPI was refounded in June 1933, the date the Communists now adopt as the founding date of their party.

The party organization was badly disrupted during World War II because of the neutrality of the South and the belligerent status of the North. In 1948, the Communists in the South founded the Irish Workers' Party and those in the North the Communist Party of Northern Ireland. At a specially convened "unity congress" held in Belfast on 15 March 1970, the two groups reunited.

The CPI is a recognized political party on both sides of the border and contests both local and national elections. It has, however, no significant support and no elected representatives.

Leadership and Organization. The CPI is divided into two geographical branches, north and south, corresponding to the political division of the country. In theory the Congress is the supreme constitutional authority of the party but in practice it tends to serve as a rubber stamp for the national executive. The innermost controlling conclave is the National Political Committee. Such little support as the CPI enjoys tends to be based on Dublin and Belfast.

Domestic Affairs. As usual the continuing political division of the country remained the main issue in 1984. The CPI participated in the discussions called Forum for a New Ireland. The CPI's submission, however, contained nothing new but simply reiterated the party's stance on unification. The party views the United Kingdom as essentially an imperialist power that gains economically from holding Ireland in a subordinate position. While continuing to advocate the creation of a single, united socialist Ireland, the party remains opposed to the use of violence and denounces the use of force by armed gangs on either side of the communal divide. In 1984 it was particularly vehement in its denunciation of the Provisional IRA's bombing of the Grand Hotel in Brighton, which nearly killed several members of the British Cabinet, including Prime Minister Margaret Thatcher herself.

The party believes Irish unification can be achieved only through bodies promoting working-class solidarity and thus overcoming the communal divide between Protestants and Catholics.

In the South the CPI's main propaganda efforts were targeted against the Labour Party, which is in the ruling coalition with Fine Gael. The CPI regards the Labour Party's support for the government's National Plan as a betrayal of working-class interests. However, although Labour Party support undoubtedly dropped in 1984, there is no evidence that any of it transferred to the CPI.

International Views. The CPI is quite untouched by the phenomenon of Eurocommunism and remains staunchly pro-Soviet. Indeed, in a country where there are several larger Marxist groups in operation, perhaps the distinctive feature of CPI attitudes is simple pro-Sovietism. The party is strongly anti-American and denounces U.S. policy in Central America, the Middle East, and elsewhere. It favors arms reduction talks in Europe and opposes the deployment of cruise and Pershing missiles and President Reagan's Strategic Defense Initiative.

The party also remains hostile to the European Economic Community, which it regards as a device for drawing Ireland into NATO planning.

Other Marxist Groups. There are numerous Marxist groups in Ireland, most of them commanding greater support than the CPI. The most important are Sinn Fein–The Workers' Party, the Irish Republican Socialist Party, and the Provisional Sinn Fein.

Richard Sim
London

Italy

Population. 56,998,000
Party. Italian Communist Party (Partito Comunista Italiano; PCI)
Founded. 1921
Membership. 1,700,000 (claimed)
Secretary General. Alessandro Natta
Secretariat. 9 members: Alessandro Natta, Gavino Angius, Gerardo Chiaromonte, Adalberto Minucci, Giancarlo Pajetta, Ugo Pecchioli, Alfredo Reichlin, Aldo Tortorella, Renato Zangheri
Directorate. 33 members
Central Control Commission. 57 members; Paolo Bufalini, chairman
Central Committee. 180 members
Status. Legal
Last Congress. Sixteenth, 2–6 March 1983, in Milan
Last Election. 1983, 29.9 percent, 198 seats in the 630-seat lower house and 107 of 315 seats in the Senate; election for the European Parliament, June 1984, 33.3 percent, 27 seats
Auxiliary Organizations. Communist Youth Federation (FGCI), General Confederation of Italian Workers (CGIL)

Publications. *L'Unità*, official daily, Emanuele Macaluso, editor, Romano Ledda, co-editor; *Rinascita*, weekly, Giuseppe Chiarante, editor; *Critica Marxista*, theoretical journal, Aldo Tortorella, editor; *Politica ed Economia*; *Riforma della Scuola*; *Democrazia e Diritto*; *Donne e Politica*; *Studi Storici*; *Nuova Rivista Internazionale*

The PCI was established in 1921 when a radical faction of the Italian Socialist Party (PSI), led by Amedeo Bordiga, Antonio Gramsci, and Palmiro Togliatti, seceded from the PSI. Declared illegal under the fascist regime, the PCI went underground, and the party headquarters was moved abroad. It reappeared on the Italian scene in 1944 and participated in governmental coalitions in the early postwar years. Excluded from office in 1947, the party has remained in opposition since then except for a brief period (summer 1976 to January 1979) when it became part of a governmental coalition but without holding cabinet posts. At the local level, the PCI has been in power in a large number of municipalities, especially in Emilia-Romagna, Tuscany, and Umbria. Alone or in coalition with the PSI, the PCI controls the administration of most major cities.

Leadership and Organization. Enrico Berlinguer, PCI secretary general since 1972, died on 11 June. Berlinguer suffered a cerebral hemorrhage on 7 June in Padua during a political rally for the election of the European Parliament. After undergoing surgery, the PCI leader fell into a coma from which he did not recover.

Born in Sassari, on the island of Sardinia, in 1922, Berlinguer had joined the PCI as a student in 1943 and by 1948 had become a member of the party's Central Committee. In 1950, he became national secretary of the Communist Youth Federation (FGCI), a post he held until 1956. Two years later he became head of the organization section of the Central Committee. Elected to parliament for the first time in 1968, Berlinguer became deputy secretary to Luigi Longo in 1969 and eventually succeeded Longo as secretary general in March 1972.

Berlinguer's name is associated with the evolution of the PCI along the line of Eurocommunism. Under his leadership, the PCI gradually asserted its autonomy vis-à-vis the Soviet Union. On a number of occasions, Berlinguer criticized the regimes of Eastern Europe and rejected the Soviet model as an appropriate solution for Italy. In 1976, at the Soviet party's Twenty-fifth Congress, Berlinguer declared: "Socialist society must be built through the contribution of different parties in a pluralistic and demo-

cratic system" (*WSJ*, 14 June). Berlinguer often criticized Soviet foreign policy, particularly with reference to events in Poland and Afghanistan. Berlinguer's policy of independence led to the reestablishment of good relations between the PCI and the Chinese Communist Party. In domestic affairs, Berlinguer developed in the early 1970s a proposal for a "historic compromise"; that is, for a coalition involving the PCI and the Christian Democratic Party (DC) or other political groups. This policy led the PCI to support DC-led cabinets between 1976 and 1979. After the unsatisfactory outcome of that experiment, Berlinguer proposed a "left alternative," an alliance with the PSI and other groups of the center-left.

Berlinguer was a very popular figure in Italy and was widely respected even outside communist circles. At the announcement of his death, there was an outpouring of feelings of sympathy. A Vatican statement said that Pope John Paul II shared the general view of Berlinguer as a man "esteemed for the seriousness of his enterprise and for the drive that motivated him" (*NYT*, 12 June). Berlinguer's funeral was attended by all major Italian political leaders, including the president, and by many foreign delegations, among these a high-level Soviet delegation led by Mikhail Gorbachev, member of the Politburo and Secretariat. Messages were sent to the PCI by a number of East European leaders. János Kádár, on behalf of the Hungarian party, declared that Berlinguer had been "an outstanding personality of the international communist movement." The message sent by Romanian authorities spoke of Berlinguer as a politician "working for the promotion of new types of relations in the communist and working class movement." Messages from the USSR were sent by both the Central Committee and by Soviet leader Konstantin Chernenko. (BBC, 12 June.)

There was considerable speculation about Berlinguer's successor. The names most frequently mentioned as likely candidates were Alessandro Natta, the 66-year-old chairman of the Central Control Commission; Luciano Lama, 63, head of the trade union federation associated with the PCI; Renato Zangheri, 59, a university professor and former mayor of Bologna; and Giorgio Napolitano, 59, the head of the PCI parliamentary group in the lower house. Two weeks after Berlinguer's death, a joint meeting of the Central Committee and of the Central Control Commission was held to elect the new party leader. A committee of eight party officials canvassed the members of the two bodies and nominated Natta as the only official candidate. Of the 238 PCI officials casting ballots, 227 voted for Natta. The other 11 abstained. There were no votes against the proposed candidate. (*NYT*, 27 June.)

Alessandro Natta, a former high school teacher, was born in Liguria and joined the PCI after World War II. In the course of his party career, he worked closely with party secretaries Palmiro Togliatti and Luigi Longo. Natta has been a member of parliament since 1948 and has occupied various important posts within the party. Among others, he has been the head of the PCI parliamentary group, editor of the party weekly *Rinascita*, and head of the press section of the Central Committee. Known for his loyalty to the party, in 1969 he was given the job of attacking a dissident New Left group that had sprung up inside the PCI. Natta had a very close relationship with Berlinguer.

It is widely believed that the choice of Natta was a compromise acceptable to the various factions within the party but that it represented only a temporary solution. Most observers believe that a definitive choice will be made at the next party congress. In his first official statement as new party secretary, Natta vowed to continue the policies of his predecessor (ANSA, 29 June).

A number of other new appointments to important party posts were made in 1984. In February, Gavino Angius was appointed by the Central Committee and the Central Control Commission as head of the Party Affairs Department to replace the late Adriana Seroni. In this new capacity, Angius was also asked to join the Secretariat. In addition, six party members were co-opted into the Central Committee (Aureliana Alberici, chief of the School and University Section; Paolo Cantelli, secretary of the Florence federation; Ugo Mazza, secretary of the Bologna federation; Graziano Mazzarello, secretary of the Genoa federation; Mario Pani, regional secretary for Sardinia; and Luciano Violante, chief of the Justice and Anticrime Section). (*L'Unità*, 21 February.) In October, Paolo Bufalini was chosen as new chairman of the Central Control Commission to replace Alessandro Natta. In the same period, Giglia Tedesco, Gianni Pellicani, and Fabio Mussi were elected members of the Directorate, Renato Sandri was co-opted into the Central

Committee, and Flavio Bertone became a member of the Central Control Commission. (Ibid., 4 October.)

Another personnel change of significance was the announcement that Luciano Lama, for many years head of the communist union CGIL, would leave his post in 1985. Observers speculated about a possible role for Lama at the top of the party in the near future. An outspoken critic of the communist regimes of Eastern Europe, Lama has often defined himself as a "reformist." Late in the year, Lama provoked some controversies by declaring that the PCI should acknowledge that de facto it had become more or less a social-democratic party (*Panorama*, 24 December).

The party's budget for fiscal 1983 and the projected budget for 1984 were approved in a meeting of the PCI Directorate in January. The deficit for fiscal 1983 was set at 3.6 billion lire, a considerably smaller figure than that of the year before. Added to the deficits from previous years, however, this produced a cumulative deficit of 24 billion lire or approximately one-fourth of the party's income for the year. The decrease in the deficit was attributed to the fact that income had risen faster than expenditures (21.4 percent and 17.8 percent, respectively). The improvement was seen as "a first sign of a reversal of the trend, even though the basic problems that have made it impossible to balance the budget remain." As in previous years, the deficit was blamed mostly on inflation and the high cost of borrowing money. The losses incurred by the party's daily also constituted a substantial burden. The main sources of revenue were membership dues (25 billion lire), assessments paid by PCI members of parliament (5 billion lire), the annual quota from the state contribution (26 billion), and L'Unità festivals and press fund drives. In urging organizational units to strive for a balanced budget, the Directorate suggested that party members be asked "to contribute a membership assessment equal to one day of work, in application of the principle that each must contribute according to economic needs." (*L'Unità*, 29 January.)

Steps were taken in 1984 to solve the financial problems of the party's daily, *L'Unità*. The paper, with a circulation of 200,000 copies daily and 600,000 on Sunday, has been losing money for the past few years and has been heavily subsidized by the party. Blaming the deficit on low proceeds from advertising and the high cost of printing the paper in its own printing shop, the editors decided to close the shop and turned to commercial printers. Moreover, it was announced in the summer that in order to raise fresh capital party members and local branches would be encouraged to purchase shares of the publishing company (*Corriere della Sera*, 12 August). By the end of the year, over 7 billion lire had been raised (*L'Unità*, 12 January 1985).

Another problem bearing on the effectiveness of the party organization came to the surface in 1984. In the early 1970s, the Youth Federation (FGCI) had almost half a million members. By 1977 membership had declined to 127,000, and in 1984 it was down to less than 50,000. This gradual decline was the object of a special session of the PCI Central Committee. The party is considering a reorganization of the FGCI. It would no longer be a unitary organization but rather a federation of leagues, each of which would be active in specific areas, such as secondary school students, university students, young women, and others. (*Corriere della Sera*, 29 November.)

Domestic Affairs. The line pursued by the party on the domestic front requires PCI leaders to take a mixed posture vis-à-vis the PSI. On the one hand, the PCI continues to envisage the PSI as a possible future ally in the left alternative. On the other hand, it sees the PSI as a key component of the five-party coalition currently in power—the more so since the cabinet led by PSI secretary Bettino Craxi adopted in the first part of 1984 a series of austerity measures designed to curb inflation and reduce or at least stabilize the huge deficit. The PCI continued to press the PSI to leave the center-left coalition and, at the same time, took a hard line toward measures proposed by the government. (ANSA, 21 February.)

A specific target of the PCI attack was a governmental decree issued in February limiting the cost of living adjustment to wages and salaries. In response to the decree, the 4.5 million–member CGIL, the PCI-controlled union, called a major national strike. Since the other major unions, which are aligned with other parties, refused to go along with the strike, the twelve-year-old alliance among the unions appeared to be in danger (*WSJ*, 23 February). In March, the PCI sponsored a huge rally that brought 750,000 people to Rome. When the governmental decree came up for discussion in parliament, the PCI mounted a successful filibuster of the measures and prevented its passage (*WP*, 17 April). The PCI opposition to the measure did not

relent when the decree was reintroduced by the cabinet, and another parliamentary battle pitching the PCI against the PSI-led government followed (ANSA, 21 May). Eventually, the government won the point on a vote of confidence, but the issue had given the PCI the opportunity to claim that the PSI was no longer a party of the left (*L'Unità*, 27 April).

All Italian politicians viewed the elections to the European Parliament on 17 June as a contest with considerable significance for domestic politics. According to observers, the main issue was not representation in Strasbourg but leadership in Rome (*Economist*, London, 9 June). Speaking at a session of the Central Committee at the end of April, party leader Achille Occhetto said: "From the June election we are expecting a sign—that is, a vote for the PCI—that will grant further strength to our party as a real rallying point for a broad, modern, reformist alignment both in Italy and in Europe" (*L'Unità*, 27 April).

The PCI gained 33.3 percent of the popular vote, just enough for the party to overtake, for the first time in Italian history, the Christian Democrats, who received 33.0 percent. The results of the election were probably affected by the death of Berlinguer a few days before. According to some observers, the PCI was the beneficiary of a "sympathy vote" (*CSM*, 28 June). It also seems likely that the success of the PCI was due, in part, to differences in turnout rates among supporters of different parties. It is possible that a number of centrist voters did not deem the election to be an important one and did not show up at the polls. Conversely, a massive mobilization effort by the PCI allowed the party to receive a plurality of the votes cast.

The results were greeted by PCI leaders as an "event of historical importance that changes the political situation and confirms the option of a democratic alternative . . . A new chapter must now be opened in the country's history. The government, undermined from within by conflicts and ruptures, was already in a situation of crisis before the election. Following the electoral defeat, this crisis must not and cannot be concealed . . . pretending that nothing is changed is unacceptable. The crisis must be faced openly and resolved." (*L'Unità*, 19 June.)

The PCI's electoral success in the contest for the European Parliament was destined to remain purely symbolic, however. The returns had no impact on the five-party governmental coalition. Despite internal conflicts over some critical issues, the Craxi cabinet managed to survive. And despite its success, the PCI ran the risk of becoming politically isolated, as PCI leader Natta openly admitted (*La Repubblica*, 29 September). For the balance of the year, the PCI alternated between postures of opposition and moves designed to reinstate the party's influence in the political dialogue.

Foreign Affairs. Preoccupation with the deterioration in the international situation was prominent in the pronouncements of PCI leaders in 1984. Toward the end of January, Berlinguer called on both the United States and the Soviet Union to stop deploying nuclear weapons in Europe and urged them to resume negotiations. "From the West," he said, "we seek a blocking of nuclear weapons. No more U.S. missiles should be deployed in Europe. From the East we seek an end to the countermeasures and a reinstatement of the moratorium on the SS-20s. Those SS-20s which surpass a certain limit, to be agreed by the two superpowers, must be destroyed." (*NYT*, 31 January.)

The PCI's strong opposition to the deployment of U.S. missiles in Sicily remained unchanged. When at the end of March Defense Minister Giovanni Spadolini announced that the new missiles would shortly be operational, the PCI Directorate issued a strong statement arguing that the installation of the missiles constituted an obstacle to the resumption of negotiations between the two superpowers. The PCI announced that it would continue to press the government to hold a national referendum "calling on the Italians to express themselves on the escalation of nuclear missiles in Italy" (ANSA, 27 March).

In the second half of 1983, the PCI had concluded that the presence of a multilateral military force in Lebanon was no longer useful in solving that conflict. Accordingly, the party began to press for the withdrawal of the Italian troops stationed in Lebanon. Calls for withdrawal were renewed early in 1984 (ibid., 1 January).

As in previous years, there were a number of polemics involving the PCI and communist parties loyal to Moscow. In January, the PCI daily published a series of articles on Afghanistan by the *L'Unità* correspondent in Moscow, Giulietto Chiesa, who had been given permission to travel to Afghanistan. The Afghan party found these articles, which reported human rights violations documented by Amnesty International, very offensive. This led to an "open letter" from the Afghan Communists to the PCI Central Committee published in the Soviet journal *New Times*. The letter accused

the PCI of giving an assessment of the Afghan situation "which coincides with the positions of Western imperialist quarters" (BBC, 9 February). An editorial in *L'Unità* (22 May) focused on the Sakharov case and clearly attacked the Soviet newspaper *Izvestiia*'s comments on the latest development of the case:

> Let us suppose that Mrs. Bonner [Sakharov's wife] is the embodiment of all the disgraces described by the Soviet newspaper. Why on earth if she "wants to flee to the West," should she have to do so "over her husband's dead body"? Is it possible that the Soviet newspaper is unaware that this is an admission of an intolerable state of affairs? Just as it is intolerable that the world has to be told about Sakharov's whereabouts by the French citizen [and French party leader Georges] Marchais, who in turn had to approach the highest Soviet authorities to discover this. Is it possible in 1984, in a major state that has carried out the greatest revolution of the century, that a great scientist who disagrees with his government's policy has to live under these conditions? Anyone can agree or disagree with Sakharov's ideas . . . but one cannot fail to protest certain methods that constitute a violation not only of the most basic human freedoms but of common sense.

At the end of May, the regular parliamentary assembly of NATO countries met in Luxembourg, and for the first time the Italian delegation included PCI representatives. Directorate member Giorgio Napolitano participated in the political discussions, and Gianni Cervetti in the military discussions. Afterwards Napolitano commented that "the U.S. representative . . . maintained a prudent stance . . . and . . . there was an immediate, apparent convergence between our assessments and positions and the positions taken by representatives of various socialist and social-democratic parties" (*L'Unità*, 2 June).

International Party Contacts. The PCI has traditionally maintained far-ranging contacts with communist and socialist parties throughout the world. In January, Berlinguer met with Willy Brandt, chairman of the Socialist International. Asked for an assessment, Berlinguer stated, "I perceive a very broad convergence with the stances of our party . . . it is significant that forces of different orientations are motivated by the same anxieties and assessments to create . . . the conditions for a resumption of international dialogue and negotiations." (Ibid., 24 January.) In late January, Berlinguer traveled to Greece for a visit with Prime Minister Andreas Papandreou and other Greek leaders. The central topic was the implications of the suspension of the U.S.-Soviet talks in Geneva. It appeared that the PCI and the Greek socialist government shared common views on the requirements for world peace and disarmament. Papandreou commended Berlinguer for his party's peace proposals and recalled his own government's moves to promote nuclear disarmament (ANSA, 31 January). In February, a delegation of the Polisario Front met with Berlinguer in Rome. The PCI leader voiced his party's "complete and steadfast support." (L'Unità, 4 February.) A similar declaration was issued in March when José Pasos Marcial of the Sandinista National Liberation Front met in Rome with Antonio Rubbi, member of the PCI Central Committee and chief of the Foreign Affairs Section. Rubbi reaffirmed "the broadest solidarity of Italian Communists with the Nicaraguan people in the face of escalating attacks on Nicaragua's independence" (ibid., 15 March). In the same period, two Soviet officials, Leonid Zamyatin of the Central Committee and Nikolai Cherkov, met with Berlinguer to discuss major international problems. The meeting was also attended by Soviet ambassador to Italy Nikolai Lunkov. (Ibid., 14 March.) Another meeting with a Soviet delegation, headed by Stepan Chervonenko of the Central Committee, took place in Rome in the early part of May (ibid., 10 May). At the end of March, a PCI Central Committee delegation, led by PCI Directorate member and Rinascita editor Giuseppe Chiarante, visited Warsaw at the invitation of the Polish Central Committee. No statement on the nature of these talks was issued. (Ibid., 31 March.) In early May, PCI Directorate member and speaker of the Lower House, Nilde Jotti, received a delegation of the Foreign Affairs Institute of the People's Republic of China (ibid., 8 May). In June, Jotti received Horst Sindermann, president of the East German legislature (ADN, 14 June). The visit was returned in August when PCI official Armando Cossutta traveled to Berlin and conferred with East German Politburo member Herbert Häber (ibid., 9 August).

After his inauguration as general secretary following Berlinguer's death, Alessandro Natta held talks with visiting foreign officials and party representatives. In June, he had talks with Bayardo Arce Castano of the Sandinista Front. In August it was announced that Natta would travel to the USSR and China, but no dates were set for these trips (ANSA, 9 August). In September, Natta met with Boris Stukalin, head of the Propaganda Department of the Soviet Central Committee. (Tass, 18 September.) He also met with a representative of the Central Committee of the Chinese Communist Party and "expressed the hope to develop further friendly relations" (NCNA, 19 September). Shortly afterwards, Natta held talks with Ali Šukrija, president of the Yugoslav party Presidium (Tanjug, 28 September).

Other Communist Groups. In October the Party of Proletarian Unity for Communism (PDUP), which was composed largely of former Communists and left-wing Socialists, decided to merge with the PCI (La Repubblica, 1 October). The operation was formally approved by the PCI Central Committee at the meeting on 29 November. The merger was largely a formal matter since the PDUP had already presented joint lists of candidates with the PCI in the parliamentary election of June 1983. The five PDUP members of the lower house were expected to join the PCI parliamentary group.

The disappearance of the PDUP leaves Proletarian Democracy (DP) as the only other group competing with the PCI on the left wing of the political spectrum. In the election of June 1983, the DP received 1.5 percent of the popular vote and obtained seven seats in the 630-member lower house. The DP also participated in the June elections for the European Parliament. It received 1.4 percent of the vote and one representative.

Terrorist Groups. In 1984, there was a further decline of terrorism carried out by self-styled true communist groups. Some episodes of violence did, however, occur. In February, representatives of the Fighting Communist Party claimed responsibility for the assassination of a U.S. diplomat and a director general of the multinational force in Egypt's Sinai peninsula (NYT, 15 February).

During the year, a number of alleged terrorists were arrested, and others were brought to trial. In March, a Red Brigades terrorist hideout complete with weapons, explosives, and lists of names was discovered in Rome (ANSA, 24 March).

In April, a group of 36 Italian magistrates who had been working on cases of terrorism warned that underground groups were in the process of reforming. According to magistrates, the terrorist groups were establishing ties with organized crime. (Ibid., 9 April.)

Further evidence of a resurgence of terrorist

groups surfaced later in the year. In December, two Red Brigade commandos attempted to carry out armed robberies in Rome and Bologna. Their plans failed, and two terrorists were killed by police. (*Corriere della Sera*, 16 December.) In late December a bomb exploded on the Naples-Milan express, killing fourteen people and injuring many others. No group claimed responsibility for the bombing. At the funeral for the victims held in Bologna, the communist mayor of that city attacked the government for its inability to stop acts of terrorism carried out by right-wing elements. The episode exacerbated further the already tense relations between the PCI and the PSI. (Ibid., 29 December.)

Giacomo Sani
Ohio State University

Luxembourg

Population. 366,000
Party. Communist Party of Luxembourg (Parti communiste luxembourgeois; CPL)
Founded. 1921
Membership. 600 (estimated)
Chairman. René Urbany
Honorary Chairman. Dominique Urbany
Executive Committee. 10 members: Aloyse Bisdorff, François Hoffmann, Fernand Hübsch, Marianne Passeri, Marcel Putz, René Urbany, Jean Wesquet, Serge Urbany, André Moes, Babette Ruckert
Secretariat. 2 members: René Urbany, Dominique Urbany
Central Committee. 31 full and 7 candidate members
Status. Legal
Last Congress. Twenty-fourth, 4–5 February 1984
Last Election. 1979, 5.0 percent, 2 of 59 seats
Auxiliary Organizations. Jeunesse communiste luxembourgeoise; Union des femmes luxembourgeoises
Publications. *Zeitung vum Lëtzeburger Vollek*, official CPL organ, daily, 1,000–1,500 copies (CPL's claim: 15,000–20,000)

The pro-Soviet CPL played an insignificant political role in Luxembourg prior to World War II. After 1945, the CPL's position improved. Communists were elected to serve in parliament and in several communities. From 1945 to 1947, Luxembourg's cabinet included one communist minister. The best election results were achieved in 1968. In elections in 1974 and 1979, the communist vote declined steadily. In 1979, the CPL received 5 percent of the vote. On 10 June 1979, in the first elections to the European Parliament, the CPL obtained 5.1 percent. At the second elections to the European Parliament on 17 June 1984, the communist vote share declined to 4.1 percent. In municipal elections in 1981, the CPL received 7.2 percent, compared with 16 percent in 1975.

The CPL held its Twenty-fourth Congress on 4–5 February. It was attended by nearly 200 delegates and delegations from eleven fraternal parties, including a Soviet delegation led by Anatoli S. Chernayev, alternate member of the Central Committee and deputy head of the International Department of the Central Committee. The congress elected a new Central Committee, consisting of 31 full and seven candidate members. CPL Chairman René Urbany was re-elected. The Central Committee elected a ten-member Executive Committee and a two-member Secretariat. Chairman René Urbany reported to the congress about the growing, communist-supported peace movement, which is fighting against dangerous military preparations and the use of Luxembourg's territory for aggressive purposes by NATO and the United States. He spoke highly of the consistent, peace-loving foreign policy of the socialist countries, above all of the Soviet Union. (Tass, 4 February; *FBIS*, 8 February.) The congress adopted a resolution "Communists—for Social Equality, for Peaceful and Democratic Luxembourg." It expresses the CPL's opposition to the militarization of Luxembourg and its support for the intensification of the people's struggle for peace. (Tass, 6 February; *FBIS*, 8 February.)

The CPL leadership is dominated by the Urbany family. René Urbany succeeded his father, Dominique, as chairman at the first meeting of the Central Committee after the Twenty-second Congress in 1977. Dominique Urbany remained as honorary chairman of the CPL. Members of the Urbany family hold many key positions in the party and its auxiliaries. René Urbany is also the director of the party press.

The CPL, like other communist parties in Western Europe, supported Soviet foreign policy objectives in its "mass publications" and its effort to promote "joint actions against the threat of war."

Contacts with fraternal parties were maintained during 1984. René Urbany visited Bulgarian leader Todor Zhivkov (Sofia domestic service, 9 August; *FBIS*, 10 August) and met in Moscow with Boris Ponomarev, alternate member of the Soviet Politburo and secretary of the Central Committee, and Vladim Zagladin, member of the Central Committee and first deputy head of the International Department (Tass, 5 November; *FBIS*, 6 November).

COPE, the CPL's publishing company, prints the French edition of the *World Marxist Review*. COPE's new and modern technical equipment and production facilities, which exceed local requirements by far, serve communist parties and organizations in several other countries.

Eric Waldman
University of Calgary

Malta

Population. 329,599 (Malta Central Office of Statistics)
Party. Communist Party of Malta (Partit Komunista Malti; CPM)
Founded. 1969
Membership. 100 (estimated)
Secretary General. Anthony Vassallo
Central Committee. 11 members: Anthony Baldacchino (president), Lino Vella (vice-president), Anthony Vassallo (secretary general), Karmenu Gerada (international secretary), Mario Mifsud (financial secretary), Mario Vella (propaganda secretary), Victor Degiovanni (assistant secretary general), Joseph Cachia (assistant international secretary), Dominic Zammit (assistant financial secretary), Michael Schembri (assistant propaganda secretary), Paul Agius

Status. Legal

Last Congress. Extraordinary Congress, 18–25 May 1984

Last Election. 1981 (CPM did not contest)

Auxiliary Organizations. Peace and Solidarity Council of Malta, Joseph V. Muscat, president; Malta-USSR Friendship and Cultural Society, Anton Cassar, president; Malta-Czechoslovakia Friendship and Cultural Society, Karmenu Gerada, president; Malta-Cuba Friendship and Cultural Society, Mario Mifsud, president; Communist Youth League (CYL), John Vassallo, president

Publications. *Zminijietna* or *Our Times*, monthly tabloid, part in English and part in Maltese; *International Political Review*, monthly, English-language edition of *World Marxist Review*; *Problemi ta Paci u Socjalizmu*, Maltese-language abstract of same; *Bridge of Friendship and Culture Malta-USSR*, issued by the Malta-USSR Friendship and Cultural Society, quarterly in English; *Bandiera Hamra* (Red flag), issued by CYL

The CPM was formed in 1969 after a series of private meetings in Valletta and elsewhere, attended by individuals holding extreme left-wing views and by disgruntled Malta Labor Party (MLP) members. From the year of foundation, its leading personality has been Anthony Vassallo, CPM secretary general since the beginning. Vassallo joined the World Federation of Democratic Youth during the late 1940s. When his communist affiliation became public knowledge, he encountered criticism and was forced by circumstances to maintain a low profile. As an engineer, he worked in a civilian capacity for the British Air Ministry establishment in Malta and later as a teacher at a government technical school. All the while, he continued to be active in the labor movement, particularly in the General Workers Union (GWU) and in sports organizations. As the communist party began to build up its infrastructure, he began to work for the party fulltime. Legal since its inception, the CPM has never been successful in recruiting a strong membership. But it has used a variety of tactics to spread its influence and infiltrate the labor movement, the drydocks, youth organizations, and, to some extent, the University of Malta. Its influence is much larger than its membership. Although it has no visible source of funds, the CPM has a complex of offices in a prime site in Valletta. It issues three regular publications, largely distributed free, and is assisted by front organizations as well as by a "progressive" bookshop and travel agency.

At the CPM's Second Congress (February 1979), Vassallo gave notice that the CPM intended to participate in the 1981 general elections. In the end, the CPM abstained from doing so. The MLP won 34 seats in the 65-seat parliament. The opposition Nationalist Party won an absolute majority of votes but secured only 31 seats under a system of proportional representation.

Leadership and Organization. In May 1984, the CPM held an extraordinary congress and elected a new Central Committee. The meeting was held behind closed doors. The delegates "approved amendments to the party statute and after a deep and long discussion approved a short-term programme which should serve to guide the party's activities." A number of resolutions were also approved. (*Zminijietna*, May/June.) The statutory amendments were not published. Various excerpts from the approved program were published in *Zminijietna*. Originally programmed to run from 18 to 20 May, the CPM extraordinary congress overshot the official schedule with additional sessions on 24 and 25 May. Members of the CPM children's organization made their first appearance on the occasion of the congress, when they distributed carnations to the delegates.

One outstanding feature of the congress was the demotion of the international secretary, Paul Agius, who was succeeded by a relatively obscure newcomer, Karmenu Gerada. Agius, a dedicated Communist with a flair for business, had been the active front man for the CPM since its foundation. He retained his post as first vice-president of the Malta-USSR Friendship and Cultural Society. Like Agius, Gerada joined the CPM after a period of residence in Australia.

The CPM monthly organ indicated well in advance of the congress that an internal party reorganization was in the offing and that an exercise in self-criticism and a reassessment of party strategy and tactics were anticipated (ibid., March). During the following month, the same journal declared editorially that the duty of the new Central Committee was "to watch the conduct of CPM members and contest every activity that could be harmful to the party." It alleged that "there are people in the CPM who are lacking in discipline and even go to the extent, perhaps unwittingly, of harming the party." By coincidence or by design, the March issue of *Zminijietna* also published the full text of a message of greetings from the Central Committee of the Communist Party of the Soviet Union to Secretary General Vassallo on the occasion of his sixtieth birthday. The message praised "the principled position of a staunch Marxist-Leninist, of an ardent propagandist of communist ideas."

The CPM secretary general is known for his insistence on maintaining the purity of party doctrine and for upholding a hard line in conformity with the Kremlin's definition of proletarian internationalism. In his opening address to the extraordinary congress, Vassallo referred to past recruitment of "ideologically weak" members. He expressed concern about the infiltration of undesirable elements into the CPM, implying that these elements might be spies rather than genuine militants. The reconstituted Central Committee is expected to protect the CPM from this danger, and while ensuring the existence of an autonomous communist presence in Malta, it would also make certain that this presence is loyal to the cause of proletarian internationalism in close alliance with the Communist Party of the Soviet Union.

In the course of his address to the congress, the CPM secretary general disclosed that since the Second Congress, the CPM had exchanged delegations and issued joint communiqués with the communist parties of the Soviet Union, Cuba, Hungary, Greece, and Cyprus. CPM representatives attended party congresses in the Soviet Union, Bulgaria, Czechoslovakia, Poland, the German Democratic Republic, Italy, France, Greece, Cyprus, West Germany, and others. They also participated in party meetings in France and Belgium and at ideological and commemorative gatherings elsewhere, as well as in peace rallies of front movements. The selection of Malta as the site for congresses of the Afro-Asian Peoples' Solidarity Organization and the International Association of Democratic Lawyers provides solid evidence of the steady buildup of the CPM in the international communist movement and of the increasing interest in Maltese affairs by overseas communist parties—an interest disproportionate to the size and importance of the CPM. It also suggests that the CPM may already have become a springboard for international communist activities. The publication of a Maltese edition of *World Marxist Review* is certainly one such activity.

Published excerpts from the party program and the resolutions approved by the extraordinary congress contained no new ideas; they all harped on the issues of peace and détente, on turning the Mediterranean into a zone "free from nuclear weapons," on unemployment, the improvement of social services, and the introduction of constitutional safeguards to ensure the continuity of nonalignment, full sovereignty, and political independence (ibid., July/August).

Domestic Affairs. Since the end of the extraordinary congress, the CPM has kept a surprisingly low profile. The party press has visibly restrained its criticism of the MLP. At the same time, it stepped up its peace and anti-American propaganda and threw its weight behind the government media in the campaign for free education and against church schools. This last issue mushroomed on occasion into anti-Vatican and anticlerical skirmishes of above-average ferocity. Since the introduction of a weekly air service by Aeroflot between Moscow and Casablanca, with stops at Budapest and Malta, Novosti Press Agency literature has begun to arrive in great quantities, and the CPM has helped to flood the island with propaganda literature. CPM publications advertise other communist literature, such as the *Information Bulletin* of the *World Marxist Review*. Village groups of CPM members mimeograph leaflets and small publications for local distribution, generally to exploit local grievances or to voice neighborhood aspirations. The strategy is to gain influence, to infiltrate local organizations, and to add to the number of fellow travelers.

This effort focuses on the grey area of Maltese politics: no one seems to know the strength of the CPM beyond the insignificant number of card-carrying members. It is certain that sympathizers, and possibly secret members, have infiltrated the labor movement and in particular the news media. There is clear evidence that communist influence at the drydocks has increased. The party line has been clearly expressed in reasonably unmistakable terms: "Because of the special circumstances prevailing in Malta, where the CPM has more or less to collaborate with members of the Labor Party and members of the GWU, we must watch continuously against every form of opportunism, because whilst we may influence labor supporters, these could similarly exercise their influence on us" (ibid.).

The CPM claims that these tactics are paying dividends. Its most outspoken claim was made after a 28 September march into Valletta by demonstrating drydock workers armed with red flags, iron bars, and rocks. The demonstrators had earlier been addressed by a government minister and asked to return to work. Instead, they drove into the capital city, invaded the law courts, and ransacked the archbishop's curia, desecrating two chapels in the process. The CPM newspaper claimed that the workers experienced a true awakening and, disobeying their leaders, instilled terror among the enemies of the workers. (Ibid., October.) The police did not apprehend or prosecute any of the demonstrators, and nobody knows the loyalties of the ringleaders.

Auxiliary and Front Organizations. By far the most important auxiliary organization is the Malta-USSR Friendship and Cultural Society. Its president, Anton Cassar, is the administrative head of the GWU newspaper staff. Cassar is the author of a book in Maltese, entitled *The Russians Say It with Flowers*, describing his impressions of visits to the Soviet Union. The secretary of the society is Remig Sacco, an MLP activist and a member of the Malta Peace and Solidarity Council. They have the assistance of a Soviet citizen who has a work permit as a Russian-language teacher and interpreter. The society offers annual scholarships to the USSR; organizes trips to the Soviet Union for its members; sponsors competitions, exhibitions, film shows, lectures, and social functions; and distributes literature.

The Malta-Czechoslovakia and Malta-Cuba friendship and cultural societies were not consistently active and existed more as dormant partners to be raised on special occasions.

The Peace and Solidarity Council of Malta received a delegation from the Soviet Peace Committee. At the end of the visit, a formal communiqué was issued in support of the Soviet and Maltese governments' efforts to strengthen security and cooperation in the Mediterranean region. (Ibid., October.)

Peace and liberation movements from 60 countries, which included known Communists, attended the International Conference of Peace and Liberation, organized by the Pope John XXIII Peace Laboratory—a noncommunist Maltese organization. The conference concentrated on protests against nuclear weapons. A proposal was advanced to set up a radio station in Malta to be called the Voice of Peace and Liberation. (*Weekend Chronicle*, Malta, 17 March.)

International Views and Activities. The CPM adopted a lower profile and worked quietly behind the scenes, but the Soviet embassy came prominently into the limelight. The most important development was the signing of a trade accord in early March, providing for the purchase by the USSR of up to $400 million worth of Maltese goods and services until 1986. A Tass report stated that Soviet purchases from Malta under the agreement were "to balance out the two countries' trade" (ibid., 3 March). The text of the agreement was not published. Among other things, Malta agreed to purchase cars, coal, oil products, and cement. On the Soviet side, a formal undertaking was made to set up a surgical instruments factory in Malta; to buy clothing, shoes, iron castings, and other products; and to give shipbuilding and repair orders to the Malta drydocks. The increase in the tempo of two-way trade during 1984 remained modest.

The Soviet commerical counselor complained at a meeting of the Malta-USSR Friendship and Cultural Society on 29 June that there is a roughly $11.5 million trade imbalance in favor of Malta (*Commercial Courier*, Malta, 23 July) and that the slow and tightfisted method of import licensing by the Malta Department of Trade had to be reassessed (*Times*, Malta, 21 November).

In an effort to encourage more trade, the Soviet foreign advertising agency organized an information exhibit at a leading hotel in Valletta during the last week of November under the personal charge of its deputy director general. A team of six high-level trade experts flew to Malta from Moscow for the exhibition. One of them was Mikhail Filipov, executive secretary of the Department of Trade with Western Countries.

There are indications, however, that an advanced stage has been reached for the construction of a number of small vessels at the drydocks to fill Soviet orders, but there was no reference to this in the Malta government budget announced on 28 November (*Commercial Courier*, 17 December).

On the cultural front, the USSR has been much more successful. Hundreds of books were presented to the national, university, and Malta drydocks libraries; more films, newsclips, and propaganda appeared in Maltese media; and sport trainers and facilities for exchanges with Maltese sport groups were provided.

Soviet ambassador to Malta Viktor N. Smirnov spelled out his country's policy: "We are working hard towards the development of all-round mutually beneficial relations between the Soviet Union and the Republic of Malta in all spheres of human endeavor—be it tourism, trade, sports, education and so on" (*Times*, 2 September).

The president of the MLP Young Socialist League visited the USSR in October to attend a youth conference and to have talks at the Komsomol secretariat (*Orizzont*, Malta, 25 October).

A new area of communist influence was opened with the launching of a scheme to send relays of Maltese workers to Czechoslovakia for training in trade unionism. This was the result of a formal agreement between the GWU, which is affiliated with the International Confederation of Free Trade Unions, and the Czechoslovak Central Council of Trade Unions, a senior partner in the World Federation of Trade Unions (a communist front organization). (*Torca*, Malta, 11 November.)

The Maltese government took certain economic initiatives vis-à-vis the communist world. From its point of view, the highest priority is to attract investment, create employment, and secure help as a demonstration of friendship. Its efforts have not been remarkably successful.

Deputy Prime Minister Carmelo Mifsud Bonnici declared at a party meeting in June that the government was planning joint projects with a number of countries, including Albania, Bulgaria, Czechoslovakia, the Soviet Union, and Hungary. He added that in a short time the fruits of the government's efforts would be visible (*Orizzont*, 25 June).

The Bulgarian deputy minister for heavy machinery and electronics arrived with another delegation to further strengthen relations between the two countries (*Times*, 18 January). It was later reported that the Bulgarians identified products to be ordered from Malta and agreed to expand a joint factory scheduled to produce electric fittings (*Weekend Chronicle*, 21 January).

After attending Andropov's funeral in Moscow, the president of the Republic of Malta, Agatha Barbara, visited the German Democratic Republic, Czechoslovakia, and Bulgaria. Possibilities for improved trade relations were discussed (*Sunday Times*, Malta, 26 February). No improvements have since been reported.

The international secretary of the MLP, while opening an exhibition on Cuba at one of his party's clubs, forecast the imminent announcement of a plan for cooperative action between the peoples of Cuba and Malta (*Orizzont*, 2 April). The announcement is still awaited.

A top-level delegation from Romania. led by Central Committee secretary Ion Coman, arrived for talks to study bilateral cooperation (*Times*, 1 May). The study phase has not led to any results.

Malta has a special relationship with North Korea, strengthened at the end of 1983 by a secret agreement that involved the supply of arms. Although only a small number of Maltese ambassadors are stationed abroad, one is resident in Pyongyang. North Korea has an embassy in Valletta with five accredited representatives. A number of Korean specialists served in Malta during 1984. A small team helped the Maltese government with the country's electric utility system; another aided the police department. As a gesture to Pyongyang, the Malta government ordered the closure of the South Korean vice-consulate in Valletta (*Democrat*, Malta, 14 April). Prime Minister Dom Mintoff and Foreign Minister Alex Sceberras Trigona visited North Korea and concluded a cultural cooperation agreement and an agreement on economic and technical cooperation.

The People's Republic of China has more solid relations with the Mintoff government, going back to 1982 when the Maltese prime minister visited Beijing and negotiated a $35 million loan from China. Since that time, China has become a partner of the Maltese government in a number of projects.

Chinese experts are currently engaged on a large project—the construction of a harbor and breakwater on the southeast part of the island. China has ordered two small ships from the Malta dockyard, to be financed by the repayment of the loan advanced to Malta in 1982. The managing director of the China Harbor Engineering Company visited Malta in October and disclosed that a joint company had been formed by China and Malta for projects in the Mediterranean region and Africa (*Times*, 30 October).

In November, the president of China, Li Xiannian, paid a five-day visit to Malta, where he was awarded Malta's highest honor. Maltese president Barbara lauded Chinese efforts at the United Nations (ibid., 23 November).

This last point highlights the nature of Malta's tightrope performance in the sphere of foreign policy with regard to the Soviet Union and China. Its declared foreign policy is based on the aspiration of making the Mediterranean stable and secure—a "lake of peace." Malta stubbornly pursued this policy at the Conference on Security and Cooperation in Europe at Helsinki and at the follow-on meetings at Belgrade, Madrid, and Stockholm. In pursuit of this policy, the Mintoff government has urged the superpowers to withdraw their fleets from the Mediterranean and to make that sea a region of peace and cooperation. Beijing considers that Malta's stand in the Mediterranean conforms with Chinese policy against hegemonism.

When Malta signed its neutrality agreement with the Soviet Union in October 1981, the two sides defined the area of their agreement. A joint communiqué issued at the time stated that both sides favored international agreements concerning extension to the Mediterranean of confidence-building measures in the military field, reductions in armed forces in the region, withdrawal from the Mediterranean of nuclear-weapon-carrying ships, renunciation of the deployment of nuclear weapons in the territories of nonnuclear countries in the region, and the obligation to be assumed by nuclear powers not to use nuclear weapons against any Mediterranean country that does not allow the development of such weapons on its territory (*WMR*, August 1981).

There is a seed of potential friction between Malta and the USSR. When the former's foreign minister addressed the U.N. General Assembly on 28 September, he declared: "We cannot feel free and secure as long as our seas remain the playground for the American Sixth Fleet to flex its muscles when it desires, as long as the Soviet Navy uses our sea as its backyard, as long as two major navies and a number of small ones use our sea as the domain of their ever enlarging war games, as long as our region is riddled with staging points for rapid troop deployment, and as long as nuclear weapons beneath and above our stars, and even on the adjoining mainland, remain the frightening daily reality."

During the second half of December, there was a series of rapid but important developments. Foreign Minister Sceberras Trigona informed parliament that the Soviet Union had agreed to help clear Malta's Grand Harbor of wartime bombs and wrecks and that a Soviet team of experts and a survey ship were expected to arrive soon (*Financial Times*, London, 12 December). The experts arrived the following day, and the survey ship on 15 December (*Sunday Times*, 16 December). The Maltese government turned to the Soviet Union for this help after protracted negotiations with the British government, which were still going on when the Maltese foreign minister made his announcement.

Prime Minister Mintoff announced his resignation from the office of prime minister (but not his membership in the Malta House of Representatives) on 22 December. A few days earlier he had informed parliament that Malta's neutrality agreement with Italy was no longer in effect "because its protocols on financial and economic assistance had run their course" (*Times*, 7 December). This immediately gave rise to a question whether the Mintoff government had ceased to adhere to its declared policy of equidistance from the superpowers since the neutrality accord with the Soviet Union was still operative.

Mintoff's career as prime minister had its grand finale in the form of an official visit to the Soviet Union, where he was given the red carpet treatment, including rounds of meetings with Konstantin Chernenko, Nikolai Tikhonov, and Andrei Gromyko.

The trip was called a "cooperation visit" and the final communiqué after the rounds of talks at the Kremlin yielded little that was new. The two sides formally agreed to expand the process of consultations "at various levels" and "expressed a readiness" to "continue mutually beneficial cooperation in the commercial and economic fields, as well as in science and technology, culture, public health, sports and in other activities."

Mintoff is reported to have referred to "the new convergence of views in a common Sino-Soviet Mediterranean approach" and to have stated: "Verily I say new times are emerging which, shrewdly exploited for the Mediterranean, could bring about still happier relations between the Mediterranean states and the Soviet Union and the People's Republic of China. May this new convergence of views in a common Sino-Soviet Mediterranean approach augur the beginning of a friendly solution of Sino-Soviet problems in the best interest of Socialism and world peace." (*Weekend Chronicle*, 22 December.) There was no reference at all to this matter in the final communiqué.

Mintoff's valedictory speech in the Malta House of Representatives on 22 December raised a number of questions, not the least of which is whether he has really decided to distance himself from active politics or whether he will continue to exercise influence by a form of remote control. He has handed the reins of office to Karmenu Mifsud Bonnici, who was co-opted as a member of parliament without ever contesting a popular election and who, therefore, owes his appointment to Mintoff and not to the electorate.

J. G. E. Hugh
Valletta, Malta

Netherlands

Population. 14,437,000
Party. Communist Party of the Netherlands (Communistische Partij van Nederland; CPN)
Founded. 1909
Membership. 10,000 (estimated)
Chairperson. Elli Izeboud
Executive Committee. 10 members: Elli Izeboud, Frank Biesboer, Fenna Bolding, Ina Brouwer, John Geelen (secretary), Siem van der Helm, Ton van Hoek, Karel Hoogkamp, Boe Thio, Jaap Wolff
Secretariat. 3 members
Central Committee. 55 members (John Geelen, secretary; Ton van Hoek, spokesman)
Status. Legal
Last Congress. Extraordinary Congress, 4, 5, 12, and 27 February 1984; Twenty-ninth Congress scheduled for 1–3 March 1985
Last Election. 1982, 1.9 percent, 3 of 150 seats; European Parliament elections, 14 June 1984, Green Progressive Accord, 5.6 percent
Auxiliary Organizations. General Netherlands Youth Organization, Netherlands Women's Movement, People's Congress Committee, Stop the N-Bomb/Stop the Nuclear Arms Race, Women Against Nuclear Weapons, CPN Youth Platform
Publications. *De Waarheid* (Truth), official daily, circulation 13,000 copies; *CPN-Leden krant*, published 10 times yearly for CPN members; *Politiek en Cultuur*, theoretical journal published 10 times yearly; *Komma*, quarterly, issued by CPN's Institute for Political and Social Research. CPN owns Pegasus Publishers.

The CPN was founded in 1909 as the Social Democratic Party (Sociaal-Democratische Partij) by radical Marxists. It assumed the name Communist Party of Holland (Communistische Partij Holland) in 1919 when the party affiliated with the Comintern. The present name dates from 1935. Except during World War II, the party has always been legal.

The most important development within the CPN during 1984 was the acceptance by the Extraordinary Congress on 26 February of a new amended party program, the first new program since World War II, as official policy of the CPN. This meant, for the time being, that there would be no official split within the party between those advocating "renewal" and those stressing the traditional CPN position. The prevention of a split within the party occurred despite the formation by a hard core of orthodox Communists on 25 February in Amsterdam of the Alliance of Communists in the Netherlands (Verbond van Communisten in Nederland; VCN), an organization distinct from the CPN.

The Executive Committee under the leadership of Chairperson Elli Izeboud, while being criticized from all sides as weak and ineffectual, was able to control the congress in such a way that neither the reformists nor the orthodox Marxists left the party. This was a delicate task as the issues dividing the two potential splinter groups ran across-the-board: whether Marxism-Leninism was the sole source of party inspiration and authority, the organizational principle of democratic centralism, the importance of the class struggle vis-à-vis women's rights, relations with the socialist countries, and cooperation with other left-wing parties. On each issue, the reformist tendency within the party won the day by a small majority.

The current problems of the CPN began in 1977 when devastating electoral results revealed serious shortcomings with respect to the traditional power base of the CPN—workers in the textile, mining, cardboard, and shipbuilding industries and in the agricultural sector in the provinces of Groningen and North Holland. These industries were disappearing in the Netherlands and the workers were going on the unemployment roles. In addition to structural changes in the economy of the Netherlands, the CPN was faced with the problem of a lack of a credible "center" for the communist movement, a waning of the popularity achieved in the resistance during World War II, a change in social forces, and the recognition by most CPN members that there is no Dutch way to socialism.

With these changes came a change in leadership; the CPN leadership is now composed of intellectuals and social workers who received their enlightenment during the democratization process in the Netherlands in the early 1970s. At the same time, many orthodox CPN members see the new CPN as "feministic, antiworker, and anti-Russian" (*Het Parool*, 9 October). This reaction received formal recognition in the founding of the Horizontal Consultation of Communists (HOC), comprising about one-quarter of the CPN's membership, in 1982 and of its successor, the VCN, in February. The year, therefore, has been dominated by this internecine struggle. The radical reformers, comprising about one-third of the CPN's membership, cast doubt on the viability of a CPN independent of other left-wing parties, while the expected creation in 1985 of a new communist party in the Netherlands threatens the existence of an already sectarian party. The remaining CPN members retain a sentiment for the traditional CPN position, but tend toward the position of "renewal" because they acknowledge the need to replace the party's traditional electoral base.

The attempt of the CPN to forge ahead with its coalition policy with parties to the left of the Labor Party (PvdA) was successful in that the joint list, the Green Progressive Accord (GPA), formed by the CPN, the Green Party of the Netherlands (GPN), the Pacifist Socialist Party (PSP) and the Political Radical Party (PPR), received 5.6 percent of the vote in the elections for the European Parliament on 14 June compared with 5.06 percent in

1979. The coalition list received two seats in the European Parliament (versus none in 1979). The best performance for the coalition in this election was in North Holland with 9.2 percent of the vote and in Amsterdam with 14.6 percent of the vote (ibid., 18 June).

Internal Party Affairs. In accordance with the mandate of the Twenty-eighth Congress, the CPN drew up a draft party program, which was presented, together with some 3,000 amendments, to the February congress. The draft program, containing the resolutions adopted at the Twenty-eighth Congress on party "renewal," became the object of intense political infighting in all CPN districts in the period leading up to the congress. In Groningen, Nico Broekema, the head of the CPN fraction in the city council, resigned from his party position because of a political move by the dominant orthodox Communists in Groningen to exclude all but three reformists from the Groningen CPN delegation of 72 to the congress (ibid., 18 January). In Amsterdam, Marcus Bakker, former veteran CPN parliamentarian, led a group of 130 CPN members who wished to preclude any split in the party either from the HOC or the reformist wings, but HOC adherents in Amsterdam were raging because of "manipulations" by leaders of the reform wing at the Amsterdam district meeting over the selection of delegates to the congress. The reform wing introduced a list of 400 names as recommendations for the district, and most of the 250 delegates chosen from Amsterdam were on the list. The radical reform wing received about 100 delegates while some 65 HOC adherents were chosen (ibid., 23 January). Members of the HOC in Amsterdam, including its founders, Laurens Meerten and René Dammen, subsequently joined Marcus Bakker's campaign for a "revolutionary and resolute Marxist party" (*Handelsblad*, 20 January). A pamphlet appeal, signed by 1,000 CPN members, was secretly placed in the party newspaper, *De Waarheid*, in support of the traditional CPN position (*Het Parool*, 20 January). In return, the reformists complained of harassment and expressed fear for the fate of the draft party program at the congress.

On 4 February, Elli Izeboud, CPN chairperson, opened the congress by criticizing the delegates for creating a polarized atmosphere. The effect, she said, of the hostility generated during the discussions on the draft program was simply to bring into doubt the desirability of attempting to create "a communist party of a new type" (*Handelsblad*, 4

February). The focal point of the first two days of the congress was the first 200 lines of the draft party program dealing with the principles of Marxism-Leninism and democratic centralism. The age composition of the delegates was 23 percent younger than 30, 58 percent between the ages of 31 and 50, and 19 percent over the age of 51.

Crucial to the success of the draft program was a majority vote on amendments pertaining to the ultimate source of inspiration for the party; that is, the basic principles of the party. An amendment presented by members of the HOC group together with the centrist group headed by Marcus Bakker and Fré Meis (a veteran CPN strike leader from Groningen) containing language to the effect that the CPN would "continue to work" on the basis of Marxism and would "stand open" to feminist ideas appeared unsatisfactory to the feminists because it upgraded Marxism at the expense of feminism. The original author of the draft party program, Henk Hoekstra, then intervened on behalf of the feminists by stating: "I had, in my text two years ago, based the CPN on Marxism. I then agreed to go along with the compromise of the commission. They persuaded me that one can come to the same point of departure from ideas other than Marxism. The text now before us is good, but the demands of the women must be met." (*Het Parool*, 6 February.) The successful formula therefore reads that the CPN will not only "continue to work on the basis of Marxist views and theories, but also on feminism," thereby placing feminism on a par with Marxism. The vote defeating the HOC-Bakker amendment was 396 against and 318 for. Bakker's attempt to retain the language of the HOC on principles was justified, he said, because "a program without a party is nothing."

During the second session of the congress on 12 February, which dealt with socioeconomic issues, the language was less theological than that of the first session, but the adoption of a "25-hour workweek with retention of wages" equal to a 40-hour workweek, by a vote of 53 percent for and 44 percent against with 3 percent abstaining, angered members of the Working Group for Communism and Trade Unions and the orthodox Communists so much they walked out of the conference hall. The choice facing the delegates was one of maintaining purchasing power or redistributing work and income. The feminists rejected the phrase "retention of wages" because they wanted a new incomes policy favoring women, while, on the other hand, those who left the hall were mad because the phrase

"25-hour workweek" was not realistic and was intended not in the first place to help the workers, but to achieve feminist goals. (Ibid., 13 February.)

Earlier, the congress had accepted the principle that in the future the CPN will accept "the majority standpoint as the point of departure for action." In addition, "minority opinions will be recognized and respected" and differences of opinion within the party are no longer subject to "disciplinary methods." (*De Waarheid*, 13 February.) Passages in the draft program relating to relations with the communist countries were accepted. These differed from the positions of the orthodox and the radical "reformist" wings. The CPN will maintain contacts with socialist opposition groups in Eastern Europe, but will not place the Soviet Union on a par with the United States concerning the causes of the international crisis. (*Handelsblad*, 13 February.)

At the last session of the congress on 26 February, the congress accepted the remaining draft text on social welfare, the democratic path to socialism, and the coalition policy without rancor, but this apparent peace was upset by the fact that a meeting on the previous day of 600 CPN members and non-CPN members in Amsterdam had led to the establishment of the VCN to replace the HOC and to provide the basis for a new political party in the Netherlands. The leaders of the new group, Laurens Meerten and René Dammen, founded the new organization to provoke the CPN leadership and to attempt a complete takeover of the HOC. The CPN leadership did not recognize the group at the congress, but later the Executive Committee stated that membership in the VCN was incompatible with membership in the CPN (*Vrij Nederland*, 3 March). The Executive Committee of the VCN is made up of Laurens Meerten, René Dammen, Ineke Jansen, Koos Verweymeren, Rinze Visser, Ries Adriaanse, Rinus van Driel, Emmy Luis, Bob Vrins, and Wil van de Klift. The meeting also resulted in a collection of f7,000, which is to be used in financing the VCN biweekly, *Manifest*. Meerten says there is a "political-ideological break" in the CPN, but no organizational split as yet. John Geelen, the secretary of the Central Committee, warned, in his closing speech to the congress, which approved the party program by a vote of 392 for, 142 against, and more than 200 abstentions, against a follow-up struggle concerning interpretations of the congress's decisions. The VCN, however, failed to persuade most of the prominent HOC adherents such as Fré Meis of Groningen to join the organization.

Subsequent to the congress several members of

the VCN were dropped by the CPN, but the reformists became increasingly frustrated over the inability of party leaders to carry out the directives of the Twenty-eighth Congress and to ward off attacks from the VCN. The foreign editor at *De Waarheid* quit, saying that the reform wing had not been successful in gaining control of the CPN. Policy, instead, has been to keep the CPN afloat. The party is now torn between "Stalinists and supporters of Solidarnosc." (*Het Parool*, 22 September.) *De Waarheid* supports the policy of "renewal" in its attempt to reach out to the "small left" parties in Holland, but does not, as a matter of editorial policy, advocate factional standpoints within the party. The editor of the paper, Constant Vecht, says the discussions during the congress were public, they were taken seriously, and the whole operation showed the ability of the CPN to accept compromises in order to avoid a split in the party. Nico Broekema quit the CPN in Groningen, Onno Bosma left the Central Committee after 22 years, and eight other reformers have left the Central Committee since the last congress.

On 6 and 7 October, 350 persons attending the first congress of the VCN agreed to found a new political party in October 1985. This group appears not only to be opposed to the radical reformers, but also to the Consultation of Enhuizen, which is led by Marcus Bakker. Bakker's group is attempting to formulate a new party program more in line with orthodox Marxism in order to influence CPN policy.

In preparation for the Twenty-ninth Congress of the CPN on 1–3 March 1985, *CPN Leden krant* has published a six-part draft resolution entitled "Concentration of Forces Against the Policies of the Right; for a Strong CPN and for a Strong Alternative." The number of accredited delegates to the Twenty-ninth Congress will total 500, with 50 alternates. The yearend party financial disclosures in *CPN Leden krant* indicate a ƒ300,000 deficit suffered because of loss of membership and contributions.

The CPN thus suffers from sectarianism or splinter group politics, a typical Dutch phenomenon. Although one can say the party leadership has kept true to the new rules and has acted fairly with respect to minority standpoints, it has itself admitted that it has not been effective in preparing and carrying out party initiatives and actions because of its continual involvement in intraparty squabbling. The greatest threat to the reform wing of the party is simply its staying power. Given the desire of those in the VCN and Bakker's Consultation of Enhuizen to return the party to a semblance of its Stalinist past, the prognosis for the new-style CPN is doubtful at best. On the other hand, while persons on either of the extremes will leave the party, it appears the CPN is preferred by the Soviet Union over any new party in the Netherlands, and most of the important personalities within the CPN support the new strategy of the party irrespective of their dislike for some of its aspects.

Domestic Affairs. The first priority of the CPN remains the prevention of nuclear war and the prevention of the deployment of cruise missiles in the Netherlands. The CPN participates in the national peace movement umbrella organization, the Cruise Missile No Committee, through its organization, Stop the N-Bomb/Stop the Nuclear Arms Race. This CPN organization is headed by Nico Schouten, and it spokesman is Gijs von der Fuhr. The organization participated in the 6–12 May action week against the deployment of 48 cruise missiles, which concluded with demonstrations on 12 May at, among others, the Soesterberg Air Field, a U.S. Air Force base near Hilversum.

The decision of the center-right coalition government of Liberals and Christian Democrats led by Prime Minister Ruud Lubbers to postpone a decision on the deployment of cruise missiles until 1 November 1985 and making that decision dependent on whether the Soviet Union deploys more SS-20 missiles than had been stationed on 1 June 1984 has effectively stymied the Cruise Missile No Committee (KKN) and its primary member organization, the Interchurch Peace Council. Spokesman Gijs von der Fuhr said the KKN must reconsider the situation and in lieu of this pause would not make any decision regarding potential activities in the immediate future (*Het Parool*, 26 June). Von der Fuhr earlier stated, however, that support will be sought among workers to boycott eventual work in preparing the Woensdrecht missile base for deployment of the cruise missiles (*Handelsblad*, 8 February).

On the socioeconomic front, the CPN had limited means to carry out any direct action program and relied, for the most part, on attempts to publicize its point of view with respect to combating the centrist-right coalition government over what is perceived by the CPN as an attempt to dismantle the social security system. The CPN organized several activities against the government decision to reduce benefits on 1 July. The CPN also organized activities against racism, the right-wing Center Party, and anti-Semitism, and for feminism and women's rights. Preparations are now under way for collective bargaining sessions with large industries, and the CPN will use this opportunity to demand a 35–36–hour workweek.

The problem for the CPN over the years with respect to coalition politics has been its pretensions of possessing a superior, scientifically based view of politics, which meant that its desire for coalition was never taken seriously by other parties. This problem for the CPN emerged early in 1984 when the Evangelical People's Party (EVP), a small left-wing Christian party, decided against joining the Green Progressive Accord because of CPN participation. Nevertheless, the CPN, led by the radical reformers, met with representatives of the other small left-wing parties and some members of the Federation of Netherlands Trade Unions (FNV) in early 1984 to promote cooperation for the purpose of agreeing on a joint list and, more ambitiously, to explore the possibility of forming a party that would stand to the left of the Labor Party. The CPN, PPR, PSP, and some members of the FNV formed the Foundation for a Leftist Breakthrough (Stichting voor een linkse doorbraak) and elected Onno Bosma of the CPN as its first chairman. Although the left-wing parties did cooperate together in the Green Progressive Accord, its Second Congress, held on 26 October in Amsterdam, revealed that the most that could be accomplished would be a joint list for the next parliamentary election, which is scheduled for 1986, if not earlier. The plight of the effort is symbolized by the fact that the CPN did not replace Onno Bosma when he resigned from the Central Committee of the CPN. Neither the PSP nor the PPR is able to make agreements with the CPN, given the uncertainty concerning the outcome of the internal power struggle. The PSP is, in any case, unlikely to agree to a joint list, not to mention a common program, because of opposition from its present leader, even though the PSP party congress agreed to exploratory talks on this subject with the CPN (*De Volkskrant*, 27 October).

Foreign Affairs and International Party Contacts. The new program adopted by the CPN calls for for "a reorientation of foreign policy toward withdrawal from NATO." Further, the CPN will not attempt to intensify relations with communist parties in Eastern Europe, but it does claim that the United States is responsible for the arms race and the Soviet Union shares responsibility for contin-

uing the arms race. With respect to support for dissident groups in the East, the party rejected a motion to remove the condition "socialist" from groups that the CPN would support, thereby giving support only to those groups that sought "democracy and national independence" from a "socialist and peace-loving perspective." (*De Waarheid*, 3 February.)

Relations with the international communist movement were restricted primarily to several meetings with the East Germans and the Soviet Union. Jaap Wolff, a member of the CPN Executive Committee, and Liesbeth Wever of the Central Committee paid a visit to the German Democratic Republic (GDR) in January where they were met by Hermann Axen and Heinz Lehmann of the German party. In February, a delegation of the CPN Youth Platform met with the secretary of the Free German Youth Central Council, to prepare for the Twelfth World Festival of Games for Youth and Students in Moscow in 1985. In mid-October, upon returning from a trip to Cuba and Nicaragua, CPN Chairperson Elli Izeboud and Anne de Boer, a member of the Central Committee, paid a short visit to the GDR where they met Hermann Axen. On 3 July, John Geelen of the Executive Committee met with GDR foreign minister Oskar Fischer, who was on an official visit to the Netherlands.

The first contact in 1984 with the Soviet Union occurred when a delegation from the Communist Party of the Soviet Union (CPSU), led by Vasili I. Konotop, a member of the Central Committee and first secretary of the Moscow regional party, paid a five-day visit to the Netherlands (16–21 April) upon the invitation of the Central Committee of the CPN. A CPN delegation informed the Soviets of the results of the congress.

The second engagement with Soviet officials occurred when Ina Brouwer, chairman of the CPN's three-person parliamentary group, organized a joint letter of protest to the Soviet ambassador in the Netherlands against the treatment of Andrei Sakharov and Elena Bonner. In mid-December, Elli Izeboud, Ton van Hoek, and Jan Berghuis, traveled to Moscow where they were met by Boris N. Ponomarev, candidate member of the CPSU Politburo, and Vadim V. Zagladin, deputy head of the Central Committee's International Department. Discussions concerned the Dutch decision to postpone the deployment of cruise missiles. The CPN delegation objected to countermeasures taken by the Soviet Union in deploying new nuclear missiles in the GDR and Czechoslovakia after NATO had begun deploying new Euromissiles. For Izeboud, the relationship of the CPN to the CPSU was similar to that of the Labor Party to the Soviet Union. "For us there does not exist an exclusive tie." The delegation complained that the discussions were not open, and both sides agreed to see what could be done to better improve this state of affairs. Berghuis, who had expected information over the condition of workers in discussions with Soviet trade union officials, was disappointed.

The CPN was represented at the German Communist Party congress in January and at the Athens Peace Conference in February, but was not represented at the *World Marxist Review* conference in Prague in December. The CPN also organized fund-raising collections for striking British mineworkers.

Robert I. Weitzel
Amsterdam

Norway

Population. 4,145,000
Parties. Norwegian Communist Party (Norges Kommunistiske Parti; NKP); Socialist Left Party (Sosialistisk Venstreparti; SV); Workers' Communist Party (Arbeidernes Kommunistiske Parti; AKP), runs as Red Electoral Alliance (Rod Valgallians; RV) in elections
Founded. NKP: 1923; SV: 1976; AKP: 1973
Membership. NKP: 500; SV: 2,000; AKP: 1,000 (all estimated)
Chairman. NKP: Hans I. Kleven; SV: Theo Koritzinsky; AKP: Paal Steigan
Central Committee. NKP. 14 full members: Hans I. Kleven, Ingrid Negard (deputy chairman), Bjorn Naustvik (organizational secretary), Arne Jorgensen (editor of *Friheten*), Trygve Horgen, Grete Trondsen, Asmund Langsether, Rolf Dahl, Gunnar Wahl, Kare Andre Nilsen, Arvid Borglund, Gunnar Sorbo, Kirsti Kristiansen, Ornulf Godager (*Friheten*, 20 September); 6 alternate members: Martin Gunnar Knutsen (former party chairman), L. Hammerstad, H. P. Hansen, Sturla Indregard, Fredrik Kristensen, Knut Johansen
Status. Legal
Last Congress. NKP: Eighteenth, 30 March–2 April 1984, in Oslo; SV: 11–13 March 1983, in Oslo; AKP: Third (RV), 4–5 April 1983, in Oslo
Last Election. 1981, NKP: 0.3 percent, no representation; SV: 4.9 percent, 4 of 155 representatives; AKP: 0.7 percent, no representation
Auxiliary Organizations. NKP: Norwegian Communist Youth League (NKU)
Publications. NKP: *Friheten* (Freedom), semiweekly; *Vart Arbeid*, internal organ; AKP: *Klassekampen* (Class struggle), daily

Norwegian Communist Party. The NKP began as a small splinter group of radical trade unionists and politicians who left the Norwegian Labor Party (Det Norske Arbeiderparti; DNA) in 1923. It experienced many lean years until after World War II, when NKP support for the war effort against Nazi Germany and the Soviet liberation of northern Norway boosted NKP popularity at the polls (eleven seats in the first postwar parliament). However, NKP fortunes fell with the onset of the cold war.

The electoral weakness of the NKP is due, in large part, to its 1975 decision to remain a staunchly pro-Soviet, Stalinist party. Its numbers and popularity dwindled when Reidar Larsen, then its chairman, and several other leaders left the NKP and formed the SV.

Although differences still exist between the NKP and the SV, NKP leader Hans I. Kleven looks favorably upon Theo Koritzinsky's call for a broad united front of left-wing parties in Norway. Kleven believes that it is especially important to establish unity of action in the labor movement, both in the unions themselves and in the political parties close to labor—the DNA, SV, and NKP.

In addition, Kleven supports Koritzinsky's proposal for electoral cooperation between the NKP and the SV. Kleven has suggested running SV and NKP candidates on joint election lists. Kleven also has backed Koritzinsky's proposal for the NKP and SV to cooperate on specific issues in order to reshape Norwegian society in a socialist direction.

The NKP continues to be one of the weakest communist parties in Western Europe. It received a mere 7,025 votes (0.3 percent) in the 1981 parliamentary elections, far short of the number needed to win a seat in the Storting. In the local elections of September 1983, the NKP captured only 0.4 percent of the vote.

The Nuclear Issue. At its Seventeenth Congress in 1981, the NKP formally adopted a peace offensive. Its essence was the struggle against the deployment of new nuclear weapons in Europe and for a nuclear-free zone in Northern Europe encompassing Norway, Sweden, Denmark, and Finland, formalized by a treaty guaranteed by the great powers. (*WMR*, April 1983.)

The NKP was active in the twenty-day Peace March 1983. The slogans, predictably, were "No to nuclear weapons in Norway" and "No to the deployment of new missiles in Europe." NKP-affiliated sponsors of the march included the Women's Committee for Peace (which also organized antiwar marches in Europe in 1981 and 1982) and the Norwegian Peace Committee (a branch of the Soviet-controlled World Peace Council).

Despite its anger over the Storting vote in support of NATO's decision to deploy new U.S. nuclear missiles in Europe, the NKP sometimes has associated with DNA positions on nuclear issues.

The NKP supported the unsuccessful October 1982 vote by the Social Democrats against NATO infrastructure appropriations needed to prepare sites for the new missiles. Moreover, the NKP praised the January 1983 findings of a DNA commission that was studying that party's armaments policy. The commission came out against the deployment of U.S. Pershing II and cruise missiles in Western Europe and in favor of a nuclear freeze and the creation of nuclear-free zones in Northern Europe.

According to the NKP, the Conservative Party, which took power in 1981, accentuated the pro-U.S. trend in Norway's foreign affairs. The NKP believes that the Conservatives have made Norway even more subordinate to the United States and have exacerbated relations between Norway and the Soviet Union. Kleven says that these relations are especially important because of Norway's geographic location and its shared border with the USSR.

The NKP has strongly accused the Norwegian government of allowing foreign airfields, radio direction-finding stations, and submarine bases on Norway's territory (charges totally unfounded in fact), as well as permitting the United States to preposition military hardware in central Norway for use by U.S. Marines in the event of a major conflict. Kleven has complained that decisions on using Norwegian territory for military purposes are made in Washington rather than in Oslo.

Predictably, the NKP has castigated Norway's military budget, which has increased in recent years. The NKP advocates continued resistance "to the escalation of war preparations" in Norway and the Norwegian involvement in "U.S. militarist plans." The NKP wants the country to pursue an "independent security and defense policy." (Ibid.; *Aftenposten*, 9 March 1983; *JPRS*, 20 April 1983.)

Differences have emerged between the NKP and the DNA on the issue of Soviet responsibility for the growing nuclear threat in Europe. In particular, the NKP has criticized the DNA's call for reductions in Soviet medium-range missiles on the continent. The NKP also backed the ongoing appeal by the Soviet bloc to the United States to follow the Soviet example and pledge no-first-use of atomic weapons.

At the beginning of 1984 a subtle shift in the NKP's position on nuclear issues became apparent. On 8 January, *Aftenposten* printed a lengthy statement by Kleven, who had just chaired an NKP Politburo session on missiles and the peace movement in Europe. The bulk of Kleven's statement was strongly anti-American, and he demanded the withdrawal of the missiles and a return to the status quo that existed in Europe before their deployment. Nevertheless, he stipulated that, parallel to the withdrawal of the U.S. missiles, "counterefforts by the Warsaw Pact [to deploy its own missiles] must cease" and there must be a "halt to all testing, production, and deployment of new nuclear weapons," presumably by the Soviets as well as the Americans.

Shortly afterward, the NKP Central Committee presented a series of proposals on weapons, stating above all that "the American missiles for Europe must be returned and the Warsaw Pact lands must stop their countermoves." The NKP's stance was not tantamount to blaming the superpowers equally for the nuclear danger, but it represented a step away from its previous position that the United States was endangering peace while the USSR was defending it.

The NKP has continued to push an October 1982 directive from the Central Board of Communists in the trade unions to link the struggle for better working and living conditions with demands for cuts in military spending. The NKP advocates switching funds earmarked for military purposes to civilian needs. The party contends that arms expenditures lead to greater unemployment.

The Eighteenth NKP Congress and Its Aftermath. Peace and jobs were the major themes at the NKP's Eighteenth Congress, held 30 March– 2 April. On the opening day of the congress, Kleven raised the familiar issues of U.S. nuclear missiles in Europe and the need for a nuclear-free zone in Northern Europe. He proposed a conference of European communist parties to discuss concrete measures to ease world tension. At the same time, he urged the Norwegian government to initiate negotiations with the other Scandinavian countries to bring about a treaty for a Nordic nuclear-free zone. Kleven strongly attacked NATO, arguing that "this military power does not give us protection; it means increased danger instead." Nevertheless, he conceded that the majority of Norwegian citizens favor continued participation in the alliance. (*Arbeiderbladet,* 31 March.)

Kleven's speech expressed optimism that there was a good possibility of averting war. He cited the alleged shift in the "correlation of forces" away from "imperialism," the peace initiatives of the Soviet bloc, and the upsurge of the antiwar movement in Europe. Terminating the deployment of American missiles on the continent and forcing the with-

drawal of those already deployed would remain the key task of the peace movement, Kleven declared. (Tass, 30 March.)

Vladimir Ptitsyn, a member of the Central Committee of the Soviet party and first secretary of the Murmansk district committee of the party, headed the Soviet delegation to the NKP congress. He echoed Kleven's sentiments on peace, disarmament, and the removal of U.S. missiles from Europe. Ptitsyn's address to the gathering also noted the upcoming fortieth anniversary of the Soviet army's liberation of northern Norway from the Nazis. He evidently believed that this occasion could be used to foster closer relations between Norway and the USSR and between their respective communist parties. (Ibid., 31 March.)

On the issue of jobs, NKP Vice-Chairman Trygve Horgen reminded the congress of the party's ten-point program to fight unemployment and of its pressure on the government to uphold the right to work. He also reiterated the labor movement's responsibility to struggle against war and militarism. On 3 April, the day after the close of the congress, the NKP organ *Friheten* published an editorial headlined "To Work, Comrades!" The NKP called for a short-term program of creating a national plan to deal with unemployment—a program to be financed by the government to the tune of 5 billion kroner annually. Over the longer term, the NKP cited the need "to abolish the capitalist system and bring in a socialist planned economy in which such crises will not take place."

On international issues, the NKP supported the Soviet stance not only on European issues but also on areas of crisis around the world. For example, the congress adopted a unanimous resolution of solidarity with Central America in its struggle against the allegedly aggressive actions of the United States (*Pravda,* 3 April). A plenum of the NKP's Central Committee in May passed resolutions opposing the Pol Pot insurgents in Kampuchea and the persecution of Communists in Iran, to cite examples of the party's international concerns (ibid., 9 May).

Aside from the NKP's specific tasks in the domestic and international arenas, as outlined by the speeches and statements at the congress, Kleven emphasized that the party had been too "introverted" and had to adopt a higher profile. The *Friheten* editorial mentioned above declared: "To set out the party's main line in practice is not only an organizational task, but a political task also. It demands that the members . . . be familiar with the party line, that they master a collective, unified consciousness. It demands that the entire party have a unified will to go out more in the Norwegian countryside, actively participate in the national class struggle . . . The NKP's profile must be that it is also a party of struggle, an action party . . . There is a need to strengthen the NKP politically, ideologically, and organizationally."

Kleven was re-elected party chairman at the congress, but elections for most of the NKP's other leading officials were postponed as a result of sharp personality conflicts. The post of deputy chairman, for example, was the object of a contest between Asmund Langsether, an academic backed by Kleven, and Trygve Horgen, a workingman supported by *Friheten* editor Arne Jorgensen, among others. Another contentious issue was Kleven's reported proposal to exclude Martin Gunnar Knutsen, the former party chairman, from the Central Committee. (*Arbeiderbladet*, 1 June.)

Central Committee member John Atle Krogstad sent a remarkable letter to Norwegian newspapers in June that reflected disillusionment with the interparty struggles. "There is an atmosphere of distrust among leading party members," he wrote. "The . . . personality conflicts in the [Central Committee] have convinced me to withdraw from the party . . . The party is permeated with personality conflicts, despite the unanimous agreements at the national congress . . . and despite the fact that the chairman was chosen unanimously." Krogstad wrote that "the NKP is digging its own grave . . . [because of] the party's lack of ability to discuss and solve its differences." (Ibid., 16 June.)

On 19 June, Kleven published a "Letter to Members of the Norwegian Communist Party" in *Friheten*. It acknowledged the damage done to the NKP by "internal conflicts and disputes, which in most instances have generally been personal rather than political and ideological differences . . . It is most regrettable that we are losing members and officeholders who support the party's policies and ideology. We cannot afford this. We can only solve our differences in a productive manner . . . by means of open, objective, and thorough debate." Kleven appointed a temporary eight-man Central Committee, including Horgen, to serve until final selections could be made.

On 8 September the NKP's National Committee, which is empowered to choose the Central Committee, met to make its selections. Written ballots reportedly were used. The results of the voting indicated that the party leadership was virtually polarized. For example, Ingrid Negard (Kleven's candidate) received eighteen votes to seventeen for Horgen in balloting for the post of deputy chairman. Similarly, Bjorn Naustvik won the post of organizational secretary by eighteen votes to seventeen for his rival Kare Andre Nilsen. The campaign by some members of the National Committee to exclude Martin Gunnar Knutsen from the Central Committee was carried to the point of an accusation by National Committee official Age Fjeld that Knutsen had passed Norwegian military secrets to the Soviet Union. The atmosphere at the National Committee meeting was described as "tumultuous"—or, as Naustvik put it, as a meeting of "strong feelings." (*Aftenposten*, 16 October.)

Magne Mortensen, the NKP's national director, sent a letter to *Friheten* (13 September) that summed up the leadership crisis as it evolved during 1984. The letter, entitled "NKP Is Now in Serious Danger," accused Kleven of divisive tactics as well as overweening personal ambition. Mortensen charged that the chairman had transformed normal differences and conflicts among party members on various issues into a debilitating contest of personalities.

Kolbjorn Harbu, the NKP's secretary for trade union issues, also wrote a letter to *Friheten* (20 September) expressing deep concern over the intraparty struggle. "With regard to the difficulties our party now finds itself in, I would say that they are political in nature," he wrote. "That is why the discussion now should be concerned with policies and not with personalities. Harbu went on to propose an extraordinary party congress for the spring of 1985 that would attempt to straighten out the NKP's internal affairs so that it could make a good showing in the Storting election campaign the following autumn. In addition, Harbu recommended that the NKP amend its bylaws to enable the congress to elect the party's chairman, deputy chairman, organizational secretary, newspaper editor, and Central Committee members.

Knutsen, who, along with his followers, was denied full membership on the Central Committee, joined the fray in the party press by accusing the Kleven group of abusing its authority. According to Knutsen, Kleven engineered the elections of Negard and Naustvik by a one-vote majority. Knutsen took up the cudgels for a new national congress to change the party's leadership. Arne Jorgensen, *Friheten*'s editor, has been a supporter of Knutsen and clearly was in favor of airing the party's disagreements in the press. Jorgensen himself has portrayed the intraparty situation as the NKP's worst crisis in recent memory and as a "seething cauldron" (*Aftenposten*, 16 October).

On 18 October the Central Committee passed a resolution that the party's dirty linen could no longer be washed in the pages of *Friheten*. The resolution was justified in the name of "democratic centralism." The decision to gag *Friheten* reportedly was taken in the face of four no votes in the Central Committee. Jorgensen was one of the four dissenters, but he decided to remain as *Friheten's* editor. He declared that "the political debate will carry on in the paper's columns. But if it is decided that such a debate will not be permitted, well, then I will have to go." (Ibid.) Jorgensen apparently was placing his hopes in the convening of an extraordinary congress in the spring of 1985.

The NKP's international links revolve largely around meetings of the Nordic communist parties and consultations with the Soviet and East European parties. The wide-ranging issues discussed at the Nordic gatherings were typified by a communiqué published after the parley of Northern European communist parties in Finland in November 1982. The document covered, among other topics, the inability of capitalism to solve unemployment problems in Scandinavia; the campaign for peace, disarmament, and a Nordic nuclear-free zone; and the right of the Palestinians to establish a state of their own (*IB*, February 1983).

In October Kleven led a party delegation to Sofia, where he held talks with Todor Zhivkov. They reportedly focused special attention on issues relating to peace and security in Europe (BTA, Sofia, 26 October). In December, the NKP participated in a meeting in Czechoslovakia of world communist parties under the auspices of the journal *Problems of Peace and Socialism* (*World Marxist Review*). The gatherings occur periodically to assess the status of the international situation and the world communist movement. (*Rudé právo*, Prague, 7 December.)

Socialist Left Party. The SV is the strongest Marxist party to the left of the DNA. In the 1981 parliamentary elections, it received 4.9 percent of the vote and four seats in the Storting. The SV campaigned as a parliamentary ally of the DNA in the local elections of September 1983. It received 5.2 percent of the vote.

Leadership and Organization. In January 1983 party leader Berge Furre was replaced by Theo Koritzinsky, who had been chairman of the Socialist Youth League. The SV congress in March of that year produced almost a completely new leadership. Koritzinsky was confirmed as chairman, Tora Houg and Einar Nyheim were selected as the new deputy chairmen, Erik Solheim continued to serve as party secretary, and a new Executive Committee was formed, including veteran Finn Gustavsen.

In the summer of 1984 a struggle broke out between Koritzinsky and Gustavsen (called "a social democrat in a red coat" by his detractors) over who would be nominated to fill an upcoming vacancy in the Oslo delegation to the Storting (*Aftenposten*, 2 June). The struggle revolved around personalities as well as policies. Women's groups within the SV, for example, announced their opposition to Gustavsen because he opposed SV participation in the campaign against pornography.

Views and Activities. In January 1983, just before his replacement as party leader, Berge Furre presented the SV Executive Committee's draft for a working program for the 1980s. The program called for stronger state power, increased state subsidies, and a further expansion of the public sector. It demanded higher taxes and wages, more housing and nationalizations, and "self-sufficiency" and increased "power for the workers" (ibid., 29 January 1983; *JPRS*, 23 February 1983).

Shortly after he assumed the party chairmanship, Koritzinsky came out in favor of broad case-by-case cooperation within the left, especially between the SV and the NKP. Koritzinsky has advocated cooperation among peace, environmental, women's, and labor groups. He has emphasized, however, that such cooperation must be under the control of local party groups and must not be aimed at party unifications. (*Friheten*, 26 January 1983; *JPRS*, 3 March 1983.)

Unlike the NKP, the SV favors reforms rather than total rejection of current Norwegian institutions. Nevertheless, Koritzinsky stresses that reforms must be structural in nature, with a transfer of power to popularly elected delegates and organized labor. This program implies greater municipal and county authority and stronger company democracy. Koritzinsky says that the SV is considering the concept of wage-earner funds, which would give unions and elected delegates more control over capital. In general, however, the SV's "new" working program appears to be simply a repackaging of old ideas.

Koritzinsky wants to make the SV a livelier

party. He has indicated that the SV is too far removed from the masses. He also stated that SV work can no longer consist of "sheets of paper and words"; the party must "appeal to the emotions" of the people. (*Aftenposten*, 29 July 1983; *JPRS*, 31 August 1983.)

The SV congress in March 1983 passed a resolution urging party members to participate in local peace marches against several airports in Norway that the SV claims are a part of U.S. nuclear strategy, "so that the civilian population in the districts concerned understands the dangers they are exposed to" (*Aftenposten*, 14 March 1983; *JPRS*, 20 April 1983). The congress also focused on the struggle against growing unemployment in Norway and the struggle for women's equality (*FBIS*, 14 March 1983).

On the international front, the SV, in a strongly worded statement, condemned the Soviet war in Afghanistan. However, there was disagreement at the congress over what relationship the SV ought to have with the country's committee on Afghanistan. It was finally agreed to support the committee's work, but the vote on this issue was very close. (*Aftenposten*, 14 March 1983; *JPRS*, 20 April 1983.)

Workers' Communist Party. The AKP was born in the late 1960s as an amalgam of various Maoist organizations that were disenchanted with the Soviet economic model and with Soviet foreign policy. The AKP was founded as a formal organization in 1973. Its electoral front has not fared well. In the 1981 parliamentary elections, the front—the RV—captured only 0.7 percent of the vote. This total was slightly better than the NKP's share of the vote but was far short of the amount necessary for a seat in the Storting.

Red Electoral Alliance. The RV is no longer simply an offshoot of the AKP. It is a coalition of the AKP and independent socialists. The RV has 25 elected representatives on municipal and county councils. The third annual RV congress was held in Oslo in April 1983. The independent socialists in the RV and some AKP members pushed through a resolution guaranteeing "real, not just formal" democratic rights for working people after the revolution in Norway. The electoral manifesto of the RV stipulates that a postrevolutionary socialist government must allow "freedom of speech and organi-

zation, independent trade unions, the right to strike, legal protection, and control by the workers over state and production organs" (*Aftenposten*, 18 April 1983).

On the question of security policy, a debate developed at the congress over Norway's membership in NATO. A motion on the country's withdrawal from the alliance was defeated by a vote of 54 to 35 (ibid.). As part of its manifesto, the RV agreed on a plank calling for strengthening the conventional defenses of Western Europe and building a strong independent defense system outside NATO. The RV argued that "the prospect of being rescued from across the Atlantic is doubtful. For this reason, the RV proposes that Norway must get out of NATO's integrated military cooperation." (Ibid., 16 April 1983.)

The RV discounts the Soviet "guarantee" not to use nuclear arms against the Nordic region. The RV also warns against relying on Soviet advocacy of arms reduction and argues for strong international pressure on the USSR to force it to destroy its SS-20 missiles under international supervision. The RV's manifesto is critical of both superpowers, but, according to the RV, the Soviet Union is the most aggressive superpower. Soviet power is regarded as ascendant and U.S. power as in decline. Thus, with no counterforce to Soviet combativeness, the threats of Soviet occupation of Europe and of a new world war are becoming greater. (Ibid.)

The RV manifesto maintains that real socialism can be introduced in Norway only through a socialist revolution in which the working class assumes state power after a prolonged struggle. The RV, therefore, is ultimately a revolutionary rather than a reform-minded party. Although it participates in elections, it contends that Norway "will never get socialism through the ballot box." (Ibid., 13 April 1983.)

A recent book by AKP member Dag Solstad provides a rare glimpse of life inside the party. Entitled *High School Teacher Pedersen's Account of the Big Political Revival in Our Country*, the book maintains that constant squabbling characterized the AKP during the early 1980s. The party appears to be seeking in vain for some sense of purpose and direction. It may face an inevitable period of decline and even a collapse in the near future.

Marian Leighton
Defense Intelligence Agency

Portugal

Population. 10,045,000
Party. Portuguese Communist Party (Partido Comunista Português; PCP)
Founded. 1921
Membership. Over 200,000, up from 115,000 in 1976 (*Economist*, London, 30 June)
Secretary General. Álvaro Cunhal (since 1961)
Secretariat. 8 full members: Álvaro Cunhal, Carlos Costa, Domingos Abrantes, Fernando Blanqui Teixeira, Joaquim Gomes, Jorge Araújo, Octávio Pato, Sérgio Vilarigues; 2 alternate members: Jaime Félix, Luísa Araújo
Political Secretariat. 5 members: Álvaro Cunhal, Carlos Brito, Carlos Costa, Domingos Abrantes, Octávio Pato
Political Commission. 18 full members: Álvaro Cunhal, Ângelo Veloso, Dias Lourenço, António Gervásio, Carlos Brito, Carlos Costa, Diniz Miranda, Domingos Abrantes, Fernando Blanqui Teixeira, Jaime Serra, Joaquim Gomes, Jorge Araújo, José Soeiro, José Casanova, José Vitoriano, Octávio Pato, Raimundo Cabral, Sérgio Vilarigues; 7 alternate members: António Lopes, António Orcinha, Artur Vidal Pinto, Bernardina Sebastião, Carlos Ramildes, Edgar Correia, Zita Seabra
Central Committee. 91 full and 74 alternate members
Status. Legal
Last Congress. Tenth, 8–11 December 1983, in Oporto
Last Election. 1983, United People's Alliance (communist coalition), 18 percent, 44 of 250 seats
Auxiliary Organizations. General Confederation of Portuguese Workers (Confederação Geral de Trabalhadores Portugueses–Intersindical Nacional; CGTP), Portugal's largest labor grouping; National Confederation of Farmers (Confederação Nacional de Agricultores), comprising 400 peasant organizations; Collective Unity of Production, representing the farm cooperatives in Alentejo (*NYT*, 21 March); Popular Democratic Movement (Movimento Democrático Popular; MDP), said to be a communist-front "satellite" party
Publications. *Avante!* weekly newspaper; *O Militante*, theoretical journal; and *O Diário*, semiofficial daily newspaper (all published in Lisbon)

Western Europe's most Stalinist, most pro-Soviet party dominates the communist movement in Portugal, controls most of the labor unions, and has appreciable political impact. Nevertheless, its influence has declined since an aborted 1976 coup attempt. Most radical-left groups, which thrived after 1974 and which opposed the "revisionist" PCP, have faded in recent years. A terrorist group active since 1980 and condemned by the PCP is the Popular Forces of the 25th of April (Fôrças Populares do 25 de Abril; FP-25).

Domestic Affairs. Despairing of the government's continuing "frontal attack" on the "revolutionary gains of the people," the PCP's Álvaro Cunhal abandoned in 1984 any further attempts at "dialogue" with Prime Minister Mário Soares. The Portuguese people were "not some wild beast to be tamed by alternate use of sweets and the whip," he said. The PCP then launched a campaign for the "urgent resignation" of the Socialist–Social Democratic cabinet in favor of a nonpartisan caretaker "government of national salvation" to address the nation's profound economic crisis while new elections were being organized. (*Avante!* 1 March; *JPRS*, 4 April, 11 July; *Diário de Notícias*, 13 June; Lisbon domestic service, 4 November; *FBIS*, 10 September, 5 November.)

Cunhal rejected claims that the crisis derived from the impact of nationalizations, land reform, and labor legislation launched after the 1974 revolution; the cause, he charged, was the systematic dismantling of those advances, attempts to impose a totalitarian state, and Portugal's increasing "dependence" on American imperialism. He denounced the "formation and growing intervention of special repressive forces" and the introduction in parliament of an internal security bill that contained "indelible" features of PIDE, the totalitarian police apparatus extinguished by the 1974 revolution. This new plan, he charged, promised to make violence and persecution of citizens a standard of Portuguese life. (*Avante!* 19 January; Moscow domestic service, 6 June; *FBIS*, 7 June; *O Jornal*, 21 June; *JPRS*, 16 March, 4 April, 20 July.)

Concluding that the Soares government was not going to resign or "fall automatically," the PCP began appealing for its "overthrow." Such a change required the cooperation of many dissident Socialists, Cunhal noted. (EFE, Madrid, 17 June; *FBIS*, 18 June.) To weaken the Socialist Party further, the PCP also appeared to support the launching at midyear of a new political force—the Eanista Movement, which hoped to become a formal political party led by António Ramalho Eanes following his tenure as president. There were charges that the movement was being infiltrated by Communists. (*A Tarde*, 10 July; *O Diabo*, 10 July, 7 August; *JPRS*, 10 August, 3 October.)

Some government officials also expressed concern over alleged communist influence in a new organization called the 25 April Association. Founded in October 1982, it purported to be a "cultural association" of members of the armed forces aimed at promoting the "liberating" spirit of the 1974 revolution. The group was seen by some as "riddled with Communists" spoiling to politicize the army and again use it as an instrument for a left-wing coup. (*NYT*, 18 February; *Economist*, London, 30 June.)

Communist deputies voted with Socialists to legalize abortion in certain cases; their own stronger bill had been rejected (*NYT*, 28 January).

Auxiliary and Front Organizations. The CGTP protested that 150,000 workers were owed back salaries, some for as much as nineteen months' work. Because of this and the government's austerity measures, the CGTP threatened in May to intensify "mass action" until the government fell. However, such action was limited to mass parades; no crippling general strike was attempted during the year. (Ibid., 8 January; *WSJ*, 27 April; *Economist*, 30 June.)

The Collective Unity of Production demanded that 1977 legislation be altered to strip the Ministry of Agriculture of its "excessive" power to decide how much land to return to former estate owners. It complained that 50,000 jobs had been lost in the Alentejo area over the past five years as cooperatives were broken up. It was reported that of the 600 collective farms originally created, only 350 have survived in an area said to be perhaps the most solidly communistic belt of rural land in Western Europe today. (*NYT*, 21 March; *Economist*, 30 June.)

At its Fifth Congress, the Portuguese Democratic Movement tentatively agreed to a renewed alliance with the PCP in future elections—"unless the general political situation changes." The party was smarting from "slanderous campaigns" that dismissed it as a "simple satellite" of the PCP and from the latter's tendency to "accept or even encourage" such an identification. Members said it was time for the party to assert its own identity and to achieve complete autonomy. (*Expresso*, 2 June; EFE, Madrid, 4 June; *FBIS*, 5 June; *JPRS*, 11 July.) Later in the year, Cunhal rebuked the party for proposing a "dialogue" with the government; such an initiative at this time "must be viewed not merely as surprising but, indeed, inopportune," he said. (Lisbon domestic service, 4 November; *FBIS*, 5 November.)

International Views and Activities. The PCP charged that the prime minister was selling out the country to U.S. imperialism. Evidence of this "shameful policy" was Soares's visit to "fascist" South Korea as well as the reception given in Portugal to visiting "dictator" José Napoleón Duarte of El Salvador and to "apartheid" leader Pieter Botha of South Africa. Cunhal described the foreign aid sought by Soares as serving his own political needs rather than those of Portugal per se. (Lisbon domestic service, 18 March; *Avante!* 26 July; *FBIS*, 19 March, 1 August.) Communists also accused the government of allowing Angolan rebel activities to take place in Portugal and of not wishing to cooperate with the Luanda government. Pointing out that the state had no intelligence service with which to monitor such activities, officials suggested that the PCP should supply "tangible proof" of activities justifying expulsions. (*Diário de Notícias*, 1 February; ANGOP, Angola, 22 February; *FBIS*, 21 and 24 February.)

PCP delegations conferred during the year with communist leaders in the Soviet Union, Poland, Czechoslovakia, Romania, Bulgaria, Yugoslavia, Cuba, and Syria as well as with Sandinista leaders in Nicaragua. The PCP was visited in Lisbon by a Sandinista leader and by a delegation of the Palestine Communist Party. Some friction was noted following Cunhal's visit to Romania in February. A "one-sided and faulty" account of the talks appeared in a Romanian weekly, according to the PCP, which charged that the report gave the impression that it was a joint communiqué, the draft of which the PCP delegation had in fact rejected. (*Avante!* 1 March; *FBIS*, 9 March.)

The interest expressed by Prime Minister Soares in February in developing relations with the USSR was described by Cunhal as a "significant novelty"; Cunhal said he doubted that anything would come of it (*Diário de Notícias*, 18 February; *FBIS*, 28 February).

A former PCP member who abandoned the party in 1976, Cândida Ventura, speculated in a newspaper interview that the PCP would remain faithfully pro-Moscow under Cunhal's successor. She explained that this was a consequence of the PCP's continuing economic and political dependence on the Soviet Union. (*Diário de Notícias*, 2 September; *JPRS*, 9 October.)

Other Far-Left Groups. A police dragnet in June turned up caches of weapons, explosives, and money and some 42 suspected members of an urban guerrilla group, the Popular Forces of the 25th of April (FP-25). The group has taken responsibility for a series of bombings, shootings, and bank robberies since 1980. (*NYT*, 21 and 22 June.) The group was charged in 1983 with being a terrorist tool of the PCP (see *YICA*, 1984, p. 513), but no legal evidence of the link could be established. In fact, many of the arrested suspects were found to have been members of the now defunct Revolutionary Party of the Proletariat, a far-left group hostile to the PCP (*NYT*, 20 December 1983; Lisbon domestic service, 18 July; *FBIS*, 18 July). The FP-25 was also said to have ties with Basque terrorists (ETA-Militar) and with the Irish Republican Army (Madrid domestic service, 22 June; *FBIS*, 25 June; *WSJ*, 15 August).

The most well-known suspect detained by police was Lt. Col. Otelo Saraiva de Carvalho, hero of the 1974 Revolution, founder of the left-wing Forces of Popular Unity (Fôrças de Unidade Popular; FUP), and unsuccessful candidate for president in 1976 and 1980. Police were convinced that the FP-25 was connected with the FUP. The latter denied this, insisting that the charges and the police raids were trumped up to justify two internal security bills being considered in parliament. One bill would establish an intelligence-gathering service, and the other would expand police powers to combat terrorism. (*NYT*, 21 and 22 June, 28 July; *Economist*, 30 June.)

H. Leslie Robinson
University of the Pacific

Spain

Population. 38,435,000
Party. Spanish Communist Party (Partido Comunista de España; PCE)
Founded. 1920
Membership. 84,000 (estimated), down from 240,000 in 1977
Secretary General. Gerardo Iglesias
President. Dolores Ibárruri (legendary La Pasionaria of Civil War days)
Secretariat. 11 members: Andreu Claret Serra, José María Coronas, Enrique Curiel Alonso, Francisco Frutos, Gerardo Iglesias, Francisco Palero, Juan Francisco Pla, Pedro Antonio Ríos, Francisco Romero Marín, Simón Sánchez Montero, Nicolás Sartorius
Executive Committee. 28 members
Central Committee. 102 members
Status. Legal
Last Congress. Eleventh, 14–18 December 1983, in Madrid
Last Election. 1982, 3.8 percent, 4 of 350 seats
Auxiliary Organization. Workers' Commissions (Comisiones Obreras; CC OO), Marcelino Camacho, chairman
Publications. *Mundo Obrero* (Labor world), weekly; *Nuestra Bandera* (Our flag), bimonthly ideological journal; both published in Madrid

The Spanish communist movement has been greatly debilitated since 1977, when it reached its peak post-Franco strength, by the expulsion or resignation of the reformist Eurocommunists for Renewal, orthodox pro-Soviet militants, and regional members rebelling against centralized party rule. The movement is now split into two main rival groups, a mainstream Eurocommunist party and one with a hard-line pro-Soviet alignment. Marxist Basques, said to have foreign communist and terrorist connections, continue their guerrilla activities.

Organization and Leadership. The PCE was further weakened during 1984, not only by the continuing struggle between *Gerardistas*—supporters of Secretary General Gerardo Iglesias—and *Carrillistas*—followers of Santiago Carrillo—but by the formation in January of a rival Communist Party (Partido Comunista; PC). Numerous pro-

Soviet dissidents who had earlier resigned or been expelled from the PCE were absorbed into the new grouping. (*RFE Research*, 27 January.)

Dismissing the "parallel party" as an "exercise in dead theory," Iglesias accused it of "sowing confusion and dividing the working class," thereby actually serving the interests of the right (*NYT*, 16 January; *WP*, 18 January). At the same time, he may have been comforted by the expectation that the new party's activities would further weaken Carrillo by competing with the militant positions that the latter had assumed since resigning as party chief in 1982. Carrillo had sought with his new line to lure back into the party—under his aegis—pro-Soviet dissidents such as the Party of Communists of Catalonia, which instead merged into the new PC. Though Iglesias had outmaneuvered Carrillo at the PCE's Eleventh Congress in December 1983 (see *YICA*, 1984, P. 515) by securing comfortable

control of the Central and Executive committees and, shortly afterwards, by completely purging Carrillistas from the party Secretariat, Carrillistas still dominated many regional organizations, including that of Madrid. They quite ignored Iglesias's call in January for "pacification" within the party and continued to oppose his bid to attract Eurorenewalists back into the PCE. (*RFE Research*, 30 December 1983, 27 January; *Mundo Obrero*, 6–12 January; Madrid domestic service, 31 January; *FBIS*, 1 February.)

Domestic Affairs. Communists cited as an "unmistakable" sign of the government's erosion a July cabinet reshuffle by Prime Minister Felipe González. The crisis was produced, according to Iglesias, because the Socialists had abandoned their goal of a "real change," which could create employment, in favor of "faltering pragmatism," severe austerity, and worker dismissals dictated by national and international conservative forces. (*Mundo Obrero*, 5–11 July; *Diario 16*, Madrid, 6 July; *FBIS*, 1 August.) PCE attacks on "deficiencies" of government policies were, however, kept moderate by Iglesias's stated fear that excessive denunciation of the Socialists could alienate workers. The right, not the Spanish Socialist Workers' Party (Partido Socialista Obrero Español; PSOE), was the main enemy, he said. (*RFE Research*, 30 December 1983.) Iglesias followed up such comments by expressing the hope that the PCE could participate in a "wide electoral front"—presumably with the PSOE—in the 1986 general elections (ibid., 8 October). He felt that the Communists were gaining strength, having increased their public support from 4 to 9 percent of voters; meanwhile some public polls suggested a decline in overall Socialist backing by as much as a third (*WSJ*, 18 October). On the other hand, Basque and Catalan Communists made no gains in regional elections in February and May, but Socialists improved their standing in the Basque vote (*Economist*, London, 3 March, 5 May).

Auxiliary Organizations. The González government's labor policies along with extensive industrial job losses were protested with strikes and marches throughout Spain by both the communist-led CC OO and the Socialist-affiliated Union of General Workers (UGT). A one-day, mass protest by 200,000 workers in February was described by the CC OO as the biggest challenge to date to plans to regenerate industry with improved labor productivity. (*WP*, 3 February; *NYT*, 3 February.) A national wave of strikes followed that led to virtually daily confrontations with police. Government officials were reportedly not very apprehensive about serious disruption from unions since only a fifth of the work force was unionized, unions lacked funds to survive long strikes, and workers were fearful of losing their jobs in the face of an unemployment rate of nearly 20 percent of the labor force. (*WSJ*, 18 October; *Economist*, 27 October; *NYT*, 19 November.)

In October, the prime minister persuaded the UGT to sign a two-year agreement fixing guidelines for economic policy. Wage increases in 1985 would be limited to 6.5 and 7.5 percent respectively for the public and private sectors. The UGT also agreed to make it easier for firms to hire workers parttime or on short contracts, but it resisted proposals—to be studied by a commission—to make it easier and cheaper to fire workers. Refusing to sign the labor pact, CC OO leader Marcelino Camacho complained that González had "sold his soul to the devil." (*WSJ*, 18 October.)

International Views and Activities. Alarmed at the Soviet Union's undisguised support for the newly formed rival Communist Party, the PCE vigorously protested this "overt interference" in the party's problems and "assistance to those seeking its division." Iglesias then conferred with a number of other communist parties, especially those in sympathetic Yugoslavia, Romania, Hungary, and China, as well as with the Soviet party, seeking support for the PCE and reiterating the party's determination to follow an independent line without any foreign tutelage. (*RFE Research*, 23 May.) "Autonomous attitudes" and "centrifugal tendencies" in the communist world were expected by a former PCE official, Manuel Azcárate, to be further encouraged by the continuing "transitional uncertainty" in the Soviet leadership. Eurorenewalist Azcárate was the party's specialist in foreign affairs before he left the PCE in late 1981 following an unsuccessful reformist challenge to Carrillo. (Ibid., 28 September; *El País*, 16 September.)

PCE spokesmen continued to press for the dismantling of foreign bases in Spain, withdrawal from NATO, and the referendum on NATO long postponed by the prime minister. U.S. President Reagan's "bellicose foreign policy" was cited as a decisive factor exacerbating international tensions. (*Mundo Obrero*, 5–11 July; *FBIS*, 1 January, 12 July.)

Rival Communist Party. After withdrawing from the PCE in late 1983, veteran communist Ignacio Gallego organized a three-day congress of dissidents in January 1984 to found the rival Communist Party. An alternate name was chosen—Spanish Peoples' Communist Party (Partido Comunista de los Pueblos de España)—in case the PCE were to challenge successfully the legality of its first choice. The 900 delegates unanimously elected Gallego secretary general and chose a Central Committee of 101 members. Disenchanted with a Eurocommunist PCE that had "lost touch with its roots," they affirmed their pro-Soviet, Marxist-Leninist commitment. Merging to form the PC were some half-dozen splinter parties; 76 percent of the delegates were said to be former members of the PCE. (*ABC*, 16 January; *NYT*, 16 January; *WP*, 18 January; *RFE Research*, 27 January; *FBIS*, 28 February; *Nuevo Rumbo*, Madrid, 14 March.) In June, some members of the Communist Party of the Balearic Islands also defected to Gallego's group (Madrid domestic service, 6 June; *FBIS*, 7 June). In December former CPE secretary general Jaime Ballesteros and four other PCE Central Committee members defected to the PC (*La Vanguardia*, Barcelona, 18 December; *FBIS*, 27 December). Pro-Moscow Enrique Lister chose not to affiliate his Communist Party of Spanish Workers (Partido Comunista de Obreros de España; PCOE) with the PC. The PC claimed a membership of 25,000, compared to 80,000 card-carrying members in the PCE. (*RFE Research*, 29 December 1983; *Los Angeles Times*, 16 January.)

The new party was expected to have far less impact on future Spanish general elections than on the trade union movement. Several prominent members of the CC OO were elected to the PC's Central Committee, and 76 percent of the party's members were said to belong to the CC OO. It was suggested that their challenge to the leadership of Marcelino Camacho, a supporter of Iglesias, might weaken the Workers' Commissions. (*WP*, 18 January; *RFE Research*, 27 January.)

There were immediate repercussions abroad from the formation of the PC. The party's founding congress was attended and enthusiastically endorsed by Soviet, Czechoslovak, East German, and Polish "observer" delegations. *Pravda* exulted that the PC would "decisively unmask Eurocommunism as a revisionist and social-democratic tendency"; at the same time, the Soviets discreetly sought to continue ties with the PCE. Several months later, Gallego headed a PC delegation on a visit to the Soviet Union, but Chernenko did not receive it personally. (*WP*, 18 January; *RFE Research*, 27 January, 25 May, 1 June; *Borba*, Belgrade, 24 May; *FBIS*, 24 and 29 May.)

Meanwhile, many other communist parties—the Chinese, most West European, the Yugoslav, Romanian, and Hungarian parties—boycotted or criticized the PC's congress. Even the pro-Soviet Portuguese Communist Party did not send a delegation. One critic alleged that this "small group" of PC "Afghans" was receiving "substantial aid" from a "foreign, invisible hand." (*Politika*, Belgrade, 4 February; *FBIS*, 9 February; *Tanjug*, Belgrade, 7 February; *RFE Research*, 23 May.)

Left-Wing Terrorist Groups. Spanish officials expressed cautious optimism that they were winning the political and military war against the Basque terrorist group, Basque Homeland and Liberty (Euzkadi ta Askatasuna; ETA). Though acknowledging that there were 43 ETA assassinations in 1983, they noted that this figure was lower than in the peak period of terrorism in 1979–1980. The figure dropped to 28 for the first ten months of 1984. Authorities were encouraged by the cumulative effects of a new French attitude of cooperation in moving against ETA refugees in the French Basque region, the increasing effectiveness of Spanish police action, and the decreasing support for the terrorists among the Basque population. (*NYT*, 5 February, 6 May; *CSM*, 22 October.)

Finally responding to Spanish entreaties, the French government began in January to deport or to confine in northern France scores of known or suspected Spanish guerrillas. In September, it extradited three to Madrid. French officials claimed the sweep was undertaken because of "the climate of progressive violence" in the border area. Several ETA leaders had been killed by a mysterious new right-wing group calling itself the Antiterrorist Group of Liberation (Grupo Antiterrorista de Liberación; GAL). Charging that the GAL was an arm of the Spanish police, Basque militants warned that the González government would "face its day of judgment." (*CSM*, 17 January, 25 September, 22 October; *WSJ*, 3 October.)

Guerrilla activities were also said to be increasingly hampered by Spanish police raids on arms caches, ambushes of militants, tighter patrol of the border, and improved intelligence (*NYT*, 6 May). Prime Minister González's stand against terrorism—stronger than that of previous governments—was said to have won the respect of the military, even though disgruntled officers still felt that more should be done (*WP*, 29 January; *NYT*, 5 February).

As the ETA and GAL vowed to avenge each killing by the other group, there was a fresh rash of violence that included the assassination of an army general and a Socialist senator running for re-election to the Basque regional parliament. The major parties suspended their campaigning, and a 24-hour strike was held to protest the latter's death. Responsibility for his killing was claimed by the Autonomous Anticapitalist Commandos, an anarchist faction that splintered from the ETA in 1977. (*NYT*, 30 January, 25 and 27 February; *Los Angeles Times*, 27 February.) A five-man Commando detail was liquidated in March by Spanish security forces as it tried to steal into Spain from southern France by rubber boat (*NYT*, 25 March). The November killing of the leader of the Herri Batasuna party, which is regarded as the ETA's political front, was protested by a general strike backed by all political parties and unions (*NYT*, 23 November).

Some felt that popular disgust with the violence played a part in boosting the Socialists into second place in the Basque vote count, up from 14 percent in 1980 elections to 23 percent. Herri Batasuna dropped only slightly, from 16 to 15 percent. The party announced that its deputies would continue to boycott parliament in protest against the Basques' "inadequate" autonomy. (Ibid., 27 February; *WP*, 28 February; *Economist*, 3 March.)

Leaders of the mainstream Basque Nationalist Party (PNV), which won 42 percent of the vote, continued to insist that the ETA could be isolated from the little popular support it has only by a stepped-up policy of transferring power to the Basque government. They were resentful that since 1981 Madrid seems to have abandoned the process of granting the region more autonomy. (*NYT*, 28 February, 6 May.)

The PCE's Iglesias continued to condemn the ETA's terrorism and to favor "any appropriate legal measure" to combat it. He also expressed his approval, in direct contrast with the French Communist Party's disapproval, of the new French policy of extraditing guerrillas to Spain. The PCE said at the same time that it would be an error to believe violence could be ended only with these measures and by the "dirty war" actions of the GAL on both sides of the border; the party said that concessions strengthening Basque autonomous institutions would be needed as well. (*Mundo Obrero*, 24 February–1 March, 27 September–3 October; *FBIS*, 14 March; *RFE Research*, 8 October.)

The history of the ETA's extensive international activities—including the financing of revolutionary armies in Central America and the training of European terrorists—was documented in January by a study financed by Spain's Interior Ministry. It detailed the group's connections in Cuban, Algerian, Lebanese, and South Yemen training camps. (*CSM*, 17 January.) In November, Madrid hosted a secret meeting of West European specialists on terrorism to coordinate antiterrorist activities (*NYT*, 18 November).

Biography. *Ignacio Gallego.* A former swineherd and Spanish Civil War veteran who led republican units in his native Andalusia, PC Secretary General Ignacio Gallego later helped organize underground resistance to the Franco dictatorship and was a leading member of the PCE Executive Committee for nearly 30 years. Following the death of Franco, he was elected a deputy of the lower house of the Spanish parliament representing Córdoba and acted, until 1982, as its deputy chairman.

In late 1983, Gallego resigned from the Central and Executive committees and withdrew from the PCE. He blamed the party's political decline on its Eurocommunist policies, its denial of its own revolutionary Marxist-Leninist traditions, and its critical attitude toward the Soviet Union. He organized dissidents into a Commission for Communist Unity, which in January launched the new Communist Party to compete with the PCE for Spanish communist loyalties. (Sources: *WP*, 18 January; *Rudé právo*, Prague, 19 January; *FBIS*, 23 January; *RFE Research*, 27 January.)

H. Leslie Robinson
University of the Pacific

Sweden

Population. 8,335,000
Party. Left Party Communists (Vansterpartiet Kommunisterna; VPK)
Founded. 1921 (VPK, 1967)
Membership. 17,500, principally in the far north, Stockholm, and Goteborg
Chairman. Lars Werner
Executive Committee. 9 members: Lars Werner, Eivor Marklund (vice-chairman), Bo Hammar (secretary), Lennart Beijer, Viola Claesson, Bror Engstrom, Kenneth Kvist, Bertil Mabrink, Margo Ingvardsson
Party Board. 35 members
Status. Legal
Last Congress. Twenty-sixth, 20–24 November 1981
Last Election. 1982, 5.6 percent, 20 of 349 seats
Auxiliary Organizations. Communist Youth (KU), Communist Women's Organization
Publications. *Ny Dag* (New day), semiweekly; *Socialistisk Debatt* (Socialist debate), monthly; both published in Stockholm

The ancestor of the VPK, Sweden's Communist Party (Sveriges Kommunistiska Partiet), was established in 1921, but a number of divisions adversely affected it in the 1920s. Its greatest moment came right after World War II when it obtained 11.2 percent of the vote in local elections. This result was largely due to the popularity of the Soviet Union at the end of the war. Since then, the communist party has usually garnered around 4–5 percent of the vote. The party has had a marginal influence in Swedish politics. It has never made a truly major contribution to communist history. Perhaps its most important role has been to allow the Social Democrats to govern during much of Sweden's recent history. During the past half-century, the Social Democrats have been Europe's most dominant social-democratic party, and during many of their years in power, they have relied on a combined majority with the Communists in the Riksdag (parliament). The Communists have, however, never been part of the government.

In Sweden, a party has to clear a 4 percent threshold in order to be represented in parliament, and after the bitter reaction to the Soviet invasion of Czechoslovakia in 1968, the VPK went under the 4 percent mark and was not represented. In the 1970 and 1976 elections, it received 4.8 percent, and in 1979 and 1982, 5.6 percent of the vote. The next election is scheduled for 1985.

The Communists changed both the name and the direction of the party congress in 1967. Blue-collar workers constituted the majority of the communist electorate in previous years, but increasingly the VPK is attracting white-collar workers and younger people. Voting studies indicate no significant age differentials among the voters of various parties, except for the VPK. In the 1979 election, approximately half of of the VPK voters were under the age of 30. Most of the party's new white-collar supporters are in cultural, educational, and health-related occupations.

The VPK projects a Marxist image, even though it has disassociated itself from Moscow and is generally regarded as one of the more moderate Western European communist parties. Its program states: "The party's foundation is scientific socialism, the revolutionary theory of Marx and Lenin. It seeks to apply this theory, develop it, infuse it with the struggle of the Swedish working class. The party's goal is to have the struggle of the working class and of the people, guided by the ideas of revolutionary socialism, lead to victory over capitalism and to a classless society."

Party Internal Affairs. In an interview published in the Helsinki communist paper *Kansan Uutiset* (7 May), VPK Chairman Werner said, in summing up the past ten years, "We are more stable now . . . and we have achieved a greater degree of unity now as a result . . . of the departure of a small faction from the party [in March 1977]. It is indeed nice to be unanimous on a chief party line when new issues come up. Then one can afford to maneuver [in a way] that was not possible before."

In the same interview, Werner said that party membership has remained the same, although there are "many new young people." He also claimed that more than half of the new members are now women. He focused his criticism on domestic issues and said that the gap between the rich and the poor has become greater. The VPK chairman also said that "relations between the Social Democrats and the communist party are less tense than before."

Domestic Affairs. For the first time since the summer of 1983, the combined support for the ruling Social Democratic Party and the VPK has outstripped that for the nonsocialist parties, 49 percent to 48.5 percent, according to the respected SIFO poll (*Svenska Dagbladet*, 1 April). The Social Democrats, under the leadership of Prime Minister Olof Palme, registered 44.5 percent, a two-point gain from the previous month of February. The VPK received the support of 4.5 percent of the voters, a half-point gain, but still perilously close to the 4 percent electoral threshold, and 1.1 percent less than what it received in the 1982 election. The Conservatives received 27.5 percent of the sample's support, a half-point drop from the previous poll. The two middle parties have weakened in the past several years. In another analysis of voters based on polls taken between January and May by *Dagens Nyheter* and the Institute for Market Research, the number of VPK voters loyal to the party slipped from 84 percent in the spring of 1983 to 67 percent a year later. According to the analysis, 0.7 percent of the gain of the Social Democrats has come from the VPK. Some former VPK support has gone to the new Environment Party. (*Dagens Nyheter*, 8 July.) The next elections are scheduled for the early autumn of 1985.

In a wide-ranging article in *Dagens Nyheter* (16 July), Carl Hermansson, the chief ideologist and former party chairman of the VPK, spoke of the party's priorities in 1984 and also leveled some attacks on the Social Democrats. Hermansson said that the major disappointment of the party was that the government "did not implement more effective and goal-oriented policies in order to bring down the extensive unemployment." He said that the government should expand the public sector and "achieve a substantial industrialization program for Sweden." The former party leader also listed a number of measures that the VPK deemed "necessary": a transition to a six-hour workday; supplementary education as a right for everyone; and a one-time tax on substantial private wealth. He criticized the conditions that were leading to a new underclass, "from which it is increasingly difficult to escape."

Despite his criticism of the Social Democrats, Hermansson did say that he was encouraged by his party's coming to an agreement with the Social Democrats on improving child subsidies and on increasing food subsidies. He also said that "the so-called turn toward the right is a surface phenomenon, perceived above all by the mass media. There are deep-reaching processes that are totally contrary to those conservative ripples on the surface."

Foreign Affairs. One of the main sources of domestic debate, however, was of foreign origin. Ever since the dramatic 1981 incident in which a Soviet Whisky-class submarine ran aground near the naval base of Karlskrona in southern Sweden, alleged Soviet submarine incursions in Swedish territorial waters have been a major issue. In 1983, a governmental report concluded that the intruders (including a bottom-crawling midget submarine) were Russian. The intrusions have continued, and more resources have been put into antisubmarine defenses. What has spurred acrimonious debate is that, even as incursions continued, Prime Minister Palme has stated his government's intention to normalize relations with the USSR (*Economist*, London, 6 October). In March, a senior Swedish official was flown to Moscow, just after frogmen had been sighted and fired upon, and in May the Soviet minister of agriculture was a guest in Stockholm. In August, however, when a Soviet fighter chased a Swedish passenger aircraft over the island of Gotland, the government did protest.

Shortly thereafter, the influential conservative paper, *Svenska Dagbladet* (8 September) carried an editorial that said, "Now that Sweden has protested the violation, the Soviet Union has the impudence simply to say that its own authorities have been unable to confirm that any violation took place. Sweden's verbal protest has been waved away. Despite this, Palme obviously considers that the exchange of visits between Sweden and the Soviet Union should continue. It is normalization that contains the longer-term message. The Social Democrats' reaction to the airspace violation and the subsequent Soviet reaction seem nearly incomprehensible." The *Svenska Dagbladet* editorial mirrored the opinion of many in Sweden.

The Soviet incursions in Swedish airspace and waters have had a profound impact on public opinion. Polls suggest that four out of five Swedes think that the Soviet Union is "unfriendly," compared with only one out of five who held the same view a few years ago (*Economist*, 6 October). All of this has had an effect on one of Sweden's most sacred cows—neutrality. The Conservatives, along with the smaller Center and Liberal parties, have alleged that the Social Democrats have not made the Soviet Union respect Sweden's neutrality. The Social Democrats, for their part, have accused the Conservatives of attempting to abandon neutrality. (Ibid., 6 October.)

VPK Chairman Werner admitted in an interview in *Dagens Nyheter* (21 March) that the submarine hunt is a sensitive political issue and yet expressed surprise that the issue has not hurt his party as much as the Soviet invasions of Hungary in 1956 and of Czechoslovakia in 1968. He said, however, "But you must not underestimate the effect on our party. People are fed day after day with reports, many of them incorrect, about what the Soviets are allegedly up to." The VPK has been critical of Soviet activities in Swedish waters, but has said that some of the so-called evidence has been misleading. Werner has said that he completely supports the government's line toward the Soviet Union; that is, criticize incursions but strive for a normalization of relations. Had the VPK not joined the criticism of the Soviet Union, it most surely would have lost substantial support. When the Swedes protested the Soviet violation of Swedish airspace on 9 August, Werner said on Swedish radio, "As for the clear violation that has taken place, one cannot be satisfied with the statement that their competent authorities were unable to find any border violation. There was a clear border violation; there are documents to prove it." (Swedish international service, 6 September.)

International Party Contacts. Werner visited Budapest in mid-July and met with Hungarian leader János Kádár in order to discuss a range of issues, including "further extending bilateral relations and the cause of peace" (MTI, Budapest, 13 July). V. G. Afanasyev, chief editor of *Pravda* and chairman of the Soviet committee for ties with peace-loving forces, met with I. Anderson, editor of the VPK organ, *Ny Dag*, on 15 March (*Pravda*, 16 March).

Rival Communist Groups. The pro-Soviet Communist Workers' Party (Arbetarpartiet Kommunisterna; APK) was founded in 1977. At a plenary session of the APK in Stockholm in late January, Chairman Rolf Hagel told the group that "the international situation is sharply aggravated due to the deployment in Europe of American medium-range nuclear missiles." The plenum adopted a unanimous resolution supporting the policies of the Soviet Union in Europe. (Tass, 22 January.) *Norskenflamman* (Northern lights) is the party paper. In 1982, the party won 0.1 percent of the vote and twelve local government seats, mainly in the north of Sweden. The APK claims 5,000 members.

The pro-Chinese Sweden's Communist Party (Sveriges Kommunistiska Partiet) was founded as the Communist League of Marxists-Leninists (KFML) in 1967 and was especially vocal during the Vietnam war. It changed its name in 1969. Its chairman is Roland Pettersson, and it publishes *M-L Gnistan* (The spark). It won eight seats in local elections in 1982.

The Marxist-Leninist Communist Party, Revolutionary (Kommunistiska Partiet Marxist-Leninisterna, Revolutionerna), the pro-Albanian group, was founded in 1970 because its members perceived the KFML as not being radical enough. Its chairman is Frank Baude. The party issues the weekly *Proletaren*. It won three seats in the 1982 local elections.

The Socialist Party (Socialistiska Partiet) was founded in the early 1970s as the Communist Workers' League and changed to its present name in 1982. It is the Swedish section of the Trotskyist Fourth International and is directed by the Executive Committee of the International. It publishes *Internationalen*. It received about 3,900 votes in the 1982 election but won no seats.

Peter Grothe
Monterey Institute of International Studies

Switzerland

Population. 6,477,000
Party. Swiss Labor Party (Partei der Arbeit der Schweiz/Parti suisse du travail/Partito Svizzero del Lavoro; PdAS)
Founded. 1921; outlawed 1940; re-established 1944
Membership. 4,500 (estimated)
General Secretary. Armand Magnin
Politburo. 14 members
Secretariat. 5 members.
Central Committee. 50 members
Status. Legal
Last Congress. Twelfth, 21–22 May 1983
Last Election. 1983, 0.9 percent, 1 of 200 seats
Auxiliary Organizations. Communist Youth League of Switzerland (KVJS), Marxist Student League, Swiss Women's Organization for Peace and Progress, Swiss Peace Movement, Swiss–Soviet Union Society, Swiss-Cuban Society, Central Sanitaire Swiss
Publications. *Voix Ouvrière* (Geneva), weekly, circulation 8,000 copies; *Vorwärts* (Basel), weekly, circulation 6,000 copies; *Il Lavatore*, Italian-language edition; *Zunder*, KVJS organ

Switzerland has three communist parties with some significance: the Swiss Labor Party (PdAS), strongest in the western part of Switzerland and in Basel; the Progressive Organizations Switzerland (POCH), whose new party statutes no longer refer to Marxism-Leninism but follow the Green concepts; and the Socialist Workers' Party (SAP), active only in a few urban centers. During 1984, the communist parties lost influence. Those of the extreme left who did not adapt quickly enough to the "Green wave" lost members and sympathizers to various splinter groups. Furthermore, Soviet propaganda lost credibility and thus influence.

The pro-Soviet PdAS is the oldest communist party in Switzerland. It was founded on 5 March 1921 as the Swiss Communist Party. The party was outlawed in 1940 and re-established on 15 October 1944 under its present name. The PdAS is in a deep crisis as a result of election defeats on the federal, canton, and local levels. The party's vote share in the 1983 federal elections was 0.9 percent, compared with 2.2 percent in 1979. The PdAS lost two

of its three seats in the lower house (Nationalrat); one was that held by General Secretary Armand Magnin, a member of the old guard. He assumed the seat in the Nationalrat vacated by the elected member. Additional reasons for the decline are the advanced age of the leadership, the Poland and Afghanistan policies of the Soviet Union, and the recent disclosures of a Soviet diplomat formerly stationed at the Soviet embassy in Bern (*Neue Zürcher Zeitung* [*NZZ*], 2 November) who revealed the close relations between the Soviet embassy and high officials of the PdAS and the Swiss–Soviet Union Society. The PdAS received yearly 300,000 Swiss francs and the Swiss–Soviet Union Society yearly 100,000 Swiss francs from Moscow to support their activities and publications. The PdAS received directives for its work from Moscow. These directives were repeated in the "decisions" of the party's Central Committee and in the party's press. (*Die Weltwoche*, 1 November; *NZZ*, 6 November.)

On the fortieth anniversary of the PdAS's re-establishment, it received congratulatory messages from several fraternal parties, including the Soviet and East German parties (*Neues Deutschland*, East Berlin, 15 October; *Pravda*, 14 October; *FBIS*, 18 and 19 October).

Hans Stebler, president of the Swiss Peace Movement (SFB), one of the founding members of the PdAS and SFB, was elected to the presidium of the Soviet front World Peace Council (*Vorwärts*, 9 February).

During the 1960s, followers of the New Left who refused to join the PdAS founded several Marxist parties, such as the POCH, the Revolutionary Marxist League (presently the SAP), the Autonomous Socialist Party (PSA), and various Maoist parties.

The POCH was founded in 1972 by student dissidents from the PdAS who rejected the party's adherence to the world communist movement and were opposed to the sterile policies of the old party. In spite of POCH's emphasis on its independence, it pursues pro-Soviet policies. During its founding phase, the Progressive Organizations Basel occupied the leadership position; however, since 1973, the party's secretariat has been located in Zürich. The POCH's membership is kept secret, but is estimated at 10,000. It publishes *POCH-Zeitung*.

The change of the party statutes and the recent redirection of POCH's professionally conducted propaganda along Green lines proved successful. The gains, however, could not make up for the losses of the other communist groups. POCH's aggressive and professional leadership was able to attain active followers in the academic professions. In the 1983 federal elections, POCH increased its representation from two to three seats. Its vote share increased from 1.7 percent in 1979 to 2.2 percent. Only Lucerne brought favorable results in canton elections. (*Informationsgruppe Schweiz*, Zürich, November.)

A POCH subsidiary, the Organization for Women's Affairs, is the most important women's group in Switzerland. It emerged from Progressive Women Switzerland. The organization's magazine is the weekly *Emanzipation*. Other organizations affiliated with POCH are the Solidarity Committee for Africa, Asia, and Latin America and the Swiss Society for Social Health.

The SAP (Sozialistische Arbeiterpartei/Parti socialiste ouvrière) adopted its new name at the Fifth Congress of the Revolutionary Marxist League in 1980. The league was founded in 1969 by a group of young Trotskyists who left the PdAS. The SAP is the Swiss section of the Fourth International

(Trotskyist) headquartered in Brussels. The party emphasizes the revolutionary class struggle in production centers. Its goal is the eventual capture of control of enterprises, a policy resembling former revolutionary syndicalism. Its leading theoretician is Fritz Osterwalder. Membership is about 500. The youth organization of the SAP, Maulwurf (Mole), disbanded in the late 1970s. In 1983, it was reinstated as the Revolutionary Socialist Youth Organization (RSJ). In the federal elections of 1983, the SAP obtained 0.4 percent of the vote. The party did not participate in the 1979 elections. SAP publications include *Bresche* (German), *La Brèche* (French), *Rosso* (Italian), and *Roja* (Spanish). At the occasion of the fifteenth anniversary of *Bresche*, the SAP held a two-day festival in Geneva. Speakers included, in addition to SAP members, representatives of the Trotskyist International and of the Socialist Party of Switzerland.

The SAP strengthened its influence in the organizations of the anti–nuclear power plant movement, such as the National Coordination of Anti–Nuclear Power Plants Opponents, which has about twelve groups, and the Nonviolent Action Against Nuclear Power Plant Kaiseraugst. One of the actions of the RSJ was the occupation of the Honduran Consulate-General in Zürich to protest U.S. support of the Honduran counterrevolution.

The PSA (Autonome Sozialistische Partei/Parti socialiste autonome/Partito Socialista Autonomo) is the outcome of a split within the Socialist Party of the canton of Tessin in 1960. Even though the dissidents obtained the support of a majority at the party congress in 1966, they were unable to assert themselves against the entrenched leadership and in April 1969 founded the PSA. Its membership is about 1,000. The PSA's influence is limited to the Italian section of Switzerland. The party considers itself an autonomous component of the world communist movement and rejects social democracy, Trotskyism, and spontaneity. In the federal elections in 1983, the PSA received 10 percent of the vote in Tessin, giving it one seat in the Nationalrat. This brought the strength of the PdAS/POCH/PSA parliamentary fraction to five seats. The PSA publishes *Politika Nuova*.

The Communist Party of Switzerland Marxist-Leninist (KPS/ML), founded on 2 January 1972, has about 200 members and a thousand sympathizers. The KPS/ML is the only pro-Chinese party that survives of the several Maoist organizations that emerged following the Soviet-Sino split. The party considers itself a part of the international communist movement and maintains close relations with the Chinese Communist Party, the Albanian Party of Labor, and other Marxist-Leninist parties. The Workers' and Soldiers' Organization Offensive is an affiliated organization that favors a strong Swiss military establishment and opposes Soviet aspirations for hegemony. The KPS/ML publishes *Oktober* (in various languages).

In addition, there are numerous alternative and ideologically diffuse groups that emerged as a result of the rejection of strict organizational forms by many young adherents of the protest movement. These groups collaborate with the political parties of the left for progressive, antinuclear, ecological, peace, and women's issues. For example, the demonstration on 3 November in Bern for "Peace for Central America and the Caribbean—Stop U.S. Intervention" was supported also by the PdAS, POCH, SAP, RSJ, Socialist Party of Switzerland (SPS), and Young Socialists (Jusos). A working group of left-wing forces was set up in Geneva, proposed by the local organization of the PdAS, to study ways and means to stop the curtailment of production and the mass dismissals of workers. Represented in the group are, in addition to the Communists, the Geneva organization of the SPS and a number of trade unions. Left-wing SPS members and trade unions cooperate with Communists on a regular basis. At the invitation of the SPS, a delegation from the Central Committee of the Socialist Unity Party of (East) Germany (SED) visited Switzerland (4–6 June). The SPS is a major party in Switzerland. SPS leader Helmut Hubacher and other leading members of the party met with the SED delegation, headed by Klaus Gäbler, chief of the SED's Propaganda Department. In a joint press release, both sides advocated "collaboration of communist and social-democratic parties, and all others interested in the preservation of peace, in a broad coalition of reason." (*NZZ*, 15 June.)

The League of Swiss Students (Verband der Schweizerischen Studentenschaft; VSS) elected Martin Schwander as general secretary. He was a military service resister, a functionary in the communist youth organization of the PdAS, and former employee of the Soviet news agency Novosti, which was involved in subversive activities in Switzerland. (*Schweizerzeit*, 20 January.)

The fourth plenary meeting of the Group for a Switzerland Without Military (Gruppe Schweiz ohne Armee; GSoA) on 30 September decided to launch in March 1985 a people's plebiscite to abolish the Swiss military establishment. The GSoA was started when about a hundred representatives of left-wing parties and of the peace movement formed on 12 September 1982 a committee to prepare an initiative to abolish the Swiss military. The originator of this idea were the Jusos. The GSoA has about 900 members and 1,000 sympathizers who are ready to collect the 100,000 signatures required for a plebiscite. In June, at a meeting organized by the SAP organization of Zürich, representatives of the Swiss Peace Council, Soldiers' Committee, Green Alternative Zürich, POCH, RSJ, and SAP expressed their support for the GSoA. (*Bresche*, 17 September.)

Since an anarchist group, headed by Hans Rudolf Hess, started in February 1982, to revitalize anarchism in Switzerland with the assistance of anarchists abroad, anarchist activities have increased. A national conference, held on 8–9 September, was one of the preparatory meetings for the International Anarchist Meeting in Venice on 24–30 September. One of the co-organizers of the international meeting, which was attended by about 5,000 persons, was the International Anarchist Research Center in Geneva.

Eric Waldman
University of Calgary

Turkey

Population. 50,207,000
Party. Communist Party of Turkey (TCP)
Founded. 1920
Membership. Negligible
Secretary General. Haydar Kutlu
Leading Bodies. No data
Status. Illegal
Last Congress. Fifth, October or November 1983
Last Election. N/a
Auxiliary Organizations. No data
Publications. None known; Our Radio and Voice of the Turkish Communist Party broadcast TCP propaganda.

Two major issues dominated politics in Turkey during 1984: the transition from military to civilian rule and continuing security and human rights problems. The illegal Turkish Communist Party, led by Secretary General Haydar Kutlu, continued to operate underground and abroad. Its presence was felt primarily through commentaries broadcast over the Voice of the Turkish Communist Party and over Our Radio, based in Eastern Europe. In addition, the Turkish military authorities periodically reported the arrest and prosecution of alleged TCP members.

The transition from military to civilian rule was given a decisive boost by the parliamentary election of November 1983, which produced a government based on a parliamentary majority of 211 out of 400 seats organized by the Motherland Party (MP), led by Turgut Ozal. The election results were significant primarily for two reasons: they produced the first clear parliamentary majority in fourteen years; and the winning party was openly opposed by President Kenan Evren, the leader of the military junta.

Two points quickly became very clear: the military was still very much involved in the daily conduct of government, and the newly organized political parties would need time to sort themselves out. The military authorities retained control of security

matters through the continuation of martial law in most provinces, including the largest cities and the southeastern region, which is inhabited predominantly by Kurds. Trials of those arrested under the junta continued, new trials were begun, and additional groups of alleged terrorists were apprehended throughout 1984. Press censorship was also maintained under military authority, largely through self-enforcement.

The sorting-out of the political parties resulted in part from the strict limits imposed by the junta on the parliamentary elections of 1983. Only three parties were allowed to compete in those elections. Although Ozal's MP won a clear plurality of the votes and a majority of seats in the new parliament, it was vulnerable to the charge that its victory was illegitimate because several potentially popular parties had been barred from competing, particularly the Social Democratic Party (SODEP) led by Professor Erdal Inonu, and the True Path Party (TPP), widely viewed as successor to the outlawed Justice Party of former premier Suleyman Demirel. Ozal moved decisively to deflate these charges by scheduling nationwide local and municipal elections for 25 March. These elections confirmed the MP's position as the leading party in the country. It garnered 41 percent of the vote and won mayoralties in

50 of 67 provincial centers. The elections seriously weakened the two parliamentary opposition parties, the Populist Party (PP) and the Nationalist Democracy Party (NDP), which together polled 16 percent of the vote; the PP won no mayoral races in any provincial centers, and the NDP only three. The two major extraparliamentary parties fared better. SODEP won 23 percent of the vote to become the second-largest party in the country, and the TPP won 13 percent of the vote (*FBIS*, 2 April). The local elections could thus be (and were widely) interpreted as confirming broad support for Turgut Ozal, his party, and his policies of strongly emphasizing economic liberalization, scaling back bureaucratic regulations and personnel, and opening the economy to the world by stimulating exports and welcoming foreign investments. It seemed clear that there would be no early parliamentary elections. Indeed, if Ozal is successful in implementing his economic policies, he might well remain in power for the full five-year parliamentary term.

Security problems persisted throughout 1984. Arrests of groups of alleged terrorists were frequently reported throughout the year, particularly in the southeast, indicating that restiveness among the Kurdish population had not by any means been overcome. There were even reports of open shootouts between government forces and dissidents, reminiscent of the disorders of the late 1970s (e.g., ibid., 31 January). With few exceptions, those arrested were identified as leftists, including alleged members of the TCP. The Turkish government also manifested anxiety concerning dissident Kurdish activity across the border in Iran and Iraq. By mid-1984, trials of dissidents of both extremes had reportedly resulted in 300 death sentences (although apparently only 25 executions had been carried out so far) and large numbers of severe prison sentences. Those convicted included many who were accused of such crimes as organizing to establish a Marxist-Leninist state; noninvolvement

in violence was apparently insufficient to merit leniency or clemency at the hands of military tribunals.

The TCP's interpretation of Turkish developments was made clear initially in a statement of the Central Committee broadcast in February. The 1983 parliamentary election was regarded as a sham that left a basically fascist military autocracy in place, although it was acknowledged that the extremely poor showing of the NDP was a dramatic defeat for the military junta and a positive omen for "the working class and all the democratic forces" (ibid., 17 February). The TCP accused the Ozal government of implementing an economic policy designed to "eliminate the last remnants of economic independence . . . and . . . placing the load of the economic crisis on the shoulders of the working class, the workers, the middle strata, and the small and medium-sized capitalists" (ibid., 14 February). In fact, the TCP labeled the Ozal government "the most antinational and collaborationist government in the history of the republic . . . a Pentagon government . . . the government of IMF officials, multinational monopolies, and their middlemen, the holding companies" (ibid., 15 February). The party urged its followers to maintain solidarity with the workers, Kurdish nationalists, and all the oppressed groups in the country, including the petite bourgeoisie, for the purpose of building a united front against the forces of fascism represented by the Evren-Ozal regime. It even allowed for cooperation with democratic parties of the left, such as SODEP, provided such parties continued to oppose the regime.

The party's position was less clear in the wake of Ozal's attendance at Andropov's funeral in Moscow and the official visit of Soviet prime minister Nikolai Tikhonov to Ankara in late December.

Frank Tachau
University of Illinois at Chicago

Select Bibliography, 1983–1984

GENERAL

Adelman, Jonathan R., ed. *Terror and Communist Politics: The Rise of the Secret Police in Communist States.* Boulder, Colo.: Westview Press, 1984. 292 pp.

Amnesty International. *Amnesty International Report, 1983.* New York: Dodd, Mead, 1983. 351 pp.

———. *Torture in the Eighties.* An Amnesty International Report. London: Amnesty International Publications, 1984. 263 pp.

Atienza, Manuel. *Marx y los derechos humanos.* Madrid: Mezquita, 1983. 280 pp.

Bekerman, Gérard. *Marx and Engels: A Conceptual Concordance.* Oxford: Blackwell, 1983. 205 pp.

Berki, R. N. *Insight and Vision: The Problem of Communism in Marx's Thought.* London: J. M. Dent, 1983. 204 pp.

Bottomore, Tom, ed. *A Dictionary of Marxist Thought.* Cambridge, Mass.: Harvard University Press, 1983. 587 pp.

Bousson, Michel. *Une Lecture bourgeoise de Karl Marx.* Paris: Editions France Empire, 1983. 222 pp.

Brenkert, George C. *Marx's Ethics of Freedom.* Boston: Routledge & Kegan Paul, 1983. 263 pp.

Callinicos, Alex. *The Revolutionary Ideas of Karl Marx.* London: Bookmarks, 1983. 208 pp.

Carnoy, Martin. *The State and Political Theory.* Princeton, N.J.: Princeton University Press, 1984. 282 pp.

Carver, Terrell. *Marx and Engels: The Intellectual Relationship.* Bloomington: Indiana University Press, 1983. 172 pp.

Cernushi, Alberto. *The Constructive Manifesto.* New York: Philosophical Library, 1983. 103 pp.

Chirkin, Veniamin Evgenevich, and Yu. Yudin. *A Socialist-Oriented State.* Moscow: Progress Publishers, 1983. 237 pp.

Cline, Ray S., and Yonah Alexander. *Terrorism: The Soviet Connection.* New York: Crane, Russak (with Georgetown University, Center for Strategic and International Studies), 1984. 165 pp.

Clouscard, Michel. *La Bête sauvage: Métamorphose de la société capitaliste et stratégie révolutionnaire.* Paris: Editions Sociales, 1983. 242 pp.

Crozier, Brian, and Arthur Seldon. *Socialism Explained.* London: Sherwood Press, 1984. 135 pp.

Crozier, Brian; Drew Middleton; and Jeremy Murray-Brown. *This War Called Peace.* London: Sherwood Press, 1984. 307 pp.

Daniels, Robert V., ed. *A Documentary History of Communism.* Rev. ed. Hanover, N.H.: University Press of New England, 1984. 2 vols.

Degenhardt, Henry W. *Policial Dissent: An International Guide to Dissent, Extra Parliamentary, Guerrilla and Illegal Political Movements.* Edited by Alan J. Day. Harlow, Eng.: Longman (distributed by Gale Research), 1983. 592 pp.

Dunn, Dennis J., ed. *Religion and Communist Society.* Selected papers from the Second World Congress for Soviet and East European Studies. Berkeley, Calif.: Berkeley Slavic Specialities, 1983. 165 pp.

Emden, Horst. *Der Marxismus und seine Pädagogik: Anspruch und Wirklichkeit.* Sankt Augustin: H. Richarz, 1983. 113 pp.

Felix, David. *Marx as Politician.* Carbondale: Southern Illinois University Press, 1983. 308 pp.

Geras, Norman. *Marx and Human Nature: Refutation of a Legend.* London: Verso Editions and NLB, 1983. 126 pp.

Gouldner, Alvin Ward. *Los dos marxismos: Contradicciones y anomalias en el desarrollo de la teoría.* Madrid: Alianza Editorial, 1983. 418 pp.

Gouverneur, Jacques. *Contemporary Capitalism and Marxist Economics.* Totowa, N.J.: Barnes & Noble, 1983. 300 pp.

Gumbrell, Colin. *Karl Marx.* New York: St. Martin's Press, 1984. 95 pp.

Harding, Neil, ed. *The State in Socialist Society.* Albany: State University of New York Press, 1984. 316 pp.

Hoffman, John. *The Gramscian Challenge: Coercion and Consent in Marxist Political Theory.* Oxford: Blackwell, 1984. 230 pp.

Jähn, Gisela, et al., eds. *Die kommunistische Internationale, 1919–1943: Ihr weltweites Wirken für Frieden, Demokratie, nationale Befreiung und Sozialismus in Bildern und Dokumenten.* East Berlin: Dietz Verlag, 1984. 363 pp.

Jain, Ajit, and Alexander J. Matejko, eds. *Marx and Marxism.* New York: Praeger, 1984. 309 pp.

Kellner, Douglas. *Herbert Marcuse and the Crisis of Marxism.* Berkeley: University of California Press, 1984. 505 pp.

Krejci, Jaroslav. *The Great Revolutions Compared.* Brighton, Eng.: Harvester Press, 1983. 256 pp.

Kriegel, Annie. *Le Système communiste mondial.* Paris: Presses Universitaires de France, 1984. 271 pp.

Kulichenko, Mykhailo Ivanovych. *Nations and Social Progress.* Translated by Galina Glagoleva. Moscow: Progress Publishers, 1984. 230 pp.

Kuz'min, N. F., et al., eds. *Zakonomernosti razvitiia marksistsko-leninskoi partii.* Moscow: Mysl', 1983. 319 pp.

Linden, Ronald H., and Bert A. Rockman, eds. *Elite Studies and Communist Politics: In Memory of Carl Beck.* Pittsburgh, Pa.: University of Pittsburgh Press, 1984. 352 pp.

Mattick, Paul, ed. *Marxism: The Last Refuge of the Bourgeoisie?* Armonk, N.Y.: M. E. Sharpe, 1983. 321 pp.

McGregor, David. *The Communist Ideal in Hegel and Marx.* Toronto: University of Toronto Press, 1984. 312 pp.

McHale, Vincent, and Sharon Skowronski, eds. *Political Parties of Europe.* Westport, Conn.: Greenwood Press, 1983. 2 vols.

Meissner, Boris, and Axel Seeberg, eds. *Kontinuität und Wandel in den Ost-West Beziehungen.* Cologne: Markus Verlag, 1983. 395 pp.

Meyer, Alfred G. *Communism.* 4th ed. New York: Random House, 1984. 195 pp.

Moshniaga, Viktor Panteleevich, et al. *Aktualnye voprosy mezhdunarodnogo dvizheniia.* Moscow: Molodaia gvardia, 1983. 239 pp.

Mullaney, Marie M. *Revolutionary Women: Gender and the Socialist Revolutionary Role.* New York: Praeger, 1983. 401 pp.

Neznanov, Viktor. *The Transition from Capitalism to Socialism.* Moscow: Progress Publishers, 1983. 173 pp.

Pirogov, G. G. *The Socialist World System.* Moscow: Progress Publishers, 1983. 131 pp.

Plimak, E. G. *The Way Society Develops.* Moscow: Progress Publishers, 1983. 142 pp.

Ponomarev, Boris N. *Marxism-Leninism in Today's World: A Living and Effective Teaching. A Reply to Critics.* New York: Pergamon Press, 1983. 174 pp.

Revel, Jean-François. *Comment les démocraties finissent.* Paris: Grasset, 1983. 332 pp.

Riddell, John, ed. *Lenin's Struggle for a Revolutionary International.* New York: Monad Press, 1984. 604 pp.

Robinson, Cedric J. *Black Marxism.* London: Zed Press, 1983. 487 pp.

Roche, John P. *The History and Impact of Marxist-Leninist Organizational Theory: "Useful Idiots," "Innocents' Clubs," and "Transmissions Belts."* Cambridge, Mass.: Institute of Foreign Policy Analysis, 1984. 75 pp.

Simons, William B., ed. *The Constitutions of the Communist World.* The Hague: Martinus Nijhoff, 1984. 644 pp.

———, and Stephen White, eds. *The Party Statutes of the Communist World.* The Hague: Martinus Nijhoff, 1984. 554 pp.

Skliarov, Yu. A., et al., eds. *Partii nauchnogo sotsializma v Azii i Afrike.* Prague: Mir i sotsializm, 1983. 190 pp.

Smith, Thomas B., *The Other Establishment: An In-depth Study of What Individual Life Is Really Like in Communist-Controlled Countries.* Chicago: Regnery/Gateway, 1984. 205 pp.

Staar, Richard F., ed. *Yearbook on International Communist Affairs, 1984: Parties and Revolutionary Movements.* Stanford: Hoover Institution Press, 1984. 578 pp.

Sterling, Claire. *The Time of the Assassins.* New York: Holt, Rinehart & Winston, 1983. 264 pp.

Sturmthal, Adolf F. *Left of Center: European Labor Since World War II.* Champaign: University of Illinois Press, 1983. 303 pp.

Turner, Denys. *Marxism and Christianity.* Totowa, N.J.: Barnes & Noble, 1983. 256 pp.

United States. Central Intelligence Agency. *Chiefs of State and Cabinet Members of Foreign Governments.* Washington, D.C.: National Technical Information Service, 1984. 149 pp.

Vinogradov, V. D. *Partiia v sisteme sotsialisticheskogo obschchestva.* Leningrad: Nauka, 1983. 150 pp.

Wells, David. *Marxism and the Modern State: An Analysis of Fetishism in Capitalist Society.* New Delhi: Select Book Service Syndicate, 1983. 214 pp.

Wheatcroft, Andrew. *The World Atlas of Revolutions.* New York: Simon & Schuster, 1983. 196 pp.

Yudin, Yu. A., et al., eds. *Partii v politicheskoi sisteme.* Moscow: Nauka, 1983. 249 pp.

Zagladin, V. V. *Istoricheskaia missiia sotsialisticheskogo obshchestva.* 2d rev. ed. Moscow: Politizdat, 1984. 222 pp.

———, and B. I. Koval', chief eds. *Mezdhunarodnoe raboche dvizhenie: Spravochnik.* Moscow: Politizdat, 1984. 463 pp.

Ziegler, Jean. *Les Rebelles: Contre l'ordre du monde. Mouvements armés de libération nationale du tiers monde.* Paris: Editions du Seuil, 1983. 413 pp.

Zinner, Paul E. *East-West Relations in Europe.* Boulder, Colo.: Westview Press, 1984. 164 pp.

Zinoviev, Alexander. *The Reality of Communism.* New York: Schocken Books, 1984. 320 pp.

AFRICA

Achebe, Chinua. *The Trouble with Nigeria.* Enugu, Nigeria: Fourth Dimension, 1983. 68 pp.

Akademiia nauk SSSR. Institut Afriki. *Aktual'nye problemy mezhafrikanskikh otnoshenii.* Moscow: Mezhdunarodnye otnosheniia, 1983. 314 pp.

Ansprenger, Franz. *Die SWAPO: Profil einer afrikanischen Befreiungsbewegung.* Bonn: Katholischer Arbeitskreis Entwicklung und Frieden, 1983. 160 pp.

Astrow, Andre. *Zimbabwe: A Revolution That Lost Its Way?* London: Zed Press, 1983. 254 pp.

Awosika, V. O. *A New Political Philosophy for Nigeria.* Lagos: African Literary and Scientific Publications, 1983. 80 pp.

Bissell, Richard E., and Michael S. Radu, eds. *Africa in the Post-Colonization Era.* New Brunswick, N.J.: Transaction Books, 1984. 263 pp.

Blanchet, G. *Elites et changements en Afrique et au Sénégal.* Paris: OSTROM, 1983. 408 pp.

Cartwright, John R. *Political Leadership in Africa.* New York: St. Martin's Press, 1983. 310 pp.

Daly, M. W. *Sudan.* Santa Barbara, Calif.: ABC-Clio Press, 1983. 175 pp.

Davidson, Basil. *Modern Africa.* New York: Longman, 1983. 234 pp.

Doro, Marion. *Rhodesia/Zimbabwe: A Bibliographic Guide to the Nationalist Period.* Boston: G. K. Hall, 1984. 247 pp.

Gavshon, Arthur L. *Crisis in Africa: Battleground of East and West.* Boulder, Colo.: Westview Press, 1984. 320 pp.

Gailey, Harry A. *Africa: The Troubled Continent.* Melbourne, Fla.: Robert Krieger, 1984. 149 pp.

Geldenhuys, Deon. *The Diplomacy of Isolation: South African Foreign Policy Making.* New York: St. Martin's Press, 1984. 295 pp.

Gorbunov, Iu. I., and A. V. Pritvorov. *Namibia: Problemy dostizhenia nezavisimosti.* Moscow: Nauka, 1983. 125 pp.

Griffiths, Ieuan L. L. *An Atlas of African Affairs.* London: Methuen, 1984. 200 pp.

Haarlow, Jens. *Labour Regulations and Black Workers' Struggles in South Africa.* Uppsala: Scandinavian Institute of African Studies, 1983. 80 pp.

Hancock, Ian. *White Liberals, Moderates, and Radicals in Rhodesia, 1953–1980.* New York: St. Martin's Press, 1984. 230 pp.

Hanlon, Joseph. *Mozambique: Revolution Under Fire.* London: Zed Press, 1984. 290 pp.

Hodder-Williams, Richard. *Conflict in Zimbabwe: The Matabeleland Problem.* London: Institute for the Study of Conflict, 1983. 20 pp.

Isaacman, Allen, and Barbara Isaacman, *Mozambique: From Colonialism to Revolution.* Boulder, Colo.: Westview Press, 1983. 235 pp.

Kühne, Winrich. *Die Politik der Sowjetunion in Afrika: Bedingungen und Dynamik ihres ideologischen, ökonomischen und militärischen Engagements.* Baden-Baden: Nomos Verlag, 1983. 299 pp.

Lefort, Rene. *Ethiopia: An Heretical Revolution?* London: Zed Press, 1983. 301 pp.

Leonard, Richard. *South Africa at War: White Power and the Crisis in Southern Africa.* Westport, Conn.: Lawrence Hill, 1983. 280 pp.

Lipman, Beata, ed. *We Make Freedom: Women in South Africa.* London: Pandora Press, 1984. 141 pp.

Magubane, Bernard, and Nzongola-Ntalaja. *Proletarization and Class Struggle in Africa.* San Francisco: Synthesis Publications, 1983. 185 pp.

Moleah, Alfred T. *Namibia: The Struggle for Liberation.* Wilmington, Del.: Disa Press, 1983. 341 pp.

Nation, Craig, and Mark V. Kauppi, eds. *The Soviet Impact in Africa.* Lexington, Mass.: Lexington Books, 1984. 275 pp.

Nelson, Harold D., ed. *Zimbabwe: A Country Study.* 2d ed. Washington, D.C.: American University Foreign Area Studies, 1983. 360 pp.

Nkomo, Joshua. *Nkomo: The Story of My Life.* London: Methuen, 1984. 270 pp.

Nyquist, Thomas E. *African Middle Class Elite.* Grahamstown, South Africa: Rhodes University, Institute of Social and Economic Research, 1983. 303 pp.

Phillips, Claude S. *The African Political Dictionary.* Santa Barbara, Calif.: ABC-Clio Press, 1984. 245 pp.

Rubenson, Sven, ed. *International Conference on Ethiopian Studies: Proceedings of the Seventh Conference, University of Lund, 26–29 April 1982.* Addis Ababa: Institute of Ethiopian Studies; East Lansing: Michigan State University, African Studies Center, 1984. 710 pp.

Sine, Babacar. *Le Marxisme devant les sociétés africaines contemporaines.* Paris: Présence africaine, 1983. 202 pp.

Spencer, John H. *Ethiopia at Bay: A Personal Account.* Algonac, Mich.: Reference Publications, 1984. 395 pp.

The Whole Truth About SWAPO: Idealistic Christians and Heroes of Freedom and Justice? Or Instruments of International Communist Aggression? Pleasantville, N.Y.: American Society for the Defense of Tradition, Family and Property, 1984. 66 pp.

Wolfers, Michael, and Jane Bergerol. *Angola in the Frontline.* London: Zed Press, 1983. 238 pp.

THE AMERICAS

Ambursley, Fitzroy, and Robin Cohen. *Crisis in the Caribbean.* New York: Monthly Review Press, 1983. 271 pp.

Arévalo, Óscar. *Qué es el socialismo científico?* Buenos Aires: Editorial Anteo, 1983. 174 pp.

———. *Victorio Codovilla y los comunistas de Buenos Aires.* Buenos Aires: Editorial Anteo, 1983. 30 pp.

Arnaud, Pascal. *Amerique latine: La formation de l'économie nationale, Argentine et Mexique.* Paris: Publisud, 1983. 154 pp.

Bishop, Maurice. *Maurice Bishop Speaks to the Workers.* New York: Pathfinder Press, 1983. 48 pp.

———. *One Caribbean.* London: British-Grenada Friendship Society, 1983. 32 pp.

Brundenius, Claes. *Revolutionary Cuba: The Challenge of Economic Growth with Equity.* Boulder, Colo.: Westview Press, 1984. 224 pp.

Burrowes, Reynold A. *The Wild Coast: An Account of Politics in Guyana.* Cambridge, Mass.: Schenkman, 1984. 348 pp.

Carr, Raymond. *Puerto Rico: A Colonial Experiment.* New York: Vintage Books, 1984. 477 pp.

Castro, Fidel. *Building Socialism in Cuba.* New York: Pathfinder Press, 1983. 367 pp.

———. *Cuba Cannot Export Revolution, Nor Can the United States Prevent It.* Havana: Editora Política, 1984. 19 pp.

———. *Fidel Castro Talks with US and French Journalists, July–August 1983.* Havana: Editora Política, 1983. 58 pp.

———. *A Pyrrhic Military Victory and a Profound Moral Defeat.* Havana: Editoria Política, 1983. 19 pp.

Chernin, Kim. *In My Mother's House.* New York: Harper & Row, 1983. 307 pp.

Churchill, Ward, ed. *Marxism and Native Americans.* Boston: South End Press, 1983. 221 pp.

Cifuentes, Robert. *Zur Typologie politischer Parteien in Lateinamerika: Die Fälle Chile und Argentinien.* Heidelberg: Esprint-Verlag, 1983. 328 pp.

Comisión Nacional de Educación del Partido Comunista. Escuela de Primer Nivel. *El partido comunista: Su programa, su linea, su organización.* Buenos Aires: Editorial Anteo, 1983. 46 pp.

Corbiere, Emilio J. *Origines del comunismo argentino: El Partido Socialista Internacional.* Buenos Aires: Centro Editor de America Latina, 1984. 175 pp.

Crawley, Eduardo. *Nicaragua in Perspective.* New York: St. Martin's Press, 1984. 200 pp.

Cuevas Diaz, J. Aurelio. *El Partido Comunista Mexicano, 1963–1973.* Mexico City: Editorial Linea, 1984. 204 pp.

Del Aguila, Juan M. *Cuba: Dilemmas of a Revolution.* Boulder, Colo.: Westview Press, 1984. 193 pp.

Doig Kline, Germán. *Iglesia y marxismo.* Lima: APRODEA, 1983. 215 pp.

Dunkerley, James. *Rebellion in the Veins: Political Struggle in Bolivia, 1952–1982.* New York: Schocken Books, 1984. 385 pp.

Erisman, H. Michael, ed. *The Caribbean Challenge: U.S. Policy in a Volatile Region.* Boulder, Colo.: Westview Press, 1984. 208 pp.

Falcoff, Mark, and Robert Royal, eds. *U.S. Policy in Central America and the Caribbean.* Washington, D.C.: Ethics and Public Policy Center, 1984. 491 pp.

Falcón, Jorge. *Mariategui, Marx-marxismo: El productor y su producto.* Lima: Empresa Editora Amauta, 1983. 103 pp.

Fava, Athos. *Después de la dictadura: Consolidar una democracia verdadera y estable.* Buenos Aires: Editorial Anteo, 1984. 63 pp.

———. *Qué opinamos los comunistas: Propuestas para transición a la democracia.* Buenos Aires: Editorial Anteo, 1983. 92 pp.

Foner, Philip S. *The Workingmen's Party of the United States: A History of the First Marxist Party in the Americas.* Minneapolis, Minn.: MEP Publications, 1984. 148 pp.

Franqui, Carlos. *Family Portrait with Fidel.* New York: Random House, 1984. 262 pp.

Furci, Carmelo. *The Chilean Communist Party and the Road to Socialism.* London: Zed Press, 1984. 204 pp.

Green, Gil. *Cuba at 25: The Continuing Revolution.* New York: International Publishers, 1983. 117 pp.

Hall, Gus. *For Peace, Jobs, Equality: Report to the 23rd Convention of the Communist Party, USA.* New York: New Outlook Publishers, 1983. 92 pp.

———. *Karl Marx: Beacon for Our Times.* New York: International Publishers, 1983. 94 pp.

Hyfler, Robert. *Prophets of the Left: American Socialist Thought in the Twentieth Century.* Westport, Conn.: Greenwood Press, 1984. 187 pp.

Jonas, Susanne; Ed McCaughan; and Elizabeth Sutherland Martinez, eds. *Guatemala: Tyranny on Trial. Testimony of the Permanent People's Tribunal.* San Francisco: Synthesis Publication, 1984. 301 pp.

Khachaturov, Karen Armenovich. *Latinskaia Amerika: Ideologiia i vneshniaia politika.* Moscow: Mezhdunarodnye otnosheniia, 1983. 318 pp.

Kivisto, Peter. *Immigrant Socialists in the United States: The Case of Finns and the Left.* Rutherford, N.J.: Farleigh Dickinson University Press, 1984. 243 pp.

Kopilow, David J. *Castro, Israel and the PLO.* Washington, D.C.: Cuban-American National Foundation, 1984. 44 pp.

Liss, Sheldon B. *Marxist Thought in Latin America.* Berkeley: University of California Press, 1984. 374 pp.

Martínez Verdugo, Arnoldo. *El proyecto socialista: Selección de discursos de la Marcha por la Democracia, diciembre de 1981–junio de 1982.* Mexico City: Ediciones del Comité Central del Partido Socialista Unificado de México (PSUM), 1983. 323 pp.

Midgett, Douglas. *Eastern Caribbean Elections, 1950–1982: Antigua, Dominica, Grenada, St. Kitts–Nevis, St. Lucia and St. Vincent.* Iowa City: University of Iowa, Center for Development Studies, Institute of Urban and Regional Research, 1983. 193 pp.

Montaner, Carlos Alberto. *Fidel Castro y la revolución cubana.* Barcelona: Plaza & Janes, 1984. 280 pp.

Munck, Ronaldo. *Revolutionary Trends in Latin America.* Montreal: McGill University, Centre for Developing Area Studies,1984. 154 pp.

Muñoz, Herald, and Joseph S. Tulchin. *Latin American Nations in World Politics.* Boulder, Colo.: Westview Press, 1984. 278 pp.

Munroe, Trevor. *Grenada: Revolution, Counterrevolution.* Kingstown, Jamaica: Vanguard Press, 1983. 165 pp.

Nolan, David. *FSLN: The Ideology of the Sandinistas and the Nicaraguan Revolution.* Coral Gables, Fla.: University of Miami, Institute of Inter-American Studies, 1984. 204 pp.

Nyrop, Richard F., ed. *Guatemala: A Country Study.* 2d ed. Washington, D.C.: American University Foreign Area Studies, 1983. 261 pp.

Pacheco, Eliezer. *Partido Comunista Brasileiro (1922–1964).* São Paulo: Editora Alfa-Omega. 1984. 236 pp.

Partido Comunista de Bolivia Marxista Leninista. Congreso Nacional Extraordinario (2d: 1983). *Linea política y programa: Aprobados en el II Congreso Nacional Extraordinario, julio 1983.* N.p.: Comisión Nacional de la Prensa, 1983. 41 pp.

Partido Comunista del Perú. *V Congreso nacional: Documentos.* Lima: Ediciones Patria Roja, 1984. 365 pp.

———. *Militante: Manual de educación para las celulas y organismos intermedios.* Lima: Comisiones Nacional del Educación del PCP, 1984. 19 pp.

Payne, Anthony. *The International Crisis in the Caribbean.* Baltimore, Md.: Johns Hopkins University Press, 1984. 177 pp.

———, Paul Sutton, and Tony Thorndike. *Grenada: Revolution and Invasion.* New York: St. Martin's Press, 1984. 233 pp.

Pereyra, Jorge. *Construir una fuerza real y operativa en marcha hacia un partido comunista de masas: Informe rendido en la reunión del Comité Central del 24 y 30 de agosto de 1984.* Buenos Aires: Editorial Anteo, 1984. 30 pp.

Prestes, Luis Carlos. *Prestes hoje.* Rio de Janeiro: Editora Codecri, 1983. 132 pp.

Revueltas, Jose. *El fracaso histórico del Partido Comunista en México.* Mexico City: Ediciones Era, 1984. 3 vols.

Schneiderman, William. *Dissent on Trial: The Story of a Political Life.* Minneapolis, Minn.: MEP Publications, 1983. 250 pp.

Schulz, Donald E., and Douglas H. Graham, eds. *Revolution and Counterrevolution in Central America and the Caribbean.* Boulder, Colo.: Westview Press, 1984. 555 pp.

Searle, Chris. *Grenada: The Struggle Against Destabilization.* London: Writers & Readers, 1983. 164 pp.

Shul'govskii, A. F., et al., eds. *Sovremennye ideologicheskie techeniia v Latinskoi Amerike*. Moscow: Nauka, 1983. 352 pp.

Spadofora, Hugo. *La derrota comunista en Nicaragua*. N.p.: Alianza Revolucionaria Democratica, 1983. 61 pp.

Thomas, Hugh S.; Georges A. Fauriol; and Juan Carlos Weiss. *The Cuban Revolution*. Boulder, Colo.: Westview Press, 1984. 69 pp.

Urdaneta Laverde, Fernando. *Mi vida en el mundo comunista*. Bogotá: Universidad la Gran Colombia, 1983. 141 pp.

Vacs, Aldo César. *Discreet Partners: Argentina and the USSR Since 1981*. Pittsburgh, Pa.: University of Pittsburgh Press, 1984. 278 pp.

Vladimirov, B. Kh. *Kuba v mezhamerikanskikh otnosheniiakh*. Moscow: Mezhdunarodnye otnosheniia, 1984. 304 pp.

Weisbord, Merrily. *The Strangest Dream: Canadian Communists, the Spy Trials, and the Cold War*. Toronto: Lester & Orpen Dennys, 1983. 255 pp.

Wiarda, Howard J. *In Search of a Policy: The United States and Latin America*. Washington, D.C.: American Enterprise Institute, 1984. 147 pp.

———, ed. *Rift and Revolution: The Central American Imbroglio*. Washington, D.C.: American Enterprise Institute, 1984. 392 pp.

ASIA AND THE PACIFIC

An, Tai Sung. *North Korea: A Political Handbook*. Wilmington, Del.: Scholarly Resources, 1983. 294 pp.

Barkan, Lenore. *Nationalists, Communists and Rural Leaders: Political Dynamics in a Chinese County, 1927–37*. Ann Arbor, Mich.: University Microfilms International, 1983. 598 pp.

Bartke, Wolfgang, and Peter Schier. *China's New Party Leadership: Biographies and Analysis of the Twelfth Central Committee of the Chinese Communist Party*. Armonk, N.Y.: M. E. Sharpe, 1985. 289 pp.

Baryshnikova, O. G., ed. *Iugovostochnaia Azia: Gosudartsvo i ekonomika*. Moscow: Nauka, 1983. 231 pp.

Bonavia, David. *The Verdict in Peking: The Trial of the Gang of Four*. New York: G. P. Putnam's Sons, 1984. 225 pp.

Braestrup, Peter, ed. *Vietnam as History: Ten Years After the Paris Peace Accords*. Washington, D.C.: University Press of America. 1984. 160 pp.

Bulletin of Concerned Asian Scholars, eds. *China from Mao to Deng: The Politics and Economics of Social Development*. Armonk, N.Y.: M. E. Sharpe, 1983. 91 pp.

Bunge, Frederica M., ed. *Burma: A Country Study*. 3d ed. Washington, D.C.: American University Foreign Area Studies, 1983. 326 pp.

———, ed. *Indonesia: A Country Study*. 4th ed. Washington, D.C.: American University Foreign Area Studies, 1983. 343 pp.

———, ed. *Philippines: A Country Study*. 3d ed. Washington, D.C.: American University Foreign Area Studies, 1984. 367 pp.

Byung Chul Koh. *The Foreign Policy Systems of North and South Korea*. Berkeley: University of California Press, 1984. 274 pp.

Chan, Anita; Richard Madsen; and Jonathan Unger. *Chen Village: The Recent History of a Peasant Community in Mao's China*. Berkeley: University of California Press, 1984. 294 pp.

Chandra, Bipan, ed. *The Indian Left: Critical Appraisals*. New Delhi: Vikas, 1983. 452 pp.

Cheah, Boon Kheng. *Red Star over Malaya: Resistance and Social Conflict During and After the Japanese Occupation of Malaya, 1941–1946*. Singapore: Singapore University Press, 1983. 366 pp.

Cheng, Peter. *China*. World Bibliographical Series, vol. 35. Santa Barbara, Calif.: ABC-Clio Press, 1984. 371 pp.

China Directory, 1984. Tokyo: Radio Press, 1984. 357 pp.

Crump, John. *The Origins of Socialist Thought in Japan*. New York: St. Martin's Press, 1983. 374 pp.

Dutton, Michael Robert. *The Crisis of Marxism in China*. Nathan, Australia: Griffith University, School of Modern Asian Studies, 1983. 84 pp.

Etcheson, Craig. *The Rise and Demise of Democratic Kampuchea*. Boulder, Colo.: Westview Press, 1984. 284 pp.

Gall, Sandy. *Behind Russian Lines: An Afghan Journal*. New York: St. Martin's Press, 1984. 194 pp.

Goodman, David S. G., ed. *Groups and Politics in the People's Republic of China*. Armonk, N.Y.: M. E. Sharpe, 1984. 217 pp.

Gurevich, Naum Manuilovich. *Afganistan: Nekotorye osobennosti sotsial'no-ekonomicheskogo razvitiia, 20–50–e gody*. Moscow: Nauka, 1983. 127 pp.

Hammond, Thomas T. *Red Flag over Afghanistan*. Boulder, Colo.: Westview Press, 1984. 261 pp.

Hardgrave, Robert L., Jr. *India Under Pressure: Prospects for Political Stability*. Boulder, Colo.: Westview Press, 1984. 214 pp.

Harding, Harry, ed. *China's Foreign Relations in the 1980's*. New Haven, Conn.: Yale University Press, 1984. 240 pp.

Hill, Gerald N., and Kathleen Hill. *Aquino Assassination*. Sonoma, Calif.: Hilltop Publishing, 1984. 223 pp.

Hua, Wu Yin. *Class and Communalism in Malaysia: Politics in a Dependent Capitalist State*. London: Zed Press, in conjunction with Marram Books, 1983. 230 pp.

Hyman, Anthony. *Afghanistan Under Soviet Domination*. New York: St. Martin's Press, 1984. 247 pp.

Johnson, U. Alexis; George R. Packard; and Alfred D. Wilhelm, Jr. *China Policy for the Next Decade*. Boston: Oelgeschlager, Gunn & Hain, 1984. 445 pp.

Karnow, Stanley. *Vietnam: A History*. New York: Viking Press, 1983. 752 pp.

Kartunova, Anastasia Ivanovna. *Politika kompartii Kitaia v rabochem voprose nakanune revoliutsii, 1925–1927 godov*. Moscow: Nauka, 1983. 188 pp.

Khan, Zillur R. *Leadership in the Least Developed Nation: Bangladesh*. Syracuse, N.Y.: Syracuse University, Maxwell School of Citizenship & Public Affairs, 1983. 209 pp.

Lawson, Don. *The Long March: Red China Under Chairman Mao*. New York: Crowell, 1983. 181 pp.

Lim, Joo-Jock, and Vani S., eds. *Armed Communist Movements in Southeast Asia*. New York: St. Martin's Press, 1984. 204 pp.

Lindsay, Michael. *The Influence of Marxist-Leninist Ideology on the Chinese Communist Party*. Washington, D.C.: American University, Center for Asian Studies, 1983. 47 pp.

Mancall, Mark. *China at the Center: 300 Years of Foreign Policy*. New York: Free Press, 1984. 540 pp.

Millar, T. B., ed. *International Security in the Southeast Asian and Southwest Pacific Region*. St. Lucia, Australia: University of Queensland Press, 1984. 317 pp.

Nyrop, Richard F., ed. *Pakistan: A Country Study*. Washington, D.C.: American University Foreign Area Studies, 1984. 372 pp.

Phak Pasason Pativat Lao. Congress (3rd: 1982, Viangchan, Laos). *III s"ezd Narodno-revoliutsionnoi partii Laosa*. Moscow: Politizdat, 1983. 119 pp.

Poole, Fred, and Max Vanzi. *The Revolution in the Philippines*. New York: McGraw-Hill, 1984. 343 pp.

Robert, Thomas C. *The Chinese People's Militia and the Doctrine of the People's War*. Washington, D.C.: National Defense University Press, 1983. 146 pp.

Salisbury, Harrison E., ed. *Vietnam Reconsidered: Lessons from a War*. New York: Harper & Row, 1984. 335 pp.

Sapozhnikov, Boris G. *Narodno-osvoboditel'naia voina v Kitae, 1946–1950 gg*. Moscow: Voennoe izdatel'stvo, 1984. 158 pp.

Schram, Stuart R. *Mao Zedong: A Preliminary Reassessment*. Hong Kong: Chinese University Press; New York: St. Martin's Press, 1984. 104 pp.

Sharma, T. R. *Communism in India: The Politics of Fragmentation*. New Delhi: Sterling, 1984. 224 pp.

Shawcross, William. *The Quality of Mercy*. New York: Simon & Schuster, 1984. 464 pp.

Sheridan, Mary, and Janet W. Salaff, eds. *Lives: Chinese Working Women*. Bloomington: Indiana University Press, 1984. 258 pp.

Sherkovina, R. I. *Politicheskie partii i politicheskaia bor'ba v Pakistane*. Moscow: Nauka, 1983. 264 pp.

Shur, V. G. *Molodezhnoe dvizhenie v Bangladeshe*. Moscow: Nauka, 1983. 133 pp.

Smith, Charles. *The Burmese Communist Party in the 1980's*. Singapore: Institute of Southeast Asian Studies, 1984. 264 pp.

Stranahan, Patricia. *Yan'an Women and the Communist Party*. Berkeley: University of California, Center for Chinese Studies, 1983. 130 pp.

Sukharchuk, G. D. *Sotsial'no-ekonomicheskie vzgliady politicheskikh liderov Kitaia pervoi poloviny XX v.: Sravnitel'nyi analiz*. Moscow: Nauka, 1983. 227 pp.

Taylor, Robert H. *Marxism and Resistance in Burma, 1942–1945*. Athens: Ohio University Press, 1984. 326 pp.

Teiwes, Frederick C. *Leadership, Legitimacy and Conflict in China*. Armonk, N.Y.: M. E. Sharpe, 1984. 167 pp.

Terrill, Ross. *The White-Boned Demon: A Biography of Madam Mao Zedong*. New York: William Morrow, 1984. 446 pp.

Thomas, S. B. *Labor and the Chinese Revolution: Class Strategies and Contradictions of Chinese Communism, 1928–48*. Ann Arbor: University of Michigan, Center for Chinese Studies, 1983. 341 pp.

Tien Chen-Ya. *The Mass Militia System and Chinese Modernization*. Oakville, Ontario: Mosaic Press, 1983. 180 pp.

Tien Hung-mao. *The Communist Party of China: Party Powers and Group Politics from the Third Plenum to the Twelfth Party Congress*. Baltimore: University of Maryland, School of Law, 1984. 56 pp.

Timmerman, Heinz. *Pekings "eurokommunistische" Wende: Zur Widereinschaltung der KP Chinas in das internationale kommunistische Parteiensystem*. Cologne: Bundesinstitut für Ostwissenschaftliche und Internationale Studien, 1983. 43 pp.

Tornquist, Olle. *Dilemmas of Third World Communism: The Destruction of the PKI in Indonesia*. London: Zed Press, 1984. 272 pp.

Tsui, Tien-hua. *The Sino-Soviet Border Dispute in the 1970s*. Oakville, Ontario: Mosaic Press, 1984. 151 pp.

United States. Central Intelligence Agency. *Directory of Chinese Officials: Provincial Organizations*. Washington, D.C.: National Technical Information Service, 1984. 313 pp.

———. *Directory of Officials in Vietnam*. Washington, D.C.: National Technical Information Service, 1983. 133 pp.

Wang, N. T. *China's Modernization and Transactional Corporations*. Lexington, Mass.: Lexington Books, 1984. 189 pp.

Whyte, Martin King, and William L. Parish. *Urban Life in Contemporary China*. Chicago: University of Chicago Press, 1984. 312 pp.

Wilson, Dick. *Chou: The Story of Zhou Enlai, 1898–1976*. London: Hutchinson, 1984. 349 pp.

Yang Jiang. *A Cadre School Life: Six Chapters*. Hong Kong: Joint Publishing Co., 1984. 91 pp.

Young Whan Kihl. *Politics and Policies in Divided Korea*. Boulder, Colo.: Westview Press, 1984. 148 pp.

EASTERN EUROPE

Amburtsumov, E. A., and O. T. Bogomolov, chief eds. *Sotsialisticheskaia Respublika Rumyniia*. Moscow: Nauka, 1984. 368 pp.

August, Frantisek, and David Rees. *Red Star over Prague*. London: Sherwood Press, 1984. 175 pp.

Banac, Ivo. *The National Question in Yugoslavia: Origins, History, Politics*. Ithaca, N.Y.: Cornell University Press, 1984, 452 pp.

Barberini, Giovanni. *Stato socialista e chisea cattolica in Polonia*. Bologna: Centro Studi Europa Orientale, 1983. 223 pp.

Barecki, Jozef, ed. *Rocznik polityczny i gospodarczy, 1981–1983*. Warsaw: Panstwowe Wydawnictwo Ekonomiczne, 1984. 464 pp.

Bensi, G.; L. Roitman; and L. Predtechevsky. *Sachalin: Befehl zum Mord*. Munich: Roitman Verlag, 1983. 160 pp.

Bentley, Raymond. *Technological Change in the German Democratic Republic*. Boulder, Colo.: Westview Press, 1984. 296 pp.

Beyme, Klaus von, and Hartmut Zimmerman, eds. *Policymaking in the German Democratic Republic*. New York: St. Martin's Press, 1983. 401 pp.

Bogomolov, O. T., chief ed. *Narodnaia Respublika Bolgariia*. Moscow: Nauka, 1983. 333 pp.

Boll, Michael M. *Cold War in the Balkans: American Foreign Policy and the Emergence of Communist Bulgaria*. Lexington: University Press of Kentucky, 1984. 250 pp.

Bolz, Klaus, ed. *Die wirtschaftliche Entwicklung in ausgewählten sozialistischen Ländern Osteuropas zur Jahreswende 1982/83*. Hamburg: Verlag Weltarchiv, 1983. 312 pp.

Brandt, Hans-Jürgen. *Die Kandidatenaufstellung zu der Volkskammerwahlen der DDR: Entscheidungsprozesse und Auswahlkriterien*. West Berlin: Nomos Verlag, 1983. 410 pp.

Brandt, P. *Karrieren eines Aussenseiters: Leo Bauer zwischen Kommunismus und Sozialdemokratie, 1912–1972*. East Berlin: Dietz Verlag, 1983. 359 pp.

Brandys, Kazimierz. *Warsaw Diary, 1978–1981*. New York: Random House, 1984. 260 pp.

Braun, Aurel. *Small State Security in the Balkans*. Totowa, N.J.: Barnes & Noble, 1983. 334 pp.

Bromke, Adam. *Poland: The Protracted Crisis*. Oakville, Ontario: Mosaic Press, 1983. 280 pp.

Büscher, Barbara, et al., eds. *Solidarność*. Cologne: Bund Verlag, 1983. 450 pp.

Ceauşescu, Ilie, ed. *War, Revolution and Society in Romania: The Road to Independence*. Boulder, Colo.: Social Science Monographs, 1983. 298 pp.

Chapignac, Pierre. *La Poudrière polonaise: Eloge critique de l'autolimitation*. Paris: Editions de la Différence, 1983. 287 pp.

Checinski, Michael. *Terror and Politics in Communist Poland*. Jerusalem: Hebrew University of Jerusalem, Soviet and East European Research Centre, 1983. 113 pp.

Council for Mutual Economic Assistance. *Sotrudnichestvo stran-chlenov SEV v oblasti standartizatsii*. Moscow: 1983. 35 pp.

———. Secretariat. *CMEA: Figures, Facts, Arguments*. Moscow: n.p., 1983. 56 pp.

Curry, Jane Leftwich, ed. and trans. *The Black Book of Polish Censorship*. New York: Random House, 1984. 433 pp.

Dawisha, Karen. *The Kremlin and the Prague Spring*. Berkeley: University of California Press, 1984. 426 pp.

Djilas, Milovan. *Jahre der Macht*. Munich: Verlag Molden; Stuttgart: S. Seewald, 1983. 472 pp.

———. *The New Class: An Analysis of the Communist System*. San Diego Calif.: Harcourt Brace Jovanovich, 1983. 214 pp.

Dragoicheva, Tsola Nincheva. *Defeat to Victory: Notes of a Bulgarian Revolutionary*. Sofia: Sofia Press, 1983. 526 pp.

Eckart, Karl. *Polen: Regionale und strukturelle Entwicklungsprobleme eines sozialistischen Landes*. Paderborn, FRG: F. Schöning, 1983. 231 pp.

Fedoseev, P. N., and Zh. P. Pakh, eds. *Velikii Oktiabr' i Vengerskaia Sovetskaia Respublika*. Moscow: Nauka, 1983. 280 pp.

Fehér, Ferenc; Agnes Heller; and György Marcus. *Dictatorship over Needs*. New York: St. Martin's Press, 1983. 312 pp.

Fischer, H. *DDR-Indien: Ein Diplomat berichtet*. East Berlin: Staatsverlag der DDR, 1984. 94 pp.

Fomin, V. N. *SEV i drugie mezhdunarodnye organizatsii*. Moscow: Nauka, 1983. 174 pp.

Fricke, Karl Wilhelm. *Opposition und Widerstand in der DDR*. Cologne: Verlag Wissenschaft und Politik, 1984. 240 pp.

Gabriel, Richard A., ed. *NATO and the Warsaw Pact*. Fighting Armies, vol. 1. Westport, Conn.: Greenwood Press, 1983. 252 pp.

Garton Ash, Timothy. *The Polish Revolution: Solidarity*. New York: Charles Scribner's Sons, 1983. 388 pp.

Gerner, Kristian. *The Soviet Union and Central Europe in the Post-war Era*. Lund: Swedish Institute of International Affairs, 1984. 238 pp.

Glowacki, Janusz. *Give Us This Day*. Translated by Konrad Brodzinski. New York: St. Martin's Press, 1983. 121 pp.

Grot-Kwasniewski, Jerzy. *Society and Deviance in Communist Poland: Attitudes Toward Social Control*. New York: St. Martin's Press, 1984, 210 pp.

Gruenwald, Oskar. *The Yugoslav Search for Man: Marxist Humanism in Contemporary Yugoslavia*. South Hadley, Mass.: J. F. Bergin, 1983. 438 pp.

Gumpel, Werner. *Sozialistische Wirtschaftssysteme*. Munich: Günter Olzog Verlag, 1983. 223 pp.

Gutmann, Gernot, et al., eds. *Das Wirtschaftssystem der DDR: Wirtschaftspolitische Gestaltungsprobleme*. Stuttgart: Gustav Fischer Verlag, 1983. 458 pp.

Haase, N., et al. *VEB Nachwuchs: Jugend in der DDR*. Reinbek, FRG: Rowohlt Verlag, 1983. 250 pp.

Hacker, Jens. *Der Ostblock: Entstehung, Entwicklung und Struktur, 1939–1980*. Baden-Baden: Nomos Verlag, 1983. 900 pp.

Hager, Kurt, ed. *Gesetzmässigkeiten unserer Epoche: Triebkräfte und Werte der Sozialismus*. Rede der Gesellschaftwissenschaftlichen Konferenz der ZK der SED am 14. und 15. Dezember 1983 in Berlin. East Berlin: Dietz Verlag, 1983. 80 pp.

Henkys, Reinhard. *Gottes Volk im Sozialismus: Wie Christen in der DDR leben*. West Berlin: Wichern Verlag, 1983. 127 pp.

Hollos, Marida, and Béla C. Maday, eds. *New Hungarian Peasants: An East-Central European Experience with Collectivization*. New York: Brooklyn College Press, 1983. 341 pp.

Holloway, David, and Jane M. O. Sharp, eds. *Warsaw Pact: Alliance in Transition?* Ithaca, N.Y.: Cornell University Press, 1984. 229 pp.

Hutchings, Robert L. *Soviet–East European Relations: Consolidation and Conflict*. Madison: University of Wisconsin Press, 1984. 314 pp.

Johnson, A. Ross, and Barbara Kliszewski. *The Polish Military After Martial Law: Report of a Rand Conference, October 14, 1982*. Santa Monica, Calif.: Rand Corporation (for the U.S. Air Force), 1983. 33 pp.

Kegel, Gerhard. *In den Stürmen des Jahrhunderts: Ein deutscher Kommunist über sein ungewöhnliches Leben*. East Berlin: Dietz Verlag, 1983. 543 pp.

Konrad, George. *Antipolitics*. San Diego, Calif.: A Helen and Kurt Wolf Book/Harcourt Brace Jovanovitch, 1983. 243 pp.

Labedz, Leopold, ed. *Poland Under Jaruzelski*. New York: Charles Scribner's Sons, 1984. 432 pp.

Lebedev, N. I. *Krakh fashizma v Rumynii*. 2d ed. Moscow: Nauka, 1983. 550 pp.

Loest, Erich. *Der vierte Zensor: Vom Entstehen und Sterben eines Romans in der DDR*. Cologne: Verlag Wissenschaft und Politik, 1984. 96 pp.

Lydall, Harold. *Yugoslav Socialism: Theory and Practice*. Oxford: Clarendon Press, 1984. 392 pp.

Mackiewicz, Jozef. *Katyń: Ungesühntes Verbrechen*. Frankfurt/Main: Possev Verlag, 1983. 244 pp.

Malcher, George C. *Poland's Politicized Army: Communists in Uniform*. New York: Praeger, 1984. 287 pp.

Mallinckrodt, Anita M. *Das kleine Massenmedium: Soziale Funktion und politische Rolle der Heftreihenliteratur in der DDR*. Cologne: Verlag Wissenschaft und Politik, 1984. 323 pp.

Markov, Georgi. *The Truth That Killed*. New Haven, Conn.: Ticknor & Fields, 1984. 280 pp.

McCauley, Martin. *The German Democratic Republic Since 1945*. London: Macmillan, 1983. 282 pp.

Neef, Helmut, et al. *Die nationale Front der DDR: Geschichtlicher Überblick*. East Berlin: Dietz Verlag, 1984, 255 pp.

Nelson, Daniel N. ed. *The Warsaw Pact and the Issue of Reliability*. Boulder, Colo.: Westview Press, 1984. 237 pp.

Nelson, Harold D., ed. *Poland: A Country Study*. Washington, D.C.: American University Foreign Area Studies, 1983. 483 pp.

Nick, Harry. *Karl Marx und die Gestaltung der entwickelten sozialistischen Gesellschaft der DDR*. East Berlin: Verlag Zeit im Bild, 1983. 70 pp. (Unnumbered pages.)

Nitsche, Hellmuth. *Zwischen Kreuz und Sowjetstern: Zeugnisse des Kirchenkampfes in der DDR, 1945–1981*. Aschaffenburg, FRG: Pattloch, 1983. 276 pp.

Péteri, György. *Effects of World War I: War Communism in Hungary*. New York: Brooklyn College Press, 1984. 229 pp.

Rakowska-Harmstone, Teresa. *Communism in Eastern Europe*. 2d ed. Bloomington: Indiana University Press, 1984. 391 pp.

Rigby, T. H., and Bohdan Harasymiw, eds. *Leadership Selection and Patron-Client Relations in the USSR and Yugoslavia*. Boston: Allen & Unwin, 1983. 246 pp.

Sanford, Gregory W. *From Hitler to Ulbricht: The Communist Reconstruction of East Germany, 1945–46*. Princeton, N.J.: Princeton University Press, 1983. 313 pp.

Schaff, Adam. *Polen heute*. Vienna: Europaverlag, 1984. 236 pp.

Scharf, C. Bradley. *Politics and Change in East Germany*. Boulder, Colo.: Westview Press, 1984. 219 pp.

Schinke, Eberhard, and Zdenek Hunacek. *Der Anteil der privaten Landwirtschaft an der Agrarproduktion in den RGW-Ländern*. West Berlin: Duncker und Humblot, 1983. 97 pp.

Schönfeld, Roland, ed. *RGW-Integration und Südosteuropa*. Munich: Oldenbourg Verlag, 1984. 298 pp.

Shabalin, A. Ya., ed. *Germanskaia Demokraticheskaia Respublika*. Moscow: Nauka, 1983. 358 pp.

Shmelev, N. P., ed. *Ekonomicheskie otnosheniia stran SEV s Zapadom*. Moscow: Nauka, 1983. 230 pp.

Simon, Jeffrey. *Cohesion and Discussion in Eastern Europe*. New York: Praeger, 1983. 235 pp.

Sobell, Vladimir. *The Red Market*. Aldershot, Eng.: Gower, 1984. 265 pp.

Staniszkis, Jadwiga. *Poland's Self-Limiting Revolution*. Edited by Jan T. Gross. Princeton, N.J.: Princeton University Press, 1984. 352 pp.

Stoph, Willi. *DDR: Staat des Sozialismus und des Friedens*. East Berlin: Dietz Verlag, 1984. 491 pp.

Tigrid, Pavel. *Arbeiter gegen den Arbeiterstaat: Widerstand in Osteuropa*. Cologne: Bund-Verlag, 1983. 160 pp.

United States. Central Intelligence Agency. Directorate of Intelligence. *Directory of East German Officials*. Washington, D.C.: National Technical Information Service, 1984. 176 pp.

———. *Directory of Officials of the Bulgarian People's Republic*. Washington, D.C.: National Technical Information Service, 1984. 132 pp.

———. *Directory of Officials of the Socialist Federal Republic of Yugoslavia*. Washington, D.C.: National Technical Information Service, 1983. 220 pp.

Voronkov, V. I., et al. *Polskaia Narodnaia Respublika: Spravochnik*. 3d ed. Moscow: Politizdat, 1984. 124 pp.

Vosske, Heinz. *Walter Ulbricht: Biographischer Abriss*. East Berlin: Dietz Verlag, 1983. 421 pp.

Wehling, Hans-Georg, ed. *DDR: Bürger im Staat*. Stuttgart: Verlag Walter Sperling and Verlag Kohlhammer, 1983. 240 pp.

Weschler, Lawrence. *The Passion of Poland: From Solidarity Through a State of War*. New York: Pantheon Books, 1984. 263 pp.

Wilhelmi, Jutta. *Jugend in der DDR: Der Weg zur "sozialistischen Persönlichkeit."* West Berlin: Holzapfel, 1983. 141 pp.

William, Lothar. *Überflug: Die DDR aus Vogelperspektive*. Leipzig: Brockhaus Verlag, 1983. 189 pp.

Zhelitski, B. I. *Rabochii klass sotsialisticheskoi Vengrii*. Moscow: Nauka, 1984. 336 pp.

USSR

Akhmedov, Ismail. *In and Out of Stalin's GRU: A Tatar's Escape from Red Army Intelligence*. Frederick, Md.: University Publications of America, 1984. 222 pp.

Akiner, Shirin. *Islamic Peoples of the Soviet Union*. Boston: Routledge & Kegan Paul, 1983. 462 pp.

Aksyutin, Yuri. *V. I. Lenin: Pages from a Life of Struggle*. Moscow: Novosti Press Agency Publishing House, 1983. 79 pp.

Andreev, P. P. *Partiia kommunisticheskogo sozidaniia*. Moscow: Mysl', 1984. 212 pp.

Atkinson, Dorothy. *The End of the Russian Land Commune, 1905–1930*. Stanford: Stanford University Press, 1983. 457 pp.

Bermann, Robert P., and John C. Baker. *Soviet Strategic Forces: Requirements and Responses*. Washington, D. C.: Brookings Institute, 1983. 171 pp.

Binyon, Michael. *Life in Russia*. New York: Pantheon Books, 1983. 286 pp.

Brucan, Silviu. *The Post-Brezhnev Era: An Insider's View*. New York: Praeger, 1983. 126 pp.

Bundesinstitut für Ostwissenschaftliche und Internationale Studien, ed. *Sowjetunion, 1982/83: Ereignisse, Probleme, Perspektiven*. Munich: Hanser Verlag, 1983, 366 pp.

Chernenko, Konstantin U. *Speeches and Writings*. 2d enl. ed. New York: Pergamon Press, 1984. 256 pp.

Chernov, Mikhail Pavlovich. *XVII s"ezd VKP(b)*. Moscow: Politizdat, 1984. 94 pp.

Cline, Ray S., and Yonah Alexander. *Terrorism: The Soviet Connection*. New York: Crane, Russak, 1984. 161 pp.

Colton, Timothy J. *The Dilemma of Reform in the Soviet Union*. New York: Council on Foreign Relations, 1984. 113 pp.

Cracraft, James, ed. *The Soviet Union Today*. Chicago: *Bulletin of the Atomic Scientists*, Educational Foundation for Nuclear Science (distributed by University of Chicago Press), 1983. 348 pp.

Crankshaw, Edward. *Putting up with the Russians*. New York: Viking, 1984. 269 pp.

Dahm, Helmut. *Marx-Lenin-Andropov: Ideologischer Lagebericht nach dem Führungswechsel in Moskau*. Cologne: Bundesinstitut für Ostwissenschaftliche und Internationale Studien, 1983. 69 pp.

Daniels, Robert V., ed. *Communism in Russia*. A Documentary History of Communism, vol. 1. Hanover, N.H.: University Press of New England, 1984. 425 pp.

————, ed., *Communism in the World*. A Documentary History of Communism, vol. 2. Hanover, N.H.: University Press of New England, 1984. 448 pp.

Desai, Padma, ed. *Marxism, Central Planning and the Soviet Economy: Economic Essays in Honor of Alexander Ehrlich*. Cambridge, Mass.: MIT Press, 1983. 285 pp.

Egorov, A. G., and K. M. Bogoliubov, eds. *Kommunisticheskaia Partiia Sovetskogo Soiuza v rezoliutsiiakh i resheniiakh s"ezdov, konferentsii i plenumov, TsK, 1898–1982*. Moscow: Politizdat, 1983. 3 vols.

Ellison, Herbert J., ed. *Soviet Policy Toward Western Europe: Implications for the Atlantic Alliance*. Seattle: University of Washington Press, 1984. 340 pp.

Ezergailis, Andrew. *The Latvian Impact on the Bolshevik Revolution: The First Phase, September 1917–1918*. Boulder, Colo.: East European Monographs, 1983. 419 pp.

Ezik, E. M. *Bol'shevistskie konferentsii nakanune Oktiabria: Avgust-oktiabr' 1917 g*. Moscow: Izdatel'stvo Moskovskogo universiteta, 1983. 285 pp.

Fateev, P. S. *Pervye russkie marksisty*. Moscow: Politizdat, 1983. 175 pp.

Frankel, Jonathan. *The Soviet Regime and Anti-Zionism: An Analysis*. Jerusalem: Hebrew University of Jerusalem, 1984. 82 pp.

Freedman, Robert O. *Soviet Jewry in the Decisive Decade, 1971–1980*. Durham, N.C.: Duke University Press, 1984. 167 pp.

Friedgut, Theodore H. *Soviet Anti-Zionism and Anti-Semitism: Another Cycle*. Jerusalem: Hebrew University of Jerusalem, 1984. 31 pp.

Gabriel, Richard. *The Antagonists: A Comparative Assessment of the Soviet and American Soldier*. Westport, Conn.: Greenwood Press, 1984. 208 pp.

Gelman, Harry. *The Brezhnev Politburo and the Decline of Détente*. Ithaca, N.Y.: Cornell University Press, 1984. 288 pp.

Getzler, Israel. *Kronstadt, 1917–1921: The Fate of Soviet Democracy*. New York: Cambridge University Press, 1983. 296 pp.

Goren, Roberta. *The Soviet Union and Terrorism*. Winchester, Mass.: Allen & Unwin, 1984. 280 pp.

Gustafson, Thane. *The Soviet Gas Campaign: Politics and Policy in Soviet Decisionmaking*. Santa Monica, Calif.: Rand Corporation, 1983. 118 pp.

Harasymiw, Bohdan. *Political Elite Recruitment in the Soviet Union*. New York: St. Martin's Press, 1984. 277 pp.

Hazard, John N.; William E. Butler; and Peter B. Maggs. *The Soviet Legal System: The Law in the 1980's*. New York: Oceana Publications (for Columbia University, Parker School of Foreign and Comparative Law), 1984. 424 pp.

Hedlund, Stefan. *Crisis in Soviet Agriculture*. New York: St. Martin's Press, 1984. 228 pp.

Hewett, Edward A., ed. *Energy, Economics, and Foreign Policy in the Soviet Union*. Washington, D.C.: Brookings Institution, 1984. 228 pp.

Hoffman, Erik P., and Robbin F. Laird, eds. *The Soviet Polity in the Modern Era*. Hawthorne, N.Y.: Aldine Publishing, 1984. 942 pp.

Hutchings, Raymond. *The Soviet Budget*. Albany: State University of New York Press, 1983. 204 pp.

Institut Marksizma-Leninizma pri TsK KPSS. *Fond dokumentov V. I. Lenina*. 2d ed. Moscow: Politizdat, 1984. 306 pp.

Ivanov, N. N., ed. *Karl Marks: Zhizn' i deiatel'nost', dokumenty i fotografii*. Moscow: Progress, 1983. 415 pp.

Jelen, Christian. *L'Aveuglement*. Paris: Flammarion, 1984. 278 pp.

Klose, Kevin. *Russia and the Russians: Inside the Closed Society*. New York: W. W. Norton, 1984. 350 pp.

Kneen, Peter. *Soviet Scientists and the State*. London: Macmillan (with University of Birmingham, Centre for Russian and East European Studies), 1984. 138 pp.

Kommunisticheskaia Partiia Sovetskogo Soiuza. *Ustav Kommunisticheskoi Partii Sovetskogo Soiuza: Utverzhden XXII s"ezdom, chastichnye izmeneniia vneseny XXIII i XXIV s"ezdami KPSS*. Moscow: Izdatel'stvo politicheskoi literatury, 1984, 61 pp.

Kostecki, M. M., ed. *The Soviet Impact on Commodity Markets*. New York: St. Martin's Press, 1984. 271 pp.

Krawchenko, Bohdan, ed. *Ukraine After Shelest*. Edmonton: University of Alberta, Canadian Institute of Ukrainian Studies, 1983. 119 pp.

Linden, Carl A. *The Soviet Party-State: The Politics of Ideocratic Despotism*. New York: Praeger, 1983. 174 pp.

Lopata, P. P., et al. *Aktual'nye voprosy nauchnogo kommunizma: Razvitie marksistsko-leninskoi teorii XXVI s"ezdom KPSS*. Moscow: Izdatel'stvo politicheskogo literatury, 1983. 302 pp.

Mace, James E. *Communism and the Dilemmas of National Liberation: National Communism in Soviet Ukraine, 1918–1933*. Cambridge, Mass.: Harvard Ukrainian Research Institute, 1983. 334 pp.

Marrese, Michael, and Jan Vanous. *Soviet Subsidization of Trade with Eastern Europe*. Berkeley: University of California Press, 1983. 254 pp.

McCauley, Martin. *Octobrists to Bolsheviks: Imperial Russia, 1905–1917*. London: E. Arnold, 1984. 226 pp.

———. *The Soviet Union After Brezhnev*. New York: Holmes & Meier, 1983. 160 pp.

———. *Stalin and Stalinism*. Harlow, Eng.: Longman, 1983. 128 pp.

McCrea, Barbara P.; Jack C. Plano; and George Klein. *The Soviet and East European Political Dictionary*. Santa Barbara, Calif.: ABC-Clio Press, 1984. 367 pp.

Medvedev, Roy. *All Stalin's Men*. New York: Doubleday, 1984. 292 pp.

Meissner, Boris. *Sowjetische Kurskorrekturen: Breshnew und seine Erben*. Zurich: Edition Interfrom, 1984. 143 pp.

Miller, R. F., and F. Fehér, eds. *Khrushchev and the Communist World*. Totowa, N.J.: Barnes & Noble, 1984. 243 pp.

Nerlich, Uwe, ed. *Soviet Power and Western Negotiating Policies*, vol. 1, *The Soviet Asset*; vol. 2, *The Western Panacea*. Cambridge, Mass.: Ballinger, 1983. 2 vols.

O'Connor, Timothy Edward. *The Politics of Soviet Culture: Anatolii Lunacharskii*. Ann Arbor, Mich.: UMI Research Press, 1983. 193 pp.

Orlova, Raisa. *Memoirs*. New York: Random House, 1984. 366 pp.

Os'movoi, M. N. ed. *Vneshneekonomicheskie sviazi SSSR so stranami Severnoi Evropy*. Moscow: Izdatel'stvo Moskovskogo universiteta, 1983. 151 pp.

Osnovin, Viktor Stepanovich. *Gorodskoi sovet: Organ sotsial'nogo upravleniia*. Moscow: Iuridicheskaia literatura, 1983. 126 pp.

Pankov, Yu. N., and Yu. K. Kharlamov, eds. *Communists and Youth: Study of Revolutionary Education*. Moscow: Progress, 1984. 254 pp.

Parks, J. D. *Culture, Conflict and Coexistence: American-Soviet Cultural Relations, 1917–1958*. Jefferson, N.C.: McFarland, 1983. 231 pp.

Pipes, Richard. *Survival Is Not Enough: Soviet Realities and America's Future*. New York: Simon & Schuster, 1984. 302 pp.

Poliakov, Leon. *De Moscou à Beyrouth: Essai sur la désinformation*. Paris: Calmann-Lévy, 1983. 194 pp.

Porter, Bruce D. *The USSR in Third World Conflicts*. New York: Cambridge University Press, 1984. 225 pp.

Ra'anan, Gavriel D. *International Policy Formation in the USSR: Factional "Debates" During the Zhdanovshchina*. Hamden, Conn.: Archon Books, 1983. 248 pp.

Radziejowski, Janusz. *The Communist Party of Western Ukraine, 1919–1929*. Edmonton: Canadian Institute of Ukrainian Studies, 1983. 224 pp.

Rodonov, P. A., chief ed. *Partiinaia rabota v usloviiakh proizvodstvennykh ob"edinenii*. Moscow: Politizdat, 1984. 327 pp.

Ro'i, Yaacov, ed. *The USSR and the Muslim World*. Winchester, Mass.: Allen & Unwin, 1984. 298 pp.

Schapiro, Leonard B. *1917: The Russian Revolutions and the Origins of Present-day Communism*. New York: Basic Books, 1984. 239 pp.

———, and Joseph Godson, eds. *The Soviet Worker: From Lenin to Andropov*. New York: St. Martin's Press, 1984. 326 pp.

Segal, Gerald, ed. *The Soviet Union and East Asia*. London: Heinemann; Boulder, Colo.: Westview Press, 1983. 150 pp.

Shaffer, Harry G., ed. *The Soviet System in Theory and Practice: Western and Soviet Views*. New York: F. Ungar, 1984. 451 pp.

Shipler, David K. *Russia: Broken Idols, Solemn Dreams*. New York: Times Books, 1983. 404 pp.

Shmelev, N. P., ed. *Ekonomicheskie otnosheniia stran SEV s Zapadom: Strategiia, dolgosrochnye interesy, perspektivy*. Moscow: Nauka, 1983. 227 pp.

Shultz, Richard H., and Roy Godson. *Dezinformatsia: Active Measures in Soviet Strategy*. Washington, D.C.: Pergamon-Brassey's (for the National Strategy Information Center), 1984. 210 pp.

Smith, Stephen Anthony. *Red Petrograd: Revolution in the Factories, 1917–18*. New York: Cambridge University Press, 1983. 347 pp.

Solomon, Susan Gross, ed. *Pluralism in the Soviet Union*. New York: St. Martin's Press, 1984. 179 pp.

Solov'ev, A. A. *S"ezdy i konferentsii KPSS*. Moscow: Politizdat, 1983. 320 pp.

Steele, Jonathan. *Soviet Power*. New York: Simon & Schuster, 1983. 287 pp.

———. *World Power: Soviet Foreign Policy Under Brezhnev and Andropov*. London: Michael Joseph, 1983. 287 pp.

———, and Eric Abraham. *Andropov in Power: From Komsomol to Kremlin*. Oxford: M. Robertson, 1983. 216 pp.

Stiller, Pavel. *Sozialpolitik der UdSSR, 1950–1980*. Baden-Baden: Nomos Verlag, 1983. 335 pp.

Suvorov, Viktor. *Inside Soviet Military Intelligence*. New York: Macmillan, 1984. 193 pp.

Talbott, Strobe. *The Russians and Reagan*. New York: Vintage Books, 1984. 140 pp.

Tel'pukhovskii, B. S. *KPSS vo glave stroitel'stva vooruzhennykh sil SSSR: Oktiabr' 1917–1982 g*. Moscow: Politizdat, 1983. 285 pp.

Teplinskii, L. B. *USSR-DRA: Good Neighbourliness and Fraternal Friendship*. Moscow: Novosti Press Agency Publishing House, 1983. 71 pp.

Terry, Sarah Micklejohn, ed. *Soviet Policy in Eastern Europe*. New Haven, Conn.: Yale University Press, 1984. 375 pp.

Timofeev, T. T., et al., eds. *Rabochii klass v proshlom i nastoiashchem: Problemy istorii i istoriographii*. Moscow: Nauka, 1984. 255 pp.

Tsedenbal, Yumjaagyn. *Izbrannye stat'i i rechi: Aprel' 1973–dekabr' 1982 goda*. Moscow: Politizdat, 1983. 528 pp.

United States. Central Intelligence Agency. Directorate of Intelligence. *Appearances of Soviet Leaders, January–December 1983*. Washington, D.C.: National Technical Information Service, 1984. 188 pp.

———. *Directory of Soviet Officials: National Organizations*. Washington, D.C.: National Technical Information Service, 1984. 371 pp.

———. *Directory of Soviet Officials: Science and Education*. Washington, D.C.: National Technical Information Service, 1984. 409 pp.

United States. Congress. House of Representatives. Committee on Foreign Affairs. Subcommittee on Europe and the Middle East and on Asian and Pacific Affairs. *The Soviet Role in Asia: Hearings, July 19–October 19, 1983*. Washington, D.C.: Committee on Foreign Affairs, 1983. 576 pp.

Vidali, Vittorio. *Diary of the Twentieth Congress of the Communist Party of the Soviet Union*. Westport, Conn.: L. Hill, 1984. 192 pp.

Volchikhin, V. G., and A. P. Mal'tsev, eds. *Spravochnik komsomol'skogo aktivista*. 3d ed. Moscow: Molodaia gvardia. 1983. 270 pp.

Voslensky, Michael. *Nomenklatura: The Soviet Ruling Class*. New York: Doubleday, 1984. 455 pp.

Werth, Nicolas. *La Vie quotidienne des paysans russes de la révolution à la collectivisation, 1917–1939*. Paris: Hachette, 1984. 410 pp.

Whelan, Joseph G. *Andropov and Reagan as Negotiators: Context and Styles in Contrast*. Library of Congress, Congressional Research Service, Report no. 83–141S. Washington, D.C., 1983. 135 pp.

Yodfat, Aryeh. *The Soviet Union and Revolutionary Iran*. London: Croom Helm, 1984. 168 pp.

Young, Brigitta. *Prospects for Soviet Grain Production*. Boulder, Colo.: Westview Press, 1983. 216 pp.

Zarodov, Konstantin I. *Tri revoliutsii v Rossii i nashe vremia*. 3d ed. Moscow: Mysl', 1983. 639 pp.

Zhukov, Georgii K. *Vospominaniia i razmyshleniia*. 5th ed. Moscow: Novosti, 1983. 3 vols.

THE MIDDLE EAST

Bakhash, Shaul. *The Reign of the Ayatollahs: Iran and the Islamic Revolution*. New York: Basic Books, 1984. 276 pp.

Brown, L. Carl. *International Politics and the Middle East*. Princeton, N.J.: Princeton University Press, 1984. 363 pp.

Cobban, Helena. *The Palestinian Liberation Organization: People, Power, Politics*. New York: Cambridge University Press, 1984. 305 pp.

Darius, Robert G.; John W. Amos, II; and Ralph H. Magnus, eds. *Gulf Security into the 1980s: Perceptual and Strategic Dimensions*. Stanford: Hoover Institution Press, 1984. 134 pp.

Gerasimov, O. G. *Irak*. Moscow: Mysl', 1984. 112 pp.

Haddad, Yvonne Yazbeck; Byron Haines; and Ellison Findlay. *The Islamic Impact*. New York: Syracuse University Press, 1984. 249 pp.

Islami, Reza S., and Rostam Mehraban Kavoussi. *The Political Economy of Saudi Arabia*. Seattle: University of Washington Press, 1984. 124 pp.

Korany, Bahgat, and Ali E. Hillal Dessouki. *The Foreign Policy of the Arab States.* Boulder, Colo.: Westview Press, 1984. 354 pp.

Kostiner, Joseph. *The Struggle for South Yemen.* New York: St. Martin's Press, 1984. 195 pp.

Parker, Richard B. *North Africa: Regional Tensions and Strategic Concerns.* New York: Praeger, 1984. 179 pp.

Polisario. *Dix ans de lutte contre le colonialisme et l'expansionisme (20 mai 1973–20 mai 1983): Front Polisario.* [France?]: Ministère de l'Information de la Culture de la R.A.S.D., 1983. 165 pp.

Sowayegh, Abdulaziz al-, *Arab Petropolitics.* New York: St. Martin's Press, 1984. 207 pp.

Stookey, Robert W., ed. *The Arabian Peninsula: Zone of Ferment.* Stanford: Hoover Institution Press, 1984. 151 pp.

Val'kova, L. V., et al., eds. *Noveishaia istoriia Iemena, 1917–1982 gg.* Moscow: Nauka, 1984. 230 pp.

Who's Who in Saudi Arabia, 1983–1984. 3d ed. Jidda: Tihama (distributed by Gale Research), 1984. 375 pp.

Ziring, Lawrence. *The Middle East Political Dictionary.* Santa Barbara, Calif.: ABC-Clio Press, 1984. 452 pp.

WESTERN EUROPE

Accornero, A., et al. *L'Identitá comunista: I militanti, le strutture, la cultura del PCI.* Rome: Editori Riuniti, 1983. 551 pp.

Alexander, Yonah. *Terrorism in Ireland.* London: Croom Helm, 1983. 208 pp.

Andrade, Juan. *Recuerdos personales.* Barcelona: Ediciones del Serbal, 1983. 234 pp.

Arasa, Daniel. *Años 40: Los maquis y el PCE.* Barcelona: Argos Vergara, 1984. 327 pp.

Attfield, John, and Stephen Williams. *1939: The Communist Party of Great Britain and the War.* London: Lawrence & Wishart, 1984. 192 pp.

Bahro, Rudolph. *From Red to Green. Interviews with "New Left Review."* London: *New Left Review*, 1984. 238 pp.

Bambach, Ralf. *Der französische Frühsozialismus.* Opladen, FRG: Westdeutscher Verlag, 1984. 756 pp.

Beaud, Michel. *La Politique économique de la gauche, mai 1981–décembre 1982.* Le Mirage de croissance, vol. 1. Paris: Syros, 1983. 214 pp.

Bedeschi, Giuseppe. *La parabola del marxismo in Italia, 1945–1983.* Bari: Laterza, 1983. 181 pp.

Bell, D. S., and Eric Shaw, eds. *The Left in France: Towards the Socialist Republic.* Nottingham, Eng.: Spokesman, 1983. 192 pp.

Bruhat, Jean. *Il n'est jamais trop tard.* Paris: Albin Michel, 1983. 292 pp.

Bruneau, Thomas C. *Politics and Nationhood: Postrevolutionary Portugal.* New York: Praeger, 1984. 174 pp.

Bruns, Wilhelm. *Deutsch-deutsche Beziehungen.* Opladen, FRG: Budrich und Leske, 1984. 212 pp.

Cacares, Benigno. *Le Mouvement ouvrier.* Paris: Editions du Seuil, 1984. 215 pp.

Callaghan, John. *British Trotskyism: Theory and Practice.* Oxford: Blackwell, 1984. 255 pp.

Capra, Fritjof. *Green Politics.* New York: E. P. Dutton, 1984. 244 pp.

Carr, Edward Hallett. *The Comintern and the Spanish Civil War.* London: Macmillan, 1984. 111 pp.

Carrère d'Encausse, Hélène. *Le Grand frère: L'Union Soviétique et l'Europe soviétisée.* Paris: Flammarion, 1983. 381 pp.

Carrillo, Santiago. *Le Communisme malgré tout: Entretiens avec Lilly Marcou.* Paris: Presses Universitaires de France, 1984. 1984 pp.

———. *Memoirs of the Transition.* Barcelona: Grijalbo, 1983. 257 pp.

Le CDFT en questions: La Réponse d'Edmond Maire. Paris: Gallimard, 1984. 246 pp.

Chiti-Batelli, Andrea. *Elezioni europee 1984 e riforma delle comunista: Una nuove strategia nella battaglia per l'Europa.* Milano: Giuffre, 1984. 197 pp.

Confederation Général du Travail. Centre Confédéral d'Etudes Economiques et Sociales. *La C.G.T. propose une nouvelle coopération internationale.* Paris: C.G.T., 1983. 31 pp.

Cowden, Morton H. *Russian Bolshevism and British Labor, 1917–1921.* Boulder, Colo.: East European Monographs, 1984. 238 pp.

Crick, Michael. *Militant.* London: Faber & Faber, 1984. 242 pp.

Depretto, J. P. *Le Communisme à l'usine: Vie ouvrière et mouvement ouvrier chez Renault, 1920–39.* Roubaix, France: Edires, 1984. 284 pp.

Downey, James. *Them and Us: Britain, Ireland and the Northern Question, 1969–82.* Dublin: Ward River, 1983. 258 pp.

Duncker, Hermann. *Über das Manifest der Kommunistischen Partei.* East Berlin: Verlag Tribüne, 1983. 191 pp.

Finnegan, Richard B. *Ireland: The Challenge of Conflict and Change.* Boulder, Colo.: Westview Press, 1983. 166 pp.

Fitzmaurice, John. *The Politics of Belgium.* New York: St. Martin's Press, 1983. 256 pp.

Fourrier, Jules. *Graine rouge.* Paris: La Brèche, 1984. 175 pp.

Fowkes, Ben. *Communism in Germany Under the Weimar Republic.* London: St. Martin's Press, 1984. 246 pp.

Garin, Eugenio. *Tra due secoli: Socialismo e filosofia in Italia dopo "L'Unità."* Bari: De Donato, 1983. 379 pp.

Garrigues, Juan Miguel. *L'Eglise, la société libre et le communisme.* Paris: Julliard, 1984. 168 pp.

Giovanni, Fabio. *I communisti e l'universita: Il PCI e la questione universitaria della constituente agli anni ottanta.* Bari: Dedalo, 1983. 191 pp.

Goguel, François. *Chroniques éléctorales: La Cinquième République après de Gaulle.* Paris: Presses de la Fondation Nationale des Sciences Politiques, 1983. 197 pp.

Gomes, Mattos. *A decáda bastarda, abril 1974 a abril 1984: Dez anos de destruição revolucionaria.* Lisbon: Editorial F. Pereira, 1984. 215 pp.

Gremetz, Maxime. *La Situation internationale et la lutte pour la paix et le désarmement: Rapport au comité central du PCF, 17, 18, 19 janvier 1984.* Paris: *Cahiers du Communisme,* 1984. 29 pp.

Guitton, Jean. *Pages brulées.* Paris: Albin Michel, 1984. 208 pp.

Hitchens, Christopher. *Cyprus.* London: Melbourne, 1984. 192 pp.

Iivonen, Jyrki. *A Ruling Non-ruling Communist Party in the West: The Finnish Communist Party.* Paper prepared for ECPR joint sessions of workshops, Freiburg, 21–25 March, 1983. Tampere: Tampereen yliopisto Jaljennepalvelu, 1983. 32 leaves.

Jerome, Jean. *Le Part des hommes: Souvenirs d'un témoin.* Paris: Acropole, 1983. 288 pp.

Kaase, Max, and Hans-Dieter Klingemann, eds. *Wahlen und politisches System.* Opladen, FRG: Westdeutscher Verlag, 1983. 651 pp.

Kellmann, Klaus. *Pluralistischer Kommunismus?* Stuttgart: Klett-Cotta, 1984. 398 pp.

Kol'chil, V. A. *Portugal'skaia Kompartiia v bor'be za demokratiiu i sotsial'nyi progress.* Moscow: Mysl', 1984. 236 pp.

Kolinsky, Eva. *Parties, Opposition and Society in West Germany.* New York: St. Martin's Press, 1984. 357 pp.

Kommunistikon Komme tès Hellados. Congress (11th: 1982, Athens, Greece). *XI s"ezd Kommunisticheskoi partii Gretsii, 12–19 dekabria 1982 goda.* Moscow: Izdatel'stvo politicheskoi literatury, 1983. 139 pp.

Laroque, Michel. *Politiques sociales dans la France contemporaine: Le social face à la crise.* Paris: Editions S.T.H., 1984. 311 pp.

Lee, A. McLung. *Terrorism in Northern Ireland.* Bayside, N.Y.: General Hall, 1983. 235 pp.

Letamendia, Pierre. *Les Partis politiques en Espagne.* Paris: Presses Universitaires de France, 1983. 127 pp.

Lister, Enrique. *Así destruyo Carrillo el PCE.* Barcelona: Planeta, 1983. 277 pp.

Louça, Francisco. *Ensaio para uma revolução 25 de abril: Dez anos de lições.* Lisbon: Edições cadernos marxistas, 1984. 85 pp.

Macridis, Roy C. *Greek Politics at a Crossroads*. Stanford: Hoover Institution Press, 1984. 72 pp.

Massenet, Michel. *La France après la gauche*. Paris: Robert Laffont, 1984. 281 pp.

Meyer zu Natrup, Friedhelm B. *Roter Gaullismus?* Paderborn, FRG: Ferdinand Schöningh, 1983. 389 pp.

Michalet, Charles Albert. *Le Défi du développement*. Paris: Editions Rochevignes, 1983. 188 pp.

Mieli, Renato. *Il PCI allo specchio*. Milan: Rizzoli, 1983. 806 pp.

Milotte, Mike. *Communism in Modern Ireland*. New York: Holmes & Meier, 1984. 326 pp.

Moreton, Edwina, and Gerald Segal, eds. *Soviet Strategy Toward Western Europe*. Winchester, Mass.: Allen & Unwin, 1984. 296 pp.

Morin, Edgar. *Le Rose et le noir*. Paris: Galilée, 1984. 130 pp.

Mortimer, Edward. *The Rise of the French Communist Party*. London: Faber & Faber, 1984. 431 pp.

Muhlen, Patrik v. zur. *Spanien war ihre Hoffnung: Die deutsche Linke im Spanischen Bürgerkrieg, 1936–1939*. Bonn: Verlag Neue Gesellschaft, 1983. 304 pp.

Nikulin, N. M. *Germanskaia Kommunisticheskaia Partiia v bor'be za mir i sotsial'nyi progress*. Moscow: Mysl', 1983. 237 pp.

Österreich und die Sowjetunion, 1918–1955: Historikerprotokoll. Vienna: Österreich-Sowjetische Gesellschaft, 1984. 189 pp.

Pajetta, Giancarlo. *Il ragazzo rosso*. Milan: A Mondadori, 1983. 316 pp.

Papadakis, Elim. *The Green Movement in West Germany*. London: Croom Helm, 1984. 230 pp.

Partito Comunista Italiano. *16. Congresso del Partito Comunista Italiano: Atti, risoluzioni, documenti*. Rome: Editori Riuniti, 1983. 722 pp.

Pike, David Wingate. *Jours de gloire, jour de honte: Le Parti communiste d'Espagne en France depuis son arrivée en jusq'à son départ en 1950*. Paris: Société d'édition d'enseignement supérieur, 1984. 311 pp.

Piro, Franco. *Comunisti al potere: Economia, societá e sistema politico in Emilia-Romagna, 1945–1965*. Venice: Marsilio, 1983. 321 pp.

Rabinbach, Anson. *The Crisis of Austrian Socialism: From Red Vienna to Civil War, 1927–1934*. Chicago: University of Chicago Press, 1983. 296 pp.

The Revolutionary Road to Communism in Britain: Manifesto of the Revolutionary Communist Group. London: Larkin Publications, 1984. 159 pp.

Robrieux, Philippe. *Histoire intérieure du Parti communiste français*. Vol. 4. Paris: Fayard, 1984. 974 pp.

Rousseau, René. *Les Femmes rouges*. Paris: Albin Michel, 1983. 293 pp.

Sacristán, Manuel. *Sobre Marx y marxismo*. Barcelona: Icaria, 1983. 428 pp.

Selle, Per. *Norges Kommunistiske Parti, 1945–50*. Bergen: Universitetsforlaget, 1983. 222 pp.

Sesenta años en la historia del Partido Comunista de España. Madrid: Fundación de Investigaciones Marxistas, 1983. 6 vols.

Smith, Gordon. *Politics in Western Europe: A Comparative Analysis*. 4th ed. New York: Holmes & Meier, 1984. 346 pp.

Speer, Monika. *Petra Kelly: Politikerin aus Betroffenheit*. Munich: Bertelsmann, 1983. 221 pp.

Thellung, Fabrizio. *Antonio Gramsci: La strategia rivoluzionaria nei paesi a capitalismo avanzato*. Geneva: Tilgher, 1983. 143 pp.

Timmermann, Heinz. *Griechenlands "Eurokommunisten": Anmerkungen zum Programm und Profil der Inlands-KP*. Cologne: Bundesinstitut für Ostwissenschaftliche und Internationale Studien, 1984. 22 pp.

Touraine, Alain. *Le Mouvement ouvrier*. Paris: Fayard, 1984. 438 pp.

Ventura, Cândida. *O socialismo que eu vivi: A ruptura dolorosa*. Lisbon: Edições "O Jornal," 1984. 272 pp.

Verdes-Leroux, Jeannine. *Au Service du parti*. Paris: Fayard, 1983. 585 pp.

Villa, Nora. *La Piccola: Grande signora del PCI*. Milan: Rizzoli, 1983. 201 pp.

Whiteley, Paul. *The Labour Party in Crisis*. London: Methuen, 1983. 318 pp.

Zaccaria, Guelfo. *A Mosca senza ritorno: Duecento comunisti italiani fra le vittime dello stalinismo*. Milan: Sugarco, 1983. 135 pp.

Index of Biographies

Alia, Ramiz	Albania	1983, pp. 247–48
Aliev, Geidar A.	USSR	1983, p. 364
Andropov, Yuri V.	USSR	1983, p. 364
Arce Castano, Bayardo	Nicaragua	1985, pp. 114–15
Bakhdash, Khalid	Syria	1984, pp. 68–69
Batmonh, Jambyn	Mongolia	1985, pp. 218–19
Berlinguer, Enrico	Italy	1983, pp. 454–55
Bishop, Maurice	Grenada	1982, p. 106
Borge Martínez, Tomás	Nicaragua	1982, pp. 129–30
Brezhnev, Leonid I.	USSR	1983, pp. 365–66
Çarçani, Adil	Albania	1983, pp. 248–49
Carrillo, Santiago	Spain	1983, p. 474
Cayetano Carpio, Salvador	El Salvador	1983, pp. 89–90
Chandra, Romesh	India	1979, p. 449
Chebrikov, Viktor M.	USSR	1983, p. 366
Chernenko, Konstantin U.	USSR	1979, p. 450; 1985, p. 366
Deng Xiaoping	China–PRC	1983, pp. 168–69
Dolanc, Stane	Yugoslavia	1979, p. 450
Dolgikh, Vladimir I.	USSR	1983, p. 365
Fedorchuk, Vitali V.	USSR	1983, pp. 366–67
Fuwa, Tetsuzo	Japan	1983, pp. 182–83
Gallego, Ignacio	Spain	1985, p. 526
Gorbachev, Mikhail S.	USSR	1980, p. 449
Grabski, Tadeusz	Poland	1983, pp. 318–19
Hall, Gus	USA	1985, p. 133
Handal, Shafik Jorge	El Salvador	1983, p. 90
Heng Samrin	Kampuchea	1980, p. 449
Herrmann, Joachim	GDR	1979, p. 451
Hu Yaobang	China–PRC	1981, pp. 464–65

Iglesias, Gerardo	Spain	1983, p. 475
Jaruzelski, Wojciech	Poland	1982, pp. 449–50
Kania, Stanislaw	Poland	1981, p. 463
Karmal, Babrak	Afghanistan	1980, p. 450
Kaysone Phomvihane	Laos	1985, pp. 209–10
Kim Chong-il	Korea, North	1981, p. 465
Kim Il-song	Korea, North	1983, p. 191
Kiselev, Tikhon Y.	USSR	1981, pp. 463–64
Langer, Felicia	Israel	1984, p. 34
Le Duc Tho	Vietnam	1985, p. 244
Ligachev, Egor K.	USSR	1984, p. 401
Machel, Samora Moisés	Mozambique	1982, p. 42
Marchais, Georges	France	1983, pp. 427–28
Mengistu Haile Mariam	Ethiopia	1982, pp. 17–18
Muhyi al-Din, Khalid	Egypt	1984, pp. 20–21
Núñez Tellez, Carlos	Nicaragua	1985, p. 115
Ortega Saavedra, Daniel	Nicaragua	1982, p. 130
Ortega Saavedra, Humberto	Nicaragua	1982, p. 130
Petkoff, Teodoro	Venezuela	1982, pp. 151–52
Pol Pot	Kampuchea	1979, p. 451
Poungi, Ange Edouard	Congo	1985, pp. 11–12
Romanov, Grigori V.	USSR	1984, p. 401
Santos, José Eduardo dos	Angola	1983, pp. 9–10
Sinuraya, Thomas	Indonesia	1985, pp. 189–90
Sokolov, Serge Leonidovich	USSR	1985, p. 367
Solomentsev, Mikhail S.	USSR	1984, pp. 401–2
Souvanna Phouma	Laos	1985, p. 209
Sychev, Vyacheslav	USSR (CMEA)	1984, p. 416
Tikhonov, Nikolai A.	USSR	1980, pp. 450–51
Truong Chin	Vietnam	1984, pp. 285–86
Villalobos, Joaquín	El Salvador	1985, p. 84
Vorotnikov, Vitali I.	USSR	1984, p. 402
Wheelock Román, Jaime	Nicaragua	1982, pp. 130–31
Zhao Ziyang	China–PRC	1981, p. 464

Index of Names

Aalto, Arvo, 365, 449, 467, 468
Aarotainen, Paivi, 391
Abbud, Ibrahim, 33
Abdallah, Abu, 432
Abdullah, Farooq, 182
Abdullayeh, R. Kh., 18
Abe, Shintaro, 359
Abebe, Alenu, 12
Abi-Ackel, Ibrahim, 52
Abouchar, Jacques, 153
Abrams, Elliot, 326
Abrantes, Domingos, 520
Abrasimov, Piotr A., 355
Abu-Shamas, Mahmud, 418
Acevedo, Óscar, 84
Achenbach, Vera, 475
Aczél, György, 295, 304
Adhikary, Man Mohan, 219, 220, 222
Adhikary, Mohan Chandra, 219, 221
Adiyaa, Gelegiyn, 216
Adjibade, Tiamiou, 9
Adjitorop, Jusuf, 187
Adriaanse, Ries, 511
Afanasyev, Viktor G., 246, 349, 365, 529
Agafonov, A. N., 242
Aganbegyan, Abel, 246
Agca, Mehmet Ali, 270
Agius, Paul, 503, 504
Agolli, Dritero, 252, 256
Aguiñada Carranza, Mario, 82, 84
Ah Leng, 210
Ahmad, Ali, 418
Ahmed, Muzaffar, 158
Ahrens, Dietmar, 482, 483
Aitamurto, Aarno, 467, 468
Aivazov, Todor, 270
Ajajai, Yusuf al-Hassan al-, 403

Akhromeyev, Sergei F., 334, 340
Akl, Joseph Abu, 428
Alaoui, Ismail, 430
Alberici, Aureliana, 498
Alevras, Yiannis, 490
Alexandersson, Skuli, 493
Alexandrov, Chudomir, 263–68 passim
Alfonsín, Raúl, 45, 46
'Ali, Bashir Hadj, 402
Ali, Nasim, 158
Ali, Sardar Shaukat, 226
Alia, Ramiz, 250–58 passim, 262, 263
Aliev, Geidar A., 333, 337, 341, 344, 345, 359, 360, 435
Alladaye, Michel, 8
Allende, Salvador, 59, 60
Alliluyeva, Svetlana, 246, 353
Almeida, Roberto António de, 4, 6
Almeida Bosque, Juan, 72
Almeidau, Freddy, 79
Almeyda, Clodomiro, 59
Almeyda, Manuel, 59
Alocer Villanueva, Jorge, 106
Altamirano, Carlos, 60
Altamirano, Eli, 111
Altangerel, Bat-Ochirym, 216
Althusser, Louis, 31
Altunin, Y. N., 363
Alushani, Ajli, 261
Alva, César, 120
Alvarez Fiallo, Efraín, 79
Amado Peña, Luis, 113
Amarales, Andrés, 66
Amatya, Tulsi Lal, 219, 220
Amazonas, João, 263
Ambartsumov, Evgeni, 246
Ambatielos, Andonis, 487
Amelin, Isnelle, 24

Amin, Hafizullah, 144
Amir, Izz-al Din Ali, 32
An Sung-hak, 197, 199
Andersen, G. H. "Bill," 222, 223
Andersen, Jan, 462
Anderson, I., 529
Andrade, Joaquim dos Santos, 53
Andrade, Joaquim Pinto de, 5, 54
Andrade, Mario de, 4
Andrei, Stefan, 318, 321, 325–32 passim
Andreotti, Giulio, 316, 354
Andres Pérez, Carlos, 42
Andrianarivo, R. T., 361
Andropov, Yuri V., 72, 114, 133, 138, 160, 175, 191, 193, 196, 202, 209, 218, 228, 235, 243–50 passim, 270, 287, 290, 293, 330, 335–42 passim, 345–51 passim, 355, 356, 357, 366, 395, 435, 461, 474, 507, 534
Angelov, Ivan, 270
Angenfort, Jupp, 475
Angius, Gavino, 496, 498
Anozie, Chaika, 21
Ansart, Gustave, 469
Antonescu, Ion, 329
Antonov, Sergei Ivanov, 270, 273, 274
Anwar, Rosihan, 190
Aquino, Benigno, Jr., 230, 231, 232
Arafat, Yassir, 173, 202, 328, 360, 390, 401, 408, 416, 417, 420, 421, 436
Araújo, Jorge, 520
Araújo, Luísa, 520
Arauz, Virgilio, 118
Arbatov, Georgi, 480
Arbenz, Jacobo, 89

Arce Castano, Bayardo, 111, 114–15, 501
Ardito Barletta, Nicolás, 115–19 passim
Arenas, Jacobo, 63
Arévalo, Óscar, 45
Arias Londoño, Gustavo, 66
Arias Madrid, Arnulfo, 115, 116, 117
Arismendi, Rodney, 135, 136
Arkhipov, Ivan V., 175, 176, 177, 247, 334, 350, 357, 358, 364
Armacost, Michael, 292
Arnalds, Ragnar, 491
Arnot, Page, 485
Arns, Paulo Evaristo, 54
Arrizola, José, 61, 65
Arroyo, Arístides, 78
Arteaga, Miguel, 391
Arthit Kamlang-ek, 236
Ary Yee Chong Tchi-Kan, 22, 24
Arze, Amadeo, 49
Asad, A. al-, 390
Asad, Hafiz al-, 360, 401, 413, 435, 436
Asad, Rif'at al-, 360, 435
Asfaw, Legesse, 12
Ashhab, Na'im Abbas-al, 418–22 passim
Ashton, Jack, 484
Aslam, C. R., 226
Assogba, Affo Frederic, 8
Atanasov, Georgi, 263, 264
Aubuisson, Roberto d', 42
Augustine, Fennis, 85
Aukhadiev, Kenes, 342
Aurich, Eberhard, 285
Aust, Ernst, 481
Avakian, Bob, 134
Avnery, Uri, 416
Awdah, Dhamin, 418
Axen, Hermann, 285, 287, 373, 417, 513
Ayala, Jaime, 126
Ayele, Embibel, 12
Azcárate, Manuel, 524
Aziz, Mohammed, 145
Aziz, Tafeq, 413
Azonhiho, Martin Dohou, 8

Babikar, Ali al-Tijani al-Tayyib, 32

Bachmann, Kurt, 475
Bai Jinian, 170
Baibakov, Nikolai K., 330, 334, 343
Bains, Hardial, 55
Bakalli, Mahmut, 369
Bakhdash, Khalid, 401, 433–36 passim
Bakker, Marcus, 510, 511, 512
Bakri, Ibrahim, 433, 434
Bakti, Razik, 227
Balabani, Simon, 255
Balaguer, Joaquín, 78
Balasingham, A. S., 234
Baldacchino, Anthony, 503
Baldrige, Malcolm, 177
Balev, Milko, 263, 266, 468
Balhaajab, Tserenpilyn, 216
Ballesteros, Jaime, 525
Baluku, Beqir, 255
Banc, Iosif, 318, 321
Bandaranaike, Sirimavo, 234
Bangash, Afzal, 226
Bangou, Henri, 88
Banias, Yiannis, 490
Barabas, Miklós, 390
Barabash, Yuri, 417
Barbara, Agatha, 507
Barcikowski, Kazimierz, 305
Barghuti, Bashir, 418, 419
Bariamikael, Assefau, 14
Barkauskas, Antanas, S., 361
Barnes, Jack, 134
Barnett, A. Doak, 173
Barr, Andrew, 495
Barrantes Lingán, Alfonso, 120, 121, 127
Barrera, César, 122
Barria, Ricardo, 118
Bartoshevich, G. G., 364
Baryalai, Mahmoud, 143, 144
Basir, Isahak, 96
Bassiuoni, Salah, 360
Basu, Jyoti, 184, 186
Batalla, Hugo, 136
Bateman Cayón, Jaime, 66
Batmonh, Jambyn, 176, 216–19 passim
Baude, Frank, 529
Bauer, Tamás, 299
Bayih, Berhanu, 12
Baylosis, Rafael, 228, 229
Beauvois, Pierre, 454

Bechetti, Arnold, 131
Begin, Menachim, 416
Beijer, Lennart, 527
Bejger, Stanislaw, 305
Bekteshi, Besnik, 251
Belaúnde Terry, Fernando, 121–26 passim
Belete, Shewandagn, 12
Belgrave, Cyril, 96
Belonogov, Aleksandr, 360
Belov, Yuri, 338
Belovski, Dimče, 367–70 passim
Ben Bella, Mohamed, 430
Benda, Václav, 281
Benjedid, Chadli, 361, 402, 403
Benke, Valéria, 295
Beno, Mikuláš, 275
Bentoumi, Amar, 391
Berecz, János, 299, 302
Berend, Iván T., 299
Berg, Max van den, 274
Berghuis, Jan, 513
Beria, Lavrenty, 337
Berlinguer, Enrico, 193, 333, 366, 443, 446, 474, 497–501 passim
Bermudez, Julio, 116
Bernales, Enrique, 121, 122
Bernov, Y. V., 175
Bertone, Flavio, 498
Bertrand, Mireille, 469
Betancur, Belisario, 62–68 passim, 84
Betancur, Modesto, 90
Betancur, Alvarez, Diego, 66
Bezymenski, Lev, 293
Bhagwan, Moses, 96
Bhagwandaas, Paul, 129
Bhashani, Maulana, 158
Bhattarai, K. P., 221
Bhutto, Begum Nusrat, 224
Bhutto, Benazir, 224, 225
Biesboer, Frank, 509
Bil'ák, Vasil, 275, 281, 438, 489
Bilić, Jure, 367
Birendra (king), 220, 222
Bîrlea, Ştefan, 318
Birri, Nabih, 427
Bisdorff, Aloyse, 502
Bishop, Alimenta, 86
Bishop, Maurice, 85, 86, 89, 98, 103
Bismarck, Otto von, 289

Biton, Charlie, 416, 418
Bizenjo, Ghaus Bux, 226
Bjornsdottir, Margret, 490
Blanco, Jorge, 77, 78
Bo Yibo, 165
Bobovikov, Ratmir, 388–89
Bobrzik, Irmgard, 475
Bobu, Emil, 318, 330
Boer, Anne de, 513
Boevereen, Etienne, 129
Bogolyubov, Klavdii M., 334
Bogomolov, Oleg T., 376, 379
Bokamba-Yangguma, Jean-
  Michel, 10
Boksteen, Lothar, 129
Bolanos Sánchez, Bolívar, 79
Bolding, Fenna, 509
Bolton, George, 484, 486
Bondarenko, Ivan, 338
Bonde, Jens Peter, 465
Bonev, Stanish, 263, 264
Bongou, Camille, 10
Bonifert, Ádám, 297
Bonin, Khristo, 265
Bonino, Carlos, 120
Bonner, Elena, 346, 347, 500,
  513
Bonnici, Carmelo Mifsud, 507
Bonnici, Karmenu Mifsud, 508
Bordiga, Amedeo, 497
Borge Martínez, Tomás, 111–14
  passim
Borglund, Arvid, 514
Borisov, Grigori, 279
Borja, Rodrigo, 80
Borodkina, Bella, 345
Bosch, Juan, 78
Bosma, Onno, 512, 513
Botha, Pieter, 31, 521
Botorog, Mihai, 391
Bou Thang, 194
Boumediene, Houari, 402
Bourguiba, Habib, 437
Bourquia, Abdeslem, 430
Bouterse, Desi, 129, 130
Bovin, Aleksandr, 351
Bowden, Maggie, 484
Bozhinov, Todor, 263, 266
Brahimi, Abdelhamid, 403
Brandt, Willy, 114, 273, 476, 500
Breitman, George, 133
Brezhnev, Leonid, 245, 247, 262,

270, 335, 340, 345, 346, 347,
  366, 476
Briones, Alejandro, 229
Briones, Carlos, 60
Brito, Carlos, 520
Brizola, Leonel, 53
Broekema, Nico, 510, 512
Brouwer, Ina, 509, 513
Brutents, Karen, 360, 364, 427,
  428, 434–37 passim
Brzezinski, Zbigniew, 203, 247,
  387
Buda, Aleks, 259
Bufalini, Paolo, 496, 498
Bui Quang Tao, 241
Bui Thanh Khiet, 241
Bukhali, Larbi, 402
Bunyen Worthong, 237–38
Burbano Burbano, Ghandi, 79
Burnett, John, 354
Burnham, Forbes, 96, 98
Burnstein, David, 414
Burrows, Vini, 132
Burt, Richard, 292, 302
Buschmann, Martha, 475
Bush, George, 351, 369, 397
Butenko, Anatoli, 246, 348

Cabaço José Luís, 16
Caballero Mendez, Asunción,
  120
Cabral, Raimundo, 520
Cachia, Joseph, 503
Cafe, Maria Mambo, 4
Caicedo, Jaime, 61, 64
Calderón, Cecilia, 80
Calero, Adolfo, 43, 113
Calvo, Óscar William, 65, 66
Camacho, Marcelino, 523, 524,
  525
Camacho, Aguilera, Julio, 72
Camara, Sadio, 25
Camejo, Peter, 133, 134
Çami, Foto, 251–58 passim
Campa Salazar, Valentín, 106
Campbell, Ronald, 352
Cano, Alfonso, 63
Cantelli, Paola, 498
Capegsan, Ignacio, 229
Capria, Nicola, 261
Caraballo, Francisco, 65

Carazo, Rodrígo, 69
Çarçani, Adil, 250–56 passim,
  260
Cardenal Martínez, Ernesto, 111,
  114
Cardenal Martínez, Fernando,
  111, 113
Cardenas, Raymundo, 108
Cardoza Aguilar, José, 93
Carías Andino, Tiburcio, 100
Carreira, Henrique Teles, 5
Carrillo, Santiago, 447, 523, 524
Carrión, Carlos, 111
Carrión Cruz, Luís, 111, 114
Carter, James E., 116, 117
Carter, Pete, 484
Carvajal, Carlos, 49
Carvalho, Otelo Saraiva de, 522
Casanova, José, 520
Cassar, Anton, 504, 406
Casteneda, Eduardo Sancho, see
  Cienfuegos, Fermán
Castillo, Adolfo, 83
Castillo, Alfredo, 79
Castillo, Fabio, 82
Castro, António, 93
Castro Ruz, Fidel, 31, 41, 70–75
  passim, 86, 103, 104, 129,
  138, 218, 332, 374
Castro Ruz, Raúl, 72
Cayetano Carpio, Salvador, 82
Cazacu, Virgil, 318, 321
Ceauşescu, Elena, 249, 318–23
  passim, 328, 331
Ceauşescu, Ilie, 320, 329
Ceauşescu, Marin, 328
Ceauşescu, Nicolae, 249, 271,
  294, 303, 318–33 passim,
  363, 374, 385, 417
Ceauşescu, Nicu, 3, 249, 318,
  320
Céleste, Christian, 88
Çeliku, Hajredin, 250, 258, 259
Cepeda, Manuel, 61, 64
Çerava, Vangjel, 251–54 passim
Cervetti, Gianni, 500
Césaire, Aimé, 105
Chacón, Lenin, 69
Chacón, Miller, 61
Chae Hui-chong, 197, 199
Chakarov, Toncho, 266
Chakravarty, Nripen, 185

Chamorro, Pedro Joaquín, 42, 43
Chan Phin, 194
Chan Si, 194, 196, 272, 364
Chand, Lokendra Bahadur, 220, 222
Chandarpal, Indra, 96
Chandarpal, Navin, 96
Chandra, Romesh, 181
Chang Chun, 210, 211
Chang Marin, Carlos, 115, 116, 117
Chapman, Frank, 132
Chatcharin Chaiwat, 236
Chater, Tony, 485
Chavez, Fidelio, 120
Chawalit Yongchaiyut, 236
Chea Sim, 194
Chea Soth, 194
Chebrikov, Viktor M., 333, 334, 337
Checa, Víctor, 120
Chen Muhua, 165, 173
Chen Pixian, 165
Chen Yun, 165
Cherkov, Nikolai, 501
Chernenko, Konstantin U., 13, 14, 72, 175, 176, 193, 203, 209, 218, 245, 246, 247, 262, 270, 293, 302, 303, 314, 316, 330–66 passim, 372, 374, 389, 394, 396, 417, 421, 435, 441, 474, 489, 497, 508, 525
Chernyayev, Anatoli, 365, 502–3
Chervernkov, Vulko, 264
Chervonenko, Stepan V., 366, 501
Cheysson, Claude, 273
Chi Chang-ik, 199
Chiarante, Giuseppe, 497, 501
Chiaromonte, Gerardo, 496
Chiesa, Giulietto, 152, 500
Chin Peng, 210, 211, 212
Chinamano, Josiah, 39
Chin-a-sen, Henk, 130
Chipande, Alberto, 16
Chipenda, Daniel, 5, 6
Chirac, Jacques, 472, 473
Chirskov, Vladimir, 341
Chissano, Joaquim Alberto, 16, 75
Chňoupek, Bohuslav, 283
Cho Se-ung, 197, 199
Choe Il-pong, 199

Choe Kwang, 197, 199
Choe Pong-man, 199
Choe Yong-nim, 197, 199
Chon Chin-su, 199
Chon Ho-kyun, 199
Chon Mun-sop, 197, 199
Chon Pyong-ho, 197
Chong Chun-ki, 197, 199
Chong Kyong-hui, 197
Chouaib, Mohamed Rifi, 430
Chu Chang-chun, 199
Chu Huy Man, 238
Chun Doo-Hwan, 192, 201, 206
Chundramun, Leetoraj, 3
Churbanova, Galina, 345
Chuthai Saengthawip, 236
Cid, Carlos del, 116, 117
Cienfuegos, Fermán, 82, 84
Cienfuegos Gorrián, Osmany, 72
Cieslak, Werner, 475
Ciobanu, Lina, 318, 320, 321
Cissoko, Seydou, 25
Čkrebić, Dušan, 367
Claesson, Viola, 527
Clancy, Pat, 142, 156
Claret Serra, Andreu, 523
Coard, Bernard, 103
Cohen, William S., 349
Collado, Fausto, 78
Collymore, Clinton, 96
Colotka, Petr, 275, 282
Colpin, Jean, 469
Coman, Ion, 318, 507
Combo-Matsiona, Bernard, 10
Concepción, Elson, 391
Constantin, Leonard, 318
Constantin, Nicolae, 318, 321
Contreras, Lourdes, 78
Conyers, John, 86
Cordera Campos, Rolando, 106, 109
Córdova Rivas, Rafael, 111
Cordovez, Diego, 152, 206
Coronas, José María, 523
Correa, Hercules, 51, 53
Correia, Edgar, 520
Cortázar, Julio, 114
Corvalán, Luís, 59, 60
Cossutta, Armando, 501
Costa, Carlos, 520
Couteau, Marcel, 454
Craig, Cheryl Allen, 132
Crain, Irving, 132

Craxi, Bettino, 261, 292, 302, 499
Criales de la Rosa, Humberto, 64
Cristescu, Poliana, 320
Crockett, George, 132
Crone, Stuart, 134
Cruz, Arturo, 42, 43, 113
Cruz, Viriato da, 4
Cserveny, Vilmos, 390
Csikós-Nagy, Béla, 299
Cuadra Chamorro, Joaquín, 111
Cuevas, Raúl, 78
Çuko, Lenka, 251
Ćulafić, Dobroslav, 367, 368
Cunhal, Álvaro, 274, 333, 447, 520, 521, 522
Curiel Alonso, Enrique, 523
Curticeanu, Silviu, 318, 320
Czechowicz, Tadeusz, 305
Czyrek, Jozef, 305, 363

Dabrowski, Bronislaw, 310
Dadoo, Yusef, 27, 28, 30, 31
Dahl, Rolf, 514
Dalton García, Roque, 84
Damdin, Paavangiyn, 216
Dammen, René, 510, 511
Dammert, Manuel, 121
Dan Hong, see Dang Van Dinh
Danesh, Mohammed Ismail, 143
Danfaka, Mady, 25
Dang Van Dinh, 242
Daniels, George, 97
Daninthe, Guy, 87, 88, 89
Dansoko, Amath, 25
Daoud, Mohammed, 144
Darag, Sudi, 32
Darío Paredes, Rubén, 118
Darío Sousa, Rubén, 115
Darwish, Yusuf, 404, 405
Dăscălescu, Constantin, 318, 326, 328, 332
Dash, M., 216
Dauto, Ossumane Ali, 17
David, Gheorghe, 318, 321
Davis, Angela, 44, 131, 132
Davis, Tricia, 484
Debarge, Marcel, 205
Debray, Regis, 114
Debrouwere, Jan, 274, 454
Degiovanni, Victor, 503
Dejid, Bujyn, 216

De León Escobar, Rosalio, 91
De León Espinoza, César
  Agusto, 115, 116
Dellums, Ronald, 86, 132
Delmotte, Filip, 454
del Valle Jiménez, Sergio 72
Demeke, Tesfaye, 14
Demichev, Piotr N., 333
Demirel, Suleyman, 533
Demszky, Gábor, 301
Deng Liqun, 165, 167
Deng Xiaoping, 141, 165–71
  passim, 174, 204, 490
Deng Yingchao, 165, 166, 167
Denktash, Rauf, 460
Dennis, Gene, 133
Desie, Wubeset, 12
Desta, Fisseha, 12, 14
Deumlich, Gerd, 475
De Vera, Benjamin, 229
Dias, Giocondo, 51
Díaz, Carmelo, 94
Díaz Rangel, Eleazar, 139
Díez Canseco, Javier, 121, 126
Dimitrov, Stanko, 265
Dinca, Ion, 318, 325, 332
Diouf, Abdou, 25
Dishoni, Sharif, 32
Dixon, Felix, 115
Dixon, Graciela J., 119
Dizdarević, Raif, 368
Djilas, Milovan, 371
Djuranović, Veselin, 368
Do Muoi, 239, 240
Doan Trong Truyen, 241
Dobrescu, Miu, 318, 320, 321,
  333
Dobrynin, Anatoli, 352, 362
Doder, Dusko, 246, 353
Doering, Uwe, 482
Dogan, Hosnu, 261
Dohlus, Horst, 285, 454
Dolanc, Stane, 368
Dolgikh, Vladimir I., 333, 334,
  337, 354
Dolinski, Helga, 482
Domic, Marco, 49, 50
Dong Sy Nguyen, 239
Douglas, Ken, 223
Douieb, Abdelmajid, 430
Doynov, Ognyan, 263, 266
Dragosavac, Dušan, 367, 371
Dragoycheva, Tsola, 264

Driel, Rinus van, 511
Duarte, Efraín, 100
Duarte, José Napoleón, 41, 42,
  82, 84, 521
Duarte, Ozeas, 54
Dubček, Alexander, 276
Dufeal, Philibert, 105
Duić, Dane, 367
Duném, Afonso van, 4
Dunn, Bill, 484
Dupuy, Ben, 99
Duray, Miklós, 282, 304
Dussart, Robert, 454
Duvalier, François, 99, 100
Duvalier, Jean-Claude, 99
Dyulgerov, Petur, 263, 264, 269
Dzerzhinsky, Felix, 154
Dzhagarov, Georgi, 269
Dzhemilyev, Mustafa, 347
Dzhurov, Dobri, 263, 272
Dzúr, Martin, 279, 385

Eanes, António Ramalho, 521
Efros, Anatoli, 349
Eisenburger, Eduard, 318
Elezi, Mehmet, 251, 256
El Fassi, Omar, 430
Elisario, Paulo, 51
Emanuel, Poul, 365, 462, 463,
  465
Emmanuel, Dany, 105
Enache, Marin, 318
Enache, Petru, 318, 321
Engstrom, Bror, 521
Enrile, Juan Ponce, 320
Erlich, Wolf, 414, 417
Ershad, Hussain Mohammed,
  158, 159, 160
Escalona, Julio, 137
Escoricio, Herminio, 5
Escoto Brockman, Miguel d',
  111, 112, 114
Espinoza Montesinos, Gustavo,
  120
Espriella, Ricardo de la, 115, 117
Evans, Richard, 169
Evren, Kenan, 533, 534

Fabius, Laurent, 88, 105, 446,
  471
Fadeyev, Y., 359

Falin, Valentin, 396
Faluvégi, Lajos, 299, 303, 325
Fandis, Andreas, 458
Fang Yi, 165
Farakos, Grigoris, 487, 488
Farhad, Muhammed, 157, 158,
  160
Faría, Jesús, 137, 138
Farkha, Ramu, 433
Farrakhan, Louis, 132
Fatogun, Dapo, 21
Fauntroy, Walter, 132
Fava, Athos, 45, 46, 47
Fayad, Alvaro, 66
Faysal, Yusuf, 433, 434, 435
Fazekas, Ludovic, 318
Febres Cordero, León, 79, 80,
  81, 362
Fedorchuk, Vitali V., 334
Fedoseyev, Piotr, 364
Fejti, György, 299
Felfe, Werner, 285, 486
Félix, Jaime, 520
Fendt, Detlef, 482
Ferge, Zsuzsa, 298
Fernández, Freddy, 391
Fernández Vargas, Leopoldo, 391
Ferraro, Geraldine, 132
Ferreira Aldunate, Wilson, 135,
  136
Ferreto Segura, Arnaldo, 68, 69,
  70
Feske, Klaus, 482
Figueiredo, João Baptista, 51,
  173
Figueroa, Jaime, 120
Filho, David Capistrano, 52
Filipov, Grisha, 11, 263, 271,
  272, 273
Filipov, Mikhail, 506
Finogenov, Pavel V., 334
Firmenich, Mario, 47, 48
Fischer, Oskar, 292, 293, 513
Fiszbin, Henri, 471
Fiterman, Charles, 469, 471, 472
Fitte-Duval, Solange, 106
Fjeld, Age, 517
Flichtbeil, Harry, 482
Florakis, Kharilaos, 274, 304,
  461, 474–75, 487–90 passim
Flores, Aldo, 49
Florijančič, Jože, 368
Fojtík, Jan, 275

Fokin, Yuri Y., 362
Fomin, Sergei, 391
Fonseca, María, 196
Forero, Teofilo, 61
Foster, Joe, 31
Frati, Regis, 51, 52
Frederick the Great, 289
Freire, Roberto, 51, 62
Fresno, Juan Francisco, 61
Frimannsdottir, Margret, 490, 491
Fritsch, Kurt, 475
Frutos, Francisco, 523
Fuentes, Antonio, 93
Fuentes, Olac, 108
Fuhr, Gijs von der, 512
Fulgsang, Villy, 462
Furre, Berge, 518
Fuwa, Tetsuzo, 190, 193

Gabdulin, Mikhail, 25
Gäbler, Bernd, 475, 477
Gäbler, Klaus, 532
Gâdea, Suzana, 318
Gado, Guiriguissou, 9
Gäinuşe, Alexandrina, 318
Galbraith, Evan, 88, 473
Gallagher, Norm, 157
Gallardo Meltiz, Gilberto Rincon, 106
Gallego, Ignacio, 366, 447, 525, 526
Gallegos Mancera, Eduardo, 137, 138
Gamarra, Isidoro, 120
Gandhi, Indira, 133, 138, 142, 152, 160, 179–86 passim, 209, 272, 353, 358, 398, 473
Gandhi, Rajiv, 179–85 passim, 272, 357, 358
Ganga-Zandzou, Jean, 10
Ganguli, Dev Kumar, 390
Gannon, Craig, 134
Garang, John, 34
Garang, Joseph, 34, 35
Garaycoa Ortíz, Xavier, 79
Garbuzov, Vasili F., 334
García, Alán, 126
García, Edgardo, 111
García, Julio, 91
García Frías, Guillermo, 72
García Ponce, Guillermo, 140

García Solis, Ivan, 106
Garg, G. K., 181
Garzón, Angelino, 61, 65
Gascon Mercado, Alejandro, 109
Gáspár, Sándor, 295, 297, 390
Gautier, Hermann, 475, 476
Gaye, Bouma, 25
Gayssot, Jean-Claude, 469
Gaži, Pavle, 368
Geelen, John, 509, 511
Geng Biao, 169
Genoino, José, 54
Genscher, Hans-Dietrich, 283, 302, 316, 351, 354, 356
Georgiev, Georgi, 265
Gerada, Karmenu, 503, 504
Gere, Mihai, 318
Gerhardt, Andre, 391
Gerns, Willi, 475
Gerö, Ernö, 296
Gerson, Si, 131
Gertel, Noé, 53
Gervásio, António, 520
Gestsson, Svavar, 490–94 passim
Gharti, Mohan Bikram, 219, 220, 221
Gheorghiu-Dej, Gheorghe, 319
Ghiţulică, Maria, 318, 321
Gierek, Edward, 307, 311
Gill, Ken, 448
Giosan, Nicolae, 318, 325
Giscard d'Estaing, Valéry, 354, 472
Gjegprifti, Llambi, 251
Gjerløv, Mette, 462
Gjizari, Niko, 252
Glackin, Eddie, 495
Glemp, Jozef, 309, 310
Glezon, Manolis, 263
Glowczyk, Jan, 305
Godager, Ornulf, 514
Godinez, Eliseo, 83
Godoy Rivas, Virgilio, 114
Goma, Louis Sylvain, 10
Gombojab, Damdiny, 216
Gomes, Joaquim, 520
Gómez Alvarez, Pablo, 106–10 passim
Goncharov, Georgi, 391
Gondikas, Dimitris, 487
Gonen, Benjamin, 414
Gonzáles, Óscar, 390
González, Andrea, 129, 134

González, Carlos, 89, 93, 94
González, Felipe, 524, 525
González, Leonel, 81
González, Macario, 139
González Moscoso, Hugo, 49
González Ramírez, Eduardo, 106
González Regus, Miguel, 390
González Urdaneta, Adelso, 140
Gonzalo Torres, Pedro, 93
Goodby, James, 386
Goodluck, Wahab, 21
Gorbachev, Mikhail S., 245–48 passim, 262, 266, 271, 273, 302, 303, 333–38 passim, 341–44 passim, 348, 355, 363, 365, 366, 446, 480, 486, 497
Gorbacheva, Raisa, 355
Gorywoda, Manfred, 305
Gotob, D., 216
Gotsev, Boris, 380
Gouk, Arkady V., 354
Graber, Michael, 451, 452
Gramsci, Antonio, 497
Granowski, Margot, 482
Gratz, Leopold, 317, 453
Grebe López, Horst, 49
Grebenyuk, Vasili, 342
Gremetz, Maxime, 469, 473, 474
Gribkov, Anatoli I., 279, 383
Grigorov, Georgi, 265
Grimsson, Olafur, 494
Grinevsky, Oleg, 386
Grishin, Viktor V., 217, 218, 245, 274, 333, 336, 337, 363
Grličkov, Kiro, 370
Gromyko, Andrei A., 14, 175, 176, 218, 274, 302, 329, 330, 333–37 passim, 350–54 passim, 359–64 passim, 394–97 passim, 409, 416, 508
Grosso, Carlos, 47
Grossu, Semyon, 340, 342
Groza, Petru, 319
Grünberg, Heinz, 482
Grzyb, Zofia, 305
Gu Mu, 165
Guaraca, Jaime, 63
Guardado y Guardado, Facundo, 84
Gudmundsdottir, Soffia, 490
Gudmundsson, Helgi, 490, 491
Gudmundsson, Olafur, 490

Guebuza, Armando Emilio, 2, 16, 17, 18
Gueye, Semou Pathe, 25
Guissani, Pablo, 48
Gulabzoy, Sayed Mohammed, 147
Gumede, Archie, 391
Gupta, Indrajit, 186
Gurbadam, T., 216
Gustavsen, Finn, 518
Gustov, Ivan S., 364
Gutiérrez, Bernardo, 65
Gutiérrez, Rodrigo, 69
Gutmann, Francis, 205
Guttormsson, Hjorleifur, 491, 493
Guzmán Reyenoso, Abimael, 123
Gylfasson, Vilmundur, 492

Haakmat, Andre, 130
Habash, George, 428
Häber, Herbert, 282, 292, 294, 355, 475, 501
Habibi, Emile, 414, 417
Habr, George, 428
Hadjeres, Sadiq, 402
Hadži-Vasilev, Kiro, 367
Haeninen, Olavi, 467
Hagel, Rolf, 365, 529
Hager, Franz, 451
Hager, Kurt, 285, 287
Haider, Iqbal, 225
Haiducu, Matei, 327
Hájek, Jiří, 282
Hajji, Salah al-, 437
Hajn, Jaroslav, 275
Halberg, Arvo, 133
Hall, Gus, 44, 130–33 passim
Hallgrimsson, Geir, 493, 494
Halpin, Kevin, 484
Halverson, Ron, 484, 485
Halyard, Helen, 135
Haman, Josef, 275
Hamid, Salim, 432
Hamid, Sulayman, 32
Hammami, Khalid, 433, 435, 436
Hammar, Bo, 527
Hammerstad, L., 514
Hamrush, Ahmad, 390
Han Guang, 165
Han Tianshi, 165
Handal, Shafik Jorge, 82, 84

Hansen, H. P., 514
Hansen, Margit, 462
Hansen, Preben Moeller, 466
Hao Jianxiu, 165
Harbu, Kolbjorn, 517
Hardardottir, Vilborg, 490, 491
Harmel, Muhammad, 437, 438
Harms, Ronald, 352
Harn Linanond, 237
Harriot, Anthony, 103
Hart Dávalos, Armando, 72
Hartmann, Arthur A., 361
Hasani, Sinan, 368
Hassan (king), 400
Havasi, Ferenc, 295, 299
Havel, Václav, 282
Havlín, Josef, 275, 363
Hawi, George, 274, 425–29 passim, 435
Hawke, Bob, 156, 157, 173
Haya de la Torre, Agustín, 122
Hayden, Bill, 114
Hazbiu, Kadri, 253, 255
Hazboun, George, 419
He Jingzhi, 369
Healey, Dennis, 355
Hegedüs, András, 301
Heiser, Klaus-Dieter, 482
Heller, Luis, 45
Helm, Siem van der, 509
Helmes, Jesse, 274
Heng Samrin, 193, 194, 196, 238
Herljević, Franjo, 367
Hermannsson, Steingrimur, 450, 491, 492
Hermansson, Carl, 528
Hermier, Guy, 469
Hernández, Melba, 388
Hernández, Pablo, 93
Hernández Colón, Rafael, 128
Hernández Tellez, Sabino, 106
Herrera, Guillermo, 120
Herrera, Letitia, 111
Herrmann, Joachim, 285
Herzog, Chaim, 415
Herzog, Philippe, 469
Hess, Hans Rudolf, 532
Hewett, Edward, 379
Hill, Edward Fowler, 155
Hill Arboleda, Nathaniel, 117
Ho Chi Minh, 142, 196, 209, 238, 244
Ho Chong-suk, 197

Ho Tam, 197, 198, 205
Hoang Tung, 239, 243
Hoarau, Elie, 22, 24
Hoarau, Mário, 23, 24
Hoarau, Roger, 22, 24
Hoek, Ton van, 509, 513
Hoekstra, Henk, 511
Hofer, Anton, 451
Hoffman, Karel, 275, 282
Hoffman, François, 502
Hoffmann, Heinz, 285, 287, 293
Hoikka, Anneli, 468–69
Holmes, Larry, 135
Homoştean, George, 332
Honecker, Erich, 13, 18, 47, 84, 249, 250, 273, 285–94 passim, 303, 316, 327, 331, 340, 355, 356, 363, 386, 461, 474
Hong Song-nam, 197
Hong Song-yong, 197, 199
Hoogkamp, Karel, 509
Hoření, Zdeněk, 275, 276
Horgen, Trygve, 514, 516, 517
Horn, Gyula, 428
Houg, Tora, 518
Hoxha, Enver, 196, 248, 250–63 passim, 372
Hoxha, Nexhmije, 254
Hrušković, Miloslav, 275
Hu Jingtao, 165, 172
Hu Qiaomu, 165
Hu Qili, 165
Hu Yaobang, 165, 173, 175, 177, 203, 204, 332, 369
Huamán Centero, Adrián, 125
Huang Chen, 211
Huang Hua, 169
Huang Kecheng, 165
Hubacher, Helmut, 532
Hübsch, Fernand, 502
Huerta, Francisco, 80
Hun Sen, 7, 194, 196
Hurtado, Hernando, 61, 64
Hurtado, Jaime, 80
Hurtado, Jorge, 121
Hurtado, Osvaldo, 80, 81
Husák, Gústav, 248, 275, 276, 279, 284, 363
Husayn, Nuri Abd-al-Razzaq, 390
Husayn, Saddam, 361
Hussein (king), 401, 423
Huynh Tan Phat, 239

Hwang Chang-yop, 197
Hyon Mu-kwang, 197

Ibárruri, Dolores, 332, 523
Ibéné, Hégésippe, 87
Ibrahim, Fatima, 36
Ibrahim, Muhsin, 425–29 passim
Ibrahimi, Ahmed Taleb, 403
Ieng Sary, 194, 295
Iglesias, Gerardo, 332, 447, 474,
    523–26 passim
Illueca, Jorge, 115
Ilón, Gaspar, 90
Ilyichev, Leonid F., 175, 176,
    357, 361
Imashev, Sattar N., 341
Indra, Alois, 275
Indregard, Sturla, 514
Ingvardsson, Margo, 526
Inonu, Erdal, 533
Inozemstev, Nikolai, 377
Irrizarry, Franklin, 128
Isa Conde, Narciso, 77, 78
Isai, Hekuran, 251, 254
Iscaro, Rubens, 45
Ishibashi, Masashi, 205, 206
Ismail, Abd al-Fattah, 439
Ivanov, Khristofor, 265
Izeboud, Elli, 365, 509, 510, 513

Jackson, George, 222
Jackson, James, 131
Jackson, Jesse, 44, 84, 86, 114,
    132, 134, 135
Jackson, Maurice, 131
Jacobs, Roel, 454
Jacques, Martin, 484
Jagan, Cheddi, 44, 96, 97, 98
Jagan, Janet, 96
Jagbaral, Nyamin, 216
Jakab, Sándor, 297
Jakeš, Miloš, 275
Jakhar, Balram, 358
Jamil, M. A., 158
Jamsjanjab, A., 216
Jan, Baba, 145
Jansen, Ineke, 511
Jaramillo Flores, Roberto, 107,
    108
Jaroszewicz, Piotr, 307

Jarowinsky, Werner, 282, 286,
    363
Jaruzelski, Wojciech, 249, 274,
    284, 295, 304–17 passim,
    331, 363
Jasray, P., 216
Jayewardene, J. R., 234, 235
Jensen, Jørgen, 462–65 passim
Jeune, Bernard, 462
Ji Pengfei, 173
Jijon Saavedra, Milton, 79
Jiménez, Lucio, 111
Jinnah, Mohammad Ali, 225
Johansen, Knut, 514
John Paul II (pope), 43, 201,
    264, 270, 274, 282, 307, 497
Joly, Ulrick, 99
Jorge, Paulo Teixeira, 3, 5, 7,
    328
Jorgensen, Anker, 465
Jorgensen, Arne, 514, 517, 518
Josephsson, Ludvik, 490
Jospin, Lionel, 473
Jotti, Nilde, 501
Juan Carlos (king), 354
June, Volker, 482
Juquin, Pierre, 469, 471

Kabir, Mohammed, 145
Kabrhelová, Marie, 275
Kádár, János, 14, 249, 277, 294–
    97 passim, 302, 303, 304,
    325, 327, 428, 472, 486, 489,
    497, 529
Kadungura, Ernest, 37
Kahane, Meir, 415
Kaiser, Robert, 245
Kajonoja, Juoko, 449, 467, 468,
    469
Kalashnikov, Vladimir, 338
Kalb, Marvin, 396
Káldy, Zoltán, 301
Kalkus, Stanislaw, 305
Kaloudhis, Nikos, 487, 488, 489
Kalt, Hans, 451, 454
Kamil, Michel, 404, 405, 407
Kamil, Najib, 404
Kamilarov, Emil, 269
Kamppainen, Arvo, 467
Kaneko, Mitsuhiro, 364
Kang Hui-won, 197

Kang Keqing, 165
Kang Song-san, 173, 197–200
    passim, 204
Kang Sun-hui, 199
Kanstrup, Gunnar, 462
Kapek, Antonín, 275
Kapitonov, Ivan V., 334
Kapitsa, Mikhail S., 176, 198,
    203, 204
Kaplani, Muhamed, 260
Kapo, Hysni, 259
Kapo, Vito, 259
Kápolyi, László, 297
Karamanev, Georgi, 266
Karamanlis, Constantin, 328
Karami, Rashid, 428
Karamukov, Dimitur, 269
Karausinov, Rusi, 270
Kardelj, Edvard, 370
Karger, Franz, 452
Karim, Ahmad, 402, 413
Karingal, Thomas, 230
Karlin, Daniel, 471
Karlov, Vladimir A., 334
Karmal, Babrak, 143–50 passim,
    155, 364, 462
Karmal, Mahbuda, 154
Károlyi, Mihály, 296
Karran, Ram, 96
Karwal, Mir Saheb, 143
Kasem Saengmit, 237
Kashtan, William, 55, 56
Katali, François Xavier, 10
Katsouridhis, G., 458
Kaunda, Kenneth, 361
Kauppila, Erkki, 467
Kawayana, Eusi, 96
Kaysone Phomvihane, 176, 207–
    10 passim, 359, 364
Kelly, Guillermo Patricio, 48
Kelly, Petra, 292
Kempný, Josef, 275
Kena, Jacob M., 15
Kennedy, Edward, 113
Kerekou, Mathieu, 2, 8, 9
Keshtmand, Sultan Ali, 143
Keuneman, Pieter, 233, 234
Khabbad, Muhammad, 433
Khadafy, Moammar, 35, 272,
    283, 372, 431
Khalikov, Kurban A., 362
Khamis, Saliba, 414
Khamtai Siphandon, 207

Khan, Fatehyab Ali, 226
Khan, Mahbub Ali, 160
Khan, Manzuru Hasan, 158
Khan, Meraj Mohammad, 226
Khang Sarin, 194, 196
Kharkabi, Zahi, 414
Khatib, Izhaq al-, 424
Khavari, Ali, 408, 410
Khenin, David, 414, 418
Khieu Samphan, 195
Khin Maung Gyi, 161, 162
Khomeini, Ruhollah, 399, 409, 410
Khristodoulidhis, G., 458
Khristou, Kiriakos, 458
Khristov, Emil, 263, 264, 267
Khrushchev, Nikita, 474
Khuri, Issa, 433
Khyari, Thami, 430
Kianuri, Nureddin, 408, 409
Kidan, Tesfaye Gebre, 12, 361
Kim Chae-yol, 199
Kim Chang-su, 199
Kim Chol-myong, 199
Kim Chong-chun, 202
Kim Chong-il, 197, 198, 203, 320, 332
Kim Chung-nin, 197, 199
Kim Hwan, 197
Kim I-hun, 198, 199
Kim Il, 198, 199
Kim Il-song, 142, 173, 197–206 passim, 272, 295, 304, 320, 332, 358, 364, 465
Kim Ki-hwan, 201
Kim Kwan, 199
Kim Kwang-chin, 203
Kim Kwang-hak, 199
Kim Kwang-hwan, 197
Kim Man-kum, 199
Kim Pok-sin, 197, 199
Kim Pong-chu, 199
Kim Song-ku, 199
Kim Tu-nam, 197
Kim Won-chon, 199
Kim Yong-nam, 197, 198, 199, 203, 206
Kim Yong-sun, 197, 199
Kinnock, Neil, 355
Kirchschläger, Rudolf, 282
Kissinger, Henry, 83
Kississou-Boma, Jean Royal, 11
Kiszczak, Czeslaw, 305, 310

Kivisto, Kalevi, 467
Klauson, Valter, 341
Kleiber, Günther, 285, 286, 293
Klemencic, Vlado, 368
Kleven, Hans I., 274, 514–518 passim
Klift, Wil van der, 511
Knutsen, Martin Gunnar, 514, 517
Ko Tae-un, 199
Kobayashi, Eizo, 191
Koçallari, Sotir, 251, 256
Koch, Horst-Dieter, 481
Kochemasov, Vyacheslav, 355
Kohl, Helmut, 170, 286, 290–93 passim, 302, 316, 327, 353, 356, 385
Kolle Cueto, Jorge, 49, 50
Kolozov, Orestis, 487
Kong Chin-tae, 197, 199
Konotop, Vasili I., 365, 513
Konovalov, Nikolai, 339
Konrád, György, 301
Konstantinou, Dinos, 458
Köpeczi, Béla, 302
Kopp, Inge, 482, 483
Korbeci, Shane, 261
Korcák, Josef, 275
Korendyasov, Ye. N., 25
Koritzinsky, Theo, 514, 515, 518
Korom, Mihály, 295, 304
Kosev, Kiril, 266, 267
Kosolapov, Richard I., 348
Kostandov, Leonid, 246, 341
Kosygin, Aleksei, 175–76
Kotsev, Venelin, 265
Kourkoulou, Roula, 487
Kovalenko, Ivan, 364
Kozmin, Sergei, 428
Kraja, Osman, 253
Krakhmanov, 146
Krassó, György, 301, 302
Krasucki, Henri, 469, 471
Krenz, Egon, 249, 285, 287, 294, 476, 482
Kristensen, Fredrik, 514
Kristensen, Kurt, 462
Kristofinis, Dhonis, 458
Krivoruchko, L. L., 339
Krogstad, John Atle, 517
Krolikowski, Werner, 285
Kroos, Achim, 477
Kropáč, Zdeněk, 282

Kruchina, Nikolai, E., 334, 338, 339
Krunić, Boško, 369
Kubadinski, Pencho, 263, 270, 461
Kubiak, Hieronim, 305
Kučan, Milan, 367
Kuhle, Jörg, 482
Kulikov, V., 384
Kulikov, Viktor G., 271, 274, 279, 348, 385
Kun, Béla, 296
Kunaev, Dinmukhamed A., 333, 336, 359
Kunalan, Srinivasan, 390
Kurteši, Ilijaz, 367
Kurzendorfer, Herwig, 482
Kutlu, Haydar (Nabi Yagci), 533
Kuznetsov, Vasili V., 333, 358, 360, 490
Kvist, Kenneth, 527
Kya Mya, 161
Kye Ung-tae, 197
Kyin Maung, 161
Kyprianou, Spyros, 448–61 passim
Kyrkos, Leonidas, 488

Laaksonen, Timo, 467
Lagadinova, Elena, 264
Lairet, Germán, 139
Lajoinie, André, 469, 471
Lal, Pushpa, 219, 220
Lallemand, Daniel, 22, 24
Lama, Luciano, 497, 498
Lama, Nirmal, 219, 220, 221
Lambsdorff, Otto, 290
Lange, David, 224
Lange, Ingeborg, 285
Langenier, Lucet, 24
Langsether, Asmund, 514, 517
Langton, Philippa, 484, 486
Laptev, Ivan, 341
Lara, Lucio, 4
Lara Bonilla, Rodrigo, 64
Larrazábal, Radamés, 137, 138
Larrea, Fernando, 80
Larsen, Reidar, 515
Laurent, Paul, 469
Lauret, Angelo, 24
Lava, Jesus, 229
Lava, Jose, 229

Lawrence, Chris, 102
Layachi, Abdallah, 430
Laye, Mohamed, 25
Lázár, György, 274, 295, 298
Lazard, Francette, 469
Le Duan, 176, 238, 239, 242, 244
Le Duc Anh, 239
Le Duc Binh, 243
Le Duc Tho, 238, 239, 244
Le Quang Dao, 239
Lechin Oquendo, Juan, 50
Ledda, Romano, 497
Ledesma, Genero, 121
Le Guen, René, 469
Lehmann, Heinz, 513
Lekaj, Veli, 255
Lenárt, Jozef, 275
Lenin, V. I., 1, 31, 54, 73, 168, 171, 212, 214, 215, 217, 245, 247, 348, 394, 527
Leosdottir, Bjarnfridur, 490
Le Pors, Anicet, 471
Leroy, Roland, 469, 471
Lert Chaichamorn, 236
Levchenko, Stanislav, 392
Lévy, Simon, 430
Li Chang, 165
Li Desheng, 165
Li Jong-gun, 390
Li Weihan, 165
Li Xiannian, 165, 173, 220, 228, 332, 507
Liao Hanxing, 127
Ligachev, Egor K., 334, 342
Lilov, Alexander, 264
Lis, Ladislav, 281
Lister, Enrique, 525
Litomiský, Jan, 281
Liu Fuzhi, 332
Ljubičić, Nikola, 368, 372
Lobo, José Carlos, 17
Lobos Zamora, Roberto, 91
Logara, Loula, 487
Logunov, Anatoli, 342
Loistl, Gustav, 451
Longo, Luigi, 446, 497, 498
Loose, Ludo, 454
Lopata, P., 340
Lopes, António, 520
López, Fausto, 78
López, Fernando, 100
López, Raúl, 100

López, Rigoberto, 93
Lora, Silvano, 78
Lora Escobar, Guillermo, 49
Losonczi, Pál, 295
Louis, Victor, 346
Louison, Einstein, 85
Louison, George, 85
Lourenço, Dias, 520
Lovell, Frank, 133
Lubbers, Ruud, 512
Lublitz, Ruth, 414
Lubsangombo, Sonomyn, 216
Lubsantseren, B., 216, 217
Lucas García, Romeo, 94
Luers, W. H., 282
Luis, Emmy, 511
Lukanov, Andrey, 263, 490
Lundstrup, Dan, 462
Lunkov, Nikolai, 501
Luong Van Nho, 242
Lushnichenko, Nikolai, 384
Lusinchi, Jaime, 138
Lustosa, Iris, 53
Luther, Martin, 289
Lyakhov, I. A., 339
Lyubimov, Yuri, 349

Ma Guorui, 165
Mabhida, Marcos, 274
Mabhida, Moses, 26, 27, 28, 31
Mabote, Sebastião Moses, 16, 18
Mabrink, Bertil, 527
Macaluso, Emanuele, 497
Macapagal, Felicismo C., 228, 229
Machado Ventura, José Ramón, 72
Machel, Samora Moisés, 2, 11, 13, 16–19 passim, 173, 272
Machungo, Mario de Graça, 16
MacKay, Ian, 484
Madjar, Ljubomir, 370
Madrid (Madrigal?) Jiménez, Óscar, 68
Madsen, Freddy, 462
Madsen, Jørgen, 462
Magallona, Merlin, 229
Magnin, Armand, 365, 530
Mahjub, Abd al-Khaliq, 33, 34
Mahle, Hans, 482
Mahmud, Sultan, 160
Maichantan Sengmani, 207

Maidana, Antonio, 119, 120
Mainale, Radha Krishna, 219, 221
Mainali, Prakash Chandra, 221
Makhele, Vincent M., 15
Maleshova, Zejfula, 251
Malile, Reiz, 262
Malina, Salomão, 51, 52
Malki, 'Ali, 402
Malkin, Anatoli, 339
Malmierca Peoli, Isidor, 11
Mamatsis, Takis, 487
Mamula, Branko, 368
Manandhar, Bishnu Bahadur, 219, 220, 222
Manayenkov, Y. A., 339
Mane, Bajram, 255
Mănescu, Manea, 318, 320, 321, 325, 327
Manik, Saifuddin Ahmed, 158
Manley, Michael, 102, 104
Mansur, Muhammad Ibrahim Nugud, 32
Mao Mao, 169
Mao Zedong, 212, 214, 215, 220, 259, 262
Marchais, Georges, 294, 333, 446, 469–74 passim, 490, 500
Marchenko, Valeri, 347
Marchuk, Guri I., 334, 343, 362, 364
Marcos, Ferdinand, 229–32 passim
Marcy, Sam, 135
Mariategui, Sandro, 127
Mari Bras, Juan, 129
Marimoutou, Léandre, 105
Marinc, Andrej, 367, 372
Marino Ospina, Ivan, 66, 67
Marjai, József, 304
Marklund, Eivor, 527
Marko, Rita, 251, 254, 257
Markov, Georgi, 341
Marković, Dragoslav, 173, 367, 370, 372, 474
Markovski, Krste, 367
Maróthy, László, 295
Márquez, Pompeyo, 138, 139
Márquez Pérez, Lizardo, 140
Marri, Khair Bux, 226
Martella, Ilario, 270
Martens, Wilfried, 455, 456
Martín, Américo, 139, 140

Martínez, Ana Guadalupe, 82, 84
Martínez, Odalis, 78
Martínez, Pedro, 93
Martínez Verdugo, Arnaldo, 106, 107
Marulanda Vélez, Manuel, 63
Marx, Karl, 1, 117, 171, 212, 214, 215, 527
Maslennikov, Nikola, 342
Masol, Vitali, 343
Mason, Mel, 134
Massoud, Ahmad Shah, 147
Mataji, R., 15
Matamoros, Marta, 117
Matić, Petar, 367, 468
Matsinhe, Mariano de Araújo, 16, 17, 18
Mauge Mosquera, René, 79, 80, 81
Mauroy, Pierre, 353–54, 446, 470, 473
Maydar, Damdinjabyn, 216
Mayer, Josef, 475
Mazdak, Farid, 144
Mazengia, Shimelis, 12
Mazumdar, Charu, 159
Mazur, Jan, 310
Mazza, Ugo, 498
Mazzarella, Graziano, 498
Mbasogo, Teodoro Obiang Nguema, 173
Mbaye, Makhtar, 25
McGahey, Mick, 448, 485, 486
McLennan, Gordon, 484, 486
Mechini, Rodolfo, 390
Medunov, Sergei F., 345, 346
Medvedev, Vadim A., 339
Meerten, Laurens, 510, 511
Méhes, Lajos, 295, 297, 390
Mehr, Bram, 129
Meis, Fré, 511
Mejía Víctores, Óscar, 90–95 passim
Melo, Teodoro, 51, 53
Men Samon, 196
Mendis, M. G., 232
Mendoza, Elias, 126
Mengal, Ataullah, 226
Mengistu Haile Mariam, 1, 12, 13, 14, 75, 272, 362, 364, 395
Merenishchev, Mikolai, 340
Merino, José, 69

Messner, Zbigniew, 305, 377
Mesyats, Valentin K., 334
Meyers, George, 131
Miah, Malik, 134
Mi'ari, Muhammad, 416
Michael, Amanuel Amde, 12
Michaelides, Georgisos, 390
Michai Nakunkit, 237
Michalek, Zbigniew, 305
Mickiewicz, Adam, 315
Mielke, Erich, 285, 287
Mies, Herbert, 475–80 passim
Mifsud, Mario, 503, 504
Mihalache, Nicolae, 318, 321
Mihali, Qirjako, 251, 252
Mikhailidhis, A., 458
Mikhailidhis, Khambis, 458
Mikhailov, Stoyan, 263, 265
Miklós, Imre, 300
Mikulić, Branko, 368
Milatović, Veljko, 367
Milewski, Miroslaw, 305
Milez, Paul, 263
Milford (lord), 448, 484
Mindszenty, József, 296
Mino, Rapo, 257
Mintoff, Dom 507, 508
Minucci, Adalberto, 496
Miranda, Diniz, 520
Miret Prieto, Pedro, 72
Mireya Cárdenas, Rosa, 81
Mirić, Jovan, 370
Mironov, Vladimir, 342
Miroshkin, Oleg S., 361
Mishev, Misho, 265
Mishin, Viktor M., 334, 339, 349
Mishka, Pali, 251
Mitchell, Charlene, 131
Mitea, Constantin, 325
Mitran, Ion, 318
Mittag, Günter, 285, 287, 474
Mitterrand, François, 2, 105, 273, 302, 327, 354, 369, 443, 445, 446, 470–73 passim
Miyamoto, Kenji, 190, 191, 193
Mladenov, Petur, 263, 265, 271, 273
Moes, André, 502
Moga, Ioachim, 318
Mohamed, Feroze, 96
Mohammed, Nazar, 145
Mohmand, Niaz Mohammed, 143

Moi, Daniel arap, 13
Moins, Jacques, 454
Mojsov, Lazar, 368, 369, 372
Mokrzyszczak, Wlodzimierz, 305
Molczyk, Eugeniusz, 383
Moleiro, Moisés, 139
Molomjamts, Demchigiyn, 216
Molotov, Vyacheslav, 246, 339
Mondale, Walter, 132, 352
Mondlane, Eduardo, 16, 18
Monge, Luis Alberto, 71
Monsanto, Pablo, 90
Montané Oropesa, Jesús, 72
Monteiro, José Óscar, 16, 17
Monterey, Glenda, 111
Monterrosa, Domingo, 83
Montes Aliaga, Ernesto, 124
Montes Manzano, Eduardo, 106
Montoro, Franco, 54
Mora Valverde, Eduardo, 68, 69, 70
Mora Valverde, Manuel, 44, 68, 69, 70
Moraes, Sergio, 51
Morán, Rolando, 94
Moreau, Gisèle, 469
Mortensen, Magne, 517
Mortimer, James, 274
Morvan, Claude, 89
Mosley, Ian, 153
Mosotho, Jacob, 15
Mosquera, Alvaro, 61
Mosquera, Francisco, 66
Motley, Langhorne, 112
Motloheloa, John, 15
Moucharik, Mohamed, 430
Mounthault, Hilaire, 10
Moura, V., 361
Moutoussamy, Ernest, 88, 89
Mozvogoi, Ivan, 342
Mrozinski, Margot, 482
Mubarak, Hamad, 432
Mubarak, Mohammed Husni, 406, 408
Mückenberger, Erich, 285
Mudhawi, Aziz Ahmad, 403
Mugabe, Robert, 1, 13, 37–40 passim
Muhammad, Abdallah, 432
Muhammad, Abu al-Qasim (Gassim), 32
Muhammad, Aziz, 412
Muhammad, Hashim, 417

Muhammad, Jasim, 403
Muhammad, Salih Hasan, 196
Muhammad al-Hasani, Ali Nasir, 13, 272, 361, 400, 429, 438–41 *passim*
Muhri, Franz, 274, 451–54 *passim*
Muhyi al-Din, Khalid, 400, 406
Mujahid, Farid, 404
Mujica, Héctor, 137
Mukherjee, Samar, 185
Muldoon, Robert, 223
Müller, Margarete, 285
Mulroney, Brian, 56
Munangagwa, Emmerson, 37
Mundey, Judy, 155
Mungoša, Dušan, 251
Muñoz, Freddy, 138–39
Munroe, Trevor, 102, 103, 104
Mura, Prokop, 254, 255
Murad, Yusuf, 433
Murawah, Karim, 428
Murdani, Benny, 187, 188, 189
Mureşan, Ana, 318
Musa, Ahmad, 432
Musa, Jamal, 414
Musavi, Mir Hossein, 410
Musawi, Baqir Ibrahim, 412
Muscat, Joseph V., 504
Mussi, Fabio, 498
Mustafa, 'Abd al-Hamid ben, 437
Mutasa, Didymus, 37
Muttetuwegama, Sarath, 233
Mutumbuka, Dzingai, 37
Muzenda, Simon, 37
Muzorewa, Abel, 40
Myant, Chris, 484
Myerson, Michael, 132
Myftiu, Manush, 251, 254, 256, 259, 261, 262
Myo Myint, 161
Mysnichenko, Vladislav P., 365

Naarendorp, Edward, 129
Naarendorp, Harvey, 129
Nadra, Fernando, 45
Nae, Elena, 318
Nafa'a, Muhammad al-, 437, 438
Nagamootoo, Moses, 96
Nagels, Jacques, 454
Nagin, Rick, 131
Nagy, Imre, 296, 301

Najibullah (Dr.), 143
Najjab, Sulayman al-, 418, 420, 421
Nakasone, Yasuhiro, 173, 192, 204, 205, 359
Nam Sang-nak, 199
Nam Trung, *see* Nguyen Dang
Namboodiripad, E. M. S., 179, 184
Namsray, Tserendashiyn, 216, 217
Napolitano, Giorgio, 497, 500
Napuri, Ricardo, 122
Narangerel, T., 216, 217
Nashshab, Sulayman al-, 418
Nasir, Azaz, 226
Nasir, Khadir, 32
Nassar, Fu'ad, 423
Natta, Alessandro, 496–501 *passim*
Naumann, Konrad, 285, 287
Naustvik, Bjorn, 514, 517
Navarro, Antonio, 66
Nazarbaev, Nursultan, 341
Nazish, Ali, 224
Ndalo, Franca, 5
Ndhlovu, Moven, 39
Ndinga-Oba, Antoine, 10
Ndlovu, Callistus, 39
Ndongu, Seydou, 25
Nedelcu, Marin, 318
Negard, Ingrid, 514, 517
Németh, Károly, 295, 297, 300
Neto, Agostinho, 4, 5
Neto, José Paulo, 51
Neumann, Alfred, 285
Neves, Almir, 51
Neves, Tancredo, 53
Ngollo, Raymond Damasse, 10
Ngouabi, Marien, 10, 11
Nguyen Co Thach, 239, 243
Nguyen Dang, 242
Nguyen Duc Khanh, 242
Nguyen Duc Tam, 209, 239
Nguyen Huu Thu, 241
Nguyen Lam, 239, 240
Nguyen Thanh Binh, 239
Nguyen Tri Muu, *see* Kaysone Phoumvihane
Nguyen Van Ki, 390
Nguyen Van Trong, 243
Nhongo, Rex, 37
Nhongo, Teurai Ropa, 37

Ni Zhifu, 165, 186
Nicolas, Armand, 104, 105
Nicolescu, Paul, 318
Nie Rongzhen, 165
Nielsen, Anette, 462
Nieto, Luis, 122
Nikaido, Susumu, 191
Nikolov, Alexander, 266
Nikolov, Petur, 265
Nikolsky, Boris, 339
Nilsen, Kare Andre, 514, 517
Ni'mah, Daniel, 433
Niño, Avelino, 66
Nixon, Richard, 132
Nkala, Enos, 37
Nkomo, Joshua, 37, 39
Nokta, Harry Persaud, 96
Nolan, Sean, 495
Nordman, Joe, 391
Norlund, Ib, 462, 465
Nosaka, Sanzo, 190
Nouhak Phoumsavan, 207
Nowak, Mieczyslaw, 310
Nujoma, Sam, 13, 369
Numeiri, Jaafar, 3, 14, 33–36 *passim*
Núñez Téllez, Carlos, 111, 114, 115
Nuon Chea, 194
Nur Ahmad Nur, 143, 145
Nuri, Baha al-Din, 412
Nuriev, Ziya N., 334, 364
Nyagumbo, Maurice, 37
Nyers, Rezsö, 380
Nyheim, Einar, 518
Nze, Pierre, 10

O Chin-u, 197
O Kuk-yol, 197, 202
O Paek-yong, 199
Obando y Bravo, Miguel, 42, 113
Obregón Cano, Ricardo, 47
Occhetto, Achille, 499
Oduho, Joseph, 34
Ogarkov, Nikolai V., 246, 337, 340, 350, 352, 382
Ojeda, Hugo, 45
Olszowski, Stefan, 114, 153, 305, 315, 317
Olteanu, Constantin, 318
Omawale, Walter, 96

Onambwe, Henrique de Carvalho Santos, 4, 6
Onorre Jarpa, Sergio, 61
Opalko, Stanislaw, 305
Opango, Yhombi, 10, 11
Oprea, Gheorghe, 318
Oqueli, Hector, 82, 84
Orcinha, António, 520
O'Riordan, Michael, 495
Orlov, Yuri, 347
Oropesa, Jesús, 126
Ortega Diaz, Pedro, 138
Ortega Saavedra, Daniel, 42, 111–14 passim, 293, 317, 332, 362, 363, 364
Ortega Saavedra, Humberto, 11, 114, 202, 362
Orzechowski, Marian, 305
Osman, Abdul Magid, 17
Osmanczyk, Edmund, 316
Osorio, Gustavo, 61
Osorio, Roso, 61
Ossetoumba, Lekounzou, 10
Osterwalder, Fritz, 531
Osunde, Lasisi A., 21
Óvári, Miklós, 295, 303, 304, 468
Ozaki, Susumu, 388
Ozal, Turgut, 533, 534

Pabón, Rosemberg, 66
Pacepa, Ion, 327
Pacho, Valentín, 120, 123, 127
Pacoste, Cornel, 318
Padilla, Hernán, 128
Padilla Rush, Rigoberto, 100, 101
Paek Hak-im, 197
Pagmadula, L., 216
Pajetta, Giancarlo, 496
Pak Nam-ki, 197, 199
Pak Song-chol, 197, 198, 202
Pak Su-dong, 199
Pak Sung-il, 199
Palejo, Rasool Bux, 226
Palero, Francisco, 523
Palin, Velko, 265
Pallayev, Gaibnazar, 362
Palme, Olof, 114, 292, 528, 529
Panã, Gheorghe, 318
Panguene, Armando, 16
Pani, Mario, 498

Panjsheri, Ghulam Dastigir, 143
Papaioannu, Ezekias, 274, 458, 460, 461
Papandreou, Andreas, 258, 260, 271, 283, 292, 317, 488, 489, 490, 501
Papazov, Nacho, 266
Papazov, Tencho, 264
Papoulias, Karolos, 260, 263
Pascual Moncayo, Pablo, 106
Pashov, Trifon, 25
Pasos Marcial, José, 501
Passeri, Marianne, 502
Pasternak, Boris, 280
Pastor Pérez, Juan, 65
Pastora, Edén, 43, 71, 112
Paţan, Ion, 318, 321
Pato, Octávio, 520
Paulo, Julião Mateus, 4
Pavlov, Grigori, 339
Payet, Bruny, 22, 24
Paz Galarraga, Jesús Angel, 140
Pe Tint, 161, 162
Pecchioli, Ugo, 496
Peçi, Shefqet, 251, 254, 255
Peck, John, 484
Peled, Mattityahu, 416
Pellicani, Gianni, 498
Pelshe, Arvid I., 345
Pen Sovan, 194
Peña Gómez, José Francisco, 77
Peng Zhen, 165, 167
Penner, Steve, 58
Percovich, Luis, 122
Percy, Jim, 155
Peres, Aurélio, 54
Pereyra, Jorge, 45
Pérez, Camilio O., 117
Pérez, Julián, 94, 95
Pérez, Lino, 138
Pérez de Cuellar, Javier, 152, 207, 460, 489
Pérez Marte, Nelson, 78
Pérez Marcano, Héctor, 139
Peristeri, Pilo, 251, 255
Perón, Juan D., 45
Persaud, Narbada, 96
Persaud, Reepu Daman, 96
Persaud, Rohit, 96
Petas, Khristos, 458
Petersen, Gert, 465
Petkoff, Teodoro, 138, 139
Petkov, Alexander, 268

Pettersson, Roland, 529
Peza, Muslim, 254
Pham Hung, 238, 239, 244
Pham Van Dong, 176, 238, 239, 242, 244
Phan Dinh Khai, 244
Phoumi Vongvichit, 207
Phoun Sipaseut, 207
Pierre, Alfredo, 78
Pimental, Rafael, 78
Pinheiro, Ivan, 51
Pinochet, Augusto, 59, 60, 61
Pinto, Artur Vidal, 520
Piot, Hippolite, 22, 24
Piquet, René, 469
Pirun Chatwanichkul, 142, 236, 237
Pirun Chontira, 236
Pitra, František, 275
Pitra, Santana André, 4
Pittman, John, 131
Pizarro, Carlos, 66
Pla, Juan Francisco, 523
Planinc, Milka, 271, 368, 369, 372
Pliaka, Sokrat, 259, 261, 262
Plissonier, Gaston, 469, 471
Pocock, Gerry, 484, 486
Podolsky, Otto, 451, 452
Pol Pot, 193, 194, 516
Poledník, Jindřich, 275
Polikeit, Georg, 475
Pölöskei, Ferenc, 300
Ponama, Jean-Baptiste, 22
Ponomarev, Boris N., 329, 331, 334, 342, 362, 363, 364, 389, 392, 402, 427, 438, 480, 486, 503, 513
Ponomarev, Mikhail, 338, 339
Poperen, Claude, 469
Popescu, Dumitru, 318, 329
Popieluszko, Jerzy, 249, 284, 301, 304, 310
Popit, Frane, 369
Popović, Miladin, 251
Porcella Peña, Miguel Antonio, 115
Porebski, Tadeusz, 305
Portabeela Esquefa, Elisenda, 101
Posadas Segura, Marcos Leonel, 106
Postelnicu, Tudor, 318

Poulantzes, Nicos, 31
Poumbouris, Mikhail, 458
Poungui, Ange Edouard, 10, 11–12
Pozderac, Hamdija, 367
Pradhan, Sahana, 219, 220, 221
Prado, Jorge del, 120–27 *passim*
Prasit, Mod Nath, 221
Preecha Piempongsarn, 236
Prem Tinsulanond, 236
Prestes, Luiz Carlos, 52
Prichkapov, Lazar, 265
Priemer, Rolf, 475
Priscott, Dave, 484
Prokopec, Jaroslav, 277
Protozanov, Aleksandr, 339
Przemyk, Grzegorz, 311
Ptitsyn, Vladimir, 516
Puar, Yusuf Abdullah, 189
Pugo, Boris, 339
Pulgar, Juvencio, 139
Pulvar, Marc, 105
Purdeli, Abdus Sattar, 144
Purvanov, Anastas, 265
Putz, Marcel, 502
Pyon Sung-tok, 205

Qader, Abdul, 143, 145, 146
Qadir, Muhammad Abd al-, 34
Qasim, Salih Muslih, 361, 439, 441
Qian Qichen, 175, 176, 357
Qiao Shi, 165
Qin Jiwei, 165

Rab, A. S. M. Abdur, 158
Račan, Ivica, 369
Radix, Kenrick, 85, 86
Radović, Miljan, 367
Radović, Radomir, 371
Radow, Brigit, 475, 477
Radu, Constantin, 318, 320
Radu, Ion, 318, 320
Rădulescu, Gheorghe, 318, 325
Rafi, Mohammed, 143
Rafsanjani, Hashemi, 409
Ragchaa, Tumenbayaryn, 216
Rahman, Sheikj Mujibur, 160
Rajk, László (father), 296, 297, 298
Rajk, László (son), 301

Rákosi, Mátyás, 296, 298, 300
Rama Rao, N. T., 182, 183, 184
Ramdhanny, Lynden, 85
Ramildes, Carlos, 520
Ramili, Bu Jama'a, 438
Ramin, Julien, 22, 24
Ramírez, Andrea, 91
Ramírez Mercado, Sergio, 111, 113, 114
Ramos, Jorge Abelardo, 47
Rao, C. Rajeswara, 179, 181, 183, 274
Rao, Hanumantha, 186
Raoul, Alfred, 10
Rashid, Abdallah 'Ali al-, 403
Rashid, Harun-ur, 158
Ratebzad, Anahita, 143
Rawwaq, Mahmud al-, 418
Rayamajhi, Keshar Jung, 219, 220, 221, 222
Razmjo, Abdul Zaher, 143
Razumovsky, Georgi, 342
Razzak, Abdur, 158
Reagan, Ronald, 31, 41, 50, 53, 57, 65, 72, 76, 98, 110, 114–18 *passim*, 129–33 *passim*, 138, 173, 177, 191, 206, 222, 247, 279, 292, 331, 335, 350–53 *passim*, 357, 372, 394–99 *passim*, 411, 420, 431, 444, 453, 460, 461, 477, 524
Rebelo, Jorge, 16, 19
Redmond, Tom, 495
Regan, Donald, 177
Rehman, Matiur, 158
Reichlin, Alfredo, 496
Reiman, Max, 476
Reiter, Karl, 451, 454
Renan Esquivel, José, 119
Renard, Claude, 454, 455, 456
Rene, Albert F., 3
Rexha, Lumturi, 251
Reyes, Raúl, 63
Reyes, Rodrigo, 113
Reyes, Simón, 49
Reyes Matos, José María, 101
Rezende, Jo, 53
Ribeiro, Bento, 5, 6
Ribičič, Mitja, 367, 369
Riddell, John, 55
Rigoberto Arce, Santos, 101
Rigout, Marcel, 471
Rikhardsdottir, Olof, 490

Ríos, Daniel, 93
Ríos, Pedro Antonio, 523
Ríos Montt, Efraín, 92, 94
Risquet Valdés, Jorge, 72
Rivera, Brooklyn, 43, 113
Rivera, Juanito, 228, 229
Rivera y Damas, Arturo, 42, 84
Rizo Alvarez, Julián, 72
Robelo, Alfonso, 43, 112
Robert, Roland, 24
Roberto, Holden, 3, 5
Roca Calderío, Blas, 72
Rodríguez, Anastacio E., 115
Rodríguez, Carlos Rafael, 72, 274, 374
Rodríguez, Dimas, 81, 83
Rodríguez, Enrique, 136
Rodríguez, Felipe, 50
Rodríguez, Irene, 45
Rodríguez, Simón, 138
Rodríguez, Ruiz, José Napoleón, 82
Rogers, Bernard, 397
Rohlíček, Rudolf, 283, 284
Rojas, Don, 86
Rojas, Ernesto, 65, 66
Rojas, Roberto, 120
Roldos, Jaime, 80
Romanik, Jerzy, 305
Romanin, Dimitri, 339
Romanov, Grigori V., 12, 245, 246, 247, 303, 333–40 *passim*, 362–65 *passim*, 396, 470
Romero, Carlos, 61
Romero Barceló, Carlos, 128
Romero Marín, Francisco, 523
Rono, Hyder Akbar Khan, 158
Roopnarine, Rupert, 96
Rosario, Domingo, 78
Rosenthal, Joseph, 404
Rosschau, Bo, 462
Rosschau, Carl, 391
Rothstein, Andrew, 485
Roumain, Jacques, 99
Roux, Jacques, 473
Roy, Ajoy, 158
Rubbi, Antonio, 501
Rubenis, Vitalijs, 342
Ruckert, Babette, 502
Rudini (general), 188
Ruiz Hernández, Henry, 111, 112, 114, 362
Rulewski, Jan, 312

Ruminatsev, A. M., 392
Rusakov, Konstantin V., 330, 334, 357, 363, 364
Rusev, Petko, 265
Rushaydat, Nabih, 433
Ryabov, Yakov P., 334, 341, 360, 362
Ryzhkov, Nikolai I., 334, 365, 377, 452, 454

Saarinen, Aarne, 365, 449, 467
Sacco, Remig, 506
Sadat, Anwar al-, 405, 406, 407
Sadeqi, Mohammed Yaseen, 143
Sadowska, Barbara, 311
Sadr, Mohammad, 409
Sa'id, Rif'at al-, 406
Sakarev, Ivan, 266
Sakharov, Andrei, 134, 346, 347, 354, 447, 500, 513
Sakik, Hisham, 437
Salam, Abdur, 158
Salas, Rodolfo, 228, 229
Salce, Luis, 78
Salfiti, Fahmi, 423
Salgado Tamayo, Manuel, 80
Sali Vongkhamsao, 207
Salibi, Maurice, 433
Salih, Abd-al-Rahman, 432
Salih, Ali Abdullah, 361
Salim, Ahmad, 32
Salim, Elie, 428
Salim al-Sabah, Salim Sabah al-, 361
Samad, Nadim Abd al-, 427
Samayoa, Salvador, 82, 84
Sammad, Zuhayr Abd al-, 433
Samon Vi-gnaket, 207
San Cheng Ming, 210, 211
San Sen, 210, 211
Sanan Soutthichak, 208
Sánchez, Luis, 111
Sánchez, Mario, 93
Sánchez, Otto, 93, 94
Sánchez, Montero, Simón, 523
Sánchez Rebolledo, Adolfo, 106
Sandev, Vladimir, 265
Sandri, Renato, 498
Sanguinetti, Julia María, 136
Sankara, Thomas, 4
Sankatshing, Glenn, 129
Santana, Daniel, 78

Santos, Armando Khembo Gumbe dos, 18
Santos, José Eduardo dos, 2–7 passim, 13, 75, 328
Santos, Marcelino dos, 16
Sardesai, S. G., 182, 183
Sarlis, Dimitris, 487
Sarlós, István, 295
Sartorius, Nicolás, 523
Sassou-Ngouesso, Denis, 1, 10, 11
Saul, Boris, 341
Savimbi, Jonas, 3, 5, 6
Savinkin, Nikolai I., 334
Savola, Helvi, 131
Sawet Piempongsarn, 236
Say Phuthang, 194
Sayed, G. M., 226
Schabowski, Günter, 285, 286, 293, 421, 435, 496
Schaff, Adam, 249, 305, 306, 307
Scharf, Erwin, 451, 454
Schembri, Michael, 503
Schifter, Richard, 453
Schjerning, Anker, 465
Schlüter, Poul, 462
Schmidt, Helmut, 286
Schmitt, Horst, 365, 482, 483
Schneidermann, Dina, 269
Schouten, Nico, 512
Schröder, Karl-Heinz, 475
Schürer, Gerhard, 285
Schwager, Irma, 451
Schwander, Martin, 531
Scocozza, Benito, 466
Scowcroft, Brent, 245
Seabra, Zita, 520
Seaga, Edward, 102
Sebastião, Bernardina, 520
Seeger, Pete, 86
Seifert, Jaroslav, 280, 282
Sekeremayi, Sydney, 37
Selassie, Haile, 1
Selibi, Jackie, 391
Semtei, Eduardo, 139
Sen, Mohit, 181
Senderov, Valeri, 347
Serbezov, Rumen, 266
Seregni, Liber, 135, 136
Seroni, Adriana, 498
Serra, Jaime, 520
Serra, Julián, 120

Šešelj, Vojislav, 371
Shah, Jaya Govinda, 220, 221
Shahin, Rushdi, 423
Shakak, Abd-al-Majid, 32
Shakir, Sharif Zayd ibn-, 361
Shalayev, Stepan A., 334, 349
Shamuyarira, Nathan, 37
Shaposhnikov, Vitali S., 388
Sharif, Mahir al-, 418
Sharma, Rakesh, 358
Sharma, Vishnu, 484
Sharma, Yogendra, 181
Sharqawi, Abd-al-Rahman, 390
Shchelokov, Nikolai A., 346
Shcherbina, Boris, 341
Shcherbitsky, Vladimir V., 329, 331, 333, 336
Shefqet, Musaraj, 251
Shehu, Feçor, 253, 255
Shehu, Mehmet, 251, 252, 255
Sheik, Shafieh Ahmed, 33
Sheppard, Barry, 134
Shevardnadze, Eduard A., 334, 361
Shitikov, Aleksei, 342
Shkliarov, Yuri A., 392, 393
Shlaudeman, Harry, 112
Shopova, Stanka, 264, 269
Shultz, George, 112, 292, 350, 351, 352, 358, 396
Siba'i, Umar, 433
Sid, Hassan Gassim al-, 32
Sidelil, Fasika, 12
Sieveking, Monika, 482
Sihanouk, Norodom, 194, 195, 202, 372
Silbermayr, Walter, 451, 452
Siles Suazo, Hernán, 49, 50
Silva, Kattorge P., 233
Silva, Luis Ignácio da, 53, 54
Simecka, Milan, 282
Sims, Joe, 391
Sin In-ha, 199
Sin, Jaime, 174
Sindermann, Horst, 285, 501
Singh, D., 358
Singh, Durga Bahadur, 221, 358
Singh, Moni, 158, 159, 160
Sinisalo, Taisto, 468
Sinowatz, Fred, 273, 302
Sinuraya, Tomas, 187, 189, 190
Siqueira, Givaldo, 51
Siraj, Shahjahan, 158

Sisavat Keobounphan, 207
Sisomphon Lovansai, 207
Sithole, Ndabaningi, 37
Siwak, Albin, 305
Siwicki, Florian, 305
Sizenko, Yevgeny, 339, 341
Sizov, Gennadi F., 365, 483
Skiba, Ivan, 339
Slovo, Joe, 20
Smirnov, Boris, 232
Smirnov, Leonid V., 334
Smirnov, Lev, 341
Smirnov, Stefan, 468
Smirnov, V. I., 340
Smirnov, Viktor N., 506
Smirnov, Vitali S., 227
Smirtyukov, Mikhail S., 334
Smith, Ian, 37, 39
So Chol, 197
So Kwang-hui, 197
So Yun-sok, 197
Soares, Mário, 7, 447, 520, 521, 522
Sodnom, Dumaagiyn, 216
Soeiro, José, 520
Sohn, Ole, 462
Sokolov, Sergei L., 334, 337, 367
Sokolov, Yuri, 345
Solano, César, 69
Solheim, Erik, 518
Solís Castro, José, 79
Solomentsev, Mikhail S., 333, 339, 345, 365
Soloukhin, Vladimir, 246
Solstad, Dag, 519
Solzhenitsyn, Alexander, 311
Somoza Debayle, Anastasio, 42, 111, 114
Son Sann, 194, 195
Son Sen, 194
Song Renqiong, 165
Sophokles, G., 485
Sorbo, Gunnar, 514
Sorensen, Ole, 462
Sosa Castro, Jesús, 106
Sosa Navarro, Mario, 100
Soto Prieto, Lionel, 72
Souhail, Abdelwahed, 430
Souphanouvong, 207–10 passim
Souvanna Phouma (prince), 207
Souza Batista, Clito Manuel, 115–18 passim

Spadolini, Giovanni, 500
Spahiu, Xhafer, 254
Spector, Norma, 132
Spengler, Wilhelm, 475
Špiljak, Mika, 332, 372, 454
Spillman, Phil, 391
Spornic, Aneta, 322
Srebrić, Borislav, 368
Srivastava, K. G., 390
Stalin, Joseph, 246, 350, 353, 387, 411
Stanishev, Dimitur, 263, 417
Stashenkov, N. A., 363
Stathis, Konstantin, 391
Stauffenberg, Claus von, 289
Stebler, Hans, 531
Stechbarth, Horst, 384
Steele, James, 131, 132
Stefani, Simon, 251
Steigan, Paal, 514
Steiner, Johann, 454
Stepan, Miroslav, 390
Stephens García, Manuel, 106
Sterling, Claire, 270
Stewart, Edwina, 495
Stewart, James, 495
Stewart, William, 56
St-Marc, Jean, 24
Stoian, Ion, 318, 320, 363
Stoica, Gheorghe, 318, 321
Stoichkov, Grigor, 263, 264, 272
Stojanović, Nikola, 367, 369
Stolypin, Pyotr, 245
Stone, Richard, 83
Stoph, Willi, 285, 286, 287, 303
Stoyanov, Dimitur, 263, 264
Strauss, Franz-Josef, 259, 261, 290
Stroessner, Alfredo, 120
Štrougal, Lubomír, 274, 275, 278, 283
Stukalin, Boris I., 365, 454, 501
Sturmann, Werner, 475
Suazo Córdova, Roberto, 101
Sudiman, Satiadjaya, 487
Suhe-Baatar, D., 217
Sukhai, Pariag, 96
Šuković, Mijat, 368
Šukrija, Ali, 367, 368, 372, 501
Sulayman (Suleiman), Muhammad Ahmad, 32
Sundarayya, P., 186

Sunmonu, Hassan, 21
Suren, C., 216
Surjetan, Harkishan Singh, 364
Suslov, Mikhail A., 245, 246, 338, 342, 366
Swirgon, Waldemar, 305
Symon, Peter Dudley, 155, 274
Szasz, Iosif, 318
Szönyi, Tibor, 298
Szürös, Mátyás, 294, 295, 302, 303, 304, 380, 474

Ta Mok, 194
Tabari, Ehsan, 409, 410
Talas, Mustafa, 435
Talhouni, Bahjat, 425
Talyzin, Nikolai V., 330, 334, 363
Tambo, Oliver, 28
Tamkevicius, Sigitas, 347
Tammisola, Helja, 467, 468
Tan Zhenlin, 165
Tanaka, Kakuei, 191
Tanchev, Petur, 264, 269
Tarabulsi, Fawwaz, 428
Taraki, Nur Mohammed, 144
Taratuta, Vasili N., 339
Tariki, 'Abd al-Majid, 437
Tayeb, Omar Mohammed al-, 35
Taylor, Sid, 131
Tchikaya, Jean Pierre Thystere, 10
Tedesco, Giglia, 498
Tedlay, Addis, 12
Teixeira, Fernando Blanqui, 520
Teixeira, Gail, 96
Tejera Gómez, Luis, 91
Téllez, Dora María, 111
Temple, Nina, 484
Terebilov, Vladimir, 341
Terenzi, Amerigo, 390
Terpeshev, Dobri, 265
Thakin Ba Thein Tin, 161, 162
Thapa, Surya Bahadur, 220, 221
Thatcher, Margaret, 141, 169, 173, 247, 302, 353, 355, 369, 496
Thawadi, Ahmad Ibrahim Muhammad al-, 403
Théodore, René, 99

Thiam, Maguette, 25
Thiam, Samba Dioulde, 25
Thiele, Ilse, 286
Thierjung, Peter, 134
Thio, Boe, 509
Thomas, Clive, 96
Thoroddsen, Gunnar, 491
Tiamzon, Benito, 229
Tikhonov, Nikolai A., 245, 246,
    274, 333–40 passim, 344,
    358, 364, 369, 377, 378, 490,
    508, 533
Tin Yee, 161
Tindemans, Leo, 283
Tinoco, Víctor Hugo, 112
Tirado López, Víctor Manuel,
    111
Tisch, Harry, 285
Tito, Josip Broz, 251, 271, 369,
    370, 387
To Huu, 238
Toaha, Mohammed, 158
Todoriev, Nikola, 266
Todorov, Stanko, 263
Togliatti, Palmiro, 497, 498
Toledo Plata, Carlos, 66
Tolkunov, Lev, 341, 342
Tomášek, František, 281
Tong Min-kwang, 199
Tongamirai, Josiah, 37
Torres, Braulio, 78
Torres, Marcelo, 66
Torres Andrade, Antonio, 120
Torrijos, Omar, 44, 115–18
    passim
Tortorella, Aldo, 496, 497
Totu, Ion, 318
Tran Kien, 239
Tran Quynh, 242
Tran Xuan Bach, 239
Traykov, Boyan, 270
Trevett, Eric, 153
Trigona, Alex Sceberras, 507,
    508
Trondsen, Grete, 514
Trottman, Ruperto Luther, 115,
    117
Trudeau, Pierre, 55, 292, 328,
    351
Truong Chinh, 238, 239, 243,
    244
Tsanov, Vasil, 263

Tsedenbal, Yumjaagyin, 216,
    219
Tsiba, Florent, 10
Tsolakis, Kostas, 487
Tsongas, Paul, 397
Tubi, Tawfiq, 414–17 passim
Tudeb, Li, 217
Tu'ma, Emile, 414, 415, 416
Tung, Jerry, 135
Tunnerman Bernheim, Carlos,
    111, 112, 114
Turf, Jef, 454, 456
Turk, Riyad al-, 433
Turkaowsky, Marco Antonio, 124
Tyazhelnikov, Yevgeny, 330
Tyner, Jarvis, 131

U San Yu, 164, 173
'Ubaydat, Ahmad, 425
Ulanfu, 165
Ulbricht, Walter, 289
Ungo, Guillermo, 82, 83, 84
Unzueta Lorenzana, Gerardo,
    106
Upegui, Mario, 61
Urban, Jerzy, 284
Urbany, Dominique, 502, 503
Urbany, René, 502, 503
Urbany, Serge, 502
Urbrieta, Jesús, 139
Ursu, Ion, 318
Ushewonkunze, Herbert, 37
Ustinov, Dimitri F., 14, 180, 242,
    245, 248, 276, 335, 337, 358,
    359, 361–67 passim, 382,
    384, 395, 425, 441
Uthman, Al-Gazuli (Jizuli) Said,
    32

Vaca Narvaja, Fernando, 48
Vafiades, Markos, 488
Vaidyalingam, A., 233
Vainionpaeae, Esko, 467
Vaino, Karl G., 365
Vajpayee, A. B., 183
Valdés Menéndez, Ramiro, 72
Van Tien Dung, 238, 239, 242,
    359, 364
van Geyt, Louis, 365, 454

Vanous, Jan, 378
Van Vooren, Robert, 347
Varela, Alfredo, 46, 390
Vargas, Tancredo, 78
Vargas Carbonell, Humberto, 68,
    69, 70
Várkonyi, Péter, 302
Varma, K. R., 220, 221, 222
Vasilev, Zhelyo, 270
Vasiliev, Nikolai, 345
Vásquez, Alvaro, 61
Vassallo, Anthony, 503, 504, 505
Vassallo, John, 504
Vecht, Constant, 512
Vedernikov, Gennadi, 338
Velasco Muñoz, Miguel Angel,
    106
Velayati, Ali Akbar, 328, 410
Velikhov, E. P., 349
Vella, Lino, 503
Vella, Mario, 503
Veloso, Ângelo, 520
Veloso, Jacinto Soares, 16
Venizelos, Eleftherios, 260
Venkataraman, Ramaswamy, 358
Ventura, Cândida, 522
Vercaigne, Jules, 454
Verdeţ, Ilie, 318, 320, 363
Vergès, Laurence, 22, 24
Vergès, Laurent, 22, 24
Vergès, Paul, 22, 23, 105
Verner, Paul, 287
Verweymeren, Koos, 511
Veselinov, Slavko, 367
Vessey, John, 178
Viannet, Louis, 469
Vides Casanova, Eduardo, 83
Vidić, Dobrivoje, 367
Vieira, Gilberto, 62–65 passim
Vieira, Sergío, 17
Vila, Oliver, 120
Vilankulu, Artur, 18
Vilarigues, Sergio, 520
Villalobos, Joaquín, 82, 83, 84
Villegas, Cruz, 138
Villegas, Jesús, 61
Vilner, Meir, 274, 364, 414–18
    passim
Vincent, Madeleine, 469
Violante, Luciano, 498
Virapoullé, Jean-Paul, 22
Virat Angkhathavorn, 235, 236

Vire-Tuominen, Mirjam, 388
Visser, Rinze, 511
Viswam, Binoy, 390
Vitoriano, José, 520
Vlasov, Aleksandr, 338, 447
Vo Chi Cong, 238, 239
Vo Van Kiet, 238–39
Voistrichenko, A. F., 339
Voitec, Ştefan, 318
Voropaev, Mikhail, 339
Vorotnikov, Vitali I., 329, 331, 333
Voss, Avgust, E., 339, 342
Vrhovec, Josip, 367, 368, 370
Vrins, Bob, 511
Vu Mao, 239
Vukasinović, Budimir, 454
Vyas, H. K., 181

Wagner, Ingmar, 462
Wahl, Gunnar, 514
Wajed, Hasina, 160
Wakil, Abdul, 145
Walde, Werner, 285
Walesa, Lech, 284, 313
Wallach, John P., 319, 325, 326, 330
Wallenberg, Raoul, 303
Wallenrod, Konrad, 315
Wan Li, 165, 175, 357
Wanchai Chitchamnong, 237
Wang Bingnan, 175
Wang Congwu, 165
Wang Heshou, 165
Wang Zhaoguo, 165, 172
Wang, Zhen, 165
Warrad, Fa'ik, 422, 425
Watanjar, Mohammed Aslam, 143, 146
Waters, Mary-Alice, 134
Webb, Sam, 131
Weber, Ellen, 475, 480
Wei Guoqing, 165
Weinberger, Caspar, 397
Werner, Lars, 527, 528, 529
Wesquet, Jean, 502
West, James, 131
Wetherborne, José Egbert, 119
Wever, Liesbeth, 513

Whaley Martínez, Leopoldo Arthur, 106
Wheelock Román, Jaime, 111, 112, 114
Whitfield, David, 485
Wilhjelm, Preben, 466
Williams, Dessima, 86
Willoch, Kaare, 173
Wimmer, Ernst, 452
Winn, Ed, 135
Winsor, Curtin, 71
Winston, Henry, 131, 132
Winter, Helen, 131
Winter, Richard, 318
Withages, Jack, 454
Woddis, Margaret, 484
Wogderess, Fikre-Selassie, 12
Woizan (general), 9
Woldenberg Karakowsky, José, 106
Wolfe, Richard C., 222
Wolff, Jaap, 509, 513
Wozniak, Marian, 305
Wu Xueqian, 47, 173, 175, 203, 215, 332, 411

Xi Zhongxun, 165
Xoxe, Koçe, 251
Xu Shiyou, 165
Xu Xiangqian, 165
Xuan Thuy, 244

Yang Dezhi, 165, 332
Yang Shangkun, 165
Yang Yong, 165
Yanovsky, R. G., 365
Yao Yilin, 165, 176
Yasenev, V., 357
Yata, 'Ali, 430, 431
Ye Fei, 172
Ye Jianying, 165
Ye Shengtao, 357
Yeba Taik Aung, 161, 162
Yegorov, Anatoli, 347, 363, 364
Yegorov, Georgi M., 334
Yepishev, Aleksei A., 320

Yermakov, Viktor, 279
Yi Chin-su, 199
Yi Chol-pong, 199
Yi Chong-mok, 203
Yi Chong-ok, 197, 198
Yi Ki-yong, 199
Yi Kun-mo, 197
Yi Song-nok, 201
Yi Song-sil, 197
Yi Yong-ik, 198
Yigletu, Ashagre, 12
Yim Chun-chu, 197, 198
Yimenu, Hailu, 12
Ylitalo, Mirja, 467
Yon Hyong-muk, 197
Yorac, Haydee, 229
Yordanov, Georgi, 263
Yotov, Yordan, 263, 264
Young, Andrew, 114
Yovchev, Mincho, 265
Yu Qiuli, 165
Yugov, Anton, 265
Yun Chi-ho, 203
Yun Ki-pok, 199

Zagarell, Mike, 131
Zagladin, Vadim V., 284, 349, 364, 365, 366, 392, 454, 480, 503, 513
Zaikov, Lev N., 365, 470
Zakariya, Ibrahim, 32
Zammit, Dominic, 503
Zamora, Leonor, 120
Zamora, Óscar, 49
Zamora Rivas, Rubén Ignacio, 82, 84
Zamyatin, Leonid M., 335, 392, 501
Zangheri, Renato, 496, 497
Zarev, Kiril, 263, 265, 266
Žarković, Vidoje, 369
Zawde, Gelagay, 14
Zayyad, Tawfiq al-, 415
Zeary, Saleh Mohammed, 143, 144, 150
Zemljarić, Janez, 368
Zhang Aiping, 178
Zhang Guoji, 172
Zhang Tingfa, 160, 165

Zhang Xiaotian, 167
Zhao Ziyang, 165–69 *passim*,
    173, 177, 204, 206, 228, 357,
    474
Zhivkov, Todor Khristov, 198,
    248, 250, 263–74 *passim*,
    327, 331, 356, 363, 364, 386,

418, 427, 428, 454, 461, 518
Zhou Enlai, 176, 232
Zhou Nan, 169
Zhu De, 167
Zhuang Xiquan, 172
Zhuravlev, G. K., 361
Ziartidhis, Andreas, 458

Zia-ul Haq, Mohammad, 224–28
    passim, 328
Ziegler, Erich, 482
Zimiamin, Mikhail V., 274, 303,
    334, 362
Zodehougan, Edouard, 8
Zumel, Antonio, 229

Index of Subjects

Discussions that can readily be located under the subheadings within each profile are not indexed here. A reader interested in Soviet foreign relations, for example, should first consult the "International Views, Positions, and Activities" section of the USSR profile. Listed here under "USSR, foreign relations" is information on this subject that occurs in other profiles.

Advisers: Cuban military and civilian, in Angola, 6, 7; East German, in Benin, 9; Soviet, in Ethiopia, 13, 34; Cuban, in Ethiopia, 34; Soviet, in Peru, 43, 127; Chinese, in Third World, 173; North Korean, in Third World, 200; North Korean, in Libya and Angola, 202; Soviet, in Pakistan, 227; Bulgarian, in Libya, 272; Bulgarian, in Angola, 272; East German in Third World, 293; Soviet military, in Syria, 435; Soviet, in South Yemen, 441

Afghanistan, People's Democratic Party of (PDPA), 143–53; and Saudi Arabian CP, 432; and Cypriot CP, 462; and French CP, 474; and Italian CP, 500

African National Congress (ANC, South Africa), 2, 20, 24, 26–32 *Passim*

Afro-Asian Peoples' Solidarity Organization (AAPSO), 151, 388–91, 505

Agriculture: in Congo, 11; in Mozambique, 19; in Zimbabwe, 38; in Afghanistan, 148–49; in China, 169, 172; in Laos, 208; in Vietnam, 240, 241; in USSR, 245, 246, 378, 381

Albania, 258; in Bulgaria, 267, 268; in Czechoslovakia, 276; East Germany, 289; Hungary, 298; Poland, 314, 315; Romania, 321–22, 323; USSR, 342, 343–344; Yugoslavia, 368

Albania (APL), 248; and Bulgaria, 271; and Yugoslavia, 369, 372; and Greece, 489; and Malta, 507

Albanian Party of Labor, 248, 250–55; and Kampuchean party, 196; and Swiss party, 532
—pro-Albanian parties, 262–63: Brazil, 51; Canada, 55, 58; Colombia, 65; Suriname, 129; Venezuela, 138; Bangladesh, 159; New Zealand, 223; Denmark, 463, 466; West Germany, 481; Sweden, 529

Alfaro Lives! (Ecuador), 81

Algeria: and East Germany, 293; and USSR, 361

Angola: relations with South Africa, 2–3; Cuban troops in, 2–3, 75; and Congo, 11; and South African CP, 32; and Cuba, 75; and Bulgaria, 272; and Poland, 317; and Romania, 328; and USSR, 361; and Yugoslavia, 372; and CMEA, 373, 377

Angola, National Front for the Liberation of (FNLA), 3, 5

Angola, National Union for the Total Independence of (UNITA), 3, 5, 6, 7

Angola, National Union of (UNTA), 3, 4, 5–6

Angola, Popular Movement for the Liberation of– Labor Party (MPLA-PT), 2, 4–7, 13; and Bulgarian CP, 274

Antigua Caribbean Liberation Movement, 76

Anti-imperialist Patriotic Union (Dominican Republic), 77, 78

Antiterrorist Group of Liberation (GAL, Spain), 525, 526

Anyanya movement (Sudan), 33, 34

Argentina: and Nicaragua, 114; and China, 173; and USSR, 362

Argentina, Communist Party of (PCA), 44, 45–47, 49

Armed Communist Movement (Egypt), 405

Armed forces: in Ethiopia, 1, 13; in People's Republic of the Congo, 2, 10; in Mozambique, 2, 17–18; in Benin, 9; in Zimbabwe, 39; in Cuba, 73, 75; in Nicaragua, 112; in Afghanistan, 147; China, 166, 177, 178; Soviet naval exercises, 175, 242; North Korean, in Libya and Angola, 202; Soviet, in Vietnam, 242; Soviet, 246, 340–41; in Albania, 255; in Bulgaria, 266–67; WTO exercises in Czecho-

Armed forces (*continued*)
slovakia, 278–79; Czechoslovak, 279; Soviet, in Afghanistan, 356–57; of WTO states, 383–86; joint WTO maneuvers, 383–84

Armed Forces of National Liberation (FALN, Puerto Rico), 129

Armed Forces of National Resistance (FARN, El Salvador), 82

Armed People's Organization (ORPA, Guatemala), 90–91

Arms sales: U.S.-Chinese, 177, 178; Soviet, to India, 180, 358; North Korean, to Libya, 202; Soviet, to North Korea, 358; Soviet, to Syria, 360; Soviet, to Kuwait, 361

Australia: and Nicaragua, 114, 173; and Albania, 262; and Yugoslavia, 372

Australia, Communist Party of (CPA), 155–56

Australia, Communist Party of—Marxist-Leninist (CPA-ML), 155, 156–57

Australia, Socialist Party of (SPA), 155, 156; and Bulgarian CP, 274; and Saudi Arabian CP, 432

Australia and New Zealand, Spartacist League of (SLANZ), 155, 156, 157

Austria: and Nicaragua, 114; and China, 173; and Bulgaria, 273; and Czechoslovakia, 282–83; and Hungary, 298, 302, 304; and Poland, 317

Austria, Communist Party of (KPO), 451–54; and Bulgarian CP, 274; and East German party, 295; and CPSU, 365; and French CP, 475

Autonomous Anticapitalist Commandos (Spain), 526

Autonomous Socialist Party (PSA, Switzerland), 531

Bahamas, Vanguard Nationalist and Socialist Party of, 76

Bahrain National Liberation Front (NLF/B), 399–400, 403–4

Balush Students' Organization (BSO, Pakistan), 226–27

Bandera Roja (BR, Venezuela), 137–38, 140

Bangladesh, Communist Party of (CPB), 157–59

Bangladesh, Communist Party of (Marxist-Leninist), 158

Bangladesh, Revolutionary Communist Party of, 158

Bangladesh Krishak-Sramik Awami League (BAKSAL), 158

Barisan Sosialis (Singapore), 211

Base Organization (Syria), 433

Basque Homeland and Liberty (ETA, Spain), 525–26; and Portuguese terrorists, 522

Belgian Communist Party (PCB/KPB), 454–57; and Bulgarian CP, 274; and East German party, 295; and CPSU, 365; and French CP, 475; and Maltese CP, 505

Belgium: and China, 173; and Czechoslovakia, 283; and Romania, 328; and USSR, 354

Benin: and Congo, 11

Benin, Revolutionary Party of the People of (PRPB), 2, 8–9

Biplabi Communist League (Bangladesh), 159

Bolivia, 43, 44

Bolivia, Communist Party of (PCB), 49–51

Bolivia, Communist Party of, Marxist-Leninist (PCB-ML), 49

Bourkina Fasso (Upper Volta), 4; and Romania, 328

Brazil: and Nicaragua, 114; and Suriname, 130; and China, 173; and USSR, 362

Brazil, Communist Party of (PCdoB), 44, 51, 52, 54, 263

Brazilian Communist Party (PCB), 44, 49, 51–53

Brazilian Democratic Movement, Party of the (PMDB), 52, 54

Britain, New Communist Party of, 153

Brunei: and North Korea, 202; and Bulgaria, 272

Budgets: Cuba, 73; Afghanistan, 148; China, 168; North Korea, 200; Mongolia, 217; Albania, 258; Czechoslovakia, 278

Bulgaria, 248; and CMEA, 373, 376, 378, 381; and WTO, 383–86

—foreign relations: Angola, 7; Congo, 11; Ethiopia, 13, 14; Mozambique, 19; Nicaragua, 114; North Korea, 198, 204; Mongolia, 217; Vietnam, 242; Bulgaria, 260; Romania, 331; USSR, 356; Yugoslavia, 369, 372; Algeria, 403; South Yemen, 441; Cyprus, 461; Malta, 507

Bulgarian Agrarian National Union (BANU), 264, 269

Bulgarian Communist Party (BCP), 263–66, 274; and Senegalese CP, 25; and South African CP, 31; and Zimbabwan party, 40; and Panamanian party, 118; and Sri Lanka CP, 235; and CPSU, 363–64; and Israeli CP, 417, 418; and Palestine CP, 421; and Lebanese CP, 427, 428; and Syrian CP, 434, 435, 436; and Austrian CP, 452, 454; and Cypriot CP, 461; and Finnish CP, 468; and Greek CP, 489, 490; and Luxembourg CP, 503; and Maltese CP, 505; and Norwegian CP, 518; and Portuguese, CP, 522

Burma: and China, 173
Burmese Communist Party (BCP), 161–64

Canada: and China, 173; and East Germany, 292;
  and Romania, 328; and USSR, 351
Canada, Communist Party of (CPC), 55, 56–57
Canada, Communist Party of (Marxist-Leninist)
  (CPC-ML), 55, 57–58
Caribbean Revolutionary Alliance (ARC, French
  Overseas Departments), 88
Central American Revolutionary Workers' Party
  (PRTC, El Salvador), 82
Central American Workers, Revolutionary Party of
  (PRTC, Honduras), 100, 101
Chad, 9, 11
Chile, Communist Party of (CPC), 43, 49, 59–61
China, foreign relations: Benin, 9; Mozambique,
  19; Zimbabwe, 40; Argentina, 47; Ecuador, 81;
  Peru, 127; Suriname, 130; Bangladesh, 160;
  Burma, 164; India, 180; Indonesia, 189; North
  Korea, 203–4; Japan, 204; Malaysia, 215;
  Nepal, 220; Pakistan, 228; Sri Lanka, 235;
  Thailand, 238; Vietnam, 243; Albania, 259,
  262; East Germany, 295; Hungary, 304;
  Poland, 317; Romania, 332; USSR, 357;
  Yugoslavia, 372; and Algeria, 403; Iran, 411;
  Italy, 501; Malta, 507–8
Chinese Communist Party (CCP), 164–66; and
  Indian parties, 180, 181, 186; and Japanese CP,
  193; and Nepalese parties, 220; and CPSU,
  364; and Yugoslav party, 369, 372; and Belgian
  CP, 455; and French CP, 474; and Italian CP,
  501; and Spanish CPs, 524, 525; and Swiss
  party, 532
—pro-Chinese parties: Sudan, 33, 44; Bolivia, 49;
  Colombia, 62, 65–66; Ecuador, 79, 80; Peru,
  121, 123; U.S., 134; Australia, 157;
  Bangladesh, 158–59; Burma, 161–62, 164;
  Indonesia, 187–89; Kampuchea, 196; Malay-
  sia, 211, 215; Nepal, 219, 220; New Zealand,
  223; Philippines, 232; Lebanon, 429; Den-
  mark, 463; Sweden, 529; Switzerland, 531–32
Christian Peace Conference (CPC), 388–91
Church-state relations: in Zimbabwe, 39; in Nic-
  aragua, 42–43, 113; in Chile, 61; in
  Afghanistan, 149–50; in Czechoslovakia, 281;
  East Germany, 287, 288; Hungary, 300–301;
  Poland, 306, 309–11; Romania, 323;
  Yugoslavia, 370–71
Collectif de militantes et de militants pour le
  socialisme (Canada), 58

Colombia, 43; and Nicaragua, 114; and USSR,
  362
Colombia, Communist Party of (PCC), 49, 61–
  62, 63–65
Colombia, Communist Party of, Marxist-Leninist
  (PCC-ML), 62, 65–66
Colombia, Marxist-Leninist League of, 65
Colombia, Revolutionary Armed Forces of
  (FARC), 62–63, 64
Committee for a New Beginning (Canada), 58
Committee of Patriotic Unity (CGUP, Guatemala),
  91
Committees of Popular Struggle (CLP, Venezuela),
  138, 140
Communist Combatant Cells (Belgium), 455
Communist Labor Organization (Lebanon), 429
Communist League (KB, West Germany), 481
Communist Left Unity (Mexico), 109
Communist Party for Independence and Socialism
  (Martinique), 105
Communist Party/Marxist-Leninist (Panama), 118
Communist Revolutionary Party (PRC, Brazil),
  52, 54
Communist Workers Nucleus (Dominican Re-
  public), 78
Communist Workers' Party (KAP, Denmark), 463,
  466
Communist Workers' Party (APK, Sweden), 529;
  and CPSU, 365
Communist Workers Party (U.S.), 135
Congo: and Bulgaria, 272
Congolese Party of Labor (PCT), 1, 10–11; and
  Bulgarian CP, 274; and Yugoslav party, 372
Congresses (1984): South African party, 2: Con-
  golese party, 10, 11; Ethiopian party, 12–13;
  Senegalese party, 25; Zimbabwe party, 37, 38;
  Brazilian CP, 51, 52; Chilean CP, 59, 60;
  Colombian CP, 61, 64–65; Costa Rica CPs, 68,
  70; Guadeloupan CP, 87–88; Jamaican party,
  102–3; U.S. party, 134; Sri Lankan CP, 233,
  235; Thai CP, 235; Romanian CP, 318, 319;
  Palestine CP, 419; Saudi Arabian CP, 432;
  Austrian CP, 452–53; Finnish CP, 467–68;
  West German CP, 476; Luxembourg CP,
  502–3; Maltese CP, 504–5; Dutch CP, 509,
  510–12; Norwegian CP, 514, 516–18
Corruption: in Hungary, 296–97; in USSR,
  345–46
Costa Rican People's Party (PCC), 44
Costa Rican Socialist Party (PSC), 68, 70
Council for Mutual Economic Assistance
  (CMEA), 248; and Cuba, 74; and Afghanistan,

CMEA (*continued*)
   153; and Laos, 209; and Mongolia, 217; and
   Vietnam, 242; and Czechoslovakia, 283; and
   Hungary, 299, 302; and Romania, 326, 329,
   330; and Yugoslavia, 372
Crime: in China, 171; Czechoslovakia, 277
Cuba, 41; troops in Angola, 2–3, 6; troops in
   Ethiopia, 14, 34; aid to Nicaragua, 41; foreign
   aid to, 41–42; economy, 41–42; indebtedness,
   42; training of Bolivian Communists in, 50
—foreign relations; and Angola, 7; and Congo,
   11; and Colombia, 65; and Ecuador, 81; and
   Suriname, 130; and Mongolia, 218; and Albania, 260; and Bulgaria, 273; and Romania,
   332; and CMEA, 373, 377; and Algeria, 403;
   Malta, 507
Cuba, Communist Party of (PCC), 31, 47, 49,
   71–73, 76, 98; and Colombian CP, 64; and
   Grenadian party, 86; and Guadeloupan CP, 87;
   and Guyanese party, 98; and Jamaican party,
   103; and Peruvian CP, 127; and Venezuelan CP,
   138; and Japanese CP, 193; and Kampuchean
   party, 196; and Bulgarian CP, 274; and East
   German party, 295; and French CP, 474; and
   Maltese CP, 505; and Dutch CP, 513; and
   Portuguese CP, 522
—pro-Cuban parties, 44, 62, 78, 79, 130, 223
Cultural organizations: North Korea, 197;
   Albania, 252, 256
Culture: in USSR, 246–47, 349; in Bulgaria, 269;
   in Czechoslovakia, 280; in East Germany, 288–
   89; Romania, 324
Curacao Socialist Movement, 76, 98
Cyprus: and Czechoslovakia, 283
Czechoslovakia, 248; and CMEA, 373, 374, 376,
   381; and WTO, 383–86
—foreign relations: Angola, 7; Nicaragua, 114;
   North Korea, 204; Vietnam, 242; Albania,
   260; Bulgaria, 272, 274; East Germany, 294;
   Hungary, 303, 304; Romania, 331; and Al-
   geria, 403; and Greece, 490; and Malta, 507
Czechoslovakia, Communist Party of (KSČ), 275–
   76; and Senegalese party, 25; and CPSU, 363;
   and Israeli CP, 417; and Palestine CP, 422; and
   Lebanese CP, 427; and Syrian CP, 435; and
   Tunisian CP, 438; and Austrian CP, 452; and
   French CP, 474; and Greek CP, 489; and
   Maltese CP, 505; and Portuguese CP, 522; and
   Spanish CP, 525

Democratic Front Against Repression
   (Guatemala), 91, 92

Democratic National Front (FDN, Nicaragua), 43
Democratic Revolutionary Alliance (ARDE, Nic-
   aragua), 43
Democratic Revolutionary Front (FDR, El Sal-
   vador), 42, 82–84
Demography: Bulgaria, 268; Czechoslovakia, 277;
   Hungary, 300; Romania, 323
Denmark: and China, 173; and Albania, 259
Denmark, Communist Party of (DKP), 462–65;
   and CPSU, 365
Directorate of the National Committee of Labor
   Unity (Guatemala), 91
Dissent: in Bulgaria, 266; in Czechoslovakia,
   281–82; East Germany, 287–88, 289; Hungary,
   301; Poland, 306, 313; USSR, 346–47; in
   Yugoslavia, 370–71
Djibouti: and East Germany, 293
Dominica Liberation Movement, 77
Dominican Communist Party (DCP), 77, 78; and
   Bulgarian CP, 274
Dominican Liberation Movement Alliance, 98
Dominican Republic, United Left of the, 77, 78
Dominican Workers Party, 77, 78

Economic growth rates: Cuba, 73, 379; Bulgaria,
   267; East Germany, 289; Hungary, 298, 378–
   79; Poland, 314; Romania, 321; USSR, 343,
   378; Yugoslavia, 368, 370; in CMEA states,
   378–79
Economic plans: Cuba, 74; Nicaragua, 111–12;
   China, 168, 170; North Korea, 200; Laos, 208;
   Mongolia, 217; Albania, 258; Bulgaria, 268;
   Czechoslovakia, 278; Hungary, 298; Poland,
   313–15; Romania, 321, 323; Yugoslavia, 368;
   intra-CMEA coordination of, 374–75
Economy: Angola, 6; Benin, 9; Mozambique, 19;
   Zimbabwe, 38–39; Cuba, 41–42, 73–75; Nicaragua, 43, 111–12; Peru, 122; Uruguay, 135,
   136; Afghanistan, 148–49; China, 167–68,
   170; North Korea, 199–200; Laos, 208;
   Mongolia, 217; Vietnam, 240, 241; USSR,
   245, 246, 342–44; Albania, 258–59; Bulgaria,
   267–68; Czechoslovakia, 277–78; East Germany, 289–90; Hungary, 298–300; Romania,
   321–23; Yugoslavia, 368, 370
Ecuador, 44; and Nicaragua, 114; and USSR, 362
Ecuador, Communist Party of (PCE), 49, 79, 80–
   81; and Yugoslav party, 372
Ecuador, Communist Party of, Marxist-Leninist
   (PCE-ML), 79
Ecuador, Revolutionary Socialist Party of (PSRE),
   79

Education: of Angolans in Czechoslovakia, 7; in Ethiopia, 13; of Dominicans in Soviet bloc, 77; of Grenadians in Cuba, 86; of Peruvians in USSR, 127; of Afghanis in USSR, 154–55; of Chinese in USSR, 175; in North Korea, 200; of North Koreans in USSR, 202–3; of Vietnamese in USSR and Eastern Europe, 242; of Albanians in Western Europe, 259; in Bulgaria, 268–69; of Nigerians in Bulgaria, 272; in Czechoslovakia, 280–81; of Third World students in East Germany, 293; in USSR, 344–45; in Yemen, 439

Egypt: and Bulgaria, 272; and Romania, 328; and USSR, 360

Egyptian Communist Party (ECP), 25, 400, 404–8

Egyptian Communist Party–8 January, 405

Egyptian Communist Workers' Party, 405

8 October Revolutionary Movement (MR-8, Brazil), 51, 53, 54

Ekota Party (Bangladesh), 158

Elections (1984): in Benin, 2, 8; in Lesotho, 2; in Congo, 11; in Réunion, 22; in El Salvador, 42; in Nicaragua, 42; in Latin America, 44; in Canada, 55, 56, 58; in Colombia, 61, 64, 66; in Ecuador, 79–80; in El Salvador, 83; in Grenada, 85; in Guatemala, 91; in Nicaragua, 111, 112–14; in Panama, 115, 116, 117; in Puerto Rico, 128–29; in U.S., 129–35 passim; in Uruguay, 135–36; in Venezuela, 139; in Bangladesh, 159–60; India, 179–86 passim; Japan, 192–93; Philippines, 230, 231–32; East Germany, 289; Poland, 311; in USSR, 341; Egypt, 406–7; Iraq, 413; Israel, 416–17; Morocco, 430, 431; Austria, 451–52; Cyprus, 460; Denmark, 462–63; France, 470, 472, 473; West Germany, 478; Greece, 488, 489; Italy, 496, 499, 501; Luxembourg, 502; Netherlands, 509, 510; Spain, 524, 526; Turkey, 533–34

El Salvador, 42

El Salvador, Communist Party of (PCES), 82; and East German party, 295

Energy: Cuba, 74; Afghanistan, 148; North Korea, 200; Hungary, 298; Poland, 314; Romania, 322; Yugoslavia, 368; in CMEA states, 374–81 passim

Equatorial Guinea: and China, 173

Eritrean Liberation Front–Revolutionary Council, 14

Espionage: Soviet, in Bangladesh, 160; Albanian, in Greece, 260; Romanian, in France, 327; Romanian, in West Germany 327–28; Soviet, in Western Europe, 354

Ethiopia, 32, 34, 40, 75; and Mongolia, 218; and Bulgaria, 272; and East Germany, 292; and USSR, 362, 364; and CMEA, 373, 377

Ethiopia, Commission to Organize the Party of the Working People of (COPWE), 1, 12–13

Ethiopia, Workers' Party of (WPE), 1, 12–13, 75; and Bulgarian CP, 274; and Hungarian party, 304; and Romanian CP, 333; and CPSU, 364; and Yugoslav party, 372

Eurocommunist parties, 443–44; Australia, 156; Japan, 193; Belgium, 455, 456, 457; Greece, 487, 488; Italy, 497; Spain, 523

Factionalism: in Angolan party, 2–3, 5; in Mozambican party, 17, 18; in Sudanese CP, 33–34; in Brazilian CP, 52; in Costa Rican CP, 69–70; in Guatemalan party, 93; in Martinique CP, 105; in Mexican party, 107–8; in Afghan party, 143, 144, 146; in Indian CP, 181–82; in Nepalese CP, 220–21; in New Zealand parties, 223; in Polish party, 307; in USSR, 336; in Yemeni party, 439; and Austrian CP, 452; in Finnish CP, 467–68; in French CP, 471–72; in British CP, 485; in Dutch CP, 510–12; in Spanish CP, 523–24

Faeroe Communist Party, 464

Farabundo Martí Front of National Liberation (FMLN, El Salvador), 42, 77, 81–84

February 18th Movement (Trinidad and Tobago), 77, 98

Federation of Violence-free Action Groups (FoGA, West Germany), 482

Fighting Communist Party (Italy), 501

Finland: and Mongolia, 218; and Bulgaria, 273; and East Germany, 292; and CMEA, 373

Finnish Communist Party (SKP), 467–69; and Bulgarian CP, 274; and East German party, 295; and Hungarian party, 304; and CPSU, 365

Forces of Popular Unity (FUP, Portugal), 522

Forward Readers Group (FRG, Canada), 55, 58

Fourth International (Trotskyist): Canadian affiliate, 58; U.S. affiliate, 133, 134; Danish affiliate, 463, 466; West German affiliate, 481; Swedish affiliate, 529; Swiss affiliate, 531

France: and Angola, 7; and Congo, 11; and Réunion, 22, 23; and Martinique, 105; and Nicaragua, 114; and China, 173; and North Korea, 205; and Mongolia, 218; and Albania, 261; and Bulgaria, 273; and Czechoslovakia, 282; and Hungary, 302; and Poland, 317; and Romania, 320, 327; and USSR, 353–54; and Yugoslavia, 369

Free Workers' Union (FAU, West Germany), 482

Free Workers' Union/Council Communists (FAU/K, West Germany), 482

Free Workers' Union/Students (FAUST, West Germany), 481

Freedom and Struggle (Brazil), 51, 54

French Communist Party, 373, 469–75; and Martinique CP, 105; and Afghan party, 153; and East German party, 294; and CPSU, 365; and Yugoslav party, 369; and Austrian CP, 452; and Greek CP, 490; and Maltese CP, 505

Frente de Izquierda Popular (Argentina), 47

German Communist Party (DKP), 475–80; and CPSU, 365; and Austrian CP, 452; and Cypriot CP, 461; and Maltese CP, 505; and Dutch CP, 514

German Democratic Republic (GDR), 248–49; and CMEA, 373, 379, 381; and WTO, 383–86

—foreign relations: Seychelles, 3; Benin, 9; Ethiopia, 14; Mozambique, 19; Cuba, 74; Salvadoran guerrillas, 84; Nicaragua, 114; North Korea, 204; Mongolia, 217; Vietnam, 242; Albania, 261; Hungary, 303; Poland, 316; Romania, 331; USSR, 354, 355–56; Yugoslavia, 372; and Algeria, 403; South Yemen, 441; Greece, 490; Italy, 501; Malta, 507

Germany, Communist League of (KBW, West Germany), 481

Germany, Communist Party of (Marxist-Leninist) (KPD, West Germany), 481

Germany, Federal Republic of (FRG): and Nicaragua, 114; and Albania, 259, 261; and Bulgaria, 273–74; and Czechoslovakia, 283; and East Germany, 286–92 *passim*; and USSR, 294–95, 351, 353, 354; and Hungary, 298, 301–2; and Poland, 316–17; 327–28

Germany, International Socialists of (ISD, West Germany), 481

Germany, Marxist-Leninist Party of (MLPD, West Germany), 481

Ghana: and Bulgaria, 272

Great Britain: and China, 169–70, 173; and Albania, 261; and Hungary, 302; and USSR, 353, 355

Great Britain, Communist Party of (CPGB), 484–86; and French CP, 475

Greece: and Albania, 258, 259, 260; and Bulgaria, 271; and Czechoslovakia, 283; and East Germany, 292; and Poland, 317; and Romania, 328; and USSR, 354; and Italian CP, 501

Greece, Communist Party of (KKE), 25, 373, 487–90; and Bulgarian CP, 274; and Hungarian party, 304; and Yugoslav party, 369; and Cypriot CP, 461; and French CP, 474–75; and Maltese CP, 505

Greece, Communist Party of–Interior (KKE-Interior), 487, 488, 490

Greece, Marxist-Leninist Communist Party of, 490

Greece, Revolutionary Communist Party of, 490

Group of International Marxists (GIM, West Germany), 481

Guadeloupe, Communist Party of (PCG), 44, 77, 87–89, 98, 100; and CPSU, 364

Guadeloupe, Movement for an Independent, 88

Guadeloupe, Union for the Liberation of, 88

Guatemala, 43

Guatemalan National Revolutionary Alliance (URNG), 91, 92, 93, 95

Guatemalan National Revolutionary Unity, 77

Guatemalan Party of Labor (PGT), 89, 90, 92–94

Guatemalan Party of Labor–Leadership Nucleus (PGT-LN), 93

Guerrilla Army of the Poor (EGP, Guatemala), 91, 94–95

Guerrillas: in Mozambique, 2, 18, 20; in Angola, 3, 5; in Sudan, 3, 34–35; in Ethiopia, 14; in Zimbabwe, 38, 39; in Latin America, 42–44; in Bolivia, 50; Chile, 60; Colombia, 62–68 *passim*; in Ecuador, 81; in El Salvador, 82–83, 120; in Guadeloupe, 88; in Guatemala, 90–92, 94–95; in Honduras, 101; in Nicaragua, 111, 112; in Peru, 123–26; in Venezuela, 137, 140; in Afghanistan, 146–47; Burma, 163–64; Kampuchea, 195; in Malaysia, 212, 213–214; Philippines, 229, 230–31; Sri Lanka, 234, 235; Thailand, 236–38; Spain, 525–26; Turkey, 534

Guiana (French), Socialist Party of, 77, 87

Guinea, Republic of, 3; and Congo, 11; and Romania, 328

Guinea and Cape Verde Islands, African party for the Independence of, 3–4

Guinea-Bissau, 3

Guyana: and Bulgaria, 273

Haitian Communists, Unified Party of (PUCH), 77, 87, 99–100

Honduran Communist Party (PCH, Honduras), 100, 101

Honduran Liberation, Morazanista Front of (FMLH), 100, 101

Honduran Revolutionary Movement (MHR), 100, 101

Honduras, 43

Hong Kong, 169–70, 173

Horizontal Consultation of Communists (HOC, Netherlands), 510, 511

Housing: Cuba, 72, 73, 75; Czechoslovakia, 278; East Germany, 289; Hungary, 300

Human rights: Albania, 257–58, 260; Czechoslovakia, 281–82; Poland, 311; Romania, 326

Hungarian Socialist Workers' Party (HSWP), 295–98, 304; and Israeli CP, 417; and Palestine CP, 421; and Lebanese CP, 427, 428; and Austrian CP, 452, 454; and French CP, 474; and British CP, 486; and Greek CP, 489; and Italian CP, 497; and Maltese CP, 505; and Spanish CPs, 524, 525; and Swedish party, 529

Hungary, 249; and CMEA, 373–81 passim; and WTO, 383–86

—foreign relations: Ethiopia, 14; North Korea, 204; Mongolia, 218; Bulgaria, 272, 274; Czechoslovakia, 277; and East Germany, 294; Romania, 325, 331; France, 327; and Algeria, 403; Malta, 507

Income, personal: China, 170; Bulgaria, 267, 268; Czechoslovakia, 278; East Germany, 289; Hungary, 298–99; Poland, 314; Romania, 322; Yugoslavia, 370

Indebtedness, foreign: Mozambique, 19, 20; Cuba, 42, 74; Nicaragua, 43; Peru, 43; Argentina, 45; Dominican Republic, 78; Ecuador, 81; Peru, 122; Uruguay, 136; Czechoslovakia, 283–84; East Germany, 291; Hungary, 298; Poland, 314, 315; Romania, 325–26; Yugoslavia, 370; of CMEA states, 381

Independence and Labor Party (PIT, Senegal), 3, 25

Independent Revolutionary Workers' Movement (MOIR, Colombia), 66

India: and China, 173; and Laos, 209; and Mongolia, 218; and Nepal, 220; and Bulgaria, 273; and USSR, 357–58; and Soviet propaganda, 398

India, Communist Party of (CPI), 25, 179–84; and Bulgarian CP, 274; and CPSU, 364

India, Communist Party of–Marxist (CPM), 179–80, 184–86, 220

Indonesian Communist Party (PKI), 187–89

Industry: in Afghanistan, 149; in Albania, 258; in Bulgaria, 267, 268; East Germany, 289; Hungary, 298, 299–300; Poland, 314; Romania,
321, 322; USSR, 343; Yugoslavia, 368

Inflation: in Czechoslovakia, 278; in Poland, 314; in Yugoslavia, 368, 370

Initiative Free Workers' Union (I.FAU, West Germany), 482

International Association of Democratic Lawyers (IADL), 388–91, 505

International Institute of Peace (IIP), 388

International meetings: December Prague meeting of CPs to discuss WMR, 3, 36, 56, 110, 118, 187, 404, 432; Caribbean CPs (Guyana, March), 41, 89, 98, 104, 106; Central American and Caribbean CPs (Havana, June), 41, 72, 76–77, 86, 106; South American CPs (Buenos Aires, July), 41, 47, 48–49, 53, 81, 118, 127; Mediterranean parties and movements (Belgrade, July), 373; Arab parties (Damascus?, June), 404, 407, 421, 432, 436

International Monetary Fund (IMF): and Mozambique, 16, 20; and Sudan, 36; and Zimbabwe, 40; Argentina, 45, 46; and Mongolia, 217; and Dominican Republic, 78, 79; and Guyana, 97; and Jamaica, 102; and Suriname, 130; Hungary, 298; and Poland, 314; and Romania, 326; and Yugoslavia, 370

International Organization of Journalists (IOJ), 86, 279, 388–91

International Socialists (Canada), 59

International Socialist Workers' Party (SAP, Denmark), 463, 466

International Union of Students (IUS), 15, 32, 117, 279, 388–91

International Workers' League (Puerto Rico), 129

Investment: China, 168; Albania, 258; East Germany, 289; Hungary, 299; Poland, 314; Romania, 321

Iran: and Nicaragua, 114; and USSR and Afghanistan, 155, 399; and China, 173; and Albania, 262; and Romania, 328; and USSR, 361; and Middle Eastern states, 399, 400

Iraq: and East Germany, 293; and Romania, 328; and USSR, 360–61; and CMEA, 373

Iraqi Communist Party (ICP), 399, 412–14; and USSR, 361; and Greek CP, 489

Ireland, Communist Party of (CPI), 495–96

Irish Republican Army (IRA), 236, 522

Irish Republican Socialist Party, 494

Islamic Brotherhood Party (Paperi, Malaysia), 211, 214

Israel: and Benin, 9; and Romania, 328

Israel, Communist Party of (CPI), 401, 414–18; and Bulgarian CP, 274; and East German party, 295; and CPSU, 364

Italian Communist Party (PCI), 373, 496–501; and Afghan party, 152–53; and Japanese CP, 193; and East German party, 294; and Romanian CP, 332–33; and CPSU, 366; and Yugoslav party, 369, 372; and Austrian CP, 452; and Danish party, 466; and French CP, 474; and Maltese CP, 505

Italy: and Angola, 7; and Nicaragua, 114; and China, 173; and Albania, 259, 261; and Bulgaria, 270, 273; and East Germany, 292; Hungary, 298, 302; and USSR, 354; and Malta, 508

Ivory Coast, 14; and Czechoslovakia, 283

Jamaica, Workers' Party of (WPJ), 77, 87, 98, 102–4, 387

Jamaica Communist Party, 102

Janamukti Party (Bangladesh), 158

Japan: and China, 173–74, 204; and North Korea, 205–6; and Bulgaria, 273; and USSR, 358–59

Japan Communist Party (JCP), 190–93; and Yugoslav party, 372

Jatiya Samjtantrik Dal (JSD, Bangladesh), 158

Jordan: and China, 173; and USSR, 361; and Greece, 490

Jordan, Communist Party of (CPJ), 401, 422–25

Jordan, Communist Party of–Leninist Cadre, 423

Kachin Independence Army (KIA, Burma), 163

Kampuchea: and Angola, 7; and North Korea, 202; and Thailand, 238; and Vietnam, 243–44; and Bulgaria, 272; and USSR, 359, 364; and Yugoslavia, 372

Kampuchean Communist Party (KCP), 194, 195, 196

Kampuchean People's Revolutionary Party (KPRP), 194–96; and Japanese CP, 193

Karen National Union (KNU, Burma), 163

Kayah New People's Party (Burma), 163

Kenya, 13

Korea, People's Democratic Republic of: foreign trade, 200, 202; aid to Third World countries, 200

—foreign relations: Seychelles, 3; Mozambique, 19; Nicaragua, 114; and China, 173; Albania, 261; Bulgaria, 272; East Germany, 295; Hungary, 304; Romania, 320, 332; USSR, 358; Yugoslavia, 369; and CMEA, 373; South Yemen, 441; Malta, 507

Korea, Republic of: and North Korea, 200–202

Korean Workers' Party (KWP), 197–99, 204–5; and Japanese CP, 193, 196; and Kampuchean party, 196; and Albanian party, 263; and Yugoslav party, 372; and Syrian CP, 436; and Danish CP, 465

Kurdish Democratic Party/Iraq (KDP/I), 413

Kurdistan, United Socialist Party of (Iraq), 413

Kuwait: and China, 173; and USSR, 361

Labor productivity: Albania, 258, 259; Bulgaria, 267; Czechoslovakia, 277; East Germany, 289; Hungary, 299; Romania, 323; USSR, 342, 343; Yugoslavia, 368, 370

Labor unions: Angola, 4, 5–6; Congo, 10, 11; Ethiopia, 12; Nigeria, 21; Réunion, 22; Sudan, 32, 33, 35; Bolivia, 44, 50, 51; Argentina, 46; Brazil, 53; Canada, 55; Chile, 59, 60; Colombia, 62, 65; Costa Rica, 68, 69, 70–71; Cuba, 72; Ecuador, 79, 80; Guadeloupe, 87, 88, 89; Guatemala, 89, 90, 92, 93; Guyana, 97; Honduras, 101; Jamaica, 102, 103; Martinique, 104, 105–6; Mexico, 107; Nicaragua, 111; Panama, 115, 117; Peru, 121, 123, 125; U.S., 131, 132; Uruguay, 136; Venezuela, 138, 140; Afghanistan, 144; Australia, 156, 157; Bangladesh, 158; China, 165; India, 179, 184, 186; Kampuchea, 194; North Korea, 197; Mongolia, 216, 217; Nepal, 220; New Zealand, 223; Pakistan, 224; Philippines, 229; Sri Lanka, 233; Vietnam, 242; Albania, 251, 253, 256; Bulgaria, 264, 269–70; Czechoslovakia, 275, 279; East Germany, 285; Hungary, 295, 297; Romania, 318; USSR, 334, 349; Yugoslavia, 368; Algeria, 402; Bahrain, 403; Jordan, 424; Lebanon, 426; Yemen, 439; Austria, 452; Belgium, 456–57; Cyprus, 458, 460; Denmark, 463, 464; France, 470, 472; West Germany, 479; Great Britain, 484, 485, 486; Iceland, 492; Italy, 496, 498, 499; Malta, 504; Portugal, 520, 521; Spain, 523, 524, 525

Labour Party (Bangladesh), 158

Labour Party (UK): and Bulgarian CP, 274; and USSR, 355

Lanka Sama Samaja Party (LSSP, Sri Lanka), 234

Lao People's Revolutionary Party (LPRP), 207–10

Laos: and Thailand, 237, 238; and USSR, 359, 364; and CMEA, 373, 377

Lebanese Communist Party (LCP), 401, 425–28, 429; and Senegalese party, 25; and Bulgarian CP, 274; and Yugoslav party, 369; and South Yemen, 440

Lebanese Communist Union, 429
Lebanese National Movement (LNM), 426, 427, 428
Lebanon, Organization of Communist Unity in (OCAL), 401, 425, 428–29
Left Party Communists (VPK, Sweden), 527–29; and Danish party, 466
Left Socialist Party (VS, Denmark), 463, 466
Lesotho, Communist Party of (CPL), 2, 15
Liberation Tigers of Tamil Eelam (Sri Lanka), 234
Libya: and Seychelles, 3; and Benin, 9; and Sudan, 34, 35; and terrorists in Guadeloupe, 88; and Nicaragua, 114; and North Korea, 202; and Bulgaria, 272; and Czechoslovakia, 283; and Romania, 328; and Yugoslavia, 369, 372; and Morocco, 431; and Greece, 490
Lorenzo Zelaya People's Revolutionary Front (FPR-LZ, Honduras), 100
Luxembourg, Communist Party of (CPL), 502–3; and CPSU, 365; and French CP, 475

M-19 (Colombia), 62, 64, 66–67
Madagascar, 32; and USSR, 361
Malay Nationalist Revolutionary Party of Malaya (MNRPM), 211, 214
Malaya, Communist Party of–Revolutionary Faction (CPM/RF), 211
Malaya, Communist Party of (CPM), 210–15
Malaya, Communist Party of—Marxist-Leninist (CPM/M-L), 211
Malayan National Liberation Front (MNLF), 214
Malayan People's Army (MPA), 211, 213
Malayan People's Liberation Front (MPLF), 211, 214
Malaysia: and China, 173; and Thailand, 237
Malaysia, Communist Party of (MCP), 210–15
Malasyian People's Liberation Army (MPLA), 213
Malaysian People's Liberation League (MPLL), 211, 214
Malta: and China, 173
Malta, Communist Party of (CPM), 503–7
Manuel Rodríguez Patriotic Front (FPMR, Chile), 43, 60
Martinique Communist Party (PCM), 44, 77, 87, 98, 104–6
Martinique Progressive party, 77
Marxist Group (MG, West Germany), 481
Marxist-Leninist Communist Party, Revolutionary (Sweden), 529
Marxist-Leninist Party (MLP, Denmark), 463, 466

Maurice Bishop Patriotic Movement (MBPM, Grenada), 44, 77, 85–87
Mauritius, Communist Party of, 3
Mazdoor Kisan Party (MKP, Pakistan), 226
Mexican Communist Party (PCM), 107
Mexican People's Party (PPM), 107, 109
Mexico: and Nicaragua, 114; and China, 173; and East Germany, 293; and CMEA, 373, 377
Mexico, Unified Socialist Party of (PSUM), 106–10; and Yugoslav party, 372
Militant (Great Britain), 487
Militia: in Angola, 5; in Benin, 8, 9; in Mozambique, 19; in Zimbabwe, 37; in Cuba, 72, 73; in Nicaragua, 111, 112; in Afghanistan, 151; in Bulgaria, 264
Minority groups: in Ethiopia, 14; in Sudan, 34; in Zimbabwe, 38, 39; Greek, in Albania, 257–58, 260, 489; Macedonian, in Bulgaria, 271; Hungarian, in Czechoslovakia, 276–77, 301, 304; Hungarian, in Romania, 301, 302, 319, 325; German, in Hungary, 302; Hungarian, in Yugoslavia, 304; German, in Poland, 316–17; German, in Romania, 319, 325; in USSR, 347; Albanian, in Yugoslavia, 369, 371; Kurdish, in Iraq, 413
Mongolia: and CMEA, 373; and South Yemen, 441
Mongolian People's Revolutionary Party (MPRP), 216–18
Montoneros (Argentina), 47–48
Moro National Liberation Front ((MNLF, Philippines), 231
Morocco: and Yugoslavia, 372
Movement for National Liberation (MONALI, Barbados), 76, 98
Movement for National Unity (Saint Vincent and the Grenadines), 77
Movement for Socialism (Dominican Republic), 78
Movement of Revolutionary Unity (MUR, Honduras), 100
Movement of the New Republic (MNR, Costa Rica), 68, 70
Movement of the Revolutionary Left (MIR, Chile), 43, 59, 60
Movement to Socialism (MAS, Venezuela), 44, 137, 138–39
Mozambique: relations with South Africa, 2; and Congo, 11; and South African CP, 29; and Zimbabwe, 40; and Cuba, 75; and Bulgaria, 272; and East Germany, 293; and Romania, 329; and USSR, 361; and CMEA, 373, 377

Mozambique, Front for the Liberation of (FRELIMO), 2, 13, 16–21
Mozambique National Resistance (MNR), 2, 18, 20

Namibia, 5
National Awami League (NAL, Bangladesh), 158, 159
National Democratic Front (NDF, Philippines), 229, 231–32
National Liberation Army (ELN, Colombia), 62, 67, 140
National Patriotic Committee (COPAN, Costa Rica), 68
National People's Army (NPA, Philippines), 229–32
National Progressive Unionist Party (NPUP, Egypt), 400, 406–7
National Revolutionary Movement (MNR, El Salvador), 82
National Unified Directorate (DRU, Honduras), 100
National Unity of the Revolutionary Left (UNIR, Peru), 121, 122
Natural gas: in Benin, 9; in USSR, 377
Nepal: and China, 173
Nepal Communist Party (NCP), 219–22
Nepal Communist Party (Marxist-Leninist) (NCP[ML]), 219–22
Netherlands: and Albania, 262; and Romania, 328
Netherlands, Alliance of Communists in the (VCN), 509, 510, 511–12
Netherlands, Communist Party of the (CPN), 509–14; and Bulgarian CP, 274; and CPSU, 365; and Yugoslav party, 369
New Alternative (NA, Venezuela), 137, 140
New Jewel Movement (NJM, Grenada), 85, 86. See also Maurice Bishop Patriotic Movement
New Zealand, Communist Party of (CPNZ), 222, 223
Nicaragua, 41, 42–43; and Benin, 9; and Ethiopia, 14; and Colombia, 65; and Costa Rica, 71; and Ecuadoran guerrilla organizations, 81; and Ecuador, 81; and Suriname, 130; and Japanese CP, 193; and North Korea, 202; and East Germany, 293; and Poland, 317; and Romania, 332; and USSR, 362, 364; and Yugoslav party, 372; and CMEA, 373, 377; and Finland, 468; and France, 468; and Dutch CP, 513
Nicaragua, Communist Party of (PCN), 111, 113
Nicaraguan Socialist Party (PSN), 111, 113

Nigeria: and Bulgaria, 272
Nkomati Accord, 2, 20, 29
Nonaligned movement: and India, 180; and Romania, 329
Norway: and China, 173; and USSR, 354
Norwegian Communist Party (NKP), 514–18; and Bulgarian CP, 274; and CPSU, 365
Nuclear-free zones: Balkans, 271, 328; Mediterranean, 505; northern Europe, 515, 516

Oil: in Angola, 6; in Benin, 9; in Nigeria, 20; in Sudan, 35; Cuban imports of Soviet, 74; in China, 177; in Vietnam, 242; Soviet sales to Czechoslovakia, 278; Soviet sales to Poland, 314; Soviet sales to Romania, 330; in USSR, 343; Uruguayan imports of Soviet, 362; shortages in Yugoslavia, 368; Soviet sales to CMEA partners, 380; Iranian sales to East Germany, 381; Soviet sales to Iceland, 494
Olympics (Los Angeles) boycott: Angola, 7; Ethiopia, 14; North Korea, 201, 206; Mongolia, 218; Vietnam, 242–43; Bulgaria, 274; East Germany, 294; Hungary, 303; Poland, 316; Romania, 326, 330; USSR, 352
Oman: and South Yemen, 439
Organization for African Unity (OAU), 40
Organization of Arab Communists (Lebanon), 429
Organization of Solidarity with the Peoples of Africa, Asia, and Latin America (AALAPSO), 388

Pakistan: and USSR and Afghanistan, 155; and China, 173; and Romania, 328
Pakistan, Communist Party of (CPP), 224
Pakistan Progressive Party, 226
Pak Mai (Thailand), 209, 237
Palestine Communist Party (PCP), 401, 418–22; and East German party, 295; and South Yemen, 440
Palestine Liberation Organization (PLO), 24, 373, 401; and China, 173; and North Korea, 202; and Romania, 328; and USSR, 360; and Israeli CP, 416, 417, 418; and Palestine CP, 420–21; and Lebanese CP, 426–27; and Syrian CP, 436; and South Yemen, 440
Palung Liberation Army (Burma), 163
Panama: and Nicaragua, 114
Panama, People's Party of (PPP), 44, 49, 115–18; and Yugoslav party, 372
Paraguayan Communist Party (PCP), 119–20

Party of Progress and Socialism (PPS, Morocco), 400, 430–31

Party of Proletarian Unity for Communism (PDUP, Italy), 501

Peace movement: Canada, 55–56, 57; India, 179, 180; Japan, 192; East Germany, 287, 288; Hungary, 301; and international fronts, 388–90; and Austrian CP, 453; and Belgian CP, 455, 457; Denmark, 465; West Germany, 477–78, 479; Great Britain, 486; Italy, 500; Luxembourg, 503; Malta, 505, 506; Netherlands, 512; Norway, 515–16

Peace organizations: Lesotho, 15; Réunion, 22, 24; Sudan, 32; Canada, 55; Costa Rica, 68; Panama, 115, 117; U.S., 131; Afghanistan, 143, 144; Bangladesh, 160; Japan, 190; New Zealand, 222; Philippines, 232; Albania, 251; Czechoslovakia, 275, 279, 282; Iraq, 413; Lebanon, 426, 429; Saudi Arabia, 432; Cyprus, 458; France, 470; West Germany, 478, 480; Iceland, 491; Malta, 504; Netherlands, 509, 512; Norway, 515; Switzerland, 530, 531, 532

Peasants' organizations: Ethiopia, 12; Colombia, 62; Costa Rica, 68; Cuba, 72; Mexico, 107; Nicaragua, 111; Peru, 125; Afghanistan, 144; Bangladesh, 158; India, 179, 183; North Korea, 197; Nepal, 220; Philippines, 229; Yemen, 439; Cyprus, 458; Portugal, 520, 521

People's Alliance (AB, Iceland), 490–94

People's Democratic Union (Yemen), 439

People's Electoral Movement (MEP, Venezuela), 137, 139–40

People's Liberation Army (EPL, Colombia), 62, 64, 65–66

People's Liberation Organization (Singapore), 211

People's National Congress (PNC, Guyana), 77

People's National Party (PNP, Jamaica), 102

People's Popular Movement (Trinidad and Tobago), 77, 87, 98

People's Progressive Party (PPP, Guyana), 25, 44, 49, 77, 87, 96–97, 98; and Bulgarian CP, 274

Personality cults: in Cuba, 73; in Afghanistan, 148; in North Korea, 198; in Albania, 252, 254; in Romania, 319–20

Peru, 43; and Nicaragua, 114

Peruvian Communist Party (PCP), 43, 49, 120–27 passim; and Yugoslav party, 372

Peruvian Communist Party–Huaycacholo, 124

Peruvian Communist Party–Puka Llacta, 124

Peruvian Communist Party–Red Flag, 123

Philippines Communist Party (PKP), 228–29, 232

Philippines, Communist Party of the, Marxist-Leninist (CPP-ML), 215, 228–32

Poland, 249; and CMEA, 373, 377, 378, 381; and WTO, 383–86

—foreign relations: Angola, 7; and Nicaragua, 114; Peru, 127; Afghanistan, 153; North Korea, 204; Mongolia, 217; Albania, 261; Bulgaria, 271–72; Czechoslovakia, 284; Hungary, 304; Romania, 331; Greece, 490

Polisario Front, 373, 501

Polish United Workers' Party (PZPR), 305, 307–9; and Angolan party, 3; and Bulgarian CP, 274; and East German party, 295; and CPSU, 363; and Palestine CP, 422; and Lebanese CP, 427; and Austrian CP, 452, 454; and Italian CP, 501; and Maltese CP, 505; and Portuguese CP, 522; and Spanish CP, 525

Popular Action Movement (MAP, Mexico), 107

Popular Action Movement—Marxist-Leninist (MAP-ML, Nicaragua), 111, 113

Popular Christian Social Party (PPSC, Nicaragua), 111, 113

Popular Democratic Movement (MDP, Ecuador), 44, 80

Popular Democratic Movement (MDP, Portugal), 520, 521

Popular Democratic Union (UDP, Peru), 122

Popular forces of the 25th of April (FP-25, Portugal), 520, 522

Popular Liberation Forces (FPL, El Salvador), 81, 82

Popular Liberation Movement (MLP, Honduras), 100

Popular Movement (Egypt), 405

Popular Revolutionary Army (ERP, El Salvador), 82, 84

Popular Social Christian Movement (MPSC, El Salvador), 82

Popular Socialist Party (PPS, Mexico), 109

Popular Vanguard Party (PVP, Costa Rica), 44, 68–71

Portugal: and Angola, 7; and Mozambique, 20; and Nicaragua, 114; and China, 173

Portuguese Communist Party (PCP), 520–22; and Angolan party, 5; and Bulgarian CP, 274; and Romanian CP, 333; and CPSU, 366; and Yugoslav party, 373; and Palestine CP, 421; and Spanish CPs, 525

Prices: Afghanistan, 149; China, 178; Czechoslovakia, 278; East Germany, 289; Hungary, 298, 299; Poland, 313, 314; Romania, 322; USSR, 343; Yugoslavia, 370

Progressive Labor Party (St. Lucia), 77, 87

Progressive Organizations Switzerland (POCH), 530, 531, 532

Progressive Party of the Working People (AKEL, Cyprus), 458–62; and Bulgarian CP, 274; and Lebanese CP, 428; and Maltese CP, 505

Progressive Socialist Organization of the Mediterranean, 373

Proletarian Democracy (DP, Italy), 501

Proletariat Party (Bangladesh), 158

Provisional Sinn Fein (Ireland), 494

Puerto Rican Communist Party (PCP), 128, 129

Puerto Rican Socialist League, 129

Puerto Rican Socialist Party (PSP), 77, 128, 129

Purbo Banglar Communist Party (Marxist-Leninist) (Bangladesh), 159

Purbo Banglar Sarbahara Party (Bangladesh), 159

Purges: China, 167, 170; North Korea, 198; Albania, 255–56; Poland, 307

Quebec, Communist Party of, 55

Radical Cause (Venezuela), 137

Radical Democratic Party (PRD, Costa Rica), 68, 69

Radio Moscow, 393

Radio Peace and Progress, 393

Rebel Armed Forces (FAR, Guatemala), 90

Red Brigades (Italy), 501–2

Red Electoral Alliance (RV, Norway), 514, 519

Réunion Communist Party (PCR), 2, 22–24

Revolutionary Armed Forces (Guatemala), 90

Revolutionary Cells (RZ, West Germany), 482

Revolutionary Communist League (Dominican Republic), 78

Revolutionary Communist Party (Argentina), 47

Revolutionary Communist Party (Lebanon), 429

Revolutionary Communist Party (PCR, Peru), 121

Revolutionary Communist Party (RCP, U.S.), 134

Revolutionary Current (Egypt), 405

Revolutionary Democratic Front (El Salvador), 77

Revolutionary Internationalist Movement (RIM, U.S.), 134

Revolutionary Left Movement (MIR, Venezuela), 137, 139, 140

Revolutionary Marxist League (Jamaica), 104

Revolutionary Movement of the Left (MIR, Peru), 121

Revolutionary People's Army (Argentina), 48

Revolutionary People's Command (Honduras), 101

Revolutionary People's Party (RVP, Suriname), 129

Revolutionary Socialst League (U.S.), 104

Revolutionary Socialist Party (PSR, Mexico), 107

Revolutionary Socialist (PSR, Peru), 121, 122, 126

Revolutionary Vanguard (VR, Peru), 121

Revolutionary Workers' League (RWL, Canada), 55, 58

Revolutionary Workers' Movement–Salvador Cayetano Carpio (MOR-SCC, El Salvador), 82

Revolutionary Workers Party (POR, Bolivia), 49, 51

Romania, 249–50; and CMEA, 373–81 passim; and WTO, 383–86

—foreign relations: Angola, 7; Mozambique, 19; Argentina, 47; Dominican Republic, 79: China, 173; North Korea, 204; Nepal, 220; and Bulgaria, 271; and East Germany, 294; Hungary, 303–4; Malta, 507

Romanian Communist Party (RCP), 318–21, 332–34; and Angolan party, 3; and Mauritius party, 3; and Bulgarian CP, 274; and CPSU, 363; and Yugoslav party, 372; and Israeli CP, 417; and Austrian CP, 452, 454; and French CP, 474; and Greek CP, 490; and Italian CP, 497; and Portuguese CP, 522; and Spanish CPs, 524, 525

Saharan Arab Democratic Republic: and Yugoslavia, 372; and Morocco, 431

Salvadoran Revolutionary Party (PRS, El Salvador), 82

Samyabadi Dal (SD, Bangladesh), 158

Sandinista Front of National Liberation (FSLN, Nicaragua), 42–43, 47, 49, 77, 110–15; and Mexican party, 110; and Peruvian CP, 127; and Kampuchean party, 196; and French CP, 473; and Greece, 490; and Italian CP, 500; and Portuguese CP, 522

São Tomé and Principe, 3

Saudi Arabia, Communist Party of (CPSA), 400, 432

Science and technology: in North Korea, 200; in Romania, 320; in CMEA, 374

Sendero Luminoso (Peru), 43, 123–26

Seychelles: relations with communist states, 3

Shan State Nationalities Liberation Organization (Burma), 163

Shan United Army (Burma), 164

Sindhi Awami Tehrik (SAT, Pakistan), 226

Sinn Fein–The Workers' Party (Ireland), 494
Slovakia, Communist Party of (KSS), 275
Socialist Action (U.S.), 133–34
Socialist Action and Unity (MAUS, Mexico), 107
Socialist Action League (SAL, New Zealand), 222, 223
Socialist Bloc (Dominican Republic), 77, 78
Socialist Challenge Organization (Canada), 58
Socialist Current (Mexico), 109
Socialist Front (Ecuador), 44
Socialist International, 25, 114, 500
Socialist Labor League (SLL, Australia), 155, 156, 157
Socialist League (LS, Venezuela), 137, 139
Socialist Left Party (SV, Norway), 514, 515, 518–19; and Danish party, 466; and Icelandic party, 494
Socialist Party (Dominican Republic), 78
Socialist Party (Sweden), 529
Socialist People's Party (SF, Denmark), 463, 465–66; and Icelandic party, 494
Socialist Revolution Group (Guadeloupe), 89
Socialist Unity Party (SED, East Germany), 285–87, 295; and Ethiopian party, 13; and Senegalese party, 25; and Argentine CP, 47; and Jamican party, 104; and Bulgarian CP, 274; and CPSU, 363; and Yugoslav party, 373; and Israeli CP, 417; and Palestine CP, 421; and Syrian CP, 435; and Austrian CP, 452, 454; and Cypriot CP, 461; and Finnish CP, 468–69; and French CP, 474; and West German CP, 476–77, 478, 480; and West Berlin party, 483; and British CP, 486; and Greek CP, 490; and Italian CP, 501; and Maltese CP, 505; and Dutch CP, 513; and Spanish CPs, 525; and Swiss party, 531
Socialist Unity Party (SUP, New Zealand), 222, 223
Socialist Vanguard Party (PAGS, Algeria), 400–401, 402
Socialist Workers Movement (Domincan Republic), 78
Socialist Workers Party (SWP, Australia), 155, 156, 157
Socialist Workers' Party (SWP, Great Britain), 487
Socialist Workers Party (PST, Mexico), 109
Socialist Workers' Party (PST, Panama), 118
Socialist Workers Party (PST, Peru), 122
Socialist Workers' Party (SAP, Switzerland), 530, 531, 532
Socialist Workers' Party (SWP, U.S.), 44, 129, 133–34, 135

Socialist Working People's Party (SWPP, Nigeria), 3, 21
Socialist Youth Foundation (Brazil), 51, 54
Social problems: Albania, 253, 255–57; Czechoslovakia, 277, 280; Hungary, 300–301
Somalia, 14
South Africa: and Mozambique, 2, 16, 17, 20; and Angola, 2–3, 5, 7; and Zimbabwe, 40
South African Communist Party (SACP), 2, 26–32; and Bulgarian CP, 274
South-West African People's Organization (SWAPO), 7, 13, 40; and Yugoslav party, 369
Soviet Union, Communist Party of the (CPSU), 333–40, 362–66; and Congolese CP, 2, 11; and Ethiopian party, 12–13; and Mozambican party, 20; and Senegalese CP, 25; and South African CP, 31; and Colombian CP, 64; and Guadeloupan CP, 87; and Guyanese party, 97; and Jamaican party, 104; and Mexican party, 110; and Indian CP, 181–82; and Japanese CP, 193; and Mongolian party, 217; and Nepalese CP, 220; and New Zealand party, 223; and Philippine CPs, 232; and Sri Lankan CP, 235; and Bulgarian CP, 274; and Yugoslav party, 369; and international fronts, 387–88; propaganda organs, 392–93; and Iraqi CP, 412; and Israeli CP, 417, 418; and Palestine CP, 421, 422; and Lebanese CP, 427, 428, 429; and Syrian CP, 435–36; and Tunisian CP, 438; and Austrian CP, 452, 454; and Cypriot CP, 461; and Danish CP, 465; and Finnish CP, 468, 469; and French CP, 473–74; and West German CP, 477, 480; and West Berlin party, 483; and British CP, 486; and Greek CP, 489; and Italian CP, 497, 501; and Luxembourg CP, 502–3; and Maltese CP, 505; and Dutch CP, 513–14; and Norwegian CP, 516; and Portuguese CP, 522; and Spanish CPs, 524, 525; and Swedish party, 529; and Swiss party, 530–31
Spain: and Angola, 7; and Nicaragua, 114; and China, 173; and Albania, 261; and USSR, 354
Spain, Communist Party of (PC), 525; and CPSU, 366, 525
Spanish Communist Party (PCE), 523–24; and East German party, 294; and Hungarian party, 304; and Romanian CP, 332; and French CP, 474
Spanish Workers, Communist Party of (PCOE), 525
Sramik-Krishak Samajbadi Dal (Bangladesh), 158
Sri Lanka, Communist Party of (CPSL), 233–35
Student organizations: Lesotho, 15; Sudan, 32;

Student organizations (*continued*)
Ecuador, 79; Guatemala, 93; Panama, 115, 117; Bangladesh, 158; India, 179, 184; Japan, 190; Nepal, 220; Pakistan, 224, 226, 227; Philippines, 229; Bahrain, 403, 404; Lebanon, 426; Belgium, 454; Cyprus, 458; Denmark, 462, 464, West Germany, 475, 477; West Berlin, 483; Switzerland, 530

Sudan: and Ethiopia, 14; and Romania, 328

Sudanese Communist Party (SCP), 3, 25, 32–36

Sudanese People's Liberation Army (SPLA), 34–35

Sudanese People's Liberation Movement (SPLM), 3, 34–35

Suriname, Communist Party of (CPS), 129

Sweden: and Nicaragua, 114; and China, 173; and East Germany, 292

Sweden's Communist Party, 529

Swiss Labor Party (PdAS), 530–31, 532; and CPSU, 365; and Austrian CP, 452

Switzerland: and Albania, 262

Switzerland, Communist Party of, Marxist-Leninist (KPS/ML), 531–32

Syria: and North Korea, 202; and Czechoslovakia, 283; and East Germany, 293; and Romania, 328; and USSR, 360; and Iraqi CP, 413; and Greece, 490

Syrian Communist Party (SCP), 401, 433–36; and Lebanese CP, 428; and South Yemen, 440; and Portuguese CP, 522

Tamil United Liberation Front (TULF, Sri Lanka), 234

Tanzania, 32; and Bulgaria, 272

Tendencia (Panama), 118

Thailand: and Laos, 208–9; and Vietnam, 243; and USSR, 359–60

Thailand, Communist Party of (CPT), 235–37

Tigre Popular Liberation Front (Ethiopia), 14

Togo: and Romania, 328

Trade: Congolese with West, 11; Zimbabwan, 40; Soviet–Argentine, 46; Cuban, 74; Soviet–Peruvian, 126; Soviet–Afghan, 153, 154; Soviet–Bangladeshi, 160; Chinese, 174; Soviet–Chinese, 175, 176–77, 357; U.S.–Chinese, 178; Chinese–Indian, 180; North Korean, 200, 201; North Korea–Libyan, 202; North Korean–Soviet, 202; Chinese–Japanese, 204; Soviet–Mongolian, 217; Romanian–Nepalese, 220; Soviet–Vietnamese, 242; Albanian, 258; Soviet–Bulgarian, 270;

Albanian–Bulgarian, 271; Bulgarian–Libyan, 272; Bulgarian–Egyptian, 272; Bulgarian–Indian, 273; Bulgarian–Cuban, 273; FRG–Bulgarian, 274; U.S.–Bulgarian, 274; Czechoslovak, 283; East German, 289, 291; Hungarian, 298, 301–2, Polish, 314–15; Romanian, 321, 325, 326, 330, 332; Soviet–Uruguayan, 362; Yugoslav, 370, 372; of CMEA states, 374–81 *passim*; Soviet–Yemeni, 441; Soviet–Icelandic, 494; Soviet–Maltese, 506

Treaties and agreements: Soviet–Angolan, 6; Cuban–Angolan, 6; Congolese–Soviet parties, 11; Congo, with Mozambique, Angola, Benin, Guinea, Cuba, USSR, 11; Soviet–Ethiopian, 13; Soviet–Mozambican, 20, 361; Soviet–Cuban, 74; GDR–Cuban, 74; Soviet–Chinese, 175, 176, 357; U.S.–Chinese, 177, 178; Soviet–North Korean, 203; North Korean–Japanese, 206; Soviet–Mongolian, 217; Mongolia, with Finland, France, India, Ethiopia, Yemen, Hungary, Cuba, 218; Romanian–Nepalese, 220; Albanian–Yugoslav, 260; Albanian–Vietnamese, 261; Albanian–Italian, 261; Albanian–Turkish, 261; Albanian–Swedish, 261–62; Soviet–Bulgarian, 270; Polish–Bulgarian, 272; Bulgarian–Mozambican, 272; Bulgarian–African, 272; Bulgarian–Kampuchean, 272; Bulgarian–Guyanese, 273; U.S.–Bulgarian, 274; Soviet–Czechoslovak–GDR–Hungarian, 277–78; East German economic with Third World, 293; Soviet–West German, 294–95; East German–North Korean, 295; East German–Chinese, 295; Hungarian–Austrian, 302; Soviet–Polish, 314; Soviet–Yemeni, 361, 441; Soviet with CMEA partners, 380

Trotskyist League (TL, Canada), 55, 58

Trotskyist parties: Argentina, 47; Bolivia, 49, 51; Brazil, 51, 54; Canada, 55, 58; Colombia, 62; Jamaica, 104; Panama, 119; Peru, 121, 122; Puerto Rico, 129; U.S. 133–34; Australia, 156, 157; Burma, 161; New Zealand, 224; Sri Lanka, 234; Lebanon, 429; Denmark, 463; West Germany, 481; Great Britain, 487; Sweden, 529; Switzerland, 531

Tudeh Party (Iran), 399, 408–11; and Syrian CP, 436

Tunisia: and China, 173

Tunisian Communist Party (TCP), 437–38

Tupac Amaru Revolutionary Movement (MRTA), 43, 124

Turkey: and China, 173; and Albania, 259, 261; and Bulgaria, 271; and Romania, 328
Turkey, Communist Party of (TCP), 533, 534
25 February Movement (25FM, Suriname), 129, 130

Umkhonto We Sizwe (South Africa), 27
Unified Mariateguista Party (PUM, Peru), 121, 122
Union Common List (Denmark), 466
Union of Soviet Socialist Republics: spy facilities in Cuba, 73; succession, 245–47, 335–36; economy, 245, 246, 342–44; agriculture, 245, 246; ideology, 246, 247; culture, 246–47; and CMEA, 373–81 *passim*; and WTO, 383–86; propaganda budget, 391; propaganda agencies, 392–93
—foreign aid: Ethiopia, 13, 14; Mozambique, 18; Nicaragua, 41, 112; Cuba, 41–42, 73, 74; Peru, 127; Suriname, 130; Afghanistan, 153–54; North Korea, 203; Mongolia, 217; Pakistan, 227; Vietnam, 242; Czechoslovakia, 282, 283
—foreign relations, 246, 350–51; Seychelles, 3; Angola, 6–7; Benin, 9; Congo, 11; Ethiopia, 13, 14; Lesotho, 15; Mozambique, 20; Peru, 43, 126; Argentina, 47; Bolivia, 51; Cuba, 72, 74; Nicaragua, 114; Suriname, 130; Afghanistan, 153–55; Bangladesh, 160; China, 174–77; India, 179–80, 183; Indonesia, 189; Kampuchea, 196; North Korea, 198, 202–3; Laos, 209; Mongolia, 217, 218; Pakistan, 227–28; Philippines, 232; Sri Lanka, 235; Vietnam, 242; Albania, 259, 262; Bulgaria, 266, 270–71; Czechoslovakia, 276; East Germany, 286, 287, 291, 293–95; Hungary, 298, 302–3; Poland, 314, 315–16; Romania, 320, 329–31; Yugoslavia, 369, 372; Middle East, 399–401; Algeria, 402–3; Egypt, 407; Iran, 408–11 *passim*; Iraq, 413–14; Jordan, 425; Lebanon, 428; Syria, 434–45; Yemen, 440, 441; Finland, 469; Greece, 490; Iceland, 494; Malta, 505–8 *passim*; Sweden, 528–29; Turkey, 534
—foreign trade: Argentina, 46; Peru, 126; Afghanistan, 153, 154; Bangladesh, 160; China, 175, 176–77, 357; North Korea, 202; Mongolian, 217; Vietnam, 242; Bulgaria, 270; Czechoslovakia, 283; East Germany, 289; Hungary, 298; Poland, 314; Romania, 330; Uruguay, 362; Iceland, 494; Yemen, 441; Malta, 506

—military: in Seychelles, 3; in São Tomé and Principe, 3; in Guinea, 3; in Ethiopia, 34; in Afghanistan, 145, 151; naval exercises in Southeast Asia, 175, 242; in Vietnam, 242
—treaties and agreements: with Angola, 6; with Congo, 11; with Ethiopia, 13; with Mozambique, 20, 361; with Cuba, 74; with China, 175, 176, 357; with North Korea, 203; with Mongolia, 217; with Bulgaria, 270; with West Germany, 294–95; with Poland, 314; with Yemen, 361, 441; with CMEA partners, 380
United Dominica Labor Party, 76–77
United Nations: and Afghanistan, 152; and North Korea, 206–7; annd Romania, 329
United People's Movement (St. Vincent and the Grenadines), 77, 98
United People's Party (Bangladesh), 159
United Revolutionary Directorate (DRU, El Salvador), 82
United Revolutionary Front (Guatemala), 91
United States: and Angola, 5, 7; and Ethiopia, 13, 14; and Sudan, 14; and Nicaragua, 43, 71, 112–13; and Costa Rica, 71; and Cuba, 75–76; and Honduras, 100–101; and China, 173, 177–78; North Korea, 206; and Sri Lanka, 235; and Albania, 259, 262; and Bulgaria, 274; and East Germany, 292; and Hungary, 298, 302; and Poland, 314, 317; and Romania, 326–27; and USSR, 351–53; and Yugoslavia, 369, 372; and Soviet propaganda, 394–97; and Austrian CP, 453
Upper Volta, 4; and Romania, 328
Uruguay: and USSR, 362
Uruguay, Communist Party of (PCU), 44, 49, 135, 136; and East German party, 295
USA, Communist Party (CPUSA), 44, 129, 130–33, 206

Vatican: and China, 173; and Poland, 309, Romania, 324
Venezuela, 43; and Nicaragua, 114; and China, 173; and Czechoslovakia, 283; and USSR, 362
Venezuela, Communist Party of (PCV), 44, 49, 87, 137, 138, 139; and Yugoslav party, 372
Vietnam: and CMEA, 373
—foreign relations: Mozambique, 19; China, 173; Indonesia, 189; Kampuchea, 194–95, 196; North Korea, 202; Laos, 208–9; Thailand, 237, 238; Albania, 261; Czechoslovakia, 283; Poland, 317; USSR, 359, 364
Vietnamese Communist Party (VCP), 31, 238–40;

VCP (*continued*)
and Japanese CP, 193; and Laotian party, 209; and Albanian party, 263; and Palestine CP, 422; and Greek CP, 490

Violence-free Action Groups–Grass-roots Movement (West Germany), 482

Warsaw Treaty Organization (WTO), 247–48; and Bulgaria, 271–72; and Romania, 329

West Berlin, Socialist Unity Party of (SEW), 482–83; and CPSU, 365

West German Communists, Maoist League of (BWK), 481

Women's International Democratic Federation (WIDF), 117, 279, 388–91

Women's organizations: Angola, 4; Benin, 8, 9; Congo, 10, 11; Ethiopia, 12; Mozambique, 16, 17; Réunion, 22, 24; Senegal, 25; Canada, 55; Cuba, 72; Guadeloupe, 87, 89; Guyana, 96; Jamaica, 102; Martinique, 104, 106; Nicaragua, 111; Panama, 115, 117; U.S., 131, 132; Afghanistan, 143, 144, 150; China, 165; Japan, 190; North Korea, 197; Mongolia, 216, 218; Vietnamese, 218; New Zealand, 222; Philippines, 229; Sri Lanka, 233; Albania, 251, 256; Bulgaria, 264; Czechoslovakia, 275, 279; East Germany, 285–86; Romania, 319; Bahrain, 403; Yemen, 439; Cyprus, 458; Finland, 468; West Berlin, 483; Luxembourg, 502; Netherlands, 509; Sweden, 527; Switzerland, 530, 531

Worker, Peasant, Student, and Popular Front (FOCEP, Peru), 121

Workers Communist League (WCL, New Zealand), 222, 223

Workers Communist Party (Canada), 58

Workers' Communist Party (AKP, Norway), 514, 519

Workers League (U.S.), 135

Workers' League for the Reconstruction of the KPD (AB, West Germany), 481

Workers Party (WP, Bangladesh), 158

Workers' Party (PT, Brazil), 51–52, 54

Workers' Revolutionary Movement (St. Lucia), 77, 98

Workers' Revolutionary Party (WRP, Great Britain), 487

Workers' Revolutionary Party (PRT, Panama), 119

Workers' Self-Defense Movement (ADO, Colombia), 62, 64

Workers World Party (U.S.), 135

Working People's Alliance, (WPA, Guyana), 96, 98

World Bank: and Mozambique, 16, 20; and

Zimbabwe, 40

World Federation of Democratic Youth (WFDY), 96, 117, 388–91

World Federation of Scientific Workers (WFSW), 388–91

World Federation of Teachers' Unions (FISE), 388

World Federation of Trade Unions (WFTU), 24, 32, 62, 117, 157, 186, 297, 388–91

World Marxist Review (*WMR*), 32, 372, 387, 392, 503, 505

—December meeting of CPs to discuss, 3, 36, 56, 110, 118, 187, 404, 432

World Peace Council (WPC), 24, 32, 56, 232, 388–91

—affiliates: Lesotho, 15; Réunion, 24; Argentina, 45, 46; Canada, 56; Philippines, 232; Lebanon, 429; Norway, 515

Yemen, People's Democratic Republic of: and Ethiopia, 14; and Sudan, 34; and Mongolia, 218; and Bulgaria, 272; and Czechoslovakia, 283; and USSR, 361; and CMEA, 377

Yemen Arab Republic: and South Yemen, 439–40

Yemen Socialist Party (YSP), 400, 438–40; and Ethiopian party, 13; and Kampuchean party, 196; and East Germany, 293; and Lebanese CP, 427, 429; and French CP, 474

Youth organizations: Angola, 4; Benin, 8, 9; Congo, 10, 11; Ethiopia, 12; Mozambique, 16, 17; Réunion, 22, 23; Sudan, 32; Argentina, 45, 47; Bolivia, 49; Canada, 55, 56; Chile, 59; Colombia, 62; Cuba, 72; Guadeloupe, 87, 89; Guatemala, 89; Guyana, 96; Jamaica, 102; Mexico, 107; Nicaragua, 111; Panama, 115, 117; U.S., 131, 132, 134; Afghanistan, 144, 150; China, 165, 172; Japan, 191; Kampuchea, 194; North Korea, 197; Mongolia, 216, 217; New Zealand, 222, 223; Philippines, 229; Sri Lanka, 233; Vietnam, 239; Albania, 251, 255–56; Bulgaria, 264; Czechoslovakia, 275, 279; East Germany, 285; Hungary, 295, 300; Romania, 319; USSR, 334, 349; Yugoslavia, 368; Algeria, 402; Bahrain, 403; Israel, 414, 417; Saudi Arabia, 432; Tunisia, 437, 438; Yemen, 439; Belgium, 454; Cyprus, 458, 459; Denmark, 462, 464; Finland, 467; France, 470; West Germany, 475, 477, 480, 482; West Berlin, 482, 483; Great Britain, 484, 486; Greece, 487, 488, 489; Ireland, 495; Italy, 496, 499; Luxembourg, 502; Malta, 504, 507; Netherlands, 509; Norway, 514; Sweden, 527; Switzerland, 530, 531, 532

Yugoslavia, 250; and CMEA, 373, 377
—foreign relations: Angola, 7; China, 173; North
    Korea, 204; Albania, 259–60; Bulgaria, 271;
    Czechoslovakia, 283; Hungary, 304; Romania,
    331–32; USSR, 356; and Algeria, 403
Yugoslavia, League of Communist of (LCY),
    367–70, 372–73; and Angolan party, 3; and
    Japanese CP, 193; and Kampuchean party, 196;
    and Czechoslovak CP, 284; and CPSU, 364;
    and Austrian CP, 452, 454; and Finnish CP,
    468; and French CP, 474; and Greek CP, 489;
    and Italian CP, 501; and Portuguese CP, 522;
    and Spanish CPs, 524, 525

Zimbabwe: and Bulgaria, 272; and Czecho-
    slovakia, 283; and Romania, 329
Zimbabwe African National Union (ZANU), 1,
    13, 37–40
Zimbabwe African Peoples' Union (ZAPU), 37, 39
Zones of peace: Indian Ocean, 24; Mediterranean,
    373